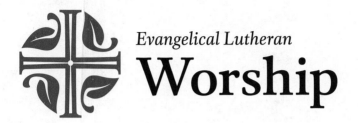

Evangelical Lutheran
Worship

Evangelical Lutheran

Worship

Published by Augsburg Fortress

Evangelical Lutheran Worship is commended for use in the Evangelical Lutheran
Church in America.

Evangelical Lutheran Worship is approved for use in the Evangelical Lutheran
Church in Canada and is commended to this church as its primary worship
resource.

Evangelical Lutheran Worship
Pew Edition

Copyright © 2006 Evangelical Lutheran Church in America
Published by Augsburg Fortress, Publishers

Manufactured in the U.S.A.

ISBN 978-0-8066-5618-2

Fifth Printing, March 2007

Contents

INTRODUCTION	6

THE CHURCH YEAR

Calendar	14
Propers	18
Prayers for Worship	64
Additional Prayers	72

HOLY COMMUNION

Setting One	94
Setting Two	116
Setting Three	138
Setting Four	147
Setting Five	156
Setting Six	165
Setting Seven	175
Setting Eight	184
Setting Nine	193
Setting Ten	203
Service of the Word	210

HOLY BAPTISM

Holy Baptism	227
Welcome to Baptism	232
Affirmation of Baptism	234
Corporate Confession and Forgiveness	238
Individual Confession and Forgiveness	243

LENT AND THE THREE DAYS

Ash Wednesday	251
Sunday of the Passion	256
Maundy Thursday	258
Good Friday	262
Vigil of Easter	266

LIFE PASSAGES

Healing	276
Funeral	279
Marriage	286

DAILY PRAYER

Morning Prayer	298
Evening Prayer	309
Night Prayer	320
Responsive Prayer	328

ASSEMBLY SONG

Psalms	#1–150
Service Music	#151–238
Hymns	#239–886
National Songs	#887–893

ADDITIONAL RESOURCES

Daily Lectionary	1121
Scripture and Worship	1154
Small Catechism	1160
Indexes	1169

Introduction

Jesus Christ is the living and abiding Word of God. By the power of the Spirit, this very Word of God, which is Jesus Christ, is read in the scriptures, proclaimed in preaching, announced in the forgiveness of sins, eaten and drunk in the Holy Communion, and encountered in the bodily presence of the Christian community. . . . God gives the Word and the sacraments to the church and by the power of the Spirit thereby creates and sustains the church among us. . . . God calls the church to exercise care and fidelity in its use of the means of grace, so that all people may hear and believe the gospel of Jesus Christ and be gathered into God's own mission for the life of the world.

The Use of the Means of Grace, *principles 1 and 2*

The Lutheran confessions describe the church in terms of the worshiping assembly. "It is also taught that at all times there must be and remain one holy, Christian church. It is the assembly of all believers among whom the gospel is purely preached and the holy sacraments are administered according to the gospel" (*Augsburg Confession*, 7). *Assembly* expresses well the nature of the church as *ekklesia*, a biblical term for the church that has at its root the meaning "called out." The common pattern for worship underscores this understanding of the church: The Holy Spirit gathers the people of God around Jesus Christ present in the word of God and the sacraments, so that the Spirit may in turn send them into the world to continue the ingathering mission of God's reign.

Worship takes place in particular assemblies within particular contexts. Yet every assembly gathered by the Holy Spirit for worship is connected to the whole church. Worship unites the people of God in one time and place with the people of God in every time and place. We use patterns, words, actions, and songs handed down through the ages to express this unity and continuity. The Lutheran confessions affirm this commitment to the treasury of Christian worship: "We do not abolish the mass but religiously keep and defend it . . . We keep traditional liturgical forms" (*Apology to the Augsburg Confession*, 24).

The Christian assembly also worships in the midst of an ever-changing world. And because the worship that constitutes the church is also the fundamental expression of the mission of

God in the world, worship is regularly renewed in order to be both responsible and responsive to the world that the church is called to serve.

At the beginning of the twenty-first century, *Evangelical Lutheran Worship* continues the renewal of worship that has taken place over the three centuries Lutherans have been on the North American continent and in the Caribbean region. During this time, renewal efforts have been marked by a movement from a variety of Lutheran immigrant traditions toward a greater similarity of liturgical forms and a more common repertoire of song. The liturgy set out in 1748 by Henry Melchior Muhlenberg and the Common Service of 1888 are two earlier milestones along this path. In the twentieth century, the consolidation of various immigrant Lutheran church bodies and those more established on this continent was reflected in the primary worship books used by mid-century, namely *Service Book and Hymnal* and *The Lutheran Hymnal*. In 1978 *Lutheran Book of Worship* was published, the fruit of an ambitious inter-Lutheran project that sought to unite most North American Lutherans in the use of a single worship book with shared liturgical forms and a common repertoire of hymnody.

The years since the publication of *Lutheran Book of Worship* have seen many changes within the church and the world. Advances in communication and technology have led to the increasing use of electronic and digital resources within the church and its worship. A growing awareness of the interrelatedness of the world, coupled with new understandings of the world's diverse cultures, has had implications also for the church as the one body of Christ throughout the world. The use of language continues to develop in response to context and societal change, as does the use of more than one language in worship. Forms of musical expression have blossomed, and churches have embraced many of these forms for use in worship.

Evangelical Lutheran Worship bears the rich tradition of Christian worship practiced among Lutherans and, at the same time, seeks to renew that tradition in response to a generation of change in the church and in the world. Its identity and its content reveal several goals.

Evangelical Lutheran Worship is a core rather than a comprehensive resource. The collection of materials is more expansive than its predecessor; it reflects a body of prayer and song that our churches consider worthy to hold in common; and, in many contexts, it will provide most or all of what is needed for the assembly's worship. Still, it is not possible or necessary for a single worship book to contain all the expressions of worship desired in every context by an increasingly diverse church. The book contains notable representatives of a wide variety of liturgical texts and musical forms that point to larger repertoires outside this volume.

Evangelical Lutheran Worship is grounded in Lutheran convictions about the centrality of the means of grace. The word of God, read, preached, and sung by the assembly, is essential to the orders of service. Baptism is set within the principal gathering for worship, and its themes are reflected in other services. Materials are newly included to help congregations welcome adults and children to formation in faith, to baptism, and to the baptismal life. Ten musical settings of Holy Communion highlight both the increased diversity of expression in the church as well as the commitment to gathering regularly around both God's word and the holy supper.

Evangelical Lutheran Worship promotes the principle that worship leadership is a shared task among those who carry out various roles in the assembly. At the same time, it affirms that the ministry of the people of God is carried out in their various vocations in the world, not merely in the church.

Evangelical Lutheran Worship continues to emphasize that "freedom and flexibility in worship is a Lutheran inheritance, and there is room for ample variety in ceremony, music, and liturgical form" (*Lutheran Book of Worship,* Introduction). And, through its design and through a variety of interpretive materials herein, it seeks to make more transparent the principle of fostering unity without imposing uniformity.

Evangelical Lutheran Worship represents the gifts of the breadth of the church of Christ, and prizes the words and songs we hold in common with other Christians. At the same time, it treasures and extends the particular accents of our Lutheran inheritance as gifts to the whole church.

Evangelical Lutheran Worship is the title of this book, but *Evangelical Lutheran Worship* is much more than this book. The pew edition stands alongside a leaders edition and musical accompaniment editions in print, all of which are needed in order for this worship book to be used to its fullest. Beyond these related volumes, *Evangelical Lutheran Worship* is also the beginning of an unfolding family of resources in forms reflecting an evolving variety of media, intended to respond to the developing needs of the church in mission.

Supporting this mission of the church, which is the mission of God in Christ for the world, is an ultimate goal of *Evangelical Lutheran Worship.* Through liturgy and song the people of God participate in that mission, for here God comes with good news to save. And through liturgy and song, God nourishes us for that mission and goes with us to bear the creative and redeeming Word of God, Jesus Christ, to the whole world.

Evangelical Lutheran Worship is the outcome of efforts toward the renewal of worship that have taken place over a decade and more. Extensive study and conversation led to statements on the practice of word and sacrament in both the Evangelical Lutheran Church in Canada (*Statement on Sacramental Practices,* 1991) and the Evangelical Lutheran Church in America (*The Use of the Means of Grace,* 1997). The preparation of supplemental and provisional resources has been accompanied by wide participation from across the churches in setting the direction and shaping the contents of a primary resource for renewing worship. In 2005 both church bodies affirmed the completion of *Evangelical Lutheran Worship* and commended its use.

May this book of the church, and the materials that support and extend it, be servants through which the Holy Spirit will call out the church, gather us around Jesus Christ in word and sacrament, and send us, enlivened, to share the good news of life in God.

General Notes

The arrangement of *Evangelical Lutheran Worship* reflects a pattern familiar to many worshipers. First are materials related to the church year. The orders of service follow, including integrated liturgical music. The numbering in this part of the book is at the bottom of each page, and red tabs at the outside edge of the pages divide the major sections.

The second part of the book consists of resources for assembly song. Psalms for singing are followed by other service music choices for the various services. The hymns are then arranged by categories beginning with the church year and continuing with thematic categories. Hymns intended for part-singing are presented with a singable harmony. Several national songs are appended at the end. The numbering in this part of the book uses large numerals at the top of each item: red numbers for the psalms, black numbers for the service music, hymns, and songs.

Additional resources include a daily lectionary, a description of the use of scripture in worship, and the Small Catechism of Martin Luther. Various indexes will be helpful especially to worship planners.

The orders of service in *Evangelical Lutheran Worship* identify the person leading worship as the *presiding minister*, when that person is normally an ordained pastor, and as the *leader*, when that person may be either lay or ordained. *Assisting ministers* are usually lay people who are selected to carry out other roles in worship, such as the readings and the prayers of intercession. The people gathered for worship are referred to as the *assembly*.

Throughout the services, notes in red italics are intended as helpful guides for worshipers and leaders. Some of these notes are instructions for worshipers' actions or postures. Recognizing that some individuals may not participate in these actions or postures, these notes describe the action of the assembly as a whole. So, for example, "the assembly sings" or "the assembly stands" are notes affirming what the whole body is doing on behalf of all who are gathered—even though the action may not be possible for some of us.

In the orders of service, the words that are spoken by a leader are in regular type. Words spoken by the assembly are in boldface type. When a particular service music item includes both a leader and an assembly part, the words are similarly distinguished. Otherwise, the words in regular type are sung by all.

The Church Year

Time is a gift of God's creation. People order time in various ways, often based on the rhythms of nature. The church organizes time by the church year. It tells the story of God, who is beyond time, acting in history—above all through the life, death, and resurrection of Jesus Christ.

All Sundays of the year are festivals of our Lord Jesus Christ. In a profound sense, Sunday—the first day and the eighth day of the week, the weekly celebration of the day of resurrection—is the primary Christian festival. Other principal festivals and observances are the Nativity of Our Lord and the Epiphany of Our Lord; Ash Wednesday and the days of Holy Week; the Three Days of Maundy Thursday, Good Friday, and the Resurrection of Our Lord; the Sundays of Easter, the Ascension of Our Lord, and the Day of Pentecost; and The Holy Trinity.

The church year includes the Christmas and Easter cycles of seasons and the periods of time after Epiphany and after Pentecost. The Christmas cycle begins with the first Sunday of Advent, four Sundays before December 25, and concludes with the Epiphany of Our Lord on January 6. The Easter cycle begins with Ash Wednesday forty days before Easter and concludes with the Day of Pentecost on the fiftieth day of Easter. The weekly progression of Sundays characterizes the Time after Epiphany and the Time after Pentecost.

Lesser festivals are additional days when we celebrate the life of Christ, the witness of those who accompanied and testified to him, and the gifts of God in the church. Commemorations illuminate various aspects of the church's life and mission through the lives of women and men who have followed Christ in succeeding generations.

The propers include scripture readings and other texts that are chosen to support the church year. Many Christian churches unite around a three-year set of Bible readings, the Revised Common Lectionary. Other propers include the prayer of the day. Additional prayers for assembly worship and devotional use are also located in this section.

Calendar

Sundays and Principal Festivals

Advent

First Sunday of Advent B*
Second Sunday of Advent B
Third Sunday of Advent B
Fourth Sunday of Advent B

Christmas

Nativity of Our Lord W
   Christmas Eve
   Christmas Day
First Sunday of Christmas W
Second Sunday of Christmas W
Epiphany of Our Lord W

Time after Epiphany

Baptism of Our Lord W
   First Sunday after Epiphany
Sundays after Epiphany G
Transfiguration of Our Lord W
   Last Sunday after Epiphany

Lent

Ash Wednesday P
First Sunday in Lent P
Second Sunday in Lent P
Third Sunday in Lent P
Fourth Sunday in Lent P
Fifth Sunday in Lent P
Sunday of the Passion S/P
   Palm Sunday

Monday in Holy Week S/P
Tuesday in Holy Week S/P
Wednesday in Holy Week S/P

The Three Days

Maundy Thursday S/W
Good Friday
Resurrection of Our Lord W/Go
   Vigil of Easter
   Easter Day

Easter

Resurrection of Our Lord W/Go
Second Sunday of Easter W
Third Sunday of Easter W
Fourth Sunday of Easter W
Fifth Sunday of Easter W
Sixth Sunday of Easter W
Ascension of Our Lord W
Seventh Sunday of Easter W
Pentecost R
   Vigil of Pentecost
   Day of Pentecost

Time after Pentecost

The Holy Trinity W
   First Sunday after Pentecost
Sundays after Pentecost G
Christ the King W
   Last Sunday after Pentecost G

*The letters indicate the suggested colors: B=blue, W=white, G=green, P=purple, S=scarlet, Go=gold, R=red.

Lesser Festivals and Commemorations

January

- **1** NAME OF JESUS* W
- **2** Johann Konrad Wilhelm Loehe, renewer of the church, 1872 W
- **15** Martin Luther King Jr., renewer of society, martyr, 1968 S/R
- **17** Antony of Egypt, renewer of the church, c. 356 W
  Pachomius, renewer of the church, 346 W
- **18** CONFESSION OF PETER W
  Week of Prayer for Christian Unity begins
- **19** Henry, Bishop of Uppsala, martyr, 1156 S/R
- **21** Agnes, martyr, c. 304 S/R
- **25** CONVERSION OF PAUL W
  Week of Prayer for Christian Unity ends
- **26** Timothy, Titus, and Silas, missionaries W
- **27** Lydia, Dorcas, and Phoebe, witnesses to the faith W
- **28** Thomas Aquinas, teacher, 1274 W

February

- **2** PRESENTATION OF OUR LORD W
- **3** Ansgar, Bishop of Hamburg, missionary to Denmark and Sweden, 865 W
- **5** The Martyrs of Japan, 1597 S/R
- **14** Cyril, monk, 869; Methodius, bishop, 885; missionaries to the Slavs W
- **18** Martin Luther, renewer of the church, 1546 W
- **23** Polycarp, Bishop of Smyrna, martyr, 156 S/R
- **25** Elizabeth Fedde, deaconess, 1921 W

March

- **1** George Herbert, hymnwriter, 1633 W
- **2** John Wesley, 1791; Charles Wesley, 1788; renewers of the church W
- **7** Perpetua and Felicity and companions, martyrs at Carthage, 202 S/R
- **10** Harriet Tubman, 1913; Sojourner Truth, 1883; renewers of society W
- **12** Gregory the Great, Bishop of Rome, 604 W
- **17** Patrick, bishop, missionary to Ireland, 461 W
- **19** JOSEPH, GUARDIAN OF JESUS W

- **21** Thomas Cranmer, Bishop of Canterbury, martyr, 1556 S/R
- **22** Jonathan Edwards, teacher, missionary to American Indians, 1758 W
- **24** Oscar Arnulfo Romero, Bishop of El Salvador, martyr, 1980 S/R
- **25** ANNUNCIATION OF OUR LORD W
- **29** Hans Nielsen Hauge, renewer of the church, 1824 W
- **31** John Donne, poet, 1631 W

April

- **4** Benedict the African, confessor, 1589 W
- **6** Albrecht Dürer, 1528; Matthias Grünewald, 1529; Lucas Cranach, 1553; artists W
- **9** Dietrich Bonhoeffer, theologian, 1945 W
- **10** Mikael Agricola, Bishop of Turku, 1557 W
- **19** Olavus Petri, priest, 1552; Laurentius Petri, Bishop of Uppsala, 1573; renewers of the church W
- **21** Anselm, Bishop of Canterbury, 1109 W
- **23** Toyohiko Kagawa, renewer of society, 1960 W
- **25** MARK, EVANGELIST S/R
- **29** Catherine of Siena, theologian, 1380 W

May

- **1** PHILIP AND JAMES, APOSTLES S/R
- **2** Athanasius, Bishop of Alexandria, 373 W
- **4** Monica, mother of Augustine, 387 W
- **8** Julian of Norwich, renewer of the church, c. 1416 W
- **9** Nicolaus Ludwig von Zinzendorf, renewer of the church, hymnwriter, 1760 W
- **14** MATTHIAS, APOSTLE S/R
- **18** Erik, King of Sweden, martyr, 1160 S/R
- **21** Helena, mother of Constantine, c. 330 W
- **24** Nicolaus Copernicus, 1543; Leonhard Euler, 1783; scientists W
- **27** John Calvin, renewer of the church, 1564 W
- **29** Jiři Tranovský, hymnwriter, 1637 W
- **31** VISIT OF MARY TO ELIZABETH W

Lesser festivals are listed in small capital letters. The other listings are commemorations. Dates after names indicate year of death.

June

1 Justin, martyr at Rome, c. 165 S/R
3 The Martyrs of Uganda, 1886 S/R
  John XXIII, Bishop of Rome, 1963 W
5 Boniface, Bishop of Mainz, missionary to
  Germany, martyr, 754 S/R
7 Seattle, chief of the Duwamish
  Confederacy, 1866 W
9 Columba, 597; Aidan, 651; Bede, 735;
  renewers of the church W
11 BARNABAS, APOSTLE S/R
14 Basil the Great, Bishop of Caesarea, 379 W
  Gregory, Bishop of Nyssa, c. 385 W
  Gregory of Nazianzus, Bishop of
  Constantinople, c. 389 W
  Macrina, teacher, c. 379 W
21 Onesimos Nesib, translator, evangelist,
  1931 W
24 JOHN THE BAPTIST W
25 Presentation of the Augsburg Confession,
  1530 W
  Philipp Melanchthon, renewer of the
  church, 1560 W
27 Cyril, Bishop of Alexandria, 444 W
28 Irenaeus, Bishop of Lyons, c. 202 W
29 PETER AND PAUL, APOSTLES S/R

July

1 Catherine Winkworth, 1878; John Mason
  Neale, 1866; hymn translators W
3 THOMAS, APOSTLE S/R
6 Jan Hus, martyr, 1415 S/R
11 Benedict of Nursia, Abbot of Monte
  Cassino, c. 540 W
12 Nathan Söderblom, Bishop of Uppsala,
  1931 W
17 Bartolomé de Las Casas, missionary to the
  Indies, 1566 W
22 MARY MAGDALENE, APOSTLE W
23 Birgitta of Sweden, renewer of the church,
  1373 W
25 JAMES, APOSTLE S/R
28 Johann Sebastian Bach, 1750; Heinrich
  Schütz, 1672; George Frederick Handel,
  1759; musicians W
29 Mary, Martha, and Lazarus of Bethany W
  Olaf, King of Norway, martyr, 1030 S/R

August

8 Dominic, founder of the Order of
  Preachers (Dominicans), 1221 W
10 Lawrence, deacon, martyr, 258 S/R
11 Clare, Abbess of San Damiano, 1253 W
13 Florence Nightingale, 1910; Clara Maass,
  1901; renewers of society W
14 Maximilian Kolbe, 1941; Kaj Munk, 1944;
  martyrs S/R
15 MARY, MOTHER OF OUR LORD W
20 Bernard, Abbot of Clairvaux, 1153 W
24 BARTHOLOMEW, APOSTLE S/R
28 Augustine, Bishop of Hippo, 430 W
  Moses the Black, monk, martyr, c. 400 S/R

September

2 Nikolai Frederik Severin Grundtvig,
  bishop, renewer of the church, 1872 W
9 Peter Claver, priest, missionary to
  Colombia, 1654 W
13 John Chrysostom, Bishop of
  Constantinople, 407 W
14 HOLY CROSS DAY S/R
16 Cyprian, Bishop of Carthage, martyr,
  c. 258 S/R
17 Hildegard, Abbess of Bingen, 1179 W
18 Dag Hammarskjöld, renewer of society,
  1961 W
21 MATTHEW, APOSTLE AND EVANGELIST S/R
29 MICHAEL AND ALL ANGELS W
30 Jerome, translator, teacher, 420 W

October

4 Francis of Assisi, renewer of the church,
  1226 W
  Theodor Fliedner, renewer of society,
  1864 W
6 William Tyndale, translator, martyr,
  1536 S/R
7 Henry Melchior Muhlenberg, pastor in
  North America, 1787 W
15 Teresa of Avila, teacher, renewer of the
  church, 1582 W
17 Ignatius, Bishop of Antioch, martyr,
  c. 115 S/R
18 LUKE, EVANGELIST S/R
23 James of Jerusalem, martyr, c. 62 S/R

26 Philipp Nicolai, 1608; Johann
   Heermann, 1647; Paul Gerhardt, 1676;
   hymnwriters W
28 SIMON AND JUDE, APOSTLES S/R
31 REFORMATION DAY R

24 Justus Falckner, 1723; Jehu Jones, 1852;
   William Passavant, 1894; pastors in
   North America W
25 Isaac Watts, hymnwriter, 1748 W
30 ANDREW, APOSTLE S/R

November

1 ALL SAINTS DAY W
3 Martín de Porres, renewer of society,
   1639 W
7 John Christian Frederick Heyer, 1873;
   Bartholomaeus Ziegenbalg, 1719;
   Ludwig Nommensen, 1918;
   missionaries W
11 Martin, Bishop of Tours, 397 W
   Søren Aabye Kierkegaard, teacher,
   1855 W
17 Elizabeth of Hungary, renewer of society,
   1231 W
23 Clement, Bishop of Rome, c. 100 W
   Miguel Agustín Pro, martyr, 1927 S/R

December

3 Francis Xavier, missionary to Asia,
   1552 W
4 John of Damascus, theologian and
   hymnwriter, c. 749 W
6 Nicholas, Bishop of Myra, c. 342 W
7 Ambrose, Bishop of Milan, 397 W
13 Lucy, martyr, 304 S/R
14 John of the Cross, renewer of the church,
   1591 W
20 Katharina von Bora Luther, renewer of
   the church, 1552 W
26 STEPHEN, DEACON AND MARTYR S/R
27 JOHN, APOSTLE AND EVANGELIST W
28 THE HOLY INNOCENTS, MARTYRS S/R

Propers

Sundays and Principal Festivals

Advent

First Sunday of Advent

A

Isaiah 2:1-5
Psalm 122 (1)*
Romans 13:11-14
Matthew 24:36-44

Stir up your power, Lord Christ, and come. By your merciful protection save us from the threatening dangers of our sins, and enlighten our walk in the way of your salvation, for you live and reign with the Father and the Holy Spirit, one God, now and forever. **Amen.**

B

Isaiah 64:1-9
Psalm 80:1-7, 17-19 (7)
1 Corinthians 1:3-9
Mark 13:24-37

Stir up your power, Lord Christ, and come. By your merciful protection awaken us to the threatening dangers of our sins, and keep us blameless until the coming of your new day, for you live and reign with the Father and the Holy Spirit, one God, now and forever. **Amen.**

C

Jeremiah 33:14-16
Psalm 25:1-10 (1)
1 Thessalonians 3:9-13
Luke 21:25-36

Stir up your power, Lord Christ, and come. By your merciful protection alert us to the threatening dangers of our sins, and redeem us for your life of justice, for you live and reign with the Father and the Holy Spirit, one God, now and forever. **Amen.**

Second Sunday of Advent

A

Isaiah 11:1-10
Psalm 72:1-7, 18-19 (7)
Romans 15:4-13
Matthew 3:1-12

Stir up our hearts, Lord God, to prepare the way of your only Son. By his coming nurture our growth as people of repentance and peace; through Jesus Christ, our Savior and Lord, who lives and reigns with you and the Holy Spirit, one God, now and forever. **Amen.**

*The appointed psalm refrain is from the verse in parentheses.

B

Isaiah 40:1-11
Psalm 85:1-2, 8-13 (13)
2 Peter 3:8-15a
Mark 1:1-8

Stir up our hearts, Lord God, to prepare the way of your only Son. By his coming strengthen us to serve you with purified lives; through Jesus Christ, our Savior and Lord, who lives and reigns with you and the Holy Spirit, one God, now and forever. **Amen.**

C

Malachi 3:1-4
or Baruch 5:1-9
Luke 1:68-79 (78)
Philippians 1:3-11
Luke 3:1-6

Stir up our hearts, Lord God, to prepare the way of your only Son. By his coming give to all the people of the world knowledge of your salvation; through Jesus Christ, our Savior and Lord, who lives and reigns with you and the Holy Spirit, one God, now and forever. **Amen.**

Third Sunday of Advent

A

Isaiah 35:1-10
Psalm 146:5-10 (8)
or Luke 1: 46b-55 (47)
James 5:7-10
Matthew 11:2-11

Stir up the wills of all who look to you, Lord God, and strengthen our faith in your coming, that, transformed by grace, we may walk in your way; through Jesus Christ, our Savior and Lord, who lives and reigns with you and the Holy Spirit, one God, now and forever. **Amen.**

B

Isaiah 61:1-4, 8-11
Psalm 126 (3)
or Luke 1: 46b-55 (52)
1 Thessalonians 5:16-24
John 1:6-8, 19-28

Stir up the wills of your faithful people, Lord God, and open our ears to the words of your prophets, that, anointed by your Spirit, we may testify to your light; through Jesus Christ, our Savior and Lord, who lives and reigns with you and the Holy Spirit, one God, now and forever. **Amen.**

C

Zephaniah 3:14-20
Isaiah 12:2-6 (6)
Philippians 4:4-7
Luke 3:7-18

Stir up the wills of your faithful people, Lord God, and open our ears to the preaching of John, that, rejoicing in your salvation, we may bring forth the fruits of repentance; through Jesus Christ, our Savior and Lord, who lives and reigns with you and the Holy Spirit, one God, now and forever. **Amen.**

Fourth Sunday of Advent

A

Isaiah 7:10-16
Psalm 80:1-7, 17-19 (7)
Romans 1:1-7
Matthew 1:18-25

Stir up your power, Lord Christ, and come. With your abundant grace and might, free us from the sin that hinders our faith, that eagerly we may receive your promises, for you live and reign with the Father and the Holy Spirit, one God, now and forever. **Amen.**

B

2 Samuel 7:1-11, 16
Luke 1:46b-55 (52)
or Psalm 89:1-4, 19-26 (1)
Romans 16:25-27
Luke 1:26-38

Stir up your power, Lord Christ, and come. With your abundant grace and might, free us from the sin that would obstruct your mercy, that willingly we may bear your redeeming love to all the world, for you live and reign with the Father and the Holy Spirit, one God, now and forever. **Amen.**

C
Micah 5:2-5a
Luke 1:46b-55 (52)
or Psalm 80:1-7 (7)
Hebrews 10:5-10
Luke 1:39-45 [46-55]

Stir up your power, Lord Christ, and come. With your abundant grace and might, free us from the sin that binds us, that we may receive you in joy and serve you always, for you live and reign with the Father and the Holy Spirit, one God, now and forever. **Amen.**

Christmas

Nativity of Our Lord

A, B, C
I *Particularly appropriate for*
Christmas Eve
Isaiah 9:2-7
Psalm 96 (11)
Titus 2:11-14
Luke 2:1-14 [15-20]

Almighty God, you made this holy night shine with the brightness of the true Light. Grant that here on earth we may walk in the light of Jesus' presence and in the last day wake to the brightness of his glory; through your Son, Jesus Christ our Lord, who lives and reigns with you and the Holy Spirit, one God, now and forever. **Amen.**

A, B, C
II *Particularly appropriate for*
Christmas Day
Isaiah 62:6-12
Psalm 97 (11)
Titus 3:4-7
Luke 2:[1-7] 8-20

All-powerful and unseen God, the coming of your light into our world has brightened weary hearts with peace. Call us out of darkness, and empower us to proclaim the birth of your Son, Jesus Christ, our Savior and Lord, who lives and reigns with you and the Holy Spirit, one God, now and forever. **Amen.**

A, B, C
III *Particularly appropriate for*
Christmas Day
Isaiah 52:7-10
Psalm 98 (3)
Hebrews 1:1-4 [5-12]
John 1:1-14

Almighty God, you gave us your only Son to take on our human nature and to illumine the world with your light. By your grace adopt us as your children and enlighten us with your Spirit, through Jesus Christ, our Redeemer and Lord, who lives and reigns with you and the Holy Spirit, one God, now and forever. **Amen.**

First Sunday of Christmas

A
Isaiah 63:7-9
Psalm 148 (13)
Hebrews 2:10-18
Matthew 2:13-23

O Lord God, you know that we cannot place our trust in our own powers. As you protected the infant Jesus, so defend us and all the needy from harm and adversity, through Jesus Christ, our Savior and Lord, who lives and reigns with you and the Holy Spirit, one God, now and forever. **Amen.**

B
Isaiah 61:10—62:3
Psalm 148 (13)
Galatians 4:4-7
Luke 2:22-40

Almighty God, you wonderfully created the dignity of human nature and yet more wonderfully restored it. In your mercy, let us share the divine life of the one who came to share our humanity, Jesus Christ, your Son, our Lord, who lives and reigns with you and the Holy Spirit, one God, now and forever. **Amen.**

C

1 Samuel 2:18-20, 26
Psalm 148 (13)
Colossians 3:12-17
Luke 2:41-52

Shine into our hearts the light of your wisdom, O God, and open our minds to the knowledge of your word, that in all things we may think and act according to your good will and may live continually in the light of your Son, Jesus Christ, who lives and reigns with you and the Holy Spirit, one God, now and forever. **Amen.**

When January 1 falls on a Sunday, the Name of Jesus is normally celebrated on that day.

Second Sunday of Christmas

A, B, C

Jeremiah 31:7-14
or Sirach 24:1-12
Psalm 147:12-20 (12)
or Wisdom 10:15-21 (20)
Ephesians 1:3-14
John 1:[1-9] 10-18

Almighty God, you have filled all the earth with the light of your incarnate Word. By your grace empower us to reflect your light in all that we do, through Jesus Christ, our Savior and Lord, who lives and reigns with you and the Holy Spirit, one God, now and forever. **Amen.**

OR

O God our redeemer, you created light that we might live, and you illumine our world with your beloved Son. By your Spirit comfort us in all darkness, and turn us toward the light of Jesus Christ our Savior, who lives and reigns with you and the Holy Spirit, one God, now and forever. **Amen.**

Epiphany of Our Lord

If celebration of the Epiphany of Our Lord is not possible on January 6, it may be observed on the second Sunday of Christmas (January 2 or later). When January 6 falls on a Sunday, it is celebrated as the Epiphany of Our Lord.

A, B, C

Isaiah 60:1-6
Psalm 72:1-7, 10-14 (11)
Ephesians 3:1-12
Matthew 2:1-12

O God, on this day you revealed your Son to the nations by the leading of a star. Lead us now by faith to know your presence in our lives, and bring us at last to the full vision of your glory, through your Son, Jesus Christ our Lord, who lives and reigns with you and the Holy Spirit, one God, now and forever. **Amen.**

OR

Almighty and ever-living God, you revealed the incarnation of your Son by the brilliant shining of a star. Shine the light of your justice always in our hearts and over all lands, and accept our lives as the treasure we offer in your praise and for your service, through Jesus Christ, our Savior and Lord, who lives and reigns with you and the Holy Spirit, one God, now and forever. **Amen.**

OR

Everlasting God, the radiance of all faithful people, you brought the nations to the brightness of your rising. Fill the world with your glory, and show yourself to all the world through him who is the true light and the bright morning star, your Son, Jesus Christ, our Savior and Lord, who lives and reigns with you and the Holy Spirit, one God, now and forever. **Amen.**

Time after Epiphany

The lectionary number refers to the appointed set of lectionary readings and propers, ordered in sequence beginning with the Sundays in the Time after Epiphany and continuing again in the Time after Pentecost.

Baptism of Our Lord

First Sunday after Epiphany   Sunday, January 7–13   Lectionary 1

A

Isaiah 42:1-9
Psalm 29 (3)
Acts 10:34-43
Matthew 3:13-17

O God our Father, at the baptism of Jesus you proclaimed him your beloved Son and anointed him with the Holy Spirit. Make all who are baptized into Christ faithful to their calling to be your daughters and sons, and empower us all with your Spirit, through Jesus Christ, our Savior and Lord, who lives and reigns with you and the Holy Spirit, one God, now and forever. **Amen.**

B

Genesis 1:1-5
Psalm 29 (3)
Acts 19:1-7
Mark 1:4-11

Holy God, creator of light and giver of goodness, your voice moves over the waters. Immerse us in your grace, and transform us by your Spirit, that we may follow after your Son, Jesus Christ, our Savior and Lord, who lives and reigns with you and the Holy Spirit, one God, now and forever. **Amen.**

C

Isaiah 43:1-7
Psalm 29 (3)
Acts 8:14-17
Luke 3:15-17, 21-22

Almighty God, you anointed Jesus at his baptism with the Holy Spirit and revealed him as your beloved Son. Keep all who are born of water and the Spirit faithful in your service, that we may rejoice to be called children of God, through Jesus Christ, our Savior and Lord, who lives and reigns with you and the Holy Spirit, one God, now and forever. **Amen.**

Second Sunday after Epiphany

Sunday, January 14–20   Lectionary 2

A

Isaiah 49:1-7
Psalm 40:1-11 (8)
1 Corinthians 1:1-9
John 1:29-42

Holy God, our strength and our redeemer, by your Spirit hold us forever, that through your grace we may worship you and faithfully serve you, follow you and joyfully find you, through Jesus Christ, our Savior and Lord. **Amen.**

B

1 Samuel 3:1-10 [11-20]
Psalm 139:1-6, 13-18 (1)
1 Corinthians 6:12-20
John 1:43-51

Thanks be to you, Lord Jesus Christ, most merciful redeemer, for the countless blessings and benefits you give. May we know you more clearly, love you more dearly, and follow you more nearly, day by day praising you, with the Father and the Holy Spirit, one God, now and forever. **Amen.**

C

Isaiah 62:1-5
Psalm 36:5-10 (8)
1 Corinthians 12:1-11
John 2:1-11

Lord God, source of every blessing, you showed forth your glory and led many to faith by the works of your Son, who brought gladness and salvation to his people. Transform us by the Spirit of his love, that we may find our life together in him, Jesus Christ, our Savior and Lord. **Amen.**

Third Sunday after Epiphany

Sunday, January 21–27   Lectionary 3

A

Isaiah 9:1-4
Psalm 27:1, 4-9 (1)
1 Corinthians 1:10-18
Matthew 4:12-23

Lord God, your lovingkindness always goes before us and follows after us. Summon us into your light, and direct our steps in the ways of goodness that come through the cross of your Son, Jesus Christ, our Savior and Lord. **Amen.**

B

Jonah 3:1-5, 10
Psalm 62:5-12 (6)
1 Corinthians 7:29-31
Mark 1:14-20

Almighty God, by grace alone you call us and accept us in your service. Strengthen us by your Spirit, and make us worthy of your call, through Jesus Christ, our Savior and Lord. **Amen.**

C

Nehemiah 8:1-3, 5-6, 8-10
Psalm 19 (7)
1 Corinthians 12:12-31a
Luke 4:14-21

Blessed Lord God, you have caused the holy scriptures to be written for the nourishment of your people. Grant that we may hear them, read, mark, learn, and inwardly digest them, that, comforted by your promises, we may embrace and forever hold fast to the hope of eternal life, through your Son, Jesus Christ our Lord. **Amen.**

Fourth Sunday after Epiphany *(if before Transfiguration)*

Sunday, January 28–February 3   Lectionary 4

A

Micah 6:1-8
Psalm 15 (1)
1 Corinthians 1:18-31
Matthew 5:1-12

Holy God, you confound the world's wisdom in giving your kingdom to the lowly and the pure in heart. Give us such a hunger and thirst for justice, and perseverance in striving for peace, that in our words and deeds the world may see the life of your Son, Jesus Christ, our Savior and Lord. **Amen.**

B

Deuteronomy 18:15-20
Psalm 111 (10)
1 Corinthians 8:1-13
Mark 1:21-28

Compassionate God, you gather the whole universe into your radiant presence and continually reveal your Son as our Savior. Bring wholeness to all that is broken and speak truth to us in our confusion, that all creation will see and know your Son, Jesus Christ, our Savior and Lord. **Amen.**

C

Jeremiah 1:4-10
Psalm 71:1-6 (6)
1 Corinthians 13:1-13
Luke 4:21-30

Almighty and ever-living God, increase in us the gifts of faith, hope, and love; and that we may obtain what you promise, make us love what you command, through your Son, Jesus Christ, our Savior and Lord. **Amen.**

When February 2 falls on a Sunday, the Presentation of Our Lord is normally celebrated on that day.

Fifth Sunday after Epiphany *(if before Transfiguration)*

Sunday, February 4–10   Lectionary 5

A

Isaiah 58:1-9a [9b-12]
Psalm 112:1-9 [10] *(4)*
1 Corinthians 2:1-12 [13-16]
Matthew 5:13-20

Lord God, with endless mercy you receive the prayers of all who call upon you. By your Spirit show us the things we ought to do, and give us the grace and power to do them, through Jesus Christ, our Savior and Lord. **Amen.**

B

Isaiah 40:21-31
Psalm 147:1-11, 20c *(3)*
1 Corinthians 9:16-23
Mark 1:29-39

Everlasting God, you give strength to the weak and power to the faint. Make us agents of your healing and wholeness, that your good news may be made known to the ends of your creation, through Jesus Christ, our Savior and Lord. **Amen.**

C

Isaiah 6:1-8 [9-13]
Psalm 138 *(2)*
1 Corinthians 15:1-11
Luke 5:1-11

Most holy God, the earth is filled with your glory, and before you angels and saints stand in awe. Enlarge our vision to see your power at work in the world, and by your grace make us heralds of your Son, Jesus Christ, our Savior and Lord. **Amen.**

Sixth Sunday after Epiphany *(if before Transfiguration)*

Sunday, February 11–17   Lectionary 6

A

Deuteronomy 30:15-20
or Sirach 15:15-20
Psalm 119:1-8 *(1)*
1 Corinthians 3:1-9
Matthew 5:21-37

O God, the strength of all who hope in you, because we are weak mortals we accomplish nothing good without you. Help us to see and understand the things we ought to do, and give us grace and power to do them, through Jesus Christ, our Savior and Lord. **Amen.**

B

2 Kings 5:1-14
Psalm 30 *(2)*
1 Corinthians 9:24-27
Mark 1:40-45

Almighty and ever-living God, with mercy you look upon our weaknesses. Stretch out your wondrous hand to protect us from danger and restore us to health, through Jesus Christ, our Savior and Lord. **Amen.**

C

Jeremiah 17:5-10
Psalm 1 *(3)*
1 Corinthians 15:12-20
Luke 6:17-26

Living God, in Christ you make all things new. Transform the poverty of our nature by the riches of your grace, and in the renewal of our lives make known your glory, through Jesus Christ, our Savior and Lord. **Amen.**

Seventh Sunday after Epiphany *(if before Transfiguration)*

Sunday, February 18–24   Lectionary 7

A

Leviticus 19:1-2, 9-18
Psalm 119:33-40 *(33)*
1 Corinthians 3:10-11, 16-23
Matthew 5:38-48

Holy God of compassion, you invite us into your way of forgiveness and peace. Lead us to love our enemies, and transform our words and deeds to be like his through whom we pray, Jesus Christ, our Savior and Lord. **Amen.**

B

Isaiah 43:18-25
Psalm 41 (4)
2 Corinthians 1:18-22
Mark 2:1-12

Almighty God, in signs and wonders your Son revealed the greatness of your saving love. Renew us with your grace, and sustain us by your power, that we may stand in the glory of your name, through Jesus Christ, our Savior and Lord. **Amen.**

C

Genesis 45:3-11, 15
Psalm 37:1-11, 39-40 (11)
1 Corinthians 15:35-38,
   42-50
Luke 6:27-38

O Lord Jesus, make us instruments of your peace, that where there is hatred, we may sow love, where there is injury, pardon, and where there is despair, hope. Grant, O divine master, that we may seek to console, to understand, and to love in your name, for you live and reign with the Father and the Holy Spirit, one God, now and forever. **Amen.**

Eighth Sunday after Epiphany *(if before Transfiguration)*

Sunday, February 25–March 1   Lectionary 8

A

Isaiah 49:8-16a
Psalm 131 (2)
1 Corinthians 4:1-5
Matthew 6:24-34

God of tender care, like a mother, like a father, you never forget your children, and you know already what we need. In all our anxiety give us trusting and faithful hearts, that in confidence we may embody the peace and justice of your Son, Jesus Christ, our Savior and Lord. **Amen.**

B

Hosea 2:14-20
Psalm 103:1-13, 22 (8)
2 Corinthians 3:1-6
Mark 2:13-22

Loving God, by tender words and covenant promise you have joined us to yourself forever, and you invite us to respond to your love with faithfulness. By your Spirit may we live with you and with one another in justice, mercy, and joy, through Jesus Christ, our Savior and Lord. **Amen.**

C

Isaiah 55:10-13
or Sirach 27:4-7
Psalm 92:1-4, 12-15 (12)
1 Corinthians 15:51-58
Luke 6:39-49

O God our rock, your word brings life to the whole creation and salvation from sin and death. Nourish our faith in your promises, and ground us in your strength, through Jesus Christ, our Savior and Lord. **Amen.**

Transfiguration of Our Lord

Last Sunday after Epiphany

A

Exodus 24:12-18
Psalm 2 (7)
or Psalm 99 (9)
2 Peter 1:16-21
Matthew 17:1-9

O God, in the transfiguration of your Son you confirmed the mysteries of the faith by the witness of Moses and Elijah, and in the voice from the bright cloud declaring Jesus your beloved Son, you foreshadowed our adoption as your children. Make us heirs with Christ of your glory, and bring us to enjoy its fullness, through Jesus Christ, our Savior and Lord, who lives and reigns with you and the Holy Spirit, one God, now and forever. **Amen.**

B

2 Kings 2:1-12
Psalm 50:1-6 (2)
2 Corinthians 4:3-6
Mark 9:2-9

Almighty God, the resplendent light of your truth shines from the mountaintop into our hearts. Transfigure us by your beloved Son, and illumine the world with your image, through Jesus Christ, our Savior and Lord, who lives and reigns with you and the Holy Spirit, one God, now and forever. **Amen.**

C

Exodus 34:29-35
Psalm 99 (9)
2 Corinthians 3:12—4:2
Luke 9:28-36 [37-43]

Holy God, mighty and immortal, you are beyond our knowing, yet we see your glory in the face of Jesus Christ. Transform us into the likeness of your Son, who renewed our humanity so that we may share in his divinity, Jesus Christ our Lord, who lives and reigns with you and the Holy Spirit, one God, now and forever. **Amen.**

Lent

Ash Wednesday

A, B, C
Joel 2:1-2, 12-17
or Isaiah 58:1-12
Psalm 51:1-17 (1)
2 Corinthians 5:20b—6:10
Matthew 6:1-6, 16-21

Almighty and ever-living God, you hate nothing you have made, and you forgive the sins of all who are penitent. Create in us new and honest hearts, so that, truly repenting of our sins, we may receive from you, the God of all mercy, full pardon and forgiveness through your Son, Jesus Christ, our Savior and Lord, who lives and reigns with you and the Holy Spirit, one God, now and forever. **Amen.**

OR

Gracious God, out of your love and mercy you breathed into dust the breath of life, creating us to serve you and our neighbors. Call forth our prayers and acts of kindness, and strengthen us to face our mortality with confidence in the mercy of your Son, Jesus Christ, our Savior and Lord, who lives and reigns with you and the Holy Spirit, one God, now and forever. **Amen.**

First Sunday in Lent

A
Genesis 2:15-17; 3:1-7
Psalm 32 (10)
Romans 5:12-19
Matthew 4:1-11

Lord God, our strength, the struggle between good and evil rages within and around us, and the devil and all the forces that defy you tempt us with empty promises. Keep us steadfast in your word, and when we fall, raise us again and restore us through your Son, Jesus Christ, our Savior and Lord, who lives and reigns with you and the Holy Spirit, one God, now and forever. **Amen.**

B

Genesis 9:8-17
Psalm 25:1-10 (10)
1 Peter 3:18-22
Mark 1:9-15

Holy God, heavenly Father, in the waters of the flood you saved the chosen, and in the wilderness of temptation you protected your Son from sin. Renew us in the gift of baptism. May your holy angels be with us, that the wicked foe may have no power over us, through Jesus Christ, our Savior and Lord, who lives and reigns with you and the Holy Spirit, one God, now and forever. **Amen.**

C

Deuteronomy 26:1-11
Psalm 91:1-2, 9-16 (11)
Romans 10:8b-13
Luke 4:1-13

O Lord God, you led your people through the wilderness and brought them to the promised land. Guide us now, so that, following your Son, we may walk safely through the wilderness of this world toward the life you alone can give, through Jesus Christ, our Savior and Lord, who lives and reigns with you and the Holy Spirit, one God, now and forever. **Amen.**

Second Sunday in Lent

A

Genesis 12:1-4a
Psalm 121 (1, 2)
Romans 4:1-5, 13-17
John 3:1-17

O God, our leader and guide, in the waters of baptism you bring us to new birth to live as your children. Strengthen our faith in your promises, that by your Spirit we may lift up your life to all the world through your Son, Jesus Christ, our Savior and Lord, who lives and reigns with you and the Holy Spirit, one God, now and forever. **Amen.**

B

Genesis 17:1-7, 15-16
Psalm 22:23-31 (27)
Romans 4:13-25
Mark 8:31-38

O God, by the passion of your blessed Son you made an instrument of shameful death to be for us the means of life. Grant us so to glory in the cross of Christ that we may gladly suffer shame and loss for the sake of your Son, Jesus Christ, our Savior and Lord, who lives and reigns with you and the Holy Spirit, one God, now and forever. **Amen.**

C

Genesis 15:1-12, 17-18
Psalm 27 (5)
Philippians 3:17—4:1
Luke 13:31-35

God of the covenant, in the mystery of the cross you promise everlasting life to the world. Gather all peoples into your arms, and shelter us with your mercy, that we may rejoice in the life we share in your Son, Jesus Christ, our Savior and Lord, who lives and reigns with you and the Holy Spirit, one God, now and forever. **Amen.**

Third Sunday in Lent

A

Exodus 17:1-7
Psalm 95 (1)
Romans 5:1-11
John 4:5-42

Merciful God, the fountain of living water, you quench our thirst and wash away our sin. Give us this water always. Bring us to drink from the well that flows with the beauty of your truth through Jesus Christ, our Savior and Lord, who lives and reigns with you and the Holy Spirit, one God, now and forever. **Amen.**

B

Exodus 20:1-17
Psalm 19 *(8)*
1 Corinthians 1:18-25
John 2:13-22

Holy God, through your Son you have called us to live faithfully and act courageously. Keep us steadfast in your covenant of grace, and teach us the wisdom that comes only through Jesus Christ, our Savior and Lord, who lives and reigns with you and the Holy Spirit, one God, now and forever. **Amen.**

C

Isaiah 55:1-9
Psalm 63:1-8 *(1)*
1 Corinthians 10:1-13
Luke 13:1-9

Eternal God, your kingdom has broken into our troubled world through the life, death, and resurrection of your Son. Help us to hear your word and obey it, and bring your saving love to fruition in our lives, through Jesus Christ, our Savior and Lord, who lives and reigns with you and the Holy Spirit, one God, now and forever. **Amen.**

Fourth Sunday in Lent

A

1 Samuel 16:1-13
Psalm 23 *(5)*
Ephesians 5:8-14
John 9:1-41

Bend your ear to our prayers, Lord Christ, and come among us. By your gracious life and death for us, bring light into the darkness of our hearts, and anoint us with your Spirit, for you live and reign with the Father and the Holy Spirit, one God, now and forever. **Amen.**

B

Numbers 21:4-9
Psalm 107:1-3, 17-22 *(19)*
Ephesians 2:1-10
John 3:14-21

O God, rich in mercy, by the humiliation of your Son you lifted up this fallen world and rescued us from the hopelessness of death. Lead us into your light, that all our deeds may reflect your love, through Jesus Christ, our Savior and Lord, who lives and reigns with you and the Holy Spirit, one God, now and forever. **Amen.**

C

Joshua 5:9-12
Psalm 32 *(11)*
2 Corinthians 5:16-21
Luke 15:1-3, 11b-32

God of compassion, you welcome the wayward, and you embrace us all with your mercy. By our baptism clothe us with garments of your grace, and feed us at the table of your love, through Jesus Christ, our Savior and Lord, who lives and reigns with you and the Holy Spirit, one God, now and forever. **Amen.**

Fifth Sunday in Lent

A

Ezekiel 37:1-14
Psalm 130 *(5)*
Romans 8:6-11
John 11:1-45

Almighty God, your Son came into the world to free us all from sin and death. Breathe upon us the power of your Spirit, that we may be raised to new life in Christ and serve you in righteousness all our days, through Jesus Christ, our Savior and Lord, who lives and reigns with you and the Holy Spirit, one God, now and forever. **Amen.**

B

Jeremiah 31:31-34
Psalm 51:1-12 (10)
  or Psalm 119:9-16 (11)
Hebrews 5:5-10
John 12:20-33

O God, with steadfast love you draw us to yourself, and in mercy you receive our prayers. Strengthen us to bring forth the fruits of the Spirit, that through life and death we may live in your Son, Jesus Christ, our Savior and Lord, who lives and reigns with you and the Holy Spirit, one God, now and forever. **Amen.**

C

Isaiah 43:16-21
Psalm 126 (5)
Philippians 3:4b-14
John 12:1-8

Creator God, you prepare a new way in the wilderness, and your grace waters our desert. Open our hearts to be transformed by the new thing you are doing, that our lives may proclaim the extravagance of your love given to all through your Son, Jesus Christ, our Savior and Lord, who lives and reigns with you and the Holy Spirit, one God, now and forever. **Amen.**

Sunday of the Passion

Palm Sunday

A
Procession with Palms
Matthew 21:1-11

Isaiah 50:4-9a
Psalm 31:9-16 (5)
Philippians 2:5-11
Matthew 26:14—27:66
  or Matthew 27:11-54

A, B, C

Everlasting God, in your endless love for the human race you sent our Lord Jesus Christ to take on our nature and to suffer death on the cross. In your mercy enable us to share in his obedience to your will and in the glorious victory of his resurrection, who lives and reigns with you and the Holy Spirit, one God, now and forever. **Amen.**

B
Procession with Palms
Mark 11:1-11
  or John 12:12-16

Isaiah 50:4-9a
Psalm 31:9-16 (5)
Philippians 2:5-11
Mark 14:1—15:47
  or Mark 15:1-39 [40-47]

OR

Sovereign God, you have established your rule in the human heart through the servanthood of Jesus Christ. By your Spirit, keep us in the joyful procession of those who with their tongues confess Jesus as Lord and with their lives praise him as Savior, who lives and reigns with you and the Holy Spirit, one God, now and forever. **Amen.**

C
Procession with Palms
Luke 19:28-40

Isaiah 50:4-9a
Psalm 31:9-16 (5)
Philippians 2:5-11
Luke 22:14—23:56
  or Luke 23:1-49

OR

O God of mercy and might, in the mystery of the passion of your Son you offer your infinite life to the world. Gather us around the cross of Christ, and preserve us until the resurrection, through Jesus Christ, our Savior and Lord, who lives and reigns with you and the Holy Spirit, one God, now and forever. **Amen.**

Monday in Holy Week

A, B, C

Isaiah 42:1-9
Psalm 36:5-11 (7)
Hebrews 9:11-15
John 12:1-11

O God, your Son chose the path that led to pain before joy and to the cross before glory. Plant his cross in our hearts, so that in its power and love we may come at last to joy and glory, through Jesus Christ, our Savior and Lord, who lives and reigns with you and the Holy Spirit, one God, now and forever. **Amen.**

Tuesday in Holy Week

A, B, C

Isaiah 49:1-7
Psalm 71:1-14 (6)
1 Corinthians 1:18-31
John 12:20-36

Lord Jesus, you have called us to follow you. Grant that our love may not grow cold in your service, and that we may not fail or deny you in the time of trial, for you live and reign with the Father and the Holy Spirit, one God, now and forever. **Amen.**

Wednesday in Holy Week

A, B, C

Isaiah 50:4-9a
Psalm 70 (1)
Hebrews 12:1-3
John 13:21-32

Almighty God, your Son our Savior suffered at human hands and endured the shame of the cross. Grant that we may walk in the way of his cross and find it the way of life and peace, through Jesus Christ, our Savior and Lord, who lives and reigns with you and the Holy Spirit, one God, now and forever. **Amen.**

The Three Days

Maundy Thursday

A, B, C

Exodus 12:1-4 [5-10] 11-14
Psalm 116:1-2, 12-19 (13)
1 Corinthians 11:23-26
John 13:1-17, 31b-35

Holy God, source of all love, on the night of his betrayal, Jesus gave us a new commandment, to love one another as he loves us. Write this commandment in our hearts, and give us the will to serve others as he was the servant of all, your Son, Jesus Christ, our Savior and Lord, who lives and reigns with you and the Holy Spirit, one God, now and forever. **Amen.**

OR

Eternal God, in the sharing of a meal your Son established a new covenant for all people, and in the washing of feet he showed us the dignity of service. Grant that by the power of your Holy Spirit these signs of our life in faith may speak again to our hearts, feed our spirits, and refresh our bodies, through Jesus Christ, our Savior and Lord, who lives and reigns with you and the Holy Spirit, one God, now and forever. **Amen.**

Good Friday

A, B, C

Isaiah 52:13—53:12
Psalm 22 *(1)*
Hebrews 10:16-25
or Hebrews 4:14-16; 5:7-9
John 18:1—19:42

Almighty God, look with loving mercy on your family, for whom our Lord Jesus Christ was willing to be betrayed, to be given over to the hands of sinners, and to suffer death on the cross; who now lives and reigns with you and the Holy Spirit, one God, forever and ever. **Amen.**

OR

Merciful God, your Son was lifted up on the cross to draw all people to himself. Grant that we who have been born out of his wounded side may at all times find mercy in him, Jesus Christ, our Savior and Lord, who lives and reigns with you and the Holy Spirit, one God, now and forever. **Amen.**

Resurrection of Our Lord

The Resurrection of Our Lord, the last of the Three Days, is also the first of the fifty days of Easter.

Vigil of Easter

A, B, C

See the list of vigil readings and responses, p. 269.
Romans 6:3-11
John 20:1-18

Eternal giver of life and light, this holy night shines with the radiance of the risen Christ. Renew your church with the Spirit given us in baptism, that we may worship you in sincerity and truth and may shine as a light in the world, through your Son, Jesus Christ our Lord, who lives and reigns with you and the Holy Spirit, one God, now and forever. **Amen.**

OR

O God, you are the creator of the world, the liberator of your people, and the wisdom of the earth. By the resurrection of your Son free us from our fears, restore us in your image, and ignite us with your light, through Jesus Christ, our Savior and Lord, who lives and reigns with you and the Holy Spirit, one God, now and forever. **Amen.**

Easter Day

A

Acts 10:34-43
or Jeremiah 31:1-6
Psalm 118:1-2, 14-24 *(24)*
Colossians 3:1-4
or Acts 10:34-43
Matthew 28:1-10
or John 20:1-18

A, B, C

O God, you gave your only Son to suffer death on the cross for our redemption, and by his glorious resurrection you delivered us from the power of death. Make us die every day to sin, that we may live with him forever in the joy of the resurrection, through your Son, Jesus Christ our Lord, who lives and reigns with you and the Holy Spirit, one God, now and forever. **Amen.**

B
Acts 10:34-43
or Isaiah 25:6-9
Psalm 118:1-2, 14-24 (24)
1 Corinthians 15:1-11
or Acts 10:34-43
Mark 16:1-8
or John 20:1-18

OR

God of mercy, we no longer look for Jesus among the dead, for he is alive and has become the Lord of life. Increase in our minds and hearts the risen life we share with Christ, and help us to grow as your people toward the fullness of eternal life with you, through Jesus Christ, our Savior and Lord, who lives and reigns with you and the Holy Spirit, one God, now and forever. **Amen.**

C
Acts 10:34-43
or Isaiah 65:17-25
Psalm 118:1-2, 14-24 (24)
1 Corinthians 15:19-26
or Acts 10:34-43
Luke 24:1-12
or John 20:1-18

The following propers may be used for a service on the evening of Easter Day.
A, B, C
Isaiah 25:6-9
Psalm 114 (7)
1 Corinthians 5:6b-8
Luke 24:13-49

O God, whose blessed Son made himself known to his disciples in the breaking of bread, open the eyes of our faith, that we may behold him in all his redeeming work, Jesus Christ, our Savior and Lord, who lives and reigns with you and the Holy Spirit, one God, now and forever. **Amen.**

Easter

The following propers may be used for a service on Easter Monday or on another day during Easter week.
A, B, C
Daniel 12:1-3
Psalm 16:8-11 (9)
Acts 2:14, 22b-32
Matthew 28:9-15a

Almighty God, you give us the joy of celebrating our Lord's resurrection. Give us also the joys of life in your service, and bring us at last to the full joy of life eternal, through Jesus Christ, our Savior and Lord, who lives and reigns with you and the Holy Spirit, one God, now and forever. **Amen.**

Second Sunday of Easter

A
Acts 2:14a, 22-32
Psalm 16 (11)
1 Peter 1:3-9
John 20:19-31

Almighty and eternal God, the strength of those who believe and the hope of those who doubt, may we, who have not seen, have faith in you and receive the fullness of Christ's blessing, who lives and reigns with you and the Holy Spirit, one God, now and forever. **Amen.**

B
Acts 4:32-35
Psalm 133 (1)
1 John 1:1—2:2
John 20:19-31

Almighty God, with joy we celebrate the day of our Lord's resurrection. By the grace of Christ among us, enable us to show the power of the resurrection in all that we say and do, through Jesus Christ, our Savior and Lord, who lives and reigns with you and the Holy Spirit, one God, now and forever. **Amen.**

C

Acts 5:27-32
Psalm 118:14-29 (28)
or Psalm 150 (6)
Revelation 1:4-8
John 20:19-31

O God of life, you reach out to us amid our fears with the wounded hands of your risen Son. By your Spirit's breath revive our faith in your mercy, and strengthen us to be the body of your Son, Jesus Christ, our Savior and Lord, who lives and reigns with you and the Holy Spirit, one God, now and forever. **Amen.**

Third Sunday of Easter

A

Acts 2:14a, 36-41
Psalm 116:1-4, 12-19 (13)
1 Peter 1:17-23
Luke 24:13-35

O God, your Son makes himself known to all his disciples in the breaking of bread. Open the eyes of our faith, that we may see him in his redeeming work, who lives and reigns with you and the Holy Spirit, one God, now and forever. **Amen.**

B

Acts 3:12-19
Psalm 4 (3)
1 John 3:1-7
Luke 24:36b-48

Holy and righteous God, you are the author of life, and you adopt us to be your children. Fill us with your words of life, that we may live as witnesses to the resurrection of your Son, Jesus Christ, our Savior and Lord, who lives and reigns with you and the Holy Spirit, one God, now and forever. **Amen.**

C

Acts 9:1-6 [7-20]
Psalm 30 (11)
Revelation 5:11-14
John 21:1-19

Eternal and all-merciful God, with all the angels and all the saints we laud your majesty and might. By the resurrection of your Son, show yourself to us and inspire us to follow Jesus Christ, our Savior and Lord, who lives and reigns with you and the Holy Spirit, one God, now and forever. **Amen.**

Fourth Sunday of Easter

A

Acts 2:42-47
Psalm 23 (1)
1 Peter 2:19-25
John 10:1-10

O God our shepherd, you know your sheep by name and lead us to safety through the valleys of death. Guide us by your voice, that we may walk in certainty and security to the joyous feast prepared in your house, through Jesus Christ, our Savior and Lord, who lives and reigns with you and the Holy Spirit, one God, now and forever. **Amen.**

B

Acts 4:5-12
Psalm 23 (1)
1 John 3:16-24
John 10:11-18

O Lord Christ, good shepherd of the sheep, you seek the lost and guide us into your fold. Feed us, and we shall be satisfied; heal us, and we shall be whole. Make us one with you, for you live and reign with the Father and the Holy Spirit, one God, now and forever. **Amen.**

C

Acts 9:36-43
Psalm 23 (1)
Revelation 7:9-17
John 10:22-30

O God of peace, you brought again from the dead our Lord Jesus Christ, the great shepherd of the sheep. By the blood of your eternal covenant, make us complete in everything good that we may do your will, and work among us all that is well-pleasing in your sight, through Jesus Christ, our Savior and Lord, who lives and reigns with you and the Holy Spirit, one God, now and forever. **Amen.**

Fifth Sunday of Easter

A

Acts 7:55-60
Psalm 31:1-5, 15-16 *(5)*
1 Peter 2:2-10
John 14:1-14

Almighty God, your Son Jesus Christ is the way, the truth, and the life. Give us grace to love one another, to follow in the way of his commandments, and to share his risen life with all the world, for he lives and reigns with you and the Holy Spirit, one God, now and forever. **Amen.**

B

Acts 8:26-40
Psalm 22:25-31 *(27)*
1 John 4:7-21
John 15:1-8

O God, you give us your Son as the vine apart from whom we cannot live. Nourish our life in his resurrection, that we may bear the fruit of love and know the fullness of your joy, through Jesus Christ, our Savior and Lord, who lives and reigns with you and the Holy Spirit, one God, now and forever. **Amen.**

C

Acts 11:1-18
Psalm 148 *(13)*
Revelation 21:1-6
John 13:31-35

O Lord God, you teach us that without love, our actions gain nothing. Pour into our hearts your most excellent gift of love, that, made alive by your Spirit, we may know goodness and peace, through your Son, Jesus Christ, our Savior and Lord, who lives and reigns with you and the Holy Spirit, one God, now and forever. **Amen.**

Sixth Sunday of Easter

A

Acts 17:22-31
Psalm 66:8-20 *(8)*
1 Peter 3:13-22
John 14:15-21

Almighty and ever-living God, you hold together all things in heaven and on earth. In your great mercy receive the prayers of all your children, and give to all the world the Spirit of your truth and peace, through Jesus Christ, our Savior and Lord, who lives and reigns with you and the Holy Spirit, one God, now and forever. **Amen.**

B

Acts 10:44-48
Psalm 98 *(4)*
1 John 5:1-6
John 15:9-17

O God, you have prepared for those who love you joys beyond understanding. Pour into our hearts such love for you that, loving you above all things, we may obtain your promises, which exceed all we can desire; through Jesus Christ, your Son and our Lord, who lives and reigns with you and the Holy Spirit, one God, now and forever. **Amen.**

C

Acts 16:9-15
Psalm 67 *(4)*
Revelation 21:10, 22—22:5
John 14:23-29
or John 5:1-9

Bountiful God, you gather your people into your realm, and you promise us food from your tree of life. Nourish us with your word, that empowered by your Spirit we may love one another and the world you have made, through Jesus Christ, our Savior and Lord, who lives and reigns with you and the Holy Spirit, one God, now and forever. **Amen.**

Ascension of Our Lord

A, B, C

Acts 1:1-11
Psalm 47 (5)
or Psalm 93 (2)
Ephesians 1:15-23
Luke 24:44-53

Almighty God, your only Son was taken into the heavens and in your presence intercedes for us. Receive us and our prayers for all the world, and in the end bring everything into your glory, through Jesus Christ, our Sovereign and Lord, who lives and reigns with you and the Holy Spirit, one God, now and forever. **Amen.**

OR

Almighty God, your blessed Son, our Savior Jesus Christ, ascended far above all heavens that he might fill all things. Mercifully give us faith to trust that, as he promised, he abides with us on earth to the end of time, who lives and reigns with you and the Holy Spirit, one God, now and forever. **Amen.**

Seventh Sunday of Easter

If the Ascension is not celebrated on the previous Thursday, it may be observed on this day.

A

Acts 1:6-14
Psalm 68:1-10, 32-35 (4)
1 Peter 4:12-14; 5:6-11
John 17:1-11

O God of glory, your Son Jesus Christ suffered for us and ascended to your right hand. Unite us with Christ and each other in suffering and in joy, that all the world may be drawn into your bountiful presence, through Jesus Christ, our Savior and Lord, who lives and reigns with you and the Holy Spirit, one God, now and forever. **Amen.**

B

Acts 1:15-17, 21-26
Psalm 1 (6)
1 John 5:9-13
John 17:6-19

Gracious and glorious God, you have chosen us as your own, and by the powerful name of Christ you protect us from evil. By your Spirit transform us and your beloved world, that we may find our joy in your Son, Jesus Christ, our Savior and Lord, who lives and reigns with you and the Holy Spirit, one God, now and forever. **Amen.**

C

Acts 16:16-34
Psalm 97 (12)
Revelation 22:12-14, 16-17,
    20-21
John 17:20-26

O God, form the minds of your faithful people into your one will. Make us love what you command and desire what you promise, that, amid all the changes of this world, our hearts may be fixed where true joy is found, your Son, Jesus Christ our Lord, who lives and reigns with you and the Holy Spirit, one God, now and forever. **Amen.**

Pentecost

Vigil of Pentecost

A, B, C

Exodus 19:1-9
or Acts 2:1-11
Psalm 33:12-22 (20)
or Psalm 130 (4)
Romans 8:14-17, 22-27
John 7:37-39

Almighty and ever-living God, you fulfilled the promise of Easter by sending the gift of your Holy Spirit. Look upon your people gathered in prayer, open to receive the Spirit's flame. May it come to rest in our hearts and heal the divisions of word and tongue, that with one voice and one song we may praise your name in joy and thanksgiving; through Jesus Christ, our Savior and Lord, who lives and reigns with you and the Holy Spirit, one God, now and forever. **Amen.**

Day of Pentecost

The fiftieth day of Easter

A

Acts 2:1-21
or Numbers 11:24-30
Psalm 104:24-34, 35b (30)
1 Corinthians 12:3b-13
or Acts 2:1-21
John 20:19-23
or John 7:37-39

O God, on this day you open the hearts of your faithful people by sending into us your Holy Spirit. Direct us by the light of that Spirit, that we may have a right judgment in all things and rejoice at all times in your peace, through Jesus Christ, your Son and our Lord, who lives and reigns with you and the Holy Spirit, one God, now and forever. **Amen.**

B

Acts 2:1-21
or Ezekiel 37:1-14
Psalm 104:24-34, 35b (30)
Romans 8:22-27
or Acts 2:1-21
John 15:26-27; 16:4b-15

Mighty God, you breathe life into our bones, and your Spirit brings truth to the world. Send us this Spirit, transform us by your truth, and give us language to proclaim your gospel, through Jesus Christ, our Savior and Lord, who lives and reigns with you and the Holy Spirit, one God, now and forever. **Amen.**

C

Acts 2:1-21
or Genesis 11:1-9
Psalm 104:24-34, 35b (30)
Romans 8:14-17
or Acts 2:1-21
John 14:8-17 [25-27]

God our creator, the resurrection of your Son offers life to all the peoples of earth. By your Holy Spirit, kindle in us the fire of your love, empowering our lives for service and our tongues for praise, through Jesus Christ, our Savior and Lord, who lives and reigns with you and the Holy Spirit, one God, now and forever. **Amen.**

Time after Pentecost

With the exception of The Holy Trinity, which is always celebrated on the first Sunday after Pentecost, the propers for the Sundays after Pentecost are determined by calendar date. The lectionary number refers to the appointed set of lectionary readings and propers, ordered in sequence beginning with the Sundays in the Time after Epiphany and continuing again in the Time after Pentecost.

Beginning with Lectionary 9, two series of readings are provided for each Sunday. In the first series, the Old Testament reading and psalm are chosen to be complementary with the gospel reading. The second series uses Old Testament readings ordered semicontinuously, with psalms that relate to these readings. Both series use the same second reading and gospel, which are listed only once. The goals of the lectionary are best realized when one series or the other is used consistently throughout the Time after Pentecost.

The Holy Trinity
First Sunday after Pentecost

A

Genesis 1:1—2:4a
Psalm 8 *(1)*
2 Corinthians 13:11-13
Matthew 28:16-20

B

Isaiah 6:1-8
Psalm 29 *(2)*
Romans 8:12-17
John 3:1-17

C

Proverbs 8:1-4, 22-31
Psalm 8 *(2)*
Romans 5:1-5
John 16:12-15

Almighty Creator and ever-living God: we worship your glory, eternal Three-in-One, and we praise your power, majestic One-in-Three. Keep us steadfast in this faith, defend us in all adversity, and bring us at last into your presence, where you live in endless joy and love, Father, Son, and Holy Spirit, one God, now and forever. **Amen.**

OR

God of heaven and earth, before the foundation of the universe and the beginning of time you are the triune God: Author of creation, eternal Word of salvation, life-giving Spirit of wisdom. Guide us to all truth by your Spirit, that we may proclaim all that Christ has revealed and rejoice in the glory he shares with us. Glory and praise to you, Father, Son, and Holy Spirit, now and forever. **Amen.**

Sunday, May 24–28 *(if after Holy Trinity)*
Time after Pentecost—Lectionary 8

A

Isaiah 49:8-16a
Psalm 131 *(2)*
1 Corinthians 4:1-5
Matthew 6:24-34

God of tender care, like a mother, like a father, you never forget your children, and you know already what we need. In all our anxiety give us trusting and faithful hearts, that in confidence we may embody the peace and justice of your Son, Jesus Christ, our Savior and Lord. **Amen.**

B

Hosea 2:14-20
Psalm 103:1-13, 22 *(8)*
2 Corinthians 3:1-6
Mark 2:13-22

Loving God, by tender words and covenant promise you have joined us to yourself forever, and you invite us to respond to your love with faithfulness. By your Spirit may we live with you and with one another in justice, mercy, and joy, through Jesus Christ, our Savior and Lord. **Amen.**

C

Isaiah 55:10-13
or Sirach 27:4-7
Psalm 92:1-4, 12-15 (12)
1 Corinthians 15:51-58
Luke 6:39-49

O God our rock, your word brings life to the whole creation and salvation from sin and death. Nourish our faith in your promises, and ground us in your strength, through Jesus Christ, our Savior and Lord. **Amen.**

Sunday, May 29–June 4 *(if after Holy Trinity)*

Time after Pentecost—Lectionary 9

A

Deuteronomy 11:18-21,
    26-28
Psalm 31:1-5, 19-24 (3)
Romans 1:16-17; 3:22b-28
    [29-31]
Matthew 7:21-29
Semicontinuous reading and psalm
Genesis 6:9-22; 7:24; 8:14-19
Psalm 46 (7)

O God our rock, you offer us a covenant of mercy, and you provide the foundation of our lives. Ground us in your word, and strengthen our resolve to be your disciples, through Jesus Christ, our Savior and Lord. **Amen.**

B

Deuteronomy 5:12-15
Psalm 81:1-10 (1)
2 Corinthians 4:5-12
Mark 2:23—3:6
Semicontinuous reading and psalm
1 Samuel 3:1-10 [11-20]
Psalm 139:1-6, 13-18 (1)

Almighty and ever-living God, throughout time you free the oppressed, heal the sick, and make whole all that you have made. Look with compassion on the world wounded by sin, and by your power restore us to wholeness of life, through Jesus Christ, our Savior and Lord. **Amen.**

C

1 Kings 8:22-23, 41-43
Psalm 96:1-9 (3)
Galatians 1:1-12
Luke 7:1-10
Semicontinuous reading and psalm
1 Kings 18:20-21 [22-29]
    30-39
Psalm 96 (7)

Merciful Lord God, we do not presume to come before you trusting in our own righteousness, but in your great and abundant mercies. Revive our faith, we pray; heal our bodies, and mend our communities, that we may evermore dwell in your Son, Jesus Christ, our Savior and Lord. **Amen.**

Sunday, June 5–11 *(if after Holy Trinity)*

Time after Pentecost—Lectionary 10

A

Hosea 5:15—6:6
Psalm 50:7-15 (15)
Romans 4:13-25
Matthew 9:9-13, 18-26
Semicontinuous reading and psalm
Genesis 12:1-9
Psalm 33:1-12 (12)

O God, you are the source of life and the ground of our being. By the power of your Spirit bring healing to this wounded world, and raise us to the new life of your Son, Jesus Christ, our Savior and Lord. **Amen.**

B

Genesis 3:8-15
Psalm 130 (7)
2 Corinthians 4:13—5:1
Mark 3:20-35
Semicontinuous reading and psalm
1 Samuel 8:4-11 [12-15]
    16-20 [11:14-15]
Psalm 138 (8)

All-powerful God, in Jesus Christ you turned death into life and defeat into victory. Increase our faith and trust in him, that we may triumph over all evil in the strength of the same Jesus Christ, our Savior and Lord. **Amen.**

C

1 Kings 17:17-24
Psalm 30 (2)
Galatians 1:11-24
Luke 7:11-17
Semicontinuous reading and psalm
1 Kings 17:8-16 [17-24]
Psalm 146 (8)

Compassionate God, you have assured the human family of eternal life through Jesus Christ. Deliver us from the death of sin, and raise us to new life in your Son, Jesus Christ, our Savior and Lord. **Amen.**

Sunday, June 12–18 *(if after Holy Trinity)*

Time after Pentecost—Lectionary 11

A

Exodus 19:2-8a
Psalm 100 (3)
Romans 5:1-8
Matthew 9:35—10:8 [9-23]
Semicontinuous reading and psalm
Genesis 18:1-15 [21:1-7]
Psalm 116:1-2, 12-19 (13)

God of compassion, you have opened the way for us and brought us to yourself. Pour your love into our hearts, that, overflowing with joy, we may freely share the blessings of your realm and faithfully proclaim the good news of your Son, Jesus Christ, our Savior and Lord. **Amen.**

B

Ezekiel 17:22-24
Psalm 92:1-4, 12-15 (12)
2 Corinthians 5:6-10 [11-13]
    14-17
Mark 4:26-34
Semicontinuous reading and psalm
1 Samuel 15:34—16:13
Psalm 20 (6)

O God, you are the tree of life, offering shelter to all the world. Graft us into yourself and nurture our growth, that we may bear your truth and love to those in need, through Jesus Christ, our Savior and Lord. **Amen.**

C

2 Samuel 11:26—12:10,
    13-15
Psalm 32 (5)
Galatians 2:15-21
Luke 7:36—8:3
Semicontinuous reading and psalm
1 Kings 21:1-10 [11-14]
    15-21a
Psalm 5:1-8 (8)

O God, throughout the ages you judge your people with mercy, and you inspire us to speak your truth. By your Spirit, anoint us for lives of faith and service, and bring all people into your forgiveness, through Jesus Christ, our Savior and Lord. **Amen.**

Sunday, June 19–25 *(if after Holy Trinity)*

Time after Pentecost—Lectionary 12

A

Jeremiah 20:7-13
Psalm 69:7-10 [11-15]
    16-18 *(16)*
Romans 6:1b-11
Matthew 10:24-39

Semicontinuous reading and psalm
Genesis 21:8-21
Psalm 86:1-10, 16-17 *(16)*

Teach us, good Lord God, to serve you as you deserve, to give and not to count the cost, to fight and not to heed the wounds, to toil and not to seek for rest, to labor and not to ask for reward, except that of knowing that we do your will, through Jesus Christ, our Savior and Lord. **Amen.**

B

Job 38:1-11
Psalm 107:1-3, 23-32 *(29)*
2 Corinthians 6:1-13
Mark 4:35-41

Semicontinuous reading and psalm
1 Samuel 17:[1a, 4-11, 19-23]
    32-49
Psalm 9:9-20 *(9)*
or 1 Samuel 17:57—18:5,
    10-16
    Psalm 133 *(1)*

O God of creation, eternal majesty, you preside over land and sea, sunshine and storm. By your strength pilot us, by your power preserve us, by your wisdom instruct us, and by your hand protect us, through Jesus Christ, our Savior and Lord. **Amen.**

C

Isaiah 65:1-9
Psalm 22:19-28 *(22)*
Galatians 3:23-29
Luke 8:26-39

Semicontinuous reading and psalm
1 Kings 19:1-4 [5-7] 8-15a
Psalms 42 and 43 *(43: 3)*

O Lord God, we bring before you the cries of a sorrowing world. In your mercy set us free from the chains that bind us, and defend us from everything that is evil, through Jesus Christ, our Savior and Lord. **Amen.**

Sunday, June 26–July 2

Time after Pentecost—Lectionary 13

A

Jeremiah 28:5-9
Psalm 89:1-4, 15-18 *(1)*
Romans 6:12-23
Matthew 10:40-42

Semicontinuous reading and psalm
Genesis 22:1-14
Psalm 13 *(5)*

O God, you direct our lives by your grace, and your words of justice and mercy reshape the world. Mold us into a people who welcome your word and serve one another, through Jesus Christ, our Savior and Lord. **Amen.**

B

Lamentations 3:22-33
or Wisdom 1:13-15; 2:23-24
Psalm 30 (1)
2 Corinthians 8:7-15
Mark 5:21-43
Semicontinuous reading and psalm
2 Samuel 1:1, 17-27
Psalm 130 (1)

Almighty and merciful God, we implore you to hear the prayers of your people. Be our strong defense against all harm and danger, that we may live and grow in faith and hope, through Jesus Christ, our Savior and Lord. **Amen.**

C

1 Kings 19:15-16, 19-21
Psalm 16 (8)
Galatians 5:1, 13-25
Luke 9:51-62
Semicontinuous reading and psalm
2 Kings 2:1-2, 6-14
Psalm 77:1-2, 11-20 (15)

Sovereign God, ruler of all hearts, you call us to obey you, and you favor us with true freedom. Keep us faithful to the ways of your Son, that, leaving behind all that hinders us, we may steadfastly follow your paths, through Jesus Christ, our Savior and Lord. **Amen.**

Sunday, July 3–9

Time after Pentecost—Lectionary 14

A

Zechariah 9:9-12
Psalm 145:8-14 (8)
Romans 7:15-25a
Matthew 11:16-19, 25-30
Semicontinuous reading and psalm
Genesis 24:34-38, 42-49,
    58-67
Psalm 45:10-17 (7)
or Song of Solomon 2:8-13 (10)

You are great, O God, and greatly to be praised. You have made us for yourself, and our hearts are restless until they rest in you. Grant that we may believe in you, call upon you, know you, and serve you, through your Son, Jesus Christ, our Savior and Lord. **Amen.**

B

Ezekiel 2:1-5
Psalm 123 (2)
2 Corinthians 12:2-10
Mark 6:1-13
Semicontinuous reading and psalm
2 Samuel 5:1-5, 9-10
Psalm 48 (1)

God of the covenant, in our baptism you call us to proclaim the coming of your kingdom. Give us the courage you gave the apostles, that we may faithfully witness to your love and peace in every circumstance of life, in the name of Jesus Christ, our Savior and Lord. **Amen.**

C

Isaiah 66:10-14
Psalm 66:1-9 (4)
Galatians 6:[1-6] 7-16
Luke 10:1-11, 16-20
Semicontinuous reading and psalm
2 Kings 5:1-14
Psalm 30 (2)

O God, the Father of our Lord Jesus, you are the city that shelters us, the mother who comforts us. With your Spirit accompany us on our life's journey, that we may spread your peace in all the world, through your Son, Jesus Christ, our Savior and Lord. **Amen.**

Sunday, July 10–16

A

Isaiah 55:10-13
Psalm 65:[1-8] 9-13 (11)
Romans 8:1-11
Matthew 13:1-9, 18-23
Semicontinuous reading and psalm
Genesis 25:19-34
Psalm 119:105-112 (105)

Almighty God, we thank you for planting in us the seed of your word. By your Holy Spirit help us to receive it with joy, live according to it, and grow in faith and hope and love, through Jesus Christ, our Savior and Lord. **Amen.**

B

Amos 7:7-15
Psalm 85:8-13 (8)
Ephesians 1:3-14
Mark 6:14-29
Semicontinuous reading and psalm
2 Samuel 6:1-5, 12b-19
Psalm 24 (7)

O God, from you come all holy desires, all good counsels, and all just works. Give to us, your servants, that peace which the world cannot give, that our hearts may be set to obey your commandments; and also that we, being defended from the fear of our enemies, may live in peace and quietness, through Jesus Christ, our Savior and Lord. **Amen.**

C

Deuteronomy 30:9-14
Psalm 25:1-10 (4)
Colossians 1:1-14
Luke 10:25-37
Semicontinuous reading and psalm
Amos 7:7-17
Psalm 82 (8)

O Lord God, your mercy delights us, and the world longs for your loving care. Hear the cries of everyone in need, and turn our hearts to love our neighbors with the love of your Son, Jesus Christ, our Savior and Lord. **Amen.**

Sunday, July 17–23

A

Isaiah 44:6-8
or Wisdom 12:13, 16-19
Psalm 86:11-17 (11)
Romans 8:12-25
Matthew 13:24-30, 36-43
Semicontinuous reading and psalm
Genesis 28:10-19a
Psalm 139:1-12, 23-24 (1)

Faithful God, most merciful judge, you care for your children with firmness and compassion. By your Spirit nurture us who live in your kingdom, that we may be rooted in the way of your Son, Jesus Christ, our Savior and Lord. **Amen.**

B

Jeremiah 23:1-6
Psalm 23 (1)
Ephesians 2:11-22
Mark 6:30-34, 53-56
Semicontinuous reading and psalm
2 Samuel 7:1-14a
Psalm 89:20-37 (1)

O God, powerful and compassionate, you shepherd your people, faithfully feeding and protecting us. Heal each of us, and make us a whole people, that we may embody the justice and peace of your Son, Jesus Christ, our Savior and Lord. **Amen.**

C
Genesis 18:1-10a
Psalm 15 (1)
Colossians 1:15-28
Luke 10:38-42
Semicontinuous reading and psalm
Amos 8:1-12
Psalm 52 (8)

Eternal God, you draw near to us in Christ, and you make yourself our guest. Amid the cares of our lives, make us attentive to your presence, that we may treasure your word above all else, through Jesus Christ, our Savior and Lord. **Amen.**

Sunday, July 24–30
Time after Pentecost—Lectionary 17

A
1 Kings 3:5-12
Psalm 119:129-136 (130)
Romans 8:26-39
Matthew 13:31-33, 44-52
Semicontinuous reading and psalm
Genesis 29:15-28
Psalm 105:1-11, 45b (1, 45)
or Psalm 128 (1)

Beloved and sovereign God, through the death and resurrection of your Son you bring us into your kingdom of justice and mercy. By your Spirit, give us your wisdom, that we may treasure the life that comes from Jesus Christ, our Savior and Lord. **Amen.**

B
2 Kings 4:42-44
Psalm 145:10-18 (16)
Ephesians 3:14-21
John 6:1-21
Semicontinuous reading and psalm
2 Samuel 11:1-15
Psalm 14 (5)

Gracious God, you have placed within the hearts of all your children a longing for your word and a hunger for your truth. Grant that we may know your Son to be the true bread of heaven and share this bread with all the world, through Jesus Christ, our Savior and Lord. **Amen.**

C
Genesis 18:20-32
Psalm 138 (8)
Colossians 2:6-15 [16-19]
Luke 11:1-13
Semicontinuous reading and psalm
Hosea 1:2-10
Psalm 85 (13)

Almighty and ever-living God, you are always more ready to hear than we are to pray, and you gladly give more than we either desire or deserve. Pour upon us your abundant mercy. Forgive us those things that weigh on our conscience, and give us those good things that come only through your Son, Jesus Christ, our Savior and Lord. **Amen.**

Sunday, July 31–August 6
Time after Pentecost—Lectionary 18

A
Isaiah 55:1-5
Psalm 145:8-9, 14-21 (16)
Romans 9:1-5
Matthew 14:13-21
Semicontinuous reading and psalm
Genesis 32:22-31
Psalm 17:1-7, 15 (15)

Glorious God, your generosity waters the world with goodness, and you cover creation with abundance. Awaken in us a hunger for the food that satisfies both body and spirit, and with this food fill all the starving world, through your Son, Jesus Christ, our Savior and Lord. **Amen.**

B

Exodus 16:2-4, 9-15
Psalm 78:23-29 (24, 25)
Ephesians 4:1-16
John 6:24-35

Semicontinuous reading and psalm
2 Samuel 11:26—12:13a
Psalm 51:1-12 (1)

O God, eternal goodness, immeasurable love, you place your gifts before us; we eat and are satisfied. Fill us and this world in all its need with the life that comes only from you, through Jesus Christ, our Savior and Lord. **Amen.**

C

Ecclesiastes 1:2, 12-14;
    2:18-23
Psalm 49:1-12 (3)
Colossians 3:1-11
Luke 12:13-21

Semicontinuous reading and psalm
Hosea 11:1-11
Psalm 107:1-9, 43 (8)

Benevolent God, you are the source, the guide, and the goal of our lives. Teach us to love what is worth loving, to reject what is offensive to you, and to treasure what is precious in your sight, through Jesus Christ, our Savior and Lord. **Amen.**

Sunday, August 7–13

Time after Pentecost—Lectionary 19

A

1 Kings 19:9-18
Psalm 85:8-13 (8)
Romans 10:5-15
Matthew 14:22-33

Semicontinuous reading and psalm
Genesis 37:1-4, 12-28
Psalm 105:1-6, 16-22, 45b (1, 45)

O God our defender, storms rage around and within us and cause us to be afraid. Rescue your people from despair, deliver your sons and daughters from fear, and preserve us in the faith of your Son, Jesus Christ, our Savior and Lord. **Amen.**

B

1 Kings 19:4-8
Psalm 34:1-8 (8)
Ephesians 4:25—5:2
John 6:35, 41-51

Semicontinuous reading and psalm
2 Samuel 18:5-9, 15, 31-33
Psalm 130 (1)

Gracious God, your blessed Son came down from heaven to be the true bread that gives life to the world. Give us this bread always, that he may live in us and we in him, and that, strengthened by this food, we may live as his body in the world, through Jesus Christ, our Savior and Lord. **Amen.**

C

Genesis 15:1-6
Psalm 33:12-22 (22)
Hebrews 11:1-3, 8-16
Luke 12:32-40

Semicontinuous reading and psalm
Isaiah 1:1, 10-20
Psalm 50:1-8, 22-23 (23)

Almighty God, you sent your Holy Spirit to be the life and light of your church. Open our hearts to the riches of your grace, that we may be ready to receive you wherever you appear, through Jesus Christ, our Savior and Lord. **Amen.**

Sunday, August 14–20

A

Isaiah 56:1, 6-8
Psalm 67 (3)
Romans 11:1-2a, 29-32
Matthew 15:[10-20] 21-28
Semicontinuous reading and psalm
Genesis 45:1-15
Psalm 133 (1)

God of all peoples, your arms reach out to embrace all those who call upon you. Teach us as disciples of your Son to love the world with compassion and constancy, that your name may be known throughout the earth, through Jesus Christ, our Savior and Lord. **Amen.**

B

Proverbs 9:1-6
Psalm 34:9-14 (10)
Ephesians 5:15-20
John 6:51-58
Semicontinuous reading and psalm
1 Kings 2:10-12; 3:3-14
Psalm 111 (10)

Ever-loving God, your Son gives himself as living bread for the life of the world. Fill us with such a knowledge of his presence that we may be strengthened and sustained by his risen life to serve you continually, through Jesus Christ, our Savior and Lord. **Amen.**

C

Jeremiah 23:23-29
Psalm 82 (8)
Hebrews 11:29—12:2
Luke 12:49-56
Semicontinuous reading and psalm
Isaiah 5:1-7
Psalm 80:1-2, 8-19 (14, 15)

O God, judge eternal, you love justice and hate oppression, and you call us to share your zeal for truth. Give us courage to take our stand with all victims of bloodshed and greed, and, following your servants and prophets, to look to the pioneer and perfecter of our faith, your Son, Jesus Christ, our Savior and Lord. **Amen.**

Sunday, August 21–27

A

Isaiah 51:1-6
Psalm 138 (8)
Romans 12:1-8
Matthew 16:13-20
Semicontinuous reading and psalm
Exodus 1:8—2:10
Psalm 124 (7)

O God, with all your faithful followers of every age, we praise you, the rock of our life. Be our strong foundation and form us into the body of your Son, that we may gladly minister to all the world, through Jesus Christ, our Savior and Lord. **Amen.**

B

Joshua 24:1-2a, 14-18
Psalm 34:15-22 (15)
Ephesians 6:10-20
John 6:56-69
Semicontinuous reading and psalm
1 Kings 8:[1, 6, 10-11] 22-30, 41-43
Psalm 84 (1)

Holy God, your word feeds your people with life that is eternal. Direct our choices and preserve us in your truth, that, renouncing what is false and evil, we may live in you, through your Son, Jesus Christ, our Savior and Lord. **Amen.**

C
Isaiah 58:9b-14
Psalm 103:1-8 (4)
Hebrews 12:18-29
Luke 13:10-17
Semicontinuous reading and psalm
Jeremiah 1:4-10
Psalm 71:1-6 (6)

O God, mighty and immortal, you know that as fragile creatures surrounded by great dangers, we cannot by ourselves stand upright. Give us strength of mind and body, so that even when we suffer because of human sin, we may rise victorious through your Son, Jesus Christ, our Savior and Lord. **Amen.**

Sunday, August 28–September 3

Time after Pentecost—Lectionary 22

A
Jeremiah 15:15-21
Psalm 26:1-8 (3)
Romans 12:9-21
Matthew 16:21-28
Semicontinuous reading and psalm
Exodus 3:1-15
Psalm 105:1-6, 23-26, 45b (1, 45)

O God, we thank you for your Son, who chose the path of suffering for the sake of the world. Humble us by his example, point us to the path of obedience, and give us strength to follow your commands, through Jesus Christ, our Savior and Lord. **Amen.**

B
Deuteronomy 4:1-2, 6-9
Psalm 15 (1)
James 1:17-27
Mark 7:1-8, 14-15, 21-23
Semicontinuous reading and psalm
Song of Solomon 2:8-13
Psalm 45:1-2, 6-9 (7)

O God our strength, without you we are weak and wayward creatures. Protect us from all dangers that attack us from the outside, and cleanse us from all evil that arises from within ourselves, that we may be preserved through your Son, Jesus Christ, our Savior and Lord. **Amen.**

C
Proverbs 25:6-7
or Sirach 10:12-18
Psalm 112 (4)
Hebrews 13:1-8, 15-16
Luke 14:1, 7-14
Semicontinuous reading and psalm
Jeremiah 2:4-13
Psalm 81:1, 10-16 (16)

O God, you resist those who are proud and give grace to those who are humble. Give us the humility of your Son, that we may embody the generosity of Jesus Christ, our Savior and Lord. **Amen.**

Sunday, September 4–10

Time after Pentecost—Lectionary 23

A
Ezekiel 33:7-11
Psalm 119:33-40 (35)
Romans 13:8-14
Matthew 18:15-20
Semicontinuous reading and psalm
Exodus 12:1-14
Psalm 149 (1)

O Lord God, enliven and preserve your church with your perpetual mercy. Without your help, we mortals will fail; remove far from us everything that is harmful, and lead us toward all that gives life and salvation, through Jesus Christ, our Savior and Lord. **Amen.**

B

Isaiah 35:4-7a
Psalm 146 (2)
James 2:1-10 [11-13] 14-17
Mark 7:24-37
Semicontinuous reading and psalm
Proverbs 22:1-2, 8-9, 22-23
Psalm 125 (1)

Gracious God, throughout the ages you transform sickness into health and death into life. Open us to the power of your presence, and make us a people ready to proclaim your promises to the whole world, through Jesus Christ, our healer and Lord. **Amen.**

C

Deuteronomy 30:15-20
Psalm 1 (3)
Philemon 1-21
Luke 14:25-33
Semicontinuous reading and psalm
Jeremiah 18:1-11
Psalm 139:1-6, 13-18 (1)

Direct us, O Lord God, in all our doings with your continual help, that in all our works, begun, continued, and ended in you, we may glorify your holy name; and finally, by your mercy, bring us to everlasting life, through Jesus Christ, our Savior and Lord. **Amen.**

Sunday, September 11–17

Time after Pentecost—Lectionary 24

A

Genesis 50:15-21
Psalm 103:[1-7] 8-13 (8)
Romans 14:1-12
Matthew 18:21-35
Semicontinuous reading and psalm
Exodus 14:19-31
Psalm 114 (7)
or Exodus 15:1b-11, 20-21 (1)

O Lord God, merciful judge, you are the inexhaustible fountain of forgiveness. Replace our hearts of stone with hearts that love and adore you, that we may delight in doing your will, through Jesus Christ, our Savior and Lord. **Amen.**

B

Isaiah 50:4-9a
Psalm 116:1-9 (9)
James 3:1-12
Mark 8:27-38
Semicontinuous reading and psalm
Proverbs 1:20-33
Psalm 19 (7)
or Wisdom 7:26—8:1 (28)

O God, through suffering and rejection you bring forth our salvation, and by the glory of the cross you transform our lives. Grant that for the sake of the gospel we may turn from the lure of evil, take up our cross, and follow your Son, Jesus Christ, our Savior and Lord. **Amen.**

C

Exodus 32:7-14
Psalm 51:1-10 (1)
1 Timothy 1:12-17
Luke 15:1-10
Semicontinuous reading and psalm
Jeremiah 4:11-12, 22-28
Psalm 14 (2)

O God, overflowing with mercy and compassion, you lead back to yourself all those who go astray. Preserve your people in your loving care, that we may reject whatever is contrary to you and may follow all things that sustain our life in your Son, Jesus Christ, our Savior and Lord. **Amen.**

Sunday, September 18–24

Time after Pentecost—Lectionary 25

A

Jonah 3:10—4:11
Psalm 145:1-8 (8)
Philippians 1:21-30
Matthew 20:1-16
Semicontinuous reading and psalm
Exodus 16:2-15
Psalm 105:1-6, 37-45 (1, 45)

Almighty and eternal God, you show perpetual lovingkindness to us your servants. Because we cannot rely on our own abilities, grant us your merciful judgment, and train us to embody the generosity of your Son, Jesus Christ, our Savior and Lord. **Amen.**

B

Jeremiah 11:18-20
or Wisdom 1:16—2:1, 12-22
Psalm 54 (4)
James 3:13—4:3, 7-8a
Mark 9:30-37
Semicontinuous reading and psalm
Proverbs 31:10-31
Psalm 1 (3)

O God, our teacher and guide, you draw us to yourself and welcome us as beloved children. Help us to lay aside all envy and selfish ambition, that we may walk in your ways of wisdom and understanding as servants of your Son, Jesus Christ, our Savior and Lord. **Amen.**

C

Amos 8:4-7
Psalm 113 (7)
1 Timothy 2:1-7
Luke 16:1-13
Semicontinuous reading and psalm
Jeremiah 8:18—9:1
Psalm 79:1-9 (9)

God among us, we gather in the name of your Son to learn love for one another. Keep our feet from evil paths. Turn our minds to your wisdom and our hearts to the grace revealed in your Son, Jesus Christ, our Savior and Lord. **Amen.**

Sunday, September 25–October 1

Time after Pentecost—Lectionary 26

A

Ezekiel 18:1-4, 25-32
Psalm 25:1-9 (6)
Philippians 2:1-13
Matthew 21:23-32
Semicontinuous reading and psalm
Exodus 17:1-7
Psalm 78:1-4, 12-16 (4)

God of love, giver of life, you know our frailties and failings. Give us your grace to overcome them, keep us from those things that harm us, and guide us in the way of salvation, through Jesus Christ, our Savior and Lord. **Amen.**

B

Numbers 11:4-6, 10-16, 24-29
Psalm 19:7-14 (8)
James 5:13-20
Mark 9:38-50
Semicontinuous reading and psalm
Esther 7:1-6, 9-10; 9:20-22
Psalm 124 (7)

Generous God, your Son gave his life that we might come to peace with you. Give us a share of your Spirit, and in all we do empower us to bear the name of Jesus Christ, our Savior and Lord. **Amen.**

C
Amos 6:1a, 4-7
Psalm 146 (7)
1 Timothy 6:6-19
Luke 16:19-31

O God, rich in mercy, you look with compassion on this troubled world. Feed us with your grace, and grant us the treasure that comes only from you, through Jesus Christ, our Savior and Lord. **Amen.**

Semicontinuous reading and psalm
Jeremiah 32:1-3a, 6-15
Psalm 91:1-6, 14-16 (2)

Sunday, October 2–8

Time after Pentecost—Lectionary 27

A
Isaiah 5:1-7
Psalm 80:7-15 (14, 15)
Philippians 3:4b-14
Matthew 21:33-46

Beloved God, from you come all things that are good. Lead us by the inspiration of your Spirit to know those things that are right, and by your merciful guidance, help us to do them, through Jesus Christ, our Savior and Lord. **Amen.**

Semicontinuous reading and psalm
Exodus 20:1-4, 7-9, 12-20
Psalm 19 (8)

B
Genesis 2:18-24
Psalm 8 (5)
Hebrews 1:1-4; 2:5-12
Mark 10:2-16

Sovereign God, you have created us to live in loving community with one another. Form us for life that is faithful and steadfast, and teach us to trust like little children, that we may reflect the image of your Son, Jesus Christ, our Savior and Lord. **Amen.**

Semicontinuous reading and psalm
Job 1:1; 2:1-10
Psalm 26 (3)

C
Habakkuk 1:1-4; 2:1-4
Psalm 37:1-9 (5)
2 Timothy 1:1-14
Luke 17:5-10

Benevolent, merciful God: When we are empty, fill us. When we are weak in faith, strengthen us. When we are cold in love, warm us, that with fervor we may love our neighbors and serve them for the sake of your Son, Jesus Christ, our Savior and Lord. **Amen.**

Semicontinuous reading and psalm
Lamentations 1:1-6
Lamentations 3:19-26 (23)
or Psalm 137 (7)

Sunday, October 9–15

Time after Pentecost—Lectionary 28

A
Isaiah 25:1-9
Psalm 23 (5)
Philippians 4:1-9
Matthew 22:1-14

Lord of the feast, you have prepared a table before all peoples and poured out your life with abundance. Call us again to your banquet. Strengthen us by what is honorable, just, and pure, and transform us into a people of righteousness and peace, through Jesus Christ, our Savior and Lord. **Amen.**

Semicontinuous reading and psalm
Exodus 32:1-14
Psalm 106:1-6, 19-23 (4)

B

Amos 5:6-7, 10-15
Psalm 90:12-17 (12)
Hebrews 4:12-16
Mark 10:17-31
Semicontinuous reading and psalm
Job 23:1-9, 16-17
Psalm 22:1-15 (1)

Almighty and ever-living God, increase in us your gift of faith, that, forsaking what lies behind and reaching out to what lies ahead, we may follow the way of your commandments and receive the crown of everlasting joy, through Jesus Christ, our Savior and Lord. **Amen.**

C

2 Kings 5:1-3, 7-15c
Psalm 111 (1)
2 Timothy 2:8-15
Luke 17:11-19
Semicontinuous reading and psalm
Jeremiah 29:1, 4-7
Psalm 66:1-12 (9)

Almighty and most merciful God, your bountiful goodness fills all creation. Keep us safe from all that may hurt us, that, whole and well in body and spirit, we may with grateful hearts accomplish all that you would have us do, through Jesus Christ, our Savior and Lord. **Amen.**

Sunday, October 16–22

Time after Pentecost—Lectionary 29

A

Isaiah 45:1-7
Psalm 96:1-9 [10-13] (7)
1 Thessalonians 1:1-10
Matthew 22:15-22
Semicontinuous reading and psalm
Exodus 33:12-23
Psalm 99 (5)

Sovereign God, raise your throne in our hearts. Created by you, let us live in your image; created for you, let us act for your glory; redeemed by you, let us give you what is yours, through Jesus Christ, our Savior and Lord. **Amen.**

B

Isaiah 53:4-12
Psalm 91:9-16 (9)
Hebrews 5:1-10
Mark 10:35-45
Semicontinuous reading and psalm
Job 38:1-7 [34-41]
Psalm 104:1-9, 24, 35b (24)

Sovereign God, you turn your greatness into goodness for all the peoples on earth. Shape us into willing servants of your kingdom, and make us desire always and only your will, through Jesus Christ, our Savior and Lord. **Amen.**

C

Genesis 32:22-31
Psalm 121 (2)
2 Timothy 3:14—4:5
Luke 18:1-8
Semicontinuous reading and psalm
Jeremiah 31:27-34
Psalm 119:97-104 (103)

O Lord God, tireless guardian of your people, you are always ready to hear our cries. Teach us to rely day and night on your care. Inspire us to seek your enduring justice for all this suffering world, through Jesus Christ, our Savior and Lord. **Amen.**

Sunday, October 23–29

Time after Pentecost—Lectionary 30

A

Leviticus 19:1-2, 15-18
Psalm 1 (2)
1 Thessalonians 2:1-8
Matthew 22:34-46

Semicontinuous reading and psalm
Deuteronomy 34:1-12
Psalm 90:1-6, 13-17 (16)

O Lord God, you are the holy lawgiver, you are the salvation of your people. By your Spirit renew us in your covenant of love, and train us to care tenderly for all our neighbors, through Jesus Christ, our Savior and Lord. **Amen.**

B

Jeremiah 31:7-9
Psalm 126 (5)
Hebrews 7:23-28
Mark 10:46-52

Semicontinuous reading and psalm
Job 42:1-6, 10-17
Psalm 34:1-8 [19-22] (8)

Eternal light, shine in our hearts. Eternal wisdom, scatter the darkness of our ignorance. Eternal compassion, have mercy on us. Turn us to seek your face, and enable us to reflect your goodness, through Jesus Christ, our Savior and Lord. **Amen.**

C

Jeremiah 14:7-10, 19-22
or Sirach 35:12-17
Psalm 84:1-7 (5)
2 Timothy 4:6-8, 16-18
Luke 18:9-14

Semicontinuous reading and psalm
Joel 2:23-32
Psalm 65 (11)

Holy God, our righteous judge, daily your mercy surprises us with everlasting forgiveness. Strengthen our hope in you, and grant that all the peoples of the earth may find their glory in you, through Jesus Christ, our Savior and Lord. **Amen.**

Sunday, October 30–November 5

Time after Pentecost—Lectionary 31

A

Micah 3:5-12
Psalm 43 (3)
1 Thessalonians 2:9-13
Matthew 23:1-12

Semicontinuous reading and psalm
Joshua 3:7-17
Psalm 107:1-7, 33-37 (8)

O God, generous and supreme, your loving Son lived among us, instructing us in the ways of humility and justice. Continue to ease our burdens, and lead us to serve alongside of him, Jesus Christ, our Savior and Lord. **Amen.**

B

Deuteronomy 6:1-9
Psalm 119:1-8 (2)
Hebrews 9:11-14
Mark 12:28-34

Semicontinuous reading and psalm
Ruth 1:1-18
Psalm 146 (8)

Almighty God, you have taught us in your Son that love fulfills the law. Inspire us to love you with all our heart, our soul, our mind, and our strength, and teach us how to love our neighbor as ourselves, through Jesus Christ, our Savior and Lord. **Amen.**

C

Isaiah 1:10-18
Psalm 32:1-7 (6)
2 Thessalonians 1:1-4, 11-12
Luke 19:1-10
Semicontinuous reading and psalm
Habakkuk 1:1-4; 2:1-4
Psalm 119:137-144 (144)

Merciful God, gracious and benevolent, through your Son you invite all the world to a meal of mercy. Grant that we may eagerly follow his call, and bring us with all your saints into your life of justice and joy, through Jesus Christ, our Savior and Lord. **Amen.**

Sunday, November 6–12

Time after Pentecost—Lectionary 32

A

Amos 5:18-24
or Wisdom 6:12-16
Psalm 70 (5)
or Wisdom 6:17-20 (17)
1 Thessalonians 4:13-18
Matthew 25:1-13
Semicontinuous reading and psalm
Joshua 24:1-3a, 14-25
Psalm 78:1-7 (4)

O God of justice and love, you illumine our way through life with the words of your Son. Give us the light we need, and awaken us to the needs of others, through Jesus Christ, our Savior and Lord. **Amen.**

B

1 Kings 17:8-16
Psalm 146 (8)
Hebrews 9:24-28
Mark 12:38-44
Semicontinuous reading and psalm
Ruth 3:1-5; 4:13-17
Psalm 127 (3)

O God, you show forth your almighty power chiefly by reaching out to us in mercy. Grant us the fullness of your grace, strengthen our trust in your promises, and bring all the world to share in the treasures that come through your Son, Jesus Christ, our Savior and Lord. **Amen.**

C

Job 19:23-27a
Psalm 17:1-9 (8)
2 Thessalonians 2:1-5, 13-17
Luke 20:27-38
Semicontinuous reading and psalm
Haggai 1:15b—2:9
Psalm 145:1-5, 17-21 (3)
or Psalm 98 (9)

O God, our eternal redeemer, by the presence of your Spirit you renew and direct our hearts. Keep always in our mind the end of all things and the day of judgment. Inspire us for a holy life here, and bring us to the joy of the resurrection, through Jesus Christ, our Savior and Lord. **Amen.**

Sunday, November 13–19

Time after Pentecost—Lectionary 33

A

Zephaniah 1:7, 12-18
Psalm 90:1-8 [9-11] 12 (12)
1 Thessalonians 5:1-11
Matthew 25:14-30
Semicontinuous reading and psalm
Judges 4:1-7
Psalm 123 (2)

Righteous God, our merciful master, you own the earth and all its peoples, and you give us all that we have. Inspire us to serve you with justice and wisdom, and prepare us for the joy of the day of your coming, through Jesus Christ, our Savior and Lord. **Amen.**

B
Daniel 12:1-3
Psalm 16 (9)
Hebrews 10:11-14 [15-18]
    19-25
Mark 13:1-8
Semicontinuous reading and psalm
1 Samuel 1:4-20
1 Samuel 2:1-10 (1)

Almighty God, your sovereign purpose brings salvation to birth. Give us faith to be steadfast amid the tumults of this world, trusting that your kingdom comes and your will is done through your Son, Jesus Christ, our Savior and Lord. **Amen.**

C
Malachi 4:1-2a
Psalm 98 (9)
2 Thessalonians 3:6-13
Luke 21:5-19
Semicontinuous reading and psalm
Isaiah 65:17-25
Isaiah 12:2-6 (6)

O God, the protector of all who trust in you, without you nothing is strong, nothing is holy. Embrace us with your mercy, that with you as our ruler and guide, we may live through what is temporary without losing what is eternal, through Jesus Christ, our Savior and Lord. **Amen.**

Christ the King *Sunday, November 20–26*
Last Sunday after Pentecost—Lectionary 34

A
Ezekiel 34:11-16, 20-24
Psalm 95:1-7a (7)
Ephesians 1:15-23
Matthew 25:31-46
Semicontinuous reading and psalm
Ezekiel 34:11-16, 20-24
Psalm 100 (3)

O God of power and might, your Son shows us the way of service, and in him we inherit the riches of your grace. Give us the wisdom to know what is right and the strength to serve the world you have made, through Jesus Christ, our Savior and Lord, who lives and reigns with you and the Holy Spirit, one God, now and forever. **Amen.**

B
Daniel 7:9-10, 13-14
Psalm 93 (2)
Revelation 1:4b-8
John 18:33-37
Semicontinuous reading and psalm
2 Samuel 23:1-7
Psalm 132:1-12 [13-18] (9)

Almighty and ever-living God, you anointed your beloved Son to be priest and sovereign forever. Grant that all the people of the earth, now divided by the power of sin, may be united by the glorious and gentle rule of Jesus Christ, our Savior and Lord, who lives and reigns with you and the Holy Spirit, one God, now and forever. **Amen.**

C
Jeremiah 23:1-6
Psalm 46 (10)
Colossians 1:11-20
Luke 23:33-43
Semicontinuous reading and psalm
Jeremiah 23:1-6
Luke 1:68-79 (69)

O God, our true life, to serve you is freedom, and to know you is unending joy. We worship you, we glorify you, we give thanks to you for your great glory. Abide with us, reign in us, and make this world into a fit habitation for your divine majesty, through Jesus Christ, our Savior and Lord, who lives and reigns with you and the Holy Spirit, one God, now and forever. **Amen.**

Lesser Festivals, Commemorations, and Occasions

Lesser Festivals

Andrew, Apostle November 30

Ezekiel 3:16-21
Psalm 19:1-6 (4)
Romans 10:10-18
John 1:35-42

Almighty God, you gave your apostle Andrew the grace to obey the call of your Son and to bring his brother to Jesus. Give us also, who are called by your holy word, grace to follow Jesus without delay and to bring into his presence those who are near to us, for he lives and reigns with you and the Holy Spirit, one God, now and forever. **Amen.**

Stephen, Deacon and Martyr December 26

2 Chronicles 24:17-22
Psalm 17:1-9, 15 (6)
Acts 6:8—7:2a, 51-60
Matthew 23:34-39

We give you thanks, O Lord of glory, for the example of Stephen the first martyr, who looked to heaven and prayed for his persecutors. Grant that we also may pray for our enemies and seek forgiveness for those who hurt us, through Jesus Christ, our Savior and Lord, who lives and reigns with you and the Holy Spirit, one God, now and forever. **Amen.**

John, Apostle and Evangelist December 27

Genesis 1:1-5, 26-31
Psalm 116:12-19 (15)
1 John 1:1—2:2
John 21:20-25

Merciful God, through John the apostle and evangelist you have revealed the mysteries of your Word made flesh. Let the brightness of your light shine on your church, so that all your people, instructed in the holy gospel, may walk in the light of your truth and attain eternal life, through Jesus Christ, our Savior and Lord, who lives and reigns with you and the Holy Spirit, one God, now and forever. **Amen.**

The Holy Innocents, Martyrs December 28

Jeremiah 31:15-17
Psalm 124 (7)
1 Peter 4:12-19
Matthew 2:13-18

We remember today, O God, the slaughter of the innocent children of Bethlehem by order of King Herod. Receive into the arms of your mercy all innocent victims. By your great might frustrate the designs of evil tyrants and establish your rule of justice, love, and peace, through Jesus Christ, our Savior and Lord, who lives and reigns with you and the Holy Spirit, one God, now and forever. **Amen.**

Name of Jesus January 1

Numbers 6:22-27
Psalm 8 (1)
Galatians 4:4-7
or Philippians 2:5-11
Luke 2:15-21

Eternal Father, you gave your incarnate Son the holy name of Jesus to be a sign of our salvation. Plant in every heart the love of the Savior of the world, Jesus Christ our Lord, who lives and reigns with you and the Holy Spirit, one God, now and forever. **Amen.**

Confession of Peter January 18

Acts 4:8-13
Psalm 18:1-6, 16-19 (2, 3)
1 Corinthians 10:1-5
Matthew 16:13-19

Almighty God, you inspired Simon Peter to confess Jesus as the Messiah and Son of the living God. Keep your church firm on the rock of this faith, so that in unity and peace it may proclaim one truth and follow one Lord, your Son, Jesus Christ our Savior, who lives and reigns with you and the Holy Spirit, one God, now and forever. **Amen.**

Conversion of Paul January 25

Acts 9:1-22
Psalm 67 (3)
Galatians 1:11-24
Luke 21:10-19

O God, by the preaching of your apostle Paul you have caused the light of the gospel to shine throughout the world. Grant that we may follow his example and be witnesses to the truth of your Son, Jesus Christ, our Savior and Lord, who lives and reigns with you and the Holy Spirit, one God, now and forever. **Amen.**

Presentation of Our Lord February 2

Malachi 3:1-4
Psalm 84 (1)
or Psalm 24:7-10 (7)
Hebrews 2:14-18
Luke 2:22-40

Almighty and ever-living God, your only-begotten Son was presented this day in the temple. May we be presented to you with clean and pure hearts by the same Jesus Christ, our great high priest, who lives and reigns with you and the Holy Spirit, one God, now and forever. **Amen.**

Joseph, Guardian of Jesus March 19

2 Samuel 7:4, 8-16
Psalm 89:1-29 (2)
Romans 4:13-18
Matthew 1:16, 18-21, 24a

O God, from the family of your servant David you raised up Joseph to be the guardian of your incarnate Son and the husband of his blessed mother. Give us grace to imitate his uprightness of life and his obedience to your commands, through Jesus Christ, our Savior and Lord, who lives and reigns with you and the Holy Spirit, one God, now and forever. **Amen.**

Annunciation of Our Lord March 25

Isaiah 7:10-14
Psalm 45 (17)
or Psalm 40:5-10 (8)
Hebrews 10:4-10
Luke 1:26-38

Pour your grace into our hearts, O God, that we who have known the incarnation of your Son, Jesus Christ, announced by an angel, may by his cross and passion be brought to the glory of his resurrection; for he lives and reigns with you, in the unity of the Holy Spirit, one God, now and forever. **Amen.**

Mark, Evangelist April 25

Isaiah 52:7-10
Psalm 57 (9)
2 Timothy 4:6-11, 18
Mark 1:1-15

Almighty God, you have enriched your church with Mark's proclamation of the gospel. Give us grace to believe firmly in the good news of salvation and to walk daily in accord with it, through Jesus Christ, our Savior and Lord, who lives and reigns with you and the Holy Spirit, one God, now and forever. **Amen.**

Philip and James, Apostles May 1

Isaiah 30:18-21
Psalm 44:1-3, 20-26 (26)
2 Corinthians 4:1-6
John 14:8-14

Almighty God, you gave to your apostles Philip and James grace and strength to bear witness to your Son. Grant that we, remembering their victory of faith, may glorify in life and death the name of our Lord Jesus Christ, who lives and reigns with you and the Holy Spirit, one God, now and forever. **Amen.**

Matthias, Apostle May 14

Isaiah 66:1-2
Psalm 56 (12)
Acts 1:15-26
Luke 6:12-16

Almighty God, you chose your faithful servant Matthias to be numbered among the twelve. Grant that your church may always be taught and guided by faithful and true pastors, through Jesus Christ our shepherd, who lives and reigns with you and the Holy Spirit, one God, now and forever. **Amen.**

Visit of Mary to Elizabeth May 31

1 Samuel 2:1-10
Psalm 113 (2)
Romans 12:9-16b
Luke 1:39-57

Mighty God, by whose grace Elizabeth rejoiced with Mary and greeted her as the mother of the Lord: look with favor on your lowly servants that, with Mary, we may magnify your holy name and rejoice to acclaim her Son as our Savior, who lives and reigns with you and the Holy Spirit, one God, now and forever. **Amen.**

Barnabas, Apostle June 11

Isaiah 42:5-12
Psalm 112 (1)
Acts 11:19-30; 13:1-3
Matthew 10:7-16

We praise you, O God, for the life of your faithful servant Barnabas, who, seeking not his own renown but the well-being of your church, gave generously of his life and possessions for the relief of the poor and the spread of the gospel. Grant that we may follow his example and by our actions give glory to you, Father, Son, and Holy Spirit, now and forever. **Amen.**

John the Baptist June 24

Malachi 3:1-4
Psalm 141 (8)
Acts 13:13-26
Luke 1:57-67 [68-80]

Almighty God, by your gracious providence your servant John the Baptist was born to Elizabeth and Zechariah. Grant to your people the wisdom to see your purpose and the openness to hear your will, that the light of Christ may increase in us, through Jesus Christ, our Savior and Lord, who lives and reigns with you and the Holy Spirit, one God, now and forever. **Amen.**

Peter and Paul, Apostles June 29

Acts 12:1-11
Psalm 87:1-3, 5-7 (3)
2 Timothy 4:6-8, 17-18
John 21:15-19

Almighty God, we praise you that your blessed apostles Peter and Paul glorified you by their martyrdoms. Grant that your church throughout the world may always be instructed by their teaching and example, be knit together in unity by your Spirit, and ever stand firm upon the one foundation who is Jesus Christ our Lord, for he lives and reigns with you and the Holy Spirit, one God, now and forever. **Amen.**

Thomas, Apostle July 3

Judges 6:36-40
Psalm 136:1-4, 23-26 (1)
Ephesians 4:11-16
John 14:1-7

Ever-living God, you strengthened your apostle Thomas with firm and certain faith in the resurrection of your Son. Grant that we too may confess our faith in Jesus Christ, our Lord and our God, who lives and reigns with you and the Holy Spirit, one God, now and forever. **Amen.**

Mary Magdalene, Apostle July 22

Ruth 1:6-18
_or_ Exodus 2:1-10
Psalm 73:23-28 (28)
Acts 13:26-33a
John 20:1-2, 11-18

Almighty God, your Son first entrusted the apostle Mary Magdalene with the joyful news of his resurrection. Following the example of her witness, may we proclaim Christ as our living Lord and one day see him in glory, for he lives and reigns with you and the Holy Spirit, one God, now and forever. **Amen.**

James, Apostle July 25

1 Kings 19:9-18
Psalm 7:1-10 (10)
Acts 11:27—12:3a
Mark 10:35-45

Gracious God, we remember before you today your servant and apostle James, the first among the twelve to be martyred for the name of Jesus Christ. Pour out on the leaders of your church that spirit of self-denying service which is the true mark of authority among your people, through Jesus Christ our servant, who lives and reigns with you and the Holy Spirit, one God, now and forever. **Amen.**

Mary, Mother of Our Lord August 15

Isaiah 61:7-11
Psalm 34:1-9 (3)
Galatians 4:4-7
Luke 1:46-55

Almighty God, in choosing the virgin Mary to be the mother of your Son, you made known your gracious regard for the poor, the lowly, and the despised. Grant us grace to receive your word in humility, and so to be made one with your Son, Jesus Christ our Savior and Lord, who lives and reigns with you and the Holy Spirit, one God, now and forever. **Amen.**

Bartholomew, Apostle August 24

Exodus 19:1-6
Psalm 12 (6)
1 Corinthians 12:27-31a
John 1:43-51

Almighty and everlasting God, you gave to your apostle Bartholomew grace truly to believe and courageously to preach your word. Grant that your church may proclaim the good news to the ends of the earth, through Jesus Christ, our Savior and Lord, who lives and reigns with you and the Holy Spirit, one God, now and forever. **Amen.**

Holy Cross Day September 14

Numbers 21:4b-9
Psalm 98:1-4 (1)
_or_ Psalm 78:1-2, 34-38 (35)
1 Corinthians 1:18-24
John 3:13-17

Almighty God, your Son Jesus Christ was lifted high upon the cross so that he might draw the whole world to himself. To those who look upon the cross, grant your wisdom, healing, and eternal life, through Jesus Christ, our Savior and Lord, who lives and reigns with you and the Holy Spirit, one God, now and forever. **Amen.**

Matthew, Apostle and Evangelist September 21

Ezekiel 2:8—3:11
Psalm 119:33-40 (33)
Ephesians 2:4-10
Matthew 9:9-13

Almighty God, your Son our Savior called a despised tax collector to become one of his apostles. Help us, like Matthew, to respond to the transforming call of Jesus Christ, who lives and reigns with you and the Holy Spirit, one God, now and forever. **Amen.**

Michael and All Angels September 29

Daniel 10:10-14; 12:1-3
Psalm 103:1-5, 20-22 (20, 21)
Revelation 12:7-12
Luke 10:17-20

Everlasting God, you have wonderfully established the ministries of angels and mortals. Mercifully grant that as Michael and the angels contend against the cosmic forces of evil, so by your direction they may help and defend us here on earth, through your Son, Jesus Christ our Lord, who lives and reigns with you and the Holy Spirit, one God whom we worship and praise with angels and archangels and all the company of heaven, now and forever. **Amen.**

Luke, Evangelist October 18

Isaiah 43:8-13
or Isaiah 35:5-8
Psalm 124 (8)
2 Timothy 4:5-11
Luke 1:1-4; 24:44-53

Almighty God, you inspired your servant Luke to reveal in his gospel the love and healing power of your Son. Give your church the same love and power to heal, and to proclaim your salvation among the nations to the glory of your name, through Jesus Christ, your Son, our healer, who lives and reigns with you and the Holy Spirit, one God, now and forever. **Amen.**

Simon and Jude, Apostles October 28

Jeremiah 26:[1-6] 7-16
Psalm 11 (1)
1 John 4:1-6
John 14:21-27

O God, we thank you for the glorious company of the apostles, and especially on this day for Simon and Jude. We pray that, as they were faithful and zealous in your mission, so we may with ardent devotion make known the love and mercy of our Savior Jesus Christ, who lives and reigns with you and the Holy Spirit, one God, now and forever. **Amen.**

Reformation Day October 31

Jeremiah 31:31-34
Psalm 46 (7)
Romans 3:19-28
John 8:31-36

Almighty God, gracious Lord, we thank you that your Holy Spirit renews the church in every age. Pour out your Holy Spirit on your faithful people. Keep them steadfast in your word, protect and comfort them in times of trial, defend them against all enemies of the gospel, and bestow on the church your saving peace, through Jesus Christ, our Savior and Lord, who lives and reigns with you and the Holy Spirit, one God, now and forever. **Amen.**

OR

Gracious Father, we pray for your holy catholic church. Fill it with all truth and peace. Where it is corrupt, purify it; where it is in error, direct it; where in anything it is amiss, reform it; where it is right, strengthen it; where it is in need, provide for it; where it is divided, reunite it; for the sake of your Son, Jesus Christ, our Savior, who lives and reigns with you and the Holy Spirit, one God, now and forever. **Amen.**

All Saints Day November 1

A

Revelation 7:9-17
Psalm 34:1-10, 22 (9)
1 John 3:1-3
Matthew 5:1-12

B

Isaiah 25:6-9
or Wisdom 3:1-9
Psalm 24 (5)
Revelation 21:1-6a
John 11:32-44

C

Daniel 7:1-3, 15-18
Psalm 149 (1)
Ephesians 1:11-23
Luke 6:20-31

A, B, C

Almighty God, you have knit your people together in one communion in the mystical body of your Son, Jesus Christ our Lord. Grant us grace to follow your blessed saints in lives of faith and commitment, and to know the inexpressible joys you have prepared for those who love you, through Jesus Christ, our Savior and Lord, who lives and reigns with you and the Holy Spirit, one God, now and forever. **Amen.**

Commemorations

Saints

Micah 6:6-8
Psalm 9:1-10 (10)
1 Corinthians 1:26-31
Luke 6:20-23

Lord God, you have surrounded us with so great a cloud of witnesses. Grant that we [*encouraged by the example of your servant/s___name/s___*] may persevere in the course that is set before us and, at the last, share in your eternal joy with all the saints in light, through Jesus Christ, our Savior and Lord, who lives and reigns with you and the Holy Spirit, one God, now and forever. **Amen.**

Martyrs

Ezekiel 20:40-42
Psalm 5 (11)
Revelation 6:9-11
Mark 8:34-38

Gracious God, in every age you have sent men and women who have given their lives in witness to your love and truth. Inspire us with the memory of___*name*___, whose faithfulness led to the way of the cross, and give us courage to bear full witness with our lives to your Son's victory over sin and death, for he lives and reigns with you and the Holy Spirit, one God, now and forever. **Amen.**

Missionaries

Isaiah 62:1-7
Psalm 48 (10)
Romans 10:11-17
Luke 24:44-53

God of grace and glory, we praise you for your servant/s ___*name/s*___ , who made the good news known [*in place of missionary work*]. Raise up, we pray, in every country, heralds of the gospel, so that the world may know the immeasurable riches of your love, and be drawn to worship you, Father, Son, and Holy Spirit, one God, now and forever. **Amen.**

Renewers of the Church

Jeremiah 1:4-10
Psalm 46 (7)
1 Corinthians 3:11-23
Mark 10:35-45

Almighty God, we praise you for your servant/s ___name/s___, through whom you have called the church to its tasks and renewed its life. Raise up in our own day teachers and prophets inspired by your Spirit, whose voices will give strength to your church and proclaim the reality of your reign, through Jesus Christ, our Savior and Lord, who lives and reigns with you and the Holy Spirit, one God, now and forever. **Amen.**

Renewers of Society

Hosea 2:18-23
Psalm 94:1-15 (14)
Romans 12:9-21
Luke 6:20-36

O God, your Son came among us to serve and not to be served, and to give his life for the life of the world. Lead us by his love to serve all those to whom the world offers no comfort and little help. Through us give hope to the hopeless, love to the unloved, peace to the troubled, and rest to the weary, through Jesus Christ, our Savior and Lord, who lives and reigns with you and the Holy Spirit, one God, now and forever. **Amen.**

OR

Holy and righteous God, you created us in your image. Grant us grace to contend fearlessly against evil and to make no peace with oppression. Help us, like your servant ___name___, to work for justice among people and nations, to the glory of your name, through Jesus Christ, our Savior and Lord, who lives and reigns with you and the Holy Spirit, one God, now and forever. **Amen.**

Pastors and Bishops

Ezekiel 34:11-16
or Acts 20:17-35
Psalm 84 (2)
1 Peter 5:1-4
or Ephesians 3:14-21
John 21:15-17
or Matthew 24:42-47

Heavenly Father, shepherd of your people, we thank you for your servant ___name___, who was faithful in the care and nurture of your flock. We pray that, following *her/his* example and the teaching of *her/his* holy life, we may by your grace attain our full maturity in Christ, through the same Jesus Christ, our Savior and Lord, who lives and reigns with you and the Holy Spirit, one God, now and forever. **Amen.**

OR

Almighty God, you have raised up faithful bishops of your church, including your servant ___name___. May the memory of *her/his* life be a source of joy for us and a bulwark of our faith, so that we may serve and confess your name before the world, through Jesus Christ, our Savior and Lord, who lives and reigns with you and the Holy Spirit, one God, now and forever. **Amen.**

Theologians and Teachers

Proverbs 3:1-7
or Wisdom 7:7-14
Psalm 119:89-104 (103)
1 Corinthians 2:6-10, 13-16
or 1 Corinthians 3:5-11
John 17:18-23
or Matthew 13:47-52

Almighty God, your Holy Spirit gives to one the word of knowledge, and to another the insight of wisdom, and to another the steadfastness of faith. We praise you for the gifts of grace imparted to your servant ___*name*___, and we pray that by *her/his* teaching we may be led to a fuller knowledge of the truth we have seen in your Son Jesus, our Savior and Lord, who lives and reigns with you and the Holy Spirit, one God, now and forever. **Amen.**

Artists and Scientists

Isaiah 28:5-6
or Hosea 14:5-8
or 2 Chronicles 20:20-21
Psalm 96 (9)
Philippians 4:8-9
or Ephesians 5:18b-20
Matthew 13:44-52

Almighty God, beautiful in majesty, majestic in holiness: You have shown us the splendor of creation in the work of your servant/s ___*name/s*___. Teach us to drive from the world all chaos and disorder, that our eyes may behold your glory, and that at last everyone may know the inexhaustible richness of your new creation in Jesus Christ our Lord, who lives and reigns with you and the Holy Spirit, one God, now and forever. **Amen.**

Occasions

Day of Thanksgiving

A
Deuteronomy 8:7-18
Psalm 65 (11)
2 Corinthians 9:6-15
Luke 17:11-19

A, B, C
Almighty God our Father, your generous goodness comes to us new every day. By the work of your Spirit lead us to acknowledge your goodness, give thanks for your benefits, and serve you in willing obedience, through Jesus Christ, our Savior and Lord. **Amen.**

B
Joel 2:21-27
Psalm 126 (3)
1 Timothy 2:1-7
Matthew 6:25-33

C
Deuteronomy 26:1-11
Psalm 100 (4)
Philippians 4:4-9
John 6:25-35

Christian Unity

Isaiah 2:2-4
Psalm 133 (1)
Ephesians 4:1-6
John 17:15-23

God our Father, your Son Jesus prayed that his followers might be one. Make all Christians one with him as he is one with you, so that in peace and concord we may carry to the world the message of your love, through Jesus Christ, our Savior and Lord. **Amen.**

Dedication or Anniversary of a Church

1 Kings 8:22-30
Psalm 84 (1)
1 Peter 2:1-9
John 10:22-30

Most High God, whom the heavens cannot contain, we give you thanks for the gifts of those who have built this house of prayer to your glory; we praise you for the fellowship of those who by their use *will make it / have made it* holy; and we pray that all who seek you here may find you and be filled with joy and peace, through Jesus Christ, our Savior and Lord, who lives and reigns with you and the Holy Spirit, one God, now and forever. **Amen.**

OR

O God, you have promised through your Son to be with your church forever. We give you thanks for those who founded this community of believers and for the signs of your presence in our congregation. Increase in us the spirit of faith and love, and make our fellowship an example to all believers and to all nations. We pray through Jesus Christ, our Savior and Lord, who lives and reigns with you and the Holy Spirit, one God, now and forever. **Amen.**

Harvest

Deuteronomy 26:1-11
Psalm 65 (11)
2 Corinthians 9:6-15
Matthew 13:24-30 [36-43]

O Lord, maker of all things, you open your hand and satisfy the desire of every living creature. We praise you for crowning the fields with your blessings and enabling us once more to gather in the fruits of the earth. Teach us to use your gifts carefully, that our land may continue to yield its increase, through Jesus Christ, our Savior and Lord. **Amen.**

Day of Penitence

Nehemiah 1:4-11a
Psalm 6 (2)
1 John 1:5—2:2
Luke 15:11-32

Lord God, accept our humble confession of the wrongs we have done, the injustice to which we have been party, and the countless denials of your mercy we have expressed. Turn us toward the love offered in your Son, and cleanse us by your grace, through Jesus Christ, our Savior and Lord. **Amen.**

OR

Almighty God, in penitence we come before you, acknowledging the sin that is within us. We share the guilt of all those who, bearing the name Christian, slay their fellow human beings because of race or faith or nation. Forgive us and change us by your love, that your word of hope may be heard clearly throughout the world, through Jesus Christ, our Savior and Lord. **Amen.**

Day of Mourning

Jonah 3:10—4:5, 11
Psalm 140 (7)
Ephesians 2:1-7 [8-10]
Luke 10:25-37

O God, strength of those who believe in you, give comfort and clarity of vision to us in this time of need. Open our ears to hear your voice and obey your will; open our hearts that true justice and wisdom may abound; and open our hands that violent resolution of conflict may cease, through Jesus Christ, our Savior and Lord. **Amen.**

Merciful God, you teach us in your holy word that you do not willingly afflict or grieve your children. Look with pity on us in our time of sorrow. Remember us in mercy. Strengthen us in patience, comfort us with the memory of your goodness, let your presence shine on us, and give us peace, through Jesus Christ, our Savior and Lord. **Amen.**

National Holiday

Jeremiah 29:4-14
Psalm 20 (6)
Romans 13:1-10
Mark 12:13-17

Lord of all the worlds, guide this nation by your Spirit to go forward in justice and freedom. Give to all our people the blessings of well-being and harmony, but above all things give us faith in you, that our nation may bring glory to your name and blessings to all peoples, through Jesus Christ, our Savior and Lord. **Amen.**

Peace

Micah 4:1-5
Psalm 85 (10)
Ephesians 2:13-18
John 15:9-12

Almighty God, all thoughts of truth and peace come from you. Kindle in the hearts of all your children the love of peace, and guide with your wisdom the leaders of the nations, so that your kingdom will go forth in peace and the earth will be filled with the knowledge of your love, through Jesus Christ, our Savior and Lord. **Amen.**

Stewardship of Creation

Job 38:1-11, 16-18
Psalm 104:1, 13-23 (24)
or Psalm 104:24-35 (24)
1 Timothy 6:6-10, 17-19
Luke 12:13-21

Almighty God, Lord of heaven and earth, we humbly pray that your gracious providence may give and preserve to our use the fruitfulness of the land and the seas, and may prosper all who labor therein; that we, who are constantly receiving good things from your hand, may always give you thanks, through Jesus Christ, our Savior and Lord. **Amen.**

OR

Merciful Creator, your hand is open wide to satisfy the needs of every living creature. Make us always thankful for your loving providence; and grant that we, remembering the account that we must one day give, may be faithful stewards of your good gifts, through Jesus Christ, our Savior and Lord. **Amen.**

New Year's Eve

Ecclesiastes 3:1-13
Psalm 8 (1)
Revelation 21:1-6a
Matthew 25:31-46

Eternal God, you have placed us in a world of space and time, and through the events of our lives you bless us with your love. Grant that in the new year we may know your presence, see your love at work, and live in the light of the event that gives us joy forever—the coming of your Son, Jesus Christ our Lord, who lives and reigns with you and the Holy Spirit, one God, now and forever. **Amen.**

# Prayers for Worship

Offering Prayer

Advent

God of abundance, we bring before you the precious fruits of your creation, and with them our very lives. Teach us patience and hope as we care for all those in need until the coming of your Son, our Savior and Lord. **Amen.**

Christmas

Good and loving God, we rejoice in the birth of Jesus, who came among the poor to bring the riches of your grace. As you have blessed us with your gifts, let them be blessing for others. With the trees of the field, with all earth and heaven, we shout for joy at the coming of your Son, Jesus Christ our Lord. **Amen.**

Lent

God our provider, you have not fed us with bread alone, but with words of grace and life. Bless us and these your gifts, which we receive from your bounty, through Jesus Christ our Lord. **Amen.**

Easter

Blessed are you, O God, ruler of heaven and earth. Day by day you shower us with blessings. As you have raised us to new life in Christ, give us glad and generous hearts, ready to praise you and to respond to those in need, through Jesus Christ, our Savior and Lord. **Amen.**

General

God of mercy and grace, the eyes of all wait upon you, and you open your hand in blessing. Fill us with good things at your table, that we may come to the help of all in need, through Jesus Christ, our redeemer and Lord. **Amen.**

General

Merciful God, as grains of wheat scattered upon the hills were gathered together to become one bread, so let your church be gathered together from the ends of the earth into your kingdom, for yours is the glory through Jesus Christ, now and forever. **Amen.**

Prayer after Communion

Advent

God for whom we wait, in this meal you give us a foretaste of that day when the hungry will be fed with good things. Send us forth to make known your deeds and to proclaim the greatness of your name, through Jesus Christ, our Savior and Lord. **Amen.**

Christmas

Radiant God, with our eyes we have seen your salvation, and in this meal we have feasted on your grace. May your Word take flesh in us, that we may be your holy people, revealing your glory made known to us in Jesus Christ, our Savior and Lord. **Amen.**

Lent

Compassionate God, you have fed us with the bread of heaven. Sustain us in our Lenten pilgrimage: may our fasting be hunger for justice; our alms, a making of peace; and our prayer, the song of grateful hearts, through Jesus Christ, our Savior and Lord. **Amen.**

Easter

Life-giving God, in the mystery of Christ's resurrection you send light to conquer darkness, water to give new life, and the bread of life to nourish your people. Send us forth as witnesses to your Son's resurrection, that we may show your glory to all the world, through Jesus Christ, our risen Lord. **Amen.**

General

Gracious God, in this meal you have drawn us to your heart, and nourished us at your table with food and drink, the body and blood of Christ. Now send us forth to be your people in the world, and to proclaim your truth this day and evermore, through Jesus Christ, our Savior and Lord. **Amen.**

General

O God, our life, our strength, our food, we give you thanks for sustaining us with the body and blood of your Son. By your Holy Spirit, enliven us to be his body in the world, that more and more we will give you praise and serve your earth and its many peoples, through Jesus Christ, our Savior and Lord. **Amen.**

Thanksgiving at the Table

Forms I–IV are in Settings One and Two of Holy Communion.

V

Holy, mighty, and merciful Lord, heaven and earth are full of your glory.

In great love you sent to us Jesus, your Son, who reached out to heal the sick and suffering, who preached good news to the poor, and who, on the cross, opened his arms to all.

In the night in which he was betrayed, our Lord Jesus took bread, and gave thanks; broke it, and gave it to his disciples, saying: Take and eat; this is my body, given for you. Do this for the remembrance of me.

Again, after supper, he took the cup, gave thanks, and gave it for all to drink, saying: This cup is the new covenant in my blood, shed for you and for all people for the forgiveness of sin. Do this for the remembrance of me.

Remembering, therefore, his death, resurrection, and ascension, we await his coming in glory.

Pour out upon us the Spirit of your love, O Lord, and unite the wills of all who share this heavenly food, the body and blood of Jesus Christ our Lord; to whom, with you and the Holy Spirit, be all glory and honor, now and forever.
Amen.

VI

Holy God, mighty Lord, gracious Father: Endless is your mercy and eternal your reign. You have filled all creation with light and life; heaven and earth are full of your glory.

We praise you for the grace shown to your people in every age: the promise to Israel, the rescue from Egypt, the gift of the promised land, the words of the prophets; and, at this end of all the ages, the gift of your Son, who proclaimed the good news in word and deed and was obedient to your will, even to giving his life.

In the night in which he was betrayed, our Lord Jesus took bread, and gave thanks; broke it, and gave it to his disciples, saying: Take and eat; this is my body, given for you. Do this for the remembrance of me.

Again, after supper, he took the cup, gave thanks, and gave it for all to drink, saying: This cup is the new covenant in my blood, shed for you and for all people for the forgiveness of sin. Do this for the remembrance of me.

For as often as we eat of this bread and drink from this cup, we proclaim the Lord's death until he comes.
Christ has died. Christ is risen. Christ will come again.

Therefore, O God, with this bread and cup we remember the life our Lord offered for us. And, believing the witness of his resurrection, we await his coming in power to share with us the great and promised feast.
Amen. Come, Lord Jesus.

Send now, we pray, your Holy Spirit, that we who share in Christ's body and blood may live to the praise of your glory and receive our inheritance with all your saints in light.
Amen. Come, Holy Spirit.

Join our prayers with those of your servants of every time and every place, and unite them with the ceaseless petitions of our great high priest until he comes as victorious Lord of all. Through him, with him, in him, in the unity of the Holy Spirit, all glory and honor is yours, almighty Father, now and forever.
Amen.

VII

Holy God, holy and mighty, holy and immortal: you we praise and glorify, you we worship and adore. You formed the earth from chaos; you encircled the globe with air; you created fire for warmth and light; you nourish the lands with water. You molded us in your image, and with mercy higher than the mountains, with grace deeper than the seas, you blessed the Israelites and cherished them as your own. That also we, estranged and dying, might be adopted to live in your Spirit, you called to us through the life and death of Jesus.

In the night in which he was betrayed, our Lord Jesus took bread, and gave thanks; broke it, and gave it to his disciples, saying: Take and eat; this is my body, given for you. Do this for the remembrance of me.

Again, after supper, he took the cup, gave thanks, and gave it for all to drink, saying: This cup is the new covenant in my blood, shed for you and for all people for the forgiveness of sin. Do this for the remembrance of me.

Together as the body of Christ, we proclaim the Lord's death until he comes.
Christ has died. Christ is risen. Christ will come again.

With this bread and cup we remember your Son, the first-born of your new creation. We remember his life lived for others, and his death and resurrection, which renews the face of the earth. We await his coming, when, with the world made perfect through your wisdom, all our sins and sorrows will be no more.
Amen. Come, Lord Jesus.

Holy God, holy and merciful, holy and compassionate, send upon us and this meal your Holy Spirit, whose breath revives us for life, whose fire rouses us to love. Enfold in your arms all who share this holy food. Nurture in us the fruits of the Spirit, that we may be a living tree, sharing your bounty with all the world.
Amen. Come, Holy Spirit.

Holy and benevolent God, receive our praise and petitions, as Jesus received the cry of the needy, and fill us with your blessing, until, needy no longer and bound to you in love, we feast forever in the triumph of the Lamb: through whom all glory and honor is yours, O God, O Living One, with the Holy Spirit, in your holy church, now and forever.
Amen.

VIII

God of our weary years, God of our silent tears, you have brought us this far along the way. In times of bitterness you did not abandon us, but guided us into the path of love and light. In every age you sent prophets to make known your loving will for all humanity. The cry of the poor has become your own cry; our hunger and thirst for justice is your own desire. In the fullness of time, you sent your chosen servant to preach good news to the afflicted, to break bread with the outcast and despised, and to ransom those in bondage to prejudice and sin.

In the night in which he was betrayed, our Lord Jesus took bread, and gave thanks; broke it, and gave it to his disciples, saying: Take and eat; this is my body, given for you. Do this for the remembrance of me.

Again, after supper, he took the cup, gave thanks, and gave it for all to drink, saying: This cup is the new covenant in my blood, shed for you and for all people for the forgiveness of sin. Do this for the remembrance of me.

For as often as we eat of this bread and drink from this cup, we proclaim the Lord's death until he comes.
Christ has died. Christ is risen. Christ will come again.

Remembering, therefore, his death and resurrection, we await the day when Jesus shall return to free all the earth from the bonds of slavery and death. Come, Lord Jesus! And let the church say, Amen.
Amen.

Send your Holy Spirit, our advocate, to fill the hearts of all who share this bread and cup with courage and wisdom to pursue love and justice in all the world. Come, Spirit of freedom! And let the church say, Amen.
Amen.

Join our prayers and praise with your prophets and martyrs of every age, that, rejoicing in the hope of the resurrection, we might live in the freedom and hope of your Son. Through him, with him, in him, in the unity of the Holy Spirit, all glory and honor is yours, almighty Father, now and forever.
Amen.

IX

Holy God, you alone are holy, you alone are God. The universe declares your praise: beyond the stars; beneath the sea; within each cell; with every breath.
We praise you, O God.

Generations bless your faithfulness: through the water; by night and day; across the wilderness; out of exile; into the future.
We bless you, O God.

We give you thanks for your dear Son: at the heart of human life; near to those who suffer; beside the sinner; among the poor; with us now.
We thank you, O God.

In the night in which he was betrayed, our Lord Jesus took bread, and gave thanks; broke it, and gave it to his disciples, saying: Take and eat; this is my body, given for you. Do this for the remembrance of me.

Again, after supper, he took the cup, gave thanks, and gave it for all to drink, saying: This cup is the new covenant in my blood, shed for you and for all people for the forgiveness of sin. Do this for the remembrance of me.

Remembering his love for us on the way, at the table, and to the end, we proclaim the mystery of faith.
Christ has died. Christ is risen. Christ will come again.

We pray for the gift of your Spirit: in our gathering; within this meal; among your people; throughout the world.

Blessing, praise, and thanks to you, holy God, through Christ Jesus, by your Spirit, in your church, without end.
Amen.

X

O God most mighty, O God most merciful, O God our rock and our salvation, hear us as we praise, call us to your table, grant us your life.

When the world was a formless void, you formed order and beauty. When Abraham and Sarah were barren, you sent them a child. When the Israelites were enslaved, you led them to freedom. Ruth faced starvation, David fought Goliath, and the psalmists cried out for healing, and full of compassion, you granted the people your life.

You entered our sorrows in Jesus our brother. He was born among the poor, he lived under oppression, he wept over the city. With infinite love, he granted the people your life.

In the night in which he was betrayed, our Lord Jesus took bread, and gave thanks; broke it, and gave it to his disciples, saying: Take and eat; this is my body, given for you. Do this for the remembrance of me.

Again, after supper, he took the cup, gave thanks, and gave it for all to drink, saying: This cup is the new covenant in my blood, shed for you and for all people for the forgiveness of sin. Do this for the remembrance of me.

Remembering his death, we cry out Amen. [**Amen.**]
Celebrating his resurrection, we shout Amen. [**Amen.**]
Trusting his presence in every time and place, we plead Amen. [**Amen.**]

O God, you are Breath: send your Spirit on this meal. O God, you are Bread: feed us with yourself. O God, you are Wine: warm our hearts and make us one. O God, you are Fire: transform us with hope.

O God most majestic, O God most motherly, O God our strength and our song, you show us a vision of a tree of life with fruits for all and leaves that heal the nations. Grant us such life, the life of the Father to the Son, the life of the Spirit of our risen Savior, life in you, now and forever. **Amen.**

XI

We give you thanks, Father, through Jesus Christ, your beloved Son, whom you sent in this end of the ages to save and redeem us and to proclaim to us your will.

He is your Word, inseparable from you, through whom you created all things, and in whom you take delight. He is your Word, sent from heaven to a virgin's womb. He there took on our nature and our lot and was shown forth as your Son, born of the Holy Spirit and of the virgin Mary. He, our Lord Jesus, fulfilled all your will and won for you a holy people; he stretched out his hands in suffering in order to free from suffering those who trust you.

He is the one who, handed over to a death he freely accepted, in order to destroy death, to break the bonds of the evil one, to crush hell underfoot, to give light to the righteous, to establish his covenant, and to show forth the resurrection, taking bread and giving thanks to you, said: Take and eat; this is my body, given for you. Do this for the remembrance of me.

In the same way he took the cup, gave thanks, and gave it for all to drink, saying: This cup is the new covenant in my blood, shed for you and for all people for the forgiveness of sin. Do this for the remembrance of me.

Remembering, then, his death and resurrection, we take this bread and cup, giving you thanks that you have made us worthy to stand before you and to serve you as your priestly people.

Send your Spirit upon these gifts of your church; gather into one all who share this bread and wine; fill us with your Holy Spirit to establish our faith in truth, that we may praise and glorify you through your Son Jesus Christ; through whom all glory and honor are yours, almighty Father, with the Holy Spirit, in your holy church, both now and forever.
Amen.

Thanksgiving at the Font

Thanksgiving I is in the order of Holy Baptism.

II

Blessed are you, O God, maker and ruler of all things. Your voice thundered over the waters at creation. You water the mountains and send springs into the valleys to refresh and satisfy all living things.

Through the waters of the flood you carried those in the ark to safety. Through the sea you led your people Israel from slavery to freedom. In the wilderness you nourished them with water from the rock, and you brought them across the river Jordan to the promised land.

By the baptism of his death and resurrection, your Son Jesus has carried us to safety and freedom. The floods shall not overwhelm us, and the deep shall not swallow us up, for Christ has brought us over to the land of promise. He sends us to make disciples, baptizing in the name of the Father, and of the Son, and of the Holy Spirit.

Pour out your Holy Spirit; wash away sin in this cleansing water; clothe the baptized with Christ; and claim your daughters and sons, no longer slave and free, no longer male and female, but one with all the baptized in Christ Jesus, who lives and reigns with you in the unity of the Holy Spirit, one God, now and forever.
Amen.

III

Blessed are you, holy God. You are the creator of the waters of the earth. You are the fire of rebirth. You poured out your Spirit on your people Israel. You breathe life into our dry bones. Your Son Jesus promised to send the Spirit to us that the world may know your peace and truth.

Pour out your Holy Spirit, and breathe new life into those who are here baptized. By your Spirit adopt us all as your children, through our Savior Jesus Christ, who lives and reigns with you and the Holy Spirit, one God, now and forever.
Amen.

IV

Holy God, mighty Lord, gracious Father: We give you thanks, for in the beginning your Spirit moved over the waters and you created heaven and earth. By the gift of water you nourish and sustain us and all living things.
Blessed be God now and forever.

By the waters of the flood you condemned the wicked and saved those whom you had chosen, Noah and his family. You led Israel by the pillar of cloud and fire through the sea, out of slavery into the freedom of the promised land.
Blessed be God now and forever.

In the waters of the Jordan your Son was baptized by John and anointed with the Spirit. By the baptism of his own death and resurrection your beloved Son has set us free from the bondage to sin and death, and has opened the way to the joy and freedom of everlasting life. He made water a sign of the kingdom and of cleansing and rebirth. In obedience to his command, we make disciples of all nations, baptizing them in the name of the Father, and of the Son, and of the Holy Spirit.
Blessed be God now and forever.

Pour out your Holy Spirit, so that those who are here baptized may be given new life. Wash away the sin of all those who are cleansed by this water and bring them forth as inheritors of your glorious kingdom.

To you be given praise and honor and worship through your Son, Jesus Christ our Lord, in the unity of the Holy Spirit, now and forever.
Amen.

V

Holy God, holy and merciful, holy and mighty, you are the river of life, you are the everlasting wellspring, you are the fire of rebirth.

Glory to you for oceans and lakes, for rivers and streams. Honor to you for cloud and rain, for dew and snow. Your waters are below us, around us, above us: our life is born in you. You are the fountain of resurrection.

Praise to you for your saving waters: Noah and the animals survive the flood, Hagar discovers your well. The Israelites escape through the sea, and they drink from your gushing rock. Naaman washes his leprosy away, and the Samaritan woman will never be thirsty again.

At this font, holy God, we pray: Praise to you for the water of baptism and for your Word that saves us in this water. Breathe your Spirit into all who are gathered here and into all creation. Illumine our days. Enliven our bones. Dry our tears. Wash away the sin within us, and drown the evil around us.

Satisfy all our thirst with your living water, Jesus Christ, our Savior, who lives and reigns with you and the Holy Spirit, one God, now and forever.
Amen.

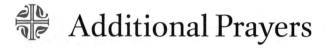 # Additional Prayers

Worship

Before worship

God of grace, you have given us minds to know you, hearts to love you, and voices to sing your praise. Fill us with your Spirit, that we may celebrate your glory and worship you in spirit and truth, through Jesus Christ, our Savior and Lord. Amen.

Grace to receive the word

Blessed Lord God, you have caused the holy scriptures to be written for the nourishment of your people. Grant that we may hear them, read, mark, learn, and inwardly digest them, that, comforted by your promises, we may embrace and forever hold fast to the hope of eternal life, which you have given us in Jesus Christ, our Savior and Lord. Amen.

Before holy communion

Merciful God, we do not presume to come to your table trusting in our own righteousness, but in your abundant mercy. Grant us, therefore, gracious Lord, so to eat and drink the body and blood of your dear Son, Jesus Christ, that we may live in him and he in us, now and forever. Amen.

After holy communion

Almighty God, you provide the true bread from heaven, your Son, Jesus Christ our Lord. Grant that we who have received the sacrament of his body and blood may abide in him and he in us, that we may be filled with the power of his endless life, now and forever. Amen.

Sending of communion to the sick and homebound

Gracious God, loving all your family with a mother's tender care: As you sent the angel to feed Elijah with heavenly bread, assist us in this ministry on which we set forth. In your love and care, nourish and strengthen those to whom we bring this sacrament, that through the body and blood of your Son we all may know the comfort of your abiding presence. Amen.

After worship

Almighty God, grant that your holy word which has been proclaimed this day may enter into our hearts through your grace, that it may produce in us the fruit of the Spirit for witness and service in the world and to the praise and honor of your name, through Jesus Christ, our Savior and Lord. Amen.

After worship

Grant, O Lord Jesus, that the ears which have heard the voice of your songs may be closed to the voice of dispute; that the eyes which have seen your great love may also behold your blessed hope; that the tongues which have sung your praise may speak the truth in love; that the feet which have walked in your courts may walk in the region of light; and that the bodies which have received your living body may be restored in newness of life. Glory to you for your inexpressible gift; for you live and reign with the Father and the Holy Spirit, one God, now and forever. Amen.

The Church

The church

Gracious Father, we pray for your holy catholic church. Fill it with all truth and peace. Where it is corrupt, purify it; where it is in error, direct it; where in anything it is amiss, reform it; where it is right, strengthen it; where it is in need, provide for it; where it is divided, reunite it; for the sake of Jesus Christ, your Son, our Lord. Amen.

Church unity

Most high and holy God, pour out upon us your one and unifying Spirit, and awaken in every confession of the whole church a holy hunger and thirst for unity in you; through Jesus Christ, our Savior and Lord. Amen.

The saints

We thank you, O God, for all your servants and witnesses of times past: for Abraham and Sarah, Moses and Miriam, Deborah and Gideon, Samuel and Hannah; for Isaiah and the prophets; for Mary, mother of our Lord; for Mary Magdalene, Peter, Paul, and for all the apostles, for Stephen and Phoebe, and for all the martyrs and saints in every time and in every land. In your mercy, give us, as you gave them, the hope of salvation and the promise of eternal life through Jesus Christ, our Savior and Lord. Amen.

Pastors and bishops

Ever-living God, strengthen and sustain pastors and bishops [especially___name/s___], that with patience and understanding they may love and care for your people. Grant that together they may follow in the way of Jesus Christ, our Savior and Lord, who lives and reigns with you and the Holy Spirit, one God, now and forever. Amen.

Associates in ministry

God of unity and peace, you give each of us grace through the gift of Christ. We give you thanks for associates in ministry [especially___name/s___], through whom your people are equipped for the work of ministry and for building up the body of Christ. With your Holy Spirit empower your servants in their calling, so that together we come to the unity of the faith and to the measure of the full stature of Jesus Christ, our Savior and Lord. Amen.

Diaconal ministry

God of compassion, your Son came among us not to be served but to serve. We give you thanks for the women and men whom you have called to the diaconal ministry of word and service [especially___name/s___]. Give them faith to serve you with gladness; sustain them with a living hope, especially in the time of despair; and kindle in them your love, so that they see in every neighbor the face of Jesus Christ our Lord, in whose name we pray. Amen.

Lay professional leaders

Gracious God, as you have called workers to varied tasks in the world and in your church, so you have called these servants to this ministry of _____. Grant them joy and a spirit of bold trust, that their work may stir up each of us to a life of fruitful service; through your Son, Jesus Christ our Lord. Amen.

Church musicians

O God of majesty, whom saints and angels delight to worship: Pour out your Spirit on your servants who, with the gifts of music, enliven our praises and proclaim your word with power. Through this ministry give us new awareness of your beauty and grace, and join our voices with all the choirs of heaven, both now and forever; through your Son, Jesus Christ our Lord. Amen.

Church artists

God of glory, we long to see your face, yet our vision is clouded by brokenness and sin. Breathe your creating Spirit into the hearts and hands of those who, through their work in the visual arts, desire to serve you. Through this ministry draw us to your truth and beauty, and bring us to the perfect fulfillment of standing in your unveiled glory, through your Son, Jesus Christ our Lord. Amen.

Teachers

O God of wisdom, in your goodness you provide faithful teachers for your church. By your Holy Spirit give all teachers insight into your holy word, lives that are examples to us all, and the courage to know and do the truth; through your Son, Jesus Christ our Lord. Amen.

Seminaries

We give you thanks, O God, for all of life and for our common calling as your servants, for the work of your church and for the ministries of word, sacrament, and service. We give you thanks for women and men whom you call to be leaders in your church and for teachers who form them for service. Through the witness and mission of our seminaries may the church join courageously in your work of compassion, mercy, justice, and peace; through Jesus Christ, our Savior and Lord. Amen.

General thanksgiving

Almighty God, Father of all mercies, we humbly thank you for your goodness to us and to all that you have made. We praise you for your creation, for keeping us and all things in your care, and for all the blessings of life. Above all we bless you for your immeasurable love in redeeming the world by our Lord Jesus Christ, for the means of grace, and for the hope of glory. And, we pray, give us such an awareness of your mercies that with thankful hearts we praise you, not only with our lips but in our lives, by giving ourselves to your service and by living in your gifts of holiness and righteousness all our days; through Jesus Christ our Lord, to whom, with you and the Holy Spirit, be all worship and praise, now and forever. Amen.

General intercession

Keep watch, dear Lord, with those who work or watch or weep, and give your angels charge over those who sleep. Tend the sick, give rest to the weary, bless the dying, soothe the suffering, comfort the afflicted, shield the joyous; and all for your love's sake. Amen.

Congregational Life

Those preparing for baptism

Merciful and most high God, creator and giver of life, you have called all people from darkness into light, from error into truth, from death into life. Grant grace to ___*name/s*___ and bless *them*. Raise *them* by your Spirit. Revive *them* by your word. Form *them* by your hand. Bring *them* to the water of life and to the bread and cup of blessing, that with all your people *they* may bear witness to your grace and praise you forever, through Jesus Christ our Lord. Amen.

New members

Almighty God, by the love of Jesus Christ you draw people to yourself and welcome them into the household of faith. May we show your joy by embracing new brothers and sisters as we bear your creative and redeeming word to all the world. Keep us close together in your Spirit, in the breaking of bread and the prayers, and in service to others, following the example of Jesus Christ, our servant and Lord. Amen.

Farewell and Godspeed

Eternal God, we thank you for ___*name/s*___ and for our life together in this congregation and community. As *they have* been a blessing to us, so now send *them* forth to be a blessing to others; through Jesus Christ, our Savior and Lord. Amen.

Founders and previous leaders of a congregation

We thank you, Lord God, for brave and believing people who planted your message in this place. We praise you for the gift of your Holy Spirit, who worked in them to gather and give order to this community, and who still sustains it. Remembering all those who have gone before us, we pray that we may follow as they followed, in the way, the truth, and the life, Jesus Christ, our Savior and Lord. Amen.

Mission

Spread of the gospel

By your word, eternal God, your creation sprang forth, and we were given the breath of life. By your word, eternal God, death is overcome, Christ is raised from the tomb, and we are given new life in the power of your Spirit. May we boldly proclaim this good news in our words and our deeds, rejoicing always in your powerful presence; through Jesus Christ, our risen Lord. Amen.

Global mission

Almighty God, you sent your Son Jesus Christ to reconcile the world to yourself. We praise and bless you for those whom you have sent in the power of the Spirit to preach the gospel to all nations. We thank you that in all parts of the earth a community of love has been gathered together by their prayers and labors, and that in every place your servants call upon your name; for the kingdom and the power and the glory are yours forever. Amen.

The mission of the church

Draw your church together, O God, into one great company of disciples, together following our teacher Jesus Christ into every walk of life, together serving in Christ's mission to the world, and together witnessing to your love wherever you will send us; for the sake of Jesus Christ our Lord. Amen.

Congregational ministries

Almighty God, your Holy Spirit equips the church with a rich variety of gifts. Grant that we may use them to bear witness to Christ in lives that are built on faith and love. Make us ready to live the gospel and eager to do your will, so that we may share with all your church in the joys of eternal life; through Jesus Christ, our Savior and Lord. Amen.

Those seeking deeper knowledge of God

Gracious and holy God, give us diligence to seek you, wisdom to perceive you, and patience to wait for you. Grant us, O God, a mind to meditate on you; eyes to behold you; ears to listen for your word; a heart to love you; and a life to proclaim you; through the power of the Spirit of Jesus Christ, our Savior and Lord. Amen.

Civic Life, Government, Nations

Peace

O God, it is your will to hold both heaven and earth in a single peace. Let the design of your great love shine on the waste of our wraths and sorrows, and give peace to your church, peace among nations, peace in our homes, and peace in our hearts; through your Son, Jesus Christ our Lord. Amen.

Peace

Gracious and holy God, lead us from death to life, from falsehood to truth. Lead us from despair to hope, from fear to trust. Lead us from hate to love, from war to peace. Let peace fill our hearts, our world, our universe; through Jesus Christ, our Savior and Lord. Amen.

Peace among the nations

Gracious God, grant peace among nations. Cleanse from our own hearts the seeds of strife: greed and envy, harsh misunderstandings and ill will, fear and desire for revenge. Make us quick to welcome ventures in cooperation among the peoples of the world, so that there may be woven the fabric of a common good too strong to be torn by the evil hands of war. In the time of opportunity, make us be diligent; and in the time of peril, let not our courage fail; through Jesus Christ our Lord. Amen.

National distress

Eternal God, amid all the turmoil and changes of the world your love is steadfast and your strength never fails. In this time of danger and trouble, be to us a sure guardian and rock of defense. Guide the leaders of our nation with your wisdom, comfort those in distress, and grant us courage and hope to face the future; through Jesus Christ, our Savior and Lord. Amen.

Time of conflict, crisis, disaster

God, our refuge and strength, you have bound us together in a common life. In all our conflicts, help us to confront one another without hatred or bitterness, to listen for your voice amid competing claims, and to work together with mutual forbearance and respect; through Jesus Christ our Lord. Amen.

Time of conflict, crisis, disaster

O God, where hearts are fearful and constricted, grant courage and hope. Where anxiety is infectious and widening, grant peace and reassurance. Where impossibilities close every door and window, grant imagination and resistance. Where distrust twists our thinking, grant healing and illumination. Where spirits are daunted and weakened, grant soaring wings and strengthened dreams. All these things we ask in the name of Jesus Christ, our Savior and Lord. Amen.

Time of civic mourning

God our creator, through whose providing care we enjoy all goodness and life, turn our eyes to your mercy in this time of confusion and loss. Comfort this nation as we mourn; shine your light on those whose only companion is darkness; and teach us all so to number our days that we may apply our hearts to your wisdom; through Jesus Christ, our Savior and Lord. Amen.

The nation

Almighty God, you have given us this good land as our heritage. Make us always remember your generosity and constantly do your will. Bless our land with honesty in the workplace, truth in education, and honor in daily life. Save us from violence, discord, and confusion; from pride and arrogance; and from every evil course of action. When times are prosperous, let our hearts be thankful; and, in troubled times, do not let our trust in you fail. We pray in the name of Jesus Christ our Lord. Amen.

The nation

Holy Trinity, one God, you show us the splendor of diversity and the beauty of unity in your own divine life. Make us, who came from many nations with many languages, a united people that delights in our many different gifts. Defend our liberties, and give those whom we have entrusted with authority the spirit of wisdom, that there might be justice and peace in our land. We pray in the name of Jesus Christ, our sovereign and our Savior. Amen.

State, provincial, local governments

Almighty God, we lift before you all who govern this *state/province/city/town* _____. May those who hold power understand that it is a trust from you to be used, not for personal glory or profit, but for the service of the people. Drive from us cynicism, selfishness, and corruption; grant in your mercy just and honest government; and give us grace to live together in unity and peace; through Jesus Christ our Lord. Amen.

Responsible citizenship

Lord God, you call your people to honor those in authority. Help us elect trustworthy leaders, participate in wise decisions for our common life, and serve our neighbors in local communities. Bless the leaders of our land, that we may be at peace among ourselves and a blessing to other nations of the earth; through Jesus Christ, our Savior and Lord. Amen.

Those in civil authority

Almighty God, our heavenly Father, bless the public servants in the government of this *state/province/city/town* _____, that they may do their work in a spirit of wisdom, charity, and justice. Help them use their authority to serve faithfully and to promote our common life; through your Son, Jesus Christ our Lord. Amen.

Courts of justice

Lord of all, you have declared what is right: to seek justice, to love kindness, and to walk humbly with you. Bless judges and courts, juries and law officers throughout our land. Guard them from retribution and from corruption. Give them the spirit of wisdom, that they may perceive the truth and administer the law impartially as instruments of your divine will. We pray in the name of the one who will come to be our judge, your Son, Jesus Christ our Lord. Amen.

Those in the armed forces

Almighty God, we commend to your gracious care and keeping all the men and women of our armed forces at home and abroad. Defend them day by day with your heavenly grace; strengthen them in their trials and temptations; give them courage to face the perils that surround them; and grant them a sense of your abiding presence wherever they may be; through Jesus Christ, our Savior and Lord. Amen.

Cities

Gracious God, bless our cities and make them places of safety for all people, rich and poor. Give us grace to work for cities where neighborhoods remain vibrant and whole, where the lost and forgotten in society are supported, and where the arts flourish. Make the diverse fabric of the city a delight to all who live and visit there and a strong bond uniting people around common goals for the good of all; through Jesus Christ, our Savior and Lord. Amen.

The gifts of agriculture

God our creator, you have ordered seedtime and harvest, sunshine and rain. Give to all who work the land fair compensation for the work of their hands. Grant that the people of this and every nation may give thanks to you for food, drink, and all that sustains life; may use with care the land and water from which these good things come; and may honor the laborers who produce them; through your Son, Jesus Christ our Lord. Amen.

The neighborhood

God our creator, by your holy prophet Jeremiah you taught your ancient people to seek the welfare of the cities in which they lived. We commend our neighborhood to your care, that it might be kept free from social strife and decay. Give us strength of purpose and concern for others, that we may create here a community of justice and peace where your will may be done; through your Son, Jesus Christ our Lord. Amen.

Schools

O God, source of all goodness: We give you thanks for the gift of reason and the opportunity for education. Bless our schools, that they may be places of learning and safety where teachers challenge the minds and nurture the hearts of students. Grant that teachers and students may work together in mutual respect and find joy in the challenges of academic life; through Jesus Christ, our Savior and Lord. Amen.

Schools

Eternal God, bless all schools, colleges, and universities [*especially*_____], that they may be lively places for sound learning, new discovery, and the pursuit of wisdom; and grant that those who teach and those who learn may find you to be the source of all truth; through Jesus Christ, our Savior and Lord. Amen.

Teachers

God of wisdom, your Son came among us as a teacher. Send your blessing on all who are engaged in the work of education: give them clearness of vision and freshness of thought, and enable them so to train the hearts and minds of their students that they may grow in wisdom and be prepared to face the challenges of life; through Jesus Christ our Lord. Amen.

Commerce and labor

Almighty God, your Son Jesus Christ dignified our labor by sharing our toil. Guide us with your justice in the workplace, so that we may never value things above people, or surrender honor to love of gain or lust for power. Prosper all efforts to put an end to work that brings no joy, and teach us how to govern the ways of business to the harm of none and for the sake of the common good; through Jesus Christ our Lord. Amen.

Social Ministry

The human family

O God of all, with wonderful diversity of languages and cultures you created all people in your image. Free us from prejudice and fear, that we may see your face in the faces of people around the world; through Jesus Christ, our Savior and Lord. Amen.

The human family

O God, you made us in your own image and redeemed us through Jesus your Son. Look with compassion on the whole human family; take away the arrogance and hatred that infect our hearts; break down the walls that separate us; unite us in bonds of love; and, through our struggle and confusion, work to accomplish your purposes on earth; so that, in your good time, every people and nation may serve you in harmony around your heavenly throne; through Jesus Christ, our Savior and Lord. Amen.

Social justice

Grant, O God, that your holy and life-giving Spirit may move every human heart; that the barriers dividing us may crumble, suspicions disappear, and hatreds cease; and that, with our divisions healed, we might live in justice and peace; through your Son, Jesus Christ our Lord. Amen.

The unemployed

God of justice, we remember before you those who suffer want and anxiety from lack of work. Guide the people of this land so to use our wealth and resources that all people may find suitable and fulfilling employment and receive just payment for their labor; through your Son, Jesus Christ our Lord. Amen.

The neglected

Almighty and most merciful God, we call to mind before you all whom it is easy to forget: those who are homeless, destitute, sick, isolated, and all who have no one to care for them. May we bring help and healing to those who are broken in body or spirit, that they may have comfort in sorrow, company in loneliness, and a place of safety and warmth; through Jesus Christ our Lord. Amen.

The poor

God of compassion, whose Son became poor for our sake: Help us to see the face of Christ in those who are poor, and in serving them to serve you. Give us generous hearts so that those living in poverty may have adequate food, clothing, and shelter. By your Spirit move us to affirm the dignity of all people and to work for just laws that protect the most vulnerable in society; through Jesus Christ, our Savior and Lord. Amen.

The oppressed

Look with mercy, gracious God, upon people everywhere who live with injustice, terror, disease, and death as their constant companions. Rouse us from our complacency and help us to eliminate cruelty wherever it is found. Strengthen those who seek equality for all. Grant that everyone may enjoy a fair portion of the abundance of the earth; through your Son, Jesus Christ our Lord. Amen.

Prisons and correctional institutions

God of justice, for our sake your Son was condemned as a criminal. Visit our jails and prisons with your judgment and mercy. Remember all prisoners; bring the guilty to repentance and amendment of life according to your will; and give hope for the future. When any are held unjustly, raise up for them advocates to bring them release, and give us the wisdom to improve our system of justice. Watch over those who work in these institutions; give them strength and compassion, and keep them from becoming brutal or callous. Lead us to do for those in prison what we would do for Christ, in whose name we pray. Amen.

Those who suffer for the sake of conscience

God of faithfulness, you bless those who are persecuted. Strengthen those who suffer for the sake of conscience. When they are accused, save them from speaking in hate; when they are rejected, save them from bitterness; when they are imprisoned, save them from despair. Give us grace to respect their witness and to discern the truth, that our society may be cleansed and strengthened; for the sake of our merciful and righteous judge, Jesus Christ our Lord. Amen.

Our enemies

Gracious God, your Son called on you to forgive his enemies while he was suffering shame and death. Lead our enemies and us from prejudice to truth; deliver them and us from hatred, cruelty, and revenge; and in your good time enable us all to stand reconciled before you; through Jesus Christ, our Savior and Lord. Amen.

Stewardship

Stewardship of natural resources

Almighty God, in giving us dominion over things on earth, you made us coworkers in your creation. Give us wisdom and reverence to use the resources of nature so that no one may suffer from our abuse of them, and that generations yet to come may continue to praise you for your bounty; through your Son, Jesus Christ our Lord. Amen.

Renewal of mind and body

O God, we thank you for times of refreshment and peace in the course of this busy life. Grant that we may so use our leisure for the renewal of our bodies and minds that our spirits may be opened to the goodness of your creation; through Jesus Christ, our Savior and Lord. Amen.

The proper use of wealth

O God, in your love you have given the people of this land gifts of abundance beyond what our forebears knew or could imagine. Mercifully grant that we may not be so occupied with material things that we forget spiritual gifts, and thus, even though we have gained the whole world, lose our souls; through Jesus Christ, our Savior and Lord. Amen.

The proper use of wealth

God of abundance, you have poured out a large measure of earthly blessings: our table is richly furnished, our cup overflows, and we live in safety and security. Teach us to set our hearts on you and not these material blessings. Keep us from becoming captivated by prosperity, and grant us in wisdom to use your blessings to your glory and to the service of humankind; through Jesus Christ our Lord. Amen.

Creation

Agriculture

Abundant God, we give you thanks for the fruitful earth, which produces what is needed for life. Bless those who work in the fields; grant favorable weather to all engaged in agriculture; and help us to ensure that all people share the fruits of the earth, rejoicing in your goodness; through your Son, Jesus Christ our Lord. Amen.

Thanks for the harvest

Most gracious God, according to your wisdom the deep waters are opened up and clouds drop gentle moisture. We praise you for the return of planting and harvest seasons, for the fertility of the soil, for the harvesting of the crops, and for all other blessings that you in your generosity pour out on all people. Give us a full understanding of your mercy, that our lives may show respect and care for your creation; through Jesus Christ, our Savior and Lord. Amen.

In time of scarce rainfall

O God, giver and sustainer of life, in this time of need send us the gift of rain, so that we may receive the fruits of the earth for our benefit and for your praise; through Jesus Christ, our Savior and Lord. Amen.

Creation and new creation

Sovereign of the universe, your first covenant of mercy was with every living creature. When your beloved Son came among us, the waters of the river welcomed him, the heavens opened to greet his arrival, the animals of the wilderness drew near as his companions. With all the world's people, may we who are washed into new life through baptism seek the way of your new creation, the way of justice and care, mercy and peace; through Jesus Christ, our Savior and Lord. Amen.

Creation's praise

Praise to you, Lord Jesus Christ, who in your self-emptying love gathered up and reconciled all creation to the Father. Innumerable galaxies of the heavens worship you. Creatures that grace the earth rejoice in you. All those in the deepest seas bow to you in adoration. As with them we give you praise, grant that we may cherish the earth, our home, and live in harmony with this good creation, for you live and reign with the Father and the Holy Spirit, one God, now and forever. Amen.

Life Passages

Birth of a child

O Lord our God, creator of all that exists, we thank you for the joy of watching new life begin and for the privilege of sharing with you in your continuing creation. In your mercy grant that these blessings may continue to us and even to our children's children, that generations yet unborn may bless your holy name; through Jesus Christ, our Savior and Lord. Amen.

Adoption of a child

Merciful God, because of your love for us in Jesus Christ we have become brothers and sisters, daughters and sons in your family, the church. We thank you for the love which welcomes _child's name_ into this household. As you have blessed _name/s of parent/s_ with this child, give *them* the joy of caring for *her/him*, and increase our joy as members of your family in Jesus Christ our Lord. Amen.

Remembrance of the faithful departed

Eternal God, your love is stronger than death, and your passion more fierce than the grave. We rejoice in the lives of those whom you have drawn into your eternal embrace. Keep us in joyful communion with them until we join the saints of every people and nation gathered before your throne in your ceaseless praise, through your Son, Jesus Christ our Lord. Amen.

Those preparing for marriage

We praise you, O God, that your children ___names___ have been drawn together in love for one another. Strengthen their hearts, so that they will keep faith with each other, please you in all things, and come to the joy of celebrating their marriage; through Jesus Christ our Lord. Amen.

Marriage

Eternal God, without your grace no promise is sure. Strengthen ___names___ with patience, kindness, gentleness, and all other gifts of your Spirit, so that they may fulfill the vows they have made. Keep them faithful to each other and to you. Fill them with such love and joy that they may build a home of peace and welcome. Guide them by your word to serve you all their days; through Jesus Christ our Lord. Amen.

Those whose marriage has ended

God of compassion and grace, in your steadfast love accompany ___name/s___ . As you ever work to restore and renew your people, overcome bitterness with your joy, hatred with your love, brokenness with your life; and give us hope through the death and resurrection of your Son, Jesus Christ our Lord. Amen.

Those entering retirement

Gracious God, we thank you for the work and witness of your servant ___name___ , who has enriched this community and brought gladness to friends and family. Now bless and preserve *her/him* at this time of transition. Day by day, guide *her/him* and give *her/him* what is needed, friends to cheer *her/his* way, and a clear vision of that to which you are now calling *her/him*. By your Holy Spirit be present in *her/his* pilgrimage, that *she/he* may travel with the one who is the way, the truth, and the life, Jesus Christ our Lord. Amen.

Daily Life

Vocation in daily life

O God, give us grace to set a good example to all among whom we live, to be just and true in all our dealings, to be strict and conscientious in the discharge of every duty; pure and temperate in all enjoyment, gracious and generous and courteous toward all; so that the mind of Jesus Christ may be formed in us and all may know that we are his disciples; in whose name we pray. Amen.

The care of children

Almighty God, with a mother's love and a father's care you have blessed us with the joy and responsibility of children. As we bring them up, give us gracious love, calm strength, and patient wisdom, that we may teach them to love whatever is just and true and good, following the example of Jesus Christ, our Savior. Amen.

Young persons

God of all good gifts, your Son gathered children into his arms and blessed them. Help us to understand our youth as they grow in years and in knowledge of your world. Give us compassion when they face temptations and experience failures. Teach us to encourage their search for truth and value in their lives. Help us to appreciate their ideals and sympathize with their frustrations; that with them we may look for a better world than either we or they have known; through Jesus Christ our Lord. Amen.

Young persons

Lord God of our ancestors, we thank you for what you have done and will continue to do with our daughters and sons. Walk with them in life, and keep the evil one from obstructing their path. You see all; you know where the water is deep. Keep them from danger. Order their steps and guide their feet while they run the race of faith. May the good work that you have begun in them be brought to completion at the day of Jesus Christ, in whose name we pray. Amen.

Families

Triune God, whose will it is that humans live in community, bless family life everywhere and fill all homes with respect, joy, laughter, and prayer. Strengthen the commitment of husbands and wives to one another, that they may mirror your covenant faithfulness; pour out your Spirit on parents, that through them their children may taste your unconditional love; and empower all family members to live in your grace and forgiveness; through Jesus Christ our Lord. Amen.

Those who live alone

Gracious God, none who trust in your Son can be separated from your love. Give to those who live alone peace and contentment in their solitude, hope and fulfillment in their love of you, and joy and companionship in their relations with others; through Jesus Christ our Lord. Amen.

The elders of the community

Blessed are you, O Lord our God, maker of heaven and earth. From everlasting you are God, our dwelling place in all generations. You are the source of holy wisdom, and the fountain of all truth. We give thanks to you for the elders among us. We are graced by their wisdom and seasoning. We are touched by their knowledge and faith. Bless them, O God, as they are a blessing to us. Pour out your Spirit, that our elders may continue to dream dreams and testify to the Light of their salvation, Jesus Christ. May we find inspiration in their years of faithfulness. May we follow their example by serving you with steadfastness and singleness of heart; through Jesus Christ, our Savior and Lord. Amen.

Affirmation of Christian Vocation

Within the sending rite of the service, this affirmation may be made by individuals or groups, and may be introduced by a description of the area of service to be affirmed. Or, the affirmation may be made by the whole assembly.

The presiding minister addresses those affirming Christian vocation.
[Sisters and brothers]/[___name/s___], both your work and your rest are in God. Will you endeavor to pattern your life on the Lord Jesus Christ, in gratitude to God and in service to others, at morning and evening, at work and at play, all the days of your life?
Response: I will, and I ask God to help me.

The presiding minister continues.
Almighty God, by the power of the Spirit you have knit these your servants into the one body of your Son, Jesus Christ. Look with favor upon them in their commitment to serve in Christ's name. Give them courage, patience, and vision; and strengthen us all in our Christian vocation of witness to the world and of service to others; through Jesus Christ our Lord. Amen.

The service concludes with the blessing and dismissal.

Healing

Health of body and soul

By your power, great God, our Lord Jesus healed the sick and gave new hope to the hopeless. Though we cannot command or possess your power, we pray for those who want to be healed. Mend their wounds, soothe fevered brows, and make broken people whole again. Help us to welcome every healing as a sign that, though death is against us, you are for us, and have promised renewed and risen life in Jesus Christ the Lord. Amen.

Those in affliction

Lord Christ, you came into the world as one of us, and suffered as we do. As we go through the trials of life, help us to realize that you are with us at all times and in all things; that we have no secrets from you; and that your loving grace enfolds us for eternity. In the security of your embrace we pray. Amen.

Those in emotional distress

Merciful God, you give us the grace that helps in time of need. Surround ___name___ with your steadfast love and lighten *her/his* burden. By the power of your Spirit, free *her/him* from distress and give *her/him* a new mind and heart made whole in the name of the risen Christ. Amen.

Those who suffer abuse and violence

Holy One, you do not distance yourself from the pain of your people, but in Jesus you bear that pain with all who suffer at others' hands. With your cleansing love bring healing and strength to ___name___; and by your justice, lift *her/him* up, that in body, mind, and spirit, *she/he* may again rejoice. In Jesus' name we pray. Amen.

Those in trouble or bereavement

Almighty God, your love never fails, and you can turn the shadow of death into daybreak. Help us to receive your word with believing hearts, so that, confident in your promises, we may have hope and be lifted out of sorrow into the joy and peace of your presence; through Jesus Christ, our Savior and Lord. Amen.

Those suffering from addiction

O blessed Jesus, you ministered to all who came to you. Look with compassion upon all who through addiction have lost their health and freedom. Restore to them the assurance of your unfailing mercy; remove the fears that attack them; strengthen those who are engaged in the work of recovery; and to those who care for them, give honesty, understanding, and persevering love; for your mercy's sake. Amen.

The chronically ill and those who support them

Loving God, your heart overflows with compassion for your whole creation. Pour out your Spirit on all people living with illness for which there is no cure, as well as their families and loved ones. Help them to know that you claim them as your own and deliver them from fear and pain; for the sake of Jesus Christ, our healer and Lord. Amen.

Caregivers and others who support the sick

God, our refuge and strength, our present help in time of trouble, care for those who tend the needs of [the sick]/[___name/s___]. Strengthen them in body and spirit. Refresh them when weary; console them when anxious; comfort them in grief; and hearten them in discouragement. Be with us all, and give us peace at all times and in every way; through Christ our peace. Amen.

Health care providers

Merciful God, your healing power is everywhere about us. Strengthen those who work among the sick; give them courage and confidence in all they do. Encourage them when their efforts seem futile or when death prevails. Increase their trust in your power even to overcome death and pain and crying. May they be thankful for every sign of health you give, and humble before the mystery of your healing grace; through Jesus Christ our Lord. Amen.

Emergency workers

God of earth and air, water and fire, height and depth, we pray for those who work in danger, who rush in to bring hope and help and comfort when others flee to safety, whose mission is to seek and save, serve and protect, and whose presence embodies the protection of the Good Shepherd. Give them caution and concern for one another, so that in safety they may do what must be done, under your watchful eye. Support them in their courage and dedication that they may continue to save lives, ease pain, and mend the torn fabric of lives and social order; through Jesus Christ our Lord. Amen.

Recovery from sickness

Almighty and merciful God, you are the only source of health and healing; you alone can bring calmness and peace. Grant to us, your children, an awareness of your presence and a strong confidence in you. In our pain, our weariness, and our anxiety, surround us with your care, protect us by your loving might, and permit us once more to enjoy health and strength and peace; through Jesus Christ, our Savior and Lord. Amen.

Restoration of health

O Lord, your compassions never fail and your mercies are new every morning. We give you thanks for giving our sister/brother [___name___] both relief from pain and hope of health renewed. Continue in her/him the good work you have begun; that she/he, daily increasing in bodily strength and rejoicing in your goodness, may so order her/his life and conduct that she/he may always think and do those things that please you; through Jesus Christ our Lord. Amen.

Spiritual Life

Daily renewal

Almighty God, by our baptism into the death and resurrection of your Son, Jesus Christ, you turn us from the old life of sin. Grant that we who are reborn to new life in him may live in righteousness and holiness all our days, through your Son, Jesus Christ our Lord. Amen.

Enlightenment of the Holy Spirit

God Almighty, Father of our Lord Jesus Christ: Grant us, we pray, to be grounded and settled in your truth by the coming of the Holy Spirit into our hearts. That which we know not, reveal; that which is wanting in us, fill up; that which we know, confirm; and keep us blameless in your service; through Jesus Christ our Lord. Amen.

Commitment

Into your hands, almighty God, we place ourselves: our minds to know you, our hearts to love you, our wills to serve you, for we are yours. Into your hands, incarnate Savior, we place ourselves: receive us and draw us after you, that we may follow your steps; abide in us and enliven us by the power of your indwelling. Into your hands, O hovering Spirit, we place ourselves: take us and fashion us after your image; let your comfort strengthen, your grace renew, and your fire cleanse us, soul and body, in life and in death, in this world of shadows and in your changeless world of light eternal, now and forever. Amen.

Commitment

Almighty and eternal God, so draw our hearts to you, so guide our minds, so fill our imaginations, so control our wills, that we may be wholly yours, utterly dedicated to you; and then use us, we pray, as you will, but always to your glory and the welfare of your people, through our Lord and Savior, Jesus Christ. Amen.

Answer to prayer

Almighty God, you have given us grace at this time to make our common prayer to you, and you have promised through your Son that where two or three are gathered together in his name, you will be in the midst of them. Fulfill now, O Lord, our desires and petitions as may be best for us, granting us, in this world, knowledge of your truth and, in the age to come, life everlasting. Amen.

Guidance

Direct us, Lord God, in all our doings with your most gracious favor, and extend to us your continual help; that in all our works begun, continued, and ended in you, we may glorify your holy name; and finally, by your mercy, bring us to everlasting life; through Jesus Christ, our Savior and Lord. Amen.

Protection through life

O God, full of compassion, we commit and commend ourselves to you, in whom we live and move and have our being. Be the goal of our pilgrimage, and our rest by the way. Give us refuge from the turmoil of worldly distractions beneath the shadow of your wings. Let our hearts, so often a sea of restless waves, find peace in you, O God; through Jesus Christ our Lord. Amen.

For a peaceful night

Dear Jesus, as a hen covers her chicks with her wings to keep them safe, protect us this night under your golden wings; for your mercy's sake. Amen.

A prayer of Augustine of Hippo

O loving God, to turn away from you is to fall, to turn toward you is to rise, and to stand before you is to abide forever. Grant us, dear God, in all our duties your help; in all our uncertainties your guidance; in all our dangers your protection; and in all our sorrows your peace; through Jesus Christ our Lord. Amen.

A prayer attributed to Francis of Assisi

Lord, make us instruments of your peace. Where there is hatred, let us sow love; where there is injury, pardon; where there is discord, union; where there is doubt, faith; where there is despair, hope; where there is darkness, light; where there is sadness, joy. Grant that we may not so much seek to be consoled as to console; to be understood as to understand; to be loved as to love. For it is in giving that we receive; it is in pardoning that we are pardoned; and it is in dying that we are born to eternal life. Amen.

A prayer of Catherine of Siena

Power of the eternal Father, help me. Wisdom of the Son, enlighten the eye of my understanding. Tender mercy of the Holy Spirit, unite my heart to yourself. Eternal God, restore health to the sick and life to the dead. Give us a voice, your own voice, to cry out to you for mercy for the world. You, light, give us light. You, wisdom, give us wisdom. You, supreme strength, strengthen us. Amen.

A prayer of Julian of Norwich

In you, Father all-mighty, we have our preservation and our bliss. In you, Christ, we have our restoring and our saving. You are our mother, brother, and savior. In you, our Lord the Holy Spirit, is marvelous and plenteous grace. You are our clothing; for love you wrap us and embrace us. You are our maker, our lover, our keeper. Teach us to believe that by your grace all shall be well, and all shall be well, and all manner of things shall be well. Amen.

A prayer of Martin Luther

Behold, Lord, an empty vessel that needs to be filled. My Lord, fill it. I am weak in the faith; strengthen me. I am cold in love; warm me and make me fervent, that my love may go out to my neighbor. I do not have a strong and firm faith; at times I doubt and am unable to trust you altogether. O Lord, help me. Strengthen my faith and trust in you. In you I have sealed the treasure of all I have. I am poor; you are rich and came to be merciful to the poor. I am a sinner; you are upright. With me, there is an abundance of sin; in you is the fullness of righteousness. Therefore I will remain with you, of whom I can receive, but to whom I may not give. Amen.

A prayer of Mother Teresa of Calcutta

Make us worthy, Lord, to serve our fellow human beings throughout the world who live and die in poverty and hunger. Give them through our hands this day their daily bread, and by our understanding love, give peace and joy. Amen.

⳩ Holy Communion

Pattern for Worship

In the principal service of Christian worship, the Holy Spirit gathers people around the means of grace—the saving Word of God and the sacraments. From the table of communion where Jesus Christ comes with forgiveness, life, and salvation, God sends us out to share the good news and to care for those in need.

The basic pattern of this service—gathering, word, meal, sending—is a structure that allows for freedom and flexibility in the ways worship may be shaped locally, while focusing on what the church holds in common. The whole people of God are joined by the same gifts of grace, for the sake of the same mission of the gospel, into the life of the one triune God.

Gathering

The Holy Spirit calls us together as the people of God.

Confession and Forgiveness
OR
Thanksgiving for Baptism

On the day of Christ's resurrection, and at other times, God gathers us in Christian assembly. We confess our sin and hear God's word of forgiveness. We give thanks for God's mercy in the gift of baptism.

Gathering Song
    Hymn or Psalm
    Kyrie
    Canticle of Praise

Singing at the gathering may include hymns old and new; a prayer for God's mercy to fill the church and the world; a canticle of praise to God's glory revealed in Jesus Christ.

Greeting
Prayer of the Day

During the gathering, the presiding minister and the assembly greet each other in the name of the triune God. The presiding minister gathers the assembly into prayer.

Word

God speaks to us in scripture reading, preaching, and song.

First Reading
Psalm
Second Reading
Gospel Acclamation
Gospel
Sermon

The word of God is proclaimed within and by the gathered assembly. The first Bible reading, usually from the Old Testament, is followed by a psalm sung in response. The second reading, usually from the New Testament letters, bears the witness of the early church. We acclaim the living Word, Jesus Christ, present in the gospel reading. Preaching brings God's word of law and gospel into our time and place to awaken and nourish faith.

Hymn of the Day
Creed
Prayers of Intercession
Peace

God's word is further proclaimed as we sing and as we confess our faith with the whole church. After praying for the whole world, we receive and extend to one another the gift of Christ's peace.

Central elements of the liturgy are noted in bold type; other elements support the essential shape of Christian worship.

Meal

God feeds us with the presence of Jesus Christ.

Offering
Setting the Table
Offering Prayer

A collection of material goods for the church's mission, including the care of those in need, is a sign of the giving of our whole selves in grateful response for all God's gifts. The table is set with bread and wine.

Great Thanksgiving
    Dialogue and Preface
    Holy, Holy, Holy

Before the Lord's supper is shared, the presiding minister leads us into thanksgiving. With the whole creation, we join the angels' song.

    Thanksgiving at the Table
    with **Words of Institution**
    OR
    Words of Institution

    Lord's Prayer

The grace of God's gift is always proclaimed in Jesus' own words of command and promise at the table. A full thanksgiving also includes praise to God for creation and salvation; remembrance of the crucified and risen Christ; and prayer for the Holy Spirit in this meal. The thanksgiving concludes with the prayer our Lord Jesus taught us.

Communion
    Communion Song
    Prayer after Communion

In Christ's body and blood given to us, God forgives us and nourishes us for mission. We sing as the bread is broken and as the meal is shared. We ask God to send us in witness to the world.

Sending

God blesses us and sends us in mission to the world.

Sending of Communion
Blessing
Sending Song
Dismissal

God's mission includes the gifts of grace that we share in worship and take also to the absent; now, we are sent to continue our participation in God's mission. With the blessing of God, we go out to live as Christ's body in the world.

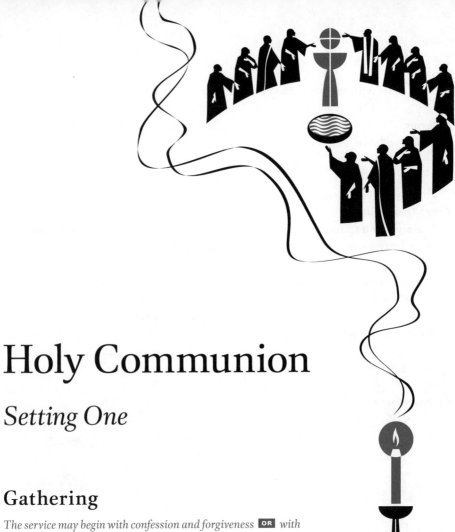

Holy Communion

Setting One

Gathering

The service may begin with confession and forgiveness **OR** *with thanksgiving for baptism (p. 97). Either order may be led at the baptismal font.*

Confession and Forgiveness
The assembly stands. All may make the sign of the cross, the sign that is marked at baptism, as the presiding minister begins.

OR

In the name of the Father, and of the ✝ Son, and of the Holy Spirit. **Amen.**	Blessed be the holy Trinity, ✝ one God, who forgives all our sin, whose mercy endures forever. **Amen.**

The presiding minister may lead one of the following or another prayer of preparation.

God of all mercy and consolation,
come to the help of your people,
turning us from our sin
to live for you alone.
Give us the power of your Holy Spirit
that we may confess our sin,
receive your forgiveness,
and grow into the fullness
of Jesus Christ, our Savior and Lord.
Amen.

OR

Almighty God,
to whom all hearts are open,
all desires known,
and from whom no secrets are hid:
cleanse the thoughts of our hearts
by the inspiration of your Holy Spirit,
that we may perfectly love you
and worthily magnify your holy name,
through Jesus Christ our Lord.
Amen.

One of the following or another confession is prayed.
Let us confess our sin in the presence of God and of one another.

The assembly kneels or stands. Silence is kept for reflection.

Most merciful God,
we confess
that we are captive to sin
and cannot free ourselves.
We have sinned against you
in thought, word, and deed,
by what we have done
and by what we have left undone.
We have not loved you
with our whole heart;
we have not loved
our neighbors as ourselves.
For the sake
of your Son, Jesus Christ,
have mercy on us.
Forgive us, renew us, and lead us,
so that we may delight in your will
and walk in your ways,
to the glory of your holy name.
Amen.

OR

Gracious God,
have mercy on us.
We confess
that we have turned from you
and given ourselves
into the power of sin.
We are truly sorry
and humbly repent.
In your compassion
forgive us our sins,
known and unknown,
things we have done
and things we have failed to do.
Turn us again to you,
and uphold us by your Spirit,
so that we may live and serve you
in newness of life
through Jesus Christ,
our Savior and Lord.
Amen.

OR

In the mercy of almighty God,
Jesus Christ was given to die for us,
and for his sake
God forgives us all our sins.
As a called and ordained minister
of the church of Christ,
and by his authority,
I therefore declare to you
the entire forgiveness of all your sins,
in the name of the Father,
and of the + Son,
and of the Holy Spirit.
Amen.

God, who is rich in mercy, loved us
even when we were dead in sin,
and made us alive
together with Christ.
By grace you have been saved.
In the name of + Jesus Christ,
your sins are forgiven.
Almighty God
strengthen you with power
through the Holy Spirit,
that Christ may live in your hearts
through faith.
Amen.

The assembly stands.

The service continues with gathering song (p. 98).

Thanksgiving for Baptism

The assembly stands. All may make the sign of the cross, the sign marked at baptism, as the presiding minister begins.

In the name of the Father,
and of the + Son,
and of the Holy Spirit.
Amen.

Blessed be the holy Trinity, + one God,
the fountain of living water,
the rock who gave us birth,
our light and our salvation.
Amen.

The presiding minister addresses the assembly.
Joined to Christ in the waters of baptism,
we are clothed with God's mercy and forgiveness.
Let us give thanks for the gift of baptism.

Water may be poured into the font as the presiding minister gives thanks.
We give you thanks, O God,
for in the beginning your Spirit moved over the waters
and by your Word you created the world,
calling forth life in which you took delight.

Through the waters of the flood you delivered Noah and his family.
Through the sea you led your people Israel from slavery into freedom.
At the river your Son was baptized by John and anointed with the Holy Spirit.
By water and your Word you claim us as daughters and sons,
making us heirs of your promise and servants of all.

We praise you for the gift of water that sustains life,
and above all we praise you for the gift of new life in Jesus Christ.
Shower us with your Spirit,
and renew our lives with your forgiveness, grace, and love.

To you be given honor and praise
through Jesus Christ our Lord
in the unity of the Holy Spirit, now and forever.
Amen.

The service continues with gathering song (p. 98). As a reminder of the gift of baptism, the assembly may be sprinkled with water during the singing.

Gathering Song

The time of gathering song may be brief or extended, and may include one or more of the following: hymns, psalms; a Kyrie; a canticle of praise.

During this time, the presiding minister and the assembly greet each other.
The grace of our Lord Jesus Christ, the love of God,
and the communion of the Holy Spirit be with you all.
And also with you.

A Kyrie may be sung in dialogue between an assisting minister and the assembly.

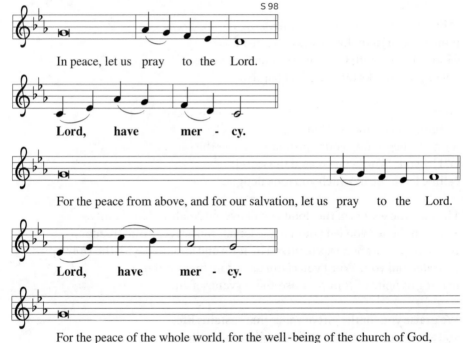

S 98

In peace, let us pray to the Lord.

Lord, have mer - cy.

For the peace from above, and for our salvation, let us pray to the Lord.

Lord, have mer - cy.

For the peace of the whole world, for the well-being of the church of God,

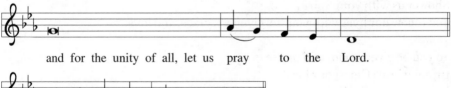

and for the unity of all, let us pray to the Lord.

Lord, have mer - cy.

For this holy house, and for all who offer here their worship and praise,

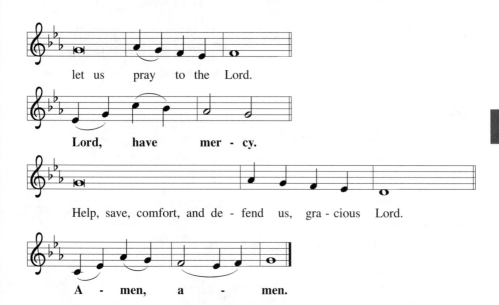

let us pray to the Lord.

Lord, have mer - cy.

Help, save, comfort, and de - fend us, gra - cious Lord.

A - men, a - men.

One of the following or another canticle of praise may be sung by all.

S 99

Glo - ry to God in the high - est, and peace to God's peo - ple on earth. Lord God, heav - en - ly King, al - might - y God and Fa - ther, we wor - ship you, we give you thanks, we praise you for your glo - ry. Lord Je - sus Christ, on - ly Son of the Fa - ther,

Lord God, Lamb of God, you take a-way the sin of the world: have mer-cy on us; you are seat-ed at the right hand of the Fa-ther: re-ceive our prayer. For you a-lone are the Ho-ly One, you a-lone are the Lord, you a-lone are the Most High, Je-sus Christ, with the Ho-ly Spir-it, in the glo-ry of God the Fa-ther. A-men. Glo-ry to God in the high-est, and peace to God's peo-ple on earth.

Refrain

This is the feast of vic-to-ry for our God.

Al - le -lu - ia, al - le-lu - ia, al - le - lu-ia, al -le - lu - ia.

1 Wor-thy is Christ, the Lamb who was slain, whose
2 Sing . . with all the peo - ple of God, and

blood set us free to be peo - ple of God.
join in the hymn of all cre - a - tion:

Pow - er and rich - es, wis - dom and strength, and
Bless-ing and hon - or, glo - ry and might be to

Refrain

hon - or and bless - ing and glo - ry are his.
God and the Lamb for - ev - er. A - men.

3 For the Lamb who was slain has be -

Refrain

gun his reign. Al - le - lu - ia.

Prayer of the Day

The presiding minister leads the prayer of the day.
Let us pray. *A brief silence is kept before the prayer.*

After the prayer the assembly responds: **Amen.**
The assembly is seated.

Word

First Reading

The reading may be announced: A reading from _____ .
The reading may be concluded: The word of the Lord. **OR** Word of God, word of life.
The assembly responds: **Thanks be to God.**

Psalm

The psalm for the day is sung.

Second Reading

The reading may be announced and concluded in the same way as the first reading.

Gospel Acclamation

The assembly stands to welcome the gospel, using this acclamation, a sung alleluia, or another appropriate song.

The proper verse may be sung, or all may sing this verse.

OR

During Lent, the acclamation of the day, this acclamation, or another appropriate song is sung.

Let your stead-fast love come to us, O Lord.

Save us as you prom-ised; we will trust your word.

Gospel

The gospel is announced:

The holy gospel according to _____ .

Glory to you, O Lord.

The gospel is proclaimed, concluding:

The gospel of the Lord.

Praise to you, O Christ.

Sermon

The assembly is seated.

Silence for reflection follows the sermon.

Hymn of the Day

The assembly stands to proclaim the word of God in song.

Creed

The Nicene Creed **OR** *the Apostles' Creed may be spoken. The Nicene Creed is appropriate during Advent, Christmas, Easter, and on festival days; the Apostles' Creed during Lent and at other times.*

Nicene Creed

We believe in one God,
   the Father, the Almighty,
   maker of heaven and earth,
   of all that is, seen and unseen.

We believe in one Lord, Jesus Christ,
   the only Son of God,
   eternally begotten of the Father,
   God from God, Light from Light,
   true God from true God,
   begotten, not made,
   of one Being with the Father;
   through him all things were made.
   For us and for our salvation
      he came down from heaven,
      was incarnate of the Holy Spirit and the virgin Mary
      and became truly human.
      For our sake he was crucified under Pontius Pilate;
      he suffered death and was buried.
      On the third day he rose again
      in accordance with the scriptures;
      he ascended into heaven
      and is seated at the right hand of the Father.
      He will come again in glory to judge the living and the dead,
      and his kingdom will have no end.

We believe in the Holy Spirit, the Lord, the giver of life,
   who proceeds from the Father and the Son,*
   who with the Father and the Son is worshiped and glorified,
   who has spoken through the prophets.
   We believe in one holy catholic and apostolic church.
   We acknowledge one baptism for the forgiveness of sins.
   We look for the resurrection of the dead,
      and the life of the world to come. Amen.

---

* *Or, "who proceeds from the Father." The phrase "and the Son" is a later addition to the creed.*

Apostles' Creed

I believe in God, the Father almighty,
    creator of heaven and earth.

I believe in Jesus Christ, God's only Son, our Lord,
    who was conceived by the Holy Spirit,
    born of the virgin Mary,
    suffered under Pontius Pilate,
    was crucified, died, and was buried;
    he descended to the dead.*
    On the third day he rose again;
    he ascended into heaven,
    he is seated at the right hand of the Father,
    and he will come to judge the living and the dead.

I believe in the Holy Spirit,
    the holy catholic church,
    the communion of saints,
    the forgiveness of sins,
    the resurrection of the body,
    and the life everlasting. Amen.

*Or, "he descended into hell," *another translation of this text in widespread use.*

Prayers of Intercession

The prayers are prepared locally for each occasion, using the following pattern or another appropriate form.

An assisting minister invites the assembly into prayer with these or similar words.
With the whole people of God in Christ Jesus,
let us pray for the church, those in need, and all of God's creation.

Prayers reflect the wideness of God's mercy for the whole world—
    for the church universal, its ministry, and the mission of the gospel;
    for the well-being of creation;
    for peace and justice in the world, the nations and those in authority, the community;
    for the poor, oppressed, sick, bereaved, lonely;
    for all who suffer in body, mind, or spirit;
    for the congregation, and for special concerns.
Additional prayers may come from the assembly.

Prayers of thanksgiving for the faithful departed may include those who recently have died and those commemorated on the church's calendar.

Each portion of the prayers ends with these or similar words.

	OR	**OR**
Lord, in your mercy,	. . . let us pray.	Hear us, O God.
hear our prayer.	**Have mercy, O God.**	**Your mercy is great.**

The presiding minister concludes the prayers with these or similar words.
Into your hands, gracious God, we commend all for whom we pray, trusting in your mercy; through Jesus Christ, our Savior.
Amen.

Peace

The presiding minister and the assembly greet each other in the peace of the risen Christ.
The peace of Christ be with you always.
And also with you.

The people may greet one another with a sign of Christ's peace and may say **Peace be with you** *or similar words.*

The assembly is seated.

Meal

Offering

An offering is gathered for the mission of the church, including the care of those in need.

During this time, the table is set. Assembly song or other music may accompany or follow the gathering of the offering (#181–188).

After the offering is gathered, the assembly stands. Bread, wine, money, and other gifts may be brought forward.

After the table is set, the assisting minister may lead one of the following or a similar prayer.

Let us pray.

Holy God, gracious and merciful, you bring forth food from the earth and nourish your whole creation. Turn our hearts toward those who hunger in any way, that all may know your care; and prepare us now to feast on the bread of life, Jesus Christ, our Savior and Lord.
Amen.

OR

God of all creation, all you have made is good, and your love endures forever. You bring forth bread from the earth and fruit from the vine. Nourish us with these gifts, that we might be for the world signs of your gracious presence in Jesus Christ, our Savior and Lord.
Amen.

OR

Blessed are you, O God, maker of all things. Through your goodness you have blessed us with these gifts: our selves, our time, and our possessions. Use us, and what we have gathered, in feeding the world with your love, through the one who gave himself for us, Jesus Christ, our Savior and Lord.
Amen.

Great Thanksgiving

The presiding minister greets the assembly and invites all present to give thanks.

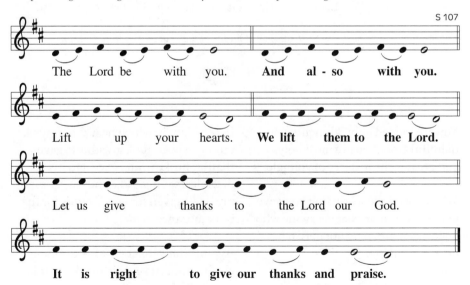

S 107

The Lord be with you. **And al - so with you.**

Lift up your hearts. **We lift them to the Lord.**

Let us give thanks to the Lord our God.

It is right to give our thanks and praise.

The presiding minister continues:

It is indeed right, our duty and our joy, that we should at all times and in all places give thanks and praise ... *Here the minister continues with the preface for the day, concluding:* ... we praise your name and join their unending hymn:

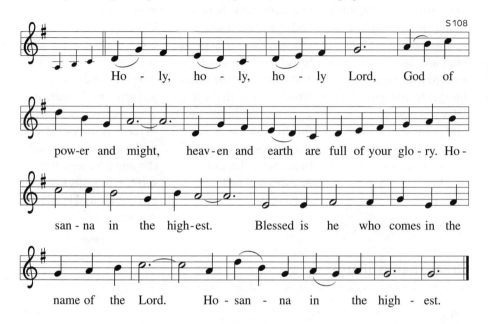

S 108

Ho - ly, ho - ly, ho - ly Lord, God of pow-er and might, heav-en and earth are full of your glo - ry. Ho - san - na in the high-est. Blessed is he who comes in the name of the Lord. Ho - san - na in the high - est.

The presiding minister continues, using one of the following or another appropriate form.

OR

I

You are indeed holy, almighty and merciful God. You are most holy, and great is the majesty of your glory.

You so loved the world that you gave your only Son, so that everyone who believes in him may not perish but have eternal life.

We give you thanks for his coming into the world to fulfill for us your holy will and to accomplish all things for our salvation.

Continue on the following page.

II

In the night in which he was betrayed, our Lord Jesus took bread, and gave thanks; broke it, and gave it to his disciples, saying: Take and eat; this is my body, given for you. Do this for the remembrance of me.

Again, after supper, he took the cup, gave thanks, and gave it for all to drink, saying: This cup is the new covenant in my blood, shed for you and for all people for the forgiveness of sin. Do this for the remembrance of me.

Continue with the Lord's Prayer (p. 112).

I, *continued*

In the night in which he was betrayed,
our Lord Jesus took bread, and gave thanks;
broke it, and gave it to his disciples, saying:
Take and eat; this is my body, given for you.
Do this for the remembrance of me.

Again, after supper, he took the cup, gave thanks,
and gave it for all to drink, saying:
This cup is the new covenant in my blood,
shed for you and for all people for the forgiveness of sin.
Do this for the remembrance of me.

For as often as we eat of this bread and drink from this cup,
we proclaim the Lord's death until he comes.

Christ has died. Christ is ris - en. Christ will come a - gain.

Remembering, therefore, his salutary command,
his life-giving passion and death, his glorious resurrection and ascension,
and the promise of his coming again,
we give thanks to you, O Lord God Almighty,
not as we ought but as we are able;
we ask you mercifully to accept our praise and thanksgiving
and with your Word and Holy Spirit to bless us, your servants,
and these your own gifts of bread and wine,
so that we and all who share in the body and blood of Christ
may be filled with heavenly blessing and grace,
and, receiving the forgiveness of sin,
may be formed to live as your holy people
and be given our inheritance with all your saints.

To you, O God, Father, Son, and Holy Spirit,
be all honor and glory in your holy church, now and forever.

A - men, a - men, a - men.

Continue with the Lord's Prayer (p. 112).

III *(Advent—Epiphany of Our Lord)*

Holy One,
the beginning and the end,
the giver of life:
Blessed are you
for the birth of creation.
Blessed are you
in the darkness and in the light.
Blessed are you
for your promise to your people.
Blessed are you
in the prophets' hopes and dreams.
Blessed are you
for Mary's openness to your will.
Blessed are you
for your Son Jesus,
the Word made flesh.

In the night in which he was betrayed,
our Lord Jesus took bread,
and gave thanks; broke it,
and gave it to his disciples,
saying: Take and eat;
this is my body, given for you.
Do this for the remembrance of me.

Again, after supper, he took the cup,
gave thanks, and gave it for all to drink,
saying: This cup
is the new covenant in my blood,
shed for you and for all people
for the forgiveness of sin.
Do this for the remembrance of me.

Let us proclaim the mystery of faith:
Christ has died.
Christ is risen.
Christ will come again.

With this bread and cup
we remember your Word
dwelling among us,
full of grace and truth.
We remember our new birth
in his death and resurrection.
We look with hope for his coming.
Come, Lord Jesus.

Holy God,
we long for your Spirit.
Come among us.
Bless this meal.
May your Word take flesh in us.
Awaken your people.
Fill us with your light.
Bring the gift of peace on earth.
Come, Holy Spirit.

All praise and glory are yours,
Holy One of Israel,
Word of God incarnate,
Power of the Most High,
one God, now and forever.
Amen.

Continue with the Lord's Prayer (p. 112).

IV *(Ash Wednesday—Day of Pentecost)*

Blessed are you,
O God of the universe.
Your mercy is everlasting
and your faithfulness endures
from age to age.

Praise to you for creating
the heavens and the earth.
Praise to you for saving the earth
from the waters of the flood.
Praise to you for bringing
the Israelites safely through the sea.
Praise to you for leading
your people through the wilderness
to the land of milk and honey.
Praise to you for the words and deeds
of Jesus, your anointed one.
Praise to you for the death and
resurrection of Christ.
Praise to you for your Spirit
poured out on all nations.

In the night in which he was betrayed,
our Lord Jesus took bread,
and gave thanks; broke it,
and gave it to his disciples,
saying: Take and eat;
this is my body, given for you.
Do this for the remembrance of me.

Again, after supper, he took the cup,
gave thanks, and gave it for all to drink,
saying: This cup
is the new covenant in my blood,
shed for you and for all people
for the forgiveness of sin.
Do this for the remembrance of me.

With this bread and cup
we remember our Lord's passover
from death to life
as we proclaim the mystery of faith:
Christ has died.
Christ is risen.
Christ will come again.

O God of resurrection and new life:
Pour out your Holy Spirit on us
and on these gifts of bread and wine.
Bless this feast.
Grace our table with your presence.
Come, Holy Spirit.

Reveal yourself to us
in the breaking of the bread.
Raise us up
as the body of Christ for the world.
Breathe new life into us.
Send us forth,
burning with justice,
peace, and love.
Come, Holy Spirit.

With *name/s and* your holy ones
of all times and places,
with the earth and all its creatures,
with sun and moon and stars,
we praise you, O God,
blessed and holy Trinity,
now and forever.
Amen.

Continue with the Lord's Prayer (p. 112).

Our Father in heaven,	**OR** Our Father, who art in heaven,
hallowed be your name,	hallowed be thy name,
your kingdom come,	thy kingdom come,
your will be done,	thy will be done,
on earth as in heaven.	on earth as it is in heaven.
Give us today our daily bread.	Give us this day our daily bread;
Forgive us our sins	and forgive us our trespasses,
as we forgive those	as we forgive those
who sin against us.	who trespass against us;
Save us from the time of trial	and lead us not into temptation,
and deliver us from evil.	but deliver us from evil.
For the kingdom, the power,	For thine is the kingdom,
and the glory are yours,	and the power, and the glory,
now and forever. Amen.	forever and ever. Amen.

For a sung version of the Lord's Prayer, see p. 163.

Communion

The presiding minister may address the assembly in these or similar words.

Taste and see	**OR** Come to the banquet,
that the Lord is good.	for all is now ready.

The assembly may be seated. The bread may be broken for the communion.

When giving the bread and cup, the communion ministers say
The body of Christ, given for you.
The blood of Christ, shed for you.
and each person may respond **Amen.**

The ministers commune either after or before others commune.

"Lamb of God" may be sung.

Lamb of God, you take a - way the sin of the world; have

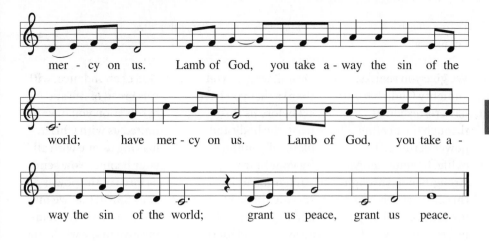

mer - cy on us. Lamb of God, you take a - way the sin of the world; have mer - cy on us. Lamb of God, you take a - way the sin of the world; grant us peace, grant us peace.

Assembly song and other music may accompany the communion.

After all have returned to their places, the assembly stands. The presiding minister may say a table blessing; the assembly responds **Amen.**

The assembly may sing the following or another suitable song.

S 113

Now, Lord, you let your ser-vant go in peace: your word has been ful - filled. My own eyes have seen the sal - va - tion which you have pre-pared in the sight of ev - 'ry peo - ple: a light to re-veal you to the na - tions and the glo - ry of your peo - ple Is - ra - el.

Now, Lord, you let your ser - vant go in peace.

The assisting minister leads one of the following or a similar prayer after communion.
Let us pray.

OR

OR

We give you thanks, almighty God, that you have refreshed us through the healing power of this gift of life. In your mercy, strengthen us through this gift, in faith toward you and in fervent love toward one another; for the sake of Jesus Christ our Lord.
Amen.

O God, we give you thanks that you have set before us this feast, the body and blood of your Son. By your Spirit strengthen us to serve all in need and to give ourselves away as bread for the hungry, through Jesus Christ our Lord.
Amen.

God of abundance, with this bread of life and cup of salvation you have united us with Christ, making us one with all your people. Now send us forth in the power of your Spirit, that we may proclaim your redeeming love to the world and continue forever in the risen life of Jesus Christ, our Lord.
Amen.

Sending

Communion ministers may be sent to take the sacrament to those who are absent.

Brief announcements may be made, especially those related to the assembly's participation in God's mission in the world. Affirmation of Christian Vocation (p. 84) may be used here.

Blessing

The presiding minister proclaims God's blessing.
Almighty God, Father, + Son, and Holy Spirit, bless you now and forever.
Amen.

OR

The Lord bless you and keep you.
The Lord's face shine on you with grace and mercy.
The Lord look upon you with favor and + give you peace.
Amen.

OR

The God of steadfastness and encouragement
grant you to live in harmony with one another,
in accordance with Christ Jesus.
Amen.
The God of hope fill you with all joy and peace in believing,
so that you may abound in hope by the power of the Holy Spirit.
Amen.
The God of all grace +bless you now and forever.
Amen.

Sending Song

If "Now, Lord, you let your servant go in peace" was not sung at the end of communion, it may be sung here, or another sending song may be sung.

Dismissal

The assisting minister may send the assembly into mission.

Go in peace. Serve the Lord.
Thanks be to God.

OR

Go in peace. Share the good news.
Thanks be to God.

OR

Go in peace. Remember the poor.
Thanks be to God.

OR

Go in peace. Christ is with you.
Thanks be to God.

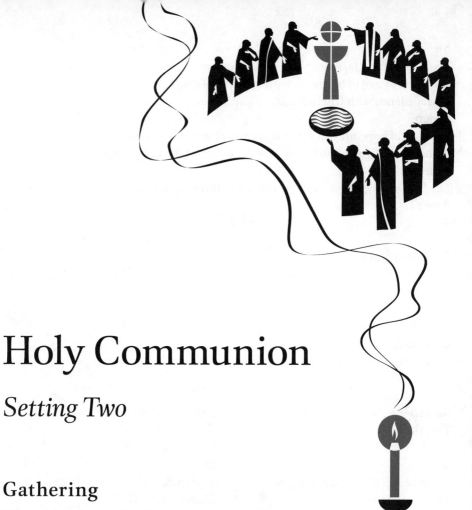

Holy Communion

Setting Two

Gathering

The service may begin with confession and forgiveness **OR** *with thanksgiving for baptism (p. 119). Either order may be led at the baptismal font.*

Confession and Forgiveness

The assembly stands. All may make the sign of the cross, the sign that is marked at baptism, as the presiding minister begins.

	OR
In the name of the Father,	Blessed be the holy Trinity, ✛ one God,
and of the ✛ Son,	who forgives all our sin,
and of the Holy Spirit.	whose mercy endures forever.
Amen.	**Amen.**

The presiding minister may lead one of the following or another prayer of preparation.

God of all mercy and consolation,
come to the help of your people,
turning us from our sin
to live for you alone.
Give us the power of your Holy Spirit
that we may confess our sin,
receive your forgiveness,
and grow into the fullness
of Jesus Christ, our Savior and Lord.
Amen.

OR

Almighty God,
to whom all hearts are open,
all desires known,
and from whom no secrets are hid:
cleanse the thoughts of our hearts
by the inspiration of your Holy Spirit,
that we may perfectly love you
and worthily magnify your holy name,
through Jesus Christ our Lord.
Amen.

One of the following or another confession is prayed.
Let us confess our sin in the presence of God and of one another.

The assembly kneels or stands. Silence is kept for reflection.

Most merciful God,
we confess
that we are captive to sin
and cannot free ourselves.
We have sinned against you
in thought, word, and deed,
by what we have done
and by what we have left undone.
We have not loved you
with our whole heart;
we have not loved
our neighbors as ourselves.
For the sake
of your Son, Jesus Christ,
have mercy on us.
Forgive us, renew us, and lead us,
so that we may delight in your will
and walk in your ways,
to the glory of your holy name.
Amen.

OR

Gracious God,
have mercy on us.
We confess
that we have turned from you
and given ourselves
into the power of sin.
We are truly sorry
and humbly repent.
In your compassion
forgive us our sins,
known and unknown,
things we have done
and things we have failed to do.
Turn us again to you,
and uphold us by your Spirit,
so that we may live and serve you
in newness of life
through Jesus Christ,
our Savior and Lord.
Amen.

The presiding minister announces God's forgiveness with these or similar words.

OR

In the mercy of almighty God,
Jesus Christ was given to die for us,
and for his sake
God forgives us all our sins.
As a called and ordained minister
of the church of Christ,
and by his authority,
I therefore declare to you
the entire forgiveness of all your sins,
in the name of the Father,
and of the + Son,
and of the Holy Spirit.
Amen.

God, who is rich in mercy, loved us
even when we were dead in sin,
and made us alive
together with Christ.
By grace you have been saved.
In the name of + Jesus Christ,
your sins are forgiven.
Almighty God
strengthen you with power
through the Holy Spirit,
that Christ may live in your hearts
through faith.
Amen.

The assembly stands.

The service continues with gathering song (p. 120).

Thanksgiving for Baptism

The assembly stands. All may make the sign of the cross, the sign marked at baptism, as the presiding minister begins.

OR

In the name of the Father,
and of the + Son,
and of the Holy Spirit.
Amen.

Blessed be the holy Trinity, + one God,
the fountain of living water,
the rock who gave us birth,
our light and our salvation.
Amen.

The presiding minister addresses the assembly.
Joined to Christ in the waters of baptism,
we are clothed with God's mercy and forgiveness.
Let us give thanks for the gift of baptism.

Water may be poured into the font as the presiding minister gives thanks.
We give you thanks, O God,
for in the beginning your Spirit moved over the waters
and by your Word you created the world,
calling forth life in which you took delight.

Through the waters of the flood you delivered Noah and his family.
Through the sea you led your people Israel from slavery into freedom.
At the river your Son was baptized by John and anointed with the Holy Spirit.
By water and your Word you claim us as daughters and sons,
making us heirs of your promise and servants of all.

We praise you for the gift of water that sustains life,
and above all we praise you for the gift of new life in Jesus Christ.
Shower us with your Spirit,
and renew our lives with your forgiveness, grace, and love.

To you be given honor and praise
through Jesus Christ our Lord
in the unity of the Holy Spirit, now and forever.
Amen.

The service continues with gathering song (p. 120). As a reminder of the gift of baptism, the assembly may be sprinkled with water during the singing.

Gathering Song

The time of gathering song may be brief or extended, and may include one or more of the following: hymns, psalms; a Kyrie; a canticle of praise.

During this time, the presiding minister and the assembly greet each other.
The grace of our Lord Jesus Christ, the love of God,
and the communion of the Holy Spirit be with you all.
And also with you.

A Kyrie may be sung in dialogue between an assisting minister and the assembly.

S 120

In peace, let us pray to the Lord. **Lord, have mer-cy.**

For the peace from above, and for our sal - va - tion, let us

pray to the Lord. **Lord, have mer - cy.**

For the peace of the whole world, for the well-being of the church of God,

and for the u - ni - ty of all, let us pray to the Lord.

Lord, have mer - cy.

For this holy house, and for all who offer here their wor-ship and praise,

let us pray to the Lord. **Lord, have mer-cy.**

Help, save, comfort, and de - fend us, gra - cious Lord.

A - **men.**

One of the following or another canticle of praise may be sung by all.

Refrain   S 121

Glo-ry to God in the high-est, and peace to God's peo-ple on earth.

1 Lord God, heav-en - ly King, al - might-y God and Fa - ther, we

wor-ship you, we give you thanks, we praise you for your glo - ry.

Refrain

Glo-ry to God in the high-est, and peace to God's peo-ple on earth.

2 Lord Je - sus Christ, on-ly Son of the Fa - ther, Lord God, Lamb of

God, you take a-way the sin of the world: have mer-cy on us; you are

seat-ed at the right hand of the Fa - ther: re- ceive our prayer.

Refrain

Glo-ry to God in the high - est, and peace to God's peo-ple on earth.

3 For you a - lone are the Ho-ly One, you a-lone are the Lord,

you a - lone are the Most High, Je - sus Christ, with the Ho - ly

Spir-it, in the glo-ry of God the Fa - ther. A - men.

Refrain

Glo-ry to God in the high - est, and peace to God's peo-ple on earth.

OR

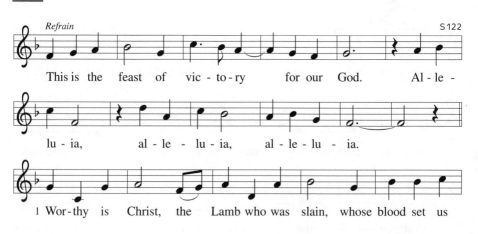

Refrain   S 122

This is the feast of vic - to-ry for our God. Al - le -

lu - ia, al - le - lu - ia, al - le - lu - ia.

1 Wor-thy is Christ, the Lamb who was slain, whose blood set us

free to be peo-ple of God. Pow-er, rich-es, wis-dom, and strength, and hon-or, bless-ing, and glo-ry are his.

Refrain

This is the feast of vic-to-ry for our God. Al - le - lu - ia, al - le - lu - ia, al - le - lu - ia.

2 Sing with all the peo-ple of God, and join in the hymn of all cre - a - tion: Bless-ing, hon-or, glo-ry, and might be to God and the Lamb for - ev - er. A - men.

Final refrain

This is the feast of vic - to-ry for our God, for the Lamb who was slain has be - gun his reign. Al - le - lu - ia, al - le - lu - ia, al - le - lu - ia.

Prayer of the Day

The presiding minister leads the prayer of the day.

Let us pray. *A brief silence is kept before the prayer.*

After the prayer the assembly responds: **Amen.**
The assembly is seated.

Word

First Reading

The reading may be announced: A reading from _____ .
The reading may be concluded: The word of the Lord. **OR** Word of God, word of life.
The assembly responds: **Thanks be to God.**

Psalm

The psalm for the day is sung.

Second Reading

The reading may be announced and concluded in the same way as the first reading.

Gospel Acclamation

The assembly stands to welcome the gospel, using this acclamation, a sung alleluia, or another appropriate song.

S 124

Al - le - lu - ia, al - le - lu - ia, al - le - lu - ia, al - le - lu - ia.

The proper verse may be sung, or all may sing this verse.

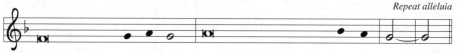

Repeat alleluia

Lord, to whom shall we go? You have the words of e - ter - nal life.

During Lent, the acclamation of the day, this acclamation, or another appropriate song is sung.

S 125

Let your stead - fast love come to us, O Lord.

Save us as you prom - ised; we will trust your word.

Save us as you prom - ised; we will trust your word.

Gospel

The gospel is announced:
The holy gospel according to _____ .
Glory to you, O Lord.

The gospel is proclaimed, concluding:
The gospel of the Lord.
Praise to you, O Christ.

Sermon

The assembly is seated.

Silence for reflection follows the sermon.

Hymn of the Day

The assembly stands to proclaim the word of God in song.

Creed

The Nicene Creed **OR** *the Apostles' Creed may be spoken. The Nicene Creed is appropriate during Advent, Christmas, Easter, and on festival days; the Apostles' Creed during Lent and at other times.*

Nicene Creed

We believe in one God,
    the Father, the Almighty,
    maker of heaven and earth,
    of all that is, seen and unseen.

We believe in one Lord, Jesus Christ,
    the only Son of God,
    eternally begotten of the Father,
    God from God, Light from Light,
    true God from true God,
    begotten, not made,
    of one Being with the Father;
    through him all things were made.
    For us and for our salvation
      he came down from heaven,
      was incarnate of the Holy Spirit and the virgin Mary
      and became truly human.
    For our sake he was crucified under Pontius Pilate;
    he suffered death and was buried.
    On the third day he rose again
    in accordance with the scriptures;
    he ascended into heaven
    and is seated at the right hand of the Father.
    He will come again in glory to judge the living and the dead,
    and his kingdom will have no end.

We believe in the Holy Spirit, the Lord, the giver of life,
    who proceeds from the Father and the Son,*
    who with the Father and the Son is worshiped and glorified,
    who has spoken through the prophets.
    We believe in one holy catholic and apostolic church.
    We acknowledge one baptism for the forgiveness of sins.
    We look for the resurrection of the dead,
      and the life of the world to come. Amen.

* Or, "who proceeds from the Father." *The phrase "and the Son" is a later addition to the creed.*

Apostles' Creed

I believe in God, the Father almighty,
    creator of heaven and earth.

I believe in Jesus Christ, God's only Son, our Lord,
    who was conceived by the Holy Spirit,
    born of the virgin Mary,
    suffered under Pontius Pilate,
    was crucified, died, and was buried;
    he descended to the dead.*
    On the third day he rose again;
    he ascended into heaven,
    he is seated at the right hand of the Father,
    and he will come to judge the living and the dead.

I believe in the Holy Spirit,
    the holy catholic church,
    the communion of saints,
    the forgiveness of sins,
    the resurrection of the body,
    and the life everlasting. Amen.

*Or, "he descended into hell," *another translation of this text in widespread use.*

Prayers of Intercession

The prayers are prepared locally for each occasion, using the following pattern or another
appropriate form.

An assisting minister invites the assembly into prayer with these or similar words.
With the whole people of God in Christ Jesus,
let us pray for the church, those in need, and all of God's creation.

Prayers reflect the wideness of God's mercy for the whole world—
    for the church universal, its ministry, and the mission of the gospel;
    for the well-being of creation;
    for peace and justice in the world, the nations and those in authority, the community;
    for the poor, oppressed, sick, bereaved, lonely;
    for all who suffer in body, mind, or spirit;
    for the congregation, and for special concerns.
Additional prayers may come from the assembly.

Prayers of thanksgiving for the faithful departed may include those who recently have died and those commemorated on the church's calendar.

Each portion of the prayers ends with these or similar words.

	OR	**OR**
Lord, in your mercy,	. . . let us pray.	Hear us, O God.
hear our prayer.	**Have mercy, O God.**	**Your mercy is great.**

The presiding minister concludes the prayers with these or similar words.
Into your hands, gracious God, we commend all for whom we pray,
trusting in your mercy; through Jesus Christ, our Savior.
Amen.

Peace

The presiding minister and the assembly greet each other in the peace of the risen Christ.
The peace of Christ be with you always.
And also with you.

The people may greet one another with a sign of Christ's peace and may say **Peace be with you** *or similar words.*

The assembly is seated.

Meal

Offering

An offering is gathered for the mission of the church, including the care of those in need.

During this time, the table is set. Assembly song or other music may accompany or follow the gathering of the offering (#181–188).

After the offering is gathered, the assembly stands. Bread, wine, money, and other gifts may be brought forward.

After the table is set, the assisting minister may lead one of the following or a similar prayer.

Let us pray.

Holy God, gracious and merciful, you bring forth food from the earth and nourish your whole creation. Turn our hearts toward those who hunger in any way, that all may know your care; and prepare us now to feast on the bread of life, Jesus Christ, our Savior and Lord.
Amen.

OR

God of all creation, all you have made is good, and your love endures forever. You bring forth bread from the earth and fruit from the vine. Nourish us with these gifts, that we might be for the world signs of your gracious presence in Jesus Christ, our Savior and Lord.
Amen.

OR

Blessed are you, O God, maker of all things. Through your goodness you have blessed us with these gifts: our selves, our time, and our possessions. Use us, and what we have gathered, in feeding the world with your love, through the one who gave himself for us, Jesus Christ, our Savior and Lord.
Amen.

Great Thanksgiving

The presiding minister greets the assembly and invites all present to give thanks.

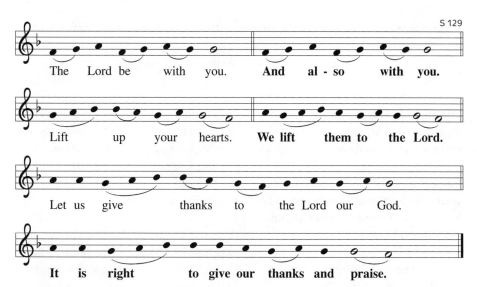

S 129

The Lord be with you. **And al - so with you.**

Lift up your hearts. **We lift them to the Lord.**

Let us give thanks to the Lord our God.

It is right to give our thanks and praise.

The presiding minister continues:

It is indeed right, our duty and our joy, that we should at all times and in all places give thanks and praise … *Here the minister continues with the preface for the day, concluding:* … we praise your name and join their unending hymn:

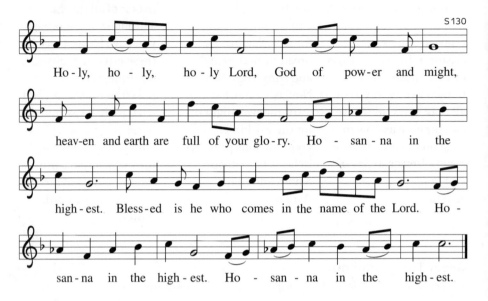

S 130

Ho - ly, ho - ly, ho - ly Lord, God of pow-er and might, heav-en and earth are full of your glo - ry. Ho - san - na in the high - est. Bless-ed is he who comes in the name of the Lord. Ho - san - na in the high - est. Ho - san - na in the high - est.

The presiding minister continues, using one of the following or another appropriate form .

OR

I

You are indeed holy, almighty and merciful God. You are most holy, and great is the majesty of your glory.

You so loved the world that you gave your only Son, so that everyone who believes in him may not perish but have eternal life.

We give you thanks for his coming into the world to fulfill for us your holy will and to accomplish all things for our salvation.

Continue on the following page.

II

In the night in which he was betrayed, our Lord Jesus took bread, and gave thanks; broke it, and gave it to his disciples, saying: Take and eat; this is my body, given for you. Do this for the remembrance of me.

Again, after supper, he took the cup, gave thanks, and gave it for all to drink, saying: This cup is the new covenant in my blood, shed for you and for all people for the forgiveness of sin. Do this for the remembrance of me.

Continue with the Lord's Prayer (p. 134).

I, *continued*

In the night in which he was betrayed,
our Lord Jesus took bread, and gave thanks;
broke it, and gave it to his disciples, saying:
Take and eat; this is my body, given for you.
Do this for the remembrance of me.

Again, after supper, he took the cup, gave thanks,
and gave it for all to drink, saying:
This cup is the new covenant in my blood,
shed for you and for all people for the forgiveness of sin.
Do this for the remembrance of me.

For as often as we eat of this bread and drink from this cup,
we proclaim the Lord's death until he comes.

Christ has died. Christ is ris-en. Christ will come a-gain.

Remembering, therefore, his salutary command,
his life-giving passion and death, his glorious resurrection and ascension,
and the promise of his coming again,
we give thanks to you, O Lord God Almighty,
not as we ought but as we are able;
we ask you mercifully to accept our praise and thanksgiving
and with your Word and Holy Spirit to bless us, your servants,
and these your own gifts of bread and wine,
so that we and all who share in the body and blood of Christ
may be filled with heavenly blessing and grace,
and, receiving the forgiveness of sin,
may be formed to live as your holy people
and be given our inheritance with all your saints.

To you, O God, Father, Son, and Holy Spirit,
be all honor and glory in your holy church, now and forever.

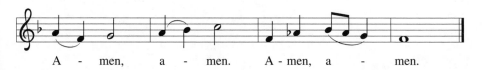

A-men, a-men. A-men, a-men.

Continue with the Lord's Prayer (p. 134).

III *(Advent—Epiphany of Our Lord)*

Holy One,
the beginning and the end,
the giver of life:
Blessed are you
for the birth of creation.
Blessed are you
in the darkness and in the light.
Blessed are you
for your promise to your people.
Blessed are you
in the prophets' hopes and dreams.
Blessed are you
for Mary's openness to your will.
Blessed are you
for your Son Jesus,
the Word made flesh.

In the night in which he was betrayed,
our Lord Jesus took bread,
and gave thanks; broke it,
and gave it to his disciples,
saying: Take and eat;
this is my body, given for you.
Do this for the remembrance of me.

Again, after supper, he took the cup,
gave thanks, and gave it for all to drink,
saying: This cup
is the new covenant in my blood,
shed for you and for all people
for the forgiveness of sin.
Do this for the remembrance of me.

Let us proclaim the mystery of faith:
Christ has died.
Christ is risen.
Christ will come again.

With this bread and cup
we remember your Word
dwelling among us,
full of grace and truth.
We remember our new birth
in his death and resurrection.
We look with hope for his coming.
Come, Lord Jesus.

Holy God,
we long for your Spirit.
Come among us.
Bless this meal.
May your Word take flesh in us.
Awaken your people.
Fill us with your light.
Bring the gift of peace on earth.
Come, Holy Spirit.

All praise and glory are yours,
Holy One of Israel,
Word of God incarnate,
Power of the Most High,
one God, now and forever.
Amen.

Continue with the Lord's Prayer (p. 134).

IV *(Ash Wednesday—Day of Pentecost)*

Blessed are you,
O God of the universe.
Your mercy is everlasting
and your faithfulness endures
from age to age.

Praise to you for creating
the heavens and the earth.
Praise to you for saving the earth
from the waters of the flood.
Praise to you for bringing
the Israelites safely through the sea.
Praise to you for leading
your people through the wilderness
to the land of milk and honey.
Praise to you for the words and deeds
of Jesus, your anointed one.
Praise to you for the death and
resurrection of Christ.
Praise to you for your Spirit
poured out on all nations.

In the night in which he was betrayed,
our Lord Jesus took bread,
and gave thanks; broke it,
and gave it to his disciples,
saying: Take and eat;
this is my body, given for you.
Do this for the remembrance of me.

Again, after supper, he took the cup,
gave thanks, and gave it for all to drink,
saying: This cup
is the new covenant in my blood,
shed for you and for all people
for the forgiveness of sin.
Do this for the remembrance of me.

With this bread and cup
we remember our Lord's passover
from death to life
as we proclaim the mystery of faith:
Christ has died.
Christ is risen.
Christ will come again.

O God of resurrection and new life:
Pour out your Holy Spirit on us
and on these gifts of bread and wine.
Bless this feast.
Grace our table with your presence.
Come, Holy Spirit.

Reveal yourself to us
in the breaking of the bread.
Raise us up
as the body of Christ for the world.
Breathe new life into us.
Send us forth,
burning with justice,
peace, and love.
Come, Holy Spirit.

With _name/s and_ your holy ones
of all times and places,
with the earth and all its creatures,
with sun and moon and stars,
we praise you, O God,
blessed and holy Trinity,
now and forever.
Amen.

Continue with the Lord's Prayer (p. 134).

Our Father in heaven,	Our Father, who art in heaven,
hallowed be your name,	hallowed be thy name,
your kingdom come,	thy kingdom come,
your will be done,	thy will be done,
on earth as in heaven.	on earth as it is in heaven.
Give us today our daily bread.	Give us this day our daily bread;
Forgive us our sins	and forgive us our trespasses,
as we forgive those	as we forgive those
who sin against us.	who trespass against us;
Save us from the time of trial	and lead us not into temptation,
and deliver us from evil.	but deliver us from evil.
For the kingdom, the power,	For thine is the kingdom,
and the glory are yours,	and the power, and the glory,
now and forever. Amen.	forever and ever. Amen.

For a sung version of the Lord's Prayer, see p. 163.

Communion

The presiding minister may address the assembly in these or similar words.

Taste and see	Come to the banquet,
that the Lord is good.	for all is now ready.

The assembly may be seated. The bread may be broken for the communion.

When giving the bread and cup, the communion ministers say
The body of Christ, given for you.
The blood of Christ, shed for you.
and each person may respond **Amen.**

The ministers commune either after or before others commune.

"Lamb of God" may be sung.

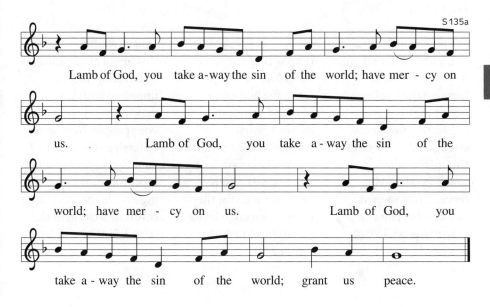

S 135a

Lamb of God, you take a-way the sin of the world; have mer - cy on us. Lamb of God, you take a - way the sin of the world; have mer - cy on us. Lamb of God, you take a - way the sin of the world; grant us peace.

Assembly song and other music may accompany the communion.

After all have returned to their places, the assembly stands. The presiding minister may say a table blessing; the assembly responds **Amen.**

The assembly may sing the following or another suitable song.

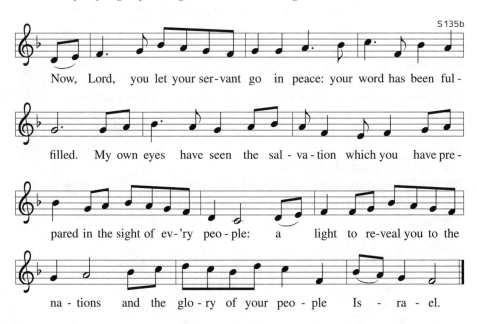

S 135b

Now, Lord, you let your ser-vant go in peace: your word has been ful - filled. My own eyes have seen the sal - va - tion which you have pre - pared in the sight of ev-'ry peo - ple: a light to re-veal you to the na - tions and the glo - ry of your peo - ple Is - ra - el.

The assisting minister leads one of the following or a similar prayer after communion.
Let us pray.

OR

OR

We give you thanks, almighty God, that you have refreshed us through the healing power of this gift of life. In your mercy, strengthen us through this gift in faith toward you and in fervent love toward one another; for the sake of Jesus Christ our Lord.
Amen.

O God, we give you thanks that you have set before us this feast, the body and blood of your Son. By your Spirit strengthen us to serve all in need and to give ourselves away as bread for the hungry, through Jesus Christ our Lord.
Amen.

God of abundance, with this bread of life and cup of salvation you have united us with Christ, making us one with all your people. Now send us forth in the power of your Spirit, that we may proclaim your redeeming love to the world and continue forever in the risen life of Jesus Christ, our Lord.
Amen.

Sending

Communion ministers may be sent to take the sacrament to those who are absent.

Brief announcements may be made, especially those related to the assembly's participation in God's mission in the world. Affirmation of Christian Vocation (p. 84) may be used here.

Blessing
The presiding minister proclaims God's blessing.
Almighty God, Father, + Son, and Holy Spirit, bless you now and forever.
Amen.

OR

The Lord bless you and keep you.
The Lord's face shine on you with grace and mercy.
The Lord look upon you with favor and + give you peace.
Amen.

The God of steadfastness and encouragement
grant you to live in harmony with one another,
in accordance with Christ Jesus.
Amen.
The God of hope fill you with all joy and peace in believing,
so that you may abound in hope by the power of the Holy Spirit.
Amen.
The God of all grace + bless you now and forever.
Amen.

Sending Song

If "Now, Lord, you let your servant go in peace" was not sung at the end of communion, it may be sung here, or another sending song may be sung.

Dismissal

The assisting minister may send the assembly into mission.

Go in peace. Serve the Lord.
Thanks be to God.

Go in peace. Share the good news.
Thanks be to God.

Go in peace. Remember the poor.
Thanks be to God.

Go in peace. Christ is with you.
Thanks be to God.

Holy Communion
Setting Three

Gathering

Confession and forgiveness (p. 94) or thanksgiving for baptism (p. 97) may begin the service.

Gathering Song

One or more of the following may be sung: hymns, psalms; a Kyrie; a canticle of praise.

During this time, the presiding minister and the assembly greet each other.
The grace of our Lord Jesus Christ, the love of God,
and the communion of the Holy Spirit be with you all.
And also with you.

A Kyrie may be sung in dialogue between an assisting minister and the assembly.

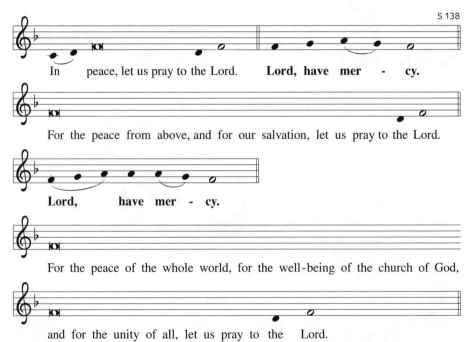

Lord, **have mer** - **cy.**

For this holy house, and for all who offer here their worship and praise,

let us pray to the Lord.   **Lord,**   **have mer** - **cy.**

Help, save, comfort, and defend us, gra - cious Lord.   **A** - **men.**

One of the following or another canticle of praise may be sung.

Assisting minister   S 139

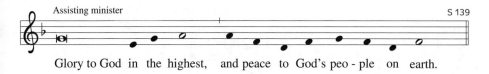

Glory to God in the highest,   and peace to God's peo - ple on earth.

All

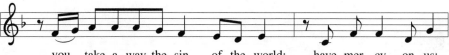

Lord God,   heav - en - ly   King, al - might - y   God and Fa - ther,

we wor-ship you,   we   give you thanks,   we praise you for your glo - ry.

Lord Je-sus Christ,   on - ly Son of the Fa-ther,   Lord God, Lamb of God,

you   take a - way the sin   of the world: have mer - cy   on us;

SETTING THREE

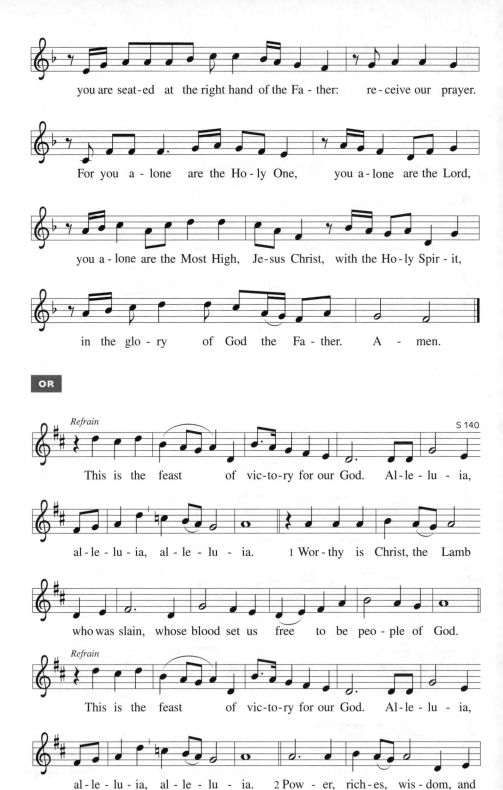

you are seat-ed at the right hand of the Fa - ther: re - ceive our prayer.

For you a - lone are the Ho - ly One, you a - lone are the Lord,

you a - lone are the Most High, Je-sus Christ, with the Ho - ly Spir - it,

in the glo - ry of God the Fa - ther. A - men.

OR

Refrain

S 140

This is the feast of vic-to-ry for our God. Al - le - lu - ia,

al - le - lu - ia, al - le - lu - ia. 1 Wor - thy is Christ, the Lamb

who was slain, whose blood set us free to be peo - ple of God.

Refrain

This is the feast of vic-to-ry for our God. Al - le - lu - ia,

al - le - lu - ia, al - le - lu - ia. 2 Pow - er, rich - es, wis - dom, and

strength, and hon - or, bless - ing, and glo - ry are his.

Refrain

This is the feast of vic-to-ry for our God. Al-le - lu - ia,

al - le - lu - ia, al - le - lu - ia. 3 Sing with all the peo - ple of

God, and join in the hymn of all cre - a - tion: Bless - ing, hon - or,

glo - ry, and might be to God and the Lamb for - ev - er. A - men.

Refrain

This is the feast of vic-to-ry for our God. Al-le - lu - ia,

al - le - lu - ia, al - le - lu - ia. 4 For the Lamb who was

slain has be - gun his reign. Al - le - lu - ia.

Final refrain

This is the feast of vic-to-ry for our God.

Al - le - lu - ia, al - le - lu - ia, al - le - lu - ia.

Prayer of the Day

Response after the prayer: **Amen.**

The assembly is seated.

Word

Readings and Psalm

Response after the conclusion of the first and the second reading: **Thanks be to God.**

The assembly stands to welcome the gospel.

Gospel Acclamation

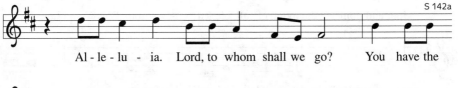

S 142a

Al - le - lu - ia. Lord, to whom shall we go? You have the words of e - ter - nal life. Al - le - lu - ia. Al - le - lu - ia.

OR

During Lent:

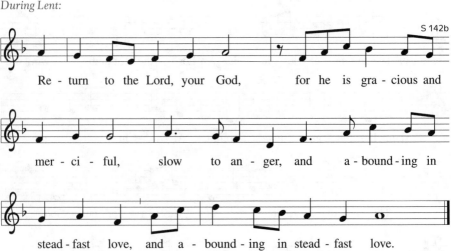

S 142b

Re - turn to the Lord, your God, for he is gra - cious and mer - ci - ful, slow to an - ger, and a - bound - ing in stead - fast love, and a - bound - ing in stead - fast love.

Gospel

Response after the announcement: **Glory to you, O Lord.**
Response after the conclusion: **Praise to you, O Christ.**

Sermon

The assembly is seated. Silence for reflection follows the sermon.

Hymn of the Day

The assembly stands to proclaim the word of God in song.

Creed

The Nicene Creed (p. 104) or the Apostles' Creed (p. 105) may be spoken.

Prayers of Intercession

Each portion of the prayers ends with these or similar words.

	OR	**OR**
Lord, in your mercy,	. . . let us pray.	Hear us, O God.
hear our prayer.	**Have mercy, O God.**	**Your mercy is great.**

Response at the conclusion of the prayers of intercession: **Amen.**

Peace

Response: **And also with you.** *The people may greet one another with a sign of Christ's peace and may say* **Peace be with you** *or similar words. Then the assembly is seated.*

Meal

An offering is gathered, and the table is set. Assembly song or other music may accompany or follow the gathering of the offering. After the offering is gathered, the assembly stands. The gifts may be brought forward. An offering prayer may be said; the assembly responds **Amen.**

Great Thanksgiving

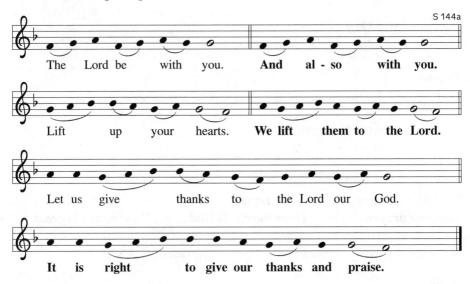

S 144a

The Lord be with you. **And al - so with you.**

Lift up your hearts. **We lift them to the Lord.**

Let us give thanks to the Lord our God.

It is right to give our thanks and praise.

The thanksgiving continues with the preface for the day or season; the assembly responds:

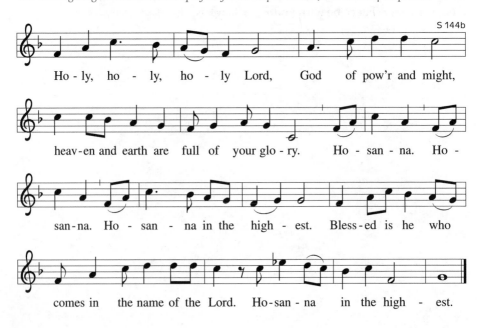

S 144b

Ho - ly, ho - ly, ho - ly Lord, God of pow'r and might,

heav-en and earth are full of your glo - ry. Ho - san - na. Ho -

san-na. Ho - san - na in the high - est. Bless-ed is he who

comes in the name of the Lord. Ho-san - na in the high - est.

The presiding minister continues, using an appropriate form.

The thanksgiving may include this acclamation.

Christ has died. Christ is ris - en. Christ will come a - gain.

The thanksgiving may include a sung Amen.

A - men, a - men, a - men.

The great thanksgiving concludes:

Our Father in heaven,
   hallowed be your name,
   your kingdom come,
   your will be done,
     on earth as in heaven.
Give us today our daily bread.
Forgive us our sins
   as we forgive those
     who sin against us.
Save us from the time of trial
   and deliver us from evil.
For the kingdom, the power,
   and the glory are yours,
   now and forever. Amen.

OR

Our Father, who art in heaven,
   hallowed be thy name,
   thy kingdom come,
   thy will be done,
     on earth as it is in heaven.
Give us this day our daily bread;
and forgive us our trespasses,
   as we forgive those
     who trespass against us;
and lead us not into temptation,
   but deliver us from evil.
For thine is the kingdom,
   and the power, and the glory,
   forever and ever. Amen.

Communion

The assembly may be seated. Music may accompany the communion and may begin with:

S 146

Lamb of God, you take a - way the sin of the world; have mer-cy on us. Lamb of God, you take a - way the sin of the world; have mer - cy on us. Lamb of God, you take a - way the sin of the world; grant us peace.

After all have returned to their places, the assembly stands. "Now, Lord, you let your servant go in peace" or another suitable song may be sung.

Prayer after Communion

Response after the prayer: **Amen.**

Sending

Blessing

Response after the blessing: **Amen.**

Sending Song

If "Now, Lord, you let your servant go in peace" was not sung at the end of communion, it may be sung here, or another sending song may be sung.

Dismissal

Response: **Thanks be to God.**

Holy Communion
Setting Four

Gathering

Confession and forgiveness (p. 94) or thanksgiving for baptism (p. 97) may begin the service.

Gathering Song

One or more of the following may be sung: hymns, psalms; a Kyrie; a canticle of praise.

During this time, the presiding minister and the assembly greet each other.
The grace of our Lord Jesus Christ, the love of God,
and the communion of the Holy Spirit be with you all.
And also with you.

A Kyrie may be sung in dialogue between an assisting minister and the assembly.

S 147

In peace, let us pray to the Lord.

Lord, have mer - cy.

For the peace from a-bove, and for our sal - vation, let us pray to the Lord.

Lord, have mer - cy.

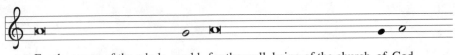

For the peace of the whole world, for the well-being of the church of God,

and for the unity of all, let us pray to the Lord.

Lord, have mer - cy.

For this holy house, and for all who offer here their wor-ship and praise,

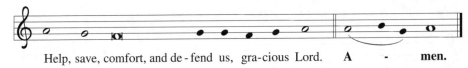

let us pray to the Lord. **Lord have mer - cy.**

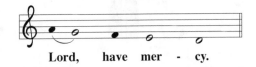

Help, save, comfort, and de-fend us, gra-cious Lord. **A - men.**

One of the following or another canticle of praise may be sung.

Assisting minister   S 148

Glo-ry to God in the high-est, and peace to God's peo-ple on earth.

All

Lord God, heav-en-ly King, al - might-y God and Fa - ther, we

wor-ship you, we give you thanks, we praise you for your glo - ry.

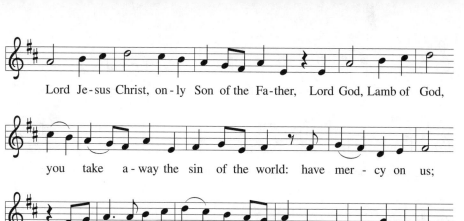

Lord Je-sus Christ, on-ly Son of the Fa-ther, Lord God, Lamb of God,

you take a-way the sin of the world: have mer-cy on us;

you are seat-ed at the right hand of the Fa-ther: re-ceive our prayer.

For you a-lone are the Ho-ly One, you a-lone are the Lord,

you a-lone are the Most High, Je-sus Christ, with the Ho-ly Spir-it,

in the glo - ry of God the Fa-ther. A - men.

OR

Refrain
Assisting minister

S 149

This is the feast of vic-to-ry for our God. Al-le-lu - ia.

All

1 Wor-thy is Christ, the Lamb who was slain, whose blood set us

free to be peo-ple of God. Pow - er and rich - es and wis - dom and

strength, and hon - or and bless-ing and glo - ry are his.

Refrain
This is the feast of vic-to-ry for our God. Al-le-lu - ia.

2 Sing with all the peo - ple of God and join in the hymn of all cre - a - tion: Bless-ing and hon - or and glo - ry and might be to God and the Lamb for - ev - er. A - men.

Final refrain
This is the feast of vic-to-ry for our God, for the Lamb who was slain has be - gun his reign. Al - le - lu - ia. Al-le - lu - ia.

Prayer of the Day

Response after the prayer: **Amen.**

The assembly is seated.

Word

Readings and Psalm

Response after the conclusion of the first and the second reading: **Thanks be to God.**

The assembly stands to welcome the gospel.

Gospel Acclamation

Al - le - lu - ia. Lord, to whom shall we go?

You have the words of e - ter - nal life. Al - le - lu - ia.

OR

During Lent:

Re - turn to the Lord, your God, for he is gra - cious and mer - ci - ful,

slow to an - ger, and a - bound - ing in stead - fast love.

Gospel

Response after the announcement: **Glory to you, O Lord.**
Response after the conclusion: **Praise to you, O Christ.**

Sermon

The assembly is seated. Silence for reflection follows the sermon.

Hymn of the Day

The assembly stands to proclaim the word of God in song.

Creed

The Nicene Creed (p. 104) or the Apostles' Creed (p. 105) may be spoken.

Prayers of Intercession

Each portion of the prayers ends with these or similar words.

	OR	**OR**
Lord, in your mercy, **hear our prayer.**	…let us pray. **Have mercy, O God.**	Hear us, O God. **Your mercy is great.**

Response at the conclusion of the prayers of intercession: **Amen.**

Peace

Response: **And also with you.** *The people may greet one another with a sign of Christ's peace and may say* **Peace be with you** *or similar words. Then the assembly is seated.*

Meal

An offering is gathered, and the table is set. Assembly song or other music may accompany or follow the gathering of the offering. After the offering is gathered, the assembly stands. The gifts may be brought forward. An offering prayer may be said; the assembly responds **Amen.**

Great Thanksgiving

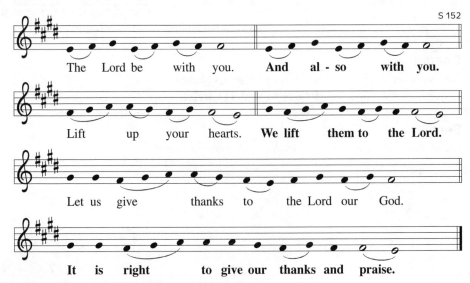

S 152

The Lord be with you. **And al-so with you.**

Lift up your hearts. **We lift them to the Lord.**

Let us give thanks to the Lord our God.

It is right to give our thanks and praise.

The thanksgiving continues with the preface for the day or season; the assembly responds:

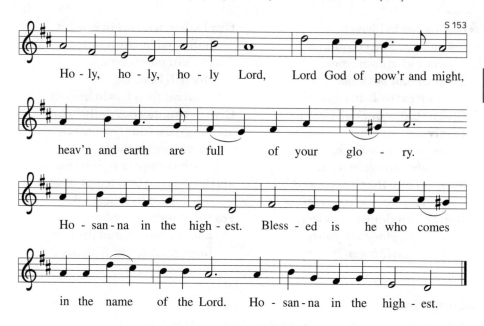

Ho - ly, ho - ly, ho - ly Lord, Lord God of pow'r and might,

heav'n and earth are full of your glo - ry.

Ho - san - na in the high - est. Bless - ed is he who comes

in the name of the Lord. Ho - san - na in the high - est.

The presiding minister continues, using an appropriate form.

The thanksgiving may include this acclamation.

Christ has died. Christ is ri - sen. Christ will come a - gain.

The thanksgiving may include a sung Amen.

A - men, a - men, a - men.

The great thanksgiving concludes:

Our Father in heaven,
   hallowed be your name,
   your kingdom come,
   your will be done,
     on earth as in heaven.
Give us today our daily bread.
Forgive us our sins
   as we forgive those
     who sin against us.
Save us from the time of trial
   and deliver us from evil.
For the kingdom, the power,
   and the glory are yours,
   now and forever. Amen.

OR

Our Father, who art in heaven,
   hallowed be thy name,
   thy kingdom come,
   thy will be done,
     on earth as it is in heaven.
Give us this day our daily bread;
and forgive us our trespasses,
   as we forgive those
     who trespass against us;
and lead us not into temptation,
   but deliver us from evil.
For thine is the kingdom,
   and the power, and the glory,
   forever and ever. Amen.

Communion

The assembly may be seated. Music may accompany the communion, and may begin with:

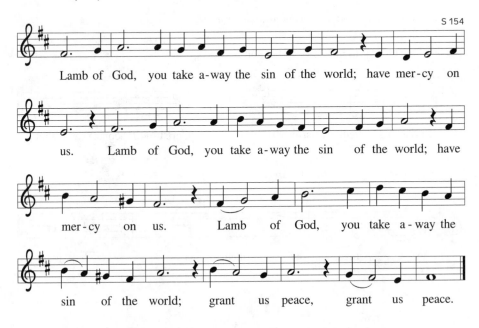

S 154

Lamb of God, you take a-way the sin of the world; have mer-cy on us. Lamb of God, you take a-way the sin of the world; have mer-cy on us. Lamb of God, you take a-way the sin of the world; grant us peace, grant us peace.

After all have returned to their places, the assembly stands. "Now, Lord, you let your servant go in peace" or another suitable song may be sung.

Prayer after Communion
Response after the prayer: **Amen.**

Sending

Blessing
Response after the blessing: **Amen.**

Sending Song
If "Now, Lord, you let your servant go in peace" was not sung at the end of communion, it may be sung here, or another sending song may be sung.

Dismissal
Response: **Thanks be to God.**

Holy Communion
Setting Five

Gathering

Confession and forgiveness (p. 94) or thanksgiving for baptism (p. 97) may begin the service.

Gathering Song

One or more of the following may be sung: hymns, psalms; a Kyrie; a canticle of praise.

During this time, the presiding minister and the assembly greet each other.
The grace of our Lord Jesus Christ, the love of God,
and the communion of the Holy Spirit be with you all.
And also with you.

A Kyrie may be sung in dialogue between an assisting minister and the assembly.

In peace, let us pray to the Lord.

Lord, have mer - cy.

For the peace from a-bove, and for our sal-va-tion, let us pray to the Lord.

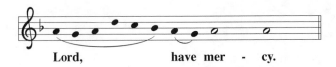

Lord, have mer - cy.

For the peace of the whole world, for the well-being of the church of God,

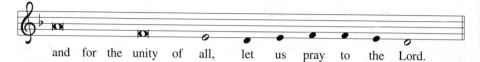

and for the unity of all, let us pray to the Lord.

Lord, have mer - cy.

For this ho-ly house, and for all who of-fer here their wor-ship and praise,

let us pray to the Lord.

Lord, have mer - cy.

Help, save, comfort, and de-fend us, gra-cious Lord.

A - men.

One of the following or another canticle of praise may be sung.

Assisting minister

S 158

Glo - ry to God in the high - est, and peace to God's peo-ple on earth.

All

Lord God, heav'n-ly King, al-might-y God and Fa - ther, we wor -

ship you, we give you thanks, we praise you for your glo - ry.

Lord Je - sus Christ, on - ly Son of the Fa - ther, O Lord God,

Lamb of God, you take a - way the sin of the world: have

mer-cy on us; you are seat - ed at the right hand of the

Fa - ther: re - ceive our prayer. For you a - lone are the

Ho - ly One, you a - lone are the Lord, you a - lone

are the Most High, Je - sus Christ, with the Ho - ly Spir - it,

in the glo - ry of God the Fa - ther. A - men.

1 All glo - ry be to God on high, and peace to earth be
2 Lord Je - sus Christ, the on - ly Son of God, cre - a - tion's
3 To you a - lone, O God, we cry, the Ho - ly One we

giv - en! Let an - gels sing, let all re - ply; good -
au - thor, O Lamb of God, your death a - lone takes
name you; for you a - lone are God most high, one

will breaks forth from heav - en! Lord God Al - might - y,
sin a - way for - ev - er. Stretch out your arms to
liv - ing God we claim you: we wor - ship you, Lord

heav - en's king, we wor - ship you, our thanks we sing, we
ev - 'ry land, and, as you reign at God's right hand, re -
Je - sus Christ, with God the Spir - it ev - er blest, in

praise you for your glo - ry.
ceive our prayer; have mer - cy.
God the Fa - ther's glo - ry. A - men.

Prayer of the Day

Response after the prayer: **Amen.**

The assembly is seated.

Word

Readings and Psalm

Response after the conclusion of the first and the second reading: **Thanks be to God.**

The assembly stands to welcome the gospel.

Gospel Acclamation

S 160a

Al-le-lu - ia, al - le-lu - ia, al - le - lu - ia.

The proper verse may be sung, or all may sing this verse.

Repeat alleluia

Lord, to whom shall we go?   You have the words of e-ter-nal life.

OR

During Lent:

S 160b

Glo - ry and praise to you, O Lord Je-sus Christ.

A proper verse may be sung; then "Glory and praise" is repeated.

Gospel

Response after the announcement: **Glory to you, O Lord.**
Response after the conclusion: **Praise to you, O Christ.**

Sermon

The assembly is seated. Silence for reflection follows the sermon.

Hymn of the Day

The assembly stands to proclaim the word of God in song.

Creed

The Nicene Creed (p. 104) or the Apostles' Creed (p. 105) may be spoken.

Prayers of Intercession

Each portion of the prayers ends with these or similar words.

	OR	**OR**
Lord, in your mercy,	. . . let us pray.	Hear us, O God.
hear our prayer.	**Have mercy, O God.**	**Your mercy is great.**

Response at the conclusion of the prayers of intercession: **Amen.**

Peace

Response: **And also with you.** *The people may greet one another with a sign of Christ's peace and may say* **Peace be with you** *or similar words. Then the assembly is seated.*

Meal

An offering is gathered, and the table is set. Assembly song or other music may accompany or follow the gathering of the offering. After the offering is gathered, the assembly stands. The gifts may be brought forward. An offering prayer may be said; the assembly responds **Amen.**

Great Thanksgiving

S 161

The Lord be with you. **And al - so with you.**

Lift up your hearts. **We lift them to the Lord.**

Let us give thanks to the Lord our God.

It is right to give our thanks and praise.

The thanksgiving continues with the preface for the day or season; the assembly responds:

S 162

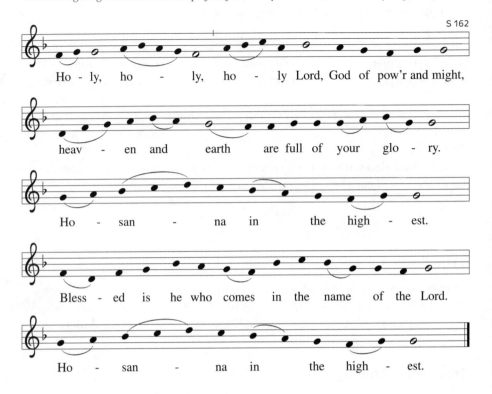

Ho - ly, ho - ly, ho - ly Lord, God of pow'r and might,

heav - en and earth are full of your glo - ry.

Ho - san - na in the high - est.

Bless - ed is he who comes in the name of the Lord.

Ho - san - na in the high - est.

The presiding minister continues, using an appropriate form.

The thanksgiving may include this acclamation.

Christ has died. Christ is ris - en. Christ will come a - gain.

The thanksgiving may include a sung Amen.

A - men, a - men. A - men, a - men.

The great thanksgiving concludes:

Our Fa-ther in heav - en, hal - lowed be your name, your king-dom come, your will be done, on earth as in heav - en. Give us to - day our dai - ly bread. For - give us our sins as we for-give those who sin a-gainst us. Save us from the time of tri - al and de - liv - er us from e - vil. For the king - dom, the pow'r, and the glo - ry are yours, now and for - ev - er. A - men.

OR

Our Father in heaven,
    hallowed be your name,
    your kingdom come,
    your will be done,
        on earth as in heaven.
Give us today our daily bread.
Forgive us our sins
    as we forgive those
        who sin against us.
Save us from the time of trial
    and deliver us from evil.
For the kingdom, the power,
    and the glory are yours,
    now and forever. Amen.

OR

Our Father, who art in heaven,
    hallowed be thy name,
    thy kingdom come,
    thy will be done,
        on earth as it is in heaven.
Give us this day our daily bread;
and forgive us our trespasses,
    as we forgive those
        who trespass against us;
and lead us not into temptation,
    but deliver us from evil.
For thine is the kingdom,
    and the power, and the glory,
    forever and ever. Amen.

Communion

The assembly may be seated. Music may accompany the communion and may begin with:

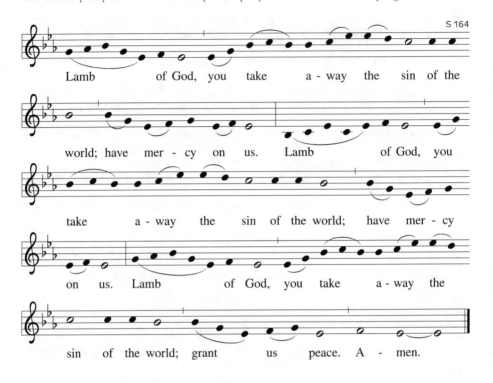

S 164

Lamb of God, you take a - way the sin of the world; have mer - cy on us. Lamb of God, you take a - way the sin of the world; have mer - cy on us. Lamb of God, you take a - way the sin of the world; grant us peace. A - men.

After all have returned to their places, the assembly stands. "Now, Lord, you let your servant go in peace" or another suitable song may be sung.

Prayer after Communion

Response after the prayer: **Amen.**

Sending

Blessing

Response after the blessing: **Amen.**

Sending Song

If "Now, Lord, you let your servant go in peace" was not sung at the end of communion, it may be sung here, or another sending song may be sung.

Dismissal

Response: **Thanks be to God.**

Holy Communion
Setting Six

Gathering

Confession and forgiveness (p. 94) or thanksgiving for baptism (p. 97) may begin the service.

Gathering Song

One or more of the following may be sung: hymns, psalms; a Kyrie; a canticle of praise.

During this time, the presiding minister and the assembly greet each other.
The grace of our Lord Jesus Christ, the love of God,
and the communion of the Holy Spirit be with you all.
And also with you.

A Kyrie may be sung in dialogue between an assisting minister and the assembly.

S 165

In peace, let us pray to the Lord.

Lord, have mer - cy.

For the peace from a - bove, and for our sal-vation, let us pray to the Lord.

Lord, have mer - cy.

For the peace of the whole world, for the well-being of the church of

God, and for the uni-ty of all, let us pray to the Lord.

Lord, have mer - cy.

For this ho - ly house, and for all who offer here their wor-ship and

praise, let us pray to the Lord.

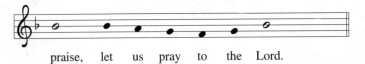

Lord, have mer - cy.

Help, save, comfort, and de - fend us, gracious Lord.

A - men.

One of the following or another canticle of praise may be sung by all.

Refrain

Glo-ry to God in the high - est, and peace

to God's peo-ple on earth. Glo-ry to God in the

high - est, and peace to God's peo-ple on earth.

1 Lord God, heav-en-ly King, al - might-y God and Fa-ther,

we wor-ship you, we give you thanks, we praise you for your glo - ry.

Refrain

Glo-ry to God in the high - est, and peace

to God's peo-ple on earth. Glo-ry to God in the

high - est, and peace to God's peo-ple on earth.

2 Lord Je - sus Christ, on - ly Son of the Fa - ther, Lord God,

Lamb of God, you take a - way the sin of the world:

have mer - cy on us; you are seat - ed at the right

hand of the Fa - ther: re - ceive our prayer.

Refrain

Glo - ry to God in the high - est, and peace

to God's peo-ple on earth. Glo - ry to God in the

high - est, and peace to God's peo-ple on earth.

3 For you a - lone are the Ho - ly One, you a - lone are the Lord, you a-

lone are the Most High, Je - sus Christ, with the Ho - ly

Spir - it, in the glo - ry of God the Fa - ther.

Final refrain

Glo - ry to God in the high - est.

A - men, a - men.

Refrain

This is the feast of vic-to-ry for our God.

Al - le - lu - ia, al - le - lu - ia.

1 Wor - thy is Christ, the Lamb who was slain, whose

blood set us free to be peo - ple of God.

Pow - er, rich - es, wis - dom, and strength, and

Refrain

hon - or, bless - ing, and glo - ry are his.

2 Sing with all the peo - ple of God, and

join in the hymn of all cre - a - tion:

Bless - ing, hon - or, glo - ry, and might be to

God and the Lamb for - ev - er. A - men.

3 For the Lamb who was slain has be -

gun his reign. Al - le - lu - ia.

Final refrain

This is the feast of vic-to-ry for our God.

Al - le - lu - ia, al - le - lu - ia.

This is the feast of vic-to-ry for our God.

Al - le - lu - ia, al - le - lu - ia.

Prayer of the Day

Response after the prayer: **Amen.**

The assembly is seated.

Word

Readings and Psalm

Response after the conclusion of the first and the second reading: **Thanks be to God.**

The assembly stands to welcome the gospel.

Gospel Acclamation

Al - le - lu - ia. Lord, to whom shall we go?

You have the words of e - ter - nal life. Al - le - lu - ia.

OR

During Lent:

Let your stead - fast love come to us, O Lord.

Save us as you prom - ised; we will trust your word.

Gospel

Response after the announcement: **Glory to you, O Lord.**
Response after the conclusion: **Praise to you, O Christ.**

Sermon

The assembly is seated. Silence for reflection follows the sermon.

Hymn of the Day

The assembly stands to proclaim the word of God in song.

Creed

The Nicene Creed (p. 104) or the Apostles' Creed (p. 105) may be spoken.

Prayers of Intercession

Each portion of the prayers ends with these or similar words.

	OR	**OR**
Lord, in your mercy,	. . . let us pray.	Hear us, O God.
hear our prayer.	**Have mercy, O God.**	**Your mercy is great.**

Response at the conclusion of the prayers of intercession: **Amen.**

Peace

Response: **And also with you.** *The people may greet one another with a sign of Christ's peace and may say* Peace be with you *or similar words. Then the assembly may be seated.*

Meal

An offering is gathered, and the table is set. Assembly song or other music may accompany or follow the gathering of the offering. After the offering is gathered, the assembly stands. The gifts may be brought forward. An offering prayer may be said; the assembly responds **Amen.**

Great Thanksgiving

The Lord be with you.
And also with you.

Lift up your hearts.
We lift them to the Lord.

Let us give thanks to the Lord our God.
It is right to give our thanks and praise.

The thanksgiving continues with the preface for the day or season; the assembly responds:

S 173

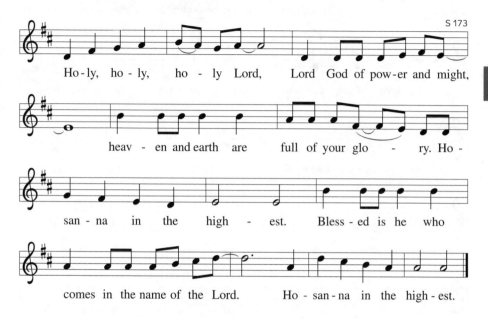

Ho-ly, ho-ly, ho-ly Lord, Lord God of pow-er and might, heav-en and earth are full of your glo - ry. Ho - san-na in the high - est. Bless-ed is he who comes in the name of the Lord. Ho - san-na in the high-est.

The presiding minister continues, using an appropriate form.

The thanksgiving may include this acclamation:
Christ has died. Christ is risen. Christ will come again.
and may conclude: **Amen.**

The great thanksgiving concludes:

OR

Our Father in heaven,	**Our Father, who art in heaven,**
hallowed be your name,	**hallowed be thy name,**
your kingdom come,	**thy kingdom come,**
your will be done,	**thy will be done,**
on earth as in heaven.	**on earth as it is in heaven.**
Give us today our daily bread.	**Give us this day our daily bread;**
Forgive us our sins	**and forgive us our trespasses,**
as we forgive those	**as we forgive those**
who sin against us.	**who trespass against us;**
Save us from the time of trial	**and lead us not into temptation,**
and deliver us from evil.	**but deliver us from evil.**
For the kingdom, the power,	**For thine is the kingdom,**
and the glory are yours,	**and the power, and the glory,**
now and forever. Amen.	**forever and ever. Amen.**

Communion

The assembly may be seated. Music may accompany the communion and may begin with:

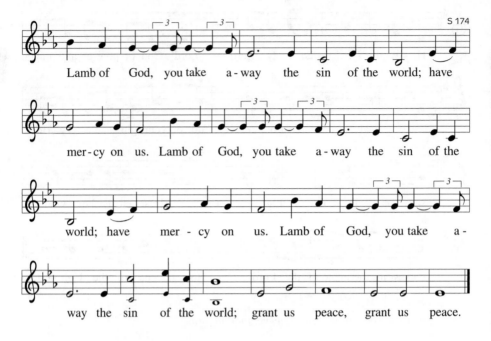

S 174

Lamb of God, you take a-way the sin of the world; have mer-cy on us. Lamb of God, you take a-way the sin of the world; have mer-cy on us. Lamb of God, you take a-way the sin of the world; grant us peace, grant us peace.

After all have returned to their places, the assembly stands. "Now, Lord, you let your servant go in peace" or another suitable song may be sung.

Prayer after Communion

Response after the prayer: **Amen.**

Sending

Blessing

Response after the blessing: **Amen.**

Sending Song

If "Now, Lord, you let your servant go in peace" was not sung at the end of communion, it may be sung here, or another sending song may be sung.

Dismissal

Response: **Thanks be to God.**

Holy Communion
Setting Seven

Gathering

Confession and forgiveness (p. 94) or thanksgiving for baptism (p. 97) may begin the service.

Gathering Song

One or more of the following may be sung: hymns, psalms; a Kyrie; a canticle of praise.

During this time, the presiding minister and the assembly greet each other.
The grace of our Lord Jesus Christ, the love of God,
and the communion of the Holy Spirit be with you all.
And also with you.

A Kyrie may be sung by all.

S 175

Se - ñor, Se - ñor, ten pie - dad;   ten pie - dad   de no -
Lord, . . have mer - cy   on   us;   O . . . Lord,   have . . .

so - tros.   Se - ñor, Se - ñor, ten pie -
mer - cy.   Lord, . . have mer - cy   on

dad;   ten pie - dad   de no - so - tros.
us;   O . . . Lord,   have . . mer - cy.

Cris - to, Cris - to, ten pie - dad;   ten pie - dad   de no -
Christ, . . have mer - cy   on   us;   O . . . Christ,   have . .

so - tros.   Cris - to, Cris - to, ten pie -
mer - cy.   Christ, . . have mer - cy   on

dad;   ten pie - dad   de no - so - tros.
us;   O . . .   Christ,   have . . mer - cy.

Se - ñor, Se - ñor, ten pie - dad;   ten pie - dad   de no -
Lord, . . have mer - cy   on   us;   O . . . Lord,   have . . .

so - tros.   Se - ñor, Se - ñor, ten pie -
mer - cy.   Lord, . . have mer - cy   on

dad;   ten pie - dad   de no - so - tros.
us;   O . . .   Lord,   have . . mer - cy.

One of the following or another canticle of praise may be sung by all.

S 176

¡Glo - ria, glo - ria, glo - ria   en   las al - tu - ras a   Dios!
Glo - ria, glo - ria, glo - ria,   glo - ry to God . . on   high!

¡Glo - ria, glo - ria, glo - ria   en   las al - tu - ras a   Dios!
Glo - ria, glo - ria, glo - ria,   glo - ry to God . . on   high!

Y en   la tie - rra   paz pa - ra a - que - llos   que a - ma el Se - ñor.
And   on earth . . . peace to God's peo - ple. Glo - ry to God.

Y en la tie - rra paz pa-ra a-que-llos que a-ma el Se - ñor.
And on earth . . peace to God's peo-ple. Glo - ry to God.

OR

Refrain   S 177

Ce - le - bre - mos la vic - to - ria de nues - tro
Cel - e - brate the feast of vic - to - ry for our

Dios. A - le - lu - ya, a - le - lu - ya.
God. Al - le - lu - ia, al - le - lu - ia.

1 *Dig - no es Cris - to, el Cor - de - ro in-mo - la - do, cu - ya*
1 Wor - thy is Christ, . . . the . . . Lamb who was slain, . . . whose . .

Refrain

san - gre nos ha li - be - ra - do, pa - ra ser el pueb - lo de Dios.
blood . . has set . . us free, ... free to be the peo - ple of God.

2 *Po - der, ri - que - zas, sa - bi - du - rí - a y fuer - za,*
2 All pow - er, rich - es, wis - dom and strength and bless - ing,

Refrain

hon - ra y a - la - ban - za y glo - ria son de él.
hon - or, thanks and praise and glo - ry to the Lamb.

3 *Can - te - mos con to - do el pueb - lo de Dios, y u -*
3 Re - joice, sing with all the peo - ple of God! Let us

na - mos nues - tras vo - ces al him - no u - ni - ver -
join our hearts and voic - es in the hymn of all . . . cre -

sal: A - la - ban - za, hon - ra, glo - ria y po -
a - tion: All . . . bless - ing, hon - or, glo - ry, and . . .

der se - an da - dos a Dios y al Cor - de - ro por siem - pre. A - mén.
might . . be giv - en to God and the Lamb . . for - ev - er. A - men.

Final refrain

Ce - le - bre - mos la vic - to - ria de nues - tro
Cel - e - brate the feast of vic - to - ry for our

Dios, ya que el Cor - de - ro in - mo - la - do ha co - men -
God, ... for the Lamb who was . . . slain has now . . be -

za - do su rei - na - do. A - le -
gun to reign in glo - ry. Al - le -

lu - ya, a - le - lu - ya.
lu - ia, al - le - lu - ia.

Prayer of the Day

Response after the prayer: **Amen.**

The assembly is seated.

Word

Readings and Psalm

Response after the conclusion of the first and the second reading: **Thanks be to God.**

The assembly stands to welcome the gospel.

Gospel Acclamation

S 179a

¡A - le - lu - ya,   a - le - lu - ya,   a - le - lu - ya!
Al - le - lu - ia,   al - le - lu - ia,   al - le - lu - ia!

¡A - le - lu - ya,   a - le - lu - ya,   a - le - lu - ya!
Al - le - lu - ia,   al - le - lu - ia,   al - le - lu - ia!

¡A - le - lu - ya,   a - le - lu - ya,
Al - le - lu - ia,   al - le - lu - ia,

a - le - lu - ya!   ¡A - le - lu - ya!
al - le - lu - ia!   Al - le - lu - ia!

OR

During Lent:

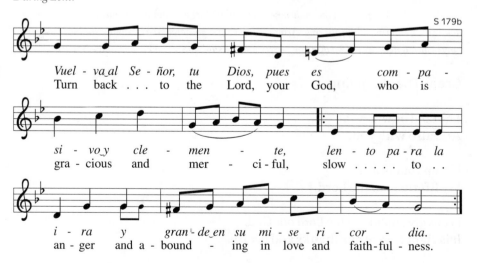

S 179b

Vuel - va_al Se - ñor,   tu   Dios,   pues   es   com - pa -
Turn   back . . . to   the   Lord,   your   God,   who   is

si - vo_y   cle - men - te,   len - to pa - ra   la
gra - cious   and   mer - ci - ful,   slow . . . . . to . .

i - ra   y   gran - de_en su mi - se - ri - cor - dia.
an - ger   and a - bound - ing in love and faith - ful - ness.

Gospel

Response after the announcement: **Glory to you, O Lord.**
Response after the conclusion: **Praise to you, O Christ.**

Sermon

The assembly is seated. Silence for reflection follows the sermon.

Hymn of the Day

The assembly stands to proclaim the word of God in song.

Creed

The Nicene Creed (p. 104) or the Apostles' Creed (p. 105) may be spoken.

Prayers of Intercession

Each portion of the prayers ends with these or similar words.

	OR	**OR**
Lord, in your mercy,	. . . let us pray.	Hear us, O God.
hear our prayer.	**Have mercy, O God.**	**Your mercy is great.**

Response at the conclusion of the prayers of intercession: **Amen.**

Peace

Response: **And also with you.** *The people may greet one another with a sign of Christ's peace and may say* **Peace be with you** *or similar words. Then the assembly may be seated.*

Meal

An offering is gathered, and the table is set. Assembly song or other music may accompany or follow the gathering of the offering. After the offering is gathered, the assembly stands. The gifts may be brought forward. An offering prayer may be said; the assembly responds **Amen.**

Great Thanksgiving

The Lord be with you.
And also with you.

Lift up your hearts.
We lift them to the Lord.

Let us give thanks to the Lord our God.
It is right to give our thanks and praise.

The thanksgiving continues with the preface for the day or season; the assembly responds:

San - to, san - to, san - to_es el Se - ñor,
Ho - ly, ho - ly, ho - ly Lord . . . . God,

Dios del u - ni - ver - so; san - to_es el Se - ñor.
God of might and pow - er; ho - ly is the Lord.

San - to, san - to, san - to, san - to_es el Se - ñor,
Ho - ly, ho - ly, ho - ly, ho - ly Lord . . . God,

Dios del u - ni - ver - so; san - to_es el Se - ñor.
God of might and pow - er; ho - ly is the Lord.

Ho - san - na en el cie - lo, ho - san - na en la
Ho - san - na in the high - est, ho - san - na here on

tie - rra. Ben - di - to el que vie - ne_en el
earth. . . . . Blest is he who comes in the

nom - bre del Se - ñor. Ho - san - na en el
name . . . of the Lord. Ho - san - na in the

cie - lo, ho - san - na en la tie - rra. Ben -
high - est, ho - san - na here on earth. . . . .

di - to el que vie - ne_en el nom - bre del Se - ñor.
Blest is he who comes in the name . . . of the Lord.

The presiding minister continues, using an appropriate form.

The thanksgiving may include this acclamation:
Christ has died. Christ is risen. Christ will come again.
and may conclude: **Amen.**

The great thanksgiving concludes:

OR

Our Father in heaven,
    hallowed be your name,
    your kingdom come,
    your will be done,
        on earth as in heaven.
Give us today our daily bread.
Forgive us our sins
    as we forgive those
        who sin against us.
Save us from the time of trial
    and deliver us from evil.
For the kingdom, the power
    and the glory are yours,
    now and forever. Amen.

Our Father, who art in heaven,
    hallowed be thy name,
    thy kingdom come,
    thy will be done,
        on earth as it is in heaven.
Give us this day our daily bread;
and forgive us our trespasses,
    as we forgive those
        who trespass against us;
and lead us not into temptation,
    but deliver us from evil.
For thine is the kingdom,
    and the power, and the glory,
    forever and ever. Amen.

Communion

The assembly may be seated. Music may accompany the communion and may begin with:

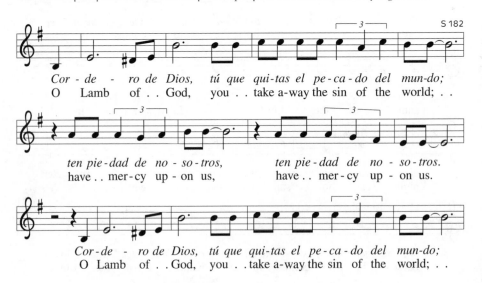

S 182

Cor - de - ro de Dios, tú que qui-tas el pe - ca - do del mun-do;
O Lamb of . . God, you . . take a-way the sin of the world; . .

ten pie - dad de no - so - tros, ten pie - dad de no - so - tros.
have . . mer-cy up - on us, have . . mer-cy up - on us.

Cor - de - ro de Dios, tú que qui-tas el pe - ca - do del mun-do;
O Lamb of . . God, you . . take a-way the sin of the world; . .

ten pie-dad de no-so-tros,   *ten pie-dad de no - so-tros.*
have .. mer-cy up-on us,   have .. mer-cy up - on us.

Cor-de - ro de Dios, tú que qui-tas el pe-ca-do del mun-do;
O Lamb of .. God, you .. take a-way the sin of the world; ..

da - nos tu paz,   *da - nos tu paz.*
grant us your peace,   grant us your peace.

After all have returned to their places, the assembly stands. "Now, Lord, you let your servant go in peace" or another suitable song may be sung.

Prayer after Communion

Response after the prayer: **Amen.**

Sending

Blessing

Response after the blessing: **Amen.**

Sending Song

If "Now, Lord, you let your servant go in peace" was not sung at the end of communion, it may be sung here, or another sending song may be sung.

Dismissal

Response: **Thanks be to God.**

Holy Communion
Setting Eight

Gathering

Confession and forgiveness (p. 94) or thanksgiving for baptism (p. 97) may begin the service.

Gathering Song

One or more of the following may be sung: hymns, psalms; a Kyrie; a canticle of praise.

During this time, the presiding minister and the assembly greet each other.
The grace of our Lord Jesus Christ, the love of God,
and the communion of the Holy Spirit be with you all.
And also with you.

A Kyrie may be sung. The assembly sings the refrain, and a leader sings the verses.

For peace in the world, for the health of the church, for the unity of all;
for this holy house, for all who worship and praise,
let us pray to the Lord, let us pray to the Lord. *Refrain*

That we may live out your impassioned response to the hungry and the poor;
that we may live out truth and justice and grace,
let us pray to the Lord, let us pray to the Lord. *Refrain*

For peace in our hearts, for peace in our homes, for friends and family;
for life and for love, for our work and our play,
let us pray to the Lord, let us pray to the Lord. *Refrain*

For your Spirit to guide; that you center our lives in the water and the Word;
that you nourish our souls with your body and blood,
let us pray to the Lord, let us pray to the Lord. *Refrain*

One of the following or another canticle of praise may be sung by all.

S 185

Refrain

Glo - ry to God in the high - est, the high - est, and
peace to God's peo - ple on earth.

1 Lord God, heav-en - ly King, al - might-y God and Fa - ther,
we wor-ship you, we give you thanks, we praise you
for your glo - ry.

Refrain

Glo - ry to God in the high-
est, the high - est, and peace to God's peo - ple on earth.

2 Lord Je - sus Christ, on - ly Son of the Fa - ther, Lord God,
Lamb of God, you take a - way the sin of the

world: have mer - cy on us; you are seat - ed at the

right hand of the Fa - ther: re - ceive our prayer.

Refrain

Glo - ry to God in the high - est, the high - est, and

peace to God's peo - ple on earth. 3 For you a -

lone are the Ho - ly One, you a - lone are the Lord,

you a - lone are the Most High, Je - sus Christ, with the

Ho - ly Spir - it, in the glo - ry of God the Fa - ther.

A - men. A - men. A - men.

Final refrain

Glo - ry to God in the high - est, the high - est, and peace to God's

peo - ple on earth. Glo - ry to God in the high-

est, the high - est, and peace to God's peo - ple on earth.

Refrain

This is the feast of vic - t'ry for our God, for the

Lamb who was slain has be - gun his reign. Al - le - lu - ia.

1 Wor-thy is Christ, the Lamb who was slain, whose blood set us free to be

peo-ple of God. Pow - er, rich - es, wis - dom, and strength, and

Refrain

hon - or, bless - ing, and glo - ry are his. This is the feast of

vic-t'ry for our God, for the Lamb who was slain has be - gun his reign. Al -

le - lu - ia. 2 Sing with all the peo - ple of God, and

join in the hymn of all cre - a - tion: Bless - ing, hon - or,

glo - ry, and might be to God and the Lamb for - ev - er. A - men.

Final refrain

This is the feast of vic - t'ry for our God, for the

Lamb who was slain has be - gun his reign. Al - le - lu - ia.

Prayer of the Day

Response to the prayer: **Amen.**

The assembly is seated.

Word

Readings and Psalm

Response after the conclusion of the first and the second reading: **Thanks be to God.**

The assembly stands to welcome the gospel.

Gospel Acclamation

S 188

Al - le - lu - ia. Lord, to whom shall we go? You have the

words of e - ter - nal life. Al - le - lu - ia.

Al - le - lu - ia, al - le - lu - ia. Al - le - lu - ia.

Al - le - lu - ia, al - le - lu - ia.

OR During Lent:

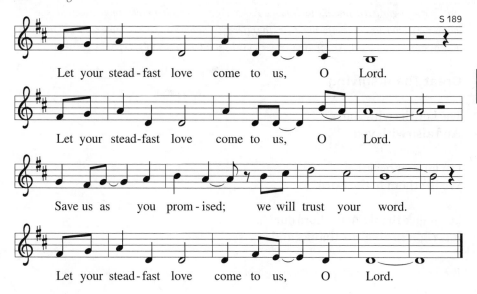

Let your stead-fast love come to us, O Lord.

Let your stead-fast love come to us, O Lord.

Save us as you prom-ised; we will trust your word.

Let your stead-fast love come to us, O Lord.

Gospel

Response after the announcement: **Glory to you, O Lord.**
Response after the conclusion: **Praise to you, O Christ.**

Sermon

The assembly is seated. Silence for reflection follows the sermon.

Hymn of the Day

The assembly stands to proclaim the word of God in song.

Creed

The Nicene Creed (p. 104) or the Apostles' Creed (p. 105) may be spoken.

Prayers of Intercession

Each portion of the prayers ends with these or similar words.

	OR	**OR**
Lord, in your mercy,	. . . let us pray.	Hear us, O God.
hear our prayer.	**Have mercy, O God.**	**Your mercy is great.**

Response at the conclusion of the prayers of intercession: **Amen.**

Peace

Response: **And also with you.** *The people may greet one another with a sign of Christ's peace and may say* **Peace be with you** *or similar words. Then the assembly is seated.*

Meal

An offering is gathered, and the table is set. Assembly song or other music may accompany or follow the gathering of the offering. After the offering is gathered, the assembly stands. The gifts may be brought forward. An offering prayer may be said; the assembly responds **Amen.**

Great Thanksgiving

The Lord be with you.
And also with you.

Lift up your hearts.
We lift them to the Lord.

Let us give thanks to the Lord our God.
It is right to give our thanks and praise.

The thanksgiving continues with the preface for the day or season; the assembly responds:

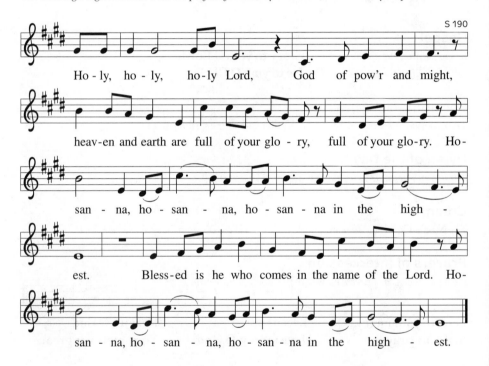

S 190

Ho - ly, ho - ly, ho - ly Lord, God of pow'r and might, heav-en and earth are full of your glo - ry, full of your glo - ry. Ho - san - na, ho - san - na, ho - san - na in the high - est. Bless-ed is he who comes in the name of the Lord. Ho - san - na, ho - san - na, ho - san - na in the high - est.

The presiding minister continues, using an appropriate form.
The thanksgiving may include this acclamation:
Christ has died. Christ is risen. Christ will come again.
and may conclude: **Amen.**

The great thanksgiving concludes:

Our Father in heaven,
    hallowed be your name,
    your kingdom come,
    your will be done,
        on earth as in heaven.
Give us today our daily bread.
Forgive us our sins
    as we forgive those
        who sin against us.
Save us from the time of trial
    and deliver us from evil.
For the kingdom, the power,
    and the glory are yours,
    now and forever. Amen.

OR

Our Father, who art in heaven,
    hallowed be thy name,
    thy kingdom come,
    thy will be done,
        on earth as it is in heaven.
Give us this day our daily bread;
and forgive us our trespasses,
    as we forgive those
        who trespass against us;
and lead us not into temptation,
    but deliver us from evil.
For thine is the kingdom,
    and the power, and the glory,
    forever and ever. Amen.

Communion

The assembly may be seated. Music may accompany the communion and may begin with:

S 191

Lamb of God, you take a-way the sin of the world; have mer-cy on us. Lamb of God, you take a-way the sin of the world; have mer-cy on us. Lamb of God, you take a-way the sin of the world; grant us peace, grant us peace, Lamb of God.

After all have returned to their places, the assembly stands. "Now, Lord, you let your servant go in peace" or another suitable song may be sung.

Prayer after Communion

Response after the prayer: **Amen.**

Sending

Blessing

Response after the blessing: **Amen.**

Sending Song

If "Now, Lord, you let your servant go in peace" was not sung at the end of communion, it may be sung here, or another sending song may be sung.

Dismissal

Response: **Thanks be to God.**

Holy Communion
Setting Nine

Gathering

Confession and forgiveness (p. 94) or thanksgiving for baptism (p. 97) may begin the service.

Gathering Song

One or more of the following may be sung: hymns, psalms; a Kyrie; a canticle of praise.

During this time, the presiding minister and the assembly greet each other.
The grace of our Lord Jesus Christ, the love of God,
and the communion of the Holy Spirit be with you all.
And also with you.

A Kyrie may be sung in dialogue between an assisting minister and the assembly.

In peace, let us pray to the Lord.

Lord, have mer - cy.

For the peace from a - bove, and for our sal - vation, let us pray to the Lord.

Lord, have mer - cy.

For the peace of the whole world, for the well-being of the church of God, and for the u-ni-ty of all, let us pray to the Lord.

Lord, have mer-cy.

For this ho-ly house, and for all who offer here their wor-ship and praise, let us pray to the Lord.

Lord, have mer-cy.

Help, save, comfort, and de-fend us, gra-cious Lord.

A - men.

One of the following or another canticle of praise may be sung by all.

S 195

Glo-ry to God in the high - est, and peace to God's peo-ple on earth.

1 Lord God, heav'n-ly King, al - might-y God and Fa-ther, we

wor-ship you, we give you thanks, we praise you for your glo-ry.

Glo-ry to God in the high - est, and peace to God's peo-ple on earth.

2 Lord Je-sus Christ, on-ly Son of the Fa-ther, Lord God, Lamb of

God, you take a-way the sin of the world: have mer-cy on us;

you are seat-ed at the right hand of the Fa-ther: re - ceive our prayer.

Glo-ry to God in the high - est, and peace to God's peo-ple on earth.

3 For you a - lone are the Ho - ly One, you a - lone are the

Lord, you a-lone are the Most High, Je-sus Christ, with the

Ho-ly Spir-it, in the glo-ry of God the Fa-ther.

A - men, a - men.

OR

Refrain   S 196

This is the feast of vic-to-ry for our God.

Al - le - lu - ia, al - le - lu - ia.

1 Wor-thy is Christ, the Lamb who was slain, whose blood set us free to be

peo-ple of God. Pow - er, rich - es, wis-dom, and strength, and

hon - or, bless - ing, and glo - ry are his.

Refrain

This is the feast of vic-to-ry for our God.

Al - le - lu - ia, al - le - lu - ia.

2 Sing with all the peo-ple of God, and join in the hymn of all cre - a - tion: Bless - ing, hon - or, glo - ry, and might be to God and the Lamb for - ev - er. A - men.

Final refrain

This is the feast of vic - to - ry for our God, for the Lamb who was slain has be - gun his reign.

Al - le - lu - ia, al - le - lu - ia, al - le - lu - ia.

Prayer of the Day

Response after the prayer: **Amen.**

The assembly is seated.

Word

Readings and Psalm

Response after the conclusion of the first and the second reading: **Thanks be to God.**

The assembly stands to welcome the gospel.

Gospel Acclamation

S 198a

Al - le - lu - ia, al - le - lu - ia.

Al - le - lu - ia, al - le - lu - ia.

The proper verse may be sung, or all may sing this verse.

Repeat alleluia

Lord, to whom shall we go? You have the words of e - ter - nal life.

During Lent:

S 198b

Let your stead - fast love come to us, O Lord.

Save us as you prom - ised; we will trust your word.

Gospel

Response after the announcement: **Glory to you, O Lord.**
Response after the conclusion: **Praise to you, O Christ.**

Sermon

The assembly is seated. Silence for reflection follows the sermon.

Hymn of the Day

The assembly stands to proclaim the word of God in song.

Creed

The Nicene Creed (p. 104) or the Apostles' Creed (p. 105) may be spoken.

Prayers of Intercession

Each portion of the prayers ends with these or similar words.

	OR	**OR**
Lord, in your mercy,	. . . let us pray.	Hear us, O God.
hear our prayer.	**Have mercy, O God.**	**Your mercy is great.**

Response at the conclusion of the prayers of intercession: **Amen.**

Peace

Response: **And also with you.** *The people may greet one another with a sign of Christ's peace, and may say* Peace be with you *or similar words. Then the assembly is seated.*

Meal

An offering is gathered, and the table is set. Assembly song or other music may accompany or follow the gathering of the offering. After the offering is gathered, the assembly stands. The gifts may be brought forward. An offering prayer may be said; the assembly responds **Amen.**

Great Thanksgiving

The thanksgiving continues with the preface for the day or season; the assembly responds:

Ho - ly, ho - ly, ho - ly Lord, God of pow-er and might, heav-en and earth are full of your glo - ry. Ho - san - na in the high-est, ho - san - na in the high - est. Bless-ed is he who comes in the name of the Lord. Ho - san - na in the high-est, ho - san - na in the high - est.

The presiding minister continues, using an appropriate form.

The thanksgiving may include this acclamation.

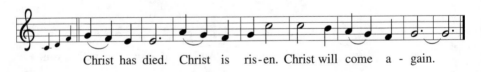

Christ has died. Christ is ris-en. Christ will come a - gain.

The thanksgiving may include a sung Amen.

A - men, a - men, a - men.

The great thanksgiving concludes:

Our Father in heaven,
  hallowed be your name,
  your kingdom come,
  your will be done,
    on earth as in heaven.
Give us today our daily bread.
Forgive us our sins
  as we forgive those
    who sin against us.
Save us from the time of trial
  and deliver us from evil.
For the kingdom, the power,
  and the glory are yours,
  now and forever. Amen.

OR

Our Father, who art in heaven,
  hallowed be thy name,
  thy kingdom come,
  thy will be done,
    on earth as it is in heaven.
Give us this day our daily bread;
and forgive us our trespasses,
  as we forgive those
    who trespass against us;
and lead us not into temptation,
  but deliver us from evil.
For thine is the kingdom,
  and the power, and the glory,
  forever and ever. Amen.

Communion

The assembly may be seated. Music may accompany the communion, and may begin with:

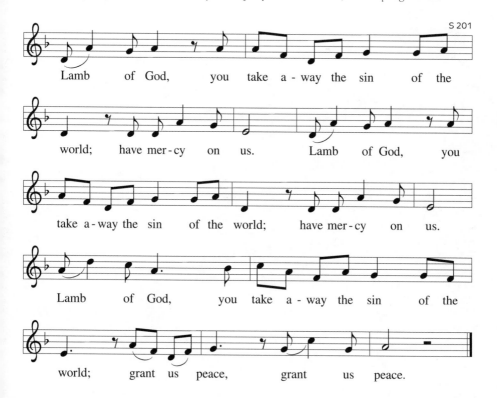

S 201

Lamb of God, you take a-way the sin of the world; have mer-cy on us. Lamb of God, you take a-way the sin of the world; have mer-cy on us. Lamb of God, you take a-way the sin of the world; grant us peace, grant us peace.

After all have returned to their places, the assembly stands. "Now, Lord, you let your servant go in peace" or another suitable song may be sung.

Prayer after Communion
Response after the prayer: **Amen.**

Sending

Blessing
Response after the blessing: **Amen.**

Sending Song
If "Now, Lord, you let your servant go in peace" was not sung at the end of communion, it may be sung here, or another sending song may be sung.

Dismissal
Response: **Thanks be to God.**

Holy Communion
Setting Ten

Gathering

Confession and forgiveness (p. 94) or thanksgiving for baptism (p. 97) may begin the service.

Gathering Song

One or more of the following may be sung: hymns, psalms; a Kyrie; a canticle of praise.

During this time, the presiding minister and the assembly greet each other.
The grace of our Lord Jesus Christ, the love of God,
and the communion of the Holy Spirit be with you all.
And also with you.

A Kyrie may be sung by all.

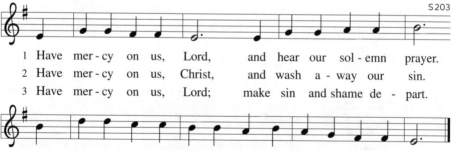

S 203

1 Have mer-cy on us, Lord, and hear our sol-emn prayer.
2 Have mer-cy on us, Christ, and wash a-way our sin.
3 Have mer-cy on us, Lord; make sin and shame de - part.

We come to hear your liv-ing word; it saves us from de-spair.
Pour out your grace and make us whole that new life may be-gin.
Re - new us with your sav-ing pow'r; cre-ate in us new hearts!

One of the following or another canticle of praise may be sung by all.

S204a

1 Glo-ry be to God in heav-en; peace, good-will to all the earth.
2 Glo-ry be to Christ for-ev-er, Lamb of God and Lord of love.
3 Ho-ly One we now ac-claim you; Lord a-lone, to you we call;

Might-y God of all cre-a-tion, Fa-ther of sur-pass-ing worth:
Son of God and gra-cious Sav-ior, you have come from heav'n a-bove;
Ho-ly One in faith we name you, God most high, yet near to all:

we ex-alt you, we a-dore you, we lift high our thanks and praise.
on the cross you died to save us; now you reign at God's right hand.
Je-sus Christ, with God the Spir-it, in the Fa-ther's splen-dor bright.

Saints and an-gels bow be-fore you; here on earth our songs we raise.
Hear our prayer; re-store, for-give us; in your prom-ise firm we stand.
For the peace that we in-her-it, glo-ry be to God on high!

OR

S204b

1 Come, let us join our cheer-ful songs with an-gels round the throne;
2 "Wor-thy the Lamb that died," they cry, "to be ex-alt-ed thus!"
3 Je-sus is wor-thy to re-ceive hon-or and pow'r di-vine;
4 Let all cre-a-tion join in one to bless the sa-cred name

ten thou-sand thou-sand are their tongues, but all their joys are one.
"Wor-thy the Lamb," our lips re-ply, "for he was slain for us!"
and bless-ings, more than we can give, be, Lord, for-ev-er thine.
of God who sits up-on the throne, and to a-dore the Lamb.

Prayer of the Day

Response after the prayer: **Amen.**

The assembly is seated.

Word

Readings and Psalm

Response after the conclusion of the first and the second reading: **Thanks be to God.**

The assembly stands to welcome the gospel.

Gospel Acclamation

S 205a

Al - le-lu - ia! Lord and Sav - ior: o - pen now your sav-ing word.

Let it burn like fire with-in us; speak un - til our hearts are stirred.

Al - le - lu - ia! Lord, we sing for the good news that you bring.

OR

During Lent:

S 205b

We are turn - ing, Lord, to hear you; you are mer - ci - ful and kind –

slow to an - ger, rich in bless - ing, and with love to us in - clined.

Gospel

Response after the announcement: **Glory to you, O Lord.**
Response after the conclusion: **Praise to you, O Christ.**

Sermon

The assembly is seated. Silence for reflection follows the sermon.

Hymn of the Day

The assembly stands to proclaim the word of God in song.

Creed

The Nicene Creed (p. 104) or the Apostles' Creed (p. 105) may be spoken.

Prayers of Intercession

Each portion of the prayers ends with these or similar words.

	OR	**OR**
Lord, in your mercy,	. . . let us pray.	Hear us, O God.
hear our prayer.	**Have mercy, O God.**	**Your mercy is great.**

Response at the conclusion of the prayers of intercession: **Amen.**

Peace

Response: **And also with you.** *The people may greet one another with a sign of Christ's peace, and may say* Peace be with you *or similar words. Then the assembly is seated.*

Meal

An offering is gathered, and the table is set. Assembly song or other music may accompany or follow the gathering of the offering. After the offering is gathered, the assembly stands. The gifts may be brought forward. An offering prayer may be said; the assembly responds **Amen.**

Great Thanksgiving

The Lord be with you.
And also with you.

Lift up your hearts.
We lift them to the Lord.

Let us give thanks to the Lord our God.
It is right to give our thanks and praise.

The thanksgiving continues with the preface for the day or season; the assembly responds:

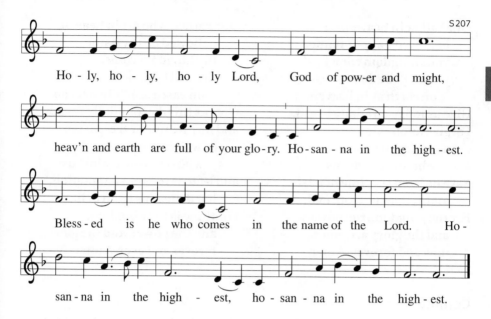

Ho - ly, ho - ly, ho - ly Lord, God of pow-er and might, heav'n and earth are full of your glo-ry. Ho-san - na in the high - est. Bless - ed is he who comes in the name of the Lord. Ho - san - na in the high - est, ho - san - na in the high - est.

The presiding minister continues, using an appropriate form.

The thanksgiving may include this acclamation.

Christ has died. Christ is ris - en. Christ will come a - gain.

The thanksgiving may include a sung Amen.

A - men, a - men, a - men.

The great thanksgiving concludes:

Our Father in heaven,
    hallowed be your name,
    your kingdom come,
    your will be done,
        on earth as in heaven.
Give us today our daily bread.
Forgive us our sins
    as we forgive those
        who sin against us.
Save us from the time of trial
    and deliver us from evil.
For the kingdom, the power,
    and the glory are yours,
    now and forever. Amen.

OR

Our Father, who art in heaven,
    hallowed be thy name,
    thy kingdom come,
    thy will be done,
        on earth as it is in heaven.
Give us this day our daily bread;
and forgive us our trespasses,
    as we forgive those
        who trespass against us;
and lead us not into temptation,
    but deliver us from evil.
For thine is the kingdom,
    and the power, and the glory,
    forever and ever. Amen.

Communion

The assembly may be seated. Music may accompany the communion, and may begin with:

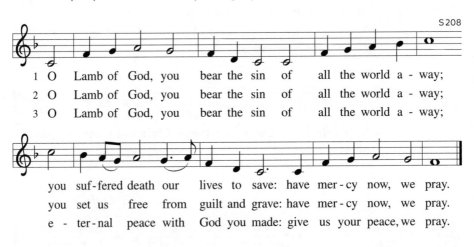

S 208

1 O Lamb of God, you bear the sin of all the world a - way;
2 O Lamb of God, you bear the sin of all the world a - way;
3 O Lamb of God, you bear the sin of all the world a - way;

you suf-fered death our lives to save: have mer - cy now, we pray.
you set us free from guilt and grave: have mer - cy now, we pray.
e - ter-nal peace with God you made: give us your peace, we pray.

After all have returned to their places, the assembly stands. "Now, Lord, you let your servant go in peace" or another suitable song may be sung.

Prayer after Communion

Response after the prayer: **Amen.**

Sending

Blessing

Response after the blessing: **Amen.**

Sending Song

If "Now, Lord, you let your servant go in peace" was not sung at the end of communion, it may be sung here, or another sending song may be sung.

Dismissal

Response: **Thanks be to God.**

Service of the Word

This Service of the Word derives its pattern from the service of Holy Communion. Although a weekly celebration of the Lord's supper is the norm, a service of the word of God is also celebrated regularly or occasionally in many places.

Gathered by the Holy Spirit, we hear and proclaim the saving word of God for all the world. We give thanks for that saving word and all the gifts of God, who then sends us to share the good news we have received and to care for those in need.

Any of the ten musical settings for Holy Communion (pp. 94–209) may be used to begin the Service of the Word. After the greeting of peace in each of those settings, the Service of the Word continues with the Thanksgiving section on p. 219.

Gathering

The service may begin with confession and forgiveness (below) or with thanksgiving for baptism (p. 97). Otherwise, the service begins with gathering song (p. 213) or with the prayer of the day (p. 215), preceded by the greeting.

Confession and Forgiveness

The assembly stands. All may make the sign of the cross, the sign marked at baptism, as the presiding minister begins.

In the name of the Father,
and of the + Son,
and of the Holy Spirit.
Amen.

OR

Blessed be the holy Trinity, + one God,
who forgives all our sin,
whose mercy endures forever.
Amen.

The presiding minister may lead one of the following or another prayer of preparation.

God of all mercy and consolation,
come to the help of your people,
turning us from our sin
to live for you alone.
Give us the power of your Holy Spirit
that we may confess our sin,
receive your forgiveness,
and grow into the fullness
of Jesus Christ, our Savior and Lord.
Amen.

OR

Almighty God,
to whom all hearts are open,
all desires known,
and from whom no secrets are hid:
cleanse the thoughts of our hearts
by the inspiration of your Holy Spirit,
that we may perfectly love you
and worthily magnify your holy name,
through Jesus Christ our Lord.
Amen.

One of the following or another confession is prayed.
Let us confess our sin in the presence of God and of one another.

The assembly kneels or stands. Silence is kept for reflection.

Most merciful God,
we confess
that we are captive to sin
and cannot free ourselves.
We have sinned against you
in thought, word, and deed,
by what we have done
and by what we have left undone.
We have not loved you
with our whole heart;
we have not loved
our neighbors as ourselves.
For the sake
of your Son, Jesus Christ,
have mercy on us.
Forgive us, renew us, and lead us,
so that we may delight in your will
and walk in your ways,
to the glory of your holy name.
Amen.

OR

Gracious God,
have mercy on us.
We confess
that we have turned from you
and given ourselves
into the power of sin.
We are truly sorry
and humbly repent.
In your compassion
forgive us our sins,
known and unknown,
things we have done
and things we have failed to do.
Turn us again to you,
and uphold us by your Spirit,
so that we may live and serve you
in newness of life
through Jesus Christ,
our Savior and Lord.
Amen.

The presiding minister announces God's forgiveness with these or similar words.

In the mercy of almighty God,
Jesus Christ was given to die for us,
and for his sake
God forgives us all our sins.
As a called and ordained minister
of the church of Christ,
and by his authority,
I therefore declare to you
the entire forgiveness of all your sins,
in the name of the Father,
and of the + Son,
and of the Holy Spirit.
Amen.

OR

God, who is rich in mercy, loved us
even when we were dead in sin,
and made us alive
together with Christ.
By grace you have been saved.
In the name of + Jesus Christ,
your sins are forgiven.
Almighty God
strengthen you with power
through the Holy Spirit,
that Christ may live in your hearts
through faith.
Amen.

The assembly stands.

*The service continues with gathering song or with the prayer of the day (p. 215), preceded by
the greeting.*

Gathering Song

*The time of gathering song may be brief or extended, and may include one or more of the
following: hymns, psalms; a Kyrie; a canticle of praise.*

During this time, the presiding minister and the assembly greet each other.
The grace of our Lord Jesus Christ, the love of God,
and the communion of the Holy Spirit be with you all.
And also with you.

A Kyrie may be sung, using Settings One–Ten, this setting, or another appropriate song.

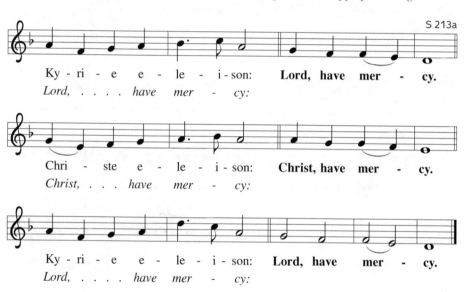

S 213a

Ky - ri - e   e - le - i - son: **Lord, have   mer - cy.**
Lord, ... have   mer - cy:

Chri - ste   e - le - i - son: **Christ, have   mer - cy.**
Christ, . . . have   mer - cy:

Ky - ri - e   e - le - i - son: **Lord, have   mer - cy.**
Lord, ... have   mer - cy:

A canticle of praise may be sung, using Settings One–Ten, this setting, or another appropriate song.

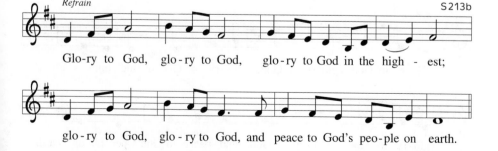

Refrain   S 213b

Glo - ry to God, glo - ry to God,   glo - ry to God in the high - est;

glo - ry to God, glo - ry to God, and peace to God's peo - ple on earth.

1 Lord God, heav-en-ly King, al - might-y God and Fa - ther, we

wor-ship you, we give you thanks, we praise you for your glo - ry.

Refrain

Glo-ry to God, glo-ry to God, glo-ry to God in the high - est;

glo-ry to God, glo - ry to God, and peace to God's peo-ple on earth.

2 Lord Je - sus Christ, on - ly Son of the Fa - ther,

Lord God, Lamb of God, you take a - way the sin of the

world: have mer-cy on us; you are seat - ed at the

right hand of the Fa - ther: re - ceive our prayer.

Refrain

Glo-ry to God, glo-ry to God, glo - ry to God in the high - est;

glo-ry to God, glo - ry to God, and peace to God's peo-ple on earth.

3 For you a-lone are the Ho - ly One, you a - lone are the Lord,

you a - lone are the Most High, Je - sus Christ, with the Ho - ly

Spir-it, in the glo - ry of God the Fa - ther. A - men.

Final refrain

Glo-ry to God, glo-ry to God, glo-ry to God in the high - est;

glo-ry to God, glo - ry to God, and peace to God's peo-ple on

earth, and peace to God's peo - ple on earth.

Prayer of the Day

The presiding minister leads the prayer of the day.
Let us pray. *A brief silence is kept before the prayer.*

After the prayer the assembly responds: **Amen.**

The assembly is seated.

Word

First Reading

The reading may be announced: A reading from _____.
The reading may be concluded: The word of the Lord. **OR** Word of God, word of life.
The assembly responds: **Thanks be to God.**

Psalm

The psalm for the day is sung.

Second Reading

The reading may be announced and concluded in the same way as the first reading.

Gospel Acclamation

The assembly stands to welcome the gospel, using the acclamations from Settings One–Ten, one of the following settings, or another appropriate song.

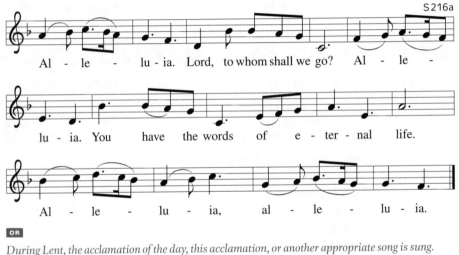

OR

During Lent, the acclamation of the day, this acclamation, or another appropriate song is sung.

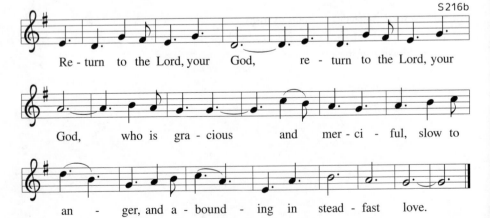

Gospel

The gospel is announced:

The holy gospel according to _____ .
Glory to you, O Lord.

The gospel is proclaimed, concluding:

The gospel of the Lord.
Praise to you, O Christ.

Sermon

The assembly is seated.

Silence for reflection follows the sermon.

Hymn of the Day

The assembly stands to proclaim the word of God in song.

Creed

The Apostles' Creed (below) or the Nicene Creed (see p. 104) may be spoken. The Nicene Creed is appropriate during Advent, Christmas, Easter, and on festival days; the Apostles' Creed during Lent and at other times.

**I believe in God, the Father almighty,
    creator of heaven and earth.**

**I believe in Jesus Christ, God's only Son, our Lord,
    who was conceived by the Holy Spirit,
    born of the virgin Mary,
    suffered under Pontius Pilate,
    was crucified, died, and was buried;
    he descended to the dead.***
    **On the third day he rose again;
    he ascended into heaven,
    he is seated at the right hand of the Father,
    and he will come to judge the living and the dead.**

**I believe in the Holy Spirit,
    the holy catholic church,
    the communion of saints,
    the forgiveness of sins,
    the resurrection of the body,
    and the life everlasting. Amen.**

---

* Or, "he descended into hell," another translation of this text in widespread use.

Prayers of Intercession

The prayers are prepared locally for each occasion, using the following pattern or another appropriate form.

An assisting minister invites the assembly into prayer with these or similar words.
With the whole people of God in Christ Jesus,
let us pray for the church, those in need, and all of God's creation.

Prayers reflect the wideness of God's mercy for the whole world—
  for the church universal, its ministry, and the mission of the gospel;
  for the well-being of creation;
  for peace and justice in the world, the nations and those in authority, the community;
  for the poor, oppressed, sick, bereaved, lonely;
  for all who suffer in body, mind, or spirit;
  for the congregation, and for special concerns.
Additional prayers may come from the assembly.
Prayers of thanksgiving for the faithful departed may include those who recently have died and those commemorated on the church's calendar.

Each portion of the prayers ends with these or similar words.

	OR	**OR**
Lord, in your mercy,	... let us pray.	Hear us, O God,
hear our prayer.	**Have mercy, O God.**	**Your mercy is great.**

The presiding minister concludes the prayers with these or similar words.
Into your hands, gracious God, we commend all for whom we pray,
trusting in your mercy; through Jesus Christ, our Savior.
Amen.

Peace

The presiding minister and the assembly greet each other in the peace of the risen Christ.
The peace of Christ be with you always.
And also with you.

The people may greet one another with a sign of Christ's peace, and may say **Peace be with you** *or similar words.*

The assembly is seated.

Thanksgiving

Offering

An offering is gathered for the mission of the church, including the care of those in need. Assembly song or other music may accompany the gathering of the offering.

After the offering is gathered, the assembly stands.

Canticle of Thanksgiving

The assembly may sing this canticle or another appropriate hymn or song.

S 219

Refrain

Sal - va-tion be-longs to our God and to Christ the Lamb for -

ev - er and ev - er. 1 Great and won-der-ful are your deeds, O

God of the u - ni - verse; just and true are your ways, O

Rul - er of all the na-tions. Who can fail to hon-or you, Lord, and

sing the glo - ry of your name? **Refrain** Sal - va-tion be-longs to our

God and to Christ the Lamb for - ev - er and ev - er.

2 For you a - lone are the Ho - ly One, and

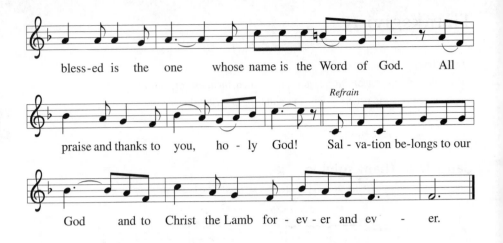

bless-ed is the one whose name is the Word of God. All

praise and thanks to you, ho-ly God! Sal-va-tion be-longs to our

God and to Christ the Lamb for-ev-er and ev - er.

Thanksgiving for the Word

The presiding minister leads one of the following or another appropriate prayer.

Let us pray.

Praise and thanks to you, holy God,
for by your Word you made all things:
you spoke light into darkness, called
forth beauty from chaos, and brought
life into being. For your Word of life,
O God,
we give you thanks and praise.

By your Word you called your people
Israel to tell of your wonderful gifts:
freedom from captivity, water on the
desert journey, a pathway home from
exile, wisdom for life with you.
For your Word of life, O God,
we give you thanks and praise.

OR

O God of justice and love, we give
thanks to you that you illumine
our way through life with the
words of your Son. Give us the
light we need, awaken us to the
needs of others, and at the end
bring all the world to your feast;
through Jesus Christ, our Savior
and Lord, to whom, with you and
the Holy Spirit, be honor and
glory forever. **Amen.**

Continue with the Lord's Prayer.

Through Jesus, your Word made flesh, you speak to us and call us to witness:
forgiveness through the cross, life to those entombed by death, the way of your
self-giving love. For your Word of life, O God,
we give you thanks and praise.

Send your Spirit of truth, O God; rekindle your gifts within us: renew our faith,
increase our hope, and deepen our love, for the sake of a world in need. Faithful to
your Word, O God, draw near to all who call on you; through Jesus Christ, our
Savior and Lord, to whom, with you and the Holy Spirit, be honor and glory forever.
Amen.

Our Father in heaven,
hallowed be your name,
your kingdom come,
your will be done,
on earth as in heaven.
Give us today our daily bread.
Forgive us our sins
as we forgive those
who sin against us.
Save us from the time of trial
and deliver us from evil.
For the kingdom, the power,
and the glory are yours,
now and forever. Amen.

OR

Our Father, who art in heaven,
hallowed be thy name,
thy kingdom come,
thy will be done,
on earth as it is in heaven.
Give us this day our daily bread;
and forgive us our trespasses,
as we forgive those
who trespass against us;
and lead us not into temptation,
but deliver us from evil.
For thine is the kingdom,
and the power, and the glory,
forever and ever. Amen.

Sending

Brief announcements may be made, especially those related to the assembly's participation in God's mission in the world. Affirmation of Christian Vocation (p. 84) may be used here.

Blessing

The presiding minister proclaims God's blessing.
Almighty God, Father, + Son, and Holy Spirit, bless you now and forever.
Amen.

OR

The Lord bless you and keep you.
The Lord's face shine on you with grace and mercy.
The Lord look upon you with favor and + give you peace.
Amen.

OR

The God of steadfastness and encouragement
grant you to live in harmony with one another,
in accordance with Christ Jesus.
Amen.
The God of hope fill you with all joy and peace in believing,
so that you may abound in hope by the power of the Holy Spirit.
Amen.
The God of all grace + bless you now and forever.
Amen.

Sending Song

A sending song may be sung.

Dismissal

The assisting minister may send the assembly into mission.

Go forth into the world to serve God with gladness; be of good courage; hold fast to that which is good; render to no one evil for evil; strengthen the fainthearted; support the weak; help the afflicted; honor all people; love and serve God, rejoicing in the power of the Holy Spirit.
Thanks be to God.

OR

Go in peace. Serve the Lord.
Thanks be to God.

OR

Go in peace. Share the good news.
Thanks be to God.

OR

Go in peace. Remember the poor.
Thanks be to God.

OR

Go in peace. Christ is with you.
Thanks be to God.

Holy Baptism

Pattern for Worship

In holy baptism the triune God delivers us from the forces of evil, puts our sinful self to death, gives us new birth, adopts us as children, and makes us members of the body of Christ, the church.

The Christian community at worship celebrates God's gift of baptism in a number of ways. The sacrament itself normally takes place in the midst of the worshiping assembly as a sign that in baptism we are made one with Christ and with the whole people of God. On behalf of the whole church, we promise support to new sisters and brothers, confess the faith with them, and welcome them into the body of Christ. Water connected to the Word—God's saving promise in Jesus Christ—is at the center of the baptismal celebration.

Although a person is baptized once, the gift of baptism continues throughout a Christian's life. Instruction in the faith for a life of discipleship is part of the preparation of those who are to be baptized or their parents and sponsors. The ongoing nurture of that faith is part of the congregation's ministries of formation, education, service, and evangelical witness. The additional orders in this section—Welcome to Baptism, Affirmation of Baptism, and Confession and Forgiveness—provide several ways by which God's people in worship may participate in the lifelong gift of baptism.

Baptism

God brings those who are baptized out of death and into life.

Presentation	*The Holy Spirit calls and invites us to receive God's grace. Sponsors present those to be baptized, and we promise our support.*
Profession of Faith	*Only by God's grace can we renounce the forces of evil and the power of sin. With the whole church, we confess our faith in the triune God.*
Thanksgiving at the Font **Baptism**	*With thanksgiving, God's saving deeds are remembered. Dying with Christ in baptism, the child of God is raised to new life through water and the Word.*
Prayer for the Holy Spirit **Sign of the Cross**	*Additional signs proclaim the meaning of baptism. We pray that the gift of the Holy Spirit sustain the baptized. The baptized are marked with the cross of Christ forever.*
Welcome	*The baptized are called to follow Jesus, the light of the world. We welcome new companions in the mission of God.*

Within the service of Holy Communion, this order normally follows the hymn of the day. Or, it may replace the thanksgiving for baptism in the gathering rite.

Holy Baptism

Presentation

Candidates for baptism, sponsors, and parents gather with the ministers at the font. The assembly may be seated.

The presiding minister may address the assembly in these or similar words.

God, who is rich in mercy and love, gives us a new birth into a living hope through the sacrament of baptism. By water and the Word God delivers us from sin and death and raises us to new life in Jesus Christ. We are united with all the baptized in the one body of Christ, anointed with the gift of the Holy Spirit, and joined in God's mission for the life of the world.

OR

In baptism our gracious heavenly Father frees us from sin and death by joining us to the death and resurrection of our Lord Jesus Christ. We are born children of a fallen humanity; by water and the Holy Spirit we are reborn children of God and made members of the church, the body of Christ. Living with Christ and in the communion of saints, we grow in faith, love, and obedience to the will of God.

Sponsors for each candidate, in turn, present the candidates.

I present ___name___ for baptism.

The presiding minister addresses candidates who are able to answer for themselves.

___Name___, called by the Holy Spirit, trusting in the grace and love of God, do you desire to be baptized into Christ?

Each candidate responds: I do.

The presiding minister addresses parents or others who bring for baptism children who are not able to answer for themselves.

Called by the Holy Spirit, trusting in the grace and love of God, do you desire to have *your children* baptized into Christ?

Response: I do.

As you bring *your children* to receive the gift of baptism, you are entrusted with responsibilities:

> to live with *them* among God's faithful people,
> bring *them* to the word of God and the holy supper,
> teach *them* the Lord's Prayer, the Creed, and the Ten Commandments,
> place in *their* hands the holy scriptures,
> and nurture *them* in faith and prayer,
> so that *your children* may learn to trust God,
> proclaim Christ through word and deed,
> care for others and the world God made,
> and work for justice and peace.

Do you promise to help *your children* grow in the Christian faith and life?

Response: I do.

The presiding minister addresses sponsors.

Sponsors, do you promise to nurture *these persons* in the Christian faith as you are empowered by God's Spirit, and to help *them* live in the covenant of baptism and in communion with the church?

Response: I do.

The presiding minister addresses the assembly.

People of God, do you promise to support ___name/s___ and pray for *them* in *their* new life in Christ?

We do.

The assembly stands.

Profession of Faith

The presiding minister addresses candidates for baptism as well as the parents and sponsors of young children. The assembly may join in the responses.

I ask you to profess your faith in Christ Jesus, reject sin, and confess the faith of the church.

Do you renounce the devil and all the forces that defy God?
Response: I renounce them.

Do you renounce the powers of this world that rebel against God?
Response: I renounce them.

Do you renounce the ways of sin that draw you from God?
Response: I renounce them.

The presiding minister addresses the candidates and the assembly.
Do you believe in God the Father?
I believe in God, the Father almighty,
  creator of heaven and earth.

Do you believe in Jesus Christ, the Son of God?
I believe in Jesus Christ, God's only Son, our Lord,
  who was conceived by the Holy Spirit,
  born of the virgin Mary,
  suffered under Pontius Pilate,
  was crucified, died, and was buried;
  he descended to the dead.*
  On the third day he rose again;
  he ascended into heaven,
  he is seated at the right hand of the Father,
  and he will come to judge the living and the dead.

Do you believe in God the Holy Spirit?
I believe in the Holy Spirit,
  the holy catholic church,
  the communion of saints,
  the forgiveness of sins,
  the resurrection of the body,
  and the life everlasting.

Or, "he descended into hell," *another translation of this text in widespread use.*

Thanksgiving at the Font

The presiding minister leads the following or another form of the thanksgiving.

The Lord be with you.
And also with you.

Let us give thanks to the Lord our God.
It is right to give our thanks and praise.

We give you thanks, O God, for in the beginning your Spirit moved over the waters and by your Word you created the world, calling forth life in which you took delight. Through the waters of the flood you delivered Noah and his family, and through the sea you led your people Israel from slavery into freedom. At the river your Son was baptized by John and anointed with the Holy Spirit. By the baptism of Jesus' death and resurrection you set us free from the power of sin and death and raise us up to live in you.

Pour out your Holy Spirit, the power of your living Word, that those who are washed in the waters of baptism may be given new life. To you be given honor and praise through Jesus Christ our Lord, in the unity of the Holy Spirit, now and forever.
Amen.

The assembly may be seated.

Baptism

The presiding minister baptizes each candidate. The candidate is immersed into the water, or water is poured on the candidate's head, as the presiding minister says:

   ___Name___ , I baptize you in the name of the Father,*
The candidate is immersed or water is poured on the candidate's head a second time:
and of the Son,
The candidate is immersed or water is poured on the candidate's head a third time:
and of the Holy Spirit.
Amen.

After each baptism, the assembly may respond with one of the following, a sung alleluia, or another acclamation (#209–213).

Blessed be God, the source of all life, the word of salvation, the spirit of mercy.

OR

You belong to Christ, in whom you have been baptized. Alleluia.

*Or, "*Name* is baptized in the name of the Father," …

Clothed with Christ in baptism, the newly baptized may receive a baptismal garment.

The presiding minister continues:
Let us pray.
We give you thanks, O God, that through water and the Holy Spirit you give your daughters and sons new birth, cleanse them from sin, and raise them to eternal life.
Laying both hands on the head of each of the newly baptized, the minister prays for each:
Sustain _____*name*_____ with the gift of your Holy Spirit: the spirit of wisdom and understanding, the spirit of counsel and might, the spirit of knowledge and the fear of the Lord, the spirit of joy in your presence, both now and forever.
Amen.

The presiding minister marks the sign of the cross on the forehead of each of the baptized.
Oil prepared for this purpose may be used. As the sign of the cross is made, the minister says:
_____*Name*_____, child of God, you have been sealed by the Holy Spirit and marked with the cross of Christ forever.
Amen.

Welcome

A lighted candle may be given to each of the newly baptized (to a sponsor of a young child) as a representative of the congregation says:

OR

Jesus said, I am the light of the world.
Whoever follows me
will have the light of life.

Let your light so shine before others
that they may see your good works
and glorify your Father in heaven.

The ministers and the baptismal group face the assembly. A representative of the congregation leads the assembly in the welcome.
Let us welcome the newly baptized.
We welcome you into the body of Christ and into the mission we share:
join us in giving thanks and praise to God
and bearing God's creative and redeeming word to all the world.

Those who have gathered at the font may return to their places. An acclamation (#209–215), psalm, or hymn may be sung.

The service continues with the prayers of intercession, or, if baptism has taken place in the gathering rite, with the greeting.

Welcome
to Baptism

Baptism includes instruction and nurture in the faith for a life of discipleship. When infants and young children are baptized, the parents and sponsors receive instruction and the children are taught throughout their development. Adults and older children receive instruction and formation for faith and ministry in the world both prior to baptism (a period that may be called the catechumenate) and following baptism.

Welcome to Baptism may be used with those who are beginning a public relationship with a Christian congregation as they inquire into Christian faith and life. Infants and children may be brought to this welcome by parents and sponsors. The order is for use within the principal gathering of the assembly. Either the presentation section or the sign of the cross section may be used, or both may be used.

Presentation

In the gathering rite, those being welcomed and their sponsors may gather with the ministers at the entrance to the church or in front of the assembly. The assembly faces them.

The presiding minister addresses the assembly.
Dear friends, we gather today with *these people* who *have* been called by God's Spirit to inquire into the Christian faith and life. Together, let us welcome *them* to this community of faith in Jesus Christ.

Those who are being welcomed are presented by name.

The presiding minister addresses the sponsors and the assembly.
People of God, will you help *these people* hear the gospel of Jesus Christ within this household of faith?
We will, and we ask God to help us.

The assisting minister addresses those who have been presented.

_____Name/s____ , gather with this community of faith and hear the word of God with us.

The service continues with gathering song. Those who have met at the entrance may join the entering procession and take their places in the assembly.

Sign of the Cross

Following the hymn of the day, those being welcomed and their sponsors come before the assembly.

A sponsor for each person being welcomed traces a cross on the person's forehead as the presiding minister says:

Receive the + sign of the cross, a sign of God's endless love and mercy for you.

The assembly responds (a musical setting is at #216):

Praise to you, O Christ, the wisdom and power of God.

A Bible may be presented to each person being welcomed.

The presiding minister blesses those who are being welcomed. At the conclusion of the prayer, the people respond **Amen.**

The assisting minister addresses those being welcomed.

God bring you in peace and joy to fullness of life in Christ
and call you to the waters of baptism.

The assembly responds (a musical setting is at #217):

**May the God of all grace, who has called you to glory,
support you and make you strong.**

Those who have come forward return to their places. The service continues with the prayers of intercession.

Affirmation
of Baptism

Affirmation of Baptism may be used at many times in the life of a baptized Christian. It is especially appropriate as part of a process of formation in faith in youth or adulthood (confirmation), at the time of beginning one's participation in a community of faith, as a sign of renewed participation in the life of the church, or at the time of a significant life passage.

The order may be adapted for use by the whole assembly. Appropriate times for use include the Baptism of Our Lord, the Vigil of Easter, the Day of Pentecost, All Saints Day, and significant occasions in the life of a congregation, such as an anniversary.

Presentation

At the conclusion of the hymn of the day, those making affirmation may gather with the ministers at the font. They may be joined by others from the assembly. The presiding minister may note briefly the occasion for this affirmation.

A sponsor or another representative of the congregation presents those making affirmation.
I present ___*name/s*___, who *desire* to make public affirmation of *their* baptism.

The presiding minister may continue with prayer.
Let us pray.
Merciful God, we thank you for *these sisters and brothers*, whom you have made your own by water and the Word in baptism. You have called *them* to yourself, enlightened *them* with the gifts of your Spirit, and nourished *them* in the community of faith. Uphold your *servants* in the gifts and promises of baptism, and unite the hearts of all whom you have brought to new birth. We ask this in the name of Christ.
Amen.

Profession of Faith

The presiding minister addresses those making public affirmation of baptism. The assembly may stand and join in the responses.

I ask you to profess your faith in Christ Jesus, reject sin, and confess the faith of the church.

Do you renounce the devil and all the forces that defy God?
Response: I renounce them.

Do you renounce the powers of this world that rebel against God?
Response: I renounce them.

Do you renounce the ways of sin that draw you from God?
Response: I renounce them.

The presiding minister addresses the assembly.
Do you believe in God the Father?
**I believe in God, the Father almighty,
     creator of heaven and earth.**

Do you believe in Jesus Christ, the Son of God?
**I believe in Jesus Christ, God's only Son, our Lord,
     who was conceived by the Holy Spirit,
     born of the virgin Mary,
     suffered under Pontius Pilate,
     was crucified, died, and was buried;
     he descended to the dead.***
     **On the third day he rose again;
     he ascended into heaven,
     he is seated at the right hand of the Father,
     and he will come to judge the living and the dead.**

Do you believe in God the Holy Spirit?
**I believe in the Holy Spirit,
     the holy catholic church,
     the communion of saints,
     the forgiveness of sins,
     the resurrection of the body,
     and the life everlasting.**

*Or, "he descended into hell," another translation of this text in widespread use.

When individuals are making public affirmation of baptism, the service continues below.
When the assembly is making affirmation of baptism, the service continues on p. 237.

Affirmation in the Presence of the Assembly

The presiding minister addresses those making public affirmation of baptism.

You have made public profession of your faith. Do you intend to continue in the covenant God made with you in holy baptism:

to live among God's faithful people,
to hear the word of God and share in the Lord's supper,
to proclaim the good news of God in Christ through word and deed,
to serve all people, following the example of Jesus,
and to strive for justice and peace in all the earth?

Each person responds: I do, and I ask God to help and guide me.

The minister addresses the assembly.

People of God, do you promise to support *these sisters and brothers* and pray for *them* in *their* life in Christ?
We do, and we ask God to help and guide us.

Those making affirmation may kneel. The presiding minister prays for God's blessing.

Let us pray.

We give you thanks, O God, that through water and the Holy Spirit you give us new birth, cleanse us from sin, and raise us to eternal life.

The blessing may be repeated for each person. The minister may lay both hands on the head of the person and say:

OR

Stir up in ___*name*___ the gift of your Holy Spirit: the spirit of wisdom and understanding, the spirit of counsel and might, the spirit of knowledge and the fear of the Lord, the spirit of joy in your presence, both now and forever.
Amen.

Father in heaven, for Jesus' sake, stir up in ___*name*___ the gift of your Holy Spirit; confirm *her/his* faith, guide *her/his* life, empower *her/him* in *her/his* serving, give *her/him* patience in suffering, and bring *her/him* to everlasting life.
Amen.

Those making public affirmation stand and face the assembly. A representative of the congregation addresses the assembly.

Let us rejoice with *these sisters and brothers* in Christ.
We rejoice with you in the life of baptism.
Together we will give thanks and praise to God
and proclaim the good news to all the world.

A hymn, song, or psalm may be sung, and may be accompanied by a reminder of baptism. The service then continues with the prayers of intercession.

Affirmation by the Assembly

When the assembly is making affirmation of baptism, the presiding minister addresses them.
You have made public profession of your faith. Do you intend to continue in the
covenant God made with you in holy baptism:
> to live among God's faithful people,
> to hear the word of God and share in the Lord's supper,
> to proclaim the good news of God in Christ through word and deed,
> to serve all people, following the example of Jesus,
> and to strive for justice and peace in all the earth?

The assembly makes affirmation:
I do, and I ask God to help and guide me.

The minister addresses the assembly.
People of God, do you promise to support and pray for one another in your life in
Christ?
We do, and we ask God to help and guide us.

The presiding minister prays for God's blessing.
Let us pray.
We give you thanks, O God, that through water and the Holy Spirit you give us
new birth, cleanse us from sin, and raise us to eternal life. Stir up in your people
the gift of your Holy Spirit: the spirit of wisdom and understanding, the spirit of
counsel and might, the spirit of knowledge and the fear of the Lord, the spirit of joy
in your presence, both now and forever.
Amen.

A hymn, song, or psalm may be sung, and may be accompanied by a reminder of baptism.
The service then continues with the prayers of intercession.

Corporate Confession and Forgiveness

Washed in water and marked with the cross, the baptized children of God are united with Christ and, through him, with other believers who together form a living community of faith. Although we are set free to live in love and faithfulness, we continue to turn away from God and from one another. Confessing our sin involves a continuing return to our baptism where our sinful self is drowned and dies; in the gift of forgiveness God raises us up again and again to new life in Jesus Christ.

Corporate Confession and Forgiveness may be used on penitential days, such as the final days of Lent, or as part of the regular schedule of the congregation. Occasions suggesting its use include the reconciliation of those estranged from one another; the confession of sharing in corporate wrongs; and a time of lament in the life of the congregation, the community, the nation, or the world. Selected portions may be used when a fuller order for confession and forgiveness within another service is desired.

Gathering

Psalm 25:1-17, Psalm 51:1-15, Psalm 103, another psalm, or an appropriate hymn or canticle may be sung as the assembly gathers.

The assembly stands. All may make the sign of the cross, the sign that is marked at baptism, as the presiding minister begins.

OR

In the name of the Father,
and of the + Son,
and of the Holy Spirit.
Amen.

Blessed be the holy Trinity, + one God,
who forgives all our sin,
whose mercy endures forever.
Amen.

The presiding minister leads one of the following or another prayer of preparation.

God of all mercy and consolation,
come to the help of your people,
turning us from our sin
to live for you alone.
Give us the power of your Holy Spirit
that we may confess our sin,
receive your forgiveness,
and grow into the fullness
of Jesus Christ, our Savior and Lord.
Amen.

OR

Almighty God,
to whom all hearts are open,
all desires known,
and from whom no secrets are hid:
cleanse the thoughts of our hearts
by the inspiration of your Holy Spirit,
that we may perfectly love you
and worthily magnify your holy name,
through Jesus Christ our Lord.
Amen.

The assembly is seated.

Word

The service includes one or more scripture readings. Responses may include a psalm in response to a reading from the Old Testament, a sung acclamation preceding a gospel reading, or other appropriate hymns, songs, and psalms.

Preaching may follow, or those present may participate in mutual conversation and consolation, guided by the minister or another leader.

Confession

The presiding minister addresses the assembly in these or similar words.

While we still were sinners,
Christ died for us.
Through the power of the Holy Spirit,
God promises to heal us and forgive us.
Let us confess our sin
in the presence of God
and of one another.

OR

If we say we have no sin,
we deceive ourselves,
and the truth is not in us.
But if we confess our sins,
God who is faithful and just
will forgive our sins
and cleanse us from all unrighteousness.

The assembly kneels or sits. Silence is kept for reflection and self-examination.

The following or another confession is prayed. The assembly's response, "Holy God," may be sung (#159–161).

Holy God, holy and mighty, holy and immortal,
have mercy on us.

For self-centered living,
and for failing to walk with humility and gentleness:
**Holy God, holy and mighty, holy and immortal,
have mercy on us.**

For longing to have what is not ours,
and for hearts that are not at rest with ourselves:
**Holy God, holy and mighty, holy and immortal,
have mercy on us.**

For misuse of human relationships,
and for unwillingness to see the image of God in others:
**Holy God, holy and mighty, holy and immortal,
have mercy on us.**

For jealousies that divide families and nations,
and for rivalries that create strife and warfare:
**Holy God, holy and mighty, holy and immortal,
have mercy on us.**

For reluctance in sharing the gifts of God,
and for carelessness with the fruits of creation:
**Holy God, holy and mighty, holy and immortal,
have mercy on us.**

For hurtful words that condemn,
and for angry deeds that harm:
**Holy God, holy and mighty, holy and immortal,
have mercy on us.**

For idleness in witnessing to Jesus Christ,
and for squandering the gifts of love and grace:
**Holy God, holy and mighty, holy and immortal,
have mercy on us.**

Forgiveness

The presiding minister addresses the assembly.

In the mercy of almighty God, Jesus Christ was given to die for us, and for his sake God forgives us all our sins. Through the Holy Spirit God cleanses us and gives us the power to proclaim the mighty acts of the one who called us out of darkness into his marvelous light. As a called and ordained minister of the church of Christ, and by his authority, I therefore declare to you the entire forgiveness of all your sins, in the name of the Father, and of the + Son, and of the Holy Spirit.
Amen.

OR

God, who is rich in mercy, loved us even when we were dead in sin, and made us alive together with Christ. By grace you have been saved. In the name of + Jesus Christ, your sins are forgiven. Almighty God strengthen you with power through the Holy Spirit, that Christ may live in your hearts through faith.
Amen.

People may come forward and kneel for the laying on of hands. The minister, laying both hands on each person's head, addresses each in turn.

In obedience to the command of our Lord Jesus Christ, I forgive you all your sins.
Response: **Amen.**

OR

In the name of Jesus Christ, your sins are forgiven. Almighty God strengthen you in all goodness and bring you to everlasting life.
Response: **Amen.**

Assembly song may accompany the laying on of hands.

After the laying on of hands, the assembly stands. The presiding minister and the assembly greet each other.
The peace of Christ be with you always.
And also with you.

The people may greet one another with a sign of Christ's peace, and may say **Peace be with you** *or similar words.*

A hymn of praise and thanksgiving may be sung.

Prayers

The prayer of the day and other prayers may be said.

The Lord's Prayer is prayed by all.

OR

Our Father in heaven,
   hallowed be your name,
   your kingdom come,
   your will be done,
     on earth as in heaven.
Give us today our daily bread.
Forgive us our sins
   as we forgive those
     who sin against us.
Save us from the time of trial
   and deliver us from evil.
For the kingdom, the power,
   and the glory are yours,
   now and forever. Amen.

Our Father, who art in heaven,
   hallowed be thy name,
   thy kingdom come,
   thy will be done,
     on earth as it is in heaven.
Give us this day our daily bread;
and forgive us our trespasses,
   as we forgive those
     who trespass against us;
and lead us not into temptation,
   but deliver us from evil.
For thine is the kingdom,
   and the power, and the glory,
   forever and ever. Amen.

Sending

Blessing

The presiding minister proclaims God's blessing.

OR

Almighty and merciful God,
Father, + Son, and Holy Spirit,
bless you now and forever.
Amen.

The Lord bless you and keep you.
The Lord's face shine on you
with grace and mercy.
The Lord look upon you with favor
and + give you peace.
Amen.

Dismissal

The assisting minister may send the assembly into mission.
Go in peace. Christ has made you free.
Thanks be to God.

Individual Confession and Forgiveness

Washed in water and marked with the cross, the baptized children of God are united with Christ and, through him, with other believers who together form a living community of faith. Although we are set free to live in love and faithfulness, we continue to turn away from God and from one another. Confessing our sin involves a continuing return to our baptism where our sinful self is drowned and dies; in the gift of forgiveness God raises us up again and again to new life in Jesus Christ.

Individual Confession and Forgiveness is a ministry of the church through which a person may confess sin and receive the assurance of God's forgiveness. This order may be used by itself at times when a congregation offers opportunity or people request the opportunity for confession. It may also be used in conjunction with pastoral care, such as to conclude a counseling session. There is a confidential nature to this order, in keeping with the discipline and practice of the Lutheran church.

Confession

The pastor begins:

OR

In the name of the Father,
and of the + Son,
and of the Holy Spirit.
Response: **Amen.**

Blessed be the holy Trinity, + one God,
who forgives all our sin,
whose mercy endures forever.
Response: **Amen.**

You have come to make confession before God.
You are free to confess before me, a pastor in the church of Christ,
sins of which you are aware and which trouble you.

The penitent may use the following form or pray in her/his own words.

Merciful God, I confess
that I have sinned in thought, word, and deed,
by what I have done and by what I have left undone.

Here the penitent may confess sins that are known and that burden her/him.

I repent of all my sins, known and unknown.
I am truly sorry, and I pray for forgiveness.
I firmly intend to amend my life,
and to seek help in mending what is broken.
I ask for strength to turn from sin
and to serve you in newness of life.

The pastor may engage the penitent in conversation, sharing admonition, counsel, and comfort from the scriptures. Psalm 51 or Psalm 103 may be spoken together.

Forgiveness

Addressing the penitent, the pastor may lay both hands on the penitent's head.

Cling to this promise: the word of forgiveness I speak to you comes from God.

OR

_____Name_____,
in obedience to the command
of our Lord Jesus Christ,
I forgive you all your sins
in the name of the Father,
and of the ☩ Son,
and of the Holy Spirit.
Response: Amen.

_____Name_____,
by water and the Holy Spirit
God gives you a new birth,
and through the death and resurrection
of Jesus Christ,
God forgives you all your sins.
Almighty God
strengthen you in all goodness
and keep you in eternal life.
Response: Amen.

The peace of God, which passes all understanding,
keep your heart and your mind in Christ Jesus.
Response: Amen.

The pastor and the penitent may share the greeting of peace.

Lent and the Three Days

Every Sunday in worship the church celebrates the life, death, and resurrection of Jesus Christ. The Holy Spirit gathers us to receive again the gifts of God that come to us through Christ, the saving Word. On several key days at the center of the church year, however, worship takes a particular shape. These central days have come to be known as the Three Days, recalling Jesus' own words to his disciples that he would be handed over to death, and that "after three days he will rise again" (Mark 10:34). The Three Days encompass the time from Maundy Thursday evening through the evening of Easter Day. In particular, the services of Maundy Thursday, Good Friday, and the Vigil of Easter unfold in a single movement, as the church each year makes the passage with Christ through death into life.

In addition to these central three days, the church has long used special orders of worship on Ash Wednesday—the first day of Lent—and on the Sunday of the Passion, Palm Sunday.

Pattern for Worship—Ash Wednesday

Ash Wednesday is a solemn day of prayer that begins the season of Lent. On this day we confess our sin in a litany of repentance. During Lent's forty days we are invited to carry out the Lenten discipline, practices of fasting, prayer, and works of love, even as we accompany people around the world who are preparing for baptism at Easter. On this day we may receive the sign of ashes. This ancient symbol of repentance reminds us of our mortality. Returning to God's mercy and grace, marked with the cross of Christ, we make our way through Lent, longing for the baptismal waters of Easter, our spiritual rebirth.

Gathering

Greeting
Prayer of the Day

Meal

or
Offering
Concluding Prayer

Word

Readings and Responses
Sermon
Hymn of the Day
Invitation to Lent
Confession of Sin
with Imposition of Ashes
Prayers of Intercession

Sending

Pattern for Worship—Sunday of the Passion (Palm Sunday)

On this day, united with Christians around the world, we mark Jesus' triumphant entry into the holy city of Jerusalem to complete the work of our salvation. We follow in his footsteps as we enter the church, our Jerusalem, acclaiming the one whose throne was the cross. In today's gospel reading we hear the passion narrative of Jesus' suffering, death, and burial for our sakes.

Gathering

Processional Gospel
Blessing of Palms
Procession
Prayer of the Day

Word

with **Reading of the Passion**

Meal and Sending

Central elements of the liturgy are noted in bold type; other elements support the essential shape of Christian worship.

Pattern for Worship—Maundy Thursday

On this night we begin the Three Days during which we participate once again in the saving power of Jesus' passing over from death into life. The Maundy Thursday service includes the words of Jesus' new commandment (*mandatum*, from which *Maundy* comes) to love one another. As a sign of our calling to follow Jesus' example of humility and service, we may wash one another's feet as Jesus washed the disciples' feet. On this night in which Jesus was handed over to death we also gather around the Lord's supper. At the service's conclusion, the altar area may be stripped of furnishings as a sign of Jesus' abandonment.

Gathering

Confession and Forgiveness
Greeting
Prayer of the Day

Meal

concluded with
Stripping of the Altar

Word

Readings and Responses
Sermon
Hymn of the Day
Footwashing
Prayers of Intercession
Peace

Pattern for Worship—Good Friday

The Good Friday service continues the journey through the Three Days of Jesus' suffering, death, and resurrection. At the heart of this service is the passion reading according to John, which celebrates Christ's victory on the cross. As Jesus draws all people to himself, we pray for the whole world for which Christ died. Finally, we honor the cross as the sign of forgiveness, healing, and salvation. With all God's people we are invited to bow before this mystery of faith. Christ has died, so that we may live.

Prayer of the Day
Readings and Responses
Sermon
Hymn of the Day
Bidding Prayer
Procession of the Cross

Pattern for Worship—Vigil of Easter

On the night before Easter Day, Christians around the world gather to celebrate Christ's passage from death to life. The service includes strong signs: new fire in darkness, light spreading from the light of Christ, the water and Word of baptism, the first resurrection meal. And powerful words: the great saving stories of Hebrew scriptures and the first Easter gospel. We keep this wondrous night in the spirit of vigil, our lamps lit, awaiting Christ's coming both now and at the end of time. Alleluia! Christ is risen! And Christ will come again.

Gathering

Greeting
Procession
Easter Proclamation
Prayer of the Day

Word

Old Testament Readings
    and Responses
New Testament Reading
Gospel with Acclamation
Sermon

Baptism

or
Affirmation of Baptism
    by the Assembly

Meal

Sending

Ash Wednesday

Gathering

The assembly gathers in silence.

The service begins with Psalm 51 or another penitential psalm, a Kyrie or another litany, or a hymn. Or, the service begins simply with the greeting.

Greeting
The assembly stands. The presiding minister and the assembly greet each other.
The Lord be with you.
And also with you.

Prayer of the Day
Response after the prayer: **Amen.**
The assembly is seated.

Word

Readings and Psalm
An assisting minister reads the first and second scripture readings. The psalm for the day follows the first reading. The psalm is Psalm 51, or Psalm 103:8-14 if Psalm 51 is sung at the gathering or during the imposition of ashes.

Response after the conclusion of the first and the second readings: **Thanks be to God.**

Gospel Acclamation

The assembly stands. The following or another appropriate acclamation may be sung.

Return to the [|] Lord, your God,
   who is gracious and merciful, slow to anger,
   and abounding in [|] steadfast love.

Gospel

Response after the announcement: **Glory to you, O Lord.**
Response after the conclusion: **Praise to you, O Christ.**

The assembly is seated.

Sermon

Silence for reflection follows.

Hymn of the Day

The assembly stands to proclaim the word of God in song.

Invitation to Lent

The assembly is seated. The presiding minister may invite the assembly into the discipline of Lent.

Confession of Sin

The presiding minister leads the following or another confession.

Let us confess our sin in the presence of God and of one another.

The assembly kneels or sits. Silence is kept for reflection and self-examination.

Most holy and merciful God,
we confess to you and to one another,
and before the whole company of heaven,
that we have sinned by our fault,
by our own fault,
by our own most grievous fault,
in thought, word, and deed,
by what we have done and by what we have left undone.

We have not loved you with our whole heart, and mind, and strength. We have not loved our neighbors as ourselves. We have not forgiven others as we have been forgiven.
Have mercy on us, O God.

We have shut our ears to your call to serve as Christ served us. We have not been true to the mind of Christ. We have grieved your Holy Spirit.
Have mercy on us, O God.

Our past unfaithfulness, the pride, envy, hypocrisy, and apathy that have infected our lives, we confess to you.
Have mercy on us, O God.

Our self-indulgent appetites and ways, and our exploitation of other people, we confess to you.
Have mercy on us, O God.

Our negligence in prayer and worship, and our failure to share the faith that is in us, we confess to you.
Have mercy on us, O God.

Our neglect of human need and suffering, and our indifference to injustice and cruelty, we confess to you.
Have mercy on us, O God.

Our false judgments, our uncharitable thoughts toward our neighbors, and our prejudice and contempt toward those who differ from us, we confess to you.
Have mercy on us, O God.

Our waste and pollution of your creation, and our lack of concern for those who come after us, we confess to you.
Have mercy on us, O God.

Restore us, O God, and let your anger depart from us.
Hear us, O God, for your mercy is great.

Imposition of Ashes

People may come forward and kneel or stand to receive the ashes.

Ministers mark the forehead of each person with a cross of ashes, saying:
Remember that you are dust, and to dust you shall return.
During this time, hymns or penitential psalms may be sung, or silence may be kept. Psalm 51 may be sung if it has not been used earlier in the service.

After those who desire ashes have received them, all may kneel or sit, and the minister continues.
Accomplish in us, O God, the work of your salvation,
that we may show forth your glory in the world.
By the cross and passion of your Son, our Savior,
bring us with all your saints to the joy of his resurrection.

The presiding minister addresses the assembly.
Almighty God have mercy on us, forgive us all our sins through our Lord Jesus Christ, strengthen us in all goodness, and by the power of the Holy Spirit keep us in eternal life.
Amen.

A service with communion continues with the prayers of intercession. The prayer, blessing, and dismissal below may be used after the communion.

OR

A service without communion concludes as follows.
> *Prayers of intercession may be spoken.*
> *An offering may be gathered for the mission of the church, including the care of those in need.*
> *"Create in me" (#185–188) may be sung after the offering is gathered.*
> *The service ends with the following prayer, the Lord's Prayer, and the sending.*

The assisting minister leads a concluding prayer.
Merciful God, accompany our journey through these forty days. Renew us in the gift of baptism, that we may provide for those who are poor, pray for those in need, fast from self-indulgence, and above all that we may find our treasure in the life of your Son, Jesus Christ, our Savior and Lord, who lives and reigns with you and the Holy Spirit, one God, now and forever.
Amen.

The Lord's Prayer is prayed by all.

Our Father in heaven,
    hallowed be your name,
    your kingdom come,
    your will be done,
      on earth as in heaven.
Give us today our daily bread.
Forgive us our sins
    as we forgive those
      who sin against us.
Save us from the time of trial
    and deliver us from evil.
For the kingdom, the power,
    and the glory are yours,
    now and forever. Amen.

OR

Our Father, who art in heaven,
    hallowed be thy name,
    thy kingdom come,
    thy will be done,
      on earth as it is in heaven.
Give us this day our daily bread;
and forgive us our trespasses,
    as we forgive those
      who trespass against us;
and lead us not into temptation,
    but deliver us from evil.
For thine is the kingdom,
    and the power, and the glory,
    forever and ever. Amen.

Sending

Blessing

The presiding minister proclaims God's blessing.
Almighty God, Father, + Son, and Holy Spirit, bless you now and forever.
Amen.

Dismissal

The assisting minister may address the assembly.
Go forth into the world to serve God with gladness;
be of good courage;
hold fast to that which is good;
render to no one evil for evil;
strengthen the fainthearted; support the weak;
help the afflicted; honor all people;
love and serve God, rejoicing in the power of the Holy Spirit.
Thanks be to God.

Sunday
of the Passion
Palm Sunday

Gathering

*If possible, the assembly gathers at a designated place outside the usual worship space,
so that all may enter in procession. Palm branches, or branches of other trees and shrubs,
are distributed before the service begins.*

The presiding minister begins (repeated one or more times).
Blessed is the one who comes in the name of the Lord.
Hosanna in the highest.

Processional Gospel
Response after the announcement: **Glory to you, O Lord.**
Response after the conclusion: **Praise to you, O Christ.**

Blessing of Palms
The presiding minister and the assembly greet each other.
The Lord be with you.
And also with you.

The presiding minister continues with the prayer of blessing, to which the people respond:
Amen.

Procession
The assisting minister addresses the assembly.
Let us go forth in peace,
in the name of Christ. Amen.

The assembly follows the ministers into the church. "All glory, laud, and honor" (#344) and other hymns, psalms, or anthems may be sung as the people process into the church or once they have taken their places.

Refrain

All glory, laud, and honor
to you, redeemer, king,
to whom the lips of children
made sweet hosannas ring.

1 You are the king of Israel
and David's royal Son,
now in the Lord's name coming,
our King and Blessed One. *Refrain*

2 The company of angels
are praising you on high;
creation and all mortals
in chorus make reply. *Refrain*

3 The multitude of pilgrims
with palms before you went.
Our praise and prayer and anthems
before you we present. *Refrain*

4 To you, before your passion,
they sang their hymns of praise.
To you, now high exalted,
our melody we raise. *Refrain*

5 Their praises you accepted;
accept the prayers we bring,
great author of all goodness,
O good and gracious king. *Refrain*

The presiding minister concludes the procession.
Blessed is the one who comes in the name of the Lord.
Hosanna in the highest.

Prayer of the Day

Response after the prayer: **Amen.**
The assembly is seated.

The service continues with the readings, including the reading of the passion gospel.

Maundy Thursday

Gathering

Confession and Forgiveness

The presiding minister invites the assembly into the confession.

Following the invitation, all kneel or sit and keep silence for reflection and self-examination.

The presiding minister leads the assembly in the confession.

Most merciful God,
we confess
that we are captive to sin
and cannot free ourselves.
We have sinned against you in thought, word, and deed,
by what we have done and by what we have left undone.
We have not loved you with our whole heart;
we have not loved our neighbors as ourselves.
For the sake of your Son, Jesus Christ, have mercy on us.
Forgive us, renew us, and lead us,
so that we may delight in your will and walk in your ways,
to the glory of your holy name.
Amen.

In the mercy of almighty God,
Jesus Christ was given to die for us,
and for his sake
God forgives us all our sins.
As a called and ordained minister
of the church of Christ,
and by his authority,
I therefore declare to you
the entire forgiveness of all your sins,
in the name of the Father,
and of the + Son,
and of the Holy Spirit.
Amen.

OR

God, who is rich in mercy, loved us
even when we were dead in sin,
and made us alive
together with Christ.
By grace you have been saved.
In the name of + Jesus Christ,
your sins are forgiven.
Almighty God
strengthen you with power
through the Holy Spirit,
that Christ may live in your hearts
through faith.
Amen.

The assembly is seated. People may come forward and kneel for the laying on of hands.

The minister, laying both hands on each person's head, addresses each in turn.
In obedience to the command of our Lord Jesus Christ, I forgive you all your sins.
The person may respond **Amen.**

Assembly song and other music may accompany the laying on of hands. Then the assembly stands.

Greeting
The presiding minister and the assembly greet each other.
The grace of our Lord Jesus Christ, the love of God,
and the communion of the Holy Spirit be with you all.
And also with you.

Prayer of the Day
Response after the prayer: **Amen.**
The assembly is seated.

Word

Readings and Psalm

An assisting minister reads the first and second scripture readings.
The psalm for the day follows the first reading.

Response after the conclusion of the first and the second reading: **Thanks be to God.**

Gospel Acclamation

The assembly stands. The following or another appropriate acclamation may be sung.
I give you a ˈ new commandment,
　　that you love one another just as I ˈ have loved you.

Gospel

Response after the announcement: **Glory to you, O Lord.**
Response after the conclusion: **Praise to you, O Christ.**

The assembly is seated.

Sermon

Silence for reflection follows.

Hymn of the Day

The assembly stands to proclaim the word of God in song.

Footwashing

When footwashing is included in the service, the assembly is seated.

The ministers and people may wash each other's feet. Assembly song and other music may accompany the footwashing. If it has not been sung as the hymn of the day, "Where charity and love" (#359, 642, 653) is especially appropriate.

Prayers of Intercession

An assisting minister invites the assembly into prayer with these or similar words.
Let us pray for new life in the church, new hope for the world, and God's love for all who are in need.

Each portion of the prayers concludes with these or similar words.

	OR	**OR**
Lord, in your mercy,	... let us pray.	Hear us, O God.
hear our prayer.	**Have mercy, O God.**	**Your mercy is great.**

The presiding minister concludes the prayers with these or similar words.
We pray to you, O God, in the name of the one who endured the cross, forgives our sin, and feeds us at his table, Jesus Christ our Lord.
Amen.

Peace
The presiding minister and the assembly greet each other in the peace of the risen Christ.
The peace of Christ be with you always.
And also with you.

The people may greet one another with a sign of Christ's peace and may say **Peace be with you** *or similar words.*

Meal
The service continues with the offering.

Stripping of the Altar

After the communion, the service may conclude with the stripping of the altar. The assembly sits or kneels. Following the prayer after communion, the sacramental elements and vessels, linens, paraments, banners, and books are removed from the worship space. Psalm 88 or Psalm 22 is sung or said by a cantor, the choir, or the assembly. Lights may be dimmed as the worship space is stripped.

All depart in silence.

Good Friday

All gather in silence.

The assembly stands when the ministers stand.

Prayer of the Day

The presiding minister begins
with the prayer of the day.
Response after the prayer: **Amen.**

The assembly is seated.

Readings and Psalm

An assisting minister reads the first and second scripture readings. The psalm for the day follows the first reading.

Response after the conclusion of the first and the second reading: **Thanks be to God.**

Gospel Acclamation

The assembly stands. The following or another appropriate acclamation may be sung.

Look to Jesus, who for the sake of the joy that was set before him
endured the cross, disregard- ˡ ing its shame,
    and has taken his seat at the right hand of the ˡ throne of God.

Gospel

The gospel is announced.

The passion of our Lord Jesus Christ according to John.

The assembly may be seated. The passion account is read or sung.

Silence for prayer and reflection follows the reading.

Sermon

Silence for reflection follows.

Hymn of the Day

The assembly stands to proclaim the word of God in song.

Bidding Prayer

The assembly kneels or sits. The assisting minister leads the invitations to prayer (the bids). Silence for prayer follows each bid. The presiding minister leads the prayers that conclude the silence. At the conclusion of each prayer, "... through Christ our Lord," *the assembly responds* **Amen.**

The assembly prays for the following:
    the church throughout the world
    leaders in the church
    those preparing for baptism
    Christians in other churches
    the Jewish people, first to hear the word of God
    those who do not share our faith in Christ
    those who do not believe in God
    God's creation
    those who serve in public office
    those in need

Finally, let us pray for all those things for which our Lord would have us ask.

OR

Our Father in heaven,	Our Father, who art in heaven,
hallowed be your name,	hallowed be thy name,
your kingdom come,	thy kingdom come,
your will be done,	thy will be done,
on earth as in heaven.	on earth as it is in heaven.
Give us today our daily bread.	Give us this day our daily bread;
Forgive us our sins	and forgive us our trespasses,
as we forgive those	as we forgive those
who sin against us.	who trespass against us;
Save us from the time of trial	and lead us not into temptation,
and deliver us from evil.	but deliver us from evil.
For the kingdom, the power,	For thine is the kingdom,
and the glory are yours,	and the power, and the glory,
now and forever. Amen.	forever and ever. Amen.

If the service does not include the procession of the cross, it ends here, and all leave in silence.

Procession of the Cross

A large cross is carried in procession through the church and placed before the assembly.
The assembly stands and faces the cross as it is brought forward.

The following dialogue is sung as the procession begins.
Behold the life-giving cross, on which was hung the Savior of ¦ the whole world.
Oh, come, let us ¦ worship him.

The dialogue is sung a second time at the midpoint of the procession.

The dialogue is sung a third time at the end of the procession.

*The assembly may be seated. Texts expressing adoration of the crucified Christ, such as
"O my people, O my church" (the solemn reproaches) and "We glory in your cross," may be
sung or said.*

*During this time, or at the end of the service, worshipers may come to the large cross to make a
sign of reverence. Reverencing the cross may include actions such as pausing before the cross,
bowing, kneeling before it for prayer, or touching it.*

When the solemn reproaches are used, "Holy God" (the Trisagion, #159–161) is sung or said:
... you have prepared a cross for your Savior.
**Holy God,
holy and mighty,
holy and immortal,
have mercy on us.**

After a brief silence, the presiding minister continues.
We adore you, O Christ, | and we bless you.
By your holy cross you have re- | deemed the world.

All stand and sing, proclaiming the triumph of the cross. "Sing, my tongue" (#355–356) and "There in God's garden" (#342) are especially appropriate.

All depart in silence. If they have not done so earlier, worshipers may reverence the cross before they depart.

Resurrection
of Our Lord
Vigil of Easter

Gathering

The service begins in darkness, after nightfall. The lighting
of a new fire takes place outside the church building, if possible.

All gather in silence.
A small unlighted candle may be given to each worshiper.

Greeting
The presiding minister and the assembly greet each other.
The grace of our Lord Jesus Christ, the love of God,
and the communion of the Holy Spirit be with you all.
And also with you.

The presiding minister may introduce and welcome the assembly to the vigil.

If it has not been burning, the new fire is lighted. A prayer over the fire may be prayed, to which the assembly responds **Amen.**

The minister may trace the inscription on the paschal candle.

Christ, yesterday and today,	+
the beginning	A
and the ending.	Ω
To Christ belongs all time	2
and all the ages;	0
to Christ belongs glory and dominion	*decade*
now and forever.	*year*
Amen.	

The presiding minister lights the paschal candle from the new fire and sings or says:
The light of Christ, rising in glory, dispel the darkness of our ˈ hearts and minds.

Procession

The procession begins, led by the assisting minister bearing the paschal candle. During or after the procession, light from the paschal candle may be passed until the peoples' candles are all lighted.

As the procession begins, the assisting minister sings:
The light ˈ of Christ.
Thanks be ˈ to God.

The procession continues, stopping at midpoint. The assisting minister lifts the paschal candle and sings on a higher tone:
The light ˈ of Christ.
Thanks be ˈ to God.

The procession continues. The assisting minister takes the paschal candle to its stand, lifts it high and sings on a still higher tone:
The light ˈ of Christ.
Thanks be ˈ to God.

The paschal candle is placed in its stand.

Easter Proclamation

An assisting minister sings the Easter proclamation. The proclamation includes this dialogue.

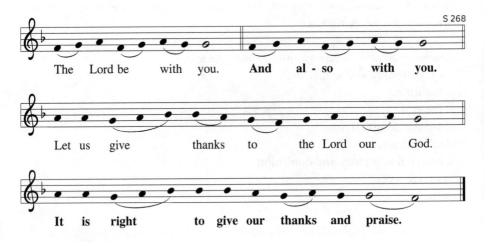

S 268

The Lord be with you. **And al - so with you.**

Let us give thanks to the Lord our God.

It is right to give our thanks and praise.

The Easter proclamation continues. The assisting minister may invite the assembly to respond in singing the following words.

This is the night!

The Easter proclamation concludes:
. . . one God, now and forever.
Amen.

Prayer of the Day

Response after the prayer: **Amen.**

The assembly is seated. Hand-held candles may be extinguished.

Word

Vigil Readings

Twelve readings are appointed. Some may be omitted. The four readings marked with an asterisk are not omitted. Each reading may be followed by a sung response. After the response there is silence for reflection, followed by a prayer, to which the assembly responds **Amen.**

*First Reading: Genesis 1:1—2:4a
Creation
Response: Psalm 136:1-9, 23-26

Second Reading: Genesis 7:1-5, 11-18; 8:6-18; 9:8-13
Flood
Response: Psalm 46

Third Reading: Genesis 22:1-18
Testing of Abraham
Response: Psalm 16

*Fourth Reading: Exodus 14:10-31; 15:20-21
Deliverance at the Red Sea
Response: Exodus 15:1b-13, 17-18

*Fifth Reading: Isaiah 55:1-11
Salvation freely offered to all
Response: Isaiah 12:2-6

Sixth Reading: Proverbs 8:1-8, 19-21; 9:4b-6
or Baruch 3:9-15, 32—4:4
The wisdom of God
Response: Psalm 19

Seventh Reading: Ezekiel 36:24-28
A new heart and a new spirit
Response: Psalms 42 and 43

Eighth Reading: Ezekiel 37:1-14
Valley of the dry bones
Response: Psalm 143

Ninth Reading: Zephaniah 3:14-20
The gathering of God's people
Response: Psalm 98

Tenth Reading: Jonah 1:1—2:1
The deliverance of Jonah
Response: Jonah 2:2-3 [4-6] 7-9

Eleventh Reading: Isaiah 61:1-4, 9-11
Clothed in the garments of salvation
Response: Deuteronomy 32:1-4, 7, 36a, 43a

*Twelfth Reading: Daniel 3:1-29
Deliverance from the fiery furnace
Response: Song of the Three 35–65

As an alternative to the following order of service, Holy Baptism or Affirmation of Baptism may be inserted here instead of after the sermon. The Litany of the Saints (#237) or a hymn may be sung as candidates for baptism, sponsors, and parents gather with the ministers at the font.

New Testament Reading: Romans 6:3-11

Gospel Acclamation

As the lights in the church are turned up, the altar candles are lighted, bells are rung, and an alleluia verse, an extended alleluia, a hymn with alleluias, or a canticle of praise ("This is the feast of victory" or "Glory to God") is sung.

Gospel

The gospel is announced:
The holy gospel according to _____.
Glory to you, O Lord.

The gospel is proclaimed, concluding:
The gospel of the Lord.
Praise to you, O Christ.

The presiding minister continues:
Alleluia. Christ is risen.
Christ is risen indeed. Alleluia.

Sermon

Silence for reflection follows.

Baptism

The Litany of the Saints (#237) or a hymn may be sung as candidates for baptism, sponsors, and parents gather with the ministers at the font.

Holy Baptism (p. 227) or Affirmation of Baptism (p. 234) follows.

Meal and Sending

After the order for Holy Baptism or Affirmation of Baptism, the service may continue with the prayers of intercession or the peace.

✠ Life Passages

In the waters of baptism, Christians make the passage with Jesus Christ through death to the new life of the resurrection. Each day of our lives is shaped by this baptismal journey. Within our lives, we mark particular occasions of transition and passage in various ways. Welcoming guests into its midst, the Christian assembly surrounds people at these times, proclaiming the good news of God's love in Christ in the context of particular circumstances in human life.

Orders of service for three principal life occasions—healing, funeral, and marriage—appear in this resource. The patterns for these rites follow closely the common pattern for the primary gathering of the Christian assembly. The order for Healing is placed within Holy Communion or the Service of the Word, following the hymn of the day. Marriage and Funeral are services in which the inclusion of the Lord's supper is encouraged.

Other prayers and blessings for particular circumstances are provided in Additional Prayers (pp. 72–87).

Pattern for Worship—Healing

Healing

God's gift of healing comes to us in word, prayer, and sign.

Prayers of Intercession
Laying On of Hands
Blessing

Gathered by the Holy Spirit around Jesus Christ, the Word of salvation, we pray for God's healing in all its dimensions. Personal prayer and a sign of healing— the laying on of hands, which may be accompanied by anointing with oil—are offered to all.

Gathering

The Holy Spirit, the comforter, gathers us in worship.

Thanksgiving for Baptism
Greeting
Prayer of the Day

Gathered by the Holy Spirit at a time of death, we proclaim Jesus Christ, the resurrection and the life. We begin in the name of the triune God and join in prayer.

Word

God speaks to us in scripture reading, preaching, and song.

Readings
Sermon
Hymn of the Day
Creed
Prayers of Intercession
Lord's Prayer

In the face of death, scripture readings and preaching witness to the resurrection and bring God's word of hope and comfort. We proclaim that word also as we sing and profess the Christian faith. Prayers for those who mourn and in thanksgiving for those who have died are followed by the prayer Jesus taught.

Meal

God gives a foretaste of the feast to come.

Sending

God blesses us and sends us out in peace.

Commendation

Into the arms of mercy God receives our loved one, and we go out in the peace of Christ.

Committal
    Reading
    Committal
    Blessing

With scripture and prayer we commit our loved one's body to its resting place and to God's love, then receive the blessing of God as we go forth.

Central elements of the liturgy are noted in bold type; other elements support the essential shape of Christian worship.

Gathering

The Holy Spirit gathers us in worship as we witness the marriage.

Entrance	*Gathered by the Holy Spirit and greeted in the name*
Greeting	*of the triune God, the assembly joins in worship. Those*
Declaration of Intention	*to be married state their intention; the assembly*
Prayer of the Day	*promises support. All are gathered into prayer.*

Word

God speaks to us in scripture reading, preaching, and song.

Readings	*Scripture readings, preaching, and song witness to*
Sermon	*the gift and vocation of marriage, bringing God's word*
Hymn of the Day	*of law and promise into this context of human life.*

Marriage

As two become one by their promises, God blesses them.

Vows	*The two pledge their love and faithfulness; the giving*
Acclamation	*of rings is a symbol of this promise. The minister an-*
Marriage Blessing	*nounces the marriage, and the assembly acclaims it.*
Prayers of Intercession	*The prayers ask God's blessing upon this marriage*
Lord's Prayer	*and remember the needs of the whole world.*

Meal

God sets out a marriage feast for all those joined to Christ.

Sending

God blesses us and sends us in mission to the world.

Peace	*Together with the newly married, we go out into the*
Blessing	*world with God's peace and blessing.*

Healing

The order for healing is an expression in worship of the church's ministry of healing. Here all who sense the need for God's healing in any aspect of their lives may join in prayer for others and themselves. Here each person may come to receive a word of blessing and prayer. Here each one may also receive a physical gesture of healing: the laying on of hands, which may be accompanied by anointing with oil. These signs, first given in baptism, tell us again that we are sealed by the Holy Spirit and marked forever with the cross of Christ, who is health and salvation for the whole world.

In its ministry of healing, the church does not replace the gifts of God that come through the scientific community nor does it promise a cure. Rather, the church offers and celebrates gifts such as these: God's presence with strength and comfort in time of suffering, God's promise of wholeness and peace, and God's love embodied in the community of faith.

Healing

This order may take place within Holy Communion or the Service of the Word, usually following the hymn of the day. The assembly may be seated.

Introduction
The presiding minister may address the assembly with these or similar words.
Our Lord Jesus healed many as a sign of the reign of God come near and sent the disciples to continue this work of healing—with prayer, the laying on of hands, and anointing. In the name of Christ, the great healer and reconciler of the world, we now entrust to God all who are in need of healing.

Prayers of Intercession

Prayers of intercession are prayed, including prayers for healing. To each petition the assembly responds with these or similar words.

In your great mercy,
hear us, O God.

The presiding minister concludes the prayers, and the assembly responds **Amen.**

Laying On of Hands

The presiding minister may address the assembly in these or similar words.

Sisters and brothers, I invite you to come and receive a sign of healing and wholeness in the name of the triune God.

Those who wish to receive laying on of hands (and anointing) approach and, as conditions permit, they may kneel.

The minister lays both hands on each person's head and may use one of these forms or similar words. The minister may also anoint the person's forehead with oil, making the sign of the cross.

_____*Name*_____, in the name of our Savior Jesus Christ, be strengthened and filled with God's grace, that you may know the healing power of the Spirit.
Response: Amen.

OR

Receive this oil as a sign of forgiveness and healing in Jesus Christ.
Response: Amen.

OR

Father in heaven, for Jesus' sake, send your Holy Spirit upon your servant, _____*name*_____; drive away all sickness of body and spirit; make whole that which is broken; deliver *her/him* from the power of evil; and preserve *her/him* in true faith, to share in the power of Christ's resurrection and to serve you with all the saints now and evermore.
Response: Amen.

The laying on of hands may be accompanied by the singing of acclamations (#218–221), psalms, hymns, and other music.

After all have returned to their places, the assembly stands, and the presiding minister continues.

Let us pray.

Living God, through the laying on of hands [*and anointing*], grant comfort in suffering to all who are in need of healing. When they are afraid, give them courage; when afflicted, give them patience; when dejected, give them hope; and when alone, assure them of the support of your holy people. We ask this through Christ our Lord.

Amen.

Blessing

The presiding minister concludes the order for healing.

Almighty God, who is a strong tower to all, to whom all things in heaven and on earth bow and obey, be now and evermore your sure defense, and help you to know that the name given to us for health and salvation is the name of our Lord and Savior, Jesus Christ.

Amen.

Peace

The presiding minister and the assembly greet each other in the peace of the risen Christ.

The peace of Christ be with you always.

And also with you.

The people may greet one another with a sign of Christ's peace and may say **Peace be with you** *or similar words.*

The assembly is seated.

The service continues with the offering.

Funeral

At a person's death, the church shares the grief of those who mourn and remembers the brevity of life on earth. At the funeral we give voice to sorrow, thank God for our loved one, and entrust this companion of ours into the hands of God. Trusting in God's promise in baptism that we are claimed by Christ forever, we rest in the sure hope of the resurrection. When the church gathers to mark the end of life, Christ crucified and risen is the witness of worship, the strength of mutual consolation, and the hope of healing.

This service may be used when the body or ashes are present, or it may be adapted for use as a memorial service. A remembrance and expression of thanksgiving for the life of the deceased may take place after the prayer of the day or before the commendation.

Gathering

The ministers may meet the coffin and the bereaved at the entrance to the church. The assembly stands and faces them.

The presiding minister may address the assembly using one or both of these paragraphs, or in similar words.

Welcome in the name of Jesus, the Savior of the world. We are gathered to worship, to proclaim Christ crucified and risen, to remember before God our *sister/brother*___*name*___ , to give thanks for *her/his* life, to commend *her/him* to our merciful redeemer, and to comfort one another in our grief.

OR

Blessed be the God and Father of our Lord Jesus Christ, the source of all mercy and the God of all consolation, who comforts us in all our sorrows so that we can comfort others in their sorrows with the consolation we ourselves have received from God.

Thanksgiving for Baptism

A thanksgiving for baptism may follow. As a sign of being clothed with Christ in baptism, a pall may be placed on the coffin by family members, pallbearers, or other assisting ministers. The minister or a representative of the congregation may say:

When we were baptized in Christ Jesus, we were baptized into his death. We were buried therefore with him by baptism into death, so that as Christ was raised from the dead by the glory of the Father, we too might live a new life. For if we have been united with him in a death like his, we shall certainly be united with him in a resurrection like his.

OR

All who are baptized into Christ have put on Christ. In *her/his* baptism, ___*name*___ was clothed with Christ. In the day of Christ's coming, *she/he* shall be clothed with glory.

The presiding minister may lead this acclamation.

Eternal God, maker of heaven and earth, who formed us from the dust of the earth, who by your breath gave us life, we glorify you.
We glorify you.

Jesus Christ, the resurrection and the life, who suffered death for all humanity, who rose from the grave to open the way to eternal life, we praise you.
We praise you.

Holy Spirit, author and giver of life, the comforter of all who sorrow, our sure confidence and everlasting hope, we worship you.
We worship you.

To you, O blessed Trinity, be glory and honor, forever and ever.
Amen.

A procession may form and enter, the ministers leading. A hymn, psalm, or anthem may be sung.

Greeting

The presiding minister and the assembly greet each other.

The grace of our Lord Jesus Christ, the love of God,
and the communion of the Holy Spirit be with you all.
And also with you.

Prayer of the Day

The presiding minister prays the prayer of the day.

Let us pray.

A brief silence is kept before the prayer.

O God of grace and glory, we remember before you today our *sister/brother*, ___*name*___. We thank you for giving *her/him* to us to know and to love as a companion in our pilgrimage on earth. In your boundless compassion, console us who mourn. Give us faith to see that death has been swallowed up in the victory of our Lord Jesus Christ, so that we may live in confidence and hope until, by your call, we are gathered to our heavenly home in the company of all your saints; through Jesus Christ, our Savior and Lord.
Amen.

OR

Almighty God, source of all mercy and giver of comfort, graciously tend those who mourn, that, casting all their sorrow on you, they may know the consolation of your love; through your Son, Jesus Christ our Lord.
Amen.

OR *(at the death of a child)*

Holy God, your beloved Son took children into his arms and blessed them. Help us to entrust ___*name*___ to your never-failing care and love. Comfort us as we bear the pain of *her/his* death, and receive us all into your everlasting arms, through Jesus Christ, our Savior and Lord.
Amen.

Word

Readings

The assembly is seated. Two or three scripture readings are proclaimed. When the service includes communion, the last is a reading from the gospels. Responses may include a psalm in response to a reading from the Old Testament, a sung acclamation preceding the reading of the gospel, or other appropriate hymns, songs, and psalms.

Sermon

Silence for reflection follows.

Hymn of the Day

The assembly stands to proclaim the word of God in song.

Creed

The Apostles' Creed may be spoken.

I believe in God the Father almighty,
    creator of heaven and earth.

I believe in Jesus Christ, God's only Son, our Lord,
    who was conceived by the Holy Spirit,
    born of the virgin Mary,
    suffered under Pontius Pilate,
    was crucified, died, and was buried;
    he descended to the dead.*
    On the third day he rose again;
    he ascended into heaven,
    he is seated at the right hand of the Father,
    and he will come to judge the living and the dead.

I believe in the Holy Spirit,
    the holy catholic church,
    the communion of saints,
    the forgiveness of sins,
    the resurrection of the body,
    and the life everlasting. Amen.

* Or, "he descended into hell," *another translation of this text in widespread use.*

Prayers of Intercession

Prayers of intercession are prayed. To each petition the assembly responds:
God of mercy,
hear our prayer.

The presiding minister concludes the prayers, and the assembly responds **Amen.**

A service with communion continues with the peace. Following the prayer after communion, the service continues with the commendation on p. 283.

OR

A service without communion continues as follows.

The Lord's Prayer is prayed by all.

OR

Our Father in heaven,
 hallowed be your name,
 your kingdom come
 your will be done,
  on earth as in heaven.
Give us today our daily bread.
Forgive us our sins
 as we forgive those
  who sin against us.
Save us from the time of trial
 and deliver us from evil.
For the kingdom, the power,
 and the glory are yours,
  now and forever. Amen.

Our Father, who art in heaven,
 hallowed be thy name,
 thy kingdom come,
 thy will be done,
  on earth as it is in heaven.
Give us this day our daily bread;
and forgive us our trespasses,
 as we forgive those
  who trespass against us;
and lead us not into temptation,
 but deliver us from evil.
For thine is the kingdom,
 and the power, and the glory,
  forever and ever. Amen.

Sending

Commendation

The ministers take their places at the coffin. The presiding minister leads the commendation.
Let us commend ___name___ to the mercy of God, our maker and redeemer.
Silence is kept.

The presiding minister may place her/his hand on the coffin during this prayer.
Into your hands, O merciful Savior, we commend your servant ___name___.
Acknowledge, we humbly beseech you, a sheep of your own fold, a lamb of your
own flock, a sinner of your own redeeming. Receive *her/him* into the arms of
your mercy, into the blessed rest of everlasting peace, and into the glorious
company of the saints in light.
Amen.

*Here or during the procession out, a farewell may be sung: "Now, Lord, you let your servant go in
peace," an acclamation (#222–223), or another hymn or song.*

If the committal occurs at another time, a blessing may precede these words of sending.
Let us go forth in peace,
in the name of Christ. Amen.

A procession may form and leave the church, the ministers leading.

Committal

The ministers precede the coffin to the place of interment. Words of comfort from the scriptures may accompany or conclude the procession.

The presiding minister greets the assembly.
Grace and peace from our Savior Jesus Christ be with you all.

Let us pray.
Holy God, holy and powerful, by the death and burial of Jesus your anointed, you have destroyed the power of death and made holy the resting places of all your people. Keep our *sister/brother* ___name___, whose body we now lay to rest, in the company of all your saints. And at the last, O God, raise *her/him* up to share with all the faithful the endless joy and peace won through the glorious resurrection of Christ our Lord, who lives and reigns with you and the Holy Spirit, one God, now and forever.
Amen.

A scripture reading may follow.

The coffin may be lowered into the grave or placed in its resting place.

Earth may be cast on the coffin as the presiding minister says:
In sure and certain hope of the resurrection to eternal life through our Lord Jesus Christ, we commend to almighty God our *sister/brother* ___name___, and we commit *her/his* body to
    the ground or *the deep* or *the elements* or *its resting place;*
earth to earth, ashes to ashes, dust to dust.

The Lord bless *her/him* and keep *her/him*.
The Lord's face shine on *her/him* with grace and mercy.
The Lord look upon *her/him* with favor and ✝ give *her/him* peace.
Amen.

The following response may be sung, or may be spoken by the minister.
Rest eternal grant *her/him*, O Lord; and let light perpetual shine upon *her/him*.

One of the following prayers may be said.

O Lord, support us all the day long of this troubled life, until the shadows lengthen and the evening comes and the busy world is hushed, the fever of life is over, and our work is done. Then, in your mercy, grant us a safe lodging, and a holy rest, and peace at the last, through Jesus Christ our Lord. **Amen.**

Merciful God, you heal the broken in heart and bind up the wounds of the afflicted. Strengthen us in our weakness, calm our troubled spirits, and dispel our doubts and fears. In Christ's rising from the dead, you conquered death and opened the gates to everlasting life. Renew our trust in you that by the power of your love we shall one day be brought together again with our *sister/brother* ___*name*___. Grant this, we pray, through Jesus Christ our Lord. **Amen.**

The Lord's Prayer may be prayed.

Our Father in heaven,
 hallowed be your name,
 your kingdom come,
 your will be done,
  on earth as in heaven.
Give us today our daily bread.
Forgive us our sins
 as we forgive those
  who sin against us.
Save us from the time of trial
 and deliver us from evil.
For the kingdom, the power,
 and the glory are yours,
  now and forever. Amen.

OR

Our Father, who art in heaven,
 hallowed be thy name,
 thy kingdom come,
 thy will be done,
  on earth as it is in heaven.
Give us this day our daily bread;
and forgive us our trespasses,
 as we forgive those
  who trespass against us;
and lead us not into temptation,
 but deliver us from evil.
For thine is the kingdom,
 and the power, and the glory,
  forever and ever. Amen.

The assembly is blessed and sent forth.

The God of peace, who brought again from the dead our Lord Jesus, the great shepherd of the sheep, by the blood of the eternal covenant, make you complete in everything good so that you may do God's will, working in you that which is well-pleasing in God's sight; through Jesus Christ, to whom be the glory forever and ever. **Amen.**

Let us go in peace.

OR

Almighty God, Father, + Son, and Holy Spirit, bless you now and forever. **Amen.**

Let us go in peace.

Marriage

Marriage is a gift of God, intended for the joy and mutual strength of those who enter it and for the well-being of the whole human family. God created us male and female and blessed humankind with the gifts of companionship, the capacity to love, and the care and nurture of children. Jesus affirmed the covenant of marriage and revealed God's own self-giving love on the cross. The Holy Spirit helps those who are united in marriage to be living signs of God's grace, love, and faithfulness.

Marriage is also a human estate, with vows publicly witnessed. The church in worship surrounds these promises with the gathering of God's people, the witness of the word of God, and prayers of blessing and intercession.

Gathering

Entrance
The assembly stands as the ministers and the wedding group enter. Music—hymn, song, psalm, instrumental music—may accompany the entrance.

Greeting
The presiding minister and the assembly greet each other.
The grace of our Lord Jesus Christ, the love of God,
and the communion of the Holy Spirit be with you all.
And also with you.

Declaration of Intention

The minister addresses the couple in these or similar words, asking each person in turn:

___Name___ , will you have___ *name* ___ to be your *wife/husband,* to live together in the covenant of marriage? Will you love *her/him,* comfort *her/him,* honor and keep *her/him,* in sickness and in health, and, forsaking all others, be faithful to *her/him* as long as you both shall live?

Response: I will.

The minister may address the assembly in these or similar words.

Will all of you, by God's grace, uphold and care for___ *name* ___ and ___ *name* ___ in their life together?

We will.

Prayer of the Day

The presiding minister leads the following or another prayer of the day.

Let us pray.

Gracious God, you sent your Son Jesus Christ into the world to reveal your love to all people. Enrich ___ *name* ___ and ___ *name* ___ with every good gift, that their life together may show forth your love; and grant that at the last we may all celebrate with Christ the marriage feast that has no end; in the name of Jesus Christ our Lord. **Amen.**

Word

Readings

The assembly is seated. Two or three scripture readings are proclaimed. When the service includes communion, the last is a reading from the gospels. Responses may include a psalm in response to a reading from the Old Testament, a sung acclamation preceding the reading of the gospel, or other appropriate hymns, songs, and psalms.

Sermon

Silence for reflection follows.

Hymn of the Day

A hymn of the day may be sung.

Marriage

Vows

The couple may join hands. Each promises faithfulness to the other in these or similar words.
I take you,___*name*___, to be my *wife/husband* from this day forward,
to join with you and share all that is to come,
and I promise to be faithful to you until death parts us.

OR

In the presence of God and this community,
I,___*name*___, take you,___*name*___, to be my *wife/husband;*
to have and to hold from this day forward,
in joy and in sorrow, in plenty and in want, in sickness and in health,
to love and to cherish, as long as we both shall live.
This is my solemn vow.

Giving of Rings

The couple may exchange rings with these or similar words.
___*Name*___, I give you this ring as a sign of my love and faithfulness.

OR

___*Name*___, I give you this ring as a symbol of my vow.
With all that I am, and all that I have, I honor you,
in the name of the Father,
and of the Son, and of the Holy Spirit.

Acclamation

The presiding minister addresses the assembly.
___*Name*___ and ___*name*___, by their promises before God and in the presence of this
assembly, have joined themselves to one another as husband and wife.
Those whom God has joined together let no one separate.
Amen. Thanks be to God.

*The assembly may offer acclamation with applause. A sung acclamation, hymn, or other music
may follow.*

Other symbols of marriage may be given or used at this time.

Marriage Blessing

The couple may kneel. The presiding minister may extend a hand over the couple while praying for God's blessing in the following or similar words.

Most gracious God, we give you thanks for your tender love in sending Jesus Christ to come among us, to be born of a human mother, and to endure the cross for our sake, that we may have abundance of life.

By the power of your Holy Spirit pour out the abundance of your blessing on ___*name*___ and ___*name*___. Defend them from every enemy. Lead them into all peace. Let your love be a seal upon their hearts, a mantle about their shoulders, and a crown upon their foreheads.

Bless them so that their lives together may bear witness to your love. Bless them in their work and in their companionship; in their sleeping and in their waking; in their joys and in their sorrows; in their life and in their death.

Finally, in your mercy, bring them to that table where your saints feast forever in your heavenly home, through Jesus Christ our Lord, who lives and reigns with you and the Holy Spirit, one God, now and forever.
Amen.

Parents or others may speak additional words of blessing and encouragement at this time.

Prayers of Intercession

The assembly stands. Prayers of intercession for the world and its needs may be prayed.

Each petition may end:
Gracious and faithful God,
hear our prayer.

The presiding minister concludes the prayers, and the assembly responds **Amen.**

A service with communion continues with the peace. After the presiding minister greets the assembly, the couple may greet each other with the kiss of peace, and the assembly may greet one another in peace.

OR

A service without communion continues as follows.

The Lord's Prayer is prayed by all.

Our Father in heaven,
    hallowed be your name,
    your kingdom come,
    your will be done,
        on earth as in heaven.
Give us today our daily bread.
Forgive us our sins
    as we forgive those
        who sin against us.
Save us from the time of trial
    and deliver us from evil.
For the kingdom, the power,
    and the glory are yours,
    now and forever. Amen.

OR

Our Father, who art in heaven,
    hallowed be thy name,
    thy kingdom come,
    thy will be done,
        on earth as it is in heaven.
Give us this day our daily bread;
and forgive us our trespasses,
    as we forgive those
        who trespass against us;
and lead us not into temptation,
    but deliver us from evil.
For thine is the kingdom,
    and the power, and the glory,
    forever and ever. Amen.

Sending

Peace
If it has not been included earlier in the service, the greeting of peace may be shared.
The peace of Christ be with you always.
And also with you.

The couple may greet one another with the kiss of peace. All present may greet one another with a gesture of peace, and may say **Peace be with you** *or similar words.*

Blessing
The presiding minister proclaims God's blessing in these or similar words.

The blessed and holy Trinity make you strong in faith and love, defend you on every side, and guide you in truth and peace, now and forever.
Amen.

OR

God Almighty send you light and truth to keep you all the days of your life. The hand of God protect you; the holy angels accompany you; and the blessing of almighty God, the Father, the + Son, and the Holy Spirit, be with you now and forever.
Amen.

Dismissal

An assisting minister may send the assembly forth in these or similar words.

Go in peace. Serve the Lord.

Thanks be to God.

A hymn may be sung or instrumental music played as the wedding group and the ministers depart.

✤ Daily Prayer

Pattern for Worship

From the gathering around word and sacrament on the first day of the week, Christians are sent by God to continue their worship each day through lives of service. St. Paul's guidance to "pray without ceasing . . . for this is the will of God in Christ Jesus for you" (1 Thess. 5:17-18) suggests that the Christian life is prayer: openness to the presence of God, responsiveness to the word of God, recognition that all of life is in Christ, and engagement in care for one another and for the whole creation. Daily prayer is a gift that nourishes growth toward living all of daily life in prayer.

Evening and morning are primary times for common prayer in various faith traditions. For Christians, Evening Prayer and Morning Prayer have an additional dimension, calling to mind Christ's passage through death to resurrection. As evening comes, we look to the light of Christ that scatters the darkness, even as we anticipate the great awakening of the resurrection. With the rising sun, we praise God for the resurrection of Jesus Christ, and we ask the Holy Spirit's help in taking up the cross to follow Jesus into another day. Night Prayer offers a time to acknowledge both the gifts and the failings of each day, and we commend ourselves and the whole world into God's hands as night comes.

Although the patterns for these times of common daily prayer are not uniform, they have several common features: the church's song, especially the singing of psalms; the reading of and reflection upon the scriptures; and prayers in a variety of forms. This basic pattern is often preceded by an opening, whether brief or extended, and concluded with the blessing of God.

In addition to prayer at these three times of day, Responsive Prayer is a simple order that may be adapted to a variety of times and contexts.

Opening

Morning
Dialogue
Doxology

Evening
Dialogue
Hymn of Light
Thanksgiving for Light

Night
Dialogue
Night Hymn
Confession and Forgiveness

We begin the pattern of daily prayer by opening our hearts and voices to the presence of God.

The words that begin morning prayer remind us that this opening is itself the gift of God: "O Lord, open my lips, and my mouth shall proclaim your praise" (Ps. 51:15).

The patterns for evening prayer and night prayer provide for an opening that may be extended: at evening prayer, with a hymn and thanksgiving for the Light that is Christ; at night prayer, with a night hymn and a communal form of confession and forgiveness.

Psalmody

Morning
Morning Psalm
Additional Psalm(s)

Evening
Evening Psalm
Additional Psalm(s)

Night
Night Psalm
Additional Psalm(s)

Morning, Evening, Night
Song

Singing the psalms is a primary element of daily prayer. Using the psalms in worship is a practice inherited from our forebears in faith, the Hebrew people. Christians through the centuries have prayed them daily.

Through the singing of psalms we express many things: adoration, praise, thanksgiving for God's deliverance, lament, confession, intercession, teaching. Used in the context of prayer, they are at the same time God's words to us and our response to God. In silence after each psalm, we continue to listen for God's voice.

We continue singing from the church's treasury of song. A hymn that reflects the time of day or the church year is especially fitting.

Central elements of the liturgy are noted in bold type; other elements support the essential shape of Christian worship.

Word

Morning
Reading(s)
Reflection
Gospel Canticle:
    Song of Zechariah

As part of daily prayer, we hear and reflect on readings from the Bible. Use of a daily lectionary helps us encounter more of the scriptures than we hear on Sundays. The reading in night prayer is typically brief, a verse or two for meditation as the day comes to a close.

Evening
Reading(s)
Reflection
Gospel Canticle:
    Song of Mary

Reflection on the reading(s) includes a time of silence, and may take other forms, too: a response through music or other arts; a brief verbal reflection such as preaching, teaching, or testimony.

Night
Brief Reading
Reflection
Gospel Canticle:
    Song of Simeon

Our response to the word of God is summed up in singing one of the great scriptural songs from the gospel of Luke. With these songs the church both proclaims and hears the liberating good news.

Prayers

Morning, Evening, Night
Prayers
Lord's Prayer
Blessing
Peace

Although all of daily prayer is in a sense praying, we conclude with intentional forms of prayer: giving thanks for the gifts of God; praying for others and for ourselves; and the Lord's Prayer. The word of God's blessing concludes daily prayer, and may be followed by the sign of peace.

OR
at **Morning Prayer**
Prayers
Lord's Prayer
Thanksgiving for Baptism
Peace

Especially on Sundays and during the Easter season, morning prayer may conclude with a thanksgiving for baptism. One form of this thanksgiving, the paschal blessing, tells the Easter story and includes the singing of "We praise you, O God."

Morning Prayer
Matins

Opening

The assembly stands.

The leader begins the dialogue, and the assembly responds, concluding with a doxology.

O Lord,   o - pen my lips,

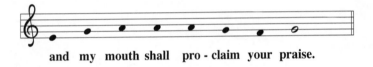

and my mouth shall pro - claim your praise.

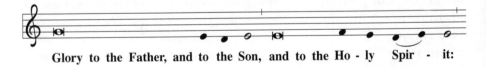

Glory to the Father, and to the Son, and to the Ho - ly   Spir - it:

as it was in the be-gin-ning, is   now, and will be for - ev - er. A - men.

The alleluia is omitted during Lent.

Al - le - lu - ia.

OR

S 299

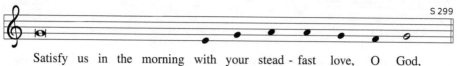

Satisfy us in the morning with your stead - fast love, O God,

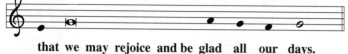

that we may rejoice and be glad all our days.

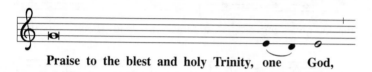

Praise to the blest and holy Trinity, one God,

who gives us life, salvation, and res - ur - rec - tion.

The alleluia is omitted during Lent.

Al - le - lu - ia.

Psalmody

The psalmody begins with a morning psalm of praise: Psalm 95:1-7a (the Venite), Psalm 63:1-8, Psalm 67, Psalm 100, or another appropriate psalm.

The psalm may be preceded and followed by a general or seasonal invitatory. When the invitatory is sung, the following or a similar tone may be used, the assembly echoing the leader.

Give glory to God, our light and our life.

Oh, come, let us wor - ship and praise.

Refrain

Come, let us sing to the Lord; let us shout for joy to the rock of our sal - va - tion. 3 Come, let us wor - ship and bow down; let us kneel be-fore the Lord our mak - er. For the Lord is our God, and we are the peo - ple of God's pas - ture and the sheep of God's hand.

Refrain

Come, let us sing to the Lord; let us shout for joy to the rock of our sal - va - tion.

Give glory to God, our light and our life.

Oh, come, let us wor - ship and praise.

The assembly is seated.

The psalmody may continue with one or more additional psalms. Each is followed by a time of silence, which may be concluded by a psalm prayer; the assembly responds **Amen.**

Song

Additional assembly song may follow the psalmody. A hymn appropriate to the time of day or the season is normally sung, the assembly standing.

Word

Readings

The assembly is seated.
The service includes one or more scripture readings. After the conclusion of each reading, the assembly may respond **Thanks be to God.**

The reading of scripture is followed by silence for reflection. Other forms of reflection may also follow, such as brief commentary, teaching, or personal witness; non-biblical readings; interpretation through music or other art forms; or guided conversation among those present.

The reflection may conclude with a scriptural dialogue. When it is sung, the following or a similar tone may be used, the assembly echoing the leader.

S302a

You have been born a - new

through the living and abiding word of God.

OR

S302b

Long ago God spoke to our ancestors in many and various ways by the prophets,

but in these last days God has spoken to us by the Son.

Gospel Canticle

The assembly stands to sing the gospel canticle for morning, the song of Zechariah, using the following or another musical version (#226, 250, 552). "We praise you, O God" (#227, 228, 414) may be used in place of the Benedictus.

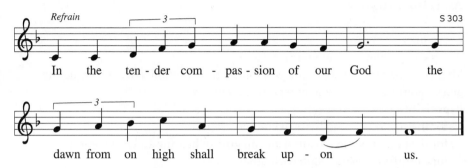

Refrain   ⌐—3—⌐   S 303

In the ten - der com - pas - sion of our God the

dawn from on high shall break up - on us.

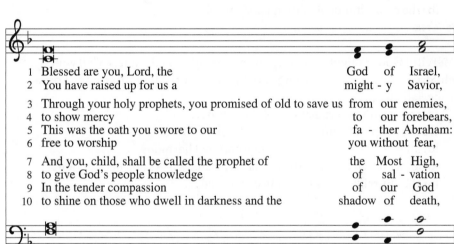

1	Blessed are you, Lord, the		God	of	Israel,
2	You have raised up for us a		might - y		Savior,
3	Through your holy prophets, you promised of old to save us	from	our		enemies,
4	to show mercy		to	our	forebears,
5	This was the oath you swore to our		fa - ther		Abraham:
6	free to worship		you	without	fear,
7	And you, child, shall be called the prophet of		the	Most	High,
8	to give God's people knowledge		of	sal -	vation
9	In the tender compassion		of	our	God
10	to shine on those who dwell in darkness and the		shadow	of	death,

1	you have come to your	people	and	set	them	free.
2	born of the	house	of your	ser -	vant	David. *Refrain*
3	from the	hands	of	all	who	hate us,
4	and to re -	member	your	ho -	ly	covenant.
5	to set us	free	from the	hands	of our	enemies,
6	holy and righteous before you,	all	the	days	of our	life. *Refrain*
7	for you will go before the	Lord	to pre -	pare	the	way,
8	by the for -	give -	ness	of	their	sins.
9	the dawn from on	high	shall	break	up -	on us,
10	and to guide our	feet	into the	way	of	peace. *Refrain*

Prayers

The assembly kneels or stands. The following or another form of the prayers may be used.

The Lord be with you.
And also with you.

Let us pray.
A brief silence for prayer follows each petition.
Mighty God of mercy, we thank you for the resurrection dawn, bringing the glory of our risen Lord who makes every day new.
Especially we thank you—
　　for the sustaining goodness of your creation ...
　　for the new creation in Christ and all gifts of healing and forgiveness ...
　　for the gifts of relationship with others ...
　　for the communion of faith in your church ...
Other thanksgivings may be added.

Merciful God of might, renew this weary world, heal the hurts of all your children, and bring about your peace for all in Christ Jesus, the living Lord.
Especially we pray—
　　for those who govern nations of the world ...
　　for the people in countries ravaged by strife or warfare ...
　　for all who work for peace and international harmony ...
　　for all who strive to save the earth from carelessness and destruction ...
　　for the church of Jesus Christ in every land ...
Other intercessions may be added.

One or more of the following prayers and other appropriate prayers may be used.
Almighty and everlasting God, you have brought us in safety to this new day. Preserve us with your mighty power, that we may not fall into sin nor be overcome in adversity. In all we do, direct us to the fulfilling of your purpose; through Jesus Christ our Lord.
Amen.

OR

O God, you have called your servants to ventures of which we cannot see the ending, by paths as yet untrodden, through perils unknown. Give us faith to go out with good courage, not knowing where we go, but only that your hand is leading us and your love supporting us; through Jesus Christ our Lord.
Amen.

OR

We give thanks to you, heavenly Father, through Jesus Christ your dear Son, that you have protected us through the night from all harm and danger. We ask that you would also protect us today from sin and all evil, so that our life and actions may please you. Into your hands we commend ourselves: our bodies, our souls, and all that is ours. Let your holy angels be with us, so that the wicked foe may have no power over us.
Amen.

The Lord's Prayer is sung or spoken.

The assembly stands.

Especially on Sundays, morning prayer may include a thanksgiving for baptism. One of the forms on pp. 307–308 may be used. If the thanksgiving for baptism is omitted, the service concludes as follows.

Blessing

Let us bless the Lord.

Thanks be to God.

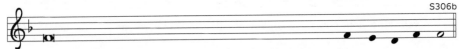

Almighty God, the Father, ✝ the Son, and the Holy Spirit, bless and pre-serve us.

A - men.

A hymn may be sung.

The greeting of peace may be shared by all.

Thanksgiving for Baptism

A baptismal hymn or canticle may be sung, and the assembly may gather at the font.

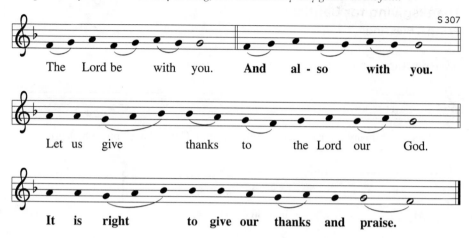

The Lord be with you. **And al - so with you.**

Let us give thanks to the Lord our God.

It is right to give our thanks and praise.

Water may be poured into the font as the leader gives thanks.

Ever-living God, author of creation, we give you thanks for your gift of water that brings life and refreshes the earth. We bless and praise you, for by water and the Word we are cleansed from sin and receive everlasting life. Join us again this day to the saving death of Christ; renew in us the living fountain of your grace; and raise us with Christ Jesus to live in newness of life; for you are merciful, and you love your whole creation, and with all your creatures we give you glory, through your Son Jesus Christ, in the unity of the Holy Spirit, now and forever. **Amen.**

As a reminder of the gift of baptism, the assembly may be sprinkled with water, and "We praise you, O God" (#227, 228, 414) or another hymn or canticle related to baptism may be sung.

The leader addresses the assembly in these or similar words.

Almighty God, who gives us a new birth by water and the Holy Spirit and forgives us all our sins, strengthen us in all goodness and by the power of the Holy Spirit keep us in eternal life through Jesus Christ our Lord. **Amen.**

The greeting of peace may be shared by all.

OR

Thanksgiving for Baptism
Paschal Blessing

A baptismal hymn or canticle may be sung, and the assembly may gather at the font.

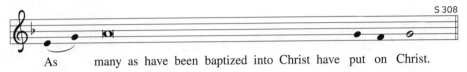

S 308

As many as have been baptized into Christ have put on Christ.

Al - le - lu - ia.

The resurrection narrative is sung or spoken.

On the first day of the week at early dawn, the women came to the tomb, taking the spices that they had prepared. They found the stone rolled away from the tomb, but when they went in they did not find the body. While they were perplexed about this, suddenly two men in dazzling clothes stood beside them. The women were terrified and bowed their faces to the ground, but the men said to them: "Why do you look for the living among the dead? Remember how he told you, while he was still in Galilee, that the Son of man must be handed over to sinners, and be crucified, and on the third day rise again."

"We praise you, O God" (#227, 228, 414) is sung. As a reminder of the gift of baptism, the assembly may be sprinkled with water during the singing of the canticle.

O God, for our redemption you gave your only Son to suffer death on the cross, and by his glorious resurrection you delivered us from the power of death. Make us die every day to sin so that we may rise to live with Christ forever; who lives and reigns with you and the Holy Spirit, one God, now and forever.
Amen.

Almighty God bless us, and direct our days and our deeds in peace.
Amen.

The greeting of peace may be shared by all.

Evening Prayer
Vespers

Opening

The assembly stands. A large, lighted candle may be carried to its place.

A dialogue may accompany or follow the procession. When it is sung, the following or a similar tone may be used, the assembly echoing the leader.

S 309

Jesus Christ is the light of the world, **the light no darkness can o-ver-come.**

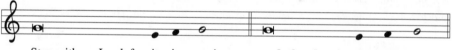

Stay with us, Lord, for it is evening, **and the day is al-most over.**

Let your light scat-ter the darkness **and illu-mine your church.**

OR

One of the following dialogues may be sung to the above or a similar tone.

General

God is our light and | our salvation,
our refuge | and our stronghold.
From the rising of the sun | to its setting,
we praise your | name, O God.
For with you is the foun- | tain of life,
and in your light | we see light.

Advent

The Spirit and the | church cry out:
Amen. | Come, Lord Jesus.
All those who await
his ap- | pearance pray:
Amen. | Come, Lord Jesus.
The whole cre- | ation pleads:
Amen. | Come, Lord Jesus.

Christmas—Baptism of Our Lord

The light shines ˈ in the darkness,
and the darkness has not ˈ overcome it.
The Word became flesh and ˈ lived among us,
and we have be- ˈ held Christ's glory.
To us a child is born, to us a ˈ Son is given.
In the Word was life, and the life was the light ˈ of all people.

Lent

Behold, now is the accept- ˈ able time;
now is the day ˈ of salvation.
Turn us again, O God of ˈ our salvation,
that the light of your face
   may ˈ shine on us.
May your justice shine ˈ like the sun;
and may the poor be ˈ lifted up.

Easter

Jesus Christ is risen ˈ from the dead.
Alleluia, alleluia, ˈ alleluia!
We are illumined
   by the brightness ˈ of his rising.
Alleluia, alleluia, ˈ alleluia!
Death has no more dominion ˈ over us.
Alleluia, alleluia, ˈ alleluia!

If the hymn of light and thanksgiving for light are omitted, the service continues with the psalmody on p. 312.

Hymn of Light

A hymn of praise to Christ the light (#229–231, 560–563) may be sung, during which candles may be lighted. When the large candle is used, other candles are lighted from its flame.

Thanksgiving for Light

The leader and the assembly give thanks, using the following or another appropriate form.

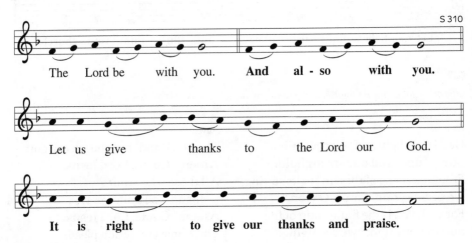

S 310

The Lord be with you. **And al - so with you.**

Let us give thanks to the Lord our God.

It is right to give our thanks and praise.

We give you thanks, O God, for in the beginning you called light in - to being,

and you set lights in the sky to govern night and day.

In a pillar of cloud by day and a pillar of fire by night

you led your peo - ple in - to freedom.

Enlighten our darkness by the light of your Christ; may your Word be

a lamp to our feet and a light to our path; for you are mer - ci - ful,

and you love your whole cre-a-tion, and with all your crea-tures we give you glory,

through your Son Je - sus Christ, in the unity of the Ho - ly Spirit,

now and for - ev - er. A - men.

The assembly is seated.

Psalmody

The psalmody begins with Psalm 141, a song of forgiveness and protection; Psalm 121; or another psalm appropriate for evening.

All (S 312)
Let my prayer rise be-fore you as in-cense;

the lift-ing up of my hands as the eve-ning sac-ri-fice.

Group One or All
O Lord, I call to you; come to me quick-ly; hear my voice when

All
I cry to you. Let my prayer rise be-fore you as in-cense;

the lift-ing up of my hands as the eve-ning sac-ri-fice.

Group Two or All
Set a watch be-fore my mouth, O Lord, and guard the door of my lips.

Group One or All
Let not my heart in-cline to an-y e-vil thing;

let me not be oc-cu-pied in wick-ed-ness with e-vil-

Group Two or All
do-ers. But my eyes are turned to you, Lord God;

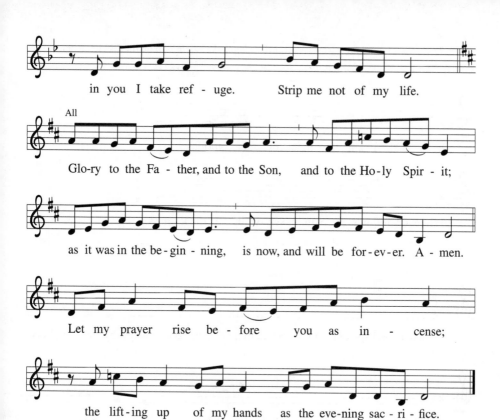

in you I take ref - uge. Strip me not of my life.

Glo-ry to the Fa - ther, and to the Son, and to the Ho-ly Spir - it;

as it was in the be-gin - ning, is now, and will be for-ev-er. A - men.

Let my prayer rise be - fore you as in - cense;

the lift-ing up of my hands as the eve-ning sac - ri - fice.

The psalmody may continue with one or more additional psalms. Each is followed by a time of silence, which may be concluded by a psalm prayer; the assembly responds **Amen.**

Song

Additional assembly song may follow the psalmody. A hymn appropriate to the time of day or the season is normally sung, the assembly standing.

Word

Readings

The assembly is seated.

The service includes one or more scripture readings. After the conclusion of each reading, the assembly may respond **Thanks be to God.**

The reading of scripture is followed by silence for reflection. Other forms of reflection may also follow, such as brief commentary, teaching, or personal witness; non-biblical readings; interpretation through music or other art forms; or guided conversation among those present.

The reflection may conclude with a scriptural dialogue. When it is sung, the following or a similar tone may be used, the assembly echoing the leader.

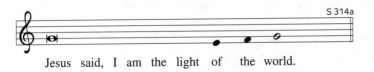

Jesus said, I am the light of the world.

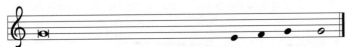

Whoever follows me will never walk in dark - ness.

OR

Long ago God spoke to our ancestors in many and various ways by the prophets,

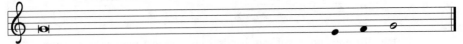

but in these last days God has spoken to us by the Son.

Gospel Canticle

The assembly stands to sing the gospel canticle for evening, the song of Mary, using the following or another musical version (#234–235; 251, 573, 723, 882).

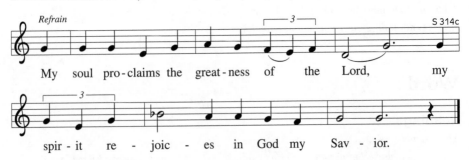

My soul pro-claims the great-ness of the Lord, my

spir - it re - joic - es in God my Sav - ior.

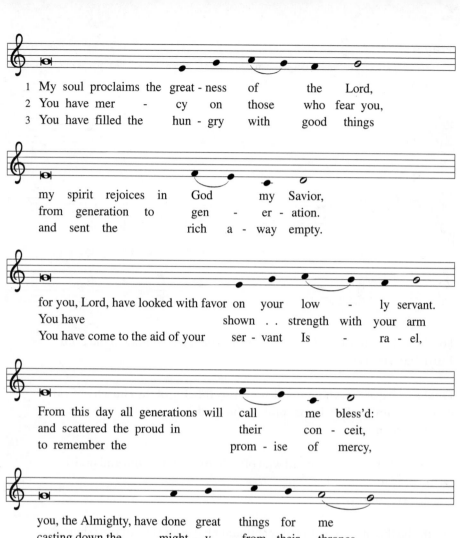

1 My soul proclaims the great-ness of the Lord,
2 You have mer - cy on those who fear you,
3 You have filled the hun-gry with good things

my spirit rejoices in God my Savior,
from generation to gen - er - ation.
and sent the rich a - way empty.

for you, Lord, have looked with favor on your low - ly servant.
You have shown .. strength with your arm
You have come to the aid of your ser - vant Is - ra - el,

From this day all generations will call me bless'd:
and scattered the proud in their con - ceit,
to remember the prom - ise of mercy,

you, the Almighty, have done great things for me
casting down the might - y from their thrones
the promise made to our . . . fore - bears,

Refrain

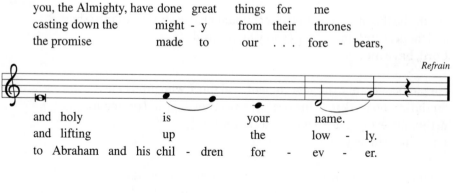

and holy is your name.
and lifting up the low - ly.
to Abraham and his chil - dren for - ev - er.

Prayers

The assembly kneels or stands. The following litany or another form of the prayers may be sung or spoken.

For the peace from above, and for our salvation, let us ⁣| pray to the Lord.
Lord, have mercy.

For the peace of the whole world, for the well-being of the church of God,
and for the unity of all, let us ⁣| pray to the Lord.
Lord, have mercy.

For this holy house, and for all who offer here their worship and praise,
let us ⁣| pray to the Lord.
Lord, have mercy.

For the health of the creation, for abundant harvests that all may share,
and for peaceful times, let us ⁣| pray to the Lord.
Lord, have mercy.

For public servants, the government, and those who protect us;
for those who work to bring peace, justice, healing, and protection
in this and every place, let us ⁣| pray to the Lord.
Lord, have mercy.

For those who travel, for those who are sick and suffering,
and for those who are in captivity, let us ⁣| pray to the Lord.
Lord, have mercy.

For deliverance in the time of affliction, wrath, danger, and need,
let us ᛁ pray to the Lord.
Lord, have mercy.

For _name/s and_ all servants of the church, for this assembly,
and for all people who await from the Lord great and abundant mercy,
let us ᛁ pray to the Lord.
Lord, have mercy.

Other petitions may be added.

Help, save, comfort, and defend us, gracious Lord.
A time of silence follows.

Giving thanks for all who have gone before us and are at rest, rejoicing in the
communion of _name/s and_ all the saints, we commend ourselves, one another, and
our whole life to you,

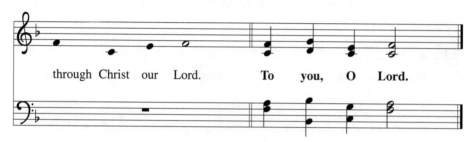

The litany may be followed by one or more additional prayers.

O God, you have called your servants to ventures of which we cannot see the
ending, by paths as yet untrodden, through perils unknown. Give us faith to go
out with good courage, not knowing where we go, but only that your hand is
leading us and your love supporting us; through Jesus Christ our Lord.
Amen.

OR

O God, from whom come all holy desires, all good counsels, and all just works:
give to us, your servants, that peace which the world cannot give, that our hearts
may be set to obey your commandments; and also that we, being defended from
the fear of our enemies, may live in peace and quietness; through Jesus Christ
our Savior, who lives and reigns with you and the Holy Spirit, God forever.
Amen.

We give thanks to you, heavenly Father, through Jesus Christ your dear Son, that you have graciously protected us today. We ask you to forgive us all our sins, where we have done wrong, and graciously to protect us tonight. Into your hands we commend ourselves: our bodies, our souls, and all that is ours. Let your holy angels be with us, so that the wicked foe may have no power over us. **Amen.**

The Lord's Prayer is sung or spoken.

S 318

Our Fa-ther in heav-en, hal-lowed be your name, your king-dom come, your will be done, on earth as in heav-en. Give us to-day our dai-ly bread. For-give us our sins as we for-give those who sin a-gainst us. Save us from the time of tri-al and de-liv-er us from e-vil. For the king-dom, the pow'r, and the glo-ry are yours, now and for-ev-er. A-men.

Blessing

Let us bless the Lord. **Thanks be to God.**

The leader continues:

The peace of God, which surpasses all understanding,

keep our hearts and our minds in Christ Je - sus. **A - men.**

OR

Almighty God, the Father, ✠ the Son, and the Holy Spirit, bless and pre-serve us.

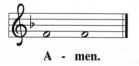

A - men.

A hymn may be sung.

The greeting of peace may be shared by all.

Night Prayer
Compline

Opening

After gathering in silence, the assembly stands.

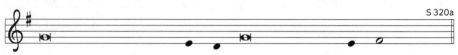

Almighty God grant us a qui - et night and peace at the last.

A - men.

One of the following dialogues is sung.

It is good to give thanks to the Lord, **to sing praise to your name, O Most High;**

to herald your love in the morning, **your truth at the close of the day.**

OR

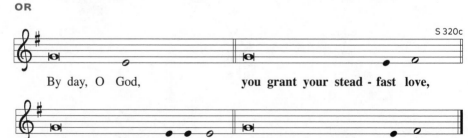

By day, O God, **you grant your stead - fast love,**

and at night your song is with me, **a prayer to the God of my life.**

Night Hymn

"All praise to thee, my God, this night" (#565) or another night hymn may be sung.

Confession and Forgiveness

The leader invites the assembly into the confession.

Let us confess our sin in the presence of God and of one another.

The assembly kneels or sits and keeps silence for self-examination.

The leader begins the confession.

Holy and gracious God,
I confess that I have sinned
against you this day.
Some of my sin I know—
the thoughts and words and deeds
of which I am ashamed—
but some is known only to you.
In the name of Jesus Christ
I ask forgiveness.
Deliver and restore me,
that I may rest in peace.

By the mercy of God
we are united with Jesus Christ,
in whom we are forgiven.
We rest now
in the peace of Christ
and rise in the morning to serve.

OR

I confess to God Almighty,
before the whole company of heaven,
and to you, my brothers and sisters,
that I have sinned by my own fault
in thought, word, and deed.
I pray God Almighty
to have mercy on me,
forgive me all my sins,
and bring me to everlasting life.
Almighty and merciful God
grant you healing, pardon, and
forgiveness of all your sins. Amen.

I confess to God Almighty, before
the whole company of heaven,
and to you,
my brothers and sisters,
that I have sinned by my own fault
in thought, word, and deed.
I pray God Almighty
to have mercy on me,
forgive me all my sins,
and bring me to everlasting life.
Almighty and merciful God
grant you healing, pardon, and
forgiveness of all your sins. Amen.

Psalmody

One or more psalms (such as 4, 33, 34, 91, 130, 134, 136) are sung or said. Each is followed by a time of silence, which may be concluded by a psalm prayer, to which the assembly responds **Amen.**

Song

A hymn or song appropriate to the time of day or the season may be sung.

Word

Reading

The service includes one of the following or another brief scripture reading.

You, O Lord, are in the midst of us, and we are called by your name; do not forsake us, O Lord our God. *(Jeremiah 14:9)*

Do not worry, saying, "What will we eat?" or "What will we drink?" or "What will we wear?" Indeed your heavenly Father knows that you need all these things. But strive first for the dominion and the righteousness of God, and all these things will be given to you as well. So do not worry about tomorrow. *(Matthew 6:31-34)*

Come to me, all you that are weary and are carrying heavy burdens, and I will give you rest. Take my yoke upon you, and learn from me; for I am gentle and humble in heart, and you will find rest for your souls. For my yoke is easy, and my burden is light. *(Matthew 11:28-30)*

Peace is my parting gift to you, my own peace, such as the world cannot give. Set your troubled hearts at rest, and banish your fears. *(John 14:27)*

I am convinced that neither death, nor life, nor angels, nor rulers, nor things present, nor things to come, nor powers, nor height, nor depth, nor anything else in all creation, will be able to separate us from the love of God in Christ Jesus our Lord. *(Romans 8:38-39)*

It is the God who said, "Let light shine out of darkness," who has shone in our hearts to give the light of the knowledge of the glory of God in the face of Jesus Christ. But we have this treasure in clay jars, so that it may be made clear that this extraordinary power belongs to God and does not come from us. *(2 Corinthians 4:6-7)*

Humble yourselves under God's mighty hand, so that God may exalt you in due time. Cast all your anxiety on the one who cares for you. Discipline yourselves, keep alert. Like a roaring lion, your adversary the devil prowls around, looking for someone to devour. Resist the devil, steadfast in your faith. *(1 Peter 5:6-9a)*

There will be no more night; the servants of God need no light of lamp or sun, for the Lord God will be their light, and they will reign forever and ever. *(Revelation 22:5)*

The reading of scripture is followed by extended silence for reflection and meditation. The silence may conclude with the following responsory.

S 323

In-to your hands, O Lord, I com - mend my spir - it.

In - to your hands I com - mend my spir - it.

You have re - deemed me, O Lord, God of truth.

In - to your hands I com - mend my spir - it.

Glory to the Fa - ther, and to the Son, and to the Ho - ly Spir - it.

In - to your hands I com - mend my spir - it.

Gospel Canticle

The assembly stands to sing the gospel canticle for night prayer, the song of Simeon, using the following or another musical version (#200–203, 313, 440). As an alternative, the canticle may be sung after the Lord's Prayer and before the concluding blessing.

Leader   S 324

Guide us wak - ing, O Lord, and guard us sleep - ing;

that a-wake we may watch with Christ and a-sleep we may rest in peace.

All

Now, Lord, you let your servant go in peace: your word has been ful-filled.

My own eyes have seen the sal - va - tion which you have prepared

in the sight of ev - 'ry peo - ple: a light to reveal you to the

na - tions and the glory of your peo - ple Is - ra - el.

Guide us wak - ing, O Lord, and guard us sleep - ing;

that a-wake we may watch with Christ and a-sleep we may rest in peace.

Prayers

Hear my prayer, O Lord; **listen to my cry.**

Keep me as the apple of your eye;

hide me in the shadow of your wings.

In righteousness I shall see you;

when I awake, your presence will give me joy.

One or more of the following prayers or other appropriate prayers may be prayed.

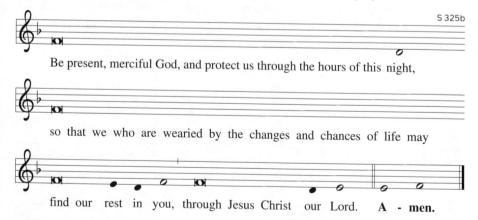

Be present, merciful God, and protect us through the hours of this night,

so that we who are wearied by the changes and chances of life may

find our rest in you, through Jesus Christ our Lord. **A - men.**

OR

O Lord, support us all the day long of this troubled life, until the shadows
lengthen and the evening comes and the busy world is hushed, the fever of life is
over, and our work is done. Then, in your mercy, grant us a safe lodging, and a
holy rest, and peace at the last, through Jesus Christ our Lord.
Amen.

OR

Be our light in the darkness, O God, and in your great mercy defend us from all perils and dangers of this night; for the love of your only Son, our Savior Jesus Christ. **Amen.**

OR

Keep watch, dear Lord, with those who work or watch or weep this night, and give your angels charge over those who sleep. Tend the sick, give rest to the weary, bless the dying, soothe the suffering, comfort the afflicted, shield the joyous; and all for your love's sake. **Amen.**

OR

Eternal God, the hours both of day and night are yours, and to you the darkness is no threat. Be present, we pray, with those who labor in these hours of night, especially those who watch and work on behalf of others. Grant them diligence in their watching, faithfulness in their service, courage in danger, and competence in emergencies. Help them to meet the needs of others with confidence and compassion; through Jesus Christ our Lord. **Amen.**

OR

Gracious God, we give you thanks for the day, especially for the good we were permitted to give and to receive; the day is now past and we commit it to you. We entrust to you the night; we rest securely, for you are our help, and you neither slumber nor sleep; through Jesus Christ our Lord. **Amen.**

The Lord's Prayer is sung or spoken.

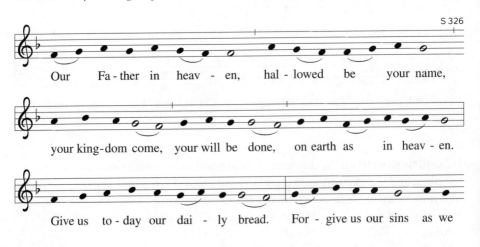

S 326

Our Fa-ther in heav-en, hal-lowed be your name, your king-dom come, your will be done, on earth as in heav-en. Give us to-day our dai-ly bread. For-give us our sins as we

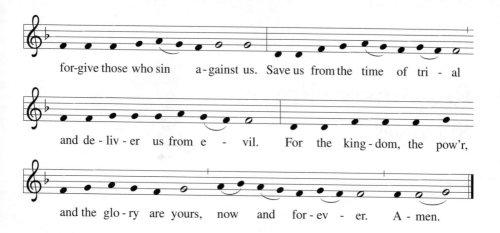

for-give those who sin a-gainst us. Save us from the time of tri - al
and de - liv - er us from e - vil. For the king - dom, the pow'r,
and the glo - ry are yours, now and for - ev - er. A - men.

Blessing

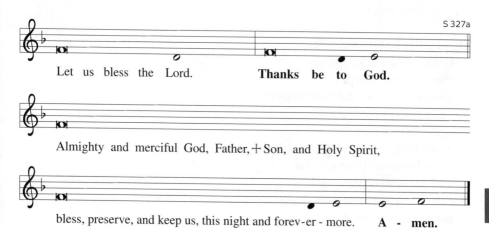

S 327a

Let us bless the Lord. **Thanks be to God.**

Almighty and merciful God, Father, + Son, and Holy Spirit,

bless, preserve, and keep us, this night and forev-er - more. **A - men.**

OR

S 327b

Now in peace I will lie down and sleep; **you alone, O God, make me se - cure.**

Let us bless the Lord. **Thanks be to God.**

The greeting of peace may be shared by all.

Responsive Prayer
Suffrages

Holy God, holy and mighty, holy and immortal,
have mercy on us.

Our Father in heaven,
   hallowed be your name,
   your kingdom come,
   your will be done, on earth as in heaven.
Give us today our daily bread.
Forgive us our sins
   as we forgive those who sin against us.
Save us from the time of trial
   and deliver us from evil.
For the kingdom, the power, and the glory are yours,
   now and forever. Amen.

I believe in God, the Father almighty,
   creator of heaven and earth.
I believe in Jesus Christ, God's only Son, our Lord,
   who was conceived by the Holy Spirit,
   born of the virgin Mary,
   suffered under Pontius Pilate,
   was crucified, died, and was buried;
   he descended to the dead.*
   On the third day he rose again;
   he ascended into heaven,
   he is seated at the right hand of the Father,
   and he will come to judge the living and the dead.

*Or, "he descended into hell," *another translation of this text in widespread use.*

I believe in the Holy Spirit,
   the holy catholic church,
   the communion of saints,
   the forgiveness of sins,
   the resurrection of the body,
   and the life everlasting. Amen.

Morning

O Lord, I cry to you for help.
In the morning
my prayer comes before you.

Let my mouth be full of your praise
and your glory all the day long.

Every day will I bless you,
and praise your name
forever and ever.

Awesome things will you show us
in your righteousness,
O God of our salvation,
O hope of all
the ends of the earth
and of the seas that are far away.

Bless the Lord, O my soul,
and all that is within me,
bless God's holy name.

You redeem my life from the grave,
and crown me with mercy
and steadfast love.

Lord, hear my prayer,
and let my cry come before you.

At other times

Show us your mercy, O God,
and grant us your salvation.

Give us the joy
of your saving help again,
and sustain us
with your bountiful Spirit.

Give peace in all the world;
for only in you can we live in safety.

Keep the nations under your care,
and guide us in the way
of justice and truth.

Let your way be known upon earth;
your saving health
among all nations.

Let not the needy be forgotten,
nor the hope of the poor
be taken away.

Create in me a clean heart, O God,
and sustain me
with your Holy Spirit.

Lord, hear my prayer,
and let my cry come before you.

The Lord be with you.
And also with you.

Let us pray.
The prayer of the day may be said.
Response after the prayer: **Amen.**

Additional prayers may be said. The final prayer is one appropriate to the time of day or the occasion.

Morning
We give thanks to you, heavenly Father, through Jesus Christ your dear Son, that you have protected us through the night from all harm and danger. We ask that you would also protect us today from sin and all evil, so that our life and actions may please you. Into your hands we commend ourselves: our bodies, our souls, and all that is ours. Let your holy angels be with us, so that the wicked foe may have no power over us.
Amen.

Noon
Gracious Jesus, our Lord and our God, at this hour you bore our sins in your own body on the tree so that we, being dead to sin, might live unto righteousness. Have mercy upon us now and at the hour of our death, and grant to us, your servants, with all others who devoutly remember your blessed Passion, a holy and peaceful life in this world and, through your grace, eternal glory in the life to come; where, with the Father and the Holy Spirit, you live and reign, God forever.
Amen.

Afternoon
O God, in you we live and move and have our being. Guide and govern us in this day by your Holy Spirit, that in all the cares and occupations of our life we may not forget you, but remember that always we are walking in your sight; through Jesus Christ our Lord.
Amen.

Evening
We give thanks to you, heavenly Father, through Jesus Christ your dear Son, that you have graciously protected us today. We ask you to forgive us all our sins, where we have done wrong, and graciously to protect us tonight. Into your hands we commend ourselves: our bodies, our souls, and all that is ours. Let your holy angels be with us, so that the wicked foe may have no power over us.
Amen.

Daily work

God our creator, you have given us work to do and call us to use our talents for the good of all. Guide us as we work, and teach us to live in the Spirit who made us your sons and daughters, in the love that made us sisters and brothers, through Jesus Christ, our Savior and Lord.
Amen.

Before travel

O God, our beginning and our end, you kept Abraham and Sarah in safety throughout the days of their pilgrimage, you led the children of Israel through the midst of the sea, and by a star you led the magi to the infant Jesus. Protect and guide us now as we set out to travel. Make our ways safe and our home-comings joyful, and bring us at last to our heavenly home, where you dwell in glory with our Lord Jesus Christ and the life-giving Holy Spirit, one God, now and forever.
Amen.

Let us bless the Lord.
Thanks be to God.

Almighty God bless us, defend us from all evil, and bring us to everlasting life.
Amen.

 # Psalms

Roots of Assembly Song

The song of the Christian assembly has its roots in the psalms of the Hebrew people, our forebears in faith. Jesus' own prayer relied on the psalms. The apostle Paul encouraged the faithful to sing "psalms, hymns, and spiritual songs to God" (Col. 3:16). Christians through the centuries have sung them daily.

Martin Luther considered the psalms the summary of all scripture, speaking to many situations and allowing the expression of a wide range of human response, such as adoration, praise, thanksgiving, lament, confession, intercession, and teaching. The psalms proclaim hope and faith, yet make room also for deep distress and questioning.

The 150 psalms presented here use a version intended for common sung prayer and proclamation, rather than a translation for study. Other singing versions of the psalms, including metrical paraphrases, are included among the service music and hymns in this volume. Translations of the psalms, such as the New Revised Standard Version, are readily available.

Singing the Psalms

The psalms are intended for singing, as their use in worship through the ages testifies. Their meaning can certainly be communicated when spoken or read silently; yet this ancient poetry is inherently musical. This psalm version is therefore pointed simply for singing by a cantor, choir, or assembly.

Each psalm verse is divided into two parts; the second half of the verse is indented. Each part has a point (ꞌ) within it. This point indicates when the singer moves from the reciting note (🔾) and continues with the rest of the melody. For example, the text of Psalm 98:4 appears as follows:

Shout with joy to the Lord, ꞌ all you lands;
lift up your voice, re- ꞌ joice, and sing.

When using tone 7, this verse is sung as follows:

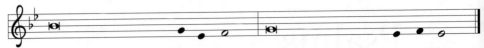

Shout with joy to the Lord, all you lands;   lift up your voice, re - joice and sing.

Whether sung by one person, a choir, or the assembly, it is important to remember that the melody is a vehicle for the natural expression of the words. The words should be sung with natural accents, as they would be if spoken. Rather than slowing down at the point ('), sing through to the end of the line.

The syllable just beyond the point is not necessarily a naturally accented syllable. In the first phrase of the example above, *Lord* naturally receives the accent instead of *all*. In the second phrase above, the natural accent falls on the second syllable of *rejoice* and therefore does receive the musical accent, although without a pause, as the singer moves from the reciting note through the rest of the melody. The same example, with natural accents underlined, may be sung as follows:

Shout with joy to the <u>Lord</u>, all you lands;   lift up your voice, re - <u>joice</u> and sing.

Singers may feel the natural accents in different places. However they are placed, it is important that the text is sung with a natural flow. A slight pause at a comma, and a slight break at a semicolon or period, will also assist in achieving this goal. The final note of each musical phrase will always correspond to the final accented syllable of the text; additional unaccented syllables that may follow are sung on the same note.

Occasionally a three-syllable word is sung to the two black notes by eliding the middle syllable. For example, *glo-ri-ous* becomes *glo-rious*, *of-fer-ing* becomes *of-f'ring*, *mar-vel-ous* becomes *mar-v'lous*. *Blessed* is sung *blest*.

Any psalm can be sung to any tone. Within a particular context, however, one tone may be a better match to the mood of the text than another. Tones 12–16 are double tones. That is, they have four phrases instead of two, so that two verses are sung to one tone. The system of singing described above is used. When using a double tone, be certain that there is an even number of verses in the psalm. Exceptions may be made if singers are prepared to use the last two phrases of the tone—or the first and last phrase—for the final, single verse.

The tones presented here are a core selection and are not meant to limit the possibilities for additional tones and musical forms the assembly may use in singing the psalms.

Psalm Tones

Psalms

1

[1] Happy are they who have not walked
in the counsel ǀ of the wicked,
  nor lingered in the way of sinners,
  nor sat in the seats ǀ of the scornful!

[2] Their delight is
in the law ǀ of the Lord,
  and they meditate
  on God's teaching
  ǀ day and night.

[3] They are like trees
planted by streams of water,
bearing fruit in due season,
with leaves that ǀ do not wither;
  everything they ǀ do shall prosper.

[4] It is not so ǀ with the wicked;
  they are like chaff
  which the wind ǀ blows away.

[5] Therefore the wicked shall not stand
upright when ǀ judgment comes,
  nor the sinner
  in the council ǀ of the righteous.

[6] For the Lord knows
the way ǀ of the righteous,
  but the way of the wicked
  shall ǀ be destroyed.

2

[1] Why are the nations ǀ in an uproar?
  Why do the peoples
  mutter ǀ empty threats?

[2] Why do the kings of the earth
rise up in revolt,
and the princes ǀ plot together,
  against the Lord and
  against the ǀ Lord's anointed?

3 "Let us break their ' yoke," they say;
  "let us cast off
    their ' bonds from us."

4 God whose throne is in heav- ' en
is laughing;
    the LORD holds them ' in derision.

5 Then in wrath God ' speaks to them
    and in rage fills ' them with terror.

6 "As for me, I have anoint- ' ed my king
    upon Zion, my ' holy mountain."

7 Let me announce
  the decree ' of the LORD,
    who said to me, "You are my son;
    this day have I be- ' gotten you.

8 Ask of me, and I will give you
  the nations for ' your inheritance
    and the ends of the earth
    for ' your possession.

9 You shall crush them with an ' iron rod
    and shatter them
    like a ' piece of pottery."

10 And now, you ' kings, be wise;
    be warned, you rulers ' of the earth.

11 Submit to the ' LORD with fear,
    and with trembling ' bow in worship;

12 lest the LORD be angry,
  and you perish
  in a sudden ' blaze of wrath.
    Happy are all
    who take ref- ' uge in God!

3

1 LORD, how many ' are my foes!
    How many there are
    who rise ' up against me!

2 How many there are who ' say to me,
    "Your God ' cannot help."

3 But you, O LORD,
  are a ' shield about me;
    you are my glory,
    the one who lifts ' up my head.

4 I call aloud to ' you, O LORD,
    and you answer me
    from your ' holy hill;

5 I lie down and ' go to sleep;
  I wake again,
    because ' you sustain me.

6 I do not fear the multi- ' tudes of people
    who set themselves
    against me ' all around.

7 Rise up, O LORD;
  set me free, ' O my God;
    surely, you will strike
    all my enemies across the face,
    you will break
    the teeth ' of the wicked.

8 Deliverance belongs ' to the LORD.
  Your blessing
    be up- ' on your people!

4

1 Answer me when I call, O God,
  defender ' of my cause;
    you set me free
    when I was in distress;
    have mercy on me
    and ' hear my prayer.

2 "You mortals, how long
  will you dishon- ' or my glory;
    how long will you love illusions
    and seek ' after lies?"

3 Know that the LORD
  does wonders ' for the faithful;
    the LORD will hear me ' when I call.

4 Tremble, then, and ' do not sin;
    speak to your heart in silence
    up- ' on your bed.

5 Offer the appointed ' sacrifices,
    and put your trust ' in the LORD.

6 Many are saying,
  "Who will show us ' any good?"
    Let the light of your face
    shine upon ' us, O LORD.

7 You have put gladness ' in my heart,
    more than when grain
    and ' wine abound.

8 In peace, I will lie ' down and sleep;
    for you alone, O LORD,
    make me ' rest secure.

5

¹ Give ear to my ⏐ words, O LORD;
 give heed ⏐ to my sighing.

² Listen to my cry for help,
 my king ⏐ and my God,
  for I ⏐ plead to you.

³ In the morning, LORD,
 you ⏐ hear my voice;
  early in the morning
  I make my appeal
  and ⏐ watch for you.

⁴ For you are not a God
 who takes plea- ⏐ sure in wickedness,
  and evil cannot ⏐ dwell with you.

⁵ Braggarts cannot stand ⏐ in your sight;
 you hate all those
  ⏐ who work wickedness.

⁶ You destroy those ⏐ who speak lies;
 the bloodthirsty and deceitful,
  O LORD, ⏐ you abhor.

⁷ But as for me,
 through the abundance
 of your steadfast love
 I will go in- ⏐ to your house;
  I will bow down
  toward your holy temple
  in ⏐ awe of you.

⁸ Lead me, LORD, in your righteousness,
 because of those
 who lie in ⏐ wait for me;
  make your way ⏐ straight before me.

⁹ For there is no truth in their mouth;
 there is destruction ⏐ in their heart;
  their throat is an open grave;
  they deceive ⏐ with their tongue.

¹⁰ Declare them guilty, O God;
 let them fall, because ⏐ of their schemes.
  Because of their many
  transgressions cast them out,
  for they have re- ⏐ belled against you.

¹¹ But all who take refuge in you
 will be glad;
 they will sing out their ⏐ joy forever.
  You will shelter them,
  so that those who love your name
  may ex- ⏐ ult in you.

¹² For you, O LORD,
 will ⏐ bless the righteous;
  you will defend them
  with your favor
  as ⏐ with a shield.

6

¹ LORD, do not rebuke me ⏐ in your anger;
 do not punish me ⏐ in your wrath.

² Have pity on me, LORD, for ⏐ I am weak;
 heal me, LORD,
  for my bones ⏐ quake in terror.

³ My spirit quakes in ⏐ awful terror;
 how long, O ⏐ LORD, how long?

⁴ Turn, O LORD, and de- ⏐ liver me;
 save me for the sake
 of your ⏐ steadfast love.

⁵ For in death no one re- ⏐ members you;
 and who will give you thanks
  ⏐ in the grave?

⁶ I grow weary because ⏐ of my groaning;
 every night I drench my pillow
 and flood my ⏐ bed with tears.

⁷ My eyes are wast- ⏐ ed with grief
 and worn away
 because of ⏐ all my enemies.

⁸ Depart from me, all ⏐ evildoers,
 for the LORD has heard
 the sound ⏐ of my weeping.

⁹ The LORD has heard my ⏐ supplication;
 the LORD ac- ⏐ cepts my prayer.

¹⁰ All my enemies shall be confounded
 and ⏐ quake with fear;
  they shall turn back
  and suddenly be ⏐ put to shame.

7

¹ O LORD my God, I take ref- ⏐ uge in you;
 save and deliver me
 from all ⏐ who pursue me;

² lest like a lion they tear ⏐ me in pieces
 and snatch me away
 with none to de- ⏐ liver me.

³ O Lord my God,
  if I have ˈ done these things:
    if there is any wickedness
    ˈ in my hands,

⁴ if I have repaid my ˈ friend with evil,
  or plundered my enemy
  ˈ without cause,

⁵ then let my enemy pursue
  and ˈ overtake me,
    trample my life into the ground,
    and lay my honor ˈ in the dust.

⁶ Stand up, O Lord, in your wrath;
  rise up against the fury
  ˈ of my enemies.
    Awake, O my God, ˈ decree justice.

⁷ Let the assembly
  of the peoples ˈ gather round you.
    Be seated on your lofty throne,
    ˈ O Most High.

⁸ O Lord, ˈ judge the nations;
  give judgment for me according
  to my righteousness, O Lord,
    and according to my innocence,
    ˈ O Most High.

⁹ Let the malice of the wicked
  come to an end,
  but estab- ˈ lish the righteous;
    for you test the mind and heart,
    O ˈ righteous God.

¹⁰ God is my shield ˈ and defense,
  the savior of the ˈ true in heart.

¹¹ God is a ˈ righteous judge;
  God sits in judgment ˈ every day.

¹² If they will not repent,
  God will sharp- ˈ en the sword,
    bend the bow and ˈ make it ready,

¹³ prepare instru- ˈ ments of death,
    and make arrows into ˈ shafts of fire.

¹⁴ Look at those
  who are in la- ˈ bor with wickedness,
    who conceive evil,
    and give birth ˈ to a lie.

¹⁵ They dig a pit and ˈ make it deep
    and fall into the hole
    that ˈ they have made.

¹⁶ Their malice turns back
  upon ˈ their own head;
    their violence falls
    on ˈ their own skull.

¹⁷ I will bear witness
  that the ˈ Lord is righteous;
    I will praise the name
    of the ˈ Lord Most High.

8

¹ O ˈ Lord our Lord,
    how majestic is your name
    in ˈ all the earth!—

² you whose glory is chanted
  above the heavens
  out of the mouths
  of in- ˈ fants and children;
    you have set up a fortress
    against your enemies,
    to silence the foe ˈ and avenger.

³ When I consider your heavens,
  the work ˈ of your fingers,
    the moon and the stars
    you have set ˈ in their courses,

⁴ what are mere mortals that you
  should be mind- ˈ ful of them,
    human beings that you
    should ˈ care for them?

⁵ Yet you have made them
  little less ˈ than divine;
    with glory and hon- ˈ or
    you crown them.

⁶ You have made them rule
  over the works ˈ of your hands;
    you have put all things
    un- ˈ der their feet:

⁷ all ˈ flocks and cattle,
    even the wild beasts ˈ of the field,

⁸ the birds of the air,
  the fish ˈ of the sea,
    and whatever passes along
    the paths ˈ of the sea.

⁹ O ˈ Lord our Lord,
    how majestic is your name
    in ˈ all the earth!

9

¹ I will give thanks to you, O Lord,
with ᴵ my whole heart;
    I will tell
    of all your ᴵ marvelous works.

² I will be glad and re- ᴵ joice in you;
I will sing to your name,
    ᴵ O Most High.

³ When my enemies are ᴵ driven back,
they will stumble and perish
    ᴵ at your presence.

⁴ For you have maintained
my right ᴵ and my cause;
    you sit upon your throne,
    O ᴵ righteous Judge.

⁵ You have rebuked the nations
and de- ᴵ stroyed the wicked;
    you have blotted out their name
    forev- ᴵ er and ever.

⁶ As for the enemy, they are finished,
in per- ᴵ petual ruin,
    their cities plowed under,
    the memory ᴵ of them perished;

⁷ but you, Lord,
are en- ᴵ throned forever;
    you have set up
    your ᴵ throne for judgment.

⁸ You rule the ᴵ world
with righteousness;
    you judge the peo- ᴵ ples
    with equity.

⁹ You, O Lord, will be a refuge
for ᴵ the oppressed,
    a refuge in ᴵ time of trouble.

¹⁰ Those who know your name
will put their ᴵ trust in you,
    for you never forsake those
    who seek ᴵ you, O Lord.

¹¹ Sing praise to the Lord,
who ᴵ dwells in Zion;
    proclaim to the peoples
    the things ᴵ God has done.

¹² The avenger of blood
will re- ᴵ member them
    and will not forget the cry
    of ᴵ the afflicted.

¹³ Be gracious to ᴵ me, O Lord;
see the misery I suffer
    from those who hate me,
    you that lift me up
    from the ᴵ gates of death;

¹⁴ so that I may tell of all your praises
and rejoice in ᴵ your salvation
    in the gates of the cit- ᴵ y of Zion.

¹⁵ The nations have fallen
into the ᴵ pit they dug;
    in the snare they set,
    their own ᴵ foot is caught.

¹⁶ The Lord is revealed
in ᴵ acts of justice;
    the wicked are trapped
    in the works of ᴵ their own hands.

¹⁷ The nations go down ᴵ to the grave,
all the peoples ᴵ that forget God.

¹⁸ For the needy
shall not always ᴵ be forgotten,
    nor shall the hope of the poor
    be tak- ᴵ en away.

¹⁹ Rise up, O Lord, let not mortals
have the ᴵ upper hand;
    let the nations
    be ᴵ judged before you.

²⁰ Put them in ᴵ fear, O Lord;
let the nations know
    they ᴵ are but mortal.

10

¹ Why do you stand so far ᴵ off, O Lord,
and hide yourself
    in ᴵ time of trouble?

² The wicked
arrogantly perse- ᴵ cute the poor,
    but they are trapped
    in the schemes they ᴵ have devised.

³ The wicked boast
of their ᴵ heart's desire;
    the covetous curse
    and re- ᴵ vile the Lord.

⁴ The wicked are so proud
that they care ᴵ not for God;
    they deny God with ᴵ every plot.

5 Their paths continually
 l twist and turn.
   Your lofty judgments
   are beyond them.
   They sneer l at their enemies.

6 They say in their heart,
 "I shall l not be shaken;
   no harm shall happen l to me ever."

7 Their mouth is full of cursing,
 deceit, l and oppression;
   under their tongue
   are mis- l chief and wrong.

8 They lurk in ambush
 in public squares,
 and in secret places
   they mur- l der the innocent;
   they spy l out the helpless.

9 They lie in wait, like a lion in cover;
 they lie in wait
 to seize up- l on the lowly;
   they seize the lowly
   and drag them away l in their net.

10 The innocent are broken
 and hum- l bled before them;
   the helpless fall
   be- l fore their power.

11 They say in their heart,
 "God l has forgotten;
   God has turned away
   and will l never notice."

12 Rise up, O Lord;
 lift up your l hand, O God;
   do not forget l the afflicted.

13 Why should the wick- l ed revile God?
   Why should they say in their heart,
   "You l do not care"?

14 Surely, you behold
 trouble and misery;
 you see it
 and take it into l your own hand.
   The helpless
   commit themselves to you,
   for you are the help- l er of orphans.

15 Break the power
 of the wick- l ed and evil;
   search out their wickedness
   until l you find none.

16 O Lord, you rule forev- l er and ever;
   the nations have vanished
   l from your land.

17 You have heard the desire
 of l the afflicted;
   you strengthen their heart
   and you listen l with your ear,

18 to give justice
 to the orphan l and oppressed,
   so that mere mortals
   may strike ter- l ror no more.

11

1 In the Lord I have l taken refuge;
   how then can you say to me,
   "Fly away like a bird l to the hilltop;

2 for see how the wicked string the bow
 and fit their arrows l to the string,
   to shoot from the shadows
   at the l true of heart.

3 When the foundations
 are be- l ing destroyed,
   what can the l righteous do?"

4 The Lord is in the holy temple,
 en- l throned in heaven.
   God's eyes keep careful watch,
   they l weigh our worth.

5 The Lord tests
 both righ- l teous and wicked
   but abhors those
   l who love violence.

6 Upon the wicked
 God shall rain coals of fire
 and l burning sulfur;
   a scorching wind shall l be their lot.

7 For the Lord is righteous,
 delighting in l righteous deeds;
   and the just shall l see God's face.

12

1 Help me, Lord,
 for there is no god- l ly one left;
   the faithful have vanished
   l from among us.

2 People tell lies ⎮ to each other;
　　they use smooth words
　　but speak from a ⎮ double heart.

3 May the LORD cut off
　all ⎮ lips that flatter,
　　and the tongues
　　⎮ that speak boastfully—

4 those who say,
　"With our tongue we ⎮ will prevail;
　　our lips are our own;
　　who is lord ⎮ over us?"

5 "Because the needy are oppressed,
　and the poor cry ⎮ out in misery,
　　I will rise up," says the LORD,
　　"and give them
　　the ⎮ help they long for."

6 The words of the ⎮ LORD are pure,
　like silver refined from ore
　and purified seven times
　⎮ in the fire.

7 O LORD, watch ⎮ over us
　and save us
　from this genera- ⎮ tion forever.

8 The wicked prowl on ⎮ every side,
　and everyone prizes
　that ⎮ which is worthless.

13

1 How long, O LORD?
　Will you forget ⎮ me forever?
　　How long
　　will you hide your ⎮ face from me?

2 How long
　shall I have perplexity in my mind,
　and grief in my heart,
　day ⎮ after day?
　　How long
　　shall my enemy triumph ⎮ over me?

3 Look upon me and answer me,
　O ⎮ LORD my God;
　　give light to my eyes,
　　lest I ⎮ sleep in death;

4 lest my enemy say,
　"I ⎮ have defeated you,"
　　and my foes rejoice
　　that ⎮ I have fallen.

5 But I trust in your un- ⎮ failing love;
　my heart is joyful
　because of your ⎮ saving help.

6 I will sing ⎮ to the LORD,
　who has dealt ⎮ with me richly.

14

1 Fools say in their hearts,
　"There ⎮ is no God."
　　They are corrupt, every deed is vile;
　　there is no one who does ⎮ any good.

2 The LORD looks down from heaven
　up- ⎮ on us all,
　　to see if there is anyone who is wise,
　　who seeks ⎮ after God.

3 They have all proved faithless;
　all alike ⎮ have turned bad;
　　there is none who does good;
　　⎮ no, not one.

4 Have they no knowledge,
　all those ⎮ evildoers
　　who eat up my people like bread
　　and do not call up- ⎮ on the LORD?

5 See how they trem- ⎮ ble with fear,
　because God is in the company
　⎮ of the righteous.

6 Your aim is to confound the plans
　of ⎮ the afflicted,
　　but the LORD ⎮ is their refuge.

7 Oh, that Israel's deliverance
　would come ⎮ out of Zion!
　　When the LORD restores
　　the fortunes of the people,
　　Jacob will rejoice
　　and Israel ⎮ will be glad.

15

1 LORD, who may dwell
　in your ⎮ tabernacle?
　　Who may abide upon your ⎮ holy hill?

2 Those who lead a blameless life
　and do ⎮ what is right,
　　who speak the truth
　　⎮ from their heart;

3 they do not slander with the tongue,
they do no evil ǀ to their friends;
    they do not cast discredit
    up- ǀ on a neighbor.

4 In their sight the wicked are rejected,
but they honor those
who ǀ fear the LORD.
    They have sworn upon their health
    and do not take ǀ back their word.

5 They do not give their money
in hope of gain,
nor do they take bribes
a- ǀ gainst the innocent.
    Those who do these things
    shall never be ǀ overthrown.

16

1 Protect me, O God,
for I take ref- ǀ uge in you;
I have said to the LORD,
"You are my Lord,
my good a- ǀ bove all other."

2 All my delight is in the godly
that are ǀ in the land,
    upon those who are noble
    a- ǀ mong the people.

3 But those who run after ǀ other gods
    shall have their troubles ǀ multiplied.

4 I will not pour out drink offerings
ǀ to such gods,
    never take their names
    up- ǀ on my lips.

5 O LORD, you are my portion
ǀ and my cup;
    it is you who up- ǀ hold my lot.

6 My boundaries
enclose a ǀ pleasant land;
    indeed, I have a ǀ rich inheritance.

7 I will bless the LORD
who ǀ gives me counsel;
    my heart teaches me
    night ǀ after night.

8 I have set the LORD
al- ǀ ways before me;
    because God is at my right hand,
    I shall ǀ not be shaken.

9 My heart, therefore, is glad,
and my spir- ǀ it rejoices;
    my body also shall ǀ rest in hope.

10 For you will not abandon me
ǀ to the grave,
    nor let your holy one ǀ see the pit.

11 You will show me the ǀ path of life;
    in your presence
    there is fullness of joy,
    and in your right hand
    are pleasures for- ǀ evermore.

17

1 Hear a just cause, O LORD;
give heed ǀ to my cry;
    listen to my prayer, which
    does not come from ǀ lying lips.

2 Let my vindication
come forth ǀ from your presence;
    let your eyes be ǀ fixed on justice.

3 Examine my heart, visit ǀ me by night,
    melt me down;
    you will find no impuri- ǀ ty in me.

4 I have not regarded what ǀ others do;
    at the word of your lips
    I have avoided
    the ways ǀ of the violent.

5 My footsteps hold fast
to your ǀ well-worn path;
    and my feet ǀ do not slip.

6 I call upon you, O God,
for you will ǀ answer me;
    incline your ear to me
    and ǀ hear my words.

7 Show me
your marvelous ǀ lovingkindness,
    O Savior of those
    who take refuge at your right hand
    from those who ǀ rise against them.

8 Keep me as the apple ǀ of your eye;
hide me
    under the shadow ǀ of your wings,

9 from the wicked ǀ who assault me,
    from my deadly enemies
    ǀ who surround me.

¹⁰ They have closed their ˈ callous hearts,
and their mouth
ˈ speaks proud things.

¹¹ They track me down;
now ˈ they surround me,
watching how they may
cast me ˈ to the ground,

¹² like a lion, greedy ˈ for its prey,
and like a young lion
lurking in ˈ secret places.

¹³ Arise, O Lord;
confront them and ˈ bring them down;
deliver me from the wicked
ˈ by your sword;

¹⁴ deliver me by your hand
from those whose portion in life
is ˈ in this world;
whose bellies you fill
with your treasure,
whose children have plenty,
who leave wealth
to their ˈ little ones.

¹⁵ But at my vindication
I shall ˈ see your face;
when I awake, I shall be satisfied,
behold- ˈ ing your likeness.

18

¹ I love you, O ˈ Lord my strength,
O Lord my stronghold,
my crag, ˈ and my haven;

² my God, my rock
in whom I ˈ put my trust,
my shield,
the horn of my salvation,
ˈ and my refuge.

³ I will call upon the Lord,
who is worthy ˈ to be praised,
and so shall I be saved
ˈ from my enemies.

⁴ The breakers of death rolled ˈ over me,
and the torrents of oblivion
made ˈ me afraid.

⁵ The cords of Sheol en- ˈ tangled me,
and the snares of death
were ˈ set for me.

⁶ I called upon the Lord in my distress
and cried out to my ˈ God for help.
From the heavens
the Lord heard my voice;
my cry ˈ reached God's ears.

⁷ The earth ˈ reeled and rocked;
the roots of the mountains shook;
they reeled because ˈ of God's anger.

⁸ Smoke rose from the Lord's nostrils
and a consuming fire
out ˈ of God's mouth;
hot burning ˈ coals blazed forth.

⁹ O Lord, you parted the heavens
ˈ and came down
with a storm cloud
un- ˈ der your feet.

¹⁰ You mounted on cheru- ˈ bim and flew;
you swooped
on the wings ˈ of the wind.

¹¹ You wrapped darkness
a- ˈ bout yourself;
you made dark waters
and thick clouds ˈ your pavilion.

¹² From the brightness of your presence,
ˈ through the clouds,
burst hailstones and ˈ coals of fire.

¹³ You thundered ˈ out of heaven;
O Most High,
you ut- ˈ tered your voice.

¹⁴ You loosed arrows
and ˈ scattered them,
hurled thunderbolts
and ˈ routed them.

¹⁵ The beds of the seas were uncovered,
and the foundations
of the ˈ world laid bare,
at your roaring, O Lord,
at the blast
of the breath ˈ of your nostrils.

¹⁶ You reached down
from on ˈ high and grasped me;
you drew me out ˈ of great waters.

¹⁷ You delivered me
from my strong enemies
and from those who ˈ hated me,
for they were too might- ˈ y for me.

¹⁸ They confronted me
   in the day of ˡ my disaster;
      but you, LORD, were ˡ my support.

¹⁹ You brought me out
   into an ˡ open place;
      you rescued me
      because you delight- ˡ ed in me.

²⁰ The LORD rewarded me
   because of my ˡ righteous dealing;
      because my hands were clean
      God re- ˡ warded me;

²¹ for I have kept the ways ˡ of the LORD
   and have not offended
      a- ˡ gainst my God;

²² for all God's judgments ˡ are before me,
   and the decrees of the LORD
      I have not put a- ˡ way from me;

²³ for I have been blame- ˡ less with God
   and have kept myself
      ˡ from iniquity;

²⁴ therefore the LORD rewarded me
   according to my ˡ righteous dealing,
      because of the cleanness
      of my hands ˡ in God's sight.

²⁵ With the faithful
   you show yourself faith- ˡ ful, O God;
      with the blameless
      you show ˡ yourself blameless.

²⁶ With the pure
   you show ˡ yourself pure,
      but with the crooked ˡ you are wily.

²⁷ Indeed, you will save a ˡ lowly people,
   but you will humble
      the ˡ haughty eyes.

²⁸ Surely you, O LORD, ˡ light my lamp;
   my God makes my ˡ darkness bright.

²⁹ With you
   I will break down ˡ an enclosure;
      with the help of my God
      I will scale ˡ any wall.

³⁰ Your way, O God, is perfect;
   your word is re- ˡ fined in fire;
      you are a shield
      to all who ˡ trust in you.

³¹ For who is God, ˡ but the LORD?
   Who is the rock, ex- ˡ cept our God?

³² It is God
   who girds me a- ˡ bout with strength
      and makes my ˡ way secure.

³³ O LORD,
   you make me sure-footed ˡ like a deer
      and let me stand firm
      ˡ on the heights.

³⁴ You train my ˡ hands for battle
   and my arms for bending
      even a ˡ bow of bronze.

³⁵ You have given me
   your ˡ shield of victory;
      your right hand also sustains me;
      your loving care ˡ makes me great.

³⁶ You lengthen my ˡ stride beneath me,
   and my ankles do ˡ not give way.

³⁷ I pursue my enemies
   and ˡ overtake them;
      I will not turn back
      till I ˡ have destroyed them.

³⁸ I strike them down,
   and they ˡ cannot rise;
      they fall defeated ˡ at my feet.

³⁹ You have girded me
   with strength ˡ for the battle;
      you have cast down
      my adversar- ˡ ies beneath me.

⁴⁰ You have put my ene- ˡ mies to flight;
   I destroy ˡ those who hate me.

⁴¹ They cry out,
   but there is ˡ none to save them;
      they cry to the LORD,
      but no ˡ answer comes.

⁴² I grind them small
   like dust be- ˡ fore the wind;
      I empty them out
      like mud in- ˡ to the streets.

⁴³ You deliver me
   from the strife of the peoples;
      you put me at the head
      ˡ of the nations;
         a people I have not ˡ known
         shall serve me.

⁴⁴ No sooner shall they hear
   than they ˡ shall obey me;
      strangers will ˡ cringe before me.

⁴⁵ The foreign peoples I will lose heart;
they shall come trembling
out I of their strongholds.

⁴⁶ The LORD lives! Blessed I is my rock!
Exalted is the God of I my salvation!

⁴⁷ This is the God who vindi- I cated me
and cast down the peo- I ples
beneath me.

⁴⁸ You rescued me from my enemies;
even over those who attacked me
I you exalted me;
you saved me from my I deadly foe.

⁴⁹ Therefore I will extol you
among the na- I tions, O LORD,
and sing praises I to your name.

⁵⁰ You multiply the victories I of your king;
you keep faith with your anointed,
with David and his descen- I dants
forever.

19

¹ The heavens declare
the glo- I ry of God,
and the sky proclaims
its I maker's handiwork.

² One day tells its tale I to another,
and one night
imparts knowledge I to another.

³ Although they have
no I words or language,
and their voices I are not heard,

⁴ their sound has gone out into all lands,
and their message
to the ends I of the world,
where God has pitched a tent
I for the sun.

⁵ It comes forth like a bridegroom
out I of his chamber;
it rejoices like a champion
to I run its course.

⁶ It goes forth
from the uttermost edge of the heavens
and runs about to the end of I it again;
nothing is hidden
from its I burning heat.

⁷ The teaching of the LORD is perfect
and re- I vives the soul;
the testimony of the LORD is sure
and gives wisdom I to the simple.

⁸ The statutes of the LORD are just
and re- I joice the heart;
the commandment of the LORD
is clear and gives light I to the eyes.

⁹ The fear of the LORD is clean
and en- I dures forever;
the judgments of the LORD
are true and righteous I altogether.

¹⁰ More to be desired are they than gold,
more than I much fine gold,
sweeter far than honey,
than honey I in the comb.

¹¹ By them also
is your ser- I vant enlightened,
and in keeping them
there is I great reward.

¹² Who can detect one's I own offenses?
Cleanse me from my I secret faults.

¹³ Above all, keep your servant
from presumptuous sins;
let them not get dominion I over me;
then shall I be whole and sound,
and innocent of a I great offense.

¹⁴ Let the words of my mouth
and the meditation of my heart
be acceptable I in your sight,
O LORD, my strength
and I my redeemer.

20

¹ May the LORD
answer you in the I day of trouble,
the name of the God of Ja- I cob
defend you;

² send you help from the I sanctuary
and strengthen you I out of Zion;

³ may the LORD
remember I all your offerings
and accept I your burnt sacrifice;

⁴ grant you your I heart's desire
and prosper I all your plans.

5 We will shout for joy at your victory
and unfurl our banners
in the name | of our God;
    may the LORD
    grant all | your requests.

6 Now I know that the LORD
gives victory to the a- | nointed one;
    God will answer out of holy heaven,
    gaining victory
    with a | strong right hand.

7 Some trust in chariots
and | some in horses,
    but we rely
    on the name of the | LORD our God.

8 They collapse | and fall down,
    but we will arise | and stand upright.

9 O LORD, give victory | to the king
and answer us | when we call.

21

1 The king rejoices in your | strength,
O LORD;
    how greatly he exults
    | in your victory!

2 You have given him his | heart's desire;
    you have not denied him
    the request | of his lips.

3 For you meet him
with blessings | of prosperity,
    and set a crown of fine gold
    up- | on his head.

4 He asked you for life,
and you gave | it to him:
    length of days, forev- | er and ever.

5 His honor is great,
because | of your victory;
    splendor and majesty
    you be- | stow upon him.

6 For you will give him
ever- | lasting blessings
    and will make him glad
    with the joy | of your presence.

7 For the king puts his trust | in the LORD;
    because of the lovingkindness
    of the Most High,
    he | will not fall.

8 Your hand will find | all your enemies;
    your right hand will find
    | all who hate you.

9 You will make them like a fiery furnace
at the time
of your appear- | ing, O LORD;
    you will swallow them up
    in your wrath,
    and fire | shall consume them.

10 You will destroy their offspring
| from the land
    and their descendants from among
    the peoples | of the earth.

11 Though they intend evil against you
and devise | wicked schemes,
    yet they shall | not prevail.

12 For you will put | them to flight
    and aim your ar- | rows at them.

13 Be exalted, O LORD, | in your might;
    we will sing and | praise your power.

22

1 My God, my God,
why have you for- | saken me?
    Why so far from saving me, so far
    from the words | of my groaning?

2 My God, I cry out by day,
but you | do not answer;
    by night, but I | find no rest.

3 Yet you are the | Holy One,
    enthroned on the prais- | es of Israel.

4 Our ancestors put their | trust in you,
    they trusted,
    and you | rescued them.

5 They cried out to you
and | were delivered;
    they trusted in you
    and were not | put to shame.

6 But as for me,
I am a worm | and not human,
    scorned by all
    and despised | by the people.

7 All who see me laugh | me to scorn;
    they curl their lips;
    they | shake their heads.

⁸ "Trust in the LORD;
 let the | LORD deliver;
  let God rescue him
  if God so de- | lights in him."

⁹ Yet you are the one
 who drew me forth | from the womb,
  and kept me safe
  on my | mother's breast.

¹⁰ I have been entrusted to you
 ever since | I was born;
  you were my God when I was still
  in my | mother's womb.

¹¹ Be not far from me,
 for trou- | ble is near,
  and there is no | one to help.

¹² Many young bulls en- | circle me;
  strong bulls of Ba- | shan
  surround me.

¹³ They open wide their | jaws at me,
  like a slashing and | roaring lion.

¹⁴ I am poured out like water;
 all my bones are | out of joint;
  my heart within my breast
  is | melting wax.

¹⁵ My strength is dried up
 like a potsherd;
 my tongue sticks to the roof
 | of my mouth;
  and you have laid me
  in the | dust of death.

¹⁶ Packs of dogs close me in,
 a band of evildoers
 | circles round me;
  they pierce my hands | and my feet.

¹⁷ I can count | all my bones
  while they stare at | me and gloat.

¹⁸ They divide my gar- | ments
 among them;
  for my clothing, | they cast lots.

¹⁹ But you, O LORD, be not | far away;
  O my help, hasten | to my aid.

²⁰ Deliver me | from the sword,
  my life from the power | of the dog.

²¹ Save me from the | lion's mouth!
  From the horns of wild bulls
  you have | rescued me.

²² I will declare your name | to my people;
  in the midst of the assembly
  | I will praise you.

²³ You who fear the LORD, give praise!
  All you of Jacob's | line, give glory.
   Stand in awe of the LORD,
   all you off- | spring of Israel.

²⁴ For the LORD does not despise
  nor abhor the poor in their poverty;
  neither is the LORD's face
  hid- | den from them;
   but when they cry out,
   | the LORD hears them.

²⁵ From you comes my praise
  in the | great assembly;
   I will perform my vows
   in the sight of those
   who | fear the LORD.

²⁶ The poor shall eat | and be satisfied.
   Let those who seek the LORD
   give praise!
   May your hearts | live forever!

²⁷ All the ends of the earth
  shall remember and turn | to the LORD;
   all the families of nations
   shall bow | before God.

²⁸ For dominion belongs | to the LORD,
   who rules o- | ver the nations.

²⁹ Indeed, all who sleep in the earth
  shall bow | down in worship;
   all who go down to the dust,
   though they be dead,
   shall kneel be- | fore the LORD.

³⁰ Their descendants
  shall | serve the LORD,
   whom they shall proclaim
   to genera- | tions to come.

³¹ They shall proclaim God's deliverance
  to a people | yet unborn,
   saying to them,
   "The | LORD has acted!"

23

1 The LORD | is my shepherd;
  I shall not | be in want.

2 The LORD makes me lie down
 | in green pastures
    and leads me be- | side still waters.

3 You restore my | soul, O LORD,
    and guide me along right pathways
     | for your name's sake.

4 Though I walk through the valley
 of the shadow of death,
 I shall | fear no evil;
    for you are with me;
    your rod and your staff,
    they | comfort me.

5 You prepare a table before me
 in the presence | of my enemies;
    you anoint my head with oil,
    and my cup is | running over.

6 Surely goodness and mercy
  shall follow me
  all the days | of my life,
    and I will dwell
    in the house of the | LORD forever.

24

1 The earth is the LORD's
 and all | that is in it,
    the world and those
    who | dwell therein.

2 For the LORD has founded it
 up- | on the seas
    and established it up- | on the rivers.

3 Who may ascend
 the mountain | of the LORD,
    and who may stand
    in God's | holy place?

4 Those of innocent hands
 and puri- | ty of heart,
    who do not swear on God's being,
    nor do they pledge by | what is false.

5 They shall receive blessing
 | from the LORD
    and righteousness
    from the God of | their salvation.

6 Such is the generation
 of those who seek | you, O LORD,
    of those who seek your face,
    O | God of Jacob.

7 Lift up your heads, O gates;
  and be lifted up, O ever- | lasting doors,
    that the King of glory | may come in.

8 Who is this | King of glory?
  The LORD, strong and mighty,
  the LORD, might- | y in battle!

9 Lift up your heads, O gates;
  and be lifted up, O ever- | lasting doors,
    that the King of glory | may come in.

10 Who is this | King of glory?
  Truly, the LORD of hosts
  is the | King of glory.

25

1 To | you, O LORD,
  I lift | up my soul.

2 My God, I put my trust in you;
  let me not be | put to shame,
    nor let my enemies
    triumph | over me.

3 Let none who look to you
  be | put to shame;
    rather let those be put to shame
     | who are treacherous.

4 Show me your | ways, O LORD,
    and teach | me your paths.

5 Lead me in your | truth and teach me,
    for you are the God of my salvation;
    in you have I trusted
    all | the day long.

6 Remember, O LORD,
  your compas- | sion and love,
    for they are from | everlasting.

7 Remember not the sins of my youth
  and | my transgressions;
    remember me
    according to your steadfast love
    and for the sake
    of your good- | ness, O LORD.

8 You are gracious and up- | right,
O Lord;
        therefore you teach sinners
        | in your way.

9 You lead the low- | ly in justice
        and teach the low- | ly your way.

10 All your paths, O Lord,
    are steadfast | love and faithfulness
        to those who keep your covenant
        and your | testimonies.

11 For your name's | sake, O Lord,
        forgive my sin, for | it is great.

12 Who are they who | fear the Lord?
        You will teach them the way
        that | they should choose.

13 They shall dwell | in prosperity,
        and their offspring
        shall inher- | it the land.

14 You, Lord, are a friend
    to | those who fear you,
        and will show | them your covenant.

15 My eyes are ever looking
    to | you, O Lord,
        for you will pluck my feet
        out | of the net.

16 Turn to me and have pit- | y on me,
        for I am left alone | and in misery.

17 The sorrows of my heart
    | have increased;
        bring me out | of my troubles.

18 Look upon my adversi- | ty and misery
        and forgive me | all my sin.

19 Look upon my enemies,
    for | they are many,
        and they bear a violent ha- | tred
        against me.

20 Protect my life and de- | liver me;
        let me not be put to shame,
        for I have trust- | ed in you.

21 Let integrity and upright- | ness
    preserve me,
        for my hope has | been in you.

22 Deliver Isra- | el, O God,
        out of | all its troubles.

26

1 Give judgment for me, O Lord,
    for I have lived | with integrity;
        I have trusted in the Lord
        and | have not faltered.

2 Test me, O | Lord, and try me;
        examine my heart | and my mind.

3 For your steadfast love
    is be- | fore my eyes;
        I have walked
        faithful- | ly with you.

4 I have not sat | with the worthless,
        nor do I consort
        with | the deceitful.

5 I have hated the company
    of | evildoers;
        I will not sit down
        | with the wicked.

6 I will wash my hands
    in inno- | cence, O Lord,
        that I may go in procession
        | round your altar,

7 singing aloud
    a song | of thanksgiving
        and recounting
        all your won- | derful deeds.

8 Lord, I love the house
    in | which you dwell
        and the place
        where your glo- | ry abides.

9 Do not sweep me a- | way
    with sinners,
        nor my life
        with those who | thirst for blood,

10 whose hands are full of | evil plots,
        and their right hands
        | full of bribes.

11 As for me, I will live | with integrity;
        redeem me,
        and be gra- | cious to me.

12 I take my stand on | level ground;
        in the full assembly
        I will | bless the Lord.

27

1 The LORD is my light and my salvation;
whom then ' shall I fear?
The LORD is the stronghold
of my life;
of whom shall I ' be afraid?

2 When evildoers close in against me
to de- ' vour my flesh,
they, my foes and my enemies,
will stum- ' ble and fall.

3 Though an army encamp against me,
my heart ' will not fear.
Though war rise up against me,
my trust will ' not be shaken.

4 One thing I ask of the LORD;
one ' thing I seek;
that I may dwell in the house
of the LORD all the days of my life;
to gaze upon the beauty of the LORD
and to seek God ' in the temple.

5 For in the day of trouble
God will ' give me shelter,
hide me in the hidden places
of the sanctuary,
and raise me high up- ' on a rock.

6 Even now my head is lifted up
above my enemies ' who surround me.
Therefore I will offer sacrifice
in the sanctuary,
sacrifices of rejoicing;
I will sing and make music
' to the LORD.

7 Hear my voice, O LORD, ' when I call;
have mercy on me and ' answer me.

8 My heart speaks your message—
' "Seek my face."
Your face, O LORD, ' I will seek.

9 Hide not your face from me,
turn not away
from your ser- ' vant in anger.
Cast me not away—
you have been my helper;
forsake me not,
O God of ' my salvation.

10 Though my father and my moth- ' er
forsake me,
the LORD will ' take me in.

11 Teach me your ' way, O LORD;
lead me on a level path,
because of ' my oppressors.

12 Subject me not to the will ' of my foes,
for they rise up against me,
false witnesses ' breathing violence.

13 This I believe—that I will see
the goodness ' of the LORD
in the land ' of the living!

14 Wait for the LORD ' and be strong.
Take heart and wait ' for the LORD!

28

1 O LORD, I call to you;
my rock, do not be deaf ' to my cry;
lest, if you do not hear me,
I become like those
who go down ' to the pit.

2 Hear the voice of my prayer
when I cry ' out to you,
when I lift up my hands
to your ho- ' ly of holies.

3 Do not snatch me away
with the wicked or with the ' evildoers,
who speak peaceably
with their neighbors,
while strife is ' in their hearts.

4 Repay them according to their deeds,
and according to the wickedness
' of their actions.
According to the work
of their hands repay them,
and give them their ' just deserts.

5 They have no understanding
of the LORD's works
or the deeds ' of God's hands;
therefore God will break them down
and not ' build them up.

6 Blessed ' be the LORD,
who has heard the voice
' of my prayer.

7 You, LORD, are my strength
and my shield; my heart trusts in you,
and I ' have been helped;
so my heart exults, and
with my song I give ' thanks to you.

8 You, Lord, are the strength
  | of your people,
    a safe refuge for | your anointed.
9 Save your people
  and bless | your inheritance;
    shepherd them
    and carry | them forever.

29

1 Ascribe to the | Lord, you gods,
  ascribe to the Lord
    glo- | ry and strength.
2 Ascribe to the Lord
  the glory | due God's name;
    worship the Lord
    in the beau- | ty of holiness.
3 The voice of the Lord
  is upon the waters;
    the God of | glory thunders;
      the Lord is upon the | mighty waters.
4 The voice of the Lord
  is a pow- | erful voice;
    the voice of the Lord
    is a | voice of splendor.
5 The voice of the Lord
  breaks the | cedar trees;
    the Lord
    breaks the ce- | dars of Lebanon;
6 the Lord makes Lebanon
  skip | like a calf,
    and Mount Hermon
    like a | young wild ox.
7 The voice | of the Lord
  bursts forth in | lightning flashes.
8 The voice of the Lord
  | shakes the wilderness;
    the Lord
    shakes the wilder- | ness of Kadesh.
9 The voice of the Lord makes the oak
  trees writhe and strips the | forests bare.
    And in the temple of the Lord
    all are | crying, "Glory!"
10 The Lord sits enthroned
  a- | bove the flood;
    the Lord sits enthroned
    as king for- | evermore.

11 O Lord, give strength | to your people;
  give them, O Lord,
    the bless- | ings of peace.

30

1 I will exalt you, O Lord,
  because you have lift- | ed me up
    and have not let my enemies
    triumph | over me.
2 O Lord my God, I cried | out to you,
  and you restored | me to health.
3 You brought me up, O Lord,
  | from the dead;
    you restored my life
    as I was going down | to the grave.
4 Sing praise to the Lord,
  | all you faithful;
    give thanks in ho- | ly remembrance.
5 God's wrath is short;
  God's favor | lasts a lifetime.
    Weeping spends the night,
    but joy comes | in the morning.
6 While I felt se- | cure, I said,
  "I shall never | be disturbed.
7 You, Lord, with your favor,
  made me as strong | as the mountains."
    Then you hid your face,
    and I was | filled with fear.
8 I cried to | you, O Lord;
  I pleaded with | my Lord, saying,
9 "What profit is there in my blood,
  if I go down | to the pit?
    Will the dust praise you
    or de- | clare your faithfulness?
10 Hear, O Lord,
  and have mer- | cy upon me;
    O Lord, | be my helper."
11 You have turned my wailing
  | into dancing;
    you have put off my sackcloth
    and clothed | me with joy.
12 Therefore my heart sings to you
  | without ceasing;
    O Lord my God,
    I will give you | thanks forever.

31

1 In you, O LORD, have I taken refuge;
let me never be ǀ put to shame;
    deliver me ǀ in your righteousness.

2 Incline your ǀ ear to me;
    make haste to de- ǀ liver me.

3 Be my strong rock,
a castle to keep me safe,
for you are my crag ǀ and my stronghold;
    for the sake of your name,
    lead ǀ me and guide me.

4 Take me out of the net
that they have secretly ǀ set for me,
    for you are my tow- ǀ er of strength.

5 Into your hands
I com- ǀ mend my spirit,
    for you have redeemed me,
    O LORD, ǀ God of truth.

6 I hate those who cling
to ǀ worthless idols,
    and I put my trust ǀ in the LORD.

7 I will rejoice and be glad
because of your ǀ steadfast love;
    for you have seen my affliction;
    you know ǀ my distress.

8 You have not handed me over
to the power ǀ of the enemy;
    you have set my feet
    in an ǀ open place.

9 Have mercy on me, O LORD,
for I ǀ am in trouble;
    my eye is consumed with sorrow,
    and also my throat ǀ and my belly.

10 For my life is wasted with grief,
and my ǀ years with sighing;
    my strength fails me
    because of affliction,
    and my bones ǀ are consumed.

11 I am the scorn of all my enemies,
a disgrace to my neighbors,
a dismay to ǀ my acquaintances;
    when they see me in the street
    ǀ they avoid me.

12 Like the dead I am forgotten,
ǀ out of mind;
    I am as useless as a ǀ broken pot.

13 For I have heard
the whispering of the crowd;
fear is ǀ all around;
    they put their heads together
    against me;
    they plot to ǀ take my life.

14 But as for me,
I have trusted in ǀ you, O LORD.
    I have said, "You ǀ are my God.

15 My times are ǀ in your hand;
    rescue me
    from the hand of my enemies,
    and from those who ǀ persecute me.

16 Let your face shine
up- ǀ on your servant;
    save me in your ǀ steadfast love."

17 LORD, let me not be put to shame,
for I have ǀ called on you;
    rather, let the wicked
    be put to shame;
    let them be silenced ǀ by the grave.

18 Let the lying lips be silenced
that speak a- ǀ gainst the righteous,
    haughtily, disdainfully,
    and ǀ with contempt.

19 How great is your goodness,
which you have laid up
for ǀ those who fear you;
    which you have done
    in the sight of all
    for those
    who put their ǀ trust in you.

20 You hide them
in the protection of your presence
from those who ǀ slander them;
    you keep them in your shelter
    from the ǀ strife of tongues.

21 Blessed are ǀ you, O LORD!
    for you have shown me
    the wonders of your love
    when I was ǀ under siege.

22 I said in my alarm,
"I have been cut off from the sight
ǀ of your eyes."
    Nevertheless,
    you heard the sound of my plea
    when I cried ǀ out to you.

23 Love the LORD, | all you saints;
    the LORD protects the faithful,
      but repays in full
      those | who act haughtily.

24 Be strong
  and let your | heart take courage,
    all you who wait | for the LORD.

32

1 Happy are they
  whose transgressions | are forgiven,
    and whose sin is | put away!

2 Happy are they
  to whom the LORD im- | putes no guilt,
    and in whose spirit
    there | is no guile!

3 While I held my tongue,
  my bones with- | ered away,
    because of my groaning
    | all day long.

4 For your hand was heavy upon me
  | day and night;
    my moisture was dried up
    as in the | heat of summer.

5 Then I acknowledged my sin to you,
  and did not con- | ceal my guilt.
    I said, "I will confess
    my transgressions to the LORD."
    Then you forgave me
    the guilt | of my sin.

6 Therefore all the faithful will make
  their prayers to you in | time of trouble;
    when the great waters overflow,
    they | shall not reach them.

7 You are my hiding-place;
  you preserve | me from trouble;
    you surround me
    with shouts | of deliverance.

8 "I will instruct you and teach you
  in the way that | you should go;
    I will guide you | with my eye.

9 Do not be like horse or mule,
  which have no | understanding;
    who must be fitted
    with bit and bridle,
    or else they will | not stay near you."

10 Great are the tribulations
  | of the wicked;
    but mercy embraces those
    who trust | in the LORD.

11 Be glad, you righteous,
  and rejoice | in the LORD;
    shout for joy,
    all who are | true of heart.

33

1 Rejoice in the | LORD, you righteous;
  praise is fitting | for the upright.

2 Praise the LORD | with the lyre;
  make music for God
    with a | ten-stringed harp.

3 Sing for the LORD | a new song;
  play your instrument skillfully
    with | joyful sounds.

4 For your word, O | LORD, is right,
  and faithful are | all your works.

5 You love righteous- | ness and justice;
  your steadfast love
    fills | the whole earth.

6 By your word were the | heavens made,
  by the breath of your mouth
    all the | hosts of heaven.

7 You gather up the waters of the ocean
  as | in a water-skin
    and store up the depths | of the sea.

8 Let all the earth | fear the LORD;
  let all who dwell in the world
    | stand in awe.

9 For God spoke, and it | came to pass;
  God commanded, and | it stood fast.

10 The LORD brings the will
  of the na- | tions to nothing
    and thwarts the designs
    | of the peoples.

11 Your will, O LORD, stands | fast forever,
  and the designs of your heart
    from | age to age.

12 Happy is the nation
  whose God | is the LORD!
    Happy the people
    chosen to | be God's heritage!

¹³ The LORD looks ᛁ down from heaven,
and sees all ᛁ humankind.

¹⁴ God sits firmly en- ᛁ throned
and watches
all who dwell ᛁ on the earth.

¹⁵ God fashions ᛁ all their hearts
and observes ᛁ all their deeds.

¹⁶ A king is not saved
by the size ᛁ of the army,
nor are warriors rescued
by ᛁ their great strength.

¹⁷ The horse gives vain ᛁ hope for victory;
despite its great strength
it ᛁ cannot save.

¹⁸ Truly, your eye is upon those
who fear ᛁ you, O LORD,
upon those
who wait for your ᛁ steadfast love,

¹⁹ to deliver their ᛁ lives from death,
and to keep them alive
in ᛁ time of famine.

²⁰ Our innermost being waits for ᛁ you,
O LORD,
our helper ᛁ and our shield.

²¹ Surely, our heart rejoic- ᛁ es in you,
for in your holy name
we ᛁ put our trust.

²² Let your lovingkindness, O LORD,
ᛁ be upon us,
even as we place our ᛁ hope in you.

34

¹ I will bless the LORD ᛁ at all times;
the praise of God
shall ever be ᛁ in my mouth.

² I will glory ᛁ in the LORD;
let the lowly hear ᛁ and rejoice.

³ Proclaim with me
the greatness ᛁ of the LORD;
let us exalt God's ᛁ name together.

⁴ I sought the LORD,
who ᛁ answered me
and delivered me
from ᛁ all my terrors.

⁵ Look upon the LORD ᛁ and be radiant,
and let not your faces ᛁ be ashamed.

⁶ I called in my affliction,
and ᛁ the LORD heard me
and saved me from ᛁ all my troubles.

⁷ The angel of the LORD encamps around
those who ᛁ fear the LORD
and de- ᛁ livers them.

⁸ Taste and see that the ᛁ LORD is good;
happy are they
who take ref- ᛁ uge in God!

⁹ Fear the LORD,
you saints ᛁ of the LORD,
for those who fear the ᛁ LORD
lack nothing.

¹⁰ The lions are in want
and ᛁ suffer hunger,
but those who seek the LORD
lack nothing ᛁ that is good.

¹¹ Come, children, and lis- ᛁ ten to me;
I will teach you reverence
ᛁ for the LORD.

¹² Who among you
takes plea- ᛁ sure in life
and desires long life
to en- ᛁ joy prosperity?

¹³ Keep your ᛁ tongue from evil
and your lips from ᛁ lying words.

¹⁴ Turn from evil ᛁ and do good;
seek peace ᛁ and pursue it.

¹⁵ The eyes of the LORD
are up- ᛁ on the righteous,
and God's ears are open
ᛁ to their cry.

¹⁶ The face of the LORD
is against those ᛁ who do evil,
to erase the remembrance of them
ᛁ from the earth.

¹⁷ The righteous cry,
and ᛁ the LORD hears them,
and delivers them
from ᛁ all their troubles.

¹⁸ The LORD is near
to the ᛁ brokenhearted
and saves those
whose spir- ᛁ its are crushed.

¹⁹ Many are the troubles ǀ of the righteous,
 but the LORD delivers them
  from ǀ every one.

²⁰ God will keep safe ǀ all their bones;
 not one of them ǀ shall be broken.

²¹ Evil will bring death ǀ to the wicked
 and those who hate the righteous
  ǀ will be punished.

²² O LORD, you redeem
 the life ǀ of your servants,
  and those who put their trust in you
  will ǀ not be punished.

35

¹ Fight those
 who fight ǀ me, O LORD;
  attack those
  who are at- ǀ tacking me.

² Take up ǀ shield and armor
 and rise ǀ up to help me.

³ Draw the sword and bar the way
 against those ǀ who pursue me;
  say to my soul,
  "I am ǀ your salvation."

⁴ Let those who seek after my life
 be ǀ shamed and humbled;
  let those who plot my ruin
  fall back and ǀ be dismayed.

⁵ Let them be like chaff
 be- ǀ fore the wind,
  and let the angel of the LORD
  drive ǀ them away.

⁶ Let their way be ǀ dark and slippery,
 and let the angel of the ǀ LORD
  pursue them.

⁷ For they have secretly
 laid a trap for me ǀ without cause;
  for no reason
  they have hunt- ǀ ed me down.

⁸ Let ruin come upon them ǀ unawares;
 let them be caught
  in the net they hid;
  let them fall into ǀ their own ruin.

⁹ Then I will be joyful in ǀ you, O LORD;
 I will glory ǀ in your victory.

¹⁰ My very bones will say,
 "LORD, ǀ who is like you?
  You deliver the poor from those
  who are too strong for them,
  the poor and needy from ǀ those
  who rob them."

¹¹ Witnesses rise up, ǀ full of malice;
 they charge me with matters
  of which ǀ I know nothing.

¹² They repay me evil
 in ex- ǀ change for good;
  my soul is full ǀ of despair.

¹³ But when they were sick
 I dressed in sackcloth
  and humbled my- ǀ self by fasting.
  I prayed with ǀ my whole heart.

¹⁴ I mourned as one would
 for a friend ǀ or a brother;
  I behaved like one
  who mourns for his mother,
  bowed ǀ down and grieving.

¹⁵ But when I stumbled,
 they rejoiced and gathered together;
  gathered together to attack,
  and I did not ǀ even know it;
  they tore me to pieces
  and ǀ would not stop.

¹⁶ Like the godless
 viciously laughing over a ǀ loaf of bread,
  they gnash their teeth ǀ over me.

¹⁷ O Lord,
 how long will ǀ you look on?
  Rescue my soul
  from their destruction,
  my precious life ǀ from these lions.

¹⁸ I will give you thanks
 in the ǀ great assembly;
  I will praise you
  in the ǀ mighty throng.

¹⁹ Do not let my treacherous foes
 rejoice ǀ over me,
  nor let those
  who hate me without cause
  wink ǀ at each other.

²⁰ For they do not ǀ plan for peace,
 but invent deceitful schemes
  against the quiet ǀ in the land.

21 They opened their mouths at ǀ me
and said,
> "Aha! we saw it
> with ǀ our own eyes."

22 You saw it, O LORD;
do ǀ not be silent;
> O Lord, be not ǀ far from me.

23 Awake, arise, ǀ to my cause,
to my defense,
> my God ǀ and my Lord!

24 Give me justice, O LORD my God,
according ǀ to your righteousness;
> do not let them gloat ǀ over me.

25 Do not let them say in their hearts,
"Aha! ǀ how delicious!"
> Do not let them say,
> "We have swal- ǀ lowed you whole."

26 Let all who rejoice at my ruin
be ashamed ǀ and disgraced;
> let those who boast against me
> be clothed with dis- ǀ may
> and shame.

27 Let those who favor my cause
sing out with joy ǀ and be glad;
> let them say always,
> "Great are you, LORD;
> you desire the well-being
> ǀ of your servant."

28 And my tongue shall be talking
ǀ of your righteousness
> and of your praise
> all ǀ the day long.

36

1 There is a voice of rebellion
deep in the heart ǀ of the wicked;
> there is no fear of God
> be- ǀ fore their eyes.

2 They flatter themselves
in ǀ their own eyes
> that their hateful sin
> will not ǀ be found out.

3 The words of their mouths
are wicked ǀ and deceitful;
> they have stopped acting wisely
> and ǀ doing good.

4 They plot wickedness upon their beds
and have set themselves
> in a way that ǀ is not good;
> they do not abhor
> that ǀ which is evil.

5 Your love, O LORD,
reaches ǀ to the heavens,
> and your faithfulness ǀ to the clouds.

6 Your righteousness
is like the strong mountains,
> your justice like ǀ the great deep;
> you save humankind and ani- ǀ mals,
> O LORD.

7 How priceless is your ǀ love, O God!
All people take refuge
> under the shadow ǀ of your wings.

8 They feast upon the abundance
ǀ of your house;
> you give them drink
> from the river of ǀ your delights.

9 For with you is the ǀ well of life,
and in your light ǀ we see light.

10 Continue your lovingkindness
to ǀ those who know you,
> and your favor
> to those who are ǀ true of heart.

11 Let not the foot of the ǀ proud
come near me,
> nor the hand of the wicked
> push ǀ me aside.

12 See how they are fallen,
those ǀ who work wickedness!
> They are cast down
> and shall not be a- ǀ ble to rise.

37

1 Do not be provoked by ǀ evildoers;
do not be jealous
> of those ǀ who do wrong.

2 For they shall soon wither
ǀ like the grass,
> and like the green grass ǀ fade away.

3 Put your trust in the LORD
ǀ and do good;
> dwell in the land
> and ǀ find safe pasture.

⁴ Take delight ˈ in the Lᴏʀᴅ,
   who shall give you
   your ˈ heart's desire.

⁵ Commit your way to the Lᴏʀᴅ;
   put your trust ˈ in the Lᴏʀᴅ,
      and see what ˈ God will do.

⁶ The Lᴏʀᴅ will make your vindication
   as clear ˈ as the light
      and the justice of your case
      like the ˈ noonday sun.

⁷ Be still before the Lᴏʀᴅ
   and wait ˈ patiently.
      Do not be provoked
      by the one who prospers,
      the one who succeeds
      in ˈ evil schemes.

⁸ Refrain from anger, leave ˈ rage alone;
      do not be provoked;
      it leads on- ˈ ly to evil.

⁹ For evildoers shall ˈ be cut off,
   but those who hope in the Lᴏʀᴅ
   shall pos- ˈ sess the land.

¹⁰ In a little while
   the wicked shall ˈ be no more;
      even if you search out their place,
      they will ˈ not be there.

¹¹ But the lowly shall pos- ˈ sess the land;
      they will delight
      in abun- ˈ dance of peace.

¹² The wicked plot
   a- ˈ gainst the righteous
      and gnash at them ˈ with their teeth.

¹³ The Lᴏʀᴅ laughs ˈ at the wicked,
      seeing that their day of judg- ˈ ment
      is coming.

¹⁴ The wicked draw their sword
   and bend their bow to strike down
   the ˈ poor and needy,
      to slaughter those
      whose ˈ ways are upright.

¹⁵ Their sword shall go
   through ˈ their own heart,
      and their bow ˈ shall be broken.

¹⁶ Better is the little
   that the ˈ righteous have
      than the great riches ˈ of the wicked.

¹⁷ For the power of the wicked
   ˈ shall be broken,
      but the Lᴏʀᴅ
      up- ˈ holds the righteous.

¹⁸ The Lᴏʀᴅ knows
   the lives ˈ of the godly,
      and their inheritance
      shall ˈ last forever.

¹⁹ They shall not wither
   in times ˈ of disaster,
      and in days of famine
      they shall be ˈ fully satisfied.

²⁰ As for the wicked, ˈ they shall perish,
      and the enemies of the Lᴏʀᴅ
      shall vanish like flowers in a field;
      they shall van- ˈ ish like smoke.

²¹ The wicked borrow and do ˈ not repay,
      but the righteous
      are gener- ˈ ous in giving.

²² Those who are blessed by God
   shall pos- ˈ sess the land,
      but those who are cursed by God
      shall ˈ be destroyed.

²³ Our steps are made firm ˈ by the Lᴏʀᴅ;
      God delights in ˈ faithful ways.

²⁴ If we stumble,
   we shall ˈ not fall headlong,
      for the Lᴏʀᴅ holds us ˈ by the hand.

²⁵ I have been young and now ˈ I am old,
      but never have I seen
      the righteous forsaken,
      or their children ˈ begging bread.

²⁶ The righteous are always generous
   ˈ in their lending,
      and their children
      shall be- ˈ come a blessing.

²⁷ Turn from evil, ˈ and do good,
      and dwell secure- ˈ ly forever.

²⁸ For the Lᴏʀᴅ loves justice,
   and will never forsake
   those ˈ who are faithful;
      they shall be kept safe forever,
      but the offspring of the wicked
      shall ˈ be destroyed.

²⁹ The righteous shall inher- ˈ it the land
      and dwell in ˈ it forever.

30 The mouths of the righteous
I utter wisdom,
and their I tongues speak justice.

31 The teaching of their God
is I in their heart,
and their footsteps I do not falter.

32 The wicked spy I on the righteous
and seek occa- I sion to kill them.

33 The Lord will not abandon the
righteous to the hand I of the wicked,
nor let them be found guilty
when I brought to trial.

34 Wait upon the Lord and keep the way
of God, who will raise you up
to pos- I sess the land;
and when the wicked are cut off,
I you will see it.

35 I have seen
the frightfully I wicked flourishing
like a tree in I native soil.

36 Suddenly they vanished
and I were not there;
I searched for them,
but they could I not be found.

37 Mark those who are blameless;
ob- I serve the upright;
for there is a future
for people who I are at peace.

38 Transgressors shall be destroyed,
I one and all;
the future of the wicked I is cut off.

39 But the deliverance of the righteous
comes from I you, O Lord;
you are their stronghold
in I time of trouble.

40 You, O Lord, will help them
and I rescue them;
you will rescue them
from the wicked and deliver them,
because in you I they seek refuge.

38

1 O Lord, do not rebuke me
I in your anger;
do not punish me
I in your wrath.

2 For your arrows
have al- I ready pierced me,
and your hand presses I hard upon me.

3 There is no health in my flesh,
because of your I indignation;
there is no soundness in my body,
because I of my sin.

4 For my iniquities I overwhelm me;
like a heavy burden
they are too much for I me to bear.

5 My wounds I stink and fester
by reason I of my foolishness.

6 I am utterly bowed I down
and prostrate;
I go about in mourning
all I the day long.

7 My loins are filled with I searing pain;
there is no health I in my body.

8 I am utterly I numb and crushed;
I wail, because of the groaning
I of my heart.

9 O Lord, you know all I my desires,
and my sighing
is not hid- I den from you.

10 My heart is pounding,
my I strength has failed me,
and the brightness of my eyes
is I gone from me.

11 My friends and companions
draw back from I my affliction;
my neighbors stand I afar off.

12 Those who seek after my life
lay I snares for me;
those who strive to hurt me
speak of my ruin
and plot treachery all I the day long.

13 But I am like the deaf who I do not hear,
like those who are mute
and do not o- I pen their mouth.

14 I have become like one
who I does not hear
and from whose mouth
comes I no defense.

15 For in you, O Lord,
have I I fixed my hope;
you will answer me,
O I Lord my God.

¹⁶ For I said, "Do not let them rejoice
at ǀ my expense,
those who gloat over me
when ǀ my foot slips."

¹⁷ Truly, I am on the ǀ verge of falling,
and my pain is al- ǀ ways with me.

¹⁸ For I admit ǀ my iniquity
and am deeply troubled
o- ǀ ver my sinfulness.

¹⁹ Many are those
who are my ǀ mortal enemies,
and numerous are those li- ǀ ars
who hate me.

²⁰ They repay e- ǀ vil for good;
they accuse me,
though I pursue ǀ what is right.

²¹ O Lord, do ǀ not forsake me;
be not far from me, ǀ O my God.

²² Make ǀ haste to help me,
O Lord of ǀ my salvation.

39

¹ I said, "I will keep watch
upon my ways,
so that I do not offend ǀ with my tongue.
I will put a muzzle on my mouth
while the wicked
are ǀ in my presence."

² So I held my tongue ǀ and said nothing;
I refrained from rash words;
but my pain be- ǀ came unbearable.

³ My heart was hot within me;
while I pondered,
the fire burst ǀ into flame;
I spoke out ǀ with my tongue:

⁴ "Lord, let me know my end
and the number ǀ of my days,
so that I may know
how ǀ short my life is.

⁵ You have given me
a mere handful of days,
and my lifetime
is as nothing ǀ in your sight;
truly, even those who stand proudly
are but a ǀ puff of wind.

⁶ We walk about like a shadow,
and in vain we ǀ are in turmoil;
we heap up riches and cannot tell
who will ǀ gather them.

⁷ So now, what ǀ is my longing?
O Lord, my hope ǀ is in you.

⁸ Deliver me from all ǀ my transgressions
and do not make me
the taunt ǀ of the fool.

⁹ I fell silent
and did not o- ǀ pen my mouth,
for surely it was ǀ you that did it.

¹⁰ Take your af- ǀ fliction from me;
I am worn down
by the blows ǀ of your hand.

¹¹ With rebukes for sin you punish us;
like a moth you eat away
ǀ all we treasure;
truly, everyone is but a ǀ puff of
wind.

¹² Hear my prayer, O Lord,
and listen to my cry;
do not shut your ears ǀ to my weeping.
For I am but a sojourner with you,
a passing guest,
as all my ǀ forebears were.

¹³ Turn your gaze from me,
that I may ǀ smile again,
before I go my way and ǀ am no more."

40

¹ I waited patiently up- ǀ on the Lord,
who stooped to me
and ǀ heard my cry.

² The Lord lifted me
out of the desolate pit,
out of the ǀ miry clay,
and set my feet upon a high cliff,
making my ǀ footing sure.

³ The Lord put a new song in my mouth,
a song of praise ǀ to our God;
many shall see, and stand in awe,
and put their trust ǀ in the Lord.

⁴ Happy are they who trust ǀ in the Lord!
They do not turn to enemies
or to those who ǀ follow lies.

5 Great are the wonders you have done,
O Lord my God!
In your plans for us,
none can be com- | pared with you!
  Oh, that I could make them known
  and tell them!
  But they are more than | I can count.

6 Sacrifice and offering
you do | not desire;
  you have opened my ears:
  burnt-offering and sin-offering
  you have | not required.

7 And so I said, "Here I | am; I come.
  In the scroll of the book
  it is writ- | ten of me:

8 'I love to do your will, | O my God;
  your law is | deep within me.'"

9 I proclaimed righteousness
in the | great assembly;
  I have not restrained my lips,
  O | Lord, you know.

10 I have not hidden your righteousness
in my heart;
  I have spoken of your faithfulness
and | your deliverance;
  I have not concealed
  your steadfast love and truth
  from the | great assembly.

11 You are the Lord;
  do not withhold your compas- | sion
  from me;
    may your steadfast love
    and your truth
    continually | keep me safe.

12 For troubles without number
  have crowded upon me;
  my sins have overtaken me,
  and I | cannot see;
    they are more than
    the hairs of my head,
    and | my heart fails me.

13 Be pleased, O Lord, to de- | liver me;
  O Lord, make | haste to help me.

14 Let them be ashamed
  and altogether dismayed
  who seek after my life | to destroy it;
    let them draw back and be disgraced
    who delight in | my misfortune.

15 Let those who say "A- | ha, aha!"
  be appalled at | their own shame.

16 Let all who seek you
  rejoice in you | and be glad;
    let those who love your salvation
    continually say,
    "Great | is the Lord!"

17 Though I am poor and afflicted,
  the Lord has | plans for me.
    You are my help and my savior;
    do not delay, | O my God.

41

1 Happy are they who re- | gard the poor!
  The Lord will deliver them
  in the | time of trouble.

2 The Lord protects and revives them,
  those blessed | in the land,
    and does not hand them over
    to the power | of their enemies.

3 The Lord sustains them
  | on their sickbed
    and ministers to them
    | in their illness.

4 I said, "Lord, be merci- | ful to me;
  heal me,
  for I have | sinned against you."

5 My enemies are saying
  wicked | things about me,
    asking when I will die,
    and | my name perish.

6 Even if they come to see me,
  they speak | empty words;
    their heart collects false rumors;
    they go out- | side and spread them.

7 All my enemies
  whisper togeth- | er about me
    and devise e- | vil against me.

8 "A deadly thing," they say,
  "has fas- | tened on him;
    he has taken to his bed
    and will never get | up again."

9 Even my best friend, whom I trusted,
  who broke | bread with me,
    has violently | turned against me.

¹⁰ But you, O LORD,
   be merciful to me and ¦ raise me up,
      and I ¦ shall repay them.
¹¹ By this I know
   you are ¦ pleased with me:
      that my enemy
         does not triumph ¦ over me.
¹² In my integrity you ¦ hold me fast,
   and shall set me
      before your ¦ face forever.
¹³ Blessed be the LORD ¦ God of Israel,
   from age to age. A- ¦ men. Amen.

42

¹ As the deer
   longs ¦ for the water-brooks,
      so longs my soul for ¦ you, O God.
² I thirst for God, for the ¦ living God;
   when shall I come to appear
      before the pres- ¦ ence of God?
³ My tears have been my food
   ¦ day and night,
      while all day long they say to me,
         "Where now ¦ is your God?"
⁴ I pour out my soul
   when I think ¦ on these things;
      how I went with the multitude
      and led them into the house of God,
      with shouts of thanksgiving,
         among those ¦ keeping festival.
⁵ Why are you so full of heaviness,
   O my soul, and why are you
   so disquiet- ¦ ed within me?
      Put your trust in God,
      for I will yet give thanks to the one
      who is my help ¦ and my God.
⁶ My soul is heav- ¦ y within me;
   therefore I will remember you
   from the land of Jordan,
   and from the peak of Mizar
      among the ¦ heights of Hermon.
⁷ One deep calls to another
   in the roar of ¦ your cascades;
      all your rapids and floods
      have gone ¦ over me.

⁸ The LORD grants lovingkindness
   ¦ in the daytime;
      in the night season
      the LORD's song is with me,
      a prayer to the God ¦ of my life.
⁹ I will say to the God of my strength,
   "Why have you re- ¦ jected me,
      and why do I wander in such gloom
      while the enemy op- ¦ presses me?"
¹⁰ While my bones are being broken,
   my enemies mock me ¦ to my face;
      all day long
      they mock me and say to me,
      "Where now ¦ is your God?"
¹¹ Why are you so full of heaviness,
   O my soul, and why are you
   so disquiet- ¦ ed within me?
      Put your trust in God,
      for I will yet give thanks to the one
      who is my help ¦ and my God.

43

¹ Give judgment for me, O God,
   and defend my cause
   against an un- ¦ godly people;
      deliver me from the deceitful
      ¦ and the wicked.
² For you are the God of my strength;
   why have you re- ¦ jected me,
      and why do I wander in such gloom
      while the enemy op- ¦ presses me?
³ Send out your light and your truth,
   that ¦ they may lead me,
      and bring me to your holy hill
      and to your ¦ sanctuary;
⁴ that I may go to the altar of God,
   to the God of my ¦ joy and gladness;
      and on the harp I will give thanks
      to you, O ¦ God my God.
⁵ Why are you so full of heaviness,
   O my soul, and why are you
   so disquiet- ¦ ed within me?
      Put your trust in God,
      for I will yet give thanks to the one
      who is my help ¦ and my God.

44

1 We have heard with our ears, O God,
our fore- ˈ bears have told us,
    what you did in their days,
    in the ˈ days of old.

2 With your hand
you drove the nations out
and plant- ˈ ed your people;
    you afflicted peoples
    ˈ and dispersed them.

3 For they did not take the land
by their sword,
nor did their arm
win the victo- ˈ ry for them;
    but your right hand, your arm,
    and the light of your face,
    because you ˈ favored them.

4 You are my king ˈ and my God;
    you command victo- ˈ ries for Jacob.

5 Through you
we pushed back our ˈ adversaries;
    through your name
    we trampled on those
    who rose ˈ up against us.

6 For I do not rely ˈ on my bow,
    and my sword
    does not give ˈ me the victory.

7 Surely, you gave us victory
over our ˈ adversaries
    and put those who hate ˈ us
    to shame.

8 Every day we glo- ˈ ried in God,
    and we will praise your ˈ name
    forever.

9 Nevertheless, you have rejected
and ˈ humbled us
    and do not go forth
    ˈ with our armies.

10 You have made us fall back
before our ˈ adversary,
    and our enemies
    have ˈ plundered us.

11 You have made us
like sheep ˈ to be eaten
    and have scattered us
    a- ˈ mong the nations.

12 You are selling your people ˈ for a trifle
and have kept your price low
    ˈ for their sale.

13 You have made us the scorn
ˈ of our neighbors,
    a mockery and derision
    to ˈ those around us.

14 You have made us a byword
a- ˈ mong the nations,
    a laughingstock a- ˈ mong the peoples.

15 My humiliation is dai- ˈ ly before me,
    and shame has cov- ˈ ered my face;

16 because of the taunts
of the mockers ˈ and blasphemers,
    because of the enemy ˈ and avenger.

17 All this has ˈ come upon us;
    yet we have not forgotten you, nor
    have we be- ˈ trayed your covenant.

18 Our heart has ˈ not turned back,
    nor have our steps strayed
    ˈ from your path;

19 though you thrust us down
into a ˈ place of misery,
    and covered us over
    ˈ with deep darkness.

20 If we have forgotten
the name ˈ of our God,
    or stretched out our hands
    to ˈ some strange god,

21 will not God ˈ find it out?
    For God knows the secrets
    ˈ of the heart.

22 Indeed, for your sake
we are being killed ˈ all day long;
    we are accounted as sheep
    ˈ for the slaughter.

23 Awake, O Lord! Why ˈ are you sleeping?
    Arise! Do not reject ˈ us forever.

24 Why have you hid- ˈ den your face
    and forgotten our affliction
    ˈ and oppression?

25 We sink down in- ˈ to the dust;
    our body cleaves ˈ to the ground.

26 Rise ˈ up, and help us,
    and save us,
    for the sake of your ˈ steadfast love.

45

¹ My heart is stirring with a noble song;
let me recite
what I have fashioned ˡ for the king;
   my tongue shall be the pen
   of a ˡ skillful writer.

² You are the noblest
a- ˡ mong the people;
   grace flows from your lips, because
   God has blessed ˡ you forever.

³ Strap your sword upon your thigh,
O ˡ mighty warrior,
   in your pride and ˡ in your majesty.

⁴ Ride out and conquer
in the cause of truth
and for the ˡ sake of justice.
   Your right hand will show you
   ˡ marvelous things.

⁵ Your arrows have been sharpened;
people fall ˡ under you;
   and the enemies of the ˡ king
   lose heart.

⁶ Your throne, O God, endures
forev- ˡ er and ever,
   a scepter of righteousness
   is the scepter ˡ of your kingdom.

⁷ You love righteousness
and ˡ hate iniquity;
   therefore God, your God,
   has anointed you
   with the oil of gladness
   above ˡ your companions.

⁸ All your garments are fragrant
with myrrh, al- ˡ oes, and cassia,
   and the music of strings
   from ivory palaces ˡ makes you glad.

⁹ Kings' daughters stand
among the ladies ˡ of the court;
   on your right hand is the queen,
   adorned with the ˡ gold of Ophir.

¹⁰ "Hear, O daughter;
consider and ˡ listen closely;
   forget your people
   and your ˡ father's house.

¹¹ The king will de- ˡ sire your beauty;
he is your master,
   so ˡ bow before him.

¹² The city of ˡ Tyre brings tribute;
the wealthiest of the people
   ˡ seek your favor."

¹³ All glorious is the princess
ˡ as she enters;
   her gown is ˡ cloth-of-gold.

¹⁴ In embroidered apparel
she is brought ˡ to the king;
   after her the bridesmaids
   follow ˡ in procession.

¹⁵ With joy and gladness
ˡ they are brought,
   and enter into the palace
   ˡ of the king.

¹⁶ "In place of ancestors, O king,
you ˡ shall have sons;
   you shall make them princes
   over ˡ all the earth.

¹⁷ I will make your name
to be remembered
   from one generation ˡ to another;
   therefore nations will praise you
   forev- ˡ er and ever."

46

¹ God is our ref- ˡ uge and strength,
a very present ˡ help in trouble.

² Therefore we will not fear,
though the ˡ earth be moved,
   and though the mountains shake
   in the depths ˡ of the sea;

³ though its waters ˡ rage and foam,
and though the mountains tremble
   ˡ with its tumult.

⁴ There is a river whose streams
make glad the cit- ˡ y of God,
   the holy habitation
   of ˡ the Most High.

⁵ God is in the midst of the city;
it shall ˡ not be shaken;
   God shall help it
   at the ˡ break of day.

⁶ The nations rage,
and the ˡ kingdoms shake;
   God speaks,
   and the earth ˡ melts away.

⁷ The LORD of ' hosts is with us;
the God of Jacob ' is our stronghold.

⁸ Come now,
regard the works ' of the LORD,
what desolations
God has brought up- ' on the earth;

⁹ behold the one who makes war to cease
in ' all the world;
who breaks the bow,
and shatters the spear,
and burns the ' shields with fire.

¹⁰ "Be still, then,
and know that ' I am God;
I will be exalted among the nations;
I will be exalted ' in the earth."

¹¹ The LORD of ' hosts is with us;
the God of Jacob ' is our stronghold.

47

¹ Clap your hands, ' all you peoples;
shout to God with a ' joyful sound.

² For the LORD Most High
is ' to be feared:
a great king over ' all the earth,

³ who subdues the ' peoples under us,
and the nations un- ' der our feet;

⁴ who chooses our inheri- ' tance for us,
the pride of Jacob,
' whom God loves.

⁵ God has gone up ' with a shout,
the LORD with the sound
' of the ram's horn.

⁶ Sing praises to ' God, sing praises;
sing praises to our ' king,
sing praises.

⁷ For God is king of ' all the earth;
sing praises ' with a song.

⁸ God reigns o- ' ver the nations;
God is en- ' throned on high.

⁹ The nobles of the peoples
have gathered
as the people of the ' God of Abraham.
The rulers of the earth
belong to God,
who is high- ' ly exalted.

48

¹ Great is the LORD,
and highly ' to be praised,
in the city of our God,
on the LORD's ' holy mountain.

² Beautiful and lofty,
the joy of all the earth, ' is Mount Zion,
the summit of the north
and city of ' the great king.

³ God is in the citadels of Jerusalem;
revealed to be the sure refuge
' of the city.

⁴ Behold, the ' kings assembled
and marched for- ' ward together.

⁵ As they looked, they ' were astounded;
dismayed, they ' fled in terror.

⁶ Trembling ' seized them there;
they writhed
like a wo- ' man in childbirth;

⁷ with an east wind you ' shattered them
like the ' ships of Tarshish.

⁸ As we have heard, so have we seen,
in the city of the LORD of hosts,
in the city ' of our God—
may God establish ' it forever!

⁹ In the midst of your tem- ' ple, O God,
we meditate on your ' steadfast love.

¹⁰ Your praise, like your name, O God,
reaches to the ends ' of the earth;
your right hand
is ' full of righteousness.

¹¹ Let Mount Zion be glad
and the towns of Ju- ' dah rejoice,
because ' of your judgments.

¹² Make the circuit of Zion;
walk ' round about it;
count the number
of the ' city's towers.

¹³ Consider well its ramparts;
exam- ' ine its strongholds;
that you may tell
those ' who come after.

¹⁴ Mark this—
God is our God forev- ' er and ever,
guiding us even ' to the end.

49

¹ Hear this, ⎪ all you peoples;
  give ear,
  all you who dwell ⎪ in the world,

² you of high de- ⎪ gree and low,
  rich and ⎪ poor together.

³ My mouth shall ⎪ speak of wisdom,
  and my heart
  shall meditate on ⎪ understanding.

⁴ I will incline my ear ⎪ to a proverb
  and set forth my riddle
  up- ⎪ on the harp.

⁵ Why should I be afraid in ⎪ evil days,
  when the wickedness
  of those at my ⎪ heels surrounds me,

⁶ the wickedness of those who trust
  in ⎪ their own prowess,
  and boast of ⎪ their great riches?

⁷ One can never re- ⎪ deem another,
  or give to God the ransom
  for an- ⎪ other's life;

⁸ for the ransom of a life ⎪ is so great
  that there would never be
  e- ⎪ nough to pay it,

⁹ in order to live forev- ⎪ er and ever
  and never ⎪ see the grave.

¹⁰ For we see that the wise die also;
  like the dull and stu- ⎪ pid they perish
  and leave their wealth
  to those who come ⎪ after them.

¹¹ Their graves shall be their homes
  forever, their dwelling places
  from generation to ⎪ generation,
  though they had named lands
  af- ⎪ ter themselves.

¹² Even though honored,
  they cannot ⎪ live forever;
  they are like the ⎪ beasts that perish.

¹³ Such is the way of self-con- ⎪ fident fools,
  and the end of those
  who delight in ⎪ their own words.

¹⁴ Like sheep they are destined to die;
  death will shep- ⎪ herd and rule them;
  straight away to the grave,
  their form wastes away,
  and Sheol is their splen- ⎪ did abode.

¹⁵ But God will ran- ⎪ som my life
  and will snatch me
  from the ⎪ grasp of death.

¹⁶ Do not be envious
  when some ⎪ become rich,
  or when the grandeur
  of their ⎪ house increases;

¹⁷ for they will carry nothing
  away ⎪ at their death,
  nor will their grandeur
  ⎪ follow them.

¹⁸ Though they think highly
  of themselves ⎪ while they live,
  and are praised for ⎪ their success,

¹⁹ they shall join the company
  ⎪ of their forebears,
  who will never see the ⎪ light again.

²⁰ Those who are honored,
  but have no ⎪ understanding,
  are like the ⎪ beasts that perish.

50

¹ The mighty one, God the ⎪ LORD,
  has spoken;
  calling the earth
  from the rising of the sun
  ⎪ to its setting.

² Out of Zion, perfect ⎪ in its beauty,
  God shines ⎪ forth in glory.

³ Our God will come
  and will ⎪ not keep silence;
  with a consuming flame before,
  and round about a ⎪ raging storm.

⁴ God calls the heavens and the earth
  ⎪ from above
  to witness the judgment
  ⎪ of the people.

⁵ "Gather before me
  my ⎪ loyal followers,
  those who have made
  a covenant with me
  and sealed ⎪ it with sacrifice."

⁶ The heavens declare
  the rightness ⎪ of God's cause,
  for it is God ⎪ who is judge.

7 "Listen, my people, and I will speak:
Israel, I will bear wit- ˡ ness
against you;
    for I am ˡ God, your God.

8 I do not accuse you
because ˡ of your sacrifices;
    your burnt offerings
    are al- ˡ ways before me.

9 I will not accept a calf
ˡ from your stalls,
    nor goats ˡ from your pens;

10 for all the wild animals of the for- ˡ est
are mine,
    the cattle on a ˡ thousand hills.

11 I know every bird ˡ of the mountains,
and the creatures of the ˡ fields
are mine.

12 If I were hungry, I ˡ would not tell you,
for the whole world is mine
and all ˡ that is in it.

13 Do you think I eat the ˡ flesh of bulls,
or drink the ˡ blood of goats?

14 Offer to God
a sacrifice ˡ of thanksgiving
    and make good your vows
    to ˡ the Most High.

15 Call upon me in the ˡ day of trouble;
I will deliver you,
and you shall ˡ honor me."

16 But to the wick- ˡ ed God says:
"Why do you recite my statutes,
    and take my covenant
    up- ˡ on your lips;

17 since you ˡ refuse discipline,
and throw my words
    be- ˡ hind your back?

18 You make friends with a thief
ˡ when you see one,
    and you cast in your lot
    ˡ with adulterers.

19 You have loosed your ˡ lips for evil,
and your tongue devis- ˡ es deceit.

20 You are always speaking evil
ˡ of your kin
    and slandering
    your own ˡ mother's child.

21 These things you have done,
and I kept still,
    and you thought that I ˡ am like you.
    I have made my accusation;
    I have put my case
    in or- ˡ der before you.

22 Consider this well,
you ˡ who forget God,
    lest I tear you apart
    and there be none to de- ˡ liver you.

23 Whoever offers me
a sacrifice of thanksgiving ˡ honors me;
    I will show the salvation of God
    to those who go ˡ the right way."

51

1 Have mercy on me, O God,
according to your ˡ steadfast love;
    in your great compassion
    blot out ˡ my offenses.

2 Wash me through and through
ˡ from my wickedness,
    and cleanse me ˡ from my sin.

3 For I know ˡ my offenses,
and my sin is ev- ˡ er before me.

4 Against you only have I sinned
and done what is evil ˡ in your sight;
    so you are justified when you speak
    and right ˡ in your judgment.

5 Indeed, I was born
ˡ steeped in wickedness,
    a sinner from my ˡ mother's womb.

6 Indeed, you delight in truth
ˡ deep within me,
    and would have me know wisdom
    ˡ deep within.

7 Remove my sins with hyssop,
and I ˡ shall be clean;
    wash me,
    and I shall be pur- ˡ er than snow.

8 Let me hear ˡ joy and gladness;
that the body you have broken
    ˡ may rejoice.

9 Hide your face ˡ from my sins,
and blot out ˡ all my wickedness.

¹⁰ Create in me a clean ⎮ heart, O God,
   and renew a right spir- ⎮ it within me.
¹¹ Cast me not away ⎮ from your presence,
   and take not your Holy Spir- ⎮ it
   from me.
¹² Restore to me the joy of ⎮ your salvation
   and sustain me
   with your boun- ⎮ tiful Spirit.
¹³ Let me teach your ways ⎮ to offenders,
   and sinners shall be re- ⎮ stored
   to you.
¹⁴ Rescue me from bloodshed,
   O God of ⎮ my salvation,
   and my tongue shall sing
   ⎮ of your righteousness.
¹⁵ O Lord, o- ⎮ pen my lips,
   and my mouth
   shall pro- ⎮ claim your praise.
¹⁶ For you take no delight in sacrifice,
   or ⎮ I would give it.
   You are not pleased
   ⎮ with burnt offering.
¹⁷ The sacrifice of God
   is a ⎮ troubled spirit;
   a troubled and broken heart, O God,
   you will ⎮ not despise.
¹⁸ Favor Zion with ⎮ your good pleasure;
   build up the walls ⎮ of Jerusalem.
¹⁹ Then you will delight
   in the appointed sacrifices,
   in burnt ⎮ and whole offerings;
   then young bulls shall be offered
   up- ⎮ on your altar.

52

¹ You mighty,
   why do you ⎮ boast of wickedness
   against the godly ⎮ all day long?
² Continually ⎮ you plot ruin;
   your tongue
   is like a sharpened razor
   that com- ⎮ mits deceit.
³ You love evil ⎮ more than good
   and lying
   more than speak- ⎮ ing the truth.

⁴ You love all words ⎮ that devour,
   O you de- ⎮ ceitful tongue.
⁵ Oh, that God would
   demol- ⎮ ish you utterly,
   topple you,
   and snatch you from your dwelling,
   and root you out
   of the land ⎮ of the living!
⁶ The righteous shall see
   ⎮ and be awestruck,
   and they shall laugh ⎮ at you,
   saying,
⁷ "This is the one
   who did not take God ⎮ for a refuge,
   but trusted in great wealth
   and found strength ⎮ in destruction."
⁸ But I am like a green olive tree
   in the ⎮ house of God;
   I trust in the steadfast love of God
   forev- ⎮ er and ever.
⁹ I will thank you forever
   for what ⎮ you have done;
   in the presence of the faithful
   I will long for your name,
   for ⎮ it is good.

53

¹ Fools say in their hearts,
   "There ⎮ is no God."
   They are corrupt,
   every deed is vile;
   there is no one
   who does ⎮ any good.
² God looks down from heaven
   up- ⎮ on us all,
   to see if there is anyone
   who is wise,
   who seeks ⎮ after God.
³ They have all proved faithless;
   all alike ⎮ have turned bad;
   there is none who does good,
   ⎮ no, not one.
⁴ Have they no knowledge,
   those ⎮ evildoers
   who eat up my people like bread
   and do not call ⎮ upon God?

5 See how greatly they tremble,
such trembling as ^l never was;
for God has scattered
the bones of the enemy;
they are put to shame,
because God has re- ^l jected them.

6 Oh, that Israel's deliverance
would come ^l out of Zion!
When God restores
the fortunes of the people,
Jacob will rejoice
and Israel ^l will be glad.

54

1 Save me, O God, ^l by your name;
in your might, de- ^l fend my cause.

2 Hear my ^l prayer, O God;
give ear to the words ^l of my mouth.

3 For strangers have risen up against me,
and the ruthless have ^l sought my life,
those who have no re- ^l gard
for God.

4 Behold, God ^l is my helper;
it is the Lord
who sus- ^l tains my life.

5 Render evil to those who ^l spy on me;
in your faithful- ^l ness,
destroy them.

6 I will offer you a ^l freewill sacrifice
and praise your name, O Lord,
for ^l it is good.

7 For you have rescued me
from ^l every trouble,
and my eye looks down
^l on my enemies.

55

1 Hear my ^l prayer, O God;
do not hide yourself
from ^l my petition.

2 Listen to me and ^l answer me;
I am restless in my complaint;
I ^l am distraught,

3 because of the noise of the enemy
and the oppression ^l of the wicked;
for they bring evil upon me
and are set against ^l me in fury.

4 My heart ^l quakes within me,
and the terrors of death
have fall- ^l en upon me.

5 Fear and trembling
have come ^l over me,
and horror ^l overwhelms me.

6 I said,
"Oh, that I had wings ^l like a dove!
I would fly away and ^l be at rest.

7 I would flee to a ^l far-off place
and make my lodging
^l in the wilderness.

8 I would hurry to find shelter
^l for myself
from the stormy ^l wind
and tempest."

9 Confuse them, Lord,
con- ^l found their speech
for I have seen violence and strife
^l in the city.

10 Day and night the sentries
make their rounds up- ^l on its walls,
but the real trouble and misery
are in the midst ^l of the city.

11 There is corruption with- ^l in the city;
its streets are never free
of oppression ^l and deceit.

12 For had it been an adversary
who taunted me,
then I ^l could have borne it;
or had it been an enemy
who rose up against me,
then I could have hidden
^l from that danger.

13 But it was you,
one after ^l my own heart,
my companion,
my own fa- ^l miliar friend,

14 with whom I kept ^l pleasant company
and walked with the throng
in the ^l house of God.

15 Let death come upon them suddenly;
   let them go down alive in- | to the grave;
      for wickedness is in their dwellings,
      in their | very midst.

16 But I will call | upon God,
   and the LORD will de- | liver me.

17 In the evening, in the morning,
   and at noonday,
   I will complain | and lament,
      and God will | hear my voice.

18 The LORD will bring me safely back
   from the battle | waged against me;
      for there are man- | y who fight me.

19 God, who is enthroned of old,
   will hear me and | bring them down;
      because they never change
      and do | not fear God.

20 This friend of mine laid | hands on me,
   and has brok- | en our covenant.

21 My friend's speech
   is smoother than butter,
   but war | lurks within;
      my friend's words,
      as soothing as lotion,
      are in | fact drawn swords.

22 Cast your burden upon the LORD,
   who | will sustain you,
      who will never
      let the | righteous stumble.

23 But you, O God,
   will bring murderers and deceivers
   down to the | lowest pit;
      they will not live out half their days,
      but I will put my | trust in you.

56

1 Have mercy on me, O God,
   for people are | hounding me;
      all day long
      they assault | and oppress me.

2 My enemies hound me all | the day long;
   truly there are many who fight
   against me | from high ground.

3 Whenever I | am afraid,
   I will put my | trust in you.

4 In God, whose word I praise,
   in God I trust and will not | be afraid,
      for what can flesh | do to me?

5 All day long they dam- | age my cause;
   their only thought
   is to | do me harm.

6 They band together; they | lie in wait;
   they spy upon my footsteps;
   because they | seek my life.

7 Deliver them o- | ver to trouble;
   O God, in your anger,
   cast | down the peoples.

8 You have noted my lamentation;
   put my tears in- | to your bottle;
      are they not recorded | in your book?

9 Whenever I call upon you,
   my enemies will be | put to flight;
      this I know, for God is | on my side.

10 In God, whose | word I praise;
   in the LORD, whose | word I praise—

11 in God I trust and will not | be afraid,
   for what can mortals | do to me?

12 I am bound by the vow
   I made to | you, O God;
      I will present to | you thank-offerings;

13 for you have rescued
   my soul from death
   and my | feet from stumbling,
      that I may walk before God
      in the light | of the living.

57

1 Be merciful to me, O God, be merciful,
   for I have taken ref- | uge in you;
      in the shadow of your wings
      will I take refuge
      until this time of trouble
      | has gone by.

2 I will call upon the | Most High God,
   the God who is with me | to the end.

3 O God, you will send from heaven
   and save me, rebuking those
   who tram- | ple upon me,
      you will send forth
      your love | and your faithfulness.

⁴ I lie in the midst of lions
   that de- ˈ vour the people;
      their teeth are spears and arrows,
      their tongue ˈ a sharp sword.
⁵ Exalt yourself above the heav- ˈ ens,
O God,
      and your glory over ˈ all the earth.
⁶ They have laid a net for my feet,
   and I ˈ am bowed low;
      they have dug a pit before me,
      but have fallen into ˈ it themselves.
⁷ My heart is steadfast, O God,
   my ˈ heart is steadfast;
      I will sing ˈ and make melody.
⁸ Wake up, my spirit;
   awake, ˈ lute and harp;
      I myself will wak- ˈ en the dawn.
⁹ I will give thanks to you
   among the peo- ˈ ples, O LORD;
      I will sing praise to you
      a- ˈ mong the nations.
¹⁰ For your steadfast love
   is greater ˈ than the heavens,
      and your faithfulness
      reaches ˈ to the clouds.
¹¹ Exalt yourself above the heav- ˈ ens,
O God,
      and your glory over ˈ all the earth.

⁵ which does not heed
   the voice ˈ of the charmer,
      no matter how skill- ˈ ful
      the charming.
⁶ O God, break their teeth
   ˈ in their mouths;
      pull the fangs of the young li- ˈ ons,
      O LORD.
⁷ Let them vanish
   like water ˈ that runs off;
      let them wither
      like ˈ trodden grass.
⁸ Let them be like the snail
   that ˈ melts away,
      like an untimely birth
      that never ˈ sees the sun.
⁹ Sooner than your pots
   can feel the heat of thorns,
      whether green ˈ or ablaze,
      may they be ˈ swept away.
¹⁰ The righteous will be glad
   when they ˈ see the vengeance;
      they will bathe their feet
      in the blood ˈ of the wicked.
¹¹ Then all will say, "Surely, there is
   a reward ˈ for the righteous;
      surely, there is a God
      who rules ˈ in the earth."

58

¹ Do you indeed decree righteous- ˈ ness,
   you gods?
      Do you judge the peo- ˈ ples
      with equity?
² No; you devise evil ˈ in your hearts,
   and your hands
      deal out violence ˈ in the earth.
³ The wicked are perverse
   ˈ from the womb;
      liars go astray ˈ from their birth.
⁴ They are as venomous
   ˈ as a serpent;
      they are like the deaf adder,
      which ˈ stops its ears,

59

¹ Rescue me from my ene- ˈ mies, O God;
   protect me from those
      who rise ˈ up against me.
² Rescue me from ˈ evildoers
   and save me from those
      who thirst ˈ for my blood.
³ See how they lie in wait for my life,
   how the mighty gather togeth- ˈ er
against me;
      not for any offense or fault
      of ˈ mine, O LORD.
⁴ Though I did no wrong,
   they run around ˈ and prepare;
      rouse yourself,
      come to my ˈ side, and see.

⁵ For you, Lord God of hosts,
  are ˈ Israel's God.
    Awake, and attend
    to all the nations;
    show no mercy to those
    who are faith- ˈ less and evil.

⁶ They go to and fro ˈ in the evening;
  they snarl like dogs
  and run a- ˈ bout the city.

⁷ Their mouths spew forth,
  with swords be- ˈ tween their lips;
    "For who," they ˈ say, "will hear us?"

⁸ But you, O Lord, you ˈ laugh at them;
  you laugh all the na- ˈ tions to scorn.

⁹ I will watch for you, ˈ O my strength;
  for you, O God, ˈ are my fortress.

¹⁰ My merciful God ˈ comes to meet me;
  God will let me look in triumph
    ˈ on my enemies.

¹¹ Slay them, O God,
  lest my peo- ˈ ple forget;
    send them reeling by your might
    and put them down,
    O ˈ Lord our shield.

¹² For the sins of their mouths,
  for the words of their lips,
  for the cursing and lies ˈ that they utter,
    let them be caught ˈ in their pride.

¹³ Make an end of them in your wrath;
  make an end of them,
  and they shall ˈ be no more.
    Let everyone know
    that God rules in Jacob,
    and to the ends ˈ of the earth.

¹⁴ They go to and fro ˈ in the evening;
  they snarl like dogs
  and run a- ˈ bout the city.

¹⁵ They for- ˈ age for food,
  and if they are not ˈ filled, they howl.

¹⁶ For my part, I will sing of your strength;
  I will celebrate your love
  ˈ in the morning;
    for you have become my stronghold,
    a refuge in the day ˈ of my trouble.

¹⁷ To you, O my strength, ˈ I will sing;
  for you, O God, are my fortress
  and my mer- ˈ ciful God.

60

¹ O God, you have cast us off
  and ˈ broken us;
    you have been angry;
    now take us ˈ back to you.

² You have shaken the earth
  and ˈ split it open;
    repair the cracks in it,
    ˈ for it totters.

³ You have made your peo- ˈ ple
  know hardship;
    you have given us wine
    that ˈ makes us stagger.

⁴ You have set up a banner
  for ˈ those who fear you,
    to be a refuge
    from the power ˈ of the bow.

⁵ Save us by your right hand
  and ˈ answer us,
    that those who are dear to you
    may ˈ be delivered.

⁶ God spoke from the holy ˈ place
  and said:
    "I will exult and parcel out Shechem;
    I will divide the val- ˈ ley of Succoth.

⁷ Gilead is mine
  and Manas- ˈ seh is mine;
    Ephraim is my helmet
    and Ju- ˈ dah my scepter.

⁸ Moab is my washbasin;
  I throw down my sandal ˈ upon Edom,
    and over Philistia
    will I ˈ shout in triumph."

⁹ Who will carry me in procession
  into the for- ˈ tified city?
    Who will bring me ˈ into Edom?

¹⁰ Have you not cast us ˈ off, O God?
  You no longer go out, O God,
  ˈ with our armies.

¹¹ Grant us your help
  a- ˈ gainst the enemy,
    for human ˈ help is worthless.

¹² With God we will do ˈ valiant deeds;
  God shall tread our enemies
  ˈ under foot.

61

¹ Hear my ' cry, O God,
  and listen ' to my prayer.

² From the end of the earth
  I call upon you
  as my ' heart grows faint;
    set me upon the rock
    that is high- ' er than I.

³ For you have ' been my refuge,
  a strong tower a- ' gainst the enemy.

⁴ I will dwell in your ' house forever;
  I will take refuge
  under the cover ' of your wings.

⁵ For you, O God, have ' heard my vows;
  you have granted me the heritage
  of those who ' fear your name.

⁶ Add length of days
  to the life ' of the king;
    let his years extend
    over many ' generations.

⁷ Let the king sit enthroned
  before ' God forever;
    bid love and faithfulness
    watch ' over him.

⁸ So will I always sing
  the praise ' of your name,
    and day by day
    I will ful- ' fill my vows.

⁵ For God alone I ' wait in silence;
  truly, my hope ' is in God.

⁶ God alone is my rock
  and ' my salvation,
    my stronghold,
    so that I shall nev- ' er be shaken.

⁷ In God is my deliverance
  ' and my honor;
    God is my strong rock
    ' and my refuge.

⁸ Put your trust in God al- ' ways,
  O people,
    pour out your hearts
    before the one who ' is our refuge.

⁹ Those of high degree
  are but a fleeting breath;
  those of low estate can- ' not be trusted.
    Placed on the scales together
    they weigh even less ' than a breath.

¹⁰ Put no trust in extortion;
  in robbery take no ' empty pride;
    though wealth increase,
    set not your ' heart upon it.

¹¹ God has spoken once,
  twice ' have I heard it,
    that power be- ' longs to God.

¹² Steadfast love belongs to ' you, O Lord,
  for you repay all
    according ' to their deeds.

62

¹ For God alone I ' wait in silence;
  from God comes ' my salvation.

² God alone is my rock and ' my salvation,
  my stronghold,
    so that I shall nev- ' er be shaken.

³ How long will all of you
  assail ' me to crush me
    as if I were a leaning fence,
    a ' toppling wall?

⁴ They seek only to bring me down
  from my place of honor;
  they take plea- ' sure in lies.
    They bless with their lips,
    but in their ' hearts they curse.

63

¹ O God, you are my God;
  eager- ' ly I seek you;
    my soul thirsts for you,
    my flesh faints for you,
    as in a dry and weary land
    where there ' is no water.

² Therefore I have gazed upon you
  in your ' holy place,
    that I might behold your power
    ' and your glory.

³ For your steadfast love
  is better than ' life itself;
    my lips shall ' give you praise.

⁴ So will I bless you as long ' as I live
  and lift up my hands ' in your name.

5 My spirit is content,
  as with the rich- | est of foods,
    and my mouth praises you
    with | joyful lips,

6 when I remember you up- | on my bed,
  and meditate on you
    in | the night watches.

7 For you have | been my helper,
  and under the shadow
  of your wings
  I | will rejoice.

8 My whole being | clings to you;
  your right hand | holds me fast.

9 May those who seek my life
  | to destroy it
    go down into the depths
    | of the earth;

10 let them be thrown
  upon the edge | of the sword,
    and let them be | food for jackals.

11 But the king will rejoice in God;
  all those who swear by God's name
  | will be glad;
    for the mouth of those
    who speak lies | shall be stopped.

64

1 Hear my voice, O God,
  when | I complain;
    protect my life
    from fear | of the enemy.

2 Hide me from the conspiracy
  | of the wicked,
    from the mob of | evildoers.

3 They sharpen their tongue
  | like a sword,
    and aim their bitter | words
    like arrows,

4 that they may shoot down
  the blame- | less from ambush;
    they shoot without warning
    and are | not afraid.

5 They hold fast to their | evil course;
  they plan how they
    may | hide their snares.

6 They say, "Who will see us?
  Who will find | out our crimes?
    We have thought out a | perfect plot."

7 The human mind and heart
  | are a mystery;
    but God will loose an arrow at them,
    and suddenly they | will be wounded.

8 God will make them trip
  o- | ver their tongues,
    and all who see them
    will | flee in horror.

9 Everyone will stand in awe
  and de- | clare God's works;
    they will ponder
    what | God has done.

10 The righteous will rejoice
  and put their trust | in the LORD,
    and all who are true of | heart
    will glory.

65

1 You are to be praised, O | God, in Zion;
  to you shall vows | be fulfilled.

2 To you, the one who | answers prayer,
  to you all | flesh shall come.

3 Our sins are strong- | er than we are,
    but you blot out
    | our transgressions.

4 Happy are they whom you choose
  and draw to your | courts
  to dwell there!
    They will be satisfied
    by the beauty of your house,
    by the holiness | of your temple.

5 Awesome things will you show us
  in your righteousness,
  O God of | our salvation,
    O hope of all the ends of the earth
    and of the oceans | far away.

6 You make firm the mountains
  | by your power;
    you are girded a- | bout with might.

7 You still the roaring | of the seas,
    the roaring of their waves,
    and the clamor | of the peoples.

8 Those who dwell
 at the ends of the earth
 will tremble at your | marvelous signs;
  you make the dawn and the dusk
  to | sing for joy.

9 You visit the earth
 and water it abundantly;
 you make it very plenteous;
 the river of God is | full of water.
  You prepare the grain,
  for so you provide | for the earth.

10 You drench the furrows
 and smooth | out the ridges;
  with heavy rain
  you soften the ground
  and | bless its increase.

11 You crown the year
 | with your goodness,
  and your paths over- | flow
  with plenty.

12 May the fields of the wilderness
 be | rich for grazing,
  and the hills be | clothed with joy.

13 May the meadows
 cover themselves with flocks,
 and the valleys
 cloak them- | selves with grain;
  let them shout for | joy and sing.

66

1 Be joyful in God, | all you lands;
  be joyful, | all the earth.

2 Sing the glory | of God's name;
  sing the glory | of God's praise.

3 Say to God,
 "How awesome | are your deeds!
  Because of your great strength
  your enemies | cringe before you.

4 All the earth bows | down before you,
  sings to you,
  sings | out your name."

5 Come now and see the | works of God,
 how awesome are God's deeds
 | toward all people.

6 God turned the sea into dry land,
 so that they went
 through the wa- | ter on foot,
  and there we re- | joiced in God.

7 Ruling forever in might,
 God keeps watch o- | ver the nations;
  let no rebels ex- | alt themselves.

8 Bless our | God, you peoples;
  let the sound of | praise be heard.

9 Our God has kept us
 a- | mong the living
  and has not allowed our | feet to slip.

10 For you, O God, have | tested us;
 you have tried us
 just as sil- | ver is tried.

11 You brought us in- | to the net;
  you laid heavy burdens
  up- | on our backs.

12 You let people ride over our heads;
 we went through | fire and water,
  but you brought us out
  into a place | of refreshment.

13 I will enter your house
 | with burnt offerings
  and will pay | you my vows—

14 those that I promised | with my lips
  and spoke with my mouth
  when I | was in trouble.

15 I will offer you burnt offerings
 of fatlings with the | smoke of rams;
  I will give you ox- | en and goats.

16 Come and listen, all you | who believe,
  and I will tell you
  what God has | done for me.

17 I called out to God | with my mouth,
  and praised the Lord
  | with my tongue.

18 If I had cherished evil | in my heart,
  the Lord would | not have heard me;

19 but in truth | God has heard me
  and has attended to the sound
  | of my prayer.

20 Blessed be God,
 who has not reject- | ed my prayer,
  nor withheld unfailing | love from me.

67

1 May God be merciful to ǀ us
and bless us;
    may the light of God's face
    ǀ shine upon us.

2 Let your way be known ǀ upon earth,
    your saving health
    a- ǀ mong all nations.

3 Let the peoples praise ǀ you, O God;
    let all the ǀ peoples praise you.

4 Let the nations be glad
and ǀ sing for joy,
    for you judge the peoples
    with equity
    and guide all the na- ǀ tions on earth.

5 Let the peoples praise ǀ you, O God;
    let all the ǀ peoples praise you.

6 The earth has brought ǀ forth
its increase;
    God, our own ǀ God, has blessed us.

7 May God ǀ give us blessing,
    and may all the ends of the earth
    ǀ stand in awe.

68

1 Let God arise,
and let God's ene- ǀ mies be scattered;
    let those who ǀ hate God flee.

2 As smoke is driven away,
so you should drive ǀ them away;
    as the wax melts before the fire,
    so let the wicked perish
    at the pres- ǀ ence of God.

3 But let the righteous be glad
and rejoice ǀ before God;
    let them also be mer- ǀ ry and joyful.

4 Sing to God,
sing praises to God's name;
exalt the one who ǀ rides the clouds;
    I Am is that name,
    rejoice ǀ before God!

5 In your holy habita- ǀ tion, O God,
    you are a father to orphans,
    defend- ǀ er of widows;

6 you give the solitary a home and
bring forth prisoners ǀ into freedom;
    but the rebels shall live
    in ǀ desert places.

7 O God, when you went forth
be- ǀ fore your people,
    when you marched
    ǀ through the wilderness,

8 the earth quaked,
and the skies poured down rain,
at the presence of God,
the ǀ God of Sinai,
    at the presence of God,
    the ǀ God of Israel.

9 You sent a bountiful ǀ rain, O God;
    you restored your inheritance
    ǀ when it languished.

10 Your people found their ǀ home in it;
    in your goodness, O God, you have
    made provision ǀ for the poor.

11 The Lord ǀ gives the word;
    great is the company of women
    who an- ǀ nounce the tidings:

12 "Kings with their armies
are flee- ǀ ing away;
    the women at home
    are divid- ǀ ing the spoils."

13 Though you lingered
a- ǀ mong the sheepfolds,
    you shall be like a dove
    whose wings are covered with silver,
    whose feathers are ǀ like green gold.

14 When the Almighty ǀ scattered kings,
    snow ǀ fell on Zalmon.

15 O mighty mountain, O ǀ hill of Bashan!
    O rugged mountain,
    O ǀ hill of Bashan!

16 Why do you look with envy,
O rugged mountain, at the hill
which God chose for a ǀ resting-place,
    where the Lord
    will re- ǀ side forever?

17 The chariots of God
are twenty thousand,
even thou- ǀ sands of thousands;
    the Lord comes in holi- ǀ ness
    from Sinai.

18 You have gone up on high
and led captivity captive;
you have received ˡ gifts from people,
from those who rebel
against the LORD ˡ God
who dwells there.

19 Blessed be the Lord
who bears us up ˡ day by day;
God is ˡ our salvation.

20 This is our God,
the God of ˡ our salvation;
God is the LORD,
by whom we ˡ escape death.

21 God shall crush the en- ˡ emies' heads,
and the hairy scalp
of those who continue
ˡ in their wickedness.

22 The LORD has said,
"I will bring them ˡ back from Bashan;
I will bring them back
from the depths ˡ of the sea;

23 that your foot may be ˡ dipped in blood,
the tongues of your dogs
in the blood ˡ of your enemies."

24 They see your proces- ˡ sion, O God,
your procession into the sanctuary,
my ˡ sovereign God:

25 the singers go before,
musicians ˡ follow after;
in the midst are maidens
playing ˡ tambourines.

26 Bless God in ˡ the assemblies;
bless the LORD,
you that are of the foun- ˡ tain
of Israel.

27 There is Benjamin,
least of the tribes, at the head;
the princes of Judah ˡ in a company;
and the princes
of Zebul- ˡ un and Naphtali.

28 Your God has or- ˡ dained
your strength;
your strength, God,
which you dis- ˡ played for us.

29 Kings shall bring ˡ gifts to you,
for your temple's sake
ˡ at Jerusalem.

30 Rebuke the wild animals
that live among the reeds,
and the herd of bulls
with the calves ˡ of the peoples.
Trample down those
who demand silver from us;
scatter the peoples
that de- ˡ light in war.

31 Let tribute be brought ˡ out of Egypt;
let Ethiopia stretch out its ˡ hands
to God.

32 Sing to God, O kingdoms ˡ of the earth;
sing praises ˡ to the Lord.

33 You ride in the heavens, O God,
in the ˡ ancient heavens;
you send forth your voice,
your ˡ mighty voice.

34 Ascribe pow- ˡ er to God,
whose majesty is over Israel;
whose strength is ˡ in the skies.

35 How wonderful you are
in your holy places, O ˡ God of Israel,
giving strength and power
to your people! ˡ Blessed be God!

69

1 Save ˡ me, O God,
for the waters have risen
up ˡ to my neck.

2 I am sinking in deep mire,
and there ˡ is no foothold.
I have come into deep waters,
and the torrent washes ˡ over me.

3 I have grown weary with my crying;
my ˡ throat is parched;
my eyes are worn out
from looking ˡ for my God.

4 Those who hate me without a cause
are more than the hairs of my head;
my lying foes who would destroy ˡ me
are mighty.
Must I then give back
what I ˡ never stole?

5 O God, you ˡ know my foolishness,
and my faults
are not hid- ˡ den from you.

6 Let not those who hope in you
be put to shame through me,
Lord | God of hosts;
let not those who seek you
be disgraced because of me,
O | God of Israel.

7 Surely, for your sake
I have suf- | fered reproach,
and shame has cov- | ered my face.

8 I have become a stranger
to | my own kindred,
an alien to my | mother's children.

9 Zeal for your house has eat- | en me up;
the scorn of those who scorn you
has fall- | en upon me.

10 I humbled my- | self with fasting,
but that was turned
to | my reproach.

11 I put on | sackcloth also,
and became a by- | word
among them.

12 Those who sit at the gate
mur- | mur against me,
and the drunkards
make | songs about me.

13 But as for me, this is my prayer to you,
at the time you have | set, O Lord:
"In your great mercy, O God,
answer me
with your un- | failing help.

14 Save me from the mire;
do not | let me sink;
let me be rescued
from those who hate me
and out of | the deep waters.

15 Let not the torrent of waters
wash over me,
neither let the deep swal- | low me up;
do not let the pit
shut its | mouth upon me.

16 Answer me, O Lord,
for your | love is kind;
in your great compassion,
| turn to me.

17 Hide not your face | from your servant;
be swift and answer me,
for I am | in distress.

18 Draw near to me | and redeem me;
because of my enemies
de- | liver me.

19 You know my reproach, my shame,
and | my dishonor;
my adversaries
are all | in your sight."

20 Reproach has broken my heart,
and I am sick | beyond healing;
I looked for sympathy,
but there was none,
for comforters,
but I | could find no one.

21 They gave me | gall to eat,
and when I was thirsty,
they gave me vine- | gar to drink.

22 Let the table before them | be a trap
and their sacred | feasts a snare.

23 Let their eyes be darkened,
that they | may not see,
and give them continual trembling
| in their loins.

24 Pour out your indigna- | tion
upon them,
and let your fierce anger
| overtake them.

25 Let their | camp be desolate,
and let there be none
to dwell | in their tents.

26 For they persecute the one
whom | you have stricken
and add to the pain of those
whom | you have pierced.

27 Lay to their charge guilt | upon guilt,
and let them not receive
your | vindication.

28 Let them be wiped out
of the book | of the living
and not be written
a- | mong the righteous.

29 As for me, I am afflicted | and in pain;
your help, O God,
will lift me | up on high.

30 I will praise your name, O | God,
in song;
I will proclaim your greatness
| with thanksgiving.

31 This will please the LORD
more than an of- | fering of oxen,
more than young bulls
with | horns and hoofs.

32 The afflicted shall see | and be glad;
you who seek God,
your | heart shall live.

33 For the LORD listens | to the needy,
and does not de- | spise
the prisoners.

34 Let the heavens and the | earth
praise God,
the seas
and all that | moves in them;

35 for God will save Zion
and rebuild the cit- | ies of Judah;
they shall live there
and have it as | their possession.

36 The children of God's servants
will in- | herit it,
and those who love God's name
will | dwell therein.

70

1 Be pleased, O God, to de- | liver me;
O LORD, make | haste to help me.

2 Let those who seek my life
be put to shame | and confounded;
let those who take pleasure
in my misfortune
draw back and | be disgraced.

3 Let those who say to me "Aha!"
and gloat | over me
turn back because | of their shame.

4 Let all who seek you
rejoice and be | glad in you;
let those who love your salvation
say forever,
"Great | is the LORD!"

5 But as for me, I am poor and needy;
come to me quick- | ly, O God.
You are my helper
and my deliverer;
O LORD, | do not tarry.

71

1 In you, O LORD, have I | taken refuge;
let me never be | put to shame.

2 In your righteousness,
deliver me and | set me free;
incline your ear to | me and save me

3 Be my strong rock,
a castle to | keep me safe;
you are my crag
| and my stronghold.

4 Deliver me, my God,
from the hand | of the wicked,
from the clutches of the evildoer
and | the oppressor.

5 For you are my hope, | O Lord GOD,
my confidence since | I was young.

6 I have been sustained by you
ever since I was born;
from my mother's womb
you have | been my strength;
my praise shall be al- | ways of you.

7 I have become a por- | tent to many;
but you are my refuge
| and my strength.

8 Let my mouth be full | of your praise
and your glory all | the day long.

9 Do not cast me off in | my old age;
forsake me not
when | my strength fails.

10 For my enemies are talk- | ing
against me,
and those who lie in wait for my life
take coun- | sel together.

11 They say, "Pursue and seize that one
whom God | has forsaken;
because there is none
| who will save."

12 O God, be not | far from me;
come quickly to help me,
| O my God.

13 May my accusers be put to shame
and | waste away;
let those who seek my misfortune
be engulfed by scorn | and reproach.

14 But I shall always | wait in patience,
    and shall praise you
    | more and more.
15 My mouth shall recount
    your mighty acts and saving deeds
    | all day long;
        though I cannot | know
        their number.
16 I will begin with the mighty works
    of | the Lord GOD;
        I will recall your righteousness,
        | yours alone.
17 O God, you have taught me
    since | I was young,
        and to this day
        I tell of your won- | derful works.
18 Now that I am old and gray-headed,
    O God, do | not forsake me,
        till I make known your strength
        to this generation
        and your power
        to all who | are to come.
19 Your righteousness, O God,
    reaches | to the heavens;
        you have done great things;
        who is like | you, O God?
20 You have shown me
    great troubles | and adversities,
        but you will restore my life
        and bring me up again
        from the deep places | of the earth.
21 You strengthen me | more and more;
    you enfold and | comfort me.
22 Therefore I will praise you
    upon the lyre
    for your faithfulness, | O my God;
        I will sing to you with the harp,
        O Holy | One of Israel.
23 My lips will sing with joy
    when I | play to you,
        and so will my soul,
        which you | have redeemed.
24 My tongue will proclaim
    your righteousness | all day long,
        for they are shamed and disgraced
        who sought to | do me harm.

72

1 Give the king your jus- | tice, O God,
    and your righteousness
    to | the king's son;
2 that he may rule
    your | people righteously
        and the | poor with justice;
3 that the mountains
    may bring prosperity | to the people,
        and the | hills, in righteousness.
4 Let him defend the needy
    a- | mong the people,
        rescue the poor,
        and crush | the oppressor.
5 May he live as long
    as the sun and | moon endure,
        from one generation | to another.
6 Let him come down like rain
    upon | the mown field,
        like showers that wa- | ter the earth.
7 In his time
    may the | righteous flourish;
        and let there be
        an abundance of peace
        till the moon shall | be no more.
8 May he rule from | sea to sea,
    and from the river Euphrates
    to the ends | of the earth.
9 May his foes bow | down before him,
    and his enemies | lick the dust.
10 May the kings of Tarshish
    and of the | isles pay tribute,
        and the kings of Sheba and Seba
        | offer gifts.
11 May all kings bow | down before him,
    and all the nations | do him service.
12 For the king delivers the poor
    who cry out | in distress,
        the oppressed,
        and those who | have no helper.
13 He has compassion
    on the low- | ly and poor,
        and preserves the lives
        | of the needy.

¹⁴ From oppression and violence
he re- [|] deems their lives,
    and precious is their blood
    [|] in his sight.

¹⁵ Long may he live!
And may there be given to him
[|] gold of Sheba;
    may prayer be made for him always,
    and may they bless him
    all [|] the day long.

¹⁶ May there be an abundance of grain
in the land, growing thick
even [|] on the hilltops;
    may its fruit flourish like Lebanon,
    and may people flourish in cities
    like the grass [|] of the field.

¹⁷ May the king's name remain forever
and be established
as long as the [|] sun endures;
    may all the nations
    bless themselves in him
    and [|] call him blessed.

¹⁸ Blessed are you, LORD God,
the [|] God of Israel;
    you alone do [|] wondrous deeds!

¹⁹ And blessed be your glorious [|] name
forever,
    and may all the earth
    be filled with your glory.
    A- [|] men. Amen.

73

¹ Truly, God is [|] good to Israel,
to those who are [|] pure in heart.

² But as for me,
my feet had [|] nearly slipped;
    I had almost [|] tripped and fallen;

³ because I en- [|] vied the proud
and saw the prosperity
[|] of the wicked.

⁴ For their entire lives
seem [|] free of pain,
    and they have their [|] fill to eat;

⁵ in the misfortunes of others
they [|] have no share;
    they are not afflicted as [|] others are;

⁶ therefore they wear their pride
[|] like a necklace
    and wrap their violence about them
    [|] like a cloak.

⁷ Their iniquity
comes [|] from gross minds,
    and their hearts overflow
    with [|] wicked thoughts.

⁸ They scoff and [|] speak maliciously;
out of their haughtiness
    they [|] plan oppression.

⁹ They set their mouths
a- [|] gainst the heavens,
    and their evil speech
    runs [|] through the world.

¹⁰ Therefore the people [|] turn to them
and they enjoy full- [|] ness of days.

¹¹ They say, "How [|] should God know?
Is there knowledge
    in [|] the Most High?"

¹² So then, these [|] are the wicked;
always at ease,
    they in- [|] crease their wealth.

¹³ In vain have I kept [|] my heart clean,
and washed my [|] hands
    in innocence.

¹⁴ I have been afflicted [|] all day long,
and punished [|] every morning.

¹⁵ Had I gone on speak- [|] ing this way,
I should have betrayed
    the generation [|] of your children.

¹⁶ When I tried to under- [|] stand
these things,
    it was too [|] hard for me;

¹⁷ until I entered God's [|] sanctuary
and discerned the end [|] of the wicked.

¹⁸ Surely, you set them in [|] slippery places;
you cast them [|] down in ruin.

¹⁹ Oh, how suddenly
do they come [|] to destruction,
    come to an end,
    and per- [|] ish from terror!

²⁰ Like a dream when one awak- [|] ens,
O Lord,
    when you arise
    you will make their [|] image vanish.

²¹ When my mind be- ' came embittered,
  I was sorely wounded ' in my heart.
²² I was stupid
  and had no ' understanding;
    I was like a brute beast
    ' in your presence.
²³ Yet I am al- ' ways with you;
  you hold me by ' my right hand.
²⁴ You will guide me ' by your counsel,
  and afterwards
    receive ' me with glory.
²⁵ Whom have I in heav- ' en but you?
  And having you,
    I desire nothing ' upon earth.
²⁶ Though my flesh and my heart
  should ' waste away,
    God is the strength of my heart
    and my por- ' tion forever.
²⁷ Truly, those who forsake ' you
  will perish;
    you destroy all who ' are unfaithful.
²⁸ But it is good for me to ' be near God;
  I have made you
    my refuge, Lord GOD,
    to tell of ' all your works.

74

¹ O God,
  why have you utterly ' cast us off?
    Why is your wrath so hot
    against the sheep ' of your pasture?
² Remember your congregation
  that you purchased ' long ago,
    the tribe you redeemed
    to be your inheritance,
    and Mount Zion ' where you dwell.
³ Turn your steps
  toward the ' endless ruins;
    the enemy has laid waste everything
    in your ' sanctuary.
⁴ Your adversaries roared
  in your ' holy place;
    they set up their standards
    as sym- ' bols of victory.
⁵ They came like people ' bearing axes
  to cut down a ' grove of trees.

⁶ They broke down
  all ' your carved work
    with hatch- ' ets and hammers.
⁷ They set fire to your ' holy place;
  they defiled
    the dwelling-place of your name
    and razed it ' to the ground.
⁸ They said to themselves,
  "Let us destroy them ' altogether."
    They burned down
    all the meeting-places of God
    ' in the land.
⁹ There are no signs for us to see;
  there is no ' prophet left;
    there is not one among us
    who ' knows how long.
¹⁰ How long, O God,
  will the adver- ' sary scoff?
    Will the enemy
    blaspheme your ' name forever?
¹¹ Why do you draw ' back your hand?
  Why does your right hand
    lie weary ' in your bosom?
¹² Yet God is my king
  from ' ancient times,
    victorious in the midst ' of the earth.
¹³ You divided the sea ' by your might
  and shattered the heads
    of the dragons up- ' on the waters;
¹⁴ you crushed the heads ' of Leviathan
  and gave it to desert crea- ' tures
    for food.
¹⁵ You split open ' spring and torrent;
  you dried up ever- ' flowing rivers.
¹⁶ Yours is the day,
  yours al- ' so the night;
    you established
    the moon ' and the sun.
¹⁷ You fixed all the boundaries
  ' of the earth;
    you made both sum- ' mer
    and winter.
¹⁸ Remember, O LORD,
  how the en- ' emy scoffed,
    how a foolish people
    de- ' spised your name.

19 Do not hand over
the life of your dove | to wild beasts;
never forget the lives | of your poor.

20 Look up- | on your covenant;
the dark places of the earth
are | haunts of violence.

21 Let not the oppressed be | put to shame;
let the poor and needy
| praise your name.

22 Arise, O God, main- | tain your cause;
remember how fools revile you
| all day long.

23 Forget not the clamor
of your | adversaries,
the continuous tumult
raised | by your enemies.

75

1 We give you thanks, O God,
we | give you thanks,
calling upon your name and
declaring all your won- | derful deeds.

2 "I will appoint a | time," says God;
"I will | judge with equity.

3 Though the earth
and all its inhab- | itants crumble,
I will make its | pillars fast.

4 I will say to the boasters,
| 'Boast no more,'
and to the wicked,
'Do not | lift your horns;

5 do not lift your | horns so high,
nor speak with | a proud neck.'"

6 For exaltation comes neither
from the east nor | from the west,
nor does it come
| from the wilderness.

7 It is | God who judges,
who puts down one
and lifts | up another.

8 For in the LORD's hand there is a cup
full of spiced and | foaming wine;
the LORD will pour it out,
and all the wicked of the earth
shall drink and | drain the dregs.

9 But I will re- | joice forever;
I will sing praises
to the | God of Jacob.

10 "I will break off all the horns
| of the wicked;
but the horns of the righteous
shall | be exalted."

76

1 In Judah, O God, | you are known;
your name is | great in Israel.

2 At Salem is your | tabernacle,
and your dwelling | is in Zion.

3 There you broke the | flashing arrows,
the shield, the sword,
and the weap- | ons of battle.

4 How glo- | rious you are!
More splendid
than the ever- | lasting mountains!

5 The strong of heart
have been despoiled;
they sink | into sleep;
none of the warriors can | lift a hand.

6 At your rebuke, O | God of Jacob,
both horse and rid- | er lie stunned.

7 What terror | you inspire!
Who can stand before you
when | you are angry?

8 From heaven
you | pronounced judgment;
the earth was afraid | and was still,

9 when God rose | up to judgment
and to save all the oppressed
| of the earth.

10 Surely, human wrath
gives | praise to you,
and the survivor of your wrath
| you restrain.

11 Make a vow to the LORD your | God
and keep it;
let all around bring gifts
to the one | who is awesome,

12 who breaks the spir- | it of princes,
and strikes terror
in the rulers | of the earth.

77

¹ I will cry a- ǀ loud to God;
　I will cry aloud,
　　and ǀ God will hear me.

² In the day of my trouble
　I ǀ sought the Lord;
　　my hand was stretched out by night
　　and did not tire;
　　I refused ǀ to be comforted.

³ I think of God, ǀ I am restless,
　I ponder, and my ǀ spirit faints.

⁴ You will not let my ǀ eyelids close;
　I am troubled and I ǀ cannot speak.

⁵ I consider the ǀ days of old;
　I remember the ǀ years long past;

⁶ I commune with my heart
　ǀ in the night;
　　I ponder and ǀ search my mind:

⁷ "Will the Lord cast me ǀ off forever
　and never again ǀ show me favor?"

⁸ Has God's steadfast love
　come to an ǀ end forever?
　　Has the Lord's promise failed
　　ǀ for all time?

⁹ Has God forgotten ǀ to be gracious,
　and in anger with- ǀ held compassion?

¹⁰ And I said, "My ǀ grief is this:
　The right hand of the Most ǀ High
　has changed."

¹¹ I will remember
　the works ǀ of the Lord,
　　and call to mind
　　your won- ǀ ders of old.

¹² I will meditate on ǀ all your acts
　and ponder your ǀ mighty deeds.

¹³ Your way, O ǀ God, is holy;
　who is so great a god
　ǀ as our God?

¹⁴ You are the God ǀ who works wonders
　and have declared your power
　a- ǀ mong the peoples.

¹⁵ By your strength
　you have re- ǀ deemed your people,
　　the descendants of Ja- ǀ cob
　　and Joseph.

¹⁶ The waters saw you, O God;
　the waters saw ǀ you and trembled;
　　the very ǀ depths were shaken.

¹⁷ The clouds poured out water;
　ǀ the skies thundered;
　　your lightning bolts
　　flashed ǀ to and fro;

¹⁸ the sound of your thunder
　was in the whirlwind;
　　your lightnings lit ǀ up the world;
　　the earth trem- ǀ bled and shook.

¹⁹ Your way was in the sea,
　and your paths in ǀ the great waters,
　　yet your footsteps ǀ were not seen.

²⁰ You led your people ǀ like a flock
　by the hand of Mo- ǀ ses and Aaron.

78

¹ Hear my teaching, ǀ O my people;
　incline your ears
　　to the words ǀ of my mouth.

² I will open my mouth ǀ in a parable;
　I will declare the mysteries
　　of ǀ ancient times—

³ that which we have heard and known,
　and what our fore- ǀ bears have told us,
　　we will not hide
　　ǀ from their children.

⁴ We will recount to generations to come
　the praiseworthy deeds
　and the power ǀ of the Lord,
　　and the wonderful works
　　ǀ God has done.

⁵ The Lord gave a decree in Jacob
　and established a ǀ law in Israel,
　　commanding our ancestors
　　to teach it ǀ to their children;

⁶ that the generations to come might know,
　and the children ǀ yet unborn;
　　that they in their turn
　　might tell it ǀ to their children;

⁷ so that they might
　put their ǀ trust in God,
　　and not forget the deeds of God,
　　but keep ǀ God's commandments,

8 and not be like their ancestors,
 a stubborn and rebellious | generation,
  a generation
   whose heart was not steadfast,
   and whose spirit was not faith- | ful
   to God.

9 The people of Ephraim,
 armed | with the bow,
  turned back in the | day of battle;

10 they did not keep the cove- | nant of God,
 and refused to walk | in God's law;

11 they forgot what | God had done,
 and the wonders
  that | had been shown them.

12 God worked marvels
 in the sight | of their ancestors,
  in the land of Egypt,
  in the | field of Zoan,

13 splitting open the sea
 and letting | them pass through;
  making the waters stand | up
  like walls;

14 leading them with a | cloud by day,
 and all the night with a | glow of fire;

15 splitting the rocks | in the wilderness
  and giving them drink
  as | from the deep;

16 bringing streams out | of a rock,
  making them flow down
  | like a river.

17 But they went on sinning | against God,
  rebelling in the desert
  against | the Most High.

18 They tested God | in their hearts,
  demanding food | for themselves.

19 They railed against | God and said,
  "Can God set a table
  | in the wilderness?

20 True, God struck the rock,
  the waters gushed out,
  and the torrents | overflowed;
   but is God able to give bread
   or to provide meat | for this people?"

21 Hearing this,
  the LORD was | full of wrath;
   a fire was kindled against Jacob,
   and anger mounted | against Israel;

22 for they had no | faith in God,
  nor did they put their trust
  in God's | saving power.

23 So God commanded the | clouds above
  and opened the | doors of heaven,

24 raining down manna upon | them to eat
  and giving them | grain from heaven.

25 So mortals ate the | bread of angels;
  God provided for them | food enough.

26 The LORD caused the east wind
 to blow | in the heavens
  and powerfully led out
  | the south wind,

27 raining down flesh upon | them like dust
  and flying birds
  like the sand | of the seas,

28 letting them fall in the midst | of the camp
  and round a- | bout the dwellings.

29 So the people ate and | were well filled,
  for God gave them
  | what they craved.

30 But before they had satis- | fied
  their craving,
   while the food
   was still | in their mouths,

31 God's anger mount- | ed against them;
  God slew their strongest men
  and laid low the | youth of Israel.

32 In spite of all this,
  they | went on sinning
   and had no faith
   in God's won- | derful works.

33 So the LORD brought their days
 to an end | like a breath
  and their years in | sudden terror.

34 Whenever God slew them,
  | they would seek God,
   and repent,
   and diligently | search for God.

35 They would remember
  that God | was their rock,
   and the Most High God
   | their redeemer.

36 But they flattered God
  | with their mouths
   and lied to God | with their tongues.

37 Their heart ⏐ was not steadfast,
    and they were not faithful
    ⏐ to the covenant.
38 Yet God, being merciful,
    forgave their sins
    and did ⏐ not destroy them;
      holding back anger many times
      and not giving ⏐ way to wrath;
39 remembering that they ⏐ were but flesh,
    a breath that goes forth
    and does ⏐ not return.
40 How often the people disobeyed
    ⏐ in the wilderness
    and offended ⏐ in the desert!
41 Again and again they ⏐ tested God
    and provoked
    the Holy ⏐ One of Israel.
42 They did not remem- ⏐ ber God's power
    in the day when they were ransomed
    ⏐ from the enemy;
43 how God showed ⏐ signs in Egypt
    and omens in the ⏐ fields of Zoan,
44 turning their rivers ⏐ into blood,
    so that they could not drink
    ⏐ of their streams,
45 sending swarms of flies among them,
    which ⏐ ate them up,
    and frogs, ⏐ which destroyed them,
46 giving their crops to the ⏐ caterpillar,
    the fruit of their toil ⏐ to the locust,
47 killing their ⏐ vines with hail
    and their syca- ⏐ mores with frost,
48 delivering their cat- ⏐ tle to hailstones
    and their livestock
    to ⏐ bolts of lightning.
49 God poured out upon them
    ⏐ blazing anger:
      fury, indignation, and distress,
      a troop of de- ⏐ stroying angels.
50 Giving full rein to anger,
    God did not spare ⏐ them from death,
      but delivered their lives ⏐ to the plague,
51 striking down
    all the first- ⏐ born of Egypt,
      the flower of youth
      in the dwell- ⏐ ings of Ham.

52 God led out the peo- ⏐ ple like sheep
    and guided them in the wilderness
    ⏐ like a flock.
53 God led them to safety,
    and they were ⏐ not afraid;
      but the sea
      over- ⏐ whelmed their enemies.
54 God brought them to the ⏐ holy hill,
    the mountain won
    by ⏐ God's right hand.
55 The LORD drove out nations
    before them
    and apportioned an inheritance
    to ⏐ them by lot,
      settling the tribes of Israel
      ⏐ in their tents.
56 But they tested the Most High God,
    ⏐ and rebelled,
      and did not keep ⏐ God's decrees.
57 They turned away
    and were disloyal ⏐ like their ancestors;
      they were undependable
      like ⏐ a warped bow.
58 They grieved God
    with ⏐ their high places
      and provoked displeasure
      ⏐ with their idols.
59 Hearing this, the ⏐ LORD was angry
    and utterly re- ⏐ jected Israel;
60 forsaking the taberna- ⏐ cle at Shiloh,
    the tent where God lived
    ⏐ among mortals,
61 delivering the ark in- ⏐ to captivity
    and glory into the adver- ⏐ sary's hand;
62 handing over the people ⏐ to the sword
    and becoming angry
    against ⏐ God's own heritage.
63 The fire consumed ⏐ their young men;
    there were no wedding songs
    ⏐ for their maidens.
64 Their priests fell ⏐ by the sword,
    and their widows
    made no ⏐ lamentation.
65 Then the LORD woke
    as ⏐ though from sleep,
      like a warrior ⏐ flushed with wine.

66 God beat | back the enemies
   and put them to per- | petual shame.

67 God rejected the | tent of Joseph
   and did not choose
     the | tribe of Ephraim,

68 choosing instead the | tribe of Judah
   and Mount Zion,
     be- | loved by God,

69 where a sanctuary was built
   like the | heights of heaven,
     like the ever- | lasting earth.

70 God chose David | to be servant,
   and took him away
     | from the sheepfolds,

71 bringing him
   from tending the | nursing ewes
     to be a shepherd
       over God's people Jacob,
       over the inheri- | tance of Israel.

72 So David shepherded them
   with a | blameless heart
     and guided them
       with | skillful hands.

79

1 O God, the nations have come
   into your inheritance;
     they have profaned your | holy temple;
     they have made Jerusalem
       a | heap of rubble.

2 They have given the bodies
   of your servants as food
   for the birds | of the air,
     and the flesh of your faithful ones
     to the beasts | of the field.

3 They have shed their blood like water
   on every side | of Jerusalem,
     and there was no one
     to | bury them.

4 We have become a reproach
   | to our neighbors,
     an object of scorn and derision
     to | those around us.

5 How long will you be an- | gry, O Lord?
   Will your fury blaze
     like | fire forever?

6 Pour out your wrath upon the nations
   who | have not known you
     and upon the kingdoms that
     have not called up- | on your name.

7 For they have de- | voured Jacob
   and made his dwell- | ing a ruin.

8 Remember not our past sins;
   let your compassion
   be | swift to meet us;
     for we have been brought | very low.

9 Help us, O God our Savior,
   for the glory | of your name;
     deliver us and forgive us our sins,
     | for your name's sake.

10 Why should the nations say,
   "Where | is their God?"
     Let it be known among the nations
     and in our sight
     that you avenge the shedding
     of your | servants' blood.

11 Let the sorrowful sighing
   of the prisoners | come before you,
     and by your great might spare those
     who are con- | demned to die.

12 Pay back sevenfold
   into the bosom | of our neighbors
     the mockery with which
     they mocked | you, O Lord.

13 For we are your people
   and the sheep | of your pasture;
     we will give you thanks forever
     and show forth your praise
     from | age to age.

80

1 Hear, O Shepherd of Israel,
   leading Joseph | like a flock;
     shine forth, you that are enthroned
     up- | on the cherubim.

2 In the presence of Ephraim, Benjamin,
   | and Manasseh,
     stir up your strength
     and | come to help us.

3 Restore | us, O God;
   let your face shine upon us,
     and we | shall be saved.

4 O LORD | God of hosts,
　　how long will your anger fume
　　when your | people pray?

5 You have fed them
　with the | bread of tears;
　　you have given them
　　bowls of | tears to drink.

6 You have made us
　the derision | of our neighbors,
　　and our enemies
　　laugh | us to scorn.

7 Restore us, O | God of hosts;
　　let your face shine upon us,
　　and we | shall be saved.

8 You have brought a vine
　| out of Egypt;
　　you cast out the nations
　　and | planted it.

9 You cleared the | ground for it;
　　it took root and | filled the land.

10 The mountains were covered
　| by its shadow
　　and the towering cedar trees
　　| by its boughs.

11 You stretched out its tendrils
　| to the sea
　　and its branches | to the river.

12 Why have you broken | down its wall,
　　so that all who pass by
　　pluck | off its grapes?

13 The wild boar of the forest
　has | ravaged it,
　　and the beasts of the field
　　have | grazed upon it.

14 Turn now, O | God of hosts,
　　look | down from heaven;

15 behold and | tend this vine;
　　preserve what your right | hand
　　has planted.

16 They burn it with | fire like rubbish;
　　at the rebuke of your countenance
　　| let them perish.

17 Let your hand be upon the one
　at | your right hand,
　　the one you have made so strong
　　| for yourself.

18 And so will we never
　turn a- | way from you;
　　give us life,
　　that we may call up- | on your name.

19 Restore us, O LORD | God of hosts;
　　let your face shine upon us,
　　and we | shall be saved.

81

1 Sing with joy to | God our strength
　　and raise a loud shout
　　to the | God of Jacob.

2 Raise a song and | sound the timbrel,
　　the merry harp, | and the lyre.

3 Blow the ram's horn at | the new moon,
　　and at the full moon,
　　the day | of our feast;

4 for this is a stat- | ute for Israel,
　　a law of the | God of Jacob.

5 God laid it
　as a solemn charge upon Joseph,
　going out over the | land of Egypt,
　　where I heard a voice
　　I | did not know:

6 "I eased your shoulder
　| from the burden;
　　your hands were set free
　　from the grave- | digger's basket.

7 You called on me in trouble,
　and I de- | livered you;
　　I answered you
　　from the secret place of thunder
　　and tested you
　　at the wa- | ters of Meribah.

8 Hear, O my people,
　and I will ad- | monish you:
　　O Israel,
　　if you would but lis- | ten to me!

9 There shall be no strange | god
　among you;
　　you shall not worship a | foreign god.

10 I am the LORD your God,
　who brought you
　out of the | land of Egypt.
　　Open your mouth wide,
　　and I | I will fill it.

¹¹ Yet my people did not | hear my voice,
and Israel would | not obey me.

¹² So I gave them over
to the stubbornness | of their hearts,
to follow their | own devices.

¹³ Oh, that my people would lis- | ten to me,
that Israel would walk | in my ways!

¹⁴ I would quickly sub- | due their enemies
and turn my hand
a- | gainst their foes.

¹⁵ Those who hate the LORD
would | cringe in fear,
and their punishment
would | last forever.

¹⁶ But I would feed you
with the | finest wheat
and satisfy you
with honey | from the rock."

82

¹ God stands to charge
the divine coun- | cil assembled,
giving judgment
in the midst | of the gods:

² "How long will you | judge unjustly,
and show favor | to the wicked?

³ Save the weak | and the orphan;
defend the hum- | ble and needy;

⁴ rescue the weak | and the poor;
deliver them
from the power | of the wicked.

⁵ They do not know,
neither do they understand;
they wander a- | bout in darkness;
all the foundations of the | earth
are shaken.

⁶ Now I say to you, | 'You are gods,
and all of you children
of | the Most High;

⁷ nevertheless,
you shall | die like mortals,
and fall like | any prince.'"

⁸ Arise, O God, and | rule the earth,
for you shall take all nations
| for your own.

83

¹ O God, do | not be silent;
do not keep still
nor hold your | peace, O God;

² for your enemies | are in tumult,
and those who hate you
have lifted | up their heads.

³ They take secret counsel
a- | gainst your people
and plot against those
whom | you protect.

⁴ They have said,
"Come, let us wipe them out
| as a people;
let the name of Israel
be remem- | bered no more."

⁵ With one mind
they have con- | spired together;
they have made an alli- | ance
against you:

⁶ the tents of Edom | and the Ishmaelites;
the Moabites | and the Hagarenes;

⁷ Gebal, and Am- | mon, and Amalek;
the Philistines
and those who | dwell in Tyre.

⁸ The Assyrians
al- | so have joined them,
empowering the descen- | dants
of Lot.

⁹ Do to them as you | did to Midian,
to Sisera, and to Jabin
at the riv- | er of Kishon:

¹⁰ they were de- | stroyed at Endor;
they became like dung
up- | on the ground.

¹¹ Make their leaders
like Or- | eb and Zeeb,
and all their commanders
like Zebah | and Zalmunna,

¹² who said, "Let us take | for ourselves
the fields of God
as | our possession."

¹³ O my God,
make them like | whirling dust
and like chaff be- | fore the wind.

¹⁴ As fire burns | down a forest,
 as flames set moun- | tains ablaze,

¹⁵ so drive them | with your tempest
 and terrify them | with your storm;

¹⁶ cover their faces with | shame, O LORD,
 that they may | seek your name.

¹⁷ Let them be disgraced
 and terri- | fied forever;
  let them be put to confu- | sion
  and perish.

¹⁸ Let them know that you,
 whose name | is I AM—
  you alone are the Most High
  over | all the earth.

84

¹ How dear to me | is your dwelling,
 O | LORD of hosts!

² My soul has a desire and longing
 for the courts | of the LORD;
  my heart and my flesh rejoice
  in the | living God.

³ Even the sparrow has found a home,
 and the swallow a nest
 where she may | lay her young,
  by the side of your altars,
  O LORD of hosts,
  my king | and my God.

⁴ Happy are they
 who dwell | in your house!
  They will always be | praising you.

⁵ Happy are the people
 whose strength | is in you,
  whose hearts are set
  on the | pilgrims' way.

⁶ Those who go
 through the balsam valley
 will find it a | place of springs,
  for the early rains have covered it
  with | pools of water.

⁷ They will climb from | height to height,
 and the God of gods
 will be | seen in Zion.

⁸ LORD God of hosts, | hear my prayer;
 give ear, O | God of Jacob.

⁹ Behold our defend- | er, O God;
 and look upon the face
 of | your anointed.

¹⁰ For one day in your courts is better
 than a | thousand elsewhere.
  I would rather stand at the threshold
  of the house of my God than dwell
  in the tents | of the wicked.

¹¹ For the LORD God
 is both sun and shield,
 bestowing | grace and glory;
  no good thing will the LORD withhold
  from those who walk | with integrity.

¹² O | LORD of hosts,
 happy are they
 who put their | trust in you!

85

¹ You have been gracious to your | land,
 O LORD;
  you have restored
  the good for- | tune of Jacob.

² You have forgiven the iniquity
 | of your people
  and blotted out | all their sins.

³ You have withdrawn | all your fury
 and turned yourself
 from your wrathful | indignation.

⁴ Restore us then, O | God our Savior;
 let your anger de- | part from us.

⁵ Will you be displeased with | us
 forever?
  Will you prolong your anger
  from | age to age?

⁶ Will you not give us | life again,
 that your people
 may re- | joice in you?

⁷ Show us your steadfast | love, O LORD,
 and grant us | your salvation.

⁸ I will listen
 to what the LORD | God is saying;
  for you speak peace
  to your faithful people
  and to those
  who turn their | hearts to you.

⁹ Truly, your salvation is very near
to ˈ those who fear you,
 that your glory
 may dwell ˈ in our land.

¹⁰ Steadfast love and faithfulness
have ˈ met together;
 righteousness and peace
 have ˈ kissed each other.

¹¹ Faithfulness shall spring up
 ˈ from the earth,
 and righteousness
 shall look ˈ down from heaven.

¹² The LORD will indeed ˈ grant prosperity,
and our land will ˈ yield its increase.

¹³ Righteousness
shall go be- ˈ fore the LORD
 and shall prepare for ˈ God a pathway.

86

¹ Bow down your ear, O LORD,
and ˈ answer me,
 for I am poor ˈ and in misery.

² Keep watch over my life,
for ˈ I am faithful;
 save your servant
 who ˈ trusts in you.

³ Be merciful to me, O LORD,
for you ˈ are my God;
 I call upon you all ˈ the day long.

⁴ Gladden the soul ˈ of your servant,
for to you, O Lord,
 I lift ˈ up my soul.

⁵ For you, O Lord,
are good ˈ and forgiving,
 and abundant in mercy
 to all who ˈ call upon you.

⁶ Give ear, O LORD, ˈ to my prayer,
and attend to the voice
 of my ˈ supplications.

⁷ In the time of my trouble
I will ˈ call upon you,
 for you will ˈ answer me.

⁸ Among the gods
there is none like ˈ you, O Lord,
 nor anything ˈ like your works.

⁹ All the nations you have made
will come and worship ˈ you, O Lord,
 and glori- ˈ fy your name.

¹⁰ For you are great;
you do ˈ wondrous things;
 and you a- ˈ lone are God.

¹¹ Teach me your way, O LORD,
and I will walk ˈ in your truth;
 give me an undivided heart
 to re- ˈ vere your name.

¹² I will thank you, O Lord my God,
with ˈ all my heart,
 and glorify your name
 for- ˈ evermore.

¹³ For great is your ˈ love toward me;
you have delivered me
 from the ˈ pit of death.

¹⁴ The arrogant rise up
against me, O God,
and a band of violent people
 ˈ seeks my life;
 they have not set you
 be- ˈ fore their eyes.

¹⁵ But you, O Lord, are gracious
and full ˈ of compassion,
 slow to anger,
 and full of kind- ˈ ness and truth.

¹⁶ Turn to me and have mer- ˈ cy on me;
give your strength
 to your servant,
 and save the child
 ˈ of your handmaid.

¹⁷ Show me a sign of your favor,
so that those who hate me may see it
and be ˈ put to shame;
 because you, Lord, have helped me
 and com- ˈ forted me.

87

¹ On the ˈ holy mountain
 stands the city ˈ God has founded;

² the LORD loves the ˈ gates of Zion
 more than all the dwell- ˈ ings
 of Jacob.

³ Glorious things are spo- ˈ ken of you,
 O city ˈ of our God.

4 I count Egypt and Babylon
  among ǀ those who know me;
      behold Philistia, Tyre, and Ethiopia:
      in Zion ǀ were they born.

5 Of the city it shall be said,
  "Everyone was ǀ born in Zion,
      and the Most High
      shall sus- ǀ tain the city."

6 Enrolling the nations,
  the ǀ LORD records:
      "These al- ǀ so were born there."

7 The singers and the danc- ǀ ers will say,
  "All my fresh springs ǀ are in you."

88

1 O LORD, my ǀ God, my Savior,
  by day and night I ǀ cry to you.

2 Let my prayer
  enter in- ǀ to your presence;
      incline your ear to my ǀ lamentation.

3 For I am ǀ full of trouble;
  my life is at the brink ǀ of the grave.

4 I am counted among those
  who go down ǀ to the pit;
      I have become like one
      who ǀ has no strength;

5 lost among the dead,
  like the slain who lie ǀ in the grave,
      whom you remember no more,
      for they are cut off ǀ from your hand.

6 You have laid me in the depths
  ǀ of the pit,
      in dark places, and in ǀ the abyss.

7 Your anger weighs up- ǀ on me heavily,
  and all your great waves
      ǀ overwhelm me.

8 You have put my friends far from me;
  you have made me
  to be ab- ǀ horred by them;
      I am in prison and can- ǀ not get free.

9 My sight has failed me
  be- ǀ cause of trouble;
      LORD, I have called upon you daily;
      I have stretched out my ǀ hands
      to you.

10 Do you work wonders ǀ for the dead?
      Will those who have died
      stand up and ǀ give you thanks?

11 Will your lovingkindness
  be declared ǀ in the grave,
      your faithfulness
      in the land ǀ of destruction?

12 Will your wonders
  be known ǀ in the dark
      or your righteousness
      in the country where all ǀ is forgotten?

13 But as for me, O LORD,
  I cry to ǀ you for help;
      in the morning
      my prayer ǀ comes before you.

14 LORD, why have you re- ǀ jected me?
      Why have you hidden your ǀ face
      from me?

15 Ever since my youth,
  I have been wretched
  and at the ǀ point of death;
      I have borne your terrors
      ǀ and am helpless.

16 Your blazing anger has swept ǀ over me;
      your terrors ǀ have destroyed me;

17 they surround me all day long
  ǀ like a flood;
      they encompass me on ǀ every side.

18 My friend and my neighbor
  you have put a- ǀ way from me,
      and darkness
      is my on- ǀ ly companion.

89

1 Your love, O LORD, forever ǀ will I sing;
      from age to age my mouth
      will pro- ǀ claim your faithfulness.

2 For I am persuaded
  that your steadfast love
  is estab- ǀ lished forever;
      you have set your faithfulness
      firmly ǀ in the heavens.

3 "I have made a covenant
  with my ǀ chosen one;
      I have sworn an oath
      to Da- ǀ vid my servant:

⁴ 'I will establish your ˈ line forever,
  and preserve your throne
    for all ˈ generations.'"

⁵ The heavens praise your won- ˈ ders,
  O LORD,
    and your faithfulness
    in the assembly of the ˈ holy ones;

⁶ for who in the skies
  can be compared ˈ to the LORD?
    Who is like the LORD
    a- ˈ mong the gods?—

⁷ a God who is feared
  in the council of the ˈ holy ones,
    great and awesome
    to those ˈ all around.

⁸ Who is like you, LORD ˈ God of hosts?
  O mighty LORD,
    your faithfulness is ˈ all around you.

⁹ You rule the raging ˈ of the sea
  and still the surging ˈ of its waves.

¹⁰ You have crushed Rahab
  with a ˈ deadly wound;
    you have scattered your enemies
    with your ˈ mighty arm.

¹¹ Yours are the heavens;
  the earth al- ˈ so is yours;
    you laid the foundations of the world
    and all ˈ that is in it.

¹² You have made the north ˈ and the south;
  Tabor and Hermon
    rejoice ˈ in your name.

¹³ You have a ˈ mighty arm;
  strong is your hand
    and high is ˈ your right hand.

¹⁴ Righteousness and justice
  are the foundations ˈ of your throne;
    love and truth go be- ˈ fore your face.

¹⁵ Happy are the people
  who know the ˈ festal shout!
    They walk, O LORD,
    in the light ˈ of your presence.

¹⁶ They rejoice daily ˈ in your name;
  they are jubilant
    ˈ in your righteousness.

¹⁷ For you are the glory ˈ of their strength,
  and by your favor
    our might ˈ is exalted.

¹⁸ Truly, our shield belongs ˈ to the LORD;
  our king to the Holy ˈ One of Israel.

¹⁹ You spoke once in a vision
  and said to your ˈ faithful people:
    "I have set the crown upon a warrior
    and have exalted one
    chosen out ˈ of the people.

²⁰ I have found Da- ˈ vid my servant;
  with my holy oil
    I have a- ˈ nointed him.

²¹ My hand will ˈ hold him fast
  and my arm will ˈ make him strong.

²² No enemy ˈ shall deceive him,
  nor shall the wicked ˈ bring him down.

²³ I will crush his ˈ foes before him
  and strike down ˈ those who hate him.

²⁴ My faithfulness and steadfast ˈ love
  are with him,
    and he shall be victorious
    ˈ through my name.

²⁵ I will set his hand ˈ on the sea,
  and his right hand ˈ on the rivers.

²⁶ He will say to me,
  'You ˈ are my father,
    my God,
    and the rock of ˈ my salvation.'

²⁷ I will make ˈ him my firstborn
  and higher than the kings
    ˈ of the earth.

²⁸ I will keep my love for ˈ him forever,
  and my covenant
    will stand ˈ firm for him.

²⁹ I will establish his ˈ line forever
  and his throne as the ˈ days of heaven.

³⁰ If his children for- ˈ sake my teaching
  and do not walk
    according ˈ to my judgments;

³¹ if they ˈ break my statutes
  and do not keep
    ˈ my commandments;

³² I will punish their transgressions
  ˈ with a rod
    and their iniquities ˈ with the lash;

³³ but I will not take my ˈ love from him,
  nor let my faithful- ˈ ness
    prove false.

³⁴ I will not | break my covenant,
  nor change
  what has gone out | of my lips.
³⁵ Once for all
  I have sworn | by my holiness:
  I will not | lie to David.
³⁶ His line shall en- | dure forever
  and his throne
  as the | sun before me;
³⁷ it shall stand fast forevermore
  | like the moon,
  the abiding witness | in the sky."
³⁸ But you have cast off
  and rejected | your anointed;
  you have become en- | raged at him.
³⁹ You have broken your covenant
  | with your servant,
  defiled his crown,
  and hurled it | to the ground.
⁴⁰ You have breached | all his walls
  and laid his strong- | holds in ruins.
⁴¹ All who pass by | plunder him;
  he has become
  the scorn | of his neighbors.
⁴² You have exalted
  the right hand | of his foes
  and made all his ene- | mies rejoice.
⁴³ You have turned back
  the edge | of his sword
  and have not sustained | him
  in battle.
⁴⁴ You have put an end | to his splendor
  and cast his throne | to the ground.
⁴⁵ You have cut short
  the days | of his youth
  and have covered | him with shame.
⁴⁶ How long
  will you hide yourself, O Lord?
  Will you hide your- | self forever?
  How long
  will your anger | burn like fire?
⁴⁷ Remember, Lord, how | short life is,
  how frail you have | made all mortals.
⁴⁸ Who can live and | not see death?
  Who can escape
  the power | of the grave?

⁴⁹ Where, Lord,
  is your steadfast | love of old,
  which you promised David
  | in your faithfulness?
⁵⁰ Remember, Lord,
  how your ser- | vants are mocked,
  how I carry in my bosom
  the taunts of | many peoples,
⁵¹ the taunts your enemies have | hurled,
  O Lord,
  which they hurled at the heels
  of | your anointed.
⁵² Blessed be the | Lord forever!
  Amen | and Amen.

90

¹ Lord, you have | been our refuge
  from one generation | to another.
² Before the mountains
  were brought forth,
  or the land and the | earth were born,
  from age to age | you are God.
³ You turn us back to the | dust and say,
  "Turn back, O chil- | dren of earth."
⁴ For a thousand years in your sight
  are like yesterday when | it is past
  and like a watch | in the night;
⁵ you sweep them away | like a dream,
  they fade away suddenly
  | like the grass:
⁶ in the morning
  it is | green and flourishes;
  in the evening
  it is dried | up and withered.
⁷ For we are consumed | by your anger;
  we are afraid
  because | of your wrath.
⁸ Our iniquities
  you have | set before you,
  and our secret sins
  in the light | of your countenance.
⁹ When you are angry,
  all our | days are gone;
  we bring our years to an end
  | like a sigh.

10 The span of our life is seventy years,
perhaps in strength | even eighty;
yet the sum of them
is but labor and sorrow,
for they pass away quickly
and | we are gone.

11 Who regards the power | of your wrath?
Who rightly fears
your | indignation?

12 So teach us to num- | ber our days
that we may apply our | hearts
to wisdom.

13 Return, O LORD;
how long | will you tarry?
Be gracious | to your servants.

14 Satisfy us by your steadfast love
| in the morning;
so shall we rejoice and be glad
| all our days.

15 Make us glad as many days
as you af- | flicted us
and as many years
as we suf- | fered adversity.

16 Show your ser- | vants your works,
and your splendor | to their children.

17 May the graciousness of the Lord
our God | be upon us;
prosper the work of our hands;
pros- | per our handiwork.

91

1 You who dwell in the shelter
of | the Most High,
who abide in the shadow
of | the Almighty—

2 you will say to the LORD,
"My refuge | and my stronghold,
my God in whom I | put my trust."

3 For God will rescue you
from the snare | of the hunter
and from the | deadly plague.

4 God's wings will cover you,
and you will find ref- | uge
beneath them;
God's faithfulness will be your
shield | and defense.

5 You shall not fear
any terror | in the night,
nor the arrow that | flies by day;

6 nor the plague
that stalks | in the darkness,
nor the sickness
that lays | waste at noon.

7 A thousand may fall at your side
and ten thousand at | your right hand,
but it will | not come near you.

8 You will only have to look
| with your eyes,
and you will see the reward
| of the wicked.

9 Because you have made the | LORD
your refuge,
and the Most High your | habitation,

10 no evil | will befall you,
nor shall affliction
come | near your dwelling.

11 For God will give the angels
charge | over you,
to guard you in | all your ways.

12 Upon their hands
they will | bear you up,
lest you strike your foot
a- | gainst a stone.

13 You will tread
upon the lion | cub and viper;
you will trample down
the lion | and the serpent.

14 I will deliver those who | cling to me;
I will uphold them,
because they | know my name.

15 They will call me,
and I will | answer them;
I will be with them in trouble;
I will rescue and | honor them.

16 With long life will I | satisfy them,
and show them | my salvation.

92

1 It is a good thing
to give thanks | to the LORD,
to sing praise to your name,
| O Most High;

² to herald your love ˈ in the morning
 and your faithful- ˈ ness at night;

³ on the psaltery, and ˈ on the lyre,
 and to the melody ˈ of the harp.

⁴ For you have made me glad
 by your ˈ acts, O LORD;
  and I shout for joy
  because of the works
  ˈ of your hands.

⁵ LORD, how great ˈ are your works!
 Your thoughts are ˈ very deep.

⁶ The dullard ˈ does not know,
 nor does the fool ˈ understand,

⁷ that though the wicked
 grow like weeds,
 and all the workers of iniq- ˈ uity
 flourish,
  they flourish only
  to be de- ˈ stroyed forever;

⁸ but ˈ you, O LORD,
 are exalted for- ˈ evermore.

⁹ For lo, your enemies, O LORD,
 lo, your ene- ˈ mies shall perish,
  and all the workers of iniquity
  ˈ shall be scattered.

¹⁰ But you have raised up my horns
 like those of ˈ a wild ox;
  I am anointed ˈ with fresh oil.

¹¹ My eyes spy out
 ˈ those who watch me;
  my ears hear
  when enemies rise ˈ up against me.

¹² The righteous shall flourish
 ˈ like a palm tree,
  and shall spread abroad
  like a ce- ˈ dar of Lebanon.

¹³ Those who are planted
 in the house ˈ of the LORD
  shall flourish
  in the courts ˈ of our God;

¹⁴ they shall still bear fruit ˈ in old age;
 they shall be ˈ green and succulent;

¹⁵ that they may show
 how up- ˈ right the LORD is,
  my rock,
  in whom there is ˈ no injustice.

93

¹ The LORD is king, robed in majesty;
 the LORD is robed in majesty
 and ˈ armed with strength.
  The LORD has made the world so sure
  that it can- ˈ not be moved.

² Ever since the world began,
 your throne has ˈ been established;
  you are from ˈ everlasting.

³ The waters have lifted up, O LORD,
 the waters have lifted ˈ up their voice;
  the waters have lifted up
  their ˈ pounding waves.

⁴ Mightier than the sound of many waters,
 mightier than the breakers ˈ of the sea,
  mightier is the LORD
  who ˈ dwells on high.

⁵ Your testimonies are ˈ very sure,
 and holiness befits your house,
 O LORD, forever and for- ˈ evermore.

94

¹ O LORD, a- ˈ venging God,
 O God of vengeance, ˈ show yourself.

² Rise up, O Judge ˈ of the world;
  give to the arrogant
  their ˈ just deserts.

³ How long shall the wick- ˈ ed, O Lord,
 how long shall the ˈ wicked triumph?

⁴ They bluster ˈ in their insolence;
 all evildoers are ˈ full of boasting.

⁵ They crush your peo- ˈ ple, O Lord,
 and afflict your ˈ very own.

⁶ They kill the widow ˈ and the stranger
 and put the or- ˈ phans to death.

⁷ And they say, "The LORD ˈ does not see,
 the God of Jacob ˈ takes no notice."

⁸ Consider well,
 you most ˈ brutish people;
  you fools, when will ˈ you be wise?

⁹ Does the one who planted the ˈ ear
 not hear?
  Does the one who formed the ˈ eye
  not see?

¹⁰ Does the one
　who disciplines the na- ˈ tions
　not punish?
　　Does the one
　　who teaches all human- ˈ kind
　　lack knowledge?

¹¹ The LORD knows our ˈ human thoughts;
　how like a puff of ˈ wind they are.

¹² Happy are they
　whom you disci- ˈ pline, O LORD,
　　those whom you teach
　　ˈ from your law;

¹³ you give them rest in ˈ evil days,
　until a pit is dug ˈ for the wicked.

¹⁴ For you will not aban- ˈ don your people,
　nor will you forsake your ˈ very own.

¹⁵ For judgment will a- ˈ gain be just,
　and all the upright of heart
　will ˈ follow it.

¹⁶ Who will rise up for me
　a- ˈ gainst the wicked?
　　Who will take a stand for me
　　against the ˈ evildoers?

¹⁷ If the Lord had not ˈ been my help,
　I should soon have dwelt
　in the ˈ land of silence.

¹⁸ As often as I said,
　"My ˈ foot has slipped,"
　　your steadfast love, O ˈ LORD,
　　upheld me.

¹⁹ When anxious thoughts ˈ fill my mind,
　your consolations ˈ cheer my soul.

²⁰ Can a seat of injustice
　be al- ˈ lied with you,
　　one which frames evil ˈ into law?

²¹ They conspire
　against the life ˈ of the righteous
　　and condemn the inno- ˈ cent
　　to death.

²² But the LORD
　has be- ˈ come my stronghold,
　　my God is my ˈ rock of refuge,

²³ who will turn back
　their wickedness against them
　and destroy them in ˈ their own sin;
　　the LORD our God
　　ˈ will destroy them.

95

¹ Come, let us sing ˈ to the LORD;
　let us shout for joy
　to the rock of ˈ our salvation.

² Let us come before God's presence
　ˈ with thanksgiving
　　and raise a loud shout
　　to the ˈ LORD with psalms.

³ For you, LORD, ˈ are a great God,
　and a great ruler a- ˈ bove all gods.

⁴ In your hand
　are the caverns ˈ of the earth;
　　the heights of the hills
　　are ˈ also yours.

⁵ The sea is yours, ˈ for you made it,
　and your hands
　have molded ˈ the dry land.

⁶ Come, let us worship ˈ and bow down,
　let us kneel before the ˈ LORD
　our maker.

⁷ For the LORD is our God,
　and we are the people of God's pasture
　and the sheep ˈ of God's hand.
　　Oh, that today
　　you would ˈ hear God's voice!

⁸ "Harden ˈ not your hearts,
　as at Meribah, as on that day
　at Massah ˈ in the desert.

⁹ There your ancestors ˈ tested me,
　they put me to the test,
　though they had ˈ seen my works.

¹⁰ Forty years I loathed that gener- ˈ ation,
　saying,
　　'The heart of this people goes astray;
　　they do not ˈ know my ways.'

¹¹ Indeed I swore ˈ in my anger,
　'They shall never come ˈ to my rest.'"

96

¹ Sing to the LORD ˈ a new song;
　sing to the LORD, ˈ all the earth.

² Sing to the LORD,
　bless the name ˈ of the LORD;
　　proclaim God's salvation
　　from ˈ day to day.

³ Declare God's glory
  a- ˡ mong the nations
    and God's wonders
    a- ˡ mong all peoples.

⁴ For great is the LORD
  and greatly ˡ to be praised,
    more to be feared ˡ than all gods.

⁵ As for all the gods of the nations,
  they ˡ are but idols;
    but you, O LORD,
    have ˡ made the heavens.

⁶ Majesty and magnificence
  are ˡ in your presence;
    power and splendor
    are in your ˡ sanctuary.

⁷ Ascribe to the LORD,
  you families ˡ of the peoples,
    ascribe to the LORD
    hon- ˡ or and power.

⁸ Ascribe to the LORD the honor
  due the ˡ holy name;
    bring offerings
    and enter the courts ˡ of the LORD.

⁹ Worship the LORD
  in the beau- ˡ ty of holiness;
    tremble before the LORD,
    ˡ all the earth.

¹⁰ Tell it out among the nations:
  "The ˡ LORD is king!
    The one who made the world
    so firm that it cannot be moved
    will judge the peo- ˡ ples
    with equity."

¹¹ Let the heavens rejoice,
  and let the ˡ earth be glad;
    let the sea thunder
    and all that is in it;
    let the field be joyful
    and all that ˡ is therein.

¹² Then shall all the trees of the wood
  shout for joy
    at your com- ˡ ing, O LORD,
    for you come to ˡ judge the earth.

¹³ You will judge the ˡ world
  with righteousness
    and the peoples ˡ with your truth.

97

¹ The LORD reigns;
  let the ˡ earth rejoice;
    let the multitude of the ˡ isles
    be glad.

² Clouds and darkness
  sur- ˡ round the LORD,
    righteousness and justice
    are the foundations
    ˡ of God's throne.

³ Fire goes be- ˡ fore the LORD,
    burning up enemies
    on ˡ every side.

⁴ Lightnings light ˡ up the world;
    the earth ˡ sees and trembles.

⁵ The mountains ˡ melt like wax
    before the Lord of ˡ all the earth.

⁶ The heavens declare
  your righteous- ˡ ness, O LORD,
    and all the peoples
    ˡ see your glory.

⁷ Confounded be all
  who worship carved images
    and delight ˡ in false gods!
    Bow down before the LORD,
    ˡ all you gods.

⁸ Zion hears and is glad,
  and the cities of Ju- ˡ dah rejoice,
    because of your judg- ˡ ments,
    O LORD.

⁹ For you are the LORD,
  most high over ˡ all the earth;
    you are exalted far a- ˡ bove all gods.

¹⁰ You who love the ˡ LORD, hate evil!
    God guards the lives of the saints
    and rescues them
    from the hand ˡ of the wicked.

¹¹ Light dawns ˡ for the righteous,
    and joy for the hon- ˡ est of heart.

¹² Rejoice in the ˡ LORD, you righteous,
    and give thanks
    to God's ˡ holy name.

98

1 Sing a new song to the LORD,
who has done | marvelous things,
whose right hand and holy arm
have | won the victory.
2 O LORD, you have made | known
your victory,
you have revealed your righteousness
in the sight | of the nations.
3 You remember
your steadfast love and faithfulness
to the | house of Israel;
all the ends of the earth
have seen the victory | of our God.
4 Shout with joy to the LORD,
| all you lands;
lift up your voice, re- | joice, and sing.
5 Sing to the LORD | with the harp,
with the harp and the | voice of song.
6 With trumpets
and the sound | of the horn
shout with joy
before the | king, the LORD.
7 Let the sea roar, and | all that fills it,
the world and those
who | dwell therein.
8 Let the rivers | clap their hands,
and let the hills ring out with joy
before the LORD,
who comes to | judge the earth.
9 The LORD will judge the | world
with righteousness
and the peo- | ples with equity.

99

1 The LORD is king;
let the | people tremble.
The LORD is enthroned
upon the cherubim;
let | the earth shake.
2 The LORD, | great in Zion,
is high a- | bove all peoples.
3 Let them confess God's name,
which is | great and awesome;
God is the | Holy One.
4 O mighty king,
lover of justice,
you have es- | tablished equity;
you have executed justice
and righteous- | ness in Jacob.
5 Proclaim the greatness of the LORD
and fall down be- | fore God's footstool;
God is the | Holy One.
6 Moses and Aaron among your priests,
and Samuel among those
who call upon your | name, O LORD;
they called upon you,
and you | answered them,
7 you spoke to them
out of the pil- | lar of cloud;
they kept your testimonies
and the decree | that you gave them.
8 O LORD our God,
you answered | them indeed;
you were a God who forgave them,
yet punished them
for their | evil deeds.
9 Proclaim the greatness of the LORD
and worship upon God's | holy hill;
for the LORD our God
is the | Holy One.

100

1 Make a joyful noise to the LORD,
| all you lands!
2 Serve the LORD with gladness;
come into God's presence
| with a song.
3 Know that the LORD is God,
our maker to whom | we belong;
we are God's people
and the sheep | of God's pasture.
4 Enter the gates of the LORD
with thanksgiving
and the | courts with praise;
give thanks
and bless God's | holy name.
5 Good indeed is the LORD,
whose steadfast love is | everlasting,
whose faithfulness endures
from | age to age.

101

1 I will sing of mer- ˈ cy and justice;
    to you, O LORD, will ˈ I sing praises.

2 I will strive to follow a blameless course;
  when shall ˈ I attain it?
        I will walk with sincerity of heart
        with- ˈ in my house.

3 I will set no worthless thing
  be- ˈ fore my eyes;
        I hate the doers of evil deeds;
        they shall not re- ˈ main with me.

4 A crooked heart shall be ˈ far from me;
    I will ˈ not know evil.

5 Those who secretly
  slander their neighbors I ˈ will destroy;
        those who have a haughty look
        and a proud heart I can- ˈ not abide.

6 My eyes are upon the faithful
  in the land,
    that they may ˈ dwell with me,
        and those who walk in integrity
        shall ˈ be my servants.

7 Those who act deceitfully
  shall not dwell ˈ in my house,
        and those who tell lies
        shall not continue ˈ in my sight.

8 Morning by morning
  I will destroy all the wicked
  ˈ in the land,
        that I may root out all evildoers
        from the city ˈ of the LORD.

102

1 Hear my ˈ prayer, O LORD,
    and let my cry ˈ come before you.

2 Hide not your face from me
  when I ˈ am in trouble.
        Incline your ear to me; when I call,
        make haste to ˈ answer me,

3 for my days drift a- ˈ way like smoke,
    and my bones are hot
    as ˈ burning coals.

4 My heart is stricken like ˈ grass
  and withered,
        so that I forget to ˈ eat my bread.

5 Because of the voice ˈ of my groaning
    I am but ˈ skin and bones.

6 I have become like a vulture
  ˈ in the wilderness,
    like an owl a- ˈ mong the ruins.

7 I lie a- ˈ wake and groan;
    I am like a sparrow,
    lonely ˈ on a housetop.

8 My enemies revile me ˈ all day long,
    and those who scoff at me
    have taken an ˈ oath against me.

9 For I have eaten ash- ˈ es for bread
    and mingled my ˈ drink with weeping.

10 Because of your indigna- ˈ tion and wrath
    you have lifted me up
    and thrown ˈ me away.

11 My days pass away ˈ like a shadow,
    and I wither ˈ like the grass.

12 But you, O LORD, en- ˈ dure forever,
    and your name from ˈ age to age.

13 You will arise
  and have compassion on Zion,
  for it is time to have mercy
  up- ˈ on Jerusalem;
        indeed, the appointed ˈ time has come.

14 For your servants
  love the city's ˈ very rubble,
        and are moved to pity
        even ˈ for its dust.

15 The nations shall fear your ˈ name,
  O LORD,
        and all the rulers of the ˈ earth
        your glory.

16 For you will ˈ build up Zion,
    and your glory ˈ will appear.

17 You will look with favor
  on the prayer ˈ of the homeless;
        you will not de- ˈ spise their plea.

18 Let this be written
  for a future ˈ generation,
        so that a people yet unborn
        may ˈ praise the LORD.

19 For you looked down
  from your holy ˈ place on high;
        from the heavens
        you beheld the ˈ earth, O LORD,

20 that you might hear the groan
ǀ of the captive
and set free those
con- ǀ demned to die;

21 that they may declare your ǀ name
in Zion
and your praise ǀ in Jerusalem;

22 when the peoples
are gath- ǀ ered together,
and the kingdoms also,
to ǀ serve the LORD.

23 God has brought down my strength
be- ǀ fore my time,
shortening the number ǀ of my days;

24 and I said, "O my God,
do not take me away
in the midst ǀ of my days;
your years endure
throughout all ǀ generations."

25 Long ago, O LORD,
you laid the foundations ǀ of the earth,
and the heavens
are the work ǀ of your hands.

26 They shall perish, but you will endure;
they all shall wear out ǀ like a garment;
as clothing you will change them,
and they ǀ shall be changed;

27 but you are al- ǀ ways the same,
and your years will ǀ never end.

28 The children of your servants
ǀ shall continue,
and their descendants
shall stand fast ǀ in your sight.

103

1 Bless the LORD, ǀ O my soul,
and all that is within me,
bless God's ǀ holy name.

2 Bless the LORD, ǀ O my soul,
and forget not ǀ all God's benefits—

3 who forgives ǀ all your sins
and heals all ǀ your diseases;

4 who redeems your life ǀ from the grave
and crowns you
with steadfast ǀ love and mercy;

5 who satisfies your desires
ǀ with good things
so that your youth is renewed
ǀ like an eagle's.

6 O LORD, you provide ǀ vindication
and justice for all who ǀ are oppressed.

7 You made known your ǀ ways to Moses
and your works
to the chil- ǀ dren of Israel.

8 LORD, you are full of compas- ǀ sion
and mercy,
slow to anger
and abounding in ǀ steadfast love;

9 you will not al- ǀ ways accuse us,
nor will you keep your an- ǀ ger
forever.

10 You have not dealt with us
according ǀ to our sins,
nor repaid us
according to ǀ our iniquities.

11 For as the heavens
are high a- ǀ bove the earth,
so great is your steadfast love
for ǀ those who fear you.

12 As far as the east is ǀ from the west,
so far have you removed
our transgres- ǀ sions from us.

13 As a father has compassion
ǀ for his children,
so you have compassion
for those who fear ǀ you, O LORD.

14 For you know well how ǀ we are formed;
you remember that we ǀ are but dust.

15 As for mortals,
their days are ǀ like the grass;
they flourish
like a flower ǀ of the field;

16 when the wind passes over it, ǀ it is gone,
and its place shall know ǀ it no more.

17 But your steadfast love, O LORD,
is forever with ǀ those who fear you,
and your righteousness
is for the ǀ children's children;

18 for those who ǀ keep your covenant
and remember to do
ǀ your commandments.

¹⁹ The LORD's throne
is estab- ǀ lished in heaven;
   God's dominion rules ǀ over all.

²⁰ Bless the LORD, you angels,
you mighty ones who ǀ do God's bidding,
   who obey the voice ǀ of God's word.

²¹ Bless the LORD, all you ǀ hosts of God,
you servants who ǀ do God's will.

²² Bless the LORD, all you works of God,
in all places ǀ where God rules;
   bless the LORD, ǀ O my soul.

104

¹ Bless the LORD, O my soul;
O LORD my God,
you are ǀ very great!
   You are clothed
   with majes- ǀ ty and splendor.

² You wrap yourself with light
as ǀ with a cloak
   and stretch out the heavens
   ǀ like a tent.

³ You lay the beams of your chambers
in the wa- ǀ ters above;
   you make the clouds your chariot;
   you ride on the wings ǀ of the wind.

⁴ You make the ǀ winds your messengers
and flames of ǀ fire your servants.

⁵ You set the earth
upon ǀ its foundations,
   so that from now until forever
   it shall nev- ǀ er be moved.

⁶ You covered it with the deep
as ǀ with a garment;
   the waters stood
   a- ǀ bove the mountains.

⁷ At your rebuke the ǀ waters fled,
scattered by your ǀ voice of thunder.

⁸ They went up into the mountains
and descended down ǀ to the valleys,
   to the place
   where ǀ you assigned them.

⁹ You set the limits
that they ǀ should not pass;
   never shall they return
   to cover the ǀ earth again.

¹⁰ You made the springs ǀ into rivers
that flow be- ǀ tween the mountains.

¹¹ All the animals
drink their ǀ fill from them,
   and the wild donkeys
   ǀ quench their thirst.

¹² Beside them the birds of the air
ǀ make their nests;
   among the branches
   they ǀ lift their voice.

¹³ From your dwelling on high,
you wa- ǀ ter the mountains;
   the earth is satisfied
   with the fruit ǀ of your works.

¹⁴ You make grass grow for the cattle,
and plants to serve ǀ humankind;
   that they may bring forth food
   ǀ from the earth,

¹⁵ wine to gladden human hearts,
oil to ǀ make the face shine,
   and bread to strengthen
   the ǀ human heart.

¹⁶ The trees of the LORD are ǀ well supplied,
the cedars of Lebanon
   ǀ that you planted,

¹⁷ in which the birds ǀ build their nests,
while the stork makes the fir ǀ trees
   its dwelling.

¹⁸ The high hills belong
to the ǀ mountain goats,
   and the stony cliffs are a refuge
   ǀ for the badgers.

¹⁹ You made the moon
to ǀ mark the seasons,
   and the sun knows the time
   ǀ of its setting.

²⁰ You bring on darkness
that it ǀ may be night,
   in which all the beasts
   of the ǀ forest prowl.

²¹ The lions roar ǀ for their prey
seeking their ǀ food from God.

²² The sun rises, and ǀ they withdraw
and lay themselves down
   ǀ in their dens.

²³ People go forth ǀ to their work
and to their labor un- ǀ til the evening.

24 How manifold are your I works,
O Lord!
    In wisdom you have made them all;
    the earth is full I of your creatures.

25 Yonder is the sea, great and wide,
with its swarms too man- I y to number,
    living things both I small and great.

26 There go the ships I to and fro,
    and Leviathan,
    which you made for the I sport of it.

27 All of them I look to you
    to give them their food
    I in due season.

28 You give it to them; they I gather it;
    you open your hand,
    and they are filled I with good things.

29 When you hide your face,
    I they are terrified;
        when you take away their breath,
        they die and return I to their dust.

30 You send forth your Spirit,
    and they I are created;
        and so you renew
        the face I of the earth.

31 May the glory of the Lord
    en- I dure forever;
        O Lord, rejoice in I all your works.

32 You look at the earth I and it trembles;
    you touch the mountains
    I and they smoke.

33 I will sing to the Lord as long I as I live;
    I will praise my God
    while I I have my being.

34 May these words of I mine please God.
    I will rejoice I in the Lord.

35 Let sinners be consumed from the earth
and the wicked I be no more.
    Bless the Lord, O my soul.
    I Hallelujah!

105

1 Give thanks to the Lord
and call up- I on God's name;
    make known the deeds of the Lord
    a- I mong the peoples.

2 Sing to the I Lord, sing praises,
    and speak
    of all God's I marvelous works.

3 Glory in God's I holy name;
    let the hearts of those
    who seek the I Lord rejoice.

4 Search for the strength I of the Lord;
    continually I seek God's face.

5 Remember the marvels I God has done,
    the wonders
    and the judgments I of God's mouth,

6 O offspring of Abra- I ham,
God's servant,
    O children of Jacob,
    God's I chosen ones.

7 The Lord I is our God,
    whose judgments prevail
    in I all the world,

8 who has always been mindful
    I of the covenant,
        the promise made
        for a thousand I generations:

9 the covenant I made with Abraham,
    the oath I sworn to Isaac,

10 which God established
    as a stat- I ute for Jacob,
        an everlasting cove- I nant for Israel,

11 saying, "To you will I give
    the I land of Canaan
        to be your allot- I ted inheritance."

12 When they were I few in number,
    of little account,
    and sojourners I in the land,

13 wandering from na- I tion to nation
    and from one kingdom I to another,

14 God let no I one oppress them
    and rebuked kings I for their sake,

15 saying, "Do not touch
    my a- I nointed ones
    and do my proph- I ets no harm."

16 Then God called for a famine
    I in the land
        and destroyed the sup- I ply of bread.

17 The Lord sent a I man before them,
    Joseph, who was sold I as a slave.

¹⁸ They bruised his | feet in fetters;
  his neck they put in an | iron collar.

¹⁹ Until his prediction | came to pass,
  the word of the LORD | tested him.

²⁰ The king sent | and released him;
  the ruler of the peoples | set him free,

²¹ setting him as a master
  o- | ver his household,
    as a ruler over all | his possessions,

²² to instruct his princes
  according | to his will
    and to teach his | elders wisdom.

²³ Israel came | into Egypt,
  and Jacob became a sojourner
    in the | land of Ham.

²⁴ The LORD made the people of Israel
  | very fruitful,
    more numerous | than their enemies,

²⁵ whose hearts God turned,
  so that they hat- | ed God's people,
    and dealt unjustly
      with the ser- | vants of God.

²⁶ O LORD, you sent Mo- | ses
  your servant,
    and Aaron, your | chosen one.

²⁷ They worked your | signs among them,
  and portents in the | land of Ham.

²⁸ You sent darkness, and | it grew dark;
  but the Egyptians rebelled
    a- | gainst your words.

²⁹ You turned their waters | into blood
  and caused their | fish to die.

³⁰ Their land was over- | run by frogs,
  in the very chambers | of their kings.

³¹ You spoke,
  and there came | swarms of insects
    and gnats within | all their borders.

³² You gave them hailstones
  in- | stead of rain,
    and flames of fire
      through- | out their land.

³³ You blasted their vines
  | and their fig trees
    and shattered every tree
      | in their country.

³⁴ You spoke, and the | locust came,
  and young locusts | without number,

³⁵ which ate up all the green plants
  | in their land
    and devoured the fruit | of their soil.

³⁶ You struck down the firstborn
  | of their land,
    the firstfruits of | all their strength.

³⁷ You led out your people
  with sil- | ver and gold;
    in all their tribes
      there was not | one that stumbled.

³⁸ Egypt was glad to | see them go,
  because they were a- | fraid of them.

³⁹ You spread out a cloud | for a covering
  and a fire to give | light by night.

⁴⁰ They asked, and | you brought quail,
  and satisfied them
    with | bread from heaven.

⁴¹ You opened the rock,
  and | water flowed,
    so the river ran in | the dry places.

⁴² For you remembered your | holy word
  and Abra- | ham your servant.

⁴³ So you led forth your peo- | ple
  with gladness,
    your chosen with | shouts of joy.

⁴⁴ You gave your people
  the lands | of the nations,
    and they took the fruit
      of | others' toil,

⁴⁵ that they might | keep your statutes
  and observe your teachings.
    | Hallelujah!

106

¹ Hallelujah! Give thanks to the LORD,
  for the | LORD is good,
    for God's mercy en- | dures forever.

² Who can declare
  the mighty acts | of the LORD
    or proclaim in | full God's praise?

³ Happy are those who | act with justice
  and always do | what is right.

⁴ Remember me, O LORD,
with the favor
you have | for your people,
and visit me with | your salvation;

⁵ that I may see the prosperity
of your elect and be glad
with the gladness | of your people,
that I may glory
with | your inheritance.

⁶ We have sinned as our | forebears did;
we have done wrong
| and dealt wickedly.

⁷ In Egypt they did not consider
your marvelous works,
nor remember the abundance
of your | steadfast love;
they rebelled by the sea,
| by the Red Sea.

⁸ But you saved them
| for your name's sake,
to make your | power known.

⁹ You rebuked the Red Sea,
and | it dried up,
and you led them through the deep
as | through a desert.

¹⁰ You saved them from the hand
of those who | hated them
and redeemed them
from the hand | of the enemy.

¹¹ The waters covered | their oppressors;
not one of | them was left.

¹² Then they be- | lieved your words
and sang songs of | praise to you.

¹³ But they soon for- | got your deeds
and did not wait | for your counsel.

¹⁴ A craving seized them
| in the wilderness,
in the desert,
they put you | to the test.

¹⁵ You gave them | what they asked,
but then sent them
a wast- | ing disease.

¹⁶ When they envied Moses
| in the camp,
and Aaron, the holy one
| of the LORD,

¹⁷ the earth opened
and | swallowed Dathan
and covered
the company | of Abiram.

¹⁸ Fire blazed up a- | gainst their company,
and flames de- | voured the wicked.

¹⁹ They made a bull- | calf at Horeb
and worshiped a | molten image;

²⁰ thus they ex- | changed their glory
for the image of an ox
that | feeds on grass.

²¹ They forgot | God their Savior,
who had done great | things
in Egypt,

²² wonderful deeds in the | land of Ham,
and fearful things | at the Red Sea.

²³ So you would have destroyed them,
had not Moses your chosen
stood | in the breach,
to turn away your wrath
from con- | suming them.

²⁴ Then they refused the | pleasant land
and would not be- | lieve
your promise.

²⁵ They grumbled | in their tents
and would not obey
the voice | of the LORD.

²⁶ So your hand
was lift- | ed against them,
to cast them down
| in the wilderness,

²⁷ to cast out their seed
a- | mong the nations,
and to scatter them
through- | out the lands.

²⁸ They joined themselves to | Ba'al-Peor
and ate sacrifices
offered | to the dead.

²⁹ They provoked you to anger
| with their actions,
and a plague
broke | out among them.

³⁰ Then Phinehas stood up
and | interceded,
and the plague came | to an end.

³¹ This was reckoned to ˡ him
  as righteousness
    throughout all genera- ˡ tions
    forever.

³² Again they angered you
  at the wa- ˡ ters of Meribah,
    so that you punished Moses
    be- ˡ cause of them;

³³ for they so embit- ˡ tered his spirit
    that he spoke rash words
    ˡ with his lips.

³⁴ They did not de- ˡ stroy the peoples
    as the LORD had com- ˡ manded them;

³⁵ they intermingled ˡ with the nations
    and ˡ learned their ways.

³⁶ They wor- ˡ shiped their idols,
    which became a ˡ snare to them.

³⁷ They sacri- ˡ ficed their sons
    and their daughters to ˡ evil spirits.

³⁸ They shed innocent blood,
  the blood of their ˡ sons and daughters,
    whom they offered
    to the idols of Canaan,
    and the land was de- ˡ filed with blood.

³⁹ They became polluted
  ˡ with their ways
    and went whoring
    ˡ through their deeds.

⁴⁰ Therefore your wrath, O LORD,
  was kindled a- ˡ gainst your people
    and you abhorred
    your ˡ own inheritance,

⁴¹ giving them into the hand
  ˡ of the nations,
    and those who hated them
    ruled ˡ over them.

⁴² Their ene- ˡ mies oppressed them,
    and they were humbled
    un- ˡ der their hand.

⁴³ Many times you delivered them,
  but they rebelled
    through ˡ their own schemes,
    and were brought down
    in ˡ their iniquity.

⁴⁴ Nevertheless, you saw ˡ their distress,
    and heard their ˡ lamentation.

⁴⁵ You remembered
  your cove- ˡ nant with them
    and relented
    out of your ˡ steadfast love.

⁴⁶ You won for ˡ them compassion
    by all who ˡ held them captive.

⁴⁷ Save us, O LORD our God, and
  gather us from a- ˡ mong the nations,
    that we may give thanks
    to your holy name
    and glory ˡ in your praise.

⁴⁸ Blessed be the LORD, the God of Israel,
  from everlasting to ˡ everlasting;
    and let all the people say,
    "Amen!" ˡ Hallelujah!

107

¹ Give thanks to the LORD,
  for the ˡ LORD is good,
    for God's mercy en- ˡ dures forever.

² Let the redeemed of the ˡ LORD proclaim
    that God redeemed them
    from the hand ˡ of the foe,

³ gathering them in ˡ from the lands;
    from the east and from the west,
    from the north and ˡ from the south.

⁴ Some wandered in ˡ desert wastes;
    they found no path to a city
    where ˡ they might dwell.

⁵ They were hun- ˡ gry and thirsty;
    their spirits lan- ˡ guished
    within them.

⁶ Then in their trouble
  they cried ˡ to the LORD,
    and you delivered them
    from ˡ their distress.

⁷ You led them ˡ on a straight path
    to go to a city
    where ˡ they might dwell.

⁸ Let them give thanks to you, LORD,
  for your ˡ steadfast love
    and your wonderful works
    ˡ for all people.

⁹ For you satisfy the ˡ thirsty soul
    and fill the hungry ˡ with good things.

¹⁰ Some dwelt in dark- ˈ ness and gloom,
  prisoners in miser- ˈ y and irons;

¹¹ because they rebelled
against the ˈ words of God
  and despised the counsel
  of ˈ the Most High.

¹² So you humbled their hearts
ˈ with hard labor;
  they stumbled,
  and there was ˈ none to help.

¹³ Then in their trouble
they cried ˈ to the Lord,
  and you delivered them
  from ˈ their distress.

¹⁴ You led them out of dark- ˈ ness
and gloom,
  and broke their ˈ bonds asunder.

¹⁵ Let them give thanks to you, Lord,
for your ˈ steadfast love
  and your wonderful works
  ˈ for all people.

¹⁶ For you shatter the ˈ doors of bronze
  and break the iron ˈ bars in two.

¹⁷ Some were fools
and took re- ˈ bellious paths;
  through their sins
  they ˈ were afflicted.

¹⁸ They loathed all man- ˈ ner of food
  and drew near ˈ to death's door.

¹⁹ Then in their trouble
they cried ˈ to the Lord
  and you delivered them
  from ˈ their distress.

²⁰ You sent forth your ˈ word
and healed them
  and rescued them ˈ from the grave.

²¹ Let them give thanks to you, Lord,
for your ˈ steadfast love
  and your wonderful works
  ˈ for all people.

²² Let them offer sacrifices
ˈ of thanksgiving
  and tell of your deeds
  with ˈ shouts of joy.

²³ Some went down to the ˈ sea in ships,
  plying their trade ˈ in deep waters.

²⁴ They beheld the works ˈ of the Lord,
  God's wonderful works
  ˈ in the deep.

²⁵ Then God spoke,
and a stormy ˈ wind arose,
  which tossed high
  the waves ˈ of the sea.

²⁶ They mounted up to the heavens
and descended ˈ to the depths;
  their souls melted away
  ˈ in their peril.

²⁷ They staggered and ˈ reeled
like drunkards,
  and all their skill was of ˈ no avail.

²⁸ Then in their trouble
they cried ˈ to the Lord,
  and you delivered them
  from ˈ their distress.

²⁹ You stilled the storm ˈ to a whisper
  and silenced the waves ˈ of the sea.

³⁰ Then were they glad
when ˈ it grew calm,
  when you guided them
  to the harbor ˈ they desired.

³¹ Let them give thanks to you, Lord,
for your ˈ steadfast love
  and your wonderful works
  ˈ for all people.

³² Let them exalt you
in the assembly ˈ of the people;
  in the council of the elders,
  let them sing ˈ hallelujah!

³³ You change rivers ˈ into deserts,
  and water-springs
  into ˈ thirsty ground,

³⁴ fruitful land into ˈ salty waste,
  because of the wickedness
  of ˈ those who dwell there.

³⁵ You change deserts into ˈ pools of water
  and dry land into ˈ water-springs.

³⁶ You settle the ˈ hungry there,
  and they establish a cit- ˈ y to dwell in.

³⁷ They sow fields ˈ and plant vineyards,
  and bring in a ˈ fruitful harvest.

³⁸ By your blessing they ˈ increase greatly;
  you do not let their ˈ herds decrease.

³⁹ Yet when they are diminished
 | and brought low,
    through oppression, trou- | ble,
    and sorrow,

⁴⁰ you pour con- | tempt on princes
    and make them wander
    in | trackless wastes;

⁴¹ but you lift up the poor | out of misery
    and multiply their families
    like | flocks of sheep.

⁴² The upright see this | and rejoice,
    but all wickedness | shuts its mouth.

⁴³ Whoever is wise
  will pon- | der these things,
    and consider well
    the Lord's | steadfast love.

108

¹ My heart is steadfast, O God,
  my | heart is steadfast;
    I will sing | and make melody.

² Wake up, my spirit;
  awake, | lute and harp;
    I myself will wak- | en the dawn.

³ I will give thanks to you, O Lord,
  a- | mong the peoples;
    I will sing praise to you
    a- | mong the nations.

⁴ For your steadfast love
  is greater | than the heavens,
    and your faithfulness
    reaches | to the clouds.

⁵ Exalt yourself above the heav- | ens,
  O God,
    and your glory over | all the earth.

⁶ Save us by your right hand
  and | answer us,
    that those who are dear to you
    may | be delivered.

⁷ God spoke from the holy | place
  and said:
    "I will exult and parcel out Shechem;
    I will divide the val- | ley of Succoth.

⁸ Gilead is mine and Manas- | seh is mine;
  Ephraim is my helmet
    and Ju- | dah my scepter.

⁹ Moab is my washbasin;
  I throw down my sandal | upon Edom,
    and over Philistia
    will I | shout in triumph."

¹⁰ Who will carry me in procession
  into the for- | tified city?
    Who will bring me | into Edom?

¹¹ Have you not cast us | off, O God?
  You no longer go out, O God,
    | with our armies.

¹² Grant us your help a- | gainst the enemy,
    for human | help is worthless.

¹³ With God we will do | valiant deeds;
    God shall tread our enemies
    | under foot.

109

¹ O God | of my praise,
    do | not be silent!

² For the mouth of the wicked,
  the mouth of the deceitful,
  is o- | pened against me;
    they have spoken against me
    with | lying tongues.

³ With hateful words,
  they en- | compass me;
    they attack me | without cause.

⁴ Despite my love, | they accuse me;
    even though I | pray for them.

⁵ They repay me e- | vil for good,
    and hatred | for my love.

⁶ Set wicked li- | ars against them;
    and let accusers stand
    at | their right hand.

⁷ When they are judged,
  let them | be found guilty,
    and let their prayer
    be count- | ed as sin.

⁸ Let their | days be few,
    and let others | take their offices.

⁹ Let their children | lack their presence,
    and their spouses | mourn their death.

¹⁰ Let their children be | waifs and beggars;
    let them be driven
    from the ruins | of their homes.

¹¹ Let the creditor seize
every- ᴵ thing they have;
may strangers plun- ᴵ der their gains.

¹² May there be no one
to ᴵ show them mercy,
and none to pity
their ᴵ orphaned children.

¹³ May their descendants ᴵ be cut off,
and their name be blotted out
in the next ᴵ generation.

¹⁴ May the wickedness of their fathers
be remembered be- ᴵ fore the LORD,
and their mothers' sin
not be ᴵ blotted out.

¹⁵ Let the LORD
always remem- ᴵ ber their sin
and erase their memory
ᴵ from the earth;

¹⁶ because they did not remember
ᴵ to show mercy,
but hounded to death the poor,
the needy, and the ᴵ brokenhearted.

¹⁷ My accusers loved cursing;
let it ᴵ come upon them.
They took no delight in blessing;
let it be ᴵ far from them.

¹⁸ They clothed themselves with cursing
as ᴵ with their garments;
let it soak into their bodies like water,
like oil in- ᴵ to their bones;

¹⁹ let it be to them like the cloaks
they wrap a- ᴵ round themselves,
and like the belts
that they ᴵ wear continually.

²⁰ Let this be the LORD's payment
to ᴵ my accusers,
to those who speak e- ᴵ vil against me.

²¹ But you, O LORD, my Lord,
deal with me according ᴵ to your name;
for your great mercy's sake,
de- ᴵ liver me.

²² For I am ᴵ poor and needy,
and my heart is ᴵ pierced within me.

²³ I have faded away
like a shad- ᴵ ow at evening;
I am shaken off ᴵ like a locust.

²⁴ My knees are ᴵ weak through fasting,
and my flesh is wast- ᴵ ed and gaunt.

²⁵ I have become a re- ᴵ proach to them;
they see and ᴵ shake their heads.

²⁶ Help me, O ᴵ LORD my God;
save me
according to your ᴵ steadfast love.

²⁷ Let them know that this ᴵ is your hand,
that you, O ᴵ LORD, have done it.

²⁸ They may curse, but ᴵ you will bless;
when they rise up
they will be put to shame,
and your servant ᴵ will rejoice.

²⁹ Let my accusers
be clothed ᴵ with disgrace
and wrap themselves in their shame
as ᴵ in a cloak.

³⁰ I will give great thanks to the LORD
ᴵ with my mouth;
in the midst of the multitude
will ᴵ I praise God,

³¹ who stands at the right hand
ᴵ of the needy,
to save them from those
ᴵ who condemn them.

110

¹ The LORD said to my Lord,
"Sit ᴵ at my right hand,
until I make your ene- ᴵ mies
your footstool."

² The LORD will extend the scepter
of your pow- ᴵ er from Zion,
saying, "Rule in the midst
ᴵ of your enemies.

³ Princely state has been yours
from the day ᴵ of your birth;
in the beauty of holiness
have I begotten you,
like dew
from the womb ᴵ of the morning."

⁴ The LORD has sworn
and will ᴵ not recant:
"You are a priest forever
after the order ᴵ of Melchizedek."

⁵ The Lord is at ⎮ your right hand,
  smiting kings in the ⎮ day of wrath;
⁶ judging the nations,
  heaping ⎮ up the corpses,
    and smashing rulers
    through- ⎮ out the earth.
⁷ The king will drink
  from the brook be- ⎮ side the way;
    therefore he will lift ⎮ high his head.

111

¹ Hallelujah!
 I will give thanks to the LORD
 with ⎮ my whole heart,
    in the assembly of the upright,
    in the ⎮ congregation.
² Great are your ⎮ works, O LORD,
  pondered by all
    who de- ⎮ light in them.
³ Majesty and splendor
 ⎮ mark your deeds,
    and your righteousness
    en- ⎮ dures forever.
⁴ You cause your wonders
  to ⎮ be remembered;
    you are gracious
    and full ⎮ of compassion.
⁵ You give food
  to ⎮ those who fear you,
    remembering forev- ⎮ er
    your covenant.
⁶ You have shown your people
  the power ⎮ of your works
    in giving them
    the lands ⎮ of the nations.
⁷ The works of your hands
  are faithful- ⎮ ness and justice;
    all of your pre- ⎮ cepts are sure.
⁸ They stand fast forev- ⎮ er and ever,
  because they are done
    in ⎮ truth and equity.
⁹ You sent redemption to your people
 and commanded your cove- ⎮ nant
 forever;
    holy and awesome ⎮ is your name.

¹⁰ The fear of the LORD
  is the begin- ⎮ ning of wisdom;
    all who practice this
    have a good understanding.
    God's praise en- ⎮ dures forever.

112

¹ Hallelujah!
 Happy are they who ⎮ fear the LORD
    and have great delight
    in ⎮ God's commandments!
² Their descendants
  will be mighty ⎮ in the land;
    the generation of the upright
    ⎮ will be blessed.
³ Wealth and riches
  will be ⎮ in their house,
    and their righteousness
    will ⎮ last forever.
⁴ Light shines in the darkness
 ⎮ for the upright;
    the righteous are merciful
    and full ⎮ of compassion.
⁵ It is good for them
  to be gener- ⎮ ous in lending
    and to manage their af- ⎮ fairs
    with justice.
⁶ For they will nev- ⎮ er be shaken;
    the righteous will be kept
    in everlast- ⎮ ing remembrance.
⁷ They will not be afraid
  of any ⎮ evil rumors;
    their heart is steadfast,
    trusting ⎮ in the LORD.
⁸ Their heart is established
  and ⎮ will not shrink,
    until they see their desire
    up- ⎮ on their enemies.
⁹ They have given freely to the poor, and
  their righteousness stands ⎮ fast forever;
    they will hold up their ⎮ head
    with honor.
¹⁰ The wicked will see it and be angry;
  they will gnash their teeth
  and ⎮ pine away;
    the desires of the wick- ⎮ ed will perish.

113

1 Hallelujah!
Give praise, you servants | of the Lord;
  praise the name | of the Lord.

2 Let the name of the | Lord be blessed,
  from this time forth for- | evermore.

3 From the rising of the sun
to its | going down
  let the name of the | Lord be praised.

4 The Lord is high a- | bove all nations,
  God's glory a- | bove the heavens.

5 Who is like the | Lord our God,
  who sits en- | throned on high,

6 but stoops | to behold
  the heavens | and the earth?

7 The Lord takes up the weak
out | of the dust
  and lifts up the poor | from the ashes,

8 enthroning them | with the rulers,
  with the rulers | of the people.

9 The Lord makes the woman
of a | childless house
  to be a joyful mother of children.
  | Hallelujah!

114

1 Hallelujah!
When Israel came | out of Egypt,
  the house of Jacob
  from a people | of strange speech,

2 Judah became God's | sanctuary
  and Israel | God's dominion.

3 The sea beheld | it and fled;
  Jordan turned | and went back.

4 The mountains | skipped like rams,
  and the little hills | like young sheep.

5 What ailed you, O sea, | that you fled,
  O Jordan, that | you turned back,

6 you mountains,
  that you | skipped like rams,
  you little hills | like young sheep?

7 Tremble, O earth,
at the presence | of the Lord,
  at the presence of the | God of Jacob,

8 who turned the hard rock
into a | pool of water
  and flint-stone into a | flowing spring.

115

1 Not to us, O Lord, not to us,
but to your | name give glory;
  because of your steadfast | love
  and faithfulness.

2 Why should the | nations say,
  "Where then | is their God?"

3 Our God | is in heaven;
  whatever God | wills, God does.

4 Their idols are sil- | ver and gold,
  the work of | human hands.

5 They have mouths,
but they | cannot speak;
  eyes they have,
  but they | cannot see;

6 they have ears, but they | cannot hear;
  noses, but they | cannot smell;

7 they have hands, but they cannot feel;
feet, but they | cannot walk;
  they make no sound
  | with their throat.

8 Those who make | them are like them,
  and so are all
  who put their | trust in them.

9 O Israel, trust | in the Lord,
  who is your help | and your shield.

10 O house of Aaron, trust | in the Lord,
  who is your help | and your shield.

11 You that fear the Lord,
trust | in the Lord,
  who is your help | and your shield.

12 The Lord has been mindful of us,
| and will bless us;
  the Lord will bless the house of Israel
  and the | house of Aaron;

13 those who fear the Lord | will be blessed,
  both small and | great together.

14 May the Lord increase you
| more and more,
  you and your | children after you.

15 May you be blessed | by the Lord,
    the maker of heav- | en and earth.
16 Heaven is the heaven | of the Lord,
    but the earth
      God entrusted | to its peoples.
17 The dead do not | praise the Lord,
    nor all those
      who go down | into silence;
18 but we will | bless the Lord,
    from this time forth forevermore.
      | Hallelujah!

116

1 I love the Lord,
  who has | heard my voice,
    and listened to my | supplication,
2 for the Lord has given | ear to me
  whenev- | er I called.
3 The cords of death entangled me;
  the anguish of the grave
  | came upon me;
    I came to | grief and sorrow.
4 Then I called upon the name
  | of the Lord:
    "O Lord, I pray you, | save my life."
5 Gracious is the | Lord and righteous;
  our God is full | of compassion.
6 The Lord watches o- | ver
  the innocent;
    I was brought low,
    | and God saved me.
7 Turn again to your rest, | O my soul.
  for the Lord
    has dealt | well with you.
8 For you have rescued my | life
  from death,
    my eyes from tears,
    and my | feet from stumbling.
9 I will walk in the presence | of the Lord
  in the land | of the living.
10 I believed, even | when I said,
    "I am great- | ly afflicted."
11 In my dis- | tress I said,
    "No one | can be trusted."

12 How shall I re- | pay the Lord
    for all the good things
      God has | done for me?
13 I will lift the cup | of salvation
    and call on the name | of the Lord.
14 I will fulfill my vows | to the Lord
    in the presence of | all God's people.
15 Precious in your | sight, O Lord,
    is the death | of your servants.
16 O Lord, truly I | am your servant;
    I am your servant,
      the child of your handmaid;
      you have freed me | from my bonds.
17 I will offer you
    the sacrifice | of thanksgiving
      and call upon the name | of the Lord.
18 I will fulfill my vows | to the Lord
    in the presence of | all God's people,
19 in the courts of | the Lord's house,
    in the midst of you, O Jerusalem.
      | Hallelujah!

117

1 Praise the Lord, | all you nations;
  extol God, | all you peoples.
2 For great is God's steadfast | love
toward us,
    and the faithfulness of the Lord
    endures forever. | Hallelujah!

118

1 Give thanks to the Lord,
  for the | Lord is good;
    God's mercy en- | dures forever.
2 Let Israel | now declare,
    "God's mercy en- | dures forever."
3 Let the house of Aar- | on declare,
    "God's mercy en- | dures forever."
4 Let those who fear the | Lord declare,
    "God's mercy en- | dures forever."
5 In distress I called | to the Lord,
    who answered by set- | ting me free.
6 The Lord is with me; I | shall not fear;
    what can anyone | do to me?

7 The LORD is with me | as my helper;
  I will look in triumph
    on | those who hate me.

8 It is better to take refuge | in the LORD
  than to | trust in mortals.

9 It is better to take refuge | in the LORD
  than to | trust in rulers.

10 All the nations sur- | rounded me;
  in the name of the LORD
  I | drove them off!

11 They surrounded me,
  indeed they sur- | rounded me;
  in the name of the LORD
  I | drove them off!

12 They surrounded me like bees
  and blazed like a | fire of thorns;
  in the name of the LORD
  I | drove them off!

13 I was pressed and pressed
  to the | point of falling,
    but the LORD came | to my help.

14 The LORD is my strength | and my song,
  and has become | my salvation.

15 Shouts of rejoicing and salvation
  echo in the tents | of the righteous:
    "The right hand of the | LORD
    acts valiantly!

16 The right hand of the LORD | is exalted!
  The right hand of the | LORD
    acts valiantly!"

17 I shall not | die, but live,
  and declare the works | of the LORD.

18 The LORD indeed
  pun- | ished me sorely,
    but did not hand me o- | ver
    to death.

19 Open for me the | gates of righteousness;
  I will enter them
    and give thanks | to the LORD.

20 "This is the gate | of the LORD;
  here the righ- | teous may enter."

21 I give thanks to you,
  for you have | answered me
    and you have become | my salvation.

22 The stone that the build- | ers rejected
  has become the chief | cornerstone.

23 By the LORD has | this been done;
  it is marvelous | in our eyes.

24 This is the day that the | LORD has made;
  let us rejoice and be | glad in it.

25 Hosanna! | O LORD, save us!
  We pray to you, LORD,
    pros- | per our days!

26 Blessed is the one
  who comes in the name | of the LORD;
  we bless you
    from the house | of the LORD.

27 The LORD is God
  and has giv- | en us light.
    Form a procession with branches
    up to the corners | of the altar.

28 You are my God, and | I will thank you;
  you are my God, and I | will exalt you.

29 Give thanks to the LORD,
  for the | LORD is good;
    God's mercy en- | dures forever.

119

Alef א
1 Happy are they
  whose | way is blameless,
    who follow the teaching | of the
    LORD!

2 Happy are they
  who observe | your decrees
    and seek you with | all their hearts,

3 who never do | any wrong,
  but always walk | in your ways.

4 You laid down | your commandments,
  that we should | fully keep them.

5 Oh, that my ways were made | so direct
  that I might | keep your statutes!

6 Then I should not be | put to shame,
  when I regard
    all | your commandments.

7 I will thank you with | a true heart,
  when I have learned
    your | righteous judgments.

8 I will | keep your statutes;
  do not utter- | ly forsake me.

Bet ב

⁹ How shall the young
keep ˈ their way clean?
By keeping ˈ to your word.

¹⁰ With my whole ˈ heart I seek you;
let me not stray
from ˈ your commandments.

¹¹ I treasure your promise ˈ in my heart,
that I may not ˈ sin against you.

¹² Blessed are ˈ you, O LORD;
instruct me ˈ in your statutes.

¹³ With my lips ˈ I recite
all the judgments
ˈ of your mouth.

¹⁴ I take greater delight
in the way of ˈ your decrees
than in all man- ˈ ner of riches.

¹⁵ I will meditate
on ˈ your commandments
and give attention ˈ to your ways.

¹⁶ My delight is ˈ in your statutes;
I will not for- ˈ get your word.

Gimel ג

¹⁷ Deal kindly ˈ with your servant,
that I may live and ˈ keep your word.

¹⁸ Open my eyes, that ˈ I may see
the wonders ˈ of your teaching.

¹⁹ I am a stranger ˈ here on earth;
do not hide
your command- ˈ ments from me.

²⁰ My soul is consumed ˈ at all times
with longing ˈ for your judgments.

²¹ You have re- ˈ buked the insolent;
cursed are they who stray
from ˈ your commandments!

²² Take away from me
their scorn ˈ and contempt,
for I have kept ˈ your decrees.

²³ Even though rulers
sit and ˈ plot against me,
your servant will meditate
ˈ on your statutes.

²⁴ For your decrees are ˈ my delight,
and they ˈ are my counselors.

Dalet ד

²⁵ My soul cleaves ˈ to the dust;
give me life according ˈ to your word.

²⁶ I have recounted my ways,
and you ˈ answered me;
instruct me ˈ in your statutes.

²⁷ Make me understand
the way of ˈ your commandments,
that I may meditate
on your ˈ marvelous works.

²⁸ My soul melts a- ˈ way from sorrow;
sustain me according ˈ to your word.

²⁹ Take from me the ˈ way of lying;
let me find grace
ˈ through your teaching.

³⁰ I have chosen the ˈ way of faithfulness;
I set your judg- ˈ ments before me.

³¹ I hold fast to ˈ your decrees;
O LORD, do not put ˈ me to shame.

³² I will run the way
of ˈ your commandments,
for you increase my ˈ heart's capacity.

He ה

³³ Teach me, O LORD,
the way ˈ of your statutes,
and I shall keep it ˈ to the end.

³⁴ Give me understanding,
and I shall ˈ keep your teaching;
I shall keep it with ˈ all my heart.

³⁵ Lead me in the path
of ˈ your commandments,
for that is ˈ my desire.

³⁶ Incline my heart to ˈ your decrees
and not to ˈ unjust gain.

³⁷ Turn my eyes
from be- ˈ holding falsehood;
give me life ˈ in your way.

³⁸ Fulfill your promise ˈ to your servant,
which is for ˈ those who fear you.

³⁹ Turn away the reproach ˈ that I dread,
because your judg- ˈ ments are good.

⁴⁰ Behold, I long
for ˈ your commandments;
by your righteousness en- ˈ liven me.

Vav ו

⁴¹ Let your steadfast love
come to ǀ me, O Lᴏʀᴅ,
and your salvation,
according ǀ to your promise.

⁴² Then shall I have a word
for ǀ those who taunt me,
because I trust ǀ in your word.

⁴³ Do not take the word of truth
out ǀ of my mouth,
for my hope is ǀ in your judgments.

⁴⁴ I will always ǀ keep your teaching,
forev- ǀ er and ever.

⁴⁵ I will ǀ walk at liberty,
because I study
ǀ your commandments.

⁴⁶ I will tell of your decrees ǀ before kings
and will not ǀ be ashamed.

⁴⁷ I will delight in ǀ your commandments,
your commandments ǀ that I love.

⁴⁸ I will lift up my hands
to ǀ your commandments,
and I will meditate
ǀ on your statutes.

Zayin ז

⁴⁹ Remember your word ǀ to your servant,
because you have giv- ǀ en me hope.

⁵⁰ This is my comfort ǀ in my trouble:
that your promise en- ǀ livens me.

⁵¹ The proud have derid- ǀ ed me cruelly,
but I have not turned
ǀ from your teaching.

⁵² When I remember
your judg- ǀ ments of old,
O Lᴏʀᴅ, I ǀ take great comfort.

⁵³ I am filled with a ǀ burning rage,
because of the wicked
who for- ǀ sake your teaching.

⁵⁴ Your statutes have been
like ǀ songs to me
wherever ǀ I have lived.

⁵⁵ I remember your name
in the ǀ night, O Lᴏʀᴅ,
and o- ǀ bey your teaching.

⁵⁶ This is how it has ǀ been with me,
because I have kept
ǀ your commandments.

Khet ח

⁵⁷ You are my por- ǀ tion, O Lᴏʀᴅ;
I have promised to ǀ keep your words.

⁵⁸ I entreat you with ǀ all my heart:
Be merciful to me
according ǀ to your promise.

⁵⁹ I have consid- ǀ ered my ways
and turned my feet
toward ǀ your decrees.

⁶⁰ I hasten and do ǀ not delay
to keep ǀ your commandments.

⁶¹ Though the cords of the wicked
en- ǀ tangle me,
I do not for- ǀ get your teaching.

⁶² At midnight I will rise
to ǀ give you thanks
for your ǀ righteous judgments.

⁶³ I am a companion of ǀ all who fear you
and of those
who keep ǀ your commandments.

⁶⁴ Your love, O Lᴏʀᴅ, ǀ fills the earth;
teach ǀ me your statutes.

Tet ט

⁶⁵ O Lᴏʀᴅ, you have dealt graciously
ǀ with your servant,
according ǀ to your word.

⁶⁶ Teach me discern- ǀ ment
and knowledge,
for I have believed
in ǀ your commandments.

⁶⁷ Before I was afflicted I ǀ went astray,
but now I ǀ keep your word.

⁶⁸ You are good
and you ǀ bring forth good;
teach ǀ me your statutes.

⁶⁹ The proud have smeared ǀ me with lies,
but I will keep your commandments
with ǀ my whole heart.

⁷⁰ Their heart is con- ǀ gealed like fat,
but my delight is ǀ in your teaching.

⁷¹ It is good for me
that I have ᴵ been afflicted,
that I might ᴵ learn your statutes.

⁷² The teaching of your mouth
is dear- ᴵ er to me
than thousands in ᴵ gold and silver.

Yod ׳

⁷³ Your hands have made me
and ᴵ fashioned me;
give me understanding, that I may
learn ᴵ your commandments.

⁷⁴ Those who fear you will be glad
ᴵ when they see me,
because I trust ᴵ in your word.

⁷⁵ I know, O LORD,
that your judg- ᴵ ments are right
and that in faithfulness
you have af- ᴵ flicted me.

⁷⁶ Let your lovingkindness
ᴵ be my comfort,
as you have promised
ᴵ to your servant.

⁷⁷ Let your compassion come to me,
that ᴵ I may live,
for your teaching is ᴵ my delight.

⁷⁸ Let the arrogant be put to shame,
for they wrong ᴵ me with lies;
but I will meditate
on ᴵ your commandments.

⁷⁹ Let those who fear you re- ᴵ turn to me,
those who know ᴵ your decrees.

⁸⁰ Let my heart be sound ᴵ in your statutes,
that I may not be ᴵ put to shame.

Kaf כ

⁸¹ I have longed for ᴵ your salvation;
I have put my hope ᴵ in your word.

⁸² My eyes have failed
from watching ᴵ for your promise,
and I say,
"When will you ᴵ comfort me?"

⁸³ I have become
like a water-skin ᴵ dried in smoke,
but I have not forgot- ᴵ ten
your statutes.

⁸⁴ How long can your ᴵ servant live?
When will you give judgment
against my ᴵ persecutors?

⁸⁵ The proud have dug ᴵ pits for me;
they who do not ᴵ keep
your teaching.

⁸⁶ All your command- ᴵ ments are true;
help me,
for they persecute ᴵ me with lies.

⁸⁷ They had almost
made an end of ᴵ me on earth,
but I have not forsaken
ᴵ your commandments.

⁸⁸ In your lovingkind- ᴵ ness, revive me,
that I may keep
the decrees ᴵ of your mouth.

Lamed ל

⁸⁹ O LORD, your word is ᴵ everlasting;
it stands firm ᴵ in the heavens.

⁹⁰ Your faithfulness remains
from one generation ᴵ to another;
you established the earth,
and ᴵ it abides.

⁹¹ By your decree
these continue ᴵ to this day,
for all things ᴵ are your servants.

⁹² If my delight
had not been ᴵ in your teaching,
I would have perished
in ᴵ my affliction.

⁹³ I will never forget
ᴵ your commandments,
because by them you ᴵ gave me life.

⁹⁴ O LORD, ᴵ I am yours;
save me,
for I study ᴵ your commandments.

⁹⁵ Though the wicked
lie in wait for me ᴵ to destroy me,
I will apply my mind
to ᴵ your decrees.

⁹⁶ I see that all things come ᴵ to an end,
but your commandment
ᴵ has no bounds.

Mem מ

97 Oh, how I ǀ love your teaching!
All the day long it is ǀ in my mind.

98 Your commandment
has made me wiser ǀ than my enemies,
for it is ǀ always with me.

99 I have more understanding
than ǀ all my teachers,
for your decrees ǀ are my study.

100 I am wiser ǀ than the elders,
because I observe
ǀ your commandments.

101 I restrain my feet from every ǀ evil way,
that I may ǀ keep your word.

102 I do not turn aside
ǀ from your judgments,
because you your- ǀ self
have taught me.

103 How sweet are your words
ǀ to my taste!
They are sweeter than honey
ǀ to my mouth.

104 Through your commandments
I gain ǀ understanding;
therefore I hate every ǀ lying way.

Nun נ

105 Your word is a lamp ǀ to my feet
and a light up- ǀ on my path.

106 I have sworn and ǀ am determined
to keep your ǀ righteous judgments.

107 I am ǀ deeply troubled;
preserve my life, O Lord,
according ǀ to your word.

108 Accept, O Lord,
the willing tribute ǀ of my lips,
and teach ǀ me your judgments.

109 My life is al- ǀ ways in danger,
yet I do not for- ǀ get your teaching.

110 The wicked have set a ǀ trap for me,
but I have not strayed
from ǀ your commandments.

111 Your decrees
are my inheri- ǀ tance forever;
truly, they are the joy ǀ of my heart.

112 I have applied my heart
to ful- ǀ fill your statutes
forever and ǀ to the end.

Samekh ס

113 I hate ǀ crooked people,
but your teach- ǀ ing I love.

114 You are my ref- ǀ uge and shield;
I hope ǀ for your word.

115 Turn away from ǀ me, you wicked,
so I can keep the commandments
ǀ of my God.

116 Sustain me according to your promise,
that ǀ I may live,
and do not ǀ thwart my hope.

117 Hold me up, and I ǀ shall be safe,
and I shall always pay heed
ǀ to your statutes.

118 You spurn all
who stray ǀ from your statutes;
their deceitfulness ǀ is in vain.

119 You clear away
all the wicked of the ǀ earth like dross;
therefore I love ǀ your decrees.

120 My flesh trembles with ǀ dread of you;
I am afraid ǀ of your judgments.

Ayin ע

121 I have done what is ǀ just and right;
do not deliver me
to ǀ my oppressors.

122 Guarantee your ǀ servant's good;
let not the ǀ proud oppress me.

123 My eyes have failed
from watching for ǀ your salvation
and for your ǀ righteous promise.

124 Deal with your servant
according to your ǀ steadfast love,
and teach ǀ me your statutes.

125 I am your servant;
grant me ǀ understanding,
that I may know ǀ your decrees.

126 It is time to act ǀ for the Lord,
for they have violat- ǀ ed
your teaching.

¹²⁷ Truly, I love | your commandments
more than gold,
even the | purest gold.

¹²⁸ Truly, I hold all your commandments
to be | right for me;
all paths of falsehood | I abhor.

Pe   פ

¹²⁹ Your de- | crees are wonderful;
therefore I obey them
with | all my heart.

¹³⁰ When your word is opened
| it gives light;
it gives understanding | to the simple.

¹³¹ I open my | mouth and pant
because I long
for | your commandments.

¹³² Turn to me and be gra- | cious to me,
as you always do
to those who | love your name.

¹³³ Order my footsteps | in your word;
let no iniquity
have dominion | over me.

¹³⁴ Rescue me from those | who oppress me,
and I will keep
| your commandments.

¹³⁵ Let your face shine up- | on your servant
and teach | me your statutes.

¹³⁶ My eyes shed | streams of tears,
because people
do not | keep your teaching.

Tsade   צ

¹³⁷ You are righ- | teous, O LORD,
and upright | are your judgments.

¹³⁸ You commanded your de- | crees
in righteousness
and | in all faithfulness.

¹³⁹ My indignation | has consumed me,
because my enemies
for- | get your words.

¹⁴⁰ Your word is | very pure,
and your | servant loves it.

¹⁴¹ I am small and of lit- | tle account,
yet I do not forget
| your commandments.

¹⁴² Your righteousness is | everlasting
and your teach- | ing is true.

¹⁴³ Trouble and distress
have | come upon me,
yet your commandments
are | my delight.

¹⁴⁴ The righteousness of your decrees
is | everlasting;
grant me understanding,
that | I may live.

Kof   ק

¹⁴⁵ I call with | my whole heart;
answer me, O LORD,
that I may | keep your statutes.

¹⁴⁶ I call | to you; save me!
I will keep | your decrees.

¹⁴⁷ I arise early in the morning
and I cry | out to you,
I hope | for your word.

¹⁴⁸ My eyes are open in
| the night watches,
that I may meditate
up- | on your promise.

¹⁴⁹ Hear my voice, O LORD,
according to your | steadfast love;
according to your ways,
| give me life.

¹⁵⁰ They who pursue mal- | ice draw near;
they are very far
| from your teaching.

¹⁵¹ You, O LORD, are | near at hand,
and all your command- | ments
are true.

¹⁵² I have known of your de- | crees of old
that you have established | them
forever.

Resh   ר

¹⁵³ Behold my affliction and de- | liver me,
for I do not for- | get your teaching.

¹⁵⁴ Plead my cause | and redeem me;
according to your promise,
| give me life.

¹⁵⁵ Deliverance is far | from the wicked,
for they do not stud- | y your statutes.

156 Great is your compas- I sion, O LORD;
   preserve my life
   according I to your ways.

157 There are many
   who persecute I and oppress me,
      yet I have not swerved
      from I your decrees.

158 I look at the treacher- I ous
   with loathing,
      they who have not I kept your word.

159 See how I love I your commandments!
   O LORD, preserve me
   by your I steadfast love.

160 The sum of your I word is truth;
   your righteous justice I is eternal.

Shin   ש

161 Rulers have persecuted me
   I without cause;
      my heart stands in awe I of your word.

162 I rejoice o- I ver your promise
   as one who I finds great spoils.

163 Lies I hate I and abhor,
   your teach- I ing I love.

164 I praise you seven I times a day
   for your I righteous judgments.

165 Great peace have they
   who I love your teaching;
      for them there is no I stumbling block.

166 I have hoped
   for your salva- I tion, O LORD,
   and I have fulfilled
   I your commandments.

167 I have kept I your decrees
   and I have I loved them deeply.

168 I have kept your commandments
   I and decrees,
      indeed, all my ways I are before you.

Tav   ת

169 Let my cry come before I you, O LORD;
   give me understanding,
   according I to your word.

170 Let my supplication I come before you;
   deliver me,
   according I to your promise.

171 My lips shall pour I forth your praise,
   when you teach I me your statutes.

172 My tongue shall sing I of your promise,
   for all your command- I ments
   are righteous.

173 Let your hand be read- I y to help me,
   for I have chosen
   I your commandments.

174 I long for your salva- I tion, O LORD,
   and your teaching is I my delight.

175 Let me live, and I I will praise you,
   and let your I judgments help me.

176 I have gone astray
   like a sheep I that is lost;
      search for your servant,
      for I do not forget
      I your commandments.

120

1 When I I was in trouble,
   I called to the LORD,
   who I answered me.

2 Deliver me, O LORD, from I lying lips
   and from the de- I ceitful tongue.

3 What shall be done to you,
   and what I more besides,
      O you de- I ceitful tongue?—

4 the sharpened arrows I of a warrior,
   along with hot I glowing coals!

5 How hateful it is
   that I must I lodge in Meshech
   and dwell
      among the I tents of Kedar!

6 Too long have I I had to live
   among the ene- I mies of peace.

7 I am on the I side of peace,
   but when I speak of it,
   they I are for war.

121

1 I lift up my eyes I to the hills;
   from where is my I help to come?

2 My help comes I from the LORD,
   the maker of heav- I en and earth.

³ The Lord will not let
your ⎮ foot be moved
nor will the one
who watches over you ⎮ fall asleep.

⁴ Behold, the keep- ⎮ er of Israel
will neither slum- ⎮ ber nor sleep;

⁵ the Lord watches ⎮ over you;
the Lord is your shade
at ⎮ your right hand;

⁶ the sun will not strike ⎮ you by day,
nor the ⎮ moon by night.

⁷ The Lord will preserve you
⎮ from all evil
and will ⎮ keep your life.

⁸ The Lord will watch over
your going out and your ⎮ coming in,
from this time forth
for- ⎮ evermore.

122

¹ I was glad when they ⎮ said to me,
"Let us go
to the house ⎮ of the Lord."

² Now our ⎮ feet are standing
within your gates, ⎮ O Jerusalem.

³ Jerusalem is built ⎮ as a city
that is at unity ⎮ with itself;

⁴ to which the tribes go up,
the tribes ⎮ of the Lord,
the assembly of Israel,
to praise the name ⎮ of the Lord.

⁵ For there are the ⎮ thrones of judgment,
the thrones of the ⎮ house of David.

⁶ Pray for the peace ⎮ of Jerusalem:
"May they pros- ⎮ per who love you.

⁷ Peace be with- ⎮ in your walls
and quietness with- ⎮ in your towers.

⁸ For the sake
of my kindred ⎮ and companions,
I pray for ⎮ your prosperity.

⁹ Because of the house
of the ⎮ Lord our God,
I will seek to ⎮ do you good."

123

¹ To you I lift ⎮ up my eyes,
to you enthroned ⎮ in the heavens.

² As the eyes of servants
look to the hand of their masters,
and the eyes of a maid
to the hand ⎮ of her mistress,
so our eyes look to you,
O Lord our God,
until you show ⎮ us your mercy.

³ Have mercy upon us, O ⎮ Lord,
have mercy,
for we have had
more than enough ⎮ of contempt,

⁴ too much of the scorn
of the in- ⎮ dolent rich,
and of the derision ⎮ of the proud.

124

¹ If the Lord
had not been ⎮ on our side,
let Isra- ⎮ el now say;

² if the Lord
had not been ⎮ on our side,
when enemies rose ⎮ up against us,

³ then would they have
swallowed us ⎮ up alive
in their fierce ⎮ anger toward us;

⁴ then would the waters
have ⎮ overwhelmed us
and the torrent gone ⎮ over us;

⁵ then would the ⎮ raging waters
have gone right ⎮ over us.

⁶ Blessed ⎮ be the Lord
who has not given us over
to be a prey ⎮ for their teeth.

⁷ We have escaped like a bird
from the snare ⎮ of the fowler;
the snare is broken,
and we ⎮ have escaped.

⁸ Our help is in the name ⎮ of the Lord,
the maker of heav- ⎮ en and earth.

125

[1] Those who trust in the LORD
are | like Mount Zion,
which cannot be moved,
but stands | fast forever.

[2] The mountains sur- | round Jerusalem;
so you surround
your people, O LORD,
from this time forth for- | evermore.

[3] The scepter of the wicked
shall not hold sway
over the land allotted | to the just,
so that the just
shall not put their | hands to evil.

[4] Show your goodness, O LORD,
to those | who are good
and to those who are | true of heart.

[5] As for those
who turn aside to crooked ways,
the LORD will lead them away
with the | evildoers;
but peace be | upon Israel.

126

[1] When the LORD restored
the for- | tunes of Zion,
then were we
like | those who dream.

[2] Then was our mouth
filled with laughter,
and our tongue with | shouts of joy.
Then they said among the nations,
"The LORD has done
great | things for them."

[3] The LORD has done great | things for us,
and we are | glad indeed.

[4] Restore our for- | tunes, O LORD,
like the watercourses | of the Negeb.

[5] Those who | sowed with tears
will reap with | songs of joy.

[6] Those who go out weeping,
carry- | ing the seed,
will come again with joy,
shoulder- | ing their sheaves.

127

[1] Unless the LORD builds the house,
their labor is in | vain who build it.
Unless the LORD
watches over the city,
in vain the senti- | nel keeps vigil.

[2] It is in vain to rise so early
and go to | bed so late;
vain, too, to eat the bread of toil;
for you, LORD, give sleep
to | your beloved.

[3] Children are a heritage
| from the LORD,
and the fruit of the womb | is a gift.

[4] Like arrows in the hand | of a warrior
are the children | of one's youth.

[5] Happy is the one
whose quiver is | full of them!
Such a one will not be put to shame
when contending with enemies
| in the gate.

128

[1] Happy are they all
who | fear the LORD,
and who follow | in God's ways!

[2] You shall eat the fruit | of your labor;
happiness and prosperity
| shall be yours.

[3] Your wife shall be like a fruitful vine
with- | in your house,
your children like olive shoots
round a- | bout your table.

[4] The one who | fears the LORD
shall thus in- | deed be blessed.

[5] The LORD bless | you from Zion,
and may you see
the prosperity of Jerusalem
all the days | of your life.

[6] May you live to see
your | children's children;
may peace be | upon Israel.

129

1 "Greatly have they oppressed me
 | since my youth,"
   let Isra- | el now say;

2 "Greatly have they oppressed me
 | since my youth,
     but they have not pre- | vailed
     against me."

3 The farmers plowed up- | on my back
     and made their | furrows long.

4 The LORD, the | Righteous One,
     has cut the cords | of the wicked.

5 Let them be put to shame
 | and thrown back,
     all those who are ene- | mies of Zion.

6 Let them be like grass
 up- | on the housetops,
     which withers
     before it | can be plucked;

7 which does not fill the hand | of the reaper,
     nor the arms of the one
     who | binds the sheaves;

8 so that those who go by do not say,
   "The blessing of the LORD | be upon you.
     We bless you
     in the name | of the LORD."

130

1 Out | of the depths
     I cry to | you, O LORD;

2 O LORD, | hear my voice!
     Let your ears be attentive
     to the voice of my | supplication.

3 If you were to keep watch | over sins,
     O LORD, | who could stand?

4 Yet with you | is forgiveness,
     in order that you | may be feared.

5 I wait for you, O LORD; | my soul waits;
     in your word | is my hope.

6 My soul waits for the Lord
  more than those who keep watch
 | for the morning,
     more than those who keep watch
     | for the morning.

7 O Israel, wait for the LORD,
   for with the LORD
   there is | steadfast love;
     with the LORD
     there is plen- | teous redemption.

8 For the LORD shall | redeem Israel
     from | all their sins.

131

1 O LORD, I am not proud;
   I have no | haughty looks.
     I do not occupy myself
     with great matters,
     or with things
     that are too | hard for me.

2 But I still my soul and make it quiet,
   like a child upon its | mother's breast;
     my soul is quiet- | ed within me.

3 O Israel, wait up- | on the LORD,
     from this time forth for- | evermore.

132

1 LORD, re- | member David,
     and all the hardships | he endured;

2 how he swore an oath | to the LORD
     and vowed a vow
     to the Mighty | One of Jacob:

3 "I will not come under the roof
 | of my house,
     nor climb up in- | to my bed;

4 I will not allow my | eyes to sleep,
     nor let my | eyelids slumber;

5 until I find a place | for the LORD,
     a dwelling
     for the Mighty | One of Jacob."

6 "The ark! We heard it | was
   in Ephrathah;
     we found it in the | fields of Ja'ar.

7 Let us go to God's | dwelling-place;
     let us fall upon our knees
     be- | fore God's footstool."

8 Arise, O LORD,
   into your | resting-place,
     you and the ark | of your strength.

⁹ Let your priests be | clothed
with righteousness;
let your faithful people | sing with joy.

¹⁰ For your servant | David's sake,
do not turn away
the face of | your anointed.

¹¹ The LORD has sworn an oath to David,
and in truth, | will not break it:
"A son, the fruit of your body,
will I set up- | on your throne.

¹² If your children keep my covenant
and my testimonies
that | I shall teach them,
their children will sit
upon your throne for- | evermore."

¹³ For the LORD has | chosen Zion,
desiring Jerusalem for a | habitation:

¹⁴ "This shall be my resting- | place forever;
here will I dwell, for I de- | light in Zion.

¹⁵ I will surely bless the cit- | y's provisions,
and satisfy the | poor with bread.

¹⁶ I will clothe the priests | with salvation,
and the faithful in Zion
will re- | joice and sing.

¹⁷ There will I make
the horn of | David flourish;
I have prepared a lamp
for | my anointed.

¹⁸ As for his enemies,
I will clothe | them with shame;
but as for him, his | crown will shine."

133

¹ How good and how pleas- | ant it is
when kindred
live togeth- | er in unity!

² It is like fine oil upon the head,
flowing down up- | on the beard,
upon the beard of Aaron,
flowing down
upon the collar | of his robe.

³ It is like the dew of Hermon
flowing down upon the | hills of Zion.
For there the LORD
has commanded the blessing:
life for- | evermore.

134

¹ Behold now! Bless the LORD,
all you servants | of the LORD,
you that stand by night
in the house | of the LORD.

² Lift up your hands in the | holy place
and | bless the LORD.

³ The LORD who made heav- | en
and earth
bless you | out of Zion.

135

¹ Hallelujah!
Praise the name | of the LORD;
give praise,
you servants | of the LORD,

² you who stand
in the house | of the LORD,
in the courts
of the house | of our God.

³ Praise the LORD, for the | LORD is good;
sing praises to God's name,
for | it is lovely!

⁴ For the Lord has | chosen Jacob,
and Israel for | a possession.

⁵ For I know that the | LORD is great,
and that our Lord
is a- | bove all gods.

⁶ Whatever the LORD pleases,
the LORD does,
in the heavens and | on the earth,
in the seas and | all the deeps,

⁷ raising up clouds
from the ends | of the earth;
making lightning for the rain,
and bringing out the wind
| from its storehouse.

⁸ The LORD struck down
the first- | born of Egypt,
the firstborn,
both hu- | man and animal,

⁹ sending signs and wonders
into the midst of | you, O Egypt,
against Pharaoh
and | all his servants.

¹⁰ The LORD struck down | many nations
    and killed | mighty kings:

¹¹ Sihon, king of the Amorites,
    and Og, the | king of Bashan,
      and all the royal- | ty of Canaan,

¹² giving their land to be | an inheritance,
    an inheritance
      for the peo- | ple of Israel.

¹³ O LORD, your name is | everlasting;
    your renown, O LORD,
      endures from | age to age.

¹⁴ For you, O LORD,
    cham- | pion your people
    and show compassion
    | to your servants.

¹⁵ The idols of the nations
    are sil- | ver and gold,
      the work of | human hands.

¹⁶ They have mouths,
    but they | cannot speak;
      eyes they have,
      but they | cannot see.

¹⁷ They have ears, but they | cannot hear;
    neither is there any breath
    | in their mouths.

¹⁸ Those who make | them are like them,
    and so are all
    who put their | trust in them.

¹⁹ O house of Israel, | bless the LORD,
    O house of Aaron, | bless the LORD.

²⁰ O house of Levi, | bless the LORD!
    you who fear the LORD,
    | bless the LORD.

²¹ Blessed from Zion | be the LORD,
    who dwells in Jerusalem.
    | Hallelujah!

136

¹ Give thanks to the LORD,
    for the | LORD is good,
      for God's mercy en- | dures forever.

² Give thanks to the | God of gods,
    for God's mercy en- | dures forever.

³ Give thanks to the | Lord of lords,
    for God's mercy en- | dures forever;

⁴ who alone | does great wonders,
    for God's mercy en- | dures forever;

⁵ who by wisdom | made the heavens,
    for God's mercy en- | dures forever;

⁶ who spread out the earth
    up- | on the waters,
      for God's mercy en- | dures forever;

⁷ who made | the great lights—
    for God's mercy en- | dures forever;

⁸ the sun to gov- | ern the day,
    for God's mercy en- | dures forever;

⁹ the moon and the stars
    to gov- | ern the night,
      for God's mercy en- | dures forever;

¹⁰ who struck down
    the first- | born of Egypt,
      for God's mercy en- | dures forever;

¹¹ and brought out Israel
    | from their midst,
      for God's mercy en- | dures forever;

¹² with a mighty hand
    and an | outstretched arm,
      for God's mercy en- | dures forever;

¹³ who divided the Red | Sea in two,
    for God's mercy en- | dures forever;

¹⁴ and made Israel
    to pass | through the middle,
      for God's mercy en- | dures forever;

¹⁵ but swept Pharaoh and his army
    in- | to the Red Sea,
      for God's mercy en- | dures forever;

¹⁶ who led the people
    | through the wilderness,
      for God's mercy en- | dures forever;

¹⁷ who struck | down great kings,
    for God's mercy en- | dures forever;

¹⁸ and slew | mighty kings,
    for God's mercy en- | dures forever;

¹⁹ Sihon, king | of the Amorites,
    for God's mercy en- | dures forever;

²⁰ and Og, the | king of Bashan,
    for God's mercy en- | dures forever;

²¹ and gave away their lands
    for | an inheritance,
      for God's mercy en- | dures forever;

²² an inheritance for Isra- ǀ el,
God's servant,
for God's mercy en- ǀ dures forever;

²³ who remembered us in our ǀ low estate,
for God's mercy en- ǀ dures forever;

²⁴ and rescued us ǀ from our enemies,
for God's mercy en- ǀ dures forever;

²⁵ who gives food ǀ to all creatures,
for God's mercy en- ǀ dures forever.

²⁶ Give thanks to the ǀ God of heaven,
for God's mercy en- ǀ dures forever.

137

¹ By the waters of Babylon
we sat ǀ down and wept,
when we remembered ǀ you, O Zion.

² As for our harps, we ǀ hung them up
on the trees
in the midst ǀ of that land.

³ For those who led us away captive
asked us for a song,
and our oppressors ǀ called for mirth:
"Sing us one of the ǀ songs of Zion."

⁴ How shall we sing ǀ the LORD's song
upon an ǀ alien soil?

⁵ If I forget you, ǀ O Jerusalem,
let my right hand for- ǀ get its skill.

⁶ Let my tongue
cleave to the roof of my mouth
if I do not re- ǀ member you,
if I do not set Jerusalem
above my ǀ highest joy.

⁷ Remember the day of Jerusalem,
O LORD,
against the peo- ǀ ple of Edom,
who said, "Down with it!
down with it!
even ǀ to the ground!"

⁸ O daughter of Babylon,
doomed ǀ to destruction,
happy shall they be who repay you
for what you have ǀ done to us!

⁹ Happy shall they be
who take your ǀ little ones
and dash them a- ǀ gainst the rock!

138

¹ I will give thanks to you, O LORD,
with ǀ my whole heart;
before the gods
I will ǀ sing your praise.

² I will bow down
toward your holy temple
and praise your name,
because of your steadfast ǀ love
and faithfulness;
for you have glorified your name
and your word a- ǀ bove all things.

³ When I called, you ǀ answered me;
you increased my ǀ strength
within me.

⁴ All the rulers of the earth
will praise ǀ you, O LORD,
when they have heard
the words ǀ of your mouth.

⁵ They will sing of the ways ǀ of the LORD,
that great is the glory ǀ of the LORD.

⁶ The LORD is high,
yet cares ǀ for the lowly,
perceiving the haughty ǀ from afar.

⁷ Though I walk in the midst of trouble,
you ǀ keep me safe;
you stretch forth your hand
against the fury of my enemies;
your right ǀ hand shall save me.

⁸ You will make good
your pur- ǀ pose for me;
O LORD,
your steadfast love endures forever;
do not abandon the works
ǀ of your hands.

139

¹ LORD, you have ǀ searched me out;
O LORD, ǀ you have known me.

² You know my sitting down
and my ǀ rising up;
you discern my thoughts ǀ from afar.

³ You trace my journeys
and my ǀ resting-places
and are acquainted with ǀ all my ways.

⁴ Indeed, there is not a word ' on my lips,
  but you, O LORD,
    know it ' altogether.

⁵ You encompass me,
  behind ' and before,
    and lay your ' hand upon me.

⁶ Such knowledge
  is too wonder- ' ful for me;
    it is so high
    that I cannot at- ' tain to it.

⁷ Where can I go then ' from your Spirit?
  Where can I flee
  ' from your presence?

⁸ If I climb up to heaven, ' you are there;
  if I make the grave my bed,
  you ' are there also.

⁹ If I take the wings ' of the morning
  and dwell in the uttermost parts
  ' of the sea,

¹⁰ even there your ' hand will lead me
  and your right hand ' hold me fast.

¹¹ If I say,
  "Surely the darkness will ' cover me,
  and the light around me
  ' turn to night,"

¹² darkness is not dark to you;
  the night is as bright ' as the day;
    darkness and light
    to you are ' both alike.

¹³ For you yourself
  created my ' inmost parts;
    you knit me together
    in my ' mother's womb.

¹⁴ I will thank you
  because I am mar- ' velously made;
    your works are wonderful,
    and I ' know it well.

¹⁵ My body was not hid- ' den from you,
  while I was being made in secret
    and woven in the depths
    ' of the earth.

¹⁶ Your eyes beheld my limbs,
  yet unfinished in the womb;
    all of them were written ' in your book;
    my days were fashioned
    before they ' came to be.

¹⁷ How deep I find your ' thoughts,
  O God!
    How great is the ' sum of them!

¹⁸ If I were to count them,
  they would be more in number
  ' than the sand;
    to count them all,
    my life span would need
    to ' be like yours.

¹⁹ Oh, that you
  would slay the wick- ' ed, O God!
    You that thirst for blood,
    de- ' part from me.

²⁰ They speak despiteful- ' ly against you;
  your enemies
    take your ' name in vain.

²¹ Do I not hate those, O ' LORD,
  who hate you?
    And do I not loathe those
    who rise ' up against you?

²² I hate them with a ' perfect hatred;
  they have become
  ' my own enemies.

²³ Search me out, O God,
  and ' know my heart;
    try me
    and know my ' restless thoughts.

²⁴ Look well
  whether there be
    any wicked- ' ness in me
      and lead me in the way
      that is ' everlasting.

140

¹ Deliver me, O LORD, from ' evildoers;
  protect me ' from the violent,

² who devise evil ' in their hearts
  and stir up strife ' all day long.

³ They have sharpened their tongues
  ' like a serpent;
    adder's poison is un- ' der their lips.

⁴ Keep me, O LORD,
  from the hands ' of the wicked;
    protect me from the violent,
    who are determined to ' trip me up.

⁵ The proud have hidden a snare for me
and stretched out a ǀ net of cords;
    they have set traps for me
    a- ǀ long the path.

⁶ I have said to the LORD,
"You ǀ are my God;
    listen, O LORD, to my ǀ supplication.

⁷ O Lord GOD,
the strength of ǀ my salvation,
    you have covered my head
    in the ǀ day of battle.

⁸ Do not grant the desires
of the wick- ǀ ed, O LORD,
    nor let their e- ǀ vil plans prosper.

⁹ Let not those who surround me
lift ǀ up their heads;
    let the evil of their lips
    ǀ overwhelm them.

¹⁰ Let hot burning coals ǀ fall upon them;
    let them be cast into the mire,
    never to rise ǀ up again."

¹¹ A slanderer
shall not be established ǀ on the earth,
    and evil shall hunt ǀ down the lawless.

¹² I know that the LORD
maintains the cause ǀ of the poor
    and renders justice ǀ to the needy.

¹³ Surely, the righteous
will give thanks ǀ to your name,
    and the upright
    shall continue ǀ in your sight.

141

¹ O LORD, I call to you;
come ǀ to me quickly;
    hear my voice when I ǀ cry to you.

² Let my prayer rise before ǀ you as incense,
the lifting up of my hands
    as the ǀ evening sacrifice.

³ Set a watch before my ǀ mouth, O LORD,
and guard the door ǀ of my lips.

⁴ Let not my heart
incline to any ǀ evil thing.
    Let me not be occupied
    in wickedness with evildoers,
    nor eat of ǀ their sweet foods.

⁵ Let the righteous strike me;
their rebukes,
as oil upon the head,
are not to ǀ be refused.
    Yet my prayers are continually
    against the deeds ǀ of the wicked.

⁶ Let their rulers
be thrown down up- ǀ on the stones,
    that they may hear my words,
    for ǀ they are sweet.

⁷ Just as one who tills the earth
ǀ breaks the rock,
    so let their bones be scattered
    at the mouth ǀ of the grave.

⁸ But my eyes are turned to ǀ you,
Lord GOD;
    in you I take refuge;
    strip me not ǀ of my life.

⁹ Guard me from the trap
that they have ǀ laid for me
    and from the snares of ǀ evildoers.

¹⁰ Let the wicked fall into ǀ their own nets,
    while I a- ǀ lone pass through.

142

¹ I cry to the LORD ǀ with my voice;
to the LORD
I make loud ǀ supplication:

² I pour out my com- ǀ plaint before you
and tell you ǀ all my trouble.

³ When my spirit languishes within me,
you ǀ know my path;
    in the way wherein I walk
    they have hidden a ǀ trap for me.

⁴ I look to my right hand
and find no ǀ one who knows me;
    I have no place to flee to,
    and no one ǀ cares for me.

⁵ I cry out to ǀ you, O LORD;
I say, "You are my refuge,
my portion
in the land ǀ of the living."

⁶ Listen to my cry for help,
for I have been brought ǀ very low;
    save me from those who pursue me,
    for they are too ǀ strong for me.

⁷ Bring me out of prison,
  that I may give thanks ˥ to your name;
    when you have dealt
    bountifully with me,
    the righteous will gath- ˥ er
    around me.

143

¹ LORD, hear my prayer,
  and in your faithfulness
  heed my ˥ supplications;
    answer me ˥ in your righteousness.

² Enter not into judgment
  ˥ with your servant,
    for in your sight
    shall no one liv- ˥ ing be justified.

³ For my enemy has sought my life
  and has crushed me ˥ to the ground,
    making me live in dark places
    like those who ˥ are long dead.

⁴ My spirit ˥ faints within me;
    my heart within ˥ me is desolate.

⁵ I remember the time past;
  I ponder ˥ all your deeds;
    I consider
    the works ˥ of your hands.

⁶ I spread out my ˥ hands to you;
    my soul gasps to you
    like a ˥ thirsty land.

⁷ O LORD, make haste to answer me;
  my ˥ spirit fails me;
    do not hide your face from me,
    or I shall be like those
    who go down ˥ to the pit.

⁸ Let me hear of your lovingkindness
  in the morning,
    for I put my ˥ trust in you;
    show me the road that I must walk,
    for I lift up my ˥ soul to you.

⁹ Deliver me
  from my ene- ˥ mies, O LORD,
    for I flee to ˥ you for refuge.

¹⁰ Teach me to do what pleases you,
  for you ˥ are my God;
    let your good Spirit
    lead me on ˥ level ground.

¹¹ Revive me, O LORD,
  ˥ for your name's sake;
    for your righteousness' sake,
    bring me ˥ out of trouble.

¹² In your steadfast love,
  destroy my enemies
    and bring all my ˥ foes to naught,
    for truly I ˥ am your servant.

144

¹ Blessed be the ˥ LORD my rock,
    who trains my hands to fight
    and my fin- ˥ gers to battle;

² my help and my fortress,
  my stronghold and ˥ my deliverer,
    my shield in whom I trust,
    who subdues the peoples
    ˥ under me.

³ O LORD, what are human beings
  that you should ˥ care for us,
    mere mortals
    that you should ˥ think of us?

⁴ We are like a ˥ puff of wind;
    our days are like
    a ˥ passing shadow.

⁵ Bow your heavens, O LORD,
  ˥ and come down;
    touch the mountains,
    and ˥ they shall smoke.

⁶ Hurl the lightning and ˥ scatter them;
    shoot out your ar- ˥ rows
    and rout them.

⁷ Stretch out your hand ˥ from on high;
    rescue me and deliver me
    from the great waters,
    from the hand of ˥ foreign peoples,

⁸ whose mouths ˥ speak deceitfully
    and whose right hand
    is ˥ raised in falsehood.

⁹ O God,
  I will sing to you ˥ a new song;
    I will play to you
    on a ˥ ten-stringed lyre.

¹⁰ You give victo- ˥ ry to rulers
    and have rescued
    Da- ˥ vid your servant.

¹¹ Rescue me from the hurtful sword
and deliver me
from the hand of ^I foreign peoples,
  whose mouths speak deceitfully
  and whose right hand
  is ^I raised in falsehood.

¹² May our sons be like plants
well nurtured ^I from their youth,
  and our daughters
  like sculptured corners ^I of a palace.

¹³ May our barns be filled
with crops of ^I every kind;
  may the flocks in our pastures
  increase by thousands
  and ^I tens of thousands.

¹⁴ May our cattle be ^I fat and sleek.
  may there be no breaching of the walls,
  no going into exile,
  no wailing in the ^I public squares.

¹⁵ Happy are the people of whom ^I this is so!
Happy are the people
whose God ^I is the LORD!

145

¹ I will exalt you, my ^I God and king,
and bless your name
  forev- ^I er and ever.

² Every day ^I will I bless you
and praise your name
  forev- ^I er and ever.

³ Great is the LORD
and greatly ^I to be praised!
  There is no end ^I to your greatness.

⁴ One generation
shall praise your works ^I to another
and shall de- ^I clare your power.

⁵ I will speak of the glorious splendor
^I of your majesty
  and all your ^I marvelous works.

⁶ They shall tell of the might
of your ^I wondrous acts,
  and I will re- ^I count your greatness.

⁷ They shall publish the remembrance
of ^I your great goodness;
  they shall sing joyfully
  ^I of your righteousness.

⁸ The LORD is gracious
and full ^I of compassion,
  slow to anger and
  abounding in ^I steadfast love.

⁹ LORD, you are ^I good to all,
and your compassion
  is over ^I all your works.

¹⁰ All your works
shall praise ^I you, O LORD,
  and your faithful ^I ones
  shall bless you.

¹¹ They shall tell of the glory
^I of your kingdom
  and speak ^I of your power,

¹² that all people
may know ^I of your power
  and the glorious splendor
  ^I of your kingdom.

¹³ Your kingdom is an everlasting kingdom;
your dominion endures
  through- ^I out all ages.
    You, LORD,
    are faithful in all your words,
    and loving in ^I all your works.

¹⁴ The Lord upholds all ^I those who fall
and lifts up those
  who ^I are bowed down.

¹⁵ The eyes of all wait upon ^I you, O LORD,
and you give them their food
  ^I in due season.

¹⁶ You open ^I wide your hand
and satisfy the desire
  of every ^I living thing.

¹⁷ You are righteous in ^I all your ways
and loving in ^I all your works.

¹⁸ You are near to all who ^I call upon you,
  to all who call up- ^I on you faithfully.

¹⁹ You fulfill the desire
of ^I those who fear you;
  you hear their ^I cry and save them.

²⁰ You watch over all ^I those who love you,
  but all the wicked you ^I shall destroy.

²¹ My mouth shall speak
the praise ^I of the LORD;
  let all flesh bless God's holy name
  forev- ^I er and ever.

146

1 Hal- ǀ lelujah!
Praise the LORD, ǀ O my soul!
2 I will praise the LORD as long ǀ as I live;
I will sing praises to my God
while I ǀ have my being.
3 Put not your ǀ trust in rulers,
in mortals in whom there ǀ is no help.
4 When they breathe their last,
they re- ǀ turn to earth,
and in that day ǀ their thoughts perish.
5 Happy are they who have
the God of Jacob ǀ for their help,
whose hope is in the ǀ LORD their God;
6 who made heaven and earth, the seas,
and all that ǀ is in them;
who keeps promis- ǀ es forever;
7 who gives justice to those
who are oppressed,
and food to ǀ those who hunger.
The LORD sets the ǀ captive free.
8 The LORD opens the eyes of the blind;
the LORD lifts up those
who ǀ are bowed down;
the LORD ǀ loves the righteous.
9 The LORD cares ǀ for the stranger;
the LORD sustains
the orphan and widow,
but frustrates the way ǀ of the wicked.
10 The LORD shall ǀ reign forever,
your God, O Zion, throughout
all generations. ǀ Hallelujah!

147

1 Hallelujah! How good it is
to sing praises ǀ to our God!
How pleasant it is
to honor ǀ God with praise!
2 The LORD re- ǀ builds Jerusalem,
and gathers the ex- ǀ iles of Israel.
3 The LORD heals the ǀ brokenhearted
and binds ǀ up their wounds.
4 The LORD counts the number ǀ of the stars
and calls them all ǀ by their names.
5 Great is our LORD
and might- ǀ y in power;
there is no limit ǀ to God's wisdom.
6 The LORD lifts ǀ up the lowly,
but casts the wicked ǀ to the ground.
7 Sing to the LORD ǀ with thanksgiving;
make music upon the harp
ǀ to our God,
8 who covers the heav- ǀ ens with clouds
and prepares rain for the earth,
making grass to grow
up- ǀ on the mountains.
9 God provides food ǀ for the cattle
and for the young ravens
ǀ when they cry.
10 God is not impressed
by the might ǀ of a horse,
and has no pleasure
in the speed ǀ of a runner,
11 but finds pleasure
in those who ǀ fear the LORD,
in those who await
God's ǀ steadfast love.
12 Worship the LORD, ǀ O Jerusalem;
praise your ǀ God, O Zion,
13 who has strengthened
the bars ǀ of your gates
and has blessed
your chil- ǀ dren within you.
14 God has established peace
ǀ on your borders
and satisfies you
with the ǀ finest wheat.
15 God sends out a command
ǀ to the earth,
a word that runs ǀ very swiftly.
16 God gives ǀ snow like wool,
scattering ǀ frost like ashes.
17 God scatters ǀ hail like bread crumbs.
Who can stand
a- ǀ gainst God's cold?
18 The LORD sends forth the ǀ word
and melts them;
the wind blows, and the ǀ waters flow.
19 God declares the ǀ word to Jacob,
statutes and judg- ǀ ments to Israel.

20 The LORD has not done so
to any | other nation;
they do not know God's judgments.
| Hallelujah!

148

1 Hallelujah!
Praise the LORD | from the heavens;
praise God | in the heights.

2 Praise the LORD, | all you angels;
sing praise, all you | hosts of heaven.

3 Praise the LORD, | sun and moon;
sing praise, all you | shining stars.

4 Praise the LORD, heav- | en of heavens,
and you waters a- | bove the heavens.

5 Let them praise the name | of the LORD,
who commanded,
and they | were created,

6 who made them stand fast
forev- | er and ever,
giving them a law
that shall not | pass away.

7 Praise the LORD | from the earth,
you sea monsters | and all deeps;

8 fire and hail, | snow and fog,
tempestuous wind,
do- | ing God's will;

9 mountains | and all hills,
fruit trees | and all cedars;

10 wild beasts | and all cattle,
creeping things and | flying birds;

11 sovereigns of the earth | and all peoples,
princes and all rulers | of the world;

12 young | men and maidens,
old and | young together.

13 Let them praise the name | of the LORD,
whose name only is exalted,
whose splendor
is over | earth and heaven.

14 The LORD has raised up
strength for the people
and praise for all | faithful servants,
the children of Israel,
a people who are near the LORD.
| Hallelujah!

149

1 Hallelujah!
Sing to the LORD | a new song,
God's praise
in the assembly | of the faithful.

2 Let Israel rejoice | in their maker;
let the children of Zion
be joyful | in their ruler.

3 Let them praise their maker's | name
with dancing;
let them sing praise
with tambou- | rine and harp.

4 For the LORD takes pleasure | in the people
and adorns the | poor with victory.

5 Let the faithful re- | joice in triumph;
let them sing for joy | on their beds.

6 Let the praises of God be | in their throat
and a two-edged sword | in their hand,

7 to wreak vengeance | on the nations
and punishment | on the peoples,

8 to bind their | kings in chains
and their nobles with | links of iron,

9 to inflict on them
the judg- | ment decreed;
this is glory for all God's faithful ones.
| Hallelujah!

150

1 Hallelujah!
Praise God in the | holy temple;
praise God in the | mighty firmament.

2 Praise God for | mighty acts;
praise God for ex- | ceeding greatness.

3 Praise God with | trumpet sound;
praise God with | lyre and harp.

4 Praise God with tambou- | rine and dance
praise God with | strings and pipe.

5 Praise God with re- | sounding cymbals;
praise God
with loud- | clanging cymbals.

6 Let everything | that has breath
praise the LORD. | Hallelujah!

Contents

SERVICE MUSIC

Holy Communion

Kyrie	151–158
Holy God (Trisagion)	159–161
Canticle of Praise	162–167
Gospel Acclamation	168–177
Prayer Response	178–180
Offering Song	181–188
Holy, Holy, Holy	189–193
Lamb of God	194–199
Sending Song	200–208

Holy Baptism	209–217
Life Passages	
Healing	218–221
Funeral	222–223
Daily Prayer	
Morning Prayer	224–228
Evening Prayer	229–236
Litanies	237–238

HYMNS

Advent	239–267	Evening	560–573
Christmas	268–300	Vocation, Ministry	574–584
Epiphany	301–303	Marriage	585–586
Time after Epiphany	304–318	Grace, Faith	587–598
Lent	319–343	Confession, Forgiveness	599–609
Holy Week, Three Days	344–360	Healing	610–617
Easter	361–394	Hope, Assurance	618–639
Pentecost, Holy Spirit	395–407	Community in Christ	640–659
Holy Trinity	408–415	Witness	660–677
Festivals, Commemorations	416–432	Stewardship	678–696
End Time	433–441	Lament	697–704
Holy Baptism	442–459	Justice, Peace	705–729
Holy Communion	460–502	Creation	730–740
Word of God	503–519	Prayer	741–754
Gathering	520–533	Trust, Guidance	755–795
Sending	534–551	Commitment, Discipleship	796–818
Morning	552–559	Praise, Thanksgiving	819–886

NATIONAL SONGS

	887–893

Service Music

151   Kyrie

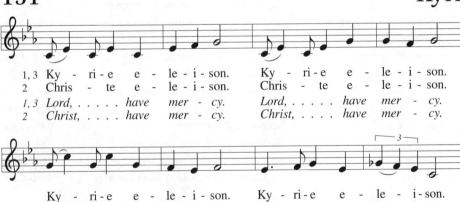

1, 3	Ky - ri - e e - le - i - son.	Ky - ri - e e - le - i - son.
2	Chris - te e - le - i - son.	Chris - te e - le - i - son.
1, 3	*Lord, ... have mer - cy.*	*Lord, ... have mer - cy.*
2	*Christ, ... have mer - cy.*	*Christ, ... have mer - cy.*

Ky - ri - e e - le - i - son.	Ky - ri - e e - le - i - son.
Chris - te e - le - i - son.	Chris - te e - le - i - son.
Lord, ... have mer - cy.	*Lord, ... have mer - cy.*
Christ, . . . have mer - cy.	*Christ, . . . have mer - cy.*

Music: Dinah Reindorf, b. c. 1927
Music © 1987 Dinah Reindorf, admin. Augsburg Fortress

Kyrie

Lord, have mer - cy. Lord, have mer - cy.

Lord, have mer - cy. Lord, have mer - cy.

Christ, have mer - cy. Christ, have mer - cy.

Christ, have mer - cy. Christ, have mer - cy.

Lord, have mer - cy. Lord, have mer - cy.

Lord, have mer - cy. Lord, have mer - cy.

Lord, have mer - cy, have mer - cy.

Lord, have mer - cy, have mer - cy.

Music: *Deutsche Messe,* Franz Schubert, 1797–1828; adapt. Richard Proulx, b. 1937
Adapt. © 1985, 1989 GIA Publications, Inc.

Kyrie

153
Nkosi, Nkosi

Nko - si, Nko - si, yi - ba nen - ce - ba.
Lord, have mer - cy, have mer - cy up - on us.

Kres - tu, Kres - tu, yi - ba nen - ce - ba.
Christ, have mer - cy, have mer - cy up - on us.

Nko - si, Nko - si, yi - ba nen - ce - ba.
Lord, have mer - cy, have mer - cy up - on us.

Text: South African
Music: G. M. Kolisi
Music © 1984 Utryck, admin. Walton Music Corp.

154

Kyrie

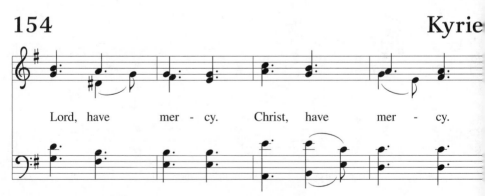

Lord, have mer - cy. Christ, have mer - cy.

Music: *Mass No. 1*, Avon Gillespie
Music © 1987 GIA Publications, Inc.

Lord, have mer - cy; have mer - cy, O Lord.

Kyrie   155

1, 3 Ky - ri - e e - lei - son.   Ky - ri - e e - lei - son.
2   Chris - te e - lei - son.   Chris - te e - lei - son.
1, 3 *Lord, . . . have mer - cy.   Lord, ... have mer - cy.*
2   *Christ, . . . have mer - cy.   Christ, ... have mer - cy.*

Ky - ri - e e - le - i - son.
Chris - te e - le - i - son.
Lord, . . . have mer - cy.
Christ, . . . have mer - cy.

Music: Russian Orthodox traditional

Kyrie   156

Leader   Assembly

Lord, have mer - cy.   **Lord, have mer - cy.**

Christ, have mer - cy.   **Christ, have mer - cy.**

Lord, have mer - cy.   **Lord, have mer - cy.**

Music: Plainsong

157

Kyrie

Leader

In peace, in peace, let us pray to the Lord.

Assembly

Lord, have mer - cy. Christ, have

For the reign of God, and for

mer - cy. Lord, have mer - cy.

peace through-out the world, for the u-ni-ty of all, let us pray to the

Lord.

For your

Lord, have mer - cy. Christ, have mer - cy. Lord, have mer - cy.

peo - ple here who have come to give you praise, for the strength to live your

Text: *Lutheran Book of Worship*, adapt. Marty Haugen, b. 1950
Music: *Now the Feast and Celebration*, Marty Haugen
Text and music © 1990 GIA Publications, Inc.

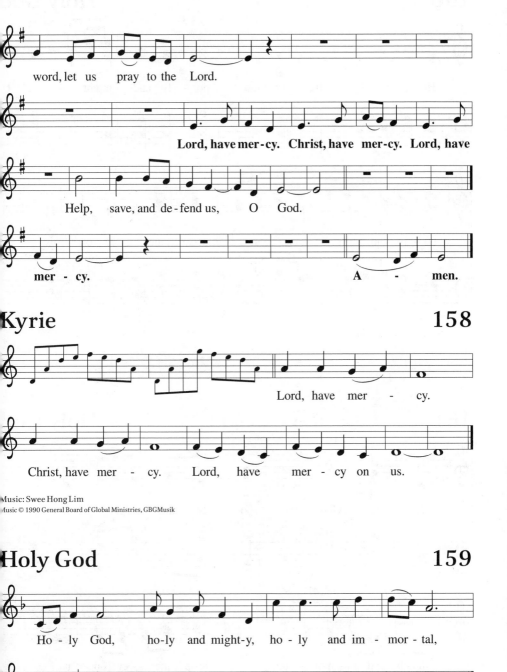

word, let us pray to the Lord.

Lord, have mer-cy. Christ, have mer-cy. Lord, have

Help, save, and de-fend us, O God.

mer - cy. A - men.

Kyrie 158

Lord, have mer - cy.

Christ, have mer - cy. Lord, have mer - cy on us.

Music: Swee Hong Lim
Music © 1990 General Board of Global Ministries, GBGMusik

Holy God 159

Ho - ly God, ho-ly and might-y, ho - ly and im - mor - tal,

have mer - cy up - on us.

Music: *Mass for Grace*, Carl Haywood, b. 1949
Music © 1997 Carl Haywood

160

Holy God

Ho - ly, ho - ly, ho - ly God, ho - ly and might - y, ho - ly and im - mor - tal, have mer - cy on us.

Music: Russian Orthodox traditional

161

Holy God

Ho - ly God, ho - ly and might - y, ho - ly and im - mor - tal, have mer - cy on us.

Music: Mark Mummert, b. 1965

Glory to God

Glo-ry to God in the high-est, and peace to God's peo-ple on earth.

Lord God, heav-en-ly King, al-might-y God and Fa - ther,

we wor-ship you, we give you thanks, we praise you for your glo - ry.

Lord Je - sus Christ, on - ly Son of the Fa - ther,

Lord God, Lamb of God, you take a-way the sin of the world:

have mer-cy on us; you are seat-ed at the right hand of the Fa-ther:

re-ceive our prayer. For you a-lone are the Ho-ly One,

you a-lone are the Lord, you a-lone are the Most High,

Je - sus Christ, with the Ho-ly Spir - it,

in the glo-ry of God the Fa-ther. A - men.

Music: *New Plainsong Mass*, David Hurd, b. 1950
Music © 1981 GIA Publications, Inc.

163

Glory to God

Glo-ry to God in the high - est, and peace to God's peo - ple on earth. Lord God, heav-en-ly King, al - might - y God and Fa-ther, we wor-ship you, we give you thanks, we praise you for your glo-ry. Lord Je - sus Christ, on - ly Son of the Fa - ther, Lord God, Lamb of God, you take a - way the sin of the world: have mer - cy on us; you are seat-ed at the right hand of the Fa - ther: re - ceive our prayer. For you a - lone are the Ho - ly One, you a - lone are the Lord, you a - lone are the Most High, Je - sus Christ, with the Ho - ly Spir-it, in the glo-ry of God the Fa - ther. A - men.

Music: Thomas Pavlechko, b. 1962
Music © 2006 Augsburg Fortress

Glory to God, Glory in the Highest

Leader
Glo-ry to God, glo-ry to God, glo-ry in the high-est!

All
Glo-ry to God, glo-ry to God, glo-ry in the high-est!

Leader To God be glo-ry for-ev-er! **All** To God be glo-ry for-ev-er!

Leader Al-le-lu-ia! A-men! **Leader** Al-le-lu-ia! A-men!

Group 1 Al-le-lu-ia! A-men! Al-le-lu-ia! A-men! **Group 1, 2** Al-le-lu-ia! A-men!

Leader Al-le-lu-ia! A-men!

Group 1, 2, 3
Al-le-lu-ia! A-men! Al-le-lu-ia! A-men! Al-le-lu-ia! A-men! Al-le-lu-ia! A-men!

Music: Peruvian traditional

165

This Is the Feast

Refrain

This is the feast of vic - to - ry for our God.

Al - le - lu - ia, al - le - lu - ia.

1 Wor - thy is Christ, the Lamb who was slain, whose

blood set us free to be peo - ple of God. *Refrain*

2 Pow - er, rich - es, wis - dom, and strength, and

hon - or, bless - ing, and glo - ry are his. *Refrain*

3 Sing with all the peo - ple of God, and

join in the hymn of all cre - a - tion. *Refrain*

Music: Peter Hallock, b. 1924
Text © 1978 *Lutheran Book of Worship*, admin. Augsburg Fortress
Music © 1987 Ionian Arts, Inc.

4 Bless-ing, hon - or, glo-ry, and might be to

God and the Lamb for - ev - er. A - men. *Refrain*

5 For the Lamb who was slain has be - gun his

reign. Al - le - lu - ia. *Refrain*

This Is the Feast 166

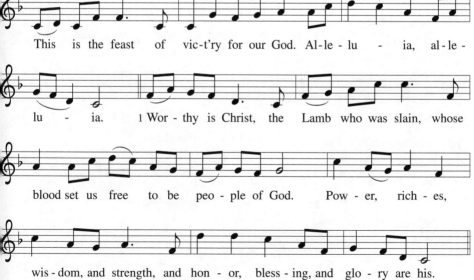

Refrain

This is the feast of vic-t'ry for our God. Al-le-lu - ia, al-le-

lu - ia. 1 Wor - thy is Christ, the Lamb who was slain, whose

blood set us free to be peo - ple of God. Pow - er, rich - es,

wis - dom, and strength, and hon - or, bless - ing, and glo - ry are his.

Music: Robert Buckley Farlee, b. 1950

Text © 1978 *Lutheran Book of Worship*, admin. Augsburg Fortress and music © 2006 Augsburg Fortress

Refrain

This is the feast of vic-t'ry for our God. Al-le-lu - ia, al-le-

lu - ia. 2 Sing with all the peo - ple of God, and

join in the hymn of all cre - a - tion: Bless-ing and hon - or,

glo - ry and might be to God and the Lamb for - ev - er. A-men.

Refrain

This is the feast of vic-t'ry for our God. Al-le-lu - ia, al-le-

lu - ia. 3 For the Lamb who was slain has be -

gun his reign. Al-le-lu - ia, al-le-lu - ia.

Final refrain

This is the feast of vic-t'ry for our God. Al-le-

lu - ia, al-le-lu - ia.

Now the Feast and Celebration

Refrain

Now the feast and cel - e - bra-tion, all of cre - a - tion

sings for joy to the God of life and love and free-dom;

praise and glo - ry for - ev - er - more!

1 Now is the feast of the Lamb once slain, whose blood has

freed and u - nit-ed us to be one great peo-ple of God. *Refrain*

2 Pow - er and rich-es, wis-dom and might, all hon - or and

glo - ry to Christ for - ev - er. *Refrain*

3 For God has come to dwell with us, to make us peo-ple of

God; to make all things new. *Refrain*

Text and music: Marty Haugen, b. 1950
Text and music © 1990 GIA Publications, Inc.

168   Gospel Acclamation

Al - le - lu - ia,   al - le - lu - ia,   al - le - lu - ia.

The proper verse may be sung, or all may sing this verse.   *Repeat allelu*

Lord, to whom shall we go?   You have the words of e - ter - nal life.

Music: Plainsong mode VI

169   Gospel Acclamation

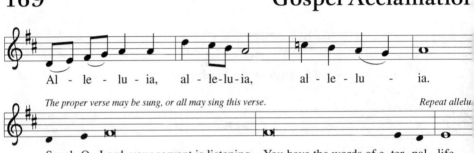

Al - le - lu - ia,   al - le - lu - ia,   al - le - lu - ia.

The proper verse may be sung, or all may sing this verse.   *Repeat allelu*

Speak, O Lord, your servant is listening.   You have the words of e - ter - nal life.

Music: Bob Moore, b. 1962
Music © 2006 Augsburg Fortress

170   Gospel Acclamation

Al - le - lu - ia,   al - le - lu - ia,   al - le - lu - ia,   al - le - lu - ia.

Al - le - lu - ia,   al - le - lu - ia,   al - le - lu - ia,   al - le - lu - ia.

The proper verse may be sung, or all may sing this verse.   *Repeat allelu*

Lord, to whom shall we go?   You have the words of e - ter - nal life.

Music: Thomas Pavlechko, b. 1962
Music © 2006 Thomas Pavlechko, admin. Augsburg Fortress

Hallelujah
Heleluyan

171

He - le - lu - yan, he - le - lu - yan; he - le, he - le - lu - yan.
Hal - le - lu - jah, hal - le - lu - jah; hal - le, hal - le - lu - jah.

He - le - lu - yan, he - le - lu - yan; he - le, he - le - lu - yan.
Hal - le - lu - jah, hal - le - lu - jah; hal - le, hal - le - lu - jah.

May be sung in canon.

Music: Muscogee (Creek) Indian; transc. Charles H. Webb, b. 1933
Transcription © 1989 The United Methodist Publishing House, admin. The Copyright Company

Halle, Halle, Hallelujah

172

Hal - le, hal - le, hal - le - lu - jah. Hal - le, hal - le, hal -

- le - lu - jah. Hal - le, hal - le, hal - le -
Hal - le - lu - jah.

lu - jah. Hal - le - lu - jah. Hal - le - lu - jah.

Music: Caribbean traditional; arr. Mark Sedio, b. 1954
Arr. © 1995 Augsburg Fortress

173

Gospel Acclamation

Hal - le - lu - jah, hal - le - lu - jah,

Hal - le - lu - jah, hal - le - lu,

Hal - le - lu - jah, hal - le - lu - jah,

hal - le - lu - jah, hal - le - lu - jah.

hal - le - lu - jah, hal - le - lu - jah.

hal - le - lu - jah, hal - le - lu - jah.

The proper verse may be sung, or all may sing this verse.   *Repeat halleluja*

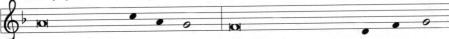

Lord, to whom shall we go?   You have the words of e - ter - nal   life.

Music: Abraham Maraire
Music © United Methodist Church Music Service, Zimbabwe

Gospel Acclamation
Celtic Alleluia

174

Al - le - lu - ia,   al - le - lu - ia.

Al - le - lu - ia,   al - le - lu - ia.

Verses may be sung by a leader. Then the alleluia is repeated.

Music: Fintan O'Carroll and Christopher Walker
Music © 1985 Fintan O'Carroll and Christopher Walker, admin. OCP Publications, Inc.

Gospel Acclamation
175

Al-le - lu - ia, al - le - lu - ia, al - le - lu - ia.

Al-le - lu - ia, al - le - lu - ia, al - le - lu - ia.

Verses may be sung by a leader. Then the alleluia is repeated.

Music: "Alleluia 7," Jacques Berthier, 1923–1994, and the Taizé Community
Music © 1984 Les Presses de Taizé, admin. GIA Publications, Inc.

Lenten Acclamation
176

Let your stead - fast love come to us, O Lord.

Save us as you prom-ised; we will trust your word.

Music: Robert Buckley Farlee, b. 1950
Text and music © 2006 Augsburg Fortress

Lenten Acclamation
177

Glo - ry to you, O Word of God, Lord Je - sus Christ.

The proper verse may be sung by a leader. Then the acclamation is repeated.

Music: Richard Proulx, b. 1937
Music © 1975 GIA Publications, Inc.

178
Hear Our Prayer

Hear our prayer, hear our prayer, Lord, make us whole:
peace to all peo - ple, hope for each soul.
God of grace, in this place, hear now our prayer.

Text and music: Paul Andress, b. 1956
Text and music © 2006 Augsburg Fortress

179
O Lord, Hear Our Prayer

O Lord, hear our prayer we of-fer up to you; O Lord, hear our prayer.

Text and music: Ralph C. Sappington, b. 1952
Text and music © 1999 Augsburg Fortress

180
The Spirit Intercedes for Us

The Spir - it in - ter - cedes for us with
End
sighs too deep for words to ex - press. Oh, oh.

Text and music: Romans 8:26, adapt. Larry Olson
Text and music © 1989 Dakota Road Music, admin. Augsburg Fortress

Additional prayer responses: #751–75:

Let the Vineyards Be Fruitful

181

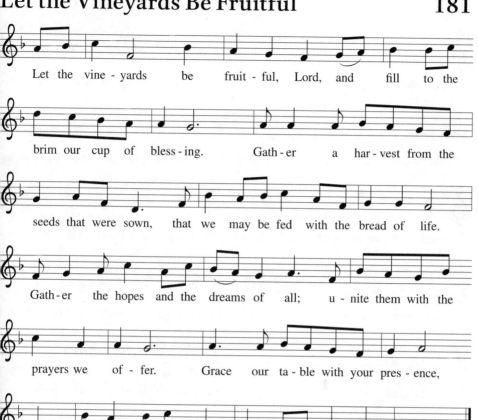

Let the vine-yards be fruit-ful, Lord, and fill to the

brim our cup of bless-ing. Gath-er a har-vest from the

seeds that were sown, that we may be fed with the bread of life.

Gath-er the hopes and the dreams of all; u-nite them with the

prayers we of-fer. Grace our ta-ble with your pres-ence,

and give us a fore-taste of the feast to come.

Music: Marty Haugen, b. 1950
Text © 1978 Lutheran Book of Worship, admin. Augsburg Fortress and music © 2004 Augsburg Fortress

182   Let the Vineyards Be Fruitful

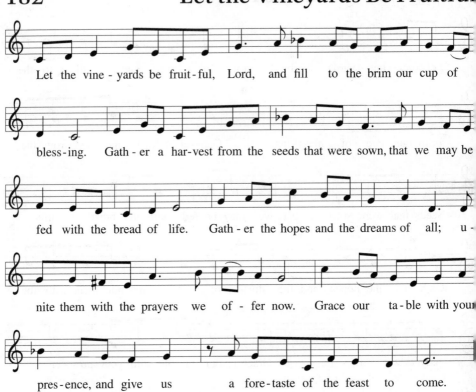

Let the vine - yards be fruit - ful, Lord, and fill   to the brim our cup of

bless - ing.   Gath - er a har-vest from the seeds that were sown, that we may be

fed with the bread of life.   Gath - er the hopes and the dreams of all;   u -

nite them with the prayers we of - fer now.   Grace our ta - ble with your

pres - ence, and give us   a fore-taste of the feast to come.

Music: Richard W. Hillert, b. 1923
Text and music © 1978 *Lutheran Book of Worship*, admin. Augsburg Fortress

183   Let the Vineyards Be Fruitful

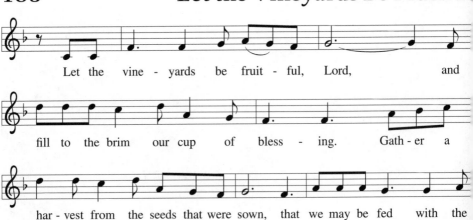

Let the   vine - yards   be fruit - ful,   Lord,   and

fill to the brim   our cup   of   bless - ing.   Gath - er a

har - vest from   the seeds that were sown,   that we may be fed   with the

Music: *Liturgy of Joy,* James M. Capers, b. 1948
Text © 1978 *Lutheran Book of Worship,* admin. Augsburg Fortress and music © 1993 Augsburg Fortress

bread of life. Gath-er the hopes and the dreams of all; u-

nite them with the prayers we of-fer. Grace our ta-ble with your

pres-ence, and give us a fore-taste of the feast to come.

Let the Vineyards Be Fruitful 184

Let the vine-yards be fruit-ful, Lord, and fill to the brim our cup of

bless-ing. Gath-er a har-vest from the seeds that were sown, that

we may be fed with the bread of life. Gath-er the hopes and dreams of

all; u-nite them with the prayers we of-fer. Grace our ta-ble

with your pres-ence, and give us a fore-taste of the feast to come.

Music: Ronald A. Nelson, b. 1927
Text and music © 1978 Lutheran Book of Worship, admin. Augsburg Fortress

185

Create in Me a Clean Heart

Cre-ate in me a clean heart, O God, and re - new a right spir-it with - in me. Cast me not a - way from your pres-ence, and take not your Ho - ly Spir - it from me. Re - store to me the joy of your sal - va - tion, and up - hold me with your free Spir - it. Cre-ate in me a clean heart, O God, and re - new a right spir - it with - in me.

Music: *Liturgy of Joy*, James M. Capers, b. 1948
Music © 1993 Augsburg Fortress

186

Create in Me a Clean Heart

Cre-ate in me a clean heart, O God, and re - new a right spir-it with-in me. Cast me not a-way from your pres-ence, and take

Music: Richard W. Hillert, b. 1923
Music © 1978 *Lutheran Book of Worship*, admin. Augsburg Fortress

not your Ho - ly Spir - it from me. Re-store to me the joy of

your sal - va - tion, and up-hold me with your free Spir - it.

Create in Me a Clean Heart 187

Cre-ate in me a clean heart, O God, and re -

new a right spir - it with - in me.

Cast me not a - way from your pres - ence, and take not your

Ho - ly Spir - it from me. Re -

store to me the joy of your sal - va - tion,

and up - hold me with your free Spir - it.

Music: *River of Life*, Tillis Butler, d. 2002
Music © 1999 Augsburg Fortress

188   Create in Me a Clean Heart

Music: J. A. Freylinghausen, 1670–1739

Holy, Holy, Holy
Acclamation and Amen

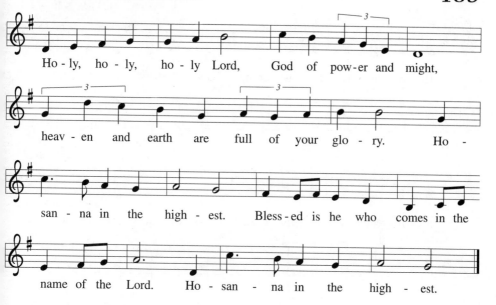

Ho - ly, ho - ly, ho - ly Lord, God of pow-er and might,

heav - en and earth are full of your glo - ry. Ho -

san - na in the high - est. Bless-ed is he who comes in the

name of the Lord. Ho - san - na in the high - est.

The thanksgiving may include this acclamation.

Christ has died. Christ is ris - en. Christ will come a - gain.

The thanksgiving may conclude with a sung Amen.

A - men, a - men, a - men.

Music: Paul D. Weber, b. 1949
Music © 2006 Augsburg Fortress

Holy, Holy, Holy
Acclamation and Amen

Ho - ly, ho - ly, ho - ly Lord, God of pow'r and might,

ho - ly, ho - ly, ho - ly Lord, God of pow'r and might,

heav-en and earth are full, full of your glo - ry.

Ho - san - na in the high - est, ho - san - na in the high - est.

Bless-ed is he who comes in the name of the Lord.

Music: *Deutsche Messe*, Franz Schubert, 1797–1828; adapt. Richard Proulx, b. 1937
Adapt. © 1985, 1989 GIA Publications, Inc.

Ho - san - na in the high - est, ho - san - na in the high - est.

The thanksgiving may include this acclamation.

Christ has died. Christ is ris'n. Christ will come a - gain.

The thanksgiving may conclude with a sung Amen.

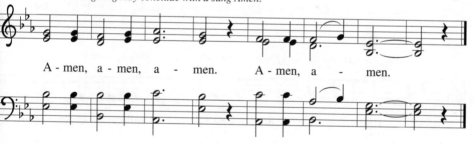

A - men, a - men, a - men. A - men, a - men.

Holy, Holy, Holy
Acclamation and Amen

Ho - ly, ho - ly, ho - ly are you, God of pow - er and might; heav - en and earth are filled with your glo - ry. Ho - san - na in the high - est. Bless - ed is the one who comes in your name. Ho - san - na in the high - est, ho - san - na in the high - est.

The acclamation may be sung first by the presiding minister, then repeated by all.

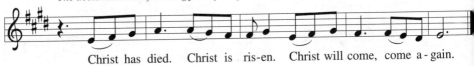

Christ has died. Christ is ris-en. Christ will come, come a-gain.

The thanksgiving may conclude with a sung Amen.

A - men, a - men. A - men, a - men.

Music: *Now the Feast and Celebration*, Marty Haugen, b. 1950
Music © 1990 GIA Publications, Inc.

Holy, Holy, Holy
Acclamation and Amen

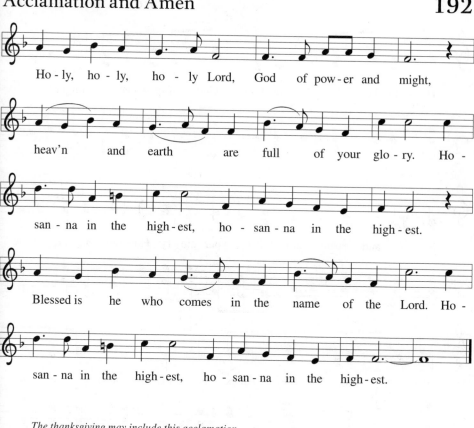

Ho - ly, ho - ly, ho - ly Lord, God of pow - er and might,

heav'n and earth are full of your glo - ry. Ho -

san - na in the high - est, ho - san - na in the high - est.

Blessed is he who comes in the name of the Lord. Ho -

san - na in the high - est, ho - san - na in the high - est.

The thanksgiving may include this acclamation.

Christ has died. Christ is ris - en. Christ will come a - gain.

The thanksgiving may conclude with a sung Amen.

A - men, a - men, a - men.

Music: *A Community Mass*, Richard Proulx, b. 1937
Music © 1971, 1977 GIA Publications, Inc.

Holy, Holy, Holy
Acclamation and Amen

Ho - ly, ho - ly, ho - ly Lord, God of pow - er and might,

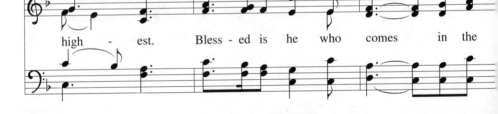

heav - en and earth are full of your glo - ry. Ho - san - na in the

high - est. Bless - ed is he who comes in the

name of the Lord. Ho - san - na in the

high - est, ho - san - na in the high - est.

Music: Per Harling, b. 1948
Music © 2004 Augsburg Fortress

The thanksgiving may include this acclamation.

Christ has died. Christ is ris - en. Christ will come a - gain.

The thanksgiving may conclude with a sung Amen.

A - men, a - men, a - men.

Lamb of God
Agnus Dei

194

A - gnus De - i, qui tollis pec-ca-ta mun - di: mi - se - re - re no - bis.
Lamb of God, . . you take away the sin of the world; have . . mer-cy on . . us.

A - gnus De - i, qui tollis pec-ca-ta mun - di: mi - se - re - re no - bis.
Lamb of God, . . you take away the sin of the world; have . . mer-cy on . . us.

A - gnus De - i, qui tollis pec-ca-ta mun - di: do - na no - bis pa - cem.
Lamb of God, . . you take away the sin of the world; grant . . us . . . . peace.

Music: Plainsong, Mass XVIII

195   # Lamb of God

Lamb of God, you take a - way the sin of the world; have mer-cy on us. Lamb of God, you take a - way the sin of the world; have mer-cy on us. Lamb of God, you take a - way the sin of the world; grant us peace, grant us peace.

Music: *Bread of Life,* Jeremy Young, b. 1948
Music © 1995 Augsburg Fortress

196   # O Christ, Lamb of God

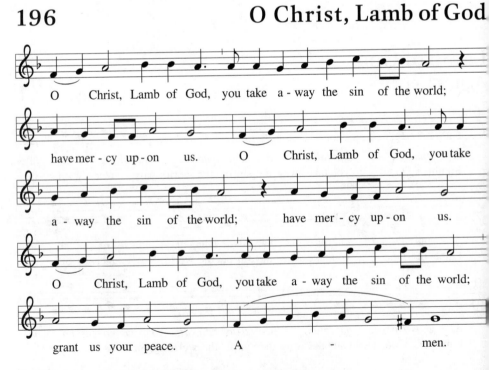

O Christ, Lamb of God, you take a - way the sin of the world; have mer - cy up-on us. O Christ, Lamb of God, you take a - way the sin of the world; have mer - cy up-on us. O Christ, Lamb of God, you take a - way the sin of the world; grant us your peace. A - men.

Music: J. Bugenhagen, *Christliche Ordnung,* 1528

O Lamb of God
Oi, Jumalan Karitsa

Oi, Ju - ma - lan Ka - rit - sa, io - ka pois o - tat maa - il - man
O Lamb .. of God, you take ... a - way ... the sin of the

syn - nin, ar - mah - da mei - tä, ar - mah - da mei - tä.
world; .. have mer - cy on us, mer - cy on us.

Oi, Ju - ma - lan Ka - rit - sa, io - ka pois o - tat maa - il - man syn - nin,
O Lamb of God, you take .. a - way .. the sin of the world; . . .

an - na meil - le rau - ha - si ja siu - na - uk - se - si.
grant us vi - sion, grant us jus - tice, grant us your own true peace.

Music: Matti Rantatalo
Music © 1992 Matti Rantatalo

O Lamb of God

197 198

O Lamb of God, you take a - way the sin of the world;

have mer - cy on us. O Lamb of God, you take a - way the

sin of the world; have mer - cy on us. O Lamb of God,

you take a - way the sin of the world; grant us your peace.

Music: Mabel Wu
Music © 1992 Mabel Wu, admin. Augsburg Fortress

199

Jesus, Lamb of God

Je - sus, Lamb of God, have mer - cy on us.

Je - sus, bear - er of our sins, have mer - cy on us.

Je - sus, re - deem - er, re - deem - er of the world,

grant us peace, grant us peace.

Music: *Deutsche Messe*, Franz Schubert, 1797–1828; adapt. Richard Proulx, b. 1937
Adapt. © 1985, 1989 GIA Publications, Inc.

Now, Lord

Now, Lord, you let your ser - vant go in peace: your word has been ful - filled. My own eyes have seen the sal - va - tion which you have pre - pared in the sight of all peo-ple: a light to re - veal you to the na-tions and the glo - ry of your peo-ple Is - ra - el. Glo - ry to the Fa-ther, and to the Son, and to the Ho - ly Spir - it, as it was in the be - gin - ning, is now, and will be for - ev - er. A - men.

Music: *Detroit Folk Mass*, Tillis Butler, d. 2002, and James Harris
Music © 1986 Fortress Press

201

Now, Lord

Now, Lord, you let your ser - vant go in peace: your word has been ful - filled. My own eyes have seen the sal - va - tion which you have pre - pared in the sight of ev - 'ry peo - ple: a light to re - veal you to the na - tions and the glo - ry of your peo - ple Is - ra - el. Glo - ry to the Fa - ther, and to the Son, and to the Ho - ly Spir - it, as it was in the be - gin - ning, is now, and will be for - ev - er. A - men.

Music: Plainsong, adapt. *Lutheran Book of Worship*
Music © 1978 *Lutheran Book of Worship*, admin. Augsburg Fortress

Now, Lord

Leader
Free to go in peace as you have prom - ised.

All
Free to go in peace as you have prom - ised.

Leader or All
Now, Lord, you have set your ser - vant free, free to go in peace as you have

All
prom - ised. Free to go in peace as you have prom - ised.

Leader or All
For these eyes of mine have seen the Savior

whom you have prepared for all the world to see:

All
Free to go in peace as you have prom - ised.

Leader or All
a light to en - lighten the nations, and the glory of your peo - ple Is - ra - el.

All
Free to go in peace as you have prom - ised.

Music: Russell Schulz-Widmar, b. 1944
Music © 2006 Augsburg Fortress

At Last, Lord
Ahora, Señor

A - ho - ra, Se - ñor, se - gún tu pro - me - sa,
At last, Lord, your word of prom - ise ful - fill - ing,

pue - des de - jar a tu sier - vo ir - se en paz.
you let your ser - vant go forth in free - dom and peace.

Por - que mis o - jos han vis - to a tu Sal - va - dor,
With my own eyes I have seen the sal - va - tion

a quien has pre - sen - ta - do an - te to - dos los
you have pre - pared . . . in the sight of all of the

pue - blos: luz pa - ra a - lum - brar a las na -
peo - ples: a light that will re - veal you to the

cio - nes y glo - ria de tu pue - blo Is - ra - el.
na - tions and the glo - ry of your peo - ple Is - ra - el.

Music: Gerhard M. Cartford, b. 1923
Text and music © 1998 Augsburg Fortress

Thankful Hearts and Voices Raise 204

Thank-ful hearts and voic - es raise; tell ev-'ry-one what God has done.

Let all who seek the Lord re - joice and bear Christ's ho - ly name.

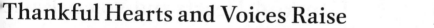

Send us with your prom - is - es and lead your peo - ple forth in joy with

shouts of thanks-giv - ing. Al - le - lu - ia. Al-le-lu - ia.

Music: Richard W. Hillert, b. 1923
Text and music © 1978, 1995 Augsburg Fortress

Thankful Hearts and Voices Raise 205

Thank-ful hearts and voic-es raise; tell ev-'ry-one what God has done.

Let all who seek the Lord re-joice and bear Christ's ho - ly name.

Send us with your prom - is - es, O God, and lead us forth in

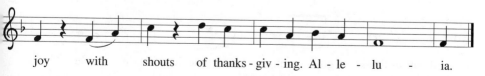

joy with shouts of thanks-giv - ing. Al - le - lu - ia.

Music: *Liturgy of Joy*, James M. Capers, b. 1948
Text © 1978, 1995 and music © 1993 Augsburg Fortress

206 Thankful Hearts and Voices Raise

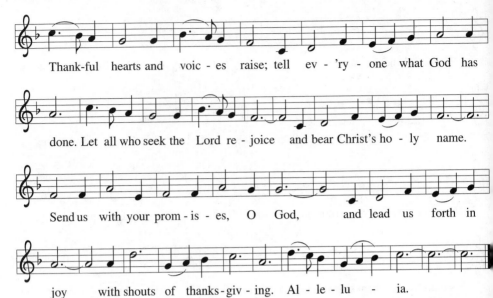

Thank-ful hearts and voic - es raise; tell ev - 'ry - one what God has

done. Let all who seek the Lord re - joice and bear Christ's ho - ly name.

Send us with your prom - is - es, O God, and lead us forth in

joy with shouts of thanks - giv - ing. Al - le - lu - ia.

Music: *Bread of Life*, Jeremy Young, b. 1948
Text © 1978, 1995 and music © 1995 Augsburg Fortress

207 Thankful Hearts and Voices Raise

Thank-ful hearts and voic-es raise; tell ev-'ry-one what God has done. Let

ev - 'ry-one who seeks the Lord re - joice and bear the name of Christ.

Send us with your prom - is - es and lead your peo - ple forth in joy with

shouts of thanks - giv - ing. Al - le - lu - ia, al - le - lu - ia.

Music: Ronald A. Nelson, b. 1927
Text and music © 1978, 1995 Augsburg Fortress

Praise to You, O God of Mercy

1 Praise to you, O God of mer - cy: thanks be to you for -
2 From of old you loved and sought us: thanks be to you for -
3 Praise to you, O God of mer - cy: thanks be to you for -

ev - er! Rais - ing high the weak and low - ly:
ev - er! Truth and jus - tice you have taught us:
ev - er! Rais - ing high the weak and low - ly:

3rd time to Coda

|1
thanks be to you for - ev - er!
thanks be to you for -
thanks be to you for -

|2
ev - er!

Strong is your faith - ful-ness, strong is your love, re -

to stanza 3

mem - b'ring your cov - e -nant of life with us.

Coda

ev - er! Thanks be to you for - ev - er!

Text and music: *Now the Feast and Celebration*, Marty Haugen, b. 1950
Text and music © 1990 GIA Publications, Inc.

209   Blessed Be God, the Source of All Life

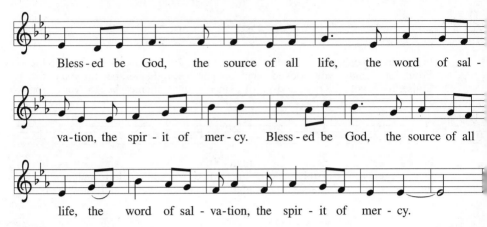

Bless-ed be God, the source of all life, the word of sal-va-tion, the spir-it of mer-cy. Bless-ed be God, the source of all life, the word of sal-va-tion, the spir-it of mer-cy.

Music: Rawn Harbor
Text © 2002 and music © 2003 Augsburg Fortress

210   Blessed Be God, the Source of All Life

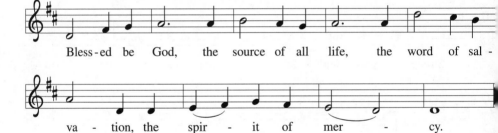

Bless-ed be God, the source of all life, the word of sal-va - tion, the spir - it of mer - cy.

Music: Carl F. Schalk, b. 1929
Text © 2002 and music © 2003 Augsburg Fortress

211   You Have Put On Christ

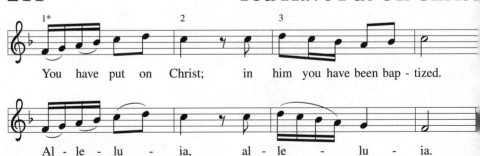

You have put on Christ; in him you have been bap - tized. Al - le - lu - ia, al - le - lu - ia.

* May be sung in two or three part canon.

Text: International Commission on English in the Liturgy
Music: Howard Hughes, b. 1930
Text © 1969 and music © 1977 International Commission on English in the Liturgy

You Belong to Christ

212

You be-long to Christ, in whom you have been bap - tized.

al - le - lu - ia.

Al - le - lu - ia, al - le - lu - ia, al - le - lu - ia.

Music: Robert A. Hobby, b. 1962
Text © 2002 and music © 2003 Augsburg Fortress

You Belong to Christ

213

You be-long to Christ, in whom you have been bap - tized.

You be-long to Christ, in whom you have been bap - tized.

Al - le - lu - ia, al - le - lu - ia.

You be-long to Christ, in whom you have been bap - tized.

Music: Ralph C. Sappington, b. 1952
Text © 2002 and music © 2003 Augsburg Fortress

214   Springs of Water, Bless the Lord

Refrain – All

Springs of wa - ter, bless the Lord.

Give God glo - ry and praise for - ev - er.

Leader or All   *Refrain*

1   Buried with Christ in death, you are raised with him to life.
2   Bathed in the foun-tain of life, you are born to a liv - ing hope.
3   You are God's work of art, cre - ated in Christ Jesus.
4   You be - long to Christ, in whom you have been bap - tized.
5   All of you are one, u - nited in Christ Jesus.
6   Re - joice, all you bap-tized, called to be chil-dren of God.

Music: Robert Buckley Farlee, b. 1950
Text and music © 1997 Augsburg Fortress

215   Blessed Be God, Who Chose You

Bless - ed be God, who chose you in Christ.

Live in love as Christ loved us.

Music: Anne Krentz Organ, b. 1960
Text © 1997 and music © 2003 Augsburg Fortress

216   Praise to You, O Christ

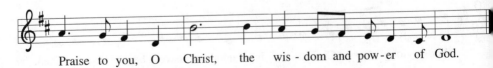

Praise to you, O Christ, the wis - dom and pow - er of God.

Music: Robert Buckley Farlee, b. 1950
Text and music © 1997 Augsburg Fortress

May the God of All Grace

217

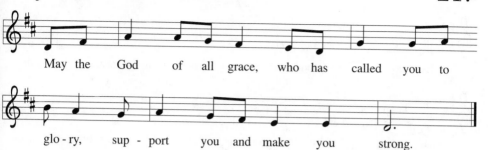

May the God of all grace, who has called you to glo - ry, sup - port you and make you strong.

Music: Robert Buckley Farlee, b. 1950
Text and music © 1997 Augsburg Fortress

You Anoint My Head

218

You a - noint my head with oil and my cup is run - ning o - ver.

Music: May Schwarz, b. 1945
Text © 2002 and music © 2003 Augsburg Fortress

219   Healer of Boundless Compassion

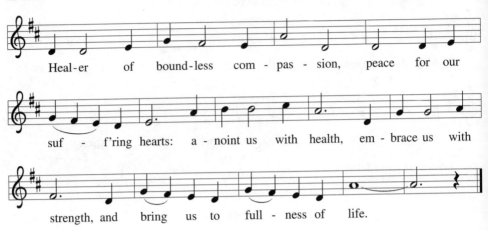

Heal-er of bound-less com - pas - sion, peace for our
suf - f'ring hearts: a - noint us with health, em - brace us with
strength, and bring us to full - ness of life.

Music: Russell Schulz-Widmar, b. 1944
Text © 2002 and music © 2003 Augsburg Fortress

220   May the God of All Healing

May the God of all heal-ing en - fold us in love,
fill us with peace, and lead us to whole-ness and strength.

Music: Jayne Southwick Cool, b. 1947
Text © 2002 and music © 2003 Augsburg Fortress

221   Blessed Be God, Who Forgives

Bless-ed be God, who for - gives all our sins, who
heals all our ills, who crowns us with mer - cy and love.

Music: Anne Krentz Organ, b. 1960
Text © 2002 and music © 2003 Augsburg Fortress

Into Paradise May the Angels Lead You 222

In-to par-a-dise may the an-gels lead you. At your com-ing may the mar-tyrs re-ceive you and lead you in-to the ho-ly cit-y, Je-ru-sa-lem, Je-ru-sa-lem. May a choir of an-gels wel-come you, and where Laz-a-rus is poor no more, may you have ev-er-last-ing rest, may you have ev-er-last-ing rest, may you have ev-er-last-ing rest.

Music: Rawn Harbor
Music © 2003 Augsburg Fortress

All of Us Go Down to the Dust 223

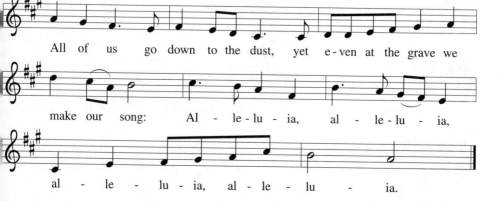

All of us go down to the dust, yet e-ven at the grave we make our song: Al-le-lu-ia, al-le-lu-ia, al-le-lu-ia, al-le-lu-ia.

Music: Mark Mummert, b. 1965
Music © 2003 Augsburg Fortress

224 Come, Let Us Sing to the Lord

1 Come, let us sing to the Lord; let us shout for joy to the rock of our sal - va - tion. Let us come be-fore God's pres-ence with thanks-giv - ing and raise a loud shout to God with psalms.

2 For the Lord is a great God, and a great rul-er o'er all gods. It is God who holds the cav - erns of the earth, and the heights of the moun-tains al - so.

3 It is God who rules the seas, whose hands have mold-ed the dry land. Come, let us bow down and bend the knee, and kneel be-fore the Lord our mak - er.

Text: Psalm 95:1-7
Music: Jack Noble White
Music © 1971 Walton Music Corp.

4 For this great one is our God, who choos-es a peo - ple and tends them, and whose hand will guide them like sheep. Oh, that to - day you would hear-ken to God's voice.

Come, Ring Out Your Joy 225

Refrain — All

Come, ring out your joy to the Lord!

Come, ring out your joy to the Lord!

Leader or All

	1	Come, let us sing	to	the	Lord;
	2	Let us come before God's presence	with	thanks -	giving,
	3	For you, Lord,	are	a	great God,
	4	In your hand are the caverns	of	the	earth;
	5	The sea is yours,	for	you	made it;
	6	Come, let us worship	and	bow	down;
	7	For the Lord	is	our	God,

	1	let us shout for joy to the rock of	our	sal -	vation.
	2	and raise a loud shout to the	Lord	with	psalms. *Refrain*
	3	and a great ruler a -	bove	all	gods.
	4	the heights of the hills are	al - so		yours.
	5	and your hands have molded	the	dry	land. *Refrain*
	6	let us kneel before the	Lord	our	maker.
	7	and we are the people of God's pasture and the sheep	of	God's	hand. *Refrain*

Text: Psalm 95:1-7a
Music: Rawn Harbor
Text © 2006 and music © 1999 Augsburg Fortress

226

Blessed Are You, Lord

Bless-ed are you, Lord, the God of Is - ra - el,
you have come to your peo-ple and set them free. You have raised
up for us a might-y Sav - ior, born of the house of your
ser-vant Da - vid. Through your ho - ly proph-ets,
you prom-ised of old to save us from our en - e-mies, from the
hands of all who hate us; you prom-ised to show mer-cy to our
fore - bears and to re - mem-ber your ho - ly cov-e-nant.
This was the oath you swore to our fa-ther A - bra-ham: to
set us free from the hands of our en - e - mies, free to

Music: Anne Krentz Organ, b. 1960
Music © 2004 Augsburg Fortress

227

We Praise You, O God

We praise you, O God, we ac-claim you as Lord; all cre-a-tion wor-ships you, the Fa-ther ev-er-last-ing. To you all an-gels, all the pow-ers of heav'n, the cher-u-bim and ser-a-phim, sing in end-less praise: Ho-ly, ho-ly, ho-ly Lord, God of pow'r and might, heav-en and earth are full of your glo-ry, full of your glo-ry.

The glo-rious com-pa-ny of a-pos-tles praise you.

The no-ble fel-low-ship of proph-ets praise you.

The white-robed ar-my of mar-tyrs praise you.

Through-out the world the ho-ly church ac-claims you: Fa-ther, of

Music: Robert Buckley Farlee, b. 1950
Music © 2001 Robert Buckley Farlee, admin. Augsburg Fortress

maj-es - ty un - bound-ed; your true and on - ly Son, wor-thy of all

praise; the Ho - ly Spir - it, ad - vo-cate and guide. You, Christ,

are the king of glo-ry, the e - ter-nal Son of the Fa - ther. When you

took our flesh to set us free you hum-bly chose the Vir - gin's womb.

You o - ver-came the sting of death and o - pened the king-dom of heav'n to

all be - liev - ers. You are seat - ed at God's right hand in glo-ry. We be-

lieve that you will come to be our judge. Come, then, Lord,

and help your peo-ple, bought with the price of your own blood,

and bring us with your saints to glo-ry ev - er - last - ing.

228

We Praise You, O God

1 We praise you, O God, we ac - claim you as Lord;
3 Holy, holy, holy Lord, God of pow'r and might,
5 The white–robed army of martyrs praise. . . . . . you.

1 all creation worships you, the Fa-ther ev - er - last - ing.
3 heaven and earth are full of your glo - ry.
5 Throughout the world the ho - ly church ac - claims you:

2 To you all angels, all the pow'rs of heav'n,
4 The glorious company of apostles praise . . . you.
6 Father, of majesty unbounded; your true and only Son, worthy of all praise;
7 You, Christ, are the king of glo - ry,

2 the cherubim and sera - phim, sing in end - less praise:
4 The noble fellowship of proph - ets praise . . . you.
6 the Holy Spir - it, ad - vo - cate and guide.
7 the eter - nal Son of the Fa - ther.

Music: Henry Lawes, 1596–1662; George W. Cooke

8 When you took our flesh to set us free
10 You are seat - ed

8 you humbly chose the Vir - gin's womb.
10 at God's right hand in glo - ry.

9 You overcame the sting of death
11 We believe that you will come

9 and opened the kingdom of heaven to all be - liev - ers.
11 to be . . . our . . . judge.

12 Come, then, Lord, and help your peo - ple,
*14 Save your people, Lord, and bless your in - her - i - tance.
16 Keep us today, Lord, from all sin.

12 bought with the price of your own blood,
14 Govern and uphold them now and al - ways.
16 Have mercy on us, Lord, have mer - cy.

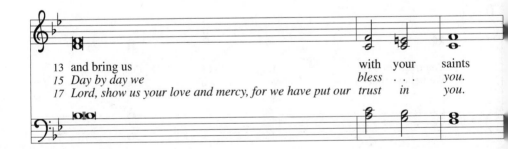

13 and bring us with your saints
15 Day by day we bless . . . you.
17 Lord, show us your love and mercy, for we have put our trust in you.

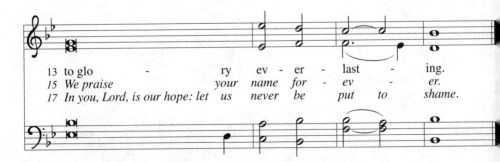

13 to glo - ry ev - er - last - ing.
15 We praise your name for - ev - er.
17 In you, Lord, is our hope: let us never be put to shame.

* The verses in italics are not part of the original canticle but have often been appended.

Joyous Light of Glory

Leader
Joy-ous light of glo - ry:

All
of the im - mor - tal Fa - ther; heav - en - ly, ho - ly, bless - ed Je - sus Christ. We have come to the set - ting of the sun, and we look to the eve - ning light. We sing to God, the Fa - ther, Son, and Ho - ly Spir - it: You are wor - thy of be - ing praised with pure voic - es for - ev - er. O Son of God, O giv - er of life: The u - ni - verse pro - claims your glo - ry.

Text: Greek hymn, 3rd cent.; tr. Roger T. Petrich, b. 1938
Music: Roger T. Petrich
Text and music © 1978 Lutheran Book of Worship, admin. Augsburg Fortress

230

Joyous Light of Glory

Joy - ous light of glo - ry, shine a - mong your

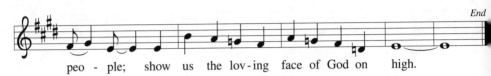

peo - ple; show us the lov - ing face of God on high.

Je - sus Christ our Sav - ior, bring us here to - geth - er as

set - ting sun gives way to eve - ning light.

We sing to God, Fa - ther, Son, and Spir - it,

wor - thy of praise for - ev - er and ev - er.

O Son of God, you give us life e - ter - nal; the

u - ni - verse pro - claims your glo - ry.

Text: Greek hymn, 3rd cent.; tr. *Worship and Praise*, 1999
Music: Ralph C. Sappington, b. 1952
Text and music © 1999 Augsburg Fortress

O Gracious Light

O gra - cious Light, pure bright-ness of the ev - er - liv - ing
Fa-ther in heav - en, O Je - sus Christ, ho - ly and bless-ed!
Now as we come to the set - ting of the sun,
and our eyes be - hold the ves - per light,
we sing your prais-es, O God: Fa - ther, Son, and Ho - ly Spir - it.
You are wor - thy at all times to be praised by hap - py
voic - es, O Son of God, O giv - er of life,
and to be glo - ri-fied through all the worlds.

Text: Greek hymn, 3rd cent.; tr. *Book of Common Prayer*
Music: Ronald Arnatt, b. 1930
Music © 1985 Church Pension Fund

232

Let My Prayer Rise Up

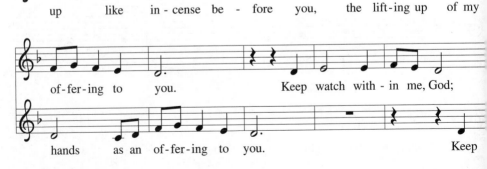

All

Let my prayer rise up like in-cense be-fore you, the
lift-ing up of my hands as an of-fer-ing to you.

Leader or Group One

O God, I call to you, come to me now; oh, hear my

All or Group Two

O God, I call to you, come to me

voice when I cry to you. Let my prayer rise up like

now; oh, hear my voice when I cry to you. Let my prayer rise

in - cense be - fore you, the lift-ing up of my hands as an

up like in - cense be - fore you, the lift-ing up of my

of-fer-ing to you. Keep watch with - in me, God;

hands as an of-fer-ing to you. Keep

Text: *Holden Evening Prayer*, Marty Haugen, b. 1950, based on Psalm 141
Music: Marty Haugen
Text and music © 1990 GIA Publications, Inc.

deep in my heart may the light of your love be burn - ing

watch with - in me, God; deep in my heart may the light of your

bright. Let my prayer rise up like in - cense be -

love be burn - ing bright. Let my prayer rise up like

fore you, the lift-ing up of my hands as an of-fer-ing to

in - cense be - fore you, the lift-ing up of my hands as an

you. All praise to the God of all— Cre - a - tor of

of-fer-ing to you. All praise to the

life; all praise be to Christ and the Spir - it of love.

God of all— Cre - a - tor of life; all praise be to Christ and the

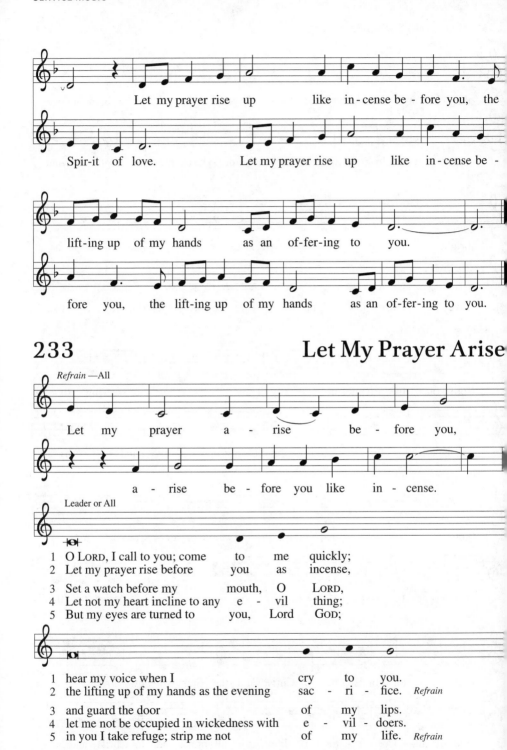

233   **Let My Prayer Arise**

Refrain —All

Let my prayer a - rise be - fore you,

a - rise be - fore you like in - cense.

Leader or All

1 O LORD, I call to you; come to me quickly;
2 Let my prayer rise before you as incense,

3 Set a watch before my mouth, O LORD,
4 Let not my heart incline to any e - vil thing;
5 But my eyes are turned to you, Lord GOD;

1 hear my voice when I cry to you.
2 the lifting up of my hands as the evening sac - ri - fice. *Refrain*

3 and guard the door of my lips.
4 let me not be occupied in wickedness with e - vil - doers.
5 in you I take refuge; strip me not of my life. *Refrain*

Text: Psalm 141:1-4, 8
Music: Leon C. Roberts, 1950–1999
Music © 1999 Augsburg Fortress

My Soul Proclaims
the Greatness of the Lord

My soul proclaims the greatness of the Lord, my spirit rejoices

in God my Sav-ior, for you, Lord, have looked with favor on your low-ly ser-vant.

From this day all generations will call me bless-ed: you, the Almighty,

have done great things for me, and ho-ly is your name. You have mercy

on those who fear you, from generation to gen-er-a-tion. You have shown

strength with your arm and scattered the proud in their con-ceit,

cast-ing down the might-y from their thrones and lift-ing up the low-ly.

You have filled the hun-gry with good things and sent the rich a -

way emp-ty. You have come to the aid of your ser-vant Is-ra-el,

Music: Plainsong, tonus peregrinus

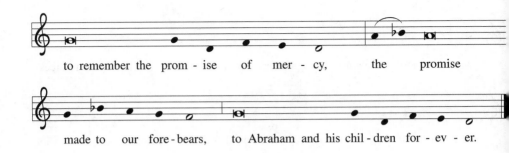

to remember the prom - ise of mer - cy, the promise

made to our fore - bears, to Abraham and his chil - dren for - ev - er.

235 My Soul Proclaims the Greatness of the Lord

My soul proclaims the greatness of the Lord,

my spirit rejoices in God my Sav - ior,

for you, Lord, have looked with favor on your low - ly ser - vant.

From this day all generations will call me blessed:

you, the Al - mighty, have done great things for me, and holy is your name.

You have mercy on those who fear you, from generation to gen - er - a - tion.

Music: Bob Moore, b. 1962
Music © 2004 Augsburg Fortress

You have shown strength with your arm and scattered the proud in their

conceit, casting down the mighty from their thrones and lift-ing up the low-ly.

You have filled the hungry with good things and sent the rich a - way empty.

You have come to the aid of your servant Israel, to remember the

prom - ise of mer - cy, the promise made to our forebears,

to Abraham and his chil - dren for - ev - er.

Magnificat

236

Canon

Ma- gni-fi-cat, ma-gni-fi-cat, ma-gni-fi-cat a-ni-ma me-a Do-mi-num.

Ma - gni-fi-cat, ma-gni-fi-cat, ma-gni-fi-cat a-ni-ma me - a!

Text: Luke 1:46; Taizé Community
Music: Jacques Berthier, 1923–1994
Text and music © 1978 Les Presses de Taizé, admin. GIA Publications, Inc.

237

Litany of the Saints

Leader .... Assembly

Lord, have mercy. **Lord, have mercy.**
Christ, have mercy. **Christ, have mercy.**
Lord, have mercy. **Lord, have mercy.**

Be gra - cious to us: **Hear us, O God.**
De - liv - er your people: **Hear us, O God.**

You loved us before the world was made: **Hear us, O God.**
You rescued the people of your promise: **Hear us, O God.**
You spoke through your prophets: **Hear us, O God.**
You gave your only Son for the life of the world: **Hear us, O God.**

For us and for our salvation he came down from heaven: **Great is your love.**
and was born of the vir - gin Mary: **Great is your love.**
who by his cross and suffering re - deemed the world: **Great is your love.**
and has washed us from our sins: **Great is your love.**
who on the third day rose from the dead: **Great is your love.**
and has given us the vic - to - ry: **Great is your love.**
who ascend - ed on high: **Great is your love.**
and intercedes for us at the right hand of God: **Great is your love.**

For the gift of the Ho - ly Spirit: **Thanks be to God.**
For the one holy catholic and apos - tol - ic church: **Thanks be to God.**
For the great cloud of witnesses
into which we are bap - tized: **Thanks be to God.**

For Sarah and Abraham, Isaac and Re - bekah: **Thanks be to God.**
For Gideon and Deborah, Da - vid and Esther: **Thanks be to God.**
For Moses and Isaiah, Jeremi - ah and Daniel: **Thanks be to God.**
For Miriam and Rahab, Abi - gail and Ruth: **Thanks be to God.**

Text and music: *Welcome to Christ*, 1997
Text and music © 1997 Augsburg Fortress

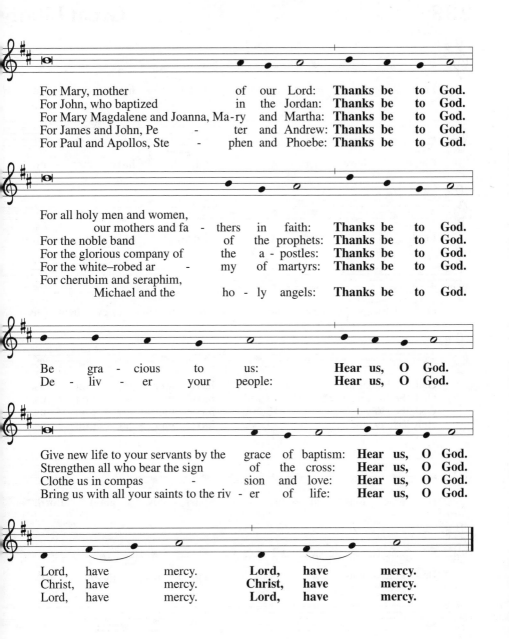

For Mary, mother of our Lord: **Thanks be to God.**
For John, who baptized in the Jordan: **Thanks be to God.**
For Mary Magdalene and Joanna, Ma-ry and Martha: **Thanks be to God.**
For James and John, Pe - ter and Andrew: **Thanks be to God.**
For Paul and Apollos, Ste - phen and Phoebe: **Thanks be to God.**

For all holy men and women,
　　our mothers and fa - thers in faith: **Thanks be to God.**
For the noble band of the prophets: **Thanks be to God.**
For the glorious company of the a - postles: **Thanks be to God.**
For the white–robed ar - my of martyrs: **Thanks be to God.**
For cherubim and seraphim,
　　Michael and the ho - ly angels: **Thanks be to God.**

Be gra - cious to us: **Hear us, O God.**
De - liv - er your people: **Hear us, O God.**

Give new life to your servants by the grace of baptism: **Hear us, O God.**
Strengthen all who bear the sign of the cross: **Hear us, O God.**
Clothe us in compas - sion and love: **Hear us, O God.**
Bring us with all your saints to the riv - er of life: **Hear us, O God.**

Lord, have mercy. **Lord, have mercy.**
Christ, have mercy. **Christ, have mercy.**
Lord, have mercy. **Lord, have mercy.**

238

Great Litany

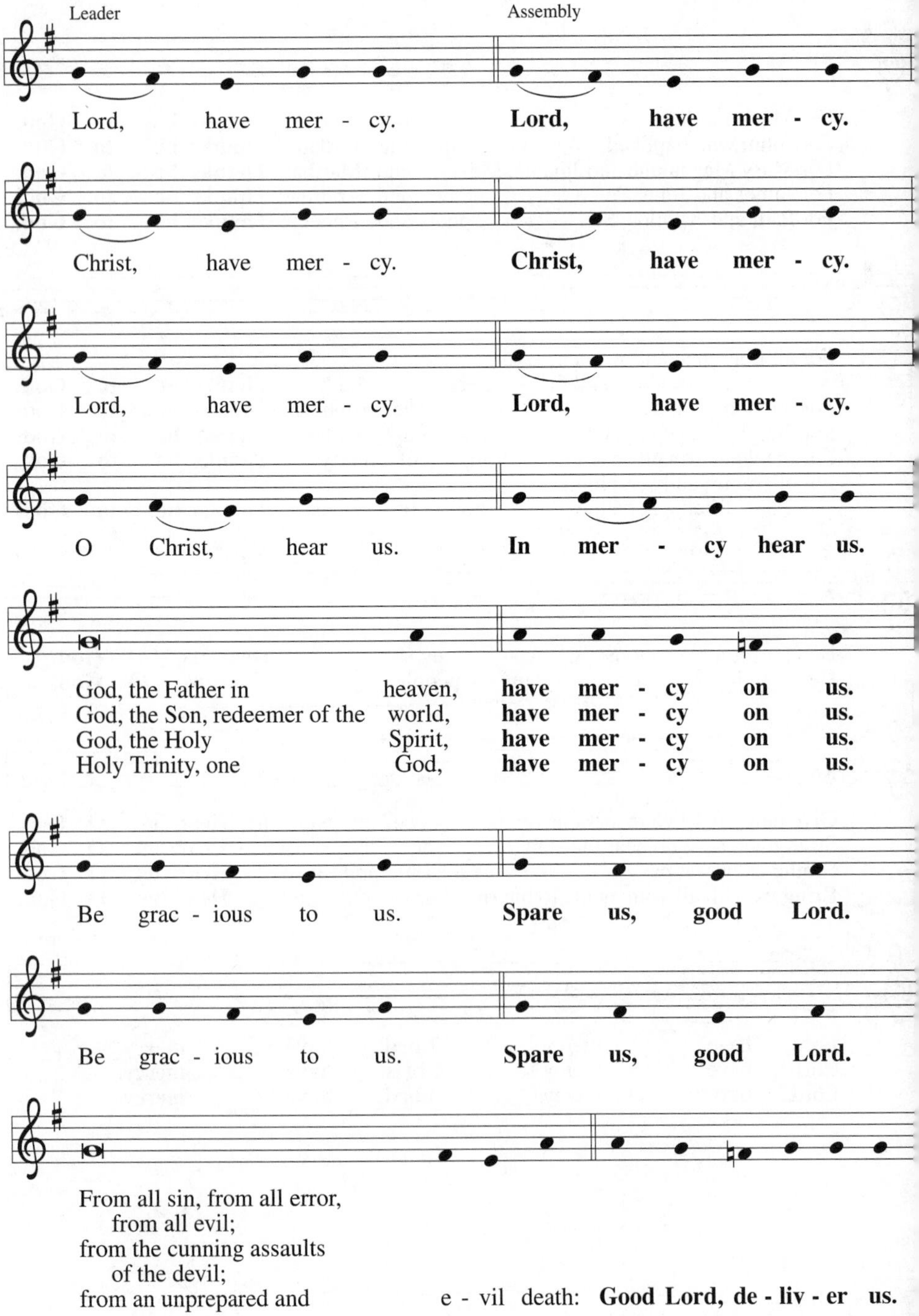

Leader | **Assembly**

Lord, have mer - cy. | **Lord, have mer - cy.**

Christ, have mer - cy. | **Christ, have mer - cy.**

Lord, have mer - cy. | **Lord, have mer - cy.**

O Christ, hear us. | **In mer - cy hear us.**

God, the Father in heaven, | **have mer - cy on us.**
God, the Son, redeemer of the world, | **have mer - cy on us.**
God, the Holy Spirit, | **have mer - cy on us.**
Holy Trinity, one God, | **have mer - cy on us.**

Be grac - ious to us. | **Spare us, good Lord.**

Be grac - ious to us. | **Spare us, good Lord.**

From all sin, from all error,
from all evil;
from the cunning assaults
of the devil;
from an unprepared and | e - vil death: **Good Lord, de - liv - er us.**

From war, bloodshed, and violence;
from corrupt and unjust government;
from sedi   -   tion and treason: **Good Lord, de - liv - er us.**

From epidemic, drought, and famine;
from fire and flood, earthquake,
    lightning, and storm,
and from ever   -   last - ing death: **Good Lord, de - liv - er us.**

By the mystery of your incarnation; by your ho - ly birth: **Help us, good Lord.**

By your baptism, fasting, and temptation;
by your agony and bloody sweat;
by your cross and suffering; by your   death and burial: **Help us, good Lord.**

By your resurrection and ascension;
by the gift of the   Ho - ly Spirit: **Help us, good Lord.**

In all time of our tribulation;
in all time of our prosperity;
in the hour of death; and in the day   of judg - ment: **Save us, good Lord.**

Though unworthy,   we im - plore you   **to hear us, Lord our God.**

To rule and govern your holy catholic church;
to guide all servants of your church
    in the love of your word and in holiness of life;
to put an end to all schisms
    and causes of offense to those who would believe;
and to bring into the way of truth all who have   gone   a - stray:

We im - plore you to hear us, good Lord.

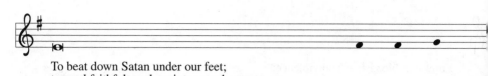

To beat down Satan under our feet;
to send faithful workers into your harvest;
to accompany your word with your Spirit and power;
to raise up those who fall
    and to strengthen those who stand;
and to comfort and help the fainthearted and   the   dis - tressed:

We im - plore you   to   hear   us,   good Lord.

To give to all nations justice and peace;
to preserve our country from discord and strife;
to direct and guard those who have civil authority;
and to bless and guide   all   our   peo - ple:

We im - plore you   to   hear   us,   good Lord.

To behold and help all who are in danger, need, or tribulation;
to protect and guide all who travel;
to preserve and provide for all women in childbirth;
to watch over children and to guide the young;
to heal the sick and to strengthen their families and friends;
to bring reconciliation to families in discord;
to provide for the unemployed and for all in need;
to be merciful to all who are imprisoned;
to support, comfort, and guide
    all orphans, widowers, and widows;
and to have mercy on   all   your peo - ple:

We im - plore you   to   hear   us,   good Lord.

To forgive our enemies, persecutors, and slanderers,
and to reconcile us to them;
to help us use wisely the fruits and treasures
of the earth, the sea, and the air;
and graciously to hear our prayers:

We im - plore you to hear us, good Lord.

Lord Jesus Christ, Son of God, we im - plore you to hear us.

Lamb of God, you take away the sin of the world; have mer - cy on us.

Lamb of God, you take away the sin of the world; have mer - cy on us.

Lamb of God, you take away the sin of the world; give us peace. A - men.

O Christ, hear us. In mer - cy hear us.

Lord, have mer - cy. Lord, have mer - cy.

Christ, have mer - cy. Christ, have mer - cy.

Lord, have mer - cy. Lord, have mer - cy.

Hymns

239   Hark, the Glad Sound!

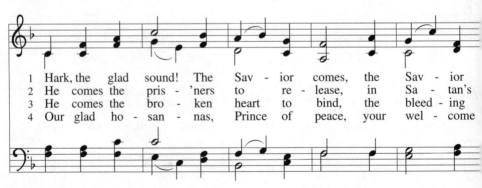

1 Hark, the glad sound! The Sav - ior comes, the Sav - ior
2 He comes the pris - 'ners to re - lease, in Sa - tan's
3 He comes the bro - ken heart to bind, the bleed - ing
4 Our glad ho - san - nas, Prince of peace, your wel - come

Text: Philip Doddridge, 1702–1751
Music: Thomas Haweis, 1734–1820

CHESTERFIELD
CM

prom - ised long; let ev - 'ry heart pre -
bond - age held. The gates of brass be -
soul to cure, and with the trea - sures
shall pro - claim, and heav'n's e - ter - nal

pare a throne and ev - 'ry voice a song.
fore him burst, the i - ron fet - ters yield.
of his grace to en - rich the hum - ble poor.
arch - es ring with your be - lov - ed name.

Light One Candle to Watch for Messiah   240

1 Light one can-dle to watch for Mes-si - ah: let the light ban-ish dark - ness.
2 Light two can-dles to watch for Mes-si - ah: let the light ban-ish dark - ness.
3 Light three can-dles to watch for Mes-si - ah: let the light ban-ish dark - ness.
4 Light four can-dles to watch for Mes-si - ah: let the light ban-ish dark - ness.

He shall bring sal - va - tion to Is - ra - el, God ful - fills the prom - ise.
He shall feed the flock like a shep-herd, gent - ly lead them home-ward.
Lift your heads and lift high the gate-way for the King of glo - ry.
He is com - ing, tell the glad tid - ings. Let your lights be shin - ing!

Text: Wayne L. Wold, b. 1954
Music: Yiddish folk tune
Text © 1984 Fortress Press

TIF IN VELDELE
10 7 96

241   O Lord, How Shall I Meet You

1 O Lord, how shall I meet you, how wel - come you a - right?
2 I lay in fet - ters, groan - ing; you came to set me free.
3 Love caused your in - car - na - tion; love brought you down to me.
4 Re - joice, then, you sad - heart - ed, who sit in deep - est gloom,

Your peo - ple long to greet you, my hope, my heart's de - light!
I stood, my shame be - moan - ing; you came to hon - or me.
Your thirst for my sal - va - tion pro - cured my lib - er - ty.
who mourn your joys de - part - ed and trem - ble at your doom.

Oh, kin - dle, Lord most ho - ly, your lamp with - in my breast
A glo - rious crown you give me, a trea - sure safe on high
Oh, love be - yond all tell - ing, that led you to em - brace
All hail the Lord's ap - pear - ing! O glo - rious Sun, now come,

to do in spir - it low - ly all that may please you best.
that will not fail or leave me as earth - ly rich - es fly.
in love, all love ex - cel - ling, our lost and fall - en race.
send forth your beams so cheer - ing and guide us safe - ly home.

Text: Paul Gerhardt, 1607–1676; tr. composite
Music: Johann Crüger, 1598–1662

WIE SOLL ICH DICH EMPFANGEN
7676

Awake! Awake, and Greet the New Morn 242

1 A - wake! A - wake, and greet the new morn, for
2 To us, to all in sor - row and fear, Em -
3 In dark - est night his com - ing shall be, when
4 Re - joice, re - joice, take heart in the night, though

an - gels her - ald its dawn - ing. Sing out your joy, for
man - u - el comes a - sing - ing, his hum - ble song is
all the world is de - spair - ing, as morn - ing light so
dark the win - ter and cheer - less, the ris - ing sun shall

soon he is born, be - hold! the Child of our long - ing.
qui - et and near, yet fills the earth with its ring - ing;
qui - et and free, so warm and gen - tle and car - ing.
crown you with light, be strong and lov - ing and fear - less.

Come as a ba - by weak and poor, to bring all hearts to -
mu - sic to heal the bro - ken soul and hymns of lov - ing -
Then shall the mute break forth in song, the lame shall leap in
Love be our song and love our prayer and love our end - less

geth - er, he o - pens wide the heav'n - ly door and
kind - ness, the thun - der of his an - thems roll to
won - der, the weak be raised a - bove the strong, and
sto - ry; may God fill ev - 'ry day we share and

lives now in - side us for - ev - er.
shat - ter all ha - tred and blind - ness.
weap - ons be bro - ken a - sun - der.
bring us at last in - to glo - ry.

Text: Marty Haugen, b. 1950
Music: Marty Haugen
Text and music © 1983 GIA Publications, Inc.

REJOICE, REJOICE
98988789

243

Lost in the Night

1 Lost in the night do the peo - ple yet lan - guish,
2 Must we be vain - ly a - wait - ing the mor - row?
3 Sor - row - ing wan - d'rers, in dark - ness yet dwell - ing,
4 Light o'er the land of the need - y is beam - ing;

long - ing for morn - ing the dark - ness to van - quish,
Shall those who have light no light let us bor - row,
dawned has the day of a ra - diance ex - cel - ling,
riv - ers of life through its des - erts are stream - ing,

plain - tive - ly sigh - ing with hearts full of an - guish.
giv - ing no heed to our bur - den of sor - row?
death's deep - est shad - ows for - ev - er dis - pel - ling.
bring - ing all peo - ples a Sav - ior re - deem - ing.

Will not day come soon? Will not day come soon?
Will you help us soon? Will you help us soon?
Christ is com - ing soon! Christ is com - ing soon!
Come and save us soon! Come and save us soon!

Text: Nordic hymn; tr. Olav Lee, 1859–1943, alt.
Music: Finnish folk tune
Text © 1932 Augsburg Publishing House

LOST IN THE NIGH
11 11 11 5

Rejoice, Rejoice, Believers

1 Re - joice, re - joice, be - liev - ers, and let your lights ap - pear;
2 The watch-ers on the moun - tain pro - claim the bride-groom near;
3 The saints, who here in pa - tience their cross and suf - f'rings bore,
4 Our hope and ex - pec - ta - tion, O Je - sus, now ap - pear;

the eve-ning is ad - vanc - ing, and dark - er night is near.
go forth as he ap - proach - es with al - le - lu - ias clear.
shall live and reign for - ev - er when sor - row is no more.
a - rise, O Sun so longed for, o'er this be - night-ed sphere.

The bride-groom is a - ris - ing and soon is draw-ing nigh.
The mar - riage feast is wait - ing; the gates wide o - pen stand.
A - round the throne of glo - ry the Lamb they shall be - hold;
With hearts and hands up - lift - ed, we plead, O Lord, to see

Up, pray and watch and wres - tle; at mid - night comes the cry.
A - rise, O heirs of glo - ry; the bride-groom is at hand.
in tri - umph cast be - fore him their di - a - dems of gold.
the day of earth's re - demp - tion that sets your peo - ple free!

Text: Laurentius Laurenti, 1660–1722; tr. Sarah B. Findlater, 1823–1907

HAF TRONES LAMPA FÄRDIG
7 6 7 6 D

Music: Swedish folk tune

245   Creator of the Stars of Night

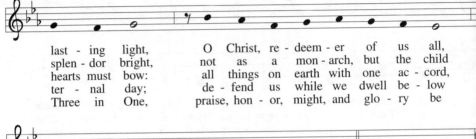

1 Cre - a - tor of the stars of night, your peo - ple's ev - er -
2 When this old world drew on toward night, you came; but not in
3 At your great name, O Je - sus, now all knees must bend, all
4 Come in your ho - ly might, we pray, re - deem us for e -
5 To God the Fa - ther, God the Son, and God the Spir - it,

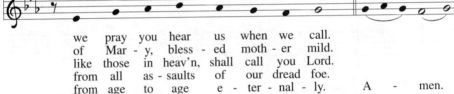

last - ing light, O Christ, re - deem - er of us all,
splen - dor bright, not as a mon - arch, but the child
hearts must bow: all things on earth with one ac - cord,
ter - nal day; de - fend us while we dwell be - low
Three in One, praise, hon - or, might, and glo - ry be

we pray you hear us when we call.
of Mar - y, bless - ed moth - er mild.
like those in heav'n, shall call you Lord.
from all as - saults of our dread foe.
from age to age e - ter - nal - ly. A - men.

Text: Latin hymn, 9th cent.; tr. *Hymnal 1940*, alt.
Music: Plainsong mode IV
Text © 1940 Church Pension Fund

CONDITOR ALME SIDERUM
LM

246   Hark! A Thrilling Voice Is Sounding!

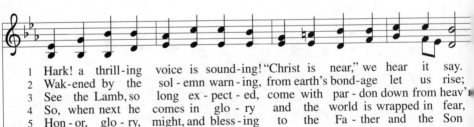

1 Hark! a thrill - ing voice is sound - ing! "Christ is near," we hear it say.
2 Wak - ened by the sol - emn warn - ing, from earth's bond - age let us rise;
3 See the Lamb, so long ex - pect - ed, come with par - don down from heav'n
4 So, when next he comes in glo - ry and the world is wrapped in fear,
5 Hon - or, glo - ry, might, and bless - ing to the Fa - ther and the Son

Text: Latin hymn, 1632; tr. Edward Caswall, 1814–1878
Music: William H. Monk, 1823–1889

MERTON
87 8

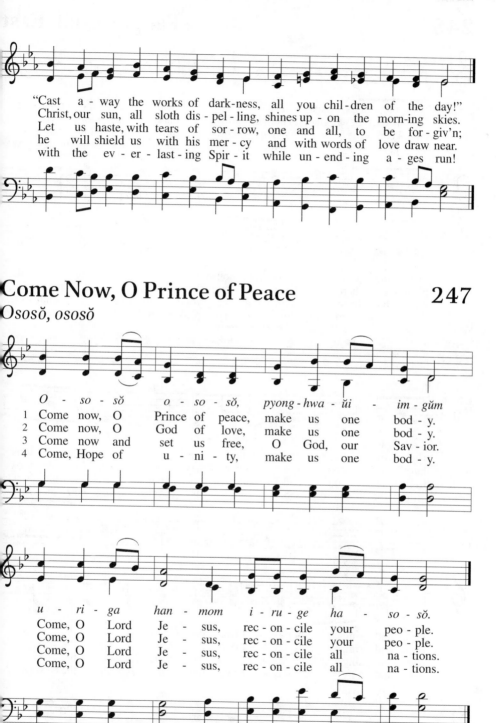

"Cast a - way the works of dark-ness, all you chil-dren of the day!"
Christ, our sun, all sloth dis - pel - ling, shines up - on the morn-ing skies.
Let us haste, with tears of sor - row, one and all, to be for - giv'n;
he will shield us with his mer - cy and with words of love draw near.
with the ev - er - last - ing Spir - it while un - end - ing a - ges run!

Come Now, O Prince of Peace 247

Ososŏ, ososŏ

O - so - sŏ   o - so - sŏ,   pyong - hwa - ŭi - im - gŭm
1 Come now, O   Prince of peace,   make us   one   bod - y.
2 Come now, O   God of love,   make us   one   bod - y.
3 Come now and   set us free,   O God,   our   Sav - ior.
4 Come, Hope of   u - ni - ty,   make us   one   bod - y.

u - ri - ga   han - mom   i - ru - ge   ha - so - sŏ.
Come, O Lord Je - sus,   rec - on - cile   your   peo - ple.
Come, O Lord Je - sus,   rec - on - cile   your   peo - ple.
Come, O Lord Je - sus,   rec - on - cile   all   na - tions.
Come, O Lord Je - sus,   rec - on - cile   all   na - tions.

Text: Geonyong Lee, b. 1947; tr. Marion Pope
Music: Geonyong Lee, b. 1947
Text and music © Geonyong Lee

OSOSŎ
6 5 5 6

248

People, Look East

1 Peo - ple, look east. The time is near of the crown - ing
2 Fur - rows, be glad. Though earth is bare, one more seed is
3 Stars, keep the watch. When night is dim, one more light the
4 An - gels an - nounce with shouts of mirth him who brings new

of the year. Make your house fair as you are a - ble,
plant - ed there. Give up your strength the seed to nour - ish,
bowl shall brim, shin - ing be - yond the frost - y weath - er,
life to earth. Set ev - 'ry peak and val - ley hum - ming

trim the hearth and set the ta - ble. Peo - ple, look
that in course the flow'r may flour - ish. Peo - ple, look
bright as sun and moon to - geth - er. Peo - ple, look
with the word, the Lord is com - ing. Peo - ple, look

east, and sing to - day— Love, the Guest, is on the way.
east, and sing to - day— Love, the Rose, is on the way.
east, and sing to - day— Love, the Star, is on the way.
east, and sing to - day— Love, the Lord, is on the way.

Text: Eleanor Farjeon, 1881–1965
Music: French carol; arr. Barry Rose, b. 1934
Text © Miss E. Farjeon Will Trust, by permission of David Higham Associates
Arr. © 1999 Novello & Co. Ltd., London

BESANÇON
87 98 8

On Jordan's Bank the Baptist's Cry

1 On Jor - dan's bank the Bap - tist's cry an - nounc - es
2 Then cleansed be ev - 'ry life from sin; make straight the
3 We hail you as our Sav - ior, Lord, our ref - uge
4 Stretch forth your hand, our health re - store, and make us
5 All praise to you, e - ter - nal Son, whose ad - vent

that the Lord is nigh; a - wake and heark - en,
way for God with - in, and let us all our
and our great re - ward; with - out your grace we
rise to fall no more; oh, let your face up -
has our free - dom won, whom with the Fa - ther

for he brings glad tid - ings of the King of kings!
hearts pre - pare for Christ to come and en - ter there.
waste a - way like flow'rs that with - er and de - cay.
on us shine and fill the world with love di - vine.
we a - dore, and Ho - ly Spir - it, ev - er - more.

Text: Charles Coffin, 1676–1749; tr. composite
Music: European tune, adapt. Michael Praetorius, 1571–1621

PUER NOBIS
LM

250

Blessed Be the God of Israel

1 Blessed be the God of Is - ra - el who comes to set us free
2 With prom-ised mer - cy will God still the cov - e - nant re - call,
3 My child, as proph-et of the Lord you will pre - pare the way,

and rais - es up new hope for us: a Branch from Da-vid's tree.
the oath once sworn to A - bra - ham, from foes to save us all;
to tell God's peo - ple they are saved from sin's e - ter - nal sway.

So have the proph-ets long de-clared that with a might-y arm
that we might wor - ship with-out fear and of - fer lives of praise
Then shall God's mer - cy from on high shine forth and nev - er cease

God would turn back our en - e - mies and all who wish us harm.
in ho - li - ness and righ - teous-ness to serve God all our days.
to drive a - way the gloom of death and lead us in - to peace.

Text: Carl P. Daw Jr., b. 1944, based on Luke 1:68-79
Music: English folk tune; arr. Ralph Vaughan Williams, 1872–1958

FOREST GREEN
CM

My Soul Proclaims Your Greatness

1 My soul pro-claims your great-ness, Lord; I sing my Sav - ior's praise!
2 To all who live in ho - ly fear your mer-cy ev - er flows.
3 To Is - ra - el, your ser - vant blest, your help is ev - er sure;

You looked up - on my low - li - ness, and I am full of grace.
With might - y arm you dash the proud, their schem-ing hearts ex - pose.
the prom - ise to our par - ents made their chil - dren will se - cure.

Now ev - 'ry land and ev - 'ry age this bless-ing shall pro - claim—
The ruth-less you have cast a - side, the low - ly throned in - stead;
Sing glo - ry to the Ho - ly One, give hon - or to the Word,

great won - ders you have done for me, and ho - ly is your name.
the hun - gry filled with all good things, the rich sent off un - fed.
and praise the Pow'r of the Most High, one God, by all a - dored.

Text: *With One Voice*, 1995, based on the Magnificat
Music: English folk tune; arr. Ralph Vaughan Williams, 1872–1958
Text © 1995 Augsburg Fortress
Arr. © Oxford University Press

KINGSFOLD
CMD

252   Each Winter As the Year Grows Older

1. Each win-ter as the year grows old-er, we each grow old-er, too. The chill sets in a lit-tle cold-er; the ver-i-ties we knew seem shak-en and un-true.
2. When race and class cry out for trea-son, when si-rens call for war, they o-ver-shout the voice of rea-son and scream till we ig-nore all we held dear be-fore.
3. Yet I be-lieve be-yond be-liev-ing that life can spring from death, that growth can flow-er from our griev-ing, that we can catch our breath and turn trans-fixed by faith.
4. So e-ven as the sun is turn-ing to jour-ney to the north, the liv-ing flame, in se-cret burn-ing, can kin-dle on the earth and bring God's love to birth.
5. O Child of ec-sta-sy and sor-rows, O Prince of peace and pain, bright-en to-day's world by to-mor-row's, re-new our lives a-gain; Lord Je-sus, come and reign!

Text: William Gay, b. 1920, alt.
Music: Annabeth Gay, b. 1925
Text and music © 1971 United Church Press

CAROL OF HOP
9 6 9 6

253   He Came Down

1. He came down that we may have love; he came down that we may have love;
2. He came down that we may have light; he came down that we may have light;
3. He came down that we may have peace; he came down that we may have peace;
4. He came down that we may have joy; he came down that we may have joy;

Text: Cameroon traditional
Music: Cameroon traditional; arr. John L. Bell, b. 1949
Arr. © 1986 Iona Community, admin. GIA Publications, Inc.

HE CAME DOW
L

he came down that we may have love;
he came down that we may have light;
he came down that we may have peace;
he came down that we may have joy;

hal - le - lu - jah for - ev - er - more.

Come, Thou Long-Expected Jesus 254

1 Come, thou long-ex - pect-ed Je - sus, born to set thy peo-ple free;
2 Born thy peo-ple to de - liv-er, born a child, and yet a king;

from our fears and sins re - lease us; let us find our rest in thee.
born to reign in us for - ev - er, now thy gra-cious king-dom bring.

Is-rael's strength and con-so - la-tion, hope of all the earth thou art,
By thine own e - ter-nal Spir-it rule in all our hearts a - lone;

dear de - sire of ev-'ry na-tion, joy of ev-'ry long-ing heart.
by thine all - suf - fi - cient mer-it raise us to thy glo-rious throne.

Text: Charles Wesley, 1707–1788
Music: W. Walker, *Southern Harmony*, 1835

JEFFERSON
8 7 8 7 D

255 There's a Voice in the Wilderness

1 There's a voice in the wil-der-ness cry-ing, a
2 O Je - ru - sa-lem, her-ald good tid-ings, as -
3 But the word of our Sav-ior is faith-ful, the

call from the ways un-trod: Pre - pare in the des-ert a
cend to the heights and sing! Pro - claim to a des-o-late
arm of our God is strong, who stands in the midst of the

high - way, a high - way for our God!
peo - ple the com - ing of their king.
na - tions and soon will right the wrong.

The val - leys shall be ex - alt - ed, the
Like flow'rs of the field we per - ish, like
Lord, feed your flock like a shep - herd, the

loft - y hills brought low; make straight all the crook - ed
grass our works de - cay; the pow'r and the pomp of
lambs so gent - ly hold; in pas - tures of peace now

plac - es where God, our God, may go!
na - tions shall pass like a dream a - way.
lead them, and bring them to your fold.

Text: James Lewis Milligan, 1876–1961, alt.
Music: Henry Hugh Bancroft, 1904–1988
Music © Estate of Eldred Bancroft, admin. B. Burrows

ASCENSIO
P

Comfort, Comfort Now My People

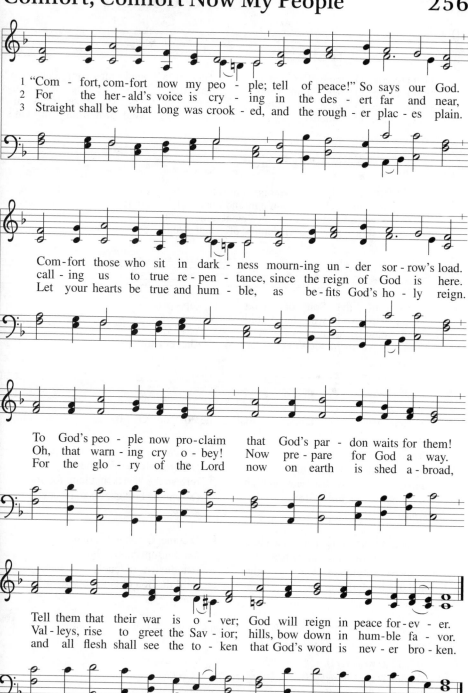

1 "Com - fort, com-fort now my peo - ple; tell of peace!" So says our God.
2 For the her - ald's voice is cry - ing in the des - ert far and near,
3 Straight shall be what long was crook - ed, and the rough - er plac - es plain.

Com-fort those who sit in dark - ness mourn-ing un - der sor - row's load.
call - ing us to true re - pen - tance, since the reign of God is here.
Let your hearts be true and hum - ble, as be - fits God's ho - ly reign.

To God's peo - ple now pro-claim that God's par - don waits for them!
Oh, that warn - ing cry o - bey! Now pre - pare for God a way.
For the glo - ry of the Lord now on earth is shed a - broad,

Tell them that their war is o - ver; God will reign in peace for-ev - er.
Val - leys, rise to greet the Sav - ior; hills, bow down in hum-ble fa - vor.
and all flesh shall see the to - ken that God's word is nev - er bro-ken.

Text: Johann G. Olearius, 1635–1711; tr. Catherine Winkworth, 1827–1878, alt.
Music: *Trente quatre pseaumes de David*, Geneva, 1551

FREU DICH SEHR
87 87 77 88

257   O Come, O Come, Emmanuel

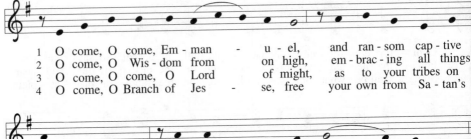

1 O come, O come, Em - man - u - el, and ran - som cap - tive
2 O come, O Wis - dom from on high, em - brac - ing all things
3 O come, O come, O Lord of might, as to your tribes on
4 O come, O Branch of Jes - se, free your own from Sa - tan's

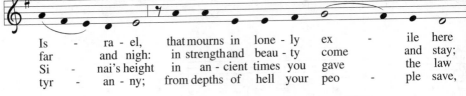

Is - ra - el, that mourns in lone - ly ex - ile here
far and nigh: in strength and beau - ty come and stay;
Si - nai's height in an - cient times you gave the law
tyr - an - ny; from depths of hell your peo - ple save,

un - til the Son of God ap - pear.
teach us your will and guide our way.   Re-joice!   Re-joice!
in cloud, and maj - es - ty, and awe.
and give them vic - t'ry o'er the grave.

Em - man - u - el shall come to you, O Is - ra - el.

5 O come, O Key of David, come,
and open wide our heav'nly home;
make safe the way that leads on high,
and close the path to misery.
Refrain

6 O come, O Dayspring, come and cheer;
O Sun of justice, now draw near
Disperse the gloomy clouds of night,
and death's dark shadow put to flight.
Refrain

7 O come, O King of nations, come,
O Cornerstone that binds in one:
refresh the hearts that long for you;
restore the broken, make us new.
Refrain

8 O come, O come, Emmanuel,
and ransom captive Israel,
that mourns in lonely exile here
until the Son of God appear.
Refrain

One stanza of this paraphrase of the great O Antiphons may be sung on
each of the last days of Advent, as follows:

Dec. 17: O Wisdom (2)
Dec. 18: O Lord of might (3)
Dec. 19: O Branch of Jesse (4)
Dec. 20: O Key of David (5)

Dec. 21: O Dayspring (6)
Dec. 22: O King of nations (7)
Dec. 23: O Emmanuel (8)

Text: *Psalteriolum Cantionum Catholicarum*, Köln, 1710; tr. composite
Music: French processional, 15th cent.
Text sts. 2, 6, 7 © 1997 Augsburg Fortress

VENI, EMMANUE
88888

Unexpected and Mysterious

1 Un - ex - pect - ed and mys - te - rious is the gen - tle
2 In a mo - men - tar - y meet - ing of e - ter - ni -
3 We are called to pon - der mys - t'ry and a - wait the

word of grace. Ev - er - lov - ing and sus - tain -
ty and time, Mar - y learned that she would car -
com - ing Christ, to em - bod - y God's com - pas -

ing is the peace of God's em - brace. If we fal - ter
ry both the mor - tal and di - vine. Then she learned of
sion for each frag - ile hu - man life. God is with us

in our cour - age and we doubt what we have known, God is
God's com - pas - sion, of E - liz - a-beth's great joy, and she
in our long - ing to bring heal - ing to the earth, while we

faith - ful to con-sole us as a moth - er tends her own.
ran to greet the wom - an who would rec - og-nize her boy.
watch with joy and won - der for the prom-ised Sav-ior's birth.

Text: Jeannette M. Lindholm, b. 1961
Music: Calvin Hampton, 1938–1984
Text © 2002 Jeannette M. Lindholm, admin. Augsburg Fortress
Music © 1977 GIA Publications, Inc.

ST. HELENA
8 7 8 7 D

259

Fling Wide the Door

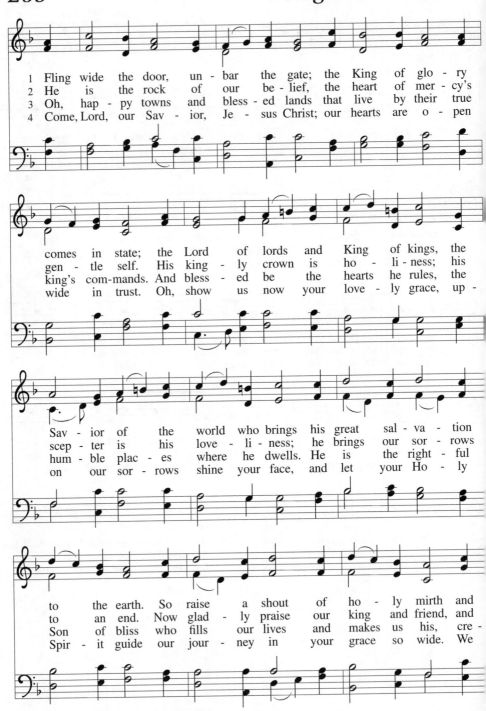

1 Fling wide the door, un - bar the gate; the King of glo - ry
2 He is the rock of our be - lief, the heart of mer - cy's
3 Oh, hap - py towns and bless - ed lands that live by their true
4 Come, Lord, our Sav - ior, Je - sus Christ; our hearts are o - pen

comes in state; the Lord of lords and King of kings, the
gen - tle self. His king - ly crown is ho - li - ness; his
king's com-mands. And bless - ed be the hearts he rules, the
wide in trust. Oh, show us now your love - ly grace, up -

Sav - ior of the world who brings his great sal - va - tion
scep - ter is his love - li - ness; he brings our sor - rows
hum - ble plac - es where he dwells. He is the right - ful
on our sor - rows shine your face, and let your Ho - ly

to the earth. So raise a shout of ho - ly mirth and
to an end. Now glad - ly praise our king and friend, and
Son of bliss who fills our lives and makes us his, cre -
Spir - it guide our jour - ney in your grace so wide. We

Text: Georg Weissel, 1590–1635; tr. Gracia Grindal, b. 1943
Music: J. A. Freylinghausen, *Geistreiches Gesangbuch*, 1704; arr. hymnal version
Text © 1978 *Lutheran Book of Worship*, admin. Augsburg Fortress
Arr. © 2006 Augsburg Fortress

MACHT HOCH DIE TÜ?
8 8 8 8 8 8 6

praise our God and Lord, Cre - a - tor, Spir - it, Word.
wor - ship him with song for sav - ing us from wrong.
a - tor of the world, our on - ly strength for good.
praise your ho - ly name, from age to age the same!

The King Shall Come 260

1 The King shall come when morn-ing dawns and light tri - um-phant breaks,
2 Not as of old a lit - tle child, to bear and fight and die,
3 Oh, bright - er than the ris - ing morn when Christ, vic - to - rious, rose
4 Oh, bright - er than that glo - rious morn shall dawn up - on our race
5 The King shall come when morn-ing dawns and light and beau - ty brings.

when beau - ty gilds the east - ern hills and life to joy a - wakes.
but crowned with glo - ry like the sun that lights the morn-ing sky.
and left the lone-some place of death, de - spite the rage of foes.
the day when Christ in splen-dor comes, and we shall see his face.
Hail, Christ the Lord! Your peo - ple pray: come quick-ly, King of kings.

Text: John Brownlie, 1859–1925
Music: A. Davisson, *Kentucky Harmony*, 1816; arr. Theodore A. Beck, 1929–2003
Arr. © 1969 Concordia Publishing House

CONSOLATION
CM

261

As the Dark Awaits the Dawn

1 As the dark a - waits the dawn,
2 As the blue ex - pec - tant hour
3 As the moon re - flects the sun
4 Shine your fu - ture on this place,

so we a - wait your light. O Star of
be - fore the sil - v'ring skies, we long to
un - til the night's de - crease, may we your
en - light - en ev - 'ry guest, that through us

prom - ise, scat - ter night, lov - ing bright, lov - ing
see your day a - rise, whole and wise, whole and
heal - ing light re - lease, liv - ing peace, liv - ing
stream your ho - li - ness, bright and blest, bright and

bright, till shades of fear are gone.
wise, O lu - cent Morn - ing Star.
peace, un - to your ho - ly dawn.
blest; come dawn, O Sun of grace.

Text: Susan Palo Cherwien, b. 1953
Music: Carl F. Schalk, b. 1929
Text © 1996 Susan Palo Cherwien, admin. Augsburg Fortress
Music © 1997 Augsburg Fortress

LUCENT
76866

262

Wait for the Lord

Wait for the Lord, whose day is near.

Text: Taizé Community
Music: Jacques Berthier, 1923–1994
Text and music © 1984 Les Presses de Taizé, admin. GIA Publications, Inc.

WAIT FOR THE LORD
88

Wait for the Lord: be strong, take heart!

Savior of the Nations, Come 263

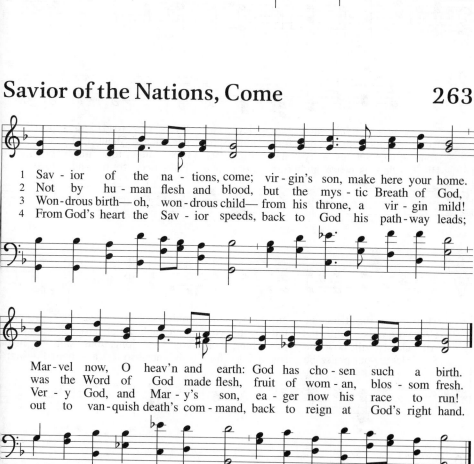

1 Sav - ior of the na - tions, come; vir - gin's son, make here your home.
2 Not by hu - man flesh and blood, but the mys - tic Breath of God,
3 Won - drous birth— oh, won - drous child— from his throne, a vir - gin mild!
4 From God's heart the Sav - ior speeds, back to God his path - way leads;

Mar - vel now, O heav'n and earth: God has cho - sen such a birth.
was the Word of God made flesh, fruit of wom - an, blos - som fresh.
Ver - y God, and Mar - y's son, ea - ger now his race to run!
out to van - quish death's com - mand, back to reign at God's right hand.

5 Now your manger, shining bright,
hallows night with newborn light.
Night cannot this light subdue;
let our faith shine ever new.

6 Praise we sing to Christ the Lord,
virgin's son, incarnate Word!
To the holy Trinity
praise we sing eternally!

Text: attr. Ambrose of Milan, 340–397; Martin Luther, 1483–1546; tr. hymnal version
Music: J. Walter, *Geistliche Gesangbüchlein*, 1524
Text © 2006 Augsburg Fortress

NUN KOMM, DER HEIDEN HEILAND
7777

264   Prepare the Royal Highway

1 Pre - pare the roy - al high - way; the King of kings is near!
2 God's peo - ple, see him com - ing: your own e - ter - nal king!
3 Then fling the gates wide o - pen to greet your prom - ised king!
4 His is no earth - ly king - dom; it comes from heav'n a - bove.

Let ev - 'ry hill and val - ley a lev - el road ap - pear!
Palm branch - es strew be - fore him! Spread gar - ments! Shout and sing!
Your king, yet ev - 'ry na - tion its trib - ute too may bring.
His rule is peace and free - dom and jus - tice, truth, and love.

Then greet the King of glo - ry, fore - told in sa - cred sto - ry,
God's prom - ise will not fail you! No more shall doubt as - sail you!
All lands will bow be - fore him; their voic - es join your sing - ing:
So let your praise be sound - ing for kind - ness so a - bound - ing:

Refrain

Ho - san - na to the Lord, for he ful - fills God's word!

Text: Frans Mikael Franzén, 1772–1847; tr. *Lutheran Book of Worship*
Music: Swedish folk tune, 17th cent.
Text © 1978 *Lutheran Book of Worship*, admin. Augsburg Fortress

BEREDEN VÄG FÖR HERRAN
7676776

The Angel Gabriel from Heaven Came 265

1 The an - gel Ga - bri - el from heav - en came,
2 "For know a bless - ed moth - er thou shalt be,
3 Then gen - tle Mar - y meek - ly bowed her head;
4 Of her, Em - man - u - el, the Christ, was born

with wings as drift - ed snow, with eyes as flame:
all gen - er - a - tions laud and hon - or thee;
"To me be as it pleas - eth God," she said.
in Beth - le - hem all on a Christ - mas morn,

"All hail to thee, O low - ly maid - en Mar - y,
thy son shall be Em - man - u - el, by seers fore - told,
"My soul shall laud and mag - ni - fy God's ho - ly name."
and Chris - tian folk through - out the world will ev - er say:

most high - ly fa - vored la - dy."
most high - ly fa - vored la - dy."
Most high - ly fa - vored la - dy,   Glo - ri - a!
"Most high - ly fa - vored la - dy."

Text: Basque carol; para. Sabine Baring-Gould, 1834–1924
Music: Basque carol; arr. C. Edgar Pettman, 1865–1943, and John Wickham
arr. © 1955, 1983 E.H. Freeman, Ltd, admin. Glenwood Music Corp.

GABRIEL'S MESSAGE
10 10 12 10

All Earth Is Hopeful
Toda la tierra

To - da la tie - rra | es - pe - ra al Sal - va - dor
1 All earth is hope - ful, | the Sav - ior comes at last!
2 Peo - ple of Is - rael, | you heard the proph - et tell:
3 Moun - tains and val - leys | will have to be pre - pared;
4 We first saw Je - sus | a ba - by in a crib.

y el sur - co a - bier - to, | la ob - ra del Se - ñor; | es el
Fur - rows lie o - pen | for God's cre - a - tive task: | this, the
"A vir - gin moth - er | will bear Em - man - u - el"; | she con -
new high - ways o - pened, | new pro - to - cols de - clared. | Al - most
This same Lord Je - sus | to - day has come to live | in our

mun - do que lu - cha | por la li - ber - tad, | re -
la - bor of peo - ple | who strug - gle to see | how
ceived him, "God with us," | our broth - er, whose birth | re -
here! God is near - ing, | in beau - ty and grace! | All
world; he is pres - ent, | in neigh - bors we see | our

1–3 *4*

cla - ma jus - ti - cia | y bus - ca la ver - dad. | dar - nos li - ber - tad.
God's truth and jus - tice | set ev - 'ry - bod - y free.
stores hope and cour - age | to chil - dren of this earth.
clear ev - 'ry gate - way, | in haste, come out in haste!
Je - sus is with us, and | ev - er sets us free.

2 *Dice el profeta al pueblo de Israel:*
"De madre virgen ya viene Emmanuel,"
será "Dios con nosotros," hermano será,
con él la esperanza al mundo volverá.

3 *Montes y valles habrá que preparar;*
nuevos caminos tenemos que trazar.
Él está ya muy cerca, venidlo a encontrar
y todas las puertas abrid de par en par

4 *En una cueva Jesús apareció,*
pero en el mundo está presente hoy.
Vive en nuestros hermanos, con ellos está;
y vuelve de nuevo a darnos libertad.

Text: Alberto Taulé, b. 1932; tr. Madeleine Forell Marshall, b. 1946
Music: Alberto Taulé
Spanish text and tune © 1993 and tr. © 1995 Centro de Pastoral Litúrgica, admin. OCP Publications

TODA LA TIERRA
11 11 12 12

Joy to the World

1 Joy to the world, the Lord is come! Let earth re-
2 Joy to the earth, the Sav - ior reigns! Let all their
3 No more let sin and sor - row grow nor thorns in -
4 He rules the world with truth and grace and makes the

ceive her king; let ev - 'ry heart pre - pare him
songs em - ploy, while fields and floods, rocks, hills, and
fest the ground; he comes to make his bless - ings
na - tions prove the glo - ries of his righ - teous -

room and heav'n and na - ture sing, and heav'n and na - ture
plains re - peat the sound-ing joy, re - peat the sound-ing
flow far as the curse is found, far as the curse is
ness and won - ders of his love, and won - ders of his

and heav'n and na - ture sing, and

sing, and heav'n, and heav'n and na - ture sing.
joy, re - peat, re - peat the sound - ing joy.
found, far as, far as the curse is found.
love, and won - ders, won - ders of his love.

heav'n and na - ture sing,

Text: Isaac Watts, 1674–1748
Music: English melody, 18th cent.; arr. Lowell Mason, 1792–1872

ANTIOCH
CM and repeat

268

From Heaven Above

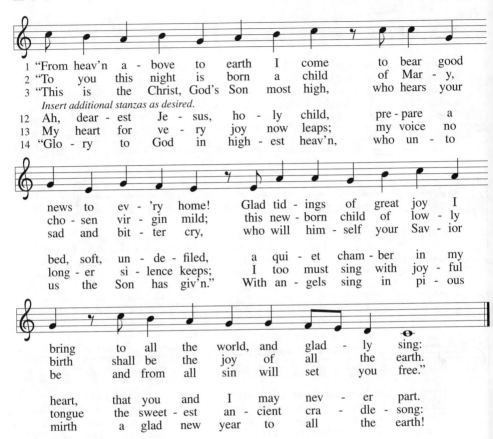

1 "From heav'n a - bove to earth I come to bear good
2 "To you this night is born a child of Mar - y,
3 "This is the Christ, God's Son most high, who hears your

Insert additional stanzas as desired.

12 Ah, dear - est Je - sus, ho - ly child, pre - pare a
13 My heart for ve - ry joy now leaps; my voice no
14 "Glo - ry to God in high - est heav'n, who un - to

news to ev - 'ry home! Glad tid - ings of great joy I
cho - sen vir - gin mild; this new - born child of low - ly
sad and bit - ter cry, who will him - self your Sav - ior

bed, soft, un - de - filed, a qui - et cham - ber in my
long - er si - lence keeps; I too must sing with joy - ful
us the Son has giv'n." With an - gels sing in pi - ous

bring to all the world, and glad - ly sing:
birth shall be the joy of all the earth.
be and from all sin will set you free."

heart, that you and I may nev - er part.
tongue the sweet - est an - cient cra - dle - song:
mirth a glad new year to all the earth!

4 "The blessing that the Father planned
the Son holds in his infant hand,
that in his kingdom, bright and fair,
you may with us his glory share."

5 "These are the signs that you will see
to let you know that it is he:
in manger-bed, in swaddling clothes
the child who all the earth upholds."

6 Now let us all with joyful cheer
go with the shepherds and draw near
to see this wondrous gift of God,
the blessed child to us bestowed.

7 Look, look, dear friends, look over there!
What lies within that manger bare?
Who is that lovely little one?
The baby Jesus, God's dear Son.

8 Welcome to earth, O noble Guest,
through whom this sinful world is blest!
You turned not from our needs away;
how can our thanks such love repay?

9 O Lord, you have created all!
How did you come to be so small,
to sweetly sleep in manger-bed
where lowing cattle lately fed?

Text: Martin Luther, 1483–1546; tr. *Lutheran Book of Worship*
Music: attr. Martin Luther; V. Schumann, *Geistliche Lieder*, 1539
Text © 1978 *Lutheran Book of Worship*, admin. Augsburg Fortress

VOM HIMMEL HOCH
LM

10 Were earth a thousand times as fair
and set with gold and jewels rare,
still such a cradle would not do
to rock a prince so great as you.

11 For velvets soft and silken stuff
you have but hay and straw so rough
on which as king so rich and great
to be enthroned in humble state.

Once in Royal David's City

269

1 Once in roy - al Da - vid's cit - y stood a low - ly cat - tle shed,
2 He came down to earth from heav-en who is God and Lord of all,
3 And our eyes at last shall see him, through his own re - deem-ing love;
4 Not in that poor low - ly sta - ble, with the ox - en stand-ing by,

where a moth-er laid her ba - by in a man - ger for his bed:
and his shel - ter was a sta - ble, and his cra - dle was a stall;
for that child so dear and gen - tle is our Lord in heav'n a - bove;
we shall see him; but in heav - en, set at God's right hand on high;

Mar - y was that moth-er mild, Je - sus Christ, her lit - tle child.
with the poor and meek and low-ly, lived on earth our Sav-ior ho - ly.
and he leads his chil - dren on to the place where he is gone.
there his chil - dren gath - er round, bright like stars, with glo - ry crowned.

Text: Cecil Frances Alexander, 1818–1895
Music: Henry J. Gauntlett, 1805–1876

IRBY
878777

270 Hark! The Herald Angels Sing

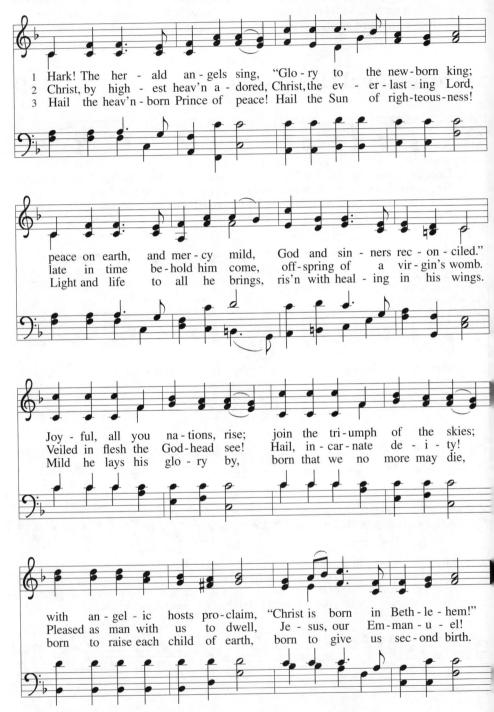

1 Hark! The her - ald an - gels sing, "Glo - ry to the new-born king;
2 Christ, by high - est heav'n a - dored, Christ, the ev - er - last - ing Lord,
3 Hail the heav'n - born Prince of peace! Hail the Sun of righ-teous-ness!

peace on earth, and mer - cy mild, God and sin - ners rec - on - ciled."
late in time be - hold him come, off - spring of a vir - gin's womb.
Light and life to all he brings, ris'n with heal - ing in his wings.

Joy - ful, all you na - tions, rise; join the tri - umph of the skies;
Veiled in flesh the God-head see! Hail, in - car - nate de - i - ty!
Mild he lays his glo - ry by, born that we no more may die,

with an - gel - ic hosts pro - claim, "Christ is born in Beth - le - hem!"
Pleased as man with us to dwell, Je - sus, our Em - man - u - el!
born to raise each child of earth, born to give us sec - ond birth.

Text: Charles Wesley, 1707–1788, alt.
Music: Felix Mendelssohn, 1809–1847; arr. William H. Cummings, 1831–1915

MENDELSSOHN
7 7 7 7 D and refrain

Refrain

Hark! The her-ald an-gels sing, "Glo-ry to the new-born king!"

I Am So Glad Each Christmas Eve
Jeg er så glad hver julekveld

271

Jeg er så glad hver ju - le - kveld, ti da blev Je - sus født;

1 I am so glad each Christ-mas Eve, the night of Je - sus' birth!
2 The lit - tle child in Beth - le - hem, he was a king in - deed!
3 He dwells a - gain in heav - en's realm, the Son of God to - day;
4 I am so glad each Christ-mas Eve! His prais - es then I sing;
5 And so I love each Christ-mas Eve, and I love Je - sus too;

da lys - te stjer - nen som en sol, og eng - ler sang så sødt.

Then like the sun the star shone forth, and an - gels sang on earth.
For he came down from heav'n a - bove to help a world in need.
and still he loves his lit - tle ones and hears them when they pray.
he o - pens now for ev - 'ry child the pal - ace of the king.
and that he loves me ev - 'ry day I know so well is true.

Text: Marie Wexelsen, 1832–1911; tr. Peter A. Sveeggen, 1881–1959
Music: Peder Knudsen, 1819–1863
Text © 1932 Augsburg Publishing House

JEG ER SÅ GLAD
CM

272   Lo, How a Rose E'er Blooming

1 Lo, how a rose e'er bloom-ing from ten-der stem hath
2 I - sai - ah had fore-told it, the rose I have in
3 This flow'r, whose fra-grance ten - der with sweet-ness fills the
4 O Sav - ior, child of Mar - y, who felt our hu - man

sprung! Of Jes - se's lin - eage com - ing as
mind; with Mar - y we be - hold it, the
air, dis - pels with glo - rious splen - dor the
woe; O Sav - ior, king of glo - ry, who

seers of old have sung, it came, a flow'r so bright, a -
vir - gin moth - er kind. To show God's love a - right, she
dark-ness ev - 'ry - where. True man, yet ver - y God, from
dost our weak - ness know: bring us at length, we pray, to

mid the cold of win - ter, when half-spent was the night.
bore to us a Sav - ior, when half-spent was the night.
sin and death he saves us and light-ens ev - 'ry load.
the bright courts of heav - en and in - to end - less day.

Text: German carol, 15th cent.; tr. Theodore Baker, 1851–1934, sts. 1–2; Harriet R. Krauth, 1845–1925, st. 3; John C. Mattes, 1876–1948, st. 4
Music: *Alte catholische geistliche Kirchengesänge*, Köln, 1599; arr. Michael Praetorius, 1571–1621

ES IST EIN ROS
7 6 7 6 6 7

All My Heart Again Rejoices

1 All my heart a - gain re - joic - es as I hear, far and
2 Je - sus' voice from low - ly man - ger soft - ly thus calls to
3 Come, then, let us has - ten yon - der; here let all, great and
4 You, dear Lord, I'll ev - er cher - ish; though my breath fail in

near, sweet-est an - gel voic - es; "Christ is born," their choirs are
us: "You are safe from dan - ger; come and see; from all that
small, kneel in awe and won - der; love him who with love is
death, I will nev - er per - ish: by your side in light e -

sing - ing, till the air ev - 'ry - where now with joy is ring - ing.
grieves you you are freed; all you need I will sure - ly give you."
yearn - ing; hail the star that from far bright with hope is burn - ing.
ter - nal I shall be end - less - ly filled with joy su - per - nal.

Text: Paul Gerhardt, 1607–1676; tr. Catherine Winkworth, 1827–1878, alt.
Music: Johann G. Ebeling, 1637–1676

WARUM SOLLT ICH
866 866

274

On Christmas Night

1 On Christ-mas night all Chris-tians sing to hear the news the
2 Then why should we on earth be sad, since our re - deem - er
3 When sin de - parts be - fore his face, then life and health come
4 All out of dark - ness we have light, which made the an - gels

an - gels bring. On Christ - mas night all Chris - tians sing to
made us glad? Then why should we on earth be sad, since
in its place. When sin de - parts be - fore his face, then
sing this night. All out of dark - ness we have light, which

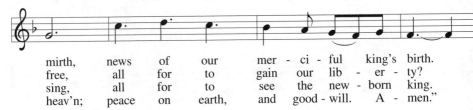

hear the news the an - gels bring: news of great joy, news of great
our re - deem - er made us glad, when from our sin he set us
life and health come in its place. An - gels re - joice with us and
made the an - gels sing this night: "Glo - ry to God in high - est

mirth, news of our mer - ci - ful king's birth.
free, all for to gain our lib - er - ty?
sing, all for to see the new - born king.
heav'n; peace on earth, and good - will. A - men."

Text: Luke Wadding, d. 1686, alt.
Music: English traditional

SUSSEX CAROL
8 8 8 8 8 8

275

Angels, from the Realms of Glory

1 An - gels, from the realms of glo - ry, wing your flight o'er all the earth;
2 Shep-herds, in the fields a - bid-ing, watch-ing o'er your flocks by night,
3 Sa - ges, leave your con - tem-pla-tions, bright-er vi - sions beam a - far;
4 All cre - a - tion, join in prais-ing God, the Fa - ther, Spir - it, Son,

Text: James Montgomery, 1771–1854, alt., sts. 1–3; *Salisbury Hymn Book*, 1857, st. 4
Music: Henry T. Smart, 1813–1879

REGENT SQUARE
8 7 8 7 8 7

once you sang cre - a - tion's sto - ry, now pro - claim Mes - si - ah's birth:
God with us is now re - sid - ing, yon - der shines the in - fant light.
seek the great de - sire of na - tions, you have seen his na - tal star.
ev - er - more your voic - es rais - ing to the e - ter - nal Three in One.

Refrain

Come and wor-ship, come and wor-ship, wor-ship Christ, the new-born king.

Infant Holy, Infant Lowly 276

1 In - fant ho - ly, in - fant low - ly, for his bed a cat - tle stall;
2 Flocks were sleep-ing, shep-herds keep-ing vig - il till the morn-ing new

ox - en low - ing, lit - tle know-ing Christ the child is Lord of all.
saw the glo - ry, heard the sto - ry, tid - ings of a gos - pel true.

Swift-ly wing-ing, an - gels sing-ing, bells are ring-ing, tid - ings bring-ing:
Thus re - joic - ing, free from sor - row, prais-es voic-ing, greet the mor - row:

Christ the child is Lord of all! Christ the child is Lord of all!
Christ the child was born for you! Christ the child was born for you!

Text: Polish carol; tr. Edith M. G. Reed, 1885–1933, alt.
Music: Polish carol

W ŻŁOBIE LEŻY
87 87 88 77

277

Away in a Manger

1 A - way in a man - ger, no crib for his bed, the lit - tle Lord
2 The cat - tle are low - ing; the ba - by a - wakes, but lit - tle Lord
3 Be near me, Lord Je - sus; I ask you to stay close by me for -

Je - sus laid down his sweet head; the stars in the bright sky looked
Je - sus, no cry - ing he makes. I love you, Lord Je - sus; look
ev - er and love me, I pray. Bless all the dear chil - dren in

down where he lay, the lit - tle Lord Je - sus a - sleep on the hay.
down from the sky and stay by my cra - dle till morn - ing is nigh.
your ten - der care and fit us for heav - en, to live with you there.

Text: North American, 19th cent.
Music: James R. Murray, 1841–1905

AWAY IN A MANGER
11 11 11 11

Away in a Manger

1 A - way in a man - ger, no crib for his bed,
2 The cat - tle are low - ing; the ba - by a - wakes,
3 Be near me, Lord Je - sus; I ask you to stay

the lit - tle Lord Je - sus laid down his sweet head;
but lit - tle Lord Je - sus, no cry - ing he makes.
close by me for - ev - er and love me, I pray.

the stars in the bright sky looked down where he lay,
I love you, Lord Je - sus; look down from the sky
Bless all the dear chil - dren in your ten - der care

the lit - tle Lord Je - sus a - sleep on the hay.
and stay by my cra - dle till morn - ing is nigh.
and fit us for heav - en, to live with you there.

Text: North American, 19th cent.
Music: William J. Kirkpatrick, 1838–1921; arr. David Willcocks, b. 1919
Arr. © Oxford University Press

CRADLE SONG
11 11 11 11

279   O Little Town of Bethlehem

1 O lit - tle town of Beth - le - hem, how still we see thee lie!
2 For Christ is born of Mar - y, and, gath - ered all a - bove
3 How si - lent - ly, how si - lent - ly the won - drous gift is giv'n!
4 O ho - ly child of Beth - le - hem, de - scend to us, we pray;

A - bove thy deep and dream-less sleep the si - lent stars go by;
while mor-tals sleep, the an - gels keep their watch of won-d'ring love.
So God im-parts to hu - man hearts the bless - ings of his heav'n.
cast out our sin, and en - ter in, be born in us to - day.

yet in thy dark streets shin - eth the ev - er - last - ing light.
O morn-ing stars, to - geth - er pro - claim the ho - ly birth,
No ear may hear his com - ing; but, in this world of sin,
We hear the Christ-mas an - gels the great glad tid - ings tell;

The hopes and fears of all the years are met in thee to - night.
and prais - es sing to God the king, and peace to all the earth!
where meek souls will re - ceive him, still the dear Christ en - ters in.
oh, come to us, a - bide with us, our Lord Im - man - u - el!

Text: Phillips Brooks, 1835–1893
Music: Lewis H. Redner, 1831–1908

ST. LOUIS
8 6 8 6 7 6 8 6

Midnight Stars Make Bright the Skies

Mingxing canlan ye wei yang

280

1 *Ming - xing can - lan ye wei yang,* *Bo - li - heng cheng*
2 *Ming - xing can - lan ye wei yang,* *gu - deng ying - ying*
1 Mid - night stars make bright the skies, Beth - le - hem in
2 Mid - night slum - ber lies o'er all, one lone bright lamp

zai shui - xiang; *ye - wai mu - ren*
zhao ke - chuang; *qu lai jiu - bu*
slum - ber lies: glis - t'ning heav'n sends
lights the stall. Choose old cloth - ing,

jian yi - xiang, tian - shang jiao - ran fa da - guang;
zuo qiang - pao, ma - cao quan dang yu - er - chuang;
forth a great light, shep - herds see a won - drous sight!
wrap him warm - ly, man - ger shall his cra - dle be.

tian - shi lie - dui tong ge - chang, mu - ren jian zhi xian jing - huang;
wei yu jiu - shi zheng xian - ni, dao cheng ren - shen zhen - li zhang;
An - gel ranks in cho - rus sing. Silk - en sounds from heav - en ring.
Born to save us from our sin, Word made flesh, our lives to win,

hu - wen lun - yin ban jiu - xiao, xuan - yan Sheng - zi jiang xia - fang:
cai li di - zuo lin xia - jie, ren - shih jian - xin yi bei - chang.
Fright-ened shep - herds hear them say: "Christ is born on earth to - day!"
came to earth from heav - en's throne, mor - tals' sin to bear a - lone.

Refrain

Zhi - gao rong - yao gui Shang - zhu, quan - di ren - min fu wu - jiang.
Glo - ry be to God on high, blest are all be - neath the sky.

Text: Jing-qiu Yang, 1912–1966; tr. Mildred A. Wiant, 1898–2001
Music: Qi-fang Liang, b. 1934
Text and music © 1977 Chinese Christian Literature Council Ltd., Hong Kong

HUAN-SHA-XI
7 7 7 7 D and refrain

Silent Night, Holy Night!
Stille Nacht, heilige Nacht!

281

Stil - le Nacht, hei - li-ge Nacht! Al - les schläft,
1 Si - lent night, ho - ly night! All is calm,
2 Si - lent night, ho - ly night! Shep - herds quake
3 Si - lent night, ho - ly night! Son of God,

ein - sam wacht nur das trau - te, hoch - hei - li - ge Paar.
all is bright round yon vir - gin moth - er and child.
at the sight; glo - ries stream from heav - en a - far,
love's pure light ra - diant beams from your ho - ly face,

Hol - der Kna - be im lok - ki-gen Haar, schlaf in himm - li-scher
Ho - ly In - fant, so ten - der and mild, sleep in heav - en-ly
heav'n-ly hosts . . . sing, al - le - lu - ia! Christ, the Sav - ior, is
with the dawn of re - deem - ing grace, Je - sus, Lord, at your

Ruh, schlaf in himm - li - scher Ruh.
peace, sleep in heav - en-ly peace.
born! Christ, the Sav - ior, is born!
birth, Je - sus, Lord, at your birth.

Text: Joseph Mohr, 1792–1849; tr. John F. Young, 1820–1885
Music: Franz Gruber, 1787–1863

STILLE NACHT
Irregular

It Came upon the Midnight Clear

282

1 It came up-on the mid-night clear, that glo - rious song of old,
2 Still through the clo - ven skies they come with peace-ful wings un - furled,
3 And you, be - neath life's crush-ing load, whose forms are bend - ing low,
4 For lo! The days are has - t'ning on, by proph-ets seen of old,

from an - gels bend - ing near the earth to touch their harps of gold:
and still their heav'n-ly mu - sic floats o'er all the wea - ry world.
who toil a - long the climb-ing way with pain - ful steps and slow:
when with the ev - er - cir - cling years shall come the time fore - told,

"Peace on the earth, good will to all, from heav'n's all - gra - cious king."
A - bove its sad and low - ly plains they bend on hov - 'ring wing,
look now, for glad and gold-en hours come swift - ly on the wing;
when peace shall o - ver all the earth its an - cient splen-dors fling,

The world in sol - emn still-ness lay to hear the an - gels sing.
and ev - er o'er its ba - bel sounds the bless-ed an - gels sing.
oh, rest be - side the wea - ry road and hear the an - gels sing!
and all the world give back the song which now the an - gels sing.

Text: Edmund H. Sears, 1810–1876
Music: Richard S. Willis, 1819–1900

CAROL
CMD

283

O Come, All Ye Faithful

1 O come, all ye faith-ful, joy-ful and tri - um-phant! O
2 The high - est, most ho - ly, light of light e - ter - nal,
3 Sing, choirs of an - gels, sing in ex-ul - ta - tion,
4 Yea, Lord, we greet thee, born this hap-py morn - ing;

come ye, O come ye to Beth - le - hem;
born of a vir - gin, a mor - tal he comes;
sing, all ye cit-i-zens of heav - en a - bove!
Je - sus, to thee be . . . glo - ry giv'n!

come and be - hold him, born the king of an - gels:
Son of the Fa - ther now in flesh ap - pear - ing!
Glo - ry to God . . . . in . . . the . . . high - est:
Word of the Fa - ther, now in flesh ap - pear - ing:

Refrain

Ve - ni - te a - do - re - mus, ve - ni - te a - do - re - mus,
O come, let us a - dore him, O come, let us a - dore him,

Text: attr. John Francis Wade, 1711–1786; tr. Frederick Oakeley, 1802–1880, sts. 1, 3–4;
   tr. unknown, st. 2
Music: attr. John Francis Wade

ADESTE FIDELES
Irregular

ve - ni - te a - do - re - mus   Do - mi - num.
O come, let us a - dore him,   Christ the Lord!

'Twas in the Moon of Wintertime   284

1 'Twas in the moon of win - ter - time when all the birds had fled, that
2 With - in a lodge of bro - ken bark the ten - der babe was found; a
3 The ear - liest moon of win - ter - time is not so round and fair as
4 O chil - dren of the for - est free, the an - gel - song is true; the

*God the Lord of all the earth sent an - gel choirs in - stead; be -
rag - ged robe of rab - bit skin en - wrapped his beau - ty round; but
was the ring of glo - ry on the help - less in - fant there. The
ho - ly child of earth and heav'n is born to - day for you. Come,

fore their light the stars grew dim, and wan - d'ring hunt - ers heard the hymn:
as the hunt - er braves drew nigh, the an - gel song rang loud and high:
chiefs from far be - fore him knelt with gifts of fox and bea - ver pelt.
kneel be - fore the ra - diant boy, who brings you beau - ty, peace, and joy.

Refrain

Je - sus your king is born! Je - sus is born, in ex - cel - sis glo - ri - a!

* original: "mighty Gitchi Manitou"

Text: Jean de Brébeuf, 1593–1649; tr. Jesse E. Middleton, 1872–1960, alt.
Music: French folk tune, c. 16th cent.
Text © 1927 The Frederick Harris Music Company

UNE JEUNE PUCELLE
86 86 88 and refrain

285

Peace Came to Earth

1 Peace came to earth at last that cho-sen night
2 And who could be the same for hav-ing held
3 You show the Fa-ther none has ev-er seen,
4 How else could I have known you, O my God!

when an-gels clove the sky with song and light
the in-fant in their arms, and lat-er felt
in flesh and blood you bore our griefs and pains,
How else could I have loved you, O my God!

and God em-bod-ied love and sheathed his might—
the wound-ed hands and side, all doubts dis-pelled—
in bread and wine you vis-it us a-gain—
How else could I em-brace you, O my God!

Who could but gasp: Im-man-u-el!
Who could but sigh: Im-man-u-el!
Who could but see Im-man-u-el!
Who could but pray: Im-man-u-el!

Who could but sing: Im-man-u-el!
Who could but shout: Im-man-u-el!
Who could but thrill: Im-man-u-el!
Who could but praise Im-man-u-el!

Text: Jaroslav J. Vajda, b. 1919
Music: Paul Manz, b. 1919
Text © 1984 Concordia Publishing House
Music © 1991 Birnamwood Publications, a div. of MorningStar Music Publishers, Inc.

SCHNEIDER
10 10 10 8 8

Your Little Ones, Dear Lord

286

1 Your lit - tle ones, dear Lord, are we, and
2 With songs we has - ten you to greet, and
3 Oh, draw us whol - ly to you, Lord, and
4 Un - til at last we too pro - claim, with

come your low - ly bed to see; en - light - en ev - 'ry
kiss the ground be - fore your feet. Oh, bless - ed hour, oh,
to us all your grace ac - cord; true faith and love to
all your saints, your glo - rious name; in par - a - dise our

soul and mind, that we the way to you may find.
sweet-est night that gave you birth, our soul's de - light.
us im - part, that we may hold you in our heart.
songs re - new, and praise you as the an - gels do.

Text: Hans A. Brorson, 1694–1764; tr. Harriet Krauth Spaeth, 1845–1925, alt.
Music: Johann A. P. Schulz, 1747–1800

HER KOMMER DINE ARME SMÅ
LM

287   Let All Together Praise Our God

1 Let all to - geth - er praise our God be - fore the
2 From God's right hand the Son de - scends, is born an
3 O ten - der Child, you veil in flesh the splen - dor
4 Your moth - er feeds you ten - der - ly, sings you a

high - est throne; to - day God o - pens heav'n a - gain and
in - fant small, and lies in pov - er - ty, his bed a
of your might; a ser - vant's garb now wraps the one who
lul - la - by, while an - gels, hail - ing Da - vid's heir, your

sends the on - ly Son, and sends the on - ly Son.
man - ger in a stall, a man - ger in a stall.
clothed the sky with light, who clothed the sky with light.
glo - ry mag - ni - fy, your glo - ry mag - ni - fy.

5 A wonderful exchange you make:
   you take our flesh and blood,
   and in return give us to share
   the shining realm of God,
   the shining realm of God.

6 Unlock the door again today
   that leads to paradise;
   the angel bars the way no more.
   To God let praises rise,
   to God let praises rise!

Text: Nikolaus Herman, 1480–1561; tr. hymnal version
Music: Nikolaus Herman
Text © 2006 Augsburg Fortress

LOBT GOTT, IHR CHRISTEN
86 866

Good Christian Friends, Rejoice

288

1 Good Chris-tian friends, re - joice with heart and soul and voice;
2 Good Chris-tian friends, re - joice with heart and soul and voice;
3 Good Chris-tian friends, re - joice with heart and soul and voice;

give ye heed to what we say: Je - sus Christ is born to - day;
now ye hear of end - less bliss: Je - sus Christ was born for this!
now ye need not fear the grave; Je - sus Christ was born to save!

ox and ass be - fore him bow, and he is in the man-ger now.
He has o - pened heav-en's door, and we are blest for - ev - er - more.
Calls you one and calls you all to gain the ev - er - last-ing hall.

Christ is born to - day! Christ is born to - day!
Christ was born for this! Christ was born for this!
Christ was born to save! Christ was born to save!

Text: Medieval Latin carol; tr. John Mason Neale, 1818–1866
Music: German carol, 14th cent.; arr. Robert L. Pearsall, 1795–1856

IN DULCI JUBILO
66 77 78 55

289   Angels We Have Heard on High

1 An - gels we have heard on high, sweet - ly sing - ing o'er the plains,
2 Shep-herds, why this ju - bi - lee? Why your joy - ous strains pro - long?
3 Come to Beth - le - hem and see him whose birth the an - gels sing;

and the moun-tains in re - ply, ech - o - ing their joy - ous strains.
What the glad-some tid - ings be which in - spire your heav'n - ly song?
come, a - dore on bend - ed knee Christ the Lord, the new - born king.

Refrain

Glo - ri - a

in ex - cel - sis De - o; glo -

Text: French carol; tr. H. F. Hemy, *The Crown of Jesus Music*, 1864
Music: French carol; arr. Edward S. Barnes, 1887–1958

GLORIA
7 7 7 7 and refrain

ri - a   in ex-cel-sis   De -   o.

Go Tell It on the Mountain   290

Refrain

Go   tell   it on the moun - tain,   o - ver the hills and ev - 'ry - where;

go   tell   it on the moun - tain   that   Je - sus   Christ is   born!

1 While shep-herds kept   their watch-ing   o'er   si - lent flocks by   night,
2 The   shep-herds feared and trem-bled   when, lo,   a - bove the   earth
3 Down in   a   lone - ly man - ger   the   hum - ble Christ was   born;

Refrain

be - hold, through-out the   heav-ens   there shone a   ho - ly   light.
rang out   the   an - gel   cho - rus   that hailed our Sav - ior's birth.
and God   sent   us   sal - va - tion   that bless - ed Christ-mas morn.

Text: African American spiritual, refrain; John W. Work Jr., 1872–1925, stanzas, alt.
Music: African American spiritual

GO TELL IT
78 76 76 76

291 Let Our Gladness Have No End

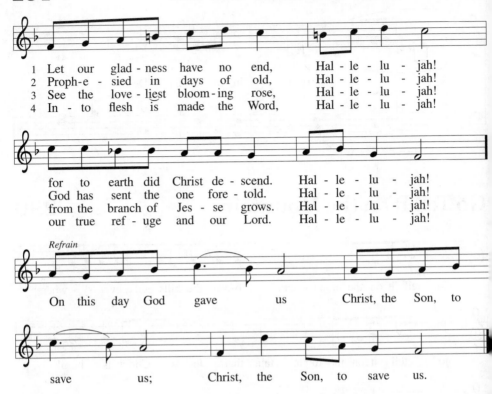

1 Let our glad - ness have no end, Hal - le - lu - jah!
2 Proph-e - sied in days of old, Hal - le - lu - jah!
3 See the love - liest bloom - ing rose, Hal - le - lu - jah!
4 In - to flesh is made the Word, Hal - le - lu - jah!

for to earth did Christ de - scend. Hal - le - lu - jah!
God has sent the one fore - told. Hal - le - lu - jah!
from the branch of Jes - se grows. Hal - le - lu - jah!
our true ref - uge and our Lord. Hal - le - lu - jah!

Refrain

On this day God gave us Christ, the Son, to

save us; Christ, the Son, to save us.

Text: Bohemian carol, 15th cent.; tr. unknown
Music: Bohemian carol, 15th cent.

NARODIL SE KRISTUS PÁN
7 4 7 4 6 6 6

292 Love Has Come

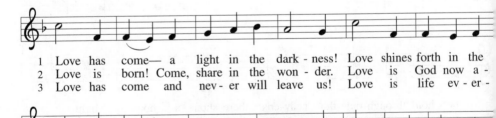

1 Love has come— a light in the dark - ness! Love shines forth in the
2 Love is born! Come, share in the won - der. Love is God now a -
3 Love has come and nev - er will leave us! Love is life ev - er -

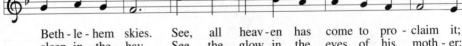

Beth - le - hem skies. See, all heav -en has come to pro - claim it;
sleep in the hay. See the glow in the eyes of his moth - er;
last - ing and free. Love is Je - sus with - in and a - mong us.

Text: Ken Bible, b. 1950
Music: F. Seguin, *Recueil de noëls composés en langue provençale,* 1856
Text © 1996 Integrity's Hosanna! Music

UN FLAMBEAU
9 9 10 9 9 8

hear how their song of joy a - ris - es: Love! Love! Born un - to
what is the name her heart is say - ing? Love! Love! Love is the
Love is the peace our hearts are seek - ing. Love! Love! Love is the

you, a Sav - ior! Love! Love! Glo - ry to God on high.
name she whis - pers; Love! Love! Je - sus, Im - man - u - el.
gift of Christ - mas. Love! Love! Praise to you, God on high!

That Boy-Child of Mary 293

Refrain

That boy - child of Mar - y was born in a sta - ble,

a man - ger his cra - dle in Beth - le - hem.

1 What shall we call him, child of the man - ger?
2 His name is Je - sus, God ev - er with us,
3 How can he save us, how can he help us,
4 Gift of the Fa - ther, to hu - man moth - er,

Refrain

What name is giv - en in Beth - le - hem?
God giv - en for us in Beth - le - hem.
born here a - mong us in Beth - le - hem?
makes him our broth - er in Beth - le - hem.

5 One with the Father, he is our Savior,
   heaven-sent helper in Bethlehem.
   Refrain

6 Gladly we praise him, love and adore him,
   give ourselves to him in Bethlehem.
   Refrain

Text: Tom Colvin, 1925–2000
Music: Malawi traditional; adapt. Tom Colvin
Text and music © 1969 Hope Publishing Company

BLANTYRE
5 5 5 4 and refrain

294

In the Bleak Midwinter

1 In the bleak mid - win - ter, frost - y wind made moan,
2 Heav - en can - not hold him, nor . . . . earth sus - tain;
3 What . . . can I give him, poor . . . . as I am?

earth stood hard as i - ron, wa - ter like a stone;
heav'n and earth shall flee a - way when he comes to reign;
If I were a shep - herd I would bring a lamb;

snow had fall - en, snow on snow, snow on snow,
in the bleak mid - win - ter a sta - ble place suf - ficed
if I were a wise . . . man I would do my part;

in the bleak mid - win - ter, long a - go.
the Lord . . . God al - might - y, Je - sus Christ.
yet what I can I give him— give my heart.

Text: Christina Georgina Rossetti, 1830–1894
Music: Gustav Holst, 1874–1934

CRANHAM
Irregula

Of the Father's Love Begotten

1 Of the Fa - ther's love be - got - ten ere the worlds be -
2 Oh, that birth for - ev - er bless - ed, when the vir - gin,
3 This is he whom seers in old time chant - ed of with
4 Let the heights of heav'n a - dore him; an - gel hosts, his
5 Christ, to thee, with God the Fa - ther, and, O Ho - ly

gan to be, he is Al - pha and O - me - ga,
full of grace, by the Ho - ly Ghost con - ceiv - ing,
one ac - cord, whom the voic - es of the proph - ets
prais - es sing; pow'rs, do - min - ions, bow be - fore him
Ghost, to thee, hymn and chant and high thanks - giv - ing

he the source, the end - ing he, of the things that are, that
bore the Sav - ior of our race, and the babe, the world's re -
prom-ised in their faith - ful word; now he shines, the long - ex -
and ex - tol our God and King; let no tongue on earth be
and un - wea - ried prais - es be: hon - or, glo - ry, and do -

have been, and that fu - ture years shall see,
deem - er, first re - vealed his sa - cred face,
pect - ed; let cre - a - tion praise its Lord
si - lent, ev - 'ry voice in con - cert ring
min - ion, and e - ter - nal vic - to - ry

ev - er - more and ev - er - more.
ev - er - more and ev - er - more.
ev - er - more and ev - er - more.
ev - er - more and ev - er - more.
ev - er - more and ev - er - more! A - men.

Text: Marcus Aurelius Clemens Prudentius, 348–413; tr. composite
Music: Plainsong mode V, 13th cent.

DIVINUM MYSTERIUM
8 7 8 7 8 7 7

296

What Child Is This

1 What child is this, who, laid to rest, on Mar-y's lap is sleep-ing?
2 Why lies he in such mean es-tate where ox and ass are feed-ing?
3 So bring him in-cense, gold, and myrrh; come, peas-ant, king, to own him.

Whom an-gels greet with an-thems sweet while shep-herds watch are keep-ing?
Good Chris-tian, fear; for sin-ners here the si-lent Word is plead-ing.
The King of kings sal-va-tion brings; let lov-ing hearts en-throne him.

This, this is Christ the king, whom shep-herds guard and an-gels sing;
Nails, spear shall pierce him through, the cross be borne for me, for you;
Raise, raise the song on high, the vir-gin sings her lul-la-by;

haste, haste to bring him laud, the babe, the son of Mar-y!
hail, hail the Word made flesh, the babe, the son of Mar-y!
joy, joy, for Christ is born, the babe, the son of Mar-y!

Text: William C. Dix, 1837–1898
Music: English ballad, 16th cent.

GREENSLEEVES
8787686

Jesus, What a Wonderful Child

Jesus, Jesus, oh, what a won-der-ful child.

Jesus, Jesus, so ho-ly, meek, and

mild; new life, new hope the child will bring.

Lis-ten to the an-gels sing: "Glo-ry, glo-ry,

glo - ry," let the heav - ens ring!

Text: African American traditional, alt.
Music: African American traditional; arr. Jeffrey Radford, 1953–2002
Arr. © 1992 Pilgrim Press

WONDERFUL CHILD
PM

The Bells of Christmas

Det kimer nu til julefest

	Det	*ki - mer*	*nu*	*til*	*ju - le - fest,*	*det*	*ki - mer*
1	The bells	of	Christ - mas	chime	once more;	the	heav'n - ly
2	This world,	though	wide and	far	out - spread,	could	scarce - ly
3	Now let	us	go with	qui - et	mind,	the	swad - dled
4	Oh, join	with	me, in	glad - ness	sing,	to	keep our

	for	*den*	*høj - e*	*gæst,*	*som*	*steg*	*til*	*la - ve*
	guest	is	at the	door.	He	comes	to	earth - ly
	find	for	you a	bed.	Your	cra - dle	was	a
	babe	with	shep - herds	find,	to	gaze	on	him who
	Christ - mas	with	our	king,	un - til	our	song,	from

	hyt - ter	*ned*	*med*	*nyt - års - ga - ver:*	*fryd*	*og*	*fred.*
	dwell - ings	still	with	new year gifts	of	peace, good	will.
	man - ger	stall,	no	pearl nor silk	nor	king - ly	hall.
	glad - dens	them,	the	love - liest flow'r	of	Jes - se's	stem.
	lov - ing	souls,	like	rush - ing might - y	wa - ter	rolls!

5 O patriarchs' Joy, O prophets' Song,
   O Dayspring bright, awaited long,
   O Son of Man, incarnate Word,
   great David's Son, great David's Lord:

6 Come, Jesus, glorious heav'nly guest,
   and keep your Christmas in our breast;
   then David's harpstrings, hushed so long,
   shall swell our jubilee of song.

Text: Nikolai F. S. Grundtvig, 1783–1872; tr. Charles Porterfield Krauth, 1823–1883, alt.
Music: Carl C. N. Balle, 1806–1855

DET KIMER NU TIL JULEFEST
LM

Cold December Flies Away

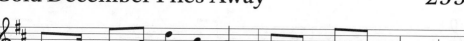

1 Cold De - cem - ber flies a - way at the rose - red splen - dor.
2 In the hope - less time of sin shad - ows deep had fall - en.
3 Now the bud has come to bloom, and the world a - wak - ens.

A - pril's crown - ing glo - ry breaks while the whole world won - ders
All the world lay un - der death. Eyes were closed in sleep - ing.
In the lil - y's pur - est flow'r dwells a won - drous fra - grance.

at the ho - ly un - seen pow'r of the tree which bears the
But, when all seemed lost in night, came the sun whose gold - en
And it spreads to all the earth from the mo - ment of its

flow'r. On the bless - ed tree blooms the red - dest flow'r. On the tree blooms the
light brings un - end - ing joy, brings the end - less joy of our hope, high - est
birth; and its beau - ty lives. In the flow'r it lives, in the flow'r, and it

rose here in love's own gar - den, full and strong in glo - ry.
hope, of our hope's bright dawn - ing, Son be - lov'd of heav - en.
spreads in its heav'n - ly bright - ness sweet per - fume de - light - ful.

Text: Catalonian carol; tr. Howard Hawhee, b. 1953
Music: Catalonian carol
Text © 1978 Lutheran Book of Worship, admin. Augsburg Fortress

EL DESEMBRE CONGELAT
PM

300

The First Noel

1 The first No - el the an - gel did say was to
2 They look - ed up and saw . . a star shin-ing
3 And by the light of that . . same star three . .
4 This star drew near to the . . north - west, o'er . .
5 Then en - tered in those wise . . men three, full . .

cer - tain poor shep - herds in fields as they lay; in fields where
in . . . the east . . be - yond . . them far; and to the
wise . . men came . . from coun - try far; to seek for a
Beth - le - hem . . it took . . its rest; and there it
rev - 'rent - ly . . . up - on . . . their knee, and of - fered

they lay, keep - ing their sheep, on a cold win - ter's
earth it gave . . . great light, and . . so it con -
king was their . . . in - tent, and to fol - low the
did both stop . . . and stay right . . o - ver the
there in his . . . pres - ence their . . gold, ... and

Text: English traditional
Music: English traditional; arr. John Stainer, 1840–1901

THE FIRST NOWEL
Irregula

night that was so deep.
tin-ued both day and night.
star wher - ev - er it went. No - el, No - el, No -
place where Je - sus lay.
myrrh, and frank - in - cense.

el, No - el! Born is the King of Is - ra - el.

301 Bright and Glorious Is the Sky

1 Bright and glo - rious is the sky, ra - diant are the
2 On that ho - ly Christ - mas night through the dark - ness
3 Sa - ges from the east a - far, when they saw this
4 Him they found in Beth - le - hem, yet he wore no

heav - ens high where the gold - en stars are shin - ing.
beamed a light; all the stars a - bove were pal - ing,
won - drous star, went to find the king of na - tions
di - a - dem; there they saw a maid - en low - ly

All their rays to earth in - clin - ing beck - on us to
all their lus - ter slow - ly fail - ing as the won - drous
and to of - fer their ob - la - tions to the child, the
with an in - fant pure and ho - ly rest - ing in her

heav'n a - bove, beck - on us to heav'n a - bove.
star drew nigh, as the won - drous star drew nigh.
new - born king, to the child, the new - born king.
lov - ing arms, rest - ing in her lov - ing arms.

Text: Nikolai F. S. Grundtvig, 1783–1872; tr. Jens Christian Aaberg, 1877–1970, alt.
Music: Danish, 19th cent.
Text © 1958 *Service Book and Hymnal*, admin. Augsburg Fortress

DEJLIG ER DEN HIMMEL BL.
77 88 7

5 Guided by the star, they found
him whose praise the ages sound.
We too have a star to guide us,
which forever will provide us
with the light to find our Lord,
with the light to find our Lord.

6 And this star, as bright as day,
that will never lead astray
with its message so appealing,
is the word of God, revealing
Christ, the way, the truth, the life,
Christ, the way, the truth, the life.

As with Gladness Men of Old 302

1 As with glad - ness men of old did the guid-ing star be - hold;
2 As with joy - ful steps they sped, Sav - ior, to thy low - ly bed,
3 As they of - fered gifts most rare at thy cra - dle, rude and bare,
4 Ho - ly Je - sus, ev - 'ry day keep us in the nar - row way;
5 In the heav'n - ly coun-try bright need they no cre - a - ted light;

as with joy they hailed its light, lead - ing on - ward, beam-ing bright;
there to bend the knee be - fore thee, whom heav'n and earth a - dore;
so may we with ho - ly joy, pure and free from sin's al - loy,
and when earth-ly things are past, bring our ran - somed souls at last
thou its light, its joy, its crown, thou its sun which goes not down;

so, most gra-cious Lord, may we ev - er - more be led by thee.
so may we with will - ing feet ev - er seek thy mer - cy seat.
all our cost-liest trea - sures bring, Christ, to thee, our heav'n-ly king.
where they need no star to guide, where no clouds thy glo - ry hide.
there for - ev - er may we sing al - le - lu - ias to our king.

Text: William C. Dix, 1837–1898, alt.
Music: Conrad Kocher, 1786–1872

DIX
7 7 7 7 7 7

303 Brightest and Best of the Stars

1. Bright-est and best of the stars of the morn - ing,
2. Cold on his cra - dle the dew - drops are shin - ing;
3. What shall we give him, in cost - ly de - vo - tion?
4. Vain - ly we of - fer each am - ple ob - la - tion,
5. Bright-est and best of the stars of the morn - ing,

dawn on our dark - ness and lend us your aid.
low lies his head with the beasts of the stall;
Shall we bring in - cense and of - f'rings di - vine,
vain - ly with gifts would his fa - vor se - cure;
dawn on our dark - ness and lend us your aid.

Star of the east, the ho - ri - zon a - dorn - ing,
an - gels a - dore him in slum - ber re - clin - ing,
gems of the moun - tain and pearls of the o - cean,
rich - er by far is the heart's ad - o - ra - tion,
Star of the east, the ho - ri - zon a - dorn - ing,

guide where our in - fant re - deem - er is laid.
mak - er and mon - arch and sav - ior of all.
myrrh from the for - est or gold from the mine?
dear - er to God are the prayers of the poor.
guide where our in - fant re - deem - er is laid.

Text: Reginald Heber, 1783–1826, alt.
Music: James P. Harding, 1850–1911, adapt.

MORNING STA
11 10 11 1

Christ, When for Us You Were Baptized   304

1 Christ, when for us you were bap - tized, God's Spir - it on you
2 God called you, "My be - lov - ed Son"; you are God's ser - vant
3 Straight- way and stead - fast un - til death you then o - beyed the
4 Bap - tize us with your Spir - it, Lord; your cross on us be

came, as peace - ful as a dove, and yet as
true, sent to pro - claim the reign of heav'n, God's
call to serve with free and will - ing heart, to
signed, that like - wise in God's ser - vice we may

ur - gent as a flame, as ur - gent as a flame.
ho - ly will to do, God's ho - ly will to do.
give your life for all, to give your life for all.
per - fect free - dom find, may per - fect free - dom find.

Text: F. Bland Tucker, 1895–1984, alt.
Music: Nikolaus Herman, 1480–1561
Text © 1985 The Church Pension Fund

LOBT GOTT, IHR CHRISTEN
86 866

305 When Jesus Came to Jordan

1 When Je - sus came to Jor - dan to be bap-tized by John,
2 He came to share temp - ta - tion, our ut - most woe and loss,
3 Come, Ho - ly Spir - it, aid us to keep the vows we make;

he did not come for par - don but as the Sin - less One.
for us and our sal - va - tion to die up - on the cross.
this ver - y day in - vade us, and ev - 'ry bond-age break.

He came to share re - pen - tance with all who mourn their sins,
So when the dove de - scend - ed on him, the Son of Man,
Come, give our lives di - rec - tion, the gift we cov - et most:

to speak the vi - tal sen - tence with which good news be - gins.
the hid - den years had end - ed, the age of grace be - gan.
to share the res - ur - rec - tion that leads to Pen - te - cost.

Text: Fred Pratt Green, 1903–2000
Music: English folk tune
Text © 1980 Hope Publishing Company

KING'S LYNN
7676D

306 Come, Beloved of the Maker

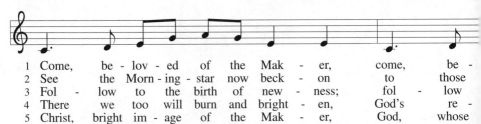

1 Come, be - lov - ed of the Mak - er, come, be -
2 See the Morn - ing - star now beck - on to those
3 Fol - low to the birth of new - ness; fol - low
4 There we too will burn and bright - en, God's re -
5 Christ, bright im - age of the Mak - er, God, whose

Text: Susan Palo Cherwien, b. 1953
Music: David Cherwien, b. 1957
Text © 2001 Susan Palo Cherwien, admin. Augsburg Fortress
Music © 2002 Augsburg Fortress

JIL
878

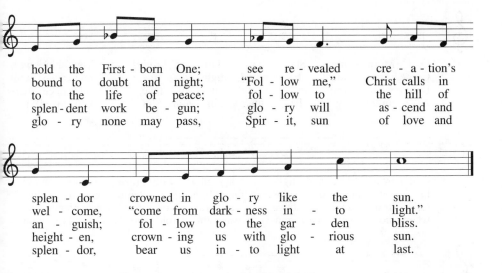

hold	the	First - born	One;	see	re - vealed	cre - a - tion's
bound	to	doubt	and	night;	"Fol - low	me,"	Christ calls	in
to	the	life	of	peace;	fol - low	to	the	hill	of
splen - dent	work	be - gun;	glo - ry	will	as - cend	and
glo - ry	none	may	pass,	Spir - it,	sun	of	love	and

splen - dor	crowned in	glo - ry	like	the	sun.
wel - come,	"come from	dark - ness	in - to	light."
an - guish;	fol - low	to	the	gar - den	bliss.
height - en,	crown - ing	us	with	glo - rious	sun.
splen - dor,	bear	us	in - to	light	at	last.

Light Shone in Darkness   307

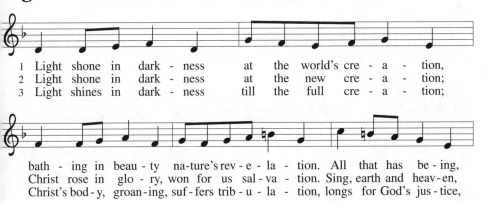

1 Light shone in dark - ness at the world's cre - a - tion,
2 Light shone in dark - ness at the new cre - a - tion;
3 Light shines in dark - ness till the full cre - a - tion;

bath - ing in beau - ty na-ture's rev - e - la - tion. All that has be - ing,
Christ rose in glo - ry, won for us sal - va - tion. Sing, earth and heav - en,
Christ's bod - y, groan-ing, suf - fers trib - u - la - tion, longs for God's jus - tice,

cry in ad - o - ra - tion, "Praise for the light. A - men!"
hymns of ju - bi - la - tion, praise for the light. A - men!
glob - al trans-for - ma - tion, prays for the light. A - men!

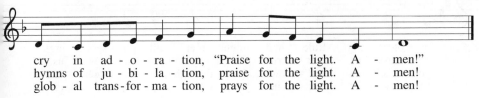

Text: Delores Dufner, OSB, b. 1939
Music: Mark Sedio, b. 1954
Text © 2001, 2003 GIA Publications, Inc.
Music © 2003 Augsburg Fortress

LUX IN TENEBRIS
11 11 11 6

308   O Morning Star, How Fair and Bright!

1 O Morn-ing Star, how fair and bright! You shine with
2 Come, pre-cious dia-mond, light di-vine, and deep with-
3 Lord, when you look on us in love, at once there
4 Al-might-y Fa-ther, in your Son you loved us,

God's own truth and light, a-glow with grace and mer-cy!
in our hearts now shine; there light a flame un-dy-ing!
falls from God a-bove a ray of pur-est plea-sure.
when not yet be-gun was this old earth's foun-da-tion!

Of Ja-cob's line, King Da-vid's son, our Lord and Sav-ior,
In your one bod-y let us be as liv-ing branch-es
Your word and Spir-it, flesh and blood re-fresh our souls with
Your Son has ran-somed us in love to live in him here

you have won our hearts to serve you on-ly! Low-ly,
of a tree, your life our lives sup-ply-ing. Now, though
heav'n-ly food. You are our dear-est trea-sure! Let your
and a-bove: this is your great sal-va-tion. Al-le-

ho-ly! Great and glo-rious, all vic-to-rious, rich
dai-ly earth's deep sad-ness may per-plex us and
mer-cy warm and cheer us! Oh, draw near us! For
lu-ia! Christ the liv-ing, to us giv-ing life

in bless-ing! Rule and might o'er all pos-sess-ing!
dis-tress us, yet with heav'n-ly joy you bless us.
you teach us God's own love through you has reached us.
for-ev-er, keeps us yours and fails us nev-er!

Text: Philipp Nicolai, 1556–1608; tr. *Lutheran Book of Worship*
Music: Philipp Nicolai
Text © 1978 *Lutheran Book of Worship*, admin. Augsburg Fortress

WIE SCHÖN LEUCHTE
P/

5 Oh, let the harps break forth in sound!
Our joy be all with music crowned,
our voices gaily blending!
For Christ goes with us all the way—
today, tomorrow, ev'ry day!
His love is never ending!
Sing out! Ring out!
Jubilation! Exultation!
Tell the story!
Praise to Christ, who reigns in glory!

6 What joy to know, when life is past,
the Lord we love is first and last,
the end and the beginning!
He will one day, oh, glorious grace,
transport us to that happy place
beyond all tears and sinning!
Amen! Amen!
Come, Lord Jesus! Crown of gladness!
We are yearning
for the day of your returning.

The Only Son from Heaven   309

1 The on-ly Son from heav-en, fore-told by an-cient seers,
2 Oh, time of God ap-point-ed, oh, bright and ho-ly morn!
3 A-wak-en, Lord, our spir-it to know and love you more,
4 O Fa-ther, here be-fore you with God the Ho-ly Ghost,

by God the Fa-ther giv-en, in hu-man form ap-pears.
He comes, the king a-noint-ed, the Christ, the vir-gin-born,
in faith to stand un-shak-en, in spir-it to a-dore,
and Je-sus, we a-dore you, O pride of an-gel-host:

No sphere his light con-fin-ing, no star so bright-ly
grim death to van-quish for us, to o-pen heav'n be-
that we, through this world mov-ing, each glimpse of heav-en
be-fore you mor-tals low-ly cry, "Ho-ly, ho-ly,

shin-ing as he, our Morn-ing Star.
fore us and bring us life a-gain.
prov-ing, may reap its full-ness there.
ho-ly, O bless-ed Trin-i-ty!"

Text: Elizabeth Cruciger, 1500–1535; tr. Arthur T. Russell, 1806–1874, alt.
Music: Enchiridion, Erfurt, 1524

HERR CHRIST, DER EINIG GOTTS SOHN
7676776

310

Songs of Thankfulness and Praise

1 Songs of thank-ful - ness and praise, Je - sus, Lord, to thee we raise;
2 Man - i - fest at Jor - dan's stream, proph-et, priest, and king su - preme;
3 Man - i - fest in mak - ing whole weak-ened bod - y, faint-ing soul;
4 Grant us grace to see thee, Lord, pres - ent in thy ho - ly word;

man - i - fest - ed by the star to the sa - ges from a - far,
and at Ca - na wed - ding guest in thy God-head man - i - fest;
man - i - fest in val - iant fight, quell-ing all the dev - il's might;
grace to im - i - tate thee now and be pure, as pure art thou;

branch of roy - al Da - vid's stem in thy birth at Beth - le - hem:
man - i - fest in pow'r di - vine, chang-ing wa - ter in - to wine,
man - i - fest in gra - cious will, ev - er bring-ing good from ill:
that we might be - come like thee at thy great e - piph - a - ny,

an - thems be to thee ad-dressed,
an - thems be to thee ad-dressed,
an - thems be to thee ad-dressed, God in flesh made man - i - fest.
and may praise thee, ev - er blest,

Text: Christopher Wordsworth, 1807–1885, alt.
Music: Jakob Hintze, 1622–1702; arr. Johann Sebastian Bach, 1685–1750

SALZBUR(
7 7 7 7

Hail to the Lord's Anointed

1 Hail to the Lord's a - noint - ed, great Da - vid's great - er Son!
2 You come with res - cue speed - y to those who suf - fer wrong,
3 You shall come down like show - ers up - on the fruit - ful earth;
4 Kings shall fall down be - fore you, and gold and in - cense bring;

Hail, in the time ap - point - ed, your reign on earth be - gun!
to help the poor and need - y, and bid the weak be strong;
love, joy, and hope, like flow - ers, spring in your path to birth.
all na - tions shall a - dore you, your praise all peo - ple sing.

You come to break op - pres - sion, to set the cap - tive
to give them songs for sigh - ing, their dark - ness turn to
Be - fore you on the moun - tains shall peace, the her - ald,
To you shall prayer un - ceas - ing and dai - ly vows as -

free, to take a - way trans - gres - sion and
light, whose souls, con - demned and dy - ing, are
go; and righ - teous - ness in foun - tains from
cend; your king - dom still in - creas - ing, a

rule in eq - ui - ty.
pre - cious in your sight.
hill to val - ley flow.
king - dom with - out end.

Text: James Montgomery, 1771–1854, alt.
Music: Leonhart Schröter, 1540–1602

FREUT EUCH, IHR LIEBEN
7 6 7 6 D

312

Jesus, Come! For We Invite You

1 Je - sus, come! for we in - vite you, guest and mas - ter,
friend and Lord; now, as once at Ca - na's wed - ding,
speak and let us hear your word: lead us through our need or
doubt - ing, hope be born and joy re - stored.

2 Je - sus, come! trans-form our plea - sures, guide us in - to
paths un - known; bring your gifts, com-mand your ser - vants,
let us trust in you a - lone: though your hand may work in
se - cret, all shall see what you have done.

3 Je - sus, come! in new cre - a - tion, heav'n brought near in
pow'r di - vine; give your un - ex - pect - ed glo - ry,
chang-ing wa - ter in - to wine: rouse the faith of your dis -
ci - ples— come, our first and great - est Sign!

4 Je - sus, come! sur - prise our dull - ness, make us will - ing
to re - ceive more than we can yet im - ag - ine,
all the best you have to give: let us find your hid - den
rich - es, taste your love, be - lieve, and live!

Text: Christopher Idle, b. 1938
Music: Harold Friedell, 1905–1958
Text © 1982 Jubilate Hymns, admin. Hope Publishing Company
Music © 1957, 1985 H. W. Gray, admin. CPP/Belwin

UNION SEMINA
87 87 8

Alternate tune: REGENT SQUA

O Lord, Now Let Your Servant

313

1 O Lord, now let your ser - vant de - part in heav'n-ly peace,
2 Then grant that I may fol - low your gleam, O glo - rious Light,

for I have seen the glo - ry of your re - deem - ing grace:
till earth-ly shad-ows scat - ter, and faith is changed to sight;

a light to lead the na - tions un - to your ho - ly hill,
till rap-tured saints shall gath - er up - on that shin-ing shore,

the glo - ry of your peo - ple, your cho - sen Is - ra - el.
where Christ, the bless-ed day - star, shall light them ev - er - more.

Text: Ernest E. Ryden, 1886–1981, alt., based on the Nunc dimittis
Music: Finnish folk tune; arr. hymnal version
Text © 1925 Board of Publication, Lutheran Church in America
arr. © 2006 Augsburg Fortress

KUORTANE
76 76 D

Alternate tune: MUNICH

314

Arise, Your Light Has Come!

1 A - rise, your light has come! The Spir - it's call o - bey;
2 A - rise, your light has come! Fling wide the pris - on door;
3 A - rise, your light has come! All you in sor - row born,
4 A - rise, your light has come! The moun - tains burst in song!

show forth the glo - ry of your God which shines on you to - day.
pro - claim the cap - tive's lib - er - ty, good tid - ings to the poor.
bind up the bro - ken - heart - ed ones and com - fort those who mourn.
Rise up like ea - gles on the wing, God's pow'r will make us strong.

Text: Ruth Duck, b. 1947
Music: William H. Walter, 1825–1893
Text © 1992 GIA Publications, Inc.

FESTAL SONG
S M

315

How Good, Lord, to Be Here

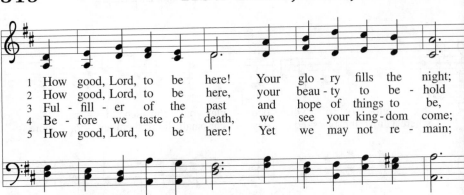

1 How good, Lord, to be here! Your glo - ry fills the night;
2 How good, Lord, to be here, your beau - ty to be - hold;
3 Ful - fill - er of the past and hope of things to be,
4 Be - fore we taste of death, we see your king - dom come;
5 How good, Lord, to be here! Yet we may not re - main;

Text: Joseph A. Robinson, 1858–1933, alt.
Music: W. Mercer, *The Church Psalter and Hymn Book*, 1854

POTSDA
S

your face and gar-ments, like the sun, shine with un-bor-rowed light.
where Mo-ses and E-li-jah stand, your mes-sen-gers of old.
we hail your bod-y glo-ri-fied and our re-demp-tion see.
we long to hold the vi-sion bright and make this hill our home.
but since you bid us leave the mount, come with us to the plain.

Oh, Wondrous Image, Vision Fair 316

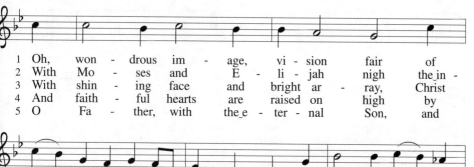

1 Oh, won - drous im - age, vi - sion fair of
2 With Mo - ses and E - li - jah nigh the in -
3 With shin - ing face and bright ar - ray, Christ
4 And faith - ful hearts are raised on high by
5 O Fa - ther, with the e - ter - nal Son, and

glo - ry that the church may share, which Christ up-on the
car - nate Lord holds con-verse high, and from the cloud, the
deigns to man - i - fest to - day what glo - ry shall be
this great vi - sion's mys - ter - y; for which in joy - ful
Ho - ly Spir - it ev - er one, we pray you, bring us

moun-tain shows, where bright - er than the sun he glows!
Ho - ly One says, "This is my be - lov - ed Son."
theirs a - bove who joy in God with per - fect love.
song we raise the voice of prayer, the hymn of praise.
by your grace to see your glo - ry face to face.

Text: Sarum, 15th cent.; tr. John Mason Neale, 1818–1866, alt.
Music: English ballad, 15th cent.

DEO GRACIAS
LM

317   # Jesus on the Mountain Peak

1 Je - sus on the moun-tain peak stands a - lone in
2 Trem-bling at his feet we saw Mo - ses and E -
3 Swift the cloud of glo - ry came, God pro - claim - ing
4 This is God's be - lov - ed Son! Law and proph - ets

glo - ry blaz - ing; let us, if we dare to speak,
li - jah speak - ing. All the proph-ets and the law
in its thun - der Je - sus as the Son by name!
sing be - fore him, first and last and on - ly One.

join the saints and an - gels prais - ing.
shout through them their joy - ful greet - ing:
Na - tions, cry a - loud in won - der:
All cre - a - tion shall a - dore him!

Al - le - lu - ia, al - le - lu - ia!

Text: Brian A. Wren, b. 1936
Music: Mark Sedio, b. 1954
Text © 1977, rev. 1995 Hope Publishing Company
Music © 2006 Augsburg Fortress

BETHOL
7 8 7 8

Alleluia, Song of Gladness

1 Al - le - lu - ia, song of glad - ness, voice of joy that can - not die;
2 Al - le - lu - ia you are sound - ing, true Je - ru - sa - lem and free;
3 Al - le - lu - ia can - not al - ways be our song while here be - low;
4 In our hymns we pray with long - ing: Grant us, bless - ed Trin - i - ty,

al - le - lu - ia is the an - them ev - er dear to choirs on high;
al - le - lu - ia, joy - ful moth - er, bring us to your ju - bi - lee;
al - le - lu - ia our trans - gres - sions make us for a while for - go;
at the last to keep glad Eas - ter with the faith - ful saints on high;

in the house of God a - bid - ing thus they sing e - ter - nal - ly.
here by Bab - y - lon's sad wa - ters mourn - ing ex - iles still are we.
for the sol - emn time is com - ing when our tears for sin shall flow.
there to you for - ev - er sing - ing al - le - lu - ia joy - ful - ly.

Text: Latin hymn, 11th cent.; tr. John Mason Neale, 1818–1866, alt.
Music: John Goss, 1800–1880

PRAISE, MY SOUL
8 7 8 7 8 7

319   O Lord, throughout These Forty Days

1 O Lord, through-out these for-ty days you
2 You strove with Sa-tan, and you won; your
3 Though parched and hun-gry, yet you prayed and
4 Be with us through this sea-son, Lord, and

prayed and kept the fast; in - spire re - pen - tance
faith - ful - ness en - dured; lend us your nerve, your
fixed your mind a - bove; so teach us to de -
all our earth - ly days, that when the fi - nal

for our sin, and free us from our past.
skill and trust in God's e - ter - nal word.
ny our - selves that we may know God's love.
Eas - ter dawns, we join in heav - en's praise.

Text: based on Claudia F. Hernaman, 1838–1898; para. Gilbert E. Doan Jr., b. 1930
Music: A. Davisson, *Kentucky Harmony*, 1816; arr. Theodore A. Beck, 1929–2003
Text © 1978 *Lutheran Book of Worship*, admin. Augsburg Fortress
Arr. © 1969 Concordia Publishing House

CONSOLATIO
C

The Glory of These Forty Days

1 The glo - ry of these for - ty days we cel - e -
2 A - lone and fast - ing Mo - ses saw the lov - ing
3 So Dan - iel trained his mys - tic sight, de - liv - ered
4 Then grant, O God, that we may, too, re - turn in

brate with songs of praise; for Christ, through whom all
God who gave the law; for and to E - li - jah,
from the li - ons' might; and John, the Bride - groom's
fast and prayer to you. Our spir - its strength - en

things were made, him - self has fast - ed and has prayed.
fast - ing, came the steeds and char - i - ots of flame.
friend, be - came the her - ald of Mes - si - ah's name.
with your grace, and give us joy to see your face.

ext: Latin hymn, 11th cent.; tr. Maurice F. Bell, 1862–1947, alt.
usic: J. Klug, *Geistliche Lieder*, 1543
xt © Oxford University Press

ERHALT UNS, HERR
LM

321 Eternal Lord of Love, Behold Your Church

1 E - ter - nal Lord of love, be - hold your church
2 So dai - ly dy - ing to the way of self,
3 If dead in you, so in you we a - rise,

walk - ing once more the pil - grim way of Lent,
so dai - ly liv - ing in your way of love,
you the first - born of all the faith - ful dead;

led by your cloud by day, by night your fire,
we walk the road, Lord Je - sus, that you trod,
and as through ston - y ground the green shoots break,

moved by your love and toward your pres - ence bent:
know - ing our - selves bap - tized in - to your death:
glo - rious in spring - time dress of leaf and flow'r,

Text: Thomas H. Cain, 1931–2003
Music: *Trente quatre pseaumes de David*, Geneva, 1551
Text © Thomas H. Cain

OLD 124T
10 10 10 10 10

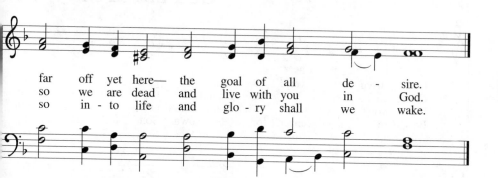

far off yet here— the goal of all de - sire.
so   we   are dead   and live with you in God.
so   in - to life   and glo - ry shall we wake.

Oh, Love, How Deep

322

1 Oh, love, how deep, how broad, how high, be - yond all
2 God sent no an - gel to our race, of high - er
3 For us bap - tized, for us he bore his ho - ly
4 For us he prayed; for us he taught; for us his

thought and fan - ta - sy, that God, the Son of
or of low - er place, but wore the robe of
fast and hun - gered sore; for us temp - ta - tion
dai - ly works he wrought, by words and signs and

God, should take our mor - tal form for mor - tals' sake!
hu - man frame, in Christ our Lord to this world came.
sharp he knew; for us the tempt - er o - ver - threw.
ac - tions thus still seek - ing not him - self, but us.

5 For us by wickedness betrayed,
 for us, in crown of thorns arrayed,
 he bore the shameful cross and death;
 for us he gave his dying breath.

6 For us he rose from death again;
 for us he went on high to reign;
 for us he sent his Spirit here
 to guide, to strengthen, and to cheer.

7 All glory to our Lord and God
 for love so deep, so high, so broad:
 the Trinity whom we adore
 forever and forevermore.

Text: Thomas á Kempis, 1380–1471; tr. Benjamin Webb, 1819–1885, alt.
Music: English ballad, 15th cent.

DEO GRACIAS
LM

323   God Loved the World

1 God loved the world so that he gave his on - ly
2 Christ Je - sus is the ground of faith, who was made
3 If you are ill, if death draws near, this truth your
4 Be of good cheer, for God's own Son for - gives all
5 All glo - ry to the Fa - ther, Son, and Ho - ly

Son the lost to save, that all who would in
flesh and suf - fered death; all who con - fide in
trou - bled heart can cheer: Christ Je - sus res - cues
sins that you have done, and jus - ti - fied by
Spir - it, Three in One! To you, O bless - ed

him be - lieve should ev - er - last - ing life re - ceive.
Christ a - lone are built on this chief cor - ner - stone.
us from death; that is the firm - est ground of faith.
Je - sus' blood, your bap - tism grants the high - est good.
Trin - i - ty, be praise now and e - ter - nal - ly!

Text: *Gesangbuch*, Bollhagen, 1791; tr. August Crull, 1846–1923, alt.
Music: Edward Miller, 1731–1807, adapt.

ROCKINGHAM OL
L

In the Cross of Christ I Glory

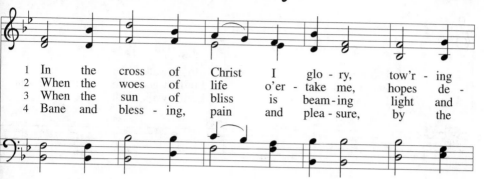

1 In the cross of Christ I glo - ry, tow'r - ing
2 When the woes of life o'er - take me, hopes de -
3 When the sun of bliss is beam - ing light and
4 Bane and bless - ing, pain and plea - sure, by the

o'er the wrecks of time. All the light of
ceive, and fears an - noy, nev - er shall the
love up - on my way, from the cross the
cross are sanc - ti - fied; peace is there that

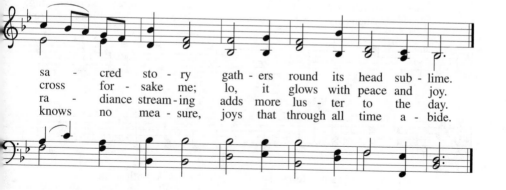

sa - cred sto - ry gath - ers round its head sub - lime.
cross for - sake me; lo, it glows with peace and joy.
ra - diance stream - ing adds more lus - ter to the day.
knows no mea - sure, joys that through all time a - bide.

Text: John Bowring, 1792–1872
Music: Ithamar Conkey, 1815–1867

RATHBUN
8 7 8 7

325   I Want Jesus to Walk with Me

Text: African American spiritual
Music: African American spiritual; arr. hymnal version
Arr. © 2006 Augsburg Fortress

SOJOURNE
Irregula

Bless Now, O God, the Journey

1 Bless now, O God, the jour - ney that all your peo - ple make,
2 Bless so - journ-ers and pil - grims who share this wind-ing way;
3 Di - vine e - ter - nal lov - er, you meet us on the road.

the path through noise and si - lence, the way of give and take.
your hope burns through the ter - rors, your love sus - tains the day.
We wait for lands of prom - ise where milk and hon - ey flow,

The trail is found in des - ert and winds the moun-tain round,
We yearn for ho - ly free - dom while of - ten we are bound;
but wait-ing not for plac - es, you meet us all a - round.

then leads be - side still wa - ters, the road where faith is found.
to - geth - er we are seek - ing the road where faith is found.
Our cov - e - nant is writ - ten on roads, as faith is found.

Text: Sylvia G. Dunstan, 1955–1993
Music: Welsh tune, 19th cent.
Text © 1991 GIA Publications, Inc.

LLANGLOFFAN
7676D

327 Through the Night of Doubt and Sorrow

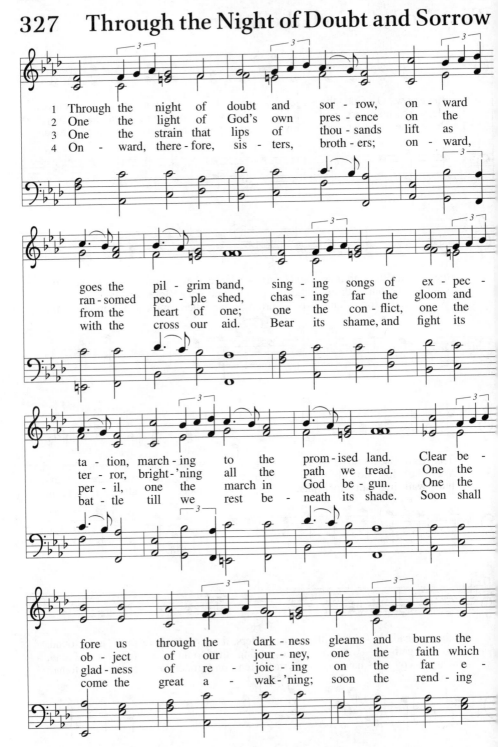

1 Through the night of doubt and sor - row, on - ward
2 One the light of God's own pres - ence on the
3 One the strain that lips of thou - sands lift as
4 On - ward, there - fore, sis - ters, broth - ers; on - ward,

goes the pil - grim band, sing - ing songs of ex - pec -
ran - somed peo - ple shed, chas - ing far the gloom and
from the heart of one; one the con - flict, one the
with the cross our aid. Bear its shame, and fight its

ta - tion, march - ing to the prom - ised land. Clear be -
ter - ror, bright - 'ning all the path we tread. One the
per - il, one the march in God be - gun. One the
bat - tle till we rest be - neath its shade. Soon shall

fore us through the dark - ness gleams and burns the
ob - ject of our jour - ney, one the faith which
glad - ness of re - joic - ing on the far e -
come the great a - wak - 'ning; soon the rend - ing

Text: Bernhardt S. Ingemann, 1789–1862; tr. Sabine Baring-Gould, 1834–1924, alt.
Music: Thomas J. Williams, 1869–1944; arr. Richard W. Hillert, b. 1923
Arr. © 1969 Concordia Publishing House

EBENEZE
8 7 8 7

guid - ing light; pil - grim clasps the hand of
nev - er tires, one the ear - nest look - ing
ter - nal shore, where the one al - might - y
of the tomb! Then the scat - t'ring of all

pil - grim step - ping fear - less through the night.
for - ward, one the hope our God in - spires.
Fa - ther reigns in love for - ev - er - more.
shad - ows, and the end of toil and gloom.

Restore in Us, O God 328

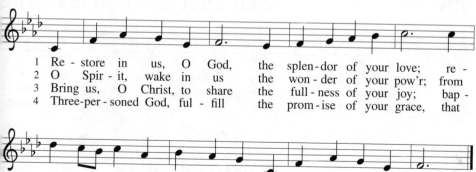

1 Re - store in us, O God, the splen-dor of your love; re -
2 O Spir - it, wake in us the won - der of your pow'r; from
3 Bring us, O Christ, to share the full - ness of your joy; bap -
4 Three-per - soned God, ful - fill the prom-ise of your grace, that

new your im - age in our hearts, and all our sins re - move.
fruit-less fear un - furl our lives like spring-time bud and flow'r.
tize us in the ris - en life that death can - not de - stroy.
we, when all our search-ing ends, may see you face to face.

Text: Carl P. Daw Jr., b. 1944
Music: Hal H. Hopson, b. 1933
Text © 1989 Hope Publishing Company
Music © 1985 Hope Publishing Company

BAYLOR
SM

Alternate tune: SOUTHWELL

329

As the Sun with Longer Journey

1 As the sun with long-er jour-ney melts the win-ter's snow and ice,
2 Through the days of wait-ing, watch-ing, in the des-ert of our sin,
3 Praise be giv-en to the mak-er of the sea-sons' year-ly round:

with its slow-ly grow-ing ra-diance warms the seed be-neath the earth,
search-ing on the far ho-ri-zon for a sign of cloud or wind,
Fa-ther, Son, and Ho-ly Spir-it— Source, Sus-tain-er, Lord of life,

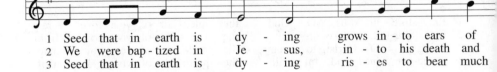

may the sun of Christ's up-ris-ing gent-ly bring our hearts to life.
we a-wait the heal-ing wa-ters of our Sav-ior's vic-to-ry.
as the ev-er turn-ing a-ges roll to their e-ter-nal rest.

Text: John Patrick Earls, OSB, b. 1935
Music: Carl F. Schalk, b. 1929
Text © 1981 Order of Saint Benedict, admin. Liturgical Press
Music © 1995 Augsburg Fortress

NAGEL
878787

330

Seed That in Earth Is Dying

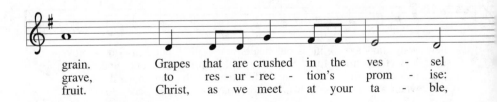

1 Seed that in earth is dy-ing grows in-to ears of
2 We were bap-tized in Je-sus, in-to his death and
3 Seed that in earth is dy-ing ris-es to bear much

grain. Grapes that are crushed in the ves-sel
grave, to res-ur-rec-tion's prom-ise:
fruit. Christ, as we meet at your ta-ble,

Text: Svein Ellingsen, b. 1929; tr. Hedwig T. Durnbaugh, b. 1929
Music: Harald Herresthal, b. 1944
Tr. © Hedwig T. Durnbaugh
Music © Norsk Musikforlag

SÅKORN SOM DØR I JORDE
76 76 87

turn in - to gold - en wine. God, through this mys - ter - y grant us
praise and e - ter - nal life. Heav-en's own prais - es be - gin here
give us the bread of life. Lord, we do thank and a - dore you!

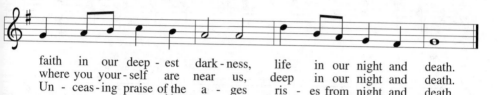

faith in our deep - est dark - ness, life in our night and death.
where you your - self are near us, deep in our night and death.
Un - ceas-ing praise of the a - ges ris - es from night and death.

As the Deer Runs to the River 331

1 As the deer runs to the riv - er, parched and wea - ry from the chase,
2 When your Is - rael crossed the des - ert where no stream or spring was seen,
3 "Come and drink," I - sa - iah sum-moned, "all who for God's mer - cy plead!
4 Christ, we come from des - ert plac - es, deep - est thirst un - sat - is - fied.

we have come from hurt and hur - ry, thirst-ing for your heal - ing grace.
Mo - ses struck the rock, and wa - ter flowed for them, re - fresh - ing, clean.
God's for - give - ness, like a foun-tain, flows to sat - is - fy your need."
Lead us to the wa - ters flow-ing from the cross on which you died.

Refrain

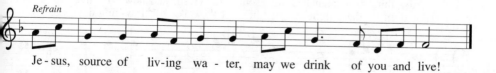

Je - sus, source of liv-ing wa - ter, may we drink of you and live!

Text: Herman G. Stuempfle Jr., b. 1923
Music: David Hurd, b. 1950
Text © 2002 GIA Publications, Inc.
Music © 1983 GIA Publications, Inc.

JULION
8 7 8 7 8 7

Alternate tune: PICARDY

332   I Heard the Voice of Jesus Say

1 I heard the voice of Je-sus say, "Come un-to me and rest;
2 I heard the voice of Je-sus say, "Be-hold, I free-ly give
3 I heard the voice of Je-sus say, "I am this dark world's light;

lay down, O wea-ry one, lay down your head up-on my breast."
the liv-ing wa-ter, thirst-y one; stoop down and drink and live."
look un-to me, your morn shall rise, and all your day be bright."

I came to Je-sus as I was, so wea-ry, worn, and sad;
I came to Je-sus, and I drank of that life-giv-ing stream;
I looked to Je-sus, and I found in him my star, my sun;

I found in him a rest-ing place, and he has made me glad.
my thirst was quenched, my soul re-vived, and now I live in him.
and in that light of life I'll walk till trav-'ling days are done.

Text: Horatius Bonar, 1808–1889
Music: Thomas Tallis, 1505–1585

THIRD MODE MELOD
CM

Alternate tune: KINGSFO

Jesus Is a Rock in a Weary Land

Refrain – All

Je - sus is a rock in a wea - ry land, a wea - ry land, a wea - ry land; my Je - sus is a rock in a wea - ry land, a shel - ter in the time of storm.

Leader or All

1 No one can do like Je - sus, not a
2 When Je - sus was on earth, ... the . .
3 Yon - der comes my Sav - ior, him . .

mum - bling word he said; he went walk - ing down to Laz-
flesh was ver - y weak; . . he took a towel and gird-
whom I love so well; . . he has the palm of vic -

Refrain

- a - rus' grave, and he raised him from the dead.
ed him - self and he washed his dis - ci - ples' feet.
- to - ry and the keys of death and hell.

Text: African American spiritual
Music: African American spiritual

WEARY LAND
Irregular

334   Tree of Life and Awesome Mystery

1 Tree of Life and awe - some mys - t'ry, in your
2 We re - mem - ber truth once spo - ken, love passed
3 Christ, you lead and we shall fol - low, stum - bling

death we are re - born; though you die in all of
on through act and word; ev - 'ry per - son lost and
though our steps may be; one with you in joy and

his - t'ry, still you rise with ev - 'ry morn, still you
bro - ken, wears the bod - y of our Lord, wears the
sor - row, we the riv - er, you the sea, we the

rise with ev - 'ry morn.
bod - y of our Lord.
riv - er, you the sea.

One of the following may be sung as the final stanza at the appropriate time.

General
Light of life beyond conceiving,
mighty Spirit of our Lord;
give new strength to our believing,
give us faith to live your word.

Lent 1
From the dawning of creation
you have loved us as your own;
stay with us through all temptation,
make us turn to you alone.

Lent 2
In our call to be a blessing,
may we be a blessing true;
may we live and die confessing
Christ as Lord of all we do.

Lent 3
Living Water of salvation,
be the fountain of each soul;
springing up in new creation,
flow in us and make us whole.

Lent 4
Give us eyes to see you clearly;
make us children of your light.
Give us hearts to live more nearly
as your gospel shining bright.

Lent 5
God of all our fear and sorrow,
God who lives beyond our death,
hold us close through each tomorrow,
love as near as ev'ry breath.

Text: Marty Haugen, b. 1950
Music: Marty Haugen
Text and music © 1984 GIA Publications, Inc.

THOMA
8787

Jesus, Keep Me Near the Cross

1 Je - sus, keep me near the cross, there's a pre - cious foun - tain;
2 Near the cross, a trem - bling soul, love and mer - cy found me;
3 Near the cross! O Lamb of God, bring its scenes be - fore me;
4 Near the cross I'll watch and wait, hop - ing, trust - ing ev - er,

free to all, a heal - ing stream flows from Cal - v'ry's moun - tain.
there the bright and morn - ing star sheds its beams a - round me.
help me walk from day to day with its shad - ow o'er me.
till I reach the gold - en strand just be - yond the riv - er.

Refrain

In the cross, in the cross be my glo - ry ev - er;

till my ran - somed soul shall find rest be - yond the riv - er.

Text: Fanny J. Crosby, 1820–1915
Music: William H. Doane, 1832–1915

NEAR THE CROSS
7 6 7 6 and refrain

Lamb of God
Your Only Son

336

1 Your on-ly Son, no sin to hide, but you have
2 Your gift of love we cru-ci-fied. We laughed and
3 I was so lost, I should have died, but you have

sent him from your side to walk up-on this guilt-y
scorned him as he died. The hum-ble king we named a
brought me to your side to be led by your staff and

sod and to be-come the Lamb of God.
fraud and sac-ri-ficed the Lamb of God.
rod and to be called a lamb of God.

Refrain

O Lamb of God, sweet Lamb of God, I love the ho-ly Lamb of God. Oh, wash me

in your pre-cious blood, my Je-sus Christ, the Lamb of God.

Text: Twila Paris, b. 1958
Music: Twila Paris
Text and music © 1985 Straightway Music/Mountain Spring Music

YOUR ONLY SO
LM

Alas! And Did My Savior Bleed

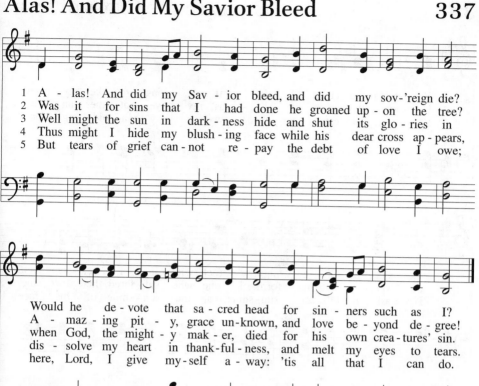

1 A - las! And did my Sav - ior bleed, and did my sov-'reign die?
2 Was it for sins that I had done he groaned up - on the tree?
3 Well might the sun in dark - ness hide and shut its glo - ries in
4 Thus might I hide my blush - ing face while his dear cross ap - pears,
5 But tears of grief can - not re - pay the debt of love I owe;

Would he de - vote that sa - cred head for sin - ners such as I?
A - maz - ing pit - y, grace un-known, and love be - yond de - gree!
when God, the might - y mak - er, died for his own crea - tures' sin.
dis - solve my heart in thank-ful - ness, and melt my eyes to tears.
here, Lord, I give my - self a - way: 'tis all that I can do.

Text: Isaac Watts, 1674–1748, alt.
Music: Hugh Wilson, 1764–1824

MARTYRDOM
CM

338

Beneath the Cross of Jesus

1 Be - neath the cross of Je - sus I long to take my stand;
2 Up - on the cross of Je - sus, my eye at times can see
3 I take, O cross, your shad - ow for my a - bid - ing place;

the shad - ow of a might - y rock with - in a wea - ry land,
the ver - y dy - ing form of one who suf - fered there for me.
I ask no oth - er sun - shine than the sun - shine of his face;

a home with-in a wil - der - ness, a rest up - on the way,
And from my con - trite heart, with tears, two won - ders I con - fess:
con - tent to let the world go by, to know no gain nor loss,

from the burn - ing of the noon - tide heat and bur - dens of the day.
the . . . won - der of his glo - rious love and my un - wor - thi - ness.
my . . . sin - ful self my on - ly shame, my glo - ry all, the cross.

Text: Elizabeth C. Clephane, 1830–1869
Music: Frederick C. Maker, 1844–1927

ST. CHRISTOPHER
7686868

Christ, the Life of All the Living

1 Christ, the life of all the liv-ing, Christ, the death of death, our foe,
2 You have suf-fered great af-flic-tion and have borne it pa-tient-ly,
3 Then, for all that bought my par-don, for the sor-rows deep and sore,

Christ, your-self for me once giv-ing to the dark-est depths of woe:
e - ven death by cru-ci-fix-ion, ful - ly to a - tone for me;
for the an-guish in the gar-den, I will thank you ev - er-more;

through your suf-f'ring, death, and mer - it life e - ter - nal I in - her - it.
for you chose to be tor-ment-ed that my doom should be pre-vent-ed.
thank you for the groan-ing, sigh-ing, for the bleed-ing and the dy - ing,

Thou-sand, thou-sand thanks are due, dear - est Je - sus, un - to you.
Thou-sand, thou-sand thanks are due, dear - est Je - sus, un - to you.
for that last tri - um - phant cry, praise you ev - er - more on high.

Text: Ernst Christoph Homburg, 1605–1681; tr. Catherine Winkworth, 1827–1878, alt.
Music: *Das grosse Cantional*, Darmstadt, 1687

JESU, MEINES LEBENS LEBEN
87 87 88 77

340   A Lamb Goes Uncomplaining Forth

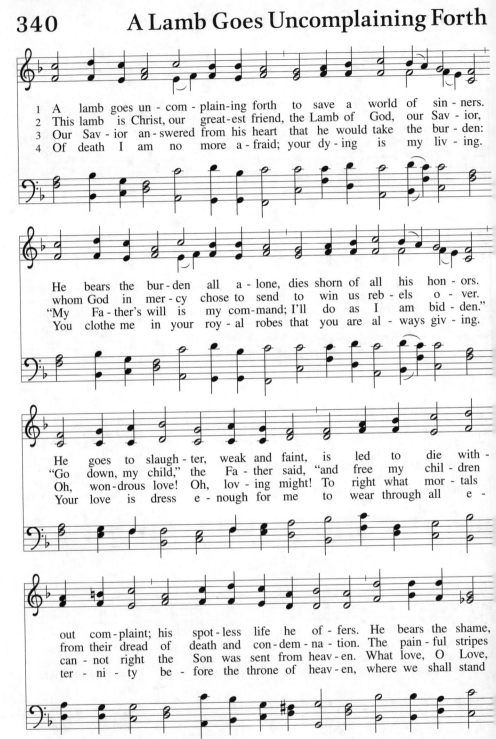

1 A lamb goes un-com-plain-ing forth to save a world of sin-ners.
2 This lamb is Christ, our great-est friend, the Lamb of God, our Sav-ior,
3 Our Sav-ior an-swered from his heart that he would take the bur-den:
4 Of death I am no more a-fraid; your dy-ing is my liv-ing.

He bears the bur-den all a-lone, dies shorn of all his hon-ors.
whom God in mer-cy chose to send to win us reb-els o-ver.
"My Fa-ther's will is my com-mand; I'll do as I am bid-den."
You clothe me in your roy-al robes that you are al-ways giv-ing.

He goes to slaugh-ter, weak and faint, is led to die with-
"Go down, my child," the Fa-ther said, "and free my chil-dren
Oh, won-drous love! Oh, lov-ing might! To right what mor-tals
Your love is dress e-nough for me to wear through all e-

out com-plaint; his spot-less life he of-fers. He bears the shame,
from their dread of death and con-dem-na-tion. The pain-ful stripes
can-not right the Son was sent from heav-en. What love, O Love,
ter-ni-ty be-fore the throne of heav-en, where we shall stand

Text: Paul Gerhardt, 1607–1676; tr. *Lutheran Book of Worship*, alt.
Music: Wolfgang Dachstein, c. 1487–1553
Text © 1978 *Lutheran Book of Worship*, admin. Augsburg Fortress

AN WASSERFLÜSSEN BABYLO
P

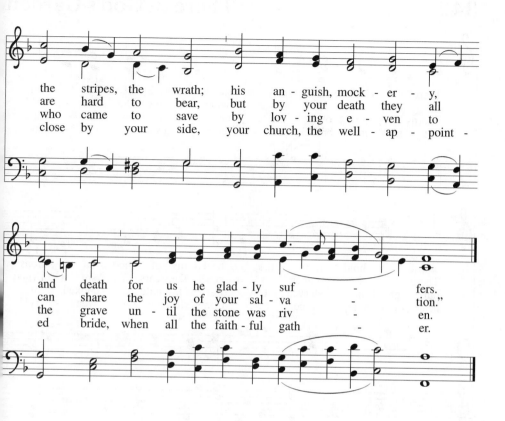

the stripes, the wrath; his an - guish, mock - er - y,
are hard to bear, but by your death they all
who came to save by lov - ing e - ven to
close by your side, your church, the well - ap - point -

and death for us he glad - ly suf - fers.
can share the joy of your sal - va - tion."
the grave un - til the stone was riv - en.
ed bride, when all the faith - ful gath - er.

Now Behold the Lamb 341

1 Now be - hold the Lamb, the pre - cious Lamb of God, who
2 Ho - ly is the Lamb, the pre - cious Lamb of God. Why
3 Thank you for the Lamb, the pre - cious Lamb of God. Be -

bore all my sin, that I may live a - gain: the pre-cious Lamb of God.
you love me so, Lord, I shall nev - er know; the pre-cious Lamb of God.
cause of your grace I can fin - ish the race; the pre-cious Lamb of God.

Text: Kirk Franklin, b. 1970
Music: Kirk Franklin; arr. Keith Hampton, b. 1957
Text and music © 1996 Lilly Mack Music

NOW BEHOLD THE LAMB
5 6 56 6

342

There in God's Garden

1 There in God's gar - den stands the Tree of Wis - dom,
2 Its name is Je - sus, name that says, "Our Sav - ior!"
3 Thorns not its own are tan - gled in its fo - liage;
4 See how its branch - es reach to us in wel - come;

whose leaves hold forth the heal - ing of the na - tions:
There on its branch - es see the scars of suf - f'ring;
our greed has starved it, our de - spite has choked it.
hear what the Voice says, "Come to me, ye wea - ry!

Tree of all knowl - edge, Tree of all com -
see there the ten - drils of our hu - man
Yet, look! it lives! its grief has not de -
Give me your sick - ness, give me all your

pas - sion, Tree of all beau - ty.
self - hood feed on its life - blood.
stroyed it nor fire con - sumed it.
sor - row, I will give bless - ing."

Text: Király Imre von Pécselyi, c. 1590–c. 1641; tr. Erik Routley, 1917–1982
Music: K. Lee Scott, b. 1950
Text © 1976 Hinshaw Music, Inc.
Music © 1987 Birnamwood Publications, a div. of MorningStar Music Publishers, Inc.

SHADES MOUNTAI
11 11 11

5 This is my ending,
   this my resurrection;
   into your hands,
   Lord, I commit my spirit.
   This have I searched for;
   now I can possess it.
   This ground is holy.

6 All heav'n is singing,
   "Thanks to Christ whose passion
   offers in mercy
   healing, strength, and pardon.
   Peoples and nations,
   take it, take it freely!"
   Amen! My Master!

My Song Is Love Unknown

343

1 My song is love un - known, my Sav - ior's love to
2 He came from his blest throne sal - va - tion to be -
3 Some - times we strew his way and his sweet prais - es
4 We cry out, we will have our dear Lord made a -

me, love to the love - less shown that they might
stow; the world that was his own would not its
sing; re - sound - ing all the day ho - san - nas
way, a mur - der - er to save, the prince of

love - ly be. Oh, who am I that
Sav - ior know. But, oh, my friend, my
to our king. Then "Cru - ci - fy!" is
life to slay. Yet cheer - ful he to

for my sake my Lord should take frail flesh and die?
friend in - deed, who at my need his life did spend!
all our breath, and for his death we thirst and cry.
suf - f'ring goes that he his foes from thence might free.

5 In life no house, no home
   my Lord on earth might have;
   in death no friendly tomb
   but what a stranger gave.
   What may I say? Heav'n was his home
   but mine the tomb wherein he lay.

6 Here might I stay and sing—
   no story so divine!
   Never was love, dear King,
   never was grief like thine.
   This is my friend, in whose sweet praise
   I all my days could gladly spend!

Text: Samuel Crossman, 1624–1683, alt.
Music: John Ireland, 1879–1962
Music © 1924 John Ireland, admin. The John Ireland Trust

LOVE UNKNOWN
6 6 6 6 4 4 8

Alternate tune: RHOSYMEDRE

344   All Glory, Laud, and Honor

Refrain

All glo-ry, laud, and hon-or to you, re-deem-er, king, to whom the lips of chil-dren made sweet ho-san-nas ring.

1 You are the king of Is - rael and Da - vid's roy - al Son,
2 The com - pa - ny of an - gels are prais-ing you on high;
3 The mul - ti - tude of pil - grims with palms be - fore you went;
4 To you, be - fore your pas - sion, they sang their hymns of praise.
5 Their prais-es you ac - cept - ed; ac - cept the prayers we bring,

Refrain

now in the Lord's name com - ing, our King and Bless-ed One.
cre - a - tion and all mor - tals in cho - rus make re - ply.
our praise and prayer and an - thems be - fore you we pre - sent.
To you, now high ex - alt - ed, our mel - o - dy we raise.
great au - thor of all good - ness, O good and gra - cious King.

Text: Theodulph of Orleans, c. 760–821; tr. John Mason Neale, 1818–1866, alt.
Music: Melchior Teschner, 1584–1635

VALET WILL ICH DIR GEBE
7676

Jesus, I Will Ponder Now

1 Je - sus, I will pon - der now on your ho - ly pas - sion;
2 Make me see your great dis - tress, an - guish, and af - flic - tion,
3 Yet, O Lord, not thus a - lone make me see your pas - sion,
4 Let me view your pain and loss with re - pen - tant griev - ing,

let your Spir - it now en - dow me for med - i - ta - tion.
bonds and blows and wretch-ed - ness and your cru - ci - fix - ion;
but its cause to me make known and its ter - mi - na - tion.
nor pre - pare a - gain your cross by un - ho - ly liv - ing.

Grant that I in love and faith may the im - age cher - ish
make me see how scourge and rod, spear and nails, did wound you,
For I al - so and my sin wrought your deep af - flic - tion;
May I give you love for love! Hear me, O my Sav - ior,

of your suf - f'ring, pain, and death, that I may not per - ish.
how you died for those, O God, who with thorns had crowned you.
this the shame-ful cause has been of your cru - ci - fix - ion.
that I may in heav'n a - bove sing your praise for - ev - er.

Text: Sigismund von Birken, 1626–1681; tr. August Crull, 1846–1923, alt.
Music: Melchior Vulpius, 1570–1615

JESU KREUZ, LEIDEN UND PEIN
7676 D

346

Ride On, Ride On in Majesty!

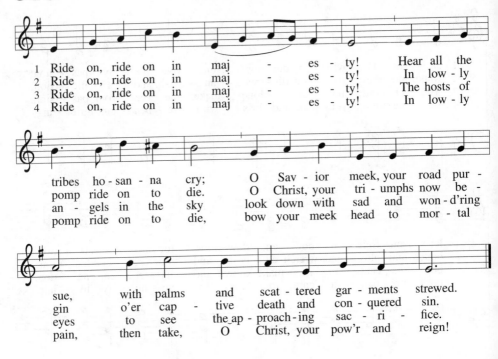

1 Ride on, ride on in maj - es - ty! Hear all the
2 Ride on, ride on in maj - es - ty! In low - ly
3 Ride on, ride on in maj - es - ty! The hosts of
4 Ride on, ride on in maj - es - ty! In low - ly

tribes ho - san - na cry; O Sav - ior meek, your road pur -
pomp ride on to die. O Christ, your tri - umphs now be -
an - gels in the sky look down with sad and won - d'ring
pomp ride on to die, bow your meek head to mor - tal

sue, with palms and scat - tered gar - ments strewed.
gin o'er cap - tive death and con - quered sin.
eyes to see the ap - proach-ing sac - ri - fice.
pain, then take, O Christ, your pow'r and reign!

Text: Henry H. Milman, 1791–1868, alt.
Music: Graham George, 1912–1993
Music © 1941 The H.W. Gray Co., Inc.

THE KING'S MAJESTY
LM

Alternate tune: TRURO

347

Go to Dark Gethsemane

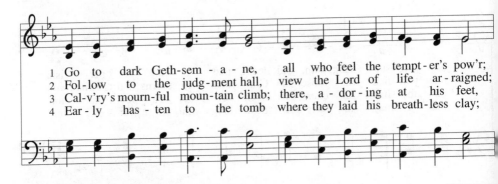

1 Go to dark Geth-sem - a - ne, all who feel the tempt-er's pow'r;
2 Fol-low to the judg-ment hall, view the Lord of life ar - raigned;
3 Cal-v'ry's mourn-ful moun-tain climb; there, a - dor - ing at his feet,
4 Ear - ly has - ten to the tomb where they laid his breath-less clay;

Text: James Montgomery, 1771–1854
Music: Richard Redhead, 1820–1901

GETHSEMANE
777777

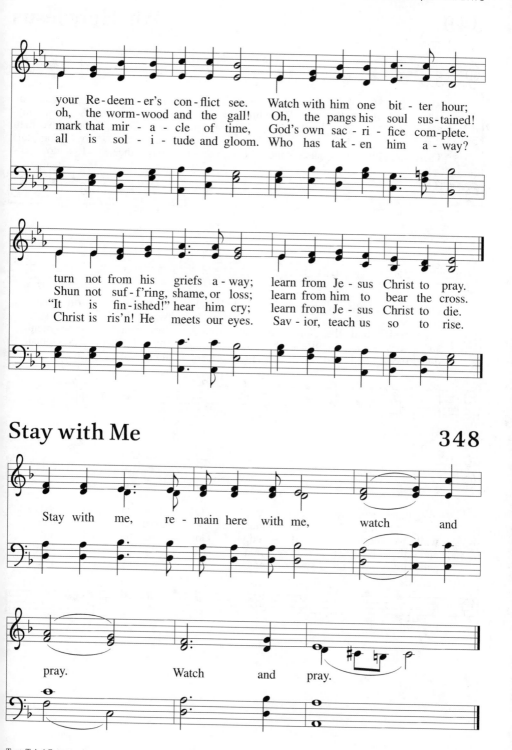

your Re-deem-er's con-flict see. Watch with him one bit-ter hour;
oh, the worm-wood and the gall! Oh, the pangs his soul sus-tained!
mark that mir - a - cle of time, God's own sac-ri - fice com-plete.
all is sol - i - tude and gloom. Who has tak-en him a - way?

turn not from his griefs a - way; learn from Je - sus Christ to pray.
Shun not suf-f'ring, shame, or loss; learn from him to bear the cross.
"It is fin-ished!" hear him cry; learn from Je - sus Christ to die.
Christ is ris'n! He meets our eyes. Sav - ior, teach us so to rise.

Stay with Me

348

Stay with me, re-main here with me, watch and

pray. Watch and pray.

Text: Taizé Community
Music: Jacques Berthier, 1923–1994
Text & music © 1984 Les Presses de Taizé, admin. GIA Publications, Inc.

STAY WITH ME
PM

349

Ah, Holy Jesus

1 Ah, ho-ly Je-sus, how hast thou of-fend-ed that we to judge thee have in hate pre-tend-ed? By foes de-rid-ed, by thine own re-ject-ed, O most af-flict-ed.

2 Who was the guilt-y? Who brought this up-on thee? A-las, my trea-son, Je-sus, hath un-done thee. 'Twas I, Lord Je-sus, I it was de-nied thee; I cru-ci-fied thee.

3 Lo, the Good Shep-herd for the sheep is of-fered; the slave hath sin-ned, and the Son hath suf-fered; for our a-tone-ment, while we noth-ing heed-ed, God in-ter-ced-ed.

4 For me, kind Je-sus, was thine in-car-na-tion, thy mor-tal sor-row, and thy life's ob-la-tion; thy death of an-guish and thy bit-ter pas-sion, for my sal-va-tion.

5 There-fore, kind Je-sus, since I can-not pay thee, I do a-dore thee, and will ev-er pray thee; think on thy pit-y and thy love un-swerv-ing, not my de-serv-ing.

Text: Johann Heermann, 1585–1647; tr. Robert Bridges, 1844–1930, alt.
Music: Johann Crüger, 1598–1662

HERZLIEBSTER JESU
11 11 11 5

They Crucified My Lord

1 They cru - ci - fied my Lord, and he nev - er said a mum-ba-lin' word;
2 They nailed him to a tree, and he nev - er said a mum-ba-lin' word;
3 They pierced him in the side, and he nev - er said a mum-ba-lin' word;
4 The blood came stream-in' down, and he nev - er said a mum-ba-lin' word;
5 He hung his head and died, and he nev - er said a mum-ba-lin' word;

they cru - ci - fied my Lord, and he nev - er said a mum-ba-lin' word;
they nailed him to a tree, and he nev - er said a mum-ba-lin' word;
they pierced him in the side, and he nev - er said a mum-ba-lin' word;
the blood came stream-in' down, and he nev - er said a mum-ba-lin' word;
he hung his head and died, and he nev - er said a mum-ba-lin' word;

not a word, not a word, not a word.

mumbalin' = complaining

Text: African American spiritual
Music: African American spiritual

SUFFERER
6 10 6 10 9

351 O Sacred Head, Now Wounded

1 O sa - cred head, now wound - ed, with grief and shame weighed down,
2 How pale thou art with an - guish, with sore a - buse and scorn;
3 What lan - guage shall I bor - row to thank thee, dear - est friend,
4 Lord, be my con - so - la - tion; shield me when I must die;

now scorn - ful - ly sur - round - ed with thorns, thine on - ly crown;
how does thy face now lan - guish, which once was bright as morn!
for this thy dy - ing sor - row, thy pit - y with - out end?
re - mind me of thy pas - sion when my last hour draws nigh.

O sa - cred head, what glo - ry, what bliss till now was thine!
Thy grief and bit - ter pas - sion were all for sin - ners' gain;
Oh, make me thine for - ev - er, and should I faint - ing be,
These eyes, new faith re - ceiv - ing, from thee shall nev - er move;

Yet, though de - spised and gor - y, I joy to call thee mine.
mine, mine was the trans - gres - sion, but thine the dead - ly pain.
Lord, let me nev - er, nev - er out - live my love to thee.
for all who die be - liev - ing die safe - ly in thy love.

Text: Paul Gerhardt, 1607–1676, based on Arnulf of Louvain, d. 1250; tr. composite
Music: German melody, c. 1500; adapt. Hans Leo Hassler, 1564–1612;
    arr. Johann Sebastian Bach, 1685–1750

HERZLICH TUT MICH VERLANGEN
7676 D

O Sacred Head, Now Wounded

352

1 O sa - cred head, now wound-ed, with grief and shame weighed down,
2 How pale thou art with an - guish, with sore a - buse and scorn;
3 What lan - guage shall I bor - row to thank thee, dear - est friend,
4 Lord, be my con - so - la - tion; shield me when I must die;

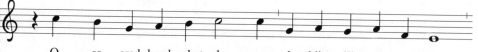

now scorn - ful - ly sur-round - ed with thorns, thine on - ly crown;
how does thy face now lan - guish, which once was bright as morn!
for this thy dy - ing sor - row, thy pit - y with - out end?
re - mind me of thy pas - sion when my last hour draws nigh.

O sa - cred head, what glo - ry, what bliss till now was thine!
Thy grief and bit - ter pas - sion were all for sin - ners' gain;
Oh, make me thine for - ev - er, and should I faint-ing be,
These eyes, new faith re - ceiv - ing, from thee shall nev - er move;

Yet, though de-spised and gor - y, I joy to call thee mine.
mine, mine was the trans-gres - sion, but thine the dead - ly pain.
Lord, let me nev - er, nev - er out - live my love to thee.
for all who die be - liev - ing die safe - ly in thy love.

Text: Paul Gerhardt, 1607–1676, based on Arnulf of Louvain, d. 1250; tr. composite
Music: German melody, c. 1500; adapt. Hans Leo Hassler, 1564–1612

HERZLICH TUT MICH VERLANGEN
7676D

353

Were You There

1 Were you there when they cru - ci - fied my Lord? Were you there?
2 Were you there when they nailed him to the tree?
3 Were you there when they pierced him in the side?
4 Were you there when the sun re - fused to shine?
5 Were you there when they laid him in the tomb? Were you there?

Were you there when they cru - ci - fied my Lord? Were you there?
Were you there when they nailed him to the tree?
Were you there when they pierced him in the side?
Were you there when the sun re - fused to shine?
Were you there when they laid him in the tomb? Were you there?

Refrain

Oh, some-times it caus-es me to trem-ble, trem-ble, trem-ble.

Were you there when they cru - ci - fied my Lord? Were you there?
Were you there when they nailed him to the tree?
Were you there when they pierced him in the side?
Were you there when the sun re - fused to shine?
Were you there when they laid him in the tomb? Were you there?

Text: African American spiritual
Music: African American spiritual
Arr. © 1999 Augsburg Fortress

WERE YOU THERE
10 10 14 10

Calvary

Every Time I Think about Jesus

Refrain

Cal - va - ry, Cal - va - ry,
1 Ev - 'ry time I think a-bout Je - sus,
2 Sin - ner, do you love . . . . my Je - sus?
3 Don't you hear him say, "It is fin - ished!"
4 Je - sus fur - nished my . . . . sal - va - tion,

Cal - va - ry, Cal - va - ry,
ev - 'ry time I think a-bout Je - sus,
Sin - ner, do you love . . . . my Je - sus?
Don't you hear him say, "It is fin - ished!"
Je - sus fur - nished my . . . . sal - va - tion,

Cal - va - ry, Cal - va - ry,
ev - 'ry time I think a-bout Je - sus;
Sin - ner, do you love . . . . my Je - sus?
Don't you hear him say, "It is fin - ished!"
Je - sus fur - nished my . . . . sal - va - tion;

sure - ly he died on Cal - va - ry.
sure - ly he died on Cal - va - ry. *Refrain*
Sure - ly he died on Cal - va - ry. *Refrain*
Sure - ly he died on Cal - va - ry. *Refrain*
sure - ly he died on Cal - va - ry. *Refrain*

Text: African American spiritual
Music: African American spiritual

CALVARY
Irregular

355

Sing, My Tongue

1 Sing, my tongue, the glo - rious bat - tle; tell the
2 God in mer - cy saw us fal - len, sunk in
3 Tell how, when at length the full - ness of the ap -
4 Thir - ty years a - mong us dwell - ing, Je - sus
5 Bend your boughs, O tree of glo - ry, your re -

tri - umph far and wide; tell a - loud the won-drous
shame and mis - er - y, felled to death in E - den's
point - ed time was come, Christ, the Word, was born of
went from Naz - a - reth, des - tined, ded - i - cat - ed,
lax - ing sin - ews bend; for a while the an - cient

sto - ry of the cross, the Cru - ci - fied;
gar - den, where in pride we claimed the tree;
wom - an, left for us the heav - 'nly home,
will - ing, did his work, and met his death;
rig - or that your birth be - stowed, sus - pend;

tell how Christ, the world's re - deem - er, van - quished
then an - oth - er tree was chos - en, which the
blazed the path of true o - be - dience, shone as
like a lamb he humb - ly yield - ed on the
and the Lord of heav'n - ly beau - ty gent - ly

death the day he died.
world from death would free.
light a - midst the gloom.
cross his dy - ing breath.
on your arms ex - tend. (7) A - men.

6 Faithful cross, true sign of triumph,
be for all the noblest tree;
none in foliage, none in blossom,
none in fruit your equal be;
symbol of the world's redemption,
for your burden makes us free.

7 Unto God be praise and glory;
to the Father and the Son,
to the eternal Spirit honor
now and evermore be done;
praise and glory in the highest,
while the timeless ages run. Amen.

Text: Venantius Honorius Fortunatus, 530–609; tr. John Mason Neale, 1818–1866, alt.
Music: Plainsong mode III, Vatican collection

PANGE LINGUA
8 7 8 7 8 7

Sing, My Tongue

356

1 Sing, my tongue, the glo - rious bat - tle; tell the tri - umph
2 God in mer - cy saw us fall - en, sunk in shame and
3 Tell how, when at length the full - ness of the ap - point - ed
4 Thir - ty years a - mong us dwell - ing, Je - sus went from
5 Bend your boughs, O tree of glo - ry, your re - lax - ing

far and wide; tell a - loud the won - drous sto - ry
mis - er - y, felled to death in E - den's gar - den,
time was come, Christ, the Word, was born of wom - an,
Naz - a - reth, des - tined, ded - i - cat - ed, will - ing,
sin - ews bend; for a while the an - cient rig - or

of the cross, the Cru - ci - fied; tell how Christ, the
where in pride we claimed the tree; then an - oth - er
left for us the heav'n - ly home, blazed the path of
did his work, and met his death; like a lamb he
that your birth be - stowed, sus - pend; and the Lord of

world's re - deem - er, van - quished death the day he died.
tree was cho - sen, which the world from death would free.
true o - be - dience, shone as light a - midst the gloom.
hum - bly yield - ed on the cross his dy - ing breath.
heav'n - ly beau - ty gent - ly on your arms ex - tend.

6 Faithful cross, true sign of triumph,
be for all the noblest tree;
none in foliage, none in blossom,
none in fruit your equal be;
symbol of the world's redemption,
for your burden makes us free.

7 Unto God be praise and glory;
to the Father and the Son,
to the eternal Spirit honor
now and evermore be done;
praise and glory in the highest,
while the timeless ages run.

Text: Venantius Honorius Fortunatus, 530–609; tr. John Mason Neale, 1818–1866, alt.
Music: Carl F. Schalk, b. 1929
Music © 1967 Concordia Publishing House

FORTUNATUS NEW
878787

357   Lamb of God, Pure and Sinless

Lamb of God, pure and sin - less, once on the cross an of - f'ring,

pa - tient, low - ly, guilt - less, for - sak - en in your suf - f'ring:

from sin's grasp you have torn us, from gloom to hope have borne us.

1 Grant us your mer - cy, O Je - sus.
2 Grant us your mer - cy, O Je - sus.
3 Your peace be with us, O Je - sus. A - men.

Text: Nikolaus Decius, 1485–1550; tr. composite
Music: Nikolaus Decius
Text © 1978, 1999 Augsburg Fortress

O LAMM GOTTES, UNSCHULDIG
7 7 6 7 7 7 8

Great God, Your Love Has Called Us   358

1 Great God, your love has called us here, as we, by love, for
2 We come with self - in - flict - ed pains of bro - ken trust and
3 Great God, in Christ you call our name and then re - ceive us
4 Then take the towel, and break the bread, and hum - ble us, and
5 Great God, in Christ you set us free your life to live, your

love were made. Your liv - ing like - ness still we bear,
cho - sen wrong, half - free, half - bound by in - ner chains,
as your own, not through some mer - it, right, or claim,
call us friends. Suf - fer and serve till all are fed,
joy to share. Give us your Spir - it's lib - er - ty

though marred, dis - hon - ored, dis - o - beyed. We come, with all our
by so - cial forc - es swept a - long, by pow'rs and sys - tems
but by your gra - cious love a - lone. We strain to glimpse your
and show how grand - ly love in - tends to work till all cre -
to turn from guilt and dull de - spair, and of - fer all that

heart and mind your call to hear, your love to find.
close con - fined, yet seek - ing hope for hu - man - kind.
mer - cy seat and find you kneel - ing at our feet.
a - tion sings, to fill all worlds, to crown all things.
faith can do while love is mak - ing all things new.

Text: Brian A. Wren, b. 1936
Music: Norman Cocker, 1889–1953
Text © 1977, rev. 1995 Hope Publishing Company
Music © Oxford University Press

RYBURN
88 88 88

359 Where Charity and Love Prevail

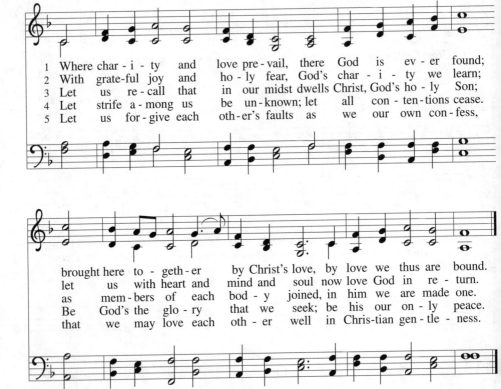

1 Where char - i - ty and love pre - vail, there God is ev - er found;
2 With grate-ful joy and ho - ly fear, God's char - i - ty we learn;
3 Let us re - call that in our midst dwells Christ, God's ho - ly Son;
4 Let strife a - mong us be un - known; let all con - ten - tions cease.
5 Let us for - give each oth-er's faults as we our own con - fess,

brought here to - geth-er by Christ's love, by love we thus are bound.
let us with heart and mind and soul now love God in re - turn.
as mem-bers of each bod - y joined, in him we are made one.
Be God's the glo - ry that we seek; be his our on - ly peace.
that we may love each oth - er well in Chris-tian gen - tle - ness.

Text: Latin hymn, 9th cent.; tr. Omer Westendorf, 1916–1997, alt.
Music: attr. Lucius Chapin, 1760–1842
Text © 1960 World Library Publications

TWENTY-FOURTH
CM

360 Love Consecrates the Humblest Act

1 Love consecrates the humblest act
and haloes mercy's deeds;
it sheds a benediction sweet
and hallows human needs.

2 When in the shadow of the cross
Christ knelt and washed the feet
of his disciples, he gave us
a sign of love complete.

3 Love serves and willing stoops to serve;
what Christ in love so true
has freely done for one and all,
let us now gladly do!

Text: Silas B. McManus, 1845–1917

TWENTY-FOURTH
CM

The Day of Resurrection!

1 The day of res - ur - rec - tion! Earth, tell it out a - broad,
2 Let hearts be purged of e - vil that we may see a - right
3 Now let the heav'ns be joy - ful, let earth its song be - gin,
4 All praise to God the Fa - ther, all praise to Christ the Son,

the pass - o - ver of glad - ness, the pass - o - ver of God.
the Lord in rays e - ter - nal of res - ur - rec - tion light,
the round world keep high tri - umph and all that is there - in.
all praise to God the Spir - it, e - ter - nal Three in One!

From death to life e - ter - nal, from sin's do - min - ion free,
and lis - t'ning to his ac - cents, may hear, so calm and plain,
Let all things, seen and un - seen, their notes of glad - ness blend;
Let all the ran - somed num - ber fall down be - fore the throne,

our Christ has brought us o - ver with hymns of vic - to - ry.
his own "All hail!" and hear - ing, may raise the glad re - frain.
for Christ the Lord has ris - en, our joy that has no end!
and hon - or, pow'r, and glo - ry as - cribe to God a - lone!

Text: John of Damascus, c. 696–c. 754; tr. John Mason Neale, 1818–1866, alt.
Music: German melody, 18th cent.; adapt. X. L. Hartig, *Melodien zum Mainzer Gesangbuche*, 1833

ELLACOMBE
7 6 7 6 D

362 At the Lamb's High Feast We Sing

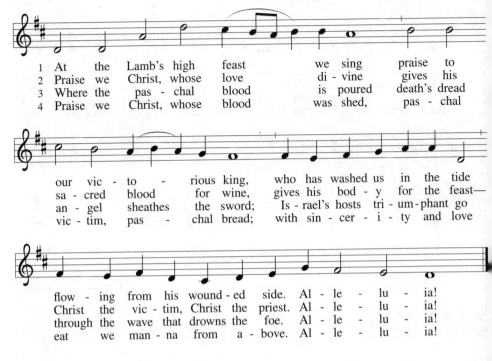

1 At the Lamb's high feast we sing / praise to
2 Praise we Christ, whose love di - vine / gives his
3 Where the pas - chal blood is poured / death's dread
4 Praise we Christ, whose blood was shed, / pas - chal

our vic - to - rious king, / who has washed us in the tide
sa - cred blood for wine, / gives his bod - y for the feast—
an - gel sheathes the sword; / Is - rael's hosts tri - um - phant go
vic - tim, pas - chal bread; / with sin - cer - i - ty and love

flow - ing from his wound - ed side. Al - le - lu - ia!
Christ the vic - tim, Christ the priest. Al - le - lu - ia!
through the wave that drowns the foe. Al - le - lu - ia!
eat we man - na from a - bove. Al - le - lu - ia!

5 Mighty victim from the sky,
   hell's fierce pow'rs beneath you lie;
   you have conquered in the fight,
   you have brought us life and light.
   Alleluia!

6 Now no more can death appall,
   now no more the grave enthrall;
   you have opened paradise,
   and your saints in you shall rise.
   Alleluia!

7 Easter triumph, Easter joy,
   this alone can sin destroy!
   From sin's pow'r, Lord, set us free,
   newborn souls in you to be.
   Alleluia!

8 Father, who the crown shall give,
   Savior, by whose death we live,
   Spirit, guide through all our days:
   Three in One, your name we praise.
   Alleluia!

Text: Latin hymn, 17th cent.; tr. Robert Campbell, 1814–1868, alt.
Music: Bohemian Brethren, *Kirchengeseng*, 1566

SONNE DER GERECHTIGKEIT
7 7 7 7 4

Come, You Faithful, Raise the Strain

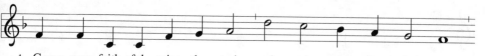

1 Come, you faith - ful, raise the strain of tri - um - phant glad - ness!
2 'Tis the spring of souls to - day: Christ has burst his pris - on,
3 Now the queen of sea - sons, bright with the day of splen - dor,
4 Nei - ther could the gates of death, nor the tomb's dark por - tal,
5 Al - le - lu - ia! now we cry to our Lord im - mor - tal,

God has brought forth Is - ra - el in - to joy from sad - ness,
and from three days' sleep in death as a sun has ris - en.
with the roy - al feast of feasts comes its joy to ren - der;
nor the watch - ers, nor the seal, hold you as a mor - tal:
who tri - um - phant burst the bars of the tomb's dark por - tal;

loosed from Pha - raoh's bit - ter yoke Ja - cob's sons and daugh - ters;
All the win - ter of our sins, long and dark, is fly - ing
comes to glad Jer - u - sa - lem, who with true af - fec - tion
but to - day, a - mong your own, you ap - pear, be - stow - ing
Al - le - lu - ia! with the Son God the Fa - ther prais - ing;

led them with un - moist - ened foot through the Red Sea wa - ters.
from the Light to whom we give laud and praise un - dy - ing.
wel - comes in un - wea - ried strain Je - sus' res - ur - rec - tion!
your deep peace, which ev - er - more pass - es hu - man know - ing.
Al - le - lu - ia! yet a - gain to the Spir - it rais - ing.

Text: John of Damascus, c. 696–c. 754; tr. John Mason Neale, 1818–1866, alt.
Music: Johann Horn, 1490–1547

GAUDEAMUS PARITER
76 76 D

Christ Has Arisen, Alleluia
Mfurahini, haleluya

M - fu - ra - hi - ni,   ha - le - lu - ya,
1 Christ has a - ris - en,   al - le - lu - ia.
2 For three long days   the grave did its worst
3 The an - gel said to   them, "Do not fear.

m - ko - mbo - zi   a - me - fu - fu - ka.
Re - joice and praise   him, al - le - lu - ia.
un - til its strength   by God was dis - persed.
You look for Je - sus   who is not here.

A - me - fu - fu - ka,   ha - le - lu - ya,
For our re - deem - er   burst from the tomb,
He who gives life   did death un - der - go,
See for your - selves   the tomb is all bare.

m - si - fu - ni   sa - sa yu ha - i.
e - ven from death,   dis - pel - ling its gloom.
and in its con - quest   his might did show.
On - ly the grave - clothes   are ly - ing there."

Text: Bernard Kyamanywa, b. 1938; tr. Howard S. Olson, b. 1922
Music: Tanzanian traditional
Text © 1968 Lutheran Theological College, Makumira, Tanzania, admin. Augsburg Fortress
Tr. © 1977 Howard S. Olson, admin. Augsburg Fortress

MFURAHINI, HALELUYA
9 9 9 9 and refrain

Refrain

Tu - mwi - mbi - e so - te kwa fu - ra - ha.
Let us sing praise to him with end - less joy.

Ye - su a - me - to - ka ka - bu - ri - ni.
Death's fear - ful sting he has come to de - stroy.

Ka - shi - nda ki - fo, ha - le - lu - ya;
Our sin for - giv - ing, al - le - lu - ia!

ha - le - lu - ya, Ye - su yu ha - i.
Je - sus is liv - ing, al - le - lu - ia!

4 "Go spread the news: he's not in the grave.
   He has arisen this world to save.
   Jesus' redeeming labors are done.
   Even the battle with sin is won."
   Refrain

5 Christ has arisen to set us free.
  Alleluia, to him praises be.
  Jesus is living! Let us all sing;
  he reigns triumphant, heavenly king.
  Refrain

365   Jesus Christ Is Risen Today

1 Je - sus Christ is ris'n to - day, Al - le - lu - ia!
2 Hymns of praise then let us sing, Al - le - lu - ia!
3 But the pains which he en - dured, Al - le - lu - ia!
4 Sing we to our God a - bove, Al - le - lu - ia!

our tri - um - phant ho - ly day, Al - le - lu - ia!
un - to Christ, our heav'n - ly king, Al - le - lu - ia!
our sal - va - tion have pro - cured; Al - le - lu - ia!
praise e - ter - nal as his love; Al - le - lu - ia!

who did once up - on the cross, Al - le - lu - ia!
who en - dured the cross and grave, Al - le - lu - ia!
now a - bove the sky he's king, Al - le - lu - ia!
praise him, all you heav'n - ly host, Al - le - lu - ia!

suf - fer to re - deem our loss. Al - le - lu - ia!
sin - ners to re - deem and save. Al - le - lu - ia!
where the an - gels ev - er sing. Al - le - lu - ia!
Fa - ther, Son, and Ho - ly Ghost. Al - le - lu - ia!

Text: Latin carol, 14th cent., sts. 1–3; tr. J. Walsh, *Lyra Davidica*, 1708, alt.;
   Charles Wesley, 1707–1788, st. 4
Music: J. Walsh, *Lyra Davidica*, 1708

EASTER HYMN
7 7 7 7 and alleluias

The Strife Is O'er, the Battle Done   **366**

Al - le - lu - ia, al - le - lu - ia, al - le - lu - ia!

1 The strife is o'er, the bat - tle done; now is the vic - tor's
2 The pow'rs of death have done their worst; Je - sus their le - gions
3 The three sad days have quick - ly sped, Christ ris - es glo - rious
4 Christ closed the yawn - ing gates of hell; the bars from heav'n's high
5 Lord, by the stripes which wound - ed you, from death's sting free your

tri - umph won! Now be the song of praise be - gun. Al - le - lu - ia!
has dis - persed. Let shouts of ho - ly joy out - burst. Al - le - lu - ia!
from the dead. All glo - ry to our ris - en head! Al - le - lu - ia!
por - tals fell. Let hymns of praise his tri - umph tell. Al - le - lu - ia!
ser - vants too, that we may live and sing to you. Al - le - lu - ia!

After the final stanza

Al - le - lu - ia, al - le - lu - ia, al - le - lu - ia!

Text: *Symphonia Sirenum*, Köln, 1695; tr. Francis Pott, 1832–1909
Music: Giovanni Pierluigi da Palestrina, 1525–1594; arr. William H. Monk, 1823–1889

VICTORY
8 8 8 with alleluias

367   Now All the Vault of Heaven Resounds

1 Now all the vault of heav'n re - sounds
2 E - ter - nal is the gift he brings,
3 Oh, fill us, Lord, with daunt - less love;
4 A - dor - ing prais - es now we bring

in praise of love that still a - bounds: "Christ has
there - fore our heart with rap - ture sings: "Christ has
set heart and will on things a - bove that we
and with the heav'n-ly bless - ed sing: "Christ has

tri - umphed! He is liv - ing!" Sing, choirs of
tri - umphed! He is liv - ing!" Now still he
con - quer through your tri - umph; grant grace suf -
tri - umphed! Al - le - lu - ia!" Be to the

an - gels, loud and clear! Re - peat their song of glo - ry
comes to give us life and by his pres - ence stills all
fi - cient for life's day that by our lives we tru - ly
Fa - ther, and our Lord, to Spir - it blest, most ho - ly

here: "Christ has tri - umphed! He is liv - ing!"
strife. "Christ has tri - umphed! He is liv - ing!"
say: "Christ has tri - umphed! He is liv - ing!"
God, all the glo - ry, nev - er end - ing!

Al - le - lu - ia, al - le - lu - ia, al - le - lu - ia!

Text: Paul Z. Strodach, 1876–1947, alt.
Music: *Geistliche Kirchengesänge*, Köln, 1623
Text © 1958 *Service Book and Hymnal*, admin. Augsburg Fortress

LASST UNS ERFREUEN
888 888 and alleluias

With High Delight Let Us Unite

368

1 With high de - light let us u - nite in songs of great ju - bi - la - tion. You pure in heart, all bear your part, sing Je - sus Christ, our sal - va - tion. To set us free for - ev - er, he is ris'n and sends to all earth's ends good news to save ev - 'ry na - tion.

2 True God, he first from death has burst forth in - to life, all sub - du - ing. His en - e - my now van - quished see; his death has been death's un - do - ing. "And yours shall be like vic - to - ry o'er death and grave," says he, who gave his life for us, life re - new - ing.

3 Let prais - es ring; give thanks, and bring to Christ our Lord ad - o - ra - tion. His hon - or speed by word and deed to ev - 'ry land, ev - 'ry na - tion. So shall his love give us a - bove, from mis - er - y and death set free, all joy and full con - so - la - tion.

Text: Georg Vetter, 1536–1599; tr. Martin H. Franzmann, 1907–1976, alt.
Music: Medieval European tune
Text © 1969 Concordia Publishing House

MIT FREUDEN ZART
8 8 8 8 8 8 8

369 Christ the Lord Is Risen Today; Alleluia!

1 Christ the Lord is ris'n to - day; Al - le - lu - ia!
2 For the sheep the Lamb has bled, Al - le - lu - ia!
3 Christ, the vic - tim un - de - filed, Al - le - lu - ia!
4 Chris - tians, on this ho - ly day, Al - le - lu - ia!

Chris - tians, has - ten on your way; Al - le - lu - ia!
sin - less in the sin - ner's stead. Al - le - lu - ia!
God and sin - ners rec - on - ciled, Al - le - lu - ia!
all your grate - ful hom - age pay; Al - le - lu - ia!

of - fer praise with love re - plete, Al - le - lu - ia!
Christ the Lord is ris'n on high; Al - le - lu - ia!
when con - tend - ing death and life, Al - le - lu - ia!
Christ the Lord is ris'n on high; Al - le - lu - ia!

at the pas - chal vic - tim's feet. Al - le - lu - ia!
now he lives, no more to die. Al - le - lu - ia!
met in strange and awe - some strife. Al - le - lu - ia!
now he lives, no more to die. Al - le - lu - ia!

Text: attr. Wipo of Burgundy, d. c. 1050; tr. Jane E. Leeson, 1807–1882, alt.
Music: Robert Williams, 1781–1821

LLANFAIR
7 7 7 7 and alleluias

Christ Jesus Lay in Death's Strong Bands   370

1 Christ Je - sus lay in death's strong bands for our of - fens - es giv - en;
2 Our Sav - ior Je - sus, God's own Son, here in our stead de - scend - ed;
3 Here the true Pas - chal Lamb we see, whom God so free - ly gave us,
4 So let us keep the fes - ti - val to which the Lord in - vites us;
5 Then let us feast this Eas - ter day on Christ the bread of heav - en;

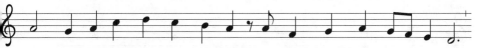

but now at God's right hand he stands and brings us life from heav-en.
the knot of sin has been un-done, the claim of death is end - ed.
who died on the ac - curs - ed tree— so strong God's love!—to save us.
Christ is the ver - y joy of all, the sun that warms and lights us.
the Word of grace has purged a - way the old and e - vil leav-en.

There-fore let us joy - ful be and sing to God right thank - ful - ly
Christ has crushed the pow'r of hell; now there is naught but death's gray shell—
See, his blood now marks our door; faith points to it; death pas - ses o'er,
Now his grace to us im-parts e - ter - nal sun - shine to our hearts;
Christ a - lone, our ho - ly meal, the hun - gry soul will feed and heal;

loud songs of hal - le - lu - jah! Hal - le - lu - jah!
its sting is lost for - ev - er. Hal - le - lu - jah!
and Sa - tan can - not harm us. Hal - le - lu - jah!
the night of sin is end - ed. Hal - le - lu - jah!
faith lives up - on no oth - er! Hal - le - lu - jah!

Text: Martin Luther, 1483–1546; tr. composite
Music: J. Walter, *Geistliche Gesangbüchlein*, 1524
Text st. 2 © 1999 Augsburg Fortress

CHRIST LAG IN TODESBANDEN
87 87 78 74

371 Christians, to the Paschal Victim

1 Chris-tians, to the pas-chal vic-tim of-fer your thank-ful prais-es—
a lamb the sheep re-deem-ing, Christ, who on-ly is sin-less,
rec-on-cil-ing sin-ners to the Fa-ther. Death and life have con-tend-ed
in that com-bat stu-pen-dous; the prince of life, who died, reigns im-mor-tal.

2 Speak, Mar-y, de-clar-ing what you saw when way-far-ing.
"The tomb of Christ, who is liv-ing, the glo-ry of Je-sus' res-ur-rec-tion;
bright an-gels at-test-ing, the shroud and nap-kin rest-ing.
My Lord, my hope, is a-ris-en; to Gal-i-lee he goes be-fore you."

3 Christ in-deed from death is ris-en, our new life ob-tain-ing.
Have mer-cy, vic-tor King, ev-er reign-ing! A - men.

Text: attr. Wipo of Burgundy, d. c. 1050; tr. composite
Music: Plainsong mode I; attr. Wipo of Burgundy

VICTIMAE PASCHAL
PM

Christ Is Arisen

1 Christ is a - ris - en from the grave's dark pris - on. So let our joy rise

full and free; Christ our com-fort true will be. Al - le - lu - ia!

2 Were Christ not a - ris - en, then death were still our

pris - on. Now, with him to life re - stored, we praise

the Fa - ther of our Lord. Al - le - lu - ia!

3 Al - le - lu - ia, al - le - lu - ia,

al - le - lu - ia! So let our joy rise full and free;

Christ our com - fort true will be. Al - le - lu - ia!

Text: German hymn, c. 1100; tr. Martin L. Seltz, 1909–1967
Music: J. Klug, *Geistliche Lieder*, 1543
Text © 1969 Concordia Publishing House

CHRIST IST ERSTANDEN
PM

373   Christ the Lord Is Risen Today!

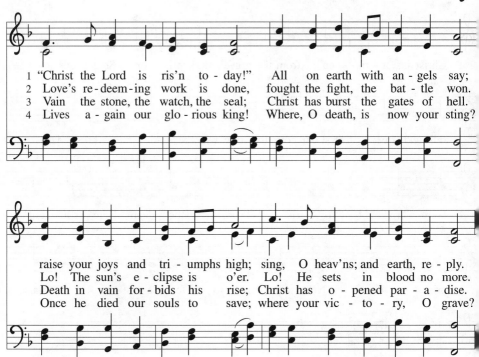

1 "Christ the Lord is ris'n to-day!" All on earth with an-gels say;
2 Love's re-deem-ing work is done, fought the fight, the bat-tle won.
3 Vain the stone, the watch, the seal; Christ has burst the gates of hell.
4 Lives a-gain our glo-rious king! Where, O death, is now your sting?

raise your joys and tri-umphs high; sing, O heav'ns; and earth, re-ply.
Lo! The sun's e-clipse is o'er. Lo! He sets in blood no more.
Death in vain for-bids his rise; Christ has o-pened par-a-dise.
Once he died our souls to save; where your vic-to-ry, O grave?

5 Hail the Lord of earth and heav'n!
Praise to thee by both be giv'n.
Thee we greet triumphant now:
hail, the resurrection, thou!

6 King of glory, soul of bliss,
everlasting life is this:
thee to know, thy pow'r to prove,
thus to sing, and thus to love!

Text: Charles Wesley, 1707–1788, alt.
Music: Pierre de Corbeil, d. 1222, arr. Lutheran Book of Worship
Arr. © 1978 Lutheran Book of Worship, admin. Augsburg Fortress

ORIENTIS PARTIBUS
7 7 7 7

Day of Arising

1 Day of a - ris - ing, Christ on the road - way,
2 When we are walk - ing, doubt - ful and dread - ing,
3 Lo, I am with you, Je - sus has spo - ken.
4 Christ, our com - pan - ion, hope for the jour - ney,

un - known com - pan - ion walks with his own.
blind - ed by sad - ness, slow - ness of heart,
This is Christ's prom - ise, this is Christ's sign:
bread of com - pas - sion, o - pen our eyes.

When they in - vite him, as fades the first day,
yet Christ walks with us, ev - er a - wait - ing
when the church gath - ers, when bread is bro - ken,
Grant us your vi - sion, set all hearts burn - ing

and bread is bro - ken, Christ is made known.
our in - vi - ta - tion: Stay, do not part.
there Christ is with us in bread and wine.
that all cre - a - tion with you may rise.

Text: Susan Palo Cherwien, b. 1953
Music: Carl F. Schalk, b. 1929
Text © 1996 Susan Palo Cherwien, admin. Augsburg Fortress
Music © 1999 Augsburg Fortress

RAABE
5 5 5 4 D

Alternate tune: BUNESSAN

Alleluia! Christ Is Arisen
¡Aleluya! Cristo resucitó

Refrain/Estribillo

¡A - le - lu - ya! Cris - to re - su - ci - tó
Al - le - lu - ia! Christ is a - ris - en.

de ma - dru - ga - da el do - min - go.
Bright is the dawn-ing of the Lord's day.

1 Fue - ron mu - jer - es al se - pul - cro. La pie - dra,_un
1 Run, faith - ful wom-en, to the grave-side. Mar - vel, the
2 Rise, Mag - da - len - a, from your weep-ing; Christ stands be -
3 Gath - er, dis - ci - ples, in the eve - ning: sud - den - ly
4 Thom-as, where were you on that eve - ning? "I'll not be -

án - gel re - mo - vió; les di - jo: "Ha re - su - ci -
stone is rolled a - way! Hear from the an - gel, "He is
fore your ver - y eyes. Quick - ly re - turn to the dis -
Christ your Lord ap - pears. "Look, it is I, your wound-ed
lieve un - less I see." Christ comes a - gain, and ev - 'ry

Refrain/Estribillo

ta - do." Y_al ir - se, les sa - lió_el Se - ñor.
ris - en." Christ goes be - fore you all the way.
ci - ples; bear the good news: "He is a - live."
Sav - ior. Peace be with you, and do not fear."
Lord's day: "Touch me and see; have faith in me."

2 La Magdalena fue_a llorarlo
y Cristo se le_apareció;
le pidió ir a sus hermanos
con un encargo que le dio. Estribillo

3 A los discípulos, de tarde,
Cristo también se presentó.
Les enseño las cinco_heridas;
dando la paz los saludó. Estribillo

4 Tomás no_estaba_en ese_encuentro;
y ver, pidió, para creer.
Cristo volvió, le dijo: "Mira,
palpa mi herida_y ten fe." Estribillo

Text: Luis Bojos, b. 1937; tr. Martin A. Seltz, b. 1951
Music: Luis Bojos
Text and music © 1974, 2000 Luis Bojos, admin. OCP Publications

SANTO DOMINGO
9 8 9 8 and refrain

Thine Is the Glory

1 Thine is the glo - ry, ris - en, con-qu'ring Son; end - less is the
2 Lo, Je - sus meets thee, ris - en from the tomb! Lov-ing - ly he
3 No more we doubt thee, glo - rious Prince of life; life is naught with-

vic - t'ry thou o'er death hast won! An - gels in bright rai - ment
greets thee, scat - ters fear and gloom; let his church with glad - ness
out thee; aid us in our strife; make us more than con - qu'rors,

rolled the stone a - way, kept the fold - ed grave - clothes
hymns of tri - umph sing, for the Lord now liv - eth;
through thy death - less love; bring us safe through Jor - dan

Refrain

where thy bod - y lay.
death hath lost its sting! Thine is the glo - ry, ris - en, con-qu'ring
to thy home a - bove.

Son; end - less is the vic - t'ry thou o'er death hast won!

Text: Edmond Budry, 1854–1932; tr. R. Birch Hoyle, 1875–1939

Music: George Frideric Handel, 1685–1759

JUDAS MACCABAEUS

5 5 6 5 6 5 65 and refrain

377

Alleluia! Jesus Is Risen!

1 Al - le - lu - ia! Je - sus is ris - en!
2 Walk - ing the way, Christ in the cen - ter
3 Je - sus the vine, we are the branch - es;
4 Weep - ing, be gone; sor - row, be si - lent:
5 Cit - y of God, Eas - ter for - ev - er,

Trum - pets re - sound - ing in glo - ri - ous light!
tell - ing the sto - ry to o - pen our eyes;
life in the Spir - it the fruit of the tree;
death put a - sun - der, and Eas - ter is bright.
gold - en Je - ru - sa - lem, Je - sus the Lamb,

Splen - dor, the Lamb, heav - en for - ev - er!
break - ing our bread, giv - ing us glo - ry!
heav - en to earth, Christ to the peo - ple,
Cher - u - bim sing: O grave, be o - pen!
riv - er of life, saints and arch - an - gels,

Oh, what a mir - a - cle God has in sight!
Je - sus our bless - ing, our con - stant sur - prise.
gift of the fu - ture now flow - ing to me.
Clothe us in won - der, a - dorn us in light.
sing with cre - a - tion to God the I Am!

Refrain

Je - sus is ris - en and we shall a - rise.

Give God the glo - ry! Al - le - lu - ia!

Text: Herbert F. Brokering, b. 1926
Music: David N. Johnson, 1922–1987
Text © 1995 Augsburg Fortress
Music © 1969 *Contemporary Worship 1*, admin. Augsburg Fortress

EARTH AND ALL STARS
45 10 45 10 and refrain

Awake, My Heart, with Gladness

1 A - wake, my heart, with glad - ness, see what to - day is done;
2 Now hell, its prince, the dev - il, of all their pow'r are shorn;
3 This is a sight that glad - dens— what peace it does im - part!
4 Now I will cling for - ev - er to Christ, my Sav - ior true;
5 Christ brings me to the por - tal that leads to bliss un - told,

now, af - ter gloom and sad - ness, comes forth the glo - rious sun.
now I am safe from e - vil, and sin I laugh to scorn.
Now noth - ing ev - er sad - dens the joy with - in my heart.
my Lord will leave me nev - er, what - e'er he pass - es through.
where - on this rhyme im - mor - tal is found in script of gold:

My Sav - ior there was laid where our bed must be made
For Christ a - gain is free; in glo - rious vic - to - ry
No gloom shall ev - er shake, no foe shall ev - er take,
He rends death's i - ron chain; he breaks through sin and pain;
"Who there my cross has shared finds here a crown pre - pared;

when, as on wings in flight, we soar to realms of light.
he who is strong to save has tri - umphed o'er the grave.
the hope which God's own Son in love for me has won.
he shat - ters hell's grim thrall; I fol - low him through all.
who there with me has died shall here be glo - ri - fied."

Text: Paul Gerhardt, 1607–1676; tr. John Kelly, 1833–1890, alt.
Music: Johann Crüger, 1598–1662

AUF, AUF, MEIN HERZ
76766666

379

Now the Green Blade Rises

1 Now the green blade ris - es from the bur - ied grain,
2 In the grave they laid him, love by ha - tred slain,
3 Forth he came at Eas - ter like the ris - en grain,
4 When our hearts are win - try, griev - ing, or in pain,

wheat that in dark earth man - y days has lain;
think - ing that he would nev - er wake a - gain,
he that for three days in the grave had lain;
your touch can call us back to life a - gain,

love lives a - gain, that with the dead has been;
laid in the earth like grain that sleeps un - seen;
raised from the dead, my liv - ing Lord is seen;
fields of our hearts that dead and bare have been;

love is come a - gain like wheat a - ris - ing green.

Text: John MacLeod Campbell Crum, 1872–1958
Music: French carol
Text © Oxford University Press

NOËL NOUVELE
11 10 10 1

380

Hallelujah! Jesus Lives

1 Hal - le - lu - jah! Je - sus lives! He is now the Liv - ing One;
2 Je - sus lives! Why do you weep? Why that sad and mourn-ful sigh?
3 Je - sus lives! And thus, my soul, life e - ter - nal waits for you;
4 Je - sus lives! Let all re - joice. Praise him, ran-somed of the earth.
5 Hal - le - lu - jah! An - gels, sing! Join with us in hymns of praise.

Text: Carl B. Garve, 1763–1841; tr. Jane L. Borthwick, 1813–1897, alt.
Music: Ludvig M. Lindeman, 1812–1887

FRED TIL BO
77777

from the gloom-y halls of death Christ, the con - quer - or, has gone,
Christ who died our broth - er here lives our broth-er still on high,
joined to Christ, your liv - ing head, where he is, you shall be too;
Praise him in a no - bler song, cher - u - bim of heav'n-ly birth.
Let your cho - rus swell the strain which our fee - bler voic - es raise:

bright fore - run - ner to the skies of his peo - ple, yet to rise.
lives for - ev - er to be - stow bless-ings on his church be - low.
with the Lord, at God's right hand, as a vic - tor you shall stand.
Praise the vic - tor king, whose sway sin and death and hell o - bey.
Glo - ry to our God a - bove and on earth his peace and love!

Peace, to Soothe Our Bitter Woes 381

1 Peace, to soothe our bitter woes,
   God in Christ on us bestows;
   Jesus bought our peace with God
   with his holy, precious blood;
   peace in him for sinners found
   is the gospel's joyful sound.

2 Peace within the church still dwells
   in our welcomes and farewells;
   and through God's baptismal pow'r
   peace surrounds our dying hour.
   Peace be with you, full and free,
   now and through eternity.

Text: Nikolai F. S. Grundtvig, 1783–1872; tr. George T. Rygh, 1860–1943, alt.

FRED TIL BOD
7 7 7 7 7 7

382

Christ Is Risen! Alleluia!

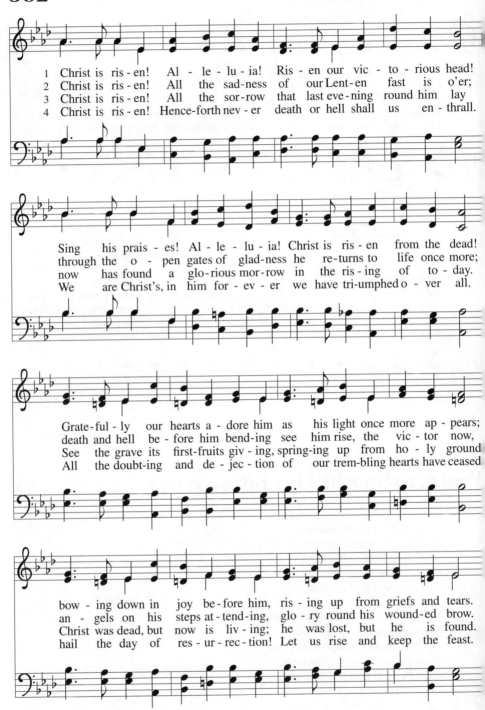

1 Christ is ris - en! Al - le - lu - ia! Ris - en our vic - to - rious head!
2 Christ is ris - en! All the sad-ness of our Lent-en fast is o'er;
3 Christ is ris - en! All the sor-row that last eve-ning round him lay
4 Christ is ris - en! Hence-forth nev - er death or hell shall us en - thrall.

Sing his prais - es! Al - le - lu - ia! Christ is ris - en from the dead!
through the o - pen gates of glad-ness he re-turns to life once more;
now has found a glo-rious mor-row in the ris - ing of to - day.
We are Christ's, in him for - ev - er we have tri-umphed o - ver all.

Grate-ful - ly our hearts a - dore him as his light once more ap - pears;
death and hell be - fore him bend-ing see him rise, the vic - tor now,
See the grave its first-fruits giv - ing, spring-ing up from ho - ly ground
All the doubt-ing and de - jec - tion of our trem-bling hearts have ceased

bow - ing down in joy be-fore him, ris - ing up from griefs and tears.
an - gels on his steps at - tend-ing, glo - ry round his wound-ed brow.
Christ was dead, but now is liv - ing; he was lost, but he is found.
hail the day of res - ur - rec - tion! Let us rise and keep the feast.

Text: John S. B. Monsell, 1811–1875, alt.
Music: Frederick C. Maker, 1844–1927

MORGENLIE
87 87 D and refrai

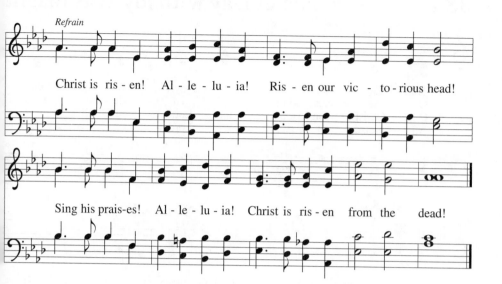

Refrain

Christ is ris - en! Al - le - lu - ia! Ris - en our vic - to - rious head!

Sing his prais-es! Al - le - lu - ia! Christ is ris - en from the dead!

Christ Is Risen! Shout Hosanna!   383

1 Christ is ris - en! Shout Ho - san - na! Cel - e - brate this day of days!
2 Christ is ris - en! Raise your spir - its from the cav - erns of de - spair.
3 Christ is ris - en! Earth and heav - en nev - er-more shall be the same.

Christ is ris - en! Hush in won - der: all cre - a - tion is a - mazed.
Walk with glad-ness in the morn-ing. See what love can do and dare.
Break the bread of new cre - a - tion where the world is still in pain.

In the des - ert all - sur-round-ing, see, a spread-ing tree has grown.
Drink the wine of res - ur - rec - tion, not a ser - vant, but a friend.
Tell its grim, de - mon - ic chor - us: "Christ is ris - en! Get you gone!"

Heal-ing leaves of grace a - bound-ing bring a taste of love un - known.
Je - sus is our strong com-pan - ion. Joy and peace shall nev - er end.
God the First and Last is with us. Sing Ho - san - na, ev - 'ry - one!

Text: Brian A. Wren, b. 1936
Music: Thomas Pavlechko, b. 1962
Text © 1986 Hope Publishing Company
Music © 2006 Thomas Pavlechko, admin. Augsburg Fortress

TURNBULL
8787D

384   That Easter Day with Joy Was Bright

1 That Eas - ter day with joy was bright; the
2 O Je - sus, king of gen - tle - ness, with
3 O Christ, you are the Lord of all in
4 All praise, O ris - en Lord, we give to

sun shone out with fair - er light when, to their long - ing
con - stant love our hearts pos - sess; to you our lips will
this our Eas - ter fes - ti - val, for you will be our
you, once dead, but now a - live! To God the Fa - ther

eyes re - stored, the a - pos - tles saw their ris - en Lord!
ev - er raise the trib - ute of our grate - ful praise.
strength and shield from ev - 'ry weap - on death can wield.
e - qual praise, and God the Spir - it, now we raise!

Text: Latin hymn, 5th cent.; tr. John Mason Neale, 1818–1866, alt.
Music: European tune, adapt. Michael Praetorius, 1571–1621

PUER NOBIS
LM

Good Christian Friends, Rejoice and Sing! 385

1 Good Chris - tian friends, re - joice and sing! Now is the tri - umph
2 The Lord of life is ris'n this day; death's might - y stone is
3 Praise we in songs of vic - to - ry that love, that life which
4 Your name we bless, O ris - en Lord, and sing to - day with

of our king! To all the world glad news we bring:
rolled a - way; let all the earth re - joice and say:
can - not die, and sing with hearts up - lift - ed high:
one ac - cord, the life laid down, the life re - stored:

Al - le - lu - ia, al - le - lu - ia, al - le - lu - ia!
Al - le - lu - ia, al - le - lu - ia, al - le - lu - ia!
Al - le - lu - ia, al - le - lu - ia, al - le - lu - ia!

Text: Cyril A. Alington, 1872–1955, alt.
Music: Melchior Vulpius, 1570–1615
Text © 1958, ren. 1986 *Hymns Ancient and Modern*, admin. Hope Publishing Company

GELOBT SEI GOTT
8 8 8 and alleluias

386   O Sons and Daughters, Let Us Sing

Al - le - lu - ia,   al - le - lu - ia,   al - le - lu - ia.

1 O   sons and daugh - ters, let   us   sing
2 That Eas - ter morn, at break of day,
3 An   an - gel clad in white they see,
4 That night the_a - pos - tles met in fear;

Insert stanzas 5-8 if desired.

9 On this most ho - ly day of days,

with heav'n - ly hosts to Christ our king:
the faith - ful wom - en went their way
who sits and speaks un - to the three,
a - mong them came their mas - ter dear,

be laud and ju - bi - lee and praise:

to - day the grave has lost its sting! Al - le - lu - ia!
to seek the tomb where Je - sus lay. Al - le - lu - ia!
"Your Lord will go to Gal - i - lee." Al - le - lu - ia!
and said, "My peace be with you here." Al - le - lu - ia!

to God your hearts and voic - es raise. Al - le - lu - ia!

After the final stanza

Al - le - lu - ia.   al - le - lu - ia.   al - le - lu - ia.

5 When Thomas first the tidings heard,
that they had seen the risen Lord,
he doubted the disciples' word.
Alleluia!

6 "My piercèd side, O Thomas, see,
and look upon my hands, my feet;
not faithless, but believing be."
Alleluia!

7 No longer Thomas then denied;
he saw the feet, the hands, the side;
"You are my Lord and God!" he cried.
Alleluia!

8 How blest are they who have not seen,
and yet whose faith has constant been,
for they eternal life shall win.
Alleluia!

Text: attr. Jean Tisserand, d. 1494; tr. John Mason Neale, 1818–1866, alt.
Music: French tune, 15th cent.

O FILII ET FILIAE
8 8 8 with alleluia

O Sons and Daughters, Let Us Sing 387

Alleluia, alleluia, alleluia!

1 O sons and daughters, let us sing
with heav'nly hosts to Christ our king:
today the grave has lost its sting!
Alleluia!

2 That Easter morn, at break of day,
a faithful woman went her way
to seek the tomb where Jesus lay.
Alleluia!

3 When Mary's heart was filled with gloom
and she stood weeping near the tomb,
a stranger spoke, she knew not whom.
Alleluia!

4 "Why do you weep?" his question came.
"Whose is the body you would claim?"
And then, at last, he spoke her name.
Alleluia!

5 No longer weeping, anguish-bent,
but with rejoicing Mary went,
by Christ as first apostle sent.
Alleluia!

Alleluia, alleluia, alleluia!

Text: Jean Tisserand, d. 1494, st. 1; tr. John Mason Neale, 1818–1866, alt.;
    Delores Dufner, OSB, b. 1939, sts. 2–5
Text sts. 2–5 © 1994, 2003 GIA Publications, Inc.

O FILII ET FILIAE
8 8 8 with alleluias

Be Not Afraid 388

Be not a-fraid, sing out for joy! Christ is ris-en, al-le - lu - ia!

Be not a-fraid, sing out for joy! Christ is ris-en, al-le - lu - ia!

Text: Matthew 28:5; Taizé Community
Music: Jacques Berthier, 1923–1994
Text and music © 1998 Les Presses de Taizé, admin. GIA Publications, Inc.

BE NOT AFRAID
4 4 8 D

389 Christ Is Alive! Let Christians Sing

1 Christ is a - live! Let Chris - tians sing. The cross stands
2 Christ is a - live! No long - er bound to dis - tant
3 In ev - 'ry in - sult, rift, and war, where col - or,
4 Wom - en and men, in age and youth, can feel the
5 Christ is a - live, and comes to bring good news to

emp - ty to the sky. Let streets and homes with
years in Pal - es - tine, but sav - ing, heal - ing,
scorn, or wealth di - vide, Christ suf - fers still, yet
Spir - it, hear the call, and find the way, the
this and ev - 'ry age, till earth and sky and

prais - es ring. Love, drowned in death, shall nev - er die.
here and now, and touch - ing ev - 'ry place and time.
loves the more, and lives, where e - ven hope has died.
life, the truth, re - vealed in Je - sus, freed for all.
o - cean ring with joy, with jus - tice, love, and praise.

Text: Brian A. Wren, b. 1936
Music: T. Williams, *Psalmodia Evangelica*, 1789
Text © 1975, rev. 1995 Hope Publishing Company

TRUR(
Lʌ

The Risen Christ

1 The ris - en Christ, who walks on wound-ed feet
2 The ris - en Christ, who stands with wound-ed side,
3 The ris - en Christ, who breaks with wound-ed hand
4 May we, Christ's bod - y, walk and serve and stand

from gar - den tomb through dark - ened cit - y street,
breathes out his Spir - it on them to a - bide
the bread for those who fail to un - der - stand,
with those op - pressed in this and ev - 'ry land,

un - locks the door of grief, de - spair, and fear,
whose faith still wa - vers, who dare not be - lieve;
re - veals him - self, de - spite their lin - g'ring tears,
till all are blessed and can a bless - ing be,

and speaks a word of peace to all who hear.
new grace, new strength, new pur - pose they re - ceive.
en - flames their hearts, then quick - ly dis - ap - pears.
re - stored in Christ to true hu - man - i - ty.

Text: Nigel Weaver, b. 1952
Music: Walter Greatorex, 1877–1949
Text © 1993 Nigel Weaver
Music © Oxford University Press

WOODLANDS
10 10 10 10

391

This Joyful Eastertide

1 This joy - ful Eas - ter - tide, a - way with sin and
2 My flesh in hope shall rest and for a sea - son
3 Death's flood has lost its chill since Je - sus crossed the

sor - - row! My love, the Cru - ci - fied, has
slum - - ber till trump from east to west shall
riv - - er. Lov - er of souls, from ill my

sprung to life this mor - row.
wake the dead in num - ber.
pass - ing soul de - liv - er.

Refrain

Had Christ, who once was slain, not burst his three-day pris - on, our

Text: George R. Woodward, 1848–1934
Music: Dutch folk tune, 17th cent.; arr. hymnal version
Arr. © 2006 Augsburg Fortress

VRUECHTEN
6 7 6 7 and refrain

faith had been in vain. But now has Christ a - ris - en, a -

ris - en, a - ris - en, a - ris - en.

392 Alleluia! Sing to Jesus

1 Al - le - lu - ia! Sing to Je - sus; his the scep-ter,
2 Al - le - lu - ia! Not as or - phans are we left in
3 Al - le - lu - ia! Bread of heav - en, here on earth our
4 Al - le - lu - ia! King e - ter - nal, Lord om - nip - o -
5 Al - le - lu - ia! Sing to Je - sus; his the scep-ter,

his the throne; Al - le - lu - ia! his the tri - umph, his the
sor - row now; Al - le - lu - ia! he is near us; faith be -
food, our stay; Al - le - lu - ia! here the sin - ful flee to
tent we own; Al - le - lu - ia! born of Mar - y, earth your
his the throne; Al - le - lu - ia! his the tri - umph, his the

vic - to - ry a - lone. Hark! The songs of peace - ful
lieves, nor ques - tions how. Though the cloud from sight re -
you from day to day. In - ter - ces - sor, friend of
foot - stool, heav'n your throne. As with - in the veil you
vic - to - ry a - lone. Hark! The songs of peace - ful

Zi - on thun - der like a might - y flood: "Je - sus
ceived him when the for - ty days were o'er, shall our
sin - ners, earth's re - deem - er, hear our plea where the
en - tered, robed in flesh, our great high priest, here on
Zi - on thun - der like a might - y flood: "Je - sus

Text: William C. Dix, 1837–1898, alt.
Music: Rowland H. Prichard, 1811–1887

HYFRYDOL
8 7 8 7 D

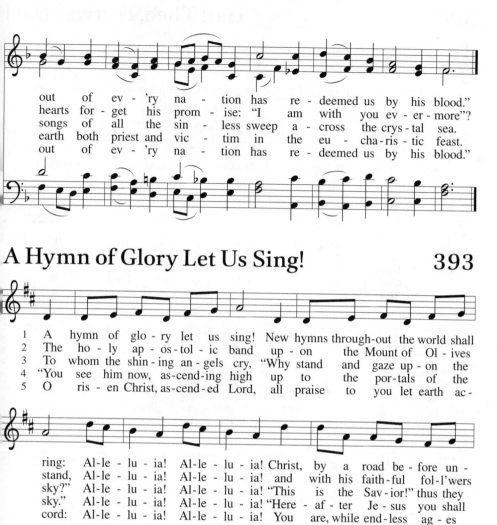

out of ev - 'ry na - tion has re - deemed us by his blood."
hearts for - get his prom - ise: "I am with you ev - er - more"?
songs of all the sin - less sweep a - cross the crys - tal sea.
earth both priest and vic - tim in the eu - cha - ris - tic feast.
out of ev - 'ry na - tion has re - deemed us by his blood."

A Hymn of Glory Let Us Sing! 393

1 A hymn of glo - ry let us sing! New hymns through-out the world shall
2 The ho - ly ap - os - tol - ic band up - on the Mount of Ol - ives
3 To whom the shin - ing an - gels cry, "Why stand and gaze up - on the
4 "You see him now, as-cend-ing high up to the por - tals of the
5 O ris - en Christ, as-cend-ed Lord, all praise to you let earth ac -

ring: Al-le - lu - ia! Al-le - lu - ia! Christ, by a road be - fore un -
stand, Al-le - lu - ia! Al-le - lu - ia! and with his faith-ful fol-l'wers
sky?" Al-le - lu - ia! Al-le - lu - ia! "This is the Sav-ior!" thus they
sky." Al-le - lu - ia! Al-le - lu - ia! "Here - af - ter Je - sus you shall
cord: Al-le - lu - ia! Al-le - lu - ia! You are, while end-less ag - es

trod, as - cends un - to the throne of God.
see their Lord as - cend in maj - es - ty.
say, "this is his glo-rious tri - umph day!" Al-le - lu - ia! Al-le -
see re - turn-ing in great maj - es - ty."
run, with Fa - ther and with Spir - it one.

lu - ia! Al-le - lu - ia, al-le - lu - ia, al-le - lu - ia!

Text: Bede, 673–735; tr. *Lutheran Book of Worship*
Music: *Geistliche Kirchengesänge*, Köln, 1623
Text © 1978 *Lutheran Book of Worship*, admin. Augsburg Fortress

LASST UNS ERFREUEN
LM and alleluias

394

Hail Thee, Festival Day!

Refrain

Hail thee, fes - ti - val day! Blest day to be hal-lowed for - ev - er;

day when our Lord was raised, break - ing the king - dom of death.

Easter 1	All	the	fair	beau - ty	of	earth	from the
Ascension 1	He	who	was	nailed	to	the	cross	is . .
Pentecost 1	Bright	and	in	like - ness	of	fire,	on . .
3	God	the	Al - might - y,	the	Lord,	the . .
5	Spir - it	of	life	and	of	pow'r,	now . .

death of the win - ter a - ris - ing! Ev - 'ry good
rul - er and Lord of all peo - ple. All things cre -
those who a - wait his ap - pear - ing, he whom the
rul - er of earth and the heav - ens, guard us from
flow in us, fount of our be - ing, light that en -

Refrain

gift of the year now with its mas - ter re - turns:
at - ed on earth sing to the glo - ry of God:
Lord had fore - told sud - den - ly, swift - ly de - scends:
harm with - out; cleanse us from e - vil with - in:
light - ens us all, life that in all may a - bide:

Text: Venantius Honorius Fortunatus, 530–609; tr. *Lutheran Book of Worship*
Music: Ralph Vaughan Williams, 1872–1958
Text © 1978 *Lutheran Book of Worship*, admin. Augsburg Fortress
Music © Oxford University Press

SALVE FESTA DIE
Irregula

Easter 2	Rise from	the	grave now,	O	Lord,	the	au - thor of
Ascension 2	Dai - ly	the	love - li - ness	grows,	a - dorned with the
Pentecost 2	Dai - ly	the	love - li - ness	grows,	a - dorned with the
4	Je - sus,	the	health of	the	world,	en - light - en	our
6	Praise to	the	giv - er	of	good!	O	Lov - er and

life	and	cre - a - tion.	Tread-ing	the	path - way of
glo - ry of	blos - som;	heav - en	its	gates now	un -
glo - ry of	blos - som;	heav - en	its	gates now	un -
minds,	great re - deem - er,	Son	of	the	Fa - ther	su -
Au - thor	of	con - cord,	pour out	your balm on	our

Refrain

death,	new	life you	give	to	us	all:
bars,	fling - ing	its	in - crease	of	light:
bars,	fling - ing	its	in - crease	of	light:
preme,	on - ly - be - got - ten	of	God:
days;	or - der	our	ways	in	your	peace:

395 Come, Holy Ghost, God and Lord

1 Come, Ho - ly Ghost, God and Lord, with all your
2 Come, ho - ly Light, guide di - vine, now cause the
3 Come, ho - ly Fire, com - fort true, grant us the

grac - es now out - poured on each be - liev - er's
word of life to shine. Teach us to know our
will your work to do and in your ser - vice

mind and heart; your fer - vent love to them im - part.
God a - right as lov - ing Fa - ther, our de - light.
to a - bide; let tri - als turn us not a - side.

Lord, by the bright - ness of your light in ho - ly
From ev - 'ry er - ror keep us free; let none but
Lord, by your pow'r pre - pare each heart and to our

faith your church u - nite; from ev - 'ry land and
Christ our teach - er be, that we in liv - ing
weak - ness strength im - part, that brave - ly here we

ev - 'ry tongue, this to your praise, O Lord, our God, be sung:
faith a - bide, in him, our Lord, with all our might con - fide.
may con - tend, through life and death to you, our Lord, as - cend.

Al - le - lu - ia! Al - le - lu - ia!

Text: German hymn, 15th cent., st. 1; Martin Luther, 1483–1546, sts. 2–3; tr. composite
Music: *Enchiridion*, Erfurt, 1524

KOMM, HEILIGER GEIST, HERRE GOTT
7 8 8 8 8 8 8 10 8

Spirit of Gentleness

396

Refrain

Spir - it, Spir - it of gen-tle-ness, blow through the wil-der-ness call-ing and free; Spir - it, Spir - it of rest-less-ness, stir me from plac-id-ness, wind, wind on the sea.

1 You moved on the wa - ters, you called to the deep,
2 You swept through the des - ert, you stung with the sand,
3 You sang in a sta - ble, you cried from a hill,
4 You call from to - mor - row, you break an-cient schemes.

then you coaxed up the moun - tains from the val - leys of sleep;
and you goad - ed your peo - ple with a law and a land;
then you whis-pered in si - lence when the whole world was still;
From the bond - age of sor - row all the cap - tives dream dreams;

and o - ver the e - ons you called to each thing:
and when they were blind - ed with i - dols and lies,
and down in the cit - y you called once a - gain,
our wom - en see vi - sions, our men clear their eyes.

Refrain

"A - wake from your slum - bers and rise on your wings."
then you spoke through your proph - ets to o - pen their eyes.
when you blew through your peo - ple on the rush of the wind.
With . . . bold new de - ci - sions your peo-ple a - rise.

Text: James K. Manley, b. 1940
Music: James K. Manley
Text and music © 1978 James K. Manley

SPIRIT
Irregular

397   # Loving Spirit

1 Lov - ing Spir-it, lov-ing Spir - it, you have cho - sen me to be—
2 Like a moth-er you en - fold me, hold my life with - in your own,
3 Like a fa - ther you pro - tect me, teach me the dis - cern - ing eye,
4 Friend and lov - er, in your close-ness I am known and held and blessed:
5 Lov - ing Spir-it, lov-ing Spir - it, you have cho - sen me to be—

you have drawn me to your won - der, you have set your sign on me.
feed me with your ver - y bod - y, form me of your flesh and bone.
hoist me up up - on your shoul-der, let me see the world from high.
in your prom - ise is my com - fort, in your pres-ence I may rest.
you have drawn me to your won - der, you have set your sign on me.

Text: Shirley Erena Murray, b. 1931
Music: W. Walker, *Southern Harmony*, 1835; arr. hymnal version
Text © 1987 The Hymn Society, admin. Hope Publishing Company
Arr. © 2006 Augsburg Fortress

RESTORATION
8 7 8 7

398   # Holy Spirit, Truth Divine

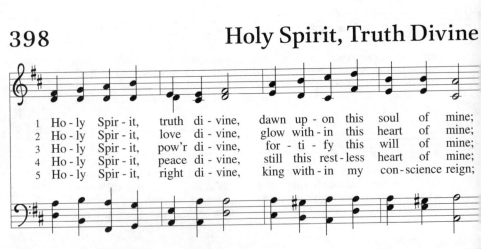

1 Ho - ly Spir - it, truth di - vine, dawn up - on this soul of mine;
2 Ho - ly Spir - it, love di - vine, glow with - in this heart of mine;
3 Ho - ly Spir - it, pow'r di - vine, for - ti - fy this will of mine;
4 Ho - ly Spir - it, peace di - vine, still this rest-less heart of mine;
5 Ho - ly Spir - it, right di - vine, king with - in my con - science reign;

Text: Samuel Longfellow, 1819–1892
Music: Orlando Gibbons, 1583–1625

SONG 1
7 7 7

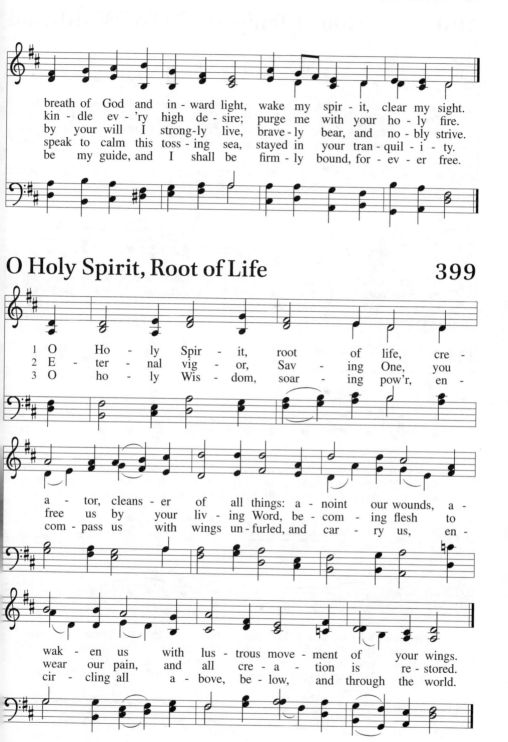

breath of God and in - ward light, wake my spir - it, clear my sight.
kin - dle ev - 'ry high de - sire; purge me with your ho - ly fire.
by your will I strong-ly live, brave - ly bear, and no - bly strive.
speak to calm this toss - ing sea, stayed in your tran - quil - i - ty.
be my guide, and I shall be firm - ly bound, for - ev - er free.

O Holy Spirit, Root of Life 399

1 O Ho - ly Spir - it, root of life, cre -
2 E - ter - nal vig - or, Sav - ing One, you
3 O ho - ly Wis - dom, soar - ing pow'r, en -

a - tor, cleans - er of all things: a - noint our wounds, a -
free us by your liv - ing Word, be - com - ing flesh to
com - pass us with wings un - furled, and car - ry us, en -

wak - en us with lus - trous move - ment of your wings.
wear our pain, and all cre - a - tion is re - stored.
cir - cling all a - bove, be - low, and through the world.

Text: Jean Janzen, b. 1933; based on Hildegard of Bingen, 1098–1179
Music: European tune; adapt. Michael Praetorius, 1571–1621; arr. hymnal version
Text © 1991 Jean Janzen, admin. Augsburg Fortress
Arr. © 2006 Augsburg Fortress

PUER NOBIS
LM

400 God of Tempest, God of Whirlwind

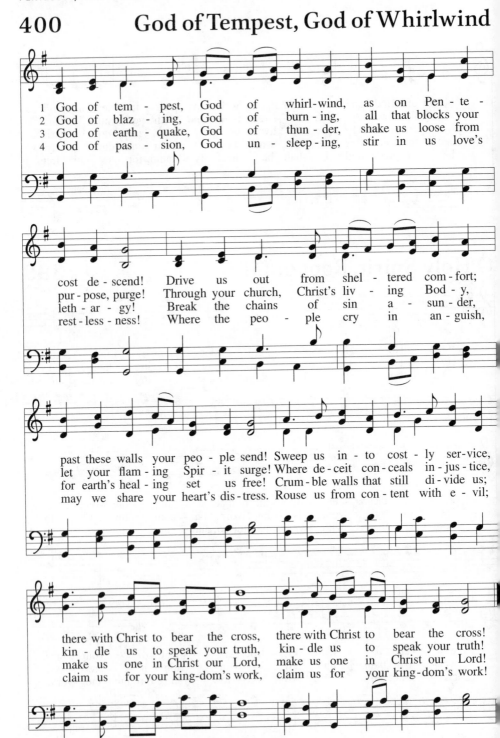

1 God of tem - pest, God of whirl-wind, as on Pen - te -
2 God of blaz - ing, God of burn - ing, all that blocks your
3 God of earth - quake, God of thun - der, shake us loose from
4 God of pas - sion, God un - sleep - ing, stir in us love's

cost de - scend! Drive us out from shel - tered com - fort;
pur - pose, purge! Through your church, Christ's liv - ing Bod - y,
leth - ar - gy! Break the chains of sin a - sun - der,
rest - less - ness! Where the peo - ple cry in an - guish,

past these walls your peo - ple send! Sweep us in - to cost - ly ser - vice,
let your flam - ing Spir - it surge! Where de - ceit con - ceals in - jus - tice,
for earth's heal - ing set us free! Crum - ble walls that still di - vide us;
may we share your heart's dis - tress. Rouse us from con - tent with e - vil;

there with Christ to bear the cross, there with Christ to bear the cross!
kin - dle us to speak your truth, kin - dle us to speak your truth!
make us one in Christ our Lord, make us one in Christ our Lord!
claim us for your king-dom's work, claim us for your king-dom's work!

Text: Herman G. Stuempfle Jr., b. 1923
Music: John Hughes, 1873–1932
Text © 2000 GIA Publications, Inc.

CWM RHONDDA
8 7 8 7 8 7 7

Gracious Spirit, Heed Our Pleading

Njoo kwetu, Roho mwema

Njo - o kwe - tu,   Ro - ho mwe - ma,   M - fa - ri - ji we - tu.

1 Gra - cious Spir - it,   heed our plead - ing,   fash - ion us all a - new.
2 Come to teach us,   come to nour - ish   those who be - lieve in Christ.
3 Guide our think - ing   and our speak-ing   done in your ho - ly name.

Tu - fu - ndi - she   ya mbi - ngu - ni,   tu - we wa - tu wa - pya.

It's your lead - ing   that we're need - ing,   help us to fol - low you.
Bless the faith - ful,   may they flour - ish,   strength-ened by grace un - priced.
Mo - ti - vate all   in their seek - ing,   free - ing from guilt and shame.

Refrain

Njo - o,   njo - o,   njo - o, Ro - ho mwe - ma.

Come,   come,   come, Ho - ly Spir - it, come.

Njo - o,   njo - o,   njo - o, Ro - ho mwe - ma.

Come,   come,   come, Ho - ly Spir - it, come.

4 Not mere knowledge, but discernment,
   nor rootless liberty;
   turn disquiet to contentment,
   doubt into certainty. *Refrain*

5 Keep us fervent in our witness,
   unswayed by earth's allure.
   Ever grant us zealous fitness,
   which you alone assure. *Refrain*

Text: Wilson Niwagila; tr. Howard S. Olson, b. 1922
Music: Wilson Niwagila; arr. Egil Hovland, b. 1924
English and Swahili text and tune © Lutheran Theological College, Makumira, Tanzania, admin. Augsburg Fortress
Arr. © Egil Hovland

NJOO KWETU, ROHO MWEMA
CM and refrain

402 Eternal Spirit of the Living Christ

1 E - ter - nal Spir - it of the liv - ing Christ, I know not how to
2 Come, pray in me the prayer I need this day; help me to see your
3 Come with the vi - sion and the strength I need to serve my God and

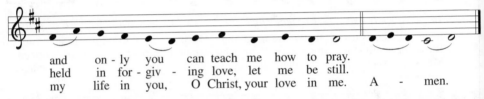

ask or what to say; I on - ly know my need, as deep as life,
pur - pose and your will, where I have failed, what I have done a - miss;
all hu - man - i - ty; ful - fill - ment of my life in love out-poured:

and on - ly you can teach me how to pray.
held in for - giv - ing love, let me be still.
my life in you, O Christ, your love in me. A - men.

Text: Frank von Christierson, 1900–1996
Music: Plainsong mode V; *Processionale*, Paris, 1697
Text © 1974 The Hymn Society, admin. Hope Publishing Company

ADORO TE DEVOTE
10 10 10 10

403 Like the Murmur of the Dove's Song

1 Like the mur - mur of the dove's song, like the chal - lenge of her
2 To the mem - bers of Christ's bod - y, to the branch - es of the
3 With the heal - ing of di - vi - sion, with the cease - less voice of

flight, like the vig - or of the wind's rush, like the
vine, to the church in faith as - sem - bled, to our
prayer, with the pow'r to love and wit - ness, with the

new flame's ea - ger might: come, Ho - ly Spir - it, come.
midst as gift and sign: come, Ho - ly Spir - it, come.
peace be - yond com - pare: come, Ho - ly Spir - it, come.

Text: Carl P. Daw Jr., b. 1944
Music: Peter Cutts, b. 1937
Text © 1982 Hope Publishing Company
Music © 1969 Hope Publishing Company

BRIDEGROOM
87 87 6

Come, Gracious Spirit, Heavenly Dove   404

1 Come, gra - cious Spir - it, heav'n - ly dove, with light and
2 The light of truth to us dis - play and make us
3 Lead us to Christ, the liv - ing way, nor let us
4 Lead us to heav'n, that we may share full - ness of

com - fort from a - bove. Come, be our guard - ian
know and choose your way; plant ho - ly fear in
from his pas - tures stray. Lead us in ho - li -
joy for - ev - er there; lead us to our e -

and our guide; o'er ev - 'ry thought and step pre - side.
ev - 'ry heart, that we from God may ne'er de - part.
ness, the road that we must take to dwell with God
ter - nal rest, to be with God for - ev - er blest.

Text: Simon Browne, 1680–1732, alt.
Music: German folk tune, 15th cent.

HERR JESU CHRIST, MEINS
LM

405

O Spirit of Life

1 O Spir - it of life, O Spir-it of God,
2 O Spir - it of life, O Spir-it of God,
3 O Spir - it of life, O Spir-it of God,
4 O Spir - it of life, O Spir-it of God,

in ev - 'ry need you bring us aid,
in - crease our faith in our dear Lord,
make us to love your sa - cred word,
en - light - en us by that same word;

pro - ceed - ing forth from heav - en's throne,
un - less your grace the pow'r should give,
the ho - ly flame of love im - part,
teach us to know God's ra - diant love,

from God, the Fa - ther and the Son;
none can be - lieve in Christ and live;
that char - i - ty may warm each heart;
lead us to Christ who reigns a - bove;

Text: Johann Niedling, 1602–1668; tr. John C. Mattes, 1876–1948, alt.
Music: *Geistliche Kirchengesänge*, Köln, 1623; arr. Johann Sebastian Bach, 1685–1750

O HEILIGER GEIST
10 8 88 10

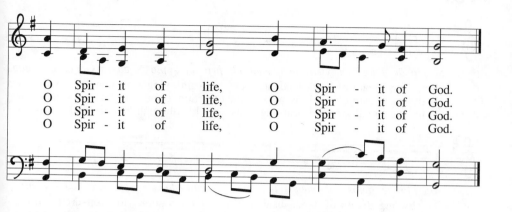

O   Spir - it   of   life,   O   Spir - it   of   God.
O   Spir - it   of   life,   O   Spir - it   of   God.
O   Spir - it   of   life,   O   Spir - it   of   God.
O   Spir - it   of   life,   O   Spir - it   of   God.

Veni Sancte Spiritus
Holy Spirit, Come to Us

406

Ostinato (repeated continuously)

Ve - ni San - cte Spi - ri - tus.   Ve - ni San - cte Spi - ri - tus.
Ho - ly Spir - it, come to us.   *Ho - ly Spir - it, come to us.*

Text: Pentecost sequence; Taizé Community
Music: Jacques Berthier, 1923–1994
Text and music © 1979, 1980, 1991 Les Presses de Taizé, admin. GIA Publications, Inc.

TAIZÉ VENI SANCTE
Irregular

O Living Breath of God
Soplo de Dios viviente

1 So-plo de Dios vi-vien-te que en el prin-ci-pio   cu-bris-te el a - gua,
1 O liv-ing Breath of God, wind at   the be-gin-ning up-on the   wa-ters;
2 O liv-ing Breath of God, by whose pow'r the Son came   to birth a - mong us;
3 O liv-ing Breath of God, bear-ing   us   to life through bap-tis-mal wa-ters;

So - plo de Dios vi - vien - te que fe - cun - da - ste la cre - a - ción:
O   liv-ing Breath of God, bear-ing the cre - a - tion to won-drous birth:
O   liv-ing Breath of God, who to the cre - a - tion gives life a - new:
O   liv-ing Breath of God, sigh-ing with cre - a - tion for free-dom's birth:

Refrain / Estribillo

Ven hoy a nues-tras al - mas, in-fún-de-nos tus do - nes;
Come now, and fill our spir - its; pour out your gifts a - bun - dant.

So - plo de Dios vi - vien - te, oh San-to E-spí - ri-tu del Se - ñor.
O   liv-ing Breath of God, Ho-ly Spir-it, breathe in us as we pray.

2 *Soplo de Dios viviente*
   por quien el Hijo se hizo hombre,
   Soplo de Dios viviente
   que renovaste la creación: Estribillo

3 *Soplo de Dios viviente*
   por quien nacemos en el bautismo,
   Soplo de Dios viviente
   que consagraste la creación: Estribillo

Text: Osvaldo Catena, 1920–1986; tr. Gerhard M. Cartford, b. 1923
Music: Swedish folk tune
Spanish text © 1979 Editorial Bonum; tr. © 1998 Augsburg Fortress

VÅRVINDAR FRISKA
8 9 8 8 and refrain

Come, Thou Almighty King 408

1 Come, thou al - might - y King, help us thy name to sing;
2 Come, thou in - car - nate Word, mer - ci - ful, might - y Lord;
3 Come, ho - ly Com - fort - er, thy sa - cred wit - ness bear
4 To thee, great One in Three, e - ter - nal prais - es be

help us to praise; Fa - ther all - glo - ri - ous, o'er all vic -
our prayer at - tend. Come and thy peo - ple bless, and give thy
in this glad hour! Thou who al - might - y art, rule now in
hence ev - er - more! Thy sov - 'reign maj - es - ty may we in

to - ri - ous, come and reign o - ver us, An - cient of Days.
word suc - cess, and let thy righ - teous-ness on us de - scend.
ev - 'ry heart, nev - er from us de - part, Spir - it of pow'r.
glo - ry see, and to e - ter - ni - ty love and a - dore.

Text: source unknown, c. 1757, alt.
Music: Felice de Giardini, 1716–1796

ITALIAN HYMN
6 6 4 6 6 6 4

409

Kyrie! God, Father

Ky - ri - e! God, Fa - ther in heav'n a - bove, you a - bound in gra - cious love, of all things the mak - er and pre - serv - er. E - le - i - son! E - le - i - son! Ky - ri - e! O Christ, our king, sal - va - tion for all you came to bring. O Lord Je - sus, God's own Son, our me - di - a - tor at the heav'n-ly throne: hear our cry and grant our sup - pli - ca - tion. E - le - i - son! E - le - i - son! Ky - ri - e! O God the Ho - ly Ghost, guard our faith, the gift we need the most, and bless our life's last hour, that we leave this sin - ful world with glad - ness. E - le - i - son! E - le - i - son! A - men.

Text: Latin hymn, c. 1100; tr. W. Gustave Polack, 1890–1950, alt.
Music: "Kyrie fons bonitatis," c. 800, adapt.
Text © 1941 Concordia Publishing House

KYRIE, GOTT VATER
PM

All Glory Be to God on High

410

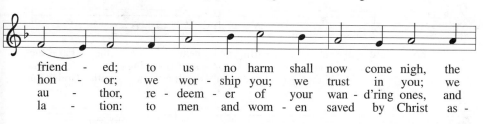

1 All glo - ry be to God on high, who has the world be -
2 O Fa - ther, for your lord - ship true we give you praise and
3 Lord Je - sus Christ, the on - ly Son of God, cre - a - tion's
4 O Ho - ly Spir - it, per - fect gift, who brings us con - so -

friend - ed; to us no harm shall now come nigh, the
hon - or; we wor - ship you; we trust in you; we
au - thor, re - deem - er of your wan - d'ring ones, and
la - tion: to men and wom - en saved by Christ as -

strife at last is end - ed. God shows good - will to
give you thanks for - ev - er. Your will is per - fect,
source of all true plea - sure; O Lamb of God, O
sure your in - spi - ra - tion. Through sick - ness, need, and

one and all, and peace when trou - bled sin - ners call. Thank
and your might re - lent - less - ly con - firms the right; your
Lord di - vine, con - form our lives to your de - sign, and
bit - ter death, grant us your warm, life - giv - ing breath; our

God for grace and mer - cy!
lord - ship is our bless - ing.
on us all have mer - cy.
lives are in your keep - ing. A - men.

Text: Nikolaus Decius, 1485–1550; tr. composite
Music: Plainsong; adapt. Nikolaus Decius
Text © 1978, 2006 Augsburg Fortress

ALLEIN GOTT IN DER HÖH
8 7 8 7 8 8 7

411 We All Believe in One True God

1 We all be - lieve in one true God,
2 We all be - lieve in Je - sus Christ,
3 We all con - fess the Ho - ly Ghost

who cre - at - ed earth and heav - en, the Fa - ther,
his own Son, our Lord, pos - sess - ing an e - qual
who, in high - est heav - en dwell - ing with God the

who to us in love has the right of chil - dren giv - en.
God-head, throne, and might, source of ev - 'ry grace and bless - ing;
Fa - ther and the Son, com-forts us be - yond all tell - ing;

He in soul and bod - y feeds us; all we need his
born of Mar - y, vir - gin moth - er, by the pow - er
who the church, his own cre - a - tion, keeps in u - ni -

hand pro - vides us; through all snares and per - ils
of the Spir - it, Word made flesh, our el - der
ty of spir - it. Here for - give - ness and sal -

leads us, watch - ing that no harm be - tide us.
broth - er; that the lost might life in - her - it,
va - tion dai - ly come through Je - sus' mer - it.

He cares for us day and
was put to death on the
All flesh shall rise; we shall

Text: Martin Luther, 1483–1546; tr. composite
Music: Latin *Credo*, c. 1300, adapt.
Text © 1941 Concordia Publishing House

WIR GLAUBEN ALL
8 8 8 8 8 8 8 8 8 8 7 8

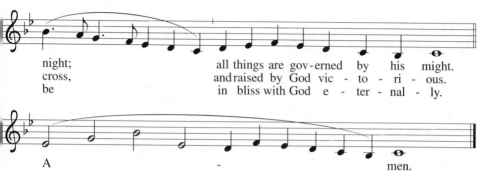

night;
cross,
be

all things are gov-erned by his might.
and raised by God vic - to - ri - ous.
in bliss with God e - ter - nal - ly.

A - men.

Come, Join the Dance of Trinity   412

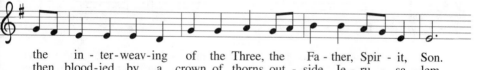

1 Come, join the dance of Trin - i - ty, be - fore all worlds be - gun—
2 Come, see the face of Trin - i - ty, new - born in Beth - le - hem;
3 Come, speak a - loud of Trin - i - ty, as wind and tongues of flame
4 With - in the dance of Trin - i - ty, be - fore all worlds be - gun,

the in - ter-weav-ing of the Three, the Fa - ther, Spir - it, Son.
then blood-ied by a crown of thorns out - side Je - ru - sa - lem.
set peo - ple free at Pen - te - cost to tell the Sav - ior's name.
we sing the prais - es of the Three, the Fa - ther, Spir - it, Son.

The u - ni - verse of space and time did not a - rise by chance,
The dance of Trin - i - ty is meant for hu - man flesh and bone;
We know the yoke of sin and death, our necks have worn it smooth;
Let voic - es rise and in - ter-weave, by love and hope set free,

but as the Three, in love and hope, made room with-in their dance.
when fear con-fines the dance in death, God rolls a - way the stone.
go tell the world of weight and woe that we are free to move!
to shape in song this joy, this life: the dance of Trin - i - ty.

Text: Richard Leach, b. 1953
Music: English folk tune
Text © 2001 Selah Publishing Co., Inc.

KINGSFOLD
CMD

413 Holy, Holy, Holy, Lord God Almighty!

1 Ho-ly, holy, ho - ly, Lord God Al-might-y!
2 Ho-ly, holy, ho - ly! All the saints a - dore thee,
3 Ho-ly, holy, ho - ly! Though the dark-ness hide thee,
4 Ho-ly, holy, ho - ly! Lord God Al-might - y!

Ear - ly in the morn - ing our song shall rise to thee.
cast - ing down their gold - en crowns a - round the glass - y sea;
though the eye of sin - ful - ness thy glo - ry may not see,
All thy works shall praise thy name in earth and sky and sea.

Ho-ly, holy, ho - ly, mer - ci - ful and might - y!
cher-u-bim and ser - a - phim fall - ing down be - fore thee,
on - ly thou art ho - ly; there is none be - side thee,
Ho-ly, holy, ho - ly, mer - ci - ful and might - y!

God in three per - sons, bless - ed Trin - i - ty!
which wert and art, and ev - er - more shalt be.
per - fect in pow'r, in love and pu - ri - ty.
God in three per - sons, bless - ed Trin - i - ty!

Text: Reginald Heber, 1783–1826, alt.
Music: John B. Dykes, 1823–1876

NICAEA
Irregular

Holy God, We Praise Your Name

1 Ho - ly God, we praise your name; Lord of all, we
2 Hark! The glad ce - les - tial hymn an - gel choirs a -
3 Lo, the ap - os - tol - ic train join your sa - cred
4 Ho - ly Fa - ther, ho - ly Son, Ho - ly Spir - it,

bow be - fore you. All on earth your scep - ter claim,
bove are rais - ing; cher - u - bim and ser - a - phim,
name to hal - low; proph - ets swell the glad re - frain,
three we name you, though in es - sence on - ly one;

all in heav'n a - bove a - dore you. In - fi - nite your
in un - ceas - ing cho - rus prais - ing, fill the heav'ns with
and the white - robed mar - tyrs fol - low; and from morn to
un - di - vid - ed God we claim you and, a - dor - ing,

vast do - main, ev - er - last - ing is your reign.
sweet ac - cord: "Ho - ly, ho - ly, ho - ly Lord!"
set of sun through the church the song goes on.
bend the knee while we own the mys - ter - y.

Text: source unknown; tr. Clarence A. Walworth, 1820–1900
Music: *Katholisches Gesangbuch*, Vienna, 1774

GROSSER GOTT
7 8 7 8 7 7

415

Father Most Holy

1 Fa - ther most ho - ly, mer - ci - ful, and ten - der; Je - sus, our
2 Trin - i - ty bless - ed, u - ni - ty un - shak - en; good - ness un -
3 Mak - er of all things, all thy crea - tures praise thee; all for thy
4 Lord God Al - might - y, un - to thee be glo - ry, one in three

Sav - ior, with the Fa - ther reign - ing; Spir - it of com - fort,
bound - ed, ver - y God of heav - en, light of the an - gels,
wor - ship were and are cre - at - ed; now, as we al - so
per - sons, o - ver all ex - alt - ed! Glo - ry we of - fer,

ad - vo - cate, de - fend - er, light nev - er wan - ing.
joy of those for - sak - en, hope of all liv - ing.
wor - ship thee de - vout - ly, hear thou our voic - es.
praise thee and a - dore thee, now and for - ev - er.

Text: Latin hymn, 10th cent.; tr. Percy Dearmer, 1867–1936, alt.
Music: Paris *Antiphoner*, 1681
Text © Oxford University Press

CHRISTE SANCTORUM
11 11 11 5

At the Name of Jesus

1 At the name of Je - sus ev - 'ry knee shall bow,
2 At his voice cre - a - tion sprang at once to sight,
3 Hum - bled for a sea - son, to re - ceive a name
4 In your hearts en - throne him; there let him sub - due
5 Chris - tians, this Lord Je - sus shall re - turn a - gain

ev - 'ry tongue con - fess him king of glo - ry now.
all the an - gel fac - es, all the hosts of light,
from the lips of sin - ners un - to whom he came,
all that is not ho - ly, all that is not true.
on the clouds of glo - ry, with his an - gel train;

It is God's good plea - sure we should call him Lord,
thrones and dom - i - na - tions, stars up - on their way,
faith - ful - ly he bore it spot - less to the last;
Crown him as your cap - tain in temp - ta - tion's hour;
for all wreaths of em - pire meet up - on his brow,

who from the be - gin - ning was the might - y Word.
all the heav'n - ly or - ders in their great ar - ray.
brought it back vic - to - rious when from death he passed.
let his will en - fold you in its light and pow'r.
and our hearts con - fess him king of glo - ry now.

Text: Caroline M. Noel, 1817–1877
Music: Ralph Vaughan Williams, 1872–1958
Music © Oxford University Press

KING'S WESTON
6565D

417

In His Temple Now Behold Him

1 In his tem - ple now be - hold him, see the long - ex -
2 In the arms of her who bore him, vir - gin pure, be -
3 Je - sus, by your pre - sen - ta - tion, when they blessed you,
4 Prince and au - thor of sal - va - tion, be your bound - less

pect - ed Lord; an - cient proph - ets had fore - told him,
hold him lie, while his a - ged saints a - dore him,
weak and poor, make us see your great sal - va - tion,
love our theme! Je - sus, praise to you be giv - en

God has sent the prom - ised Word. Now to praise him,
ere in per - fect faith they die. Al - le - lu - ia!
seal us with your prom - ise sure; and pre - sent us,
by the world you did re - deem, with the Fa - ther

his re - deem - ed shall break forth with one ac - cord.
Al - le - lu - ia! Lo, the in - car - nate God Most High!
in your glo - ry, to your Fa - ther, cleansed and pure.
and the Spir - it God of maj - es - ty su - preme!

Text: Henry J. Pye, 1825–1903, alt.
Music: Henry T. Smart, 1813–1879

REGENT SQUARE
8 7 8 7 8 7

Rejoice in God's Saints

418

1 Re - joice in God's saints to - day and all days!
2 Some march with e - vents to turn them God's way;
3 Re - joice in those saints, un - praised and un - known,
4 Re - joice in God's saints to - day and all days!

A world with - out saints for - gets how to praise.
some need to with - draw, the bet - ter to pray;
who bear some-one's cross, or shoul-der their own:
A world with - out saints for - gets how to praise.

Their faith in ac - quir - ing the hab - it of prayer,
some car - ry the gos - pel through fire and through flood:
they share our com - plain - ing, our com - forts, our cares:
In lov - ing, in liv - ing, they prove it is true:

their depth of a - dor - ing, Lord, help us to share.
our world is their par - ish, their pur - pose is God.
what pa - tience in car - ing, what cour - age is theirs!
their way of self - giv - ing, Lord, leads us to you.

Text: Fred Pratt Green, 1903–2000
Music: C. Hubert H. Parry, 1848–1918
Text © 1973 Hope Publishing Company

LAUDATE DOMINUM
10 10 11 11

419

For All the Faithful Women

1 For all the faith-ful wom-en who served in days of old,
Insert one or more of stanzas 3–11 or this general stanza 2:
2 O God, for saints and ser-vants, those named and those un-known,
Last All praise to God the Fa-ther! All praise to Christ the Son!

to you shall thanks be giv-en; to all, their stor-y told.

in whom through all the a-ges your light of glo-ry shone,
All praise to God the Spir-it, who binds the church as one!

They served with strength and glad-ness in tasks your wis-dom gave.

we of-fer glad thanks-giv-ing and fer-vent prayer we raise
With saints who went be-fore us, with saints who wit-ness still,

To you their lives bore wit-ness, pro-claimed your pow'r to save.

that, faith-ful in your ser-vice, our lives may sing your praise.
we sing glad al-le-lu-ias and strive to do your will.

Miriam

3 We praise your name for Miriam,
who sang triumphantly
while Pharaoh's vaunted army
lay drowned beneath the sea.
As Israel marched to freedom,
her chains of bondage gone,
so may we reach the kingdom
your mighty arm has won.

Hannah

4 To Hannah, praying childless
before the throne of grace,
you gave a son and called him
to serve before your face.
Grant us her perseverance;
Lord, teach us how to pray
and trust in your deliv'rance
when darkness hides our way.

Text: Herman G. Stuempfle Jr., b. 1923
Music: Finnish folk tune
Text © 1993 GIA Publications, Inc.

KUORTANE
76 76 D

Alternate tune: KING'S LYNN

Ruth

5 For Ruth, who left her homeland
and ventured forth in faith,
who pledged to serve and worship
Naomi's God till death,
we praise you, God of Israel,
and pray for hearts set free
to bind ourselves to others
in love and loyalty.

Mary, Mother of Our Lord

6 We honor faithful Mary,
fair maiden, full of grace.
She bore the Christ, our brother,
who saved our human race.
May we, with her, surrender
ourselves to your command
and lay upon your altar
our gifts of heart and hand.

Martha and Mary

7 We sing of busy Martha,
who toiled with pot and pan
while Mary sat in silence
to hear the word again.
Christ, keep our hearts attentive
to truth that you declare,
and strengthen us for service
when work becomes our prayer.

The Woman at the Well

8 Recall the outcast woman
with whom our Lord conversed:
Christ gave her living water
to quench her deepest thirst.
Like hers, our hearts are yearning;
Christ offers us his word.
Then may our lips be burning
to witness to our Lord.

Mary Magdalene

9 We praise the other Mary,
who came at Easter dawn
and near the tomb did tarry,
but found her Lord was gone.
As joyfully she saw him
in resurrection light,
may we by faith behold him,
the day who ends all night.

Dorcas

10 Lord, hear our praise of Dorcas,
who served the sick and poor.
Her hands were cups of kindness,
her heart an open door.
Send us, O Christ, your Body,
where people cry in pain,
and touch them with compassion
to make them whole again.

Eunice and Lois

11 For Eunice and for Lois,
we sing our thanks and praise.
Young Timothy they nurtured
and led him in your ways.
Raise up in ev'ry household
true teachers of your word
whose lives will bear clear witness
to Christ, our risen Lord.

420

By All Your Saints

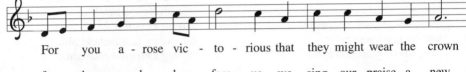

1 By all your saints still striv - ing, for all your saints at rest,

Insert appointed stanza or this general stanza 2:

2 A - pos - tles, proph - ets, mar - tyrs, and all the no - ble throng

Last Give praise to God Al - might - y, and wor - ship God the Son,

your ho - ly name, O Je - sus, for - ev - er - more be blessed!

who wear the spot - less rai - ment and raise the cease - less song—

and sing to God the Spir - it, e - ter - nal Three in One,

For you a - rose vic - to - rious that they might wear the crown

for these passed on be - fore us, we sing our praise a - new

till all the ran - somed num - ber fall down be - fore the throne,

and share the light of glo - ry re - flect - ed from your throne.

and, walk - ing in their foot - steps, would live our lives for you.

and hon - or, pow'r, and glo - ry as - cribe to God a - lone.

Andrew, Apostle + November 30

3 All praise, O Lord, for Andrew,
the first to welcome you,
whose witness to his brother
named you Messiah true.
May we, with hearts kept open
to you throughout the year,
proclaim to friend and neighbor
your advent ever near.

Stephen, Deacon and Martyr + December 26

4 All praise for Stephen, martyr,
who saw you ready stand
to help in time of torment,
to plead at God's right hand.
O Jesus, born to save us,
grant us discerning sight,
that true till death we serve you
and witness to your light.

See #421 for additional stanzas and an alternate tune.

Text: Horatio Bolton Nelson, 1823–1913, alt.; hymnal version, sts. 4, 9
Music: English folk tune
Text sts. 4, 9 © 2006 Augsburg Fortress

KING'S LYNN

7 6 7 6 D

Alternate tune: KUORTANE

John, Apostle and Evangelist + December 27

5   For John, belov'd disciple,
    exiled on Patmos' shore,
    and for John's holy gospel,
    we praise you evermore.
    Praise for the mystic vision
    these words to us unfold.
    Instill in us the longing
    your glory to behold.

The Holy Innocents, Martyrs + December 28

6   All praise for infant martyrs,
    whom you with tend'rest love
    received from Herod's bloodshed
    to share your home above.
    O Rachel, cease your weeping;
    they rest from earthbound cares.
    Lord, grant us hearts as guileless
    and crowns as bright as theirs.

Confession of Peter + January 18

7   We praise you, Lord, for Peter,
    so eager and so bold,
    thrice falling, yet repentant,
    thrice charged to feed your fold.
    Lord, make your pastors faithful
    to guard your flock from harm,
    and hold them when they waver
    with your almighty arm.

Conversion of Paul + January 25

8   Praise for the light from heaven,
    praise for the voice of awe,
    praise for the glorious vision
    the persecutor saw.
    O Lord, for Paul's enlight'ning
    we bless your name today;
    come, shine within our darkness,
    and guide us on our way.

Joseph, Guardian of Jesus + March 19

9   We sing our praise for Joseph,
    your guardian, dearest Lord;
    who, list'ning to the angel,
    once saved you from the sword.
    In temple, home, and workshop,
    he led you, honed your skill.
    So teach us, Christ our brother,
    to do our Father's will.

Mark, Evangelist + April 25

10 For Mark, O Lord, we praise you,
    whose fainting heart, made strong,
    poured forth the faithful gospel
    to animate our song.
    May we, in all our weakness,
    receive your pow'r divine,
    and all, as fruitful branches,
    grow strong in you, the vine.

Philip and James, Apostles + May 1

11 We praise your name for Philip,
    blest guide to Greek and Jew,
    and for young James, the faithful
    who heard and followed you.
    Oh, grant us grace to know you,
    the way, the truth, the life,
    and wrestle with temptation
    till victors in the strife.

Matthias, Apostle + May 14

12 Lord, your abiding presence
    directs the wondrous choice;
    the lot falls to Matthias,
    the faithful now rejoice.
    May we as true apostles
    your holy church defend,
    and by your parting promise
    be with us to the end.

421

By All Your Saints

1 By all your saints still striv - ing, for all your saints at rest,
Insert appointed stanza or this general stanza 2:
2 A - pos - tles, proph - ets, mar - tyrs, and all the no - ble throng
Last Give praise to God Al - might - y, and wor - ship God the Son,

your ho - ly name, O Je - sus, for - ev - er - more be blessed!

who wear the spot - less rai - ment and raise the cease-less song—
and sing to God the Spir - it, e - ter - nal Three in One,

For you a - rose vic - to - rious that they might wear the crown

for these passed on be - fore us, we sing our praise a - new
till all the ran - somed num - ber fall down be - fore the throne,

and share the light of glo - ry re - flect - ed from your throne.

and, walk - ing in their foot - steps, would live our lives for you.
and hon - or, pow'r, and glo - ry as - cribe to God a - lone.

Barnabas, Apostle + June 11

13 For Barnabas we praise you,
appointed by your call,
who, filled with faith and Spirit,
proclaimed your word with Paul.
Give us your grace, O Savior,
that we become the same:
companions in your mission,
who bear the Christian name.

John the Baptist + June 24

14 We praise you for the Baptist,
forerunner of the Word,
our true Elijah, making
a highway for the Lord.
The last and greatest prophet,
he saw the dawning ray
of light that grows in splendor
until the perfect day.

See #420 for additional stanzas and an alternate tune.

Text: Horatio Bolton Nelson, 1823–1913, alt.; hymnal version, sts. 13, 16, 18
Music: Finnish folk tune
Text sts. 13, 16, 18 © 2006 Augsburg Fortress

KUORTANE
7 6 7 6 D

Alternate tune: KING'S LYNN

Thomas, Apostle + July 3

15 All praise to you for Thomas,
     whose short-lived doubtings prove
     your perfect two-fold nature,
     and all your depth of love.
     May all who live with questions
     have faith in you restored;
     grant us the grace to know you,
     to say, "My God and Lord."

Mary Magdalene, Apostle + July 22

16 For Magdalene we praise you,
     steadfast at cross and tomb.
     Your "Mary!" in the garden
     dispelled her tears and gloom.
     Apostle to the apostles,
     she ran to spread the word;
     send us to shout the good news
     that we have seen the Lord.

James, Apostle + July 25

17 For James, O Lord, we praise you,
     who fell to Herod's sword,
     who drank your cup of suff'ring
     and thus fulfilled your word.
     Lord, curb our vain impatience
     for glory and for gain,
     and nerve us for such suff'rings
     as glorify your name.

Mary, Mother of Our Lord + August 15

18 Oh, magnify with Mary
     the God whom we adore;
     rejoice in Christ our Savior,
     true God whom Mary bore;
     and praise the holy Power
     in her made manifest.
     With all the generations
     acclaim this woman blest.

Bartholomew, Apostle + August 24

19 All praise for him whose candor
     through all his doubt you saw
     when Philip at the fig tree
     disclosed you in the law.
     Discern, beneath our surface,
     O Lord, what we can be,
     that by your truth made guileless,
     your glory we may see.

Matthew, Apostle, Evangelist + September 21

20 For Matthew, Lord, whose gospel
     your human life declared,
     who, worldly gain forsaking,
     your path of suff'ring shared.
     From wealth that dulls and chains us,
     oh, raise our eyes anew,
     that we, whate'er our calling,
     may rise and follow you.

Luke, Evangelist + October 18

21 For Luke, belov'd physician,
     all praise, whose gospel shows
     the healer of the nations,
     the one who shares our woes.
     Your wine and oil, O Savior,
     upon our spirits pour,
     and with true balm of Gilead
     anoint us evermore.

Simon and Jude, Apostles + October 28

22 All praise for Jude and Simon,
     who sealed their faith today;
     one love, one hope impelled them
     to tread the sacred way.
     May we with zeal as earnest
     the faith of Christ maintain,
     and foll'wing these our brothers,
     at length your rest attain.

422   # For All the Saints

1 For all the saints who from their la - bors rest, who
2 Thou wast their rock, their for - tress, and their might; thou,
Stanzas 3–5 on facing page.
6 But then there breaks a yet more glo - rious day: the
7 From earth's wide bounds, from o - cean's far - thest coast, through

thee by faith be - fore the world con - fessed, thy
Lord, their cap - tain in the well - fought fight; . . .

saints tri - um - phant rise in bright ar - ray; the
gates of pearl streams in the count - less host, . . .

name, O Je - sus, be for - ev - er blest.
thou, in the dark - ness drear, their one true light.

King of glo - ry pass - es on his way.
sing - ing to Fa - ther, Son, and Ho - ly Ghost:

Al - le - lu - ia! Al - le - lu - ia!

Text: William W. How, 1823–1897
Music: Ralph Vaughan Williams, 1872–1958
Music © Oxford University Press

SINE NOMINE
10 10 10 and alleluias

3 Oh, blest com - mu - nion, fel - low - ship di - vine,
4 And when the strife is fierce, the war - fare long,
5 The gold - en eve - ning bright-ens in the west;

we fee - bly strug - gle, they in glo - ry shine; yet
steals on the ear the dis - tant tri - umph song, and
soon, soon to faith - ful ser - vants com - eth rest; . . .

all are one in thee, for all are thine.
hearts are brave a - gain and arms are strong.
sweet is the calm of par - a - dise the blest.

Al - le - lu - ia! Al - le - lu - ia!

423

Shall We Gather at the River

1 Shall we gath-er at the riv-er, where bright an-gel feet have trod,
2 On the mar-gin of the riv-er, wash-ing up its sil-ver spray,
3 Ere we reach the shin-ing riv-er, lay we ev-'ry bur-den down;
4 Soon we'll reach the shin-ing riv-er, soon our pil-grim-age will cease;

with its crys-tal tide for-ev - er flow-ing by the throne of God?
we will walk and wor-ship ev - er, all the hap-py gold - en day.
grace our spir-its will de-liv - er, and pro-vide a robe and crown.
soon our hap-py hearts will quiv-er with the mel-o - dy of peace.

Refrain

Yes, we'll gath-er at the riv - er, the beau-ti-ful, the beau-ti-ful riv - er;

gath-er with the saints at the riv - er that flows by the throne of God.

Text: Robert Lowry, 1826–1899
Music: Robert Lowry

HANSON PLACE
8 7 8 7 and refrain

Ye Watchers and Ye Holy Ones 424

1 Ye watch - ers and ye ho - ly ones, bright
2 O high - er than the cher - u - bim, more
3 Re - spond, ye souls in end - less rest, ye
4 O friends, in glad - ness let us sing, su -

ser - aphs, cher - u - bim, and thrones, raise the glad strain:
glo - rious than the ser - a - phim, lead their prais - es:
pa - tri - archs and proph - ets blest: "Al - le - lu - ia!
per - nal an - thems ech - o - ing: "Al - le - lu - ia!

"Al - le - lu - ia!" Cry out, do - min - ions, prince - doms,
"Al - le - lu - ia!" Thou bear - er of the e - ter - nal
Al - le - lu - ia!" Ye ho - ly twelve, ye mar - tyrs
Al - le - lu - ia!" To God the Fa - ther, God the

pow'rs, arch - an - gels, vir - tues, an - gel choirs:
Word, most gra - cious, mag - ni - fy the Lord:
strong, all saints tri - um - phant, raise the song:
Son, and God the Spir - it, Three in One:

"Al - le - lu - ia! Al - le - lu - ia!" Al - le -

lu - ia, al - le - lu - ia, al - le - lu - ia!

Text: J. Athelstan Riley, 1858–1945
Music: *Geistliche Kirchengesänge*, Köln, 1623
Text © Oxford University Press

LASST UNS ERFREUEN
8 8 8 8 8 and alleluias

425   Behold the Host Arrayed in White

1 Be - hold the host ar - rayed in white like thou - sand snow - clad
2 On earth their work was not thought wise, but see them now in
3 O bless - ed saints, now take your rest; a thou - sand times shall

moun - tains bright, that stands with palms and sings its psalms be -
heav - en's eyes; be - fore God's throne of pre - cious stone they
you be blest for keep - ing faith firm un - to death and

fore the throne of light! These are the saints who
shout their vic - t'ry cries. On earth they wept through
scorn - ing world - ly trust. For now you live at

kept God's word; they are the hon - ored of the Lord. He
bit - ter years; now God has wiped a - way their tears, trans -
home with God and har - vest seeds once cast a - broad in

Text: Hans A. Brorson, 1694–1764; tr. Gracia Grindal, b. 1943, alt.
Music: Norwegian folk tune, 17th cent.; arr. Edvard H. Grieg, 1843–1907
Text © 1978 *Lutheran Book of Worship*, admin. Augsburg Fortress

DEN STORE HVIDE FLO
P

is their prince who drowned their sins, so they were cleansed, re -
formed their strife to heav'n - ly life, and freed them from their
tears and sighs. See with new eyes the pat - tern in the

stored. They now serve God both day and night; they
fears. For now they have the best at last; they
seed. The myr - iad an - gels raise their song. O

sing their songs in end - less light. Their an - thems ring when
keep their sweet e - ter - nal feast. At God's right hand our
saints, sing with that hap - py throng; lift up one voice; let

they all sing with an - gels shin - ing bright.
Lord com - mands; he is both host and guest.
heav'n re - joice in our re - deem - er's song!

426   Sing with All the Saints in Glory

1 Sing with all the saints in glo - ry, sing the res - ur - rec - tion song!
2 Oh, what glo - ry, far ex - ceed - ing all that eye has yet per - ceived!
3 Life e - ter - nal! heav'n re - joic - es: Je - sus lives who once was dead.

Death and sor - row, earth's dark sto - ry, to the for - mer days be - long.
Ho - liest hearts for a - ges plead - ing nev - er that full joy con - ceived.
Shout with joy, O death - less voic - es! Child of God, lift up your head!

All a - round the clouds are break - ing, soon the storms of time shall cease;
God has prom - ised, Christ pre - pares it, there on high our wel - come waits.
Life e - ter - nal! Oh, what won - ders crowd on faith; what joy un - known,

in God's like - ness we a - wak - en, know - ing ev - er - last - ing peace.
Ev - 'ry hum - ble spir - it shares it, Christ has passed the e - ter - nal gates.
when, a - mid earth's clos - ing thun - ders, saints shall stand be - fore the throne!

Text: William J. Irons, 1812–1883, alt.   MISSISSIPP
Music: William Bradley Roberts, b. 1947   87 87 D
Music © 1995 Augsburg Fortress

427   For All Your Saints, O Lord

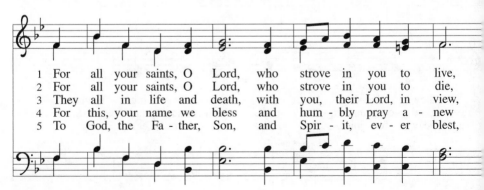

1 For all your saints, O Lord, who strove in you to live,
2 For all your saints, O Lord, who strove in you to die,
3 They all in life and death, with you, their Lord, in view,
4 For this, your name we bless and hum - bly pray a - new
5 To God, the Fa - ther, Son, and Spir - it, ev - er blest,

Text: Richard Mant, 1776–1848, alt.   FESTAL SONG
Music: William H. Walter, 1825–1893   S M

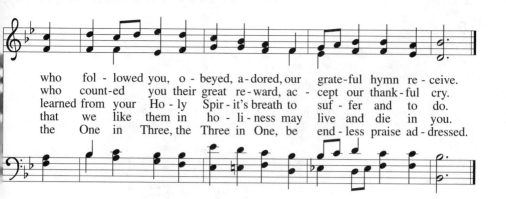

who fol-lowed you, o-beyed, a-dored, our grate-ful hymn re-ceive.
who count-ed you their great re-ward, ac-cept our thank-ful cry.
learned from your Ho-ly Spir-it's breath to suf-fer and to do.
that we like them in ho-li-ness may live and die in you.
the One in Three, the Three in One, be end-less praise ad-dressed.

Give Thanks for Saints

428

1 Give thanks for those whose faith is firm when all a-
2 Give thanks for those whose hope is clear, be-yond mere
3 Give thanks for those whose love is pure, a spar-kling
4 Give thanks for saints of a-ges past and saints a-

round seems bleak: on God's good prom-ise they re-ly, so
mor-tal sight: who seek the cit-y God has planned, the
pre-cious stone: they show by what they say and do an
live to-day: though of-ten by this world de-spised, their

while they live and when they die how force-ful
true, e-ter-nal prom-ised land, and steer on
in-ward beau-ty, warm and true, for God's con-
hearts by God are rich-ly prized. Give thanks that

ly they speak— the strong, who once were weak!
toward that light, a bea-con ev-er bright.
cerns they own— God's love through them is known.
we may say we share their pil-grim way.

Text: Martin E. Leckebusch, b. 1962
Music: C. Hubert H. Parry, 1848–1918
Text © 2003 Kevin Mayhew Ltd.

REPTON
868866

429 In Our Day of Thanksgiving

1 In our day of thanks-giv - ing one psalm let us of - fer
2 In the morn - ing of life, and at noon, and at eve - ning,
3 These stones that have ech - oed their prais - es are ho - ly,
4 Sing praise, then, and thanks that God's love here has found them

for the saints who be - fore us re - ceived the re - ward;
they were gath - ered to heav'n from our wor - ship be - low;
and dear is the ground where their feet have once trod;
whose jour - ney is end - ed, whose per - ils are past;

when the shad - ow of death fell up - on them, we sor - rowed
but not till God's love, at the font and the al - tar,
yet here they con - fessed they were strang-ers and pil - grims,
they be - lieved in the light; and its glo - ry is round them,

but now we re - joice that they rest in the Lord.
had clothed them with grace for the way they should go.
and still they were seek-ing the cit - y of God.
where the clouds of earth's sor - row are lift - ed at last.

Text: William Henry Draper, 1855–1933
Music: Richard Strutt, 1848–1927

ST. CATHERINE'S COUR
13 12 13 1

Rejoice, for Christ Is King! 430

1 Re - joice, for Christ is king! Your Lord and king a - dore;
2 Our Sav - ior Je - sus reigns, the God of truth and love;
3 His king - dom can - not fail; he rules o'er earth and heav'n;
4 He sits at God's right hand till all his foes sub - mit

re - joice, give thanks, and sing, and tri - umph ev - er - more:
when he had purged our stains, he took his seat a - bove:
the keys of death and hell are to our Je - sus giv'n:
and bow to his com - mand and fall be - neath his feet:

Refrain

Lift up your heart, lift up your voice; re -

joice, a - gain I say, re - joice!

Text: Charles Wesley, 1707–1788, alt.
Music: William E. Fischer, 1849–1936

LAUS REGIS
666688

431 O Christ, What Can It Mean for Us

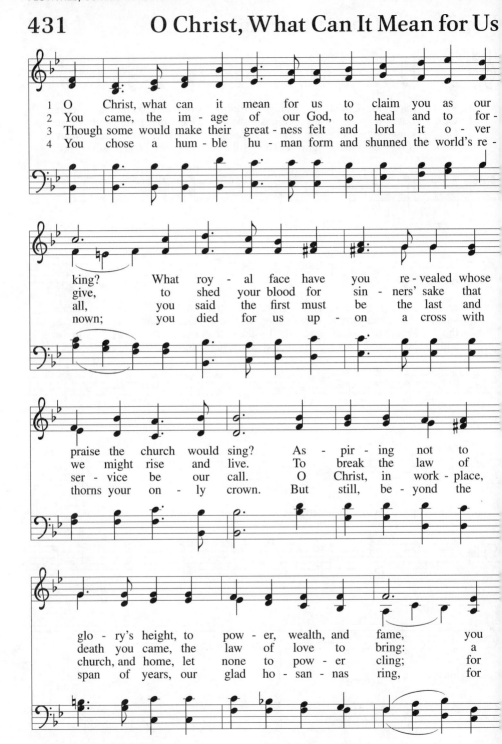

1 O Christ, what can it mean for us to claim you as our king? What roy - al face have you re - vealed whose praise the church would sing? As - pir - ing not to glo - ry's height, to pow - er, wealth, and fame, you

2 You came, the im - age of our God, to heal and to for - give, to shed your blood for sin - ners' sake that we might rise and live. To break the law of death you came, the law of love to bring: a

3 Though some would make their great - ness felt and lord it o - ver all, you said the first must be the last and ser - vice be our call. O Christ, in work - place, church, and home, let none to pow - er cling; for

4 You chose a hum - ble hu - man form and shunned the world's re - nown; you died for us up - on a cross with thorns your on - ly crown. But still, be - yond the span of years, our glad ho - san - nas ring, for

Text: Delores Dufner, OSB, b. 1939
Music: Henry S. Cutler, 1824–1902
Text © 2001, 2003 GIA Publications, Inc.

ALL SAINTS NEW
CMD

walked a   dif - f'rent, low - ly   way,   an - oth - er's   will your   aim.
dif - f'rent rule   of   righ - teous-ness,   a   dif-f'rent kind   of   king.
still, through us,   you   come   to   serve,   a   dif-f'rent kind   of   king.
now   at   God's right   hand   you reign,   a   dif-f'rent kind   of   king!

The Head That Once Was Crowned 432

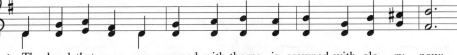

1 The head that once was crowned with thorns is crowned with glo - ry   now;
2 The high - est place that heav'n af - fords   is   his   by sov-'reign right,
3 The joy   of   all   who   dwell   a - bove, the   joy   of   all   be - low
4 To them the cross, with   all   its shame, with all   its   grace, is   giv'n;

a   roy - al   di - a - dem a - dorns the   might - y   vic - tor's   brow.
the   King of kings, and Lord of lords, and heav'n's e - ter - nal   light.
to   whom he man - i - fests his love, and grants   his   name to know;
their name, an ev - er - last - ing name, their joy,   the   joy of heav'n.

5 They suffer with their Lord below;
   they reign with him above;
   their profit and their joy to know
   the myst'ry of his love.

6 The cross he bore is life and health,
   though shame and death to him;
   his people's hope, his people's wealth,
   their everlasting theme!

Text: Thomas Kelly, 1769–1855
Music: Jeremiah Clarke, 1669–1707

ST. MAGNUS
CM

433

Blessing, Honor, and Glory

Bless - ing, hon - or, glo - ry to the Lamb.

Ho - ly, righ - teous, wor - thy is the Lamb.

Death could not hold him down, for he is ris - en!

Seat - ed up - on the throne, he is the Lamb of God!

Bless - ing, hon - or, glo - ry to the Lamb.

Ho - ly, righ - teous, wor - thy is the Lamb.

Death could not hold him down, for he is ris - en!

Seat - ed up - on the throne, he is the Lamb of God!

Bless - ing, hon - or, glo - ry to the Lamb. Ho - ly,

righ - teous, wor - thy is the Lamb of God.

Text: Geoff Bullock and David Reidy
Music: Geoff Bullock and David Reidy
Text and music © 1998 Word Music, LLC. and Maranatha! Music, admin. Music Services, Inc.

BLESSING, HONOR, AND GLOR
P.N.

Jesus Shall Reign

1 Je - sus shall reign wher - e'er the sun does its suc -
2 To him shall end - less prayer be made, and prais - es
3 Peo - ple and realms of ev - 'ry tongue dwell on his
4 Bless-ings a - bound wher - e'er he reigns: the pris-'ners
5 Let ev - 'ry crea - ture rise and bring pe - cu - liar

ces - sive jour - neys run; his king-dom stretch from
throng to crown his head; his name like sweet per -
love with sweet - est song; and in - fant voic - es
leap to lose their chains, the wea - ry find e -
hon - ors to our king; an - gels de - scend with

shore to shore, till moons shall wax and wane no more.
fume shall rise with ev - 'ry morn - ing sac - ri - fice.
shall pro - claim their ear - ly bless - ings on his name.
ter - nal rest, and all who suf - fer want are blest.
songs a - gain, and earth re - peat the loud a - men.

Text: Isaac Watts, 1674–1748, alt.
Music: attr. John Hatton, d. 1793

DUKE STREET
LM

435 Lo! He Comes with Clouds Descending

1 Lo! he comes with clouds de - scend - ing,
2 Now re - demp - tion, long - ex - pect - ed,
3 Yea, a - men, let all a - dore thee,

once for our sal - va - tion slain;
comes in sol - emn splen - dor near;
high on thine e - ter - nal throne;

thou - sand thou - sand saints at - tend - ing
all the saints this world re - ject - ed
Sav - ior, take the pow'r and glo - ry,

join to sing the glad re - frain:
thrill the trum - pet sound to hear:
claim the king - dom as thine own.

Text: Charles Wesley, 1707–1788, alt.
Music: Thomas Olivers, 1725–1799

HELMSLE
87 87 12

Al - le - lu - ia, al - le - lu - ia, al - le -
Al - le - lu - ia, al - le - lu - ia, al - le -
Al - le - lu - ia, al - le - lu - ia, al - le -

lu - ia! Christ the Lord re - turns to reign.
lu - ia! See the day of God ap - pear!
lu - ia! Thou shalt reign, and thou a - lone!

436

Wake, Awake, for Night Is Flying

1 Wake, a-wake, for night is fly - ing, the watch-men
2 Zi - on hears the watch-men sing - ing, and all her
3 Glo - ri - a! Let heav'n a - dore you! Let saints and

on the heights are cry - ing; a - wake, Je - ru - sa - lem, at last.
heart with joy is spring - ing. She wakes, she ris - es from her gloom.
an - gels sing be - fore you, with harp and cym-bal's clear-est tone.

Mid - night hears the wel - come voic - es, and at the
Her dear friend comes down, all glo - rious, the strong in
Gates of pearl, twelve por - tals gleam - ing, lead us to

thrill-ing cry re - joic - es: "Come forth, you maid-ens! Night is past.
grace, in truth vic - to - rious: her star is ris'n; her light is come.
bliss be - yond all dream - ing, with an - gel choirs a - round your throne.

Text: Philipp Nicolai, 1556–1608; tr. composite
Music: Philipp Nicolai
Text © 1999 Augsburg Fortress

WACHET AU
P /

The bride - groom comes! A - wake; your lamps with glad - ness take!"
Now come, O Bless - ed One, Lord Je - sus, God's own Son.
No eye has caught the light, no ear the thun - d'ring might

Al - le - lu - ia! Rise and pre - pare the feast to share;
Sing ho - san - na! Oh, hear the call! Come one, come all,
of such glo - ry. There we will go: what joy we'll know!

go, meet the bride - groom, who draws near.
and fol - low to the ban - quet hall.
There sweet de - light will ev - er flow.

437   On Jordan's Stormy Bank I Stand

1 On Jor-dan's storm-y bank I stand, and cast a wish-ful eye
2 All o'er those wide ex-tend-ed plains shines one e-ter-nal day;
3 No chill-ing winds or pois'nous breath can reach that health-ful shore;
4 When shall I reach that hap-py place and be for-ev-er blest?

to Ca-naan's fair and hap-py land, where my pos-ses-sions lie.
there God the Son for-ev-er reigns and scat-ters night a-way.
sick-ness and sor-row, pain and death, are felt and feared no more.
When shall I see my Sav-ior's face and in God's bos-om rest?

Refrain

I am bound for the prom-ised land, I am bound for the prom-ised land,

oh, who will come and go with me? I am bound for the prom-ised land.

Text: Samuel Stennett, 1727–1795
Music: W. Walker, *Southern Harmony*, 1835; adapt. Rigdon M. McIntosh, 1836–1899

PROMISED LAND
CM and refrain

My Lord, What a Morning 438

Refrain

My Lord, what a morn-ing; my Lord, what a morn-ing; oh,

my Lord, what a morn-ing, when the stars be-gin to fall.

1 You will hear the trum-pet sound,
2 You will hear the sin-ner cry, to wake the na-tions un-der-ground,
3 You will hear the Chris-tian shout,

look-ing to my God's right hand, when the stars be-gin to fall.

Refrain

Text: African American spiritual
Music: African American spiritual

BURLEIGH
6 8 7 7 and refrain

439
Soon and Very Soon

1 Soon and ver - y soon
2 No more cry - in' there,
3 No more dy - in' there,
4 Soon and ver - y soon
we are goin' to see the King,

soon and ver - y soon
no more cry - in' there,
no more dy - in' there,
soon and ver - y soon
we are goin' to see the King,

soon and ver - y soon
no more cry - in' there,
no more dy - in' there,
soon and ver - y soon
we are goin' to see the King.

1, 2, 3

Hal - le - lu - jah, hal - le - lu - jah, we're goin' to see the King!

Text: Andraé Crouch, b. 1945
Music: Andraé Crouch
Text and music © 1976 Bud John Songs, Inc./Crouch Music, admin. EMI Christian Music Publishing

VERY SOO
12 12 12 and refra

Coda after stanza 4

Hal - le - lu - jah, hal - le - lu -

jah, hal - le - lu - jah, hal - le - lu - jah.

In Peace and Joy I Now Depart 440

1 In peace and joy I now de - part as God is will - ing,
2 Christ Je - sus makes the way for me, my gra - cious Sav - ior;
3 The Lord is health and sav - ing light for ev - 'ry na - tion,

and faith fills all my mind and heart, calm - ing, still - ing.
with eyes of faith and trust I see God's great fa - vor.
dis - pel - ling shad - ows of the night with sal - va - tion:

God the Lord has prom-ised me that death is but a slum - ber.
When this life comes to an end, my hope is God's em - brac - ing.
Is - rael's praise and hope's de-light, my trea-sure, joy, and glo - ry.

Text: Martin Luther, 1483–1546, based on the Nunc dimittis; tr. composite
Music: Martin Luther
Text © 2000 Augsburg Fortress

MIT FRIED UND FREUD
858477

441   Oh, Happy Day When We Shall Stand

1 Oh, hap - py day when we shall stand a - mid the
2 Oh, bless - ed day when Christ shall come and show him -
3 Oh, what a might - y rush - ing flood of joy and
4 O Lord, your grace is ev - 'ry - thing; your love has

heav'n - ly throng; and sing with hosts from ev - 'ry land the
self as Lord, and thou - sands meet in their new home which
love and peace will roll down o - ver us with good and
made us free to stand a - mong the saints and sing the

new ce - les - tial song, the new ce - les - tial song.
Je - sus has pre - pared, which Je - sus has pre - pared.
bless - ed - ness and grace, and bless - ed - ness and grace.
glo - ry that we see, the glo - ry that we see.

Text: Wilhelm A. Wexels, 1797–1866; tr. composite
Music: Nikolaus Herman, 1480–1561
Text © 1958, 1978 Augsburg Fortress

LOBT GOTT, IHR CHRISTE
8 6 8 6

All Who Believe and Are Baptized 442

1 All who be-lieve and are bap-tized shall see the Lord's sal -
2 With one ac-cord, O God, we pray, grant us your Ho - ly

va - tion; bap-tized in-to the death of Christ, they are a
Spir - it; help us in our in - fir - mi - ty through Je - sus'

new cre - a - tion; through Christ's re-demp-tion they will stand a -
blood and mer - it; grant us to grow in grace each day by

mong the glo-rious heav'n-ly band of ev-'ry tribe and na - tion.
ho - ly bap-tism, that we may e - ter-nal life in-her - it.

xt: Thomas H. Kingo, 1634–1703; tr. George T. Rygh, 1860–1943, alt.
usic: *Etlich christlich Lieder*, Wittenberg, 1524

ES IST DAS HEIL
8 7 8 7 8 8 7

443

Dearest Jesus, We Are Here

1 Dear-est Je - sus, we are here, glad - ly your com -
2 Your com-mand is clear and plain, and we would o -
3 There-fore we have come to you, in our arms this
4 Gra-cious head, your mem-ber own; shep - herd, take your
5 Now in - to your heart we pour prayers that from our

mand o - bey - ing. With this child we now draw near
bey it du - ly: "You must all be born a - gain,
in - fant bear - ing; tru - ly here your grace we view;
lamb and feed it; prince of peace, make here your throne;
hearts pro - ceed - ed. Our pe - ti - tions heav'n-ward soar;

in re - sponse to your own say - ing that to you it
heart and life re - new - ing tru - ly, born of wa - ter
may this child, your mer - cy shar - ing, in your arms be
way of life, to heav - en lead it; pre - cious vine, let
may our heart's de - sires be heed - ed! Write the name we

Text: Benjamin Schmolck, 1672–1737; tr. Catherine Winkworth, 1827–1878, alt.
Music: Johann R. Ahle, 1625–1673

LIEBSTER JESU, WIR SIND HIE
78788

shall be giv - en as a child and heir of heav - en.
and the Spir - it, and my king - dom thus in - her - it."
shield-ed ev - er, yours on earth and yours for - ev - er.
noth - ing sev - er from your side this branch for - ev - er.
now have giv - en; write it in the book of heav - en!

Cradling Children in His Arm 444

Cra - dling chil - dren in his arm, Je - sus gave his bless - ing.

To our babes a wel-come warm he is yet ad - dress - ing.

Take them, Lord, give life a - new in the liv - ing wa - ters!

Keep them al - ways near to you as your sons and daugh-ters!

Text: Nikolai F. S. Grundtvig, 1783–1872; tr. Johannes H. V. Knudsen, 1902–1982
Music: Johann Horn, 1490–1547
Text © 1976 Johannes H. V. Knudsen, admin. Augsburg Fortress

GAUDEAMUS PARITER
76 76 D

445 Wash, O God, Our Sons and Daughters

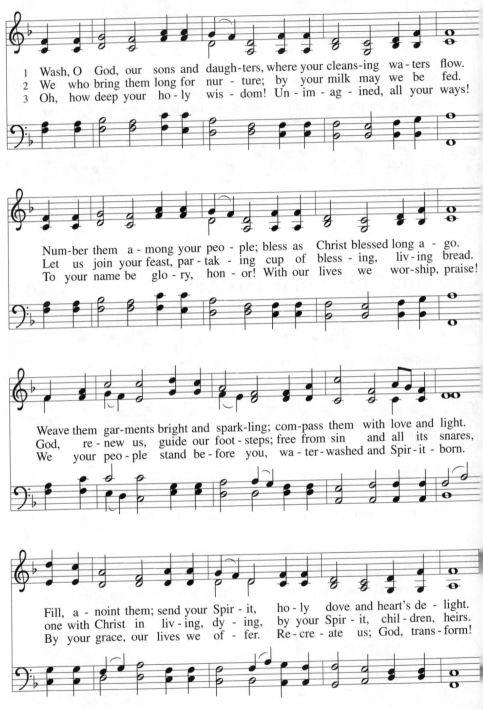

1 Wash, O God, our sons and daugh-ters, where your cleans-ing wa-ters flow.
2 We who bring them long for nur-ture; by your milk may we be fed.
3 Oh, how deep your ho-ly wis-dom! Un-im-ag-ined, all your ways!

Num-ber them a-mong your peo-ple; bless as Christ blessed long a-go.
Let us join your feast, par-tak-ing cup of bless-ing, liv-ing bread.
To your name be glo-ry, hon-or! With our lives we wor-ship, praise!

Weave them gar-ments bright and spark-ling; com-pass them with love and light.
God, re-new us, guide our foot-steps; free from sin and all its snares,
We your peo-ple stand be-fore you, wa-ter-washed and Spir-it-born.

Fill, a-noint them; send your Spir-it, ho-ly dove and heart's de-light.
one with Christ in liv-ing, dy-ing, by your Spir-it, chil-dren, heirs.
By your grace, our lives we of-fer. Re-cre-ate us; God, trans-form!

Text: Ruth Duck, b. 1947
Music: *The Sacred Harp*, Philadelphia, 1844; arr. *Selected Hymns*, 1985
Text © 1989 The United Methodist Publishing House, admin. The Copyright Company
Arr. © 1985 Augsburg Fortress

BEACH SPRING
8 7 8 7

I'm Going on a Journey

1 I'm go-ing on a jour-ney, and I'm start-ing to-day. My
head is wet, and I'm on my way. Christ's mark is on me;
it's on you, too; it says he loves me, and he loves you, too!

2 I'm be-com-ing this day a saint of God. It
real-ly does-n't mat-ter what roads I trod. Wher-ev-er I go, God's
been there, too. God's love has touched me and will car-ry me through.

3 There are oth-er saints who have said a-men. They'll
keep me faith-ful to my jour-ney's end. A-long the way
I want to be the kind of per-son that God set free.

Text: Kenneth D. Larkin
Music: Edward V. Bonnemère, 1921–1996
Text and music © 1994 Amity Music

WET SAINTS
Irregular

447

O Blessed Spring

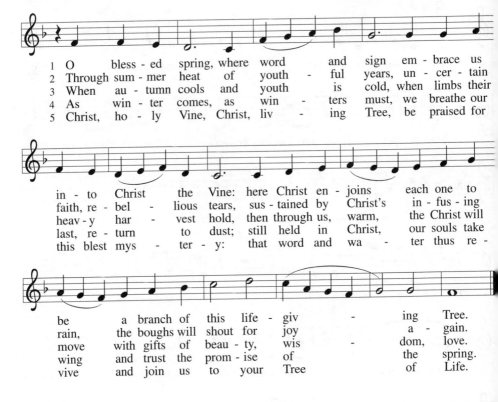

1 O bless-ed spring, where word and sign em-brace us
2 Through sum-mer heat of youth-ful years, un-cer-tain
3 When au-tumn cools and youth is cold, when limbs their
4 As win-ter comes, as win-ters must, we breathe our
5 Christ, ho-ly Vine, Christ, liv-ing Tree, be praised for

in-to Christ the Vine: here Christ en-joins each one to
faith, re-bel-lious tears, sus-tained by Christ's in-fus-ing
heav-y har-vest hold, then through us, warm, the Christ will
last, re-turn to dust; still held in Christ, our souls take
this blest mys-ter-y: that word and wa-ter thus re-

be a branch of this life-giv-ing Tree.
rain, the boughs will shout for joy a-gain.
move with gifts of beau-ty, wis-dom, love.
wing and trust the prom-ise of the spring.
vive and join us to your Tree of Life.

Text: Susan Palo Cherwien, b. 1953
Music: Robert Buckley Farlee, b. 1950
Text © 1993 Susan Palo Cherwien, admin. Augsburg Fortress
Music © 1993 Robert Buckley Farlee, admin. Augsburg Fortress

BERGLUND
LM

448

This Is the Spirit's Entry Now

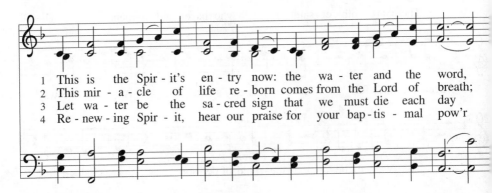

1 This is the Spir-it's en-try now: the wa-ter and the word,
2 This mir-a-cle of life re-born comes from the Lord of breath;
3 Let wa-ter be the sa-cred sign that we must die each day
4 Re-new-ing Spir-it, hear our praise for your bap-tis-mal pow'r

Text: Thomas E. Herbranson, b. 1933
Music: North American traditional; arr. hymnal version
Text © Thomas E. Herbranson
Arr. © 2006 Augsburg Fortress

LAND OF REST
CM

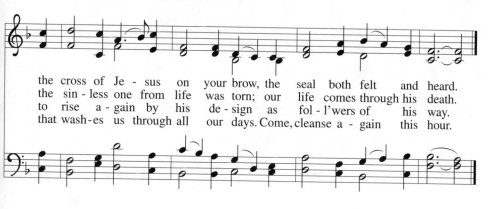

the cross of Je - sus on your brow, the seal both felt and heard.
the sin - less one from life was torn; our life comes through his death.
to rise a - gain by his de - sign as fol - l'wers of his way.
that wash-es us through all our days. Come, cleanse a - gain this hour.

We Know That Christ Is Raised 449

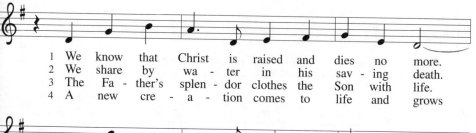

1 We know that Christ is raised and dies no more.
2 We share by wa - ter in his sav - ing death.
3 The Fa - ther's splen - dor clothes the Son with life.
4 A new cre - a - tion comes to life and grows

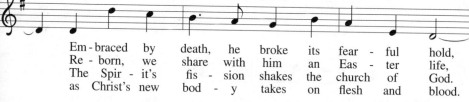

Em - braced by death, he broke its fear - ful hold,
Re - born, we share with him an Eas - ter life,
The Spir - it's fis - sion shakes the church of God.
as Christ's new bod - y takes on flesh and blood.

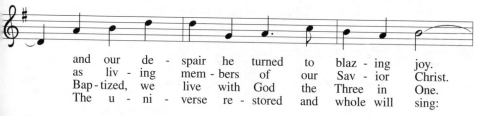

and our de - spair he turned to blaz - ing joy.
as liv - ing mem - bers of our Sav - ior Christ.
Bap - tized, we live with God the Three in One.
The u - ni - verse re - stored and whole will sing:

Hal - le - lu - jah!

Text: John B. Geyer, b. 1932
Music: Charles V. Stanford, 1852–1924
Text © John B. Geyer

ENGELBERG
10 10 10 4

450

I Bind unto Myself Today

1 I bind un-to my-self to-day the strong name
of the Trin-i-ty by in-vo-ca-tion
of the same, the Three in One and One in Three.

2 I bind this day to me for-ev-er, by pow'r of
faith, Christ's in-car-na-tion, his bap-tism in the
Jor-dan Riv-er, his cross of death for my sal-va-tion, his
burst-ing from the spic-ed tomb, his rid-ing
up the heav'n-ly way, his com-ing at the
day of doom, I bind un-to my-self to-day.

3 I bind un-to my-self to-day . . the vir-tues
of the star-lit heav-en, the glo-rious sun's life-
giv-ing ray, . . the white-ness of the moon at e-ven, the
flash-ing of the light-ning free, the whirl-ing
wind's tem-pes-tuous shocks, the sta-ble earth, the
deep salt sea, a-round the old e-ter-nal rocks.

Text: attr. Patrick, 372–466; para. Cecil Frances Alexander, 1818–1895
Music sts. 1–3, 5: Irish melody

ST. PATRICK'S BREASTPLATE
Irregula

4 Christ be with me, Christ with-in me, Christ be-hind me, Christ be-fore me,
Christ be-neath me, Christ a-bove me, Christ in qui - et, Christ in dan - ger,

Christ be-side me, Christ to win me, Christ to com - fort and re-store me,
Christ in hearts of all that love me, Christ in mouth of friend and strang-er.

5 I bind un - to my - self the name, the strong name of the

Trin - i - ty by in - vo - ca - tion of the same, the

Three in One and One in Three, of whom all na - ture has cre -

a - tion, e - ter - nal Fa - ther, Spir - it, Word. Praise to the

Lord of my sal - va-tion; sal - va - tion is of Christ the Lord!

Music st. 4: Irish melody

DEIRDRE
LM

451   We Are Baptized in Christ Jesus

1 We are bap-tized in Christ Je-sus, we are bap-tized in his death;
2 In the wa-ter and the wit-ness, in the break-ing of the bread,
3 Glo-ry be to God the Fa-ther, glo-ry be to Christ the Son,

that as Christ is raised vic-to-rious, we might live a brand new life.
in the wait-ing arms of Je-sus who is ris-en from the dead,
glo-ry to the Ho-ly Spir-it, ev-er three and ev-er one;

And if we have been u-nit-ed in a dread-ful death like his,
God has made a new be-gin-ning from the ash-es of our past;
as it was in the be-gin-ning, glo-ry now re-sounds a-gain

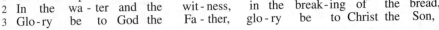

we will all be re-u-nit-ed, for he lives.
in the los-ing and the win-ning we hold fast.
in a song that has no end-ing. . . . . A-men.

Text: John C. Ylvisaker, b. 1937
Music: John C. Ylvisaker
Text and music © 1985 John C. Ylvisaker

OUIMETTE
87 87 87 11

452   Awake, O Sleeper, Rise from Death

1 A-wake, O sleep-er, rise from death, and Christ shall give you light;
2 To us on earth he came to bring from sin and fear re-lease,
3 There is one bod-y and one hope, one Spir-it and one call,
4 Then walk in love as Christ has loved, who died that he might save;
5 For us Christ lived, for us he died, and con-quered in the strife.

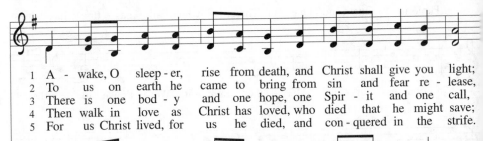

Text: F. Bland Tucker, 1895–1984
Music: Carl G. Gläser, 1784–1829
Text © 1980 Augsburg Publishing House

AZMON
CM

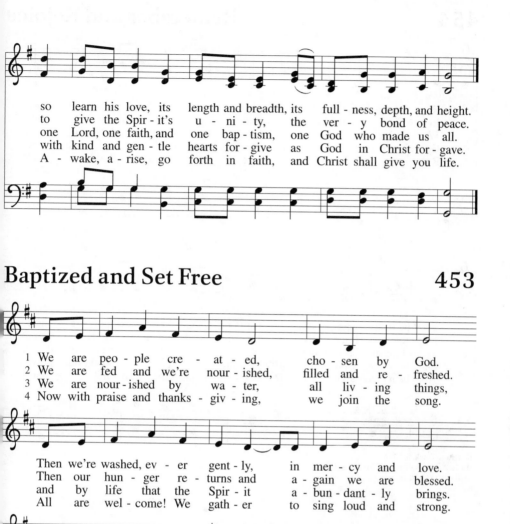

so   learn his love, its   length and breadth, its   full - ness, depth, and height.
to   give the Spir - it's   u - ni - ty,   the   ver - y   bond of peace.
one   Lord, one faith, and   one   bap - tism,   one   God who made us all.
with kind and gen - tle   hearts for - give   as   God   in Christ for - gave.
A - wake, a - rise, go   forth in faith,   and Christ shall give you life.

Baptized and Set Free   453

1 We   are   peo - ple   cre - at - ed,   cho - sen   by   God.
2 We   are   fed and we're   nour - ished,   filled and re - freshed.
3 We   are   nour - ished by   wa - ter,   all   liv - ing things,
4 Now with praise and thanks - giv - ing,   we   join   the   song.

Then we're washed, ev - er   gent - ly,   in mer - cy   and   love.
Then our   hun - ger re - turns and   a - gain we   are   blessed.
and   by   life that the   Spir - it   a - bun - dant - ly brings.
All   are   wel - come! We   gath - er   to sing loud and   strong.

Sin   has pow - er   no   more. Je - sus o - pened the   door
For   what - ev - er   the   need, God is great - er in - deed:
As   we jour - ney toward home, may your pres - ence be   known:
Not   en - slaved, but set   free! From now on,   all   will   be

to   a   foun - tain bring - ing heal - ing, and whole - ness and more.
end - less o - cean, al - ways deep - er than all   of   our   need.
pre - cious riv - er,   ev - er - flow - ing, now car - ry us   home.
one   in   Je - sus,   one in   wa - ter, bap - tized and set   free!

Text: Cathy Skogen-Soldner, b. 1956
Music: Cathy Skogen-Soldner
Text and music © 1999 Augsburg Fortress

BAPTIZED AND SET FREE
74756685

454 Remember and Rejoice

1 Re - mem - ber and re - joice, re - newed by floods of grace.
2 In life, in death, we trust in God's most ho - ly name,
3 We pledge our - selves a - new to flee the lures of hell,
4 God, bless us by your grace; re - mind us of your care.
5 Re - mem - ber and re - joice, re - newed by floods of grace.

We bear the sign of Je - sus Christ, that time can - not e - rase.
for - ev - er traced by wa - ter sign, and sealed by Spir - it flame.
to cling to Christ's com - mu - ni - ty, in jus - tice, peace to dwell.
Re - new - ing Spir - it, fill us now, in - spire our work, our prayer.
We bear the sign of Je - sus Christ, that time can - not e - rase.

Text: Ruth Duck, b. 1947
Music: Aaron Williams, 1731–1776
Text © 1992 GIA Publications, Inc.

ST. THOMAS
S M

455 Crashing Waters at Creation

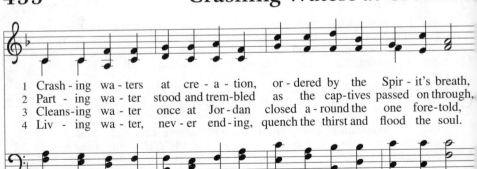

1 Crash - ing wa - ters at cre - a - tion, or - dered by the Spir - it's breath,
2 Part - ing wa - ter stood and trem - bled as the cap - tives passed on through,
3 Cleans - ing wa - ter once at Jor - dan closed a - round the one fore - told,
4 Liv - ing wa - ter, nev - er end - ing, quench the thirst and flood the soul.

Text: Sylvia G. Dunstan, 1955–1993
Music: attr. Christian F. Witt, 1660–1716; adapt. Henry J. Gauntlett, 1805–1876
Text © 1991 GIA Publications, Inc.

STUTTGART
8 7 8 7

first   to   wit - ness   day's be - gin - ning   from the bright-ness   of night's death.
wash - ing   off   the   chains of bond-age—chan-nel   to   a   life made new.
o - pened   to   re - veal   the glo - ry   ev - er new and   ev - er   old.
Well-spring, source of   life   e - ter - nal, drench our dry-ness, make us whole.

Baptized in Water   456

1 Bap-tized   in   wa - ter,   sealed by the   Spir - it,   cleansed by   the
2 Bap-tized   in   wa - ter,   sealed by the   Spir - it,   dead   in   the
3 Bap-tized   in   wa - ter,   sealed by the   Spir - it,   marked with the

blood of   Christ our   king: heirs of sal - va - tion,   trust-ing his
tomb with   Christ our   king: one with his   ris - ing,   freed and for -
sign of   Christ our   king: born of the   Spir - it,   we   are God's

prom - ise,   faith-ful - ly now   God's   praise we   sing.
giv - en,   thank-ful - ly now   God's   praise we   sing.
chil - dren;   joy-ful - ly now   God's   praise we   sing.

Text: Michael Saward, b. 1932
Music: Gaelic tune; arr. hymnal version
Text © 1982 Jubilate Hymns, admin. Hope Publishing Company
Arr. © 2006 Augsburg Fortress

BUNESSAN
5 5 8 D

457

Waterlife

Leader or All

1 Be - fore I can re - mem - ber the cov - e - nant was sealed
2 A sim - ple sweet be - gin - ning, a lov - ing place to start:
3 My hope and ex - pec - ta - tion for true com - mun - i - ty

with Fa - ther, Son, and Spir - it, in wa - ter was re-vealed.
Christ be - gan the sing - ing that swells with-in my heart.
be - gins with res - ur - rec - tion, his death and life in me.

The cleans-ing was for cer - tain, with wa - ter and the Word;
His love be-came my call - ing, his life my min - is - try.
His Spir - it fills the Bod - y: his church through wa - ter sees

gen - tle words were spo - ken, in heav - en they were heard.
His name is my a - dop - tion in - to his fam - i - ly.
prom - ise for to - mor - row, his wa - ter-life in me.

Refrain
All

They were sing-ing wa - ter-life, be - gin - ning life, wa-ter-life

all my life, wa-ter-life, Spir - it life, wa - ter - life.

Text: Handt Hanson, b. 1950
Music: Handt Hanson
Text and music © 1991 Prince of Peace Publishing, Changing Church, Inc.

SPIRIT LIF
7 6 7 6 D and refrai

Praise and Thanksgiving Be to God 458

1 Praise and thanks - giv - ing be to God our
2 Not our own ho - li - ness, nor that we have
3 Come, Ho - ly Spir - it, come in vis - i -
4 Praise to the Fa - ther, Son, and Ho - ly

mak - er, source of all bless - ing, prod - i - gal cre -
striv - en brings us the peace which you, O Christ, have
ta - tion; you are the truth, our hope, and our sal -
Spir - it: one Lord, one faith, one source of ev - 'ry

a - tor. Bap - tized and made your own, now we come be -
giv - en. Bap - tized and set a - part, strength - en us, O
va - tion. Bap - tize with joy and pow'r, give, O Dove de -
mer - it. Here now re - new your church through this sym - bol

fore you, and we a - dore you.
Sav - ior, with grace and fa - vor.
scend - ing, life nev - er end - ing.
giv - en; grant peace from heav - en.

Text: H. Francis Yardley, 1911–1990; Frank J. Whiteley, b. 1914, alt.
Music: Paris *Antiphoner*, 1681
Text © 1969 H. Francis Yardley and Frank J. Whiteley

CHRISTE SANCTORUM
11 11 12 5

459   Wade in the Water

Refrain

All

Wade in the wa - ter, wade in the wa - ter, chil - dren,

wade in the wa - ter, God's a-goin'-a trou-ble the wa - ter.

Leader   All

1 See that host all dressed in white,
2 See that band all dressed in red,   God's a-goin'-a trou-ble the
3 Look o - ver yon - der, what do I see?
4 If you don't be - lieve I've been re - deemed,

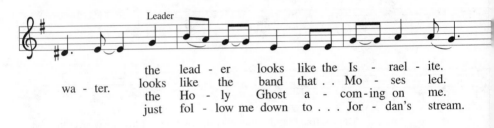

Leader

the lead - er looks like the Is - rael - ite.
wa - ter.   looks like the band that . . Mo - ses led.
the Ho - ly Ghost a - com - ing on me.
just fol - low me down to . . . Jor - dan's stream.

All   *Refrain*

God's a - goin' - a trou - ble the wa - ter.

Text: African American spiritual
Music: African American spiritual

WADE IN THE WATER
Irregula

Now the Silence

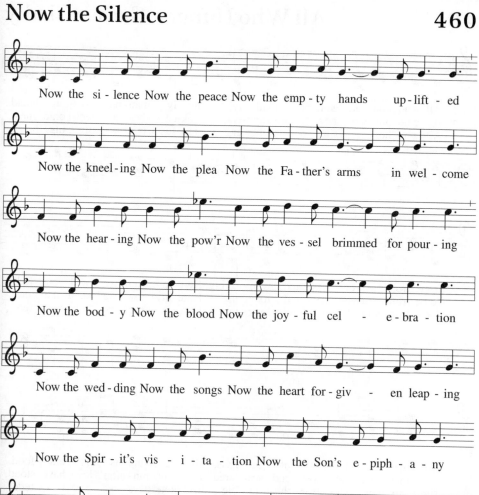

Now the si - lence Now the peace Now the emp - ty hands up - lift - ed

Now the kneel - ing Now the plea Now the Fa - ther's arms in wel - come

Now the hear - ing Now the pow'r Now the ves - sel brimmed for pour - ing

Now the bod - y Now the blood Now the joy - ful cel - e - bra - tion

Now the wed - ding Now the songs Now the heart for - giv - en leap - ing

Now the Spir - it's vis - i - ta - tion Now the Son's e - piph - a - ny

Now the Fa - ther's bless - ing Now Now Now

Text: Jaroslav J. Vajda, b. 1919
Music: Carl F. Schalk, b. 1929
Text and music © 1969 Hope Publishing Company

NOW
PM

461 All Who Hunger, Gather Gladly

1 All who hun-ger, gath-er glad - ly; ho - ly man-na is our bread.
2 All who hun-ger, nev - er strang-ers; seek-er, be a wel-come guest.
3 All who hun-ger, sing to - geth - er, Je - sus Christ is liv - ing bread.

Come from wil-der - ness and wan - d'ring. Here in truth we will be fed.
Come from rest-less - ness and roam-ing. Here in joy we keep the feast.
Come from lone - li - ness and long-ing. Here in peace we have been fed.

You that yearn for days of full-ness, all a - round us is our food.
We that once were lost and scat-tered in com - mu - nion's love have stood.
Blest are those who from this ta - ble live their days in grat-i - tude.

Taste and see the grace e - ter - nal. Taste and see that God is good.
Taste and see the grace e - ter - nal. Taste and see that God is good.
Taste and see the grace e - ter - nal. Taste and see that God is good.

Text: Sylvia G. Dunstan, 1955–1993
Music: W. Moore, *Columbian Harmony*, 1825; arr. hymnal version
Text © 1991 GIA Publications, Inc.
Arr. © 2003 Augsburg Fortress

HOLY MANNA
87 87 D

Now We Join in Celebration

462

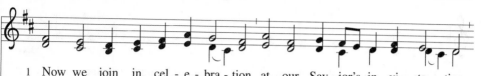

1 Now we join in cel - e - bra - tion at our Sav - ior's in - vi - ta - tion,
2 Lord, as round this feast we gath - er, fill our hearts with ho - ly rap - ture!
3 Lord, we share in this com - mu - nion as one fam - 'ly of God's chil - dren,

dressed no more in spir - it som - ber, clothed in - stead in joy and won - der;
For this bread and cup of bless - ing are for us the sure pos - sess - ing
rec - on - ciled through you, our broth - er, one in you with God our Fa - ther.

for the Lord of all ex - is - tence, put - ting off di - vine tran - scen - dence,
of your lov - ing deed on Cal - v'ry, of your liv - ing self, our vic - t'ry,
Give us grace to live for oth - ers, serv - ing all, both friends and strang - ers,

stoops a - gain in love to meet us, with his ver - y life to feed us.
pledge of your un - fail - ing pres - ence, fore - taste here of heav'n - ly glad - ness.
seek - ing jus - tice, love, and mer - cy till you come in fi - nal glo - ry.

Text: Joel W. Lundeen, 1918–1990
Music: Johann Crüger, 1598–1662
Text © Joel W. Lundeen, admin. Augsburg Fortress

SCHMÜCKE DICH
LMD

463 Lord, Who the Night You Were Betrayed

1 Lord, who the night you were be-trayed did pray that all your
2 For all your church on earth, we in-ter-cede; Lord, make our
3 And hear our prayer for wan-d'rers from your fold; re-store them,
4 So, Lord, at length when sac-ra-ments shall cease, may we be

church might be for-ev-er one: help us at
sad di-vi-sions soon to cease; draw us all
too, Good Shep-herd of the sheep, back to the
one with all your church a-bove— one with your

ev-'ry eu-cha-rist to say with will-ing heart and
clos-er, each to each, we plead, by draw-ing all to
faith your saints con-fessed of old, and to the church still
saints in one un-bro-ken peace, one with your saints in

soul, "Your will be done." Oh, may we all one bread, one
you, O Prince of peace; thus may we all one bread, one
pledged that faith to keep. Soon may we all one bread, one
one un-bound-ed love; more bless-ed still, in peace and

Text: William H. Turton, 1856–1938, alt.
Music: Orlando Gibbons, 1583–1625

SONG 1
10 10 10 10 10 10

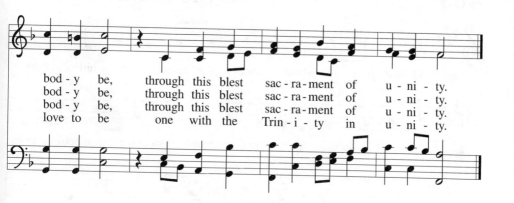

bod - y be, through this blest sac - ra - ment of u - ni - ty.
bod - y be, through this blest sac - ra - ment of u - ni - ty.
bod - y be, through this blest sac - ra - ment of u - ni - ty.
love to be one with the Trin - i - ty in u - ni - ty.

Bread of Life, Our Host and Meal 464

1 Bread of life, our host and meal, Je - sus, feed us.
2 Bread now break and wine now pour, Je - sus, feed us.
3 Grant for - give - ness in the feast— Je - sus, feed us—
4 Thank you for this gift we share. Je - sus, feed us.

Christ, by faith, to see and feel, feed us with your love.
Make us one, our hope re - store; feed us with your love.
for the great - est and the least; feed us with your love.
Save God's chil - dren ev - 'ry - where; feed us with your love.

Text: Ray Makeever, b. 1943; Rusty Edwards, b. 1955
Music: Ray Makeever; arr. Rusty Edwards
Text and music © 1996 Hope Publishing Company

JESUS, FEED US
7 4 75

465

As the Grains of Wheat

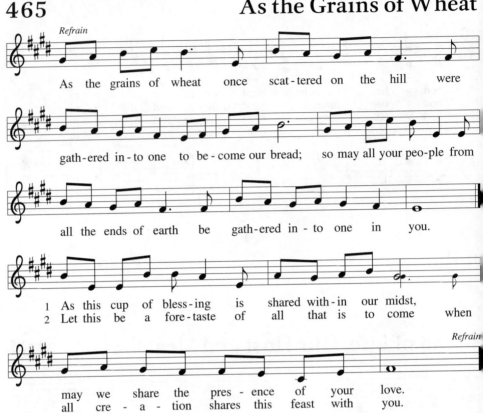

Refrain

As the grains of wheat once scat-tered on the hill were

gath-ered in-to one to be-come our bread; so may all your peo-ple from

all the ends of earth be gath-ered in-to one in you.

1 As this cup of bless-ing is shared with-in our midst,
2 Let this be a fore-taste of all that is to come when

Refrain

may we share the pres - ence of your love.
all cre - a - tion shares this feast with you.

Text: Didache, 2nd cent.; Marty Haugen, b. 1950
Music: Marty Haugen
Text and music © 1990 GIA Publications, Inc.

AS THE GRAINS
Irregular

466

In the Singing

1 In the sing-ing, in the si-lence, in the hands ex-pect-ant, o-pen,
2 In the ques-tion, in the an-swer, in the mo-ment of ac-cept-ance,

in the bless-ing, in the break-ing, in your pres-ence at this ta-ble,
in the heart's cry, in the heal-ing, in the cir-cle of your peo-ple,

Text: Shirley Erena Murray, b. 1931
Music: Carlton R. Young, b. 1926
Text and music © 1996 Hope Publishing Company

BREAD OF PEACE
LM and refrain

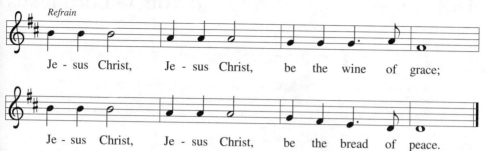

Refrain

Je - sus Christ, Je - sus Christ, be the wine of grace;

Je - sus Christ, Je - sus Christ, be the bread of peace.

We Place upon Your Table, Lord 467

1 We place up - on your ta - ble, Lord, where you by
2 With - in these sim - ple things there lie the height and
3 Ac - cept them, Lord; they come from you; we take them

grace have bid us dine, these to - kens of our dai - ly
depth of hu - man life: our pain and tears, our thoughts and
hum - bly from your hand; put these your gifts to high - er

work, the food of life, the bread and wine.
toils, our hopes and fears, our joy and strife.
use: the ho - ly meal that you com - mand.

Text: M. F. C. Wilson, 1884–1944, alt.
Music: W. Walker, *Southern Harmony*, 1835

DISTRESS
LM

468

Around You, O Lord Jesus

1 A - round you, O Lord Je - sus, your own you gath - er still
2 We hear your in - vi - ta - tion, and heed, O Lord, your call;
3 We are your own for - ev - er; un - til our fi - nal breath

to share the feast you give us with grace our lives to fill.
your word of con - so - la - tion is spo - ken here to all.
we will be true and nev - er— in joy, in grief, in death—

You say to us so lov - ing - ly, "Take, eat! This is my
It draws us to your lov - ing heart; it brings to us your
de - part from you, for you are still a - mong your peo - ple

bod - y! Take, drink! This is my blood!"
bless - ing, which nev - er will de - part.
dwell - ing, as you have said you will.

Text: Frans Mikael Franzén, 1772–1847; tr. composite
Music: H. Thomissön, *Den danske Psalmebog*, 1569
Text © 1978 *Lutheran Book of Worship*, admin. Augsburg Fortress

O JESU, ÄN DE DINA
7 6 7 6 8 7 6

By Your Hand You Feed Your People

469

1 By your hand you feed your peo - ple, food of an - gels, heav-en's bread.
2 In this meal we taste your sweet-ness, bread for hun - ger, wine of peace.
3 Send us now with faith and cour - age to the hun - gry, lost, be - reaved.

For these gifts we did not la - bor, by your grace have we been fed:
Ho - ly word and ho - ly wis - dom sat - is - fy our deep-est needs.
In our liv - ing and our dy - ing, we be - come what we re - ceive:

Refrain

Christ's own bod - y, blessed and bro - ken, cup o'er - flow-ing, life out - poured,

giv-en as a liv-ing to - ken of your world re-deemed, re - stored.

Text: Susan R. Briehl, b. 1952
Music: Marty Haugen, b. 1950
Text and music © 2002 GIA Publications, Inc.

CAMROSE
8787D

470 Draw Us in the Spirit's Tether

1 Draw us in the Spir-it's teth - er, for when hum - bly
2 As dis - ci - ples used to gath - er in the name of
3 All our meals and all our liv - ing make as sac - ra -

in your name two or three are met to - geth - er,
Christ to sup, then with thanks to God the giv - er
ments of you, that by car - ing, help-ing, giv - ing,

you are in the midst of them. Al - le - lu - ia!
break the bread and bless the cup, Al - le - lu - ia!
we may be dis - ci - ples true. Al - le - lu - ia!

Al - le - lu - ia! Touch we now your gar - ment's hem.
Al - le - lu - ia! so now bind our friend - ship up.
Al - le - lu - ia! We will serve with faith a - new.

Text: Percy Dearmer, 1867–1936, alt.
Music: Harold Friedell, 1905–1958
Text © Oxford University Press
Music © 1957, 1985 H. W. Gray, admin. CPP/Belwin

UNION SEMINARY
8 7 8 7 8 7

Let Us Break Bread Together

1 Let us break bread to - geth-er on our knees;
2 Let us drink wine to - geth-er on our knees;
3 Let us praise God to - geth-er on our knees;

let us break bread to - geth-er on our knees.
let us drink wine to - geth-er on our knees.
let us praise God to - geth-er on our knees.

Refrain

When I fall on my knees, with my face to the ris - ing

sun, O Lord, have mer-cy on me.

Text: African American spiritual
Music: African American spiritual

BREAK BREAD TOGETHER
10 10 and refrain

Eat This Bread
Jesus Christ, Bread of Life

472

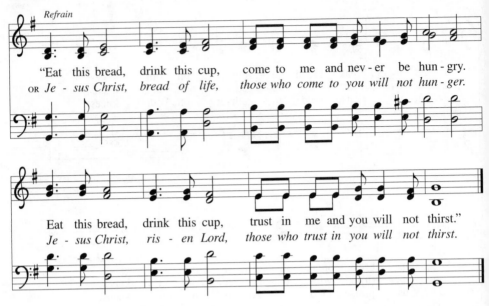

Refrain

"Eat this bread, drink this cup, come to me and nev-er be hun-gry.
OR *Je-sus Christ, bread of life, those who come to you will not hun-ger.*

Eat this bread, drink this cup, trust in me and you will not thirst."
Je-sus Christ, ris-en Lord, those who trust in you will not thirst.

Text: Taizé Community
Music: Jacques Berthier, 1923–1994
Text and music © 1984 Les Presses de Taizé, admin. GIA Publications, Inc.

BERTHIER
Irregular

Holy, Holy, Holy
Santo, santo, santo

473

San-to, san-to, san-to, mi co-ra-zón te_a-do-ra.
Ho-ly, ho-ly, ho-ly, my heart, my heart a-dores you.

Mi co-ra-zón te sa-be de-cir: San-to_e-res Se-ñor.
My heart is glad to say the words: You are ho-ly, God.

Text: Argentine traditional
Music: Argentine traditional

ARGENTINE SANTO
6785

Bread of Life from Heaven

474

Refrain

Bread of life from heav-en, your blood and bod-y giv-en,

we eat this bread and drink this cup un-til you come a-gain.

1	Break	now	the	bread	of Christ's sac-ri-fice;	giv-ing
2	Seek	not	the	food	that will pass a-way;	set your
3	Love	as	the	one	who, in love for you,	gave him-
4	Dwell	in	the	one	who now dwells in you;	make your
5	Drink	of	this	cup	and de-clare his death;	eat this

thanks, hun-gry ones, gath-er round. Eat, all of you, and be
hearts on the food that en-dures. Come, learn the true and the
self for the life of the world. Come to the one who is
home in the life-giv-ing Word. Know on-ly Christ, Ho-ly
bread and be-lieve Eas-ter morn; trust his re-turn and, with

Refrain

sat-is-fied; in Christ's pres-ence the loaves will a-bound.
liv-ing way, that the full-ness of life may be yours.
food for you, that your hun-ger and thirst be no more.
One of God, and be-lieve in the truth you have heard.
ev-'ry breath, praise the one in whom you are re-born.

Text: Susan R. Briehl, b. 1952
Music: Argentine traditional, refrain; Marty Haugen, b. 1950, stanzas
Text and music © 2001 GIA Publications, Inc.

ARGENTINE SANTO | BREAK NOW THE BREAD
9 9 9 9 and refrain

475 Lord, Enthroned in Heavenly Splendor

1 Lord, en - throned in heav'n - ly splen - dor, first - be -
2 Though the low - liest form now veil you as of
3 Pas - chal Lamb, your of - f'ring, fin - ished once for
4 Life - im - part - ing heav'n - ly man - na, strick - en

got - ten from the dead, you a - lone, our strong de -
old in Beth - le - hem, here as there your an - gels
all when you were slain, in its full - ness un - di -
rock with stream - ing side, heav'n and earth with loud ho -

fend - er, lift - ing up your peo - ple's head. Al - le -
hail you, branch and flow'r of Jes - se's stem. Al - le -
min - ished shall for - ev - er - more re - main, Al - le -
san - na wor - ship you, the Lamb who died, Al - le -

lu - ia, al - le - lu - ia, al - le - lu - ia! Je - sus, true and
lu - ia, al - le - lu - ia, al - le - lu - ia! We in wor - ship
lu - ia, al - le - lu - ia, al - le - lu - ia! cleans - ing souls from
lu - ia, al - le - lu - ia, al - le - lu - ia! ris'n, as - cend - ed,

Text: George H. Bourne, 1840–1925
Music: William Owen, 1814–1893

BRYN CALFARIA
8 7 8 7 4 4 4 7 7

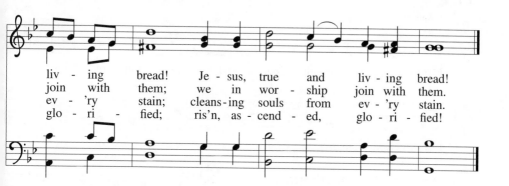

liv - ing bread! Je - sus, true and liv - ing bread!
join with them; we in wor - ship join with them.
ev - 'ry stain; cleans-ing souls from ev - 'ry stain.
glo - ri - fied; ris'n, as - cend - ed, glo - ri - fied!

Thee We Adore, O Savior 476

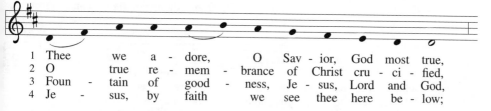

1 Thee we a - dore, O Sav - ior, God most true,
2 O true re - mem - brance of Christ cru - ci - fied,
3 Foun - tain of good - ness, Je - sus, Lord and God,
4 Je - sus, by faith we see thee here be - low;

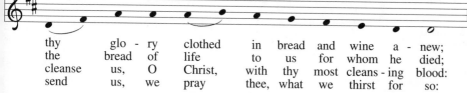

thy glo - ry clothed in bread and wine a - new;
the bread of life to us for whom he died;
cleanse us, O Christ, with thy most cleans - ing blood:
send us, we pray thee, what we thirst for so:

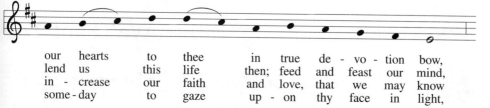

our hearts to thee in true de - vo - tion bow,
lend us this life then; feed and feast our mind,
in - crease our faith and love, that we may know
some - day to gaze up - on thy face in light,

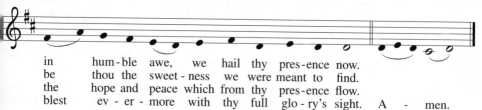

in hum - ble awe, we hail thy pres-ence now.
be thou the sweet - ness we were meant to find.
the hope and peace which from thy pres-ence flow.
blest ev - er - more with thy full glo - ry's sight. A - men.

Text: Thomas Aquinas, 1227–1274; tr. Gerard Manley Hopkins, 1844–1889,
  and James R. Woodford, 1820–1885, alt.
Music: Plainsong mode V; *Processionale*, Paris, 1697

ADORO TE DEVOTE
10 10 10 10

477   I Received the Living God

Refrain

I re-ceived the liv-ing God, and my heart is full of joy.

I re-ceived the liv-ing God, and my heart is full of joy.

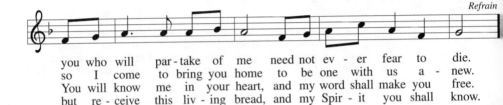

1 Je-sus said: I am the bread, knead-ed long to give you life;
2 Je-sus said: I am the way, and my Fa-ther longs for you;
3 Je-sus said: I am the truth; come and fol-low close to me.
4 Je-sus said: I am the life, far from whom no thing can grow,

Refrain

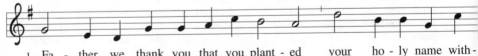

you who will par-take of me need not ev-er fear to die.
so I come to bring you home to be one with us a-new.
You will know me in your heart, and my word shall make you free.
but re-ceive this liv-ing bread, and my Spir-it you shall know.

Text: Anonymous
Music: Anonymous

LIVING GOD
7 7 7 7 and refrain

478   Father, We Thank You

1 Fa-ther, we thank you that you plant-ed your ho-ly name with-
2 Watch o'er your church, O Lord, in mer-cy, save it from e-vil,

in our hearts. Knowl-edge and faith and life im-mor-tal Je-sus your
guard it still; per-fect it in your love, u-nite it, cleansed and con-

Text: Didache, 2nd cent.; para. F. Bland Tucker, 1895–1984, alt.
Music: attr. Louis Bourgeois, 1510–1561
Text © Church Pension Fund

RENDEZ À DIEU
9 8 9 8 D

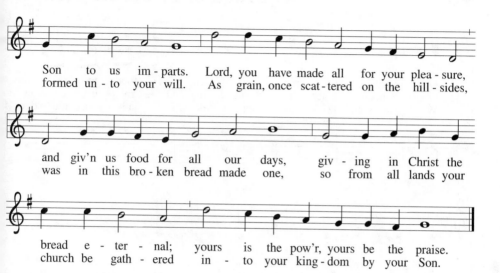

Son to us im - parts. Lord, you have made all for your plea - sure,
formed un - to your will. As grain, once scat - tered on the hill - sides,

and giv'n us food for all our days, giv - ing in Christ the
was in this bro - ken bread made one, so from all lands your

bread e - ter - nal; yours is the pow'r, yours be the praise.
church be gath - ered in - to your king - dom by your Son.

We Come to the Hungry Feast 479

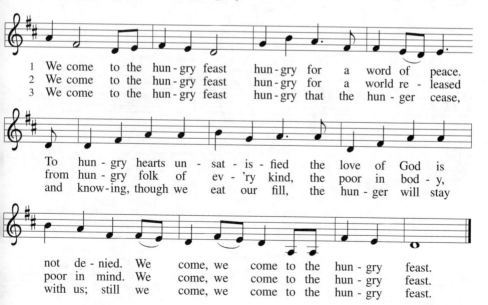

1 We come to the hun - gry feast hun - gry for a word of peace.
2 We come to the hun - gry feast hun - gry for a world re - leased
3 We come to the hun - gry feast hun - gry that the hun - ger cease,

To hun - gry hearts un - sat - is - fied the love of God is
from hun - gry folk of ev - 'ry kind, the poor in bod - y,
and know - ing, though we eat our fill, the hun - ger will stay

not de - nied. We come, we come to the hun - gry feast.
poor in mind. We come, we come to the hun - gry feast.
with us; still we come, we come to the hun - gry feast.

Text: Ray Makeever, b. 1943
Music: Ray Makeever
Text and music © 1982 Ray Makeever, admin. Augsburg Fortress

HUNGRY FEAST
77889

480   O Bread of Life from Heaven

1 O bread of life from heav - en, O food to pil - grims
2 O fount of grace re - deem - ing, O riv - er ev - er
3 We love you, Je - sus, ten - der, in all your hid - den

giv - en, O man - na from a - bove: feed
stream - ing from Je - sus' wound - ed side: come
splen - dor with - in these means of grace. Oh,

with the bless - ed sweet - ness of your di - vine com -
now, your love be - stow - ing on thirst - ing souls, and
let the veil be riv - en, and our clear eye in

plete - ness the souls that want and need your love.
flow - ing till all are ful - ly sat - is - fied.
heav - en be - hold your glo - ry face to face.

Text: Latin hymn, c. 1661; tr. Hugh T. Henry, 1862–1946, sts. 1, 3;
   tr. Philip Schaff, 1819–1893, st. 2
Music: Heinrich Isaac, 1450–1517; arr. Johann Sebastian Bach, 1685–1750

O WELT, ICH MUSS DICH LASSEN
776 778

Come to the Table

481

Come to the ta - ble of mer - cy, pre - pared with the wine and the bread.

All who are hun - gry and thirst - y, come, and your souls will be fed.

Come at the Lord's in - vi - ta - tion; re - ceive from his nail - scarred hand.

Eat of the bread of sal - va - tion; drink of the blood of the Lamb.

Text: Claire Cloninger, b. 1942
Music: Martin J. Nystrom, b. 1956
Text and music © 1991 Integrity's Hosanna! Music; Juniper Landing Music, admin. Word Music; and Word Music

COME TO THE TABLE
88 87 87 87

482   I Come with Joy

1 I come with joy, a child of God, for - giv - en, loved, and
2 I come with Chris - tians far and near to find, as all are
3 As Christ breaks bread, and bids us share, each proud di - vi - sion
4 The Spir - it of the ris - en Christ, un - seen, but ev - er
5 To - geth - er met, to - geth - er bound by all that God has

free, the life of Je - sus to re - call in
fed, the new com - mu - ni - ty of love in
ends. The love that made us, makes us one, and
near, is in such friend - ship bet - ter known, a -
done, we'll go with joy, to give the world the

love laid down for me, in love laid down for me.
Christ's com - mu - nion bread, in Christ's com - mu - nion bread.
strang - ers now are friends, and strang - ers now are friends.
live a - mong us here, a - live a - mong us here.
love that makes us one, the love that makes us one.

Text: Brian A. Wren, b. 1936
Music: W. Walker, *Southern Harmony*, 1835
Text © 1971, rev. 1995 Hope Publishing Company

DOVE OF PEACE
86 866

483   Here Is Bread

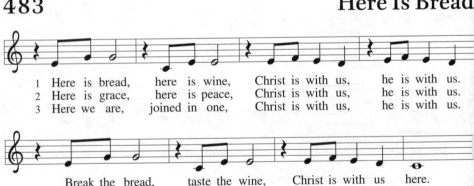

1 Here is bread, here is wine, Christ is with us, he is with us.
2 Here is grace, here is peace, Christ is with us, he is with us.
3 Here we are, joined in one, Christ is with us, he is with us.

Break the bread, taste the wine, Christ is with us here.
Know his grace, find his peace, feast on Je - sus here.
We'll pro - claim till he comes Je - sus cru - ci - fied.

Text: Graham Kendrick, b. 1950
Music: Graham Kendrick
Text and music © 1991 Make Way Music, admin. by Music Services in the Western Hemisphere

HERE IS BREAD
3 3 4 4 3 3 5 and refrain

Refrain

In this bread there is heal-ing, in this cup is life for-ev-er.

In this mo-ment, by the Spir-it, Christ is with us here.

You Satisfy the Hungry Heart
Gift of Finest Wheat

484

Refrain

You sat-is-fy the hun-gry heart with gift of fin-est wheat.

Come give to us, O sav-ing Lord, the bread of life to eat.

1 As when the shep-herd calls his sheep, they know and heed his voice;
2 With joy-ful lips we sing to you our praise and grat-i-tude
3 Is not the cup we bless and share the blood of Christ out-poured?
4 The mys-t'ry of your pres-ence, Lord, no mor-tal tongue can tell:
5 You give your-self to us, O Lord; then self-less let us be,

Refrain

so when you call your fam-'ly, Lord, we fol-low and re-joice.
that you should count us wor-thy, Lord, to share this heav'n-ly food.
Do not one cup, one loaf, de-clare our one-ness in the Lord?
whom all the world can-not con-tain comes in our hearts to dwell.
to serve each oth-er in your name in truth and char-i-ty.

Text: Omer Westendorf, 1916–1997
Music: Robert E. Kreutz, 1922–1996
Text and music © 1977 Archdiocese of Philadelphia

BICENTENNIAL
CM and refrain

485

I Am the Bread of Life

Leader or All

1 "I am the Bread of life. You who
2 "The bread that . . . I will give is my
3 "Un - less . . . . . . you . . . . eat of the
4 "I am the res - ur - rec - tion, ...
5 Yes, Lord, ... I be - lieve that . . .

come to me shall not hun - ger, and who be -
flesh for the life of the world, ... and if you
flesh of the Son of Man . . . . and . . .
I . . . . . . am the life. . . . . . . If you be -
you . . . . . . are the Christ, ... the . . .

lieve in me shall not thirst. No one can come to
eat . . . . of this bread, you shall . . live for -
drink . . . of his blood, and drink . . . . of his
lieve . . . in . . . me, e - ven . . though you
Son . . . of . . . God, who . . . have . . .

me un - less the Fa - ther beck - ons."
ev - er, ... you shall live for - ev - er."
blood, you shall not have life with - in you."
die, ... you shall live for - ev - er."
come in - to . . . the . . . . world. . . .

Refrain
All

"And I will raise you up, and I will raise you up,

Text: Suzanne Toolan, RSM, b. 1927, based on John 6
Music: Suzanne Toolan, RSM
Text and music © 1966, 1970, 1986, 1993 GIA Publications, Inc.

I AM THE BREAD
Irregular

and I will raise you up on the last day."

God Extends an Invitation
Nuestro Padre nos invita

486

Nues-tro Pa - dre nos in - vi - ta   *a la me - sa de la*
God ex - tends an in - vi - ta - tion   to the ta - ble of cre -

vi - da,   *don - de hay vi - no, luz y pan;*   *y no -*
a - tion,   where there's wine and light and bread.   Here we

so - tros nos reu - ni - mos,   *y lo nues - tro com - par - ti - mos,*   *pues a -*
gath - er in thanks - giv - ing   and we of - fer all our liv - ing.   Here the

sí es la co - mu - nión;   *pues a - sí es la co - mu - nión.*
feast of life is spread;   here the feast of life is spread.

Text: Miria T. Kolling; English and Spanish tr. Gerhard M. Cartford, b. 1923
Music: Miria T. Kolling
Tr. © 1998 Augsburg Fortress
Music © Miria T. Kolling

NUESTRO PADRE
8 8 7 8 8 7 7

487

What Feast of Love

1 What feast of love is of-fered here, what ban-quet come from heav-en?
2 What light of truth is of-fered here, what cov - e - nant from heav-en?
3 What wine of love is of-fered here, what crim-son drink from heav-en?

What food of ev - er - last-ing life, what gra - cious gift is giv - en?
What hope of ev - er - last-ing life, what won-drous word is giv - en?
What stream of ev - er - last-ing life, what pre - cious blood is giv - en?

This, this is Christ the king, the bread come down from heav - en.
This, this is Christ the king, the sun come down from heav - en.
This, this is Christ the king, the sweet - est wine of heav - en.

Oh, taste and see and sing! How sweet the man - na giv - en!
Oh, see and hear and sing! The Word of God is giv - en!
Oh, taste and see and sing! The Son of God is giv - en!

Text: Delores Dufner, OSB, b. 1939
Music: English ballad, 16th cent.
Text © 1993 Delores Dufner, admin. OCP Publications

GREENSLEEVES
87 87 67 67

Soul, Adorn Yourself with Gladness

488

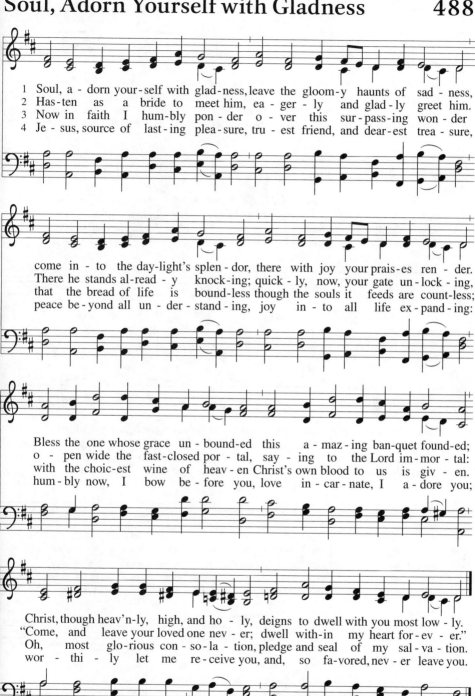

1 Soul, a - dorn your - self with glad - ness, leave the gloom - y haunts of sad - ness,
2 Has - ten as a bride to meet him, ea - ger - ly and glad - ly greet him.
3 Now in faith I hum - bly pon - der o - ver this sur - pass - ing won - der
4 Je - sus, source of last - ing plea - sure, tru - est friend, and dear - est trea - sure,

come in - to the day - light's splen - dor, there with joy your prais - es ren - der.
There he stands al - read - y knock - ing; quick - ly, now, your gate un - lock - ing,
that the bread of life is bound - less though the souls it feeds are count - less;
peace be - yond all un - der - stand - ing, joy in - to all life ex - pand - ing:

Bless the one whose grace un - bound - ed this a - maz - ing ban - quet found - ed;
o - pen wide the fast - closed por - tal, say - ing to the Lord im - mor - tal:
with the choic - est wine of heav - en Christ's own blood to us is giv - en.
hum - bly now, I bow be - fore you, love in - car - nate, I a - dore you;

Christ, though heav'n - ly, high, and ho - ly, deigns to dwell with you most low - ly.
"Come, and leave your loved one nev - er; dwell with - in my heart for - ev - er."
Oh, most glo - rious con - so - la - tion, pledge and seal of my sal - va - tion.
wor - thi - ly let me re - ceive you, and, so fa - vored, nev - er leave you.

Text: Johann Franck, 1618–1677; tr. *Lutheran Book of Worship*
Music: Johann Crüger, 1598–1662
Text © 1978 *Lutheran Book of Worship*, admin. Augsburg Fortress

SCHMÜCKE DICH
LMD

Soul, Adorn Yourself with Gladness

Vengo a ti, Jesús amado

489

1 *Ven-go a ti, Je - sús a - ma - do: lí - bra - me de mi pe - ca - do.*
1 Soul, a - dorn your- self with glad - ness, leave the gloom - y haunts of sad - ness,
2 Now in faith I hum - bly pon - der o - ver this sur - pass - ing won - der
3 Je - sus, source of last - ing plea - sure, tru - est friend, and dear - est trea - sure,

Cal - ma, Re - den - tor, mi llan - to;
come in - to the day - light's splen - dor,
that the bread of life is bound - less
peace be - yond all un - der - stand - ing,

he pe - ca - do tan - to, tan - to.
there with joy your prais - es ren - der.
though the souls it feeds are count - less;
joy in - to all life ex - pand - ing:

Con la san - gre que ver - tis - te das con - sue - lo al al - ma
Bless the one whose grace un - bound-ed this a - maz - ing ban - quet
with the choic - est wine of heav - en Christ's own blood to us is
hum - bly now, I bow be - fore you, love in - car - nate, I a -

tris - te; ham - bre tor - nas en har - tu - ra,
found-ed; Christ, though heav'n - ly, high, and ho - ly,
giv - en. Oh, most glo - rious con - so - la - tion,
dore you; wor - thi - ly let me re - ceive you,

sal - va - ción me das se - gu - ra.
deigns to dwell with you most low - ly.
pledge and seal of my sal - va - tion.
and, so fa - vored, nev - er leave you.

Text: Johann Franck, 1618–1677, stanzas; Esther Bertieaux, b. 1944, refrain; tr. composite
Music: Evy Lucío Cordova, b. 1934
Text © 1964, 1978, 1998 Augsburg Fortress
Music © 1968 Peer International Corporation of Puerto Rico

CANTO AL BORINQUEN
LMD and refrain

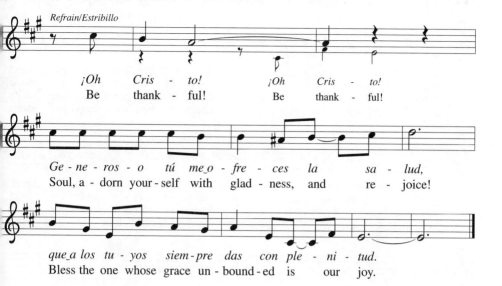

Refrain/Estribillo

¡Oh Cris - to! ¡Oh Cris - to!
Be thank - ful! Be thank - ful!

Ge - ne - ros - o tú me_o - fre - ces la sa - lud,
Soul, a - dorn your - self with glad - ness, and re - joice!

que_a los tu - yos siem - pre das con ple - ni - tud.
Bless the one whose grace un - bound - ed is our joy.

2 Vida_ofrece,_y paz preciosa
   tu palabra poderosa;
   por unirse_al elemento
   hace_el santo sacramento.
   Con el pan y vino_adquiero
   cuerpo_y sangre del Cordero.
   ¡Oh, misterio tan profundo!
   ¿Quién lo_entiende_en este mundo? Estribillo

3 Ya mi alma tú libraste,
   y_el pecado tú quitaste,
   cual preludio de tu cielo,
   hoy me gozo_en tu consuelo.
   Cielos, tierra, noche_y día
   te den gracias a porfía:
   "Por tus múltiples favores,
   ¡gracias mil y mil loores!" Estribillo

490 Let All Mortal Flesh Keep Silence

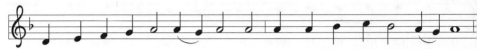

1 Let all mor-tal flesh keep si-lence,and with fear and trem-bling stand;
2 King of kings,yet born of Mar-y, as of old on earth he stood,
3 Rank on rank the host of heav-en spreads its van-guard on the way;
4 At his feet the six-winged ser-aph, cher-u-bim with sleep-less eye,

pon-der noth-ing earth-ly - mind-ed, for with bless-ing in his hand
Lord of lords in hu-man ves-ture, in the bod-y and the blood,
as the Light of light, de-scend-ing from the realms of end-less day,
veil their fac-es to the pres-ence, as with cease-less voice they cry:

Christ our God to earth de-scend - ing comes full hom-age to de-mand.
he will give to all the faith - ful his own self for heav'n-ly food.
comes,the pow'rs of hell to van - quish, as the dark-ness clears a-way.
"Al - le - lu - ia! Al - le-lu - ia! Al - le-lu-ia, Lord Most High!"

Text: Liturgy of St. James; tr. Gerard Moultrie, 1829–1885, alt.
Music: French folk tune, 17th cent.

PICARD\
87878\

491 Come, Let Us Eat

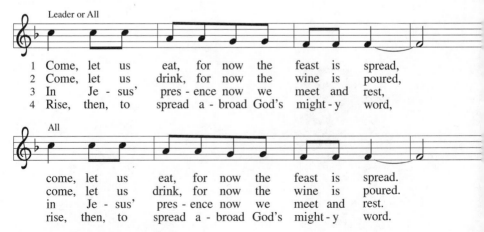

Leader or All

1 Come, let us eat, for now the feast is spread,
2 Come, let us drink, for now the wine is poured,
3 In Je - sus' pres - ence now we meet and rest,
4 Rise, then, to spread a - broad God's might-y word,

All

come, let us eat, for now the feast is spread.
come, let us drink, for now the wine is poured.
in Je - sus' pres - ence now we meet and rest.
rise, then, to spread a - broad God's might-y word.

Text: Billema Kwillia, b. 1925, sts. 1–3; Gilbert E. Doan Jr., b. 1930, st. 4, alt.;
   tr. Margaret D. Miller, b. 1927, sts. 1–3, alt.
Music: Billema Kwillia, adapt.
Text sts. 1–3 and tune © Lutheran World Federation; text st. 4 and adapt. © 1972 Contemporary Worship 4, admin. Augsburg Fortress

A VA DE\
10 10 10 1\

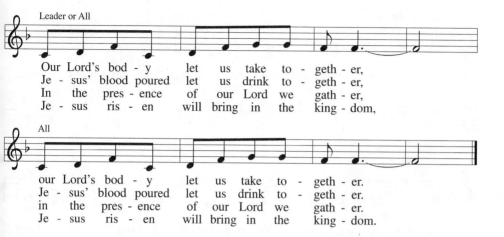

Leader or All

Our Lord's bod - y let us take to - geth - er,
Je - sus' blood poured let us drink to - geth - er,
In the pres - ence of our Lord we gath - er,
Je - sus ris - en will bring in the king - dom,

All

our Lord's bod - y let us take to - geth - er.
Je - sus' blood poured let us drink to - geth - er.
in the pres - ence of our Lord we gath - er.
Je - sus ris - en will bring in the king - dom.

Eat This Bread, Drink This Cup   492

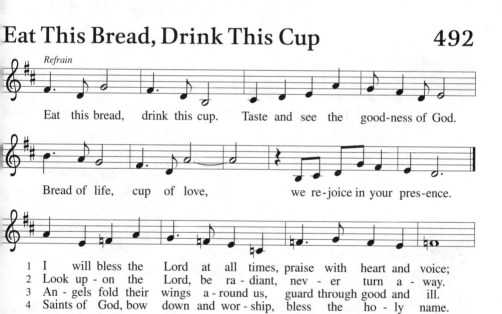

Refrain

Eat this bread, drink this cup. Taste and see the good-ness of God.

Bread of life, cup of love, we re-joice in your pres-ence.

1 I will bless the Lord at all times, praise with heart and voice;
2 Look up - on the Lord, be ra - diant, nev - er turn a - way.
3 An - gels fold their wings a - round us, guard through good and ill.
4 Saints of God, bow down and wor - ship, bless the ho - ly name.

Refrain

in my God I glo - ry for - ev - er: lis - ten and re - joice!
God will save in ev - 'ry af - flic - tion, hear us when we pray.
Those who seek the Lord will lack noth-ing; taste, and have your fill.
Rise to tell God's great-ness for - ev - er, won - drous deeds pro - claim!

Text: Jeremy Young, b. 1948, refrain; *With One Voice*, stanzas, based on Ps. 34
Music: Jeremy Young
Text and music © 1995 Augsburg Fortress

STONERIDGE
85 95 and refrain

493

Taste and See

Refrain – All

Taste and see, taste and see the good-ness of the Lord. Oh,

taste and see, taste and see the good-ness of the Lord, of the Lord.

Leader or All

1 I will bless the Lord at all times. Praise shall

al-ways be on my lips; my soul shall glo-ry in the

Lord; for God has been so good to me.

2 Glo-ri-fy the Lord with me. To-geth-er let us

all praise God's name. I called the Lord, who an-swered

Text: James E. Moore Jr., b. 1951, based on Ps. 34
Music: James E. Moore Jr.
Text and music © 1983 GIA Publications, Inc.

TASTE AND SEE
Irregular

me; from all my trou-bles I was set free.

3 Refrain

3 Wor-ship the Lord, all you peo-ple. You'll want for

noth-ing if you ask. Taste and see that the Lord is

Refrain

good; in God we need put all our trust.

For the Bread Which You Have Broken 494

1 For the bread which you have bro-ken, for the wine which you have poured,
2 By this prom-ise that you love us, by your gift of peace re-stored,
3 With the saints who now a-dore you, seat-ed at the heav'n-ly board,
4 In your ser-vice, Lord, de-fend us; in our hearts keep watch and ward;

for the words which you have spo-ken, now we give you thanks, O Lord.
by your call to heav'n a-bove us, hal-low all our lives, O Lord.
may the church still wait-ing for you keep love's tie un-bro-ken, Lord.
in the world to which you send us let your king-dom come, O Lord.

Text: Louis F. Benson, 1855–1930, alt.
Music: *Gross Catolisch Gesangbuch*, Nürnberg, 1631; arr. William Smith Rockstro, 1823–1895
Text © Robert F. Jefferys Jr.

OMNI DIE
8787

495   We Who Once Were Dead

1 We who once were dead now live, ful - ly know - ing Je - sus
2 We were lost in night, but you sought and found us. Give us
3 He be - came our bread; Je - sus died to save us. On him
4 Let us share the pain you en - dured in dy - ing; we shall

as our head. Life is o - ver - flow - ing when he breaks the bread.
strength to fight; death is all a - round us. Je - sus, be our light.
we are fed, eat - ing what he gave us, ris - ing from the dead.
then re - main liv - ing; death de - fy - ing, we shall rise a - gain.

5 Jesus, you were dead,
but you rose and, living,
made yourself our bread,
in your goodness giving
life though we were dead.

6 This is your design;
in this meal we meet you.
Be our bread and wine,
Jesus, we entreat you.
This shall be our sign.

Text: Muus Jacobse, 1909–1972; tr. composite
Music: Rik Veelenturf, b. 1936
Text and music © 1967 Gooi en Sticht, BV, Baarn, The Netherlands, admin. OCP Publications

MIDDEN IN DE DOOD
56565

496   One Bread, One Body

Refrain

One bread, one bod - y, one Lord of all; one cup of

bless - ing which we bless, and we, though man - y

Text: John Foley, SJ, b. 1939
Music: John Foley, SJ
Text and music © 1978 John B. Foley, SJ, and OCP Publications

ONE BREAD, ONE BODY
4 4 6 and refrain

through-out the earth, we are one bod - y in this one Lord.

1 Gen - tile or Jew, ser - vant or free,
2 Man - y the gifts, man - y the works,
3 Grain for the fields, scat-tered and grown,

Refrain

wom - an or man, no more.
one in the Lord of all.
gath - ered to one for all.

Strengthen for Service, Lord   497

1 Streng-then for ser - vice, Lord, the hands that ho - ly
2 The tongues that sang your ho - ly name now purge of
3 And may the feet that walked your courts be nev - er

things have ta - ken; and let the ears that heard your
all de - cep - tion; keep bright the eyes that saw your
lured to wan - der; but lead the faith - ful nour - ished

word to false - hood nev - er wak - en.
love and sharp - en their per - cep - tion.
here to jour - ney on in splen - dor.

Text: Syriac Liturgy of Malabar; tr. composite
Music: Robert A. Hobby, b. 1962
Music © 2006 Augsburg Fortress

BUCKHURST RUN
8 7 8 7

United at the Table

498

Unidos en la fiesta

Refrain / Estribillo

U - ni - dos en la fies - ta, la_a - le - grí - a
U - nit - ed at the ta - ble: all our joy is

se_ha - ce can - ción. U - ni - dos en la fe,
joined in song. U - nit - ed in the faith:

la_a - le - grí - a se_ha - ce_o - ra - ción.
all our joy to God be - longs.

1 Can - ta - re - mos al Se - ñor
1 We will praise God, we will sing
2 We will praise God, we will feast
3 We will praise God, we will play

a - le - lu - yas con him - nos y sal - mos,
al - le - lu - ias with hymns and with psalm - o - dy;
at the boun - ti - ful ta - ble of life and grace;
al - le - lu - ias with rhy - thm and in - stru - ments;

por - que gran - de_es el a - mor
we will praise God for the love
we will praise God and give thanks
we will praise God for the love

Refrain / Estribillo

que_en no - so - tros por siem - pre mos - tró.
that sus - tains us e - ter - nal - ly.
for com - mu - nion with ev - 'ry race.
that in - vites all cre - a - tion to dance.

2 Cantaremos la bondad
del Señor que nos sienta_a su mesa,
y nos llama_a comulgar
como_hermanos su vino_y su pan. *Estribillo*

3 Cantaremos al Señor
aleluyas al son de_instrumentos,
y será nuestra canción
la_alabanza que_ensalza su_amor. *Estribillo*

Text: Joaquín Madurga; tr. Angel Mattos, b. 1947, and Gerhard M. Cartford, b. 1923
Music: Joaquín Madurga
Text and music © 1979, 1998 J. Madurga and San Pablo Internacional—SSP, admin. OCP Publications

UNIDOS EN LA FIESTA
7 11 7 9 and refrain

O Lord, We Praise You

499

1 O Lord, we praise you, bless you, and a - dore you, in thanks -
2 Your ho - ly bod - y in - to death was giv - en, life to
3 Lord God, be - stow on us your grace and fa - vor, that we

giv - ing bow be - fore you. Here with your
win for us in heav - en. No great - er
fol - low Christ our Sav - ior and live to -

bod - y and your blood you nour - ish our weak souls that
love than this to you could bind us; may this feast of
geth - er here in love and u - nion, nor re - pent this

they may flour - ish. O Lord, have mer - cy!
that re - mind us! O Lord, have mer - cy!
blest com - mu - nion. O Lord, have mer - cy!

May your bod - y, Lord, born of Mar - y, that our
Lord, your kind - ness so much did move you that your
Let not your good Spir - it for - sake us; by this

sins and sor - rows did car - ry, and your blood for us plead
blood now moves us to love you. All our debt you have paid;
ho - ly ban - quet re - make us. Give your church, Lord, to see

in all tri - al, fear, and need: O Lord, have mer - cy!
peace with God once more is made. O Lord, have mer - cy!
days of peace and u - ni - ty. O Lord, have mer - cy!

Text: German hymn, 15th cent., st. 1; Martin Luther, 1483–1546, sts. 2–3; tr. composite
Music: J. Walter, *Geistliche Gesangbüchlein*, 1524

GOTT SEI GELOBET UND GEBENEDEIET
PM

500

Now We Remain

Refrain
We hold the death of the Lord deep in our hearts.

Liv-ing, now we re-main with Je-sus the Christ.

1 Once we were peo-ple a-fraid, lost in the night. Then by your

Refrain
cross we were saved; dead be-came liv-ing, life from your giv-ing.

2 Some-thing that we have known, some-thing we've touched, what we have

Refrain
seen with our eyes, this we have heard: life-giv-ing Word.

3 He chose to give of him-self, be-came our bread; bro-ken,

Refrain
that we might live; love be-yond love, pain for our pain.

4 We are the pres-ence of God; this is our call;

now to be-come bread and wine, food for the hun-gry, life for the

Text: David Haas, b. 1957
Music: David Haas
Text and music © 1983 GIA Publications, Inc.

NOW WE REMAIN
Irregular

Refrain

wea-ry; for to live with the Lord, we must die with the Lord.

Come with Us, O Blessed Jesus 501

Come with us, O bless - ed Je - sus, with us ev - er - more to be.

And, in leav - ing now thine al - tar, let us nev - er - more leave thee!

Let thy bright ce - les - tial cho - rus nev - er cease the heav'n - ly strain;

but in us, thy lov-ing chil-dren, come with peace, good will to reign.

Text: John Henry Hopkins Jr., 1820–1891
Music: Johann Schop, 1600–1665; arr. Johann Sebastian Bach, 1685–1750

WERDE MUNTER
8787D

502 The King of Love My Shepherd Is

1 The King of love my shep - herd is, whose good - ness
2 Where streams of liv - ing wa - ter flow, my ran - somed
3 Per - verse and fool - ish oft I strayed, but yet in
4 In death's dark vale I fear no ill, with thee, dear

fail - eth nev - er; I noth - ing lack if
soul he lead - eth and, where the ver - dant
love he sought me, and on his shoul - der
Lord, be - side me, thy rod and staff my

I am his and he is mine for - ev - er.
pas - tures grow, with food ce - les - tial feed - eth.
gent - ly laid, and home, re - joic - ing, brought me.
com - fort still; thy cross be - fore to guide me.

5 Thou spreadst a table in my sight;
thine unction grace bestoweth;
and, oh, what transport of delight
from thy pure chalice floweth!

6 And so, through all the length of days
thy goodness faileth never.
Good Shepherd, may I sing thy praise
within thy house forever.

Text: Henry W. Baker, 1821–1877
Music: Irish tune

ST. COLUMBA
8 7 8 7

A Mighty Fortress Is Our God 503

1 A might - y for - tress is our God,
2 No strength of ours can match his might!
3 Though hordes of dev - ils fill the land
4 God's Word for - ev - er shall a - bide,

a sword and shield vic - to - rious;
We would be lost, re - ject - ed.
all threat - 'ning to de - vour us,
no thanks to foes, who fear it;

he breaks the cruel op - pres - sor's rod
But now a cham - pion comes to fight,
we trem - ble not, un - moved we stand;
for God him - self fights by our side

and wins sal - va - tion glo - rious.
whom God him - self e - lect - ed.
they can - not o - ver - pow'r us.
with weap - ons of the Spir - it.

The old e - vil foe, sworn to work us woe,
Ask who this may be: Lord of hosts is he!
This world's prince may rage, in fierce war en - gage.
If they take our house, goods, fame, child, or spouse,

with dread craft and might he arms him - self to fight.
Christ Je - sus our Lord, God's on - ly Son, a - dored.
He is doomed to fail; God's judg - ment must pre - vail!
wrench our life a - way, they can - not win the day.

On earth he has no e - qual.
He holds the field vic - to - rious.
One lit - tle word sub - dues him.
The king - dom's ours for - ev - er!

Text: Martin Luther, 1483–1546; tr. *Lutheran Book of Worship*
Music: Martin Luther
Text © 1978 *Lutheran Book of Worship*, admin. Augsburg Fortress

EIN FESTE BURG
878755567

504

A Mighty Fortress Is Our God

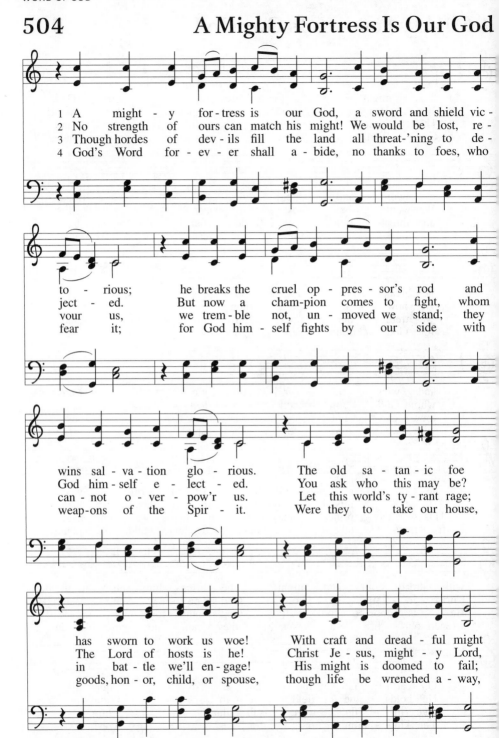

1 A might - y for - tress is our God, a sword and shield vic -
2 No strength of ours can match his might! We would be lost, re -
3 Though hordes of dev - ils fill the land all threat-'ning to de -
4 God's Word for - ev - er shall a - bide, no thanks to foes, who

to - rious; he breaks the cruel op - pres - sor's rod and
ject - ed. But now a cham-pion comes to fight, whom
vour us, we trem - ble not, un - moved we stand; they
fear it; for God him - self fights by our side with

wins sal - va - tion glo - rious. The old sa - tan - ic foe
God him - self e - lect - ed. You ask who this may be?
can - not o - ver - pow'r us. Let this world's ty - rant rage;
weap-ons of the Spir - it. Were they to take our house,

has sworn to work us woe! With craft and dread - ful might
The Lord of hosts is he! Christ Je - sus, might - y Lord,
in bat - tle we'll en - gage! His might is doomed to fail;
goods, hon - or, child, or spouse, though life be wrenched a - way,

Text: Martin Luther, 1483–1546; tr. *Lutheran Book of Worship*
Music: Martin Luther, 1483–1546
Text © 1978 *Lutheran Book of Worship*, admin. Augsburg Fortress

EIN FESTE BURG
87 87 66 66 7

he arms him - self to fight. On earth he has no e - qual.
God's on - ly Son, a - dored. He holds the field vic - to - rious.
God's judg-ment must pre - vail! One lit - tle word sub - dues him.
they can - not win the day. The king-dom's ours for - ev - er!

A Mighty Fortress Is Our God   505

1 A mighty fortress is our God,
a bulwark never failing;
our helper frees us from the flood
of mortal ills prevailing.
For still our ancient foe,
forsworn to work us woe,
with guile and dreadful might
is armed to wage the fight:
on earth there is no equal.

2 If we in our own strength confide,
our striving turns to losing;
the righteous one fights by our side,
the one of God's own choosing.
You ask who this may be:
Christ Jesus, it is he,
the Lord of hosts by name.
No other God we claim!
None else can win the battle.

3 Though all the world with devils fill
and threaten to devour us,
we tremble not, we trust God's will:
they cannot overpow'r us.
Though Satan rant and rage,
in fiercest war engage,
this tyrant's doomed to fail;
God's judgment must prevail!
One little word shall triumph.

4 God's Word shall stand above the pow'rs,
shall end all their thanksgiving.
The Spirit and the gifts are ours,
for God with us is living.
Let goods and kindred go,
this mortal life also;
though all of these be gone,
they yet have nothing won.
The kingdom's ours forever!

Text: Martin Luther, 1483–1546; tr. Frederick H. Hedge, 1805–1890, alt.
Text © 2006 Augsburg Fortress

EIN FESTE BURG
8 7 8 7 6 6 6 6 7

506 The Word of God Is Source and Seed

1 The Word of God is source and seed; it comes to
2 The Word of God is breath and life; it comes to
3 The Word of God is flesh and grace, who comes to

die and sprout and grow. So make your dark earth
heal and wake and save. So let the Spir - it
sing, to laugh and cry. So dare to be as

wel - come warm; root deep the grain God bent to sow.
touch and mend and rouse your dry bones from their grave.
Je - sus was, who came to live and love and die.

Refrain

Gau-de - a - mus Do - mi - no, gau - de - a - mus Do - mi - no,
In the Lord let us re - joice, in the Lord let us re - joice,

gau - de - a - mus Do - mi - no!
in the Lord let us re - joice!

Text: Delores Dufner, OSB, b. 1939
Music: David Hurd, b. 1950
Text © 1983, 1993 Sisters of St. Benedict, St. Joseph, MN, admin. Augsburg Fortress
Music © 1995 Augsburg Fortress

GAUDEAMUS DOMINO
LM and refrain

O God of Light

507

1 O God of light, your word, a lamp un - fail - ing,
2 From days of old, through blind and will - ful a - ges,
3 Un - dimmed by time, those words are still re - veal - ing
4 To all the world your sum - mons you are send - ing,

shall pierce the dark - ness of our earth - bound way
though we re - belled, you gent - ly sought a - gain,
to sin - ful hearts your jus - tice and your grace;
through all the earth, to ev - 'ry land and race,

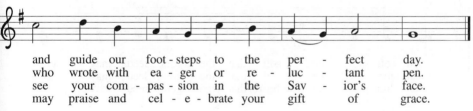

and show your grace, your plan for us un - veil - ing,
and spoke through saints, a - pos - tles, proph - ets, sa - ges,
and quest - ing spir - its, long - ing for your heal - ing,
that myr - iad tongues, in one great an - them blend - ing,

and guide our foot - steps to the per - fect day.
who wrote with ea - ger or re - luc - tant pen.
see your com - pas - sion in the Sav - ior's face.
may praise and cel - e - brate your gift of grace.

Text: Sarah E. Taylor, 1883–1954, alt.
Music: H. Barrie Cabena, b. 1933
Text © 1952, ren. 1980 The Hymn Society, admin. Hope Publishing Company
Music © 1978 Lutheran Book of Worship, admin. Augsburg Fortress

ATKINSON
11 10 11 10

508 As Rain from the Clouds

1 As rain from the clouds will your word come to earth,
2 As grain that is scat - tered your word has been sown
3 As rays of the sun shall your word light the world,

as snow from the heav - ens re - fresh - ing the land.
on rocks and on road - ways, in good earth and sand.
a - wak - ing and warm - ing and heal - ing our land.

Then soft - en our soil that the good seed may grow
Make fer - tile our soil that the good seed may grow
Then shine in our hearts that the good seed may grow

and rip - en rich fruit to re - turn to your hand.
and rip - en rich fruit to re - turn to your hand.
and rip - en rich fruit to re - turn to your hand.

Text: Delores Dufner, osb, b. 1939
Music: Jonathan E. Spilman, 1812–1896; arr. hymnal version
Text © 1983, 2003 GIA Publications, Inc.
Arr. © 2003 Augsburg Fortress

AFTON WATE
11 11 11 11 [

We praise you, our God, for the dew of your word;
We praise you, our God, for the seed of your word;
We praise you, our God, for the light of your word;

we thank you, good gar - d'ner, for your ten - der toil.
we thank you, good gar - d'ner, for your ten - der toil.
we thank you, good gar - d'ner, for your ten - der toil.

We bless you, best farm - er, for hun - dred - fold yield,
We bless you, best farm - er, for hun - dred - fold yield,
We bless you, best farm - er, for hun - dred - fold yield,

for har - vest of grace in our once - bar - ren soil.
for har - vest of grace in our once - bar - ren soil.
for har - vest of grace in our once - bar - ren soil.

509 God's Word Is Our Great Heritage

God's word is our great her - i - tage and shall be ours for - ev - er;

to spread its light from age to age shall be our chief en - deav - or.

Through life it guides our way; in death it is our stay. Lord, grant while

time shall last your church may hold it fast through - out all gen - er - a - tions

Text: Nikolai F. S. Grundtvig, 1783–1872; tr. Ole G. Belsheim, 1861–1925, alt.
Music: Martin Luther, 1483–1546

EIN FESTE BUR
87 87 6 6 66

Word of God, Come Down on Earth

510

1 Word of God, come down on earth, liv - ing rain from heav'n de-scend - ing; touch our hearts and bring to birth faith and hope and love un-end - ing. Word al-might - y, we re - vere you; Word made flesh, we long to hear you.

2 Word e - ter - nal, throned on high, Word that brought to life cre - a - tion, Word that came from heav'n to die, cru - ci - fied for our sal - va - tion, sav - ing Word, the world re - stor-ing, speak to us, your love out - pour - ing.

3 Word that speaks God's ten - der love, one with God be - yond all tell - ing, Word that sends us from a - bove God the Spir - it, with us dwell - ing, Word of truth, to all truth lead us; Word of life, with one bread feed us.

Text: James Quinn, SJ, b. 1919
Music: Johann R. Ahle, 1625–1673
Text © James Quinn, SJ, admin. Selah Publishing Co., Inc.

LIEBSTER JESU, WIR SIND HIER
787888

511

Thy Strong Word

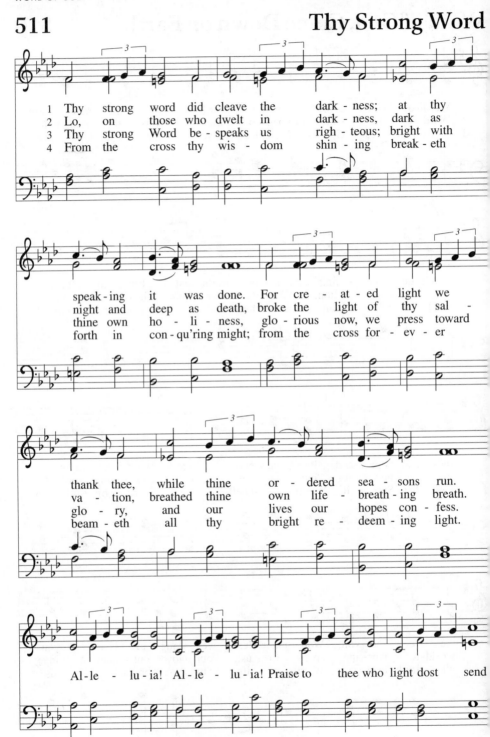

1 Thy strong word did cleave the dark - ness; at thy
2 Lo, on those who dwelt in dark - ness, dark as
3 Thy strong Word be - speaks us righ - teous; bright with
4 From the cross thy wis - dom shin - ing break - eth

speak - ing it was done. For cre - at - ed light we
night and deep as death, broke the light of thy sal -
thine own ho - li - ness, glo - rious now, we press toward
forth in con - qu'ring might; from the cross for - ev - er

thank thee, while thine or - dered sea - sons run.
va - tion, breathed thine own life - breath - ing breath.
glo - ry, and our lives our hopes con - fess.
beam - eth all thy bright re - deem - ing light.

Al - le - lu - ia! Al - le - lu - ia! Praise to thee who light dost send

Text: Martin H. Franzmann, 1907–1976
Music: Thomas J. Williams, 1869–1944; arr. Richard W. Hillert, b. 1923
Text and arr. © 1969 Concordia Publishing Housee

EBENEZER
8787

Al - le - lu - ia! Al - le - lu - ia! Al - le - lu - ia with - out end!

5   Give us lips to sing thy glory,
tongues thy mercy to proclaim,
throats that shout the hope that fills us,
mouths to speak thy holy name.
Alleluia! Alleluia!
May the light which thou dost send
fill our songs with alleluias,
alleluias without end!

6   God the Father, light-creator,
to thee laud and honor be.
To thee, Light of Light begotten,
praise be sung eternally.
Holy Spirit, light-revealer,
glory, glory be to thee.
Mortals, angels, now and ever
praise the holy Trinity!

Lord, Let My Heart Be Good Soil   512

Lord, let my heart be good soil, o-pen to the seed of your word.

Lord, let my heart be good soil, where love can grow and peace is un-der-stood.

When my heart is hard, break the stone a - way. When my heart is cold,

warm it with the day. When my heart is lost, lead me on your way.

Lord, let my heart, Lord, let my heart, Lord, let my heart be good soil.

Text: Handt Hanson, b. 1950
Music: Handt Hanson
Text and music © 1985 Prince of Peace Publishing, Changing Church, Inc.

GOOD SOIL
PM

Listen, God Is Calling

Neno lake Mungu

513

Refrain

Ne - no, ne - no la - ke Mu-ngu la - ku - i - ta we - we,
Lis - ten, lis - ten, God is call-ing, through the Word in - vit - ing,

ne - no la wo - ko - vu, te - na je - ma. ma.
of - fer - ing for - give-ness, com - fort, and joy. joy.

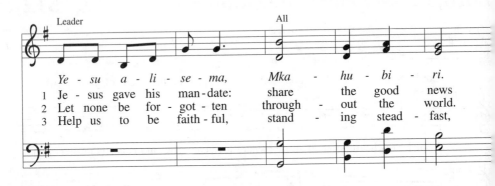

Ye - su a - li - se - ma, Mka - hu - bi - ri.
1 Je - sus gave his man-date: share the good news
2 Let none be for - got - ten through - out the world.
3 Help us to be faith-ful, stand - ing stead - fast,

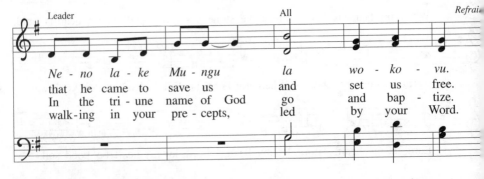

Ne - no la - ke Mu - ngu la wo - ko - vu.
that he came to save us and set us free.
In the tri - une name of God go and bap - tize.
walk-ing in your pre - cepts, led by your Word.

Text: Tanzanian traditional; tr. Howard S. Olson, b. 1922
Music: Tanzanian tune; arr. Austin C. Lovelace, b. 1919
Text © 1968 Lutheran Theological College, Makumira, Tanzania, admin. Augsburg Fortress
Arr. © 1968 Austin C. Lovelace

NENO LAKE MUNGU
6 4 6 4 and refrain

O Word of God Incarnate

514

1 O Word of God in - car - nate, O Wis - dom from on high,
2 The church from you, dear Mas - ter, re - ceived the gift di - vine;
3 Oh, make your church, dear Sav - ior, a lamp of bur - nished gold

O Truth un - changed, un - chang - ing, O Light of our dark sky:
and still that light is lift - ed o'er all the earth to shine.
to bear be - fore the na - tions your true light, as of old;

we praise you for the ra - diance that from the hal - lowed page,
It is the chart and com - pass that, all life's voy - age through,
oh, teach your wand - 'ring pil - grims by this their path to trace,

a lan - tern to our foot - steps, shines on from age to age.
mid mists and rocks and quick - sands still guides, O Christ, to you.
till, clouds and dark - ness end - ed, they see you face to face.

Text: William W. How, 1823–1897, alt.
Music: *Neuvermehrtes Gesangbuch*, Meiningen, 1693

MUNICH
76 76 D

515 Break Now the Bread of Life

1 Break now the bread of life, dear Lord, to me, as once you
2 Bless your own word of truth, dear Lord, to me, as when you
3 You are the bread of life, dear Lord, to me, your ho - ly

broke the loaves be - side the sea. Be - yond the sa - cred page
blessed the bread by Gal - i - lee. Then shall all bond - age cease,
word the truth that res - cues me. Give me to eat and live

I seek you, Lord; my spir - it waits for you, O liv - ing Word.
all fet - ters fall; and I shall find my peace, my All - in - All!
with you a - bove; teach me to love your truth, for you are love.

Text: Mary A. Lathbury, 1841–1913, alt.
Music: William F. Sherwin, 1826–1888

BREAD OF LIFE
6 4 6 4 D

516 Almighty God, Your Word Is Cast

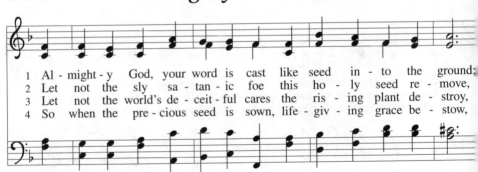

1 Al - might - y God, your word is cast like seed in - to the ground;
2 Let not the sly sa - tan - ic foe this ho - ly seed re - move,
3 Let not the world's de - ceit - ful cares the ris - ing plant de - stroy,
4 So when the pre - cious seed is sown, life - giv - ing grace be - stow,

Text: John Cawood, 1775–1852, alt.
Music: J. Day, Psalter, 1562

ST. FLAVIA
CM

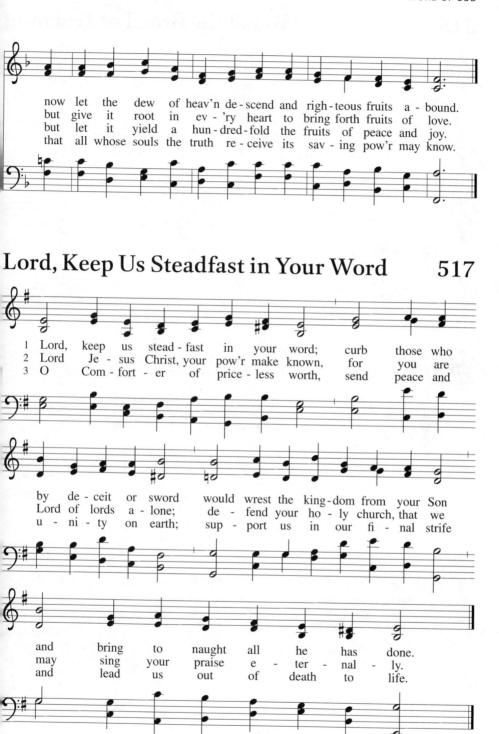

now let the dew of heav'n de - scend and righ - teous fruits a - bound.
but give it root in ev - 'ry heart to bring forth fruits of love.
but let it yield a hun - dred - fold the fruits of peace and joy.
that all whose souls the truth re - ceive its sav - ing pow'r may know.

Lord, Keep Us Steadfast in Your Word   517

1 Lord, keep us stead - fast in your word; curb those who
2 Lord Je - sus Christ, your pow'r make known, for you are
3 O Com - fort - er of price - less worth, send peace and

by de - ceit or sword would wrest the king - dom from your Son
Lord of lords a - lone; de - fend your ho - ly church, that we
u - ni - ty on earth; sup - port us in our fi - nal strife

and bring to naught all he has done.
may sing your praise e - ter - nal - ly.
and lead us out of death to life.

Text: Martin Luther, 1483–1546; tr. Catherine Winkworth, 1827–1878, alt.
Music: J. Klug, *Geistliche Lieder*, 1543

ERHALT UNS, HERR
LM

518

We Eat the Bread of Teaching

Refrain

We eat the bread of teach-ing, drink wine of wis - dom, are giv - en here a taste of the king - dom. To-geth-er joined, the great - est and the least, we all are one at Wis-dom's ho - ly feast.

1. Wis - dom calls through - out the cit - y, knows our hun - ger, and in pit - y gives her lov - ing in - vi - ta - tion to the ban - quet of sal - va - tion.

2. Sim - ple ones whose hearts are yearn - ing, come and gain from Wis-dom's learn - ing; bread and wine she is pre - par - ing, know her lov - ing in the shar - ing.

3. En - ter with de - light and sing - ing, for her rich - ness now is bring - ing us this joy - ous cel - e - bra - tion; eat and drink in ju - bi - la - tion.

Refrain

Text: Omer Westendorf, 1916–1997
Music: Jerry Ray Brubaker, b. 1946
Text and music © 1998 World Library Publications

Open Your Ears, O Faithful People

519

1 O - pen your ears, O faith-ful peo - ple, o - pen your ears and hear God's word.
2 They who have ears to hear the mes - sage, they who have ears, now let them hear;

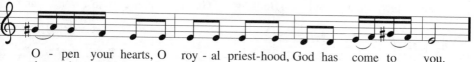

O - pen your hearts, O roy - al priest-hood, God has come to you.
they who would learn the way of wis - dom, let them hear God's word.

Refrain

To - rah o - ra, To - rah o - ra, hal - le - lu - jah!
God has spo - ken to the peo - ple, hal - le - lu - jah!

Hal-le-lu-jah!

To - rah o - ra, To - rah o - ra, hal - le - lu - jah!
God has spo - ken words of wis - dom, hal - le - lu - jah!

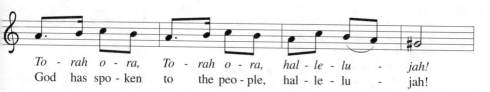

To - rah o - ra, To - rah o - ra, hal - le - lu - jah!
God has spo - ken to the peo - ple, hal - le - lu - jah!

To - rah o - ra, To - rah o - ra, hal - le - lu - jah!
God has spo - ken words of wis - dom, hal - le - lu - jah!

Text: Hasidic traditional; Willard F. Jabusch, b. 1930, English version
Music: Hasidic tune
Text © 1966, 1982 Willard F. Jabusch, admin. OCP Publications

YISRAEL V'ORAITA
98 95 and refrain

520

Dearest Jesus, at Your Word

1 Dear - est Je - sus, at your word we have come a -
2 All our knowl - edge, sense, and sight lie in deep - est
3 Ra - diance of God's glo - ry bright, Light of Light from
4 Fa - ther, Son, and Ho - ly Ghost, praise to you and

gain to hear you; let our thoughts and hearts be stirred
dark - ness shroud - ed till your Spir - it breaks the night,
God pro - ceed - ing, Je - sus, send your bless - ed light;
ad - o - ra - tion! Grant us what we need the most:

and in glow - ing faith be near you as the prom - is -
fill - ing us with light un - cloud - ed. All good thoughts and
help our hear - ing, speak - ing, heed - ing, that our prayers and
all your gos - pel's con - so - la - tion while we here on

es here giv - en draw us whol - ly up to heav - en.
all good liv - ing come but by your gra - cious giv - ing.
songs may please you, as with grate - ful hearts we praise you.
earth a - wait you, till in heav'n with praise we greet you.

Text: Tobias Clausnitzer, 1619–1684, sts. 1–3; *Gesangbuch*, Berlin, 1707, st. 4;
 tr. Catherine Winkworth, 1827–1878, adapt.
Music: Johann R. Ahle, 1625–1673

LIEBSTER JESU, WIR SIND HIER
7 8 7 8 8 8

O Day of Rest and Gladness

1 O day of rest and glad - ness, O day of joy and light,
2 On you, at earth's cre - a - tion, the light first had its birth;
3 To - day on wea - ry na - tions the heav'n-ly man - na falls;
4 New grac - es ev - er gain - ing from this our day of rest,

O balm for care and sad - ness, most beau - ti - ful, most bright:
on you, for our sal - va - tion, Christ rose from depths of earth;
to ho - ly con - vo - ca - tions the sil - ver trum - pet calls,
we reach the rest re - main - ing to spir - its of the blest.

on you the high and low - ly, through a - ges joined in tune,
on you, our Lord vic - to - rious the Spir - it sent from heav'n;
where gos - pel light is glow - ing with pure and ra - diant beams
We sing to you our prais - es, O Fa - ther, Spir - it, Son;

sing, "Ho - ly, ho - ly, ho - ly," to the great God tri - une.
and thus on you, most glo - rious, a three - fold light was giv'n.
and liv - ing wa - ter flow - ing with soul - re - fresh-ing streams.
the church its voice up - rais - es to you, blest Three in One.

Text: Christopher Wordsworth, 1807–1885, alt.
Music: German melody, 18th cent.; adapt. X. L. Hartig, *Melodien zum Mainzer Gesangbuche*, 1833

ELLACOMBE
7676D

522

As We Gather at Your Table

1 As we gath-er at your ta-ble, as we lis-ten to your word,
2 Turn our wor-ship in-to wit-ness in the sac-ra - ment of life;
3 Gra-cious Spir-it, help us sum-mon oth-er guests to share that feast

help us know, O God, your pres-ence; let our hearts and minds be stirred.
send us forth to love and serve you, bring-ing peace where there is strife.
where tri-um-phant Love will wel-come those who had been last and least.

Nour-ish us with sa-cred sto-ry till we claim it as our own;
Give us, Christ, your great com-pas-sion to for - give as you for - gave;
There no more will en - vy blind us nor will pride our peace de - stroy,

teach us through this ho - ly ban-quet how to make Love's vic - t'ry known.
may we still be - hold your im-age in the world you died to save.
as we join with saints and an-gels to re - peat the sound-ing joy.

Text: Carl P. Daw Jr., b. 1944
Music: *Oude en Nieuwe Hollantse Boerenlities en Contradansen*, 1710; arr. Julius Röntgen, 1855–1932
Text © 1989 Hope Publishing Company

IN BABILONE
8 7 8 7 D

Let Us Go Now to the Banquet
Vamos todos al banquete

Refrain / Estribillo

Va - mos to - dos al ban - que - te, a la
Let us go now to the ban - quet, to the

me - sa de la crea - ción; ca - da cual con su ta - bu -
feast of the u - ni - verse. The ta - ble's set and a place is

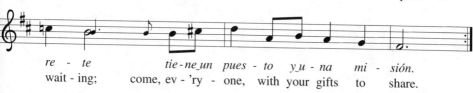

re - te tie - ne_un pues - to y_u - na mi - sión.
wait - ing; come, ev - 'ry - one, with your gifts to share.

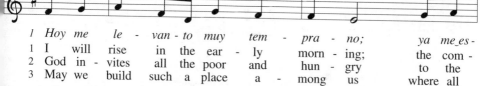

1 Hoy me le - van - to muy tem - pra - no; ya me_es -
1 I will rise in the ear - ly morn - ing; the com -
2 God in - vites all the poor and hun - gry to the
3 May we build such a place a - mong us where all

pe - ra la co - mu - ni - dad; voy su - bien - do_a - le - gre la
mu - ni - ty's wait - ing for me. With a spring in my step I'm
ban - quet of jus - tice and good where the har - vest will not be
peo - ple are e - qual in love. God has called us to work to -

Refrain / Estribillo

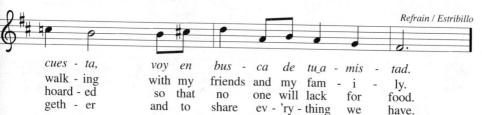

cues - ta, voy en bus - ca de tu_a - mis - tad.
walk - ing with my friends and my fam - i - ly.
hoard - ed so that no one will lack for food.
geth - er and to share ev - 'ry - thing we have.

2 Dios invita_a todos los pobres
a_esta mesa común por la fe,
donde no_hay acaparadores
y_a nadie le falta_el conqué. *Estribillo*

3 Dios nos manda_a_hacer de_este mundo
una mesa donde_haya_igualdad,
trabajando_y luchando juntos,
compartiendo la propiedad. *Estribillo*

Text: Guillermo Cuéllar, b. 1955, *Misa popular salvadoreña*; tr. Bret Hesla, b. 1957, and
William Dexheimer Pharris, b. 1956
Music: Guillermo Cuéllar, b. 1955
Text and music © 1988, 1996 GIA Publications, Inc.

VAMOS TODOS AL BANQUETE
99 98 and refrain

524

What Is This Place

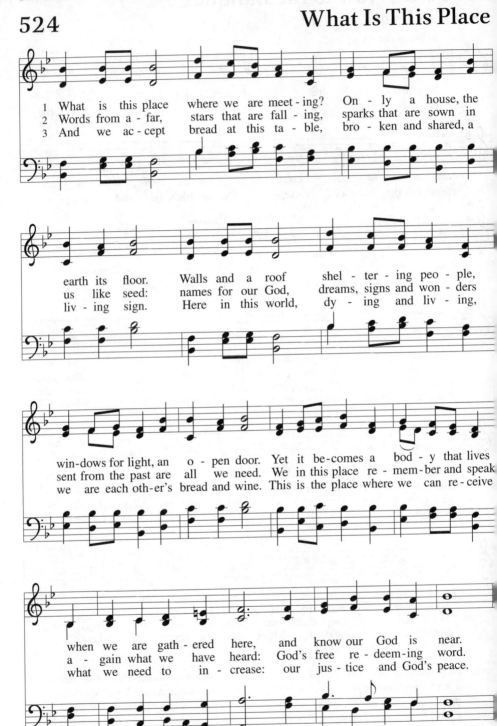

1 What is this place where we are meet-ing? On-ly a house, the
2 Words from a-far, stars that are fall-ing, sparks that are sown in
3 And we ac-cept bread at this ta-ble, bro-ken and shared, a

earth its floor. Walls and a roof shel-ter-ing peo-ple,
us like seed: names for our God, dreams, signs and won-ders
liv-ing sign. Here in this world, dy-ing and liv-ing,

win-dows for light, an o-pen door. Yet it be-comes a bod-y that lives
sent from the past are all we need. We in this place re-mem-ber and speak
we are each oth-er's bread and wine. This is the place where we can re-ceive

when we are gath-ered here, and know our God is near.
a-gain what we have heard: God's free re-deem-ing word.
what we need to in-crease: our jus-tice and God's peace.

Text: Huub Oosterhuis, b. 1933; tr. David Smith, b. 1933
Music: A. Valerius, *Nederlandtsch Gedenckclanck*, 1626; arr. Adrian Engels, b. 1906
Text and arr. © 1984 TEAM Publications, admin. OCP Publications

KOMT NU MET ZAN
98 98 96

You Are Holy
Du är helig

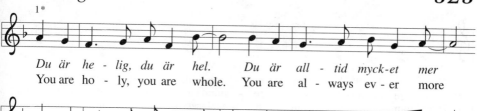

Du är he - lig, du är hel. Du är all - tid myck-et mer
You are ho - ly, you are whole. You are al - ways ev - er more

än vi nån - sin kan för - stå, du är nä - ra än - då.
than we ev - er un-der - stand. You are al - ways at hand.

Väl - sig - nad va - re du som kom - mer hit just nu,
Bless-ed are you com-ing near. Bless - ed are you com-ing here

väl - sig - na-de vår jord, blir till bröd på vår jord.
to your church in wine and bread, raised from soil, raised from dead.

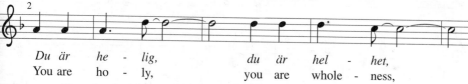

Du är he - lig, du är hel - het,
You are ho - ly, you are whole - ness,

du är när - het he - la kos - mos lo - var dig!
you are pres - ent. Let the cos - mos praise you, Lord!

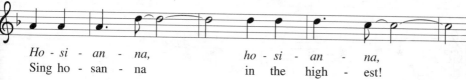

Ho - si - an - na, ho - si - an - na,
Sing ho - san - na in the high - est!

ho - si - an - na, ho - si - an - na vår Gud.
Sing ho - san - na! Sing ho - san - na to our God!

* *May be sung in canon.*

Text: Per Harling, b. 1948
Music: Per Harling
Text and music © 1990 Ton Vis Produktion AB, admin. Augsburg Fortress

DU ÄR HELIG
PM

526

God Is Here!

1 God is here! As we your peo-ple meet to of-fer
2 Here are sym-bols to re-mind us of our life-long
3 Here our chil-dren find a wel-come in the Shep-herd's
4 Lord of all, of church and king-dom, in an age of

praise and prayer, may we find in full-er mea-sure
need of grace; here are ta-ble, font, and pul-pit;
flock and fold; here as bread and wine are tak-en,
change and doubt, keep us faith-ful to the gos-pel;

what it is in Christ we share. Here, as in the
here the cross has cen-tral place. Here in hon-es-
Christ sus-tains us as of old. Here the ser-vants
help us work your pur-pose out. Here, in this day's

world a-round us, all our var-ied skills and arts
ty of preach-ing, here in si-lence, as in speech,
of the Ser-vant seek in wor-ship to ex-plore
ded-i-ca-tion, all we have to give, re-ceive;

Text: Fred Pratt Green, 1903–2000
Music: Cyril V. Taylor, 1907–1991
Text © 1979 Hope Publishing Company
Music © 1942, ren. 1970 Hope Publishing Company

ABBOT'S LEIGH
87 87 D

wait the com - ing of the Spir - it in - to o - pen minds and hearts.
here, in new - ness and re - new - al, God the Spir - it comes to each.
what it means in dai - ly liv - ing to be - lieve and to a - dore.
we, who can - not live with-out you, we a - dore you! We be - lieve!

Lord Jesus Christ, Be Present Now 527

1 Lord Je - sus Christ, be pres - ent now; our
2 Un - seal our lips to sing your praise in
3 Then shall we join the hosts that cry, "O
4 All glo - ry to the Fa - ther, Son, and

hearts in true de - vo - tion bow. Your Spir - it send with
end - less hymns through all our days; in - crease our faith and
ho - ly, ho - ly Lord Most High!" And in the light of
Ho - ly Spir - it, Three in One! To you, O bless - ed

light di - vine, and let your truth with - in us shine.
light our minds; and set us free from doubt that blinds.
that blest place we then shall see you face to face.
Trin - i - ty, be praise through-out e - ter - ni - ty!

Text: attr. Wilhelm II, 1598–1662; tr. Catherine Winkworth, 1827–1878, alt.
Music: *Cantionale Germanicum*, Gochsheim, 1628

HERR JESU CHRIST, DICH ZU UNS WEND
LM

Come and Fill Our Hearts
Confitemini Domino

Con - fi - te - mi - ni   Do - mi - no   quo - ni - am   bo - nus.
Come and fill our hearts   with your peace.   You a - lone, O Lord, are ho - ly.

Con - fi - te - mi - ni   Do - mi - no.   Al - le - lu - ia!
Come and fill our hearts   with your peace.   Al - le - lu - ia!

Text: Psalm 136:1 (Latin); Taizé Community
Music: Jacques Berthier, 1923–1994
Text and music © 1982, 1991 Les Presses de Taizé, admin. GIA Publications, Inc.

CONFITEMINI DOMINO
PM

Jesus, We Are Gathered
Jesu, tawa pano

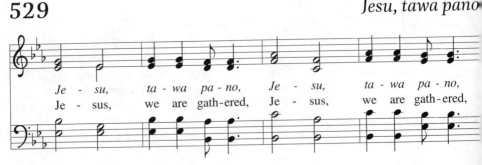

Je - su,   ta - wa pa - no,   Je - su,   ta - wa pa - no,
Je - sus,   we are gath - ered,   Je - sus,   we are gath - ered,

Text: Patrick Matsikenyiri
Music: Patrick Matsikenyiri
Text and music © 1990, 1996 General Board of Global Ministries, GBG Musik

JESU, TAWA PANO
6 6 6 9

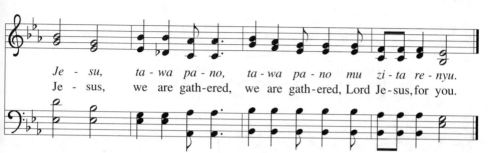

Je - su, ta - wa pa - no, ta - wa pa - no mu zi - ta re - nyu.
Je - sus, we are gath-ered, we are gath-ered, Lord Je - sus, for you.

Here, O Lord, Your Servants Gather
Sekai no tomo to te o tsunagi

530

Se - ka - i no to - mo to te o tsu - na - gi,
1 Here, O Lord, your ser - vants gath - er, hand we link with hand;
2 Man - y are the tongues we speak, scat - tered are the lands,
3 Na - ture's se - crets o - pen wide, chang - es nev - er cease.
4 Grant, O God, an age re - newed, filled with death-less love;

Jyu - ji - ka no mo - to ni ta - tsu wa - re - ra,
look - ing toward our Sav - ior's cross, joined in love we stand.
yet our hearts are one in God, one in love's de - mands.
Where, oh where, can wea - ry souls find the source of peace?
help us as we work and pray, send us from a - bove

Ka - mi no mi - ku - ni o me a te to shi,
As we seek the realm of God, we u - nite to pray:
E'en in dark - ness hope ap - pears, call - ing age and youth:
Un - to all those sore dis - tressed, torn by end - less strife:
truth and cour - age, faith and pow'r, need - ed in our strife:

Shu Ye - su no mi - chi o su - su - mi yu - kan.
Je - sus, sav - ior, guide our steps, for you are the Way.
Je - sus, teach - er, dwell with us, for you are the Truth.
Je - sus, heal - er, bring your balm, for you are the Life.
Je - sus, mas - ter, be our Way, be our Truth, our Life.

Text: Tokuo Yamaguchi, 1900–1995; tr. Everett M. Stowe
Music: Japanese Gagaku mode; Isao Koizumi, 1907–1992
Text © 1958 The United Methodist Publishing House, admin. The Copyright Company
Music © 1958 Isao Koizumi

TŌKYŌ
7575 D

The Trumpets Sound, the Angels Sing
The Feast Is Ready

1 The trum-pets sound, the an - gels sing, the feast is
2 Ta - bles are la - den with good things; oh, taste the
3 The hun - gry heart he sat - is - fies, of - fers the

read - y to be - gin. The gates of heav'n are o - pen wide,
peace and joy he brings. He'll fill you up with love di - vine;
poor his par - a - dise. Now hear all heav'n and earth ap - plaud

and Je - sus wel - comes you in - side.
he'll turn your wa - ter in - to wine.
the a - maz - ing good - ness of the Lord.

Refrain

Sing with thank - ful - ness songs of pure de - light.

Come and rev - el in heav - en's love and light.

Take your place at the ta - ble of the King.

The feast is read - y to be - gin;

the feast is read - y to be - gin.

Text: Graham Kendrick, b. 1950
Music: Graham Kendrick
Text and music © 1989 Make Way Music, admin. Music Services in the Western Hemisphere

THE FEAST IS READY
LM and refrain

Gather Us In

532

1 Here in this place the new light is stream-ing, now is the dark - ness
2 We are the young, our lives are a mys - t'ry, we are the old who
3 Here we will take the wine and the wa - ter, here we will take the
4 Not in the dark of build-ings con - fin - ing, not in some heav - en,

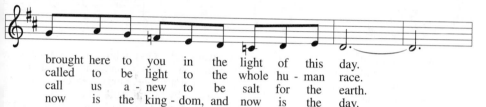

van - ished a - way; see in this space our fears and our dream-ings
yearn for your face; we have been sung through-out all of his - t'ry,
bread of new birth, here you shall call your sons and your daugh-ters,
light years a - way— here in this place the new light is shin - ing,

brought here to you in the light of this day.
called to be light to the whole hu - man race.
call us a - new to be salt for the earth.
now is the king - dom, and now is the day.

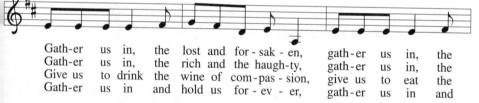

Gath-er us in, the lost and for - sak - en, gath-er us in, the
Gath-er us in, the rich and the haugh-ty, gath-er us in, the
Give us to drink the wine of com-pas - sion, give us to eat the
Gath-er us in and hold us for - ev - er, gath-er us in and

blind and the lame; call to us now, and we shall a - wak-en,
proud and the strong; give us a heart, so meek and so low - ly,
bread that is you; nour-ish us well, and teach us to fash-ion
make us your own; gath-er us in, all peo-ples to - geth-er,

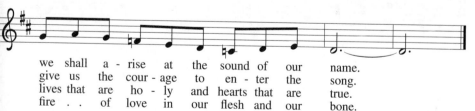

we shall a - rise at the sound of our name.
give us the cour - age to en - ter the song.
lives that are ho - ly and hearts that are true.
fire . . of love in our flesh and our bone.

Text: Marty Haugen, b. 1950
Music: Marty Haugen
Text and music © 1982 GIA Publications, Inc.

GATHER US IN
10 9 10 10 D

533 Open Now Thy Gates of Beauty

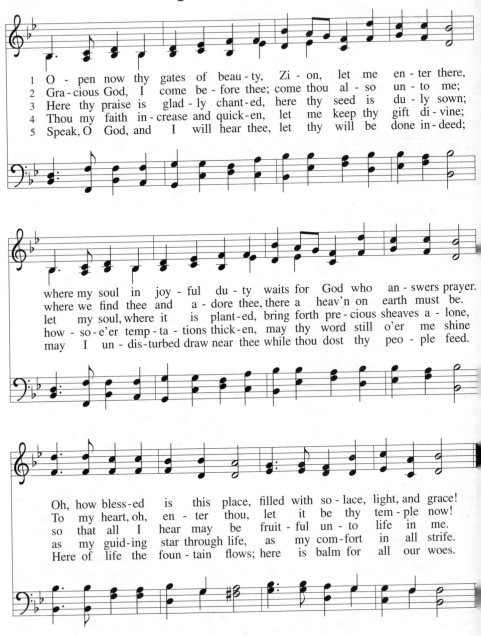

1 O - pen now thy gates of beau - ty, Zi - on, let me en - ter there,
2 Gra - cious God, I come be - fore thee; come thou al - so un - to me;
3 Here thy praise is glad - ly chant-ed, here thy seed is du - ly sown;
4 Thou my faith in - crease and quick-en, let me keep thy gift di - vine;
5 Speak, O God, and I will hear thee, let thy will be done in - deed;

where my soul in joy - ful du - ty waits for God who an - swers prayer.
where we find thee and a - dore thee, there a heav'n on earth must be.
let my soul, where it is plant-ed, bring forth pre - cious sheaves a - lone,
how - so - e'er temp - ta - tions thick-en, may thy word still o'er me shine
may I un - dis-turbed draw near thee while thou dost thy peo - ple feed.

Oh, how bless-ed is this place, filled with so - lace, light, and grace!
To my heart, oh, en - ter thou, let it be thy tem - ple now!
so that all I hear may be fruit - ful un - to life in me.
as my guid-ing star through life, as my com-fort in all strife.
Here of life the foun - tain flows; here is balm for all our woes.

Text: Benjamin Schmolck, 1672–1737; tr. Catherine Winkworth, 1827–1878, alt.
Music: Joachim Neander, 1650–1680

UNSER HERRSCHER
87 87 77

Savior, Again to Your Dear Name

534

1 Sav - ior, a - gain to your dear name we raise
2 Grant us your peace up - on our home - ward way;
3 Grant us your peace, Lord, through the com - ing night;
4 Grant us your peace through - out our earth - ly life,

with one ac - cord our part - ing hymn of praise;
with you be - gan, with you shall end the day;
for us trans - form its dark - ness in - to light.
our balm in sor - row, and our stay in strife;

once more we bless you ere our wor - ship cease,
guard all the lips from sin, the hearts from shame,
Keep us from harm and dan - ger till the dawn;
then, when your voice shall bid our con - flict cease,

then, low - ly bend - ing, wait your word of peace.
that in this house have called up - on your name.
your eve - ning pres - ence prom - ise to your own.
call us, O Lord, to your e - ter - nal peace.

Text: John Ellerton, 1826–1893, alt.
Music: Edward J. Hopkins, 1818–1901; arr. Arthur S. Sullivan, 1842–1900

ELLERS
10 10 10 10

Hallelujah! We Sing Your Praises

Haleluya! Pelo tsa rona

Refrain—sung twice each time

Ha - le - lu - ya! Pe - lo tsa ro - na, di tha -
Hal - le - lu - jah! We sing your prais - es, all our

bi - le ka - o - fe - la. Ha - le - lu - ya! Pe - lo tsa
hearts are filled with glad - ness. Hal - le - lu - jah! We sing your

End

ro - na, di tha - bi - le ka - o - fe - la.
prais - es, all our hearts are filled with glad - ness.

1 Christ the Lord to us said: I am wine, I am bread,
2 Now he sends us all out, strong in faith, free of doubt,

Repeat stanza, then sing refrain

I am wine, I am bread, give to all who thirst and hun - ger.
strong in faith, free of doubt. Tell to all the joy - ful gos - pel.

Text: South African; tr. *Freedom Is Coming*, 1984
Music: South African; arr. *Freedom Is Coming*
Tr. and arr. © 1984 Utryck, admin. Walton Music Corp.

HALELUYA! PELO TSA RONA
6 6 6 8 and refrain

God Be with You Till We Meet Again

1 God be with you till we meet a-gain; by good coun-sels guide, up-hold you,
2 God be with you till we meet a-gain; ho - ly wings se - cure-ly hide you,
3 God be with you till we meet a-gain; when life's per - ils thick con-found you,

with a shep-herd's care en-fold you;
dai - ly man - na still pro-vide you; God be with you till we meet a-gain.
put un-fail - ing arms a-round you;

Refrain

Till we meet, till we meet, till we
till we meet, till we meet a - gain,

meet at Je - sus' feet; till we meet, till we
till we meet, till we meet, till we

meet, God be with you till we meet a - gain.
meet a - gain,

Text: Jeremiah E. Rankin, 1828–1904
Music: William G. Tomer, 1833–1896

GOD BE WITH YOU
9 8 8 9 and refrain

537
On Our Way Rejoicing

1 On our way re - joic - ing glad - ly let us go.
2 Un - to God the Fa - ther joy - ful songs we sing;

Christ our Lord has con - quered; van - quished is the foe.
un - to God the Sav - ior thank - ful hearts we bring;

Christ with - out, our safe - ty; Christ with - in, our joy;
un - to God the Spir - it bow we and a - dore,

who, if we be faith - ful, can our hope de - stroy?
on our way re - joic - ing now and ev - er - more.

Refrain

On our way re - joic - ing; as we for - ward move,

Text: John S. B. Monsell, 1811–1875, alt.
Music: Frances R. Havergal, 1836–1879

HERMAS
6 5 6 5 6 5 D

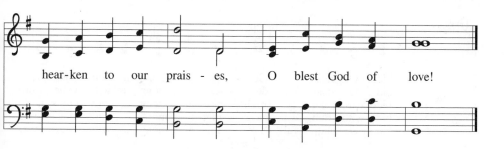

hear-ken to our prais - es, O blest God of love!

The Lord Now Sends Us Forth
Enviado soy de Dios

538

En - via - do soy de Dios, *mi ma - no lis - ta_es - tá*
The Lord now sends us forth with hands to serve and give,

pa - ra cons-truir con él *un mun - do fra - ter - nal.*
to make of all the earth a bet - ter place to live.

Los án - ge - les no son *en - via - dos a cam - biar*
The an - gels are not sent in - to our world of pain

un mun - do de do - lor *por un mun - do me - jor;*
to do what we were meant to do in Je - sus' name;

me ha to - ca - do_a mí *ha - cer - lo rea - li - dad.*
that falls to you and me and all who are made free.

A - yú - da - me, Se - ñor, *a_ha - cer tu vo - lun - tad.*
Help us, O Lord, we pray, to do your will to - day.

Text: Anonymous, Central America; tr. Gerhard M. Cartford, b. 1923
Music: Anonymous, Central America
English text © 1998 Augsburg Fortress

ENVIADO
12 12 12 12 12 12

539

Abide, O Dearest Jesus

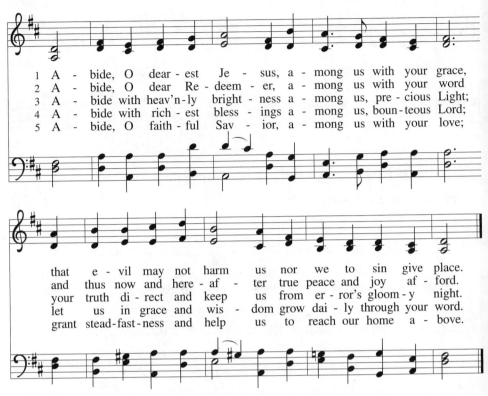

1 A - bide, O dear - est Je - sus, a - mong us with your grace,
2 A - bide, O dear Re - deem - er, a - mong us with your word
3 A - bide with heav'n - ly bright - ness a - mong us, pre - cious Light;
4 A - bide with rich - est bless - ings a - mong us, boun - teous Lord;
5 A - bide, O faith - ful Sav - ior, a - mong us with your love;

that e - vil may not harm us nor we to sin give place.
and thus now and here - af - ter true peace and joy af - ford.
your truth di - rect and keep us from er - ror's gloom - y night.
let us in grace and wis - dom grow dai - ly through your word.
grant stead-fast-ness and help us to reach our home a - bove.

Text: Josua Stegmann, 1588–1632; tr. August Crull, 1846–1923
Music: Melchior Vulpius, 1570–1615

CHRISTUS, DER IST MEIN LEBEN
7 6 7 6

540

Go, Make Disciples

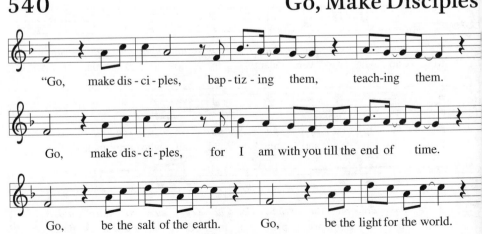

"Go, make dis - ci - ples, bap - tiz - ing them, teach-ing them.

Go, make dis - ci - ples, for I am with you till the end of time.

Go, be the salt of the earth. Go, be the light for the world.

Text: Handt Hanson, b. 1950
Music: Handt Hanson
Text and music © 1996 Prince of Peace Publishing, Changing Church, Inc.

GO, MAKE DISCIPLES
P M

Go, be a cit-y on a hill, so all can see that you're serv-ing me. Go, make dis-ci-ples."

O Jesus, Blessed Lord

541

1 O Je - sus, bless - ed Lord, to you my heart - felt
2 Break forth, my soul, in joy and say: What wealth has

thanks and praise are due; you have so lov - ing - ly be - stowed
come to me to - day! My Sav - ior dwells with - in my soul

on me your bod - y and your blood.
and makes my wound - ed spir - it whole!

Text: Thomas H. Kingo, 1634–1703; tr. Arthur J. Mason, 1851–1928, alt.
Music: Carl Nielsen, 1865–1931

UD GÅR DU NU PÅ LIVETS VEJ
LM

Alternate tune: WAREHAM

542   O Living Bread from Heaven

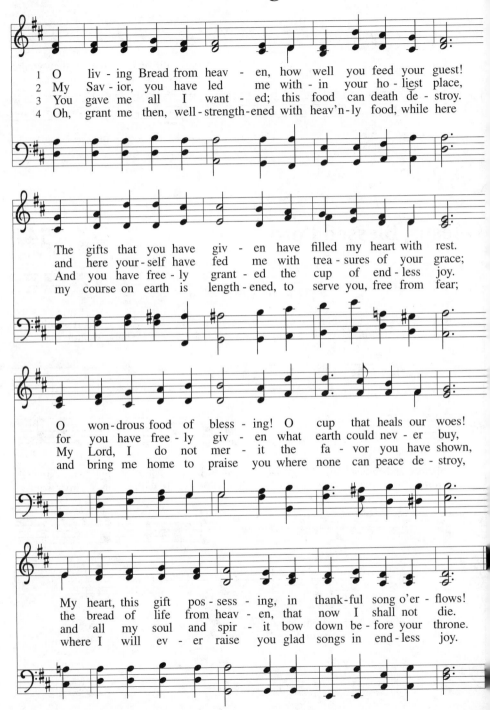

1 O liv - ing Bread from heav - en, how well you feed your guest!
2 My Sav - ior, you have led me with - in your ho - liest place,
3 You gave me all I want - ed; this food can death de - stroy.
4 Oh, grant me then, well - strength-ened with heav'n - ly food, while here

The gifts that you have giv - en have filled my heart with rest.
and here your - self have fed me with trea - sures of your grace;
And you have free - ly grant - ed the cup of end - less joy.
my course on earth is length - ened, to serve you, free from fear;

O won - drous food of bless - ing! O cup that heals our woes!
for you have free - ly giv - en what earth could nev - er buy,
My Lord, I do not mer - it the fa - vor you have shown,
and bring me home to praise you where none can peace de - stroy,

My heart, this gift pos - sess - ing, in thank - ful song o'er - flows!
the bread of life from heav - en, that now I shall not die.
and all my soul and spir - it bow down be - fore your throne.
where I will ev - er raise you glad songs in end - less joy.

Text: Johann Rist, 1607–1667; tr. Catherine Winkworth, 1827–1878, alt.
Music: Samuel S. Wesley, 1810–1876

AURELIA
7 6 7 6 D

Go, My Children, with My Blessing

1 "Go, my chil - dren, with my bless-ing, nev - er a - lone.
2 "Go, my chil - dren, sins for - giv - en, at peace and pure.
3 "Go, my chil - dren, fed and nour-ished, clos - er to me.

Wak - ing, sleep - ing, I am with you, you are my own.
Here you learned how much I love you, what I can cure.
Grow in love and love by serv - ing, joy - ful and free.

In my love's bap - tis - mal riv - er I have made you mine for - ev - er.
Here you heard my dear Son's sto - ry, here you touched him, saw his glo - ry.
Here my Spir - it's pow - er filled you, here my ten - der com-fort stilled you.

Go, my chil - dren, with my bless - ing, you are my own."
Go, my chil - dren, sins for - giv - en, at peace and pure."
Go, my chil - dren, fed and nour-ished, joy - ful and free."

Text: Jaroslav J. Vajda, b. 1919, alt.
Music: Welsh traditional; arr. Ralph Vaughan Williams, 1872–1958
Text © 1983 Concordia Publishing House
Arr. © Oxford University Press

AR HYD Y NOS
84 84 88 84

544   Praise the Lord, Rise Up Rejoicing

1 Praise the Lord, rise up re - joic - ing, wor - ship, thanks, de -
2 Scat - tered flock, one shep - herd shar - ing, lost and lone - ly,
3 Sins for - giv - en, wrongs for - giv - ing, we go forth a -

vo - tion voic - ing: glo - ry be to God on high!
one voice hear - ing, ears at - ten - tive to your word;
lert and liv - ing in your Spir - it, strong and free.

Christ, your cross and pas - sion shar - ing, by this eu - cha -
by your blood new life re - ceiv - ing, in your bod - y,
Part - ners in your new cre - a - tion, seek - ing peace in

rist de - clar - ing yours the fi - nal vic - to - ry.
firm be - liev - ing, we are yours, and you the Lord.
ev - 'ry na - tion, may we faith - ful fol - l'wers be.

Text: Howard C. A. Gaunt, 1902–1983, alt.
Music: Johann Löhner, 1645–1705, adapt.
Text © Oxford University Press

ALLES IST AN GOTTES SEGEN
887 D

545   Lord, Dismiss Us with Your Blessing

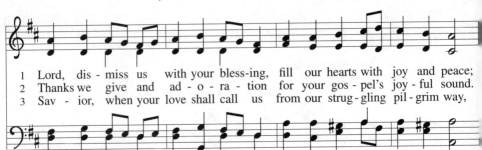

1 Lord, dis - miss us with your bless-ing, fill our hearts with joy and peace;
2 Thanks we give and ad - o - ra - tion for your gos - pel's joy - ful sound.
3 Sav - ior, when your love shall call us from our strug - gling pil - grim way,

Text: attr. John Fawcett, 1740–1817, sts. 1–2, alt.; Godfrey Thring, 1823–1903, st. 3, alt.
Music: Sicilian, 18th cent.

SICILIAN MARINERS
8 7 8 7 8 7

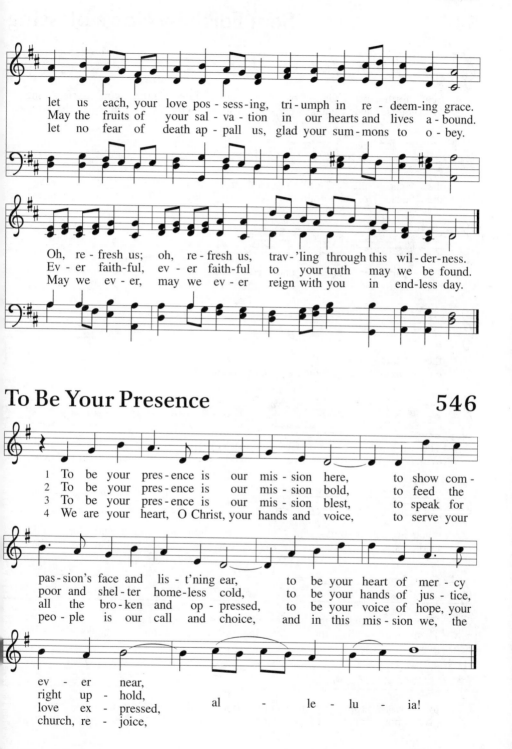

let us each, your love pos - sess-ing, tri-umph in re - deem-ing grace.
May the fruits of your sal - va - tion in our hearts and lives a - bound.
let no fear of death ap - pall us, glad your sum-mons to o - bey.

Oh, re - fresh us; oh, re - fresh us, trav - 'ling through this wil - der - ness.
Ev - er faith-ful, ev - er faith-ful to your truth may we be found.
May we ev - er, may we ev - er reign with you in end - less day.

To Be Your Presence

546

1 To be your pres - ence is our mis - sion here, to show com -
2 To be your pres - ence is our mis - sion bold, to feed the
3 To be your pres - ence is our mis - sion blest, to speak for
4 We are your heart, O Christ, your hands and voice, to serve your

pas - sion's face and lis - t'ning ear, to be your heart of mer - cy
poor and shel - ter home-less cold, to be your hands of jus - tice,
all the bro - ken and op - pressed, to be your voice of hope, your
peo - ple is our call and choice, and in this mis - sion we, the

ev - er near,
right up - hold,
love ex - pressed, al - le - lu - ia!
church, re - joice,

Text: Delores Dufner, OSB, b. 1939
Music: Charles V. Stanford, 1852–1924
Text © 2000 GIA Publications, Inc.

ENGELBERG
10 10 10 and alleluia

547

Sent Forth by God's Blessing

1 Sent forth by God's bless-ing, our true faith con - fess-ing,
2 With praise and thanks-giv-ing to God ev - er - liv-ing,

the peo - ple of God from this dwell-ing take leave.
the tasks of our ev - 'ry - day life we will face—

The sup - per is end - ed. Oh, now be ex - tend - ed
our faith ev - er shar-ing, in love ev - er car - ing,

the fruits of this ser - vice in all who be - lieve.
em - brac-ing God's chil - dren, the whole hu - man race.

The seed of Christ's teach-ing, re - cep - tive souls
With your feast you feed us, with your light now

reach-ing, shall blos - som in ac - tion for God and for all.
lead us; u - nite us as one in this life that we share.

Your grace shall in - cite us, your love shall u - nite us
Then may all the liv - ing with praise and thanks - giv - ing

to work for your king - dom and an - swer your call.
give hon - or to Christ and his name that we bear.

Text: Omer Westendorf, 1916–1997, alt.
Music: Welsh folk tune
Text © 1964 World Library Publications

THE ASH GROVE
66 11 66 11 D

Rise, O Church, like Christ Arisen

548

1 Rise, O church, like Christ a - ris - en,
2 Rise, trans - formed, and choose to fol - low
3 Rise, re - mem - ber well the fu - ture
4 Ser - vice be our sure vo - ca - tion;

from this meal of love and grace;
af - ter Christ, though wound - ed, whole;
God has called us to re - ceive;
cour - age be our dai - ly breath;

may we through such love en - vi - sion
bro - ken, shared, our lives are hal - lowed
pres - ent by God's lov - ing nur - ture,
mer - cy be our des - ti - na - tion

whose we are, and whose, our praise.
to re - lease and to con - sole.
Spir - it - ed then let us live.
from this day and un - to death.

Al - le - lu - ia, al - le - lu - ia;
Al - le - lu - ia, al - le - lu - ia;
Al - le - lu - ia, al - le - lu - ia;
Al - le - lu - ia, al - le - lu - ia.

God, the won - der of our days.
Christ, our pres - ent, past, and goal.
Spir - it, grace by whom we live.
Rise, O church, a liv - ing faith.

Text: Susan Palo Cherwien, b. 1953
Music: Timothy J. Strand, b. 1958
Text © 1997 Susan Palo Cherwien, admin. Augsburg Fortress
Music © 1997 Augsburg Fortress

SURGE ECCLESIA
878787

Alternate tune: PRAISE, MY SOUL

Send Me, Jesus
549
Thuma mina, Nkosi yam

1 *Thu - ma mi - na,*   *thu - ma mi - na,*   *thu - ma mi - na, Nko - si yam.*
2 *Ndi - ya vu - ma,*   *ndi - ya vu - ma,*   *ndi - ya vu - ma, Nko - si yam.*
1 Send me, Je - sus;   send me, Je - sus;   send me, Je - sus; send me, Lord.
2 I am will - ing;   I am will - ing;   I am will - ing, will - ing, Lord.

Thu - ma mi - na.
Send me, Je - sus.

Text: South African
Music: South African

THUMA MINA, NKOSI YAM
4 4 7

550
On What Has Now Been Sown

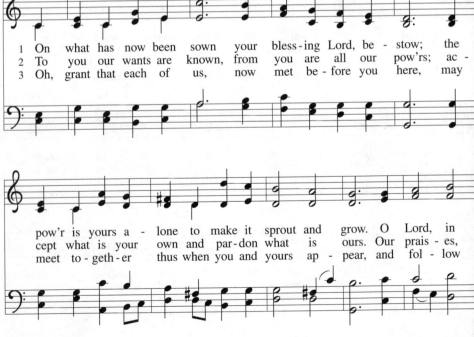

1 On what has now been sown your bless - ing Lord, be - stow; the
2 To you our wants are known, from you are all our pow'rs; ac -
3 Oh, grant that each of us, now met be - fore you here, may

pow'r is yours a - lone to make it sprout and grow. O Lord, in
cept what is your own and par - don what is ours. Our prais - es,
meet to - geth - er thus when you and yours ap - pear, and fol - low

Text: John Newton, 1725–1807, alt.
Music: John Darwall, 1731–1789

DARWALL'S 148TH
6 6 6 6 8 8

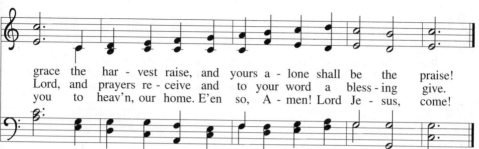

grace the har - vest raise, and yours a - lone shall be the praise!
Lord, and prayers re - ceive and to your word a bless - ing give.
you to heav'n, our home. E'en so, A - men! Lord Je - sus, come!

The Spirit Sends Us Forth to Serve   551

1 The Spir - it sends us forth to serve; we go in
2 We go to com - fort those who mourn and set the
3 We go to be the hands of Christ, to scat - ter
4 Then let us go to serve in peace, the gos - pel

Je - sus' name to bring glad tid - ings
bur - dened free; where hope is dim, to
joy like seed and, all our days, to
to pro - claim. God's Spir - it has em -

to the poor, God's fa - vor to pro - claim.
share a dream and help the blind to see.
cher - ish life, to do the lov - ing deed.
pow - ered us; we go in Je - sus' name.

Text: Delores Dufner, OSB, b. 1939
Music: attr. Thomas Haweis, 1734–1820
Text © 1993 Delores Dufner, admin. OCP Publications

CHESTERFIELD
CM

552   Blessed Be the God of Israel

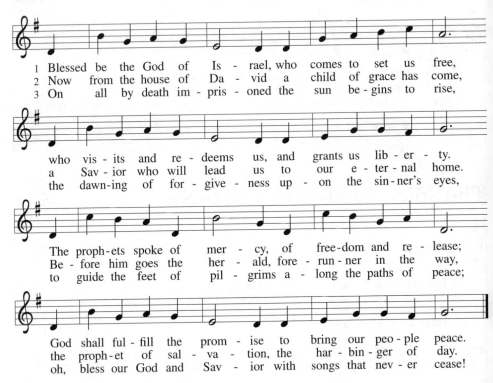

1 Blessed be the God of Is - rael, who comes to set us free,
2 Now from the house of Da - vid a child of grace has come,
3 On all by death im - pris - oned the sun be - gins to rise,

who vis - its and re - deems us, and grants us lib - er - ty.
a Sav - ior who will lead us to our e - ter - nal home.
the dawn-ing of for - give - ness up - on the sin-ner's eyes,

The proph-ets spoke of mer - cy, of free-dom and re - lease;
Be - fore him goes the her - ald, fore - run - ner in the way,
to guide the feet of pil - grims a - long the paths of peace;

God shall ful - fill the prom - ise to bring our peo - ple peace.
the proph-et of sal - va - tion, the har - bin - ger of day.
oh, bless our God and Sav - ior with songs that nev - er cease!

Text: Michael Perry, 1942–1996, based on Luke 1:68-79
Music: Hal H. Hopson, b. 1933
Text © 1973 Jubilate Hymns, admin. Hope Publishing Company
Music © 1983 Hope Publishing Company

MERLE'S TUNE
7676 D

553   Christ, Whose Glory Fills the Skies

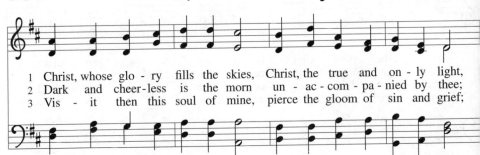

1 Christ, whose glo - ry fills the skies, Christ, the true and on - ly light,
2 Dark and cheer-less is the morn un - ac - com - pa - nied by thee;
3 Vis - it then this soul of mine, pierce the gloom of sin and grief;

Text: Charles Wesley, 1707–1788
Music: J. G. Werner, Choralbuch, 1815

RATISBON
7 7 7 7 7 7

Sun of righteousness, arise, triumph o'er the shades of night;
joyless is the day's return, till thy mercy's beams I see,
fill me, radiancy divine, scatter all my unbelief;

Dayspring from on high, be near; Daystar, in my heart appear.
till they inward light impart, glad my eyes, and warm my heart.
more and more thyself display, shining to the perfect day.

Lord, Your Hands Have Formed 554

1 Lord, your hands have formed this world, ev-'ry part is shaped by
2 Yours the soil that holds the seed, you give warmth and mois-ture,
3 Like a mat you roll out land, space to build for us and

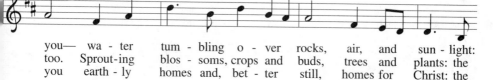

you— wa-ter tum-bling o-ver rocks, air, and sun-light:
too. Sprout-ing blos-soms, crops and buds, trees and plants: the
you earth-ly homes and, bet-ter still, homes for Christ: the

each day's signs that you make all things new.
sea-son's signs that you make all things new.
tru-est sign that you make all things new.

Text: Ramon and Sario Oliano; para. James Minchin, b. 1942; tr. Delbert Rice
Music: Ikalahan (Philippines) traditional
Text © James Minchin, admin. Asian Institute for Liturgy & Music

GAYOM NI HIGAMI
77776

Oh, Sing to God Above
Cantemos al Señor

1. Can - te - mos al Se - ñor   un him - no de a - le - grí - a,
2. Can - te - mos al Se - ñor   un him - no de a - la - ban - za
1. Oh, sing to God a - bove   a hymn of joy - ful greet-ing,
2. Oh, sing to God a - bove   a hymn of praise and bless-ing,

un cán - ti - co de a - mor   al na - cer el nue - vo dí - a.
que ex-pre - se nues-tro a-mor,   nues - tra fe y nues - tra es - pe - ran - za.
a song of grate-ful love   in the new day's light re - peat - ing:
a song of grate-ful love,   hope and faith our hearts ex - press-ing:

El hi - zo el cie - lo, el mar,   el sol y las es - tre - llas
En to - da la crea - ción   pre - go - na su gran-de - za,
you made the sea and sky,   the sun and stars in splen-dor;
cre - a - tion lifts its voice   to tell your might and glo - ry,

y vio en e - llos bon - dad,   pues sus o - bras e - ran be - llas.
a - sí nues - tro can - tar   va a - nun - cian - do su be - lle - za.
de - light shone in your eye—   all your works were filled with won-der.
and we, too, will re - joice   to pro - claim the sav - ing sto - ry.

Refrain / Estribillo

¡A - le-lu - ya!   ¡A - le-lu - ya!   Can - te - mos al Se -
Al - le-lu - ia!   Al - le-lu - ia!   Oh, sing to God a -

ñor: ¡A - le - lu - ya!   ¡A - le-lu - ya!   ¡A - le-lu -
bove: Al-le - lu - ia!   Al - le-lu - ia!   Al - le-lu -

ya!   Can - te - mos al Se - ñor: ¡A - le - lu - ya!
ia!   Oh, sing to God a - bove: Al-le - lu - ia!

Text: Carlos Rosas, b. 1939; tr. *With One Voice*
Music: Carlos Rosas
Spanish text and music © 1976 Resource Publications, Inc.
Tr. © 1995 Augsburg Fortress

ROSAS
6 7 6 8 D and refrain

Last time

Can - te - mos al   Se - ñor: ¡A - le - lu - ya!
Oh, sing   to God   a - bove: Al - le - lu - ia!

Morning Has Broken

556

1 Morn-ing has bro - ken   like the first morn - ing;   black-bird has
2 Sweet the rain's new   fall,   sun - lit from heav - en,   like the first
3 Mine is   the   sun - light!   Mine is   the   morn - ing,   born of the

spo - ken   like the first bird.   Praise for the sing - ing!   Praise for the
dew - fall   on the first grass.   Praise for the sweet - ness   of   the wet
one light   E - den saw play!   Praise with e - la - tion,   praise ev - 'ry

morn - ing!   Praise for them, spring - ing   fresh from the   Word!
gar - den,   sprung in com - plete - ness   where God's feet   pass.
morn - ing,   God's re - cre - a - tion   of   the new   day!

Text: Eleanor Farjeon, 1881–1965
Music: Gaelic tune; arr. hymnal version
Text © Miss E. Farjeon Will Trust, admin. David Higham Associates
Arr. © 2006 Augsburg Fortress

BUNESSAN
5 5 5 4 D

557   Awake, My Soul, and with the Sun

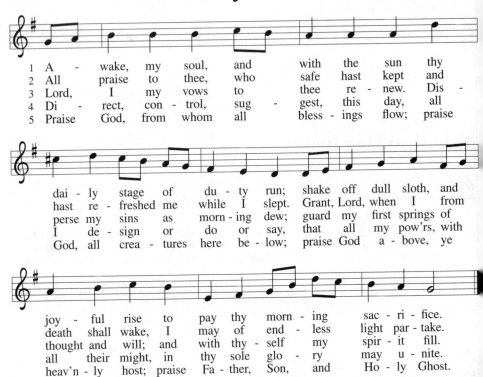

1 A - wake, my soul, and with the sun thy
2 All praise to thee, who safe hast kept and
3 Lord, I my vows to thee re - new. Dis -
4 Di - rect, con - trol, sug - gest, this day, all
5 Praise God, from whom all bless - ings flow; praise

dai - ly stage of du - ty run; shake off dull sloth, and
hast re - freshed me while I slept. Grant, Lord, when I from
perse my sins as morn - ing dew; guard my first springs of
I de - sign or do or say, that all my pow'rs, with
God, all crea - tures here be - low; praise God a - bove, ye

joy - ful rise to pay thy morn - ing sac - ri - fice.
death shall wake, I may of end - less light par - take.
thought and will; and with thy - self my spir - it fill.
all their might, in thy sole glo - ry may u - nite.
heav'n - ly host; praise Fa - ther, Son, and Ho - ly Ghost.

Text: Thomas Ken, 1637–1711, alt.
Music: François H. Barthélémon, 1741–1808

MORNING HYMN
LM

558   Lord God, We Praise You

1 Lord God, we praise you, now the night is o - ver, ac - tive and
2 Mon - arch of all things, fit us for your man - sions; ban - ish our
3 All - ho - ly Fa - ther, Son, and e - qual Spir - it, Trin - i - ty

Text: attr. Gregory I, 540–604; tr. composite
Music: Paris Antiphoner, 1681

CHRISTE SANCTORUM
11 11 11 5

watch-ful, stand - ing here be - fore you; sing - ing, we of - fer
weak-ness, health and whole-ness send - ing; bring us to heav - en,
bless - ed, send us your sal - va - tion; yours is the glo - ry,

prayer and med - i - ta - tion; thus we a - dore you.
where your saints u - nit - ed joy with-out end - ing.
gleam - ing and re - sound-ing through all cre - a - tion.

O Splendor of God's Glory Bright 559

1 O Splen - dor of God's glo - ry bright, O liv - ing Spring of light from
2 Teach us to love with all our might; drive en - vy out, re - move all
3 As dawn speeds on a - cross the sky, true Dawn, with haste come from on
4 All glo - ry be to God Most High; to God the Son let prais - es

light: come, ver - y Sun of truth and love;
spite; turn to the good each trou - bling care,
high. O Word, through whom light came to be,
rise; the Spir - it blest let us a - dore

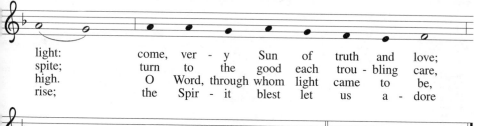

come with your ra - diance from a - bove.
and give us grace your name to bear.
come in your pow'r and set us free.
for - ev - er and for - ev - er - more. A - men.

Text: Ambrose of Milan, 340–397; tr. composite
Music: Plainsong mode I; Sarum *Antiphoner,* 15th cent.
Text © 2000 Augsburg Fortress

SPLENDOR PATERNAE
LM

560

Christ, Mighty Savior

1. Christ, might-y Sav-ior, Light of all cre-a-tion, you make the
2. Now comes the day's end as the sun is set-ting, mir-ror of
3. There-fore we come now eve-ning rites to of-fer, joy-ful-ly
4. Give heed, we pray you, to our sup-pli-ca-tion, that you may
5. Though bod-ies slum-ber, hearts shall keep their vig-il, for-ev-er

day-time ra-diant with the sun-light and to the night give
day-break, pledge of res-ur-rec-tion; while in the heav-ens
chant-ing ho-ly hymns to praise you, with all cre-a-tion
grant us par-don for of-fens-es, strength for our weak hearts,
rest-ing in the peace of Je-sus, in light or dark-ness

glit-ter-ing a-dorn-ment, stars in the heav-ens.
choirs of stars ap-pear-ing hal-low the night-fall.
join-ing hearts and voic-es, sing-ing your glo-ry.
rest for ach-ing bod-ies, sooth-ing the wea-ry.
wor-ship-ing our Sav-ior now and for-ev-er.

Text: Mozarabic, 10th cent.; tr. Alan McDougall, 1895–1964; para. Anne LeCroy, b. 1930
Music: Richard W. Dirksen, 1921–2003
Text © 1982 The United Methodist Publishing House, admin. The Copyright Company
Music © 1984 Washington National Cathedral Music Program

INNISFREE FARM
11 11 11 5

Alternate tune: CHRISTE SANCTORUM

561

Joyous Light of Heavenly Glory

1. Joy-ous light of heav'n-ly glo-ry, lov-ing glow of God's own
2. In the stars that grace the dark-ness, in the blaz-ing sun of
3. You who made the heav-en's splen-dor, ev-'ry danc-ing star of

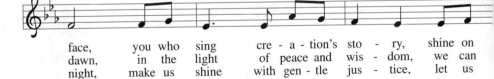

face, you who sing cre-a-tion's sto-ry, shine on
dawn, in the light of peace and wis-dom, we can
night, make us shine with gen-tle jus-tice, let us

Text: Greek hymn, 3rd cent., para. Marty Haugen, b. 1950
Music: Marty Haugen
Text and music © 1987 GIA Publications, Inc.

JOYOUS LIGHT
8 7 8 7 D

ev - 'ry land and race. Now as eve - ning falls a -
hear your qui - et song. Love that fills the night with
each re - flect your light. Might - y God of all cre -

round us, we shall raise our songs to you. God of day - break,
won - der, love that warms the wea - ry soul, love that bursts all
a - tion, gen - tle Christ who lights our way, lov - ing Spir - it

God of shad - ows, come and light our hearts a - new.
chains a - sun - der, set us free and make us whole.
of sal - va - tion, lead us on to end - less day.

O Radiant Light, O Sun Divine   562

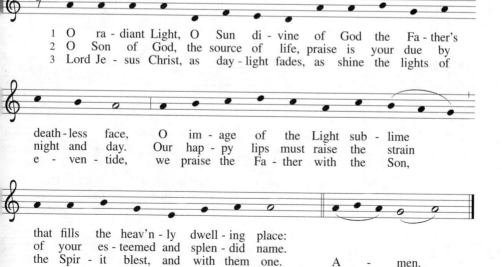

1 O ra - diant Light, O Sun di - vine of God the Fa - ther's
2 O Son of God, the source of life, praise is your due by
3 Lord Je - sus Christ, as day - light fades, as shine the lights of

death - less face, O im - age of the Light sub - lime
night and day. Our hap - py lips must raise the strain
e - ven - tide, we praise the Fa - ther with the Son,

that fills the heav'n - ly dwell - ing place:
of your es - teemed and splen - did name.
the Spir - it blest, and with them one. A - men.

Text: Greek hymn, 3rd cent.; para. William G. Storey
Music: Plainsong mode I
Text © William G. Storey

JESU DULCIS MEMORIA
LM

563   O Light Whose Splendor Thrills

1 O Light whose splen - dor thrills and glad - dens
2 As twi - light hov - ers near at sun - set,
3 In all life's bril - liant, time - less mo - ments,

with ra - diance bright - er than the sun,
and lamps are lit, and chil - dren nod,
let faith - ful voic - es sing your praise,

pure gleam of God's un - end - ing glo - ry,
in eve - ning hymns we lift our voic - es
O Son of God, our life - be - stow - er,

O Je - sus, blest A - noint - ed One:
to Fa - ther, Spir - it, Son, one God,
whose glo - ry light - ens end - less days.

Text: Greek hymn, 3rd cent.; para. Carl P. Daw Jr., b. 1944
Music: Clement C. Scholefield, 1839–1904
Text © 1989 Hope Publishing Company

ST. CLEMENT
9898

God, Who Made the Earth and Heaven 564

1 God, who made the earth and heav-en, dark - ness and light:
2 And when morn a - gain shall call us to run life's way,
3 Guard us wak - ing, guard us sleep-ing, and, when we die,
4 Ho - ly Fa - ther, throned in heav-en, all - ho - ly Son,

you the day for work have giv-en, for rest the night.
may we still, what - e'er be-fall us, your will o - bey.
may we in your might - y keep-ing all peace - ful lie.
Ho - ly Spir - it, free - ly giv-en, blest Three in One:

May your an - gel guards de - fend us, slum-ber sweet your mer - cy send us,
From the pow'r of e - vil hide us, in the nar - row path - way guide us,
When the last dread call shall wake us, then, O Lord, do not for - sake us,
grant us grace, we now im - plore you, till we lay our crowns be - fore you

ho - ly dreams and hopes at - tend us all through the night.
nev - er be your smile de - nied us all through the day.
but to reign in glo - ry take us with you on high.
and in wor - thier strains a - dore you while a - ges run.

Text: Reginald Heber, 1783–1826, st. 1, alt.; William Mercer, 1811–1873, sts. 2, 4, alt.;
Richard Whately, 1787–1863, st. 3, alt.
Music: Welsh traditional; arr. Ralph Vaughan Williams, 1872–1958
Arr. © Oxford University Press

AR HYD Y NOS
84848884

565 All Praise to Thee, My God, This Night

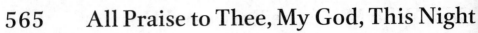

1 All praise to thee, my God, this night for all the bless-ings of the light.
2 For - give me, Lord, for thy dear Son, the ill that I this day have done;
3 Teach me to live, that I may dread the grave as lit - tle as my bed.
4 Oh, may my soul in thee re - pose, and may sweet sleep mine eye-lids close,
5 Praise God, from whom all bless-ings flow; praise God, all crea-tures here be - low;

Keep me, oh, keep me, King of kings, be-neath thine own al-might - y wings.
that with the world, my-self, and thee, I, ere I sleep, at peace may be.
Teach me to die, that so I may rise glo - rious at the awe-some day.
sleep that shall me more vig-'rous make to serve my God when I a - wake!
praise God a - bove, ye heav'n-ly host; praise Fa - ther, Son, and Ho - ly Ghost.

May be sung in canon.

Text: Thomas Ken, 1637–1711, alt.
Music: Thomas Tallis, 1505–1585

TALLIS' CANON
LM

566 When Twilight Comes

1 When twi-light comes and the sun sets, moth - er hen pre-pares for
2 One day the Rab - bi, Lord Je - sus, called the twelve to share his
3 So gath-er round once a - gain, friends, touched by fad - ing glow of

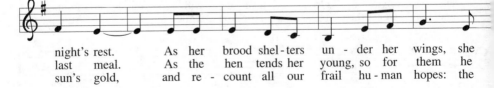

night's rest. As her brood shel-ters un - der her wings, she
last meal. As the hen tends her young, so for them he
sun's gold, and re - count all our frail hu - man hopes: the

Text: Moises B. Andrade, b. 1948; tr. James Minchin, b. 1942
Music: Francisco Feliciano, b. 1941
Tr. © James Minchin, admin. Asian Institute for Liturgy & Music
Music © Francisco Feliciano, admin. Asian Institute for Liturgy & Music

DAPIT HAPON
88999777

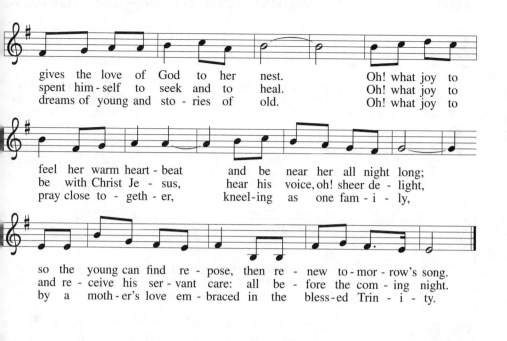

gives the love of God to her nest. Oh! what joy to
spent him - self to seek and to heal. Oh! what joy to
dreams of young and sto - ries of old. Oh! what joy to

feel her warm heart - beat and be near her all night long;
be with Christ Je - sus, hear his voice, oh! sheer de - light,
pray close to - geth - er, kneel-ing as one fam - i - ly,

so the young can find re - pose, then re - new to - mor - row's song.
and re - ceive his ser - vant care: all be - fore the com - ing night.
by a moth - er's love em - braced in the bless - ed Trin - i - ty.

To You, before the Close of Day 567

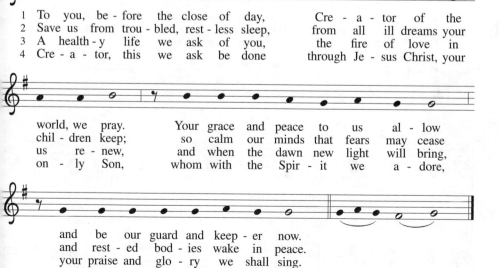

1 To you, be - fore the close of day, Cre - a - tor of the
2 Save us from trou - bled, rest - less sleep, from all ill dreams your
3 A health - y life we ask of you, the fire of love in
4 Cre - a - tor, this we ask be done through Je - sus Christ, your

world, we pray. Your grace and peace to us al - low
chil - dren keep; so calm our minds that fears may cease
us re - new, and when the dawn new light will bring,
on - ly Son, whom with the Spir - it we a - dore,

and be our guard and keep - er now.
and rest - ed bod - ies wake in peace.
your praise and glo - ry we shall sing.
with you, one God for - ev - er - more. A - men.

Text: Compline office hymn, c. 6th cent.; tr. John Mason Neale, 1818–1866, alt.
Music: Plainsong mode VI

JAM LUCIS
LM

568 Now Rest beneath Night's Shadow

1 Now rest be-neath night's shad-ow the wood-land, field,
2 Lord Je-sus, since you love me, now spread your wings
3 My loved ones, rest se-cure-ly, for God this night

and mead-ow— the world in slum-ber lies. But you, my heart,
a-bove me and shield me from a-larm. Though e-vil would
will sure-ly from per-il guard your heads. Sweet slum-ber may

a-wak-ing and prayer and mu-sic mak-ing:
as-sail me, your mer-cy will not fail me;
God send you; the an-gel hosts at-tend you

let praise to your cre-a-tor rise.
I rest in your pro-tect-ing arm.
and through the night watch o'er your beds.

Text: Paul Gerhardt, 1607–1676; tr. composite
Music: Heinrich Isaac, 1450–1517; arr. *Lutheran Book of Worship*
Arr. © 1978 *Lutheran Book of Worship*, admin. Augsburg Fortress

O WELT, ICH MUSS DICH LASSEN
776 7778

The Day You Gave Us, Lord, Has Ended 569

1 The day you gave us, Lord, has end - ed;
2 We thank you that your church, un - sleep - ing
3 As to each con - ti - nent and is - land
4 The sun, here hav - ing set, is wak - ing
5 So be it, Lord; your realm shall nev - er,

the dark - ness falls at your be - hest.
while earth rolls on - ward in - to light,
the dawn leads on an - oth - er day,
your chil - dren un - der west - ern skies,
like earth's proud em - pires, pass a - way;

To you our morn - ing hymns as - cend - ed;
through all the world its watch is keep - ing,
the voice of prayer is nev - er si - lent,
and hour by hour, as day is break - ing,
but stand and grow and rule for - ev - er,

your praise shall hal - low now our rest.
and nev - er rests by day or night.
nor dies the strain of praise a - way.
fresh hymns of thank - ful praise a - rise.
till all your crea - tures own your sway.

Text: John Ellerton, 1826–1893, alt.
Music: Clement C. Scholefield, 1839–1904

ST. CLEMENT
9898

570

Now the Day Is Over

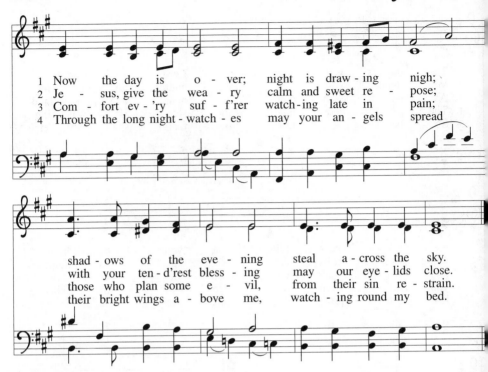

1 Now the day is o - ver; night is draw - ing nigh;
2 Je - sus, give the wea - ry calm and sweet re - pose;
3 Com - fort ev - 'ry suf - f'rer watch-ing late in pain;
4 Through the long night - watch - es may your an - gels spread

shad - ows of the eve - ning steal a - cross the sky.
with your ten - d'rest bless - ing may our eye - lids close.
those who plan some e - vil, from their sin re - strain.
their bright wings a - bove me, watch - ing round my bed.

5 When the morning wakens,
then may I arise
pure and fresh and sinless
in your holy eyes.

6 Glory to the Father,
glory to the Son,
and to you, blest Spirit,
while the ages run.

Text: Sabine Baring-Gould, 1834–1924, alt.
Music: Joseph Barnby, 1838–1896

MERRIAL
6 5 6 5

571

O Trinity, O Blessed Light

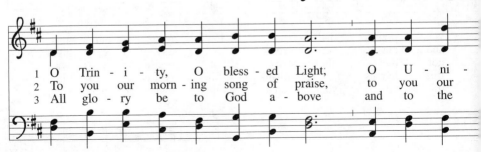

1 O Trin - i - ty, O bless - ed Light; O U - ni -
2 To you our morn - ing song of praise, to you our
3 All glo - ry be to God a - bove and to the

Text: attr. Ambrose of Milan, 340–397; tr. composite
Music: Nikolaus Herman, 1480–1561
Text © 1978 Lutheran Book of Worship, admin. Augsburg Fortress

O HEILIGE DREIFALTIGKEIT
L M

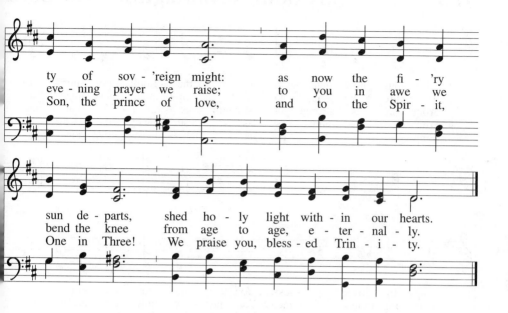

ty of sov - 'reign might: as now the fi - 'ry
eve - ning prayer we raise; to you in awe we
Son, the prince of love, and to the Spir - it,

sun de - parts, shed ho - ly light with - in our hearts.
bend the knee from age to age, e - ter - nal - ly.
One in Three! We praise you, bless - ed Trin - i - ty.

Now It Is Evening

572

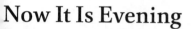

1 Now it is eve-ning: lights of the cit - y bid us re - mem-ber
2 Now it is eve-ning: food on the ta - ble bids us re - mem-ber
3 Now it is eve-ning: lit - tle ones sleep-ing bid us re - mem-ber
4 Now it is eve-ning: here in our meet-ing may we re - mem-ber

Christ is our light. Man - y are lone - ly, who will be
Christ is our life. Man - y are hun - gry, who will be
Christ is our peace. Some are ne - glect - ed, who will be
Christ is our friend. Some may be strang - ers, who will be

neigh-bor? Where there is car - ing, Christ is our light.
neigh-bor? Where there is shar - ing, Christ is our life.
neigh-bor? Where there is car - ing, Christ is our peace.
neigh-bor? Where there's a wel - come, Christ is our friend.

Text: Fred Pratt Green, 1903–2000
Music: Rusty Edwards, b. 1955
Text © 1974 Hope Publishing Company
Music © 1993 Hope Publishing Company

BOZEMAN
5 5 5 4 D
Alternate tune: BUNESSAN

573

My Soul Now Magnifies the Lord

1 My soul now mag - ni - fies the Lord; my spir - it
2 For you a - lone, O God of might, have done a -
3 Your arm is strong; your strength is great. You scat - ter
4 You feed the hun - gry as your own; the wealth - y
5 Sing glo - ry to the Ho - ly One, give hon - or

leaps, by joy pos - sessed. You keep me in your kind re -
maz - ing things for me. Your mer - cy flows; your name like
those of proud in - tent and cast them down from high es -
leave with emp - ty hands. You give your help to Is - ra -
to the in - car - nate Word, and praise the Pow'r of God most

gard; all gen - er - a - tions call me blessed.
light re - mains in time per - pet - ual - ly.
tate; then give the low your nour - ish - ment.
el; your gra - cious prom - ise al - ways stands.
high, from age to age by all a - dored.

Text: Stephanie K. Frey, b. 1952, alt., based on the Magnificat
Music: Heinrich Schütz, 1585–1672
Text © 1978, 1995 Augsburg Fortress

ICH HEB MEIN AUGEN SEHNLICH AUF
LM

Here I Am, Lord

574

1 "I, the Lord of sea and sky, I have heard my peo-ple cry.
2 "I, the Lord of snow and rain, I have borne my peo-ple's pain.
3 "I, the Lord of wind and flame, I will tend the poor and lame.

All who dwell in dark and sin my hand will save.
I have wept for love of them. They turn a-way.
I will set a feast for them. My hand will save.

I, who made the stars of night, I will make their dark-ness bright.
I will break their hearts of stone, give them hearts for love a-lone.
Fin-est bread I will pro-vide till their hearts be sat-is-fied.

Who will bear my light to them? Whom shall I send?"
I will speak my word to them. Whom shall I send?"
I will give my life to them. Whom shall I send?"

Refrain

Here I am, Lord. Is it I, Lord? I have heard you

call-ing in the night. I will go, Lord, if you

lead me. I will hold your peo-ple in my heart.

Text: Daniel L. Schutte, b. 1946
Music: Daniel L. Schutte
Text and music © 1981 OCP Publications, Inc.

HERE I AM, LORD
7 7 7 4 D and refrain

575   In Christ Called to Baptize

1. In Christ called to bap-tize, we wit-ness to grace
2. In Christ called to ban-quet, one ta-ble we share,
3. In Christ called to wit-ness, by grace we will preach
4. U-nite us, a-noint us, O Spir-it of love,

and gath-er a peo-ple from each land and race.
a ha-ven of wel-come, a cir-cle of care.
the life-giv-ing gos-pel; God's love we will teach.
for you are with-in us, a-round us, a-bove.

In deep, flow-ing wa-ters, we share in Christ's death,
Al-though we are man-y, we share in one bread.
By grace may our liv-ing give proof to our praise
E-quip us for ser-vice with gifts you be-stow.

then, ris-ing to new life, give thanks with each breath.
One cup of thanks-giv-ing pro-claims Christ, our head.
in cost-ly com-pas-sion re-flect-ing Christ's ways.
In Christ is our call-ing. In Christ may we grow.

Text: Ruth Duck, b. 1947
Music: Welsh traditional; arr. John Roberts, 1807–1876, alt.
Text © 1995 Pilgrim Press

ST. DENIO
11 11 11 11

We All Are One in Mission

576

1 We all are one in mis - sion; we all are one in call,
2 We all are called for ser - vice, to wit - ness in God's name.
3 Now let us be u - nit - ed, and let our song be heard.

our var - ied gifts u - nit - ed by Christ, the Lord of all.
Our min - is - tries are dif - f'rent; our pur - pose is the same:
Now let us be a ves - sel for God's re - deem - ing Word.

A sin - gle great com - mis - sion com - pels us from a - bove
to touch the lives of oth - ers with God's sur - pris - ing grace,
We all are one in mis - sion; we all are one in call,

to plan and work to - geth - er that all may know Christ's love.
so ev - 'ry folk and na - tion may feel God's warm em - brace.
our var - ied gifts u - nit - ed by Christ, the Lord of all.

Text: Rusty Edwards, b. 1955
Music: Finnish folk tune; arr. hymnal version
Text © 1986 Hope Publishing Company
Arr. © 2006 Augsburg Fortress

KUORTANE
7 6 7 6 D

577 Creator Spirit, Heavenly Dove

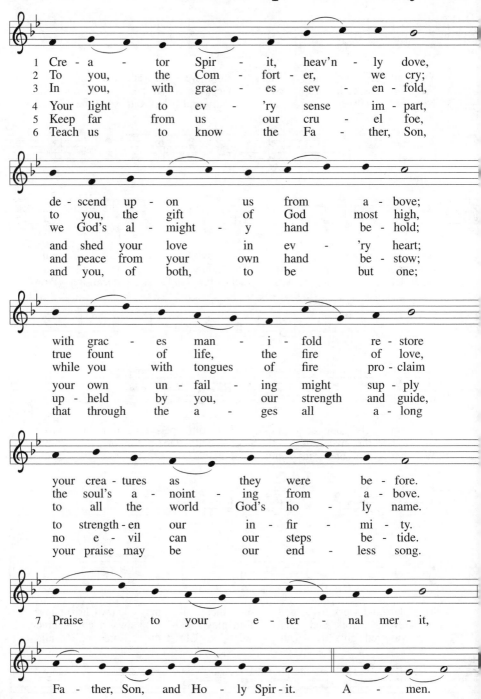

1 Cre - a - tor Spir - it, heav'n - ly dove,
2 To you, the Com - fort - er, we cry;
3 In you, with grac - es sev - en - fold,
4 Your light to ev - 'ry sense im - part,
5 Keep far from us our cru - el foe,
6 Teach us to know the Fa - ther, Son,

de - scend up - on us from a - bove;
to you, the gift of God most high,
we God's al - might - y hand be - hold;
and shed your love in ev - 'ry heart;
and peace from your own hand be - stow;
and you, of both, to be but one;

with grac - es man - i - fold re - store
true fount of life, the fire of love,
while you with tongues of fire pro - claim
your own un - fail - ing might sup - ply
up - held by you, our strength and guide,
that through the a - ges all a - long

your crea - tures as they were be - fore.
the soul's a - noint - ing from a - bove.
to all the world God's ho - ly name.
to strength - en our in - fir - mi - ty.
no e - vil can our steps be - tide.
your praise may be our end - less song.

7 Praise to your e - ter - nal mer - it,

Fa - ther, Son, and Ho - ly Spir - it. A - men.

Text: Rhabanus Maurus, 776–856; tr. composite
Music: Sarum plainsong, mode VIII

VENI CREATOR SPIRITU
LM

Creator Spirit, Heavenly Dove

578

1 Cre - a - tor Spir - it, heav'n - ly dove, de - scend
2 To you, the Com - fort - er, we cry; to you,
3 In you, with grac - es sev - en - fold, we God's
4 Your light to ev - 'ry sense im - part, and shed

up - on us from a - bove; with grac - es man - i -
the gift of God most high, true fount of life, the
al - might - y hand be - hold; while you with tongues of
your love in ev - 'ry heart; your own un - fail - ing

fold re - store your crea - tures as they were be - fore.
fire of love, the soul's a - noint - ing from a - bove.
fire pro - claim to all the world God's ho - ly name.
might sup - ply to strength - en our in - fir - mi - ty.

5 Keep far from us our cruel foe,
   and peace from your own hand bestow;
   upheld by you, our strength and guide,
   no evil can our steps betide.

6 Teach us to know the Father, Son,
   and you, of both, to be but one;
   that through the ages all along
   your praise may be our endless song.

Text: Rhabanus Maurus, 776–856; tr. composite
Music: J. Klug, Geistliche Lieder, 1543

KOMM, GOTT SCHÖPFER
LM

579   Lord, You Give the Great Commission

1 Lord, you give the great com - mis-sion: "Heal the sick and
2 Lord, you call us to your ser - vice: "In my name bap -
3 Lord, you make the com - mon ho - ly: "This my bod - y,
4 Lord, you show us love's true mea-sure: "Fa - ther, what they
5 Lord, you bless with words as - sur - ing: "I am with you

preach the word." Lest the church ne - glect its mis - sion,
tize and teach." That the world may trust your prom-ise,
this my blood." Let us all, for earth's true glo - ry,
do, for - give." Yet we hoard as pri - vate trea-sure
to the end." Faith and hope and love re - stor - ing,

and the gos - pel go un - heard, help us wit - ness
life a - bun - dant meant for each, give us all new
dai - ly lift life heav - en - ward, ask - ing that the
all that you so free - ly give. May your care and
may we serve as you in - tend and, a - mid the

to your pur - pose with re - newed in - teg - ri - ty:
fer - vor, draw us clos - er in com - mu - ni - ty:
world a - round us share your chil - dren's lib - er - ty:
mer - cy lead us to a just so - ci - e - ty:
cares that claim us, hold in mind e - ter - ni - ty:

Text: Jeffery Rowthorn, b. 1934
Music: Cyril V. Taylor, 1907–1991
Text © 1978 Hope Publishing Company
Music © 1942, ren. 1970 Hope Publishing Company

ABBOT'S LEIGH
8 7 8 7

Refrain

With the Spir-it's gifts em-pow'r us for the work of min - is - try.

How Clear Is Our Vocation, Lord 580

1 How clear is our vo - ca - tion, Lord, when once we heed your call
2 But if, for - get - ful, we should find your yoke is hard to bear;
3 We mar - vel how your saints be - come in hin - dranc-es more sure;
4 In what you give us, Lord, to do, to - geth - er or a - lone,

to live ac-cord-ing to your word and dai - ly learn, re-freshed, re - stored,
if world-ly pres-sures fray the mind and love it - self can - not un - wind
whose joy - ful vir-tues put to shame the ca - sual way we wear your name,
in old rou-tines or ven-tures new, may we not cease to look to you,

that you are Lord of all and will not let us fall.
its tan - gled skein of care: our in - ward life re - pair.
and by our faults ob - scure your pow'r to cleanse and cure.
the cross you hung up - on, all you en - deav - ored done.

Text: Fred Pratt Green, 1903–2000
Music: C. Hubert H. Parry, 1848–1918
Text © 1982 Hope Publishing Company

REPTON
8 6 8 8 6 6

581

You Are Mine

1 "I will come to you in the si - lence,
2 "I am hope for all who are hope - less,
3 "I am strength for all the de - spair - ing,
(4) am the Word that leads all to free - dom,
                                   I

I will lift you from all your fear.
I am eyes for all who long to see.
heal-ing for the ones who dwell in shame.
am the peace the world can - not give.
                       (2) In the

You will hear my voice, I claim you as my choice. Be
shad-ows of the night, I will be your light.
All the blind will see, the lame will all run free, and
I will call your name, em - brac - ing all your pain. Stand

still and know I am here. _To stanza 2_
Come and rest in me. _To refrain_
all will know my name. _To refrain_
up, now walk and live! _To refrain_

Refrain

Do not be a-fraid, I am with you. I have called you each by

name. Come and fol-low me, I will bring you home; I

To stanzas 3 and 4

love you and you are mine."

4 "I

Text: David Haas, b. 1957
Music: David Haas
Text and music © 1991 GIA Publications, Inc.

YOU ARE MINE
Irregula

Holy Spirit, Ever Dwelling

582

1 Ho-ly Spir-it, ev-er dwell-ing in the ho-liest realms of light;
2 Ho-ly Spir-it, ev-er liv-ing as the church's ver-y life;
3 Ho-ly Spir-it, ev-er work-ing through the church's min-is-try;

Ho-ly Spir-it, ev-er brood-ing o'er a world of gloom and night;
Ho-ly Spir-it, ev-er striv-ing through us in a cease-less strife;
quick-'ning, strength-'ning, and ab-solv-ing, set-ting cap-tive sin-ners free;

Ho-ly Spir-it, ev-er rais-ing those of earth to thrones on high;
Ho-ly Spir-it, ev-er form-ing in the church the mind of Christ:
Ho-ly Spir-it, ev-er bind-ing age to age and soul to soul

liv-ing, life-im-part-ing Spir-it, you we praise and mag-ni-fy.
you we praise with end-less wor-ship for your gifts and fruits un-priced.
in com-mu-nion nev-er end-ing, you we wor-ship and ex-tol.

Text: Timothy Rees, 1874–1939, alt.
Music: *Oude en Nieuwe Hollantse Boerenlities en Contradansen*, 1710; arr. Julius Röntgen, 1855–1932

IN BABILONE
8787D

Take My Life, That I May Be
Toma, oh Dios, mi voluntad

Refrain/Estribillo

To - ma, oh Dios, mi vo - lun - tad, y haz - la tu - ya, na - da más;
Take my life, that I may be con - se - crat - ed, Lord, to thee;

to - ma, sí, mi co - ra - zón y tu tro - no en él ten - drás.
take my mo - ments and my days; let them flow in cease -less praise.

1 Que mi vi - da en - te - ra es - té con - sa - gra -
1 Take my hands and let them move at the im -
2 Take my sil - ver and my gold, not a mite
3 Take my voice and let me sing al - ways, on -
4 Take my will and make it thine; it shall be

da a ti, Se - ñor; que a mis ma - nos pue -
pulse of thy love; take my feet and let
would I with - hold; take my in - tel - lect
ly for my King; take my lips and let
no lon - ger mine; take my heart, it is

Refrain/Estribillo

da guiar el im - pul - so de tu a - mor.
them be swift and beau - ti - ful for thee.
and use ev - 'ry pow'r as thou shalt choose.
them be filled with mes - sag - es from thee.
thine own; it shall be thy roy - al throne.

2 Que mis pies tan sólo en pos
de lo santo puedan ir,
y que a ti, Señor, mi voz,
se complazca en bendecir. Estribillo

3 Que mis labios al hablar
hablen sólo de tu amor;
que mis bienes dedicar
yo los quiera a ti, Señor. Estribillo

4 Que mi tiempo todo esté
consagrado a tu loor;
que mi mente y su poder
sean usados en tu honor. Estribillo

Text: Frances R. Havergal, 1836–1879, adapt.; Spanish text: Vicente Mendoza, 1875–1955
Music: William Dexheimer Pharris, b. 1956; arr. Mark Sedio, b. 1954
Music © 1999 Augsburg Fortress

TOMA MI VOLUNTA
7 7 7 7

The Son of God, Our Christ

584

1 The Son of God, our Christ, the Word, the Way,
shared hu - man life and toiled through - out the day;
from com - mon folk he called the twelve to be
co - work - ers in his sa - cred min - is - try.

2 In ev - 'ry test, in tri - als man - i - fold,
these ser - vants wit - nessed, by their faith made bold;
and with the gifts and tal - ents which they brought
the church was found - ed and God's mes - sage taught.

3 To - day, as then, Christ sum - mons us to dare
to fol - low bold - ly and his work to share,
to help and heal the sick, the blind, the lame,
de - clar - ing to the world his ho - ly name.

4 In cit - y street, in town, or on the soil,
may each serve Christ in faith - ful dai - ly toil,
and in each thought and kind - ly word and deed,
o - bey Christ's call and go where he shall lead.

5 Wher - e'er we find our wit - ness should be made,
what - e'er our task, be thou, O Christ, our aid,
that we may glad - ly give for thee our best
and find each task di - vine - ly sent and blest.

Text: Edward M. Blumenfeld, b. 1927, alt.
Music: Alfred M. Smith, 1879–1971
Text © 1957, ren. 1985 The Hymn Society, admin. Hope Publishing Company
Music © 1941 Historic Church of the Ascension, Atlantic City, NJ

SURSUM CORDA
10 10 10 10

585 Hear Us Now, Our God and Father

1 Hear us now, our God and Fa - ther, send your Spir - it
2 Give them joy to light - en sor - row, give them hope to
3 May the grace of Christ, our Sav - ior, and the Fa - ther's

from a - bove on this Chris - tian man and wom - an who here
bright - en life. Go with them to face the mor - row, stay with
bound-less love, with the Ho - ly Spir - it's fa - vor rest up -

make their vows of love. Bind their hearts in true de - vo - tion
them in ev - 'ry strife. As your word has prom - ised, ev - er
on them from a - bove. Thus may they a - bide in u - nion

end - less as the sea - shore's sands, bound-less as the
fill them with your strength and grace, so that each may
with each oth - er and the Lord, and pos - sess in

Text: Harry N. Huxhold, 1922–2006, sts. 1–2; John Newton, 1725–1807, st. 3, alt.
Music: Rowland H. Prichard, 1811–1887
Text sts. 1–2 © 1978 Lutheran Book of Worship, admin. Augsburg Fortress

HYFRYDOL
8 7 8 7

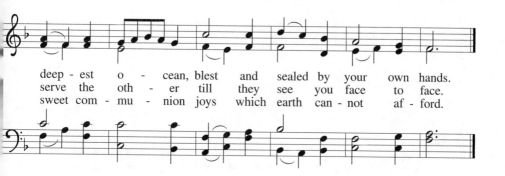

deep - est   o - cean, blest   and   sealed   by   your   own   hands.
serve   the   oth - er   till   they   see   you   face   to   face.
sweet com - mu - nion   joys   which   earth   can - not   af - ford.

This Is a Day, Lord, Gladly Awaited   586

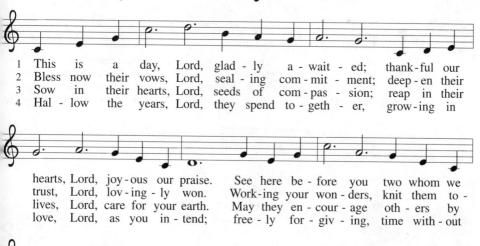

1 This   is   a   day, Lord,   glad - ly   a - wait - ed;   thank-ful   our
2 Bless   now   their   vows, Lord,   seal - ing   com - mit - ment;   deep - en   their
3 Sow   in   their   hearts, Lord,   seeds   of   com - pas - sion;   reap   in   their
4 Hal - low   the   years, Lord,   they   spend   to - geth - er,   grow - ing   in

hearts, Lord, joy-ous our praise.   See here be - fore you   two whom we
trust, Lord, lov - ing - ly   won.   Work-ing your won - ders,   knit them to -
lives, Lord, care for your earth.   May they en - cour - age   oth - ers   by
love, Lord, as you in - tend;   free - ly   for - giv - ing,   time with-out

cher - ish;   keep them be - side   you   all   of   their   days.
geth - er   so   noth - ing   sun - ders   two   be - come   one.
be - ing   signs   of   God's new   age   com - ing   to   birth.
num - ber;   self - less - ly   liv - ing,   time with-out   end.

Text: Jeffery Rowthorn, b. 1934
Music: Gaelic tune
Text © 1992 Hope Publishing Company

BUNESSAN
5 5 5 4 D

587   There's a Wideness in God's Mercy

1 There's a wide-ness
2 There is wel-come
3 For the love of
4 'Tis not all we

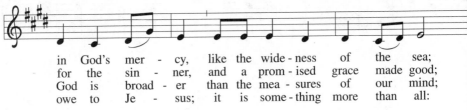

in God's mer - cy, like the wide-ness of the sea;
for the sin - ner, and a prom-ised grace made good;
God is broad - er than the mea-sures of our mind;
owe to Je - sus; it is some-thing more than all:

there's a kind - ness in God's jus - tice which is more than
there is mer - cy with the Sav - ior; there is heal - ing
and the heart of the E - ter - nal is most won - der -
great - er good be - cause of e - vil, larg - er mer - cy

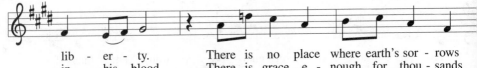

lib - er - ty. There is no place where earth's sor - rows
in his blood. There is grace e - nough for thou - sands
ful - ly kind. But we make this love too nar - row
through the fall. Make our love, O God, more faith - ful;

are more felt than up in heav'n. There is no place
of new worlds as great as this; there is room for
by false lim - its of our own; and we mag - ni -
let us take you at your word, and our lives will

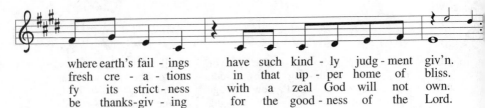

where earth's fail - ings have such kind - ly judg - ment giv'n.
fresh cre - a - tions in that up - per home of bliss.
fy its strict-ness with a zeal God will not own.
be thanks-giv - ing for the good - ness of the Lord.

Text: Frederick W. Faber, 1814–1863, alt.
Music: Calvin Hampton, 1938–1984
Music © 1977 GIA Publications, Inc.

ST. HELEN
8 7 8 7

There's a Wideness in God's Mercy 588

1 There's a wide-ness in God's mer - cy, like the wide-ness of the sea;
2 There is wel - come for the sin - ner, and a prom-ised grace made good;
3 For the love of God is broad-er than the mea - sures of our mind;
4 'Tis not all we owe to Je - sus; it is some-thing more than all:

there's a kind-ness in God's jus - tice which is more than lib - er - ty.
there is mer - cy with the Sav-ior; there is heal-ing in his blood.
and the heart of the E - ter - nal is most won-der - ful - ly kind.
great - er good be - cause of e - vil, larg - er mer - cy through the fall.

There is no place where earth's sor - rows are more felt than up in heav'n.
There is grace e - nough for thou-sands of new worlds as great as this;
But we make this love too nar - row by false lim - its of our own;
Make our love, O God, more faith - ful; let us take you at your word,

There is no place where earth's fail - ings have such kind - ly judg-ment giv'n.
there is room for fresh cre - a - tions in that up - per home of bliss.
and we mag-ni - fy its strict-ness with a zeal God will not own.
and our lives will be thanks-giv - ing for the good-ness of the Lord.

Text: Frederick W. Faber, 1814–1863, alt.
Music: North American, 19th cent.

LORD, REVIVE US
87 87 D

589

All Depends on Our Possessing

1 All de-pends on our pos-sess-ing God's free grace and con-stant bless-ing, though all earth-ly wealth de-part. They who trust with faith un-shak-en by their God are not for-sak-en and will keep a daunt-less heart.

2 God, who hith-er-to has fed me and to man-y joys has led me, is and ev-er shall be mine. God, who did so gent-ly school me and who dai-ly guides and rules me, will re-main my help di-vine.

3 When with sor-row I am strick-en, hope my heart a-new will quick-en, all my long-ing shall be stilled. To your lov-ing-kind-ness ten-der all my be-ing I sur-ren-der; Lord, on you a-lone I build.

4 Well you know what best to grant me; all the long-ing hopes that haunt me, joy and sor-row, have their day. I shall doubt your wis-dom nev-er; as you will, so be it ev-er; I com-mit to you my way.

5 If on earth my days should length-en, God, my wea-ry soul still strength-en; all my trust in you I place. Earth-ly wealth is not a-bid-ing; like a stream a-way it's glid-ing; safe I an-chor in your grace.

Text: *Gesangbuch*, Nürnberg, 1676; tr. Catherine Winkworth, 1827–1878, alt.
Music: Johann Löhner, 1645–1705, adapt.

ALLES IST AN GOTTES SEGE
887

Salvation unto Us Has Come

1 Sal - va - tion un - to us has come by God's free grace and fa - vor;
2 What God did in the law de - mand no one could keep un - fail - ing;
3 Since Christ has full a - tone-ment made and brought to us sal - va - tion,
4 Faith clings to Je - sus' cross a - lone and rests in him un - ceas - ing;

good works can - not a - vert our doom, they help and save us
great woe a - rose on ev - 'ry hand, and sin grew all - pre -
we will re - joice, we will be glad and build on this foun -
and by its fruits true faith is known, with love and hope in -

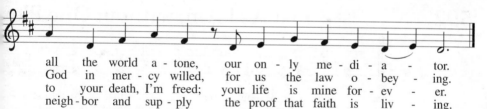

nev - er. Faith looks to Je - sus Christ a - lone, who did for
vail - ing. Be - cause the law must be ful - filled, Christ came as
da - tion. Your grace a - lone, dear Lord, I plead; bap - tized in -
creas - ing. For faith a - lone can jus - ti - fy; works serve our

all the world a - tone, our on - ly me - di - a - tor.
God in mer - cy willed, for us the law o - bey - ing.
to your death, I'm freed; your life is mine for - ev - er.
neigh-bor and sup - ply the proof that faith is liv - ing.

5 All blessing, honor, thanks, and praise
to Father, Son, and Spirit!
Lord, you have saved us by your grace;
all glory to your merit!
O triune God in heav'n above,
you have revealed your saving love;
your blessed name we hallow.

6 Your kingdom come, your will be done
in this world as in heaven;
give bread for each new day begun;
our sins be all forgiven,
as we forgive what others do;
in ev'ry trial see us through;
from evil save us. Amen.

Text: Paul Speratus, 1484–1551; tr. hymnal version
Music: *Etlich christlich Lieder*, Wittenberg, 1524
Text © 2006 Augsburg Fortress

ES IST DAS HEIL
8 7 8 7 8 8 7

591 That Priceless Grace

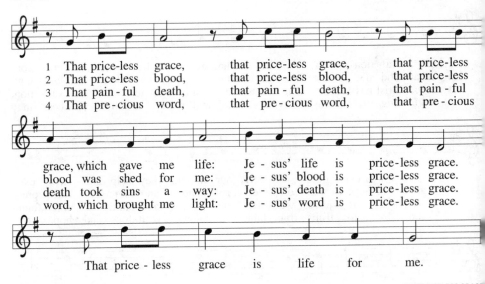

1 That price-less grace, that price-less grace, that price-less
2 That price-less blood, that price-less blood, that price-less
3 That pain-ful death, that pain-ful death, that pain-ful
4 That pre-cious word, that pre-cious word, that pre-cious

grace, which gave me life: Je - sus' life is price-less grace.
blood was shed for me: Je - sus' blood is price-less grace.
death took sins a - way: Je - sus' death is price-less grace.
word, which brought me light: Je - sus' word is price-less grace.

That price - less grace is life for me.

Text: Emmanuel F. Y. Grantson, b. 1949
Music: Ghanaian traditional
Text © 1999 Augsburg Fortress

THAT PRICELESS GRACE
4 4 8 7 8

592 Just As I Am, without One Plea

1 Just as I am, with - out one plea, but that thy blood was
2 Just as I am, though tossed a - bout with man - y a con - flict,
3 Just as I am, thou wilt re - ceive, wilt wel - come, par - don,
4 Just as I am; thy love un-known has bro - ken ev - 'ry

shed for me, and that thou bidd'st me come to thee,
man - y a doubt, fight - ings and fears with - in, with - out,
cleanse, re - lieve; be - cause thy prom - ise I be - lieve,
bar - rier down; now to be thine, yea, thine a - lone,

Text: Charlotte Elliott, 1789–1871
Music: William B. Bradbury, 1816–1868

WOODWORTH
L M

O Lamb of God, I come, I come.

Drawn to the Light

593

1 Peo - ple who walk in dark - ness have sought a light in the
2 How can we tell a heav - en from hell if ev - 'ry - one
3 Where is the sun? Oh, there will be none! The Lamb is the

heart of the dark - est night. Just when we thought all would be
dwells in the dark of night? Morn - ing dis - pels, gent - ly com -
one who is shin - ing bright, bids us to come! Life has be -

lost, we were drawn to the light of God.
pels, and we're drawn to the light of God.
gun when we're drawn to the light of God.

Refrain

Dawn is in sight! Gone is the night, drawn to the

light and the morn - ing. Glo - rious and bright, oh, what a

sight to be drawn to the light of God.

Text: John C. Ylvisaker, b. 1937
Music: John C. Ylvisaker
Text and music © 1990 John C. Ylvisaker

LA CROSSE
9 10 88 and refrain

594   Dear Christians, One and All, Rejoice

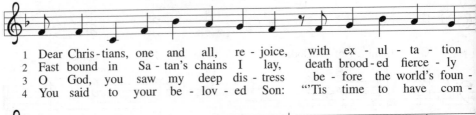

1 Dear Chris-tians, one and all, re - joice, with ex - ul - ta - tion
2 Fast bound in Sa - tan's chains I lay, death brood-ed fierce - ly
3 O God, you saw my deep dis - tress be - fore the world's foun -
4 You said to your be - lov - ed Son: "'Tis time to have com -

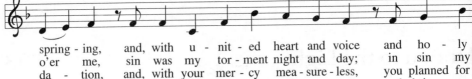

spring - ing, and, with u - nit - ed heart and voice and ho - ly
o'er me, sin was my tor - ment night and day; in sin my
da - tion, and, with your mer - cy mea - sure-less, you planned for
pas - sion. Then go, bright jew - el of my crown, and bring to

rap - ture sing - ing, pro - claim the won-ders God has done, pro -
moth-er bore me. My own good works all came to naught, free
my sal - va - tion. You turned to me a fa - ther's heart; you
all sal - va - tion; from sin and sor - row set them free; slay

claim the vic - t'ry God has won, how pre-cious was our ran - som!
will a - gainst God's judg-ment fought, so firm - ly sin pos - sessed me.
did not choose the eas - y part, but gave your dear-est trea - sure.
bit - ter death for them that they may live with you for - ev - er."

5 The Son obeyed your gracious will,
   was born of virgin mother;
  and, your good pleasure to fulfill,
   he came to be my brother.
  His royal pow'r disguised he bore,
  a servant's form, like mine, he wore,
   to lead the devil captive.

6 To me he said: "Stay close to me,
   I am your rock and castle.
  Your ransom I myself will be;
   for you I strive and wrestle.
  The foe will shed my precious blood;
  all this I suffer for your good;
   my life o'er death will triumph.

7 "Now to my Father I depart,
   from earth to heav'n ascending,
  and, gracious wisdom to impart,
   the Holy Spirit sending,
  who will in trouble comfort you,
  will teach you well, your faith renew,
   and in all truth will guide you.

8 "What I on earth have done and taught
   guide all your life and teaching;
  so shall the glorious reign of God
   increase, the whole world reaching.
  Let none the gospel gift impede;
  I make you free; be free indeed!
   This final word I leave you."

Text: Martin Luther, 1483–1546; tr. hymnal version
Music: *Etlich christlich Lieder*, Wittenberg, 1524
Text © 2006 Augsburg Fortress

NUN FREUT EUCH
878788

Jesus Loves Me!

1 Je - sus loves me! this I know, for the Bi - ble tells me so;
2 Je - sus loves me! he who died heav - en's gates to o - pen wide;
3 Je - sus loves me! he will stay close be - side me all the way;

lit - tle ones to him be - long, they are weak, but he is strong.
he will wash a - way my sin, let his lit - tle child come in.
when at last I come to die, he will take me home on high.

Refrain

Yes, Je - sus loves me, yes, Je - sus loves me,

yes, Je - sus loves me, the Bi - ble tells me so.

Text: Anna B. Warner, 1820–1915, alt.
Music: William B. Bradbury, 1816–1868

JESUS LOVES ME
7 7 7 7 and refrain

596 My Hope Is Built on Nothing Less

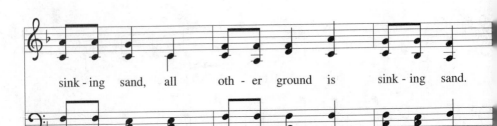

1. My hope is built on noth-ing less than Je-sus' blood and righ-teous-ness;
2. When dark-ness veils his love-ly face, I rest on his un-chang-ing grace;
3. His oath, his cov-e-nant, his blood sus-tain me in the rag-ing flood;
4. When he shall come with trum-pet sound, oh, may I then in him be found,

no mer-it of my own I claim, but whol-ly lean on Je-sus' name.
in ev-'ry high and storm-y gale my an-chor holds with-in the veil.
when all sup-ports are washed a-way, he then is all my hope and stay.
clothed in his righ-teous-ness a-lone, re-deemed to stand be-fore the throne.

Refrain

On Christ, the sol-id rock, I stand; all oth-er ground is
sink-ing sand, all oth-er ground is sink-ing sand.

Text: Edward Mote, 1797–1874, alt.
Music: William B. Bradbury, 1816–1868

THE SOLID ROCK
8 8 8 8 8 8

My Hope Is Built on Nothing Less 597

1 My hope is built on noth - ing less than
2 When dark - ness veils his love - ly face, I
3 His oath, his cov - e - nant, his blood sus -
4 When he shall come with trum - pet sound, oh,

Je - sus' blood and righ - teous - ness; no mer - it of my
rest on his un - chang - ing grace; in ev - 'ry high and
tain me in the rag - ing flood; when all sup - ports are
may I then in him be found, clothed in his righ - teous -

own I claim, but whol - ly lean on Je - sus' name.
storm - y gale my an - chor holds with - in the veil.
washed a - way, he then is all my hope and stay.
ness a - lone, re - deemed to stand be - fore the throne!

Refrain

On Christ, the sol - id rock, I stand; all oth - er ground is sink - ing sand.

Text: Edward Mote, 1797–1874, alt.
Music: John B. Dykes, 1823–1876

MELITA
888888

598   For by Grace You Have Been Saved

1 For by grace you have been saved and e - ven faith is not your
2 "So my grace is all - suf - fi - cient for each child who is my
3 So this weak - ness with con - tent - ment I'll ac - cept now in my

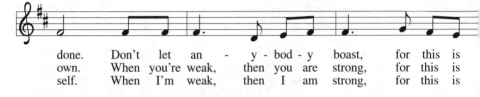

own, it's the gift of God for you and not the works that you have
own, for my strength is now made per - fect for each child who is my
self, all my hard - ships, pains, and griefs that still lie deep with - in my

done. Don't let an - y - bod - y boast, for this is
own. When you're weak, then you are strong, for this is
self. When I'm weak, then I am strong, for this is

God's great gift. A - men.
God's great gift." A - men.
God's great gift. A - men. A - men.

Text: Kari Tikka, b. 1946; tr. Michael Harper
Music: Kari Tikka
Text and music © Fennica Gehrman, admin. Boosey & Hawkes, Inc.

ARMOLAUL
15 15 1

599   Lord Jesus, Think on Me

1 Lord Je - sus, think on me, and purge a - way my sin;
2 Lord Je - sus, think on me, by anx - ious thoughts op - pressed;
3 Lord Je - sus, think on me, nor let me go a - stray;
4 Lord Je - sus, think on me, that, when the flood is past,

Text: Synesius of Cyrene, 375–430; tr. Allen W. Chatfield, 1808–1896, alt.
Music: W. Daman, *The Psalmes of Dauid*, 1579, alt.

SOUTHWEL
S

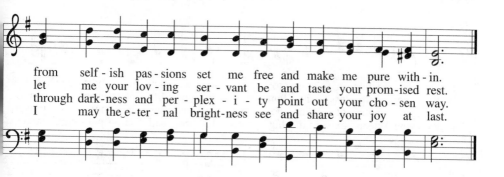

from   self - ish pas - sions set   me free and make me pure with - in.
let   me your lov - ing ser - vant be and taste your prom - ised rest.
through dark - ness and per - plex - i - ty point out your cho - sen way.
I   may the e - ter - nal bright - ness see and share your joy   at   last.

Out of the Depths I Cry to You   600

1 Out of   the depths I cry to you;   O Lord God, hear me   call - ing.
2 All things you send are full of grace; you crown our lives with fa - vor.
3 In you   a - lone, O God, we hope, and not   in   our own mer - it.
4 My soul is wait - ing for you, Lord, as one who longs for morn - ing;

In - cline your ear to my dis - tress   in spite of my re - bel - ling.
All our good works are done in vain with - out our Lord and Sav - ior.
We rest our fears in your good Word and trust your Ho - ly Spir - it.
no watch - er waits with great - er hope than I   for your re - turn - ing.

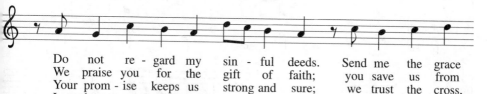

Do   not re - gard my   sin - ful deeds. Send me   the grace
We praise you for the gift of faith;   you save us from
Your prom - ise keeps us strong and sure;   we trust the cross,
I   hope as Is - rael in   the Lord, who sends re - demp -

my   spir - it needs;   with - out it   I   am noth - ing.
the grip of death;   our lives are in your keep - ing.
your sig - na - ture,   in - scribed up - on our tem - ples.
tion through the Word. Praise God for grace and mer - cy!

Text: Martin Luther, 1483–1546; tr. composite
Music: attr. Martin Luther
Text © 1978, 2006 Augsburg Fortress

AUS TIEFER NOT
87 87 887

601

Savior, When in Dust to You

1 Sav-ior, when in dust to you low we bow in hom-age due;
2 By your help-less in-fant years, by your life of want and tears,
3 By your hour of dire de-spair, by your ag-o-ny of prayer,
4 By your deep ex-pir-ing groan, by the sad se-pul-chral stone,

when, re-pen-tant, to the skies scarce we lift our weep-ing eyes;
by your days of deep dis-tress in the sav-age wil-der-ness,
by the cross, the nail, the thorn, pierc-ing spear, and tor-tur-ing scorn,
by the vault whose dark a-bode held in vain the ris-ing God,

oh, by all your pains and woe suf-fered once for us be-low,
by the dread, mys-te-rious hour of the in-sult-ing tempt-er's pow'r,
by the gloom that veiled the skies o'er the dread-ful sac-ri-fice,
oh, from earth to heav'n re-stored, might-y, re-as-cend-ed Lord,

bend-ing from your throne on high, hear our pen-i-ten-tial cry!
turn, oh, turn a fa-v'ring eye; hear our pen-i-ten-tial cry!
lis-ten to our hum-ble sigh; hear our pen-i-ten-tial cry!
bend-ing from your throne on high, hear our pen-i-ten-tial cry!

Text: Robert Grant, 1779–1838, alt.
Music: Joseph Parry, 1841–1903

ABERYSTWYTH
7 7 7 7 D

Your Heart, O God, Is Grieved
Vieme to, Pane Bože náš

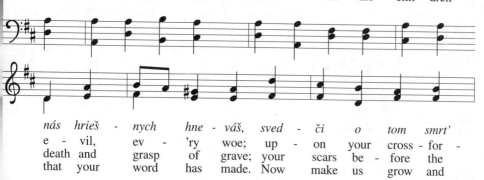

Leader

Otče nebeský, Svoritel'u sveta, Bo - že, zmi - luj sa nad na - mi.
1 O God, Father in heav - en, have mer - cy up - on us.
2 O Son of God, redeemer of the world, have mer - cy up - on us.
3 O God, Holy Spir - it, have mer - cy up - on us.

All

Vie - me to, Pa - ne Bo - že náš, že sa na
Your heart, O God, is grieved, we know, by ev - 'ry
Your arms ex - tend, O Christ, to save from sting of
O lav - ish Giv - er, come to aid the chil - dren

nás hrieš - nych hne - váš, sved - či o tom smrt'
e - vil, ev - 'ry woe; up - on your cross - for -
death and grasp of grave; your scars be - fore the
that your word has made. Now make us grow and

ne - vin - ná Tvoj - ho je - di - né - ho Sy - na.
sak - en Son our death is laid, and peace is won.
Fa - ther move his heart to mer - cy at such love.
help us pray; bring joy and com - fort, come to stay.

Text: Jiří Tranovský, 1591–1637; tr. Jaroslav J. Vajda, b. 1919
Music: *Tranoscius*, 1636; arr. Michal Kutzky, 1828–1899
Tr. © 1970 Concordia Publishing House

ZNÁME TO, PANE BOŽE NÁŠ
Irregular

603 God, When Human Bonds Are Broken

1 God, when hu-man bonds are bro-ken and we lack the love or skill
2 Through that still-ness, with your Spir-it come in-to our world of stress,
3 You in us are bruised and bro-ken: hear us as we seek re-lease
4 Send us, God of new be-gin-nings, hum-bly hope-ful in-to life.
5 Give us faith to be more faith-ful, give us hope to be more true,

to re-store the hope of heal-ing, give us grace and make us still.
for the sake of Christ for-giv-ing all the fail-ures we con-fess.
from the pain of ear-lier liv-ing; set us free and grant us peace.
Use us as a means of bless-ing: make us stron-ger, give us faith.
give us love to go on learn-ing: God, en-cour-age and re-new!

Text: Fred Kaan, b. 1929
Music: William H. Monk, 1823–1889
Text © 1989 Hope Publishing Company

MERTON
8 7 8 7

604 O Christ, Our Hope

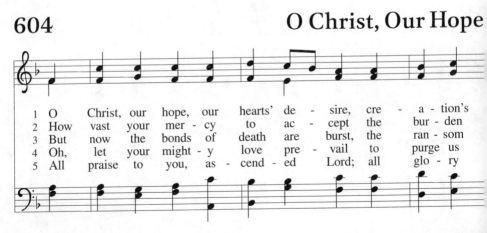

1 O Christ, our hope, our hearts' de-sire, cre-a-tion's
2 How vast your mer-cy to ac-cept the bur-den
3 But now the bonds of death are burst, the ran-som
4 Oh, let your might-y love pre-vail to purge us
5 All praise to you, as-cend-ed Lord; all glo-ry

Text: Latin hymn, c. 8th cent.; tr. John Chandler, 1806–1876, adapt.
Music: Nikolaus Herman, 1480–1561

LOBT GOTT, IHR CHRISTEN
8 6 8 6 6

might - y Lord, re - deem - er of the fall - en world, by
of our sin, and bow your head in cru - el death to
has been paid; you reign a - bove at God's right hand, in
of our pride, that we may stand be - fore your throne by
ev - er be to Fa - ther, Son, and Spir - it blest through

ho - ly love out - poured, by ho - ly love out - poured:
make us clean with - in, to make us clean with - in.
robes of light ar - rayed, in robes of light ar - rayed.
mer - cy pu - ri - fied, by mer - cy pu - ri - fied.
all e - ter - ni - ty, through all e - ter - ni - ty!

Forgive Our Sins As We Forgive   605

1 "For - give our sins as we for - give," you taught us, Lord, to pray;
2 How can your par - don reach and bless the un - for - giv - ing heart
3 In blaz - ing light your cross re - veals the truth we dim - ly knew:
4 Lord, cleanse the depths with - in our souls and bid re - sent - ment cease;

but you a - lone can grant us grace to live the words we say.
that broods on wrongs and will not let old bit - ter - ness de - part?
how tri - fling oth - ers' debts to us; how great our debt to you!
then, by your mer - cy rec - on - ciled, our lives will spread your peace.

Text: Rosamond E. Herklots, 1905–1987, alt.
Music: *The Sacred Harp*, Philadelphia, 1844
Text © Oxford University Press

DETROIT
C M

606   Our Father, We Have Wandered

1 Our Fa - ther, we have wan - dered and hid - den from your face;
2 And now at length dis - cern - ing the e - vil that we do,
3 O Lord of all the liv - ing, both ban - ished and re - stored,

in fool-ish-ness have squan - dered your leg - a - cy of grace.
be - hold us, Lord, re - turn - ing with hope and trust to you.
com-pas-sion-ate, for - giv - ing, and ev - er - car - ing Lord,

But now, in ex - ile dwell - ing, we rise with fear and shame,
In haste you come to meet us and home re - joic - ing bring,
grant now that our trans - gress - ing, our faith - less - ness may cease.

as, dis - tant but com - pel - ling, we hear you call our name.
in glad-ness there to greet us with calf and robe and ring.
Stretch out your hand in bless - ing, in par - don, and in peace.

Text: Kevin Nichols, 1929–2006
Music: Hans Leo Hassler, 1564–1612; arr. Johann Sebastian Bach, 1685–1750
Text © 1981 International Committee on English in the Liturgy, Inc.

HERZLICH TUT MICH VERLANGEN
76 76 L

Come, Ye Disconsolate

607

1 Come, ye dis - con - so - late, wher - e'er ye lan - guish;
2 Joy of the des - o - late, light of the stray - ing,
3 Here see the Bread of life; see wa - ters flow - ing

come to the mer - cy - seat, fer - vent - ly kneel.
hope of the pen - i - tent, fade - less and pure;
forth from the throne of God, pure from a - bove.

Here bring your wound - ed hearts, here tell your an - guish;
here speaks the Com - fort - er, ten - der - ly say - ing,
Come to the feast of love; come, ev - er know - ing

earth has no sor - row that heav'n can - not heal.
"Earth has no sor - row that heav'n can - not cure."
earth has no sor - row but heav'n can re - move.

Text: Thomas Moore, 1779–1852, sts. 1–2; Thomas Hastings, 1784–1872, st. 3
Music: Samuel Webbe Sr., 1740–1816

CONSOLATOR
11 10 11 10

608 Softly and Tenderly Jesus Is Calling

1. Soft - ly and ten - der - ly Je - sus is call - ing, call - ing for
2. Why should we tar - ry when Je - sus is plead - ing, plead - ing for
3. Oh, for the won - der - ful love he has prom - ised, prom - ised for

you and for me. See, on the por - tals he's wait - ing and watch-ing,
you and for me? Why should we lin - ger and heed not his mer - cies,
you and for me! Though we have sinned, he has mer - cy and par - don,

Refrain

watch-ing for you and for me. "Come home, come home!
mer - cies for you and for me? Come home, come home!
par - don for you and for me.

You who are wea - ry, come home." Ear - nest - ly, ten - der - ly,

Je - sus is call - ing, call - ing, "O sin - ner, come home!"

Text: Will L. Thompson, 1847–1909
Music: Will L. Thompson

THOMPSON
11 7 11 7 and refrain

Chief of Sinners Though I Be

1 Chief of sin - ners though I be, Je - sus shed his blood for me,
2 Oh, the height of Je - sus' love! High - er than the heav'ns a - bove,
3 On - ly Je - sus can im - part balm to heal the wound - ed heart,
4 Chief of sin - ners though I be, Christ is all in all to me;
5 O my Sav - ior, help af - ford by your Spir - it and your word!

died that I might live on high, lives that I might nev - er die.
deep - er than the depths of sea, last - ing as e - ter - ni - ty.
peace that flows from sin for - giv'n, joy that lifts the soul to heav'n,
all my wants to him are known, all my sor - rows are his own.
When my way - ward heart would stray, keep me in the nar - row way;

As the branch is to the vine, I am his, and he is mine.
Love that found me—won-drous thought—found me when I sought him not.
faith and hope to walk with God in the way that E - noch trod.
He sus - tains the hid - den life safe with him from earth - ly strife.
grace in time of need sup - ply while I live and when I die.

Text: William McComb, 1793–1870
Music: Richard Redhead, 1820–1901

GETHSEMANE
7 7 7 7 7 7

610   O Christ, the Healer, We Have Come

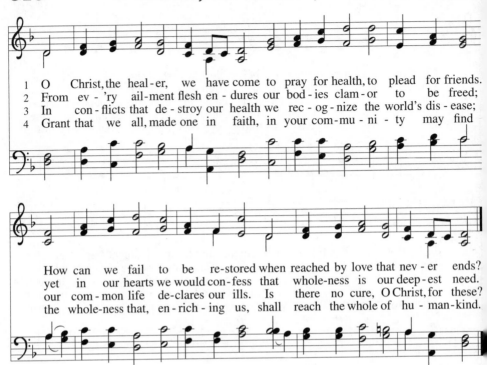

1 O Christ, the heal-er, we have come to pray for health, to plead for friends.
2 From ev-'ry ail-ment flesh en-dures our bod-ies clam-or to be freed;
3 In con-flicts that de-stroy our health we rec-og-nize the world's dis-ease;
4 Grant that we all, made one in faith, in your com-mu-ni-ty may find

How can we fail to be re-stored when reached by love that nev-er ends?
yet in our hearts we would con-fess that whole-ness is our deep-est need.
our com-mon life de-clares our ills. Is there no cure, O Christ, for these?
the whole-ness that, en-rich-ing us, shall reach the whole of hu-man-kind.

Text: Fred Pratt Green, 1903–2000
Music: W. Walker, *Southern Harmony*, 1835
Text © 1969 Hope Publishing Company

DISTRESS
LM

611   I Heard the Voice of Jesus Say

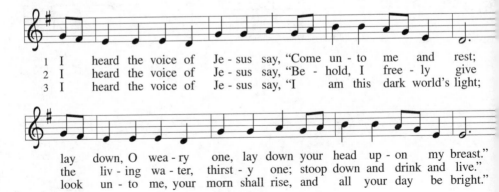

1 I heard the voice of Je-sus say, "Come un-to me and rest;
2 I heard the voice of Je-sus say, "Be-hold, I free-ly give
3 I heard the voice of Je-sus say, "I am this dark world's light;

lay down, O wea-ry one, lay down your head up-on my breast."
the liv-ing wa-ter, thirst-y one; stoop down and drink and live."
look un-to me, your morn shall rise, and all your day be bright."

Text: Horatius Bonar, 1808–1889
Music: English folk tune

KINGSFOLD
CM D

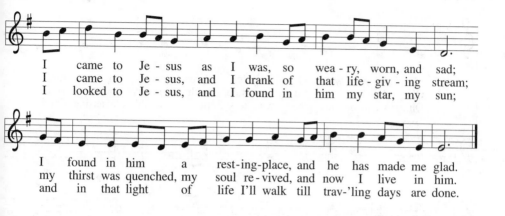

I came to Je - sus as I was, so wea - ry, worn, and sad;
I came to Je - sus, and I drank of that life - giv - ing stream;
I looked to Je - sus, and I found in him my star, my sun;

I found in him a rest-ing-place, and he has made me glad.
my thirst was quenched, my soul re - vived, and now I live in him.
and in that light of life I'll walk till trav-'ling days are done.

Healer of Our Every Ill

612

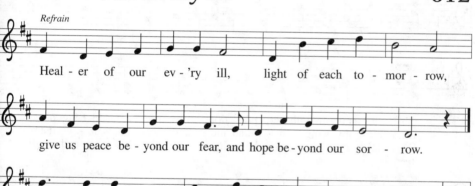

Refrain

Heal - er of our ev - 'ry ill, light of each to - mor - row,

give us peace be - yond our fear, and hope be - yond our sor - row.

1 You who know our fears and sad - ness, grace us with your
2 In the pain and joy be - hold - ing, how your grace is
3 Give us strength to love each oth - er, ev - 'ry sis - ter,
4 You who know each thought and feel - ing, teach us all your

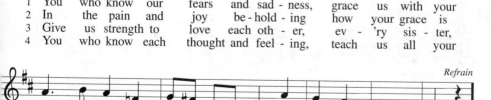

Refrain

peace and glad-ness; Spir-it of all com - fort, fill our hearts.
still un - fold - ing, give us all your vi - sion, God of love.
ev - 'ry broth - er; Spir-it of all kind-ness, be our guide.
way of heal - ing; Spir-it of com-pas - sion, fill each heart.

Text: Marty Haugen, b. 1950
Music: Marty Haugen
Text and music © 1987 GIA Publications, Inc.

HEALER OF OUR EVERY ILL
88 9 and refrain

613

Thy Holy Wings

1 Thy ho-ly wings, O Sav-ior, spread gent-ly o-ver me,
2 Oh, let me nes-tle near thee, with-in thy down-y breast
3 Oh, wash me in the wa-ters of No-ah's cleans-ing flood.

and let me rest se-cure-ly through good and ill in thee.
where I will find sweet com-fort and peace with-in thy nest.
Give me a will-ing spir-it, a heart both clean and good.

Oh, be my strength and por-tion, my rock and hid-ing place,
Oh, close thy wings a-round me and keep me safe-ly there,
Oh, take in-to thy keep-ing thy chil-dren great and small,

and let my ev-'ry mo-ment be lived with-in thy grace.
for I am but a new-born and need thy ten-der care.
and while we sweet-ly slum-ber, en-fold us one and all.

Text: Carolina Sandell Berg, 1832–1903, sts. 1, 3; Gracia Grindal, b. 1943, st. 2; tr. composite
Music: Swedish folk tune; arr. hymnal version
Text © 1983 Gracia Grindal, admin. Selah Publishing Co., Inc.
Arr. © 2006 Augsburg Fortress

BRED DINA VIDA VINGAR
7676D

There Is a Balm in Gilead

Refrain

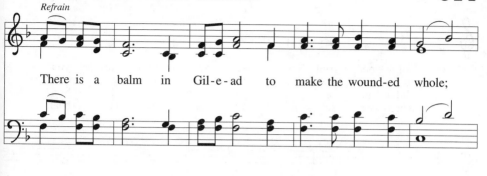

There is a balm in Gil-e-ad to make the wound-ed whole;

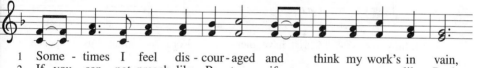

there is a balm in Gil-e-ad to heal the sin-sick soul.

1 Some - times I feel dis - cour-aged and think my work's in vain,
2 If you can - not preach like Pe - ter, if you can - not pray like Paul,
3 Don't ev - er be dis - cour-aged, for Je - sus is your friend;

Refrain

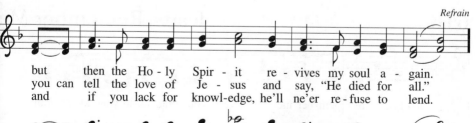

but then the Ho - ly Spir - it re - vives my soul a - gain.
you can tell the love of Je - sus and say, "He died for all."
and if you lack for knowl-edge, he'll ne'er re - fuse to lend.

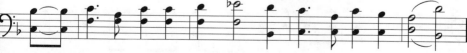

Text: African American spiritual
Music: African American spiritual

BALM IN GILEAD
Irregular

615

In All Our Grief

1 In all our grief and fear we turn to you.
2 Help us to put a - side the an - gry word,
3 You did not e - ven spare your on - ly Son.
4 God, when we suf - fer all that we can bear,

O God, you know all that we think or do,
the clench - ing fist, the wish and will to hurt.
He lived our griefs and bore all e - vil done,
then let us know that you in truth are near

you know the pain we put each oth - er through.
Teach us the way in which love best is served.
but through his cross, re - demp - tion has been won.
and will not leave us lost in all our fear.

Refrain

Lord, have mer - cy, Christ, have mer - cy, Lord, grant us peace.

Text: Sylvia G. Dunstan, 1955–1993
Music: Charles R. Anders, b. 1929
Text © 1991 GIA Publications, Inc.
Music © 1978 *Lutheran Book of Worship*, admin. Augsburg Fortress

FREDERICKTOWN
10 10 10 and refrain

616

Jesus, Remember Me

Je - sus, re - mem - ber me when you come in - to your king - dom.

Text: Luke 23:42; Taizé Community
Music: Jacques Berthier, 1923–1994
Text and music © 1981 Les Presses de Taizé, admin. GIA Publications, Inc.

REMEMBER ME
6 8 6 8

Je-sus, re-mem-ber me when you come in-to your king-dom.

We Come to You for Healing, Lord 617

1 We come to you for heal - ing, Lord, of
2 As once you walked through an - cient streets and
3 You touch us through phy - si - cians' skills, through
4 When nights are long with wake - ful - ness, through
5 We come to you, O lov - ing Lord, in

bod - y, mind, and soul, and pray that by your
reached toward those in pain, come, ris - en Christ, a -
nurs - es' gifts of care, and through the love of
days when strength runs low, grant us your gift of
our dis - tress and pain, in trust that through our

Spir - it's touch we may a - gain be whole.
mong us still with pow'r to heal a - gain.
faith - ful friends who lift our lives in prayer.
pa - tience, Lord, your calm - ing peace to know.
nights and days your grace will heal, sus - tain.

Text: Herman G. Stuempfle Jr., b. 1923
Music: Hugh Wilson, 1764–1824
Text © 2002 GIA Publications, Inc.

MARTYRDOM
CM

618   # Guide Me Ever, Great Redeemer

1 Guide me ev - er, great Re - deem - er, pil - grim through this
2 O - pen now the crys - tal foun - tain where the heal - ing
3 When I tread the verge of Jor - dan, bid my anx - ious

bar - ren land. I am weak, but you are might - y; hold me
wa - ters flow; let the fire and cloud - y pil - lar lead me
fears sub - side; death of death and hell's de - struc - tion, land me

with your pow'r - ful hand. Bread of heav - en, bread of heav - en,
all my jour - ney through. Strong de - liv - 'rer, strong de - liv - 'rer,
safe on Ca - naan's side. Songs and prais - es, songs and prais - es

feed me now and ev - er - more, ev - er - more, feed me now and ev - er - more.
shield me with your might - y arm, might - y arm, shield me with your might - y arm.
I will raise for - ev - er - more, ev - er - more, I will raise for - ev - er - more.

Text: William Williams, 1717–1791; tr. William Williams and Peter Williams, 1722–1796, alt.
Music: John Hughes, 1873–1932

CWM RHONDDA
8 7 8 7 8 7 7

I Know That My Redeemer Lives! 619

1. I know that my Re - deem - er lives! What com - fort
2. He lives tri - um - phant from the grave; he lives e -
3. He lives to grant me rich sup - ply; he lives to
4. He lives to si - lence all my fears; he lives to

this sweet sen - tence gives! He lives, he lives, who
ter - nal - ly to save; he lives ex - alt - ed,
guide me with his eye; he lives to com - fort
wipe a - way my tears; he lives to calm my

once was dead; he lives, my ev - er - liv - ing head!
throned a - bove; he lives to rule his church in love.
me when faint; he lives to hear my soul's com - plaint.
trou - bled heart; he lives all bless - ings to im - part.

5. He lives to bless me with his love;
he lives to plead for me above;
he lives my hungry soul to feed;
he lives to help in time of need.

6. He lives, my kind, wise, heav'nly friend;
he lives and loves me to the end;
he lives, and while he lives, I'll sing;
he lives, my prophet, priest, and king!

7. He lives and grants me daily breath;
he lives, and I shall conquer death;
he lives my mansion to prepare;
he lives to bring me safely there.

8. He lives, all glory to his name!
He lives, my Savior, still the same;
what joy this blest assurance gives:
I know that my Redeemer lives!

Text: Samuel Medley, 1738–1799, alt.
Music: attr. John Hatton, d. 1793

DUKE STREET
LM

620 How Sweet the Name of Jesus Sounds

1 How sweet the name of Je - sus sounds in
2 It makes the wound - ed spir - it whole and
3 Dear name! The rock on which I build, my
4 By thee my prayers ac - cep - tance gain al -

a be - liev - er's ear! It soothes our sor - rows,
calms the heart's un - rest; 'tis man - na to the
shield and hid - ing place; my nev - er - fail - ing
though with sin de - filed. The dev - il charg - es

heals our wounds, and drives a - way all fear.
hun - gry soul and to the wea - ry, rest.
trea - sury, filled with bound - less stores of grace.
me in vain, and I am owned a child.

5 O Jesus, shepherd, guardian, friend,
my prophet, priest, and king,
my Lord, my life, my way, my end,
accept the praise I bring.

6 How weak the effort of my heart,
how cold my warmest thought;
but when I see thee as thou art,
I'll praise thee as I ought.

7 Till then I would thy love proclaim
with every fleeting breath;
and may the music of thy name
refresh my soul in death!

Text: John Newton, 1725–1807, alt.
Music: Alexander R. Reinagle, 1799–1877

ST. PETER
CM

Jesus Lives, My Sure Defense

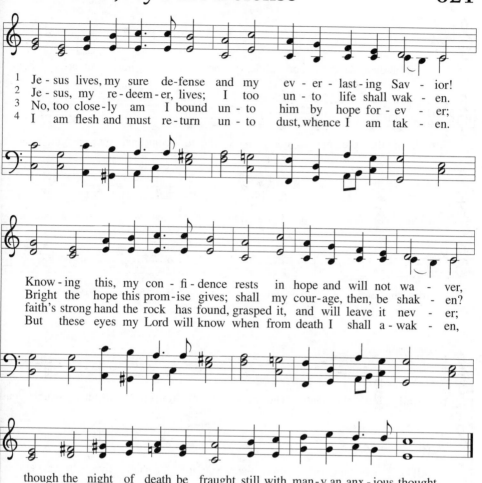

1 Je - sus lives, my sure de-fense and my ev - er - last-ing Sav - ior!
2 Je - sus, my re-deem-er, lives; I too un - to life shall wak - en.
3 No, too close-ly am I bound un - to him by hope for - ev - er;
4 I am flesh and must re-turn un - to dust, whence I am tak - en.

Know - ing this, my con - fi - dence rests in hope and will not wa - ver,
Bright the hope this prom-ise gives; shall my cour-age, then, be shak - en?
faith's strong hand the rock has found, grasped it, and will leave it nev - er;
But these eyes my Lord will know when from death I shall a - wak - en,

though the night of death be fraught still with man-y an anx - ious thought.
Shall I fear then? Can the head rise and leave his mem-bers dead?
e - ven death now can-not part from its Lord the trust - ing heart.
with my Sav - ior to a - bide in his glo - ry, at his side.

5 Then take comfort and rejoice,
  for his people Christ will cherish.
  Fear not, you will hear his voice;
  dying, you will never perish;
  for the very grave is stirred
  when the trumpet's blast is heard.

6 Here on earth, then, let your hearts
  rise from longings vain and hollow.
  Seek what Christ your Lord imparts
  while you in his footsteps follow.
  As you now still wait to rise,
  set your hearts beyond the skies!

Text: Otto von Schwerin, 1616–1679; tr. Catherine Winkworth, 1827–1878, alt.
Music: attr. Johann Crüger, 1598–1662

JESUS, MEINE ZUVERSICHT
787877

622   Neither Death nor Life

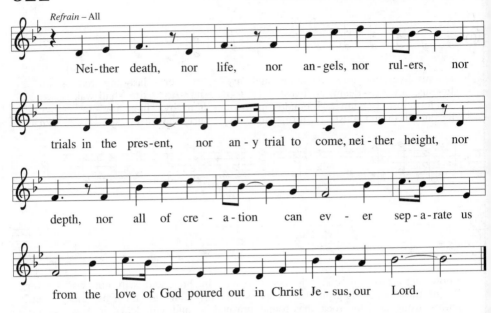

Refrain – All

Nei-ther death, nor life, nor an-gels, nor rul-ers, nor
trials in the pres-ent, nor an-y trial to come, nei-ther height, nor
depth, nor all of cre - a-tion can ev - er sep-a-rate us
from the love of God poured out in Christ Je - sus, our Lord.

Leader or All

1 Dwell in the one who raised Christ from the dead; though your
2 All who are led by the Spir-it shall live as
3 All of the suf - f'ring we now must en - dure is
4 All of cre - a - tion a - waits the new birth, the
5 Who can sep - a - rate us from the love of Christ? Will

Text: Marty Haugen, b. 1950, based on Romans 8
Music: Marty Haugen
Text and music © 2001 by GIA Publications, Inc

NEITHER DEATH NOR LIFE
Irregular

623 Rock of Ages, Cleft for Me

1 Rock of A - ges, cleft for me, let me hide my - self in thee;
2 Not the la - bors of my hands can ful - fill thy law's de - mands;
3 Noth - ing in my hand I bring; sim - ply to thy cross I cling.
4 While I draw this fleet - ing breath, when mine eye - lids close in death,

let the wa - ter and the blood, from thy riv - en side which flowed,
could my zeal no res - pite know, could my tears for - ev - er flow,
Na - ked, come to thee for dress; help - less, look to thee for grace;
when I soar to worlds un - known, see thee on thy judg - ment throne,

be of sin the dou - ble cure; cleanse me from its guilt and pow'r.
all for sin could not a - tone; thou must save, and thou a - lone.
foul, I to the foun - tain fly; wash me, Sav - ior, or I die.
Rock of A - ges, cleft for me, let me hide my - self in thee.

Text: Augustus M. Toplady, 1740–1778
Music: Thomas Hastings, 1784–1872

TOPLADY
777777

Jesus, Still Lead On

1 Je - sus, still lead on, till our rest be won; and, al-though the
2 If the way be drear, if the foe be near, let no faith - less
3 When we seek re - lief from a long-felt grief, when temp-ta - tions
4 Je - sus, still lead on, till our rest be won; heav'n-ly lead - er,

way be cheer - less, we will fol - low, calm and fear - less;
fears o'er - take us, let not faith and hope for - sake us;
come al - lur - ing make us pa - tient and en - dur - ing;
still di - rect us, still sup - port, con - sole, pro - tect us,

guide us by your hand to the prom - ised land.
safe - ly past the foe to our home we go.
show us that bright shore where we weep no more.
till we safe - ly stand in the prom - ised land.

Text: Nicolaus L. von Zinzendorf, 1700–1760; tr. Jane L. Borthwick, 1813–1897, alt.
Music: Adam Drese, 1620–1701

SEELENBRÄUTIGAM
5 5 8 8 5 5

Come, We That Love the Lord

We're Marching to Zion

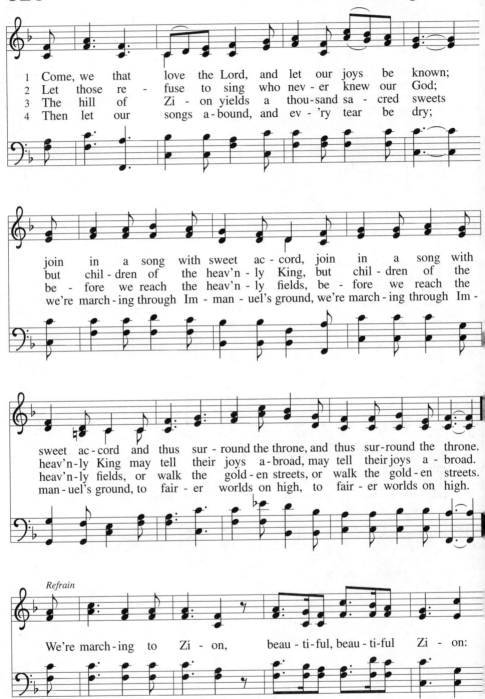

1 Come, we that love the Lord, and let our joys be known;
2 Let those re - fuse to sing who nev - er knew our God;
3 The hill of Zi - on yields a thou-sand sa - cred sweets
4 Then let our songs a-bound, and ev - 'ry tear be dry;

join in a song with sweet ac - cord, join in a song with
but chil - dren of the heav'n - ly King, but chil - dren of the
be - fore we reach the heav'n - ly fields, be - fore we reach the
we're march - ing through Im - man - uel's ground, we're march - ing through Im -

sweet ac - cord and thus sur - round the throne, and thus sur-round the throne.
heav'n - ly King may tell their joys a - broad, may tell their joys a - broad.
heav'n - ly fields, or walk the gold - en streets, or walk the gold - en streets.
man - uel's ground, to fair - er worlds on high, to fair - er worlds on high.

Refrain

We're march - ing to Zi - on, beau - ti-ful, beau - ti-ful Zi - on:

Text: Isaac Watts, 1674–1748, stanzas; Robert Lowry, 1826–1899, refrain
Music: Robert Lowry

MARCHING TO ZION
6 6 8 8 6 6 and refrain

we're march-ing up-ward to Zi - on, the beau-ti-ful cit-y of God.

By Gracious Powers

626

1 By gra - cious pow'rs so won - der - ful - ly shel - tered,
2 Yet is this heart by its old foe tor - ment - ed,
3 And when this cup you give is filled to brim - ming
4 Yet when a - gain in this same world you give us
5 By gra - cious pow'rs so faith - ful - ly pro - tect - ed,

and con - fi - dent - ly wait - ing come what may,
still e - vil days bring bur - dens hard to bear;
with bit - ter suf - f'ring, hard to un - der - stand,
the joy we had, the bright - ness of your sun,
so qui - et - ly, so won - der - ful - ly near,

we know that God is with us night and morn - ing,
oh, give our fright - ened souls the sure sal - va - tion,
we take it thank - ful - ly and with - out trem - bling
we shall re - mem - ber all the days we lived through
we live each day in hope, with you be - side us,

and nev - er fails to greet us each new day.
for which, O Lord, you taught us to pre - pare.
out of so good and so be - loved a hand.
and our whole life shall then be yours a - lone.
and go with you through ev - 'ry com - ing year.

Text: Dietrich Bonhoeffer, 1906–1945; tr. Fred Pratt Green, 1903–2000
Music: Robert Buckley Farlee, b. 1950
Tr. © 1974 Hope Publishing Company
Music © 2006 Augsburg Fortress

TELOS
11 10 11 10

627 O Day Full of Grace

1 O day full of grace that now we see ap-pear-ing on
2 O day full of grace, O bless-ed time, our Lord on the
3 For Christ bore our sins, and not his own, when he on the
4 God came to us then at Pen-te-cost, the Spir-it new
5 When we on that fi-nal jour-ney go that Christ is for

earth's ho-ri - zon, bring light from our God that we may
earth ar-riv - ing; then came to the world that light sub-
cross was hang - ing; and then he a-rose and moved the
life re-veal - ing, that we might no more in death be
us pre-par - ing, we'll gath-er in song, our hearts a-

be a-bun - dant in joy this sea - son. God, shine for us
lime, great joy for us all re-triev - ing; for Je-sus all
stone, that we, un-to him be-long - ing, might join with an-
lost, its pow'r o-ver us dis-pel - ling. This flame will the
glow, all joy of the heav-ens shar - ing, and there we will

now in this dark place; your name on our hearts em-bla - zon.
mor-tals did em-brace, all shame and des-pair re-mov - ing.
gel-ic hosts to raise our voic-es in end-less sing - ing.
mark of sin ef-face and bring to us all true heal - ing.
join God's end-less praise, with an-gels and saints a-dor - ing.

Text: Scandinavian folk hymn; tr. Gerald Thorson, 1921–2001, alt.
Music: Christoph E. F. Weyse, 1774–1842
Text © 1978 Lutheran Book of Worship, admin. Augsburg Fortress

DEN SIGNEDE DAG
989898

Alternate text, stanzas 2–4

2 How blest was that gracious midnight hour,
  when God in our flesh was given;
  then brightened the dawn with light and pow'r
  that spread o'er the darkened heaven;
  then rose o'er the world that Sun divine,
  which gloom from our hearts has driven.

3 Yea, were ev'ry tree endowed with speech,
  and were ev'ry leaflet singing,
  they never with praise God's worth could reach,
  though earth with their praise were ringing.
  Who fully could praise the Light of life
  who light to our souls is bringing?

4 As birds in the morning sing their praise,
  God's fatherly love we cherish,
  for giving to us this day of grace,
  for life that shall never perish.
  The church God has kept two thousand years,
  and hungering souls did nourish.

Text: Scandinavian folk hymn; Nikolai F. S. Grundtvig, 1783–1872; tr. composite

Jerusalem, My Happy Home   **628**

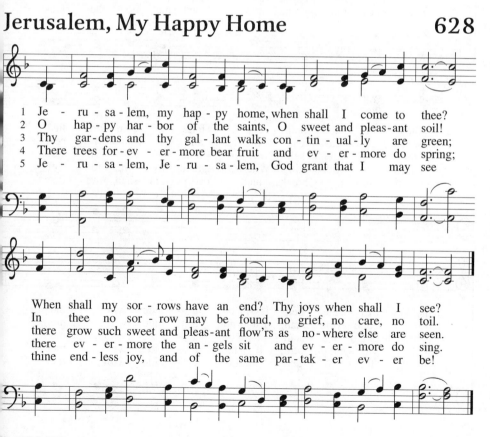

1 Je - ru - sa - lem, my hap - py home, when shall I come to thee?
2 O hap - py har - bor of the saints, O sweet and pleas - ant soil!
3 Thy gar - dens and thy gal - lant walks con - tin - ual - ly are green;
4 There trees for - ev - er - more bear fruit and ev - er - more do spring;
5 Je - ru - sa - lem, Je - ru - sa - lem, God grant that I may see

When shall my sor - rows have an end? Thy joys when shall I see?
In thee no sor - row may be found, no grief, no care, no toil.
there grow such sweet and pleas-ant flow'rs as no - where else are seen.
there ev - er - more the an - gels sit and ev - er - more do sing.
thine end - less joy, and of the same par - tak - er ev - er be!

Text: F. B. P., 16th cent.
Music: North American traditional; arr. hymnal version
Arr. © 2006 Augsburg Fortress

LAND OF REST
CM

629

Abide with Me

1 A - bide with me, fast falls the e - ven - tide.
2 Swift to its close ebbs out life's lit - tle day;
3 I need thy pres - ence ev - 'ry pass - ing hour;
4 I fear no foe, with thee at hand to bless;
5 Hold thou thy cross be - fore my clos - ing eyes,

The dark - ness deep - ens; Lord, with me a - bide.
earth's joys grow dim, its glo - ries pass a - way;
what but thy grace can foil the tempt - er's pow'r?
ills have no weight, and tears no bit - ter - ness.
shine through the gloom, and point me to the skies;

When oth - er help - ers fail and com - forts flee,
change and de - cay in all a - round I see;
Who like thy - self my guide and stay can be?
Where is death's sting? Where, grave, thy vic - to - ry?
heav'n's morn - ing breaks, and earth's vain shad - ows flee;

help of the help - less, oh, a - bide with me.
O thou who chang - est not, a - bide with me.
Through cloud and sun - shine, oh, a - bide with me.
I tri - umph still, if thou a - bide with me!
in life, in death, O Lord, a - bide with me.

Text: Henry F. Lyte, 1793–1847
Music: William H. Monk, 1823–1889

EVENTIDE
10 10 10 10

In Heaven Above

1 In heav'n a - bove, in heav'n a - bove, where God our Fa - ther dwells:
2 In heav'n a - bove, in heav'n a - bove, what glo - ry deep and bright!
3 In heav'n a - bove, in heav'n a - bove, no tears of pain are shed,
4 In heav'n a - bove, in heav'n a - bove, God has a joy pre - pared,

how bound-less there the bless - ed - ness! No tongue its great-ness tells.
The splen - dor of the noon-day sun grows pale be - fore its light.
for noth - ing there can fade or die; life's full - ness round is spread,
which mor - tal ear has nev - er heard, nor mor - tal vi - sion shared,

There face to face, and full and free, the ev - er -
The might - y sun that goes not down, be - fore whose
and like an o - cean, joy o'er - flows, and with im -
which nev - er en - tered mor - tal thought, in mor - tal

liv - ing God we see, our God, the Lord of hosts!
face clouds nev - er frown, is God, the Lord of hosts!
mor - tal mer - cy glows our God, the Lord of hosts!
dreams was nev - er sought, O God, the Lord of hosts!

Text: Laurentius L. Laurinus, 1573–1655; tr. William Maccall, 1812–1888
Music: Norwegian folk tune; arr. Elmer T. R. Hanke, 1901–1958
Arr. © 1942 Augsburg Publishing House

I HIMMELEN, I HIMMELEN
8686886

631 Love Divine, All Loves Excelling

1 Love di - vine, all loves ex - cel - ling, Joy of heav'n, to earth come down! Fix in us thy hum - ble dwell-ing, all thy faith - ful mer - cies crown. Je - sus, thou art all com - pas - sion, pure, un - bound - ed love thou art; vis - it us with

2 Breathe, oh, breathe thy lov - ing Spir - it in - to ev - 'ry trou - bled breast; let us all in thee in - her - it; let us find thy prom-ised rest. Take a - way the love of sin - ning; Al - pha and O - me - ga be; end of faith, as

3 Come, Al - might - y, to de - liv - er; let us all thy life re - ceive; sud - den - ly re - turn, and nev - er, nev - er more thy tem - ples leave. Thee we would be al - ways bless-ing, serve thee as thy hosts a - bove, pray, and praise thee

4 Fin - ish then thy new cre - a - tion, pure and spot - less let us be; let us see thy great sal - va - tion per - fect - ly re - stored in thee! Changed from glo - ry in - to glo - ry, till in heav'n we take our place, till we cast our

Text: Charles Wesley, 1707–1788
Music: Rowland H. Prichard, 1811–1887

HYFRYDOL
8787 D

thy sal - va - tion, en - ter ev - 'ry trem - bling heart.
its be - gin - ning, set our hearts at lib - er - ty.
with - out ceas - ing, glo - ry in thy per - fect love.
crowns be - fore thee, lost in won - der, love, and praise!

O God, Our Help in Ages Past 632

1 O God, our help in a - ges past, our hope for years to come,
2 Un - der the shad - ow of your throne your saints have dwelt se - cure;
3 Be - fore the hills in or - der stood or earth re - ceived its frame,
4 A thou - sand a - ges in your sight are like an eve - ning gone,

our shel - ter from the storm - y blast, and our e - ter - nal home:
suf - fi - cient is your arm a - lone, and our de - fense is sure.
from ev - er - last - ing you are God, to end - less years the same.
short as the watch that ends the night be - fore the ris - ing sun.

5 Time, like an ever-rolling stream,
bears all our years away;
they fly forgotten, as a dream
dies at the op'ning day.

6 O God, our help in ages past,
our hope for years to come,
still be our guard while troubles last
and our eternal home.

Text: Isaac Watts, 1674–1748, alt.
Music: William Croft, 1678–1727

ST. ANNE
CM

633

We've Come This Far by Faith

Refrain – All

We've come this far by faith, lean-ing on the Lord;

trust-ing in his ho-ly word, he's nev-er failed us yet.

Oh, can't turn a-round, we've come this

far by faith. We've come this far by faith.

Leader
1 Just remember
the good things God has done,
things that seemed impossible;
oh, praise him for the vict'ries he has won.
Oh! *Refrain*

Leader
2 Don't be discouraged
with trouble in your life;
he'll bear your burdens,
and move all the discord and strife.
Oh! *Refrain*

Text: Albert A. Goodson, 1883–1947
Music: Albert A. Goodson
Text and music © 1965, ren. 1993 Manna Music, Inc

THIS FAR BY FAITH
Irregular

All Hail the Power of Jesus' Name! 634

1 All hail the pow'r of Je - sus' name! Let an - gels pros - trate fall;
2 O seed of Is - rael's cho - sen race now ran - somed from the fall,
3 Hail him, you heirs of Da - vid's line, whom Da - vid Lord did call—
4 Sin - ners, whose love can ne'er for - get the worm-wood and the gall,

bring forth the roy - al di - a - dem and crown him Lord of all.
hail him who saves you by his grace and crown him Lord of all.
the God in - car - nate, man di - vine—and crown him Lord of all.
go spread your tro - phies at his feet and crown him Lord of all.

Bring forth the roy - al di - a - dem and crown him Lord of all.
Hail him who saves you by his grace and crown him Lord of all.
The God in - car - nate, man di - vine—and crown him Lord of all.
Go spread your tro - phies at his feet and crown him Lord of all.

5 Let ev'ry kindred, ev'ry tribe
on this terrestrial ball
to him all majesty ascribe
and crown him Lord of all.

6 Oh, that with yonder sacred throng
we at his feet may fall!
We'll join the everlasting song
and crown him Lord of all.

Text: Edward Perronet, 1726–1792, sts. 1–4; J. Rippon, A Selection of Hymns, 1787, sts. 5–6
Music: Oliver Holden, 1765–1844

CORONATION
868686

635   We Walk by Faith

1. We walk by faith and not by sight; with
2. We may not touch your hands and side, nor
3. Help then, O Lord, our un - be - lief; and
4. For you, O res - ur - rec - ted Lord, are
5. And when our life of faith is done, in

gra - cious words draw near,   O Christ, who spoke as
fol - low where you trod;   but in your prom - ise
may our faith a - bound   to call on you when
found in means di - vine: be - neath the wa - ter
realms of clear - er light   may we be - hold you

none e'er spoke: "My peace be with you here."
we re - joice, and cry, "My Lord and God!"
you are near and seek where you are found:
and the word, be - neath the bread and wine.
as you are, with full and end - less sight.

Text: Henry Alford, 1810–1871, alt.
Music: Marty Haugen, b. 1950
Music © 1984 GIA Publications, Inc.

SHANTI
CM

636   How Small Our Span of Life

1. How small our span of life, O God, our years from birth till death:
2. And yet our speck of life is spanned by your in - fin - i - ty;
3. O Christ, you left e - ter - ni - ty to plunge in time's swift stream,
4. We thank you, God, for kind - ling faith that lights our tran - sient years,

a sin - gle beat with - in the heart, the catch-ing of a breath,
our tick of time on earth is caught in your e - ter - ni - ty.
to share the short-ness of our span, our mor - tal lives re - deem.
il - lu - min - ing our pil-grim-age through mists of doubt and fears;

Text: Herman G. Stuempfle Jr., b. 1923
Music: English traditional
Text © 1993 GIA Publications, Inc.

KINGSFOLD
CMD

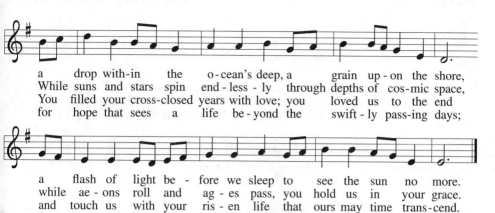

a   drop with-in   the   o-cean's deep, a   grain up-on the shore,
While   suns and stars spin   end-less-ly   through depths of cos-mic space,
You   filled your cross-closed years with love; you   loved us to the end
for   hope that sees   a   life be-yond the   swift-ly pass-ing days;

a   flash of   light be - fore we sleep to   see the sun   no more.
while   ae - ons roll   and   ag - es pass, you hold us in   your grace.
and   touch us with your   ris - en life that ours may time trans-cend.
for   love, both hu - man and di - vine, that lifts our hearts to praise.

Holy God, Holy and Glorious 637

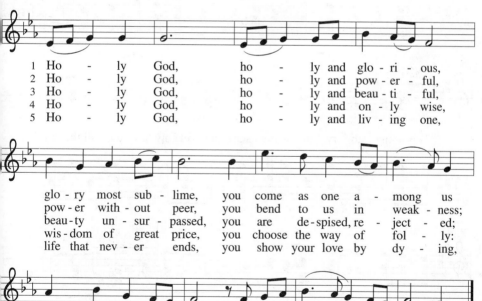

1 Ho - ly   God,   ho - ly and glo - ri - ous,
2 Ho - ly   God,   ho - ly and pow - er - ful,
3 Ho - ly   God,   ho - ly and beau - ti - ful,
4 Ho - ly   God,   ho - ly and on - ly   wise,
5 Ho - ly   God,   ho - ly and liv - ing one,

glo - ry most sub - lime,   you come as one a - mong us
pow - er with - out peer,   you bend to us in weak - ness;
beau - ty un - sur - passed, you are   de - spised, re - ject - ed;
wis - dom of   great price,   you choose the way of fol - ly:
life that nev - er   ends,   you show your love by dy - ing,

in - to hu - man time,   and we be - hold   your glo - ry.
emp - tied, you draw near,   and we be - hold   your pow - er.
scorned, you hold us fast, and we be - hold   your beau - ty.
God   the cru - ci - fied, and we be - hold   your wis - dom.
dy - ing for your friends, and we be - hold   you liv - ing.

Text: Susan R. Briehl, b. 1952
Music: Robert Buckley Farlee, b. 1950
Text © 2002 GIA Publications, Inc.
Music © 2001 Robert Buckley Farlee, admin. Augsburg Fortress

NELSON
95757

638

Blessed Assurance

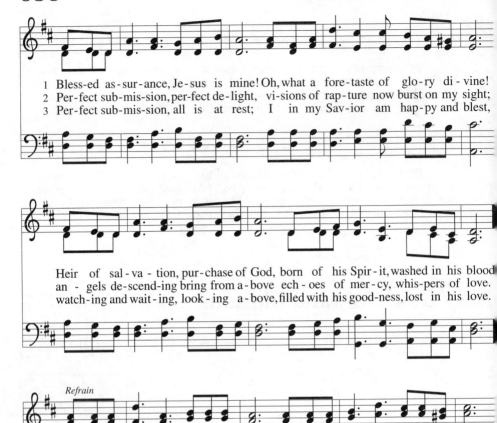

1 Bless-ed as-sur-ance, Je-sus is mine! Oh, what a fore-taste of glo-ry di-vine!
2 Per-fect sub-mis-sion, per-fect de-light, vi-sions of rap-ture now burst on my sight;
3 Per-fect sub-mis-sion, all is at rest; I in my Sav-ior am hap-py and blest,

Heir of sal-va-tion, pur-chase of God, born of his Spir-it, washed in his blood
an - gels de-scend-ing bring from a-bove ech - oes of mer-cy, whis-pers of love.
watch-ing and wait-ing, look-ing a-bove, filled with his good-ness, lost in his love.

Refrain

This is my sto - ry, this is my song, prais-ing my Sav - ior all the day long:

this is my sto - ry, this is my song, prais-ing my Sav - ior all the day long.

Text: Fanny J. Crosby, 1820–1915
Music: Phoebe P. Knapp, 1830–1908

ASSURANCE
9 10 9 9 and refrain

When We Are Living

Pues si vivimos

1 *Pues si vi - vi - mos,*   *pa - ra él vi - vi - mos,*
1 When we are liv - ing,   it is in Christ Je - sus,
2 'Mid times of sor - row   and in times of pain,. . . .
3 A - cross this wide world,   we shall al - ways find . . . .

y si mo - ri - mos   *pa - ra él mo - ri - mos.*
and when we're dy - ing,   it is in the Lord. . . .
when sens - ing beau - ty   or in love's em - brace, . . .
those who are cry - ing   with no peace of mind; . . .

Sea que vi - va - mos   *o que mu - ra - mos,*
Both in our liv - ing   and in our dy - ing,
wheth - er we suf - fer,   or sing re - joic - ing,
and when we help them,   or when we feed them,

so - mos del Se - ñor,   *so - mos del Se - ñor.*
we be - long to God,   we be - long to God.
we be - long to God,   we be - long to God.
we be - long to God,   we be - long to God.

2   *En la tristeza y en el dolor,*
   en la belleza y en el amor,
   sea que suframos o que gocemos,
   somos del Señor, somos del Señor.

3   *En este mundo por doquier habrá*
   gente que llora y sin consolar.
   Sea que_ayudemos o que_alimentemos,
   somos del Señor, somos del Señor.

Text: st. 1, based on Romans 14:8; tr. Elise S. Eslinger, b. 1942;
   st. 2–3, Roberto Escamilla, b. 1931; tr. George Lockwood, b. 1946
Music: Spanish traditional
Spanish text, sts. 2–3 © 1983 Abingdon Press and tr. © 1989 The United Methodist Publishing House, admin. The Copyright Company

SOMOS DEL SEÑOR
Irregular

640

Our Father, by Whose Name

1 Our Father, by whose name all par-ent-hood is known,
2 O Christ, your-self a child with-in an earth-ly home,
3 O Ho-ly Spir-it, bind our hearts in u-ni-ty

in love di-vine you claim each fam-'ly as your own.
with heart still un-de-filed to full a-dult-hood come:
and teach us how to find the love from self set free;

Bless moth-ers, fa-thers, guard-ing well, with con-stant love as
our chil-dren bless in ev-'ry place that they may all be-
in all our hearts such love in-crease that ev-'ry home, by

sen-ti-nel, the homes in which your peo-ple dwell.
hold your face and, know-ing you, may grow in grace.
this re-lease, may be the dwell-ing place of peace.

Text: F. Bland Tucker, 1895–1984, alt.
Music: John D. Edwards, 1806–1885
Text © Church Pension Fund

RHOSYMEDRE
6 6 6 6 888

All Are Welcome

641

1 Let us build a house where love can dwell and all can safe-ly
2 Let us build a house where proph-ets speak, and words are strong and
3 Let us build a house where love is found in wa - ter, wine and
4 Let us build a house where hands will reach be - yond the wood and
5 Let us build a house where all are named, their songs and vi - sions

live, a place where saints and chil - dren tell how
true, where all God's chil - dren dare to seek to
wheat: a ban - quet hall on ho - ly ground where
stone to heal and strength - en, serve and teach, and
heard and loved and trea - sured, taught and claimed as

hearts learn to for - give. Built of hopes and dreams and
dream God's reign a - new. Here the cross shall stand as
peace and jus - tice meet. Here the love of God, through
live the Word they've known. Here the out - cast and the
words with - in the Word. Built of tears and cries and

vi - sions, rock of faith and vault of grace; here the love of
wit - ness and as sym - bol of God's grace; here as one we
Je - sus, is re - vealed in time and space; as we share in
strang-er bear the im - age of God's face; let us bring an
laugh-ter, prayers of faith and songs of grace, let this house pro -

Refrain

Christ shall end di - vi - sions:
claim the faith of Je - sus:
Christ the feast that frees us: All   are wel - come,
end to fear and dan - ger:
claim from floor to raf - ter:

all are wel - come, all are wel - come in this place.

Text: Marty Haugen, b. 1950
Music: Marty Haugen
Text and music © 1994 GIA Publications, Inc.

TWO OAKS
9 6 8 6 8 7 10 and refrain

Ubi caritas et amor
Where True Charity and Love Abide

642

U - bi ca - ri - tas et a - mor,
Where true char - i - ty and love a - bide,

u - bi ca - ri - tas, De - us i - bi est.
God is dwell - ing there; God is dwell - ing there.

Text: Latin antiphon, 9th cent.; Taizé Community; tr. *With One Voice*
Music: Jacques Berthier, 1923–1994
Text and music © 1979 Les Presses de Taizé, admin. GIA Publications, Inc.
Tr. © 1995 Augsburg Fortress

TAIZÉ UBI CARITAS
Irregular

We Are All One in Christ
Somos uno en Cristo

643

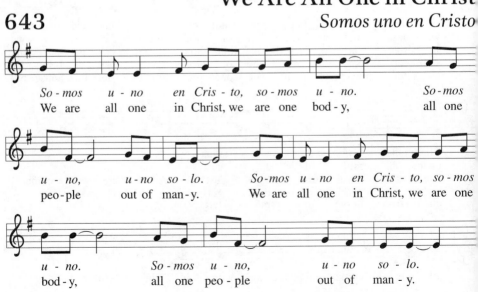

So - mos u - no en Cris - to, so - mos u - no. *So - mos*
We are all one in Christ, we are one bod - y, all one

u - no, u - no so - lo. So - mos u - no en Cris - to, so - mos
peo - ple out of man - y. We are all one in Christ, we are one

u - no. So - mos u - no, u - no so - lo.
bod - y, all one peo - ple out of man - y.

Text: Anonymous; tr. Gerhard M. Cartford, b. 1923
Music: Anonymous
English text © 1998 Augsburg Fortress

SOMOS UNO
PM

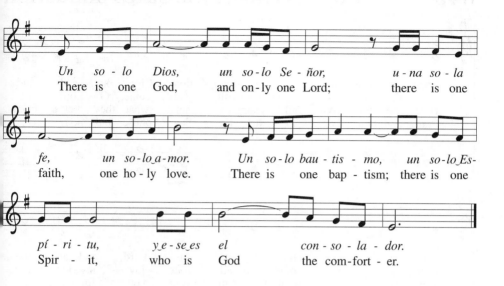

Un so - lo Dios, un so - lo Se - ñor, u - na so - la
There is one God, and on - ly one Lord; there is one

fe, un so - lo_a - mor. Un so - lo bau - tis - mo, un so - lo_Es -
faith, one ho - ly love. There is one bap - tism; there is one

pí - ri - tu, y_e - se_es el con - so - la - dor.
Spir - it, who is God the com - fort - er.

Although I Speak with Angel's Tongue   644

1 Al - though I speak with an - gel's tongue, my faith, my
2 For love is pa - tient, love is kind, and nev - er
3 For now we peer at dark - ened glass; our vi - sions
4 The gifts are man - y, the Bod - y one, and in - to

knowl - edge all sur - pass, but have no love, my gifts are
vain with boast - ing pride; love bears all things, all things en -
end; our tongues all cease. In part we know, in part now
one are all bap - tized. Be - lov - ed, share one heart, one

vain as clang - ing gong or blar - ing brass.
dures. All things must end; love will a - bide.
see: then we will see love face to face.
mind, one hope, one faith, one love in Christ.

Text: Andrew Donaldson, b. 1951
Music: English traditional
Text © 1995 Andrew Donaldson

O WALY WALY
LM

645   Christ Is Made the Sure Foundation

1 Christ is made the sure foun-da - tion, Christ, our head and
2 To this tem - ple, where we call you, come, O Lord of
3 Here be-stow on all your ser - vants what they seek from
4 Praise and hon - or to the Fa - ther, praise and hon - or

cor - ner - stone, cho - sen of the Lord and pre - cious,
hosts, and stay; come with all your lov - ing-kind - ness,
you to gain; what they gain from you, for - ev - er
to the Son, praise and hon - or to the Spir - it,

bind - ing all the church in one; ho - ly Zi - on's
hear your peo - ple as they pray; and your full - est
with the bless - ed to re - tain; and here - af - ter
ev - er three and ev - er one: one in might and

help for - ev - er and our con - fi - dence a - lone.
ben - e - dic - tion shed with-in these walls to - day.
in your glo - ry ev - er-more with you to reign.
one in glo - ry while un-end - ing a - ges run!

Text: Latin hymn, c. 7th cent.; tr. John Mason Neale, 1818–1866, alt.
Music: Henry Purcell, 1659–1695; arr. Ernest Hawkins, 1802–1868

WESTMINSTER ABBE
87 87 8 7

The Peace of the Lord
La paz del Señor

1 La paz del Se - ñor, la paz del Se - ñor, la
1 The peace of the Lord, the peace of the Lord, the
2 The peace of the Lord, the peace of the Lord, the
3 The peace of the Lord, the peace of the Lord, the

paz del Re - su - ci - ta - do: la paz del Se -
peace of the ris - en Lord Je - sus: the peace of the
peace of the ris - en Lord Je - sus: the peace of the
peace of the ris - en Lord Je - sus: the peace of the

ñor a ti y_a mí, a to - dos al - can - za -
Lord is for you and for me, and al - so for all of God's
Lord is a - mong us right now, so o - pen your - selves to re -
Lord kept with - in can - not live, so o - pen your - selves now to

rá; la paz del Se - ñor a ti y_a
chil - dren. The peace of the Lord is for you and for
ceive it. The peace of the Lord is a - mong us right
share it. The peace of the Lord kept with - in can - not

mí, a to - dos al - can - za - rá.
me, and al - so for all of God's chil - dren.
now, so o - pen your - selves to re - ceive it.
live, so o - pen your - selves now to share it.

2 La paz del Señor, la paz del Señor,
la paz del Resucitado:
se hace presente_ahora_y_aquí
apréstate_a recibirla;
se hace presente ahora_y_aquí
apréstate_a recibirla.

3 La paz del Señor, la paz del Señor,
la paz del Resucitado:
no puede vivir encerrada_en sí,
apréstate_a compartirla;
no puede vivir encerrada_en sí,
apréstate_a compartirla.

Text: Anders Ruuth; tr. Gerhard M. Cartford, b. 1923
Music: Anders Ruuth
Spanish text and music © Anders Ruuth
English text © Lutheran World Federation

LA PAZ DEL SEÑOR
10 9 11 9 11 9

647 Glorious Things of You Are Spoken

1 Glo - rious things of you are spo - ken, Zi - on, cit - y
2 See, the streams of liv - ing wa - ters, spring - ing from e -
3 Round each hab - i - ta - tion hov - 'ring, see the cloud and
4 Sav - ior, since of Zi - on's cit - y I through grace a

of our God! He whose word can - not be bro - ken
ter - nal love, well sup - ply your sons and daugh - ters,
fire ap - pear for a glo - ry and a cov - 'ring,
mem - ber am, let the world de - ride or pit - y,

formed you for his own a - bode. On the Rock of A - ges
and all fear of want re - move. Who can faint, while such a
show - ing that the Lord is near. Thus de - riv - ing from their
I will glo - ry in your name. Fad - ing are the world's vain

found - ed, what can shake your sure re - pose? With sal -
riv - er ev - er will their thirst as - suage? Grace which,
ban - ner light by night and shade by day, safe they
plea - sures, all their boast - ed pomp and show; sol - id

Text: John Newton, 1725–1807, alt.
Music: William P. Rowlands, 1860–1937

BLAENWERN
87 87 D

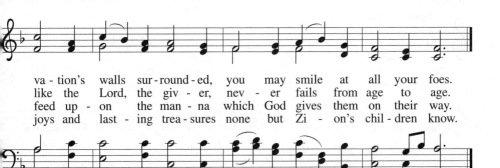

va - tion's walls sur - round - ed, you may smile at all your foes.
like the Lord, the giv - er, nev - er fails from age to age.
feed up - on the man - na which God gives them on their way.
joys and last - ing trea - sures none but Zi - on's chil - dren know.

Beloved, God's Chosen 648

1 Be - lov - ed, God's cho - sen, put on as a gar - ment
2 With - in, call forth Wis - dom, to dwell in you rich - ly;
3 Be - lov - ed, God's cho - sen, put on as a gar - ment

com - pas - sion, for - give - ness, and good - ness of heart.
let peace rule your hearts and that peace be of Christ.
com - pas - sion, for - give - ness, and good - ness of heart.

A - bove all, be - fore all, let love be your rai - ment
And from the heart's cham - ber, be - lov - ed and ho - ly,
A - bove all, be - fore all, let love be your rai - ment

that binds in - to one ev - 'ry dis - so - nant part.
let sing - ing thanks - giv - ing to God ev - er rise.
that binds in - to one ev - 'ry dis - so - nant part.

Text: Susan Palo Cherwien, b. 1953
Music: Robert A. Hobby, b. 1962
Text © 1994 Susan Palo Cherwien, admin. Augsburg Fortress
Music © 1997 Augsburg Fortress

ANDREW'S SONG
12 11 12 11

Behold, How Pleasant
Miren qué bueno

649

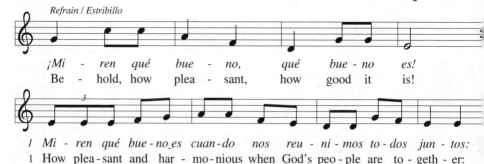

Refrain / Estribillo

¡Mi - ren qué bue - no, qué bue - no es!
Be - hold, how plea - sant, how good it is!

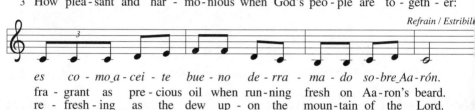

1 Mi - ren qué bue - no_es cuan-do nos reu - ni - mos to - dos jun - tos:
1 How plea - sant and har - mo - nious when God's peo - ple are to - geth - er:
2 How plea - sant and har - mo - nious when God's peo - ple are to - geth - er:
3 How plea - sant and har - mo - nious when God's peo - ple are to - geth - er:

Refrain / Estribillo

es co - mo_a - cei - te bue - no de - rra - ma - do so-bre_Aa - rón.
fra - grant as pre - cious oil when run - ning fresh on Aa - ron's beard.
re - fresh - ing as the dew up - on the moun-tain of the Lord.
there the Lord God be - stows a bless-ing— life for - ev - er - more.

2 *Miren qué bueno_es cuando*
nos reunimos todos juntos:
se parace_al rocío
sobre los montes de Sión. Estribillo

3 *Miren qué bueno_es cuando*
nos reunimos todos juntos:
porque_el Señor nos manda
vida_eterna_y bendición. Estribillo

Text: Pablo Sosa, b. 1933, based on Psalm 133
Music: Pablo Sosa
Text and music © Pablo Sosa

MIREN QUÉ BUENO
15 14 and refrain

650

In Christ There Is No East or West

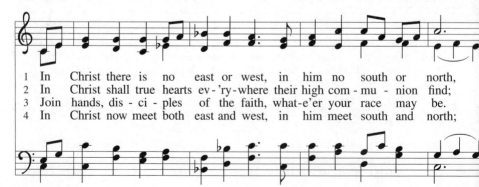

1 In Christ there is no east or west, in him no south or north,
2 In Christ shall true hearts ev - 'ry - where their high com - mu - nion find;
3 Join hands, dis - ci - ples of the faith, what-e'er your race may be.
4 In Christ now meet both east and west, in him meet south and north;

Text: John Oxenham, 1852–1941, alt.
Music: African American spiritual; adapt. Harry T. Burleigh, 1866–1949

MCKEE
CM

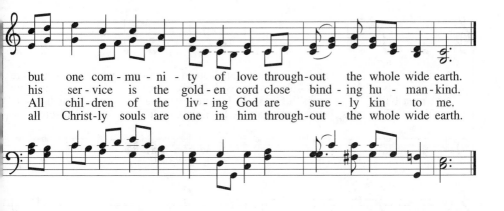

but one com-mu-ni-ty of love through-out the whole wide earth.
his ser-vice is the gold-en cord close bind-ing hu-man-kind.
All chil-dren of the liv-ing God are sure-ly kin to me.
all Christ-ly souls are one in him through-out the whole wide earth.

Oh, Praise the Gracious Power 651

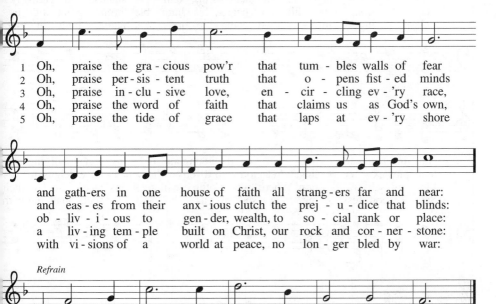

1 Oh, praise the gra-cious pow'r that tum-bles walls of fear
2 Oh, praise per-sis-tent truth that o-pens fist-ed minds
3 Oh, praise in-clu-sive love, en-cir-cling ev-'ry race,
4 Oh, praise the word of faith that claims us as God's own,
5 Oh, praise the tide of grace that laps at ev-'ry shore

and gath-ers in one house of faith all strang-ers far and near:
and eas-es from their anx-ious clutch the prej-u-dice that blinds:
ob-liv-i-ous to gen-der, wealth, to so-cial rank or place:
a liv-ing tem-ple built on Christ, our rock and cor-ner-stone:
with vi-sions of a world at peace, no lon-ger bled by war:

Refrain

We praise you, Christ! Your cross has made us one!

6 Oh, praise the pow'r, the truth,
the love, the word, the tide.
Yet more than these, oh, praise their source,
praise Christ the crucified: *Refrain*

7 Oh, praise the living Christ
with faith's bright songful voice!
Announce the gospel to the world
and with these words rejoice: *Refrain*

Text: Thomas H. Troeger, b. 1945
Music: Carol Doran, b. 1936
Text and music © 1984 Oxford University Press, Inc.

CHRISTPRAISE RAY
SM and refrain

652

Built on a Rock

1 Built on a rock the church shall stand, e - ven when stee-ples are
2 Sure - ly, in tem - ples made with hands God the Most High is not
3 Christ builds a house of liv - ing stones: we are his own hab - i -
4 Yet in this house, an earth - ly frame, Je - sus the chil-dren is

fall - ing; crum-bled have spires in ev - 'ry land, bells still are
dwell - ing— high in the heav'ns his tem - ple stands, all earth - ly
ta - tion; he fills our hearts, his hum - ble thrones, grant-ing us
bless - ing; hith - er we come to praise his name, faith in our

chim-ing and call - ing— call - ing the young and old to rest, call-ing the
tem - ples ex - cel - ling. Yet God who dwells in heav'n a - bove deigns to a -
life and sal - va - tion. Where two or three will seek his face, he in their
Sav - ior con-fess - ing. Je - sus to us his Spir - it sent, mak-ing with

souls of those dis - tressed, long - ing for life ev - er - last - ing.
bide with us in love, mak - ing our bod - ies his tem - ple.
midst will show his grace, bless-ings up - on them be - stow - ing.
us his cov - e - nant, grant-ing his chil-dren the king - dom.

Text: Nikolai F. S. Grundtvig, 1783–1872; tr. Carl Doving, 1867–1937, adapt.
Music: Ludvig M. Lindeman, 1812–1887
Text © 1958 *Service Book and Hymnal*, admin. Augsburg Fortress

KIRKEN DEN ER ET GAMMELT HUS
8888888

5   Through all the passing years, O Lord,
    grant that, when church bells are ringing,
    many may come to hear your Word,
    who here this promise is bringing:
    "I know my own, my own know me;
    you, not the world, my face shall see;
    my peace I leave with you. Amen."

Where True Charity and Love Abide
Ubi caritas et amor

653

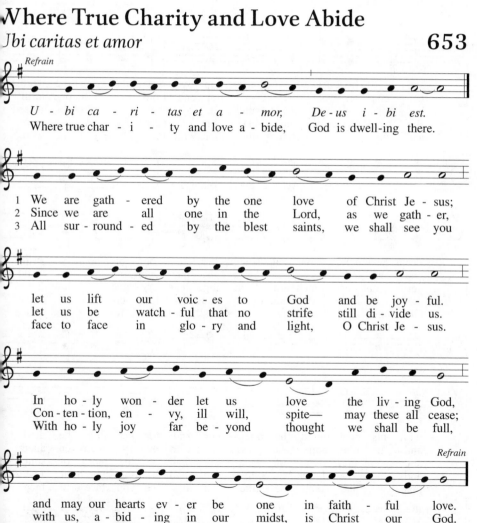

Refrain

U - bi ca - ri - tas et a - mor,   De - us i - bi est.
Where true char - i - ty and love a - bide,   God is dwell-ing there.

1 We   are gath - ered   by the one   love   of Christ Je - sus;
2 Since we are   all   one in the   Lord, as we gath - er,
3 All sur - round - ed by the blest saints, we shall see you

let us lift   our   voic - es   to   God   and be joy - ful.
let us be   watch - ful that no   strife still di - vide us.
face to face   in   glo - ry and   light, O Christ Je - sus.

In   ho - ly won - der let us   love   the liv - ing God,
Con - ten - tion, en - vy, ill will,   spite— may these all cease;
With ho - ly joy   far be - yond thought we shall be full,

Refrain

and may our hearts ev - er be   one   in faith - ful love.
with us, a - bid - ing in our midst, is Christ our God.
from age to age, world with - out end, for - ev - er - more.

Text: Latin, 9th cent.; tr. composite
Music: Plainsong mode VI
Text © 1995, 2001 Augsburg Fortress

UBI CARITAS
12 12 12 12 and refrain

654

The Church's One Foundation

1 The church's one foun - da - tion is Je - sus Christ, her Lord;
2 E - lect from ev - 'ry na - tion, yet one o'er all the earth,
3 Though with a scorn - ful won - der this world sees her op - pressed,
4 Through toil and trib - u - la - tion and tu - mult of her war,
5 Yet she on earth has u - nion with God, the Three in One,

she is his new cre - a - tion by wa - ter and the word.
her char - ter of sal - va - tion one Lord, one faith, one birth:
by schisms . . rent a - sund - er, by her - e - sies dis - tressed,
she waits the con - sum - ma - tion of peace for - ev - er - more;
and mys - tic sweet com - mu - nion with those whose rest is won.

From heav'n he came and sought her to be his ho - ly bride;
one ho - ly name she bless - es, par - takes one ho - ly food,
yet saints their watch are keep - ing; their cry goes up: "How long?"
till with the vi - sion glo - rious her long - ing eyes are blest,
Oh, bless - ed heav'n-ly cho - rus! Lord, save us by your grace,

with his own blood he bought her, and for her life he died.
and to one hope she press - es with ev - 'ry grace en - dued.
and soon the night of weep - ing shall be the morn of song.
and the great church vic - to - rious shall be the church at rest.
that we, like saints be - fore us, may see you face to face.

Text: Samuel J. Stone, 1839–1900
Music: Samuel S. Wesley, 1810–1876

AUREL
7676

Son of God, Eternal Savior

655

1 Son of God, e - ter - nal Sav - ior, source of life and truth and grace,
2 As you, Lord, have lived for oth - ers, so may we for oth - ers live.
3 Come, O Christ, and reign a - mong us, King of love and Prince of peace;
4 Son of God, e - ter - nal Sav - ior, source of life and truth and grace,

Word made flesh, whose birth a - mong us hal - lows all our hu - man race,
Free - ly have your gifts been grant - ed; free - ly may your ser - vants give.
hush the storm of strife and pas - sion, bid its cru - el dis - cords cease.
Word made flesh, whose birth a - mong us hal - lows all our hu - man race:

you our head, who, throned in glo - ry, for your own will ev - er plead:
Yours the gold and yours the sil - ver, yours the wealth of land and sea;
By your pa - tient years of toil - ing, by your si - lent hours of pain,
by your pray - ing, by your will - ing that your peo - ple should be one,

fill us with your love and pit - y, heal our wrong, and help our need.
we but stew - ards of your boun - ty held in sol - emn trust will be.
quench our fe - vered thirst of plea - sure, stem our self - ish greed of gain.
grant, oh, grant our hope's fru - i - tion: here on earth your will be done.

Text: Somerset C. Lowry, 1855–1932
Music: *Oude en Nieuwe Hollantse Boerenlities en Contradansen*, 1710; arr. Julius Röntgen, 1855–1932

IN BABILONE
8787D

656   Blest Be the Tie That Binds

1 Blest be the tie that binds our hearts in Chris - tian love;
2 Be - fore our Fa - ther's throne we pour our ar - dent prayers;
3 We share our mu - tual woes, our mu - tual bur - dens bear,
4 From sor - row, toil, and pain, and sin we shall be free;

the u - ni - ty of heart and mind is like to that a - bove.
our fears, our hopes, our aims are one, our com - forts and our cares.
and of - ten for each oth - er flows the sym - pa - thiz - ing tear.
and per - fect love and friend - ship reign through all e - ter - ni - ty.

Text: John Fawcett, 1740–1817, alt.
Music: Johann G. Nägeli, 1773–1836, adapt.

DENNIS
SM

657   Rise, O Sun of Righteousness

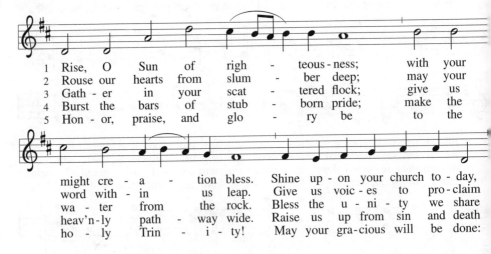

1 Rise, O Sun of righ - teous - ness; with your
2 Rouse our hearts from slum - ber deep; may your
3 Gath - er in your scat - tered flock; give us
4 Burst the bars of stub - born pride; make the
5 Hon - or, praise, and glo - ry be to the

might cre - a - tion bless. Shine up - on your church to - day,
word with - in us leap. Give us voic - es to pro - claim
wa - ter from the rock. Bless the u - ni - ty we share
heav'n - ly path - way wide. Raise us up from sin and death
ho - ly Trin - i - ty! May your gra - cious will be done:

Text: Christian David, et al.; tr. Frank W. Stoldt, b. 1958
Music: Bohemian Brethren, *Kirchengeseng*, 1566
Text © 2003 Augsburg Fortress

SONNE DER GERECHTIGKEIT
7 7 7 7

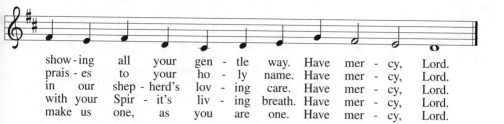

show - ing all your gen - tle way. Have mer - cy, Lord.
prais - es to your ho - ly name. Have mer - cy, Lord.
in our shep - herd's lov - ing care. Have mer - cy, Lord.
with your Spir - it's liv - ing breath. Have mer - cy, Lord.
make us one, as you are one. Have mer - cy, Lord.

O Jesus, Joy of Loving Hearts 658

1 O Je - sus, joy of lov - ing hearts, the fount of
2 We taste you, ev - er - liv - ing bread, and long to
3 For you our rest - less spir - its yearn, wher - e'er our
4 O Je - sus, ev - er with us stay! Make all our

life, the light of all: from ev - 'ry bliss that earth im -
feast up - on you still; we drink of you, the foun - tain -
chang - ing lot is cast; glad, when your smile on us you
mo - ments fair and bright! Oh, chase the night of sin a -

parts we turn, un - filled, to hear your call.
head; our thirst - ing souls from you we fill.
turn, blest, when by faith we hold you fast.
way! Shed o'er the world your ho - ly light.

Text: attr. Bernard of Clairvaux, 1091–1153; tr. Ray Palmer, 1808–1887, alt.
Music: W. Gardiner, *Sacred Melodies*, 1815

WALTON
LM

659 Will You Let Me Be Your Servant

1 Will you let me be your ser-vant, let me be as
2 We are pil-grims on a jour-ney, we are trav-'lers
3 I will hold the Christ-light for you in the night-time
4 I will weep when you are weep-ing; when you laugh I'll
5 Will you let me be your ser-vant, let me be as

Christ to you? Pray that I may have the grace to
on the road; we are here to help each oth-er
of your fear; I will hold my hand out to you,
laugh with you. I will share your joy and sor-row
Christ to you? Pray that I may have the grace to

let you be my ser - vant, too.
walk the mile and bear the load.
speak the peace you long to hear.
till we've seen this jour - ney through.
let you be my ser - vant, too.

Text: Richard Gillard, b. 1953
Music: Richard Gillard; arr. Betty Pulkingham, b. 1928
Text and music © 1977 Scripture In Song, admin. Integrity Music

THE SERVANT SONG
878

Lift High the Cross

Refrain

Lift high the cross, the love of Christ pro - claim till
all the world a - dore his sa - cred name.

1 Come, Chris - tians, fol - low where our cap - tain trod,
2 All new - born ser - vants of the Cru - ci - fied
3 O Lord, once lift - ed on the glo - rious tree,
4 So shall our song of tri - umph ev - er be:

Refrain

our king vic - to - rious, Christ, the Son of God.
bear on their brows the seal of him who died.
as thou hast prom - ised, draw us all to thee.
praise to the Cru - ci - fied for vic - to - ry!

Text: George W. Kitchin, 1827–1912; rev. Michael R. Newbolt, 1874–1956
Music: Sydney H. Nicholson, 1875–1947
Text and music © 1974 Hope Publishing Company

CRUCIFER
10 10 10 10

661

I Love to Tell the Story

1 I love to tell the sto - ry of un - seen things a - bove,
2 I love to tell the sto - ry: how pleas - ant to re - peat
3 I love to tell the sto - ry, for those who know it best

of Je - sus and his glo - ry, of Je - sus and his love.
what seems, each time I tell it, more won - der - ful - ly sweet!
seem hun - ger - ing and thirst - ing to hear it like the rest.

I love to tell the sto - ry, be - cause I know it's true;
I love to tell the sto - ry, for some have nev - er heard
And when, in scenes of glo - ry, I sing the new, new song,

it sat - is - fies my long-ings as noth - ing else would do.
the mes - sage of sal - va - tion from God's own ho - ly word.
I'll sing the old, old sto - ry that I have loved so long.

Text: Katherine Hankey, 1834–1911
Music: William E. Fischer, 1849–1936

HANKE
7 6 7 6 D and refrai

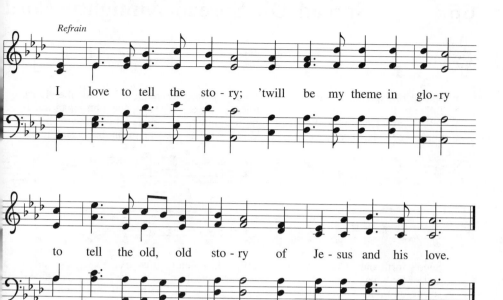

Refrain

I love to tell the sto - ry; 'twill be my theme in glo - ry

to tell the old, old sto - ry of Je - sus and his love.

Christ Is the King! 662

1 Christ is the king! O friends, re - joice; broth - ers and sis - ters,
2 Oh, mag - ni - fy the Lord, and raise an - thems of joy and
3 O Chris - tian wom - en, Chris - tian men, all the world o - ver,
4 Let Love's all - rec - on - cil - ing might your scat - tered com - pa -
5 So shall the church at last be one; so shall God's will on

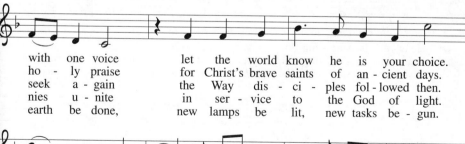

with one voice let the world know he is your choice.
ho - ly praise for Christ's brave saints of an - cient days.
seek a - gain the Way dis - ci - ples fol - lowed then.
nies u - nite in ser - vice to the God of light.
earth be done, new lamps be lit, new tasks be - gun.

Al - le - lu - ia, al - le - lu - ia, al - le - lu - ia!

Text: George K.A. Bell, 1883–1958, alt.
Music: Charles R. Anders, b. 1929
Text © Oxford University Press
Music © 1978 *Lutheran Book of Worship*, admin. Augsburg Fortress

BEVERLY
8 8 8 and alleluias

663   Spread, Oh, Spread, Almighty Word

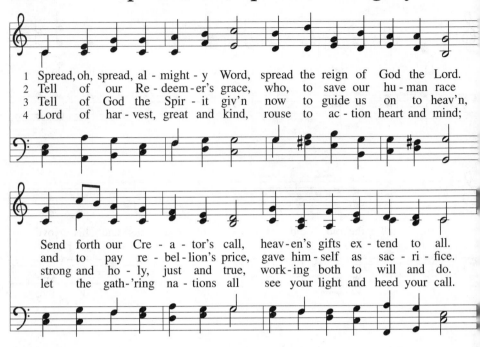

1 Spread, oh, spread, al - might - y Word, spread the reign of God the Lord.
2 Tell of our Re - deem - er's grace, who, to save our hu - man race
3 Tell of God the Spir - it giv'n now to guide us on to heav'n,
4 Lord of har - vest, great and kind, rouse to ac - tion heart and mind;

Send forth our Cre - a - tor's call, heav - en's gifts ex - tend to all.
and to pay re - bel - lion's price, gave him - self as sac - ri - fice.
strong and ho - ly, just and true, work - ing both to will and do.
let the gath - 'ring na - tions all see your light and heed your call.

Text: Jonathan F. Bahnmaier, 1774–1841; tr. *Lutheran Book of Worship*, alt.
Music: J. A. Freylinghausen, *Geistreiches Gesangbuch*, 1704
Text © 1978 *Lutheran Book of Worship*, admin. Augsburg Fortress

GOTT SEI DAN
777

664   Heaven Is Singing for Joy
El cielo canta alegría

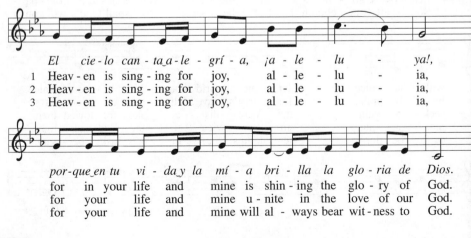

     El cie - lo can - ta_a - le - grí - a, ¡a - le - lu - ya!,
1 Heav - en is sing - ing for joy, al - le - lu - ia,
2 Heav - en is sing - ing for joy, al - le - lu - ia,
3 Heav - en is sing - ing for joy, al - le - lu - ia,

     por - que_en tu vi - da_y la mí - a bri - lla la glo - ria de Dios.
for in your life and mine is shin - ing the glo - ry of God.
for your life and mine u - nite in the love of our God.
for your life and mine will al - ways bear wit - ness to God.

Text: Pablo Sosa, b. 1933
Music: Pablo Sosa
Text and music © Pablo Sosa

ALEGRI
7 4 6 8 and refra

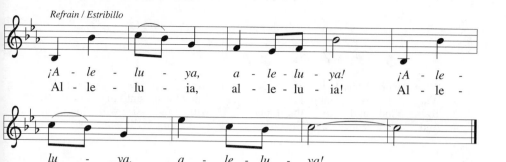

Refrain / Estribillo

¡A - le - lu - ya, a - le - lu - ya! ¡A - le -
Al - le - lu - ia, al - le - lu - ia! Al - le -

lu - ya, a - le - lu - ya!
lu - ia, al - le - lu - ia!

2 El cielo canta alegría, ¡aleluya!,
porque a tu vida y la mía
las une el amor de Dios. Estribillo

3 El cielo canta alegría, ¡aleluya!,
porque tu vida y la mía
proclamarán al Señor. Estribillo

Rise, Shine, You People!   665

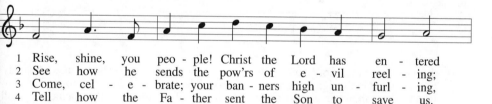

1 Rise, shine, you peo - ple! Christ the Lord has en - tered
2 See how he sends the pow'rs of e - vil reel - ing;
3 Come, cel - e - brate; your ban - ners high un - furl - ing,
4 Tell how the Fa - ther sent the Son to save us.

our hu - man sto - ry; God in him is cen - tered. He comes to
he brings us free - dom, light and life and heal - ing. All men and
your songs and prayers a - gainst the dark - ness hurl - ing. To all the
Tell of the Son, who life and free - dom gave us. Tell how the

us, by death and sin sur - round - ed, with grace un - bound - ed.
wom - en, who by guilt are driv - en, now are for - giv - en.
world go out and tell the sto - ry of Je - sus' glo - ry.
Spir - it calls from ev - 'ry na - tion God's new cre - a - tion.

Text: Ronald A. Klug, b. 1939, alt.
Music: Dale Wood, 1934–2003
Text and music © 1974 Augsburg Publishing House

WOJTKIEWIECZ
11 11 11 5

666   What Wondrous Love Is This

1 What won-drous love is this, O my soul, O my soul! What
2 When I was sink-ing down, sink-ing down, sink-ing down, when
3 To God and to the Lamb I will sing, I will sing; to
4 And when from death I'm free, I'll sing on, I'll sing on; and

won-drous love is this, O my soul! What won-drous love is this
I was sink-ing down, sink-ing down, when I was sink-ing down
God and to the Lamb I will sing; to God and to the Lamb,
when from death I'm free, I'll sing on; and when from death I'm free,

that caused the Lord of bliss to bear the dread-ful curse for my
be - neath God's righ-teous frown, Christ laid a - side his crown for my
who is the great I Aм, while mil - lions join the theme, I will
I'll sing God's love for me, and through e - ter - ni - ty I'll sing

soul, for my soul, to bear the dread-ful curse for my soul?
soul, for my soul, Christ laid a - side his crown for my soul.
sing, I will sing, while mil - lions join the theme, I will sing.
on, I'll sing on; and through e - ter - ni - ty I'll sing on.

Text: North American folk hymn, 19th cent., alt.
Music: W. Walker, *Southern Harmony*, 1835; arr. Paul J. Christiansen, 1914–1997, alt.
Arr. © 1955 Augsburg Publishing House

WONDROUS LOVE
12 9 6 6 12 9

Take Up Your Cross, the Savior Said

1 "Take up your cross," the Sav - ior said,
2 Take up your cross; let not its weight
3 Take up your cross, nor heed the shame,
4 Take up your cross and fol - low Christ,

"if you would my dis - ci - ple be;
per - vade your soul with vain a - larm;
nor let your fool - ish heart re - bel;
nor think till death to lay it down;

for - sake the past, and come this day,
his strength shall bear your spir - it up,
for you the Lord en - dured the cross
for those who hum - bly bear the cross

and hum - bly fol - low af - ter me."
sus - tain your heart, and nerve your arm.
to save your soul from death and hell.
one day will wear the glo - rious crown.

Text: Charles W. Everest, 1814–1877, alt.
Music: W. Hauser, *Hesperian Harp*, 1848; arr. hymnal version
arr. © 2006 Augsburg Fortress

BOURBON
LM

668

O Zion, Haste

1 O Zi - on, haste, your mis - sion high ful - fill - ing,
2 Pub - lish to ev - 'ry peo - ple, tongue, and na - tion
3 He comes a - gain! O Zi - on, ere you meet him,

to tell to all the world that God is light;
that God, in whom they live and move, is love;
make known to ev - 'ry heart his sav - ing grace;

that he who made all na - tions is not will - ing
tell how he stooped to save his lost cre - a - tion
let none whom he has ran - somed fail to greet him,

one soul should per - ish, lost in shades of night.
and died on earth that we might live a - bove.
through your ne - glect, un - fit to see his face.

Text: Mary A. Thomson, 1834–1923
Music: James Welch, 1837–1901

ANGELIC SONG
11 10 11 10 and refrain

Refrain

Pub - lish glad tid - ings, tid - ings of peace,

tid - ings of Je - sus, re - demp-tion, and re - lease.

Rise Up, O Saints of God! 669

1 Rise up, O saints of God! From vain am - bi - tions turn;
2 Speak out, O saints of God! De - spair en - gulfs earth's frame;
3 Rise up, O saints of God! The king-dom's task em - brace;
4 Give heed, O saints of God! Cre - a - tion cries in pain;
5 Com - mit your hearts to seek the paths which Christ has trod;

Christ rose tri - um-phant that your hearts with no - bler zeal might burn.
as heirs of God's bap - tis - mal grace, the word of hope pro - claim.
re - dress sin's cru - el con - se-quence; give jus - tice larg - er place.
stretch forth your hand of heal-ing now, with love the weak sus - tain.
and, quick-ened by the Spir-it's pow'r, rise up, O saints of God!

Text: Norman O. Forness, b. 1936
Music: William H. Walter, 1825–1893
Text © Norman O. Forness, admin. Augsburg Fortress

FESTAL SONG
SM

670

Build Us Up, Lord

1 Build us up, Lord, build us up; set in us a strong foun-da-tion. Lead us to do your ho-ly will; form and shape your new cre-a-tion. Build us up, Lord, build us up; as we guide and teach each oth-er, help us to share your love with the world: ev-'ry sis-ter, ev-'ry broth-er.

2 Build us up, Lord, build us up; let our lives re-flect your glo-ry. Cast a-way all our doubts and fears; help us tell the world your sto-ry. Build us up, Lord, build us up; help us bear good fruit for you, Lord, give us vi-sion and keep us sure. Grant us faith that's stead-fast and true.

Refrain

Grow-ing in Christ, we plant seeds for the king-dom; we fol-low in faith what's be-gun! Lord, set in our hearts the pow'r of your word to spread the news of your Son!

Text: Mark Glaeser, b. 1956, and Donna Hanna, b. 1952
Music: Mark Glaeser and Donna Hanna
Text and music © 2003 Augsburg Fortress

BUILD US U
P

Shine, Jesus, Shine

Refrain

Shine, Je-sus, shine, fill this land with the Fa-ther's glo-ry;
blaze, Spir-it, blaze, set our hearts on fire.
Flow, riv-er, flow, flood the na-tions with grace and mer-cy;
send forth your Word, Lord, and let there be light!

1 Lord, the light of your love is shin-ing, in the midst of the
2 As we gaze on your king-ly bright-ness, so our fac-es dis-

dark-ness, shin-ing; Je-sus, light of the world, shine up-on us,
play your like-ness, ev-er chang-ing from glo-ry to glo-ry,

set us free by the truth you now bring us.
mir-rored here, may our lives tell your sto-ry.

Refrain

Shine on me, shine on me:
Shine on me, shine on me:

Text: Graham Kendrick, b. 1950
Music: Graham Kendrick
Text and music © 1987 Make Way Music, admin. Music Services in the Western Hemisphere

SHINE, JESUS, SHINE
9 9 10 10 3 3 and refrain

672 Signs and Wonders

1 Signs and won - ders lead the danc - ing
2 Hope and free - dom join the cir - cle:
3 Cast a - side all fear and hid - ing;

from the heart God frees from fear;
Mar - y to the gar - den came,
hand in hand we dance the round.

wings of an - gels greet the mai - den,
saw the ra - diance of the mar - vel,
God is with us, Christ, a - bid - ing,

and God finds a dwell-ing here;
heard the Ris - en call her name;
and the Spir - it's gifts a - bound.

bold - ly may we lift our hands, bow
bold - ly may we heed Christ's call, step
Called by God to ho - li - ness, let

the head, and voice A - men;
be-yond the gar - den wall;
us bold - ly serve and bless;

thus does glo - ry shine at mid-night: o - pen hearts in - vite the star - light.
beau - ti - ful the feet pro-ceed-ing with good news of death's de-feat - ing.
and to hearts that sigh and hun - ger may our lives dance signs and won - ders.

Text: Susan Palo Cherwien, b. 1953
Music: *Trente quatre pseaumes de David*, Geneva, 1551
Text © 2005 Susan Palo Cherwien, admin. Augsburg Fortress

FREU DICH SEHR
87 87 77 88

673 God, Whose Almighty Word

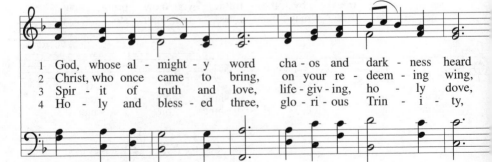

1 God, whose al - might - y word cha - os and dark - ness heard
2 Christ, who once came to bring, on your re - deem - ing wing,
3 Spir - it of truth and love, life - giv - ing, ho - ly dove,
4 Ho - ly and bless - ed three, glo - ri - ous Trin - i - ty,

Text: John Marriott, 1780–1825, alt.
Music: Felice de Giardini, 1716–1796

ITALIAN HYMN
664 6664

and took their flight: hear us, we hum-bly pray, and where the
heal-ing and sight; health to the trou-bled mind, sight where il-
speed forth your flight; move on the wa-ter's face bear-ing the
Wis-dom, Love, Might: bound-less as o-cean's tide, roll-ing in

gos-pel day sheds not its glo-rious ray, let there be light.
lu-sions blind; oh, now to hu-man-kind let there be light.
lamp of grace, and in earth's dark-est place let there be light.
full-est pride, through the earth, far and wide, let there be light.

Let Us Talents and Tongues Employ 674

1 Let us tal-ents and tongues em-ploy, reach-ing out with a shout of joy:
2 Christ is a-ble to make us one, at the ta-ble he sets the tone,
3 Je-sus calls us in, sends us out bear-ing fruit in a world of doubt,

bread is bro-ken, the wine is poured, Christ is spo-ken and seen and heard.
teach-ing peo-ple to live to bless, love in word and in deed ex-press.
gives us love to tell, bread to share: God (Im-man-u-el) ev-'ry-where!

Refrain

Je-sus lives a-gain, earth can breathe a-gain, pass the Word a-round: loaves a-bound!

Text: Fred Kaan, b. 1929
Music: Jamaican folk tune; adapt. Doreen Potter, 1925–1980
Text and music © 1975 Hope Publishing Company

LINSTEAD
LM and refrain

675 O Christ, Our Light, O Radiance True

1 O Christ, our light, O Ra - diance true, shine forth on
2 Fill with the ra - diance of your grace the wan - d'rers
3 Lord, o - pen all re - luc - tant ears and take a -
4 Lord, let your mer - cy's gen - tle ray shine down on
5 Make theirs with ours a sin - gle voice up - lift - ed,

those es-tranged from you, and bring them to your home a-
lost in er - ror's maze. Set free all those whose hearts and
way the need - less fears of those who trem - ble to ex -
oth - ers strayed a - way. To those in con - science wound - ed
ev - er to re - joice with wond-'ring grat - i - tude and

gain, where their de - light shall nev - er end.
minds some deep de - lu - sion haunts and binds.
press the faith their in - most hearts con - fess.
sore show heav - en's wait - ing, o - pen door.
praise to you, O Lord, for bound - less grace.

Text: Johann Heermann, 1585–1647; tr. composite
Music: Gesangbuch, Nürnberg, 1676
Text © 1978 Lutheran Book of Worship, admin. Augsburg Fortress

O JESU CHRISTE, WAHRES LICH
LM

Lord, Speak to Us, That We May Speak 676

1 Lord, speak to us, that we may speak in
2 Oh, lead us, Lord, that we may lead the
3 Oh, teach us, Lord, that we may teach the
4 Oh, fill us with your full - ness, Lord, un -

liv - ing ech - oes of your tone; as you have sought, so
wan-d'ring and the wa - v'ring feet; oh, feed us, Lord, that
pre - cious truths which you im - part; and wing our words, that
til our ver - y hearts o'er - flow in kin - dling thought and

let us seek your stray - ing chil - dren, lost and lone.
we may feed your hun - g'ring ones with man - na sweet.
they may reach the hid - den depths of man - y a heart.
glow - ing word, your love to tell, your praise to show.

Text: Frances R. Havergal, 1836–1879, alt.
Music: Robert Schumann, 1810–1856

CANONBURY
LM

677

This Little Light of Mine

1 This lit-tle light of mine, I'm goin'-a let it shine;
2 Ev-'ry-where I go, I'm goin'-a let it shine;
3 Je-sus gave it to me, I'm goin'-a let it shine;

oh, oh,

this lit-tle light of mine, I'm goin'-a let it shine;
ev-'ry-where I go, I'm goin'-a let it shine;
Je-sus gave it to me, I'm goin'-a let it shine;

oh,

this lit-tle light of mine, I'm goin'-a let it shine,
ev-'ry-where I go, I'm goin'-a let it shine,
Je-sus gave it to me, I'm goin'-a let it shine,

oh,

let it shine, let it shine, let it shine.
let it shine, let it shine, let it shine.
let it shine, let it shine, let it shine.

Text: African American spiritual
Music: African American spiritual; arr. Horace Clarence Boyer, b. 1935
Arr. © Horace Clarence Boyer

THIS JO
Irregula

God, Whose Giving Knows No Ending 678

1 God, whose giv-ing knows no end-ing, from your rich and end-less store:
2 Skills and time are ours for press-ing toward the goals of Christ, your Son:
3 Trea-sure, too, you have en-trust-ed, gain through pow'rs your grace con-ferred;

na-ture's won-der, Je - sus' wis-dom, cost-ly cross, grave's shat-tered door,
all at peace in health and free-dom, rac-es joined, the church made one.
ours to use for home and kin-dred, and to spread the gos - pel word.

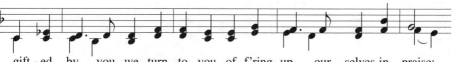

gift-ed by you, we turn to you, of-f'ring up our-selves in praise;
Now di - rect our dai-ly la-bor, lest we strive for self a - lone;
O - pen wide our hands in shar-ing, as we heed Christ's age-less call,

thank-ful song shall rise for - ev - er, gra-cious do - nor of our days.
born with tal - ents, make us ser - vants fit to an - swer at your throne.
heal - ing, teach-ing, and re - claim-ing, serv-ing you by lov-ing all.

Text: Robert L. Edwards, 1915–2006
Music: C. Hubert H. Parry, 1848–1918
Text © 1961, ren. 1989 The Hymn Society, admin. Hope Publishing Company

RUSTINGTON
8 7 8 7 D

Alternate tune: HYMN TO JOY

679   For the Fruit of All Creation

1 For the fruit of all cre-a-tion, thanks be to God.
2 In the just re-ward of la-bor, God's will is done.
3 For the har-vests of the Spir-it, thanks be to God.

For these gifts to ev-'ry na-tion, thanks be to God.
In the help we give our neigh-bor, God's will is done.
For the good we all in-her-it, thanks be to God.

For the plow-ing, sow-ing, reap-ing, si-lent growth while we are sleep-ing,
In our world-wide task of car-ing for the hun-gry and de-spair-ing,
For the won-ders that as-tound us, for the truths that still con-found us,

fu-ture needs in earth's safe-keep-ing, thanks be to God.
in the har-vests we are shar-ing, God's will is done.
most of all, that love has found us, thanks be to God.

Text: Fred Pratt Green, 1903–2000
Music: Welsh traditional; arr. Ralph Vaughan Williams, 1872–1958

AR HYD Y NOS
8 4 8 4 8 8 8

We Plow the Fields and Scatter

Aramos nuestros campos

A - ra - mos nues - tros cam - pos,   y   lue - go_el   sem - bra - dor
1 We plow the fields and scat - ter   the   good seed   on   the   land,
2 You on - ly are the mak - er   of   all things near and   far.
3 We thank you, our cre - a - tor,   for   all things bright and   good,

en   e - llos   la   si - mien - te   es - par - ce   con   a - mor.
but   it   is   fed and   wa - tered   by God's al - might - y   hand,
You   paint the way - side   flow - er,   you light the eve - ning star.
the   seed - time and the   har - vest,   our   life, our health, our food.

Mas   es   de Dios la   ma - no   que   la_ha - ce   ger - mi - nar,
who   sends the snow in   win - ter,   the   warmth to swell the grain,
The   winds and waves o - bey you,   by   you   the birds are fed;
No   gifts have we   to   of - fer   for   all   your love im - parts

ca - lor   y   llu - via   dan - do   a   to - dos por i - gual.
the   breez - es and the   sun - shine, and soft re - fresh - ing rain.
much more to   us,   your   chil - dren, you give our dai - ly bread.
but   what you most would trea - sure— our hum - ble, thank - ful hearts.

2 El hacedor supremo
de cuanto_existe_es él.
Su_aroma da_a las flores
y_a las abejas miel.
Las aves alimenta,
de peces puebla_el mar,
y da_a las gentes todas
el cotidiano pan.

3 Mil gracias, Dios, te damos
por cuanto bien nos das:
las flores y los frutos,
salud, la vida_y pan.
No hay con qué paguemos
lo que nos da tu_amor,
más que nuestro sincero
y_humilde corazón.

Text: Matthias Claudius, 1740–1815; English tr. Jane M. Campbell, 1817–1878, alt.;
Spanish tr. Ernesto Barocio, 1866–1948
Music: Luis Olivieri, b. 1937
Music © 1989 Abingdon Press, admin. The Copyright Company

SAN FERNANDO
76 76 D

681
We Plow the Fields and Scatter

1 We plow the fields and scat - ter the good seed on the land,
2 You on - ly are the mak - er of all things near and far.
3 We thank you, our cre - a - tor, for all things bright and good,

but it is fed and wa - tered by God's al - might - y hand,
You paint the way - side flow - er, you light the eve - ning star.
the seed - time and the har - vest, our life, our health, our food.

who sends the snow in win - ter, the warmth to swell the grain,
The winds and waves o - bey you, by you the birds are fed;
No gifts have we to of - fer for all your love im - parts,

the breez - es and the sun - shine, and soft re - fresh-ing rain.
much more to us, your chil - dren, you give our dai - ly bread.
but what you most would trea - sure—our hum - ble, thank-ful hearts.

Text: Matthias Claudius, 1740–1815; tr. Jane M. Campbell, 1817–1878, alt.
Music: Johann A. P. Schulz, 1747–1800

WIR PFLÜGEN
7 6 7 6 D and refrain

All good gifts a-round us are sent from heav'n a-bove.

We thank you, Lord, we thank you, Lord, for all your love.

To God Our Thanks We Give

Reamo leboga

682

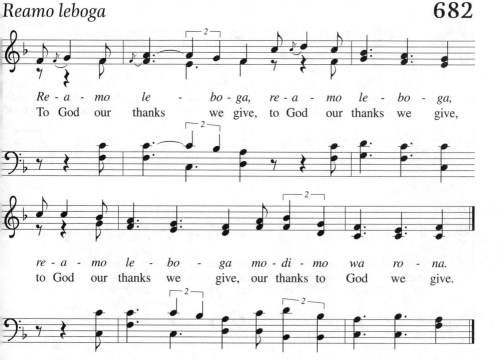

Re-a-mo le-bo-ga, re-a-mo le-bo-ga,
To God our thanks we give, to God our thanks we give,

re-a-mo le-bo-ga mo-di-mo wa ro-na.
to God our thanks we give, our thanks to God we give.

Text: Botswanan traditional, as taught by Daisy Nshakazongwe; tr. I-to Loh, b. 1936
Music: Botswanan traditional, as taught by Daisy Nshakazongwe
Text and music © 1986 World Council of Churches and the Asian Institute for Liturgy and Music

REAMO LEBOGA
6666

683 The Numberless Gifts of God's Mercies

1 The num - ber-less gifts of God's mer - cies my tongue can-not
2 Like all of the stars in the heav - ens, God's mer - cies can
3 I'll nev - er count all of God's mer - cies, but oh, I can

fath - om or tell. Like dew that ap-pears in the morn - ing,
nev - er be told. They shine through the dark - ness of mid - night;
give God my praise for all of that love, my thanks-giv - ing

they come to us shin - ing and full. The num - ber-less
their beau - ties can nev - er grow old. Like all of the
and love to the end of my days. I'll nev - er count

gifts of God's mer - cies my tongue can-not fath - om or tell.
stars in the heav - ens, God's mer - cies can nev - er be told.
all of God's mer - cies, but oh, I can give God my praise!

Text: Carolina Sandell Berg, 1832–1903; tr. Gracia Grindal, b. 1943
Music: Albert Lindström, 1853–1935
Text © 1993 Selah Publishing Co., Inc.

JAG KAN ICKE RÄKNA DEM ALLA
989898

Creating God, Your Fingers Trace 684

1 Cre - at - ing God, your fin - gers trace the bold de -
2 Sus - tain - ing God, your hands up - hold earth's mys - t'ries
3 Re - deem - ing God, your arms em - brace all now de -
4 In - dwell - ing God, your gos - pel claims one fam - 'ly

signs of far - thest space; let sun and moon and stars and
known or yet un - told; let wa - ter's frag - ile blend with
spised for creed or race; let peace, de - scend - ing like a
with a bil - lion names; let ev - 'ry life be touched by

light and what lies hid - den praise your might.
air, en - a - bling life, pro - claim your care.
dove, make known on earth your heal - ing love.
grace un - til we praise you face to face.

Text: Jeffery Rowthorn, b. 1934
Music: W. Walker, *Southern Harmony*, 1835; arr. hymnal version
Text © 1979 The Hymn Society, admin. Hope Publishing Company
Arr. © 2006 Augsburg Fortress

PROSPECT
LM

685 Take My Life, That I May Be

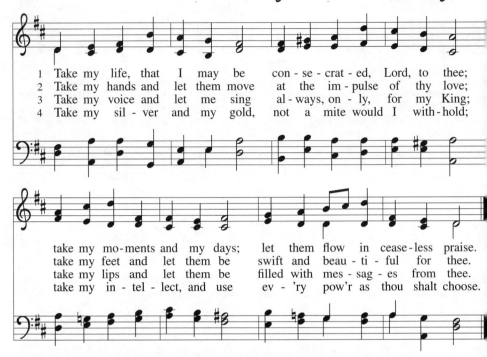

1 Take my life, that I may be con - se - crat - ed, Lord, to thee;
2 Take my hands and let them move at the im - pulse of thy love;
3 Take my voice and let me sing al - ways, on - ly, for my King;
4 Take my sil - ver and my gold, not a mite would I with - hold;

take my mo-ments and my days; let them flow in cease-less praise.
take my feet and let them be swift and beau - ti - ful for thee.
take my lips and let them be filled with mes - sag - es from thee.
take my in - tel - lect, and use ev - 'ry pow'r as thou shalt choose.

5 Take my will and make it thine;
it shall be no longer mine.
Take my heart, it is thine own;
it shall be thy royal throne.

6 Take my love; my Lord, I pour
at thy feet its treasure store;
take myself, and I will be
ever, only, all for thee.

Text: Frances R. Havergal, 1836–1879, alt.
Music: William H. Havergal, 1793–1870

PATMOS
7 7 7 7

686 We Give Thee but Thine Own

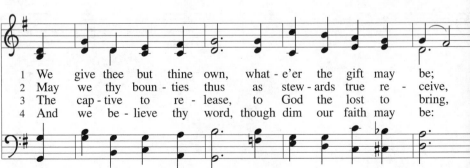

1 We give thee but thine own, what - e'er the gift may be;
2 May we thy boun - ties thus as stew - ards true re - ceive,
3 The cap - tive to re - lease, to God the lost to bring,
4 And we be - lieve thy word, though dim our faith may be:

Text: William W. How, 1823–1897, alt.
Music: L. Mason and G. Webb, Cantica Lauda, 1850

HEATH
S M

all that we have is thine a - lone, a trust, O Lord, from thee.
and glad - ly, as thou bless - est us, to thee our first - fruits give.
to teach the way of life and peace—it is a Christ-like thing.
what - e'er we do for thine, O Lord, we do it un - to thee.

Come to Us, Creative Spirit 687

1 Come to us, cre - a - tive Spir - it, in this ho - ly
2 Po - et, paint - er, mu - sic - mak - er, all your trea - sures
3 Word from God e - ter - nal spring - ing, fill our minds, we
4 In all plac - es and for - ev - er glo - ry be ex -

house; ev - 'ry hu - man tal - ent hal - low,
bring; crafts - man, ac - tor, grace - ful danc - er,
pray; and in all ar - tis - tic vi - sion
pressed to the Son, with God the Fa - ther

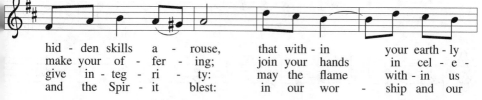

hid - den skills a - rouse, that with - in your earth - ly
make your of - fer - ing; join your hands in cel - e -
give in - teg - ri - ty: may the flame with - in us
and the Spir - it blest: in our wor - ship and our

tem - ple, wise and sim - ple may re - joice.
bra - tion: let cre - a - tion shout and sing!
burn - ing kin - dle yearn - ing day by day.
liv - ing keep us striv - ing for the best.

Text: David Mowbray, b. 1938
Music: Richard Proulx, b. 1937
Text © 1979 Stainer & Bell Ltd. and the Trustees for Methodist Church Purposes, admin. Hope Publishing Company
Music © 1986 GIA Publications, Inc.

CASTLEWOOD
85 85 843

688

Lord of Light

1 Lord of light, your name out - shin - ing all the stars and
2 By the toil of faith - ful work - ers in some far out -
3 Grant that knowl - edge, still in - creas - ing, at your feet may
4 By the prayers of faith - ful watch - ers, nev - er si - lent

suns of space, use our tal - ents in your king - dom
ly - ing field, by the cour - age where the ra - diance
low - ly kneel; with your grace our tri - umphs hal - low,
day or night; by the cross of Je - sus, bring - ing

as the ser - vants of your grace; use us to ful -
of the cross is still re - vealed, by the vic - to -
with your char - i - ty our zeal; lift the na - tions
peace to all and heal - ing light; by the love that

fill your pur - pose in the gift of Christ your Son.
ries of meek - ness, through re - proach and suf - f'ring won:
from the shad - ows to the glad - ness of the sun:
pass - es knowl - edge, mak - ing all your chil - dren one:

Text: Howell E. Lewis, 1860–1953, alt.
Music: Cyril V. Taylor, 1907–1991
Text © Union of Welsh Independents
Music © 1942, ren. 1970 Hope Publishing Company

ABBOT'S LEIGH
87 87 D

Refrain

Fa - ther, as in high - est heav - en, so on earth your will be done.

Praise and Thanksgiving   689

1 Praise and thanks - giv - ing, God, we would of - fer for all things
2 God, bless the la - bor we bring to serve you, that with our
3 Fa - ther, pro - vid - ing food for your chil - dren, by Wis - dom's
4 Then will your bless - ing reach ev - 'ry peo - ple, free - ly con -

liv - ing, you have made good: har - vest of sown fields, fruits of the
neigh - bor we may be fed. Sow - ing or till - ing, we would work
guid - ing teach us to share one with an - oth - er, so that, re -
fess - ing your gra - cious hand. Where you are reign - ing, no one will

or - chard, hay from the mown fields, blos - som and wood.
with you, har - vest - ing, mill - ing for dai - ly bread.
joic - ing with us, all oth - ers may know your care.
hun - ger; your love sus - tain - ing show - ers the land.

Text: Albert F. Bayly, 1901–1984, alt.
Music: Gaelic tune; arr. hymnal version
Text © Oxford University Press
Arr. © 2006 Augsburg Fortress

BUNESSAN
5 5 5 4 D

690   We Raise Our Hands to You, O Lord

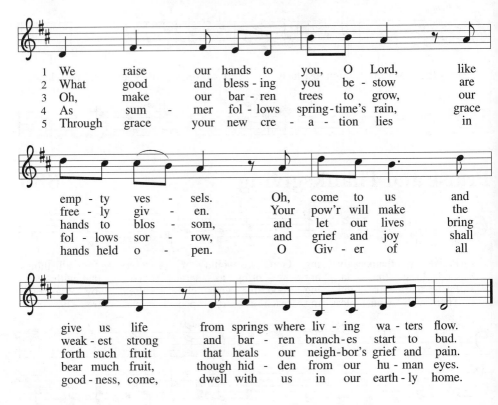

1 We raise our hands to you, O Lord, like
2 What good and bless-ing you be-stow are
3 Oh, make our bar-ren trees to grow, our
4 As sum - mer fol-lows spring-time's rain, grace
5 Through grace your new cre - a - tion lies in

emp - ty ves - sels. Oh, come to us and
free - ly giv - en. Your pow'r will make the
hands to blos - som, and let our lives bring
fol - lows sor - row, and grief and joy shall
hands held o - pen. O Giv - er of all

give us life from springs where liv - ing wa - ters flow.
weak - est strong and bar - ren branch-es start to bud.
forth such fruit that heals our neigh-bor's grief and pain.
bear much fruit, though hid - den from our hu - man eyes.
good - ness, come, dwell with us in our earth - ly home.

Text: Svein Ellingsen, b. 1929; tr. Hedwig T. Durnbaugh, b. 1929
Music: Trond Kverno, b. 1945
Tr. © Hedwig T. Durnbaugh
Music © 1978 Norsk Musikforlag

VI REKKER VÅRE HENDER FREM
8 5 8 8

691   Accept, O Lord, the Gifts We Bring

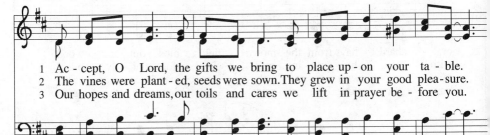

1 Ac - cept, O Lord, the gifts we bring to place up - on your ta - ble.
2 The vines were plant - ed, seeds were sown. They grew in your good plea - sure.
3 Our hopes and dreams, our toils and cares we lift in prayer be - fore you.

Text: Beth Bergeron Folkemer, b. 1957
Music: English folk tune; arr. Alice Parker, b. 1925
Text © 1990 Augsburg Fortress
Arr. © 1995 Augsburg Fortress

BARBARA ALLEN
8 7 8 7

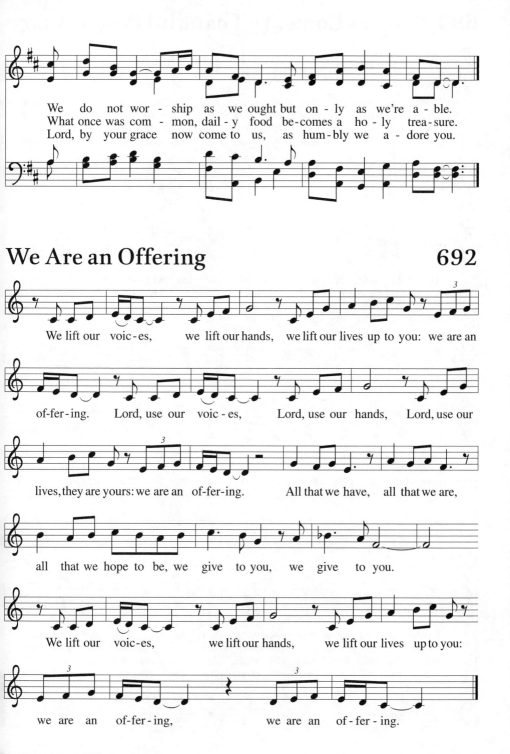

We do not wor - ship as we ought but on - ly as we're a - ble.
What once was com - mon, dail - y food be - comes a ho - ly trea - sure.
Lord, by your grace now come to us, as hum - bly we a - dore you.

We Are an Offering

692

We lift our voic - es, we lift our hands, we lift our lives up to you: we are an

of - fer - ing. Lord, use our voic - es, Lord, use our hands, Lord, use our

lives, they are yours: we are an of - fer - ing. All that we have, all that we are,

all that we hope to be, we give to you, we give to you.

We lift our voic - es, we lift our hands, we lift our lives up to you:

we are an of - fer - ing, we are an of - fer - ing.

Text: Dwight Liles, b. 1957
Music: Dwight Liles
Text and music © 1984 Word Music, LLC

OFFERING
PM

693   Come, Ye Thankful People, Come

1 Come, ye thank-ful peo - ple, come; raise the song of har - vest home.
2 All the world is God's own field, fruit un - to his praise to yield;
3 For the Lord our God shall come and shall take his har - vest home;
4 E - ven so, Lord, quick - ly come to thy fi - nal har - vest home.

All be safe - ly gath - ered in ere the win - ter storms be - gin.
wheat and tares to - geth - er sown, un - to joy or sor - row grown.
from his field shall in that day all of - fens - es purge a - way;
Gath - er then thy peo - ple in, free from sor - row, free from sin,

God, our mak - er, doth pro - vide for our wants to be sup - plied.
First the blade, and then the ear, then the full corn shall ap - pear.
give his an - gels charge at last in the fire the tares to cast,
there, for - ev - er pu - ri - fied, in thy gar - ner to a - bide.

Come to God's own tem - ple, come, raise the song of har - vest home.
Lord of har - vest, grant that we whole - some grain and pure may be.
but the fruit - ful ears to store in his gar - ner ev - er - more.
Come, with all thine an - gels, come, raise the glo - rious har - vest home!

Text: Henry Alford, 1810–1871, alt.
Music: George J. Elvey, 1816–1893

ST. GEORGE'S, WINDSOR
7777D

Sing to the Lord of Harvest

694

1 Sing to the Lord of har - vest your songs of love and praise;
2 God makes the clouds drop fat - ness, the des - erts bloom and spring,
3 Bring to this sa - cred al - tar the gifts his good-ness gave,

with joy - ful hearts and voic - es your al - le - lu - ias raise;
the hills leap up in glad - ness, the val - leys laugh and sing.
the gold-en sheaves of har - vest, the souls Christ died to save.

by him the roll - ing sea - sons in fruit - ful or - der move;
God fills them with his full - ness, all things with large in - crease,
Your hearts lay down be - fore him when at his feet you fall,

sing to the Lord of har - vest a joy - ous song of love.
and crowns the year with good - ness, with plen - ty and with peace.
and with your lives a - dore him who gave his life for all.

Text: John S. B. Monsell, 1811–1875, alt.
Music: Johann Steurlein, 1546–1613

WIE LIEBLICH IST DER MAIEN
7676D

695

As Saints of Old

1 As saints of old their first-fruits brought of or - chard, flock, and field
2 A world in need now sum-mons us to la - bor, love, and give;
3 In grat - i - tude and hum-ble trust we bring our best to - day

to God, the giv - er of all good, the source of boun-teous yield,
to make our life an of - fer - ing to God, that all may live.
to serve your cause and share your love with all a - long life's way.

so we to - day first - fruits would bring, the wealth of this good land,
The church of Christ is call - ing us to make the dream come true;
O God, who gave your - self to us in Je - sus Christ your Son,

of farm and mar - ket, shop and home, of mind and heart and hand.
a world re-deemed by Christ-like love; all life in Christ made new.
teach us to give our - selves each day un - til life's work is done.

Text: Frank von Christierson, 1900–1996, alt.
Music: English folk tune; arr. Ralph Vaughan Williams, 1872–1958
Text © 1961, ren. 1989 The Hymn Society, admin. Hope Publishing Company
Arr. © Oxford University Press

FOREST GREEN
CMD

Jesus Calls Us; o'er the Tumult

696

1 Je - sus calls us; o'er the tu - mult of our
2 As of old Saint An - drew heard it by the
3 Je - sus calls us from the wor - ship of the
4 In our joys and in our sor - rows, days of
5 Je - sus calls us! By your mer - cy, Sav - ior,

life's wild, rest - less sea, day by day his clear voice
Gal - i - le - an lake, turned from home and toil and
vain world's gold - en store, from each i - dol that would
toil and hours of ease, still he calls, in cares and
may we hear your call, give our hearts to your o -

sound - ing, say - ing, "Chris - tian, fol - low me":
kin - dred, leav - ing all for Je - sus' sake.
keep us, say - ing, "Chris - tian, love me more."
plea - sures, "Chris - tian, love me more than these."
be - dience, serve and love you best of all.

Text: Cecil Frances Alexander, 1818–1895
Music: William H. Jude, 1851–1922

GALILEE
8 7 8 7

697 Just a Closer Walk with Thee

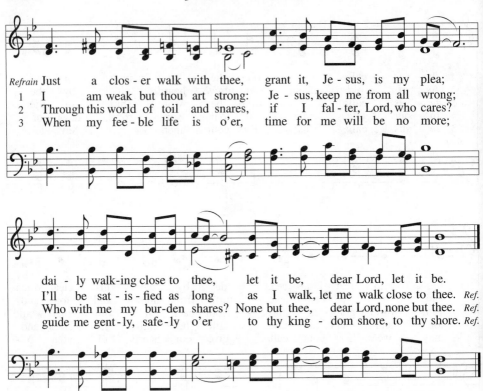

Refrain Just a clos-er walk with thee, grant it, Je-sus, is my plea;
1 I am weak but thou art strong: Je-sus, keep me from all wrong;
2 Through this world of toil and snares, if I fal-ter, Lord, who cares?
3 When my fee-ble life is o'er, time for me will be no more;

dai-ly walk-ing close to thee, let it be, dear Lord, let it be.
I'll be sat-is-fied as long as I walk, let me walk close to thee. *Ref.*
Who with me my bur-den shares? None but thee, dear Lord, none but thee. *Ref.*
guide me gent-ly, safe-ly o'er to thy king-dom shore, to thy shore. *Ref.*

Text: North American traditional
Music: North American traditional

CLOSER WALK
Irregular

698 How Long, O God

1 "How long, O God?" the psalm-ist cries, a cry we make our own,
2 The e-vil lurks with-in, with-out, it threat-ens to de-stroy
3 Your grace, O God, seems far a-way; will heal-ing ev-er come?
4 How can we hope? How can we sing? O God, set free our voice
5 "How long, O God?" the psalm-ist cries, a cry we make our own.

Text: Ralph F. Smith, 1950–1994
Music: North American traditional; arr. hymnal version
Text © 2003 Augsburg Fortress
Arr. © 2006 Augsburg Fortress

LAND OF REST
CM

for we are lost, a - lone, a - fraid, and far a - way from home.
the frag - ile cords that make us one, that bind our hearts in joy.
Our bro - ken lives lie bro - ken still; will night give way to dawn?
to name the sor - rows, name the pain, that we might yet re - joice.
Though we are lost, a - lone, a - fraid, our God will lead us home.

In Deepest Night 699

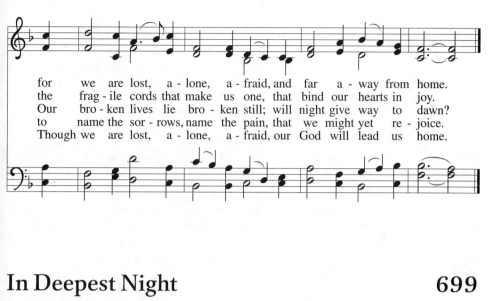

1 In deep - est night, in dark - est days, when harps are
2 When friend was lost, when love de - ceived, dear Je - sus
3 When through the wa - ters winds our path, a - round us

hung, no songs we raise, when si - lence must
wept, God was be - reaved; so with us in
pain, a - round us death: deep calls to deep,

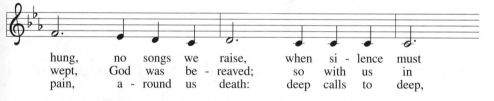

suf - fice as praise, yet sound - ing in us qui - et - ly
our grief God grieves, and round a - bout us mourn - ful - ly
a sav - ing breath, and found be - side us faith - ful - ly

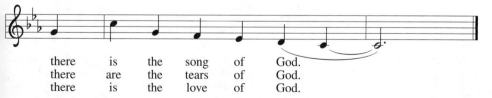

there is the song of God.
there are the tears of God.
there is the love of God.

Text: Susan Palo Cherwien, b. 1953
Music: Thomas Pavlechko, b. 1962
Text © 1995 Susan Palo Cherwien, admin. Augsburg Fortress
Music © 2002 Selah Publishing Co., Inc.

DEEP BLUE
88886

700   Bring Peace to Earth Again

1 Where ar - mies scourge the coun - try - side, and peo - ple flee in fear,
2 Where an - ger fes - ters in the heart, and strikes with cru - el hand;
3 Where homes are torn by bit - ter strife, and love dis - solves in blame;
4 O God, whose heart com - pas - sion - ate bears ev - 'ry hu - man pain,

where si - rens scream through flam - ing nights, and death is ev - er near:
where vio - lence stalks the trou - bled streets, and ter - ror haunts the land:
where walls you meant for shel - t'ring care hide deeds of hurt and shame;
re - deem this vio - lent, wound - ing world till gen - tle - ness shall reign.

Refrain

O God of mer - cy, hear our prayer: bring peace to earth a - gain!

Text: Herman G. Stuempfle Jr., b. 1923
Music: Perry Nelson, b. 1955
Text and music © 1996 World Library Publications

PACE MIO DIO
868686

701   Once We Sang and Danced

1 Once we sang and danced with glad - ness, once de - light filled ev - 'ry breath;
2 All the wil - lows bow in weep - ing, all the riv - ers rage and moan,
3 God, who came to dwell a - mong us, God, who suf - fered our dis - grace,
4 Come, O Christ, a - mong the ash - es, come to wipe our tears a - way,

now we sit a - mong the ash - es, all our dreams de - stroyed by death.
as cre - a - tion joins our plead - ing: "God, do not leave us a - lone."
from your own heart, grieved and wound - ed, come the rich - es of your grace.
death de - stroy and sor - row ban - ish; now and al - ways, come and stay.

Text: Susan R. Briehl, b. 1952, based on Psalm 137
Music: Latvian folk tune
Text © 2003 GIA Publications, Inc.

KAS DZIEDĀJA
8787

You, Dear Lord
Tú, Señor, que brillas

Refrain / Estribillo

Tú, Se - ñor, que bri - llas en las ti -
You, dear Lord, re - splen - dent with - in our

nie - blas: da - nos, da - nos tu luz.
dark - ness: grant us, grant us your light.

Mi co - ra - zón es - tá san - gran - do, me sien - to
1 This heart of mine is in deep an - guish. I feel so
2 This night I fol - low in your foot - steps, but can - not
3 We soon shall see the new day dawn - ing, shall see the

le - jos, le - jos de ti. La vi - da_es tris - te si tú nos
far - off, so far from you. How sad our life, Lord, if you should
clear - ly be - hold your light. You, Lord, must guide us through - out our
dawn - ing of_e - ter - nal light. May we in lov - ing and peace - ful

Refrain / Estribillo

de - jas, si tú nos de - jas so - los, sin luz.
leave us, if you should leave us with - out your light.
life - time, through - out our life - time to that clear light.
liv - ing be - hold to - geth - er your end - less light.

2 *En esta noche sigo tus pasos,*
   aunque no vea clara tu luz.
   Guíanos, tú, por esta vida,
   por esta vida hasta la luz. Estribillo

3 *Pronto vendrá el nuevo día,*
   amanecer de_eterna luz.
   Nace_en nosotros paz y_esperanza,
   juntos veremos la luz sin fin. Estribillo

Text: Anonymous; tr. Fred Pratt Green, 1903–2000
Music: Gerhard M. Cartford, b. 1923
English text © 1982 Hope Publishing Company
Music © Lutheran World Federation

TÚ SEÑOR
9 9 10 9 and refrain

703

O God, Why Are You Silent

1 O God, why are you si - lent? I can - not hear your voice;
2 My hope lies bruised and bat - tered, my wound-ed heart is torn;
3 Through end - less nights of weep - ing, through wea - ry days of grief,
4 May pain draw forth com - pas - sion, let wis - dom rise from loss;

the proud and strong and vio - lent all claim you and re - joice;
my spir - it spent and shat - tered by life's re - lent - less storm;
my heart is in your keep - ing, my com - fort, my re - lief.
oh, take my heart and fash - ion the im - age of your cross;

you prom-ised you would hold me with ten - der - ness and care.
will you not bend to hear me, my cries from deep with - in?
Come, share my tears and sad - ness, come, suf - fer in my pain,
then may I know your heal - ing through heal - ing that I share,

Draw near, O Love, en - fold me, and ease the pain I bear.
Have you no word to cheer me when night is clos - ing in?
oh, bring me home to glad - ness, re - store my hope a - gain.
your grace and love re - veal - ing, your ten - der - ness and care.

Text: Marty Haugen, b. 1950
Music: Hans Leo Hassler, 1564–1612; arr. Johann Sebastian Bach, 1685–1750
Text © 2003 GIA Publications, Inc.

HERZLICH TUT MICH VERLANGEN
7 6 7 6 D

When Pain of the World Surrounds Us 704

1 When pain of the world sur - rounds us with dark - ness and de -
2 We see with . . fear and trem - bling our ach - ing world in
3 The church is a ho - ly ves - sel the liv - ing wa - ters
4 We praise you . . for our jour - ney and your a - bun - dant

spair, when search - ing just con - founds us with
need, con - fess - ing to each oth - er our
fill to nour - ish all the peo - ple, God's
grace, your sav - ing word that guid - ed a

false hopes ev - 'ry - where, when lives are starved for mean - ing and
waste - ful - ness and greed. May we with stead - fast car - ing the
pur - pose to ful - fill. May we with hum - ble cour - age be
strug - gling hu - man race. O God, with all cre - a - tion, your

des - ti - ny is bare, we are called to fol - low Je - sus and
hun - gry chil - dren feed. We are called to fol - low Je - sus and
o - pen to God's will. We are called to fol - low Je - sus and
fu - ture we em - brace. We are called to fol - low Je - sus and

let God's heal - ing flow through us.
let God's jus - tice flow through us.
let God's Spir - it flow through us.
let God's chang - es flow through us.

Text: Jim Strathdee, b. 1941
Music: Jim Strathdee
Text and music © 1978 Desert Flower Music

CALLED TO FOLLOW
Irregular

705 God of Grace and God of Glory

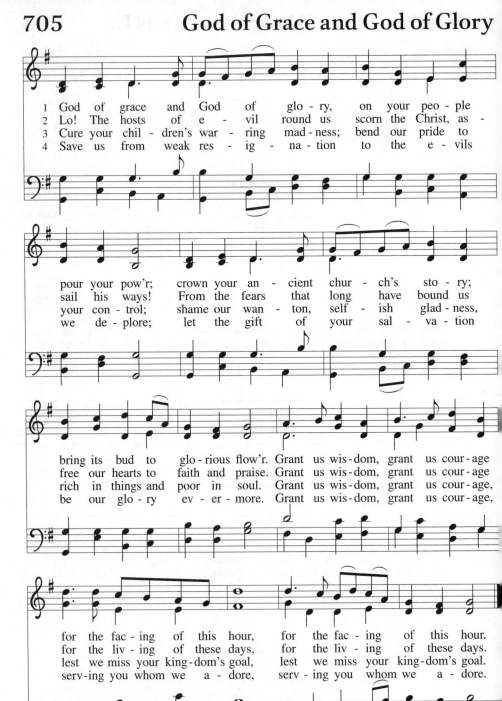

1 God of grace and God of glo - ry, on your peo - ple
2 Lo! The hosts of e - vil round us scorn the Christ, as -
3 Cure your chil - dren's war - ring mad - ness; bend our pride to
4 Save us from weak res - ig - na - tion to the e - vils

pour your pow'r; crown your an - cient chur - ch's sto - ry;
sail his ways! From the fears that long have bound us
your con - trol; shame our wan - ton, self - ish glad - ness.
we de - plore; let the gift of your sal - va - tion

bring its bud to glo - rious flow'r. Grant us wis - dom, grant us cour - age
free our hearts to faith and praise. Grant us wis - dom, grant us cour - age
rich in things and poor in soul. Grant us wis - dom, grant us cour - age,
be our glo - ry ev - er - more. Grant us wis - dom, grant us cour - age,

for the fac - ing of this hour, for the fac - ing of this hour.
for the liv - ing of these days, for the liv - ing of these days.
lest we miss your king - dom's goal, lest we miss your king - dom's goal.
serv - ing you whom we a - dore, serv - ing you whom we a - dore.

Text: Harry E. Fosdick, 1878–1969
Music: John Hughes, 1873–1932

CWM RHONDDA
8787877

The People Walk
Un pueblo que camina

Refrain / Estribillo

Un pue - blo que ca - mi - na por el mun - do gri -
The peo - ple walk through-out the world to - geth - er and

tan - do: "¡Ven, Se - ñor!" Un pue - blo que bus - ca_en es - ta
cry out, "Come, O Lord"; the peo - ple who long to claim the

vi - da la gran li - be - ra - ción.
prom - ise, God's lib - er - at - ing Word.

1 Los po - bres siem - pre_es - pe - ran el a - ma - ne - cer de_un
1 The poor ones of the world a - wait the dawn of hope, when
2 You broke the bonds of sin, un - tied the cap - tive's hands, re -
3 The life - blood of the world is shed in mind - less war; and

dí - a más jus - to y sin o - pre - sión. Los
jus - tice will shine and make op - pres - sion flee. The
leased us from fear and slav - 'ry to the law. We
fam - 'lies de - sire a home where con - flicts cease. With

Refrain / Estribillo

po - bres he - mos pues - to la_es - pe - ran - za_en ti: ¡Li - ber - ta - dor!
emp - ty hands of all are raised to you, Lord God: oh, set us free!
lift our hands in hope, we put our trust in you, O God of love.
all the world we lift our hands in hope to you, O God of peace.

2 *Salvaste nuestra vida de la_esclavitud,*
esclavos de la ley, sirviendo_en el temor.
Nosotros hemos puesto la_esperanza_en ti:
¡Dios del amor! Estribillo

3 *El mundo, por la guerra, sangra sin razón;*
familias destrozadas buscan un hogar.
El mundo tiene puesta su_esperanza_en ti:
¡Dios de la paz! Estribillo

Text: Juan A. Espinosa, b. 1940; tr. Martin A. Seltz, b. 1951
Music: Juan A. Espinosa
Text and music © 1972, 1998 Juan A. Espinosa, admin. OCP Publications

UN PUEBLO QUE CAMINA
12 11 12 4 and refrain

707 Lord of Glory, You Have Bought Us

1 Lord of glo - ry, you have bought us with your life - blood
2 Grant us hearts, dear Lord, to give you glad - ly, free - ly,
3 Won - drous hon - or you have giv - en to our hum - blest
4 Lord of glo - ry, you have bought us with your life - blood

as the price, nev - er grudg - ing for the lost ones that tre -
of your own. With the sun - shine of your good - ness melt our
char - i - ty in your own mys - te - rious sen - tence, "You have
as the price, nev - er grudg - ing for the lost ones that tre -

men - dous sac - ri - fice; and with that have free - ly giv - en
thank - less hearts of stone till our cold and self - ish na - tures,
done it all to me." Na - ked, sick, in pris - on, hun - gry—
men - dous sac - ri - fice. Give us faith to trust you bold - ly,

bless - ings count - less as the sand to the un - thank - ful
warmed by you, at length be - lieve that more hap - py
in the least, your face we view, say - ing by your
hope, to stay our souls on you: but, oh, best of

Text: Eliza S. Alderson, 1818–1889, alt.
Music: Rowland H. Prichard, 1811–1887

HYFRYDOL
8787D

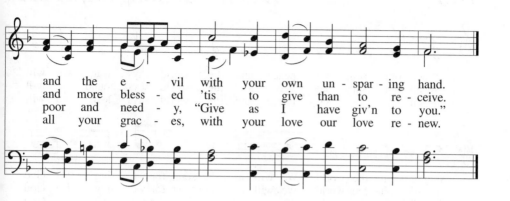

and the e - vil with your own un - spar - ing hand.
and more bless - ed 'tis to give than to re - ceive.
poor and need - y, "Give as I have giv'n to you."
all your grac - es, with your love our love re - new.

Jesu, Jesu, Fill Us with Your Love   708

Refrain

Je - su, Je - su, fill us with your love, show

us how to serve the neigh-bors we have from you.

1 Kneels at the feet of his friends, si - lent - ly wash - es their feet,
2 Neigh-bors are wealth - y and poor, var - ied in col - or and race,
3 These are the ones we will serve, these are the ones we will love;
4 Kneel at the feet of our friends, si - lent - ly wash-ing their feet:

Refrain

mas - ter who acts as a slave to them.
neigh-bors are near - by and far a - way.
all these are neigh-bors to us and you.
this is the way we will live with you.

Text: Tom Colvin, 1925–2000, alt.
Music: Ghanaian folk tune, adapt. Tom Colvin
Text and music © 1969 Hope Publishing Company

CHEREPONI
7 7 9 and refrain

709   When Our Song Says Peace

1 When our song says peace and the world says war, we will
2 When our song says free and the world says bound, we will
3 When our song says home and the world says lost, we will

sing de-spite the world. We will trust the song, for we sing of God,
sing de-spite the world. We will trust the song, for we sing of God,
sing de-spite the world. We will trust the song, for we sing of God,

who breaks the spear and sword and stills the storm of war.
who o - pens pris - on doors and sets the cap - tives free.
who brings us home at last, and gives a song to all.

Text: Richard Leach, b. 1953
Music: Thomas Pavlechko, b. 1962
Text © 1997 Selah Publishing Co., Inc.
Music © 2003 Augsburg Fortress

JENKINS
107 1066

710   Let Streams of Living Justice

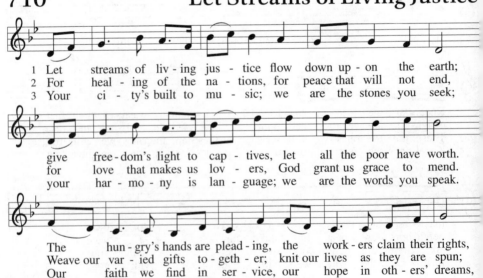

1 Let streams of liv - ing jus - tice flow down up - on the earth;
2 For heal - ing of the na - tions, for peace that will not end,
3 Your ci - ty's built to mu - sic; we are the stones you seek;

give free-dom's light to cap - tives, let all the poor have worth.
for love that makes us lov - ers, God grant us grace to mend.
your har - mo - ny is lan - guage; we are the words you speak.

The hun-gry's hands are plead-ing, the work-ers claim their rights,
Weave our var - ied gifts to - geth - er; knit our lives as they are spun;
Our faith we find in ser - vice, our hope in oth - ers' dreams,

Text: William Whitla, b. 1934
Music: Gustav Holst, 1874–1934
Text © 1989 William Whitla

THAXTED
13 13 13 13 13 13

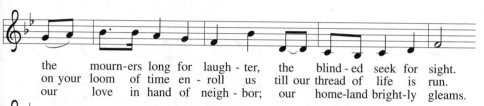

the   mourn-ers long for laugh - ter,   the   blind - ed seek for sight.
on your loom of time en - roll   us   till our thread of life   is   run.
our   love   in hand of neigh - bor;   our   home-land bright-ly gleams.

Make   lib - er - ty   a   bea - con, strike down the i - ron pow'r;
O great weav - er   of our fab - ric, bind church and world in   one;
In - scribe our hearts with jus - tice; your way—the path un - tried;

a - bol - ish an - cient ven - geance: pro - claim your peo-ple's hour.
dye our tex - ture with your ra - diance, light our col - ors with your sun.
your   truth—the heart of strang - er; your   life—the Cru - ci - fied.

O Day of Peace   711

1 O   day of peace that dim - ly shines through all our hopes and prayers and dreams,
2 Then shall the wolf dwell with the lamb,   nor shall the fierce de - vour the small;

guide us   to jus - tice, truth, and   love, de - liv-ered from our self - ish schemes.
as beasts and cat - tle calm - ly   graze, a lit - tle child shall lead them   all.

May swords of hate fall from our hands, our hearts from en - vy find re - lease,
Then en - e - mies shall learn to love,   all crea - tures find their true ac - cord;

till by God's grace our war - ring world shall see Christ's prom-ised reign of peace.
the hope of peace shall be ful - filled, for all   the   earth shall know the Lord.

Text: Carl P. Daw Jr., b. 1944
Music: C. Hubert H. Parry, 1848–1918
Text © 1982 Hope Publishing Company

JERUSALEM
LMD

712 Lord, Whose Love in Humble Service

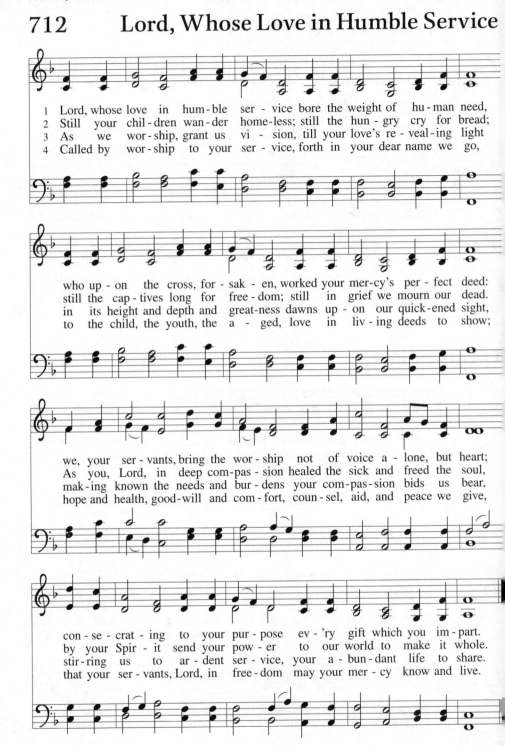

1 Lord, whose love in hum-ble ser-vice bore the weight of hu-man need,
2 Still your chil-dren wan-der home-less; still the hun-gry cry for bread;
3 As we wor-ship, grant us vi - sion, till your love's re - veal-ing light
4 Called by wor-ship to your ser-vice, forth in your dear name we go,

who up - on the cross, for - sak - en, worked your mer-cy's per - fect deed:
still the cap-tives long for free-dom; still in grief we mourn our dead.
in its height and depth and great-ness dawns up - on our quick-ened sight,
to the child, the youth, the a - ged, love in liv-ing deeds to show;

we, your ser - vants, bring the wor - ship not of voice a - lone, but heart;
As you, Lord, in deep com-pas - sion healed the sick and freed the soul,
mak-ing known the needs and bur - dens your com-pas-sion bids us bear,
hope and health, good-will and com - fort, coun - sel, aid, and peace we give,

con - se - crat - ing to your pur - pose ev - 'ry gift which you im - part.
by your Spir - it send your pow - er to our world to make it whole.
stir-ring us to ar - dent ser - vice, your a - bun-dant life to share.
that your ser - vants, Lord, in free-dom may your mer - cy know and live.

Text: Albert F. Bayly, 1901–1984
Music: The Sacred Harp, Philadelphia, 1844; arr. Selected Hymns, 1985
Text © Oxford University Press
Arr. © 1985 Augsburg Fortress

BEACH SPRING
87 87 D

O God of Every Nation

713

1 O God of ev - 'ry na - tion, of ev - 'ry race and land,
2 From search for wealth and pow - er and scorn of truth and right,
3 Lord, strength-en all who la - bor that all may find re - lease
4 Keep bright in us the vi - sion of days when war shall cease,

re - deem your whole cre - a - tion with your al - might - y hand;
from trust in bombs that show - er de - struc-tion through the night,
from fear of rat - tling sa - ber, from dread of war's in - crease;
when ha - tred and di - vi - sion give way to love and peace,

where hate and fear di - vide us and bit - ter threats are hurled,
from pride of race and sta - tion and blind-ness to your way,
when hope and cour-age fal - ter, Lord, let your voice be heard;
till dawns the morn-ing glo - rious when truth and love shall reign,

in love and mer - cy guide us and heal our strife - torn world.
de - liv - er ev - 'ry na - tion, e - ter - nal God, we pray.
with faith that none can al - ter, your ser - vants un - der - gird.
and Christ shall rule vic - to - rious o'er all the world's do - main.

Text: William W. Reid Jr., b. 1923
Music: Welsh tune, 19th cent.
Text © 1958, ren. 1986 The Hymn Society, admin. Hope Publishing Company

LLANGLOFFAN
7676 D

714

O God of Mercy, God of Light

1 O God of mer - cy, God of light, in love and
2 You sent your Son to die for all, that our lost
3 Teach us the les - son Je - sus taught: to feel for
4 For all are kin - dred, far and wide, since Je - sus

mer - cy in - fi - nite, teach us, as ev - er
world might hear your call; oh, hear us lest we
those his blood has bought, that ev - 'ry deed and
Christ for all has died; grant us the will, and

in your sight, to live our lives in you.
stray and fall! We rest our hope in you.
word and thought may work a work for you.
grace pro - vide, to love them all in you.

5 In sickness, sorrow, want, or care,
   may we each other's burdens share;
   may we, where help is needed, there
   give help as though to you.

6 And may your Holy Spirit move
   all those who live to live in love,
   till you receive in heav'n above
   all those who live in you.

Text: Godfrey Thring, 1823–1903, alt.
Music: Joseph Barnby, 1838–1896; arr. hymnal version
Arr. © 2006 Augsburg Fortress

JUST AS I AM
888 6

Christ, Be Our Light

715

1 Long-ing for light, we wait in dark-ness. Long-ing for
2 Long-ing for peace, our world is trou-bled. Long-ing for
3 Long-ing for food, man-y are hun-gry. Long-ing for
4 Long-ing for shel-ter, man-y are home-less. Long-ing for
5 Man-y the gifts, man-y the peo-ple, man-y the

truth, we turn to you. Make us your own,
hope, man-y de-spair. Your word a-lone
wa-ter, man-y still thirst. Make us your bread,
warmth, man-y are cold. Make us your build-ing,
hearts that yearn to be-long. Let us be ser-vants

your ho-ly peo-ple, light for the world to see.
has pow'r to save us. Make us your liv-ing voice.
bro-ken for oth-ers, shared un-til all are fed.
shel-ter-ing oth-ers, walls made of liv-ing stone.
to one an-oth-er, signs of your king-dom come.

Refrain

Christ, be our light! Shine in our hearts. Shine through the

dark-ness. Christ, be our light! Shine in your

church gath-ered to-day.

Text: Bernadette Farrell, b. 1957
Music: Bernadette Farrell
Text and music © 1993 Bernadette Farrell, admin. OCP Publications

CHRIST, BE OUR LIGHT
98 96 and refrain

716   Lord of All Nations, Grant Me Grace

1 Lord of all na - tions, grant me grace to love all
2 Break down the wall that would di - vide thy chil - dren,
3 For - give me, Lord, where I have erred by love - less
4 Give me thy cour - age, Lord, to speak when - ev - er
5 With thine own love may I be filled and by thy

peo - ple, ev - 'ry race; and in each per - son may I
Lord, on ev - 'ry side. My neigh - bor's good let me pur -
act and thought - less word. Make me to see the wrong I
strong op - press the weak. Should I my - self the vic - tim
Ho - ly Spir - it willed, that all I touch, wher - e'er I

see my kin - dred, loved, re - deemed by thee.
sue; let Chris - tian love bind warm and true.
do will cru - ci - fy my Lord a - new.
be, help me for - give, re - mem - b'ring thee.
be, may be di - vine - ly touched by thee.

Text: Olive Wise Spannaus, b. 1916, alt.   BEATUS VIR
Music: *Šamotulský Kancionál*, 1561   LM
Text © 1969 Concordia Publishing House

717   Let Justice Flow like Streams

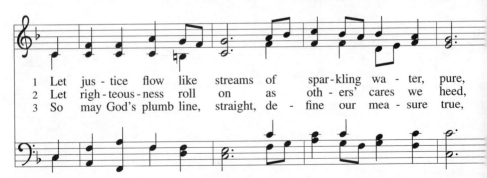

1 Let jus - tice flow like streams of spar - kling wa - ter, pure,
2 Let righ - teous - ness roll on as oth - ers' cares we heed,
3 So may God's plumb line, straight, de - fine our mea - sure true,

Text: Jane Parker Huber, b. 1926   ST. THOMAS
Music: Aaron Williams, 1731–1776   SM
Text © 1984 Jane Parker Huber, admin. Westminster John Knox Press

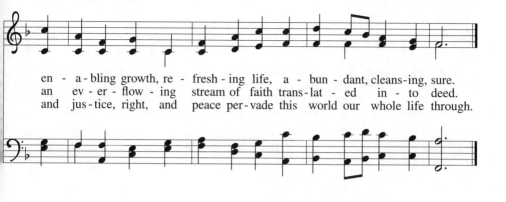

en - a - bling growth, re - fresh - ing life, a - bun - dant, cleans-ing, sure.
an ev - er - flow - ing stream of faith trans-lat - ed in - to deed.
and jus - tice, right, and peace per - vade this world our whole life through.

In a Lowly Manger Born 718

1 In a low - ly man - ger born, hum - ble life be - gun in scorn;
2 Vis - it - ing the lone and lost, stead - y - ing the tem - pest-tossed,
3 Then, to res - cue you and me, Je - sus died up - on the tree.

un - der Jo - seph's watch - ful eye, Je - sus grew as you and I;
giv - ing of him - self in love, call - ing minds to things a - bove.
See in him God's love re - vealed; by his pas - sion we are healed.

knew the suf - f'rings of the weak, knew the pa - tience of the meek,
Sin - ners glad - ly hear his call; pub - li - cans be - fore him fall,
Now he lives in glo - ry bright, lives a - gain in pow'r and might;

hun - gered as but poor folk can; this is he. Be - hold the man!
for in him new life be - gan; this is he. Be - hold the man!
come and take the path he trod, son of Mar - y, Son of God.

Text: Kō Yūki, 1896–1985; tr. composite
Music: Seigi Abe, 1891–1974
Text © 1978 Lutheran Book of Worship, admin. Augsburg Fortress
Music © Seigi Abe, admin. Christian Conference of Asia

MABUNE
7 7 7 7 D

719   Where Cross the Crowded Ways of Life

1 Where cross the crowd-ed ways of life, where sound the
2 In haunts of wretch-ed - ness and need, on shad - owed
3 From ten - der child-hood's help - less - ness, from hu - man
4 The cup of wa - ter giv'n for you still holds the

cries of race and clan, a - bove the noise of
thresh-olds dark with fears, from paths where hide the
grief and bur - dened toil, from fam - ished souls, from
fresh - ness of your grace; yet long these mul - ti -

self - ish strife, we hear your voice, O Son of Man.
lures of greed, we catch the vi - sion of your tears.
sor - row's stress, your heart has nev - er known re - coil.
tudes to view the strong com - pas - sion in your face.

5 O Master, from the mountainside
make haste to heal these hearts of pain;
among these restless throngs abide;
oh, tread the city's streets again;

6 Till all the world shall learn your love
and follow where your feet have trod,
till glorious from your heav'n above
shall come the city of our God.

Text: Frank M. North, 1850–1935, alt.
Music: W. Gardiner, *Sacred Melodies*, 1815

WALTON
LM

We Are Called

1 Come! Live in the light! Shine with the joy and the love of the
2 Come! O-pen your heart! Show your. . mer-cy to all those in
3 Sing! Sing a new song! Sing of that great day when all will be

Lord! We are called to be light for the king-dom, to
fear! We are called to be hope for the hope-less so
one! God will reign, and we'll walk with each oth-er as

live in the free-dom of the cit-y of God.
ha-tred and blind-ness . . . will be . . . no more.
sis-ters and broth-ers . . . u-nit-ed in love.

Refrain

We are called to act with jus-tice, we are called to

love ten-der-ly; we are called to serve one an-

oth-er, to walk hum-bly with God.

Text: David Haas, b. 1957
Music: David Haas
Text and music © 1988 GIA Publications, Inc.

WE ARE CALLED
Irregular

721

Goodness Is Stronger than Evil

Good-ness is stron-ger than e - vil; love is stron-ger than hate;

light is stron-ger than dark - ness; life is stron-ger than death; vic-t'ry is

Oh,

ours, vic-t'ry is ours, through God who loves us. Vic-t'ry is

vic - t'ry is ours, vic-t'ry is ours, through God who loves us. Oh,

ours, vic-t'ry is ours, through God who loves us.

vic - t'ry is ours, vic - t'ry is ours, through God who loves us.

Text: From *An African Prayer Book*, Desmond Tutu, b. 1931
Music: John L. Bell, b. 1949
Text © 1995 Desmond Tutu, admin. Random House, Inc. and Lynn C. Franklin Associates, Ltd.
Music © 1996 Iona Community, admin. GIA Publications, Inc.

O Christ, Your Heart, Compassionate

1 O Christ, your heart, com - pas - sion - ate, bore ev - 'ry hu - man pain.
2 As once you wel-comed those cast down and healed the sick, the blind,
3 O Christ, cre - ate new hearts in us that beat in time with yours,
4 O Love that made the dis - tant stars, yet marks the spar-row's fall,

Its beat - ing was the pulse of God; its breadth, God's vast do - main.
so may all bruised and bro-ken lives through us your help still find.
that, joined by faith with your great heart, be - come love's o - pen doors.
whose arms stretched wide up - on a cross em - brace and bear us all:

The heart of God, the heart of Christ com-bined in per - fect rhyme
Lord, join our hearts with those who weep that none may weep a - lone,
We are your bod - y, ris - en Christ; our hearts, our hands we yield
come, make your church a ser - vant church that walks your ser-vant ways,

to write God's love in hu - man deeds, e - ter - ni - ty in time.
and help us bear an - oth - er's pain as though it were our own.
that through our life and min - is - try your love may be re - vealed.
whose deeds of love rise up to you, a sac - ri - fice of praise!

Text: Herman G. Stuempfle Jr., b. 1923
Music: German melody, 18th cent.; adapt. X. L. Hartig, *Melodien zum Mainzer Gesangbuche*, 1833
Text © 2000 GIA Publications, Inc.

ELLACOMBE
CMD

723 Canticle of the Turning

1 My soul cries out with a joy - ful shout that the
2 Though I am small, my . . . God, my all, you . . .
3 From the halls of pow'r to the for - tress tow'r, not a
4 Though the na - tions rage from . . age to age, we re -

God of my heart is great, and my spir - it sings of the
work great . . things in me, and your mer - cy will last from the
stone will be left on stone. Let the king be - ware for your
mem - ber who holds us fast: God's mer - cy must de -

won - drous things that you bring to the ones who wait.
depths of the past to the end of the age to be.
jus - tice tears ev - 'ry ty - rant . . . from his throne.
liv - er us from the con - quer - or's crush - ing grasp.

You fixed your sight on your ser - vant's plight, and my
Your ver - y name puts the proud to shame, and to
The hun - gry poor shall . . weep no more, for the
This sav - ing word that our fore - bears heard is the

weak - ness you did not spurn, so from east to west shall my
those who would for you yearn, you will show your might, put the
food they can nev - er earn; there are ta - bles spread, ev - 'ry
prom - ise which holds us bound, till the spear and rod can be

name be blest. Could the world be a - bout to turn?
strong to flight, for the world is a - bout to turn.
mouth be fed, for the world is a - bout to turn.
crushed by God, who is turn - ing the world a - round.

Text: Rory Cooney, b. 1952, based on the Magnificat
Music: Irish traditional
Text © 1990 GIA Publications, Inc.

STAR OF COUNTY DOWN
Irregula

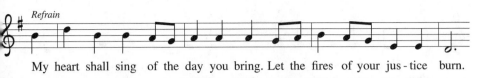

My heart shall sing of the day you bring. Let the fires of your jus - tice burn.

Wipe a - way all tears, for the dawn draws near, and the world is a-bout to turn.

All Who Love and Serve Your City 724

1 All who love and serve your cit - y, all who
2 In your day of loss and sor - row, in your
3 In your day of wealth and plen - ty, wast - ed
4 For all days are days of judg - ment, and the
5 Ris - en Lord, shall yet the cit - y be the

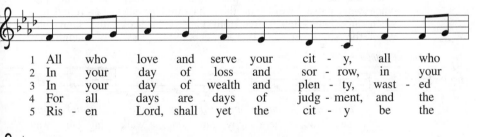

bear its dai - ly stress, all who cry for peace and
day of help - less strife, hon - or, peace, and love re -
work and wast - ed play, call to mind the word of
Lord is wait - ing still, draw - ing near a world that
cit - y of de - spair? Come to - day, our judge, our

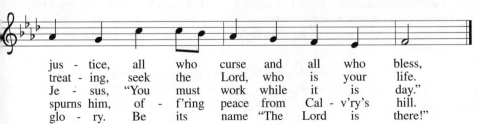

jus - tice, all who curse and all who bless,
treat - ing, seek the Lord, who is your life.
Je - sus, "You must work while it is day."
spurns him, of - f'ring peace from Cal - v'ry's hill.
glo - ry. Be its name "The Lord is there!"

Text: Erik Routley, 1917–1982
Music: Paul D. Weber, b. 1949
Text © 1969 Stainer & Bell Ltd., admin. in USA and Canada by Hope Publishing Company
Music © 2006 Augsburg Fortress

NEW ORLEANS
8 7 8 7

When the Poor Ones

725

Cuando el pobre

1 Cuan - do el po - bre   na - da   tie - ne   y aún re - par - te,
1 When   the   poor ones,   who have   noth - ing,   still   are   giv - ing;
2 When com - pas - sion   gives the   suf - f'ring   con - so - la - tion;
3 When   our   spir - its,   like   a   chal - ice,   brim with glad - ness;
4 When the good - ness   poured from heav - en   fills   our   dwell - ings;

cuan - do   al - guien   pa - sa   sed   y a - gua nos   da,
when the thirst - y   pass the   cup,   wa - ter   to   share;
when ex - pect - ing   brings to   birth   hope that was   lost;
when our voic - es,   full and   clear,   sing out the   truth;
when the na - tions   work to   change   war in - to   peace;

cuan - do el dé - bil   a su her - ma - no   for - ta - le - ce:
when the wound - ed   of - fer oth - ers   strength and heal - ing:
when we choose love,   not the ha - tred   all   a - round us:
when our long - ings,   free from en - vy,   seek   the hum - ble:
when the strang - er   is ac - cept - ed   as   our neigh - bor:

Refrain / Estribillo

Va Dios mis - mo en nues-tro   mis - mo   ca - mi - nar;
We see God,   here   by our   side,   walk - ing our   way;

va Dios mis - mo en nues-tro mis - mo   ca - mi - nar.
we see God, here   by our side, walk - ing our   way.

2 Cuando alguno sufre y logra su consuelo,
   cuando espera y no se cansa de esperar,
   cuando amamos, aunque el odio nos rodee:
   Estribillo

3 Cuando crece la alegría y nos inunda,
   cuando dicen nuestros labios la verdad,
   cuando amamos el sentir de los sencillos
   Estribillo

4 Cuando abunda el bien y llena los hogares,
   cuando alguien donde hay guerra pone paz,
   cuando "hermano" le llamamos al extraño:
   Estribillo

Text: José Antonio Olivar, b. 1939; tr. Martin A. Seltz, b. 1951
Music: Miguel Manzano, b. 1934
Text and music © 1971, 1998 J. A. Olivar, Miguel Manzano, and San Pablo Internacional—SSP, admin. OCP Publications

EL CAMINO
12 11 12 11 1

Light Dawns on a Weary World 726

1 Light dawns on a wea - ry world when eyes be - gin to
2 Love grows in a wea - ry world when hun - gry hearts find
3 Hope blooms in a wea - ry world when crea - tures, once for -

see all peo - ple's dig - ni - ty. Light dawns on a
bread and chil - dren's dreams are fed. Love grows in a
lorn, find wil - der - ness re - born. Hope blooms in a

wea - ry world: the prom - ised day of jus - tice comes.
wea - ry world: the prom - ised feast of plen - ty comes.
wea - ry world: the prom - ised green of E - den comes.

Refrain

The trees shall clap their hands; the dry lands, gush with springs;

the hills and moun - tains shall break forth with sing - ing!

We shall go out in joy, and be led forth in peace,

as all the world in won - der ech - oes sha - lom.

Text: Mary Louise Bringle, b. 1953
Music: William P. Rowan, b. 1951
Text © 2002 GIA Publications, Inc.
Music © 2000 William P. Rowan, admin. GIA Publications, Inc.

TEMPLE OF PEACE
7 6 6 7 8 and refrain

727 Lord Christ, When First You Came to Earth

1 Lord Christ, when first you came to earth, up-
2 O awe-some Love, which finds no room in
3 New ad-vent of the love of Christ, will
4 O wound-ed hands of Je-sus, build in

on a cross they bound you, and mocked your sav-ing
life where sin de-nies you, and, doomed to death, shall
we a-gain re-fuse you, till in the night of
us your new cre-a-tion; our pride is dust, our

king-ship's worth by thorns with which they crowned you. And
bring to doom the pow'r that cru-ci-fies you, till
hate and war we per-ish as we lose you? From
vaunt is stilled; we wait your rev-e-la-tion. O

still our wrongs may fash-ion now new thorns to pierce that
not a stone is left on stone, and then the na-tions'
an-cient doubts our minds re-lease to seek the king-dom
Love that tri-umphs o-ver loss, we bring our hearts be-

stead-y brow, and robe of sor-row round you.
pride, o'er-thrown, will nev-er-more de-fy you!
of your peace, by which a-lone we choose you.
fore your cross; come, fin-ish your sal-va-tion.

Text: W. Russell Bowie, 1882–1969, alt.
Music: Medieval European tune

MIT FREUDEN ZAR
878788

Blest Are They

728

Leader or All

1 Blest are they, the poor in spir - it; theirs is the
2 Blest are they, the low - ly ones; . . . they shall in -
3 Blest are they . . . . . who show mer - cy; mer - cy
4 Blest are they . . . . . who seek peace; . . they are the
5 Blest are you who suf - fer hate, . . . all . . . be -

king - dom of God. Blest are they,
her - it the earth. Blest are they who
shall . . . be theirs. Blest are they, the
chil - dren of God. Blest are they who
cause . . . of me. Re - joice, be glad,

full of sor - row; they shall be con - soled.
hun - ger and thirst; they shall have their fill.
pure of heart; they . . . . . shall see God.
suf - fer in faith; the glo - ry of God is theirs.
yours is the king - dom; shine for all to see.

Refrain
All

Re - joice and be glad!

Bless - ed are you, ho - ly are you!

Re - joice and be glad!

Yours is the king-dom of God!

Text: David Haas, b. 1957
Music: David Haas
Text and music © 1985 GIA Publications, Inc.

729 The Church of Christ, in Every Age

1 The church of Christ, in ev - 'ry age be - set by
2 A - cross the world, a - cross the street, the vic - tims
3 Then let the ser - vant church a - rise, a car - ing
4 For he a - lone, whose blood was shed, can cure the
5 We have no mis - sion but to serve in full o -

change, but Spir - it - led, must claim and test its
of in - jus - tice cry for shel - ter and for
church that longs to be a part - ner in Christ's
fe - ver in our blood, and teach us how to
be - dience to our Lord; to care for all, with -

her - i - tage and keep on ris - ing from the dead.
bread to eat, and nev - er live be - fore they die.
sac - ri - fice, and clothed in Christ's hu - man - i - ty.
share our bread and feed the starv - ing mul - ti - tude.
out re - serve, and spread his lib - er - at - ing word.

Text: Fred Pratt Green, 1903–2000
Music: William Knapp, 1698–1768
Text © 1971 Hope Publishing Company

WAREHA
L

Lord Our God, with Praise We Come 730

1 Lord our God, with praise we come be - fore you.
2 God is God, though lands were all for - sak - en.
3 Vales and hills shall move from their foun - da - tions;

Let all na - tions hum - bly now im - plore you.
God is God, though all by death were tak - en.
heav'n and earth shall crash in con - ster - na - tion;

May we en - deav - or to praise you ev - er, and
Al - though all rac - es had left no trac - es, in
moun - tains tran - scend - ing will have their end - ing. Then

ceas - ing nev - er, may we for - ev - er a - dore you.
star - ry spac - es God's love em - brac - es cre - a - tion.
Christ de - scend - ing shall bring un - end - ing sal - va - tion.

Text: Petter Dass, 1647–1707; tr. Peter A. Sveeggen, 1881–1959, alt.
Music: Norwegian traditional, arr. hymnal version
Text © 1951 Augsburg Publishing House
Arr. © 2006 Augsburg Fortress

ROMEDAL
10 10 10 5 8

731

Earth and All Stars!

1 Earth and all stars! Loud rush-ing plan - ets!
2 Trum - pet and pipes! Loud clash-ing cym - bals!
3 En - gines and steel! Loud pound-ing ham - mers!
4 Class-rooms and labs! Loud boil-ing test tubes!
5 Knowl-edge and truth! Loud sound-ing wis - dom!

Sing to the Lord a new song!
Sing to the Lord a new song!
Sing to the Lord a new song!
Sing to the Lord a new song!
Sing to the Lord a new song!

Hail, wind, and rain! Loud blow-ing snow - storm!
Harp, lute, and lyre! Loud hum-ming cel - los!
Lime - stone and beams! Loud build-ing work - ers!
Ath - lete and band! Loud cheer-ing peo - ple!
Daugh - ter and son! Loud pray-ing mem - bers!

Sing to the Lord a new song!
Sing to the Lord a new song!
Sing to the Lord a new song!
Sing to the Lord a new song!
Sing to the Lord a new song!

Refrain

God has done mar - vel - ous things.

I too sing prais - es with a new song!

Text: Herbert F. Brokering, b. 1926
Music: David N. Johnson, 1922–1987
Text and music © 1968 Augsburg Publishing House

EARTH AND ALL STAR
4 5 7 D and refrai

Borning Cry

1 "I was there to hear your born-ing cry, I'll be there when you are old.
2 "When you heard the won-der of the Word I was there to cheer you on;
3 "In the mid-dle a-ges of your life, not too old, no lon-ger young,

I re-joiced the day you were bap-tized to see your life un-fold.
you were raised to praise the liv-ing Lord, to whom you now be-long.
I'll be there to guide you through the night, com-plete what I've be-gun.

I was there when you were but a child, with a faith to suit you well;
If you find some-one to share your time and you join your hearts as one,
When the eve-ning gent-ly clos-es in and you shut your wea-ry eyes,

in a blaze of light you wan-dered off to find where de-mons dwell."
I'll be there to make your vers-es rhyme from dusk till ris-ing sun."
I'll be there as I have al-ways been, with just one more sur-prise."

4 "I was there to hear your born-ing cry, I'll be there when you are old.

I re-joiced the day you were bap-tized to see your life un-fold."

Text: John C. Ylvisaker, b. 1937
Music: John C. Ylvisaker
Text and music © 1985 John C. Ylvisaker

733

Great Is Thy Faithfulness

1 Great is thy faith-ful-ness, O God my Fa-ther; there is no
2 Sum-mer and win-ter and spring-time and har-vest, sun, moon, and
3 Par-don for sin and a peace that en-dur-eth, thine own dear

shad-ow of turn-ing with thee; thou chang-est not, thy com-
stars in their cours-es a - bove join with all na-ture in
pres-ence to cheer and to guide; strength for to - day and bright

pas-sions they fail not; as thou hast been, thou for - ev - er wilt be.
man - i - fold wit-ness to thy great faith-ful - ness, mer-cy, and love.
hope for to - mor-row, bless-ings all mine, with ten thou-sand be - side!

Refrain

Great is thy faith-ful-ness! Great is thy faith-ful-ness! Morn-ing by

Text: Thomas O. Chisholm, 1866–1960
Music: William M. Runyan, 1870–1957
Text and music © 1923, ren. 1951 Hope Publishing Company

FAITHFULNESS
11 10 11 10 and refrain

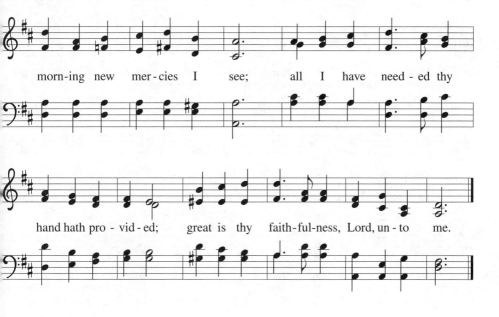

morn-ing new mer-cies I see; all I have need-ed thy

hand hath pro - vid - ed; great is thy faith-ful-ness, Lord, un - to me.

God, Whose Farm Is All Creation 734

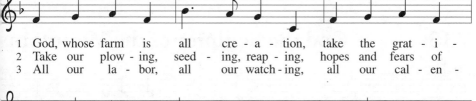

1 God, whose farm is all cre - a - tion, take the grat - i -
2 Take our plow - ing, seed - ing, reap - ing, hopes and fears of
3 All our la - bor, all our watch - ing, all our cal - en -

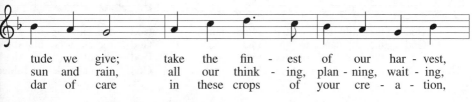

tude we give; take the fin - est of our har - vest,
sun and rain, all our think - ing, plan - ning, wait - ing,
dar of care in these crops of your cre - a - tion,

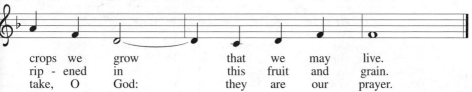

crops we grow that we may live.
rip - ened in this fruit and grain.
take, O God: they are our prayer.

Text: John Arlott, 1914–1991
Music: Larry J. Long, b. 1954
Text © Trustees of the late John Arlott
Music © 2006 Augsburg Fortress

HARVEST GIFTS
8 7 8 7

Alternate tune: OMNI DIE

735   Mothering God, You Gave Me Birth

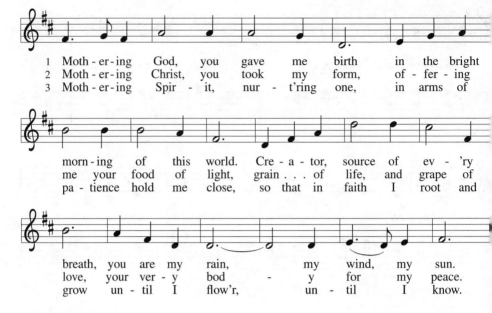

1 Moth-er-ing God, you gave me birth in the bright
2 Moth-er-ing Christ, you took my form, of-fer-ing
3 Moth-er-ing Spir-it, nur-t'ring one, in arms of

morn-ing of this world. Cre-a-tor, source of ev-'ry
me your food of light, grain... of life, and grape of
pa-tience hold me close, so that in faith I root and

breath, you are my rain, my wind, my sun.
love, your ver-y bod - y for my peace.
grow un-til I flow'r, un - til I know.

Text: Jean Janzen, b. 1933; based on Julian of Norwich, c. 1342–c. 1413
Music: Carolyn Jennings, b. 1936
Text © 1991 Jean Janzen, admin. Augsburg Fortress
Music © 1995 Augsburg Fortress

NORWIC
L M

736   God the Sculptor of the Mountains

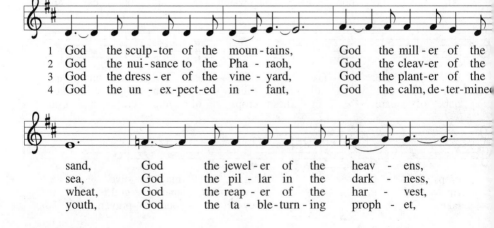

1 God the sculp-tor of the moun-tains, God the mill-er of the
2 God the nui-sance to the Pha - raoh, God the cleav-er of the
3 God the dress-er of the vine - yard, God the plant-er of the
4 God the un - ex-pect-ed in - fant, God the calm, de-ter-mined

sand, God the jewel-er of the heav - ens,
sea, God the pil - lar in the dark - ness,
wheat, God the reap - er of the har - vest,
youth, God the ta - ble-turn-ing proph - et,

Text: John Thornburg, b. 1954
Music: Amanda Husberg, b. 1940
Text © 1993 John Thornburg
Music © 1996 Abingdon Press, admin. The Copyright Company

JENNINGS–HOUSTO
87878

God the pot - ter of the land: you are womb of all cre -
God the bea - con of the free: you are fount of all de -
God the source of all we eat: you are host at ev - 'ry
God the re - sur-rect - ed truth: you are pres - ent ev - 'ry

a - tion, we are form - less; shape us now.
liv - 'rance, we are sight - less; lead us now.
ta - ble, we are hun - gry; feed us now.
mo - ment, we are search - ing; meet us now.

He Comes to Us as One Unknown 737

1 He comes to us as one un-known, a breath un - seen, un -
2 He comes when souls in si - lence lie and thoughts of day de -
3 He comes to us in sound of seas, the o - cean's fume and
4 He comes in love as once he came by flesh and blood and
5 He comes in truth when faith is grown; be - lieved, o - beyed, a -

heard; as though with - in a heart of stone, or shriv - eled seed in
part; half - seen up - on the in - ward eye, a fall - ing star a -
foam; yet small and still up - on the breeze, a wind that stirs the
birth; to bear with - in our mor - tal frame a life, a death, a
dored; the Christ in all the scrip - tures shown, as yet un - seen, but

dark - ness sown, a pulse of be - ing stirred, a pulse of be - ing stirred.
cross the sky of night with - in the heart, of night with - in the heart.
tops of trees, a voice to call us home, a voice to call us home.
sav - ing name, for ev - 'ry child of earth, for ev - 'ry child of earth.
not un - known, our Sav - ior and our Lord, our Sav - ior and our Lord.

Text: Timothy Dudley-Smith, b. 1926
Music: C. Hubert H. Parry, 1848–1918
Text © 1984 Hope Publishing Company

REPTON
868866

738 God Created Heaven and Earth

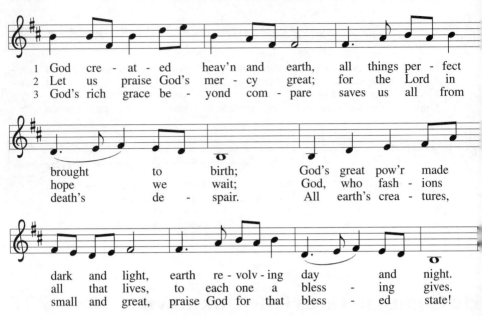

1 God cre - at - ed heav'n and earth, all things per - fect
2 Let us praise God's mer - cy great; for the Lord in
3 God's rich grace be - yond com - pare saves us all from

brought to birth; God's great pow'r made
hope we wait; God, who fash - ions
death's de - spair. All earth's crea - tures,

dark and light, earth re - volv - ing day and night.
all that lives, to each one a bless - ing gives.
small and great, praise God for that bless - ed state!

Text: Taiwanese traditional; tr. Boris Anderson, b. 1918, and Clare Anderson, b. 1923
Music: Piⁿ po melody, from Taiwanese Seng-si
Text © Boris and Clare Anderson, admin. Christian Conference of Asia

TŌA-SĪA
7 7 7 7

739 Touch the Earth Lightly

1 Touch the earth light - ly, use the earth gent - ly,
2 We who en - dan - ger, who cre - ate hun - ger,
3 Let there be green - ing, birth from the burn - ing,
4 God of all liv - ing, God of all lov - ing,

nour - ish the life of the world in our care:
a - gents of death for all crea - tures that live,
wa - ter that bless - es, and air that is sweet,
God of the seed - ling, the snow, and the sun,

Text: Shirley Erena Murray, b. 1931
Music: Colin Gibson, b. 1933
Text and music © 1992 Hope Publishing Company

TENDERNES
55 10

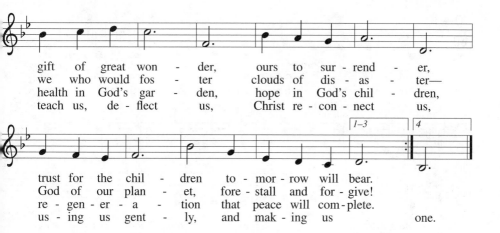

gift of great won - der, ours to sur - rend - er,
we who would fos - ter clouds of dis - as - ter—
health in God's gar - den, hope in God's chil - dren,
teach us, de - flect us, Christ re - con - nect us,

1–3   *4*

trust for the chil - dren to - mor - row will bear.
God of our plan - et, fore - stall and for - give!
re - gen - er - a - tion that peace will com - plete.
us - ing us gent - ly, and mak - ing us one.

God of the Sparrow   740

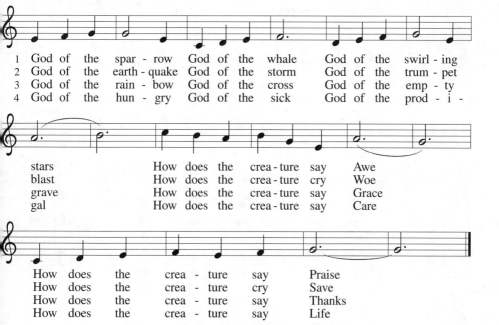

1 God of the spar - row God of the whale God of the swirl - ing
2 God of the earth - quake God of the storm God of the trum - pet
3 God of the rain - bow God of the cross God of the emp - ty
4 God of the hun - gry God of the sick God of the prod - i -

stars   How does the crea - ture say Awe
blast   How does the crea - ture cry Woe
grave   How does the crea - ture say Grace
gal   How does the crea - ture say Care

How does the crea - ture say Praise
How does the crea - ture cry Save
How does the crea - ture say Thanks
How does the crea - ture say Life

5 God of the neighbor God of the foe
God of the pruning hook
How does the creature say Love
How does the creature say Peace

6 God of the ages God near at hand
God of the loving heart
How do your children say Joy
How do your children say Home

Text: Jaroslav J. Vajda, b. 1919
Music: Carl F. Schalk, b. 1929
Text © 1983 Concordia Publishing House
Music © 1983 GIA Publications, Inc.

ROEDER
9677

Your Will Be Done
Mayenziwe

Ma - ye - nzi - we 'nta - ndo ya - kho.
Your will be done on earth, O Lord.

Ma - ye -
Your will

Ma - ye - nzi - we 'nta - ndo ya - kho.
Your will be done on earth, O Lord.

Ma - ye -
Your will

Ma - ye - nzi - we 'nta - ndo ya - kho.
Your will be done on earth, O Lord.

Ma - ye - nzi - we 'nta - ndo ya - kho.
Your will be done on earth, O Lord.

Ma - ye - nzi - we 'nta - ndo ya - kho.
Your will be done on earth, O Lord.

Text: South African, based on the Lord's Prayer
Music: South African traditional, as taught by Gobingca George Mxadana; transc. John L. Bell, b. 1949
Arr. © 1990 Iona Community, admin. GIA Publications, Inc.

MAYENZIW
8 8 8 8

What a Friend We Have in Jesus

1 What a friend we have in Je - sus,   all   our sins and griefs to bear!
2 Have we tri - als and temp-ta - tions?   Is   there trou-ble an - y-where?
3 Are we weak and heav-y - lad - en,   cum-bered with a   load of care?

What a priv - i - lege to car - ry   ev - 'ry-thing to God in prayer!
We should nev - er be dis - cour - aged— take it to the Lord in prayer.
Pre - cious Sav - ior, still our ref - uge— take it to the Lord in prayer.

Oh, what peace we of - ten for - feit;   oh, what need-less pain we bear—
Can we find a friend so faith - ful   who will all our sor-rows share?
Do your friends de-spise, for - sake you?   Take it to the Lord in prayer.

all be - cause we do not car - ry   ev - 'ry-thing to God in prayer!
Je - sus knows our ev - 'ry weak - ness— take it to the Lord in prayer.
In his arms he'll take and shield you;   you will find a so - lace there.

Text: Joseph Scriven, 1820–1886
Music: Charles C. Converse, 1832–1918

CONVERSE
8 7 8 7 D

743   Now to the Holy Spirit Let Us Pray

1 Now to the Ho - ly Spir - it let us pray
2 O sweet - est Love, your grace on us be - stow;
3 Tran - scen - dent com - fort in our ev - 'ry need,
4 Shine in our hearts, O Spir - it, pre - cious light,

for true faith, most need - ed on our way:
set our hearts with sa - cred fire a - glow,
help us nei - ther scorn nor death to heed,
that we Je - sus Christ may know a - right,

Guide us and de - fend us when life is end - ing
that with hearts u - nit - ed we love each oth - er,
that we may not fal - ter, nor cour - age fail us
cling - ing to our Sav - ior, whose blood has bought us,

and our jour - ney home-ward is tend - ing. Lord, have mer - cy!
ev - 'ry strang - er, sis - ter, and broth - er. Lord, have mer - cy!
when the foe shall taunt and as - sail us. Lord, have mer - cy!
who to our true home-land has brought us. Lord, have mer - cy!

Text: Medieval German *Leise,* st. 1; Martin Luther, 1483–1546, sts. 2–4; tr. composite
Music: J. Walter, *Geistliche Gesangbüchlein,* 1524
Text sts. 1, 4 © 2006 Augsburg Fortress
Text sts. 2–3 © 1969 Concordia Publishing House

NUN BITTEN WIR
10 9 11 9 4

744   Lord, Be Glorified

1 In my life, Lord, be glo - ri - fied, be glo - ri - fied;
2 In our song, Lord, be glo - ri - fied, be glo - ri - fied;
3 In your church, Lord, be glo - ri - fied, be glo - ri - fied;
4 In your world, Lord, be glo - ri - fied, be glo - ri - fied;

Text: Bob Kilpatrick, b. 1952
Music: Bob Kilpatrick
Text and music © 1978 Bob Kilpatrick Music, assigned 1998 to The Lorenz Corporation

BE GLORIFIED
4 4 4 4

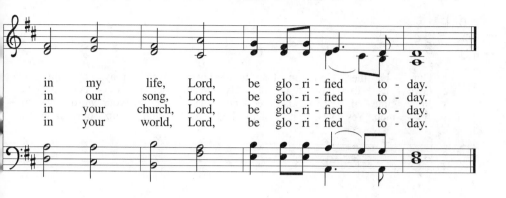

in my life, Lord, be glo - ri - fied to - day.
in our song, Lord, be glo - ri - fied to - day.
in your church, Lord, be glo - ri - fied to - day.
in your world, Lord, be glo - ri - fied to - day.

Lord, Teach Us How to Pray Aright   745

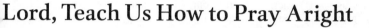

1 Lord, teach us how to pray a - right, with rev - 'rence and with fear.
2 We per - ish if we cease from prayer; oh, grant us pow'r to pray.
3 Give deep hu - mil - i - ty; the sense of god - ly sor - row give;
4 Faith in the on - ly sac - ri - fice that can for sin a - tone;
5 Give these, and then your will be done; thus strength-ened with all might,

Though dust and ash - es in your sight, we may, we must draw near.
And when to meet you we pre - pare, Lord, meet us on our way.
a strong de - sire, with con - fi - dence, to hear your voice and live;
to cast our hopes, to fix our eyes on Christ, on Christ a - lone.
we, through your Spir - it and your Son, shall pray, and pray a - right.

Text: James Montgomery, 1771–1854, alt.
Music: Orlando Gibbons, 1583–1625

SONG 67
CM

746

Our Father, God in Heaven Above

1 Our Fa - ther, God in heav'n a - bove, we pray, u - nit - ed
2 Give us to - day our dai - ly bread; let ev - 'ry - one be
3 In time of tri - al, res - cue us. Let your word give suc -
4 A - men. Yes, yes, it shall be so! Build up our faith and

in your love: Your name be hal - lowed. Help us, Lord,
clothed and fed. For - give our sins, as we for - give
cess to us when, on our left and on our right,
make it grow; be - set by doubt, help us be - lieve

in faith - ful - ness to keep your word. Your king - dom come; your
when oth - ers hurt us as we live. Help us to dwell in
temp - ta - tions chal - lenge us to fight. De - liv - er us from
what here we ask we shall re - ceive. So, by your prom - ise,

will be done on earth as there be - fore your throne.
har - mo - ny and serve each oth - er will - ing - ly.
e - vil's pow'r and com - fort us in life's last hour.
in your name, with loud A - men your Yes we claim!

Text: Martin Luther, 1483–1546, abridged; tr. hymnal version
Music: V. Schumann, *Geistliche Lieder*, 1539
Text © 2006 Augsburg Fortress

VATER UNSER
8 8 8 8 8 8

Our Father, God in Heaven Above 747

1 Our Father, God in heav'n above,
pour out on us the Spirit's love
that we unite in word and deed
and call to you in ev'ry need;
help us no thoughtless words to say,
but, as our Savior taught, to pray.

2 Your name be hallowed. Help us, Lord,
in faithfulness to keep your word,
that to the glory of your name
we walk before you free from blame.
Let no false teaching make us stray;
lead all the lost to find your way.

3 Your kingdom come: yours will it be
in time and in eternity.
Let your good Spirit from on high
our hearts with gifts of grace supply.
Break Satan's reign of hate and rage;
preserve your church from age to age.

4 Your gracious will on earth be done
as there in heav'n before your throne,
that firm in faith we may remain
in time of joy and time of pain.
Curb flesh and blood and ev'ry ill
that sets itself against your will.

5 Give us today our daily bread;
let ev'ryone be clothed and fed;
in plague and famine, war and strife,
preserve from all that threatens life;
that all the world may live in peace,
that greed be gone and love increase.

6 Forgive our sins, we now implore,
that they may trouble us no more,
and let us ev'ry sin forgive
when others hurt us as we live.
Help us to dwell in harmony
and serve each other willingly.

7 In time of trial, rescue us.
Let your word give success to us
when, on our left and on our right,
temptations challenge us to fight.
Your Spirit be the armor strong
that steels our faith to right the wrong.

8 Deliver us from evil, Lord;
in fearsome days your help afford.
Free us at last from death's grim pow'r,
and comfort us in life's last hour;
in mercy give us calm release,
breathe into us eternal peace.

9 Amen. Yes, yes, it shall be so!
Build up our faith and make it grow;
beset by doubt, help us believe
what here we ask we shall receive.
So, by your promise, in your name,
with loud Amen your Yes we claim!

Text: Martin Luther, 1483–1546; tr. hymnal version
Text © 2006 Augsburg Fortress

VATER UNSER
888888

748   O God in Heaven

1 O God in heav - en, grant to your chil - dren mer - cy and
2 Je - sus, re - deem - er, help us re - mem - ber your pain and
3 Spir - it un - end - ing, give us your bless - ing: strength for the

bless-ing, songs nev - er ceas - ing, grace to in - vite us, peace to u-
pas - sion, your res - ur - rec - tion, your call to fol - low, your love to-
wea - ry, help for the need - y, hope for the scorn-ful, peace for the

nite us— O God in heav - en, au - thor of love.
mor - row— Je - sus, re - deem - er, sav - ior, and friend.
mourn-ful— Spir - it un - end - ing, com-fort and guide.

Text: Daniel T. Niles, 1908–1970, alt.
Music: Ilonggo (Philippines) traditional, adapt. Elena G. Maquiso, 1961–2005; arr. *Cantate Domino*, 1980
Text © 1964 Christian Conference of Asia
Tune © 1962 Elena G. Maquiso; arr. © 1980 World Council of Churches

HALAD
5 5 5 5 5 5 5

O God of Love, O King of Peace

749

1 O God of love, O King of peace, make wars through-
2 Re - mem - ber, Lord, your works of old, the won - ders
3 Whom shall we trust but you, O Lord? Where rest but
4 Where saints and an - gels dwell a - bove all hearts are

out the world to cease; our greed and sin - ful wrath re - strain.
that our el - ders told; re - mem - ber not our sins' deep stain.
on your faith - ful word? None ev - er called on you in vain.
knit in ho - ly love; oh, bind us in that heav'n - ly chain.

Give peace, O God, give peace a - gain.

Text: Henry W. Baker, 1821–1877
Music: J. Klug, *Geistliche Lieder*, 1543

ERHALT UNS, HERR
LM

750   Lord, Thee I Love with All My Heart

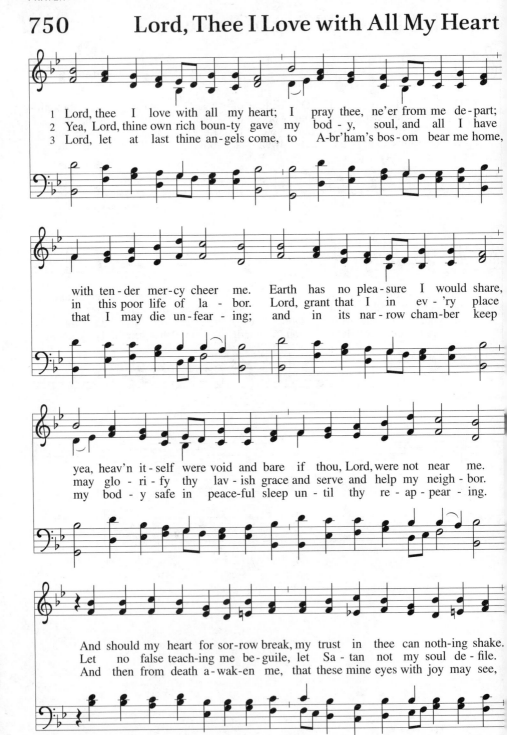

1 Lord, thee I love with all my heart; I pray thee, ne'er from me de-part;
2 Yea, Lord, thine own rich boun-ty gave my bod-y, soul, and all I have
3 Lord, let at last thine an-gels come, to A-br'ham's bos-om bear me home,

with ten-der mer-cy cheer me. Earth has no plea-sure I would share,
in this poor life of la-bor. Lord, grant that I in ev-'ry place
that I may die un-fear-ing; and in its nar-row cham-ber keep

yea, heav'n it-self were void and bare if thou, Lord, were not near me.
may glo-ri-fy thy lav-ish grace and serve and help my neigh-bor.
my bod-y safe in peace-ful sleep un-til thy re-ap-pear-ing.

And should my heart for sor-row break, my trust in thee can noth-ing shake.
Let no false teach-ing me be-guile, let Sa-tan not my soul de-file.
And then from death a-wak-en me, that these mine eyes with joy may see,

Text: Martin Schalling, 1532–1608; tr. Catherine Winkworth, 1827–1878, alt.
Music: B. Schmid, *Orgeltabulaturbuch*, 1577

HERZLICH LIEB
P M

Thou art the por - tion I have sought; thy pre - cious
Give strength and pa - tience un - to me to bear my
O Son of God, thy glo - rious face, my Sav - ior

blood my soul has bought. Lord Je - sus Christ, my God and Lord,
cross and fol - low thee. Lord Je - sus Christ, my God and Lord,
and my fount of grace. Lord Je - sus Christ, my prayer at - tend,

my God and Lord, for - sake me not! I trust thy word.
my God and Lord, in death thy com - fort still af - ford.
my prayer at - tend, and I will praise thee with - out end!

O Lord, Hear My Prayer
The Lord Is My Song

751

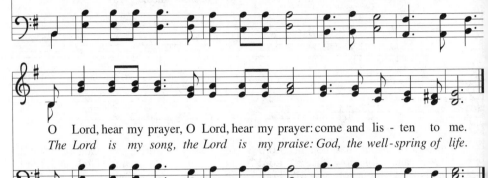

O Lord, hear my prayer, O Lord, hear my prayer: when I call, an - swer me.
OR *The Lord is my song, the Lord is my praise: all my hope comes from God.*

O Lord, hear my prayer, O Lord, hear my prayer: come and lis - ten to me.
The Lord is my song, the Lord is my praise: God, the well - spring of life.

Text: Psalm 102:1–2; Taizé Community, adapt.
Music: Jacques Berthier, 1923–1994
Text and music © 1982, 1991 Les Presses de Taizé, admin. GIA Publications, Inc.

HEAR MY PRAYER
556D

752 Lord, Listen to Your Children Praying

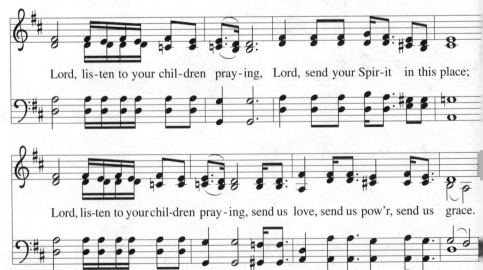

Lord, lis-ten to your chil-dren pray-ing, Lord, send your Spir-it in this place;

Lord, lis-ten to your chil-dren pray-ing, send us love, send us pow'r, send us grace.

Text: Ken Medema, b. 1943
Music: Ken Medema
Text and music © 1973 Hope Publishing Company

CHILDREN PRAYING
9899

Dona nobis pacem

753

1 *Canon*

Do-na no-bis pa-cem, pa-cem. Do-na no-bis pa - cem.

2

Do - na no - bis pa-cem. Do-na no-bis pa - cem.

3

Do - na no - bis pa-cem. Do-na no-bis pa - cem.

Text: Traditional
Music: Traditional

DONA NOBIS PACEM
86

Jesus, the Very Thought of You

754

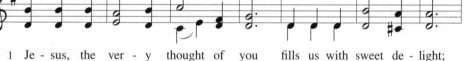

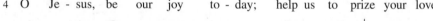

1 Je - sus, the ver - y thought of you fills us with sweet de - light;
2 No voice can sing, no heart can frame, nor can the mind re - call
3 O Hope of ev - 'ry con - trite soul, O Joy of all the meek,
4 O Je - sus, be our joy to - day; help us to prize your love;

but sweet-er far your face to view and rest with - in your light.
a sweet-er sound than your blest name, O Sav - ior of us all!
how kind you are to those who fall! How good to those who seek!
grant us at last to hear you say: "Come, share my home a - bove."

Text: attr. Bernard of Clairvaux, 1091–1153; tr. Edward Caswall, 1814–1878
Music: John B. Dykes, 1823–1876

ST. AGNES
CM

755

Jesus, Savior, Pilot Me

1 Je - sus, Sav - ior, pi - lot me o - ver
2 As a moth - er stills her child, thou canst
3 When at last I near the shore, and the

life's tem - pes - tuous sea; un - known waves be - fore me
hush the o - cean wild; bois - t'rous waves o - bey thy
fear - ful break-ers roar twixt me and the peace-ful

roll, hid - ing rock and treach-'rous shoal; chart and
will when thou say'st to them: "Be still." Won - drous
rest, then, while lean - ing on thy breast, may I

com - pass come from thee. Je - sus, Sav - ior, pi - lot me.
sov - 'reign of the sea, Je - sus, Sav - ior, pi - lot me.
hear thee say to me: "Fear not, I will pi - lot thee."

Text: Edward Hopper, 1818–1888
Music: John Edgar Gould, 1822–1875

PILOT
7 7 7 7 7 7

Eternal Father, Strong to Save 756

1 E - ter - nal Fa - ther, strong to save, whose arm has bound the
2 O Sav - ior, whose al - might - y word the winds and waves sub -
3 O Ho - ly Spir - it, who didst brood up - on the cha - os
4 O Trin - i - ty of love and pow'r, all trav - 'lers guard in

rest - less wave, who bade the might - y o - cean deep its
mis - sive heard, who walked up - on the foam - ing deep, and
dark and rude, and bid its an - gry tu - mult cease, and
dan - ger's hour from rock and tem - pest, fire and foe, pro -

own ap - point - ed lim - its keep: oh, hear us when we
calm a - mid the storm didst sleep: oh, hear us when we
give, for wild con - fu - sion, peace: oh, hear us when we
tect them where - so - e'er they go; thus ev - er - more shall

cry to thee for those in per - il on the sea.
cry to thee for those in per - il on the sea.
cry to thee for those in per - il on the sea.
rise to thee glad hymns and praise from land and sea.

Text: William Whiting, 1825–1878, alt.
Music: John B. Dykes, 1823–1876

MELITA
888888

757   All My Hope on God Is Founded

1 All my hope on God is found - ed who will all my
2 Mor - tal pride and earth - ly glo - ry, sword and crown be -
3 Great thy good-ness, e'er en - dur - ing; deep thy wis - dom,
4 Still from earth to God e - ter - nal sac - ri - fice of

trust re - new, who through change and chance will guide me,
tray our trust; what with care and toil we fash - ion,
pass - ing thought; splen - dor, light, and life at - tend thee,
praise be done, high a - bove all prais - es prais - ing

on - ly good and on - ly true. God un - known, God a -
tow'r and tem - ple, fall to dust. But thy pow'r, hour by
beau - ty spring - ing out of naught. Ev - er - more from thy
for the gift of God's own Son. Christ doth call one and

lone, call my heart to be thine own.
hour, is my tem - ple and my tow'r.
store new - born worlds rise and a - dore.
all: ye who fol - low shall not fall.

Text: Joachim Neander, 1650–1680; para. Robert Bridges, 1844–1930, alt.
Music: Herbert Howells, 1892–1983
Music © 1968 Novello & Co, Ltd., London

MICHAEL
8 7 8 7 3 3 7

758   You Are the Way

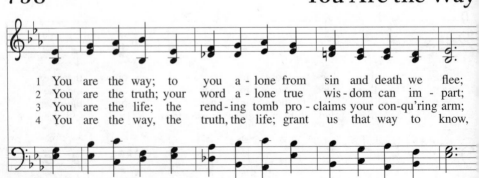

1 You are the way; to you a - lone from sin and death we flee;
2 You are the truth; your word a - lone true wis - dom can im - part;
3 You are the life; the rend-ing tomb pro - claims your con-qu'ring arm;
4 You are the way, the truth, the life; grant us that way to know,

Text: George W. Doane, 1799–1859, alt.
Music: *Psalter*, Edinburgh, 1615

DUNDEE
CM

all those who search for God, you find and by your grace set free.
you on - ly can in - form the mind and pu - ri - fy the heart.
and those who put their trust in you not death nor hell shall harm.
that truth to keep, that life to win, whose joys e - ter - nal flow.

My Faith Looks Up to Thee 759

1 My faith looks up to thee, thou Lamb of Cal - va - ry,
2 May thy rich grace im - part strength to my faint - ing heart,
3 While life's dark maze I tread and griefs a - round me spread,
4 When ends life's tran - sient dream, when death's cold, sul - len stream

Sav - ior di - vine! Now hear me while I pray, take all my
my zeal in - spire; as thou hast died for me, oh, may my
be thou my guide; bid dark - ness turn to day, wipe sor - row's
shall o'er me roll; blest Sav - ior, then, in love fear and dis -

guilt a - way, oh, let me from this day be whol - ly thine!
love to thee pure, warm, and change - less be, a liv - ing fire!
tears a - way, nor let me ev - er stray from thee a - side.
trust re - move; oh, bear me safe a - bove, a ran - somed soul!

Text: Ray Palmer, 1808–1887
Music: Lowell Mason, 1792–1872

OLIVET
6 6 4 6 6 6 4

760

O Christ the Same

1 O Christ the same, through all our sto-ry's pag - es,
2 O Christ the same, the friend of sin - ners, shar - ing
3 O Christ the same, se - cure with - in whose keep - ing

our loves and hopes, our fail - ures and our fears;
our in - most thoughts, the se - crets none can hide,
our lives and loves, our days and years re - main,

e - ter - nal Lord, the king of all the a - ges,
still as of old up - on your bod - y bear - ing
our work and rest, our wak - ing and our sleep - ing,

un - chang - ing still a - mid the pass - ing years:
the marks of love, in tri - umph glo - ri - fied:
our calm and storm, our plea - sure and our pain:

O liv - ing Word, the source of all cre - a - tion,
O Son of Man, who stooped for us from heav - en,
O Lord of love, for all our joys and sor - rows,

who spread the skies, and set the stars a - blaze,
O Prince of life, in all your sav - ing pow'r,
for all our hopes, when earth shall fade and flee,

O Christ the same, who wrought our whole sal - va - tion,
O Christ the same, to whom our hearts are giv - en,
O Christ the same, be - yond our brief to - mor - rows,

we bring our thanks for all our yes - ter - days.
we bring our thanks for this the pres - ent hour.
we bring our thanks for all that is to be.

Text: Timothy Dudley-Smith, b. 1926
Music: Carl F. Schalk, b. 1929
Text © 1984 Hope Publishing Company
Music © 2006 Augsburg Fortress

RED HILL ROAD
11 10 11 10 D

Evening and Morning

761

1 Eve - ning and morn - ing, sun - set and dawn - ing,
2 Gra - cious Lord, hear me, par - don and spare me;
3 Ills that still grieve me soon are to leave me;
4 To God in heav - en all praise be giv - en!

wealth, peace, and glad - ness, com - fort in sad - ness:
calm all my ter - rors, blot out my er - rors,
though bil - lows tow - er, and winds gain pow - er,
O God, we of - fer and glad - ly prof - fer

these are your works, rich in glo - ry di - vine!
that jus - ti - fied in your sight I may stand.
af - ter the storm the fair sun shows its face.
gifts from your hand; these a - lone you will prize:

Times with - out num - ber, a - wake or in slum - ber,
Or - der my go - ings, di - rect all my do - ings;
Joys e'er in - creas - ing and peace nev - er ceas - ing:
hearts that re - ceive you and faith to be - lieve you;

your eye ob - serves us, from dan - ger pre - serves us,
guard me and guide me and stay close be - side me;
these shall I trea - sure and share in full mea - sure
hymns that a - dore you are pre - cious be - fore you

caus - ing your mer - cy up - on us to shine.
all I com - mit to your fa - ther - ly hand.
when in your man - sions you grant me a place.
and to your throne like sweet in - cense a - rise.

Text: Paul Gerhardt, 1607–1676; tr. composite
Music: Johann G. Ebeling, 1637–1676
Text © 1930, 2006 Augsburg Fortress

DIE GÜLDNE SONNE
PM

Holy, Holy, Holy, Holy
Santo, santo, santo, santo

762

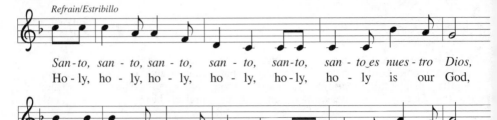

Refrain/Estribillo

San - to, san - to, san - to, san - to, san - to, san - toes nues - tro Dios,
Ho - ly, ho - ly, ho - ly, ho - ly, ho - ly, ho - ly is our God,

Se - ñor de to - da la tie - rra. San - to, san - toes nues - tro Dios.
God, the Lord of earth and heav - en. Ho - ly, ho - ly is our God.

San - to, san - to, san - to, san - to, san - to, san - toes nues - tro Dios,
Ho - ly, ho - ly, ho - ly, ho - ly, ho - ly, ho - ly is our God,

End/Fin

Se - ñor de to - da la his - to - ria. San - to, san - toes nues - tro Dios.
God, the Lord of all of his - t'ry. Ho - ly, ho - ly is our God.

Que a - com - pa - ña a nues - tro pue - blo, que vi - ve en nues - tras lu - chas,
Who ac - com - pa - nies our peo - ple, who lives with - in our strug - gles,

del u - ni - ver - so en - te - ro el ú - ni - co Se - ñor.
of all the earth and heav - en the one and on - ly Lord.

Ben - di - tos los que en su nom - bre el e - van - ge - lio a - nun - cian,
Blest are they who in the Lord's name an - nounce the ho - ly gos - pel,

Refrain/Estribillo

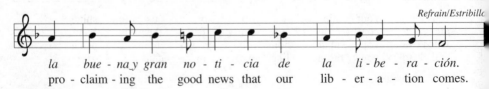

la bue - na y gran no - ti - cia de la li - be - ra - ción.
pro - claim - ing the good news that our lib - er - a - tion comes.

Text: Guillermo Cuéllar, b. 1955; tr. Linda McCrae
Music: Guillermo Cuéllar
Text and music © 1993, 1994 GIA Publications, Inc.

CUÉLLAR
P M

My Life Flows On in Endless Song

763

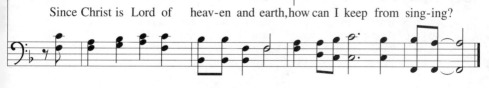

1 My life flows on in end - less song; a - bove earth's lam-en - ta - tion,
2 Through all the tu - mult and the strife, I hear that mu - sic ring - ing.
3 What though my joys and com-forts die? The Lord my Sav-ior liv - eth.
4 The peace of Christ makes fresh my heart, a foun - tain ev - er spring-ing!

I catch the sweet, though far-off hymn that hails a new cre - a - tion.
It finds an ech - o in my soul. How can I keep from sing-ing?
What though the dark - ness gath-er round? Songs in the night he giv - eth.
All things are mine since I am his! How can I keep from sing-ing?

Refrain

No storm can shake my in-most calm while to that Rock I'm cling-ing.

Since Christ is Lord of heav-en and earth, how can I keep from sing-ing?

Text: Robert Lowry, 1826–1899
Music: Robert Lowry, alt.

HOW CAN I KEEP FROM SINGING
87 87 and refrain

764   Have No Fear, Little Flock

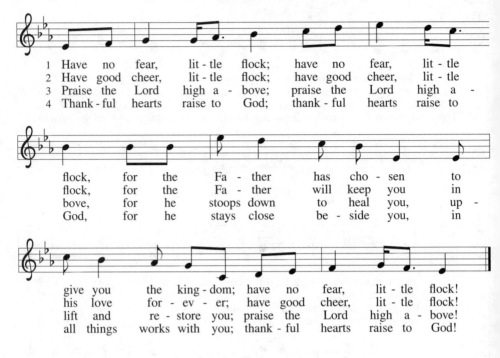

1 Have no fear, lit-tle flock; have no fear, lit-tle
2 Have good cheer, lit-tle flock; have good cheer, lit-tle
3 Praise the Lord high a-bove; praise the Lord high a-
4 Thank-ful hearts raise to God; thank-ful hearts raise to

flock, for the Fa-ther has cho-sen to
flock, for the Fa-ther will keep you in
bove, for he stoops down to heal you, up-
God, for he stays close be-side you, in

give you the king-dom; have no fear, lit-tle flock!
his love for-ev-er; have good cheer, lit-tle flock!
lift and re-store you; praise the Lord high a-bove!
all things works with you; thank-ful hearts raise to God!

Text: Luke 12:32, st. 1; Marjorie Jillson, b. 1931, sts. 2–4
Music: Heinz Werner Zimmermann, b. 1930
Text and music © 1973 Concordia Publishing House

LITTLE FLOCK
66766

765   Lord of All Hopefulness

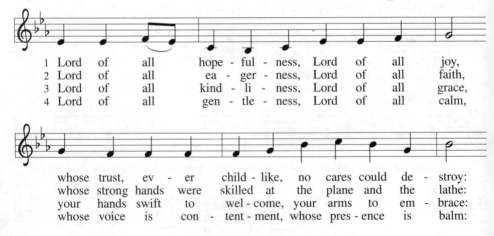

1 Lord of all hope-ful-ness, Lord of all joy,
2 Lord of all ea-ger-ness, Lord of all faith,
3 Lord of all kind-li-ness, Lord of all grace,
4 Lord of all gen-tle-ness, Lord of all calm,

whose trust, ev-er child-like, no cares could de-stroy,
whose strong hands were skilled at the plane and the lathe:
your hands swift to wel-come, your arms to em-brace:
whose voice is con-tent-ment, whose pres-ence is balm:

Text: Jan Struther, 1901–1953
Music: Irish traditional
Text © Oxford University Press

SLANE
10 11 11 12

be there at our wak - ing, and give us, we pray,
be there at our la - bors, and give us, we pray,
be there at our hom - ing, and give us, we pray,
be there at our sleep - ing, and give us, we pray,

your bliss in our hearts, Lord, at the break of the day.
your strength in our hearts, Lord, at the noon of the day.
your love in our hearts, Lord, at the eve of the day.
your peace in our hearts, Lord, at the end of the day.

Lord of Our Life 766

1 Lord of our life and God of our sal - va - tion, star of our
2 See round your ark the hun - gry bil - lows curl - ing, see how your
3 Lord, you can help when earth - ly ar - mor fails us; Lord, you can
4 Peace in our hearts, our trou - bled thoughts as - suag - ing, peace in your

night and hope of ev - 'ry na - tion: hear and re - ceive your
foes their ban - ners are un - furl - ing. Lord, while their poi - soned
save when dead - ly sin as - sails us; and, in the day when
church, where kin - dred souls are rag - ing, peace, when the world its

church's sup - pli - ca - tion, Lord God Al - might - y.
ar - rows they are hurl - ing, you can pre - serve us.
hell it - self ap - palls us, grant us your peace, Lord:
end - less war is wag - ing, peace in your heav - en.

Text: Matthäus A. von Löwenstern, 1594–1648; tr. Philip Pusey, 1799–1855, alt.
Music: Poitiers *Antiphoner*, 1746

ISTE CONFESSOR
11 11 11 5

767 Lord, Take My Hand and Lead Me

1 Lord, take my hand and lead me up-on life's way;
2 Lord, when the tem-pest ra - ges, I need not fear;
3 Lord, when the shad-ows length-en and night has come,

di - rect, pro-tect, and feed me from day to day.
for you, the Rock of A - ges, are al - ways near.
I know that you will strength-en my steps toward home,

With-out your grace and fa - vor I go a - stray;
Close by your side a - bid - ing, I fear no foe,
then noth-ing can im-pede me, O bless-ed Friend!

so take my hand, O Sav - ior, and lead the way.
for when your hand is guid - ing, in peace I go.
So, take my hand and lead me un - to the end.

Text: Julie von Hausmann, 1825–1901; tr. *Lutheran Book of Worship*
Music: Friedrich Silcher, 1789–1860
Text © 1978 *Lutheran Book of Worship*, admin. Augsburg Fortress

SO NIMM DENN MEINE HÄNDE
7 4 7 4 D

Lead Me, Guide Me

Refrain

Lead me, guide me, a - long the way;

for if you lead me, I can - not stray.

Lord, let me walk each day with thee.

Lead me, O Lord, lead me.

1 I am weak and I need thy strength and pow'r
2 Help me tread in the paths of righ - teous - ness,
3 I am lost if you take your hand from me,

to help me o - ver my weak - est hour.
be my aid when Sa - tan and sin op - press.
I am blind with - out . . . thy light to see.

Help me through the dark - ness thy face to see.
I am put - ting all . . . . my trust in thee.
Lord, just al - ways let me thy ser - vant be.

Refrain

Lead me, O Lord, lead me.

Text: Doris Akers, 1922–1995
Music: Doris Akers
Text and music © 1953 Doris Akers, admin. Unichappell Music, Inc.

LEAD ME, GUIDE ME
Irregular

769

If You But Trust in God to Guide You

1 If you but trust in God to guide you
with gen - tle
hand through all your ways,
you'll find that God is there be-
side you when cross - es come, in try - ing days.
Trust then in
God's un - chang - ing love;
build on the rock that will not move.

2 What gain is there in anx - ious weep - ing,
in help - less
an - ger and dis - tress?
If you are in your Sav - ior's
keep - ing, in sor - row will he love you less?
For Christ who
took for you a cross
will bring you safe through ev - 'ry loss.

3 The Lord our rest - less hearts is hold - ing,
in peace and
qui - et - ness con - tent.
We rest in God's good will un-
fold - ing, what wis - dom from on high has sent.
God, who has
cho - sen us by grace,
knows ver - y well the fears we face.

4 Sing, pray, and keep God's ways un - swerv - ing,
of - fer your
ser - vice faith - ful - ly.
Trust heav - en's word; though un - de-
serv - ing, you'll find God's prom - ise true to be.
This is our
con - fi - dence in - deed:
God nev - er fails in time of need.

Text: Georg Neumark, 1621–1681; tr. composite
Music: Georg Neumark
Text © 1978, 2006 Augsburg Fortress

WER NUR DEN LIEBEN GOTT
9 8 9 8 9 8

Give Me Jesus

1 In the morn-ing when I rise, in the morn-ing when I rise,
2 Dark . . . mid-night was my cry, dark . . . mid-night was my cry,
3 Just a - bout the break of day, just a - bout the break of day,
4 Oh, . . . when I come to die, oh, . . . when I come to die,
5 And . . . when I want to sing, and . . . when I want to sing,

in the morn-ing when I rise, give me Je - sus.
dark . . . mid-night was my cry, give me Je - sus.
just a - bout the break of day, give me Je - sus.
oh, . . . when I come to die, give me Je - sus.
and . . . when I want to sing, give me Je - sus.

Refrain

Give me Je - sus, give me Je - sus.

You may have all the rest, give me Je - sus.

Text: African American spiritual
Music: African American spiritual; arr. hymnal version
Arr. © 2006 Augsburg Fortress

GIVE ME JESUS
Irregular

771 God, Who Stretched the Spangled Heavens

1 God, who stretched the span - gled heav - ens in - fi - nite in time and place,
2 We have ven - tured worlds un - dreamed of since the child-hood of our race;
3 As each far ho - ri - zon beck - ons, may it chal-lenge us a - new:

flung the suns in burn-ing ra - diance through the si - lent fields of space:
known the ec - sta - sy of wing-ing through un - trav-eled realms of space;
chil - dren of cre - a - tive pur - pose, serv - ing oth - ers, hon - 'ring you.

we, your chil - dren in your like-ness, share in - ven - tive pow'rs with you;
probed the se - crets of the at - om, yield-ing un - i - mag - ined pow'r,
May our dreams prove rich with prom-ise; each en-deav-or well be - gun;

great Cre - a - tor, still cre - at - ing, show us what we yet may do.
fac - ing us with life's de - struc-tion or our most tri - um-phant hour.
great Cre - a - tor, give us guid-ance till our goals and yours are one.

Text: Catherine Cameron, b. 1927
Music: W. Walker, *Southern Harmony*, 1835
Text © 1967 Hope Publishing Company

HOLY MANNA
8 7 8 7 D

772 Oh, That the Lord Would Guide My Ways

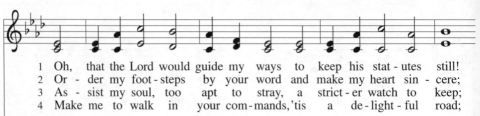

1 Oh, that the Lord would guide my ways to keep his stat - utes still!
2 Or - der my foot - steps by your word and make my heart sin - cere;
3 As - sist my soul, too apt to stray, a strict - er watch to keep;
4 Make me to walk in your com-mands, 'tis a de - light - ful road;

Text: Isaac Watts, 1674–1748, alt.
Music: William H. Havergal, 1793–1870

EVAN
CM

Oh, that my God would grant me grace to know and do his will!
let sin have no do-min-ion, Lord, but keep my con-science clear.
and should I e'er for-get your way, re-store your wan-d'ring sheep.
nor let my head or heart or hands of-fend a-gainst my God.

Precious Lord, Take My Hand   773

1 Pre-cious Lord, take my hand, lead me on, let me stand,
2 When my way grows . . drear, pre-cious Lord, lin-ger near,
3 When the dark-ness ap-pears and the night draws . . near,

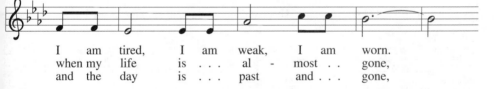

I am tired, I am weak, I am worn.
when my life is . . . al - most . . gone,
and the day is . . . past and . . . gone,

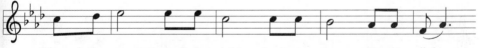

Through the storm, through the night, lead me on to the light.
hear my cry, hear my call, hold my hand lest I fall.
at the riv - er I stand, guide my feet, hold my hand.

Take my hand, pre-cious Lord, lead me home.

Text: Thomas A. Dorsey, 1899–1993
Music: George N. Allen, 1812–1877, adapt. Thomas A. Dorsey
Text and music © 1938, 1966 Unichappell Music Inc., admin. Hal Leonard Corp.

PRECIOUS LORD
Irregular

What a Fellowship, What a Joy Divine

Leaning on the Everlasting Arms

1 What a fel-low-ship, what a joy di-vine, lean-ing on the ev-er-last-ing arms;
2 Oh, how sweet to walk in this pil-grim way, lean-ing on the ev-er-last-ing arms;
3 What have I to dread, what have I to fear, lean-ing on the ev-er-last-ing arms?

what a bless-ed-ness, what a peace is mine, lean-ing on the ev-er-last-ing arms.
oh, how bright the path grows from day to day, lean-ing on the ev-er-last-ing arms.
I have bless-ed peace with my Lord so near, lean-ing on the ev-er-last-ing arms.

Refrain

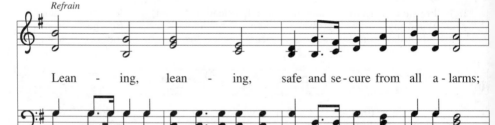

Lean - ing, lean - ing, safe and se-cure from all a-larms;

Lean - ing on Je - sus, lean-ing on Je - sus,

lean - ing, lean - ing, lean-ing on the ev - er - last-ing arms.

lean - ing on Je - sus, lean - ing on Je - sus,

Text: Elisha A. Hoffman, 1839–1929
Music: Anthony J. Showalter, 1858–1924

SHOWALTER
10 9 10 9 and refrain

Jesus, Priceless Treasure

1 Je - sus, price-less trea - sure, source of pur - est plea - sure,
2 In thine arm I rest me; foes who would mo - lest me
3 Hence, all fears and sad - ness, for the Lord of glad - ness,

tru - est friend to me: ah, how long I've pant - ed, and my heart has
can - not reach me here. Though the earth be shak - ing, ev - 'ry heart be
Je - sus, en - ters in. God, who dear - ly loves us, from all tri - al

faint - ed, thirst - ing, Lord, for thee! Thine I am, O spot - less Lamb;
quak - ing, Je - sus calms my fear. Light-nings flash and thun - ders crash;
saves us, gives sweet peace with - in. I have borne this world - ly scorn;

no - thing in this world can hide thee, naught I ask be - side thee.
yet, though sin and hell as - sail me, Je - sus will not fail me.
still in thee lies pur - est plea - sure: Je - sus, price-less trea - sure!

Text: Johann Franck, 1618–1677; tr. Catherine Winkworth, 1827–1878, alt.
Music: Johann Crüger, 1598–1662; arr. hymnal version
Arr. © 2006 Augsburg Fortress

JESU, MEINE FREUDE
665 665 786

776 What God Ordains Is Good Indeed

1 What God or-dains is good in-deed, for all life well pro-vid - ing.
2 What God or-dains is good in-deed: my light, my life, my Sav - ior!
3 What God or-dains is good in-deed. When hope seems like de - lu - sion,
4 What God or-dains is good in-deed. My Lord will nev-er fail me

The will of God is best for me, the ground of my con-fid - ing.
No ill can get the best of me; God's care will nev - er wa - ver.
I taste the bit - ter cup and plead, "Lord, quench my fear, con - fu - sion."
on dan-ger's path, in deep-est need, when death in grief shall veil me.

My faith - ful God, on ev - 'ry road you know the way un -
Through joy and pain I shall at - tain the dawn dis - clos - ing
God ends the night, re - stores de - light; by faith I face to -
My God so dear will draw me near, in lov - ing arms will

fold - ing and my hand you are hold - ing.
clear - ly that God has loved me dear - ly.
mor - row and yield to God all sor - row.
hold me, at last in light en - fold me.

Text: Samuel Rodigast, 1649–1708; tr. Martin A. Seltz, b. 1951
Music: Severus Gastorius, 1646–1682
Text © 2000 Augsburg Fortress

WAS GOTT TUT
8 7 8 7 8 7 7

Come to Me, All Pilgrims Thirsty

1 "Come to me, all pil-grims thirst-y; drink the wa-ter I will give.
2 "Come to me, all trav-'lers wea-ry; come that I may give you rest.
3 "Come to me, be-liev-ers bur-dened; find re-fresh-ment in this place.
4 "Come to me, re-pen-tant sin-ners; leave be-hind your guilt and shame.

If you knew what gift I of-fer, you would come to me and live."
Drink the cup of life I of-fer; at this ta-ble be my guest."
Come, re-ceive the gift I of-fer, turn to me and seek my face."
Come and know di-vine com-pas-sion, turn to me, I call your name."

Refrain

Je-sus, ev-er-flow-ing foun-tain, give us wa-ter from your well.

In the gra-cious gift you of-fer there is joy no tongue can tell.

5 "Come to me, distressed and needy;
   I would be your trusted friend.
   Come and seek the gift I offer,
   come, your open hands extend." *Refrain*

6 "Come to me, abandoned, orphaned;
   lonely ways no longer roam.
   Come and take the gift I offer,
   let me make in you my home." *Refrain*

Text: Delores Dufner, OSB, b. 1939
Music: *The Sacred Harp*, Philadelphia, 1844; arr. *Selected Hymns*, 1985
Text © 1992, 1996 Sisters of St. Benedict, St. Joseph, MN
Arr. © 1985 Augsburg Fortress

BEACH SPRING
8 7 8 7 D

778

The Lord's My Shepherd

1 The Lord's my shep-herd; I'll not want. He makes me down to lie
2 My soul he doth re - store a - gain, and me to walk doth make
3 Yea, though I walk in death's dark vale, yet will I fear no ill;
4 My ta - ble thou hast rich - ly spread in pres - ence of my foes;
5 Good - ness and mer - cy all my life shall sure - ly fol - low me,

in pas - tures green; he lead - eth me the qui - et wa - ters by.
with - in the paths of righ - teous - ness, e'en for his own name's sake;
for thou art with me, and thy rod and staff me com - fort still;
my head thou dost with oil a - noint, and my cup o - ver - flows.
and in God's house for - ev - er - more my dwell - ing - place shall be;

He lead - eth me, he lead - eth me the qui - et wa - ters by.
with - in the paths of righ - teous - ness, e'en for his own name's sake.
for thou art with me, and thy rod and staff me com - fort still.
My head thou dost with oil a - noint, and my cup o - ver - flows.
and in God's house for - ev - er - more my dwell - ing - place shall be.

Text: *The Psalms of David in Meeter*, Edinburgh, 1650
Music: James L. Macbeth Bain; arr. Gordon Jacob, 1895–1984
Arr. © Oxford University Press

BROTHER JAMES' AIR
86 86 86

Amazing Grace, How Sweet the Sound 779

1 A - maz - ing grace!— how sweet the sound— that saved a wretch like me! I once was lost, but now am found; was blind, but now I see.
2 'Twas grace that taught my heart to fear, and grace my fears re - lieved; how pre - cious did that grace ap - pear the hour I first be - lieved!
3 Through man - y dan - gers, toils, and snares I have al - read - y come; 'tis grace has brought me safe thus far, and grace will lead me home.
4 The Lord has prom - ised good to me; his word my hope se - cures; he will my shield and por - tion be as long as life en - dures.
5 When we've been there ten thou - sand years, bright shin - ing as the sun, we've no less days to sing God's praise than when we'd first be - gun.

Text: John Newton, 1725–1807, alt., sts. 1–4; anonymous, st. 5
Music: W. Walker, *Southern Harmony*, 1835; arr. Edwin O. Excell, 1851–1921, alt.

NEW BRITAIN
CM

780

Shepherd Me, O God

Refrain
All

Shep- herd me, O God, be - yond my wants, be - yond my fears, from

to stanzas 1, 2, 3, 5 | *to stanza 4*

death in - to life. life.

Leader or All

1 God is my shep - herd, so noth - ing shall I want, I
2 Gent - ly you raise me and heal my wea - ry soul, you
3 Though I should wan - der the val - ley of death, I

rest in the mead-ows of faith - ful - ness and love, I
lead me by path-ways of righ - teous-ness and truth, my
fear no e - vil, for you are at my side, your

Refrain

walk by the qui - et wa - ters of peace.
spir - it shall sing the mu - sic of your name.
rod and your staff, my com - fort and my hope.

Leader or All

4 You have set me a ban-quet of love in the face of

Refrain

ha-tred, crown-ing me with love be-yond my pow'r to hold.

Leader or All

5 Sure-ly your kind-ness and mer-cy fol-low me all the days of my life;

Text: Marty Haugen, b. 1950, based on Psalm 23
Music: Marty Haugen
Text and music © 1986 GIA Publications, Inc.

SHEPHERD ME
Irregular

I will dwell in the house of my God for-ev - er - more.

Final refrain
All

Shep-herd me, O God, be - yond my wants, be -

yond my fears, from death in - to life.

Children of the Heavenly Father
Tryggare kan ingen vara

781

Tryg - ga - re kan ing-en va - ra än Guds lil - la bar - na - ska - ra,
1 Chil - dren of the heav'n-ly Fa-ther safe-ly in his bo - som gath - er;
2 God his own doth tend and nour-ish, in his ho - ly courts they flour-ish.
3 Nei - ther life nor death shall ev - er from the Lord his chil - dren sev - er;
4 Though he giv - eth or he tak-eth, God his chil-dren ne'er for - sak - eth;

stjär - nan ej på him - la - fäs - tet, få - geln ej i kän - da näs - tet.
nest - ling bird nor star in heav - en such a ref - uge e'er was giv - en.
From all e - vil things he spares them, in his might - y arms he bears them.
un - to them his grace he show - eth, and their sor - rows all he know - eth.
his the lov - ing pur-pose sole - ly to pre-serve them pure and ho - ly.

Text: Carolina Sandell Berg, 1832–1903; tr. Ernst W. Olson, 1870–1958
Music: Swedish folk tune
Text © 1925 Board of Publication, Lutheran Church in America

TRYGGARE KAN INGEN VARA
LM

782 My Shepherd, You Supply My Need

1 My Shep-herd, you sup-ply my need; most ho-ly is your name.
2 When I walk through the shades of death, your pres-ence is my stay;
3 The sure pro-vi-sions of my God at-tend me all my days;

In pas-tures fresh you make me feed, be-side the liv-ing stream.
one word of your sup-port-ing breath drives all my fears a-way.
oh, may your house be my a-bode and all my work be praise.

You bring my wan-d'ring spir-it back when I for-sake your ways,
Your hand, in sight of all my foes, does still my ta-ble spread;
Here would I find a set-tled rest, while oth-ers go and come;

and lead me, for your mer-cy's sake, in paths of truth and grace.
my cup with bless-ings o-ver-flows, your oil a-noints my head.
no more a strang-er or a guest, but like a child at home.

Text: Isaac Watts, 1674–1748, alt., based on Psalm 23
Music: North American traditional

RESIGNATION
CMD

Praise and Thanks and Adoration 783

1 Praise and thanks and ad - o - ra - tion, Son of God, to you we give,
2 Hold me ev - er in your keep - ing, com - fort me in pain and strife;

for you chose to serve cre - a - tion, died that sin - ers all might live.
through my laugh - ter and my weep - ing, lift me to a no - bler life.

Dear Lord Je - sus, guide my way; faith - ful let me day by day
Draw my fer - vent love to you; con - stant hope and faith re - new

fol - low where your steps are lead - ing, find ad - ven - ture, joys ex - ceed - ing!
in your birth, your life and pas - sion, in your death and res - ur - rec - tion.

Text: Thomas H. Kingo, 1634–1703; tr. *Lutheran Book of Worship*
Music: *Trente quatre pseaumes de David*, Geneva, 1551
Text © 1978 *Lutheran Book of Worship*, admin. Augsburg Fortress

FREU DICH SEHR
87 87 77 88

Grant Peace, We Pray, in Mercy, Lord 784

Grant peace, we pray, in mer - cy, Lord; peace in our time, oh, send us!

For there is none on earth but you, none oth - er to de - fend us.

You on - ly, Lord, can fight for us. A - men.

Text: Medieval antiphon, adapt. Martin Luther, 1483–1546; tr. *Laudamus*, 1952
Music: Plainsong mode I; *Gesangbuch*, Nürnberg, 1676
Text © Lutheran World Federation

VERLEIH UNS FRIEDEN
87 87 8

When Peace like a River

It Is Well with My Soul

785

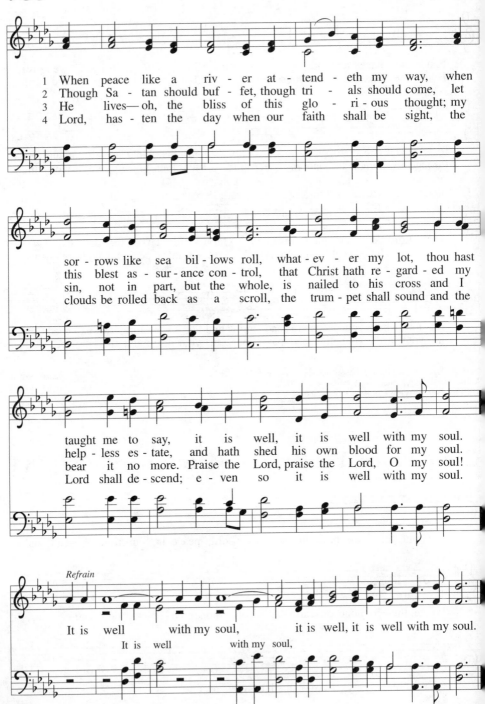

1 When peace like a riv - er at - tend - eth my way, when
2 Though Sa - tan should buf - fet, though tri - als should come, let
3 He lives—oh, the bliss of this glo - ri - ous thought; my
4 Lord, has - ten the day when our faith shall be sight, the

sor - rows like sea bil - lows roll, what - ev - er my lot, thou hast
this blest as - sur - ance con - trol, that Christ hath re - gard - ed my
sin, not in part, but the whole, is nailed to his cross and I
clouds be rolled back as a scroll, the trum - pet shall sound and the

taught me to say, it is well, it is well with my soul.
help - less es - tate, and hath shed his own blood for my soul.
bear it no more. Praise the Lord, praise the Lord, O my soul!
Lord shall de - scend; e - ven so it is well with my soul.

Refrain

It is well with my soul, it is well, it is well with my soul.
It is well with my soul,

Text: Horatio G. Spafford, 1828–1888
Music: Philip P. Bliss, 1838–1876

VILLE DU HAVRE
11 8 11 9 and refrain

O Holy Spirit, Enter In

786

1 O Ho - ly Spir - it, en - ter in, and in our hearts your
2 Left to our - selves, we sure - ly stray; oh, lead us on the
3 O might - y Rock, O Source of life, let your good Word in

work be - gin, and make our hearts your dwell - ing. Sun of the soul,
nar - row way, with wis - est coun - sel guide us; and give us stead -
doubt and strife be in us strong - ly burn - ing, that we be faith -

O Light di - vine, a - round and in us bright - ly shine, your strength
fast - ness, that we may fol - low you for - ev - er free, no mat -
ful un - to death and live in love and ho - ly faith, from you

in us up - well - ing. In your ra - diance life from heav - en now is
ter who de - rides us. Gent - ly heal those hearts now bro - ken; give some
true wis - dom learn - ing. Lord, your mer - cy on us show - er; by your

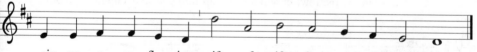

giv - en o - ver - flow - ing, gift of gifts be - yond all know - ing.
to - ken you are near us, whom we trust to light and cheer us.
pow - er Christ con - fess - ing, we will cher - ish all your bless - ing.

Text: Michael Schirmer, 1606–1673; tr. Catherine Winkworth, 1827–1878, adapt.
Music: Philipp Nicolai, 1556–1608

WIE SCHÖN LEUCHTET
PM

787

On Eagle's Wings

Leader or All

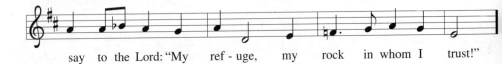

1 You who dwell in the shel-ter of the Lord, who a-bide in this shad-ow for life,

say to the Lord: "My ref - uge, my rock in whom I trust!"

Refrain
All

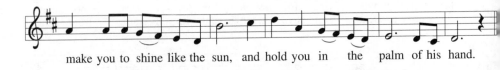

And he will raise you up on ea - gle's wings, bear you on the breath of dawn,

make you to shine like the sun, and hold you in the palm of his hand.

Leader or All

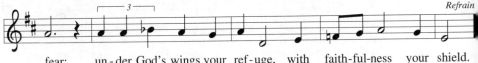

2 The snare of the fowl-er will nev-er cap-ture you, and fam-ine will bring you no

Refrain

fear; un - der God's wings your ref-uge, with faith-ful-ness your shield.

Leader or All

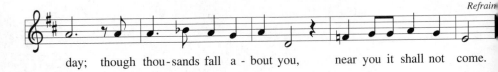

3 You need not fear the ter-ror of the night, nor the ar-row that flies by

Refrain

day; though thou-sands fall a - bout you, near you it shall not come.

Text: Michael Joncas, b. 1957
Music: Michael Joncas
Text and music © 1979 OCP Publications

ON EAGLE'S WINGS
Irregular

Leader or All

4 For to the an-gels God's giv-en a com-mand to guard you in all of your ways; up-on their hands they will bear you up, lest you dash your foot a-gainst a stone.

Final refrain
All

And he will raise you up on ea-gle's wings, bear you on the breath of dawn, make you to shine like the sun, and hold you in the palm of his hand.

And hold you, hold you in the palm of his hand.

788 If God My Lord Be for Me

1 If God my Lord be for me, I may a host de - fy;
2 I build on this foun - da - tion, that Je - sus and his blood
3 Christ Je - sus is my splen - dor, my sun, my light, a - lone;
4 For joy my heart is ring - ing; all sor - row dis - ap - pears;

for when I pray, be - fore me my foes, con - found - ed, fly.
a - lone are my sal - va - tion, the true, e - ter - nal good.
were he not my de - fend - er be - fore the judg - ment throne,
and full of mirth and sing - ing, it wipes a - way all tears.

If Christ, my head and mas - ter, be - friend me from a - bove,
With - out him all that pleas - es will vain and emp - ty prove.
I nev - er should find fa - vor and mer - cy in God's sight,
The sun that cheers my spir - it is Je - sus Christ, my king;

what foe or what di - sas - ter can drive me from his love?
The gifts I have from Je - sus a - lone are worth my love.
but be de-stroyed for - ev - er as dark - ness by the light.
the heav'n I shall in - her - it makes me re - joice and sing.

Text: Paul Gerhardt, 1607–1676; tr. Richard Massie, 1800–1887, adapt.
Music: English melody, 16th cent.; arr. hymnal version
Arr. © 2006 Augsburg Fortress

IST GOTT FÜR MICH
7 6 7 6 D

Savior, like a Shepherd Lead Us

789

1 Sav-ior like a shep-herd lead us; much we need your ten-der care.
2 We are yours; in love be-friend us, be the guard-ian of our way;
3 You have prom-ised to re-ceive us, poor and sin-ful though we be;
4 Ear-ly let us seek your fa-vor, ear-ly let us do your will;

In your pleas-ant pas-tures feed us, for our use your fold pre-pare.
keep your flock, from sin de-fend us, seek us when we go a-stray.
you have mer-cy to re-lieve us, grace to cleanse, and pow'r to free.
bless-ed Lord and on-ly Sav-ior, with your love our spir-its fill.

Bless-ed Je-sus, bless-ed Je-sus, you have bought us; we are yours.
Bless-ed Je-sus, bless-ed Je-sus, hear us chil-dren when we pray.
Bless-ed Je-sus, bless-ed Je-sus, ear-ly let us turn to you.
Bless-ed Je-sus, bless-ed Je-sus, you have loved us, love us still.

Bless-ed Je-sus, bless-ed Je-sus, you have bought us; we are yours.
Bless-ed Je-sus, bless-ed Je-sus, hear us chil-dren when we pray.
Bless-ed Je-sus, bless-ed Je-sus, ear-ly let us turn to you.
Bless-ed Je-sus, bless-ed Je-sus, you have loved us, love us still.

Text: attr. Dorothy A. Thrupp, 1779–1847
Music: William B. Bradbury, 1816–1868

BRADBURY
8787D

790

Day by Day

1 Day by day, your mer - cies, Lord, at - tend me, bring - ing com - fort
2 Day by day, I know you will pro - vide me strength to serve and
3 Oh, what joy to know that you are near me when my bur - dens

to my anx - ious soul. Day by day, the bless-ings, Lord, you send me
wis - dom to o - bey; I will seek your lov - ing will to guide me
grow too great to bear; oh, what joy to know that you will hear me

draw me near - er to my heav'n - ly goal. Love di - vine, be - yond all
o'er the paths I strug - gle day by day. I will fear no e - vil
when I come, O Lord, to you in prayer. Day by day, no mat - ter

mor - tal mea - sure, brings to naught the bur - dens of my quest; Sav - ior,
of the mor - row, I will trust in your en - dur - ing grace. Sav - ior,
what be - tide me, you will hold me ev - er in your hand. Sav - ior,

Text: Carolina Sandell Berg, 1832–1903; tr. Robert Leaf, 1936–2005
Music: Oskar Ahnfelt, 1813–1882
Text © 1992 Augsburg Fortress

BLOTT EN DAG
10 9 10 9 D

We Sing to You, O God

791

Text: Gracia Grindal, b. 1943
Music: John Ireland, 1879–1962
Text © 1993 Selah Publishing Co., Inc.
Music © 1924 John Ireland, admin. The John Ireland Trust

LOVE UNKNOWN
66 12 88

Alternate tune: RHOSYMEDRE

792
When Memory Fades

1 When mem - 'ry fades, and rec - og - ni - tion fal - ters,
2 As frail - ness grows, and youth - ful strengths di - min - ish,
3 With - in your Spir - it, good - ness lives un - fad - ing.

when eyes we love grow dim, and minds con - fused,
in wea - ry arms which worked their ear - nest fill,
The past and fu - ture min - gle in - to one.

speak to our souls of love that nev - er al - ters,
your ag - ing ser - vants la - bor now to fin - ish
All joys re - main, un - shad - owed light per - vad - ing.

speak to our hearts, by pain and fear a - bused.
their earth - ly tasks, as fits your mer - cy's will.
No val - ued deed will ev - er be un - done.

Text: Mary Louise Bringle, b. 1953
Music: Jean Sibelius, 1865–1957
Text © 2002 by GIA Publications, Inc.
Music © Breitkopf & Härtel

FINLANDIA
11 10 11 10 11 10

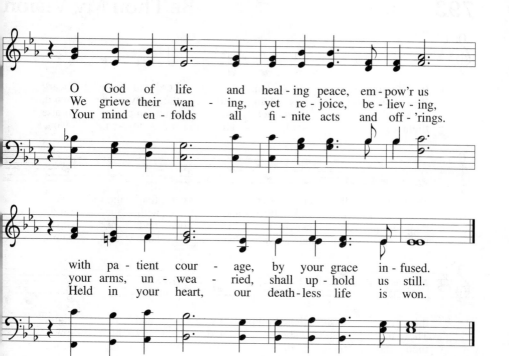

O God of life and heal-ing peace, em-pow'r us
We grieve their wan - ing, yet re - joice, be - liev - ing,
Your mind en - folds all fi - nite acts and off - 'rings.

with pa - tient cour - age, by your grace in - fused.
your arms, un - wea - ried, shall up - hold us still.
Held in your heart, our death-less life is won.

793

Be Thou My Vision

1 Be thou my vi - sion, O Lord of my heart;
2 Be thou my wis - dom, and thou my true word;
3 Rich - es I heed not, nor vain, emp - ty praise,
4 Light of my soul, af - ter vic - to - ry won,

naught be all else to me, save that thou art:
I ev - er with thee and thou with me, Lord.
thou mine in - her - i - tance, now and al - ways:
may I reach heav - en's joys, O heav - en's Sun!

thou my best thought both by day and by night,
Thou my soul's shel - ter, and thou my high tow'r,
thou and thou on - ly, the first in my heart,
Heart of my own heart, what - ev - er be - fall,

wak - ing or sleep - ing, thy pres - ence my light.
raise thou me heav'n - ward, O Pow'r of my pow'r.
great God of heav - en, my trea - sure thou art.
still be my vi - sion, O Rul - er of all.

Text: Irish, 8th cent.; vers. Eleanor H. Hull, 1860–1935, alt.; tr. Mary E. Byrne, 1880–1931
Music: Irish traditional

SLANE
10 10 10 10

Calm to the Waves 794

Calm to the waves. Calm to the wind. Je - sus whis - pers, "Peace, be still."

Balm to our hearts. Fears at an end. In still-ness, hear his voice.

Text: Mary Louise Bringle, b. 1953
Music: Thomas Pavlechko, b. 1962
Text © 2002 GIA Publications, Inc.
Music © 2002 Selah Publishing Co., Inc.

CALM SEAS
447446

God, My Lord, My Strength 795

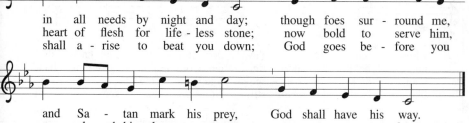

1 God, my Lord, my strength, my place of hid - ing and con - fid - ing
2 Christ in me, and I am freed for liv - ing and for - giv - ing,
3 Up, weak knees and spir - it bowed in sor - row! No to - mor-row

in all needs by night and day; though foes sur - round me,
heart of flesh for life - less stone; now bold to serve him,
shall a - rise to beat you down; God goes be - fore you

and Sa - tan mark his prey, God shall have his way.
now cheered his love to own, nev - er - more a - lone.
and an - gels all a - round; on your head a crown!

Text: *Tranoscius*, 1636; tr. Jaroslav J. Vajda, b. 1919
Music: *Gradual*, Prague, 1567
Text © 1969 Concordia Publishing House

PÁN BŮH
1047565

796

How Firm a Foundation

1 How firm a foun - da - tion, O saints of the Lord,
2 "Fear not, I am with you, oh, be not dis - mayed,
3 "When through fi - 'ry tri - als your path - way shall lie,
4 "Through - out all their life - time my peo - ple shall prove

is laid for your faith in Christ Je - sus, the Word!
for I am your God and will still give you aid;
my grace, all - suf - fi - cient, shall be your sup - ply.
my sov - 'reign, e - ter - nal, un - change - a - ble love;

What more can he say than to you he has said
I'll strength - en you, help you, and cause you to stand,
The flames shall not hurt you; I on - ly de - sign
and then, when gray hairs shall their tem - ples a - dorn,

who un - to the Sav - ior for ref - uge have fled?
up - held by my righ - teous, om - nip - o - tent hand."
your dross to con - sume and your gold to re - fine."
like lambs they shall still in my bo - som be borne."

Text: J. Rippon, *A Selection of Hymns*, 1787, alt.
Music: Early American

FOUNDATION
11 11 11 11

Blessed Be the Name

Heri ni jina

1 *He - ri ni ji - na,*   *he - ri ni ji - na,*   *he - ri ni ji - na la Ye - su.*
2 *Twe - nde kwa Ye - su,*   *twe - nde kwa Ye - su,*   *twe - nde kwa Ye - su mbi - ngu - ni.*
1 Bless - ed be the name, bless - ed be the name,   bless - ed be the name, Je - sus' name.
2 Let   us go to Je - sus, let   us go to Je - sus,   let us go to Je - sus in heav'n.

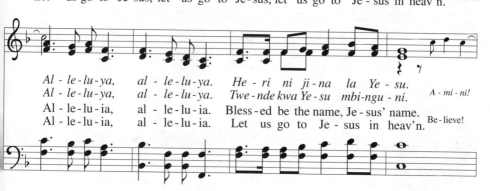

He - ri ni ji - na,   *he - ri ni ji - na,*   *he - ri ni ji - na la Ye - su.*
Twe - nde kwa Ye - su,   *twe - nde kwa Ye - su,*   *twe - nde kwa Ye - su mbi - ngu - ni.*   *A - mi - ni!*
Bless - ed be the name, bless - ed be the name, bless - ed be the name, Je - sus' name.
Let   us go to Je - sus, let   us go to Je - sus, let us go to Je - sus in heav'n. Be - lieve!

Al - le - lu - ya,   *al - le - lu - ya.*   *He - ri ni ji - na la Ye - su.*
Al - le - lu - ya,   *al - le - lu - ya.*   *Twe - nde kwa Ye - su mbi - ngu - ni.*   *A - mi - ni!*
Al - le - lu - ia,   al - le - lu - ia.   Bless - ed be the name, Je - sus' name.
Al - le - lu - ia,   al - le - lu - ia.   Let us go to Je - sus in heav'n. Be - lieve!

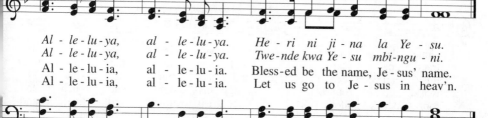

Al - le - lu - ya,   *al - le - lu - ya.*   *He - ri ni ji - na la Ye - su.*
Al - le - lu - ya,   *al - le - lu - ya.*   *Twe - nde kwa Ye - su mbi - ngu - ni.*
Al - le - lu - ia,   al - le - lu - ia.   Bless - ed be the name, Je - sus' name.
Al - le - lu - ia,   al - le - lu - ia.   Let us go to Je - sus in heav'n.

Text: East African traditional, as taught by Deogratias Mahamba
Music: East African traditional; arr. hymnal version
Text and arr. © 2003 Augsburg Fortress

HERI NI JINA
5 5 8 5 5 8 8 8 8 8

Will You Come and Follow Me
The Summons

1 "Will you come and fol - low me if I but call your name? Will you go where you don't
2 "Will you leave your - self be - hind if I but call your name? Will you care for cruel and
3 "Will you let the blind - ed see if I but call your name? Will you set the pris - 'ners
4 "Will you love the you you hide if I but call your name? Will you quell the fear in -
5 Lord, your sum - mons ech - oes true when you but call my name. Let me turn and fol - low

know and nev - er be the same? Will you let my love be shown, will you let my
kind and nev - er be the same? Will you risk the hos - tile stare, should your life at -
free and nev - er be the same? Will you kiss the lep - er clean, and do such as
side and nev - er be the same? Will you use the faith you've found to re - shape the
you and nev - er be the same. In your com - pa - ny I'll go where your love and

name be known, will you let my life be grown in you and you in me?"
tract or scare? Will you let me an - swer pray'r in you and you in me?"
this un - seen, and ad - mit to what I mean in you and you in me?"
world a - round, through my sight and touch and sound in you and you in me?"
foot - steps show. Thus I'll move and live and grow in you and you in me.

Text: John L. Bell, b. 1949
Music: Scottish traditional
Text © 1987 Iona Community, admin. GIA Publications, Inc.

KELVINGROVE
13 13 77 13

Come, Follow Me, the Savior Spake   799

1 "Come, fol - low me," the Sav - ior spake, "all in my way a -
2 "I am the light; I light the way, a god - ly life dis -
3 "I teach you how to shun and flee what harms your soul's sal -
4 Then let us fol - low Christ, our Lord, and take the cross ap -

bid - ing; de - ny your - selves, the world for - sake, o -
play - ing; I bid you walk as in the day; I
va - tion; from ev - 'ry guile your heart I free, from
point - ed, and, firm - ly cling - ing to his word, in

bey my call and guid - ing. Oh, bear the cross, what -
keep your feet from stray - ing. I am the way, and
sin and its temp - ta - tion. I am the ref - uge
suf - f'ring be un - daunt - ed. For those who bear the

e'er be - tide; take my ex - am - ple for your guide."
well I show how you should so - journ here be - low."
of the soul and lead you to your heav'n - ly goal."
bat - tle's strain the crown of heav'n - ly life ob - tain.

Text: Johann Scheffler, 1624–1677; tr. Charles W. Shaeffer, 1813–1896, alt.
Music: Bartholomäus Gesius, 1555–1613; adapt. Johann Herman Schein, 1586–1630

MACHS MIT MIR, GOTT
878788

800   Spirit of God, Descend upon My Heart

1 Spir - it of God, de - scend up - on my heart;
2 I ask no dream, no proph - et ec - sta - sies,
3 Have you not bid me love you, God and King;
4 Teach me to love you as your an - gels love,

wean it from earth, through all its puls - es move;
no sud - den rend - ing of the veil of clay,
all, all your own, soul, heart, and strength, and mind?
one ho - ly pas - sion fill - ing all my frame:

stoop to my weak - ness, strength to me im - part,
no an - gel vis - i - tant, no op - 'ning skies;
I see your cross; there teach my heart to cling.
the bap - tism of the heav'n - de - scend - ed dove,

and make me love you as I ought to love.
but take the dim - ness of my soul a - way.
Oh, let me seek you and, oh, let me find!
my heart an al - tar, and your love the flame.

Text: George Croly, 1780–1860
Music: Frederick C. Atkinson, 1841–1897

MORECAMBE
10 10 10 10

Change My Heart, O God

Refrain

Change my heart, O God; make it ev-er true.

Change my heart, O God; may I be like you.

You are the pot - ter; I am the clay.

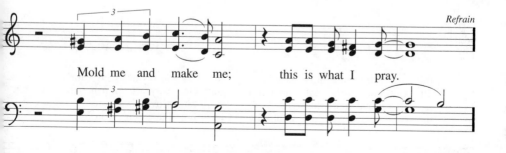

Mold me and make me; this is what I pray.

Text: Eddie Espinosa, b. 1953
Music: Eddie Espinosa
Text and music © 1982 Mercy/Vineyard Publishing, admin. Music Services

CHANGE MY HEART
PM

802

Let Us Ever Walk with Jesus

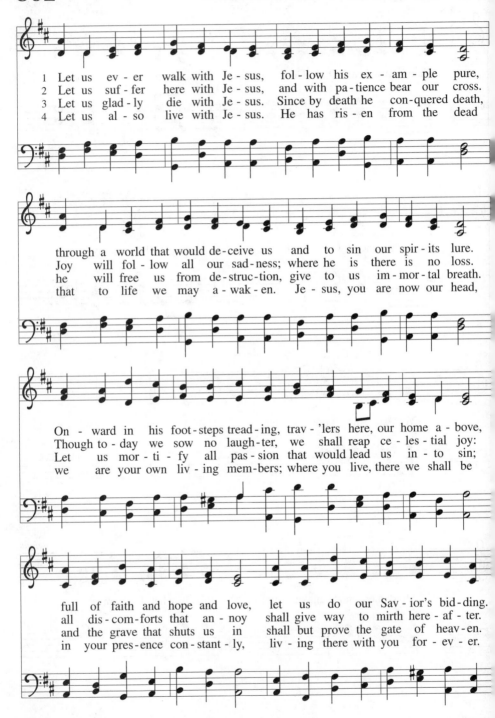

1 Let us ev-er walk with Je-sus, fol-low his ex-am-ple pure,
2 Let us suf-fer here with Je-sus, and with pa-tience bear our cross.
3 Let us glad-ly die with Je-sus. Since by death he con-quered death,
4 Let us al-so live with Je-sus. He has ris-en from the dead

through a world that would de-ceive us and to sin our spir-its lure.
Joy will fol-low all our sad-ness; where he is there is no loss.
he will free us from de-struc-tion, give to us im-mor-tal breath.
that to life we may a-wak-en. Je-sus, you are now our head,

On-ward in his foot-steps tread-ing, trav-'lers here, our home a-bove,
Though to-day we sow no laugh-ter, we shall reap ce-les-tial joy:
Let us mor-ti-fy all pas-sion that would lead us in-to sin;
we are your own liv-ing mem-bers; where you live, there we shall be

full of faith and hope and love, let us do our Sav-ior's bid-ding.
all dis-com-forts that an-noy shall give way to mirth here-af-ter.
and the grave that shuts us in shall but prove the gate of heav-en.
in your pres-ence con-stant-ly, liv-ing there with you for-ev-er.

Text: Sigismund von Birken, 1626–1681; tr. *Lutheran Book of Worship*, alt.
Music: Georg G. Boltze, 18th cent.
Text © 1978 *Lutheran Book of Worship*, admin. Augsburg Fortress

LASSET UNS MIT JESU ZIEHEN
8787877877

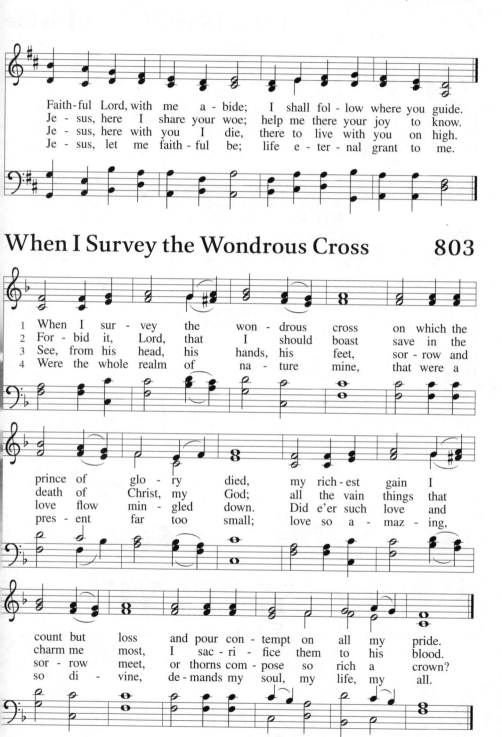

Faith-ful Lord, with me a - bide; I shall fol - low where you guide.
Je - sus, here I share your woe; help me there your joy to know.
Je - sus, here with you I die, there to live with you on high.
Je - sus, let me faith - ful be; life e - ter - nal grant to me.

When I Survey the Wondrous Cross 803

1 When I sur - vey the won - drous cross on which the
2 For - bid it, Lord, that I should boast save in the
3 See, from his head, his hands, his feet, sor - row and
4 Were the whole realm of na - ture mine, that were a

prince of glo - ry died, my rich - est gain I
death of Christ, my God; all the vain things that
love flow min - gled down. Did e'er such love and
pres - ent far too small; love so a - maz - ing,

count but loss and pour con - tempt on all my pride.
charm me most, I sac - ri - fice them to his blood.
sor - row meet, or thorns com - pose so rich a crown?
so di - vine, de - mands my soul, my life, my all.

Text: Isaac Watts, 1674–1748
Music: Lowell Mason, 1792–1872

HAMBURG
LM

Alternate tune: ROCKINGHAM OLD

804

Come Down, O Love Divine

1 Come down, O Love di - vine; seek thou this soul of mine
2 Oh, let it free - ly burn, till world - ly pas - sions turn
3 Let ho - ly char - i - ty mine out - ward ves - ture be,
4 And so the yearn - ing strong, with which the soul will long,

and vis - it it with thine own ar - dor glow - ing;
to dust and ash - es in its heat con - sum - ing;
and low - li - ness be - come mine in - ner cloth - ing;
shall far out - pass the pow'r of hu - man tell - ing;

O Com - fort - er, draw near; with - in my heart ap - pear
and let thy glo - rious light shine ev - er on my sight,
true low - li - ness of heart, which takes the hum - bler part,
no soul can guess Love's grace till it be - come the place

and kin - dle it, thy ho - ly flame be - stow - ing.
and clothe me round, the while my path il - lum - ing.
and o'er its own short - com - ings weeps with loath - ing.
where - in the Ho - ly Spir - it makes a dwell - ing.

Text: Bianco da Siena, d. 1434; tr. Richard F. Littledale, 1833–1890
Music: Ralph Vaughan Williams, 1872–1958
Music © Oxford University Press

DOWN AMPNEY
66 11 66 11

Lead On, O King Eternal!

805

1 Lead on, O King e - ter - nal! The day of march has come;
2 Lead on, O King e - ter - nal, till sin's fierce war shall cease,
3 Lead on, O King e - ter - nal: we fol - low, not with fears,

hence - forth in fields of con - quest your tents will be our home.
and ho - li - ness shall whis - per the sweet a - men of peace;
for glad - ness breaks like morn - ing wher - e'er your face ap - pears.

Through days of prep - a - ra - tion your grace has made us strong;
for not with swords loud clash - ing, nor roll of stir - ring drums,
Your cross is lift - ed o'er us; we jour - ney in its light;

and now, O King e - ter - nal, we lift our bat - tle song.
but deeds of love and mer - cy the heav'n - ly king - dom comes.
the crown a - waits the con - quest; lead on, O God of might!

Text: Ernest W. Shurtleff, 1862–1917
Music: Henry T. Smart, 1813–1879

LANCASHIRE
7676D

806

O God, My Faithful God

1 O God, my faith-ful God, true foun-tain ev - er flow - ing,
2 Give me the strength to do with read - y heart and will - ing
3 Keep me from say - ing words that lat - er need re - call - ing;
4 When dan-gers gath - er round, oh, keep me calm and fear - less;

with - out whom noth-ing is, all per - fect gifts be - stow - ing:
what - ev - er you com-mand, my call - ing here ful - fill - ing—
guard me, lest i - dle speech may from my lips be fall - ing;
help me to bear the cross when life seems dark and cheer - less;

give me a health - y frame, and may I have with - in
to do it when I ought, with all my might—and bless
but when, with - in my place, I must and ought to speak,
help me, as you have taught, to love both great and small,

a con - science free from blame, a soul un - stained by sin.
what - ev - er I have wrought, for you must give suc - cess.
then to my words give grace, lest I of - fend the weak.
and, by your Spir - it's might, to live at peace with all.

Text: Johann Heermann, 1585–1647; tr. Catherine Winkworth, 1827–1878, alt.
Music: Ahasuerus Fritsch, 1629–1701

WAS FRAG ICH NACH DER WELT
67 67 66 66

Come, Thou Fount of Every Blessing 807

1 Come, thou Fount of ev - 'ry bless-ing, tune my heart to sing thy grace;
2 Here I raise my Eb - en - e - zer: "Hith-er by thy help I've come";
3 Oh, to grace how great a debt - or dai - ly I'm con-strained to be;

streams of mer - cy, nev - er ceas-ing, call for songs of loud-est praise.
and I hope, by thy good plea-sure, safe-ly to ar - rive at home.
let that grace now like a fet - ter bind my wan-d'ring heart to thee.

While the hope of end-less glo - ry fills my heart with joy and love,
Je - sus sought me when a strang-er, wan-d'ring from the fold of God;
Prone to wan - der, Lord, I feel it; prone to leave the God I love.

teach me ev - er to a - dore thee; may I still thy good-ness prove.
he, to res - cue me from dan - ger, in - ter - posed his pre-cious blood.
Here's my heart, oh, take and seal it; seal it for thy courts a - bove.

Text: Robert Robinson, 1735–1790, alt.
Music: J. Wyeth, *Repository of Sacred Music*, Part II, 1813

NETTLETON
8787D

Lord Jesus, You Shall Be My Song

Jésus, je voudrais te chanter

808

1 *Jé - sus, je vou - drais te chan - ter sur ma rou - te,*
1 Lord Je - sus, you shall be my song as I jour - ney;
2 Lord Je - sus, I'll praise you as long as I jour - ney.
3 As long as I live, Je - sus, make me your ser - vant,
4 I fear in the dark and the doubt of my jour - ney;

Jé - sus, je vou - drais t'an - non - cer à mes voi - sins par - tout,
I'll tell ev - 'ry - bod - y a - bout you wher - ev - er I go:
May all of my joy be a faith - ful re - flec - tion of you.
to car - ry your cross and to share all your bur - dens and tears.
but cour - age will come with the sound of your steps by my side.

car toi seul es la vie et la paix et l'a - mour:
you a - lone are our life and our peace and our love.
May the earth and the sea and the sky join my song.
For you saved me by giv - ing your bod - y and blood.
And with all of the fam - 'ly you saved by your love,

Jé - sus, je vou - drais te chan - ter sur ma rou - te.
Lord Je - sus, you shall be my song as I jour - ney.
Lord Je - sus, I'll praise you as long as I jour - ney.
As long as I live, Je - sus, make me your ser - vant.
we'll sing to your dawn at the end of our jour - ney.

Text: Les Petites Soeurs de Jésus and L'Arche Community; tr. Stephen Somerville, b. 1931
Music: Les Petites Soeurs de Jésus and L'Arche Community

Text and music © Les Petites Soeurs de Jésus
Tr. © 1970 Stephen Somerville

LES PETITES SOEURS
12 14 12 12

2 Jésus, je voudrais te louer sur ma route;
  Jésus, je voudrais que ma voix soit l'écho de ta joie,
  et que chante la terre et que chante le ciel;
  Jésus, je voudrais te louer sur ma route.

3 Jésus, je voudrais te servir sur ma route,
  Jésus, je voudrais partager les soufrances de ta croix,
  car tu livres pour moi et ton corps et ton sang;
  Jésus, je voudrais te servir su ma route.

4 Jésus, je voudrais tour au long de ma route,
  entendre tes pas résonner dans le nuit près de moi,
  jusqu'à l'aube du jour où ton peuple sauvé,
  Jésus, chantera ton retour sur ma route.

Send Me, Lord
Thuma mina

809

Text: South African traditional; tr. *Freedom Is Coming*, 1984
Music: South African traditional; arr. *Freedom Is Coming*
Tr. and arr. © 1984 Utryck, admin. Walton Music Corp.

THUMA MINA
Irregular

810

O Jesus, I Have Promised

1 O Je - sus, I have prom - ised to serve you to the end;
2 Oh, let me feel you near me; the world is ev - er near.
3 Oh, let me hear you speak - ing in ac - cents clear and still
4 O Je - sus, you have prom - ised to all who fol - low you

re - main for - ev - er near me, my mas - ter and my friend.
I see the sights that daz - zle, the tempt-ing sounds I hear.
a - bove the storms of pas - sion, the mur - murs of self - will.
that where you are in glo - ry your ser - vant shall be too.

I shall not fear the bat - tle if you are by my side,
My foes are ev - er near me, a - round me and with - in;
Now speak to re - as - sure me, to has - ten or con - trol;
And Je - sus, I have prom - ised to serve you to the end;

nor wan - der from the path - way if you will be my guide.
but, Je - sus, then draw near - er to shield my soul from sin.
now speak and make me lis - ten, O Guard-ian of my soul.
oh, give me grace to fol - low, my mas - ter and my friend.

Text: John E. Bode, 1816–1874, alt.
Music: *Neuvermehrtes Gesangbuch*, Meiningen, 1693

MUNICH
76 76 D

On My Heart Imprint Your Image 811

On my heart im - print your im - age, bless-ed Je - sus, king of grace,

that life's trou-bles nor its plea-sures ev - er may your work e - rase.

Let the clear in - scrip-tion be: Je - sus, cru - ci - fied for me,

is my life, my hope's foun-da-tion, all my glo-ry and sal-va - tion!

Text: Thomas H. Kingo, 1634–1703; tr. Peer O. Strömme, 1856–1921, alt.
Music: Johann B. König, 1691–1758

DER AM KREUZ
87 87 77 88

812 Faith of Our Fathers

1 Faith of our fa - thers, liv - ing still in spite of dun - geon,
2 The mar-tyrs, chained in pris - ons dark, were still in heart and
3 Faith of our fa - thers! We will love both friend and foe in

fire, and sword. Oh, how our hearts beat high with joy
con - science free; and blest would be their chil - dren's fate
all our strife; pro-claim thee too, as love knows how,

Refrain

when-e'er we hear that glo - rious word. Faith of our fa - thers,
if they, like them, should die for thee.
by sav - ing word and faith - ful life.

ho - ly faith, we will be true to thee till death.

Text: Frederick W. Faber, 1814–1863, alt.
Music: Henri F. Hemy, 1818–1888; James G. Walton, 1821–1905, refrain

ST. CATHERINE
888888

Faith of Our Fathers

813

1 Faith of our fathers, living still
in spite of dungeon, fire, and sword.
Oh, how our hearts beat high with joy
whene'er we hear that glorious word.
Faith of our fathers, holy faith,
we will be true to you till death.

2 Faith of our mothers, daring faith,
your work for Christ is love revealed,
spreading God's word from pole to pole,
making love known and freedom real.
Faith of our mothers, holy faith,
we will be true to you till death.

3 Faith of our sisters, brothers too,
who still must bear oppression's might,
raising on high, in prisons dark,
the cross of Christ still burning bright.
Faith for today, O living faith,
we will be true to you till death.

4 Faith born of God, oh, call us yet,
bind us with all who follow you,
sharing the struggle of your cross
until the world is made anew.
Faith born of God, O living faith,
we will be true to you till death.

Text: Frederick W. Faber, 1814–1863, st. 1, alt.; Joseph R. Alfred, b. 1947, sts. 2–4
Text sts. 2–4 © Joseph R. Alfred

ST. CATHERINE
888888

Take, Oh, Take Me As I Am

814

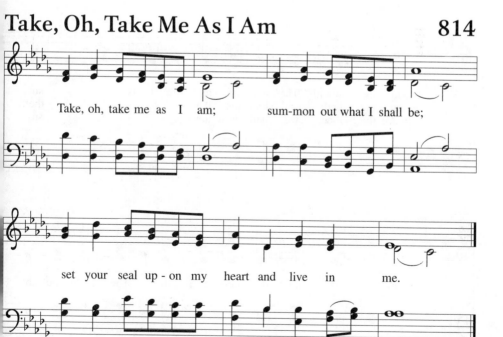

Take, oh, take me as I am; sum-mon out what I shall be;

set your seal up-on my heart and live in me.

Text: John L. Bell, b. 1949
Music: John L. Bell
Text and music © 1995 Iona Community, admin. GIA Publications, Inc.

TAKE ME AS I AM
7774

815 I Want to Walk as a Child of the Light

1 I want to walk as a child of the light. I want to
2 I want to see . . . the bright-ness of God. I want to
3 I'm look-ing for . . . the com-ing of Christ. I want to

fol - low Je - sus. God set the stars to give
look at Je - sus. Clear Sun of righ-teous-ness,
be with Je - sus. When we have run . . . . with

light to the world. The star of my life is Je - sus.
shine on my path, and show me the way to the Fa - ther.
pa - tience the race, we shall know the joy of Je - sus.

Refrain

In him there is no dark-ness at all. The night and the

Text: Kathleen Thomerson, b. 1934
Music: Kathleen Thomerson
Text and music © 1970, 1975 Celebration

HOUSTON
10 7 10 8 and refrain

day are both a - like. The Lamb is the light of the

cit - y of God. Shine in my heart, Lord Je - sus.

Come, My Way, My Truth, My Life 816

1 Come, my way, my truth, my life: such a
2 Come, my light, my feast, my strength: such a
3 Come, my joy, my love, my heart: such a

way as gives us breath; such a truth as ends all
light as shows a feast; such a feast as mends in
joy as none can move; such a love as none can

strife; such a life as kill - eth death.
length; such a strength as makes his guest.
part; such a heart as joys in love.

Text: George Herbert, 1593–1632
Music: Ralph Vaughan Williams, 1872–1958
Music © Stainer & Bell Ltd.

THE CALL
7 7 7 7

You Have Come Down to the Lakeshore
Tú has venido a la orilla

817

1 *Tú* | *has ve - ni - do_a la_o - ri - lla,* | *no_has bus -*
1 You | have come down to the lake - shore | seek - ing
2 You | know full well what I have, Lord: | nei - ther
3 You | need my hands, my ex - haus - tion, | work - ing
4 You | who have fished oth - er wa - ters; | you, the

ca - do | *ni_a sa - bios ni_a ri - cos;* | *tan só - lo*
nei - ther | the wise nor the wealth - y, | but on - ly
trea - sure | nor wea - pons for con - quest, | just these my
love for | the rest of the wea - ry— | a love that's
long - ing | of souls that are yearn - ing: | O lov - ing

quie - res | *que yo te si - ga.*
ask - ing | for me to fol - low.
fish nets | and will for work - ing.
will - ing | to go on lov - ing.
Friend, you | have come to call me.

Refrain / Estribillo

Se - ñor, | *me_has mi - ra - do_a los o - jos;* | *son - ri - en - do,*
Sweet Lord, | you have looked in - to my eyes; | kind - ly smil - ing,

has di - cho mi nom - bre. | *En la_a - re - na* | *he de - ja - do mi*
you've called out my name. . . . | On the sand I | have a - ban-doned my

bar - ca; | *jun - to_a ti* | *bus - ca - ré o - tro mar.*
small boat; | now with you, | I will seek oth - er seas.

Text: Cesáreo Gabaráin, 1936–1991; tr. Madeleine Forell Marshall, b. 1946
Music: Cesáreo Gabaráin
Text and music © 1979 Cesáreo Gabaráin, OCP Publications

PESCADOR DE HOMBRES
8 10 10 and refrain

2 Tú sabes bien lo que tengo:
   en mi barca no_hay oro no_espadas;
   tan sólo redes y mi trabajo. Estribillo

3 Tú necesitas mis manos,
   mi cansancio que_a otros descanse,
   amor que quiera seguir amando. Estribillo

4 Tú, Pescador de_otros mares,
   ansia_eterna de_almas que_esperan.
   Amigo bueno, que_así me llamas. Estribillo

O Master, Let Me Walk with You   818

1 O Mas - ter, let me walk with you in low - ly
2 Help me the slow of heart to move by some clear,
3 Teach me your pa - tience; share with me a clos - er,
4 In hope that sends a shin - ing ray far down the

paths of ser - vice true; tell me your se - cret;
win - ning word of love; teach me the way - ward
dear - er com - pa - ny, in work that keeps faith
fu - ture's broad - 'ning way, in peace that on - ly

help me bear the strain of toil, the fret of care.
feet to stay, and guide them in the home - ward way.
sweet and strong, in trust that tri - umphs o - ver wrong,
you can give; with you, O Mas - ter, let me live.

Text: Washington Gladden, 1836–1918, alt.
Music: H. Percy Smith, 1825–1898

MARYTON
LM

Come, All You People

Uyaimose

U - ya - i - mo - se, ti - na - ma - te Mwa - ri;
1 Come, all you peo - ple, come and praise the Most High;
2 Come, all you peo - ple, come and praise the Sav - ior;
3 Come, all you peo - ple, come and praise the Spir - it;

u - ya - i - mo - se, ti - na - ma - te Mwa - ri;
come, all you peo - ple, come and praise the Most High;
come, all you peo - ple, come and praise the Sav - ior;
come, all you peo - ple, come and praise the Spir - it;

u - ya - i - mo - se, ti - na - ma - te Mwa - ri;
come, all you peo - ple, come and praise the Most High;
come, all you peo - ple, come and praise the Sav - ior;
come, all you peo - ple, come and praise the Spir - it;

u - ya - i - mo - se Zvi - no.
come now and wor - ship the Lord.
come now and wor - ship the Lord.
come now and wor - ship the Lord.

Text: Alexander Gondo; tr. I-to Loh, b. 1936, alt.
Music: Alexander Gondo
Text and music © 1986 World Council of Churches and the Asian Institute of Liturgy & Music

UYAIMOSE
5 6 5 6 5 6 7

O Savior, Precious Savior

820

1 O Sav - ior, pre-cious Sav - ior, whom yet un-seen we love;
2 O bring - er of sal - va - tion, who won - drous-ly hast wrought,
3 In thee all full-ness dwell-eth, all grace and pow'r di - vine;
4 Oh, grant the con-sum - ma - tion of this our song a - bove,

O name of might and fa - vor, all oth - er names a - bove:
thy - self the rev - e - la - tion of love be-yond our thought:
the glo - ry that ex - cel - leth, O Son of God, is thine.
in end-less ad - o - ra - tion and ev - er-last-ing love;

we wor - ship thee; we bless thee; to thee a - lone we sing;
we wor - ship thee; we bless thee; to thee a - lone we sing;
We wor - ship thee; we bless thee; to thee a - lone we sing;
then shall we praise and bless thee where per - fect prais-es ring,

we praise thee and con - fess thee, our ho - ly Lord and King.
we praise thee and con - fess thee, our gra - cious Lord and King.
we praise thee and con - fess thee, our glo - rious Lord and King.
and ev - er-more con - fess thee, our Sav - ior and our King!

Text: Frances R. Havergal, 1836–1879
Music: Arthur H. Mann, 1850–1929

ANGEL'S STORY
7676 D

821

Shout to the Lord

My Je-sus, my Sav-ior, Lord, there is none like you.

All of my days I want to praise the won-ders of your might-y love.

My com-fort, my shel-ter, tow-er of ref-uge and strength;

let ev-'ry breath, all that I am nev-er cease to wor-ship you.

Shout to the Lord, all the earth; let us sing pow-er and maj-es-ty, praise

to the King. Moun-tains bow down and the seas will roar at the

sound of your name. I sing for joy at the work of your hands;

for-ev-er I'll love you, for-ev-er I'll stand.

Noth-ing com-pares to the prom-ise I have in you.

Text: Darlene Zschech, b. 1965
Music: Darlene Zschech
Text and music © 1993 Darlene Zschech/Hillsong Publishing, admin. in USA & Canada Integrity's Hosanna! Music

SHOUT TO THE LORD
PM

Oh, Sing to the Lord
Cantad al Señor

1 Can - tad al Se - ñor un cán - ti - co nue - vo.
1 Oh, sing to the Lord, oh, sing God a new song.
2 For God is the Lord, and God has done won - ders.
3 So dance for our God and blow all the trum - pets.
4 Oh, shout to our God, who gave us the Spir - it.
5 For Je - sus is Lord! A - men! Al - le - lu - ia!

Can - tad al Se - ñor un cán - ti - co nue - vo.
Oh, sing to the Lord, oh, sing God a new song.
For God is the Lord, and God has done won - ders.
So dance for our God and blow all the trum - pets.
Oh, shout to our God, who gave us the Spir - it.
For Je - sus is Lord! A - men! Al - le - lu - ia!

Can - tad al Se - ñor un cán - ti - co nue - vo.
Oh, sing to the Lord, oh, sing God a new song.
For God is the Lord, and God has done won - ders.
So dance for our God and blow all the trum - pets.
Oh, shout to our God, who gave us the Spir - it.
For Je - sus is Lord! A - men! Al - le - lu - ia!

¡Can - tad al Se - ñor, can - tad al Se - ñor!
Oh, sing to our God, oh, sing to our God.
Oh, sing to our God, oh, sing to our God.
Oh, sing to our God, oh, sing to our God.
Oh, sing to our God, oh, sing to our God.
Oh, sing to our God, oh, sing to our God.

2 Pues nuestro Señor ha hecho prodigios.
Pues nuestro Señor ha hecho prodigios.
Pues nuestro Señor ha hecho prodigios.
¡Cantad al Señor, cantad al Señor!

3 Cantad al Señor, alabadle con arpa.
Cantad al Señor, alabadle con arpa.
Cantad al Señor, alabadle con arpa.
¡Cantad al Señor, cantad al Señor!

4 Es él que nos da el_Espíritu Santo.
Es él que nos da el_Espíritu Santo.
Es él que nos da el_Espíritu Santo.
¡Cantad al Señor, cantad al Señor!

5 ¡Jesus es Señor! ¡Amén, aleluya!
¡Jesus es Señor! ¡Amén, aleluya!
¡Jesus es Señor! ¡Amén, aleluya!
¡Cantad al Señor, cantad al Señor!

Text: Brazilian folk song; tr. Gerhard M. Cartford, b. 1923, Spanish and English
Music: Brazilian folk tune
Text © Gerhard Cartford, admin. Augsburg Fortress

CANTAD AL SEÑOR
56 56 56 55

823 Praise the Lord! O Heavens

1 Praise the Lord! O heav'ns, a - dore him; praise him, an - gels, in the height;
2 Praise the Lord, for he is gra - cious; nev - er shall his prom - ise fail.

sun and moon, re - joice be - fore him; praise him, gleam - ing stars and light.
God has made his saints vic - to - rious; sin and death shall not pre - vail.

Praise the Lord, for he has spo - ken; worlds his might - y voice o - beyed;
Praise the God of our sal - va - tion; hosts on high, his pow'r pro - claim;

laws which nev - er shall be bro - ken for their guid - ance he has made.
heav'n and earth, and all cre - a - tion, laud and mag - ni - fy his name!

Text: *Foundling Hospital Collection*, London, 1796
Music: Franz Joseph Haydn, 1732–1809

AUSTRIA
8 7 8 7 D

Alternate tune: HYFRYDOL

This Is My Father's World

824

1 This is my Fa-ther's world, and to my lis-t'ning ears all
2 This is my Fa-ther's world; the birds their car-ols raise; the
3 This is my Fa-ther's world; oh, let me not for-get that,

na - ture sings, and round me rings the mu - sic of the spheres.
morn - ing light, the lil - y white, de - clare their mak - er's praise.
though the wrong seems oft so strong, God is the rul - er yet.

This is my Fa-ther's world; I rest me in the thought of
This is my Fa-ther's world; he shines in all that's fair. In the
This is my Fa-ther's world; why should my heart be sad? The

rocks and trees, of skies and seas; his hand the won - ders wrought.
rus - tling grass I hear him pass; he speaks to me ev-'ry-where.
Lord is king, let heav - en ring; God reigns, let earth be glad!

Text: Maltbie D. Babcock, 1858–1901
Music: Franklin L. Sheppard, 1852–1930, adapt.

TERRA PATRIS
SMD

825

You Servants of God

1 You ser-vants of God, your Mas-ter pro-claim, and pub-lish a-
2 As-cend-ed on high, al-might-y to save, yet still he is
3 Sal-va-tion to God who sits on the throne! Let all cry a-
4 Then let us a-dore and give him his right, all glo-ry and

broad his won-der-ful name; the name, all-vic-to-rious, of
nigh, his pres-ence we have. The great con-gre-ga-tion his
loud and hon-or the Son. The prais-es of Je-sus the
pow'r and wis-dom and might, all hon-or and bless-ing, with

Je-sus ex-tol; his king-dom is glo-rious and rules o-ver all!
tri-umph shall sing, as-crib-ing sal-va-tion to Je-sus, our king!
an-gels pro-claim, fall down on their fac-es, and wor-ship the Lamb.
an-gels a-bove, and thanks nev-er ceas-ing, and in-fin-ite love!

Text: Charles Wesley, 1707–1788, alt.
Music: attr. Johann Michael Haydn, 1737–1806

LYONS
10 10 11 11

Thine the Amen

1 Thine the a - men thine the praise al - le - lu - ias an - gels raise
2 Thine the life e - ter - nal - ly thine the prom-ise let there be
3 Thine the tru - ly thine the yes thine the ta - ble we the guest
4 Thine the king-dom thine the prize thine the won - der full sur-prise
5 Thine the glo - ry in the night no more dy - ing on - ly light

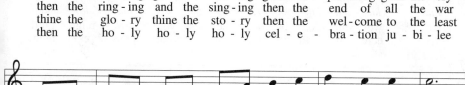

thine the ev - er - last - ing head thine the break-ing of the bread
thine the vi - sion thine the tree all the earth on bend-ed knee
thine the mer - cy all from thee thine the glo - ry yet to be
thine the ban - quet then the praise then the jus - tice of thy ways
thine the riv - er thine the tree then the Lamb e - ter - nal - ly

thine the glo - ry thine the sto - ry thine the har - vest then the cup
gone the nail - ing gone the rail - ing gone the plead-ing gone the cry
then the ring - ing and the sing-ing then the end of all the war
thine the glo - ry thine the sto - ry then the wel - come to the least
then the ho - ly ho - ly ho - ly cel - e - bra - tion ju - bi - lee

thine the vine - yard then the cup is lift - ed up lift - ed up.
gone the sigh - ing gone the dy - ing what was loss lift - ed high.
thine the liv - ing thine the lov - ing ev - er - more ev - er - more.
then the won - der all in - creas - ing at thy feast at thy feast.
thine the splen-dor thine the bright-ness on - ly thee on - ly thee.

Text: Herbert F. Brokering, b. 1926
Music: Carl F. Schalk, b. 1929
Text and music © 1983 Augsburg Publishing House

THINE
14 14 15 14

Arise, My Soul, Arise!
Nyt ylös, sieluni

Nyt y - lös, sie - lu - ni, nous' y - lös mul - last' täs - tä!
1 A - rise, my soul, a - rise! Stretch forth to things e - ter - nal
2 Now hear the harps of heav'n! Oh, hear the song vic - to - rious,

Käy jal - kain juu - reen Ju - ma - lan ja Ka - rit - san.
and has - ten to the feet of your re - deem - er God,
the nev - er - end - ing an - them sound - ing through the sky!

Ja vaikk' ei sil - mä - ni va - lo - a Her - ran kes - tä,
who, hid from mor - tal eyes, yet dwells in light su - per - nal;
To mor - tals is not giv'n to join in strains so glo - rious;

niin kui - ten - kin sä rie - mui - ten käy lau - la - maan.
so wor - ship God in hum - ble - ness, your sov - 'reign Lord.
yet here on earth we too can sing our prais - es high!

I - äi - seen i - loon ja juh - laan ja - loon
The ban - quet of love a - waits you a - bove;
Christ bought with his blood the ran - somed of God;

oot Ka - rit - san sä suu - riin häi - hin kut - sut - tu.
yet here you have a fore - taste of the feast to come!
to him be ev - er - last - ing pow'r and vic - to - ry.

Tai - va - han kun - ni - a on Her - ran ar - mos - ta
Re - joice, my soul, re - joice, to heav'n lift up your voice:
And let the great a - men re - sound through heav'n a - gain.

Text: Johan Kahl, 1721–1746; Finnish tr. *Halullisten Sjelujen Hengelliset Laulut*, 1790;
   English tr. Ernest E. Ryden, 1886–1981, alt.
Music: Finnish folk tune
Text © 1958 *Service Book and Hymnal*, admin. Augsburg Fortress

NYT YLÖS, SIELUNI
P M

sun   o - sa - si,   sun   pe - rin - tös   ja   ta - va - ras.
*Siis   rie - muit - se   ja   a - jat - te - le   au - tuut - tas.
1, 2 Al - le - lu - ia,   al - le - lu - ia,   al - le - lu - ia!

*The Finnish stanza repeats the last line of music.

Alleluia! Voices Raise

828

1 Al - le - lu - ia! Voic - es raise, sound - ing God Al -
2 Now come all be - fore God's face, in this cho - rus
3 Let, in praise of Christ, the sound run a nev - er -
4 So this huge wide orb we see shall one choir, one
5 Thus our song shall o - ver - climb all the bounds of

might - y's praise. Al - le - lu - ia, al - le - lu - ia!
take your place. Al - le - lu - ia, al - le - lu - ia!
end - ing round, Al - le - lu - ia, al - le - lu - ia!
tem - ple be. Al - le - lu - ia, al - le - lu - ia!
space and time. Al - le - lu - ia, al - le - lu - ia!

Hith - er bring in one con - sent heart and voice and in - stru -
And a - mid the mor - tal throng, be you mas - ters of the
that our songs of praise may be ev - er - last - ing, as is
In the Ho - ly Spir - it one, we will sing what God has
Al - le - lu - ia! Voic - es raise, sound - ing God Al - might - y's

ment. Al - le - lu - ia, al - le - lu - ia, al - le - lu - ia!
song. Al - le - lu - ia, al - le - lu - ia, al - le - lu - ia!
he. Al - le - lu - ia, al - le - lu - ia, al - le - lu - ia!
done. Al - le - lu - ia, al - le - lu - ia, al - le - lu - ia!
praise. Al - le - lu - ia, al - le - lu - ia, al - le - lu - ia!

Text: George Wither, 1588–1667, alt., based on Psalms 148 and 150
Music: Richard W. Hillert, b. 1923
Music © 1990, 1991 Oxford University Press, Inc.

PRINCETON
7787712

829

Have You Thanked the Lord?

Refrain

Have you thanked the Lord? Have you praised God's name?

Don't you know that no to-mor-row is quite the same?

Have you thanked the Lord? Have you knelt in prayer,

and re-joiced that, rain or sun-shine, our God is there?

1 Hal - le - lu - jah! Thank the Lord for sun, sand, and sea,
2 Hal - le - lu - jah! Par - a - dise we taste where we are;
3 Hal - le - lu - jah! Joy and peace the Sav - ior will bring.

ev - 'ry star at night that shines for you and me.
sum - mer breez - es, win - ter warmth are nev - er far.
Grace a - maz - ing! So we lift our voice and sing,

Bless - ings so man - y come our way:
God's love is ev - er on dis - play:
grate - ful when clouds are bright or gray:

Refrain

have you thanked the Lord to - day?
have you thanked the Lord to - day?
have you thanked the Lord to - day?

Text: Bill LaMotta, 1919–1980
Music: Bill LaMotta
Text and music © Bill (Wilbur) LaMotta

LAMOTTA
12 11 8 7 and refrain

How Marvelous God's Greatness 830

1 How mar-vel-ous God's great-ness, how glo-ri-ous God's might!
2 Each ti-ny flow'r-et whis-pers the great life-giv-er's name;
3 The o-cean's vast a-byss-es in one grand psalm re-cord
4 The star-ry hosts are sing-ing through all the light-strewn sky

To this the world bears wit-ness in won-ders day and night:
the might-y moun-tain mass-es his maj-es-ty pro-claim;
the deep mys-ter-ious coun-sels and mer-cies of the Lord;
of God's ma-jes-tic tem-ple and pal-ace courts on high;

in form of flow'r and snow-flake, in morn's re-splen-dent birth,
the val-leys deep are hymn-ing God's shel-ter for his own;
the ic-y waves of win-ter are thun-d'ring on the strand;
when in these out-er cham-bers such glo-ry gilds the night,

in af-ter-glow at eve-ning, in sky and sea and earth.
the snow-capped peaks are point-ing to God's al-might-y throne.
and grief's chill stream is guid-ed by God's all-gra-cious hand.
oh, what tran-scen-dent bright-ness is God's e-ter-nal light!

Text: Valdimar Briem, 1848–1930; tr. Charles V. Pilcher, 1879–1961, alt.
Music: *Koralpsalmboken*, Stockholm, 1697
Text © 1958 *Service Book and Hymnal*, admin. Augsburg Fortress

DEN BLOMSTERTID NU KOMMER
7676D

831 The God of Abraham Praise

1 The God of A-br'ham praise, who reigns en-throned a - bove;
2 The God of A-br'ham praise! At your su - preme com - mand
3 The God of A-br'ham praise! Your all - suf - fi - cient grace
4 Your prom-ise you have sworn; I on your oath de - pend.

An - cient of ev - er - last - ing days, and God of love—
from earth I rise and seek the joys at your right hand.
shall guide me all my pil - grim days in all my ways.
I shall, on ea - gle wings up - borne, to heav'n as - cend.

"I Am the One I Am"— by earth and heav'n con - fessed;
I all on earth for - sake— its wis - dom, fame, and pow'r—
You deign to call me friend; you call your - self my God!
I shall be - hold your face; I shall your pow'r a - dore,

I bow and bless the sa - cred name for - ev - er blest.
and you my on - ly por - tion make, my shield and tow'r.
And you will save me to the end through Je - sus' blood.
and sing the won - ders of your grace for - ev - er - more.

Text: Thomas Olivers, 1725–1799, alt., based on the *Yigdal*, c. 14th cent.
Music: Jewish melody; arr. Meyer Lyon, 1751–1797

YIGDAL
6 6 8 4 D

5   Though nature's strength decay,
    and earth and hell withstand,
    to Canaan's bounds I urge my way
    at your command.
    The wat'ry deep I pass,
    with Jesus in my view,
    and through the howling wilderness
    my way pursue.

6   The goodly land I see,
    with peace and plenty blest;
    a land of sacred liberty
    and endless rest.
    There milk and honey flow,
    and oil and wine abound,
    and trees of life forever grow
    with mercy crowned.

7   Before the great Three-One
    the saints exulting stand
    and tell the wonders God has done
    through all their land.
    The list'ning spheres attend
    and swell the growing fame
    and sing the songs which never end,
    the wondrous name.

8   The whole triumphant host
    give thanks to God on high.
    "Hail, Father, Son, and Holy Ghost!"
    they ever cry.
    Hail, Abr'ham's God and mine!
    I join the heav'nly lays:
    to you be glory, might divine,
    and endless praise!

My Lord of Light   832

1   My Lord of light who made the worlds, in wis-dom you have spo-ken;
2   My Lord of love who knew no sin, a sin-ner's death en-dur-ing:
3   My Lord of life who came in fire when Christ was high as-cend-ed:
4   My Lord of lords, one Trin-i-ty, to your pure name be giv-en

but those who heard your wise com-mands your ho-ly law have bro-ken.
for us you wore a crown of thorns, a crown of life se-cur-ing.
your burn-ing love is now re-leased, our days of fear are end-ed.
all glo-ry now and ev-er-more, all praise in earth and heav-en.

Text: Christopher Idle, b. 1938
Music: English folk tune; arr. Alice Parker, b. 1925
Text © 1980 by Jubilate Hymns, admin. Hope Publishing Company
Arr. © 1995 Augsburg Fortress

BARBARA ALLEN
8787

833 Oh, That I Had a Thousand Voices

1 Oh, that I had a thou - sand voic - es to praise my
2 Let ev - 'ry pow'r in me im - plant - ed a - rise, keep
3 You for - est leaves so green and ten - der that dance for
4 All crea - tures that have breath and mo - tion, that throng the
5 Cre - a - tor, hum - bly I im - plore you to lis - ten

God with thou - sand tongues! My heart, which in the Lord re -
si - lence now no more; put forth the strength that God has
joy in sum - mer air, you mead - ow grass - es, bright and
earth, the sea, the sky, come, share with me my heart's de -
to my earth - ly song un - til that day when I a -

joic - es, would then pro - claim in grate - ful songs to all, wher -
grant - ed! Your no - blest work is to a - dore! O soul and
slen - der, you flow'rs so fra - grant and so fair, you live to
vo - tion, help me to sing God's prais - es high! My ut - most
dore you, when I will join the an - gel throng and raise to

ev - er I might be, what great things God has done for me!
bod - y, join to raise with heart - felt joy your mak - er's praise!
show forth praise a - lone. Join me to make God's glo - ry known!
pow'rs can nev - er quite de - clare the won - ders of God's might!
you with joy - ful cry ten thou - sand hal - le - lu - jahs high!

Text: Johann Mentzer, 1658–1734; tr. composite
Music: Johann B. König, 1691–1758
Text © 2006 Augsburg Fortress

O DASS ICH TAUSEND ZUNGEN HÄTTE
9 8 9 8 8 8

Immortal, Invisible, God Only Wise   834

1 Im - mor - tal, in - vis - i - ble, God on - ly wise,
2 Un - rest - ing, un - hast - ing, and si - lent as light,
3 To all, life thou giv - est, to both great and small;
4 Thou reign - est in glo - ry; thou dwell - est in light;

in light in - ac - ces - si - ble hid from our eyes,
nor want - ing, nor wast - ing, thou rul - est in might;
in all life thou liv - est, the true life of all;
thine an - gels a - dore thee, all veil - ing their sight;

most bless - ed, most glo - rious, the An - cient of Days,
thy jus - tice like moun-tains high soar - ing a - bove
we blos - som and flour - ish like leaves on the tree,
all laud we would ren - der; oh, help us to see

al - might - y, vic - to - rious, thy great name we praise!
thy clouds which are foun - tains of good - ness and love.
and with - er and per - ish, but naught chang-eth thee.
'tis on - ly the splen-dor of light hid - eth thee!

Text: Walter Chalmers Smith, 1824–1908, alt.
Music: Welsh traditional; arr. John Roberts, 1807–1876

ST. DENIO
11 11 11 11

835 All Creatures, Worship God Most High!

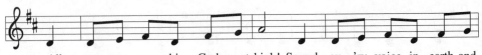

1 All crea-tures, wor-ship God most high! Sound ev-'ry voice in earth and
2 Sing, broth-er wind; with clouds and rain you grow the gifts of fruit and
3 Sing, broth-er fire, so mirth-ful, strong; drive far the shad-ows, join the
4 All who for love of God for-give, all who in pain or sor-row

sky: Al-le - lu - ia! Al-le - lu - ia! Sing, broth-er sun, in splen-dor
grain: Al-le - lu - ia! Al-le - lu - ia! Dear sis - ter wa - ter, use - ful,
throng: Al-le - lu - ia! Al-le - lu - ia! Dear moth-er earth, so rich in
grieve: Al-le - lu - ia! Al-le - lu - ia! Christ bears your bur-dens and your

bright; sing, sis - ter moon and stars of night:
clear, make mu - sic for your Lord to hear:
care, praise God in col - ors bright and rare: Al-le - lu - ia, al-le -
fears; still make your song a - mid the tears:

lu - ia, al - le - lu - ia, al - le - lu - ia, al - le - lu - ia!

5 And you, most gentle sister death,
  waiting to hush our final breath: Alleluia! Alleluia!
  Since Christ our light has pierced your gloom,
  fair is the night that leads us home.
  Alleluia, alleluia, alleluia, alleluia, alleluia!

6 O sisters, brothers, take your part,
  and worship God with humble heart: Alleluia! Alleluia!
  All creatures, bless the Father, Son,
  and Holy Spirit, Three in One:
  Alleluia, alleluia, alleluia, alleluia, alleluia!

Text: Francis of Assisi, 1182–1226; tr. composite
Music: *Geistliche Kirchengesänge*, Köln, 1623
Text © 1997 Augsburg Fortress

LASST UNS ERFREUEN
888 88 and alleluias

Joyful, Joyful We Adore Thee

836

1 Joy - ful, joy - ful we a - dore thee, God of glo - ry, Lord of love!
2 All thy works with joy sur - round thee, earth and heav'n re - flect thy rays,
3 Thou art giv - ing and for - giv - ing, ev - er bless - ing, ev - er blest,

Hearts un - fold like flow'rs be - fore thee, prais - ing thee, their sun a - bove.
stars and an - gels sing a - round thee, cen - ter of un - bro - ken praise.
well - spring of the joy of liv - ing, o - cean - depth of hap - py rest!

Melt the clouds of sin and sad - ness, drive the gloom of doubt a - way.
Field and for - est, vale and moun - tain, flow - 'ry mead - ow, flash - ing sea,
Thou our Fa - ther, Christ our broth - er, all who live in love are thine;

Giv - er of im - mor - tal glad - ness, fill us with the light of day.
chant - ing bird, and flow - ing foun - tain call us to re - joice in thee.
teach us how to love each oth - er, lift us to the joy di - vine!

Text: Henry van Dyke, 1852–1922
Music: Ludwig van Beethoven, 1770–1827, adapt.

HYMN TO JOY
8 7 8 7 D

Many and Great, O God
Wakantanka taku nitawa

Wa - kan - tan - ka   ta - ku   ni - ta - wa   tan - ka - ya
1 Man - y and   great,   O God,   are your works,   mak - er of
2 Grant un - to   us   com - mu - nion with   you,   O Star - a -

qa   o - ta.   Ma - hpi - ya   kin   e - ya - hna - ke   ca,
earth and   sky.   Your hands have set   the heav'ns   with   stars;
bid - ing   One.   Come un - to   us   and dwell   with   us;

ma - ka kin   he   du - o - wan - ca.   Mni - o - wan
your fin - gers   spread   the moun - tains and   plains.   Lo,   at your
with you are   found   the gifts   of . . .   life.   Bless   us with

ca - śbe - ya - wan - ke   cin,   he - na o - ya - ki - hi.
word   the   wa - ters   were formed;   deep seas o - bey   your   voice.
life   that   has   no . . .   end,   e - ter - nal life   with   you.

Text: Joseph R. Renville, 1779–1846; para. Philip Frazier, 1892–1964, alt.
Music: Dakota tune; arr. *Songs of the People*, 1986
Arr. © 1986 Augsburg Publishing House

LAC QUI PARLE
9 6 8 8 8 6

Beautiful Savior

838

1 Beau - ti - ful Sav - ior, King of cre - a - tion,
2 Fair are the mead - ows, fair are the wood - lands,
3 Fair is the sun - shine, fair is the moon - light,
4 Beau - ti - ful Sav - ior, Lord of the na - tions,

Son of God and Son of Man!
robed in flow'rs of bloom - ing spring;
bright the spar - kling stars on high;
Son of God and Son of Man!

Tru - ly I'd love thee, tru - ly I'd serve thee,
Je - sus is fair - er, Je - sus is pur - er,
Je - sus shines bright - er, Je - sus shines pur - er
Glo - ry and hon - or, praise, ad - o - ra - tion,

light of my soul, my joy, my crown.
he makes our sor - rowing spir - it sing.
than all the an - gels in the sky.
now and for - ev - er - more be thine!

Text: *Gesangbuch*, Münster, 1677; tr. Joseph A. Seiss, 1823–1904
Music: Silesian folk tune, 19th cent.

SCHÖNSTER HERR JESU
557558

839   Now Thank We All Our God

1 Now thank we all our God   with hearts and hands and voic - es,
2 Oh, may this boun-teous God   through all our life be near us,
3 All praise and thanks to God   the Fa - ther now be giv - en,

who won-drous things has done,   in whom this world re - joic - es;
with ev - er joy - ful hearts   and bless - ed peace to cheer us,
the Son, and Spir - it blest,   who reign in high - est heav - en,

who, from our moth - ers' arms,   has blest us on our way
and keep us all in grace,   and guide us when per - plexed,
the one e - ter - nal God,   whom earth and heav'n a - dore;

with count-less gifts of love, and   still is ours to - day.
and free us from all harm in   this world and the next.
for thus it was, is now, and   shall be ev - er - more.

Text: Martin Rinkhart, 1586–1649; tr. Catherine Winkworth, 1827–1878
Music: Johann Crüger, 1598–1662

NUN DANKET ALLE GOTT
67 67 66 66

Now Thank We All Our God

840

1 Now thank we all our God with hearts and hands and voic - es,
2 Oh, may this boun - teous God through all our life be near us,
3 All praise and thanks to God the Fa - ther now be giv - en,

who won - drous things has done, in whom this world re - joic - es;
with ev - er joy - ful hearts and bless - ed peace to cheer us,
the Son, and Spir - it blest, who reign in high - est heav - en,

who, from our moth - ers' arms, has blest us on our way
and keep us all in grace, and guide us when per - plexed,
the one e - ter - nal God, whom earth and heav'n a - dore;

with count - less gifts of love, and still is ours to - day.
and free us from all harm in this world and the next.
for thus it was, is now, and shall be ev - er - more.

Text: Martin Rinkhart, 1586–1649; tr. Catherine Winkworth, 1827–1878
Music: Johann Crüger, 1598–1662

NUN DANKET ALLE GOTT
67 67 66 66

841

Lift Every Voice and Sing

1 Lift ev - 'ry voice and sing till earth and heav - en ring,
2 Ston - y the road we trod, bit - ter the chas - t'ning rod,
3 God of our wea - ry years, God of our si - lent tears,

ring with the har - mo - nies of lib - er - ty.
felt in the days when hope un - born had died;
thou who hast brought us thus far on the way;

Let our re - joic - ing rise high as the lis - t'ning skies,
yet with a stead - y beat, have not our wea - ry feet
thou who hast by thy might led us in - to the light,

let it re - sound loud as the roll - ing sea.
come to the place for which our par - ents sighed?
keep us for - ev - er in the path, we pray.

Text: James W. Johnson, 1871–1938
Music: J. Rosamond Johnson, 1873–1954

LIFT EVERY VOICE AND SING
P M

Sing a song full of the faith that the dark past has taught us;
We have come o - ver a way that with tears has been wa - tered;
Lest our feet stray from the plac - es, our God, where we met thee;

sing a song full of the hope that the pres - ent has brought us;
we have come, tread - ing our path through the blood of the slaugh - tered,
lest, our hearts drunk with the wine of the world, we for - get thee;

fac - ing the ris - ing sun of our new day be - gun,
out from the gloom - y past, till now we stand at last
shad - owed be - neath thy hand, may we for - ev - er stand,

let us march on till vic - to - ry is won.
where the white gleam of our bright star is cast.
true to our God, true to our na - tive land.

842

Oh, Worship the King

1 Oh, wor-ship the King, all - glo-rious a - bove.
2 The earth with its store of won-ders un - told,
3 Your boun-ti - ful care what tongue can re - cite?
4 Frail chil-dren of dust, and fee-ble as frail,
5 O mea-sure-less might, in - ef - fa - ble love,

Oh, grate-ful-ly sing God's pow-er and love;
Al - might-y, your pow'r has found-ed of old;
It breathes in the air, it shines in the light,
in you do we trust, nor find you to fail;
while an-gels de-light to hymn you a - bove,

our shield and de - fend-er, the An - cient of Days,
es - tab - lished it fast by a change-less de - cree,
it streams from the hills, it de - scends to the plain,
your mer - cies, how ten - der, how firm to the end,
the hum - bler cre - a - tion, though fee - ble their lays,

pa - vil - ioned in splen-dor, and gird - ed with praise.
and round it has cast, like a man-tle, the sea.
and sweet-ly dis - tills in the dew and the rain.
our mak-er, de - fend-er, re - deem-er, and friend.
with true ad - o - ra - tion shall sing to your praise.

Text: Robert Grant, 1779–1838, alt.
Music: William Croft, 1678–1727

HANOVER
10 10 11 11

Praise the One Who Breaks the Darkness 843

1 Praise the One who breaks the dark-ness with a lib-er-at-ing light;
2 Praise the One who blessed the chil-dren with a strong yet gen-tle word;
3 Praise the one true love in-car-nate: Christ, who suf-fered in our place;

praise the One who frees the pris-'ners, turn-ing blind-ness in-to sight.
praise the One who drove out de-mons with a pierc-ing, two-edged sword.
Je - sus died and rose for man-y that we may know God by grace.

Praise the One who preached the gos-pel, heal-ing ev-'ry dread dis-ease,
Praise the One who brings cool wa-ter to the des-ert's burn-ing sand;
Let us sing for joy and glad-ness, see-ing what our God has done.

calm-ing storms and feed-ing thou-sands with the ver-y bread of peace.
from this well comes liv-ing wa-ter quench-ing thirst in ev-'ry land.
Praise the one re-deem-ing glo-ry; praise the One who makes us one.

Text: Rusty Edwards, b. 1955
Music: J. Wyeth, *Repository of Sacred Music*, Part II, 1813
Text © 1987 Hope Publishing Company

NETTLETON
8787D

Praise to the Lord
Louez l'Eternel

1 Lou - ez l'E - ter - nel, ser - vi - teurs de
2 Qui est comme no - tre Dieu, dans les cieux, sur la
1 Praise to the Lord, all of you, God's
2 There is none like our God in the heav'ns or on

Dieu. Bé - ni soit son nom, main - te - nant,
ter - re, qui ex - al - te les pauvres au rang des grands
ser - vants. Bless - ed be the name of our God
earth, who lifts the poor from the dust, seat - ing them

à ja - mais. Du le - ver du so - leil,
de son peu - ple, qui ma - ni - feste mi - sé - ri - corde?
now and ev - er. From the ris - ing of the sun,
with the might-y, who stoops to raise the weak and low:

Refrain

bé - ni soit son nom! Lou - é soit Dieu, l'E - ter - nel!
may the Lord be praised, praise to the name of the Lord!

Text: Ron Klusmeier, b. 1946, based on Psalm 113; French tr. R. Gerald Hobbs, b. 1941
Music: Ron Klusmeier
Text and music © 1972 Ron Klusmeier

RICHARDSON–BURTON
Irregular

Voices Raised to You

1 Voic - es raised to you we of - fer; tune them, God, for
2 All cre - a - tion joins to praise you; earth and sky your
3 Christ, the song of love in - car - nate, touch-ing earth with
4 Spir - it, flam - ing through cre - a - tion, kin - dle faith with -
5 How can an - y praise we of - fer mea - sure all the

songs of praise. Hearts and hands we bring in trib - ute
works dis - play. Art and mu - sic, gifts you lend us,
heav - en's grace, for your liv - ing, suf - f'ring, dy - ing,
in each heart. Lift our voic - es high in cho - rus;
thanks we owe? Take our hearts and hands and voic - es—

for your gifts through all our days. Al - le - lu - ia!
we re - turn to you to - day. Al - le - lu - ia!
for your ris - ing, hear our praise! Al - le - lu - ia!
through our hands your love im - part. Al - le - lu - ia!
gifts of love we can be - stow. Al - le - lu - ia!

Al - le - lu - ia! Tri - une God, to you we sing!
Al - le - lu - ia! God, cre - a - tor, source of life!
Al - le - lu - ia! Christ, re - deem - er, Lord of life!
Al - le - lu - ia! Spir - it, help - er, breath of life!
Al - le - lu - ia! Tri - une God, to you we sing!

Text: Herman G. Stuempfle Jr., b. 1923
Music: Carolyn Jennings, b. 1936
Text © 1997 GIA Publications, Inc.
Music © 1996 Carolyn Jennings

SONG OF PRAISE
878787

Amen, We Praise Your Name
Amen siakudumisa
846

Ma - si - thi! / A-men si - a - ku - du - mi - sa! / Ma - si - thi!
Sing prais - es! / A-men, we praise your name, O God! Sing prais - es!

A - men si - a - ku - du - mi - sa! / Ma - si - thi! / A - men, ba - wo.
A - men, we praise your name, O God! / Sing prais - es! / A - men, a - men.

A - men, ba - wo. / A - men si - a - ku - du - mi - sa! / Ma - si - thi!
A - men, a - men. / A-men, we praise your name, O God! Sing prais - es!

Text: South African traditional
Music: attr. S. C. Molefe, as taught by Gobingca George Mxadana
Music © Gobingca Mxadana

AMEN SIAKUDUMISA
PM

847 # Come, Let Us Join Our Cheerful Songs

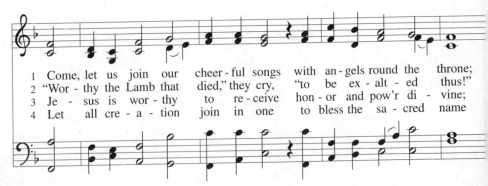

1 Come, let us join our cheer - ful songs with an - gels round the throne;
2 "Wor - thy the Lamb that died," they cry, "to be ex - alt - ed thus!"
3 Je - sus is wor - thy to re - ceive hon - or and pow'r di - vine;
4 Let all cre - a - tion join in one to bless the sa - cred name

Text: Isaac Watts, 1674–1748
Music: Johann Crüger, 1598–1662

NUN DANKET ALL
CM

ten thou-sand thou-sand are their tongues, but all their joys are one.
"Wor - thy the Lamb," our lips re - ply, "for he was slain for us!"
and bless-ings, more than we can give, be, Lord, for - ev - er thine.
of God who sits up - on the throne, and to a - dore the Lamb.

Give to Our God Immortal Praise! 848

1 Give to our God im - mor - tal praise! Mer - cy and
2 He sent his Son with pow'r to save from guilt and
3 Give to the Lord of lords re - nown; the King of

truth are all his ways. Won - ders of grace to
dark - ness and the grave. Won - ders of grace to
kings with glo - ry crown. His mer - cies ev - er

God be - long; re - peat his mer - cies in your song.
God be - long; re - peat his mer - cies in your song.
shall en - dure when lords and kings are known no more!

Text: Isaac Watts, 1674–1748
Music: attr. John Hatton, d. 1793

DUKE STREET
LM

Yours, Lord, Is the Glory
Tuya es la gloria

849

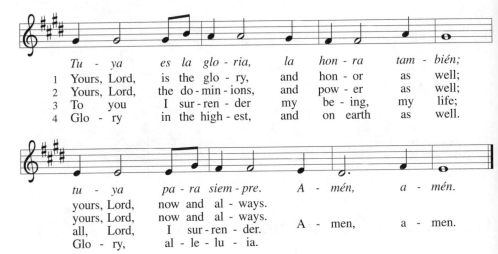

Tu - ya es la glo - ria, la hon - ra tam - bién;
1. Yours, Lord, is the glo - ry, and hon - or as well;
2. Yours, Lord, the do - min - ions, and pow - er as well;
3. To you I sur - ren - der my be - ing, my life;
4. Glo - ry in the high - est, and on earth as well.

tu - ya pa - ra siem - pre. A - mén, a - mén.
yours, Lord, now and al - ways.
yours, Lord, now and al - ways. A - men, a - men.
all, Lord, I sur - ren - der.
Glo - ry, al - le - lu - ia.

2 *Tuyos los dominios,*
los tronos también;
tuyos para siempre.
Amén, amén.

3 *A ti yo me rindo,*
te adoro también,
amo absoluto.
Amén, amén.

4 *Gloria en las alturas*
y en la tierra también;
gloria aleluya.
Amén, amén.

Text: Traditional; tr. Gerhard M. Cartford, b. 1923
Music: Traditional
Tr. © 1998 Augsburg Fortress

TUYA ES LA GLORIA
6 5 6 4

850 When in Our Music God Is Glorified

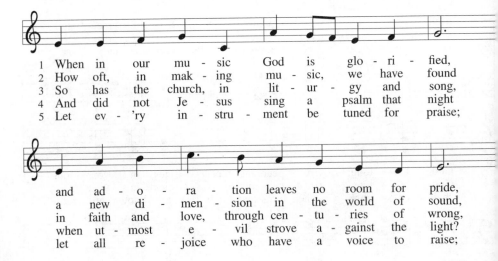

1. When in our mu - sic God is glo - ri - fied,
2. How oft, in mak - ing mu - sic, we have found
3. So has the church, in lit - ur - gy and song,
4. And did not Je - sus sing a psalm that night
5. Let ev - 'ry in - stru - ment be tuned for praise;

and ad - o - ra - tion leaves no room for pride,
a new di - men - sion in the world of sound,
in faith and love, through cen - tu - ries of wrong,
when ut - most e - vil strove a - gainst the light?
let all re - joice who have a voice to raise;

Text: Fred Pratt Green, 1903–2000
Music: Charles R. Anders, b. 1929
Test © 1972 Hope Publishing Company
Music © 1978 *Lutheran Book of Worship*, admin. Augsburg Fortress

FREDERICKTOWN
10 10 10 and alleluias

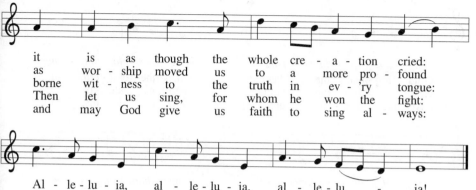

it   is   as   though the   whole   cre - a - tion   cried:
as   wor - ship   moved   us   to   a   more   pro - found
borne   wit - ness   to   the   truth   in   ev - 'ry   tongue:
Then   let   us   sing,   for   whom   he   won   the   fight:
and   may   God   give   us   faith   to   sing   al - ways:

Al - le - lu - ia,   al - le - lu - ia,   al - le - lu - ia!

When in Our Music God Is Glorified   851

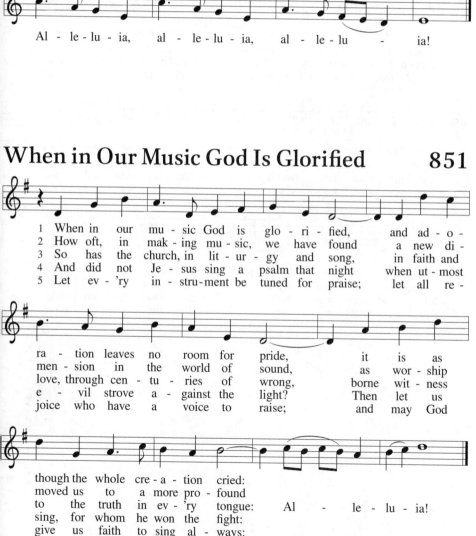

1 When in   our   mu - sic God is   glo - ri - fied,   and ad - o -
2 How oft,   in   mak - ing mu - sic, we   have found   a   new di -
3 So has   the   church, in lit - ur - gy and   song,   in faith and
4 And did   not   Je - sus sing a   psalm that night   when ut - most
5 Let ev - 'ry   in - stru-ment be   tuned for praise;   let all re -

ra - tion leaves no   room for   pride,   it   is   as
men - sion in   the   world of   sound,   as   wor - ship
love, through cen - tu - ries of   wrong,   borne wit - ness
e - vil strove   a - gainst the   light?   Then let us
joice who have   a   voice to   raise;   and may God

though the whole cre - a - tion cried:
moved us   to   a more pro - found
to   the   truth in ev - 'ry tongue: Al - le - lu - ia!
sing, for   whom he won the fight:
give   us   faith to sing al - ways:

Text: Fred Pratt Green, 1903–2000
Music: Charles V. Stanford, 1852–1924
Text © 1972 Hope Publishing Company

ENGELBERG
10 10 10 4

Golden Breaks the Dawn

Qing zao qilai kan

852

Qing zao qi - lai kan,   *hong ri chu tong - fang,*
1 Gold - en breaks the dawn,   comes the east - ern sun;
2 Ho - ly, liv - ing God,   keep me safe to - day;
3 Give me dai - ly bread,   while I do my part;

xiong - zhuang xiang yong - shi,   *mei - hao xiang xin - lang;*
like a rid - er strong,   set the course to run.
though I wea - ry plod,   make me kind, I pray.
bright skies o - ver - head,   glad - ness in my heart.

tian gao fei - niao guo,   *di kuo ye - hua xiang,*
Birds a - bove me fly,   flow - ers bloom be - low;
Let me guide our youth,   hon - or weak and old;
Sim - ple wants pro - vide,   e - vil let me shun;

zhao wo qin gong - zuo,   *Tian - fu you en - guang.*
through the earth and sky   God's great mer - cies flow.
let me serve with truth,   and God's love un - fold.
Je - sus at my side,   till the day is done.

Text: Tzu-chen Chao; para. Frank W. Price, 1885–1974
Music: Te-ngai Hu
Text and music © 1977 Chinese Christian Literature Council Ltd., Hong Kong

LE P'ING
5 5 5 5 D

When Morning Gilds the Skies

1 When morn-ing gilds the skies, my heart a - wak - ing cries:
2 When mirth for mu - sic longs, this is my song of songs:
3 No love - lier an - ti - phon in all high heav'n is known
4 Let all of hu - man - kind in this their con - cord find:
5 Sing, sun and stars of space, sing, all who see his face,

may Je - sus Christ be praised! When eve - ning shad - ows fall,
may Je - sus Christ be praised! God's ho - ly house of prayer
than "Je - sus Christ be praised!" There to the e - ter - nal Word
may Je - sus Christ be praised! Let all the earth a - round
sing, "Je - sus Christ be praised!" God's whole cre - a - tion o'er,

this rings my cur - few call: may Je - sus Christ be praised!
has none that can com - pare with "Je - sus Christ be praised!"
the e - ter - nal psalm is heard: oh, Je - sus Christ be praised!
ring joy - ous with the sound: may Je - sus Christ be praised!
to - day and ev - er - more shall Je - sus Christ be praised!

Text: German hymn, 19th cent.; tr. Robert Bridges, 1844–1930, alt.
Music: Joseph Barnby, 1838–1896

LAUDES DOMINI
666666

854

Blessing and Honor

1 Bless-ing and hon - or and glo - ry and pow'r, wis - dom and
2 Let all the heav - ens sound forth Je - sus' name; let all the
3 Ev - er as - cend - ing the song and the joy, ev - er de -
4 Give we the glo - ry and praise to the Lamb! Take we the

rich - es and strength ev - er - more, be to the Lamb who our
earth sing his glo - ry and fame. O - cean and moun - tain, stream,
scend - ing the love from on high; bless - ing and hon - or and
robe and the harp and the palm; sing we the song of the

bat - tle has won, whose are the king - dom, the crown, and the
for - est, and flow'r ech - o his prais - es and tell of his
glo - ry and praise— this is the theme of the hymns that we
Lamb who was slain, dy - ing in weak-ness and ris - ing to

throne; whose are the king - dom, the crown, and the throne!
pow'r; ech - o his prais - es and tell of his pow'r.
raise; this is the theme of the hymns that we raise.
reign; dy - ing in weak - ness and ris - ing to reign!

Text: Horatius Bonar, 1808–1889, alt.
Music: Matthias Keller, 1813–1875

AMERICAN HYMN
10 10 10 10 10

Crown Him with Many Crowns

1 Crown him with man - y crowns, the Lamb up - on his throne;
2 Crown him the vir - gin's Son, the God in - car - nate born,
3 Crown him the Lord of love— be - hold his hands and side,
4 Crown him the Lord of life, who tri - umphed o'er the grave
5 Crown him the Lord of years, the po - ten - tate of time,

hark, how the heav'n - ly an - them drowns all mu - sic but its own.
whose arm those crim - son tro - phies won which now his brow a - dorn;
rich wounds, yet vis - i - ble a - bove, in beau - ty glo - ri - fied.
and rose vic - to - rious in the strife for those he came to save.
cre - a - tor of the roll - ing spheres, in - ef - fab - ly sub - lime.

A - wake, my soul, and sing of him who died for thee,
fruit of the mys - tic rose, yet of that rose the stem,
No an - gels in the sky can ful - ly bear that sight,
His glo - ries now we sing, who died and rose on high,
All hail, Re - deem - er, hail! For thou hast died for me;

and hail him as thy match - less king through all e - ter - ni - ty.
the root whence mer - cy ev - er flows, the babe of Beth - le - hem.
but down - ward bend their burn - ing eyes at mys - ter - ies so bright.
who died, e - ter - nal life to bring, and lives that death may die.
thy praise and glo - ry shall not fail through - out e - ter - ni - ty.

Text: Matthew Bridges, 1800–1894, sts. 1–3, 5; Godfrey Thring, 1823–1903, st. 4
Music: George J. Elvey, 1816–1893

DIADEMATA
SMD

How Great Thou Art

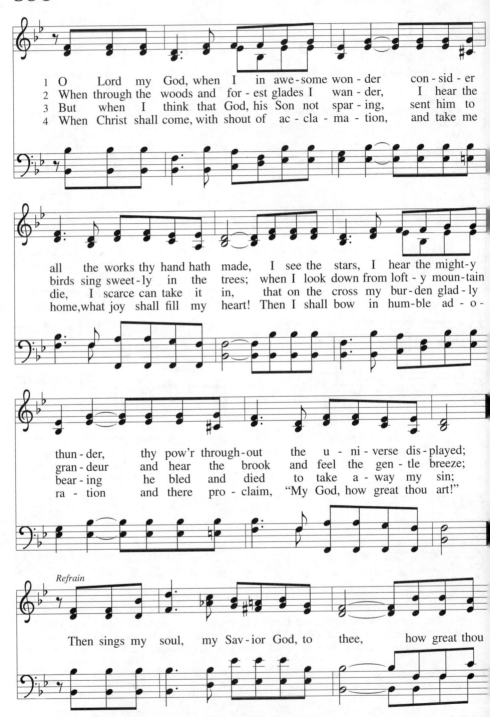

1 O Lord my God, when I in awe-some won-der, con-sid-er
2 When through the woods and for-est glades I wan-der, I hear the
3 But when I think that God, his Son not spar-ing, sent him to
4 When Christ shall come, with shout of ac-cla-ma-tion, and take me

all the works thy hand hath made, I see the stars, I hear the might-y
birds sing sweet-ly in the trees; when I look down from loft-y moun-tain
die, I scarce can take it in, that on the cross my bur-den glad-ly
home, what joy shall fill my heart! Then I shall bow in hum-ble ad-o-

thun-der, thy pow'r through-out the u-ni-verse dis-played;
gran-deur and hear the brook and feel the gen-tle breeze;
bear-ing he bled and died to take a-way my sin;
ra-tion and there pro-claim, "My God, how great thou art!"

Refrain

Then sings my soul, my Sav-ior God, to thee, how great thou

Text: Carl G. Boberg, 1859–1940; tr. and adapt. Stuart K. Hine, 1899–1989
Music: Swedish folk tune; adapt. Stuart K. Hine
Text and music © 1953, ren. 1981 S.K. Hine, assigned to Manna Music, Inc.

O STORE GUD
11 10 11 10 and refrain

art! How great thou art! Then sings my soul, my Sav-ior God, to

thee, how great thou art! How great thou art!

Lord, I Lift Your Name on High 857

Lord, I lift your name on high; Lord, I love to sing your prais-es.

I'm so glad you're in my life, I'm so glad you came to save us.

You came from heav-en to earth to show the way, from the earth

to the cross, my debt to pay, from the cross to the grave,

from the grave to the sky; Lord, I lift your name on high.

Text: Rick Founds, b. 1954
Music: Rick Founds
Text and music © 1989 Maranatha Praise, Inc., admin. Music Services

LORD, I LIFT YOUR NAME
PM

858   Praise to the Lord, the Almighty

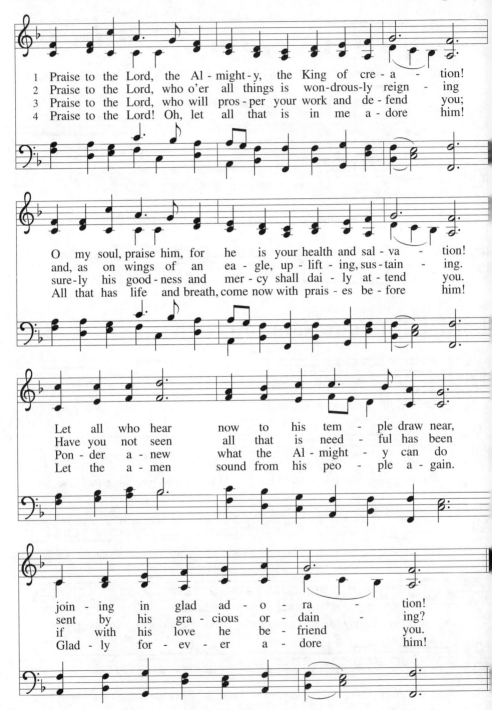

1 Praise to the Lord, the Al - might-y, the King of cre - a - tion!
2 Praise to the Lord, who o'er all things is won-drous-ly reign - ing
3 Praise to the Lord, who will pros - per your work and de - fend you;
4 Praise to the Lord! Oh, let all that is in me a - dore him!

O my soul, praise him, for he is your health and sal - va - tion!
and, as on wings of an ea - gle, up - lift - ing, sus-tain - ing.
sure - ly his good - ness and mer - cy shall dai - ly at - tend you.
All that has life and breath, come now with prais - es be - fore him!

Let all who hear now to his tem - ple draw near,
Have you not seen all that is need - ful has been
Pon - der a - new what the Al - might - y can do
Let the a - men sound from his peo - ple a - gain.

join - ing in glad ad - o - ra - tion!
sent by his gra - cious or - dain - ing?
if with his love he be - friend you.
Glad - ly for - ev - er a - dore him!

Text: Joachim Neander, 1650–1680; tr. Catherine Winkworth, 1827–1878, alt.
Music: *Ernewerten Gesangbuch*, Part II, Stralsund, 1665

LOBE DEN HERREN
14 14 4 7 8

Praise to the Lord, the Almighty

1   Praise to the Lord, the Almighty, the God of creation!
    My heart is longing to offer up sweet adoration.
    Melody make; dulcimer, harp, now awake.
    Sound forth your praise, ev'ry nation.

2   Praise the Almighty, o'er all life so wondrously reigning,
    and, as on wings of an eagle, uplifting, sustaining.
    Have you not seen? All that is needful has been
    sent by God's gracious ordaining.

3   Praise the Almighty, who prospers your work and defends you;
    see from the heavens the showers of mercy God sends you.
    Ponder anew what the Almighty can do;
    infinite Love here befriends you.

4   Praise the Almighty! In wonder my spirit is soaring!
    All that has life and breath, come now with praises outpouring.
    Let the amen sound from God's people again,
    gladly forever adoring!

Text: Joachim Neander, 1650–1680; tr. composite
Text © 2000 Augsburg Fortress

LOBE DEN HERREN
14 14 4 7 8

I'm So Glad Jesus Lifted Me

1 I'm   so   glad   I'm   so   glad
2 Sa - tan had me bound,   Je-sus lift-ed me.   Sa - tan had me bound,
3 When I was in trou - ble,   When I was in trou - ble,

                      I'm   so   glad
Je-sus lift-ed me.   Sa - tan had me bound,   Je-sus lift-ed me,
                      When I was in trou - ble,

    sing-ing glo - ry, hal - le - lu - jah!   Je - sus lift - ed me.

Text: African American spiritual
Music: African American spiritual

JESUS LIFTED ME
Irregular

When Long before Time

861

The Singer and the Song

1 When long be - fore time and the worlds were be - gun,
2 The si - lence was bro - ken when God sang the Song,
3 The sounds of the crea - tures were one with their Lord's,
4 Though down through the a - ges the Song dis - ap - peared,

when there was no earth and no sky and no sun,
and light pierced the dark - ness and rhy - thm be - gan,
their har - mo - nies sweet and be - fit - ting the Word;
its har - mo - nies bro - ken and al - most un - heard,

and all was deep si - lence and night reigned su - preme,
and with its first birth - cries cre - a - tion was born,
the Sing - er was pleased as the earth sang the Song,
the Sing - er comes to us to sing it a - gain,

and e - ven our Mak - er had on - ly a dream—
and crea - ture - ly voic - es sang praise to the morn.
the choir of the crea - tures re - ech - oed it long.
our God - is - with - us in the world now as then.

Text: Peter W. A. Davison, b. 1936
Music: Peter W. A. Davison; arr. George Black, 1931–2003
Text and tune © Peter W. A. Davison, admin. Augsburg Fortress
Arr. © George Black

THE SINGER AND THE SONG
11 11 11 11

5   The Light has returned as it came once before,
the Song of the Lord is our own song once more,
so let us all sing with one heart and one voice
the Song of the Singer in whom we rejoice.

6   To you, God the Singer, our voices we raise,
to you, Song Incarnate, we give all our praise,
to you, Holy Spirit, our life and our breath,
be glory forever, through life and through death.

Praise, Praise! You Are My Rock   862

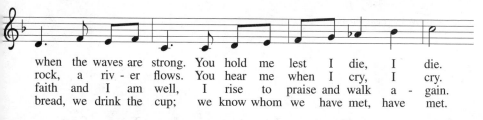

1 Praise, praise! You are my rock. The wind, the waves are high. You hold me
2 Praise, praise! You are my rock. My des - ert sand is dry. You break the
3 Praise, praise! You are my rock. You calm the fear and pain. One word of
4 Praise, praise! You are my rock. You host the ta - ble set. We break the

when the waves are strong. You hold me lest I die, I die.
rock, a riv - er flows. You hear me when I cry, I cry.
faith and I am well, I rise to praise and walk a - gain.
bread, we drink the cup; we know whom we have met, have met.

Praise, praise! O God, you are my rock.

5   Praise, praise! You are my rock.
The Easter grave is sealed;
you roll the stone—you, God, alone—
then sin and death are healed, are healed.
Praise, praise!
O God, you are my rock.

6   Praise, praise! You are my rock.
You stood high on a hill.
A holy cloud: you are on high.
Be still, my heart, be still, be still.
Praise, praise!
O God, you are my rock.

Text: Herbert F. Brokering, b. 1926
Music: Rusty Edwards, b. 1955
Text and music © 1999 Augsburg Fortress

ZACHARY WOODS ROCK
66888

863 My God, How Wonderful Thou Art

1 My God, how won-der-ful thou art, thy maj-es-ty how bright!
2 How won-der-ful, how beau-ti-ful the sight of thee must be—
3 No earth-ly fa-ther loves like thee; no moth-er, e'er so mild,
4 Yet I may love thee too, O Lord, al-might-y as thou art,
5 My God, how won-der-ful thou art, thou ev-er-last-ing friend!

How beau-ti-ful thy mer-cy seat in depths of burn-ing light!
thine end-less wis-dom, bound-less pow'r, and awe-some pu-ri-ty!
bears and for-bears as thou hast done with me, thy sin-ful child.
for thou hast stooped to ask of me the love of my poor heart.
On thee I stay my trust-ing heart till faith in vi-sion end.

Text: Frederick W. Faber, 1814–1863
Music: *Psalter*, Edinburgh, 1615

DUNDEE
CM

864 Praise, My Soul, the God of Heaven

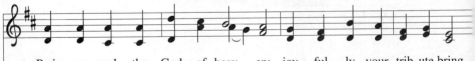

1 Praise, my soul, the God of heav-en; joy-ful-ly your trib-ute bring.
2 God be praised for grace and fa-vor to our fore-bears in dis-tress.
3 Frail as sum-mer's flow'r we flour-ish, blows the wind and it is gone;
4 An-gels sing in ad-o-ra-tion, in God's pres-ence, face to face.

Text: Henry F. Lyte, 1793–1847; alt. Walter R. Bouman, 1927–2005
Music: John Goss, 1800–1880

PRAISE, MY SOU
87 87 8

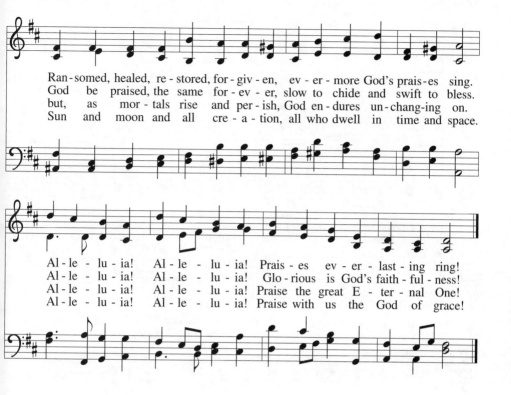

Ran - somed, healed, re - stored, for - giv - en, ev - er - more God's prais - es sing.
God be praised, the same for - ev - er, slow to chide and swift to bless.
but, as mor - tals rise and per - ish, God en - dures un - chang-ing on.
Sun and moon and all cre - a - tion, all who dwell in time and space.

Al - le - lu - ia! Al - le - lu - ia! Prais - es ev - er - last - ing ring!
Al - le - lu - ia! Al - le - lu - ia! Glo - rious is God's faith - ful - ness!
Al - le - lu - ia! Al - le - lu - ia! Praise the great E - ter - nal One!
Al - le - lu - ia! Al - le - lu - ia! Praise with us the God of grace!

Praise, My Soul, the King of Heaven 865

1 Praise, my soul, the King of heaven;
to his feet your tribute bring.
Ransomed, healed, restored, forgiven,
evermore his praises sing.
Alleluia! Alleluia!
Praise the everlasting King!

2 Praise him for his grace and favor
to our forebears in distress.
Praise him, still the same forever,
slow to chide and swift to bless.
Alleluia! Alleluia!
Glorious in his faithfulness!

3 Tenderly he shields and spares us;
well our feeble frame he knows.
In his hands he gently bears us,
rescues us from all our foes.
Alleluia! Alleluia!
Widely as his mercy flows.

4 Angels help us to adore him,
who behold him face to face.
Sun and moon bow down before him;
all who dwell in time and space.
Alleluia! Alleluia!
Praise with us the God of grace.

Text: Henry F. Lyte, 1793–1847

PRAISE, MY SOUL
8 7 8 7 8 7

We Are Marching in the Light

Siyahamba

866

Si - ya - hamb' e - ku - kha - nyen' kwen - khos', si - ya - hamb' e - ku - kha-
We are march - ing in the light of God, we are march-ing in the

nyen' kwen - khos'. Si - ya - hamb' e - ku - kha - nyen' kwen - khos',
light of God. We are march - ing in the light of God,

si - ya - hamb' e - ku - kha - nyen' kwen - khos'.
we are march-ing in the light of God.

si - ya - hamb' e - ku - kha - nyen' kwen–, kha - nyen' kwen - khos'.
we are march - ing in the light of, the light of God.

si - ya - hamb' e - ku - kha - nyen' kwen - khos'.
we are march - ing in the light of God.

Si - ya - ham - ba_____ oo_____
We are march - ing_____ oo_____

Si - ya - ham - ba, ham - ba, si - ya - ham - ba, ham - ba,
We are march - ing, march - ing, we are march - ing, march - ing,

Text: South African traditional; tr. *Freedom Is Coming*, 1984
Music: South African traditional; arr. *Freedom Is Coming*
Tr. and arr. © 1984 Utryck, admin. Walton Music Corp.

SIYAHAMBA
Irregular

si - ya - hamb' e - ku - kha - nyen' kwen - khos'.
we are march-ing in the light of God.

si - ya - hamb' e - ku - kha - nyen' kwen–, kha - nyen' kwen - khos'.
we are march - ing in the light of, the light of God.

si - ya - hamb' e - ku - kha - nyen' kwen - khos'.
we are march - ing in the light of God.

Si - ya - ham - ba_____ oo_____
We are march - ing_____ oo_____

Si - ya - ham - ba, ham - ba, si - ya - ham - ba, ham - ba,
We are march - ing, march - ing, we are march - ing, march - ing,

si - ya - hamb' e - ku - kha - nyen' kwen - khos'.
we are march-ing in the light of God.

Additional stanzas ad lib.:
We are dancing …
We are praying …
We are singing …

867

In Thee Is Gladness

1 In thee is glad-ness a-mid all sad-ness, Je-sus, sun-shine of my
2 Je-sus is ours! .. We fear no pow-ers, not of earth or sin or

heart. By thee are giv-en the gifts of heav-en, thou the
death. He sees and bless-es in worst dis-tress-es; he can

true re-deem-er art. Our souls thou wak-est; our bonds thou
change them with a breath. Where-fore the sto-ry tell of his

break-est. Who trusts thee sure-ly has built se-cure-ly
glo-ry with heart and voic-es; all heav'n re-joic-es

and stands for-ev-er: Al-le-lu-ia! Our hearts are
in him for-ev-er: Al-le-lu-ia! We shout for

pin-ing to see thy shin-ing, dy-ing or liv-ing,
glad-ness, tri-umph o'er sad-ness, love him and praise him

to thee are cleav-ing; naught can us sev-er: Al-le-lu-ia!
and still shall raise him glad hymns for-ev-er: Al-le-lu-ia!

Text: Johann Lindemann, 1549–1631; tr. Catherine Winkworth, 1827–1878, alt.
Music: Giovanni Giacomo Gastoldi, 1556–1622

IN DIR IST FREUDE
P M

Isaiah in a Vision Did of Old

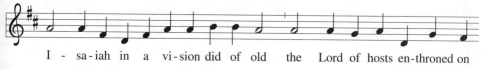

I - sa-iah in a vi-sion did of old the Lord of hosts en-throned on

high be-hold, whose splen-did train was wide out-spread un - til its stream-ing

glo-ry did the tem-ple fill. A - bove God's throne the shin-ing ser - a-phim

with six-fold wings did rev-'rence un - to him. With two each ser-aph hid his

glo-rious face, and two a-bout his feet did in - ter-lace, and with the

oth-er two he soared on high, and one un - to an-oth-er thus did cry:

"Ho - ly, ho - ly, ho - ly

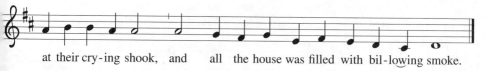

is the Lord of hosts! His glo - ry fill-eth all the earth!" The beams and lin-tels

at their cry-ing shook, and all the house was filled with bil-low-ing smoke.

Text: Martin Luther, 1483–1546; tr. Martin H. Franzmann, 1907–1976
Music: Martin Luther
Text © 1978 *Lutheran Book of Worship*, admin. Augsburg Fortress

JESAIA, DEM PROPHETEN
PM

We Have Seen the Lord
Nimemwona Bwana

869

Text: Tanzanian traditional; tr. Jeff Sartain, b. 1962
Music: Tanzanian tune; arr. Mark Sedio, b. 1954
Tr. and arr. © 2003 Concordia Publishing House

NIMEMWONA BWANA
Irregular

We Praise You, O God

1 We praise you, O God, our re - deem - er, cre - a - tor;
2 We wor - ship you, God of our fa - thers and mo - thers;
3 With voic - es u - nit - ed our prais - es we of - fer

in grate - ful de - vo - tion our trib - ute we bring.
through tri - al and tem - pest our guide you have been.
and glad - ly our songs of thanks - giv - ing we raise.

We lay it be - fore you; we kneel and a - dore you;
When per - ils o'er - take us, you will not for - sake us,
With you, Lord, be - side us, your strong arm will guide us.

we bless your ho - ly name; glad prais - es we sing.
and with your help, O Lord, our strug - gles we win.
To you, our great re - deem - er, for - ev - er be praise!

Text: Julia C. Cory, 1882–1963
Music: A. Valerius, *Nederlandtsch Gedenckclanck*, 1626

KREMSER
12 11 12 11

871   Sing Praise to God, the Highest Good

1 Sing praise to God, the high-est good, the au-thor of cre-
2 What your al-might-y pow'r has made, in mer-cy you are
3 We sought the Lord in our dis-tress; O God, in mer-cy
4 All who con-fess Christ's ho-ly name, give God the praise and

a - tion! O God of love, you un-der-stood our need for
keep - ing; by morn-ing glow or eve-ning shade, your eye is
hear us. Our Sav-ior saw our help-less-ness and came with
glo - ry! Let all God's sav-ing pow'r pro-claim; give God the

your sal-va - tion. With heal-ing balm our souls you fill;
nev-er sleep - ing; in the do-min-ion of your might
peace to cheer us. For this we thank and praise the Lord,
praise and glo - ry! Cast ev-'ry i - dol from its throne;

all our la-ment with peace you still.
all things are just and good and right. To God all praise and glo - ry!
who is by one and all a - dored.
God is the Lord, and God a - lone:

Text: Johann J. Schütz, 1640–1690; tr. Frances E. Cox, 1812–1897, adapt.
Music: Melchior Vulpius, 1570–1615

LOBT GOTT DEN HERREN, IHF
8 7 8 7 8 8 7

Praise Ye the Lord

Refrain

Praise ye the Lord, hal - le - lu - jah!

Ev - 'ry - bod - y, praise the Lord.

1 Praise God with the sound of the trum - pet;
2 Praise God with ho - ly cym - bals;
3 Praise God in the ho - ly tem - ple;
4 Praise God on top of the moun - tains;

praise God with the lute and the harp;
praise God with strings and with pipes;
praise God for al - might - y deeds;
praise God both day and night;

praise God with the tim - brel and danc - ing;
praise God with clash - ing cym - bals;
praise God for those boun - ti - ful mer - cies;
praise God down in the low val - leys;

Refrain

praise God wher - ev - er you are.
praise God with all of your might.
for God ful - fills our needs.
praise God be - cause it's all right.

Text: J. Jefferson Cleveland, 1937–1986, based on Psalm 150
Music: J. Jefferson Cleveland
Text and music © J. Jefferson Cleveland

CLEVELAND
Irregular

873

Rejoice, Ye Pure in Heart!

1 Re - joice, ye   pure in   heart!   Re - joice, give thanks, and   sing;
2 With voice as   full and   strong   as   o - cean's surg - ing praise,
3 With all   the   an - gel choirs,   with   all   the   saints on   earth
4 Still lift   your stan - dard high,   still march in   firm   ar - ray,

your fes - tal   ban - ner wave on   high, the cross   of Christ your king.
send forth the   stur - dy hymns of   old, the psalms of   an - cient days.
pour out the   strains of   joy   and bliss, true rap - ture, no - blest mirth.
as   pil - grims through the   dark - ness wend till dawns the gol - den day.

Refrain

Re - joice!   Re - joice!   Re - joice, give thanks, and   sing!

Re - joice!   Re - joice!

5 At last the march shall end;
   the wearied ones shall rest;
   the pilgrims find their home at last,
   Jerusalem the blest. *Refrain*

6 Praise God who reigns on high,
   the Lord whom we adore:
   the Father, Son, and Spirit blest,
   one God forevermore. *Refrain*

Text: Edward H. Plumptre, 1821–1891, alt.
Music: Arthur H. Messiter, 1834–1916

MARION
S M and refrain

Rejoice, Ye Pure in Heart!

1 Re - joice, ye pure in heart! Re - joice, give thanks, and sing; your
2 With voice as full and strong as o - cean's surg - ing praise, send
3 With all the an - gel choirs, with all the saints on earth pour
4 Still lift your stan - dard high, still march in firm ar - ray, as

fes - tal ban - ner wave on high, the cross of Christ your king.
forth the stur - dy hymns of old, the psalms of an - cient days.
out the strains of joy and bliss, true rap - ture, no - blest mirth.
pil - grims through the dark - ness wend till dawns the gol - den day.

Refrain

Ho - san - na! Ho - san - na! Re - joice, give thanks, and sing!

5 At last the march shall end;
the wearied ones shall rest;
the pilgrims find their home at last,
Jerusalem the blest. *Refrain*

6 Praise God who reigns on high,
the Lord whom we adore:
the Father, Son, and Spirit blest,
one God forevermore. *Refrain*

Text: Edward H. Plumptre, 1821–1891, alt.
Music: Richard W. Dirksen, 1921–2003
Music © 1974 (renewed) Harold Flammer Music, a division of Shawnee Press, Inc.

VINEYARD HAVEN
S M and refrain

875 Praise, Praise, Praise the Lord!

Praise, praise, praise the Lord! Praise God's ho - ly name. Al - le - lu - ia!

Praise, praise, praise the Lord! Praise God's ho - ly name. Al - le - lu - ia!

Praise God's ho - ly name. Al - le - lu - ia! Praise God's ho - ly name. Al - le - lu - ia!

Praise God's ho - ly name. Al - le - lu - ia! Praise God's ho - ly name. Al - le - lu - ia!

Text: Cameroon traditional, collected by Elaine Hanson
Music: Cameroon processional; arr. Ralph M. Johnson
Text and music © 1994 earthsongs

CAMEROON PRAISE
59599999

Let the Whole Creation Cry 876

1 Let the whole cre - a - tion cry, "Glo - ry to the Lord on high!"
2 Ser - vants striv - ing for the Lord, proph-ets burn - ing with the word,
3 Men and wom - en, young and old, raise the an - them loud and bold,

Heav'n and earth, a - wake and sing, "Praise to our al - might - y king!"
those to whom the arts be - long add their voic - es to the song.
and let chil-dren's hap - py hearts in this wor - ship take their parts;

Praise God, an - gel hosts a - bove, ev - er bright and fair in love;
Pow'rs of knowl-edge and of law, to the glo - rious cir - cle draw;
from the north to south-ern pole let the might - y cho - rus roll:

sun and moon, lift up your voice; night and stars, in God re - joice.
all who work and all who wait, sing, "The Lord is good and great!"
"Ho - ly, Ho - ly, Ho - ly One; glo - ry be to God a - lone!"

Text: Stopford A. Brooke, 1832–1916, alt.
Music: Jakob Hintze, 1622–1702; arr. Johann Sebastian Bach, 1685–1750, adapt.

SALZBURG
7777D

877

Praise the Almighty!

1 Praise the Al - might - y! Lord, I   a - dore   you!
2 Trust not in ru - lers; they are but mor - tal;
3 Lord, you give jus - tice in all op - pres - sion,
4 Praise, all you peo - ple, the name so ho - ly,

Yes, I will laud you un - til death;
earth - born they are and soon de - cay.
main - tain the right, set pris - 'ners free.
the Lord who does such won - drous things!

with songs and an - thems I come be - fore you
Vain are their coun - sels at life's last por - tal,
You feed the hun - gry in your com - pas - sion;
All that has be - ing, to praise God sole - ly,

as long as you al - low me breath. From you my life
when the cold grave en - gulfs its prey. Since mor - tals can
heal - ing and life flow from your tree. Hap - py are all
with hap - py heart its a - men sings! Chil - dren of God,

and all things came; all the day long I bless your name.
no help af - ford, place all your trust in Christ, our Lord.
who hope in God, whose grace is rich and deep and broad!
with saints at rest, praise Fa - ther, Son, and Spir - it blest!

Hal - le - lu - jah! Hal - le - lu - jah!

Text: Johann D. Herrnschmidt, 1675–1723; tr. hymnal version
Music: *Neuvermehrtes Christlich Seelenharpf*, Ansbach, 1665
Text © 2006 Augsburg Fortress

LOBE DEN HERREN, O MEINE SEELE
108 108 888

Soli Deo Gloria

1 O God of bless-ings, all praise to you! Your love sur-
2 All praise for proph-ets, through grace in - spired to preach and
3 All praise for mu - sic, deep gift pro - found, through hands and
4 All praise for Je - sus, best gift di - vine through word and
5 A bil - lion voic - es in one great song, now soft and

rounds us our whole life through. You are the
wit - ness with hearts on fire. Your Spir - it
voic - es in ho - ly sound; the psalms of
wit - ness, in bread and wine; in - car - nate
gen - tle, now deep and strong, in ev - 'ry

free - dom of those op - pressed; you are the com - fort of all dis-
choos-es the weak and small to sing the new reign where might - y
Da - vid, and Mar - y's praise, in word-less splen-dor and lyr - ic
love song of bound-less grace, priest, teach-er, proph-et in time and
cul - ture and style and key, from hill and val - ley, with sky and

tressed. Come now, O ho - ly and wel - come guest:
fall; with them may we live your gos - pel call:
phrase, with all cre - a - tion one song we raise:
space, your stead - fast kind - ness with hu - man face:
sea, with Christ we praise you e - ter - nal - ly:

So - li De - o glo - ri - a! So - li De - o glo - ri - a!

Text: Marty Haugen, b. 1950
Music: Marty Haugen
Text and music © 1999 GIA Publications, Inc.

SOLI DEO GLORIA
9999977

879 For the Beauty of the Earth

1 For the beau-ty of the earth, for the beau-ty of the skies,
2 For the won-der of each hour of the day and of the night,
3 For the joy of ear and eye, for the heart and mind's de-light,
4 For the joy of hu-man love, broth-er, sis-ter, par-ent, child,
5 For each per-fect gift of thine, peace on earth and joy in heav'n;

for the love which from our birth o-ver and a-round us lies:
hill and vale and tree and flow'r, sun and moon and stars of light:
for the mys-tic har-mo-ny link-ing sense to sound and sight:
friends on earth and friends a-bove; for all gen-tle thoughts and mild:
for thy-self, best gift di-vine, to our world so free-ly giv'n:

Refrain

Christ, our God, to thee we raise this our sac-ri-fice of praise.

Text: Folliott S. Pierpoint, 1835–1917, alt.
Music: Conrad Kocher, 1786–1872

DIX
777777

O God beyond All Praising

880

1 O God be-yond all prais - ing, we wor-ship you to - day
2 The flow'r of earth - ly splen - dor in time must sure - ly die,
3 Then hear, O gra - cious Sav - ior, ac - cept the love we bring,

and sing the love a - maz - ing that songs can-not re - pay;
its frag - ile bloom sur - ren - der to you, the Lord most high;
that we who know your fa - vor may serve you as our King;

for we can on - ly won - der at ev - 'ry gift you send,
but hid - den from all na - ture the e - ter - nal seed is sown—
and wheth - er our to - mor-rows be filled with good or ill,

at bless-ings with - out num - ber and mer-cies with-out end:
though small in mor - tal stat - ure, to heav-en's gar - den grown:
we'll tri - umph through our sor - rows and rise to bless you still:

we lift our hearts be - fore you and wait up - on your word,
for Christ, your gift from heav - en, from death has set us free,
to mar - vel at your beau - ty and glo - ry in your ways,

we hon - or and a - dore you, our great and might - y Lord.
and we through him are giv - en the fi - nal vic - to - ry.
and make a joy - ful du - ty our sac - ri - fice of praise.

Text: Michael Perry, 1942–1996
Music: Gustav Holst, 1874–1934
Text © 1982, 1987 Jubilate Hymns, admin. Hope Publishing Company

THAXTED
13 13 13 13 13 13

881   Let All Things Now Living

1 Let all things now liv-ing a song of thanks-giv-ing to
2 God rules all the forc-es: the stars in their cours-es and

God the cre-a-tor tri-um-phant-ly raise,
sun in its or-bit o-be-dient-ly shine;

who fash-ioned and made us, pro-tect-ed and stayed us, who
the hills and the moun-tains, the riv-ers and foun-tains, the

still guides us on to the end of our days.
deeps of the o-cean pro-claim God di-vine.

God's ban-ners are o'er us, God's light goes be-
We too should be voic-ing our love and re-

fore us, a pil-lar of fire shin-ing forth in the night,
joic-ing; with glad ad-o-ra-tion a song let us raise

till shad-ows have van-ished and dark-ness is ban-ished, as
till all things now liv-ing u-nite in thanks-giv-ing: "To

for-ward we trav-el from light in-to light.
God in the high-est, ho-san-na and praise!"

Text: Katherine K. Davis, 1892–1980, alt.
Music: Welsh folk tune
Text © 1939, 1966 E. C. Schirmer Music Company

THE ASH GROVE
6 6 11 6 6 11 D

My Soul Does Magnify the Lord 882

1 My soul does mag - ni - fy the Lord; my spir - it
2 From this day all will call me blest, from now through
3 His mer - cy touch - es those who love, and those who
4 He cast the might - y from their thrones, and he has
5 He comes to all who seek his love, for he re -
6 All glo - ry be to God on high, and to his
7 Just as it was, it is to - day, and it shall

sings of God my Sav - ior, for he has looked with
all the com - ing a - ges. The Lord has done great
serve . . . one an - oth - er. And with great strength he has
lift - ed up the low - ly. He fills the hun - gry
mem - bers the prom - ise that he had made to
Son, . . . God the Sav - ior, and to the Spir - it of
last through all to - mor - rows, and so my soul mag - ni -

love and fa - vor on his low - ly ser - vant.
things for me and ho - ly is his name.
scat - tered all the proud in their con - ceit.
with good things while oth - ers turn a - way.
A - bra - ham and to the chil - dren of God.
life and truth that burns with - in our hearts.
fies the Lord; praise God for - ev - er. A - men.

Text: Grayson Warren Brown, b. 1948, based on the Magnificat
Music: Grayson Warren Brown
Text and music © 1992 Grayson Warren Brown, admin. OCP Publications

GOSPEL MAGNIFICAT
Irregular

883 All People That on Earth Do Dwell

1 All peo-ple that on earth do dwell, sing to the
2 Know that the Lord is God in - deed; with - out our
3 Oh, en - ter then his gates with praise; ap - proach with
4 For why? The Lord our God is good: his mer - cy
5 To Fa - ther, Son, and Ho - ly Ghost, the God whom

Lord with cheer - ful voice; him serve with mirth, his
aid he did us make. We are his folk, he
joy his courts un - to; praise, laud, and bless his
is for - ev - er sure; his truth at all times
heav'n and earth a - dore, from us and from the

praise forth tell; come ye be - fore him and re - joice.
doth us feed, and for his sheep he doth us take.
name al - ways, for it is seem - ly so to do.
firm - ly stood, and shall from age to age en - dure.
an - gel host be praise and glo - ry ev - er - more.

Text: William Kethe, d. c. 1594
Music: Louis Bourgeois, 1510–1561

OLD HUNDREDTH
LM

884 Praise God, from Whom All Blessings Flow

Praise God, from whom all blessings flow;
praise him, all creatures here below;
praise him above, ye heav'nly host;
praise Father, Son, and Holy Ghost.

Text: Thomas Ken, 1637–1711

OLD HUNDREDTH
LM

Praise God, from Whom All Blessings Flow   885

Alternate text
Praise God, from whom all blessings flow;
praise God, all creatures here below;
praise God above, ye heav'nly host;
praise Father, Son, and Holy Ghost.

Text: Thomas Ken, 1637–1711, alt.

OLD HUNDREDTH
LM

Oh, for a Thousand Tongues to Sing   886

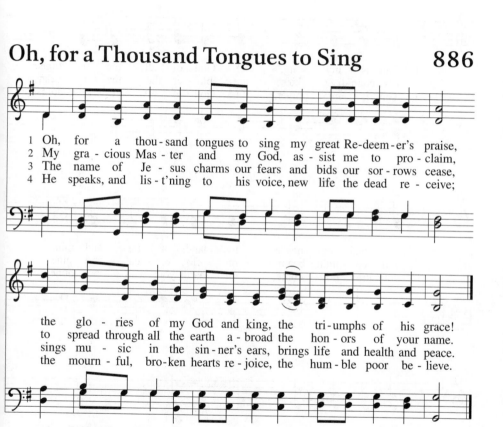

1 Oh, for a thou-sand tongues to sing my great Re-deem-er's praise,
2 My gra-cious Mas-ter and my God, as-sist me to pro-claim,
3 The name of Je-sus charms our fears and bids our sor-rows cease,
4 He speaks, and lis-t'ning to his voice, new life the dead re-ceive;

the glo-ries of my God and king, the tri-umphs of his grace!
to spread through all the earth a-broad the hon-ors of your name.
sings mu-sic in the sin-ner's ears, brings life and health and peace.
the mourn-ful, bro-ken hearts re-joice, the hum-ble poor be-lieve.

5 Look unto him, your Savior own,
   O fallen human race!
   Look and be saved through faith alone,
   be justified by grace!

6 To God all glory, praise, and love
   be now and ever giv'n
   by saints below and saints above,
   the church in earth and heav'n.

Text: Charles Wesley, 1707–1788, alt.
Music: Carl G. Gläser, 1784–1829; arr. Lowell Mason, 1792–1872

AZMON
CM

887

This Is My Song

1 This is my song, O God of all the na-tions,
2 My coun-try's skies are blu-er than the o-cean,
3 This is my prayer, O God of all earth's king-doms,

a song of peace for lands a-far and mine.
and sun-light beams on clo-ver-leaf and pine.
your king-dom come; on earth your will be done.

This is my home, the coun-try where my heart is;
But oth-er lands have sun-light too, and clo-ver,
O God, be lift-ed up till all shall serve you,

Text: Lloyd Stone, 1912–1993, sts. 1–2; Georgia Harkness, 1891–1974, st. 3
Music: Jean Sibelius, 1865–1957
Text sts. 1–2 © 1934, 1962, Lorenz Publishing Company, st. 3 © 1964 Lorenz Publishing Company
Music © Breitkopf & Härtel

FINLANDIA
11 10 11 10 11 10

here are my hopes, my dreams, my ho - ly shrine;
and skies are ev - 'ry - where as blue as mine.
and hearts u - nit - ed learn to live as one.

but oth - er hearts in oth - er lands are beat - ing
So hear my song, O God of all the na - tions,
So hear my prayer, O God of all the na - tions;

with hopes and dreams as true and high as mine.
a song of peace for their land and for mine.
my - self I give you; let your will be done.

888   O Beautiful for Spacious Skies

1 O beau - ti - ful for spa - cious skies, for am - ber waves of grain,
2 O beau - ti - ful for he - roes proved in lib - er - at - ing strife,
3 O beau - ti - ful for pa - triot dream that sees be - yond the years

for pur - ple moun-tain maj - es - ties a - bove the fruit-ed plain:
who more than self their coun-try loved, and mer - cy more than life:
thine al - a - bas - ter cit - ies gleam, un - dimmed by hu - man tears:

A - mer - i - ca! A - mer - i - ca! God shed his grace on thee,
A - mer - i - ca! A - mer - i - ca! May God thy gold re - fine,
A - mer - i - ca! A - mer - i - ca! God mend thine ev - 'ry flaw,

and crown thy good with broth - er-hood from sea to shin-ing sea.
till all suc - cess be no - ble-ness, and ev - 'ry gain di - vine.
con - firm thy soul in self - con-trol, thy lib - er - ty in law.

Text: Katherine L. Bates, 1859–1929
Music: Samuel A. Ward, 1848–1903

MATERNA
CMD

The Right Hand of God

1 The right hand of God is writ-ing in our land,
2 The right hand of God is point-ing in our land,
3 The right hand of God is strik-ing in our land,
4 The right hand of God is heal-ing in our land,

writ - ing with pow-er and with love,
point - ing the way . . . we must go,
strik-ing out at en - vy, hate, and greed.
heal-ing bro - ken bod-ies, minds, and souls,

our con - flicts and our fears, our tri-umphs and our tears
so cloud-ed is the way, so eas-i-ly we stray,
Our self-ish-ness and lust, our pride and deeds un-just
so won-drous is its touch with love that means so much,

are re-cord-ed by the right hand of God.
but we're guid-ed by the right hand of God.
are de-stroyed by the right hand of God.
when we're healed by the right hand of God.

Optional stanza

5 The right hand of God
is planting in our land,
planting seeds of freedom, hope, and love.

In these Caribbean lands,
let people all join hands,
and be one by the right hand of God.

Text: Patrick Prescod
Music: Noel Dexter
Text and music © 1981 Caribbean Conference of Churches

LA MANO DE DIOS
5 6 8 6 6 10

890 Mine Eyes Have Seen the Glory

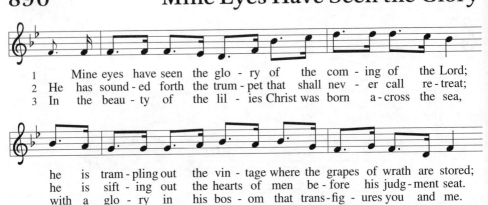

1 Mine eyes have seen the glo - ry of the com - ing of the Lord;
2 He has sound - ed forth the trum - pet that shall nev - er call re - treat;
3 In the beau - ty of the lil - ies Christ was born a - cross the sea,

he is tram - pling out the vin - tage where the grapes of wrath are stored;
he is sift - ing out the hearts of men be - fore his judg - ment seat.
with a glo - ry in his bos - om that trans - fig - ures you and me.

he has loosed the fate - ful light - ning of his ter - ri - ble swift sword:
Oh, be swift, my soul, to an - swer him; be ju - bi - lant, my feet!
As he died to make men ho - ly, let us live to make men free,

his truth is march - ing on.
Our God is march - ing on.
while God is march - ing on.

Refrain

Glo - ry, glo - ry! Hal - le - lu - jah! Glo - ry, glo - ry! Hal - le - lu - jah!

Glo - ry, glo - ry! Hal - le - lu - jah! His truth is march-ing on.

Text: Julia Ward Howe, 1819–1910
Music: North American, 19th cent.

BATTLE HYMN
15 15 15 6 and refrain

God Bless Our Native Land

891

1 God bless our na - tive land; firm may it ev - er stand
2 So shall our prayers a - rise to God a - bove the skies,

through storm and night. When the wild tem - pests rave, Rul - er of
on whom we wait. Thou who art ev - er nigh, guard-ing with

wind and wave, do thou our coun - try save by thy great might.
watch-ful eye, to thee a - loud we cry: God save the state!

Text: Charles T. Brooks, 1812–1883; John S. Dwight, 1813–1893
Music: *Thesaurus Musicus*, London, 1744

NATIONAL ANTHEM
6 6 4 6 6 6 4

892

O Canada

O Can - a - da! Our home and na - tive land!
O Can - a - da! Ter - re de nos aï - eux,

True pa - triot love in all *thy sons com - mand.
ton front est ceint de fleu - rons glo - ri - eux!

With glow-ing hearts we see thee rise, the True North strong and free!
Car ton bras sait por - ter l'é-pé - e, il sait por - ter la croix!

From far and wide, O Can - a - da, we stand on guard for thee.
Ton his-toire est une é-po-pé - e des plus bril - lants ex - ploits.

God keep our land glo - rious and free! O Can - a - da, we stand on
Et ta va - leur, de foi trem-pée, pro - té - ge - ra nos foy - ers

guard for thee. O Can - a - da, we stand on guard for thee.
et nos droits. Pro - té - ge - ra nos foy - ers et nos droits.

*or "our lives"

Text: Adolphe-Basile Routhier, 1839–1920, French; R. Stanley Weir, 1856–1926, English, alt.
Music: Calixa Lavallée, 1842–1891

O CANADA
Irregular

Before You, Lord, We Bow

1 Be - fore you, Lord, we bow, our God who reigns a - bove and
2 May ev - 'ry moun-tain height, each vale and for - est green, shine
3 Earth, hear your mak - er's voice; your great re - deem - er own; be -
4 And when in pow'r he comes, oh, may then ev - 'ry land from

rules the world be - low with bound-less pow'r and love. Our thanks we
forth in wis-dom's light, and its rich fruits be seen! May ev - 'ry
lieve, o - bey, re - joice, and wor - ship God a - lone. Cast down your
all its rend - ing tombs send forth a glo - rious band, a count-less

bring in joy and praise, our hearts we raise, to you we sing!
tongue be tuned to praise and join to raise a grate - ful song.
pride, your sin de - plore, and bow be - fore the Cru - ci - fied.
throng, with joy to sing to heav'n's high king sal - va - tion's song!

Text: Francis Scott Key, 1779–1843, alt.
Music: John Darwall, 1731–1789

DARWALL'S 148TH
666688

Additional Resources

DAILY LECTIONARY

Year A   1121

Year B   1132

Year C   1143

SCRIPTURE AND WORSHIP   1154

SMALL CATECHISM   1160

INDEXES

Acknowledgments   1169

Copyright Holders and Acknowledgments   1172

Topical Index of Hymns   1178

Source Index — Service Music and Hymns   1189

Hymn Tunes — Alphabetical   1195

Hymn Tunes — Metrical   1199

First Lines and Titles — Liturgical Music   1204

First Lines and Titles — Hymns   1205

Daily Lectionary

The foundational premise of this set of daily readings is their relationship to the Sunday lectionary. The readings are chosen so that the days leading up to Sunday (Thursday through Saturday) prepare for the Sunday readings. The days flowing out from Sunday (Monday through Wednesday) reflect upon the Sunday readings. No additional readings are assigned for Sundays and festivals; readings for those days are in the Propers section (pp. 18–63). From the body of daily readings for each week, selections may be made for the local context.

Year A

Advent 1

Th   Psalm 122
Daniel 9:15-19
James 4:1-10

F   Psalm 122
Genesis 6:1-10
Hebrews 11:1-7

Sa   Psalm 122
Genesis 6:11-22
Matthew 24:1-22

Su   *First Sunday of Advent*

M   Psalm 124
Genesis 8:1-19
Romans 6:1-11

Tu   Psalm 124
Genesis 9:1-17
Hebrews 11:32-40

W   Psalm 124
Isaiah 54:1-10
Matthew 24:23-35

Advent 2

Th   Psalm 72:1-7, 18-19
Isaiah 4:2-6
Acts 1:12-17, 21-26

F   Psalm 72:1-7, 18-19
Isaiah 30:19-26
Acts 13:16-25

Sa   Psalm 72:1-7, 18-19
Isaiah 40:1-11
John 1:19-28

Su   *Second Sunday of Advent*

M   Psalm 21
Isaiah 24:1-16a
1 Thessalonians 4:1-12

Tu   Psalm 21
Isaiah 41:14-20
Romans 15:14-21

W   Psalm 21
Genesis 15:1-18
Matthew 12:33-37

Advent 3

Th   Psalm 146:5-10
Ruth 1:6-18
2 Peter 3:1-10

F   Psalm 146:5-10
Ruth 4:13-17
2 Peter 3:11-18

Sa   Psalm 146:5-10
1 Samuel 2:1-8
Luke 3:1-18

Su   *Third Sunday of Advent*

M   Psalm 42
Isaiah 29:17-24
Acts 5:12-16

Tu   Psalm 42
Ezekiel 47:1-12
Jude 17-25

W   Psalm 42
Zechariah 8:1-17
Matthew 8:14-17, 28-34

Advent 4

Dated readings begin Dec. 22

Th   Psalm 80:1-7, 17-19
2 Samuel 7:1-17
Galatians 3:23-29

F   Psalm 80:1-7, 17-19
2 Samuel 7:18-22
Galatians 4:1-7

Sa   Psalm 80:1-7, 17-19
2 Samuel 7:23-29
John 3:31-36

Su   *Fourth Sunday of Advent*

M   1 Samuel 2:1-10
Genesis 17:15-22
Galatians 4:8-20

Tu   1 Samuel 2:1-10
Genesis 21:1-21
Galatians 4:21—5:1

W   1 Samuel 2:1-10
Genesis 37:2-11
Matthew 1:1-17

Days around Christmas

Dec 22   Luke 1:46b-55
Isaiah 33:17-22
Revelation 22:6-7, 18-20

Dec 23   Luke 1:46b-55
2 Samuel 7:18, 23-29
Galatians 3:6-14

Dec 24–25   *Nativity of Our Lord*

Dec 26	Psalm 148 Wisdom 4:7-15 Acts 7:59—8:8	Su	Baptism of Our Lord	**Epiphany 4**	
		M	Psalm 89:5-37 Genesis 35:1-15 Acts 10:44-48	Th	Psalm 15 Deuteronomy 16:18-20 1 Peter 3:8-12
Dec 27	Psalm 148 Proverbs 8:22-31 1 John 5:1-12	Tu	Psalm 89:5-37 Jeremiah 1:4-10 Acts 8:4-13	F	Psalm 15 Deuteronomy 24:17—25:4 1 Timothy 5:17-24
Dec 28	Psalm 148 Isaiah 49:13-23 Matthew 18:1-14	W	Psalm 89:5-37 Isaiah 51:1-16 Matthew 12:15-21	Sa	Psalm 15 Micah 3:1-4 John 13:31-35
Dec 29	Psalm 20 Jeremiah 31:15-22 Luke 19:41-44	**Epiphany 2**		Su	Fourth Sunday after Epiphany
Dec 30	Psalm 20 Isaiah 26:1-9 2 Corinthians 4:16-18	Th	Psalm 40:1-11 Isaiah 22:15-25 Galatians 1:6-12	M	Psalm 37:1-17 Ruth 1:1-18 Philemon 1-25
Dec 31	Psalm 20 1 Kings 3:5-14 John 8:12-19	F	Psalm 40:1-11 Genesis 27:30-38 Acts 1:1-5	Tu	Psalm 37:1-17 Ruth 2:1-16 James 5:1-6
Jan 1	Name of Jesus	Sa	Psalm 40:1-11 1 Kings 19:19-21 Luke 5:1-11	W	Psalm 37:1-17 Ruth 3:1-13; 4:13-22 Luke 6:17-26
Jan 2	Psalm 72 Genesis 12:1-7 Hebrews 11:1-12	Su	Second Sunday after Epiphany	**Epiphany 5**	
Days around Epiphany		M	Psalm 40:6-17 Exodus 12:1-13, 21-28 Acts 8:26-40	Th	Psalm 112:1-9 [10] Deuteronomy 4:1-14 1 John 5:1-5
Jan 3	Psalm 72 Genesis 28:10-22 Hebrews 11:13-22	Tu	Psalm 40:6-17 Isaiah 53:1-12 Hebrews 10:1-4	F	Psalm 112:1-9 [10] Isaiah 29:1-12 James 3:13-18
Jan 4	Psalm 72 Exodus 3:1-5 Hebrews 11:23-31	W	Psalm 40:6-17 Isaiah 48:12-21 Matthew 9:14-17	Sa	Psalm 112:1-9 [10] Isaiah 29:13-16 Mark 7:1-8
Jan 5	Psalm 72 Joshua 1:1-9 Hebrews 11:32—12:2	**Epiphany 3**		Su	Fifth Sunday after Epiphany
Jan 6	Epiphany of Our Lord	Th	Psalm 27:1-6 1 Samuel 1:1-20 Galatians 1:11-24	M	Psalm 119:105-112 2 Kings 22:3-20 Romans 11:2-10
Jan 7	Psalm 72 1 Kings 10:1-13 Ephesians 3:14-21	F	Psalm 27:1-6 1 Samuel 9:27—10:8 Galatians 2:1-10	Tu	Psalm 119:105-112 2 Kings 23:1-8, 21-25 2 Corinthians 4:1-12
Jan 8	Psalm 72 1 Kings 10:14-25 Ephesians 4:7, 11-16	Sa	Psalm 27:1-6 1 Samuel 15:34—16:13 Luke 5:27-32	W	Psalm 119:105-112 Proverbs 6:6-23 John 8:12-30
Jan 9	Psalm 72 Micah 5:2-9 Luke 13:31-35	Su	Third Sunday after Epiphany	**Epiphany 6**	
Epiphany 1		M	Psalm 27:7-14 Judges 6:11-24 Ephesians 5:6-14	Th	Psalm 119:1-8 Genesis 26:1-5 James 1:12-16
Th	Psalm 29 1 Samuel 3:1-9 Acts 9:1-9	Tu	Psalm 27:7-14 Judges 7:12-22 Philippians 2:12-18	F	Psalm 119:1-8 Leviticus 26:34-46 1 John 2:7-17
F	Psalm 29 1 Samuel 3:10—4:1a Acts 9:10-19a	W	Psalm 27:7-14 Genesis 49:1-2, 8-13, 21-26 Luke 1:67-79	Sa	Psalm 119:1-8 Deuteronomy 30:1-9a Matthew 15:1-9
Sa	Psalm 29 1 Samuel 7:3-17 Acts 9:19b-31			Su	Sixth Sunday after Epiphany

M   Psalm 119:9-16
     Exodus 20:1-21
     James 1:2-8

Tu   Psalm 119:9-16
     Deuteronomy 23:21—24:4, 10-15
     James 2:1-13

W   Psalm 119:9-16
     Proverbs 2:1-15
     Matthew 19:1-12

Epiphany 7

Th   Psalm 119:33-40
     Exodus 22:21-27
     1 Corinthians 10:23—11:1

F   Psalm 119:33-40
     Leviticus 6:1-7
     Galatians 5:2-6

Sa   Psalm 119:33-40
     Leviticus 24:10-23
     Matthew 7:1-12

Su   *Seventh Sunday*
     after Epiphany

M   Psalm 119:57-64
     Proverbs 25:11-22
     Romans 12:9-21

Tu   Psalm 119:57-64
     Genesis 31:1-3, 17-50
     Hebrews 12:14-16

W   Psalm 119:57-64
     Proverbs 3:27-35
     Luke 18:18-30

Epiphany 8

Th   Psalm 131
     Proverbs 12:22-28
     Philippians 2:19-24

F   Psalm 131
     Isaiah 26:1-6
     Philippians 2:25-30

Sa   Psalm 131
     Isaiah 31:1-9
     Luke 11:14-23

Su   *Eighth Sunday after Epiphany*

M   Psalm 104
     Deuteronomy 32:1-14
     Hebrews 10:32-39

Tu   Psalm 104
     1 Kings 17:1-16
     1 Corinthians 4:6-21

W   Psalm 104
     Isaiah 66:7-13
     Luke 12:22-31

Transfiguration

Th   Psalm 2
     Exodus 6:2-9
     Hebrews 8:1-7

F   Psalm 2
     Exodus 19:9b-25
     Hebrews 11:23-28

Sa   Psalm 2
     1 Kings 21:20-29
     Mark 9:9-13

Su   *Transfiguration of Our Lord*

M   Psalm 78:17-20, 52-55
     Exodus 33:7-23
     Acts 7:30-34

Tu   Psalm 78:17-20, 52-55
     1 Kings 19:9-18
     Romans 11:1-6

Lent 1

W   *Ash Wednesday*

Th   Psalm 51
     Jonah 3:1-10
     Romans 1:1-7

F   Psalm 51
     Jonah 4:1-11
     Romans 1:8-17

Sa   Psalm 51
     Isaiah 58:1-12
     Matthew 18:1-7

Su   *First Sunday in Lent*

M   Psalm 32
     1 Kings 19:1-8
     Hebrews 2:10-18

Tu   Psalm 32
     Genesis 4:1-16
     Hebrews 4:14—5:10

W   Psalm 32
     Exodus 34:1-9, 27-28
     Matthew 18:10-14

Lent 2

Th   Psalm 121
     Isaiah 51:1-3
     2 Timothy 1:3-7

F   Psalm 121
     Micah 7:18-20
     Romans 3:21-31

Sa   Psalm 121
     Isaiah 51:4-8
     Luke 7:1-10

Su   *Second Sunday in Lent*

M   Psalm 128
     Numbers 21:4-9
     Hebrews 3:1-6

Tu   Psalm 128
     Isaiah 65:17-25
     Romans 4:6-13

W   Psalm 128
     Ezekiel 36:22-32
     John 7:53—8:11

Lent 3

Th   Psalm 95
     Exodus 16:1-8
     Colossians 1:15-23

F   Psalm 95
     Exodus 16:9-21
     Ephesians 2:11-22

Sa   Psalm 95
     Exodus 16:27-35
     John 4:1-6

Su   *Third Sunday in Lent*

M   Psalm 81
     Genesis 24:1-27
     2 John 1-13

Tu   Psalm 81
     Genesis 29:1-14
     1 Corinthians 10:1-4

W   Psalm 81
     Jeremiah 2:4-13
     John 7:14-31, 37-39

Lent 4

Th   Psalm 23
     1 Samuel 15:10-21
     Ephesians 4:25-32

F   Psalm 23
     1 Samuel 15:22-31
     Ephesians 5:1-9

Sa   Psalm 23
     1 Samuel 15:32-34
     John 1:1-9

Su   *Fourth Sunday in Lent*

M   Psalm 146
     Isaiah 59:9-19
     Acts 9:1-20

Tu   Psalm 146
     Isaiah 42:14-21
     Colossians 1:9-14

W   Psalm 146
     Isaiah 60:17-22
     Matthew 9:27-34

Lent 5

Th   Psalm 130
     Ezekiel 1:1-3; 2:8—3:3
     Revelation 10:1-11

F   Psalm 130
     Ezekiel 33:10-16
     Revelation 11:15-19

Sa Psalm 130
Ezekiel 36:8-15
Luke 24:44-53

Su *Fifth Sunday in Lent*

M Psalm 143
1 Kings 17:17-24
Acts 20:7-12

Tu Psalm 143
2 Kings 4:18-37
Ephesians 2:1-10

W Psalm 143
Jeremiah 32:1-9, 36-41
Matthew 22:23-33

Lent 6

Th Psalm 31:9-16
1 Samuel 16:11-13
Philippians 1:1-11

F Psalm 31:9-16
Job 13:13-19
Philippians 1:21-30

Sa Psalm 31:9-16
Lamentations 3:55-66
Mark 10:32-34

Su *Sunday of the Passion*

M *Monday in Holy Week*

Tu *Tuesday in Holy Week*

W *Wednesday in Holy Week*

Three Days—Easter

Th *Maundy Thursday*

F *Good Friday*

Sa *Vigil of Easter*

Su *Resurrection of Our Lord*

M Psalm 118:1-2, 14-24
Exodus 14:10-31; 15:20-21
Colossians 3:5-11

Tu Psalm 118:1-2, 14-24
Exodus 15:1-18
Colossians 3:12-17

W Psalm 118:1-2, 14-24
Joshua 3:1-17
Matthew 28:1-10

Easter 2

Th Psalm 16
Song of Solomon 2:8-15
Colossians 4:2-5

F Psalm 16
Song of Solomon 5:9—6:3
1 Corinthians 15:1-11

Sa Psalm 16
Song of Solomon 8:6-7
John 20:11-20

Su *Second Sunday of Easter*

M Psalm 114
Judges 6:36-40
1 Corinthians 15:12-20

Tu Psalm 114
Jonah 1:1-17
1 Corinthians 15:19-28

W Psalm 114
Jonah 2:1-10
Matthew 12:38-42

Easter 3

Th Psalm 116:1-4, 12-19
Isaiah 25:1-5
1 Peter 1:8b-12

F Psalm 116:1-4, 12-19
Isaiah 26:1-4
1 Peter 1:13-16

Sa Psalm 116:1-4, 12-19
Isaiah 25:6-9
Luke 14:12-14

Su *Third Sunday of Easter*

M Psalm 134
Genesis 18:1-14
1 Peter 1:23-25

Tu Psalm 134
Proverbs 8:32—9:6
1 Peter 2:1-3

W Psalm 134
Exodus 24:1-11
John 21:1-14

Easter 4

Th Psalm 23
Exodus 2:15b-25
1 Peter 2:9-12

F Psalm 23
Exodus 3:16-22; 4:18-20
1 Peter 2:13-17

Sa Psalm 23
Ezekiel 34:1-16
Luke 15:1-7

Su *Fourth Sunday of Easter*

M Psalm 100
Ezekiel 34:17-23
1 Peter 5:1-5

Tu Psalm 100
Ezekiel 34:23-31
Hebrews 13:20-21

W Psalm 100
Jeremiah 23:1-8
Matthew 20:17-28

Easter 5

Th Psalm 31:1-5, 15-16
Genesis 12:1-3
Acts 6:8-15

F Psalm 31:1-5, 15-16
Exodus 3:1-12
Acts 7:1-16

Sa Psalm 31:1-5, 15-16
Jeremiah 26:20-24
John 8:48-59

Su *Fifth Sunday of Easter*

M Psalm 102:1-17
Exodus 13:17-22
Acts 7:17-40

Tu Psalm 102:1-17
Proverbs 3:5-12
Acts 7:44-56

W Psalm 102:1-17
Proverbs 3:13-18
John 8:31-38

Easter 6

Th Psalm 66:8-20
Genesis 6:5-22
Acts 27:1-12

F Psalm 66:8-20
Genesis 7:1-24
Acts 27:13-38

Sa Psalm 66:8-20
Genesis 8:13-19
John 14:27-29

Su *Sixth Sunday of Easter*

M Psalm 93
Genesis 9:8-17
Acts 27:39-44

Tu Psalm 93
Deuteronomy 5:22-33
1 Peter 3:8-12

W Psalm 93
Deuteronomy 31:1-13
John 16:16-24

Easter 7

Th *Ascension of Our Lord*

F Psalm 93
2 Kings 2:1-12
Ephesians 2:1-7

Sa Psalm 93
2 Kings 2:13-15
John 8:21-30

Su *Seventh Sunday of Easter*

M Psalm 99
Leviticus 9:1-11, 22-24
1 Peter 4:1-6

Tu Psalm 99
    Numbers 16:41-50
    1 Peter 4:7-11

W   Psalm 99
    1 Kings 8:54-65
    John 3:31-36

Pentecost
Th Psalm 33:12-22
    Exodus 19:1-9a
    Acts 2:1-11

F   Psalm 33:12-22
    Exodus 19:16-25
    Romans 8:14-17

Sa Psalm 33:12-22
    Exodus 20:1-21
    Matthew 5:1-12

Su *Day of Pentecost*

M   Psalm 104:24-34, 35b
    Joel 2:18-29
    Romans 8:18-24

Tu Psalm 104:24-34, 35b
    Ezekiel 39:7-8, 21-29
    Romans 8:26-27

W   Psalm 104:24-34, 35b
    Numbers 11:24-30
    John 7:37-39

Holy Trinity
Th Psalm 8
    Job 38:1-11
    2 Timothy 1:8-12a

F   Psalm 8
    Job 38:12-21
    2 Timothy 1:12b-14

Sa Psalm 8
    Job 38:22-38
    John 14:15-17

Su *The Holy Trinity*

M   Psalm 29
    Job 38:39—39:12
    1 Corinthians 12:1-3

Tu Psalm 29
    Job 39:13-25
    1 Corinthians 12:4-13

W   Psalm 29
    Job 39:26—40:5
    John 14:25-26

Sunday, May 24–28
Th Psalm 131
    Proverbs 12:22-28
    Philippians 2:19-24

F   Psalm 131
    Isaiah 26:1-6
    Philippians 2:25-30

Sa Psalm 131
    Isaiah 31:1-9
    Luke 11:14-23

Su *May 24–28 (Lectionary 8)*

M   Psalm 104
    Deuteronomy 32:1-14
    Hebrews 10:32-39

Tu Psalm 104
    1 Kings 17:1-16
    1 Corinthians 4:6-21

W   Psalm 104
    Isaiah 66:7-13
    Luke 12:22-31

The following readings relate to the complementary series of the Sunday lectionary.

Sunday, May 29–June 4
Th Psalm 31:1-5, 19-24
    Exodus 24:1-8
    Romans 2:17-29

F   Psalm 31:1-5, 19-24
    Deuteronomy 30:1-5
    Romans 9:6-13

Sa Psalm 31:1-5, 19-24
    Amos 2:6-11
    Matthew 7:1-6

Su *May 29–June 4 (Lectionary 9)*

M   Psalm 52
    Joshua 8:30-35
    Romans 2:1-11

Tu Psalm 52
    Joshua 24:1-2, 11-28
    Romans 3:9-22a

W   Psalm 52
    Job 28:12-28
    Matthew 7:13-20

Sunday, June 5–11
Th Psalm 50:7-15
    Lamentations 1:7-11
    2 Peter 2:17-22

F   Psalm 50:7-15
    Lamentations 3:40-58
    Acts 28:1-10

Sa Psalm 50:7-15
    Exodus 34:1-9
    Matthew 9:27-34

Su *June 5–11 (Lectionary 10)*

M   Psalm 40:1-8
    Leviticus 15:25-31; 22:1-9
    2 Corinthians 6:14—7:2

Tu Psalm 40:1-8
    Hosea 8:11-14; 10:1-2
    Hebrews 13:1-16

W   Psalm 40:1-8
    Hosea 14:1-9
    Matthew 12:1-8

Sunday, June 12–18
Th Psalm 100
    Exodus 4:18-23
    Hebrews 3:1-6

F   Psalm 100
    Exodus 4:27-31
    Acts 7:35-43

Sa Psalm 100
    Exodus 6:28—7:13
    Mark 7:1-13

Su *June 12–18 (Lectionary 11)*

M   Psalm 105:1-11, 37-45
    Joshua 1:1-11
    1 Thessalonians 3:1-5

Tu Psalm 105:1-11, 37-45
    1 Samuel 3:1-9
    2 Thessalonians 2:13—3:5

W   Psalm 105:1-11, 37-45
    Proverbs 4:10-27
    Luke 6:12-19

Sunday, June 19–25
Th Psalm 69:7-10 [11-15] 16-18
    Jeremiah 18:12-17
    Hebrews 2:5-9

F   Psalm 69:7-10 [11-15] 16-18
    Jeremiah 18:18-23
    Acts 5:17-26

Sa Psalm 69:7-10 [11-15] 16-18
    Jeremiah 20:1-6
    Luke 11:53—12:3

Su *June 19–25 (Lectionary 12)*

M   Psalm 6
    Micah 7:1-7
    Revelation 2:1-7

Tu Psalm 6
    Jeremiah 26:1-12
    Revelation 2:8-11

W   Psalm 6
    Jeremiah 38:1-13
    Matthew 10:5-23

Sunday, June 26–July 2

Th Psalm 89:1-4, 15-18
Jeremiah 25:1-7
Galatians 5:2-6

F   Psalm 89:1-4, 15-18
Jeremiah 25:8-14
Galatians 5:7-12

Sa Psalm 89:1-4, 15-18
Jeremiah 28:1-4
Luke 17:1-4

Su *June 26–July 2*
(Lectionary 13)

M Psalm 119:161-168
1 Kings 21:1-16
1 Thessalonians 4:9-12

Tu Psalm 119:161-168
1 Kings 21:17-29
1 John 4:1-6

W Psalm 119:161-168
Jeremiah 18:1-11
Matthew 11:20-24

Sunday, July 3–9

Th Psalm 145:8-14
Zechariah 1:1-6
Romans 7:1-6

F   Psalm 145:8-14
Zechariah 2:6-13
Romans 7:7-20

Sa Psalm 145:8-14
Zechariah 4:1-7
Luke 10:21-24

Su *July 3–9 (Lectionary 14)*

M Psalm 131
Jeremiah 27:1-11, 16-22
Romans 1:18-25

Tu Psalm 131
Jeremiah 28:10-17
Romans 3:1-8

W Psalm 131
Jeremiah 13:1-11
John 13:1-17

Sunday, July 10–16

Th Psalm 65:[1-8] 9-13
Isaiah 48:1-5
Romans 2:12-16

F   Psalm 65:[1-8] 9-13
Isaiah 48:6-11
Romans 15:14-21

Sa Psalm 65:[1-8] 9-13
Isaiah 52:1-6
John 12:44-50

Su *July 10–16 (Lectionary 15)*

M Psalm 92
Leviticus 26:3-20
1 Thessalonians 4:1-8

Tu Psalm 92
Deuteronomy 28:1-14
Ephesians 4:17—5:2

W Psalm 92
Proverbs 11:23-30
Matthew 13:10-17

Sunday, July 17–23

Th Psalm 86:11-17
Isaiah 41:21-29
Hebrews 2:1-9

F   Psalm 86:11-17
Isaiah 44:9-17
Hebrews 6:13-20

Sa Psalm 86:11-17
Isaiah 44:18-20
Matthew 7:15-20

Su *July 17–23 (Lectionary 16)*

M Psalm 75
Nahum 1:1-13
Revelation 14:12-20

Tu Psalm 75
Zephaniah 3:1-13
Galatians 4:21—5:1

W Psalm 75
Daniel 12:1-13
Matthew 12:15-21

Sunday, July 24–30

Th Psalm 119:129-136
1 Kings 1:28-37
1 Corinthians 4:14-20

F   Psalm 119:129-136
1 Kings 1:38-48
Acts 7:44-53

Sa Psalm 119:129-136
1 Kings 2:1-4
Matthew 12:38-42

Su *July 24–30 (Lectionary 17)*

M Psalm 119:121-128
1 Kings 3:16-28
James 3:13-18

Tu Psalm 119:121-128
1 Kings 4:29-34
Ephesians 6:10-18

W Psalm 119:121-128
Proverbs 1:1-7, 20-33
Mark 4:30-34

Sunday, July 31–August 6

Th Psalm 145:8-9, 14-21
Proverbs 10:1-5
Philippians 4:10-15

F   Psalm 145:8-9, 14-21
Isaiah 51:17-23
Romans 9:6-13

Sa Psalm 145:8-9, 14-21
Isaiah 44:1-5
Matthew 7:7-11

Su *July 31–August 6*
(Lectionary 18)

M Psalm 78:1-8, 17-29
Deuteronomy 8:1-10
Romans 1:8-15

Tu Psalm 78:1-8, 17-29
Deuteronomy 26:1-15
Acts 2:37-47

W Psalm 78:1-8, 17-29
Exodus 16:2-15, 31-35
Matthew 15:32-39

Sunday, August 7–13

Th Psalm 85:8-13
1 Kings 18:1-16
Acts 17:10-15

F   Psalm 85:8-13
1 Kings 18:17-19, 30-40
Acts 18:24-28

Sa Psalm 85:8-13
1 Kings 18:41-46
Matthew 16:1-4

Su *August 7–13 (Lectionary 19)*

M Psalm 18:1-19
Genesis 7:11—8:5
2 Peter 2:4-10

Tu Psalm 18:1-19
Genesis 19:1-29
Romans 9:14-29

W Psalm 18:1-19
Job 36:24-33; 37:14-24
Matthew 8:23-27

Sunday, August 14–20

Th Psalm 67
Isaiah 45:20-25
Revelation 15:1-4

F   Psalm 67
Isaiah 63:15-19
Acts 14:19-28

Sa Psalm 67
Isaiah 56:1-5
Matthew 14:34-36

Su *August 14–20*
    (Lectionary 20)

M   Psalm 87
    2 Kings 5:1-14
    Acts 15:1-21

Tu Psalm 87
    Isaiah 43:8-13
    Romans 11:13-29

W   Psalm 87
    Isaiah 66:18-23
    Matthew 8:1-13

Sunday, August 21–27
Th Psalm 138
    Ezekiel 28:11-19
    1 Corinthians 6:1-11

F   Psalm 138
    Ezekiel 31:15-18
    2 Corinthians 10:12-18

Sa Psalm 138
    Ezekiel 36:33-38
    Matthew 16:5-12

Su *August 21–27 (Lectionary 21)*

M   Psalm 18:1-3, 20-32
    1 Samuel 7:3-13
    Romans 2:1-11

Tu Psalm 18:1-3, 20-32
    Deuteronomy 32:18-20,
    28-39
    Romans 11:33-36

W   Psalm 18:1-3, 20-32
    Isaiah 28:14-22
    Matthew 26:6-13

Sunday, August 28–September 3
Th Psalm 26:1-8
    Jeremiah 14:13-18
    Ephesians 5:1-6

F   Psalm 26:1-8
    Jeremiah 15:1-9
    2 Thessalonians 2:7-12

Sa Psalm 26:1-8
    Jeremiah 15:10-14
    Matthew 8:14-17

Su *August 28–September 3*
    (Lectionary 22)

M   Psalm 17
    2 Samuel 11:2-26
    Revelation 3:1-6

Tu Psalm 17
    2 Samuel 11:27b—12:15
    Revelation 3:7-13

W   Psalm 17
    Jeremiah 17:5-18
    Matthew 12:22-32

Sunday, September 4–10
Th Psalm 119:33-40
    Ezekiel 24:1-14
    2 Corinthians 12:11-21

F   Psalm 119:33-40
    Ezekiel 24:15-27
    Romans 10:15b-21

Sa Psalm 119:33-40
    Ezekiel 33:1-6
    Matthew 23:29-36

Su *September 4–10*
    (Lectionary 23)

M   Psalm 119:65-72
    Leviticus 4:27-31; 5:14-16
    1 Peter 2:11-17

Tu Psalm 119:65-72
    Deuteronomy 17:2-13
    Romans 13:1-7

W   Psalm 119:65-72
    Leviticus 16:1-5, 20-28
    Matthew 21:18-22

Sunday, September 11–17
Th Psalm 103:[1-7] 8-13
    Genesis 37:12-36
    1 John 3:11-16

F   Psalm 103:[1-7] 8-13
    Genesis 41:53—42:17
    Acts 7:9-16

Sa Psalm 103:[1-7] 8-13
    Genesis 45:1-20
    Matthew 6:7-15

Su *September 11–17*
    (Lectionary 24)

M   Psalm 133
    Genesis 48:8-22
    Hebrews 11:23-29

Tu Psalm 133
    Genesis 49:29—50:14
    Romans 14:13—15:2

W   Psalm 133
    Genesis 50:22-26
    Mark 11:20-25

Sunday, September 18–24
Th Psalm 145:1-8
    Nahum 1:1, 14—2:2
    2 Corinthians 13:1-4

F   Psalm 145:1-8
    Nahum 2:3-13
    2 Corinthians 13:5-10

Sa Psalm 145:1-8
    Zephaniah 2:13-15
    Matthew 19:23-30

Su *September 18–24*
    (Lectionary 25)

M   Psalm 106:1-12
    Genesis 27:1-29
    Romans 16:1-16

Tu Psalm 106:1-12
    Genesis 28:10-17
    Romans 16:17-20

W   Psalm 106:1-12
    Isaiah 41:1-13
    Matthew 18:1-5

Sunday, September 25–
October 1
Th Psalm 25:1-9
    Ezekiel 12:17-28
    James 4:11-16

F   Psalm 25:1-9
    Ezekiel 18:5-18
    Acts 13:32-41

Sa Psalm 25:1-9
    Ezekiel 18:19-24
    Mark 11:27-33

Su *September 25–October 1*
    (Lectionary 26)

M   Psalm 28
    Judges 14:1-20
    Philippians 1:3-14

Tu Psalm 28
    Judges 16:1-22
    Philippians 1:15-21

W   Psalm 28
    Judges 16:23-31
    Matthew 9:2-8

Sunday, October 2–8
Th Psalm 80:7-15
    Jeremiah 2:14-22
    Colossians 2:16-23

F   Psalm 80:7-15
    Jeremiah 2:23-37
    Philippians 2:14-18; 3:1-4a

Sa Psalm 80:7-15
    Jeremiah 6:1-10
    John 7:40-52

Su *October 2–8 (Lectionary 27)*

M   Psalm 144
    Ezekiel 19:10-14
    1 Peter 2:4-10

Tu Psalm 144
    Isaiah 27:1-6
    2 Corinthians 5:17-21

W   Psalm 144
    Song of Solomon 8:5-14
    John 11:45-57

Sunday, October 9–15

Th   Psalm 23
     Isaiah 22:1-8a
     1 Peter 5:1-5, 12-14

F   Psalm 23
     Isaiah 22:8b-14
     James 4:4-10

Sa   Psalm 23
     Isaiah 24:17-23
     Mark 2:18-22

Su   *October 9–15 (Lectionary 28)*

M   Psalm 34
     Exodus 19:7-20
     Jude 17-25

Tu   Psalm 34
     Amos 9:5-15
     Philippians 3:13—4:1

W   Psalm 34
     Song of Solomon 7:10—8:4
     John 6:25-35

Sunday, October 16–22

Th   Psalm 96:1-9 [10-13]
     Judges 17:1-6
     3 John 9-12

F   Psalm 96:1-9 [10-13]
     Deuteronomy 17:14-20
     1 Peter 5:1-5

Sa   Psalm 96:1-9 [10-13]
     Isaiah 14:3-11
     Matthew 14:1-12

Su   *October 16–22*
     (Lectionary 29)

M   Psalm 98
     Daniel 3:1-18
     Revelation 18:1-10, 19-20

Tu   Psalm 98
     Daniel 3:19-30
     Revelation 18:21-24

W   Psalm 98
     Daniel 6:1-28
     Matthew 17:22-27

Sunday, October 23–29

Th   Psalm 1
     Numbers 5:5-10
     Titus 1:5-16

F   Psalm 1
     Deuteronomy 9:25—10:5
     Titus 2:7-8, 11-15

Sa   Psalm 1
     Proverbs 24:23-34
     John 5:39-47

Su   *October 23–29*
     (Lectionary 30)

M   Psalm 119:41-48
     Deuteronomy 6:1-9, 20-25
     James 2:8-13

Tu   Psalm 119:41-48
     Deuteronomy 10:10-22
     James 2:14-26

W   Psalm 119:41-48
     Proverbs 16:1-20
     Matthew 19:16-22

Sunday, October 30–November 5

Th   Psalm 43
     1 Samuel 2:27-36
     Romans 2:17-29

F   Psalm 43
     Ezekiel 13:1-16
     2 Peter 2:1-3

Sa   Psalm 43
     Malachi 1:6—2:9
     Matthew 23:13-28

Su   *October 30–November 5*
     (Lectionary 31)

M   Psalm 5
     Jeremiah 5:18-31
     1 Thessalonians 2:13-20

Tu   Psalm 5
     Lamentations 2:13-17
     Acts 13:1-12

W   Psalm 5
     Proverbs 16:21-33
     Matthew 15:1-9

Sunday, November 6–12

Th   Psalm 70
     Amos 1:1—2:5
     Revelation 8:6—9:12

F   Psalm 70
     Amos 3:1-12
     Revelation 9:13-21

Sa   Psalm 70
     Amos 4:6-13
     Matthew 24:1-14

Su   *November 6–12*
     (Lectionary 32)

M   Psalm 63
     Amos 8:7-14
     1 Corinthians 14:20-25

Tu   Psalm 63
     Joel 1:1-14
     1 Thessalonians 3:6-13

W   Psalm 63
     Joel 3:9-21
     Matthew 24:29-35

Sunday, November 13–19

Th   Psalm 90:1-8 [9-11] 12
     Ezekiel 6:1-14
     Revelation 16:1-7

F   Psalm 90:1-8 [9-11] 12
     Ezekiel 7:1-9
     Revelation 16:8-21

Sa   Psalm 90:1-8 [9-11] 12
     Ezekiel 7:10-27
     Matthew 12:43-45

Su   *November 13–19*
     (Lectionary 33)

M   Psalm 9:1-14
     Zechariah 1:7-17
     Romans 2:1-11

Tu   Psalm 9:1-14
     Zechariah 2:1-5; 5:1-4
     1 Thessalonians 5:12-18

W   Psalm 9:1-14
     Job 16:1-21
     Matthew 24:45-51

Christ the King

Th   Psalm 95:1-7a
     1 Kings 22:13-23
     Revelation 14:1-11

F   Psalm 95:1-7a
     1 Chronicles 17:1-15
     Revelation 22:1-9

Sa   Psalm 95:1-7a
     Isaiah 44:21-28
     Matthew 12:46-50

Su   *November 20–26*
     (Lectionary 34)

M   Psalm 7
     Esther 2:1-18
     2 Timothy 2:8-13

Tu   Psalm 7
     Esther 8:3-17
     Revelation 19:1-9

W   Psalm 7
     Ezekiel 33:7-20
     John 5:19-40

The following readings relate to the semicontinuous series of the Sunday lectionary.

Sunday, May 29–June 4

Th Psalm 46
    Genesis 1:1—2:4a
    Romans 2:17-29

F   Psalm 46
    Genesis 2:4b-25
    Romans 9:6-13

Sa Psalm 46
    Genesis 3:1-24
    Matthew 7:1-6

Su *May 29–June 4 (Lectionary 9)*

M   Psalm 69:1-3, 13-16, 30-36
    Genesis 4:1-16
    Romans 2:1-11

Tu Psalm 69:1-3, 13-16, 30-36
    Genesis 4:17—5:5
    Romans 3:9-22a

W   Psalm 69:1-3, 13-16, 30-36
    Genesis 11:1-9
    Matthew 7:13-20

Sunday, June 5–11

Th Psalm 33:1-12
    Genesis 13:1-18
    2 Peter 2:17-22

F   Psalm 33:1-12
    Genesis 14:17-24
    Acts 28:1-10

Sa Psalm 33:1-12
    Genesis 15:1-20
    Matthew 9:27-34

Su *June 5–11 (Lectionary 10)*

M   Psalm 119:41-48
    Genesis 16:1-15
    2 Corinthians 6:14—7:2

Tu Psalm 119:41-48
    Genesis 17:1-27
    Hebrews 13:1-16

W   Psalm 119:41-48
    Genesis 18:16-33
    Matthew 12:1-8

Sunday, June 12–18

Th Psalm 116:1-2, 12-19
    Genesis 21:1-7
    Hebrews 3:1-6

F   Psalm 116:1-2, 12-19
    Genesis 24:1-9
    Acts 7:35-43

Sa Psalm 116:1-2, 12-19
    Genesis 24:10-52
    Mark 7:1-13

Su *June 12–18 (Lectionary 11)*

M   Psalm 126
    Genesis 23:1-19
    1 Thessalonians 3:1-5

Tu Psalm 126
    Genesis 25:7-11
    2 Thessalonians 2:13—3:5

W   Psalm 126
    Nehemiah 9:1-8
    Luke 6:12-19

Sunday, June 19–25

Th Psalm 86:1-10
    Exodus 12:43-49
    Hebrews 2:5-9

F   Psalm 86:1-10
    Genesis 35:1-4
    Acts 5:17-26

Sa Psalm 86:1-10
    Ezekiel 29:3-7
    Luke 11:53—12:3

Su *June 19–25 (Lectionary 12)*

M   Psalm 86:11-17
    Genesis 16:1-15
    Revelation 2:1-7

Tu Psalm 86:11-17
    Genesis 25:12-18
    Revelation 2:8-11

W   Psalm 86:11-17
    Jeremiah 42:18-22
    Matthew 10:5-23

Sunday, June 26–July 2

Th Psalm 13
    Micah 7:18-20
    Galatians 5:2-6

F   Psalm 13
    2 Chronicles 20:5-12
    Galatians 5:7-12

Sa Psalm 13
    Genesis 26:23-25
    Luke 17:1-4

Su *June 26–July 2*
    (Lectionary 13)

M   Psalm 47
    Genesis 22:15-18
    1 Thessalonians 4:9-12

Tu Psalm 47
    1 Kings 18:36-39
    1 John 4:1-6

W   Psalm 47
    Isaiah 51:1-3
    Matthew 11:20-24

Sunday, July 3–9

Th Psalm 45:10-17
    Genesis 25:19-27
    Romans 7:1-6

F   Psalm 45:10-17
    Genesis 27:1-17
    Romans 7:7-20

Sa Psalm 45:10-17
    Genesis 27:18-29
    Luke 10:21-24

Su *July 3–9 (Lectionary 14)*

M   Song of Solomon 2:8-13
    Genesis 27:30-46
    Romans 1:18-25

Tu Song of Solomon 2:8-13
    Genesis 29:1-14
    Romans 3:1-8

W   Song of Solomon 2:8-13
    Genesis 29:31-35
    John 13:1-17

Sunday, July 10–16

Th Psalm 119:105-112
    Exodus 3:1-6
    Romans 2:12-16

F   Psalm 119:105-112
    Deuteronomy 32:1-10
    Romans 15:14-21

Sa Psalm 119:105-112
    Isaiah 2:1-4
    John 12:44-50

Su *July 10–16 (Lectionary 15)*

M   Psalm 142
    Micah 1:1-5
    1 Thessalonians 4:1-8

Tu Psalm 142
    Jeremiah 49:7-11
    Ephesians 4:17—5:2

W   Psalm 142
    Obadiah 15-21
    Matthew 13:10-17

Sunday, July 17–23

Th Psalm 139:1-12, 23-24
    Isaiah 44:1-5
    Hebrews 2:1-9

F   Psalm 139:1-12, 23-24
    Ezekiel 39:21-29
    Hebrews 6:13-20

Sa Psalm 139:1-12, 23-24
    Exodus 14:9-25
    Matthew 7:15-20

Su *July 17–23 (Lectionary 16)*

M Psalm 139:13-18
Genesis 32:3-21
Revelation 14:12-20

Tu Psalm 139:13-18
Genesis 33:1-17
Galatians 4:21—5:1

W Psalm 139:13-18
Genesis 35:16-29
Matthew 12:15-21

Sunday, July 24–30
Th Psalm 105:1-11, 45b
Genesis 29:1-8
1 Corinthians 4:14-20

F Psalm 105:1-11, 45b
Genesis 29:9-14
Acts 7:44-53

Sa Psalm 105:1-11, 45b
Genesis 29:31—30:24
Matthew 12:38-42

Su *July 24–30 (Lectionary 17)*

M Psalm 65:8-13
Genesis 30:25-36
James 3:13-18

Tu Psalm 65:8-13
Genesis 30:37-43
Ephesians 6:10-18

W Psalm 65:8-13
Genesis 46:2—47:12
Mark 4:30-34

Sunday, July 31–August 6
Th Psalm 17:1-7, 15
Isaiah 14:1-2
Philippians 4:10-15

F Psalm 17:1-7, 15
Isaiah 41:8-10
Romans 9:6-13

Sa Psalm 17:1-7, 15
Genesis 31:1-21
Matthew 7:7-11

Su *July 31–August 6*
(Lectionary 18)

M Psalm 17:1-7, 15
Genesis 31:22-42
Romans 1:8-15

Tu Psalm 17:1-7, 15
Genesis 32:3-21
Acts 2:37-47

W Psalm 17:1-7, 15
Isaiah 43:1-7
Matthew 15:32-39

Sunday, August 7–13
Th Psalm 105:1-6, 16-22, 45b
Genesis 35:22b-29
Acts 17:10-15

F Psalm 105:1-6, 16-22, 45b
Genesis 36:1-8
Acts 18:24-28

Sa Psalm 105:1-6, 16-22, 45b
Genesis 37:5-11
Matthew 16:1-4

Su *August 7–13 (Lectionary 19)*

M Psalm 28
Genesis 37:29-36
2 Peter 2:4-10

Tu Psalm 28
Genesis 39:1-23
Romans 9:14-29

W Psalm 28
Genesis 40:1-23
Matthew 8:23-27

Sunday, August 14–20
Th Psalm 133
Genesis 41:14-36
Revelation 15:1-4

F Psalm 133
Genesis 41:37-57
Acts 14:19-28

Sa Psalm 133
Genesis 42:1-28
Matthew 14:34-36

Su *August 14–20*
(Lectionary 20)

M Psalm 130
Genesis 43:1-34
Acts 15:1-21

Tu Psalm 130
Genesis 44:1-34
Romans 11:13-29

W Psalm 130
Genesis 45:16-28
Matthew 8:1-13

Sunday, August 21–27
Th Psalm 124
Genesis 49:1-33
1 Corinthians 6:1-11

F Psalm 124
Genesis 49:29—50:14
2 Corinthians 10:12-18

Sa Psalm 124
Genesis 50:15-26
Matthew 16:5-12

Su *August 21–27*
(Lectionary 21)

M Psalm 8
Exodus 1:1-7
Romans 2:1-11

Tu Psalm 8
Exodus 2:11-15a
Romans 11:33-36

W Psalm 8
Exodus 2:15b-22
Matthew 26:6-13

Sunday, August 28–September 3
Th Psalm 105:1-6, 23-26, 45b
Exodus 2:23-24
Ephesians 5:1-6

F Psalm 105:1-6, 23-26, 45b
Exodus 3:16-25
2 Thessalonians 2:7-12

Sa Psalm 105:1-6, 23-26, 45b
Exodus 4:1-9
Matthew 8:14-17

Su *August 28–September 3*
(Lectionary 22)

M Psalm 83:1-4, 13-18
Exodus 4:10-31
Revelation 3:1-6

Tu Psalm 83:1-4, 13-18
Exodus 5:1—6:13
Revelation 3:7-13

W Psalm 83:1-4, 13-18
Exodus 7:14-25
Matthew 12:22-32

Sunday, September 4–10
Th Psalm 149
Exodus 9:1-7
2 Corinthians 12:11-21

F Psalm 149
Exodus 10:21-29
Romans 10:15b-21

Sa Psalm 149
Exodus 11:1-10
Matthew 23:29-36

Su *September 4–10*
(Lectionary 23)

M Psalm 121
Exodus 12:14-28
1 Peter 2:11-17

Tu Psalm 121
Exodus 12:29-42
Romans 13:1-7

W Psalm 121
Exodus 13:1-10
Matthew 21:18-22

Sunday, September 11–17

Th Psalm 114
Exodus 13:17-22
1 John 3:11-16

F Psalm 114
Exodus 14:1-18
Acts 7:9-16

Sa Psalm 114
Exodus 15:19-21
Matthew 6:7-15

Su *September 11–17*
(Lectionary 24)

M Psalm 77
Joshua 3:1-17
Hebrews 11:23-29

Tu Psalm 77
Nehemiah 9:9-15
Romans 14:13—15:2

W Psalm 77
2 Kings 2:1-18
Mark 11:20-25

Sunday, September 18–24

Th Psalm 105:1-6, 37-45
Exodus 15:22-27
2 Corinthians 13:1-4

F Psalm 105:1-6, 37-45
Exodus 16:1-21
2 Corinthians 13:5-10

Sa Psalm 105:1-6, 37-45
Exodus 16:22-30
Matthew 19:23-30

Su *September 18–24*
(Lectionary 25)

M Psalm 119:97-104
Exodus 16:31-35
Romans 16:1-16

Tu Psalm 119:97-104
Numbers 11:1-9
Romans 16:17-20

W Psalm 119:97-104
Numbers 11:18-23, 31-32
Matthew 18:1-5

**Sunday, September 25–
October 1**

Th Psalm 78:1-4, 12-16
Isaiah 48:17-21
James 4:11-16

F Psalm 78:1-4, 12-16
Numbers 20:1-13
Acts 13:32-41

Sa Psalm 78:1-4, 12-16
Numbers 27:12-14
Mark 11:27-33

Su *September 25–October 1*
(Lectionary 26)

M Psalm 42
Exodus 18:1-12
Philippians 1:3-14

Tu Psalm 42
Exodus 18:13-27
Philippians 1:15-21

W Psalm 42
Exodus 19:9b-25
Matthew 9:2-8

Sunday, October 2–8

Th Psalm 19
Exodus 23:1-9
Colossians 2:16-23

F Psalm 19
Exodus 23:14-19
Philippians 2:14-18; 3:1-4a

Sa Psalm 19
Exodus 23:10-13
John 7:40-52

Su *October 2–8 (Lectionary 27)*

M Psalm 119:49-56
Deuteronomy 5:1-21
1 Peter 2:4-10

Tu Psalm 119:49-56
Deuteronomy 5:22—6:3
2 Corinthians 5:17-21

W Psalm 119:49-56
Deuteronomy 6:10-25
John 11:45-57

Sunday, October 9–15

Th Psalm 106:1-6, 19-23
Exodus 24:1-8
1 Peter 5:1-5, 12-14

F Psalm 106:1-6, 19-23
Exodus 24:9-11
James 4:4-10

Sa Psalm 106:1-6, 19-23
Exodus 24:12-18
Mark 2:18-22

Su *October 9–15*
(Lectionary 28)

M Psalm 97
Exodus 32:15-35
Jude 17-25

Tu Psalm 97
Exodus 33:1-6
Philippians 3:13—4:1

W Psalm 97
2 Kings 17:7-20
John 6:25-35

Sunday, October 16–22

Th Psalm 99
Exodus 33:7-11
3 John 9-12

F Psalm 99
Exodus 31:1-11
1 Peter 5:1-5

Sa Psalm 99
Exodus 39:32-43
Matthew 14:1-12

Su *October 16–22*
(Lectionary 29)

M Psalm 63:1-8
Exodus 40:34-38
Revelation 18:1-10, 19-20

Tu Psalm 63:1-8
Numbers 12:1-9
Revelation 18:21-24

W Psalm 63:1-8
Numbers 13:1-2, 17—14:9
Matthew 17:22-27

Sunday, October 23–29

Th Psalm 90:1-6, 13-17
Deuteronomy 31:14-22
Titus 1:5-16

F Psalm 90:1-6, 13-17
Deuteronomy 32:1-14, 18
Titus 2:7-8, 11-15

Sa Psalm 90:1-6, 13-17
Deuteronomy 32:44-47
John 5:39-47

Su *October 23–29*
(Lectionary 30)

M Psalm 119:41-48
Numbers 33:38-39
James 2:8-13

Tu Psalm 119:41-48
Exodus 34:29-35
James 2:14-26

W Psalm 119:41-48
Deuteronomy 26:16—27:7
Matthew 19:16-22

Sunday, October 30–November 5

Th Psalm 107:1-7, 33-37
Joshua 1:1-11
Romans 2:17-29

F Psalm 107:1-7, 33-37
Joshua 2:1-14
2 Peter 2:1-3

Sa Psalm 107:1-7, 33-37
Joshua 2:15-24
Matthew 23:13-28

Su *October 30–November 5*
    (Lectionary 31)

M   Psalm 128
    Joshua 4:1-24
    1 Thessalonians 2:13-20

Tu Psalm 128
    Joshua 6:1-16, 20
    Acts 13:1-12

W   Psalm 128
    Joshua 10:12-14
    Matthew 15:1-9

Sunday, November 6–12

Th Psalm 78:1-7
    Joshua 5:10-12
    Revelation 8:6—9:12

F   Psalm 78:1-7
    Joshua 8:30-35
    Revelation 9:13-21

Sa Psalm 78:1-7
    Joshua 20:1-9
    Matthew 24:1-14

Su *November 6–12*
    (Lectionary 32)

M   Psalm 78
    Joshua 24:25-33
    1 Corinthians 14:20-25

Tu Psalm 78
    Nehemiah 8:1-12
    1 Thessalonians 3:6-13

W   Psalm 78
    Jeremiah 31:31-34
    Matthew 24:29-35

Sunday, November 13–19

Th Psalm 123
    Judges 2:6-15
    Revelation 16:1-7

F   Psalm 123
    Judges 2:16-23
    Revelation 16:8-21

Sa Psalm 123
    Judges 5:1-12
    Matthew 12:43-45

Su *November 13–19*
    (Lectionary 33)

M   Psalm 83:1-4, 9-10, 17-18
    Judges 4:8-24
    Romans 2:1-11

Tu Psalm 83:1-4, 9-10, 17-18
    Exodus 2:1-10
    1 Thessalonians 5:12-18

W   Psalm 83:1-4, 9-10, 17-18
    Esther 7:1-10
    Matthew 24:45-51

Christ the King

Th Psalm 100
    Genesis 48:15-22
    Revelation 14:1-11

F   Psalm 100
    Isaiah 40:1-11
    Revelation 22:1-9

Sa Psalm 100
    Ezekiel 34:25-31
    Matthew 12:46-50

Su *November 20–26*
    (Lectionary 34)

M   Psalm 28
    Numbers 27:15-23
    2 Timothy 2:8-13

Tu Psalm 28
    Zechariah 11:4-17
    Revelation 19:1-9

W   Psalm 28
    Jeremiah 31:10-14
    John 5:19-40

Year B

Advent 1

Th Psalm 80:1-7, 17-19
    Zechariah 13:1-9
    Revelation 14:6-13

F   Psalm 80:1-7, 17-19
    Zechariah 14:1-9
    1 Thessalonians 4:1-18

Sa Psalm 80:1-7, 17-19
    Micah 2:1-13
    Matthew 24:15-31

Su *First Sunday of Advent*

M   Psalm 79
    Micah 4:1-5
    Revelation 15:1-8

Tu Psalm 79
    Micah 4:6-13
    Revelation 18:1-10

W   Psalm 79
    Micah 5:1-5a
    Luke 21:34-38

Advent 2

Th Psalm 85:1-2, 8-13
    Hosea 6:1-6
    1 Thessalonians 1:2-10

F   Psalm 85:1-2, 8-13
    Jeremiah 1:4-10
    Acts 11:19-26

Sa Psalm 85:1-2, 8-13
    Ezekiel 36:24-28
    Mark 11:27-33

Su *Second Sunday of Advent*

M   Psalm 27
    Isaiah 26:7-15
    Acts 2:37-42

Tu Psalm 27
    Isaiah 4:2-6
    Acts 11:1-18

W   Psalm 27
    Malachi 2:10—3:1
    Luke 1:5-17

Advent 3

Th Psalm 126
    Habakkuk 2:1-5
    Philippians 3:7-11

F   Psalm 126
    Habakkuk 3:2-6
    Philippians 3:12-16

Sa Psalm 126
    Habakkuk 3:13-19
    Matthew 21:28-32

Su *Third Sunday of Advent*

M   Psalm 125
    1 Kings 18:1-18
    Ephesians 6:10-17

Tu Psalm 125
    2 Kings 2:9-22
    Acts 3:17—4:4

W   Psalm 125
    Malachi 3:16—4:6
    Mark 9:9-13

Advent 4
Dated readings begin Dec. 22

Th Psalm 89:1-4, 19-26
    2 Samuel 6:1-11
    Hebrews 1:1-4

F   Psalm 89:1-4, 19-26
    2 Samuel 6:12-19
    Hebrews 1:5-14

Sa Psalm 89:1-4, 19-26
    Judges 13:2-24
    John 7:40-52

Su	*Fourth Sunday of Advent*	Jan 7	Psalm 110 Exodus 1:22—2:10 Hebrews 11:23-26	F	Psalm 62:5-12 Jeremiah 20:7-13 2 Peter 3:1-7

Su *Fourth Sunday of Advent*

M Luke 1:6b-55
1 Samuel 1:1-18
Hebrews 9:1-14

Tu Luke 1:46b-55
1 Samuel 1:19-28
Hebrews 8:1-13

W Luke 1:46b-55
1 Samuel 2:1-10
Mark 11:1-11

Days around Christmas
Dec 22 Psalm 96
Zephaniah 3:8-13
Romans 10:5-13

Dec 23 Psalm 96
Zephaniah 3:14-20
Romans 13:11-14

Dec 24–25 *Nativity of Our Lord*

Dec 26 Psalm 148
Jeremiah 26:1-9, 12-15
Acts 6:8-15; 7:51-60

Dec 27 Psalm 148
Exodus 33:18-23
1 John 1:1-9

Dec 28 Psalm 148
Jeremiah 31:15-17
Matthew 2:13-18

Dec 29 Psalm 148
Isaiah 49:5-15
Matthew 12:46-50

Dec 30 Psalm 148
Proverbs 9:1-12
2 Peter 3:8-13

Dec 31 Psalm 148
1 Kings 3:5-14
John 8:12-19

Jan 1 *Name of Jesus*

Jan 2 Psalm 148
Proverbs 1:1-7
James 3:13-18

Days around Epiphany
Jan 3 Psalm 110
Proverbs 1:20-33
James 4:1-10

Jan 4 Psalm 110
Proverbs 3:1-12
James 4:11-17

Jan 5 Psalm 110
Proverbs 22:1-9
Luke 6:27-31

Jan 6 *Epiphany of Our Lord*

Jan 7 Psalm 110
Exodus 1:22—2:10
Hebrews 11:23-26

Jan 8 Psalm 110
Exodus 2:11-25
Hebrews 11:27-28

Jan 9 Psalm 110
Exodus 3:7-15
John 8:39-59

Epiphany 1
Th Psalm 29
1 Samuel 3:1-21
Acts 9:10-19a

F Psalm 29
1 Samuel 16:1-13
1 Timothy 4:11-16

Sa Psalm 29
1 Kings 2:1-4, 10-12
Luke 5:1-11

Su *Baptism of Our Lord*

M Psalm 69:1-5, 30-36
Genesis 17:1-13
Romans 4:1-12

Tu Psalm 69:1-5, 30-36
Exodus 30:22-38
Acts 22:2-16

W Psalm 69:1-5, 30-36
Isaiah 41:14-20
John 1:29-34

Epiphany 2
Th Psalm 139:1-6, 13-18
Judges 2:6-15
2 Corinthians 10:1-11

F Psalm 139:1-6, 13-18
Judges 2:16-23
Acts 13:16-25

Sa Psalm 139:1-6, 13-18
1 Samuel 2:21-25
Matthew 25:1-13

Su *Second Sunday after Epiphany*

M Psalm 86
1 Samuel 9:27—10:8
2 Corinthians 6:14—7:1

Tu Psalm 86
1 Samuel 15:10-31
Acts 5:1-11

W Psalm 86
Genesis 16:1-14
Luke 18:15-17

Epiphany 3
Th Psalm 62:5-12
Jeremiah 19:1-15
Revelation 18:11-20

F Psalm 62:5-12
Jeremiah 20:7-13
2 Peter 3:1-7

Sa Psalm 62:5-12
Jeremiah 20:14-18
Luke 10:13-16

Su *Third Sunday after Epiphany*

M Psalm 46
Genesis 12:1-9
1 Corinthians 7:17-24

Tu Psalm 46
Genesis 45:25—46:7
Acts 5:33-42

W Psalm 46
Proverbs 8:1-21
Mark 3:13-19a

Epiphany 4
Th Psalm 111
Deuteronomy 3:23-29
Romans 9:6-18

F Psalm 111
Deuteronomy 12:28-32
Revelation 2:12-17

Sa Psalm 111
Deuteronomy 13:1-5
Matthew 8:28—9:1

Su *Fourth Sunday after Epiphany*

M Psalm 35:1-10
Numbers 22:1-21
Acts 21:17-26

Tu Psalm 35:1-10
Numbers 22:22-28
1 Corinthians 7:32-40

W Psalm 35:1-10
Jeremiah 29:1-14
Mark 5:1-20

Epiphany 5
Th Psalm 147:1-11, 20c
Proverbs 12:10-21
Galatians 5:2-15

F Psalm 147:1-11, 20c
Job 36:1-23
1 Corinthians 9:1-16

Sa Psalm 147:1-11, 20c
Isaiah 46:1-13
Matthew 12:9-14

Su *Fifth Sunday after Epiphany*

M Psalm 102:12-28
2 Kings 4:8-17, 32-37
Acts 14:1-7

Tu Psalm 102:12-28
2 Kings 8:1-6
Acts 15:36-41

W   Psalm 102:12-28
    Job 6:1-13
    Mark 3:7-12

Epiphany 6
Th Psalm 30
    Leviticus 13:1-17
    Hebrews 12:7-13

F   Psalm 30
    Leviticus 14:1-20
    Acts 19:11-20

Sa Psalm 30
    Leviticus 14:21-32
    Matthew 26:6-13

Su *Sixth Sunday after Epiphany*

M   Psalm 6
    2 Chronicles 26:1-21
    Acts 3:1-10

Tu Psalm 6
    2 Kings 7:3-10
    1 Corinthians 10:14—11:1

W   Psalm 6
    Job 30:16-31
    John 4:46-54

Epiphany 7
Th Psalm 41
    2 Chronicles 7:12-22
    3 John 2-8

F   Psalm 41
    Isaiah 38:1-8
    Hebrews 12:7-13

Sa Psalm 41
    Isaiah 39:1-8
    Luke 4:38-41

Su *Seventh Sunday
    after Epiphany*

M   Psalm 38
    Isaiah 30:18-26
    Acts 14:8-18

Tu Psalm 38
    Micah 4:1-7
    2 Corinthians 1:1-11

W   Psalm 38
    Lamentations 5:1-22
    John 5:19-29

Epiphany 8
Th Psalm 103:1-13, 22
    Ezekiel 16:1-14
    Romans 3:1-8

F   Psalm 103:1-13, 22
    Ezekiel 16:44-52
    2 Peter 1:1-11

Sa Psalm 103:1-13, 22
    Ezekiel 16:53-63
    John 7:53—8:11

Su *Eighth Sunday after Epiphany*

M   Psalm 45:6-17
    Hosea 3:1-5
    2 Corinthians 1:23—2:11

Tu Psalm 45:6-17
    Hosea 14:1-9
    2 Corinthians 11:1-15

W   Psalm 45:6-17
    Isaiah 62:1-5
    John 3:22-36

Transfiguration
Th Psalm 50:1-6
    1 Kings 11:26-40
    2 Corinthians 2:12-17

F   Psalm 50:1-6
    1 Kings 14:1-18
    1 Timothy 1:12-20

Sa Psalm 50:1-6
    1 Kings 16:1-7
    Luke 19:41-44

Su *Transfiguration of Our Lord*

M   Psalm 110:1-4
    Exodus 19:7-25
    Hebrews 2:1-4

Tu Psalm 110:1-4
    Job 19:23-27
    1 Timothy 3:14-16

Lent 1
W   *Ash Wednesday*

Th Psalm 25:1-10
    Daniel 9:1-14
    1 John 1:3-10

F   Psalm 25:1-10
    Daniel 9:15-25a
    2 Timothy 4:1-5

Sa Psalm 25:1-10
    Psalm 32
    Matthew 9:2-13

Su *First Sunday in Lent*

M   Psalm 77
    Job 4:1-21
    Ephesians 2:1-10

Tu Psalm 77
    Job 5:8-27
    1 Peter 3:8-18a

W   Psalm 77
    Proverbs 30:1-9
    Matthew 4:1-11

Lent 2
Th Psalm 22:23-31
    Genesis 15:1-6, 12-18
    Romans 3:21-31

F   Psalm 22:23-31
    Genesis 16:1-6
    Romans 4:1-12

Sa Psalm 22:23-31
    Genesis 16:7-15
    Mark 8:27-30

Su *Second Sunday in Lent*

M   Psalm 105:1-11, 37-45
    Genesis 21:1-7
    Hebrews 1:8-12

Tu Psalm 105:1-11, 37-45
    Genesis 22:1-19
    Hebrews 11:1-3, 13-19

W   Psalm 105:1-11, 37-45
    Jeremiah 30:12-22
    John 12:36-43

Lent 3
Th Psalm 19
    Exodus 19:1-9a
    1 Peter 2:4-10

F   Psalm 19
    Exodus 19:9b-15
    Acts 7:30-40

Sa Psalm 19
    Exodus 19:16-25
    Mark 9:2-8

Su *Third Sunday in Lent*

M   Psalm 84
    1 Kings 6:1-4, 21-22
    1 Corinthians 3:10-23

Tu Psalm 84
    2 Chronicles 29:1-11, 16-19
    Hebrews 9:23-28

W   Psalm 84
    Ezra 6:1-16
    Mark 11:15-19

Lent 4
Th Psalm 107:1-3, 17-22
    Genesis 9:8-17
    Ephesians 1:3-6

F   Psalm 107:1-3, 17-22
    Daniel 12:5-13
    Ephesians 1:7-14

Sa Psalm 107:1-3, 17-22
    Numbers 20:22-29
    John 3:1-13

Su *Fourth Sunday in Lent*

M   Psalm 107:1-16
    Exodus 15:22-27
    Hebrews 3:1-6

Tu Psalm 107:1-16
    Numbers 20:1-13
    1 Corinthians 10:6-13

W   Psalm 107:1-16
    Isaiah 60:15-22
    John 8:12-20

Lent 5

Th Psalm 51:1-12
    Isaiah 30:15-18
    Hebrews 4:1-13

F   Psalm 51:1-12
    Exodus 30:1-10
    Hebrews 4:14—5:4

Sa Psalm 51:1-12
    Habakkuk 3:2-13
    John 12:1-11

Su *Fifth Sunday in Lent*

M   Psalm 119:9-16
    Isaiah 43:8-13
    2 Corinthians 3:4-11

Tu Psalm 119:9-16
    Isaiah 44:1-8
    Acts 2:14-24

W   Psalm 119:9-16
    Haggai 2:1-9, 20-23
    John 12:34-50

Lent 6

Th Psalm 118:1-2, 19-29
    Deuteronomy 16:1-8
    Philippians 2:1-11

F   Psalm 118:1-2, 19-29
    Jeremiah 33:1-9
    Philippians 2:12-18

Sa Psalm 118:1-2, 19-29
    Jeremiah 33:10-16
    Mark 10:32-34, 46-52

Su *Sunday of the Passion*

M   *Monday in Holy Week*

Tu *Tuesday in Holy Week*

W   *Wednesday in Holy Week*

Three Days—Easter

Th *Maundy Thursday*

F   *Good Friday*

Sa *Vigil of Easter*

Su *Resurrection of Our Lord*

M   Psalm 118:1-2, 14-24
    Genesis 1:1-19
    1 Corinthians 15:35-49

Tu Psalm 118:1-2, 14-24
    Genesis 1:20—2:4a
    1 Corinthians 15:50-58

W   Psalm 118:1-2, 14-24
    Song of Solomon 3:1-11
    Mark 16:1-8

Easter 2

Th Psalm 133
    Daniel 1:1-21
    Acts 2:42-47

F   Psalm 133
    Daniel 2:1-23
    Acts 4:23-31

Sa Psalm 133
    Daniel 2:24-49
    John 12:44-50

Su *Second Sunday of Easter*

M   Psalm 135
    Daniel 3:1-30
    1 John 2:3-11

Tu Psalm 135
    Daniel 6:1-28
    1 John 2:12-17

W   Psalm 135
    Isaiah 26:1-15
    Mark 12:18-27

Easter 3

Th Psalm 4
    Daniel 9:1-19
    1 John 2:18-25

F   Psalm 4
    Daniel 10:2-19
    1 John 2:26-28

Sa Psalm 4
    Acts 3:1-10
    Luke 22:24-30

Su *Third Sunday of Easter*

M   Psalm 150
    Jeremiah 30:1-11a
    1 John 3:10-16

Tu Psalm 150
    Hosea 5:15—6:6
    2 John 1-6

W   Psalm 150
    Proverbs 9:1-6
    Mark 16:9-18

Easter 4

Th Psalm 23
    Genesis 30:25-43
    Acts 3:17-26

F   Psalm 23
    Genesis 46:28—47:6
    Acts 4:1-4

Sa Psalm 23
    Genesis 48:8-19
    Mark 6:30-34

Su *Fourth Sunday of Easter*

M   Psalm 95
    1 Samuel 16:1-13
    1 Peter 5:1-5

Tu Psalm 95
    1 Chronicles 11:1-9
    Revelation 7:13-17

W   Psalm 95
    Micah 7:8-20
    Mark 14:26-31

Easter 5

Th Psalm 22:25-31
    Amos 8:1-7
    Acts 8:1b-8

F   Psalm 22:25-31
    Amos 8:11-13
    Acts 8:9-25

Sa Psalm 22:25-31
    Amos 9:7-15
    Mark 4:30-32

Su *Fifth Sunday of Easter*

M   Psalm 80
    Isaiah 5:1-7
    Galatians 5:16-26

Tu Psalm 80
    Isaiah 32:9-20
    James 3:17-18

W   Psalm 80
    Isaiah 65:17-25
    John 14:18-31

Easter 6

Th Psalm 98
    Isaiah 49:5-6
    Acts 10:1-34

F   Psalm 98
    Isaiah 42:5-9
    Acts 10:34-43

Sa Psalm 98
    Deuteronomy 32:44-47
    Mark 10:42-45

Su *Sixth Sunday of Easter*

M   Psalm 93
    Deuteronomy 7:1-11
    1 Timothy 6:11-12

Tu Psalm 93
    Deuteronomy 11:1-17
    1 Timothy 6:13-16

W   Psalm 93
    Deuteronomy 11:18-21
    Mark 16:19-20

Easter 7

Th *Ascension of Our Lord*

F   Psalm 47
    Exodus 24:15-18
    Revelation 1:9-18

Sa Psalm 47
    Deuteronomy 34:1-7
    John 16:4-11

Su *Seventh Sunday of Easter*

M   Psalm 115
    Exodus 28:29-38
    Philippians 1:3-11

Tu Psalm 115
    Numbers 8:5-22
    Titus 1:1-9

W   Psalm 115
    Ezra 9:5-15
    John 16:16-24

Pentecost

Th Psalm 33:12-22
    Genesis 2:4b-7
    1 Corinthians 15:42b-49

F   Psalm 33:12-22
    Job 37:1-13
    1 Corinthians 15:50-57

Sa Psalm 33:12-22
    Exodus 15:6-11
    John 7:37-39

Su *Day of Pentecost*

M   Psalm 104:24-34, 35b
    Joel 2:18-29
    1 Corinthians 12:4-11

Tu Psalm 104:24-34, 35b
    Genesis 11:1-9
    1 Corinthians 12:12-27

W   Psalm 104:24-34, 35b
    Ezekiel 37:1-14
    John 20:19-23

Holy Trinity

Th Psalm 29
    Isaiah 1:1-4, 16-20
    Romans 8:1-8

F   Psalm 29
    Isaiah 2:1-5
    Romans 8:9-11

Sa Psalm 29
    Isaiah 5:15-24
    John 15:18-20, 26-27

Su *The Holy Trinity*

M   Psalm 20
    Numbers 9:15-23
    Revelation 4:1-8

Tu Psalm 20
    Exodus 25:1-22
    1 Corinthians 2:1-10

W   Psalm 20
    Numbers 6:22-27
    Mark 4:21-25

Sunday, May 24–28

Th Psalm 103:1-13, 22
    Ezekiel 16:1-14
    Romans 3:1-8

F   Psalm 103:1-13, 22
    Ezekiel 16:44-52
    2 Peter 1:1-11

Sa Psalm 103:1-13, 22
    Ezekiel 16:53-63
    John 7:53—8:11

Su *May 24–28 (Lectionary 8)*

M   Psalm 45:6-17
    Hosea 3:1-5
    2 Corinthians 1:23—2:11

Tu Psalm 45:6-17
    Hosea 14:1-9
    2 Corinthians 11:1-15

W   Psalm 45:6-17
    Isaiah 62:1-5
    John 3:22-36

The following readings relate to the complementary series of the Sunday lectionary.

Sunday, May 29–June 4

Th Psalm 81:1-10
    Exodus 31:12-18
    Acts 25:1-12

F   Psalm 81:1-10
    Leviticus 23:1-8
    Romans 8:31-39

Sa Psalm 81:1-10
    Leviticus 24:5-9
    John 7:19-24

Su *May 29–June 4 (Lectionary 9)*

M   Psalm 78:1-4, 52-72
    Exodus 16:13-26
    Romans 9:19-29

Tu Psalm 78:1-4, 52-72
    Exodus 16:27-36
    Acts 15:1-5, 22-35

W   Psalm 78:1-4, 52-72
    1 Samuel 21:1-6
    John 5:1-18

Sunday, June 5–11

Th Psalm 130
    Isaiah 28:9-13
    1 Peter 4:7-19

F   Psalm 130
    Deuteronomy 1:34-40
    2 Corinthians 5:1-5

Sa Psalm 130
    Genesis 2:4b-14
    Luke 8:4-15

Su *June 5–11 (Lectionary 10)*

M   Psalm 74
    1 Samuel 16:14-23
    Revelation 20:1-6

Tu Psalm 74
    1 Kings 18:17-40
    Revelation 20:7-15

W   Psalm 74
    Isaiah 26:16—27:1
    Luke 11:14-28

Sunday, June 12–18

Th Psalm 92:1-4, 12-15
    Genesis 3:14-24
    Hebrews 2:5-9

F   Psalm 92:1-4, 12-15
    1 Kings 10:26—11:8
    Hebrews 11:4-7

Sa Psalm 92:1-4, 12-15
    2 Kings 14:1-14
    Mark 4:1-20

Su *June 12–18 (Lectionary 11)*

M   Psalm 52
    Ezekiel 31:1-12
    Galatians 6:11-18

Tu Psalm 52
    Jeremiah 21:11-14
    Revelation 21:22—22:5

W   Psalm 52
    Jeremiah 22:1-9
    Luke 6:43-45

Sunday, June 19–25

Th Psalm 107:1-3, 23-32
    Job 29:1-20
    Acts 20:1-16

F   Psalm 107:1-3, 23-32
    Job 29:21—30:15
    Acts 21:1-16

Sa Psalm 107:1-3, 23-32
    Job 37:1-13
    Luke 21:25-28

Su *June 19–25 (Lectionary 12)*

M   Psalm 65
    Exodus 7:14-24
    Acts 27:13-38

Tu Psalm 65
    Exodus 9:13-35
    Acts 27:39-44

W   Psalm 65
    Joshua 10:1-14
    Mark 6:45-52

Sunday, June 26–July 2
Th Psalm 30
    Lamentations 1:16-22
    2 Corinthians 7:2-16

F   Psalm 30
    Lamentations 2:1-12
    2 Corinthians 8:1-7

Sa Psalm 30
    Lamentations 2:18-22
    Luke 4:31-37

Su *June 26–July 2*
    (Lectionary 13)

M   Psalm 88
    Leviticus 21:1-15
    2 Corinthians 8:16-24

Tu Psalm 88
    Leviticus 15:19-31
    2 Corinthians 9:1-5

W   Psalm 88
    2 Kings 20:1-11
    Mark 9:14-29

Sunday, July 3–9
Th Psalm 123
    Jeremiah 7:1-15
    1 Corinthians 4:8-13

F   Psalm 123
    Jeremiah 7:16-26
    2 Corinthians 10:7-11

Sa Psalm 123
    Jeremiah 7:27-34
    Matthew 8:18-22

Su *July 3–9 (Lectionary 14)*
M   Psalm 119:81-88
    Ezekiel 2:8—3:11
    2 Corinthians 11:16-33

Tu Psalm 119:81-88
    Jeremiah 16:1-13
    James 5:7-12

W   Psalm 119:81-88
    Jeremiah 16:14-21
    John 7:1-9

Sunday, July 10–16
Th Psalm 85:8-13
    Amos 2:6-16
    Colossians 2:1-5

F   Psalm 85:8-13
    Amos 3:1-12
    Colossians 4:2-18

Sa Psalm 85:8-13
    Amos 4:6-13
    Luke 1:57-80

Su *July 10–16 (Lectionary 15)*
M   Psalm 142
    Amos 5:1-9
    Acts 21:27-39

Tu Psalm 142
    Amos 9:1-4
    Acts 23:12-35

W   Psalm 142
    Amos 9:11-15
    Luke 7:31-35

Sunday, July 17–23
Th Psalm 23
    Jeremiah 10:1-16
    Colossians 1:15-23

F   Psalm 23
    Jeremiah 10:17-25
    Acts 17:16-31

Sa Psalm 23
    Jeremiah 12:1-13
    Luke 18:35-43

Su *July 17–23 (Lectionary 16)*
M   Psalm 100
    Jeremiah 50:1-7
    Hebrews 13:17-25

Tu Psalm 100
    Zechariah 9:14—10:2
    Acts 20:17-38

W   Psalm 100
    2 Samuel 5:1-12
    Luke 15:1-7

Sunday, July 24–30
Th Psalm 145:10-18
    1 Kings 19:19-21
    Colossians 1:9-14

F   Psalm 145:10-18
    2 Kings 3:4-20
    Colossians 3:12-17

Sa Psalm 145:10-18
    2 Kings 4:38-41
    John 4:31-38

Su *July 24–30 (Lectionary 17)*
M   Psalm 111
    Genesis 18:1-15
    Philippians 4:10-20

Tu Psalm 111
    Exodus 24:1-11
    Romans 15:22-33

W   Psalm 111
    Isaiah 25:6-10a
    Mark 6:35-44

Sunday, July 31–August 6
Th Psalm 78:23-29
    Exodus 12:33-42
    1 Corinthians 11:17-22

F   Psalm 78:23-29
    Exodus 12:43—13:2
    1 Corinthians 11:27-34

Sa Psalm 78:23-29
    Exodus 13:3-10
    Matthew 16:5-12

Su *July 31–August 6 (Lectionary 18)*
M   Psalm 107:1-3, 33-43
    Numbers 11:16-23, 31-32
    Ephesians 4:17-24

Tu Psalm 107:1-3, 33-43
    Deuteronomy 8:1-20
    1 Corinthians 12:27-31

W   Psalm 107:1-3, 33-43
    Isaiah 55:1-9
    Mark 8:1-10

Sunday, August 7–13
Th Psalm 34:1-8
    1 Samuel 28:20-25
    Romans 15:1-6

F   Psalm 34:1-8
    2 Samuel 17:15-29
    Galatians 6:1-10

Sa Psalm 34:1-8
    1 Kings 2:1-9
    Matthew 7:7-11

Su *August 7–13 (Lectionary 19)*
M   Psalm 81
    1 Kings 17:1-16
    Ephesians 5:1-14

Tu Psalm 81
    Ruth 2:1-23
    2 Peter 3:14-18

W   Psalm 81
    Jeremiah 31:1-6
    John 6:35-40

Sunday, August 14–20
Th Psalm 34:9-14
    Job 11:1-20
    Acts 6:8-15

F   Psalm 34:9-14
    Job 12:1-25
    Romans 16:17-20

Sa Psalm 34:9-14
    Job 13:1-19
    John 4:7-26

Su *August 14–20 (Lectionary 20)*
M   Psalm 36
    Genesis 43:1-15
    Acts 6:1-7

Tu Psalm 36
    Genesis 45:1-15
    Acts 7:9-16

W   Psalm 36
    Genesis 47:13-26
    Mark 8:14-21

Sunday, August 21–27
Th Psalm 34:15-22
    Joshua 22:1-9
    1 Thessalonians 5:1-11

F   Psalm 34:15-22
    Joshua 22:10-20
    Romans 13:11-14

Sa Psalm 34:15-22
    Joshua 22:21-34
    Luke 11:5-13

Su *August 21–27 (Lectionary 21)*

M   Psalm 119:97-104
    Nehemiah 9:1-15
    Ephesians 5:21—6:9

Tu Psalm 119:97-104
    Nehemiah 9:16-31
    Ephesians 6:21-24

W   Psalm 119:97-104
    Isaiah 33:10-16
    John 15:16-25

Sunday, August 28–September 3
Th Psalm 15
    Exodus 32:1-14
    James 1:1-8

F   Psalm 15
    Exodus 32:15-35
    James 1:9-16

Sa Psalm 15
    Exodus 34:8-28
    John 18:28-32

Su *August 28–September 3*
    (Lectionary 22)

M   Psalm 106:1-6, 13-23, 47-48
    Deuteronomy 4:9-14
    1 Timothy 4:6-16

Tu Psalm 106:1-6, 13-23, 47-48
    Deuteronomy 4:15-20
    1 Peter 2:19-25

W   Psalm 106:1-6, 13-23, 47-48
    Deuteronomy 4:21-40
    Mark 7:9-23

Sunday, September 4–10
Th Psalm 146
    Isaiah 30:27-33
    Romans 2:1-11

F   Psalm 146
    Isaiah 32:1-8
    Romans 2:12-16

Sa Psalm 146
    Isaiah 33:1-9
    Matthew 15:21-31

Su *September 4–10*
    (Lectionary 23)

M   Isaiah 38:10-20
    Joshua 6:1-21
    Hebrews 11:29—12:2

Tu Isaiah 38:10-20
    Joshua 8:1-23
    Hebrews 12:3-13

W   Isaiah 38:10-20
    Judges 15:9-20
    Matthew 17:14-21

Sunday, September 11–17
Th Psalm 116:1-9
    Joshua 2:1-14
    Hebrews 11:17-22

F   Psalm 116:1-9
    Joshua 2:15-24
    James 2:17-26

Sa Psalm 116:1-9
    Joshua 6:22-27
    Matthew 21:23-32

Su *September 11–17*
    (Lectionary 24)

M   Psalm 119:169-176
    1 Kings 13:1-10
    Romans 3:9-20

Tu Psalm 119:169-176
    1 Kings 13:11-25
    Colossians 3:1-11

W   Psalm 119:169-176
    Isaiah 10:12-20
    John 7:25-36

Sunday, September 18–24
Th Psalm 54
    Judges 6:1-10
    1 Corinthians 2:1-5

F   Psalm 54
    1 Kings 22:24-40
    Romans 11:25-32

Sa Psalm 54
    2 Kings 17:5-18
    Matthew 23:29-39

Su *September 18–24*
    (Lectionary 25)

M   Psalm 139:1-18
    2 Kings 5:1-14
    James 4:8-17

Tu Psalm 139:1-18
    2 Kings 11:21—12:16
    James 5:1-6

W   Psalm 139:1-18
    Jeremiah 1:4-10
    John 8:21-38

Sunday, September 25–October 1
Th Psalm 19:7-14
    Exodus 18:13-27
    Acts 4:13-31

F   Psalm 19:7-14
    Deuteronomy 1:1-18
    Acts 12:20-25

Sa Psalm 19:7-14
    Deuteronomy 27:1-10
    Matthew 5:13-20

Su *September 25–October 1*
    (Lectionary 26)

M   Psalm 5
    Zechariah 6:9-15
    1 Peter 1:3-9

Tu Psalm 5
    Zechariah 8:18-23
    1 John 2:18-25

W   Psalm 5
    Zechariah 10:1-12
    Matthew 18:6-9

Sunday, October 2–8
Th Psalm 8
    Genesis 20:1-18
    Galatians 3:23-29

F   Psalm 8
    Genesis 21:22-34
    Romans 8:1-11

Sa Psalm 8
    Genesis 23:1-20
    Luke 16:14-18

Su *October 2–8 (Lectionary 27)*

M   Psalm 112
    Deuteronomy 22:13-30
    1 Corinthians 7:1-9

Tu Psalm 112
    Deuteronomy 24:1-5
    1 Corinthians 7:10-16

W   Psalm 112
    Jeremiah 3:6-14
    Matthew 5:27-36

Sunday, October 9–15
Th Psalm 90:12-17
    Deuteronomy 5:1-21
    Hebrews 3:7-19

F   Psalm 90:12-17
    Deuteronomy 5:22-33
    Hebrews 4:1-11

Sa Psalm 90:12-17
    Amos 3:13—4:5
    Matthew 15:1-9

Su *October 9–15 (Lectionary 28)*

M Psalm 26
Obadiah 1-9
Revelation 7:9-17

Tu Psalm 26
Obadiah 10-16
Revelation 8:1-5

W Psalm 26
Obadiah 17-21
Luke 16:19-31

Sunday, October 16–22
Th Psalm 91:9-16
Genesis 14:17-24
Romans 15:7-13

F Psalm 91:9-16
Isaiah 47:1-9
Revelation 17:1-18

Sa Psalm 91:9-16
Isaiah 47:10-15
Luke 22:24-30

Su *October 16–22*
(Lectionary 29)

M Psalm 37:23-40
1 Samuel 8:1-18
Hebrews 6:1-12

Tu Psalm 37:23-40
1 Samuel 10:17-25
Hebrews 6:13-20

W Psalm 37:23-40
1 Samuel 12:1-25
John 13:1-17

Sunday, October 23–29
Th Psalm 126
Jeremiah 23:9-15
Hebrews 7:1-10

F Psalm 126
Jeremiah 26:12-24
Hebrews 7:11-22

Sa Psalm 126
Jeremiah 29:24-32
Mark 8:22-26

Su *October 23–29*
(Lectionary 30)

M Psalm 119:17-24
Exodus 4:1-17
1 Peter 2:1-10

Tu Psalm 119:17-24
2 Kings 6:8-23
Acts 9:32-35

W Psalm 119:17-24
Jeremiah 33:1-11
Matthew 20:29-34

Sunday, October 30–November 5
Th Psalm 119:1-8
Exodus 22:1-15
Hebrews 9:1-12

F Psalm 119:1-8
Leviticus 19:32-37
Romans 3:21-31

Sa Psalm 119:1-8
Numbers 9:9-14
Luke 10:25-37

Su *October 30–November 5*
(Lectionary 31)

M Psalm 51
Deuteronomy 6:10-25
Romans 12:17-21; 13:8-10

Tu Psalm 51
Deuteronomy 28:58—29:1
Acts 7:17-29

W Psalm 51
Micah 6:1-8
John 13:31-35

Sunday, November 6–12
Th Psalm 146
Numbers 36:1-13
Romans 5:6-11

F Psalm 146
Deuteronomy 15:1-11
Hebrews 9:15-24

Sa Psalm 146
Deuteronomy 24:17-22
Mark 11:12-14, 20-24

Su *November 6–12*
(Lectionary 32)

M Psalm 94
Ruth 1:1-22
1 Timothy 5:1-8

Tu Psalm 94
Ruth 3:14—4:6
1 Timothy 5:9-16

W Psalm 94
Ruth 4:7-22
Luke 4:16-30

Sunday, November 13–19
Th Psalm 16
Daniel 4:4-18
1 Timothy 6:11-21

F Psalm 16
Daniel 4:19-27
Colossians 2:6-15

Sa Psalm 16
Daniel 4:28-37
Mark 12:1-12

Su *November 13–19*
(Lectionary 33)

M Psalm 13
Daniel 8:1-14
Hebrews 10:26-31

Tu Psalm 13
Daniel 8:15-27
Hebrews 10:32-39

W Psalm 13
Zechariah 12:1—13:1
Mark 13:9-23

Christ the King
Th Psalm 93
Ezekiel 28:1-10
Acts 7:54—8:1a

F Psalm 93
Ezekiel 28:20-26
1 Corinthians 15:20-28

Sa Psalm 93
Daniel 7:1-8, 15-18
John 3:31-36

Su *November 20–26*
(Lectionary 34)

M Psalm 76
Daniel 7:19-27
Revelation 11:1-14

Tu Psalm 76
Ezekiel 29:1-12
Revelation 11:15-19

W Psalm 76
Ezekiel 30:20-26
John 16:25-33

The following readings relate to the semicontinuous series of the Sunday lectionary.

Sunday, May 29–June 4
Th Psalm 139:1-6, 13-18
1 Samuel 1:1-18
Acts 25:1-12

F Psalm 139:1-6, 13-18
1 Samuel 1:19-27
Romans 8:31-39

Sa Psalm 139:1-6, 13-18
1 Samuel 2:1-10
John 7:19-24

Su *May 29–June 4 (Lectionary 9)*

M Psalm 99
1 Samuel 2:11-17
Romans 9:19-29

Tu Psalm 99
1 Samuel 2:18-21
Acts 15:1-5, 22-35

W Psalm 99
1 Samuel 2:22-36
John 5:1-18

Sunday, June 5–11

Th Psalm 138
1 Samuel 4:1-22
1 Peter 4:7-19

F Psalm 138
1 Samuel 5:1-12
2 Corinthians 5:1-5

Sa Psalm 138
1 Samuel 6:1-18
Luke 8:4-15

Su *June 5–11 (Lectionary 10)*

M Psalm 108
1 Samuel 7:3-15
Revelation 20:1-6

Tu Psalm 108
1 Samuel 8:1-22
Revelation 20:7-15

W Psalm 108
1 Samuel 9:1-14
Luke 11:14-28

Sunday, June 12–18

Th Psalm 20
1 Samuel 9:15-27
Hebrews 2:5-9

F Psalm 20
1 Samuel 10:1-8
Hebrews 11:4-7

Sa Psalm 20
1 Samuel 13:1-15a
Mark 4:1-20

Su *June 12–18 (Lectionary 11)*

M Psalm 53
1 Samuel 13:23—14:23
Galatians 6:11-18

Tu Psalm 53
1 Samuel 15:10-23
Revelation 21:22—22:5

W Psalm 53
1 Samuel 15:24-31
Luke 6:43-45

Sunday, June 19–25

Th Psalm 9:9-20
1 Samuel 16:14-23
Acts 20:1-16

F Psalm 9:9-20
1 Samuel 17:55—18:5
Acts 21:1-16

Sa Psalm 9:9-20
1 Samuel 18:1-4
Luke 21:25-28

Su *June 19–25 (Lectionary 12)*

M Psalm 119:113-128
1 Samuel 18:6-30
Acts 27:13-38

Tu Psalm 119:113-128
1 Samuel 19:1-7
Acts 27:39-44

W Psalm 119:113-128
1 Samuel 19:8-17
Mark 6:45-52

Sunday, June 26–July 2

Th Psalm 130
1 Samuel 19:18-24
2 Corinthians 7:2-16

F Psalm 130
1 Samuel 20:1-25
2 Corinthians 8:1-7

Sa Psalm 130
1 Samuel 20:27-42
Luke 4:31-37

Su *June 26–July 2
(Lectionary 13)*

M Psalm 18:1-6, 43-50
1 Samuel 23:14-18
2 Corinthians 8:16-24

Tu Psalm 18:1-6, 43-50
1 Samuel 31:1-13
2 Corinthians 9:1-5

W Psalm 18:1-6, 43-50
1 Chronicles 10:1-14
Mark 9:14-29

Sunday, July 3–9

Th Psalm 48
2 Samuel 2:1-11
1 Corinthians 4:8-13

F Psalm 48
2 Samuel 3:1-12
2 Corinthians 10:7-11

Sa Psalm 48
2 Samuel 3:31-38
Matthew 8:18-22

Su *July 3–9 (Lectionary 14)*

M Psalm 21
2 Samuel 5:1-10
2 Corinthians 11:16-33

Tu Psalm 21
2 Samuel 5:11-16
James 5:7-12

W Psalm 21
2 Samuel 5:17-25
John 7:1-9

Sunday, July 10–16

Th Psalm 24
Exodus 25:10-22
Colossians 2:1-5

F Psalm 24
Exodus 37:1-16
Colossians 4:2-18

Sa Psalm 24
Numbers 10:11-36
Luke 1:57-80

Su *July 10–16 (Lectionary 15)*

M Psalm 68:24-35
2 Samuel 6:6-12a
Acts 21:27-39

Tu Psalm 68:24-35
2 Samuel 3:12-16
Acts 23:12-35

W Psalm 68:24-35
2 Samuel 6:16-23
Luke 7:31-35

Sunday, July 17–23

Th Psalm 89:20-37
1 Chronicles 11:15-19
Colossians 1:15-23

F Psalm 89:20-37
1 Chronicles 14:1-2
Acts 17:16-31

Sa Psalm 89:20-37
1 Chronicles 15:1-2, 16:4-13
Luke 18:35-43

Su *July 17–23 (Lectionary 16)*

M Psalm 61
2 Samuel 7:18-29
Hebrews 13:17-25

Tu Psalm 61
2 Samuel 8:1-18
Acts 20:17-38

W Psalm 61
2 Samuel 9:1-13
Luke 15:1-7

Sunday, July 24–30

Th Psalm 14
2 Samuel 10:1-5
Colossians 1:9-14

F Psalm 14
2 Samuel 10:6-12
Colossians 3:12-17

Sa Psalm 14
2 Samuel 10:13-19
John 4:31-38

Su *July 24–30 (Lectionary 17)*

M Psalm 37:12-22
2 Samuel 11:14-21
Philippians 4:10-20

Tu Psalm 37:12-22
2 Samuel 11:22-27
Romans 15:22-33

W Psalm 37:12-22
2 Chronicles 9:29-31
Mark 6:35-44

Sunday, July 31–August 6

Th   Psalm 51:1-12
      Exodus 32:19-26a
      1 Corinthians 11:17-22

F   Psalm 51:1-12
      Joshua 23:1-16
      1 Corinthians 11:27-34

Sa   Psalm 51:1-12
      Judges 6:1-10
      Matthew 16:5-12

Su   *July 31–August 6*
      (Lectionary 18)

M   Psalm 50:16-23
      2 Samuel 12:15-25
      Ephesians 4:17-24

Tu   Psalm 50:16-23
      2 Samuel 13:1-19
      1 Corinthians 12:27-31

W   Psalm 50:16-23
      2 Samuel 13:20-36
      Mark 8:1-10

Sunday, August 7–13

Th   Psalm 130
      2 Samuel 13:37—14:24
      Romans 15:1-6

F   Psalm 130
      2 Samuel 14:25-33
      Galatians 6:1-10

Sa   Psalm 130
      2 Samuel 15:1-13
      Matthew 7:7-11

Su   *August 7–13 (Lectionary 19)*

M   Psalm 57
      2 Samuel 15:13-31
      Ephesians 5:1-14

Tu   Psalm 57
      2 Samuel 18:19-33
      2 Peter 3:14-18

W   Psalm 57
      2 Samuel 19:1-18
      John 6:35-40

Sunday, August 14–20

Th   Psalm 111
      1 Kings 1:1-30
      Acts 6:8-15

F   Psalm 111
      1 Kings 1:28-48
      Romans 16:17-20

Sa   Psalm 111
      1 Kings 2:1-11
      John 4:7-26

Su   *August 14–20 (Lectionary 20)*

M   Psalm 101
      1 Kings 3:16-28
      Acts 6:1-7

Tu   Psalm 101
      1 Kings 7:1-12
      Acts 7:9-16

W   Psalm 101
      1 Kings 8:1-21
      Mark 8:14-21

Sunday, August 21–27

Th   Psalm 84
      1 Kings 4:20-28
      1 Thessalonians 5:1-11

F   Psalm 84
      1 Kings 4:29-34
      Romans 13:11-14

Sa   Psalm 84
      1 Kings 5:1-12
      Luke 11:5-13

Su   *August 21–27*
      (Lectionary 21)

M   Psalm 11
      1 Kings 5:13-18
      Ephesians 5:21—6:9

Tu   Psalm 11
      1 Kings 6:1-14
      Ephesians 6:21-24

W   Psalm 11
      1 Kings 6:15-38
      John 15:16-25

Sunday, August 28–September 3

Th   Psalm 45:1-2, 6-9
      Song of Solomon 1:1-17
      James 1:1-8

F   Psalm 45:1-2, 6-9
      Song of Solomon 2:1-7
      James 1:9-16

Sa   Psalm 45:1-2, 6-9
      Hosea 3:1-5
      John 18:28-32

Su   *August 28–September 3*
      (Lectionary 22)

M   Psalm 144:9-15
      Song of Solomon 3:6-11
      1 Timothy 4:6-16

Tu   Psalm 144:9-15
      Song of Solomon 5:2—6:3
      1 Peter 2:19-25

W   Psalm 144:9-15
      Song of Solomon 8:5-7
      Mark 7:9-23

Sunday, September 4–10

Th   Psalm 125
      Proverbs 1:1-19
      Romans 2:1-11

F   Psalm 125
      Proverbs 4:10-27
      Romans 2:12-16

Sa   Psalm 125
      Proverbs 8:1-31
      Matthew 15:21-31

Su   *September 4–10*
      (Lectionary 23)

M   Psalm 73:1-20
      Proverbs 8:32—9:6
      Hebrews 11:29—12:2

Tu   Psalm 73:1-20
      Proverbs 11:1-31
      Hebrews 12:3-13

W   Psalm 73:1-20
      Proverbs 14:1-9
      Matthew 17:14-21

Sunday, September 11–17

Th   Psalm 19
      Proverbs 15:1-17
      Hebrews 11:17-22

F   Psalm 19
      Proverbs 19:24-29
      James 2:17-26

Sa   Psalm 19
      Proverbs 21:1-17
      Matthew 21:23-32

Su   *September 11–17*
      (Lectionary 24)

M   Psalm 73:21-28
      Proverbs 22:1-21
      Romans 3:9-20

Tu   Psalm 73:21-28
      Proverbs 25:1-28
      Colossians 3:1-11

W   Psalm 73:21-28
      Proverbs 29:1-27
      John 7:25-36

Sunday, September 18–24

Th   Psalm 1
      Proverbs 30:1-10
      1 Corinthians 2:1-5

F   Psalm 1
      Proverbs 30:18-33
      Romans 11:25-32

Sa   Psalm 1
      Ecclesiastes 1:1-18
      Matthew 23:29-39

Su   *September 18–24*
      (Lectionary 25)

M   Psalm 128
      Proverbs 27:1-27
      James 4:8-17

Tu   Psalm 128
      Ecclesiastes 4:9-16
      James 5:1-6

W Psalm 128
Ecclesiastes 5:1-20
John 8:21-38

Sunday, September 25–October 1
Th Psalm 124
Esther 1:1-21
Acts 4:13-31

F Psalm 124
Esther 2:1-23
Acts 12:20-25

Sa Psalm 124
Esther 3:1-15
Matthew 5:13-20

Su *September 25–October 1*
(Lectionary 26)

M Psalm 140
Esther 4:1-17
1 Peter 1:3-9

Tu Psalm 140
Esther 5:1-14
1 John 2:18-25

W Psalm 140
Esther 8:1-17
Matthew 18:6-9

Sunday, October 2–8
Th Psalm 26
Job 2:11—3:26
Galatians 3:23-29

F Psalm 26
Job 4:1-21
Romans 8:1-11

Sa Psalm 26
Job 7:1-21
Luke 16:14-18

Su *October 2–8 (Lectionary 27)*

M Psalm 55:1-15
Job 8:1-22
1 Corinthians 7:1-9

Tu Psalm 55:1-15
Job 11:1-20
1 Corinthians 7:10-16

W Psalm 55:1-15
Job 15:1-35
Matthew 5:27-36

Sunday, October 9–15
Th Psalm 22:1-15
Job 17:1-16
Hebrews 3:7-19

F Psalm 22:1-15
Job 18:1-21
Hebrews 4:1-11

Sa Psalm 22:1-15
Job 20:1-29
Matthew 15:1-9

Su *October 9–15*
(Lectionary 28)

M Psalm 39
Job 26:1-14
Revelation 7:9-17

Tu Psalm 39
Job 28:12—29:10
Revelation 8:1-5

W Psalm 39
Job 32:1-22
Luke 16:19-31

Sunday, October 16–22
Th Psalm 104:1-9, 24, 35b
Job 36:1-16
Romans 15:7-13

F Psalm 104:1-9, 24, 35b
Job 37:1-24
Revelation 17:1-18

Sa Psalm 104:1-9, 24, 35b
Job 39:1-30
Luke 22:24-30

Su *October 16–22*
(Lectionary 29)

M Psalm 75
Job 40:1-24
Hebrews 6:1-12

Tu Psalm 75
Job 41:1-11
Hebrews 6:13-20

W Psalm 75
Job 41:12-34
John 13:1-17

Sunday, October 23–29
Th Psalm 34:1-8 [19-22]
2 Kings 20:12-19
Hebrews 7:1-10

F Psalm 34:1-8 [19-22]
Nehemiah 1:1-11
Hebrews 7:11-22

Sa Psalm 34:1-8 [19-22]
Job 42:7-9
Mark 8:22-26

Su *October 23–29*
(Lectionary 30)

M Psalm 28
Isaiah 59:9-19
1 Peter 2:1-10

Tu Psalm 28
Ezekiel 18:1-32
Acts 9:32-35

W Psalm 28
Ezekiel 14:12-23
Matthew 20:29-34

Sunday, October 30–November 5
Th Psalm 146
Ruth 1:18-22
Hebrews 9:1-12

F Psalm 146
Ruth 2:1-9
Romans 3:21-31

Sa Psalm 146
Ruth 2:10-14
Luke 10:25-37

Su *October 30–November 5*
(Lectionary 31)

M Psalm 18:20-30
Ruth 2:15-23
Romans 12:17-21; 13:8-10

Tu Psalm 18:20-30
Ruth 3:1-7
Acts 7:17-29

W Psalm 18:20-30
Ruth 3:8-18
John 13:31-35

Sunday, November 6–12
Th Psalm 127
Ruth 4:1-10
Romans 5:6-11

F Psalm 127
Ruth 4:11-17
Hebrews 9:15-24

Sa Psalm 127
Ruth 4:18-22
Mark 11:12-14, 20-24

Su *November 6–12*
(Lectionary 32)

M Psalm 113
Genesis 24:1-10
1 Timothy 5:1-8

Tu Psalm 113
Genesis 24:11-27
1 Timothy 5:9-16

W Psalm 113
Genesis 24:28-42
Luke 4:16-30

Sunday, November 13–19
Th 1 Samuel 2:1-10
1 Samuel 1:21-28
1 Timothy 6:11-21

F 1 Samuel 2:1-10
1 Samuel 2:18-21
Colossians 2:6-15

Sa	1 Samuel 2:1-10 1 Samuel 3:1-18 Mark 12:1-12	W	Psalm 3 1 Kings 8:22-30 Mark 13:9-23	Su	*November 20–26* *(Lectionary 34)*

Sa   1 Samuel 2:1-10
     1 Samuel 3:1-18
     Mark 12:1-12

Su   *November 13–19*
     (Lectionary 33)

M   Psalm 3
     1 Samuel 3:19—4:2
     Hebrews 10:26-31

Tu   Psalm 3
     Deuteronomy 26:5-10
     Hebrews 10:32-39

W   Psalm 3
     1 Kings 8:22-30
     Mark 13:9-23

Christ the King

Th   Psalm 132:1-12 [13-18]
     2 Kings 22:1-10
     Acts 7:54—8:1a

F   Psalm 132:1-12 [13-18]
     2 Kings 22:11-20
     1 Corinthians 15:20-28

Sa   Psalm 132:1-12 [13-18]
     2 Kings 23:1-14
     John 3:31-36

Su   *November 20–26*
     (Lectionary 34)

M   Psalm 63
     2 Kings 23:15-25
     Revelation 11:1-14

Tu   Psalm 63
     1 Samuel 17:55—18:5
     Revelation 11:15-19

W   Psalm 63
     2 Samuel 2:1-7
     John 16:25-33

Year C

Advent 1

Th   Psalm 25:1-10
     Nehemiah 9:6-15
     1 Thessalonians 5:1-11

F   Psalm 25:1-10
     Nehemiah 9:16-25
     1 Thessalonians 5:12-22

Sa   Psalm 25:1-10
     Nehemiah 9:26-31
     Luke 21:20-24

Su   *First Sunday of Advent*

M   Psalm 90
     Numbers 17:1-11
     2 Peter 3:1-18

Tu   Psalm 90
     2 Samuel 7:18-29
     Revelation 22:12-16

W   Psalm 90
     Isaiah 1:24-31
     Luke 11:29-32

Advent 2

Th   Luke 1:68-79
     Malachi 3:5-12
     Philippians 1:12-18a

F   Luke 11:68-79
     Malachi 3:13-18
     Philippians 1:18b-26

Sa   Luke 1:68-79
     Malachi 4:1-6
     Luke 9:1-6

Su   *Second Sunday of Advent*

M   Psalm 126
     Isaiah 40:1-11
     Romans 8:22-25

Tu   Psalm 126
     Isaiah 19:18-25
     2 Peter 1:2-15

W   Psalm 126
     Isaiah 35:3-7
     Luke 7:18-30

Advent 3

Th   Isaiah 12:2-6
     Amos 6:1-8
     2 Corinthians 8:1-15

F   Isaiah 12:2-6
     Amos 8:4-12
     2 Corinthians 9:1-15

Sa   Isaiah 12:2-6
     Amos 9:8-15
     Luke 1:57-66

Su   *Third Sunday of Advent*

M   Isaiah 11:1-9
     Numbers 16:1-19
     Hebrews 13:7-17

Tu   Isaiah 11:1-9
     Numbers 16:20-35
     Acts 28:23-31

W   Isaiah 11:1-9
     Micah 4:8-13
     Luke 7:31-35

Advent 4

Dated readings begin Dec. 22

Th   Psalm 80:1-7
     Jeremiah 31:31-34
     Hebrews 10:10-18

F   Psalm 80:1-7
     Isaiah 42:10-18
     Hebrews 10:32-39

Sa   Psalm 80:1-7
     Isaiah 66:7-11
     Luke 13:31-35

Su   *Fourth Sunday of Advent*

M   Psalm 113
     Genesis 25:19-28
     Colossians 1:15-20

Tu   Psalm 113
     Genesis 30:1-24
     Romans 8:18-30

W   Psalm 113
     Isaiah 42:14-21
     Luke 1:5-25

Days around Christmas

Dec 22   Luke 1:46b-55
         Micah 4:1-5
         Ephesians 2:11-22

Dec 23   Luke 1:46b-55
         Micah 4:6-8
         2 Peter 1:16-21

Dec 24–25   *Nativity of Our Lord*

Dec 26   Psalm 148
         2 Chronicles 24:17-24
         Acts 6:1-7; 7:51-60

Dec 27   Psalm 148
         Proverbs 8:32-36
         John 21:19b-24

Dec 28   Psalm 148
         Isaiah 54:1-13
         Revelation 21:1-7

Dec 29   Psalm 147:12-20
         1 Chronicles 28:1-10
         1 Corinthians 3:10-17

Dec 30   Psalm 147:12-20
         2 Chronicles 1:7-13
         Mark 13:32-37

Dec 31   Psalm 147:12-20
         1 Kings 3:5-14
         John 8:12-19

Jan 1   *Name of Jesus*

Jan | Psalm 147:12-20
2 | Proverbs 1:1-7
James 3:13-18

Days around Epiphany

Jan | Psalm 72
3 | Job 42:10-17
Luke 8:16-21

Jan | Psalm 72
4 | Isaiah 6:1-5
Acts 7:44-53

Jan | Psalm 72
5 | Jeremiah 31:7-14
John 1:[1-9] 10-18

Jan | *Epiphany of Our Lord*
6

Jan | Psalm 72
7 | Daniel 2:1-19
Ephesians 4:17—5:1

Jan | Psalm 72
8 | Daniel 2:24-49
Ephesians 5:15-20

Jan | Psalm 72
9 | Numbers 24:15-19
Luke 1:67-79

Epiphany 1

Th | Psalm 29
Ecclesiastes 1:1-11
1 Corinthians 1:18-31

F | Psalm 29
Ecclesiastes 2:1-11
1 Corinthians 2:1-10

Sa | Psalm 29
Ecclesiastes 3:1-15
1 Corinthians 2:11-16

Su | *Baptism of Our Lord*

M | Psalm 106:1-12
Judges 4:1-16
Ephesians 6:10-17

Tu | Psalm 106:1-12
Judges 5:12-21
1 John 5:13-21

W | Psalm 106:1-12
Numbers 27:1-11
Luke 11:33-36

Epiphany 2

Th | Psalm 36:5-10
Jeremiah 3:1-5
Acts 8:18-24

F | Psalm 36:5-10
Jeremiah 3:19-25
1 Corinthians 7:1-7

Sa | Psalm 36:5-10
Jeremiah 4:1-4
Luke 11:14-23

Su | *Second Sunday after Epiphany*

M | Psalm 145
Isaiah 54:1-8
Romans 12:9-21

Tu | Psalm 145
Song of Solomon 4:1-8
1 Corinthians 1:3-17

W | Psalm 145
Song of Solomon 4:9—5:1
Luke 5:33-39

Epiphany 3

Th | Psalm 19
Isaiah 61:1-7
Romans 7:1-6

F | Psalm 19
Nehemiah 2:1-10
Romans 12:1-8

Sa | Psalm 19
Nehemiah 5:1-13
Luke 2:39-52

Su | *Third Sunday after Epiphany*

M | Psalm 119:89-96
Jeremiah 36:1-10
1 Corinthians 14:1-12

Tu | Psalm 119:89-96
Jeremiah 36:11-26
2 Corinthians 7:2-12

W | Psalm 119:89-96
Jeremiah 36:27-32
Luke 4:38-44

Epiphany 4

Th | Psalm 71:1-6
2 Chronicles 34:1-7
Acts 10:44-48

F | Psalm 71:1-6
2 Chronicles 35:20-27
Acts 19:1-10

Sa | Psalm 71:1-6
2 Chronicles 36:11-21
John 1:43-51

Su | *Fourth Sunday after Epiphany*

M | Psalm 56
1 Kings 17:8-16
1 Corinthians 2:6-16

Tu | Psalm 56
2 Kings 5:1-14
1 Corinthians 14:13-25

W | Psalm 56
Jeremiah 1:11-19
Luke 19:41-44

Epiphany 5

Th | Psalm 138
Numbers 20:22-29
Acts 9:19b-25

F | Psalm 138
Numbers 27:12-23
Acts 9:26-31

Sa | Psalm 138
Judges 3:7-11
Luke 4:42-44

Su | *Fifth Sunday after Epiphany*

M | Psalm 115
Judges 5:1-11
1 Corinthians 14:26-40

Tu | Psalm 115
1 Samuel 9:15—10:1b
1 Timothy 3:1-9

W | Psalm 115
Isaiah 8:1-15
Luke 5:27-32

Epiphany 6

Th | Psalm 1
Jeremiah 13:12-19
Acts 13:26-34

F | Psalm 1
Jeremiah 13:20-27
1 Peter 1:17—2:1

Sa | Psalm 1
Jeremiah 17:1-4
Luke 11:24-28

Su | *Sixth Sunday after Epiphany*

M | Psalm 120
2 Kings 24:18—25:21
1 Corinthians 15:20-34

Tu | Psalm 120
Ezra 1:1-11
2 Corinthians 1:12-19

W | Psalm 120
Jeremiah 22:11-17
Luke 11:37-52

Epiphany 7

Th | Psalm 37:1-11, 39-40
Genesis 43:16-34
Romans 8:1-11

F | Psalm 37:1-11, 39-40
Genesis 44:1-17
1 John 2:12-17

Sa | Psalm 37:1-11, 39-40
Genesis 44:18-34
Luke 12:57-59

Su | *Seventh Sunday after Epiphany*

M | Psalm 38
Genesis 33:1-17
1 Corinthians 11:2-16

Tu | Psalm 38
1 Samuel 24:1-22
1 Corinthians 11:17-22, 27-33

W   Psalm 38
Leviticus 5:1-13
Luke 17:1-4

Epiphany 8
Th   Psalm 92:1-4, 12-15
Proverbs 13:1-12
Romans 5:12—6:2

F   Psalm 92:1-4, 12-15
Proverbs 15:1-9
1 Thessalonians 4:13-18

Sa   Psalm 92:1-4, 12-15
Isaiah 30:8-17
John 16:1-4a

Su   *Eighth Sunday after Epiphany*

M   Psalm 1
Jeremiah 24:1-10
1 Corinthians 16:1-12

Tu   Psalm 1
Jeremiah 29:10-19
1 Corinthians 16:13-24

W   Psalm 1
Proverbs 5:1-23
Luke 14:34-35

Transfiguration
Th   Psalm 99
Deuteronomy 9:1-5
Acts 3:11-16

F   Psalm 99
Deuteronomy 9:6-14
Acts 10:1-8

Sa   Psalm 99
Deuteronomy 9:15-24
Luke 10:21-24

Su   *Transfiguration of Our Lord*

M   Psalm 35:11-28
Exodus 35:1-29
Acts 10:9-23a

Tu   Psalm 35:11-28
Ezekiel 1:1—2:1
Acts 10:23b-33

Lent 1
W   *Ash Wednesday*

Th   Psalm 91:1-2, 9-16
Exodus 5:10-23
Acts 7:30-34

F   Psalm 91:1-2, 9-16
Exodus 6:1-13
Acts 7:35-42

Sa   Psalm 91:1-2, 9-16
Ecclesiastes 3:1-8
John 12:27-36

Su   *First Sunday in Lent*

M   Psalm 17
1 Chronicles 21:1-17
1 John 2:1-6

Tu   Psalm 17
Zechariah 3:1-10
2 Peter 2:4-21

W   Psalm 17
Job 1:1-22
Luke 21:34—22:6

Lent 2
Th   Psalm 27
Genesis 13:1-7, 14-18
Philippians 3:2-12

F   Psalm 27
Genesis 14:17-24
Philippians 3:17-20

Sa   Psalm 27
Psalm 118:26-29
Matthew 23:37-39

Su   *Second Sunday in Lent*

M   Psalm 105:1-15 [16-41] 42
Exodus 33:1-6
Romans 4:1-12

Tu   Psalm 105:1-15 [16-41] 42
Numbers 14:10b-24
1 Corinthians 10:1-13

W   Psalm 105:1-15 [16-41] 42
2 Chronicles 20:1-22
Luke 13:22-31

Lent 3
Th   Psalm 63:1-8
Daniel 3:19-30
Revelation 2:8-11

F   Psalm 63:1-8
Daniel 12:1-4
Revelation 3:1-6

Sa   Psalm 63:1-8
Isaiah 5:1-7
Luke 6:43-45

Su   *Third Sunday in Lent*

M   Psalm 39
Jeremiah 11:1-17
Romans 2:1-11

Tu   Psalm 39
Ezekiel 17:1-10
Romans 2:12-16

W   Psalm 39
Numbers 13:17-27
Luke 13:18-21

Lent 4
Th   Psalm 32
Joshua 4:1-13
2 Corinthians 4:16—5:5

F   Psalm 32
Joshua 4:14-24
2 Corinthians 5:6-15

Sa   Psalm 32
Exodus 32:7-14
Luke 15:1-10

Su   *Fourth Sunday in Lent*

M   Psalm 53
Leviticus 23:26-41
Revelation 19:1-8

Tu   Psalm 53
Leviticus 25:1-19
Revelation 19:9-10

W   Psalm 53
2 Kings 4:1-7
Luke 9:10-17

Lent 5
Th   Psalm 126
Isaiah 43:1-7
Philippians 2:19-24

F   Psalm 126
Isaiah 43:8-15
Philippians 2:25—3:1

Sa   Psalm 126
Exodus 12:21-27
John 11:45-57

Su   *Fifth Sunday in Lent*

M   Psalm 20
Exodus 40:1-15
Hebrews 10:19-25

Tu   Psalm 20
Judges 9:7-15
1 John 2:18-28

W   Psalm 20
Habakkuk 3:2-15
Luke 18:31-34

Lent 6
Th   Psalm 31:9-16
Isaiah 53:10-12
Hebrews 2:1-9

F   Psalm 31:9-16
Isaiah 54:9-10
Hebrews 2:10-18

Sa   Psalm 31:9-16
Leviticus 23:1-8
Luke 22:1-13

Su   *Sunday of the Passion*

M   *Monday in Holy Week*

Tu   *Tuesday in Holy Week*

W   *Wednesday in Holy Week*

Three Days—Easter
Th   *Maundy Thursday*

F   *Good Friday*

Sa   *Vigil of Easter*

Su   *Resurrection of Our Lord*

M   Psalm 118:1-2, 14-24
      Joshua 10:16-27
      1 Corinthians 5:6b-8

Tu   Psalm 118:1-2, 14-24
      Judges 4:17-23; 5:24-31a
      Revelation 12:1-12

W   Psalm 118:1-2, 14-24
      2 Samuel 6:1-15
      Luke 24:1-12

Easter 2

Th   Psalm 150
      1 Samuel 17:1-23
      Acts 5:12-16

F   Psalm 150
      1 Samuel 17:19-32
      Acts 5:17-26

Sa   Psalm 150
      1 Samuel 17:32-51
      Luke 24:36-40

Su   *Second Sunday of Easter*

M   Psalm 122
      Esther 7:1-10
      Revelation 1:9-20

Tu   Psalm 122
      Esther 8:1-17
      Revelation 2:8-11

W   Psalm 122
      Esther 9:1-5, 18-23
      Luke 12:4-12

Easter 3

Th   Psalm 30
      Isaiah 5:11-17
      Revelation 3:14-22

F   Psalm 30
      Isaiah 6:1-4
      Revelation 4:1-11

Sa   Psalm 30
      Genesis 18:1-8
      Luke 14:12-14

Su   *Third Sunday of Easter*

M   Psalm 121
      Ezekiel 1:1-25
      Acts 9:19b-31

Tu   Psalm 121
      Ezekiel 1:26—2:1
      Acts 26:1-18

W   Psalm 121
      Isaiah 6:1-8
      Luke 5:1-11

Easter 4

Th   Psalm 23
      Ezekiel 11:1-25
      Revelation 5:1-10

F   Psalm 23
      Ezekiel 20:39-44
      Revelation 6:1—7:4

Sa   Psalm 23
      Ezekiel 28:25-26
      Luke 12:29-32

Su   *Fourth Sunday of Easter*

M   Psalm 100
      Ezekiel 37:15-28
      Revelation 15:1-4

Tu   Psalm 100
      Ezekiel 45:1-9
      Acts 9:32-35

W   Psalm 100
      Jeremiah 50:17-20
      John 10:31-42

Easter 5

Th   Psalm 148
      Ezekiel 2:8—3:11
      Revelation 10:1-11

F   Psalm 148
      Daniel 7:13-14
      Revelation 11:15

Sa   Psalm 148
      Daniel 7:27
      Revelation 11:16-19

Su   *Fifth Sunday of Easter*

M   Psalm 133
      1 Samuel 20:1-23, 35-42
      Acts 11:19-26

Tu   Psalm 133
      2 Samuel 1:4-27
      Acts 11:27-30

W   Psalm 133
      Leviticus 19:9-18
      Luke 10:25-28

Easter 6

Th   Psalm 67
      Proverbs 2:1-5
      Acts 15:36-41

F   Psalm 67
      Proverbs 2:6-8
      Acts 16:1-8

Sa   Psalm 67
      Proverbs 2:9-15
      Luke 19:1-10

Su   *Sixth Sunday of Easter*

M   Psalm 93
      1 Chronicles 12:16-22
      Revelation 21:5-14

Tu   Psalm 93
      2 Chronicles 15:1-15
      Revelation 21:15-22

W   Psalm 93
      2 Chronicles 34:20-33
      Luke 2:25-38

Easter 7

Th   *Ascension of Our Lord*

F   Psalm 97
      Exodus 33:12-17
      Revelation 22:6-9

Sa   Psalm 97
      Exodus 33:18-23
      John 1:14-18

Su   *Seventh Sunday of Easter*

M   Psalm 29
      Exodus 40:16-38
      Acts 16:35-40

Tu   Psalm 29
      2 Chronicles 5:2-14
      Acts 26:19-29

W   Psalm 29
      Ezekiel 3:12-21
      Luke 9:18-27

Pentecost

Th   Psalm 104:24-34, 35b
      Isaiah 32:11-17
      Galatians 5:16-25

F   Psalm 104:24-34, 35b
      Isaiah 44:1-4
      Galatians 6:7-10

Sa   Psalm 104:24-34, 35b
      2 Kings 2:1-15a
      Luke 1:5-17

Su   *Day of Pentecost*

M   Psalm 48
      Joel 2:18-29
      1 Corinthians 2:1-11

Tu   Psalm 48
      Ezekiel 11:14-25
      1 Corinthians 2:12-16

W   Psalm 48
      Numbers 24:1-14
      Luke 1:26-38

Holy Trinity

Th   Psalm 8
      Proverbs 3:13-18
      Ephesians 1:17-19

F   Psalm 8
      Proverbs 3:19-26
      Ephesians 4:1-6

Sa   Psalm 8
      Proverbs 4:1-9
      Luke 2:41-52

Su *The Holy Trinity*

M Psalm 124
Proverbs 7:1-4
Ephesians 4:7-16

Tu Psalm 124
Proverbs 8:4-21
Ephesians 5:15-20

W Psalm 124
Daniel 1:1-21
Luke 1:46b-55

Sunday, May 24–28

Th Psalm 92:1-4, 12-15
Proverbs 13:1-12
Romans 5:12—6:2

F Psalm 92:1-4, 12-15
Proverbs 15:1-9
1 Thessalonians 4:13-18

Sa Psalm 92:1-4, 12-15
Isaiah 30:8-17
John 16:1-4a

Su *May 24–28 (Lectionary 8)*

M Psalm 1
Jeremiah 24:1-10
1 Corinthians 16:1-12

Tu Psalm 1
Jeremiah 29:10-19
1 Corinthians 16:13-24

W Psalm 1
Proverbs 5:1-23
Luke 14:34-35

The following readings relate to the complementary series of the Sunday lectionary.

Sunday, May 29–June 4

Th Psalm 96:1-9
1 Kings 6:23-38
2 Corinthians 5:11-17

F Psalm 96:1-9
1 Kings 8:14-21
2 Corinthians 11:1-6

Sa Psalm 96:1-9
1 Kings 8:31-40
Luke 4:31-37

Su *May 29–June 4 (Lectionary 9)*

M Psalm 5
Jonah 4:1-11
Acts 8:26-40

Tu Psalm 5
Nehemiah 1:1-11
Acts 3:1-10

W Psalm 5
Isaiah 56:1-8
Mark 7:24-30

Sunday, June 5–11

Th Psalm 30
2 Samuel 14:1-11
Acts 22:6-21

F Psalm 30
2 Samuel 14:12-24
Acts 26:1-11

Sa Psalm 30
2 Samuel 14:25-33
Matthew 9:2-8

Su *June 5–11 (Lectionary 10)*

M Psalm 68:1-10, 19-20
Genesis 22:1-14
Galatians 2:1-10

Tu Psalm 68:1-10, 19-20
Judges 11:29-40
Galatians 2:11-14

W Psalm 68:1-10, 19-20
Jeremiah 8:14-22
Luke 8:40-56

Sunday, June 12–18

Th Psalm 32
2 Samuel 13:23-39
James 4:1-7

F Psalm 32
2 Samuel 15:1-12
Romans 11:1-10

Sa Psalm 32
2 Samuel 18:28—19:8
Luke 5:17-26

Su *June 12–18 (Lectionary 11)*

M Psalm 130
2 Chronicles 29:1-19
Galatians 3:1-9

Tu Psalm 130
2 Chronicles 30:1-12
Galatians 3:10-14

W Psalm 130
2 Chronicles 30:13-27
Mark 2:1-12

Sunday, June 19–25

Th Psalm 22:19-28
Isaiah 56:9-12
Romans 2:17-29

F Psalm 22:19-28
Isaiah 57:1-13
Galatians 3:15-22

Sa Psalm 22:19-28
Isaiah 59:1-8
Matthew 9:27-34

Su *June 19–25 (Lectionary 12)*

M Psalm 64
Job 18:1-21
1 Corinthians 1:18-31

Tu Psalm 64
Job 19:1-22
Ephesians 2:11-22

W Psalm 64
Ezekiel 32:1-10
Luke 9:37-43a

Sunday, June 26–July 2

Th Psalm 16
Leviticus 9:22—10:11
2 Corinthians 13:5-10

F Psalm 16
2 Kings 1:1-16
Galatians 4:8-20

Sa Psalm 16
Deuteronomy 32:15-27,
39-43
Luke 9:21-27

Su *June 26–July 2 (Lectionary 13)*

M Psalm 140
Genesis 24:34-41, 50-67
1 John 2:7-11

Tu Psalm 140
Jeremiah 3:15-18
Ephesians 5:6-20

W Psalm 140
Jeremiah 23:16-22
Matthew 10:16-25

Sunday, July 3–9

Th Psalm 66:1-9
2 Kings 21:1-15
Romans 7:14-25

F Psalm 66:1-9
Jeremiah 51:47-58
2 Corinthians 8:1-7

Sa Psalm 66:1-9
Zechariah 14:10-21
Luke 9:1-6

Su *July 3–9 (Lectionary 14)*

M Psalm 119:73-80
Jeremiah 6:10-19
Acts 19:21-27

Tu Psalm 119:73-80
Jeremiah 8:4-13
Acts 19:28-41

W Psalm 119:73-80
Joshua 23:1-16
Luke 10:13-16

Sunday, July 10–16

Th Psalm 25:1-10
    Genesis 41:14-36
    James 2:14-26

F   Psalm 25:1-10
    Genesis 41:37-49
    Acts 7:9-16

Sa Psalm 25:1-10
    Leviticus 19:1-4, 32-37
    John 3:16-21

Su *July 10–16 (Lectionary 15)*

M   Psalm 25:11-20
    Job 24:1-8
    James 2:1-7

Tu Psalm 25:11-20
    Proverbs 19:1-17
    1 John 3:11-17

W   Psalm 25:11-20
    Ecclesiastes 9:13-18
    Matthew 25:31-46

Sunday, July 17–23

Th Psalm 15
    Genesis 12:10-20
    Hebrews 5:1-6

F   Psalm 15
    Genesis 13:1-18
    Ephesians 3:14-21

Sa Psalm 15
    Genesis 14:1-16
    Luke 8:4-10

Su *July 17–23 (Lectionary 16)*

M   Psalm 119:97-104
    Exodus 18:1-12
    Colossians 1:27—2:7

Tu Psalm 119:97-104
    Proverbs 9:1-18
    1 John 2:1-6

W   Psalm 119:97-104
    Deuteronomy 12:1-12
    John 6:41-51

Sunday, July 24–30

Th Psalm 138
    Esther 2:19—3:6
    Acts 1:15-20

F   Psalm 138
    Esther 3:7-15
    Acts 2:22-36

Sa Psalm 138
    Esther 4:1-17
    Luke 8:22-25

Su *July 24–30 (Lectionary 17)*

M   Psalm 55:16-23
    Esther 5:1-14
    Colossians 2:16—3:1

Tu Psalm 55:16-23
    Esther 6:1—7:6
    Romans 9:30—10:4

W   Psalm 55:16-23
    Esther 7:7—8:17
    Matthew 5:43-48

Sunday, July 31–August 6

Th Psalm 49:1-12
    Proverbs 23:1-11
    Romans 11:33-36

F   Psalm 49:1-12
    Proverbs 24:1-12
    Ephesians 4:17-24

Sa Psalm 49:1-12
    Ecclesiastes 1:1-11
    Mark 10:17-22

Su *July 31–August 6*
    (Lectionary 18)

M   Psalm 127
    Ecclesiastes 2:1-17
    Colossians 3:18—4:1

Tu Psalm 127
    Ecclesiastes 3:16—4:8
    Colossians 4:2-6

W   Psalm 127
    Ecclesiastes 12:1-8, 13-14
    Luke 12:22-31

Sunday, August 7–13

Th Psalm 33:12-22
    Job 21:1-16
    Romans 9:1-9

F   Psalm 33:12-22
    Ecclesiastes 6:1-6
    Acts 7:1-8

Sa Psalm 33:12-22
    Genesis 11:27-32
    Matthew 6:19-24

Su *August 7–13 (Lectionary 19)*

M   Psalm 89:1-18
    2 Chronicles 33:1-17
    Hebrews 11:1-7

Tu Psalm 89:1-18
    2 Chronicles 34:22-33
    Hebrews 11:17-28

W   Psalm 89:1-18
    Jeremiah 33:14-26
    Luke 12:41-48

Sunday, August 14–20

Th Psalm 82
    Joshua 7:1, 10-26
    Hebrews 10:26-31

F   Psalm 82
    1 Samuel 5:1-12
    Hebrews 10:32-39

Sa Psalm 82
    1 Samuel 6:1-16
    Matthew 24:15-27

Su *August 14–20*
    (Lectionary 20)

M   Psalm 32
    Jeremiah 23:30-40
    1 John 4:1-6

Tu Psalm 32
    Jeremiah 25:15-29
    Acts 7:44-53

W   Psalm 32
    Jeremiah 25:30-38
    Luke 19:45-48

Sunday, August 21–27

Th Psalm 103:1-8
    Numbers 15:32-41
    Hebrews 12:3-17

F   Psalm 103:1-8
    2 Chronicles 8:12-15
    Acts 17:1-9

Sa Psalm 103:1-8
    Nehemiah 13:15-22
    Luke 6:1-5

Su *August 21–27*
    (Lectionary 21)

M   Psalm 109:21-31
    Ezekiel 20:1-17
    Hebrews 3:7—4:11

Tu Psalm 109:21-31
    Ezekiel 20:18-32
    Revelation 3:7-13

W   Psalm 109:21-31
    Ezekiel 20:33-44
    Luke 6:6-11

Sunday, August 28–September 3

Th Psalm 112
    Proverbs 15:13-17
    1 Peter 3:8-12

F   Psalm 112
    Proverbs 18:6-12
    1 Peter 4:7-11

Sa Psalm 112
    Proverbs 21:1-4, 24-26
    Matthew 20:20-28

Su *August 28–September 3*
    (Lectionary 22)

M   Psalm 119:65-72
    2 Chronicles 12:1-12
    Hebrews 13:7-21

Tu Psalm 119:65-72
    Isaiah 2:12-17
    Titus 1:1-9

W   Psalm 119:65-72
     Isaiah 57:14-21
     Luke 14:15-24

Sunday, September 4–10
Th   Psalm 1
     Genesis 39:1-23
     Philippians 2:25-30

F   Psalm 1
     Deuteronomy 7:12-26
     Colossians 4:7-17

Sa   Psalm 1
     Deuteronomy 29:2-20
     Matthew 10:34-42

Su   *September 4–10*
     (Lectionary 23)

M   Psalm 101
     2 Kings 17:24-41
     1 Timothy 3:14—4:5

Tu   Psalm 101
     2 Kings 18:9-18
     1 Timothy 4:6-16

W   Psalm 101
     2 Kings 18:19-25; 19:1-7
     Luke 18:18-30

Sunday, September 11–17
Th   Psalm 51:1-10
     Genesis 6:1-6
     1 Timothy 1:1-11

F   Psalm 51:1-10
     Genesis 7:6-10; 8:1-5
     2 Peter 2:1-10a

Sa   Psalm 51:1-10
     Genesis 8:20—9:7
     John 10:11-21

Su   *September 11–17*
     (Lectionary 24)

M   Psalm 73
     Amos 7:1-6
     1 Timothy 1:18-20

Tu   Psalm 73
     Jonah 3:1-10
     2 Peter 3:8-13

W   Psalm 73
     Job 40:6-14; 42:1-6
     Luke 22:31-33, 54-62

Sunday, September 18–24
Th   Psalm 113
     Exodus 23:1-9
     Romans 3:1-8

F   Psalm 113
     Ezekiel 22:17-31
     Romans 8:31-39

Sa   Psalm 113
     Isaiah 5:8-23
     Mark 12:41-44

Su   *September 18–24*
     (Lectionary 25)

M   Psalm 12
     Proverbs 14:12-31
     Acts 4:1-12

Tu   Psalm 12
     Proverbs 17:1-5
     1 Corinthians 9:19-23

W   Psalm 12
     Proverbs 21:10-16
     Luke 20:45—21:4

Sunday, September 25– October 1
Th   Psalm 146
     Proverbs 22:2-16
     2 Corinthians 8:8-15

F   Psalm 146
     Proverbs 28:3-10
     Ephesians 2:1-10

Sa   Psalm 146
     Proverbs 28:11-28
     Luke 9:43b-48

Su   *September 25–October 1*
     (Lectionary 26)

M   Psalm 62
     Amos 6:8-14
     Revelation 3:14-22

Tu   Psalm 62
     Hosea 10:9-15
     James 5:1-6

W   Psalm 62
     Hosea 12:2-14
     Matthew 19:16-22

Sunday, October 2–8
Th   Psalm 37:1-9
     2 Kings 18:1-8, 28-36
     Revelation 2:8-11

F   Psalm 37:1-9
     2 Kings 19:8-20, 35-37
     Revelation 2:12-29

Sa   Psalm 37:1-9
     Isaiah 7:1-9
     Matthew 20:29-34

Su   *October 2–8 (Lectionary 27)*

M   Psalm 3
     Habakkuk 1:5-17
     James 1:2-11

Tu   Psalm 3
     Habakkuk 2:5-11
     1 John 5:1-5, 13-21

W   Psalm 3
     Habakkuk 2:12-20
     Mark 11:12-14, 20-24

Sunday, October 9–15
Th   Psalm 111
     Leviticus 14:33-53
     2 Timothy 1:13-18

F   Psalm 111
     Numbers 4:34—5:4
     2 Timothy 2:1-7

Sa   Psalm 111
     Numbers 12:1-15
     Luke 5:12-16

Su   *October 9–15 (Lectionary 28)*

M   Psalm 61
     2 Kings 5:15-19a
     Acts 26:24-29

Tu   Psalm 61
     2 Kings 5:19b-27
     Ephesians 6:10-20

W   Psalm 61
     2 Kings 15:1-7
     Matthew 10:5-15

Sunday, October 16–22
Th   Psalm 121
     Isaiah 54:11-17
     Acts 17:22-34

F   Psalm 121
     Genesis 31:43—32:2
     2 Timothy 2:14-26

Sa   Psalm 121
     Genesis 32:3-21
     Mark 10:46-52

Su   *October 16–22*
     (Lectionary 29)

M   Psalm 57
     1 Samuel 25:2-22
     1 Corinthians 6:1-11

Tu   Psalm 57
     1 Samuel 25:23-35
     James 5:7-12

W   Psalm 57
     1 Samuel 25:36-42
     Luke 22:39-46

Sunday, October 23–29
Th   Psalm 84:1-7
     Jeremiah 9:1-16
     2 Timothy 3:1-9

F   Psalm 84:1-7
     Jeremiah 9:17-26
     2 Timothy 3:10-15

Sa   Psalm 84:1-7
     Jeremiah 14:1-6
     Luke 1:46-55

Su   *Sunday, October 23–29*
     (Lectionary 30)

M	Psalm 84:8-12	**Sunday, November 6–12**		Su	*November 13–19*

M   Psalm 84:8-12
1 Samuel 2:1-10
1 Peter 4:12-19

Tu Psalm 84:8-12
Daniel 5:1-12
1 Peter 5:1-11

W Psalm 84:8-12
Daniel 5:13-31
Matthew 21:28-32

Sunday, October 30–November 5

Th Psalm 32:1-7
Proverbs 15:8-11, 24-33
2 Corinthians 1:1-11

F   Psalm 32:1-7
Job 22:21—23:17
2 Peter 1:1-11

Sa Psalm 32:1-7
Isaiah 1:1-9
John 8:39-47

Su *October 3–November 5*
(Lectionary 31)

M   Psalm 50
Nehemiah 13:1-3, 23-31
1 Corinthians 5:9-13

Tu Psalm 50
Zechariah 7:1-14
Jude 5-21

W Psalm 50
Amos 5:12-24
Luke 19:11-27

Sunday, November 6–12

Th Psalm 17:1-9
Deuteronomy 25:5-10
Acts 22:22—23:11

F   Psalm 17:1-9
Genesis 38:1-26
Acts 24:10-23

Sa Psalm 17:1-9
Exodus 3:13-20
Luke 20:1-8

Su *November 6–12*
(Lectionary 32)

M   Psalm 123
Job 20:1-11
2 Peter 1:16-21

Tu Psalm 123
Job 21:1, 17-34
2 John 1-13

W Psalm 123
Job 25:1—26:14
John 5:19-29

Sunday, November 13–19

Th Psalm 98
1 Samuel 28:3-19
Romans 1:18-25

F   Psalm 98
2 Samuel 21:1-14
2 Thessalonians 1:3-12

Sa Psalm 98
Ezekiel 10:1-19
Luke 17:20-37

Su *November 13–19*
(Lectionary 33)

M   Psalm 141
Ezekiel 11:14-25
Ephesians 4:25—5:2

Tu Psalm 141
Ezekiel 39:21—40:4
1 Corinthians 10:23—11:1

W Psalm 141
Ezekiel 43:1-12
Matthew 23:37—24:14

Christ the King

Th Psalm 46
2 Chronicles 18:12-22
Hebrews 9:23-28

F   Psalm 46
Zechariah 11:1-17
1 Peter 1:3-9

Sa Psalm 46
Jeremiah 22:18-30
Luke 18:15-17

Su *November 20–26*
(Lectionary 34)

M   Psalm 24
Jeremiah 46:18-28
Revelation 21:5-27

Tu Psalm 24
Isaiah 33:17-22
Revelation 22:8-21

W Psalm 24
Isaiah 60:8-16
Luke 1:1-4

The following readings relate to the semicontinuous series of the Sunday lectionary.

Sunday, May 29–June 4

Th Psalm 96
1 Kings 12:20-33
2 Corinthians 5:11-17

F   Psalm 96
1 Kings 16:29-34
2 Corinthians 11:1-6

Sa Psalm 96
1 Kings 18:1-19
Luke 4:31-37

Su *May 29–June 4 (Lectionary 9)*

M   Psalm 135
Ezekiel 8:1-18
Acts 8:26-40

Tu Psalm 135
Ezekiel 14:1-11
Acts 3:1-10

W Psalm 135
Ezekiel 14:12-23
Mark 7:24-30

Sunday, June 5–11

Th Psalm 146
Exodus 29:1-9
Acts 22:6-21

F   Psalm 146
Numbers 15:17-26
Acts 26:1-11

Sa Psalm 146
Joshua 9:1-27
Matthew 9:2-8

Su *June 5–11 (Lectionary 10)*

M   Psalm 68:1-10, 19-20
Job 22:1-20
Galatians 2:1-10

Tu Psalm 68:1-10, 19-20
Job 24:9-25
Galatians 2:11-14

W Psalm 68:1-10, 19-20
Job 31:16-23
Luke 8:40-56

Sunday, June 12–18

Th Psalm 5:1-8
1 Kings 20:1-22
James 4:1-7

F   Psalm 5:1-8
1 Kings 20:23-34
Romans 11:1-10

Sa Psalm 5:1-8
1 Kings 20:35-43
Luke 5:17-26

Su *June 12–18 (Lectionary 11)*

M   Psalm 83
Genesis 31:17-35
Galatians 3:1-9

Tu Psalm 83
2 Samuel 19:31-43
Galatians 3:10-14

W Psalm 83
Malachi 3:5-12
Mark 2:1-12

Sunday, June 19–25

Th Psalms 42 and 43
    Genesis 24:1-21
    Romans 2:17-29

F   Psalms 42 and 43
    Job 6:14-30
    Galatians 3:15-22

Sa Psalms 42 and 43
    Proverbs 11:3-13
    Matthew 9:27-34

Su *June 19–25 (Lectionary 12)*

M   Psalm 59
    2 Kings 9:1-13
    1 Corinthians 1:18-31

Tu Psalm 59
    2 Kings 9:14-26
    Ephesians 2:11-22

W   Psalm 59
    2 Kings 9:30-37
    Luke 9:37-43a

Sunday, June 26–July 2

Th Psalm 77:1-2, 11-20
    1 Kings 22:29-40, 51-53
    2 Corinthians 13:5-10

F   Psalm 77:1-2, 11-20
    2 Kings 1:1-12
    Galatians 4:8-20

Sa Psalm 77:1-2, 11-20
    2 Kings 1:13-18; 2:3-5
    Luke 9:21-27

Su *June 26–July 2 (Lectionary 13)*

M   Psalm 75
    2 Kings 2:15-22
    1 John 2:7-11

Tu Psalm 75
    2 Kings 3:4-20
    Ephesians 5:6-20

W   Psalm 75
    2 Kings 4:1-7
    Matthew 10:16-25

Sunday, July 3–9

Th Psalm 30
    2 Kings 4:8-17
    Romans 7:14-25

F   Psalm 30
    2 Kings 4:18-31
    2 Corinthians 8:1-7

Sa Psalm 30
    2 Kings 4:32-37
    Luke 9:1-6

Su *July 3–9 (Lectionary 14)*

M   Psalm 6
    2 Kings 5:15-19a
    Acts 19:21-27

Tu Psalm 6
    2 Kings 5:19b-27
    Acts 19:28-41

W   Psalm 6
    2 Kings 6:1-7
    Luke 10:13-16

Sunday, July 10–16

Th Psalm 82
    Amos 1:1—2:3
    James 2:14-26

F   Psalm 82
    Amos 2:4-11
    Acts 7:9-16

Sa Psalm 82
    Amos 2:12—3:8
    John 3:16-21

Su *July 10–16 (Lectionary 15)*

M   Psalm 7
    Amos 3:9—4:5
    James 2:1-7

Tu Psalm 7
    Amos 4:6-13
    1 John 3:11-17

W   Psalm 7
    Amos 5:1-9
    Matthew 25:31-46

Sunday, July 17–23

Th Psalm 52
    Amos 5:10-17
    Hebrews 5:1-6

F   Psalm 52
    Amos 5:18-27
    Ephesians 3:14-21

Sa Psalm 52
    Amos 6:1-14
    Luke 8:4-10

Su *July 17–23 (Lectionary 16)*

M   Psalm 119:17-32
    Amos 7:1-6
    Colossians 1:27—2:7

Tu Psalm 119:17-32
    Amos 8:13—9:4
    1 John 2:1-6

W   Psalm 119:17-32
    Amos 9:5-15
    John 6:41-51

Sunday, July 24–30

Th Psalm 85
    Hosea 4:1-19
    Acts 1:15-20

F   Psalm 85
    Hosea 5:1-15
    Acts 2:22-36

Sa Psalm 85
    Hosea 1:11—2:15
    Luke 8:22-25

Su *July 24–30 (Lectionary 17)*

M   Psalm 44
    Hosea 2:14—3:5
    Colossians 2:16—3:1

Tu Psalm 44
    Hosea 6:1-10
    Romans 9:30—10:4

W   Psalm 44
    Hosea 6:11—7:16
    Matthew 5:43-48

Sunday, July 31–August 6

Th Psalm 107:1-9, 43
    Hosea 8:1-14
    Romans 11:33-36

F   Psalm 107:1-9, 43
    Hosea 9:1-17
    Ephesians 4:17-24

Sa Psalm 107:1-9, 43
    Hosea 10:1-15
    Mark 10:17-22

Su *July 31–August 6*
    (Lectionary 18)

M   Psalm 60
    Hosea 11:12—12:14
    Colossians 3:18—4:1

Tu Psalm 60
    Hosea 13:1-16
    Colossians 4:2-6

W   Psalm 60
    Hosea 14:1-9
    Luke 12:22-31

Sunday, August 7–13

Th Psalm 50:1-8, 22-23
    Isaiah 9:8-17
    Romans 9:1-9

F   Psalm 50:1-8, 22-23
    Isaiah 9:18—10:4
    Acts 7:1-8

Sa Psalm 50:1-8, 22-23
    Isaiah 1:2-9, 21-23
    Matthew 6:19-24

Su *August 7–13 (Lectionary 19)*

M   Psalm 11
    Isaiah 2:1-4
    Hebrews 11:1-7

Tu Psalm 11
    Isaiah 24:1-13
    Hebrews 11:17-28

W   Psalm 11
    Isaiah 24:14-23
    Luke 12:41-48

Sunday, August 14–20

Th Psalm 80:1-2, 8-19
Isaiah 2:5-11
Hebrews 10:26-31

F Psalm 80:1-2, 8-19
Isaiah 3:1-17
Hebrews 10:32-39

Sa Psalm 80:1-2, 8-19
Isaiah 3:18—4:6
Matthew 24:15-27

Su *August 14–20*
(Lectionary 20)

M Psalm 74
Isaiah 5:8-23
1 John 4:1-6

Tu Psalm 74
Isaiah 5:24-30
Acts 7:44-53

W Psalm 74
Isaiah 27:1-13
Luke 19:45-48

Sunday, August 21–27

Th Psalm 71:1-6
Jeremiah 6:1-19
Hebrews 12:3-17

F Psalm 71:1-6
Jeremiah 6:20-30
Acts 17:1-9

Sa Psalm 71:1-6
Jeremiah 1:1-3, 11-19
Luke 6:1-5

Su *August 21–27 (Lectionary 21)*

M Psalm 10
Jeremiah 7:1-15
Hebrews 3:7—4:11

Tu Psalm 10
Jeremiah 7:16-26
Revelation 3:7-13

W Psalm 10
Jeremiah 7:27-34
Luke 6:6-11

Sunday, August 28–September 3

Th Psalm 81:1, 10-16
Jeremiah 11:1-17
1 Peter 3:8-12

F Psalm 81:1, 10-16
Jeremiah 12:1-13
1 Peter 4:7-11

Sa Psalm 81:1, 10-16
Jeremiah 2:1-3, 14-22
Matthew 20:20-28

Su *August 28–September 3*
(Lectionary 22)

M Psalm 58
Jeremiah 2:23-37
Hebrews 13:7-21

Tu Psalm 58
Jeremiah 3:1-14
Titus 1:1-9

W Psalm 58
Jeremiah 3:15-25
Luke 14:15-24

Sunday, September 4–10

Th Psalm 139:1-6, 13-18
Jeremiah 15:10-21
Philippians 2:25-30

F Psalm 139:1-6, 13-18
Jeremiah 16:14—17:4
Colossians 4:7-17

Sa Psalm 139:1-6, 13-18
Jeremiah 17:14-27
Matthew 10:34-42

Su *September 4–10*
(Lectionary 23)

M Psalm 2
Jeremiah 18:12-23
1 Timothy 3:14—4:5

Tu Psalm 2
Jeremiah 19:1-15
1 Timothy 4:6-16

W Psalm 2
Jeremiah 20:1-18
Luke 18:18-30

Sunday, September 11–17

Th Psalm 14
Jeremiah 13:20-27
1 Timothy 1:1-11

F Psalm 14
Jeremiah 4:1-10
2 Peter 2:1-10a

Sa Psalm 14
Jeremiah 4:13-21, 29-31
John 10:11-21

Su *September 11–17*
(Lectionary 24)

M Psalm 94
Jeremiah 5:1-17
1 Timothy 1:18-20

Tu Psalm 94
Jeremiah 5:18-31
2 Peter 3:8-13

W Psalm 94
Jeremiah 14:1-10, 17-22
Luke 22:31-33, 54-62

Sunday, September 18–24

Th Psalm 79:1-9
Jeremiah 12:14—13:11
Romans 3:1-8

F Psalm 79:1-9
Jeremiah 8:1-13
Romans 8:31-39

Sa Psalm 79:1-9
Jeremiah 8:14-17; 9:2-11
Mark 12:41-44

Su *September 18–24*
(Lectionary 25)

M Psalm 106:40-48
Jeremiah 9:12-26
Acts 4:1-12

Tu Psalm 106:40-48
Jeremiah 10:1-16
1 Corinthians 9:19-23

W Psalm 106:40-48
Jeremiah 10:17-25
Luke 20:45—21:4

Sunday, September 25–October 1

Th Psalm 91:1-6, 14-16
Jeremiah 23:9-22
2 Corinthians 8:8-15

F Psalm 91:1-6, 14-16
Jeremiah 23:23-32
Ephesians 2:1-10

Sa Psalm 91:1-6, 14-16
Jeremiah 24:1-10
Luke 9:43b-48

Su *September 25–October 1*
(Lectionary 26)

M Psalm 119:49-56
Jeremiah 32:16-35
Revelation 3:14-22

Tu Psalm 119:49-56
Jeremiah 32:36-44
James 5:1-6

W Psalm 119:49-56
Jeremiah 33:1-13
Matthew 19:16-22

Sunday, October 2–8

Th Lamentations 3:19-26
Jeremiah 52:1-11
Revelation 2:8-11

F Lamentations 3:19-26
Jeremiah 52:12-30
Revelation 2:12-29

Sa Lamentations 3:19-26
Lamentations 1:7-15
Matthew 20:29-34

Su *October 2–8 (Lectionary 27)*

M Psalm 137
Lamentations 1:16-22
James 1:2-11

Tu Psalm 137
Lamentations 2:13-22
1 John 5:1-5, 13-21

W Psalm 137
Lamentations 5:1-22
Mark 11:12-14, 20-24

Sunday, October 9–15

Th Psalm 66:1-12
Jeremiah 25:1-14
2 Timothy 1:13-18

F Psalm 66:1-12
Jeremiah 27:1-22
2 Timothy 2:1-7

Sa Psalm 66:1-12
Jeremiah 28:1-17
Luke 5:12-16

Su *October 9–15 (Lectionary 28)*

M Psalm 102:1-17
Jeremiah 29:8-23
Acts 26:24-29

Tu Psalm 102:1-17
Jeremiah 29:24-32
Ephesians 6:10-20

W Psalm 102:1-17
Jeremiah 25:15-32
Matthew 10:5-15

Sunday, October 16–22

Th Psalm 119:97-104
Jeremiah 26:1-15
Acts 17:22-34

F Psalm 119:97-104
Jeremiah 26:16-24
2 Timothy 2:14-26

Sa Psalm 119:97-104
Jeremiah 31:15-26
Mark 10:46-52

Su *October 16–22*
(Lectionary 29)

M Psalm 129
Jeremiah 38:14-28
1 Corinthians 6:1-11

Tu Psalm 129
Jeremiah 39:1-18
James 5:7-12

W Psalm 129
Jeremiah 50:1-7, 17-20
Luke 22:39-46

Sunday, October 23–29

Th Psalm 65
Joel 1:1-20
2 Timothy 3:1-9

F Psalm 65
Joel 2:1-11
2 Timothy 3:10-15

Sa Psalm 65
Joel 2:12-22
Luke 1:46-55

Su *October 23–29*
(Lectionary 30)

M Psalm 87
Joel 3:1-8
1 Peter 4:12-19

Tu Psalm 87
Joel 3:9-16
1 Peter 5:1-11

W Psalm 87
Joel 3:17-20
Matthew 21:28-32

Sunday, October 30–November 5

Th Psalm 119:137-144
Jeremiah 33:14-26
2 Corinthians 1:1-11

F Psalm 119:137-144
Habakkuk 1:5-17
2 Peter 1:1-11

Sa Psalm 119:137-144
Habakkuk 2:5-11
John 8:39-47

Su *October 3–November 5*
(Lectionary 31)

M Psalm 142
Habakkuk 2:12-20
1 Corinthians 5:9-13

Tu Psalm 142
Habakkuk 3:1-16
Jude 5-21

W Psalm 142
Habakkuk 3:17-19
Luke 19:11-27

Sunday, November 6–12

Th Psalm 145:1-5, 17-21
Zechariah 1:1-17
Acts 22:22—23:11

F Psalm 145:1-5, 17-21
Zechariah 6:9-15
Acts 24:10-23

Sa Psalm 145:1-5, 17-21
Haggai 1:1-15a
Luke 20:1-8

Su *November 6–12*
(Lectionary 32)

M Psalm 98
Haggai 2:10-19
2 Peter 1:16-21

Tu Psalm 98
Haggai 2:20-23
2 John 1-13

W Psalm 98
Zechariah 8:1-17
John 5:19-29

Sunday, November 13–19

Th Isaiah 12
Isaiah 57:14-21
Romans 1:18-25

F Isaiah 12
Isaiah 59:1-15a
2 Thessalonians 1:3-12

Sa Isaiah 12
Isaiah 59:15b-21
Luke 17:20-37

Su *November 13–19*
(Lectionary 33)

M Psalm 76
Isaiah 60:17-22
Ephesians 4:25—5:2

Tu Psalm 76
Isaiah 66:1-13
1 Corinthians 10:23—11:1

W Psalm 76
Isaiah 66:14-24
Matthew 23:37—24:14

Christ the King

Th Luke 1:68-79
Jeremiah 21:1-14
Hebrews 9:23-28

F Luke 1:68-79
Jeremiah 22:1-17
1 Peter 1:3-9

Sa Luke 1:68-79
Jeremiah 22:18-30
Luke 18:15-17

Su *November 20–26*
(Lectionary 34)

M Psalm 117
Jeremiah 30:1-17
Revelation 21:5-27

Tu Psalm 117
Jeremiah 30:18-24
Revelation 22:8-21

W Psalm 117
Jeremiah 31:1-6
Luke 1:1-4

Scripture and Worship

Worship in the Christian assembly is biblical. From ancient times the church has read publicly from the Old and New Testaments and has drawn upon the scriptures to shape the whole of worship. Biblical language and imagery have historically been adapted and shaped to form the language through which God's people pray, sing, and address both God and one another.

Public reading from the Bible, using a translation that is both current and accessible, is the most direct use of the scriptures in worship. A common lectionary—a shared list of biblical readings—connects worshiping communities through the use of the same readings on the same day, while assisting the assembly in encountering the breadth of the scriptures.

Scripture readings are usually introduced with an announcement such as, "A reading from . . ." or "The holy gospel according to . . ." They may be concluded with "The word of the Lord" or "Word of God, word of life" or "The gospel of the Lord." This framing sets the public reading of the Bible apart from other uses of biblical language and imagery in worship.

Scripture grounds not only the words but also the patterns and actions of worship. Even as the disciples learned from Jesus to pray, God's command and promise, as witnessed in the scriptures, guide the church's proclamation of the gospel and use of the sacraments.

We sing "Glory to God" with the angels from Luke's gospel or "This is the feast" using images and language from Revelation. We sing psalms and pray the Lord's Prayer. We gather around the table remembering "the night in which he was betrayed." We share the peace of Christ and with that same peace we are sent to "share the good news."

Just as biblical preaching participates in the creating and transforming power of God's own word, so biblical language, imagery, and action draw the Christian assembly into God's saving story.

The following are some of the key biblical foundations for worship within the principal services of Holy Communion and Holy Baptism.

Holy Communion

Gathering

Blow the trumpet in Zion; sanctify a fast; call a solemn assembly; gather the people . . .
(*Joel 2:15-17*)

For where two or three are gathered in my name, I am there among them. (*Matthew 18:20*)

When the day of Pentecost had come, they were all together in one place. (*Acts 2:1-13*)

Confession and Forgiveness

Go therefore and make disciples of all nations, baptizing them in the name of the Father and of
the Son and of the Holy Spirit. (*Matthew 28:19*)

Bless the LORD, O my soul . . . who forgives all your sins and heals all your diseases. (*Psalm 103:2-3*)

God's mercy endures forever. (*Psalm 136:1*)

If we say that we have no sin, we deceive ourselves, and the truth is not in us. If we confess our sins,
[God] who is faithful and just will forgive us our sins and cleanse us from all unrighteousness.
(*1 John 1:8-9*)

Jesus answered them, "Very truly, I tell you, everyone who commits sin is a slave to sin."
(*John 8:34*)

You shall love the Lord your God with all your heart, and with all your soul, and with all your
mind . . . You shall love your neighbor as yourself. (*Matthew 22:37-39*)

I will delight in your commandments. (*Psalm 119:47*)

Show me your ways, O LORD. (*Psalm 25:4*)

[Jesus] breathed on [the disciples] and said to them, "Receive the Holy Spirit. If you forgive the sins
of any, they are forgiven them; if you retain the sins of any, they are retained." (*John 20:22-23*)

But God, who is rich in mercy, out of the great love with which he loved us even when we were
dead through our trespasses, made us alive together with Christ—by grace you have been saved . . .
I pray, that according to the riches of his glory, he may grant that you may be strengthened in
your inner being with power through his Spirit, and that Christ may dwell in your hearts through
faith, as you are being rooted and grounded in love. (*Ephesians 2:4-5; 3:16-17*)

Thanksgiving for Baptism

. . . the fountain of living water, the LORD. (*Jeremiah 17:13*)

You were unmindful of the Rock that bore you; you forgot the God who gave you birth.
(*Deuteronomy 32:18*)

The LORD is my light and my salvation. (*Psalm 27:1*)

Gathering Song

Sing to the Lord a new song, God's praise in the assembly of the faithful. (*Psalm 149:1-4*)

They called out, saying, "Jesus, Master, have mercy on us!" (*Luke 17:13*)

Glory to God in the highest heaven, and on earth peace among those whom he favors! (*Luke 2:14*)

Every tongue should confess that Jesus Christ is Lord, to the glory of God the Father. (*Philippians 2:11*)

On this mountain the LORD of hosts will make for all peoples a feast . . . Let us be glad and rejoice in his salvation. (*Isaiah 25:6-9*)

Worthy is the Lamb that was slaughtered to receive power and wealth and wisdom and might and honor and glory and blessing! . . . To the one seated on the throne and to the Lamb be blessing and honor and glory and might forever and ever! (*Revelation 5:12-13*)

Greeting

The grace of the Lord Jesus Christ, the love of God, and the communion of the Holy Spirit be with all of you. (*2 Corinthians 13:13*)

[The angel] came to [Mary] and said, "Greetings, favored one! The Lord is with you." (*Luke 1:28*)

Word

Readings and Responses

So shall my word be that goes out from my mouth; it shall not return to me empty. (*Isaiah 55:10-11*)

In the beginning was the Word . . . And the Word became flesh and lived among us. (*John 1:1-5, 14*)

Let the word of Christ dwell in you richly; teach and admonish one another in all wisdom; and with gratitude in your hearts sing psalms, hymns, and spiritual songs to God. (*Colossians 3:16*)

Hear the word of the LORD. (*Jeremiah 2:4*)

Give attention to the public reading of scripture, to exhorting, to teaching. (*1 Timothy 4:13*)

No prophecy of scripture is a matter of one's own interpretation. (*2 Peter 1:20-21*)

From the throne came a voice saying, "Praise our God . . ." Then I heard what seemed to be the voice of a great multitude, like the sound of many waters and like the sound of mighty thunder-peals, crying out, "Hallelujah!" (*Revelation 19:5-6*)

Simon Peter answered him, "Lord, to whom can we go? You have the words of eternal life." (*John 6:68*)

Let your steadfast love come to me, O LORD, and your salvation according to your promise . . . I trust in your word. (*Psalm 119:41, 42*)

The LORD is slow to anger, and abounding in steadfast love. (*Numbers 14:18*)

Prayers of Intercession

First of all, then, I urge that supplications, prayers, intercessions, and thanksgivings be made for everyone, for kings and all who are in high positions, so that we may lead a quiet and peaceable life in all godliness and dignity. (*1 Timothy 2:1-2*)

Then Jesus, crying with a loud voice, said, "Father, into your hands I commend my spirit." (*Luke 23:46*)

Peace

So when you are offering your gift at the altar, if you remember that your brother or sister has something against you, leave your gift there before the altar and go; first be reconciled to your brother or sister, and then come and offer your gift. (*Matthew 5:23-24*)

On that day, the first day of the week ... Jesus came and stood among them and said, "Peace be with you." (*John 20:19*)

Greet one another with a holy kiss. All the churches of Christ greet you. (*Romans 16:16*)

Meal

They devoted themselves to the apostles' teaching and fellowship, to the breaking of bread and the prayers. (*Acts 2:42*)

Offering

Is not this the fast I choose ... to share your bread with the hungry, and bring the homeless poor into your house; when you see the naked, to cover them, and not to hide yourself from your own kin? (*Isaiah 58:6-7*)

For I was hungry and you gave me food, I was thirsty and you gave me something to drink, I was a stranger and you welcomed me. (*Matthew 25:35*)

Thanksgiving at the Table

Let us lift up our hearts as well as our hands to God in heaven. (*Lamentations 3:41*)

We must always give thanks to God for you, brothers and sisters, as is right, because your faith is growing abundantly. (*2 Thessalonians 1:3*)

[The seraphs] called to one another and said: "Holy, holy, holy is the LORD of hosts; the whole earth is full of his glory." (*Isaiah 6:3*)

The crowds that went ahead of him and that followed were shouting, "Hosanna to the Son of David! Blessed is the one who comes in the name of the Lord! Hosanna in the highest heaven!" (*Matthew 21:9*)

For I received from the Lord what I also handed on to you, that the Lord Jesus on the night when he was betrayed took a loaf of bread, and when he had given thanks, he broke it and said, "This is my body that is for you. Do this in remembrance of me." In the same way he took the cup also, after supper, saying, "This cup is the new covenant in my blood. Do this, as often as you drink it, in remembrance of me." For as often as you eat this bread and drink the cup, you proclaim the Lord's death until he comes. (*1 Corinthians 11:23-26*)

Pray then in this way: Our Father in heaven ... (*Matthew 6:9-13*)

Communion Song

The next day [John] saw Jesus coming toward him and declared, "Here is the Lamb of God who takes away the sin of the world!" *(John 1:29)*

When [Jesus] was at the table with them, he took bread, blessed and broke it, and gave it to them. Then their eyes were opened, and they recognized him. *(Luke 24:30-31)*

Simeon took [Jesus] in his arms and praised God, saying, "Master, now you are dismissing your servant in peace, according to your word; for my eyes have seen your salvation, which you have prepared in the presence of all peoples, a light for revelation to the Gentiles and for glory to your people Israel." *(Luke 2:28-32)*

Sending

Go therefore and make disciples of all nations. *(Matthew 28:19)*

As the Father has sent me, so I send you. *(John 20:21)*

So if I, your Lord and Teacher, have washed your feet, you also ought to wash one another's feet. *(John 13:1-15)*

You shall say to them, the LORD bless you and keep you; the LORD make his face to shine upon you, and be gracious to you; the LORD lift up his countenance upon you, and give you peace. *(Numbers 6:23-26)*

May the God of steadfastness and encouragement grant you to live in harmony with one another, in accordance with Christ Jesus . . . May the God of hope fill you with all joy and peace in believing. *(Romans 15:5, 13)*

[Jesus] said to the woman, "Your faith has saved you; go in peace." *(Luke 7:50)*

Do not lag in zeal, be ardent in spirit, serve the Lord. *(Romans 12:11)*

They asked only one thing, that we remember the poor. *(Galatians 2:10)*

As you go, proclaim the good news, "The kingdom of heaven has come near." *(Matthew 10:7)*

Thanks be to God, who gives us the victory through our Lord Jesus Christ. *(1 Corinthians 15:57)*

Holy Baptism

Do you not know that all of us who have been baptized into Christ Jesus were baptized into his death? Therefore we have been buried with him by baptism into death, so that, just as Christ was raised from the dead by the glory of the Father, so we too might walk in newness of life. *(Romans 6:3-4)*

[God] is the source of your life in Christ Jesus. *(1 Corinthians 1:30)*

You belong to Christ, and Christ belongs to God. *(1 Corinthians 3:23)*

As many of you as were baptized into Christ have clothed yourselves with Christ. *(Galatians 3:27)*

The spirit of the LORD shall rest on [the promised one], the spirit of wisdom and understanding, the spirit of counsel and might, the spirit of knowledge and the fear of the LORD. *(Isaiah 11:2)*

In [Christ] you also, when you had heard the word of truth, the gospel of your salvation, and had believed in him, were marked with the seal of the promised Holy Spirit. *(Ephesians 1:13-14)*

Jesus spoke to them, saying, "I am the light of the world. Whoever follows me will never walk in darkness but will have the light of life." *(John 8:12)*

Let your light shine before others, so that they may see your good works and give glory to your Father in heaven. *(Matthew 5:16)*

Small Catechism
of Martin Luther

The Ten Commandments

The First Commandment
You shall have no other gods.

What is this? **OR** *What does this mean?*
We are to fear, love, and trust God above all things.

The Second Commandment
You shall not make wrongful use of the name of the Lord your God.

What is this? **OR** *What does this mean?*
We are to fear and love God, so that we do not curse, swear, practice magic, lie, or deceive using God's name, but instead use that very name in every time of need to call on, pray to, praise, and give thanks to God.

The Third Commandment
Remember the sabbath day, and keep it holy.

What is this? **OR** *What does this mean?*
We are to fear and love God, so that we do not despise preaching or God's word, but instead keep that word holy and gladly hear and learn it.

The Fourth Commandment
Honor your father and your mother.

What is this? **OR** *What does this mean?*
We are to fear and love God, so that we neither despise nor anger our parents and others in authority, but instead honor, serve, obey, love, and respect them.

The Fifth Commandment
You shall not murder.

What is this? **OR** *What does this mean?*
We are to fear and love God, so that we neither endanger nor harm the lives of our neighbors, but instead help and support them in all of life's needs.

The Sixth Commandment

You shall not commit adultery.

What is this? **OR** *What does this mean?*
We are to fear and love God, so that we lead pure and decent lives in word and deed, and each of us loves and honors his or her spouse.

The Seventh Commandment

You shall not steal.

What is this? **OR** *What does this mean?*
We are to fear and love God, so that we neither take our neighbors' money or property nor acquire them by using shoddy merchandise or crooked deals, but instead help them to improve and protect their property and income.

The Eighth Commandment

You shall not bear false witness against your neighbor.

What is this? **OR** *What does this mean?*
We are to fear and love God, so that we do not tell lies about our neighbors, betray or slander them, or destroy their reputations. Instead we are to come to their defense, speak well of them, and interpret everything they do in the best possible light.

The Ninth Commandment

You shall not covet your neighbor's house.

What is this? **OR** *What does this mean?*
We are to fear and love God, so that we do not try to trick our neighbors out of their inheritance or property or try to get it for ourselves by claiming to have a legal right to it and the like, but instead be of help and service to them in keeping what is theirs.

The Tenth Commandment

You shall not covet your neighbor's wife, or male or female slave, or ox, or donkey, or anything that belongs to your neighbor.

What is this? **OR** *What does this mean?*
We are to fear and love God, so that we do not entice, force, or steal away from our neighbors their spouses, household workers, or livestock, but instead urge them to stay and fulfill their responsibilities to our neighbors.

What then does God say about all these commandments?
God says the following: "I, the Lord your God, am a jealous God, punishing children for the iniquity of parents, to the third and the fourth generation of those who reject me, but showing steadfast love to the thousandth generation of those who love me and keep my commandments."

What is this? **OR** *What does this mean?*
God threatens to punish all who break these commandments. Therefore we are to fear his wrath and not disobey these commandments. However, God promises grace and every good thing to all those who keep these commandments. Therefore we also are to love and trust him and gladly act according to his commands.

The Creed

The First Article: *On Creation*
I believe in God, the Father almighty, creator of heaven and earth.

What is this? **OR** *What does this mean?*
I believe that God has created me together with all that exists. God has given me and still preserves my body and soul: eyes, ears, and all limbs and senses; reason and all mental faculties.

In addition, God daily and abundantly provides shoes and clothing, food and drink, house and farm, spouse and children, fields, livestock, and all property—along with all the necessities and nourishment for this body and life. God protects me against all danger and shields and preserves me from all evil. And all this is done out of pure, fatherly, and divine goodness and mercy, without any merit or worthiness of mine at all! For all of this I owe it to God to thank and praise, serve and obey him. This is most certainly true.

The Second Article: *On Redemption*
I believe in Jesus Christ, God's only Son, our Lord, who was conceived by the Holy Spirit, born of the virgin Mary, suffered under Pontius Pilate, was crucified, died, and was buried; he descended to the dead.* On the third day he rose again; he ascended into heaven, he is seated at the right hand of the Father, and he will come to judge the living and the dead.

What is this? **OR** *What does this mean?*
I believe that Jesus Christ, true God, begotten of the Father in eternity, and also a true human being, born of the virgin Mary, is my Lord. He has redeemed me, a lost and condemned human being. He has purchased and freed me from all sins, from death, and from the power of the devil, not with gold or silver but with his holy, precious blood and with his innocent suffering and death. He has done all this in order that I may belong to him, live under him in his kingdom, and serve him in eternal righteousness, innocence, and blessedness, just as he is risen from the dead and lives and rules eternally. This is most certainly true.

The Third Article: *On Being Made Holy*
I believe in the Holy Spirit, the holy catholic church, the communion of saints, the forgiveness of sins, the resurrection of the body, and the life everlasting.

What is this? **OR** *What does this mean?*
I believe that by my own understanding or strength I cannot believe in Jesus Christ my Lord or come to him, but instead the Holy Spirit has called me through the gospel, enlightened me with his gifts, made me holy and kept me in the true faith, just as he calls, gathers, enlightens, and makes holy the whole Christian church on earth and keeps it with Jesus Christ in the one common, true faith. Daily in this Christian church the Holy Spirit abundantly forgives all sins—mine and those of all believers. On the last day the Holy Spirit will raise me and all the dead and will give to me and all believers in Christ eternal life. This is most certainly true.

*Or, "he descended into hell," another translation of this text in widespread use.

The Lord's Prayer

Introduction
Our Father in heaven.

What is this? **OR** *What does this mean?*
With these words God wants to attract us, so that we come to believe he is truly our Father and we are truly his children, in order that we may ask him boldly and with complete confidence, just as loving children ask their loving father.

The First Petition
Hallowed be your name.

What is this? **OR** *What does this mean?*
It is true that God's name is holy in itself, but we ask in this prayer that it may also become holy in and among us.

How does this come about?
Whenever the word of God is taught clearly and purely and we, as God's children, also live holy lives according to it. To this end help us, dear Father in heaven! However, whoever teaches and lives otherwise than the word of God teaches, dishonors the name of God among us. Preserve us from this, heavenly Father!

The Second Petition
Your kingdom come.

What is this? **OR** *What does this mean?*
In fact, God's kingdom comes on its own without our prayer, but we ask in this prayer that it may also come to us.

How does this come about?
Whenever our heavenly Father gives us his Holy Spirit, so that through the Holy Spirit's grace we believe God's holy word and live godly lives here in time and hereafter in eternity.

The Third Petition
Your will be done, on earth as in heaven.

What is this? **OR** *What does this mean?*
In fact, God's good and gracious will comes about without our prayer, but we ask in this prayer that it may also come about in and among us.

How does this come about?
Whenever God breaks and hinders every evil scheme and will—as are present in the will of the devil, the world, and our flesh—that would not allow us to hallow God's name and would prevent the coming of his kingdom, and instead whenever God strengthens us and keeps us steadfast in his word and in faith until the end of our lives. This is God's gracious and good will.

The Fourth Petition
Give us today our daily bread.

What is this? **OR** *What does this mean?*
In fact, God gives daily bread without our prayer, even to all evil people, but we ask in this prayer that God cause us to recognize what our daily bread is and to receive it with thanksgiving.

What then does "daily bread" mean?
Everything included in the necessities and nourishment for our bodies, such as food, drink, clothing, shoes, house, farm, fields, livestock, money, property, an upright spouse, upright children, upright members of the household, upright and faithful rulers, good government, good weather, peace, health, decency, honor, good friends, faithful neighbors, and the like.

The Fifth Petition
Forgive us our sins, as we forgive those who sin against us.

What is this? **OR** *What does this mean?*
We ask in this prayer that our heavenly Father would not regard our sins nor deny these petitions on their account, for we are worthy of nothing for which we ask, nor have we earned it. Instead we ask that God would give us all things by grace, for we daily sin much and indeed deserve only punishment. So, on the other hand, we, too, truly want to forgive heartily and to do good gladly to those who sin against us.

The Sixth Petition
Save us from the time of trial.

What is this? **OR** *What does this mean?*
It is true that God tempts no one, but we ask in this prayer that God would preserve and keep us, so that the devil, the world, and our flesh may not deceive us or mislead us into false belief, despair, and other great and shameful sins, and that, although we may be attacked by them, we may finally prevail and gain the victory.

The Seventh Petition
And deliver us from evil.

What is this? **OR** *What does this mean?*
We ask in this prayer, as in a summary, that our Father in heaven may deliver us from all kinds of evil—affecting body or soul, property or reputation—and at last, when our final hour comes, may grant us a blessed end and take us by grace from this valley of tears to himself in heaven.

Conclusion
[For the kingdom, the power, and the glory are yours, now and forever.] Amen.

What is this? **OR** *What does this mean?*
That I should be certain that such petitions are acceptable to and heard by our Father in heaven, for he himself commanded us to pray like this and has promised to hear us. "Amen, amen" means "Yes, yes, it is going to come about just like this."

The Sacrament of Holy Baptism

I

What is baptism?
Baptism is not simply plain water. Instead, it is water used according to God's command and connected with God's word.

What then is this word of God?
Where our Lord Christ says in Matthew 28, "Go therefore and make disciples of all nations, baptizing them in the name of the Father and of the Son and of the Holy Spirit."

II

What gifts or benefits does baptism grant?
It brings about forgiveness of sins, redeems from death and the devil, and gives eternal salvation to all who believe it, as the words and promise of God declare.

What are these words and promise of God?
Where our Lord Christ says in Mark 16, "The one who believes and is baptized will be saved; but the one who does not believe will be condemned."

III

How can water do such great things?
Clearly the water does not do it, but the word of God, which is with and alongside the water, and faith, which trusts this word of God in the water. For without the word of God the water is plain water and not a baptism, but with the word of God it is a baptism, that is, a grace-filled water of life and a "bath of the new birth in the Holy Spirit," as St. Paul says to Titus in chapter 3, "through the water of rebirth and renewal by the Holy Spirit. This Spirit he poured out on us richly through Jesus Christ our Savior, so that, having been justified by his grace, we might become heirs according to the hope of eternal life. The saying is sure."

IV

What then is the significance of such a baptism with water?
It signifies that the old person in us with all sins and evil desires is to be drowned and die through daily sorrow for sin and through repentance, and on the other hand that daily a new person is to come forth and rise up to live before God in righteousness and purity forever.

Where is this written?
St. Paul says in Romans 6, "We have been buried with Christ by baptism into death, so that, just as Christ was raised from the dead by the glory of the Father, so we too might walk in newness of life."

How people are to be taught to confess

What is confession?
Confession consists of two parts. One is that we confess our sins. The other is that we receive the absolution, that is, forgiveness, from the pastor as from God himself and by no means doubt but firmly believe that our sins are thereby forgiven before God in heaven.

Which sins is a person to confess?
Before God one is to acknowledge the guilt for all sins, even those of which we are not aware, as we do in the Lord's Prayer. However, before the pastor we are to confess only those sins of which we have knowledge and which trouble us.

Which sins are these?
Here reflect on your place in life in light of the Ten Commandments: whether you are father, mother, son, daughter, master, mistress, servant; whether you have been disobedient, unfaithful, lazy, whether you have harmed anyone by word or deed; whether you have stolen, neglected, wasted, or injured anything.

The Sacrament of the Altar

What is the Sacrament of the Altar?
It is the true body and blood of our Lord Jesus Christ under the bread and wine, instituted by Christ himself for us Christians to eat and to drink.

Where is this written?
The holy evangelists Matthew, Mark, and Luke, and St. Paul write thus:
"In the night in which he was betrayed, our Lord Jesus took bread, and gave thanks; broke it, and gave it to his disciples, saying: Take and eat; this is my body, given for you. Do this for the remembrance of me. Again, after supper, he took the cup, gave thanks, and gave it for all to drink, saying: This cup is the new covenant in my blood, shed for you and for all people for the forgiveness of sin. Do this for the remembrance of me."

What is the benefit of such eating and drinking?
The words "given for you" and "shed for you for the forgiveness of sin" show us that forgiveness of sin, life, and salvation are given to us in the sacrament through these words, because where there is forgiveness of sin, there is also life and salvation.

How can bodily eating and drinking do such a great thing?
Eating and drinking certainly do not do it, but rather the words that are recorded: "given for you" and "shed for you for the forgiveness of sin." These words, when accompanied by the physical eating and drinking, are the essential thing in the sacrament, and whoever believes these very words has what they declare and state, namely, "forgiveness of sin."

Who, then, receives this sacrament worthily?
Fasting and bodily preparation are in fact a fine external discipline, but a person who has faith in these words, "given for you" and "shed for you for the forgiveness of sin," is really worthy and well prepared. However, a person who does not believe these words or doubts them is unworthy and unprepared, because the words "for you" require truly believing hearts.

The Morning Blessing

In the morning, as soon as you get out of bed, you are to make the sign of the holy cross and say:
"God the Father, Son, and Holy Spirit watch over me. Amen."

Then, kneeling or standing, say the Apostles' Creed and the Lord's Prayer. If you wish, you may in addition recite this little prayer as well:
"I give thanks to you, heavenly Father, through Jesus Christ your dear Son, that you have protected me through the night from all harm and danger. I ask that you would also protect me today from sin and all evil, so that my life and actions may please you. Into your hands I commend myself: my body, my soul, and all that is mine. Let your holy angel be with me, so that the wicked foe may have no power over me. Amen."

After singing a hymn perhaps (for example, one on the Ten Commandments) or whatever else may serve your devotion, you are to go to your work joyfully.

The Evening Blessing

In the evening, when you go to bed, you are to make the sign of the holy cross and say:
"God the Father, Son, and Holy Spirit watch over me. Amen."

Then, kneeling or standing, say the Apostles' Creed and the Lord's Prayer. If you wish, you may in addition recite this little prayer as well:
"I give thanks to you, heavenly Father, through Jesus Christ your dear Son, that you have graciously protected me today. I ask you to forgive me all my sins, where I have done wrong, and graciously to protect me tonight. Into your hands I commend myself: my body, my soul, and all that is mine. Let your holy angel be with me, so that the wicked foe may have no power over me. Amen."

Then you are to go to sleep quickly and cheerfully.

Table Blessings

The children and the members of the household are to come devoutly to the table, fold their hands, and recite:
"The eyes of all wait upon you, O Lord, and you give them their food in due season. You open your hand and satisfy the desire of every living creature."

Then they are to recite the Lord's Prayer and the following prayer:
"Lord God, heavenly Father, bless us and these your gifts, which we receive from your bountiful goodness, through Jesus Christ our Lord. Amen."

Similarly, after eating they should in the same manner fold their hands and recite devoutly:
"Give thanks to the Lord, for the Lord is good, for God's mercy endures forever. God provides food for the cattle and for the young ravens when they cry. God is not impressed by the might of a horse, and has no pleasure in the speed of a runner, but finds pleasure in those who fear the Lord, in those who await God's steadfast love."

Then recite the Lord's Prayer and the following prayer:
"We give thanks to you, Lord God our Father, through Jesus Christ our Lord for all your benefits, you who live and reign forever. Amen."

Indexes

Acknowledgments

The material on pages 1–338, #1–150, and pages 1121–1167, both text and music, is covered by the copyright of *Evangelical Lutheran Worship,* unless otherwise noted. This material has been prepared by the Renewing Worship project for use in the Evangelical Lutheran Church in America and the Evangelical Lutheran Church in Canada.

Material from other sources is gratefully acknowledged and is used by permission where necessary. Every effort has been made to identify the copyright holders and administrators for copyrighted words and music. The publisher regrets any oversight that may have occurred and will make proper acknowledgment in future editions if correct information is brought to the publisher's attention.

Text Sources
A fuller listing of the sources of textual material other than the hymn texts is in *Evangelical Lutheran Worship* Leaders Edition. The following sources for these texts are particularly acknowledged.

The New Revised Standard Version Bible © 1989 Division of Christian Education of the National Council of Churches of Christ in the United States of America.

Materials prepared by the Consultation on Common Texts (CCT), published in *A Christian Celebration of Marriage* © 1995; *Revised Common Lectionary* © 1992; *Revised Common Lectionary Prayers* © 2002; and *Revised Common Lectionary Daily Readings* © 2005.

Materials prepared by the English Language Liturgical Consultation (ELLC), published in *Praying Together* © 1988: the Apostles' Creed, the Nicene Creed, the preface dialogue, the Lord's Prayer, the canticle texts "Glory to God in the highest," "Holy, holy, holy," "Lamb of God," "Now, Lord, you let your servant go in peace," "Glory to the Father," "Blessed are you, Lord," "My soul proclaims the greatness of the Lord," "We praise you, O God," and "Jesus, Lamb of God."

Book of Common Prayer 1979 according to the use of The Episcopal Church USA.

Book of Common Worship, Presbyterian Church USA and the Cumberland Presbyterian Church, © 1993 Westminister John Knox Press.

Give Us Grace: An Anthology of Anglican Prayers, compiled by Christopher L. Webber, © 2004 Morehouse Publishing.

Libro de Liturgia y Cántico © 1998 Augsburg Fortress.

Living Witnesses: The Adult Catechumenate © 1992 Evangelical Lutheran Church in Canada.

Lutheran Book of Worship and *Lutheran Book of Worship* Ministers Edition © 1978 Lutheran Church in America, The American Lutheran Church, The Evangelical Lutheran Church of Canada, and The Lutheran Church—Missouri Synod.

Statement on Sacramental Practices © 1991 Evangelical Lutheran Church in Canada.

Sundays and Seasons annual worship planning guide, 1995—, Augsburg Fortress.

The Book of Concord: The Confessions of the Evangelical Lutheran Church, edited by Robert Kolb and Timothy J. Wengert, © 2000 Fortress Press.

The Use of the Means of Grace: A Statement on the Practice of Word and Sacrament © 1997 Evangelical Lutheran Church in America. Adopted for guidance and practice by the Fifth Biennial Churchwide Assembly of the Evangelical Lutheran Church in America, 1997.

This Far by Faith: An African American Resource for Worship © 1999 Augsburg Fortress.

Welcome to Christ: Lutheran Rites for the Catechumenate © 1997 Augsburg Fortress.

With One Voice: A Lutheran Resource for Worship © 1995 Augsburg Fortress.

The Renewing Worship series © Evangelical Lutheran Church in America, admin. Augsburg Fortress: *Congregational Song: Proposals for Renewal* (vol. 1, 2001); *Principles for Worship* (vol. 2, 2002; in Spanish translation, *Principios para la Adoración,* 2003); *Holy Baptism and Related Rites* (vol. 3, 2002); *Life Passages: Marriage, Healing, Funeral* (vol. 4, 2002); *New Hymns and Songs* (vol. 5, 2003); *Holy Communion and Related Rites* (vol. 6, 2004); *Daily Prayer* (vol. 7, 2004); *The Church's Year* (vol. 8, 2004).

Music Sources
Composers of the liturgical music on pages 1–332 (all service music settings © or administered by Augsburg Fortress):

Holy Communion, Setting One © 2006: Mark Mummert, b. 1965, Kyrie, "Glory to God," "This is the feast," Lenten Acclamation; Thomas Pavlechko, b. 1962, Gospel Acclamation (Alleluia), "Holy, holy, holy"; Robert Buckley Farlee, b. 1950, "Lamb of God," "Now, Lord, you let your servant go in peace."

Holy Communion, Setting Two © 2004, 2006: Marty Haugen, b. 1950.

Holy Communion, Setting Three © 1978, 2006: Richard W. Hillert, b. 1923.

Holy Communion, Setting Four © 1978, 2006: Ronald A. Nelson, b. 1927.

Holy Communion, Setting Five © 1958, 1978, 2006: Plainsong, arr. Regina Fryxell, 1899–1993, and Richard W. Hillert, b. 1923; "All glory be to God on high," Nikolaus Decius, c. 1485–c. 1550.

Holy Communion, Setting Six © 1993, 1999, 2006: Tillis Butler, d. 2002, Kyrie, Gospel Acclamation (Alleluia), "Holy, holy, holy"; James Capers, b. 1948, "Glory to God," "This is the feast," "Lamb of God"; Rawn Harbor, Lenten Acclamation; James Harris, Gospel Acclamation (Alleluia), "Holy, holy, holy."

Holy Communion, Setting Seven © 1998, 2006: Anonymous, "Holy, holy, holy: Santo, santo, santo"; Gerhard M. Cartford, b. 1923, "Celebremos la victoria: Celebrate the feast of victory"; Victor Jortack, Gospel Acclamation (Alleluia), "Lamb of God: Cordero de Dios"; *Misa popular nicaragüense,* Kyrie; José Ruiz, b. 1956, Lenten Acclamation; Pablo Sosa, b. 1933, "Gloria, gloria, gloria" © Pablo Sosa.

Holy Communion, Setting Eight © 1970, 1990, 1995, 1999, 2006: Jay Beech, b. 1960, "Holy, holy, holy," "Lamb of God"; Robin Cain, Gospel Acclamations; Dennis Friesen-Carper, "Glory to God"; Phil Kadidlo, Gospel Acclamations; Larry Olson, "Kyrie eleison" © Dakota Road Music; John C. Ylvisaker, b. 1937, "This is the feast."

Holy Communion, Setting Nine © 2004, 2006: Joel Martinson, b. 1960.

Holy Communion, Setting Ten © 1997, 2006: hymn tunes; see source information for Southwell, #599; Hymn to Joy, #836; Nun danket all, #847; Unser Herrscher, #533; Kas dzieda¯ja, #701; Land of Rest, #448; Twenty-fourth, #359.

Service of the Word © 1995, 2006: Robert Buckley Farlee, b. 1950, "Salvation belongs to our God"; Jeremy Young, b. 1948, Kyrie, "Glory to God," Gospel Acclamations.

Morning Prayer © 2004, 2006: Carolyn Jennings, b. 1936, "Come, let us sing to the Lord"; Mark Mummert, b. 1965, "Blessed are you, Lord."

Evening Prayer © 1978, 2006: David Schack, b. 1947, "Let my prayer rise before you"; Russell Schulz-Widmar, b. 1944, "My soul proclaims the greatness of the Lord."

Night Prayer © 1978, 2006: Plainsong, arr. Carlos R. Messerli, b. 1927, alt.

Art Sources
Cover image, service and section art, and Church Year frontispiece: Nicholas T. Markell, b. 1961, Markell Studios, Inc.; Holy Communion frontispiece (*Supper at Emmaus*): He Qi, b. 1951; Holy Baptism frontispiece (*Baptism into Community*): Wayne Lacson Forte, b. 1950; Lent and the Three Days frontispiece: Julie Lonneman, b. 1954; Life Passages frontispiece: Barbara Zuber, b. 1926; Daily Prayer frontispiece (*Prayer of the Hours*): Lucinda Naylor, b. 1957; Psalms frontispiece: Tanja Butler, b. 1955; Service Music and Hymns frontispiece (*Sing!*): Christine Nicoll Parson, b. 1943.

Renewing Worship Resource Proposal Group
Susan R. Briehl, Lorraine Brugh, Michael L. Burk, Cheryl E. Dieter, Joseph A. Donnella II, Jonathan Eilert, Gordon W. Lathrop, Rafael Malpica-Padilla, Robert A. Rimbo, Thomas H. Schattauer, Martin A. Seltz, Karen Walhof.

Renewing Worship Editorial Teams
Kevin Anderson, Barbara Berry-Bailey, Karen Bockelman, Susan R. Briehl, Lorraine Brugh, James Frederick Brown, Teresa Bowers, Michael L. Burk, Dennis Bushkofsky, David Cherwien, Marcia Cox, Cheryl E. Dieter, Pablo Espinoza, Robert Buckley Farlee, Beth Bergeron Folkemer, M. Alexandra George, Mark Glaeser, Timothy Guenther, Robert Hawkins, Sarah Henrich, Paul Hoffman, Mary Hughes, Diane Jacobson, Karen Johnson-Lefsrud, Patricia Kazarow, Dirk Lange, Gordon W. Lathrop, Donald Luther, Craig Mueller, Thomas Pavlechko, Mary Preus, Gail Ramshaw, Peter Rehwaldt, Julie Ryan, Thomas H. Schattauer, Martin A. Seltz, Frank C. Senn, Frank W. Stoldt, Mark Strobel, Marilyn Kay Stulken, Scott C. Weidler, E. Louise Williams, Wayne L. Wold.

In addition to the work of the editorial teams, the development of *Evangelical Lutheran Worship* involved participants in a series of consultations that led to *Principles for Worship*; development panels that provided input to and review of the editorial teams' work; those who provided theological and liturgical review at several intervals in the process; congregations and worshiping communities that contributed to research and evaluated provisional materials; and many individuals who shared their creative gifts and offered insights and evaluation through the Renewing Worship process.

Worship Resource Development Staff
Michael L. Burk, Cheryl E. Dieter, Martin A. Seltz, project management; Ruth Allin, Kevin Anderson, Barbara Berry-Bailey, Suzanne Burke, Robert Buckley Farlee, Scott C. Weidler.

Design and Production
Staff: Jodi Gustafson, Jessica Hillstrom, Douglas Hodgeman, Laurie Ingram, Lynette Johnson, Joshua Messner, Linda Parriott, Diana Running, Ivy Palmer Skrade, Jessica Thoreson, Mark Weiler. Associates: art direction, Lynn Joyce Hunter; design, Kantor Group, Minneapolis; music engraving, Jürgen Selk (Music Graphics International, London), Mark Adler (Music Arranging and Engraving, Minneapolis).

Copyright Holders and Administrators

Augsburg Fortress
Attn: Permissions
PO Box 1209
Minneapolis MN 55440-1209
Ph: (800) 421-0239 or (612) 330-3127
Fax: (800) 722-7766 or (612) 330-3455
E-mail: copyright@augsburgfortress.org
www.augsburgfortress.org

Church Publishing, Inc.
Attn: Copyrights and Permissions
445 Fifth Ave.
New York NY 10016
Ph: (800) 223-6602 x 360
Fax: (212) 779-3392
Email: copyrights@cpg.org
www.churchpublishing.org

Concordia Publishing House
Attn: Copyrights
3558 S. Jefferson Ave.
St. Louis MO 63118-3968
Ph: (314) 268-1000 ext. 1254
Fax: (314) 268-1329
E-mail: copyrights@cph.org
www.cph.org

GIA Publications, Inc.
Attn: Reprints
7404 S. Mason Ave.
Chicago IL 60638
Ph: (800) 442-1358 ext. 56
Fax: (708) 496 3828 perms
or (708) 458-4940 (OneLicense.net)
E-mail: reprints@giamusic.com
www.onelicense.net

Hal Leonard Corporation
Attn: Copyright Department
7777 W. Bluemound Rd.
Milwaukee WI 53213
Ph: (414) 774-3630
Fax: (414) 774-3259
hlcopyright@halleonard.com

Hope Publishing Company
Attn: Copyright Department
380 S. Main Pl.
Carol Stream IL 60188
Ph: (800) 323 1049
Fax: (630) 665 2552
www.hopepublishing.com

Licensing Associates
Walton Music Corporation
935 Broad Street #31
Bloomfield NJ 07003
Ph: (973) 743-6444
Fax: (973) 743-6444
E-mail: kathleenkarcher@hotmail.com

Lutheran World Federation
Permissions
150 route de Ferney
Box 2100
CH-1211 Geneva 2
Switzerland
Ph: 011 +41 22 791 61 11
Fax: 011 +41 22 791 66 30
E-mail: eggert@lutheranworld.org
www.lutheranworld.org

Music Services, Inc.
1526 Otter Creek Rd.
Nashville TN 37215
Ph: (615) 371-1320
Fax: (615) 371-1351
E-mail: info@musicservices.org
www.musicservices.org

OCP Publications
Attn: Licensing Department
PO Box 18030
Portland OR 97218-0030
Ph: (503) 281-1191
Fax: (503) 282-3486
E-mail: liturgy@ocp.org
www.ocp.org

Oxford University Press
Attn: Rights & Permissions
198 Madison Ave.
New York NY 10016-4314
Ph: (212) 726-6000 ext. 6048
Fax: (212) 726-6441
E-mail: music.us@oup.com
www.oup.com

Selah Publishing Co.
Attn: Licensing Dept.
4143 Brownsville Rd. #2
Pittsburgh PA 15227
Ph: (412) 886-1020
Fax: (412) 886-1022
E-mail: licensing@selahpub.com
www.selahpub.com

The Copyright Company
1025 16th Ave. S.
Suite 204
Nashville TN 37212
Ph: (615) 321-1096
Fax: (615) 321-1099
E-mail: tcc@thecopyrightco.com

World Library Publications
Attn: Customer Care Dept.
3708 River Rd.
Franklin Park IL 60131-2158
Ph: (800) 566-6150
or if outside USA: 1+847-678-9300 ext. 2752
Fax: (888) 957 3291
or if outside USA: 1+847-671-5715
E-mail: wlpcs@jspaluch.com

John Ylvisaker
New Generation Publishers, Inc.
Publication Rights and Records
Box 321
Waverly IA 50677-0321
Ph: (319) 352-4396
Fax: (319) 352-0765
E-mail: fern@ylvisaker.com
www.ylvisaker.com

Current copyright and contact information is available from the publisher at www.sundaysandseasons.com.

Copyright Acknowledgments: Service Music and Hymns

Topical Index of Hymns

Adoration (see also Praise, Thanksgiving)
634   All hail the power of Jesus' name!
638   Blessed assurance
408   Come, thou almighty King
687   Come to us, creative Spirit
535   Hallelujah! We sing your praises
664   Heaven is singing for joy
414   Holy God, we praise your name
473   Holy, holy, holy
582   Holy Spirit, ever dwelling
434   Jesus shall reign
660   Lift high the cross
730   Lord our God, with praise we come
555   Oh, sing to God above
783   Praise and thanks and adoration
531   The trumpets sound, the angels sing
511   Thy strong word
525   You are holy

ADVENT, 239–267
827   Arise, my soul, arise!
552   Blessed be the God of Israel
723   Canticle of the Turning
715   Christ, Be Our Light
625   Come, we that love the Lord
501   Come with us, O blessed Jesus
593   Drawn to the Light
311   Hail to the Lord's anointed
737   He comes to us as one unknown
815   I want to walk as a child of the light
490   Let all mortal flesh keep silence
435   Lo! He comes with clouds descending
272   Lo, how a rose e'er blooming
727   Lord Christ, when first you came to earth
475   Lord, enthroned in heavenly splendor
730   Lord our God, with praise we come
631   Love divine, all loves excelling
236   Magnificat
438   My Lord, what a morning
882   My soul does magnify the Lord
573   My soul now magnifies the Lord
711   O day of peace
749   O God of love, O King of peace
279   O little town of Bethlehem
295   Of the Father's love begotten
437   On Jordan's stormy bank I stand
519   Open your ears, O faithful people
430   Rejoice, for Christ is king!
439   Soon and very soon
488, 489   Soul, adorn yourself with gladness
309   The only Son from heaven
706   The people walk
551   The Spirit sends us forth to serve
327   Through the night of doubt and sorrow
436   Wake, awake, for night is flying
510   Word of God, come down on earth

Affirmation of Baptism (see also Holy Baptism)
326   Bless now, O God, the journey
304   Christ, when for us you were baptized
799   Come, follow me, the Savior spake
404   Come, gracious Spirit, heavenly dove
332, 611   I heard the voice of Jesus say
767   Lord, take my hand and lead me
735   Mothering God, you gave me birth
810   O Jesus, I have promised
330   Seed that in earth is dying
814   Take, oh, take me as I am

720   We Are Called
581   You Are Mine

Angels
270   Hark! The herald angels sing
414   Holy God, we praise your name
490   Let all mortal flesh keep silence
787   On Eagle's Wings
265   The angel Gabriel from heaven came
531   The trumpets sound, the angels sing
424   Ye watchers and ye holy ones

Anniversary – see Dedication, Anniversary

Arts, Science
687   Come to us, creative Spirit
684   Creating God, your fingers trace
731   Earth and all stars!
771   God, who stretched the spangled heavens
881   Let all things now living
308   O Morning Star, how fair and bright!
531   The trumpets sound, the angels sing
845   Voices raised to you
850, 851   When in our music God is glorified
861   When long before time

Ascension
393   A hymn of glory let us sing!
392   Alleluia! Sing to Jesus
416   At the name of Jesus
389   Christ is alive! Let Christians sing
594   Dear Christians, one and all, rejoice
394   Hail thee, festival day!
475   Lord, enthroned in heavenly splendor
579   Lord, you give the great commission
832   My Lord of light
604   O Christ, our hope
862   Praise, praise! You are my rock
825   You servants of God

Ash Wednesday (see also Lent; Confession, Forgiveness)
793   Be thou my vision
801   Change my heart, O God
712   Lord, whose love in humble service
328   Restore in us, O God

Assurance – see Hope, Assurance

Atonement
339   Christ, the life of all the living
358   Great God, your love has called us
718   In a lowly manger born
595   Jesus loves me!
307   Light shone in darkness
596, 597   My hope is built on nothing less
343   My song is love unknown
651   Oh, praise the gracious power
591   That priceless grace
342   There in God's garden
587, 588   There's a wideness in God's mercy
803   When I survey the wondrous cross
510   Word of God, come down on earth

Baptism of our Lord
304   Christ, when for us you were baptized
455   Crashing waters at creation
450   I bind unto myself today
881   Let all things now living
322   Oh, love, how deep
249   On Jordan's bank the Baptist's cry
305   When Jesus came to Jordan

Beginning of Service – see Gathering

Bible – see Word of God

Burial – see Community in Christ; Funeral

Celebration – see Joy, Celebration

Children, Songs for
464	Bread of life, our host and meal
794	Calm to the waves
781	Children of the heavenly Father
715	Christ, Be Our Light
528	Come and fill our hearts
491	Come, let us eat
753	Dona nobis pacem
731	Earth and all stars!
879	For the beauty of the earth
540	Go, make disciples
543	Go, my children, with my blessing
290	Go tell it on the mountain
721	Goodness is stronger than evil
764	Have no fear, little flock
325	I want Jesus to walk with me
815	I want to walk as a child of the light
446	I'm going on a journey
860	I'm so glad Jesus lifted me
466	In the singing
708	Jesu, Jesu, fill us with your love
595	Jesus loves me!
616	Jesus, remember me
471	Let us break bread together
674	Let us talents and tongues employ
660	Lift high the cross
240	Light one candle to watch for Messiah
744	Lord, be glorified
857	Lord, I lift your name on high
765	Lord of all hopefulness
767	Lord, take my hand and lead me
341	Now behold the Lamb
283	O come, all ye faithful
269	Once in royal David's city
640	Our Father, by whose name
872	Praise ye the Lord
264	Prepare the royal highway
549	Send me, Jesus
439	Soon and very soon
293	That boy-child of Mary
538	The Lord now sends us forth
677	This little light of mine
613	Thy holy wings
284	'Twas in the moon of wintertime
459	Wade in the water
866	We are marching in the light
353	Were you there
286	Your little ones, dear Lord
741	Your will be done

Christ the King – see Reign of Christ

Christian Hope – see Hope, Assurance

Christian Life (see also Commitment, Discipleship; Trust, Guidance)
631	Love divine, all loves excelling
447	O blessed spring
714	O God of mercy, God of light

CHRISTMAS, 268–300 (see also Incarnation)
245	Creator of the stars of night
253	He came down
718	In a lowly manger born
267	Joy to the world
490	Let all mortal flesh keep silence

309	The only Son from heaven
487	What feast of love
861	When long before time

Church – see Community in Christ

Church Building – see Dedication, Anniversary

City (see also Justice, Peace)
724	All who love and serve your city
625	Come, we that love the Lord
572	Now it is evening
390	The risen Christ
584	The Son of God, our Christ
518	We eat the bread of teaching
719	Where cross the crowded ways of life

Close of Service – see Sending

Comfort, Rest (see also Hope, Assurance; Trust, Guidance)
560	Christ, mighty Savior
536	God be with you till we meet again
332, 611	I heard the voice of Jesus say
397	Loving Spirit
806	O God, my faithful God
381	Peace, to soothe our bitter woes
423	Shall we gather at the river
502	The King of love my shepherd is
342	There in God's garden
614	There is a balm in Gilead
255	There's a voice in the wilderness
613	Thy holy wings
617	We come to you for healing, Lord
659	Will you let me be your servant

Commemorations – see Festivals, Commemorations

COMMITMENT, DISCIPLESHIP, 796–818
(see also Service; Vocation, Ministry)
314	Arise, your light has come!
793	Be thou my vision
306	Come, beloved of the Maker
321	Eternal Lord of love, behold your church
526	God is here!
400	God of tempest, God of whirlwind
401	Gracious Spirit, heed our pleading
332, 611	I heard the voice of Jesus say
696	Jesus calls us; o'er the tumult
674	Let us talents and tongues employ
572	Now it is evening
748	O God in heaven
313	O Lord, now let your servant
454	Remember and rejoice
669	Rise up, O saints of God!
396	Spirit of Gentleness
348	Stay with me
583, 685	Take my life, that I may be
538	The Lord now sends us forth
677	This little light of mine
704	When pain of the world surrounds us
725	When the poor ones

COMMUNITY IN CHRIST, 640–659
(see also Gathering; Holy Communion)
503–505	A mighty fortress is our God
828	Alleluia! Voices raise
326	Bless now, O God, the journey
670	Build us up, Lord
395	Come, Holy Ghost, God and Lord
247	Come now, O Prince of peace
374	Day of arising
419	For all the faithful women
400	God of tempest, God of whirlwind

575	In Christ called to baptize
674	Let us talents and tongues employ
744	Lord, Be Glorified
808	Lord Jesus, you shall be my song
766	Lord of our life
579	Lord, you give the great commission
839, 840	Now thank we all our God
610	O Christ, the healer, we have come
722	O Christ, your heart, compassionate
843	Praise the One who breaks the darkness
548	Rise, O church, like Christ arisen
878	Soli Deo Gloria
729	The church of Christ, in every age
390	The risen Christ
586	This is a day, Lord, gladly awaited
327	Through the night of doubt and sorrow
576	We all are one in mission
411	We all believe in one true God
720	We Are Called
774	What a fellowship, what a joy divine

Compassion, Caring

648	Beloved, God's chosen
728	Blest are they
700	Bring peace to earth again
777	Come to me, all pilgrims thirsty
594	Dear Christians, one and all, rejoice
733	Great is thy faithfulness
612	Healer of our every ill
708	Jesu, Jesu, fill us with your love
712	Lord, whose love in humble service
631	Love divine, all loves excelling
572	Now it is evening
722	O Christ, your heart, compassionate
703	O God, why are you silent
606	Our Father, we have wandered
877	Praise the Almighty!
729	The church of Christ, in every age
546	To be your presence
704	When pain of the world surrounds us
725	When the poor ones

CONFESSION, FORGIVENESS, 599–609
(see also Grace, Faith; Healing)

331	As the deer runs to the river
626	By gracious powers
801	Change my heart, O God
777	Come to me, all pilgrims thirsty
543	Go, my children, with my blessing
323	God loved the world
358	Great God, your love has called us
482	I come with joy
328	Restore in us, O God
342	There in God's garden
566	When twilight comes
510	Word of God, come down on earth
581	You Are Mine

CREATION, 730–740 (see also Stewardship)

835	All creatures, worship God most high!
412	Come, join the dance of Trinity
879	For the beauty of the earth
771	God, who stretched the spangled heavens
852	Golden breaks the dawn
829	Have you thanked the Lord?
830	How marvelous God's greatness
836	Joyful, joyful we adore thee
561	Joyous light of heavenly glory
881	Let all things now living
876	Let the whole creation cry
837	Many and great, O God
556	Morning has broken

555	Oh, sing to God above
842	Oh, worship the King
878	Soli Deo Gloria
824	This is my Father's world
861	When long before time

Cross-bearing

338	Beneath the cross of Jesus
812, 813	Faith of our fathers
400	God of tempest, God of whirlwind
580	How clear is our vocation, Lord
324	In the cross of Christ I glory
345	Jesus, I will ponder now
335	Jesus, keep me near the cross
802	Let us ever walk with Jesus
808	Lord Jesus, you shall be my song
806	O God, my faithful God
667	Take up your cross, the Savior said
798	Will you come and follow me

Daily Life and Work (see also Vocation, Ministry)

724	All who love and serve your city
695	As saints of old
557	Awake, my soul, and with the sun
470	Draw us in the Spirit's tether
761	Evening and morning
526	God is here!
744	Lord, Be Glorified
765	Lord of all hopefulness
689	Praise and thanksgiving
548	Rise, O church, like Christ arisen
878	Soli Deo Gloria
538	The Lord now sends us forth

Death – see Heaven; Funeral

Dedication, Anniversary

645	Christ is made the sure foundation
647	Glorious things of you are spoken
526	God is here!
579	Lord, you give the great commission
839, 840	Now thank we all our God
632	O God, our help in ages past
533	Open now thy gates of beauty
654	The church's one foundation

Diaconal Ministry (see also Service; Vocation, Ministry)

358	Great God, your love has called us
708	Jesu, Jesu, fill us with your love
712	Lord, whose love in humble service

Discipleship – see Commitment, Discipleship

Diversity – see Human Family; Unity

EASTER, 361–394

433	Blessing, Honor, and Glory
474	Bread of life from heaven
419	For all the faithful women
721	Goodness is stronger than evil
619	I know that my Redeemer lives!
860	I'm so glad Jesus lifted me
621	Jesus lives, my sure defense
447	O blessed spring
604	O Christ, our hope
862	Praise, praise! You are my rock
426	Sing with all the saints in glory
646	The peace of the Lord
826	Thine the amen
451	We are baptized in Christ Jesus
869	We have seen the Lord
449	We know that Christ is raised
635	We walk by faith
495	We who once were dead

Education (see also Word of God)

793	Be thou my vision
645	Christ is made the sure foundation
577, 578	Creator Spirit, heavenly dove
731	Earth and all stars!
401	Gracious Spirit, heed our pleading
398	Holy Spirit, truth divine
805	Lead on, O King eternal!
676	Lord, speak to us, that we may speak
758	You are the way

END TIME, 433–441 (see also Judgment)

452	Awake, O sleeper, rise from death
693	Come, ye thankful people, come
246	Hark! A thrilling voice is sounding!
730	Lord our God, with praise we come
711	O day of peace
430	Rejoice, for Christ is king!
426	Sing with all the saints in glory
432	The head that once was crowned
327	Through the night of doubt and sorrow
262	Wait for the Lord

EPIPHANY, TIME AFTER EPIPHANY, 301–318
(see also Light)

275	Angels, from the realms of glory
793	Be thou my vision
728	Blest are they
715	Christ, Be Our Light
553	Christ, whose glory fills the skies
593	Drawn to the Light
253	He came down
815	I want to walk as a child of the light
280	Midnight stars make bright the skies
460	Now the silence
722	O Christ, your heart, compassionate
886	Oh, for a thousand tongues to sing
507	O God of light
322	Oh, love, how deep
651	Oh, praise the gracious power
559	O Splendor of God's glory bright
843	Praise the One who breaks the darkness
665	Rise, shine, you people!
671	Shine, Jesus, shine
300	The first Noel
706	The people walk
677	This little light of mine
576	We all are one in mission
720	We Are Called
866	We are marching in the light
798	Will you come and follow me
510	Word of God, come down on earth
581	You Are Mine
817	You have come down to the lakeshore

Evangelism (see also Justice, Peace; Witness)

535	Hallelujah! We sing your praises
513	Listen, God is calling
714	O God of mercy, God of light
886	Oh, for a thousand tongues to sing
671	Shine, Jesus, shine
729	The church of Christ, in every age
538	The Lord now sends us forth
551	The Spirit sends us forth to serve
546	To be your presence
576	We all are one in mission
725	When the poor ones

EVENING, 560–573

539	Abide, O dearest Jesus
629	Abide with me
723	Canticle of the Turning
715	Christ, Be Our Light

374	Day of arising
753	Dona nobis pacem
761	Evening and morning
770	Give Me Jesus
795	God, my Lord, my strength
815	I want to walk as a child of the light
440	In peace and joy I now depart
881	Let all things now living
765	Lord of all hopefulness
767	Lord, take my hand and lead me
882	My soul does magnify the Lord
251	My soul proclaims your greatness
658	O Jesus, joy of loving hearts
313	O Lord, now let your servant
773	Precious Lord, take my hand
671	Shine, Jesus, shine
613	Thy holy wings
702	You, dear Lord

Expanded Images for God

468	Around you, O Lord Jesus
453	Baptized and Set Free
456	Baptized in water
736	God the sculptor of the mountains
637	Holy God, holy and glorious
755	Jesus, Savior, pilot me
403	Like the murmur of the dove's song
397	Loving Spirit
735	Mothering God, you gave me birth
863	My God, how wonderful thou art
568	Now rest beneath night's shadow
480	O bread of life from heaven
399	O Holy Spirit, root of life
407	O living Breath of God
514	O Word of God incarnate
613	Thy holy wings
258	Unexpected and mysterious
445	Wash, O God, our sons and daughters
791	We sing to you, O God
566	When twilight comes
602	Your Heart, O God, Is Grieved

Faith – see Grace, Faith

Family

700	Bring Peace to Earth Again
879	For the beauty of the earth
603	God, when human bonds are broken
271	I am so glad each Christmas Eve
615	In all our grief
595	Jesus loves me!
523	Let us go now to the banquet
640	Our Father, by whose name
792	When memory fades

FESTIVALS, COMMEMORATIONS, 416–432

Forgiveness – see Confession, Forgiveness

Freedom

266	All earth is hopeful
762	Holy, holy, holy, holy
717	Let justice flow like streams
841	Lift every voice and sing
711	O day of peace
407	O living Breath of God
665	Rise, shine, you people!
672	Signs and wonders
878	Soli Deo Gloria
706	The people walk
866	We are marching in the light
666	What wondrous love is this
368	With high delight let us unite

Funeral (see also Heaven; Hope, Assurance)

377 Alleluia! Jesus is risen!
422 For all the saints
770 Give Me Jesus
721 Goodness is stronger than evil
483 Here is bread
815 I want to walk as a child of the light
429 In our day of thanksgiving
595 Jesus loves me!
409 Kyrie! God, Father
730 Lord our God, with praise we come
759 My faith looks up to thee
500 Now we remain
447 O blessed spring
760 O Christ the same
786 O Holy Spirit, enter in
313 O Lord, now let your servant
351, 352 O sacred head, now wounded
787 On Eagle's Wings
773 Precious Lord, take my hand
502 The King of love my shepherd is
778 The Lord's my shepherd
531 The trumpets sound, the angels sing
391 This joyful Eastertide
613 Thy holy wings

GATHERING, 520–533 (see also Praise, Thanksgiving)

641 All Are Welcome
461 All who hunger, gather gladly
468 Around you, O Lord Jesus
645 Christ is made the sure foundation
819 Come, all you people
395 Come, Holy Ghost, God and Lord
408 Come, thou almighty King
625 Come, we that love the Lord
470 Draw us in the Spirit's tether
415 Father most holy
401 Gracious Spirit, heed our pleading
414 Holy God, we praise your name
312 Jesus, come! For we invite you
730 Lord our God, with praise we come
460 Now the silence
627 O day full of grace
786 O Holy Spirit, enter in
821 Shout to the Lord
406 Veni Sancte Spiritus

Good Friday (see also Holy Week, Three Days)

616 Jesus, remember me
343 My song is love unknown
342 There in God's garden
803 When I survey the wondrous cross

GRACE, FAITH, 587–598 (see also Trust, Guidance)

337 Alas! And did my Savior bleed
461 All who hunger, gather gladly
326 Bless now, O God, the journey
469 By your hand you feed your people
354 Calvary
807 Come, thou Fount of every blessing
812, 813 Faith of our fathers
738 God created heaven and earth
526 God is here!
323 God loved the world
358 Great God, your love has called us
796 How firm a foundation
636 How small our span of life
332, 611 I heard the voice of Jesus say
860 I'm so glad Jesus lifted me
335 Jesus, keep me near the cross
735 Mothering God, you gave me birth
622 Neither death nor life

604 O Christ, our hope
748 O God in heaven
606 Our Father, we have wandered
864 Praise, my soul, the God of heaven
865 Praise, my soul, the King of heaven
623 Rock of ages, cleft for me
488, 489 Soul, adorn yourself with gladness
457 Waterlife
690 We raise our hands to you, O Lord
635 We walk by faith
633 We've come this far by faith
581 You Are Mine

Grief, Sorrow (see also Lament; Trust, Guidance)

468 Around you, O Lord Jesus
626 By gracious powers
553 Christ, whose glory fills the skies
790 Day by day
770 Give Me Jesus
603 God, when human bonds are broken
612 Healer of our every ill
325 I want Jesus to walk with me
788 If God my Lord be for me
769 If you but trust in God to guide you
615 In all our grief
628 Jerusalem, my happy home
624 Jesus, still lead on
712 Lord, whose love in humble service
759 My faith looks up to thee
763 My life flows on in endless song
600 Out of the depths I cry to you
285 Peace came to earth
773 Precious Lord, take my hand
439 Soon and very soon
390 The risen Christ
342 There in God's garden
614 There is a balm in Gilead
687 We raise our hands to you, O Lord

Growth

329 As the sun with longer journey
679 For the fruit of all creation
543 Go, my children, with my blessing
734 God, whose farm is all creation
554 Lord, your hands have formed
550 On what has now been sown
640 Our Father, by whose name
547 Sent forth by God's blessing
449 We know that Christ is raised
680, 681 We plow the fields and scatter

Guidance – see Trust, Guidance

Harvest – see Creation; Praise, Thanksgiving; Stewardship

HEALING, 610–617

242 Awake! Awake, and greet the new morn
607 Come, ye disconsolate
323 God loved the world
603 God, when human bonds are broken
673 God, whose almighty word
483 Here is bread
698 How long, O God
860 I'm so glad Jesus lifted me
466 In the singing
595 Jesus loves me!
808 Lord Jesus, you shall be my song
703 O God, why are you silent
606 Our Father, we have wandered
871 Sing praise to God, the highest good
704 When pain of the world surrounds us
510 Word of God, come down on earth
581 You Are Mine

Heaven (see also Funeral; Hope, Assurance)

377	Alleluia! Jesus is risen!
827	Arise, my soul, arise!
797	Blessed be the name
485	I am the Bread of life
815	I want to walk as a child of the light
440	In peace and joy I now depart
595	Jesus loves me!
616	Jesus, remember me
308	O Morning Star, how fair and bright!
441	Oh, happy day when we shall stand
423	Shall we gather at the river
426	Sing with all the saints in glory
439	Soon and very soon
831	The God of Abraham praise
826	Thine the amen

HOLY BAPTISM, 442–459

641	All Are Welcome
331	As the deer runs to the river
326	Bless now, O God, the journey
732	Borning Cry
304	Christ, when for us you were baptized
647	Glorious things of you are spoken
540	Go, make disciples
543	Go, my children, with my blessing
575	In Christ called to baptize
660	Lift high the cross
397	Loving Spirit
330	Seed that in earth is dying
423	Shall we gather at the river
502	The King of love my shepherd is
826	Thine the amen
613	Thy holy wings

HOLY COMMUNION, 460–502

641	All Are Welcome
827	Arise, my soul, arise!
522	As we gather at your table
362	At the Lamb's high feast we sing
453	Baptized and Set Free
638	Blessed assurance
854	Blessing and honor
777	Come to me, all pilgrims thirsty
607	Come, ye disconsolate
374	Day of arising
532	Gather Us In
543	Go, my children, with my blessing
535	Hallelujah! We sing your praises
575	In Christ called to baptize
312	Jesus, come! For we invite you
697	Just a closer walk with thee
523	Let us go now to the banquet
674	Let us talents and tongues employ
735	Mothering God, you gave me birth
541	O Jesus, blessed Lord
658	O Jesus, joy of loving hearts
542	O living Bread from heaven
862	Praise, praise! You are my rock
544	Praise the Lord, rise up rejoicing
330	Seed that in earth is dying
547	Sent forth by God's blessing
878	Soli Deo Gloria
390	The risen Christ
531	The trumpets sound, the angels sing
826	Thine the amen
436	Wake, awake, for night is flying
524	What is this place
566	When twilight comes
525	You are holy

Holy Cross Day

335	Jesus, keep me near the cross
660	Lift high the cross
651	Oh, praise the gracious power
355, 356	Sing, my tongue
342	There in God's garden
803	When I survey the wondrous cross

Holy Spirit – see Pentecost, Holy Spirit

HOLY TRINITY, 408–415

819	Come, all you people
684	Creating God, your fingers trace
673	God, whose almighty word
398	Holy Spirit, truth divine
450	I bind unto myself today
735	Mothering God, you gave me birth
832	My Lord of light
748	O God in heaven
328	Restore in us, O God
548	Rise, O church, like Christ arisen
657	Rise, O Sun of righteousness
511	Thy strong word
845	Voices raised to you

HOLY WEEK, THREE DAYS, 344–360 (see also Lent; Maundy Thursday; Good Friday; Vigil of Easter)

HOPE, ASSURANCE, 618–639 (see also Trust, Guidance)

266	All earth is hopeful
852	Golden breaks the dawn
721	Goodness is stronger than evil
699	In deepest night
440	In peace and joy I now depart
802	Let us ever walk with Jesus
726	Light dawns on a weary world
750	Lord, thee I love with all my heart
381	Peace, to soothe our bitter woes
877	Praise the Almighty!
672	Signs and wonders
439	Soon and very soon
826	Thine the amen
702	You, dear Lord

Human Family (see also Unity)

641	All Are Welcome
389	Christ is alive! Let Christians sing
358	Great God, your love has called us
650	In Christ there is no east or west
708	Jesu, Jesu, fill us with your love
471	Let us break bread together
496	One bread, one body
547	Sent forth by God's blessing
498	United at the table

Humility

804	Come down, O Love divine
358	Great God, your love has called us
708	Jesu, Jesu, fill us with your love
599	Lord Jesus, think on me
745	Lord, teach us how to pray aright
712	Lord, whose love in humble service
431	O Christ, what can it mean for us
725	When the poor ones

Hunger

715	Christ, Be Our Light
679	For the fruit of all creation
535	Hallelujah! We sing your praises
674	Let us talents and tongues employ
726	Light dawns on a weary world
712	Lord, whose love in humble service
572	Now it is evening

739	Touch the earth lightly
479	We come to the hungry feast
704	When pain of the world surrounds us
484	You satisfy the hungry heart

Incarnation
(see also Christmas; Epiphany, Time after Epiphany)

412	Come, join the dance of Trinity
737	He comes to us as one unknown
336	Lamb of God
490	Let all mortal flesh keep silence
857	Lord, I lift your name on high
399	O Holy Spirit, root of life
843	Praise the One who breaks the darkness
672	Signs and wonders
655	Son of God, eternal Savior
506	The Word of God is source and seed
861	When long before time
510	Word of God, come down on earth

Invitation (see also Gathering)

306	Come, beloved of the Maker
777	Come to me, all pilgrims thirsty
481	Come to the table
607	Come, ye disconsolate
492	Eat this bread, drink this cup
486	God extends an invitation
332, 611	I heard the voice of Jesus say
696	Jesus calls us; o'er the tumult
513	Listen, God is calling
608	Softly and tenderly Jesus is calling
587, 588	There's a wideness in God's mercy
518	We eat the bread of teaching

Invocation (see also Gathering; Pentecost, Holy Spirit)

804	Come down, O Love divine
408	Come, thou almighty King
577, 578	Creator Spirit, heavenly dove
414	Holy God, we praise your name
786	O Holy Spirit, enter in
305	When Jesus came to Jordan

Journey, Pilgrimage (see also Trust, Guidance)

326	Bless now, O God, the journey
625	Come, we that love the Lord
321	Eternal Lord of love, behold your church
618	Guide me ever, great Redeemer
636	How small our span of life
325	I want Jesus to walk with me
815	I want to walk as a child of the light
446	I'm going on a journey
624	Jesus, still lead on
841	Lift every voice and sing
545	Lord, dismiss us with your blessing
808	Lord Jesus, you shall be my song
514	O Word of God incarnate
327	Through the night of doubt and sorrow
866	We are marching in the light
704	When pain of the world surrounds us
659	Will you let me be your servant

Joy, Celebration (see also Praise, Thanksgiving)

728	Blest are they
731	Earth and all stars!
535	Hallelujah! We sing your praises
664	Heaven is singing for joy
477	I received the living God
267	Joy to the world
631	Love divine, all loves excelling
308	O Morning Star, how fair and bright!
555	Oh, sing to God above
531	The trumpets sound, the angels sing
436	Wake, awake, for night is flying

Judgment

266	All earth is hopeful
358	Great God, your love has called us
246	Hark! A thrilling voice is sounding!
788	If God my Lord be for me
435	Lo! He comes with clouds descending
707	Lord of glory, you have bought us
438	My Lord, what a morning
432	The head that once was crowned
260	The King shall come
342	There in God's garden
436	Wake, awake, for night is flying
666	What wondrous love is this
785	When peace like a river

JUSTICE, PEACE, 705–729

266	All earth is hopeful
522	As we gather at your table
700	Bring Peace to Earth Again
247	Come now, O Prince of peace
684	Creating God, your fingers trace
753	Dona nobis pacem
812, 813	Faith of our fathers
400	God of tempest, God of whirlwind
784	Grant peace, we pray, in mercy, Lord
530	Here, O Lord, your servants gather
561	Joyous light of heavenly glory
523	Let us go now to the banquet
882	My soul does magnify the Lord
572	Now it is evening
748	O God in heaven
749	O God of love, O King of peace
651	Oh, praise the gracious power
285	Peace came to earth
646	The peace of the Lord
889	The right hand of God
887	This is my song
546	To be your presence
479	We come to the hungry feast
524	What is this place
704	When pain of the world surrounds us
702	You, dear Lord

Justification – see Atonement; Grace, Faith; Reconciliation

Kingdom of God (see also End Time; Reign of Christ)

728	Blest are they
670	Build us up, Lord
715	Christ, Be Our Light
532	Gather Us In
400	God of tempest, God of whirlwind
311	Hail to the Lord's anointed
517	Lord, keep us steadfast in your word
711	O day of peace
255	There's a voice in the wilderness
720	We Are Called
518	We eat the bread of teaching

LAMENT, 697–704 (see also Grief, Sorrow)

696	Jesus calls us; o'er the tumult
730	Lord our God, with praise we come
381	Peace, to soothe our bitter woes

Last Things – see End Time; Judgment

LENT, 319–343 (see also Holy Week, Three Days)

801	Change my heart, O God
777	Come to me, all pilgrims thirsty
618	Guide me ever, great Redeemer
615	In all our grief
616	Jesus, remember me
624	Jesus, still lead on
802	Let us ever walk with Jesus

727	Lord Christ, when first you came to earth
857	Lord, I lift your name on high
808	Lord Jesus, you shall be my song
447	O blessed spring
811	On my heart imprint your image
606	Our Father, we have wandered
862	Praise, praise! You are my rock
601	Savior, when in dust to you
608	Softly and tenderly Jesus is calling
814	Take, oh, take me as I am
591	That priceless grace
506	The Word of God is source and seed
305	When Jesus came to Jordan
510	Word of God, come down on earth
602	Your Heart, O God, Is Grieved

Lesser Festivals – see Festivals, Commemorations

Liberation – see Freedom

Light
(see also Epiphany, Time after Epiphany; Morning; Evening)
793	Be thou my vision
715	Christ, Be Our Light
520	Dearest Jesus, at your word
593	Drawn to the Light
532	Gather Us In
738	God created heaven and earth
673	God, whose almighty word
721	Goodness is stronger than evil
332, 611	I heard the voice of Jesus say
815	I want to walk as a child of the light
768	Lead me, guide me
726	Light dawns on a weary world
843	Praise the One who breaks the darkness
657	Rise, O Sun of righteousness
671	Shine, Jesus, shine
677	This little light of mine
702	You, dear Lord

Love (see also Community in Christ)
644	Although I speak with angel's tongue
648	Beloved, God's chosen
656	Blest be the tie that binds
721	Goodness is stronger than evil
358	Great God, your love has called us
661	I love to tell the story
650	In Christ there is no east or west
708	Jesu, Jesu, fill us with your love
595	Jesus loves me!
836	Joyful, joyful we adore thee
716	Lord of all nations, grant me grace
750	Lord, thee I love with all my heart
631	Love divine, all loves excelling
292	Love has come
343	My song is love unknown
622	Neither death nor life
722	O Christ, your heart, compassionate
322	Oh, love, how deep
586	This is a day, Lord, gladly awaited
642	Ubi caritas et amor
720	We Are Called
666	What wondrous love is this
803	When I survey the wondrous cross
653	Where true charity and love abide
581	You Are Mine

MARRIAGE, 585–586
648	Beloved, God's chosen
816	Come, my way, my truth, my life
312	Jesus, come! For we invite you
836	Joyful, joyful we adore thee
839, 840	Now thank we all our God

| 308 | O Morning Star, how fair and bright! |
| 488, 489 | Soul, adorn yourself with gladness |

Mary, Mother of Our Lord
421	By all your saints
723	Canticle of the Turning
299	Cold December flies away
419	For all the faithful women
272	Lo, how a rose e'er blooming
236	Magnificat
882	My soul does magnify the Lord
573	My soul now magnifies the Lord
251	My soul proclaims your greatness
263	Savior of the nations, come
258	Unexpected and mysterious
424	Ye watchers and ye holy ones

Maundy Thursday (see also Holy Week, Three Days)
708	Jesu, Jesu, fill us with your love
333	Jesus is a rock in a weary land
463	Lord, who the night you were betrayed
712	Lord, whose love in humble service
642	Ubi caritas et amor
566	When twilight comes
653	Where true charity and love abide

Mercy
738	God created heaven and earth
733	Great is thy faithfulness
631	Love divine, all loves excelling
714	O God of mercy, God of light
606	Our Father, we have wandered
600	Out of the depths I cry to you
608	Softly and tenderly Jesus is calling
683	The numberless gifts of God's mercies
587, 588	There's a wideness in God's mercy
602	Your Heart, O God, Is Grieved

Ministry – see Vocation, Ministry

Mission – see Evangelism; Justice, Peace; Witness

Missionaries (see also Vocation, Ministry)
660	Lift high the cross
579	Lord, you give the great commission
668	O Zion, haste

MORNING, 552–559
250	Blessed be the God of Israel
790	Day by day
761	Evening and morning
770	Give Me Jesus
733	Great is thy faithfulness
413	Holy, holy, holy, Lord God Almighty!
471	Let us break bread together
438	My Lord, what a morning
844	Praise to the Lord, all of you
853	When morning gilds the skies

Music (see also Arts, Science)
828	Alleluia! Voices raise
731	Earth and all stars!
556	Morning has broken
878	Soli Deo Gloria
531	The trumpets sound, the angels sing
498	United at the table
845	Voices raised to you
850, 851	When in our music God is glorified
861	When long before time

Name of Jesus
634	All hail the power of Jesus' name!
416	At the name of Jesus
797	Blessed be the name

245   Creator of the stars of night
770   Give Me Jesus
620   How sweet the name of Jesus sounds
820   O Savior, precious Savior
886   Oh, for a thousand tongues to sing
821   Shout to the Lord
293   That boy-child of Mary

Nation (see also National Songs)
757   All my hope on God is founded
695   As saints of old
700   Bring Peace to Earth Again
841   Lift every voice and sing
711   O day of peace
713   O God of every nation

NATIONAL SONGS, 887–893 (see also Nation)

New Year
626   By gracious powers
268   From heaven above
867   In thee is gladness
282   It came upon the midnight clear
760   O Christ the same
632   O God, our help in ages past

Offering (see also Commitment, Discipleship; Stewardship)
465   As the grains of wheat
481   Come to the table
486   God extends an invitation
294   In the bleak midwinter
523   Let us go now to the banquet
674   Let us talents and tongues employ
712   Lord, whose love in humble service
500   Now We Remain
658   O Jesus, joy of loving hearts
496   One bread, one body
330   Seed that in earth is dying
583, 685   Take my life, that I may be
531   The trumpets sound, the angels sing
845   Voices raised to you
479   We come to the hungry feast
467   We place upon your table, Lord
296   What child is this

Pastors (see also Vocation, Ministry)
526   God is here!
358   Great God, your love has called us
817   You have come down to the lakeshore

PENTECOST, HOLY SPIRIT, 395–407
804   Come down, O Love divine
807   Come, thou Fount of every blessing
577, 578   Creator Spirit, heavenly dove
526   God is here!
394   Hail thee, festival day!
582   Holy Spirit, ever dwelling
752   Lord, listen to your children praying
743   Now to the Holy Spirit let us pray
627   O day full of grace
786   O Holy Spirit, enter in
800   Spirit of God, descend upon my heart
305   When Jesus came to Jordan

Pilgrimage – see Journey, Pilgrimage

PRAISE, THANKSGIVING, 819–886
(see also Adoration; Joy, Celebration)
410   All glory be to God on high
634   All hail the power of Jesus' name!
377   Alleluia! Jesus is risen!
638   Blessed assurance
250   Blessed be the God of israel
433   Blessing, Honor, and Glory

645   Christ is made the sure foundation
412   Come, join the dance of Trinity
408   Come, thou almighty King
807   Come, thou Fount of every blessing
687   Come to us, creative Spirit
693   Come, ye thankful people, come
679   For the fruit of all creation
740   God of the sparrow
535   Hallelujah! We sing your praises
414   Holy God, we praise your name
473   Holy, holy, holy
762   Holy, holy, holy, holy
582   Holy Spirit, ever dwelling
434   Jesus shall reign
660   Lift high the cross
808   Lord Jesus, you shall be my song
730   Lord our God, with praise we come
236   Magnificat
556   Morning has broken
763   My life flows on in endless song
573   My soul now magnifies the Lord
251   My soul proclaims your greatness
555   Oh, sing to God above
783   Praise and thanks and adoration
689   Praise and thanksgiving
458   Praise and thanksgiving be to God
430   Rejoice, for Christ is king!
694   Sing to the Lord of harvest
683   The numberless gifts of God's mercies
531   The trumpets sound, the angels sing
511   Thy strong word
682   To God our thanks we give
680, 681   We plow the fields and scatter
791   We sing to you, O God
525   You are holy

PRAYER, 741–754
402   Eternal Spirit of the living Christ
530   Here, O Lord, your servants gather
616   Jesus, remember me
409   Kyrie! God, Father
789   Savior, like a shepherd lead us
809   Send me, Lord
348   Stay with me
814   Take, oh, take me as I am

Presentation of Our Lord
718   In a lowly manger born
417   In his temple now behold him
440   In peace and joy I now depart
545   Lord, dismiss us with your blessing
313   O Lord, now let your servant

Preservation – see Creation

Procession
394   Hail thee, festival day!
660   Lift high the cross
651   Oh, praise the gracious power
873, 874   Rejoice, ye pure in heart!
866   We are marching in the light

Proclamation (see also Witness; Word of God)
412   Come, join the dance of Trinity
540   Go, make disciples
762   Holy, holy, holy, holy
575   In Christ called to baptize
821   Shout to the Lord
878   Soli Deo Gloria
720   We Are Called

Races and Cultures – see Community in Christ; Human Family; Justice, Peace

Reconciliation
(see also Confession, Forgiveness; Grace, Faith)

594	Dear Christians, one and all, rejoice
605	Forgive our sins as we forgive
603	God, when human bonds are broken
716	Lord of all nations, grant me grace
463	Lord, who the night you were betrayed
462	Now we join in celebration
711	O day of peace
651	Oh, praise the gracious power

Redemption (see also Atonement; Grace, Faith)

304	Christ, when for us you were baptized
336	Lamb of God
808	Lord Jesus, you shall be my song
341	Now behold the Lamb

Reformation Day
(see also Community in Christ; Word of God)

594	Dear Christians, one and all, rejoice
576	We all are one in mission

Reign of Christ

634	All hail the power of Jesus' name!
416	At the name of Jesus
433	Blessing, Honor, and Glory
389	Christ is alive! Let Christians sing
662	Christ is the king!
855	Crown him with many crowns
616	Jesus, remember me
434	Jesus shall reign
475	Lord, enthroned in heavenly splendor
760	O Christ the same
431	O Christ, what can it mean for us
507	O God of light
430	Rejoice, for Christ is king!
878	Soli Deo Gloria
439	Soon and very soon
569	The day you gave us, Lord, has ended
432	The head that once was crowned
260	The King shall come
826	Thine the amen

Repentance – see Confession, Forgiveness; Reconciliation

Rest – see Comfort, Rest

Resurrection – see Heaven; Funeral

Saints Days (see also Festivals, Commemorations)

728	Blest are they
645	Christ is made the sure foundation
625	Come, we that love the Lord
580	How clear is our vocation, Lord
758	You are the way

Scripture – see Word of God

SENDING, 534–551

516	Almighty God, your word is cast
412	Come, join the dance of Trinity
501	Come with us, O blessed Jesus
400	God of tempest, God of whirlwind
580	How clear is our vocation, Lord
661	I love to tell the story
575	In Christ called to baptize
440	In peace and joy I now depart
674	Let us talents and tongues employ
513	Listen, God is calling
839, 840	Now thank we all our God
399	O Holy Spirit, root of life
313	O Lord, now let your servant
820	O Savior, precious Savior
381	Peace, to soothe our bitter woes

783	Praise and thanks and adoration
809	Send me, Lord
531	The trumpets sound, the angels sing
677	This little light of mine
576	We all are one in mission
720	We Are Called

Service
(see also Commitment, Discipleship; Vocation, Ministry)

695	As saints of old
715	Christ, Be Our Light
679	For the fruit of all creation
705	God of grace and God of glory
400	God of tempest, God of whirlwind
852	Golden breaks the dawn
358	Great God, your love has called us
650	In Christ there is no east or west
708	Jesu, Jesu, fill us with your love
768	Lead me, guide me
712	Lord, whose love in humble service
360	Love consecrates the humblest act
572	Now it is evening
431	O Christ, what can it mean for us
722	O Christ, your heart, compassionate
548	Rise, O church, like Christ arisen
672	Signs and wonders
878	Soli Deo Gloria
655	Son of God, eternal Savior
538	The Lord now sends us forth
551	The Spirit sends us forth to serve
546	To be your presence
720	We Are Called
686	We give thee but thine own
725	When the poor ones
639	When we are living
659	Will you let me be your servant

Society – see Justice, Peace

Sorrow – see Grief, Sorrow; Lament

STEWARDSHIP, 678–696
(see also Creation; Offering; Justice, Peace)

674	Let us talents and tongues employ
714	O God of mercy, God of light
655	Son of God, eternal Savior
583	Take my life, that I may be
845	Voices raised to you
479	We come to the hungry feast
850, 851	When in our music God is glorified

Struggle – see Lament; Trust, Guidance

Suffering – see Grief, Sorrow; Lament; Trust, Guidance

Temptation

626	By gracious powers
325	I want Jesus to walk with me
769	If you but trust in God to guide you
810	O Jesus, I have promised
742	What a friend we have in Jesus

Thanksgiving – see Praise, Thanksgiving

Transfiguration of Our Lord

318	Alleluia, song of gladness
838	Beautiful Savior
715	Christ, Be Our Light
306	Come, beloved of the Maker
637	Holy God, holy and glorious
315	How good, Lord, to be here!
815	I want to walk as a child of the light
317	Jesus on the mountain peak
316	Oh, wondrous image, vision fair

671   Shine, Jesus, shine
309   The only Son from heaven

Trinity – see Holy Trinity

TRUST, GUIDANCE, 755–795
(see also Hope, Assurance; Journey, Pilgrimage)
589   All depends on our possessing
799   Come, follow me, the Savior spake
404   Come, gracious Spirit, heavenly dove
577, 578   Creator Spirit, heavenly dove
796   How firm a foundation
450   I bind unto myself today
699   In deepest night
867   In thee is gladness
696   Jesus calls us; o'er the tumult
333   Jesus is a rock in a weary land
335   Jesus, keep me near the cross
595   Jesus loves me!
697   Just a closer walk with thee
805   Lead on, O King eternal!
841   Lift every voice and sing
517   Lord, keep us steadfast in your word
750   Lord, thee I love with all my heart
596, 597   My hope is built on nothing less
811   On my heart imprint your image
600   Out of the depths I cry to you
862   Praise, praise! You are my rock
454   Remember and rejoice
821   Shout to the Lord
502   The King of love my shepherd is
613   Thy holy wings
262   Wait for the Lord
581   You Are Mine
702   You, dear Lord

Unity (see also Holy Communion; Community in Christ)
453   Baptized and Set Free
247   Come now, O Prince of peace
530   Here, O Lord, your servants gather
575   In Christ called to baptize
403   Like the murmur of the dove's song
517   Lord, keep us steadfast in your word
843   Praise the One who breaks the darkness
887   This is my song
739   Touch the earth lightly
576   We all are one in mission
720   We Are Called
581   You Are Mine

Vigil of Easter
(see also Easter; Holy Baptism; Holy Week, Three Days)
331   As the deer runs to the river
740   God of the sparrow
736   God the sculptor of the mountains
881   Let all things now living

VOCATION, MINISTRY, 574–584
(see also Commitment, Discipleship; Service)
314   Arise, your light has come!
679   For the fruit of all creation
540   Go, make disciples
526   God is here!
358   Great God, your love has called us
696   Jesus calls us; o'er the tumult
712   Lord, whose love in humble service
722   O Christ, your heart, compassionate
669   Rise up, O saints of God!

729   The church of Christ, in every age
546   To be your presence
692   We Are an Offering

Welcome (see also Gathering)
641   All Are Welcome
461   All who hunger, gather gladly
453   Baptized and Set Free
306   Come, beloved of the Maker
444   Cradling children in his arm
482   I come with joy
575   In Christ called to baptize
572   Now it is evening
381   Peace, to soothe our bitter woes
587, 588   There's a wideness in God's mercy
826   Thine the amen

Wisdom
648   Beloved, God's chosen
469   By your hand you feed your people
637   Holy God, holy and glorious
689   Praise and thanksgiving
518   We eat the bread of teaching

WITNESS, 660–677
(see also Evangelism; Justice, Peace; Sending)
314   Arise, your light has come!
508   As rain from the clouds
416   At the name of Jesus
412   Come, join the dance of Trinity
812, 813   Faith of our fathers
290   Go tell it on the mountain
400   God of tempest, God of whirlwind
401   Gracious Spirit, heed our pleading
574   Here I Am, Lord
582   Holy Spirit, ever dwelling
575   In Christ called to baptize
434   Jesus shall reign
513   Listen, God is calling
808   Lord Jesus, you shall be my song
579   Lord, you give the great commission
886   Oh, for a thousand tongues to sing
651   Oh, praise the gracious power
878   Soli Deo Gloria
497   Strengthen for service, Lord
729   The church of Christ, in every age
584   The Son of God, our Christ
576   We all are one in mission
411   We all believe in one true God
720   We Are Called
798   Will you come and follow me
825   You servants of God

WORD OF GOD, 503–519
522   As we gather at your table
301   Bright and glorious is the sky
715   Christ, Be Our Light
737   He comes to us as one unknown
796   How firm a foundation
661   I love to tell the story
533   Open now thy gates of beauty
524   What is this place

Worship (see also Adoration; Praise, Thanksgiving)
687   Come to us, creative Spirit
761   Evening and morning
490   Let all mortal flesh keep silence
460   Now the silence

Sources of Service Music and Hymns

A

A Community Mass (Proulx) 192
A Selection of Hymns (Rippon) 634, 796
Aaberg, Jens Christian 301
Abe, Seigi 718
African American spiritual 290, 325, 333, 350, 353, 354, 438, 459, 471, 614, 650, 677, 770, 860
African American traditional 297
Ahle, Johann R. 443, 510, 520
Ahnfelt, Oskar 790
Akers, Doris 768
Alderson, Eliza S. 707
Alexander, Cecil Frances 269, 450, 696
Alford, Henry 635, 693
Alfred, Joseph R. 813
Alington, Cyril A. 385
Allen, George N. 773
Alte catholische geistliche Kirch-engesänge, Köln 272
Ambrose of Milan 263, 559, 571
An African Prayerbook 721
Anders, Charles R. 615, 662, 850
Anderson, Boris 738
Anderson, Clare 738
Andrade, Moises B. 566
Andress, Paul 178
Aquinas, Thomas 476
Argentine traditional 473, 474
Arlott, John 734
Arnatt, Ronald 231
Arnulf of Louvain 351, 352
Arthur, John W. 165, 166, 181, 182, 183, 184, 204, 205, 206, 207
Atkinson, Frederick C. 800

B

Babcock, Maltbie D. 824
Bach, Johann Sebastian 310, 351, 405, 480, 501, 606, 703, 876
Bahnmaier, Jonathan F. 663
Bain, James L. Macbeth 778
Baker, Henry W. 502, 749
Baker, Theodore 272
Balle, Carl C. N. 298
Bancroft, Henry Hugh 255
Baring-Gould, Sabine 265, 327, 570
Barnby, Joseph 570, 714, 853
Barnes, Edward S. 289
Barocio, Ernesto 680
Barthélémon, François H. 557
Basque carol 265
Bates, Katherine L. 888
Bayly, Albert F. 689, 712
Beck, Theodore A. 260, 588
Bede 393
Beethoven, Ludwig van 836
Bell, George K. A. 662
Bell, John L. 253, 721, 741, 798, 814
Bell, Maurice F. 320, 368
Belsheim, Ole G. 509
Benson, Louis F. 494
Berg, Carolina Sandell 613, 683, 781, 790
Bernard of Clairvaux 658, 754

Berthier, Jacques 175, 236, 262, 348, 388, 406, 472, 528, 616, 642, 751
Bertieaux, Esther 489
Bible, Ken 292
Birken, Sigismund von 345, 802
Black, George 861
Bliss, Philip P. 785
Blumenfeld, Edward M. 584
Boberg, Carl G. 856
Bode, John E. 810
Bohemian Brethren (Kirchengeseng) 362, 657
Bohemian carol 291
Bojos, Luis 375
Boltze, Georg G. 802
Bonar, Horatius 332, 611, 854
Bonhoeffer, Dietrich 626
Bonnemère, Edward V. 446
Book of Common Prayer 231
Borthwick, Jane L. 380, 624
Botswanan traditional 682
Bouman, Walter R. 864
Bourgeois, Louis 478, 883
Bourne, George H. 475
Bowie, W. Russell 727
Bowring, John 324
Boyer, Horace Clarence 677
Bradbury, William B. 592, 595, 596, 789
Brazilian folk song 822
Brazilian folk tune 822
Bread of Life (Young) 195, 206
Brébeuf, Jean de 284
Bridges, Matthew 855
Bridges, Robert 349, 757, 853
Briehl, Susan R. 469, 474, 637, 701
Briem, Valdimar 830
Bringle, Mary Louise 726, 792, 794
Brokering, Herbert F. 377, 731, 826, 862
Brooke, Stopford A. 876
Brooks, Charles T. 891
Brooks, Phillips 279
Brorson, Hans A. 286, 425
Brown, Grayson Warren 882
Browne, Simon 404
Brownlie, John 260
Brubaker, Jerry Ray 518
Budry, Edmond 376
Bugenhagen, J. (Christliche Ordnung) 196
Bullock, Geoff 433
Burleigh, Harry T. 650
Butler, Tillis 187, 200
Byrne, Mary E. 793

C

Cabena, H. Barrie 507
Cain, Thomas H. 321
Cameron, Catherine 771
Cameroon processional 875
Cameroon traditional 253, 875
Campbell, Jane M. 680, 681
Campbell, Robert 362
Cantate Domino 748
Cantica Lauda (Mason and Webb) 686

Cantionale Germanicum, Gochsheim 527
Capers, James M. 183, 185, 205
Caribbean traditional 172
Cartford, Gerhard M. 203, 407, 486, 498, 538, 643, 646, 702, 822, 849
Caswall, Edward 246, 754
Catalonian carol 299
Catena, Osvaldo 407
Cawood, John 516
Central America 538
Chandler, John 604
Chao, Tzu-chen 852
Chapin, Lucius 359
Chatfield, Allen W. 599
Cherwien, David 306
Cherwien, Susan Palo 261, 306, 374, 447, 548, 648, 672, 699
Chisholm, Thomas O. 733
Choralbuch (Werner) 553
Christiansen, Paul J. 666
Christierson, Frank von 402, 695
Christliche Ordnung (Bugenhagen) 196
Clarke, Jeremiah 432
Claudius, Matthias 680, 681
Clausnitzer, Tobias 520
Clephane, Elizabeth C. 338
Cleveland, J. Jefferson 872
Cloninger, Claire 481
Cocker, Norman 358
Coffin, Charles 249
Columbian Harmony 461
Colvin, Tom 293, 708
Compline office hymn 567
Conkey, Ithamar 324
Converse, Charles C. 742
Cooke, George W. 228
Cool, Jayne Southwick 220
Cooney, Rory 723
Corbeil, Pierre de 373
Cory, Julia C. 870
Cox, Frances E. 871
Croft, William 632, 842
Croly, George 800
Crosby, Fanny J. 335, 638
Crossman, Samuel 343
Crouch, Andraé 439
Cruciger, Elizabeth 309
Crüger, Johann 241, 349, 378, 462, 488, 621, 775, 839, 840, 847
Crull, August 287, 323, 345, 539
Crum, John MacLeod Campbell 379
Cuéllar, Guillermo 523, 762
Cummings, William H. 270
Cutler, Henry S. 431
Cutts, Peter 403

D

Dachstein, Wolfgang 340
Dakota tune 837
Daman, W. (The Psalmes of Dauid) 599
Danish 301
Darwall, John 550, 893
Das grosse Cantional, Darmstadt 339

Dass, Petter 730
David, Christian 657
Davis, Katherine K. 881
Davison, Peter W. A. 861
Davisson, A. (*Kentucky Harmony*) 260, 319
Daw, Carl P. Jr. 250, 328, 403, 522, 563, 711
Day, J. (*Psalter*) 516
Dearmer, Percy 415, 470
Decius, Nikolaus 357, 410
Den danske Psalmebog 468
Detroit Folk Mass (Butler and Harris) 200
Deutsche Messe 152, 190, 199
Dexheimer Pharris, William 523, 583
Dexter, Noel 889
Didache 301, 465
Dirksen, Richard W. 560, 874
Dix, William C. 296, 302, 392
Doan, Gilbert E. Jr. 319, 410, 491
Doane, George W. 758
Doane, William H. 335
Doddridge, Philip 239
Donaldson, Andrew 644
Doran, Carol 651
Dorsey, Thomas A. 773
Doving, Carl 652
Draper, William Henry 429
Drese, Adam 624
Duck, Ruth 314, 445, 454, 575
Dudley-Smith, Timothy 737, 760
Dufner, Delores, OSB 307, 387, 431, 487, 506, 508, 546, 551, 777
Dunstan, Sylvia G. 326, 455, 461, 615
Durnbaugh, Hedwig T. 330, 690
Dutch folk tune 391
Dwight, John S. 891
Dykes, John B. 413, 597, 754, 756

E
Earls, John Patrick, OSB 329
Early American 796
East African traditional 797
Ebeling, Johann G. 273, 761
Edwards, John D. 640
Edwards, Robert L. 678
Edwards, Rusty 464, 572, 576, 843, 862
Ellerton, John 534, 569
Ellingsen, Svein 330, 690
Elliott, Charlotte 592
Elvey, George J. 693, 855
Enchiridion, Erfurt 309, 395
Engels, Adrian 524
English ballad 296, 316, 322, 487
English folk tune 250, 251, 305, 412, 420, 611, 691, 695, 832
English melody 267, 788
English traditional 274, 300, 636, 644
Ernewerten Gesangbuch, Part II, Stralsund 858
Escamilla, Roberto 639
Eslinger, Elise S. 639
Espinosa, Eddie 801
Espinosa, Juan A. 706
Etlich christlich Lieder, Wittenberg 442, 590, 594

European tune 249, 384, 399
Everest, Charles W. 667
Excell, Edwin O. 779

F
F. B. P. 628
Faber, Frederick W. 587, 588, 812, 813, 863
Farjeon, Eleanor 248, 556
Farlee, Robert Buckley 166, 176, 214, 216, 217, 227, 447, 626, 637
Farrell, Bernadette 715
Fawcett, John 545, 656
Feliciano, Francisco 566
Findlater, Sarah B. 244
Finnish folk tune 243, 313, 419, 421, 576, 827
Fischer, William E. 430, 661
Foley, John, SJ 496
Folkemer, Beth Bergeron 691
Forness, Norman O. 669
Fortunatus, Venantius Honorius 355, 356, 394
Fosdick, Harry E. 705
Foundling Hospital Collection, London 823
Founds, Rick 857
Francis of Assisi 835
Franck, Johann 488, 489, 775
Franklin, Kirk 341
Franzén, Frans Mikael 264, 468
Franzmann, Martin H. 368, 511, 868
Frazier, Philip 837
French carol 248, 289, 379
French folk tune 284, 490
French processional 257
French tune 386
Frey, Stephanie K. 573
Freylinghausen, J. A. 188
Freylinghausen, J. A. (*Geistreiches Gesangbuch*) 259, 663
Friedell, Harold 312, 470
Fritsch, Ahasuerus 806

G
Gabaráin, Cesáreo 817
Gaelic tune 456, 556, 586, 689
Gardiner, W. (*Sacred Melodies*) 658, 719
Garve, Carl B. 380
Gastoldi, Giovanni Giacomo 867
Gastorius, Severus 776
Gaunt, Howard C. A. 544
Gauntlett, Henry J. 269, 455
Gay, Annabeth 252
Gay, William 252
Geistliche Gesangbüchlein (Walter) 263, 370, 499, 743
Geistliche Kirchengesänge, Köln 367, 393, 405, 424, 835
Geistliche Lieder (Klug) 320, 372, 517, 578, 749
Geistliche Lieder (Schumann) 268, 746
Geistreiches Gesangbuch (Freylinghausen) 259, 663
George, Graham 346
Gerhardt, Paul 241, 273, 340, 351, 352, 378, 568, 761, 788

German carol 272, 288
German folk tune 404
German hymn 372, 395, 499, 853
German melody 351, 352, 361, 521, 722
Gesangbuch, Berlin 520
Gesangbuch, Bollhagen 323
Gesangbuch, Münster 838
Gesangbuch, Nürnberg 589, 675, 784
Gesius, Bartholomäus 799
Geyer, John B. 449
Ghanaian folk tune 708
Ghanaian traditional 591
Giardini, Felice de 408, 673
Gibbons, Orlando 398, 463, 745
Gibson, Colin 739
Gillard, Richard 659
Gillespie, Avon 156
Gladden, Washington 818
Glaeser, Mark 670
Gläser, Carl G. 452, 886
Gondo, Alexander 819
Goodson, Albert A. 633
Goss, John 318, 864, 865
Gould, John Edgar 755
Gradual, Prague 795
Grant, Robert 601, 842
Grantson, Emmanuel F. Y. 591
Greatorex, Walter 390
Greek hymn 229, 230, 231, 561, 562, 563
Green, Fred Pratt 305, 418, 526, 572, 580, 610, 626, 679, 702, 729, 850, 851
Gregory I 558
Grieg, Edvard H. 425
Grindal, Gracia 259, 425, 441, 571, 600, 613, 683, 791
Gross Catolisch Gesangbuch, Nürnberg 494
Gruber, Franz 281
Grundtvig, Nikolai F. S. 298, 301, 381, 444, 509, 627, 652

H
Haas, David 500, 581, 720, 728
Hallock, Peter 165
Halullisten Sjelujen Hengelliset Laulut 827
Hampton, Calvin 258, 587
Hampton, Keith 341
Handel, George Frideric 376
Hanke, Elmer T. R. 630
Hankey, Katherine 661
Hanna, Donna 670
Hanson, Elaine 875
Hanson, Handt 457, 512, 540
Harbor, Rawn 209, 222, 225
Harding, James P. 303
Harkness, Georgia 887
Harling, Per 193, 525
Harper, Michael 598
Harris, James 200
Hartig, X. L. (*Melodien zum Mainzer Gesangbuche*) 361, 521, 722
Hasidic traditional 519
Hasidic tune 519
Hassler, Hans Leo 351, 352, 606, 703

Hastings, Thomas 607, 623
Hatton, John 434, 619, 848
Haugen, Marty 157, 167, 181, 191,
  208, 232, 242, 334, 465, 469,
  474, 532, 561, 612, 622, 635,
  641, 703, 780, 878
Hauser, W. (*Hesperian Harp*) 667
Hausmann, Julie von 767
Havergal, Frances R. 537, 583, 676,
  685, 820
Havergal, William H. 685, 772
Haweis, Thomas 239, 551
Hawhee, Howard 299
Hawkins, Ernest 645
Haydn, Franz Joseph 823
Haydn, Johann Michael 825
Haywood, Carl 159
Heber, Reginald 303, 413, 564
Hedge, Frederick H. 505
Heermann, Johann 349, 675, 806
Hemy, Henri F. 812
Hemy, H. F. (*The Crown of Jesus
  Music*) 289
Henry, Hugh T. 480
Herbert, George 816
Herbranson, Thomas E. 448
Herklots, Rosamond E. 605
Herman, Nikolaus 287, 304, 441,
  571, 604
Hernaman, Claudia F. 319
Herresthal, Harald 330
Herrnschmidt, Johann D. 877
Hesla, Bret 523
Hesperian Harp 667
Hildegard of Bingen 399
Hillert, Richard W. 182, 186, 204,
  327, 511, 828
Hine, Stuart K. 856
Hintze, Jakob 310, 876
Hobbs, R. Gerald 844
Hobby, Robert A. 212, 497, 648
Hoffman, Elisha A. 774
Holden, Oliver 634
Holst, Gustav 294, 710, 880
Homburg, Ernst Christoph 339
Hopkins, Edward J. 534
Hopkins, Gerard Manley 476
Hopkins, John Henry Jr. 501
Hopper, Edward 755
Hopson, Hal H. 328, 552
Horn, Johann 363, 444
Hovland, Egil 401
How, William W. 422, 514, 686
Howe, Julia Ward 890
Howells, Herbert 757
Hoyle, R. Birch 376
Hu, Te-ngai 852
Huber, Jane Parker 717
Hughes, Howard 211
Hughes, John 400, 618, 705
Hull, Eleanor H. 793
Hurd, David 162, 331, 506
Husberg, Amanda 736
Huxhold, Harry N. 585
Hymnal 1940 245
Hymnal version 259, 263, 287, 313,
  325, 391, 397, 399, 420, 421, 448,
  456, 461, 508, 556, 576, 590,
  594, 613, 628, 667, 684, 689,
  698, 714, 746, 747, 770, 775, 788,
  797, 877

I
Idle, Christopher 312, 832
Ikalahan (Philippines) tradi-
  tional 554
Ilonggo (Philippines) tradi-
  tional 748
Ingemann, Bernhardt S. 327
International Commission on English
  in the Liturgy 211
Ireland, John 343, 791
Irish melody 450
Irish traditional 723, 765, 793
Irish tune 502, 793
Irons, William J. 426
Isaac, Heinrich 480, 568

J
Jabusch, Willard F. 519
Jacob, Gordon 778
Jacobse, Muus 495
Jamaican folk tune 674
Janzen, Jean 399, 735
Japanese Gagaku mode 530
Jennings, Carolyn 735, 845
Jewish melody 831
Jillson, Marjorie 764
John of Damascus 361, 363
Johnson, David N. 377, 731
Johnson, J. Rosamond 841
Johnson, James W. 841
Johnson, Ralph M. 875
Joncas, Michael 787
Jude, William H. 696
Julian of Norwich 735

K
Kaan, Fred 603, 674
Kahl, Johan 827
Katholisches Gesangbuch, Vienna
  414
Keller, Matthias 854
Kelly, John 378
Kelly, Thomas 432
Ken, Thomas 557, 565, 884, 885
Kendrick, Graham 483, 531, 671
Kentucky Harmony 260, 319
Kethe, William 883
Key, Francis Scott 893
Kilpatrick, Bob 744
Kingo, Thomas H. 442, 541, 783,
  811
Kirchengeseng (Bohemian Breth-
  ren) 362, 657
Kirkpatrick, William J. 278
Kitchin, George W. 660
Klug, J. (*Geistliche Lieder*) 320, 372,
  517, 578, 749
Klug, Ronald A. 665
Klusmeier, Ron 844
Knapp, Phoebe P. 638
Knapp, William 729
Knudsen, Johannes H. V. 444
Knudsen, Peder 271
Kocher, Conrad 302, 879
Kolisi, G. M. 153
Kolling, Miria T. 486
König, Johann B. 811, 833
Koralpsalmboken, Stockholm 830
Krauth, Charles Porterfield 298
Krauth, Harriet R. 272, 286
Kreutz, Robert E. 484

Kutzky, Michal 602
Kverno, Trond 690
Kwillia, Billema 491
Kyamanywa, Bernard 364
Kyrie fons bonitatis 409

L
LaMotta, Bill 829
L'Arche Community 808
Larkin, Kenneth D. 446
Lathbury, Mary A. 515
Latin 653
Latin antiphon 642
Latin carol 365
Latin *Credo* 411
Latin hymn 245, 246, 318, 320,
  359, 362, 384, 409, 415, 480,
  604, 645
Latvian folk tune 701
Laudamus 784
Laurenti, Laurentius 244
Laurinus, Laurentius L. 630
Lavallée, Calixa 892
Lawes, Henry 228
Leach, Richard 412, 709
Leaf, Robert 790
Leckebusch, Martin E. 428
LeCroy, Anne 560
Lee, Geonyong 247
Lee, Olav 243
Leeson, Jane E. 369
Lehenbauer, Albert 489
Les Petites Soeurs de Jésus 808
Lewis, Howell E. 688
Liang, Qi-fang 280
Liles, Dwight 692
Lim, Swee Hong 158
Lindeman, Ludvig M. 380, 652
Lindemann, Johann 867
Lindholm, Jeannette M. 258
Littledale, Richard F. 804
Liturgy of Joy (Capers) 183, 185, 205
Liturgy of St. James 490
Lockwood, George 639
Loh, I-to 682, 819
Löhner, Johann 544, 589
Long, Larry J. 734
Longfellow, Samuel 398
Lord's Prayer 741
Lovelace, Austin C. 513
Löwenstern, Matthäus A. von 766
Lowry, Robert 423, 625, 763
Lowry, Somerset C. 655
Lucío Cordova, Evy 489
Lundeen, Joel W. 462
Luther, Martin 263, 268, 370, 395,
  411, 440, 499, 503, 504, 505,
  509, 517, 594, 600, 743, 746, 747,
  784, 868
Lutheran Book of Worship 157, 201,
  238, 264, 268, 308, 340, 373,
  393, 394, 488, 489, 503, 504,
  568, 663, 767, 783, 802
Lyon, Meyer 831
Lyra Davidica 365
Lyte, Henry F. 629, 864, 865

M
Maccall, William 630
Madurga, Joaquín 498
Magnificat 251, 573, 723

Mahamba, Deogratias 797
Makeever, Ray 464, 479
Maker, Frederick C. 338, 382
Malawi traditional 293
Manley, James K. 396
Mann, Arthur H. 820
Mant, Richard 427
Manz, Paul 285
Manzano, Miguel 725
Maquiso, Elena G. 748
Maraire, Abraham 173
Marriott, John 673
Marshall, Madeleine Forell 266, 817
Mason, Arthur J. 541
Mason, L. and G. Webb (*Cantica Lauda*) 686
Mason, Lowell 267, 759, 803, 886
Massie, Richard 370, 788
Matsikenyiri, Patrick 529
Mattes, John C. 272, 405
Mattos, Angel 498
Maurus, Rhabanus 577, 578
McComb, William 609
McCrae, Linda 762
McDougall, Alan 560
McIntosh, Rigdon M. 437
McManus, Silas B. 360
Medema, Ken 752
Medieval antiphon 784
Medieval European tune 368, 727
Medieval German *Leise* 743
Medieval Latin carol 288
Medley, Samuel 619
Melodien zum Mainzer Gesangbuche (Hartig) 361, 521, 722
Mendelssohn, Felix 270
Mendoza, Vicente 583
Mentzer, Johann 833
Mercer, W. (*The Church Psalter and Hymn Book*) 315
Mercer, William 564
Messiter, Arthur H. 873
Middleton, Jesse E. 284
Miller, Edward 323
Miller, Margaret D. 491
Milligan, James Lewis 255
Milman, Henry H. 346
Minchin, James 554, 566
Misa popular salvadoreña 523
Mohr, Joseph 281
Molefe, S. C. 846
Monk, William H. 246, 366, 603, 629
Monsell, John S. B. 382, 537, 694
Montgomery, James 275, 311, 347, 745
Moore, Bob 169, 235
Moore, James E. Jr. 493
Moore, Thomas 607
Moore, W. (*Columbian Harmony*) 461
Mote, Edward 596, 597
Moultrie, Gerard 490
Mowbray, David 687
Mozarabic 560
Mummert, Mark 161, 223
Murray, James R. 277
Murray, Shirley Erena 397, 466, 739
Muscogee (Creek) Indian 171
Mxadana, Gobingca George 741, 846

N
Nägeli, Johann G. 656
Neale, John Mason 257, 288, 316, 318, 344, 355, 356, 361, 363, 384, 386, 387, 567, 645
Neander, Joachim 533, 757, 858, 859
Nederlandtsch Gedenckclanck (Valerius) 524, 870
Nelson, Horatio Bolton 420, 421
Nelson, Perry 700
Nelson, Ronald A. 184, 207
Neumark, Georg 769
Neuvermehrtes Christlich Seelenharpf, Ansbach 877
Neuvermehrtes Gesangbuch, Meiningen 514, 810
New Plainsong Mass (Hurd) 162
Newbolt, Michael R. 660
Newton, John 550, 585, 620, 647, 779
Nichols, Kevin 606
Nicholson, Sydney H. 660
Nicolai, Philipp 308, 436, 786
Niedling, Johann 405
Nielsen, Carl 541
Niles, Daniel T. 748
Niwagila, Wilson 401
Noel, Caroline M. 416
Nordic hymn 243
North American 277, 278, 588, 890
North American folk hymn 666
North American traditional 448, 628, 697, 698, 782
North, Frank M. 719
Norwegian folk tune 425, 630
Norwegian traditional 730
Now the Feast and Celebration (Haugen) 157, 167, 191, 208, 465
Nshakazongwe, Daisy 682
Nunc dimittis 440
Nystrom, Martin J. 481

O
Oakeley, Frederick 283
O'Carroll, Fintan 174
Olearius, Johann G. 256
Oliano, Ramon 554
Oliano, Sario 554
Olivar, José Antonio 725
Olivers, Thomas 435, 831
Olivieri, Luis 680
Olson, Ernst W. 781
Olson, Howard S. 364, 401, 513
Olson, Larry 180
Oosterhuis, Huub 524
Organ, Anne Krentz 215, 221, 226
Orgeltabulaturbuch (Schmid) 750
Oude en Nieuwe Hollantse Boerenlities en Contradansen 522, 582, 655
Owen, William 475
Oxenham, John 650

P
Palestrina, Giovanni Pierluigi da 366
Palmer, Ray 658, 759
Paris *Antiphoner* 415, 458, 558
Paris, Twila 336
Parker, Alice 691, 832
Parry, C. Hubert H. 418, 428, 580, 678, 711, 737

Parry, Joseph 601
Patrick 450
Pavlechko, Thomas 163, 170, 383, 699, 709, 794
Pearsall, Robert L. 288
Pécselyi, Király Imre von 342
Pentecost sequence 406
Perronet, Edward 634
Perry, Michael 552, 880
Peruvian traditional 164
Petrich, Roger T. 229
Pettman, C. Edgar 265
Pierpoint, Folliott S. 879
Pilcher, Charles V. 830
Pi^{n}po melody 738
Plainsong 156, 168, 194, 201, 234, 245, 295, 355, 371, 402, 410, 476, 559, 562, 567, 653
Plumptre, Edward H. 873, 874
Poitiers *Antiphoner* 766
Polack, W. Gustave 409
Polish carol 276
Pope, Marion 247
Pott, Francis 366
Potter, Doreen 674
Praetorius, Michael 249, 272, 384, 399
Prescod, Patrick 889
Price, Frank W. 852
Prichard, Rowland H. 392, 585, 631, 707
Processionale, Paris 402, 476
Proulx, Richard 152, 177, 190, 192, 199, 687
Prudentius, Marcus Aurelius Clemens 295
Psalmodia Evangelica (Williams) 389
Psalter (Day) 516
Psalter, Edinburgh 758, 863
Psalteriolum Cantionum Catholicarum, Köln 257
Pulkingham, Betty 659
Purcell, Henry 645
Pye, Henry J. 417

Q
Quinn, James, SJ 510

R
Radford, Jeffrey 297
Rankin, Jeremiah E. 536
Rantatalo, Matti 197
Recueil de noëls composés en langue provençale (Seguin) 292
Redhead, Richard 347, 609
Redner, Lewis H. 279
Reed, Edith M. G. 276
Rees, Timothy 582
Reid, William W. Jr. 713
Reidy, David 433
Reinagle, Alexander R. 620
Reindorf, Dinah 151
Renville, Joseph R. 837
Repository of Sacred Music, Part II (Wyeth) 807, 843
Rice, Delbert 554
Riley, J. Athelstan 424
Rinkhart, Martin 839, 840
Rippon, J. (*A Selection of Hymns*) 634, 796

Rist, Johann 542
River of Life (Butler) 187
Roberts, John 575, 834
Roberts, Leon C. 233
Roberts, William Bradley 426
Robinson, Joseph A. 315
Robinson, Robert 807
Rockstro, William Smith 494
Rodigast, Samuel 776
Röntgen, Julius 522, 582, 655
Rosas, Carlos 555
Rose, Barry 248
Rossetti, Christina Georgina 294
Routhier, Adolphe-Basile 892
Routley, Erik 342, 724
Rowan, William P. 726
Rowlands, William P. 647
Rowthorn, Jeffery 579, 586, 684
Runyan, William M. 733
Russell, Arthur T. 309
Russian Orthodox traditional 155, 160
Ruuth, Anders 646
Ryden, Ernest E. 313, 613, 827
Rygh, George T. 381, 441, 442

S

Sacred Melodies (Gardiner) 658, 719
Salisbury Hymn Book 275
Šamotulský Kancionál 716
Sandell, Carolina (Lina) 613, 683, 781, 790
Sappington, Ralph C. 179, 213, 230
Sartain, Jeff 869
Sarum 316
Sarum Antiphoner 559
Sarum plainsong 577
Saward, Michael 456
Scandinavian folk hymn 627
Schaff, Philip 480
Schalk, Carl F. 210, 261, 329, 356, 374, 460, 740, 760, 826
Schalling, Martin 750
Scheffler, Johann 799
Schein, Johann Herman 799
Schirmer, Michael 786
Schmid, B. (Orgeltabulaturbuch) 750
Schmolck, Benjamin 443, 533
Scholefield, Clement C. 563, 569
Schop, Johann 501
Schröter, Leonhart 311
Schubert, Franz 152, 190, 199
Schulz, Johann A. P. 286, 681
Schulz-Widmar, Russell 202, 219
Schumann, Robert 676
Schumann, V. (Geistliche Lieder) 268, 746
Schutte, Daniel L. 574
Schütz, Heinrich 573
Schütz, Johann J. 871
Schwarz, May 218
Schwerin, Otto von 621
Scott, K. Lee 342
Scottish traditional 798
Scriven, Joseph 742
Sears, Edmund H. 282
Sedio, Mark 172, 307, 317, 583, 869
Seguin, F. (Recueil de noëls composés en langue provençale) 292
Seiss, Joseph A. 838
Selected Hymns 445, 712, 777

Seltz, Martin A. 375, 706, 725, 776
Seltz, Martin L. 372
Shaeffer, Charles W. 799
Sheppard, Franklin L. 824
Sherwin, William F. 515
Showalter, Anthony J. 774
Shurtleff, Ernest W. 805
Sibelius, Jean 792, 887
Sicilian 545
Siena, Bianco da 804
Silcher, Friedrich 767
Silesian folk tune 838
Skogen-Soldner, Cathy 453
Smart, Henry T. 275, 417, 805
Smith, Alfred M. 584
Smith, David 524
Smith, H. Percy 818
Smith, Ralph F. 698
Smith, Walter Chalmers 834
Somerville, Stephen 808
Songs of the People 837
Sosa, Pablo 649, 664
South African 153, 535, 549, 741
South African traditional 741, 809, 846, 866
Southern Harmony 254, 397, 437, 467, 482, 610, 666, 684, 771, 779
Spaeth, Harriet Krauth 272, 286
Spafford, Horatio G. 785
Spanish traditional 639
Spannaus, Olive Wise 716
Speratus, Paul 590
Spilman, Jonathan E. 508
Stainer, John 300
Stanford, Charles V. 449, 546, 851
Stegmann, Josua 539
Stennett, Samuel 437
Steurlein, Johann 694
Stoldt, Frank W. 657
Stone, Lloyd 887
Stone, Samuel J. 654
Storey, William G. 562
Stowe, Everett M. 530
Strand, Timothy J. 548
Strathdee, Jim 704
Strodach, Paul Z. 367
Strömme, Peer O. 811
Struther, Jan 765
Strutt, Richard 429
Stuempfle, Herman G. Jr. 331, 400, 419, 617, 636, 700, 722, 845
Sullivan, Arthur S. 534
Sveeggen, Peter A. 271, 730
Swedish folk tune 244, 264, 407, 613, 781, 856
Symphonia Sirenum, Köln 366
Synesius of Cyrene, 599
Syriac Liturgy of Malabar 497

T

Taiwanese traditional 738
Taizé Community 175, 236, 262, 348, 388, 406, 472, 528, 616, 642, 751
Tallis, Thomas 332, 565
Tanzanian traditional 364, 513, 869
Tanzanian tune 513, 869
Taulé, Alberto 266
Taylor, Cyril V. 526, 579, 688
Taylor, Sarah E. 507
Teschner, Melchior 344

The Church Psalter and Hymn Book (Mercer) 315
The Crown of Jesus Music (Hemy) 289
The English Hymnal 371
The Lutheran Hymnal 411
The Psalmes of Dauid (Daman) 599
The Psalms of David in Meeter, Edinburgh 778
The Sacred Harp, Philadelphia 445, 605, 712, 777
Theodulph of Orleans 344
Thesaurus Musicus, London 891
Thomas á Kempis 322
Thomerson, Kathleen 815
Thomissön, H. (Den danske Psalmebog) 468
Thompson, Will L. 608
Thomson, Mary A. 668
Thornburg, John 736
Thorson, Gerald 627
Thring, Godfrey 545, 714, 855
Thrupp, Dorothy A. 789
Tikka, Kari 598
Tisserand, Jean 386, 387
Tomer, William G. 536
Toolan, Suzanne, RSM 485
Toplady, Augustus M. 623
Traditional 203, 753, 849
Tranoscius 602, 795
Tranovský, Jiří 602
Trente quatre pseaumes de David, Geneva 256, 321, 672, 783
Troeger, Thomas H. 651
Tucker, F. Bland 304, 452, 478, 640
Turton, William H. 463
Tutu, Desmond 721

V

Vajda, Jaroslav J. 285, 460, 543, 602, 740, 795
Valerius, A. (Nederlandtsch Gedenckclanck) 524, 870
Van Dyke, Henry 836
Vatican collection 355
Vaughan Williams, Ralph 250, 251, 394, 416, 422, 543, 564, 679, 695, 804, 816
Veelenturf, Rik 495
Vetter, Georg 368
Vulpius, Melchior 345, 385, 539, 871

W

Wadding, Luke 274
Wade, John Francis 283
Walker, Christopher 174
Walker, W. (Southern Harmony) 254, 397, 437, 467, 482, 610, 666, 684, 771, 779
Walsh, J. (Lyra Davidica) 365
Walter, J. (Geistliche Gesang-büchlein) 263, 370, 499, 743
Walter, William H. 314, 427, 669
Walton, James G. 812
Walworth, Clarence A. 414
Ward, Samuel A. 888
Warner, Anna B. 595
Watts, Isaac 267, 337, 434, 625, 632, 772, 782, 803, 847, 848

Weaver, Nigel 390
Webb, Benjamin 322
Webb, Charles H. 171
Webbe, Samuel Sr. 607
Weber, Paul D. 189, 724
Weir, R. Stanley 892
Weissel, Georg 259
Welch, James 668
Welcome to Christ 237
Welsh folk tune 547, 881
Welsh traditional 543, 564, 575,
     679, 834
Welsh tune 326, 713
Werner, J. G. (*Choralbuch*) 553
Wesley, Charles 254, 270, 365, 373,
     430, 435, 553, 631, 825, 886
Wesley, Samuel S. 542, 654
Westendorf, Omer 359, 484, 518,
     547
Wexels, Wilhelm A. 441
Wexelsen, Marie 271
Weyse, Christoph E. F. 627
Whately, Richard 564
White, Jack Noble 224
Whiteley, Frank J. 458
Whiting, William 756
Whitla, William 710
Wiant, Mildred A. 280

Wickham, John 265
Wilhelm II 527
Willcocks, David 278
Williams, Aaron 454, 717
Williams, Peter 618
Williams, Robert 369
Williams, T. (*Psalmodia Evangelica*)
     389
Williams, Thomas J. 327, 511
Williams, William 618
Willis, Richard S. 282
Wilson, Hugh 337, 617
Wilson, M. F. C. 467
Winkworth, Catherine 256, 273,
     339, 443, 517, 520, 527, 533, 542,
     589, 621, 750, 775, 786, 806,
     839, 840, 858, 867
Wipo of Burgundy 369, 371
With One Voice 251, 492, 555, 642
Wither, George 828
Witt, Christian F. 455
Wold, Wayne L. 240
Wood, Dale 665
Woodford, James R. 476
Woodward, George R. 391
Wordsworth, Christopher 310, 521
Work, John W. Jr. 290
Worship and Praise 230

Worship Supplement 743
Wren, Brian A. 317, 358, 383, 389,
     482
Wu, Mabel 198
Wyeth, J. (*Repository of Sacred Music,*
     Part II) 807, 843

Y
Yamaguchi, Tokuo 530
Yang, Jing-qiu 280
Yardley, H. Francis 458
Yiddish folk tune 240
Yigdal 831
Ylvisaker, John C. 451, 593, 732
Young, Carlton R. 466
Young, Jeremy 195, 206, 492
Young, John F. 281
Yūki, Kō 718

Z
Zimmermann, Heinz Werner 764
Zinzendorf, Nicolaus L. von 624
Zschech, Darlene 821

Alphabetical Index of Tunes

A

A va de   491
Abbot's Leigh   526, 579, 688
Aberystwyth   601
Ach bleib mit deiner Gnade   539
Adeste fideles   283
Adoro te devote   402, 476
Afton Water   508
Agincourt Hymn   316, 322
Alegría   664
All Saints New   431
Allein Gott in der Höh   S159, 410
Alles ist an Gottes Segen   544, 589
Amen siakudumisa   846
America   891
American Hymn   854
An Wasserflüssen Babylon   340
Andrew's Song   648
Angelic Songs   668
Angel's Story   820
Antioch   267
Ar hyd y nos   543, 564, 679
Argentine Santo   473, 474
Armolaulu   598
As the Grains   465
Ascension   255
Assurance   638
Atkinson   507
Auf, auf, mein Herz   378
Aurelia   542, 654
Aus tiefer Not   600
Austria   823
   Austrian Hymn   823
   Ave Maria, klarer und lichter
   Morgenstern   361, 521, 722
Away in a Manger   277
Azmon   452, 886

B

Balm in Gilead   614
Baptized and Set Free   453
Barbara Allen   691, 832
Battle Hymn   890
Baylor   328
Be Glorified   744
Be Not Afraid   388
Beach Spring   445, 712, 777
Beatus vir   716
   Behold a Host   425
Bereden väg för Herran   264
Berglund   447
Berthier   472
Besançon   248
Bethold   317
Beverly   662
Bicentennial   484
Blaenwern   647
Blantyre   293
Blessing, Honor, and Glory   433
Blest Are They   728
   Blomstertid   830
Blott en dag   790
   Borning Cry   732
Bourbon   667
Bozeman   572

Bradbury   789
   Bread of Life (Toolan)   485
Bread of Life   515
Bread of Peace   466
Break Bread Together   471
Break Now the Bread   474
Bred dina vida vingar   613
   Breslau   404
Bridegroom   403
Brother James' Air   778
Bryn Calfaria   475
Buckhurst Run   497
Build Us Up   670
Bunessan   456, 556, 586, 689
Burleigh   438

C

Called to Follow   704
Calm Seas   794
Calvary   354
Cameroon Praise   875
Camrose   469
Canonbury   676
Cantad al Señor   822
Canto al Borinquen   489
Carol   282
Carol of Hope   252
Castlewood   687
   Celestia   301
Change My Heart   801
Chereponi   708
Chesterfield   239, 551
Children Praying   752
   China   595
Christ, Be Our Light   715
Christ ist erstanden   372
Christ lag in Todesbanden   370
Christe sanctorum   415, 458, 558
   Christmas Eve   271
Christpraise Ray   651
Christus, der ist mein Leben   539
Cleveland   872
Closer Walk   697
Come to the Table   481
Conditor alme siderum   245
Confitemini Domino   528
Consolation   260, 319
Consolator   607
Converse   742
Coronation   634
Cradle Song   278
Cranham   294
Crucifer   660
   Crusader's Hymn   838
Cuéllar   762
Cwm Rhondda   400, 618, 705

D

Dapit hapon   566
Darwall's 148th   550, 893
Deep Blue   699
Deirdre   450
Dejlig er den himmel blå   301
Den blomstertid nu kommer
   830

Den signede dag   627
Den store hvide flok   425
Dennis   656
Deo gracias   316, 322
Der am Kreuz   811
Det kimer nu til julefest   298
Detroit   605
Diademata   855
Die güldne Sonne   761
Distress   467, 610
Divinum mysterium   295
Dix   302, 879
Dona nobis pacem   753
Dove of Peace   482
Down Ampney   804
Du är helig   525
Duke Street   434, 619, 848
Dundee   758, 863

E

Earth and All Stars   377, 731
   Easter Glory   380, 381
Easter Hymn   365
Ebenezer   327, 511
Ein feste Burg (isometric)   504, 505,
   509
Ein feste Burg (rhythmic)   503
El camino   725
El desembre congelat   299
Ellacombe   361, 521, 722
Ellers   534
   Emmanuel   298
Engelberg   449, 546, 851
Enviado   538
Erhalt uns, Herr   320, 517, 749
Es ist das Heil (isometric)   442
Es ist das Heil (rhythmic)   590
Es ist ein Ros   272
Evan   772
Eventide   629

F

Faithfulness   733
Festal Song   314, 427, 669
Finlandia   792, 887
Forest Green   250, 695
Fortunatus New   356
Foundation   796
   Franzén   468
Fred til bod   380, 381
Fredericktown   615, 850
Freu dich sehr   256, 672, 783
Freut euch, ihr lieben   311

G

Gabriel's Message   265
Galilee   696
Gather Us In   532
Gaudeamus Domino   506
Gaudeamus pariter   363, 444
Gayom ni higami   554
Gelobt sei Gott   385
   Genevan 98/118   478
Gethsemane   347, 609
   Gift of Finest Wheat   484

Indented lines indicate names by which tunes in this book may also be known.

Give Me Jesus   770
Gloria   289
Go, Make Disciples   540
Go Tell It   290
God Be with You   536
Good Soil   512
Goodness Is Stronger   721
Gott sei Dank   663
Gott sei gelobet und gebenedeiet   499
Great White Host   425
Greensleeves   296, 487
Grosser Gott   414

H

Haf trones lampa färdig   244
Halad   748
Haleluya! Pelo tsa rona   535
Hamburg   803
Hankey   661
Hanover   842
Hanson Place   423
Harvest Gifts   734
He Came Down   253
Healer of Our Every Ill   612
Hear My Prayer   751
Heath   686
Helmsley   435
Her kommer dine arme små   286
Here I Am, Lord   574
Here Is Bread   483
Heri ni jina   797
Hermas   537
Herr Christ, der einig Gotts Sohn   309
Herr Jesu Christ, dich zu uns wend   527
Herr Jesu Christ, meins   404
Herre Gud, dit dyre navn   730
Herzlich lieb   750
Herzlich tut mich verlangen (isometric)   351, 606, 703
Herzlich tut mich verlangen (rhythmic)   352
Herzliebster Jesu   349
Holy Manna   461, 771
Houston   815
How Can I Keep from Singing   763
Huan-sha-xi   280
Hungry Feast   479
Hyfrydol   392, 585, 631, 707
Hymn to Joy   S204a, 836

I

I Am the Bread   485
I himmelen, i himmelen   630
Ich heb mein Augen sehnlich auf   573
In Babilone   522, 582, 655
In dir ist Freude   867
In dulci jubilo   288
Innisfree Farm   560
Innsbruck   480, 568
Irby   269
Ist Gott für mich   788
Iste confessor   766
It Is Well   785
Italian Hymn   408, 673

J

Jag kan icke räkna dem alla   683
Jam lucis   567
Jefferson   254
Jeg er så glad   271
Jenkins   709
Jennings-Houston   736
Jerusalem   711
Jesaia, dem Propheten   868
Jesu dulcis memoria   562
Jesu, Joy   501
Jesu Kreuz, Leiden und Pein   345
Jesu, meine Freude   775
Jesu, meines Lebens Leben   339
Jesu, tawa pano   529
Jesus, Feed Us   464
Jesus Lifted Me   860
Jesus Loves Me   595
Jesus, meine Zuversicht   621
Jill   306
Joyous Light   561
Judas Maccabaeus   376
Julion   331
Just as I Am   714

K

Kas dziedāja   S205b, 701
Kelvingrove   798
King's Lynn   305, 420
King's Weston   416
Kingsfold   251, 412, 611, 636
Kirken den er et gammelt hus   652
Komm, Gott Schöpfer   578
Komm, Heiliger Geist, Herre Gott   395
Komt nu met zang   524
Kremser   870
Kuortane   313, 419, 421, 576
Kyrie, Gott Vater   409

L

La Crosse   593
La mano de Dios   889
La paz del Señor   646
Lac qui Parle   837
Lamb of God   336
LaMotta   829
Lancashire   805
Land of Rest   S207, 448, 628, 698
Lasset uns mit Jesu ziehen   802
Lasst uns erfreuen   367, 393, 424, 835
Laudate Dominum   418
Laudes Domini   853
Laus Regis   430
Le p'ing   852
Lead Me, Guide Me   768
Leoni   831
Les Petites Soeurs   808
Liebster Jesu, wir sind hier   443, 510, 520
Lift Every Voice and Sing   841
Light Divine   398
Linstead   674
Little Flock   764
Living God   477
Llanfair   369
Llangloffan   326, 713
Lo desembre congelat   299
Lobe den Herren   858, 859

Lobe den Herren, O meine Seele   877
Lobt Gott den Herren, ihr   871
Lobt Gott, ihr Christen   287, 304, 441, 604
Lord, I Lift Your Name   857
Lord, Revive Us   588
Lost in the Night   243
Love Unknown   343, 791
Lucent   261
Lux in tenebris   307
Lyons   825

M

Mabune   718
Machs mit mir, Gott   799
Macht hoch die Tür   259
Magnificat   882
Marching to Zion   625
Marion   873
Martyrdom   337, 617
Maryton   818
Materna   888
Mayenziwe   741
McKee   650
Melita   597, 756
Mendelssohn   270
Merle's Tune   552
Merrial   570
Merton   246, 603
Mfurahini, haleluya   364
Michael   757
Midden in de dood   495
Miren qué bueno   649
Mississippi   426
Mit Freuden zart   368, 727
Mit Fried und Freud   440
Morecambe   800
Morgenlied   382
Morning Hymn   557
Morning Star   303
Moscow   408, 673
Munich   514, 810

N

Nagel   329
Narodil se Kristus Pán   291
National Anthem   891
Neander   533
Near the Cross   335
Neither Death nor Life   622
Nelson   637
Neno lake Mungu   513
Nettleton   807, 843
New Britain   779
New Orleans   724
Nicaea   413
Nimemwona Bwana   869
Njoo kwetu, Roho mwema   401
Noël nouvelet   379
Norwich   735
Now   460
Now Behold the Lamb   341
Now We Remain   500
Nuestro Padre nos invita   486
Nun bitten wir   743
Nun danket all   S204b, 847
Nun danket alle Gott (isometric)   840
Nun danket alle Gott (rhythmic)   839

Nun freut euch 594
Nun komm, der Heiden Hei-
  land 263
  Nyland 313, 576
Nyt ylös, sieluni 827

O

O Canada 892
O dass ich tausend Zungen
  hätte 833
O filii et filiae 386, 387
O heilige Dreifaltigkeit 571
O Heiliger Geist 405
O Jesu, än de dina 468
O Jesu Christe, wahres Licht 675
  O Jesulein süss 405
O Lamm Gottes, unschuldig 357
  O sanctissima 545
O store Gud 856
O Waly Waly 644
O Welt, ich muss dich lassen
  (isometric) 480
O Welt, ich muss dich lassen
  (rhythmic) 568
Offering 692
Old 124th 321
Old Hundredth 883, 884, 885
Olivet 759
Omni die 494
On Eagle's Wings 787
One Bread, One Body 496
Orientis partibus 373
Ososŏ 247
Ouimette 451

P

Pace mio Dio 700
  Palestrina 366
Pán Bůh 795
Pange lingua 355
  Passion Chorale 351, 352, 606
Patmos 685
Pescador de hombres 817
  Petra 347, 609
Picardy 490
Pilot 755
Potsdam 315
Praise, My Soul 318, 864, 865
Precious Lord 773
Princeton 828
Promised Land 437
Prospect 684
Puer nobis 249, 384, 399

R

Raabe 374
Rathbun 324
Ratisbon 553
Reamo leboga 682
Red Hill Road 760
Regent Square 275, 417
Rejoice, Rejoice 242
Remember Me 616
Rendez à Dieu 478
Repton 428, 580, 737
Resignation 782
Restoration 397
Rhosymedre 640
Richardson-Burton 844
  Richmond 239, 551
  Rio de la Plata 849
Rockingham Old 323

Roeder 740
  Roland's Tune 788
Romedal 730
Rosas 555
  Rouen 766
Rustington 678
Ryburn 358

S

St. Agnes 754
St. Anne 632
St. Catherine 812, 813
St. Catherine's Court 429
St. Christopher 338
St. Clement 563, 569
St. Columba 502
St. Denio 575, 834
St. Flavian 516
St. George's, Windsor 693
St. Helena 258, 587
St. Louis 279
St. Magnus 432
St. Patrick's Breastplate 450
  St. Paul 442, 590
St. Peter 620
  St. Theodulph 344
St. Thomas 454, 717
Såkorn som dør i jorden 330
  Salvator natus 291
Salve festa dies 394
Salzburg 310, 876
San Fernando 680
  Sandell 781
Santo Domingo 375
Schmücke dich 462, 488
Schneider 285
Schönster Herr Jesu 838
Seelenbräutigam 624
Shades Mountain 342
Shanti 635
Shepherd Me 780
Shine, Jesus, Shine 671
Shout to the Lord 821
Showalter 774
Sicilian Mariners 545
Sine nomine 422
Siyahamba 866
Slane 765, 793
So nimm denn meine Hände 767
Sojourner 325
Soli Deo gloria 878
Somos del Señor 639
Somos uno 643
Song 1 463
Song 13 398
Song 67 745
Song of Praise 845
Sonne der Gerechtigkeit 362, 657
Southwell S309, 599
Spirit 396
Spirit Life 457
Splendor Paternae 559
Star of County Down 723
Stay with Me 348
Stille Nacht 281
Stoneridge 492
Stuttgart 455
Sufferer 350
  Suomi 827
Surge ecclesia 548
Sursum corda 584
Sussex Carol 274

T

Taizé Ubi caritas 642
Taizé Veni Sancte 406
Take Me as I Am 814
Tallis' Canon 565
Taste and See 493
  Taulé 266
  Te Deum 414
Telos 626
Temple of Peace 726
Tenderness 739
Terra Patris 824
That Priceless Grace 591
Thaxted 710, 880
The Ash Grove 547, 881
The Call 816
The Feast Is Ready 531
The First Nowell 300
The King's Majesty 346
The Servant Song 659
The Singer and the Song 861
The Solid Rock 596
Thine 826
Third Mode Melody 332
This Far by Faith 633
This Joy 677
Thomas 334
Thompson 608
Thuma mina 809
Thuma mina, Nkosi yam 549
Tif in veldele 240
Tōa-sīa 738
Toda la tierra 266
Tōkyō 530
Toma mi voluntad 583
  Ton-y-Botel 327, 511
Toplady 623
  Trouble the Water 459
Truro 389
Tryggare kan ingen vara 781
Tú Señor 702
Turnbull 383
Tuya es la gloria 849
Twenty-fourth S208, 359, 360
Two Oaks 641

U

Ubi caritas 653
Ud går du nu på livets vej 541
Un flambeau 292
Un pueblo que camina 706
Une jeune pucelle 284
Unidos en la fiesta 498
Union Seminary 312, 470
Unser Herrscher S205a, 533
Uyaimose 819

V

Valet will ich dir geben 344
Vamos todos al banquete 523
Vårvindar friska 407
Vater unser 746, 747
Veni Creator Spiritus 577
Veni, Emmanuel 257
Verleih uns Frieden 784
Very Soon 439
Vi rekker våre hender frem 690
Victimae paschali 371
Victory 366
Ville du Havre 785
Vineyard Haven 874
Vom Himmel hoch 268

Vruechten 391
Vulpius 385

W

W żłobie leży 276
Wachet auf 436
Wade in the Water 459
Wait for the Lord 262
Walton 658, 719
Wareham 729
Warum sollt ich 273
Was frag ich nach der Welt 806
Was Gott tut 776
Waterlife 732
   Waterlife (Hanson) 457

We Are Called 720
Weary Land 333
Wer nur den lieben Gott 769
Werde munter 501
Were You There 353
Westminster Abbey 645
Wet Saints 446
   Weyse 627
Wie lieblich ist der Maien 694
Wie schön leuchtet 308, 786
Wie soll ich dich empfangen 241
Wir glauben all 411
Wir pflügen 681
Wisdom's Feast 518
Wojtkiewiecz 665

Wonderful Child 297
Wondrous Love 666
Woodlands 390
Woodworth 592

Y

Yigdal 831
Yisrael v'oraita 519
You Are Mine 581
Your Only Son 336

Z

Zachary Woods Rock 862
Známe to, Pane Bože náš 602

Metrical Index of Tunes

S M (Short Meter—6 6 8 6)
Baylor 328
Dennis 656
Festal Song 314, 427, 669
Heath 686
Potsdam 315
St. Thomas 454, 717
Southwell 599

S M and refrain
Christpraise Ray 651
Marion 873
Vineyard Haven 874

S M D (Short Meter Double—6 6 8 6 6 6 8 6)
Diademata 855
Terra Patris 824

C M (Common Meter—8 6 8 6)
Azmon 452, 886
Chesterfield 239, 551
Consolation 260, 319
Detroit 605
Dundee 758, 863
Evan 772
Jeg er så glad 271
Land of Rest 448, 628, 698
Martyrdom 337, 617
McKee 650
New Britain 779
Nun danket all 847
St. Agnes 754
St. Anne 632
St. Flavian 516
St. Magnus 432
St. Peter 620
Shanti 635
Song 67 745
Twenty-fourth 359, 360

C M and refrain
Bicentennial 484
Njoo kwetu, Roho mwema 401
Promised Land 437

C M and repeat
Antioch 267

C M D (Common Meter Double—8 6 8 6 8 6 8 6)
All Saints New 431
Carol 282
Ellacombe 722
Forest Green 250. 695
Kingsfold 251, 412, 611, 636
Materna 888
Resignation 782
Third Mode Melody 332

L M (Long Meter—8 8 8 8)
Beatus vir 716
Berglund 447
Bourbon 667
Canonbury 676
Conditor alme siderum 245
Deirdre 450
Deo gracias 316, 322
Det kimer nu til julefest 298

Distress 467, 610
Duke Street 434, 619, 848
Erhalt uns, Herr 320, 517, 749
Hamburg 803
He Came Down 253
Her kommer dine arme små 286
Herr Jesu Christ, dich zu uns wend 527
Herr Jesu Christ, meins 404
Ich heb mein Augen sehnlich auf 573
Jam lucis 567
Jesu dulcis memoria 562
Komm, Gott Schöpfer 578
Maryton 818
Morning Hymn 557
Norwich 735
O heilige Dreifaltigkeit 571
O Jesu Christe, wahres Licht 675
O Waly Waly 644
Old Hundredth 883, 884, 885
Prospect 684
Puer nobis 249, 384, 399
Rockingham Old 323
Splendor Paternae 559
Tallis' Canon 565
The King's Majesty 346
Truro 389
Tryggare kan ingen vara 781
Ud går du nu på livets vej 541
Veni Creator Spiritus 577
Vom Himmel hoch 268
Walton 658, 719
Wareham 729
Woodworth 592

L M and alleluias
Lasst uns erfreuen 393

L M and refrain
Bread of Peace 466
Gaudeamus Domino 506
Linstead 674
The Feast Is Ready 531

L M D (Long Meter Double—8 8 8 8 8 8 8 8)
Jerusalem 711
Schmücke dich 462, 488
Your Only Son 336

L M D and refrain
Canto al Borinquen 489

3 3 4 4 3 3 5 and refrain
Here Is Bread 483

4 4 4 4 6
Be Glorified 744

4 4 6 and refrain
One Bread, One Body 496

4 4 7
Thuma mina, Nkosi yam 549

4 4 7 4 4 6
Calm Seas 794

4 4 8 D
Be Not Afraid 388

4 4 8 7 8
That Priceless Grace 591

4 5 7 D and refrain
Earth and All Stars 731

4 5 10 4 5 10 and refrain
Earth and All Stars 377

5 5 5 4 and refrain
Blantyre 293

5 5 5 4 D
Bozeman 572
Bunessan 556, 586, 689
Raabe 374

5 5 5 5 D
Le p'ing 852

5 5 5 5 5 5 5 4
Halad 748

5 5 6 D
Hear My Prayer 751

5 5 6 5 6 5 6 5 and refrain
Judas Maccabaeus 376

5 5 7 5 5 8
Schönster Herr Jesu 838

5 5 8 D
Bunessan 456

5 5 8 5 5 8 8 8 8
Heri ni jina 797

5 5 8 8 5 5
Seelenbräutigam 624

5 5 10 D
Tenderness 739

5 6 5 6 5
Midden in de dood 495

5 6 5 6 5 6 5 5
Cantad al Señor 822

5 6 5 6 5 6 7
Uyaimose 819

5 6 5 6 6
Now Behold the Lamb 341

5 6 8 6 6 10
La mano de Dios 889

5 9 5 9 9 9 9 9
Cameroon Praise 875

6 4 6 4 and refrain
Neno lake Mungu 513

6 4 6 4 D
Bread of Life 515

6 5 5 6
Ososŏ 247

6 5 6 4
Tuya es la gloria   849

6 5 6 5
Merrial   570

6 5 6 5 D
King's Weston   416

6 5 6 5 6 5 D
Hermas   537

6 6 4 6 6 6 4
Italian Hymn   408, 673
National Anthem   891
Olivet   759

6 6 5 6 6 5 7 8 6
Jesu, meine Freude   775

6 6 6 6
Reamo leboga   682

6 6 6 6 4 4 8
Love Unknown   343

6 6 6 6 6 6
Laudes Domini   853

6 6 6 6 8 8
Darwall's 148th   550, 893
Laus Regis   430

6 6 6 6 8 8 8
Rhosymedre   640

6 6 6 8 and refrain
Haleluya! Pelo tsa rona   535

6 6 6 9
Jesu, tawa pano   529

6 6 7 6 6
Little Flock   764

6 6 7 7 7 8 5 5
In dulci jubilo   288

6 6 8 4 D
Yigdal   831

6 6 8 8 6 6 and refrain
Marching to Zion   625

6 6 8 8 8
Zachary Woods Rock   862

6 6 11 6 6 11
Down Ampney   804

6 6 11 6 6 11 D
The Ash Grove   547, 881

6 6 12 8 8
Love Unknown   791

6 7 6 7 and refrain
Vruechten   391

6 7 6 7 6 6 6 6
Nun danket alle Gott (isometric)
   840
Nun danket alle Gott (rhythmic)
   839
Was frag ich nach der Welt   806

6 7 6 8 D and refrain
Rosas   555

6 7 8 5
Argentine Santo   473

6 8 6 8
Remember Me   616

6 8 7 7 and refrain
Burleigh   438

6 10 6 10 9
Sufferer   350

7 4 6 8 and refrain
Alegría   664

7 4 7 4 D
So nimm denn meine Hände   767

7 4 7 4 6 6 6
Narodil se Kristus Pán   291

7 4 7 5
Jesus, Feed Us   464

7 4 7 5 6 6 8 5
Baptized and Set Free   453

7 5 7 5 D
Tōkyō   530

7 6 6 7 8
Temple of Peace   726

7 6 7 6
Christus, der ist mein Leben   539

7 6 7 6 and refrain
Near the Cross   335

7 6 7 6 D
Angel's Story   820
Aurelia   542, 654
Bred dina vida vingar   613
Den blomstertid nu kommer   830
Ellacombe   361, 521
Freut euch, ihr lieben   311
Gaudeamus pariter   363, 444
Haf trones lampa färdig   244
Herzlich tut mich verlangen
   (isometric)   351, 606, 703
Herzlich tut mich verlangen
   (rhythmic)   352
Ist Gott für mich   788
Jesu Kreuz, Leiden und Pein   345
King's Lynn   305, 420
Kuortane   313, 419, 421, 576
Lancashire   805
Llangloffan   326, 713
Merle's Tune   552
Munich   514, 810
San Fernando   680
Valet will ich dir geben   344
Wie lieblich ist der Maien   694
Wie soll ich dich empfangen   241

7 6 7 6 D and refrain
Hankey   661
Spirit Life   457
Wir pflügen   681

7 6 7 6 6 6 6 6
Auf, auf, mein Herz   378

7 6 7 6 6 7 6
Es ist ein Ros   272

7 6 7 6 7 7 6
Herr Christ, der einig Gotts Sohn
   309

7 6 7 6 7 7 6 6
Bereden väg för Herran   264

7 6 7 6 8 7 6
O Jesu, än de dina   468
Såkorn som dør i jorden   330

7 6 8 6 6
Lucent   261

7 6 8 6 8 6 8 6
St. Christopher   338

7 7 6 7 7 7 8
O Lamm Gottes, unschuldig   357

7 7 6 7 7 8
O Welt, ich muss dich lassen
   (isometric)   480
O Welt, ich muss dich lassen
   (rhythmic)   568

7 7 7 4
Take Me as I Am   814

7 7 7 4 D and refrain
Here I Am, Lord   574

7 7 7 7
Gott sei Dank   663
Nun komm, der Heiden Heiland
   263
Orientis partibus   373
Patmos   685
Song 13   398
The Call   816
Tōa-sīa   738

7 7 7 7 and alleluias
Easter Hymn   365
Llanfair   369

7 7 7 7 and refrain
Gloria   289
Jesus Loves Me   595
Living God   477

7 7 7 7 D
Aberystwyth   601
Mabune   718
St. George's, Windsor   693
Salzburg   310, 876
Toma mi voluntad   583

7 7 7 7 D and refrain
Huan-sha-xi   280
Mendelssohn   270

7 7 7 7 4
Sonne der Gerechtigkeit   362, 657

7 7 7 7 6
Gayom ni higami   554

7 7 7 7 7 7
Dix   302, 879
Fred til bod   380, 381
Gethsemane   347, 609

Pilot   755
Ratisbon   553
Toplady   623

7 7 8 7 7 12
Princeton   828

7 7 8 8 7 7
Dejlig er den himmel blå   301

7 7 8 8 9
Hungry Feast   479

7 7 9 and refrain
Chereponi   708

7 8 7 6 7 6 7 6
Go Tell It   290

7 8 7 8 7 7
Grosser Gott   414
Jesus, meine Zuversicht   621

7 8 7 8 8
Bethold   317

7 8 7 8 8 8
Liebster Jesu, wir sind hier   443, 510,
    520

7 8 8 8 8 8 10 8
Komm, Heiliger Geist, Herre Gott
    395

7 11 7 9 and refrain
Unidos en la fiesta   498

8 4 8 4 8 8 8 4
Ar hyd y nos   543, 564, 679

8 5 8 4 7 7
Mit Fried und Freud   440

8 5 8 5 8 4 3
Castlewood   687

8 5 8 8
Vi rekker våre hender frem   690

8 5 9 5 and refrain
Stoneridge   492

8 6
Dona nobis pacem   753

8 6 6 8 6 6
Warum sollt ich   273

8 6 7 6 4 4 5
Goodness Is Stronger   721

8 6 8 6 6
Dove of Peace   482
Lobt Gott, ihr Christen   287, 304,
    441, 604

8 6 8 6 7 6 8 6
St. Louis   279

8 6 8 6 8 6
Brother James' Air   778
Coronation   634
Pace mio Dio   700

8 6 8 6 8 8 and refrain
Une jeune pucelle   284

8 6 8 6 8 8 6
I himmelen, i himmelen   630

8 6 8 8 6 6
Repton   428, 580, 737

8 7 8 7
Barbara Allen   691, 832
Buckhurst Run   497
Galilee   696
Harvest Gifts   734
Jill   306
Kas dziedāja   701
Merton   246, 603
New Orleans   724
Omni die   494
Rathbun   324
Restoration   397
St. Columba   502
Stuttgart   455
The Servant Song   659

8 7 8 7 and refrain
Hanson Place   423
How Can I Keep from Singing   763

8 7 8 7 D
Abbot's Leigh   526, 579, 688
Austria   823
Beach Spring   445, 712, 777
Blaenwern   647
Bradbury   789
Camrose   469
Converse   742
Ebenezer   327, 511
Holy Manna   461, 771
Hyfrydol   392, 585, 631, 707
Hymn to Joy   836
In Babilone   522, 582, 655
Jefferson   254
Joyous Light   561
Lord, Revive Us   588
Mississippi   426
Nettleton   807, 843
Rustington   678
St. Helena   258, 587
Turnbull   383
Werde munter   501

8 7 8 7 D and refrain
Morgenlied   382

8 7 8 7 3 3 7
Michael   757

8 7 8 7 4 4 4 7 7
Bryn Calfaria   475

8 7 8 7 5 5 5 6 7
Ein feste Burg (rhythmic)   503

8 7 8 7 6
Bridegroom   403

8 7 8 7 6 6 6 6 7
Ein feste Burg (isometric)   504, 505,
    509

8 7 8 7 6 7 6 7
Greensleeves   487

8 7 8 7 6 8 6 7
Greensleeves   296

8 7 8 7 7
Thomas   334

8 7 8 7 7 7
Irby   269
Unser Herrscher   533

8 7 8 7 7 7 8 8
Der am Kreuz   811
Freu dich sehr   256, 672, 783

8 7 8 7 7 8 7 4
Christ lag in Todesbanden   370

8 7 8 7 8
Verleih uns Frieden   784

8 7 8 7 8 7
Fortunatus New   356
Jennings-Houston   736
Julion   331
Nagel   329
Pange lingua   355
Picardy   490
Praise, My Soul   318, 864, 865
Regent Square   275, 417
Sicilian Mariners   545
Song of Praise   845
Surge ecclesia   548
Union Seminary   312, 470
Westminster Abbey   645

8 7 8 7 8 7 7
Cwm Rhondda   400, 618, 705
Divinum mysterium   295
Was Gott tut   776

8 7 8 7 8 7 7 8 7 7
Lasset uns mit Jesu ziehen   802

8 7 8 7 8 7 11
Ouimette   451

8 7 8 7 8 8
Machs mit mir, Gott   799

8 7 8 7 8 8 7
Allein Gott in der Höh   410
Aus tiefer Not   600
Es ist das Heil (isometric)   442
Es ist das Heil (rhythmic)   590
Lobt Gott den Herren, ihr   871
Mit Freuden zart   727
Nun freut euch   594

8 7 8 7 8 8 7 7
Jesu, meines Lebens Leben   339
Wżłobie leży   276

8 7 8 7 12 7
Helmsley   435

8 7 9 8 8 7
Besançon   248

8 8
Wait for the Lord   262

8 8 7 D
Alles ist an Gottes Segen   544, 589

8 8 7 8 8 7 7
Nuestro Padre nos invita   486

8 8 8 and alleluias
Beverly   662
Gelobt sei Gott   385

8 8 8 with alleluias
O filii et filiae   386, 387
Victory   366

8 8 8 6
Just as I Am   714

8 8 8 7 8 7 8 7
Come to the Table   481

8 8 8 8 6
Deep Blue   699

8 8 8 8 8
Mayenziwe   741

8 8 8 8 8 and alleluias
Lasst uns erfreuen   424, 835

8 8 8 8 8 8
Melita   597, 756
Ryburn   358
St. Catherine   812, 813
Sussex Carol   274
Vater unser   746, 747
Veni, Emmanuel   257

8 8 8 8 8 8 and alleluias
Lasst uns erfreuen   367

8 8 8 8 8 8 6 6
Macht hoch die Tür   259

8 8 8 8 8 8 8
Kirken den er et gammelt hus   652
Mit Freuden zart   368
The Solid Rock   596

8 8 8 8 8 8 8 8 7 8
Wir glauben all   411

8 8 9 and refrain
Healer of Our Every Ill   612

8 8 9 9 9 7 7 7
Dapit hapon   566

8 9 8 8 and refrain
Vårvindar friska   407

8 10 10 and refrain
Pescador de hombres   817

9 5 7 5 7
Nelson   637

9 6 7 7
Roeder   740

9 6 8 6 8 7 10 and refrain
Two Oaks   641

9 6 8 8 8 6
Lac qui Parle   837

9 6 9 6 6
Carol of Hope   252

9 7 9 6 D
Waterlife   732

9 8 8 9 and refrain
God Be with You   536

9 8 9 5 and refrain
Yisrael v'oraita   519

9 8 9 6 and refrain
Christ, Be Our Light   715

9 8 9 8
St. Clement   563, 569

9 8 9 8 and refrain
Santo Domingo   375

9 8 9 8 D
Rendez à Dieu   478

9 8 9 8 8 7 8 9
Rejoice, Rejoice   242

9 8 9 8 8 8
O dass ich tausend Zungen hätte
        833

9 8 9 8 9 6 6
Komt nu met zang   524

9 8 9 8 9 8
Den signede dag   627
Jag kan icke räkna dem alla   683
Wer nur den lieben Gott   769

9 8 9 9
Children Praying   752

9 9 9 8 and refrain
Vamos todos al banquete   523

9 9 9 9 and refrain
Break Now the Bread   474
Mfurahini, haleluya   364

9 9 9 9 9 7 7
Soli Deo gloria   878

9 9 10 9 and refrain
Tú Señor   702

9 9 10 9 9 8
Un flambeau   292

9 9 10 10 3 3 and refrain
Shine, Jesus, Shine   671

9 10 8 8 and refrain
La Crosse   593

9 10 9 9 and refrain
Assurance   638

10 4 7 5 6 5
Pán Bůh   795

10 7 9 6
Tif in veldele   240

10 7 10 6 6
Jenkins   709

10 7 10 8 and refrain
Houston   815

10 8 8 8 10
O Heiliger Geist   405

10 8 10 8 8 8 8
Lobe den Herren, O meine Seele
        877

10 9 10 9 and refrain
Showalter   774

10 9 10 9 D
Blott en dag   790

10 9 10 10 D
Gather Us In   532

10 9 11 9 4
Nun bitten wir   743

10 9 11 9 11 9
La paz del Señor   646

10 10 and refrain
Break Bread Together   471

10 10 10 and alleluias
Engelberg   546
Fredericktown   850
Sine nomine   422

10 10 10 and refrain
Fredericktown   615

10 10 10 4
Engelberg   449, 851

10 10 10 5 8
Romedal   730

10 10 10 8 8
Schneider   285

10 10 10 10
A va de   491
Adoro te devote   402, 476
Crucifer   660
Ellers   534
Eventide   629
Morecambe   800
Slane   793
Sursum corda   584
Woodlands   390

10 10 10 10 10 10
Old 124th   321
American Hymn   854

10 10 10 10 10 10 10
Song 1   463

10 10 11 11
Laudate Dominum   418
Lyons   825
Hanover   842

10 10 12 10
Gabriel's Message   265

10 10 14 10
Were You There   353

10 11 11 12
Slane   765

11 7 11 7 and refrain
Thompson   608

11 8 11 9 and refrain
Ville du Havre   785

11 10 10 11
Noël nouvelet   379

11 10 11 10
Atkinson   507
Consolator   607
Morning Star   303
Telos   626

11 10 11 10 and refrain
Angelic Songs   668
Faithfulness   733
O store Gud   856

11 10 11 10 D
Red Hill Road   760

11 10 11 10 11 10
Finlandia   792, 887

11 11 11 5
Christe sanctorum   415, 558
Herzliebster Jesu   349
Innisfree Farm   560
Iste confessor   766
Shades Mountain   342
Wojtkiewicz   665

11 11 11 5 5
Lost in the Night   243

11 11 11 6
Lux in tenebris   307

11 11 11 11
Away in a Manger   277
Cradle Song   278
Foundation   796
St. Denio   575, 834
The Singer and the Song   861

11 11 11 11 D
Afton Water   508

11 11 12 5
Christe sanctorum   458

11 11 12 12
Toda la tierra   266

12 9 6 6 12 9
Wondrous Love   666

12 11 8 7 and refrain
LaMotta   829

12 11 12 4 and refrain
Un pueblo que camina   706

12 11 12 11
Andrew's Song   648
Kremser   870

12 11 12 11 11
El camino   725

12 12 12 and refrain
Very Soon   439

12 12 12 12 and refrain
Ubi caritas   653

12 12 12 12 12 12
Enviado   538

12 14 12 12
Les Petites Soeurs   808

13 12 13 11
St. Catherine's Court   429

13 13 7 7 13
Kelvingrove   798

13 13 13 13 13 13
Thaxted   710, 880

14 14 4 7 8
Lobe den Herren   858, 859

14 14 15 14
Thine   826

15 14 and refrain
Miren qué bueno   649

15 15 15
Armolaulu   598

15 15 15 6 and refrain
Battle Hymn   890

Irregular
Adeste fideles   283
Amen siakudumisa   846
As the Grains   465
Balm in Gilead   614
Berthier   472
Blest Are They   728
Called to Follow   704
Calvary   354
Cleveland   872
Closer Walk   697
Cranham   294
Give Me Jesus   770
I Am the Bread   485
Jesus Lifted Me   860
Lead Me, Guide Me   768
Magnificat   882
Neither Death nor Life   622
Nicaea   413
Nimemwona Bwana   869
Now We Remain   500
O Canada   892
On Eagle's Wings   787
Precious Lord   773
Richardson-Burton   844

St. Patrick's Breastplate   450
Salve festa dies   394
Shepherd Me   780
Siyahamba   866
Sojourner   325
Somos del Señor   639
Spirit   396
Star of County Down   723
Stille Nacht   281
Taizé Ubi caritas   642
Taizé Veni Sancte   406
Taste and See   493
The First Nowell   300
This Far by Faith   633
This Joy   677
Thuma mina   809
Wade in the Water   459
We Are Called   720
Weary Land   333
Wet Saints   446
You Are Mine   581
Známe to, Pane Bože náš   602

PM (Peculiar Meter)
An Wasserflüssen Babylon   340
Ascension   255
Blessing, Honor, and Glory   433
Build Us Up   670
Change My Heart   801
Christ ist erstanden   372
Confitemini Domino   528
Cuéllar   762
Den store hvide flok   425
Die güldne Sonne   761
Du är helig   525
El desembre congelat   299
Go, Make Disciples   540
Good Soil   512
Gott sei gelobet und gebenedeiet   499
Herzlich lieb   750
In dir ist Freude   867
Jesaia, dem Propheten   868
Kyrie, Gott Vater   409
Lift Every Voice and Sing   841
Lord, I Lift Your Name   857
Now   460
Nyt ylös, sieluni   827
Offering   692
Shout to the Lord   821
Somos uno   643
Stay with Me   348
Victimae paschali   371
Wachet auf   436
Wie schön leuchtet   308, 786
Wisdom's Feast   518
Wonderful Child   297

First Lines and Titles of Liturgical Music

Agnus Dei 194
Ahora, Señor 203
All glory be to God on high S159
All of us go down to the dust 223
Alleluia! Lord and Savior S205a
At last, Lord 203

Benedictus S303, 226
Blessed are you, Lord S303, 226
Blessed be God, the source of all life 209, 210
Blessed be God, who chose you 215
Blessed be God, who forgives 221
Blessed be the Lord S303, 226

Celebrate the feast of victory S177
Celebremos la victoria S177
Celtic Alleluia 174
Come, let us join our cheerful songs S204b
Come, let us sing to the Lord S300, 224
Come, ring out your joy 225
Communion Acclamations S108, S130, S144b, S153, S162, S173, S181, S191, S200, S207, 189–193
Cordero de Dios S182
Create in me a clean heart 185–188

Evening Prayer Opening Dialogue S309

Free to go in peace as you have promised 202

Gloria, gloria, gloria S176
Glory and praise to you S160b
Glory be to God in heaven S204a
Glory to God S99, S121, S139, S148, S158, (S159), S167, S176, S185, S195, (S204a), S213b, 162–164
Glory to God, glory in the highest 164
Glory to you, O Word of God 177
Gospel Acclamation (Alleluia) S102, S124, S142a, S151a, S160a, S171a, S179a, S188, S198a, S205a, S216a, 168–175
Gospel Acclamation (Lent) *see Lenten Acclamation*
Great Litany 238

Halle, halle, hallelujah 172
Hallelujah 171
Have mercy on us, Lord S203
Healer of boundless compassion 219
Hear my prayer, O Lord S325
Hear our prayer 178
Heleluyan 171
Holy God 159–161
Holy, holy, holy S173, S181, S190
Holy, holy, holy; Christ has died; Amen S108, S130, S144b, S153, S162, S200, S207, 189–193
Hymn of Light 229–231

In peace, let us pray to the Lord S98, S120, S138, S147, S156, S165, S193, (S316), 157
Into paradise may the angels lead you 222

Jesus, Lamb of God 199
Joyous light of glory 229, 230

Kyrie S98, S120, S138, S147, S156, S165, S175, S184, S193, S203, S213a, 151–158
Kyrie eleison S184, S213a, 151, 155

Lamb of God S112, S135a, S146, S154, S164, S174, S182, S191, S201, S208, 194–199
Lenten Acclamation S103, S125, S142b, S151b, S160b, S171b, S179b, S189, S198b, S205b, S216b, 176, 177

Let my prayer arise 233
Let my prayer rise before you S312
Let my prayer rise up 232
Let the vineyards be fruitful 181–184
Let your steadfast love come to us S103, S125, S171b, S189, S198b, 176
Litany S316
Litany (Great) 238
Litany of the Saints 237
Lord, have mercy S213a, 151–156, 158
Lord, have mercy on us S175

Magnificat S314, 234–236
May the God of all grace 217
May the God of all healing 220
Morning Prayer Opening Dialogue S298, S299
My soul proclaims the greatness of the Lord S314, 234, 235

Night Prayer Opening S320a, S320b, S320c
Night Prayer Responsory S323
Nkosi, Nkosi 153
Now the feast and celebration 167
Now, Lord S113, S135b, S324, 200–203
Nunc dimittis see Now, Lord

O Christ, Lamb of God 196
O gracious light 231
O Lamb of God S182, 197, 198
O Lamb of God, you bear the sin S208
O Lord, hear our prayer 179
Offering Song 181–188
Oi, Jumalan Karitsa 197
Our Father in heaven S163, S305, S318, S326

Phos hilaron 229–231
Praise to you, O Christ 216
Praise to you, O God of mercy 208
Prayer Response 178–180
Preface dialogue (D Major) S107
Preface dialogue (E Major) S152
Preface dialogue (F Major) S129, S144a, S161, S199

Return to the Lord, your God S142b, S151b, S216b

Salvation belongs to our God S219
Santo, santo, santo S181
Señor, ten piedad S175
Springs of water, bless the Lord 214

Te Deum laudamus 227, 228
Thankful hearts and voices raise 204–207
Thanks Be to God 208
Thanksgiving for Light S310
The Spirit intercedes for us 180
This is the feast S101, S122, S140, S149, S169, (S177), S187, S196, (S204b), 165, 166
Trisagion 159–161
Turn back to the Lord S179b

Venite S300, 224, 225
Vuelva al Señor 179b

We are turning, Lord, to hear you S205b
We praise you, O God 227, 228

You anoint my head 218
You belong to Christ 212, 213
You have put on Christ 211

Indented lines indicate first lines or titles by which some songs in this book may also be known.

First Lines and Titles of Hymns

A

393	A hymn of glory let us sing!
340	A lamb goes uncomplaining forth
503–505	A mighty fortress is our God
539	Abide, O dearest Jesus
629	Abide with me
539	Abide with us, our Savior
691	Accept, O Lord, the gifts we bring
349	Ah, holy Jesus
337	Alas! And did my Savior bleed
375	*¡Aleluya! Cristo resucitó*
641	All Are Welcome
835	All creatures, worship God most high!
835	All creatures of our God and King
589	All depends on our possessing
266	All earth is hopeful
410	All glory be to God on high
344	All glory, laud, and honor
634	All hail the power of Jesus' name!
273	All my heart again rejoices
757	All my hope on God is founded
883	All people that on earth do dwell
565	All praise to thee, my God, this night
442	All who believe and are baptized
461	All who hunger, gather gladly
724	All who love and serve your city
375	Alleluia! Christ is arisen
377	Alleluia! Jesus is risen!
392	Alleluia! Sing to Jesus
318	Alleluia, song of gladness
828	Alleluia! Voices raise
516	Almighty God, your word is cast
644	Although I speak with angel's tongue
779	Amazing grace, how sweet the sound
846	*Amen siakudumisa*
846	Amen, we praise your name
888	America the Beautiful
275	Angels, from the realms of glory
289	Angels we have heard on high
680	*Aramos nuestros campos*
827	Arise, my soul, arise!
314	Arise, your light has come!
468	Around you, O Lord Jesus
508	As rain from the clouds
695	As saints of old
261	As the dark awaits the dawn
331	As the deer runs to the river
465	As the grains of wheat
329	As the sun with longer journey
522	As we gather at your table
302	As with gladness men of old
362	At the Lamb's high feast we sing
416	At the name of Jesus
242	Awake! Awake, and greet the new morn
378	Awake, my heart, with gladness
557	Awake, my soul, and with the sun
452	Awake, O sleeper, rise from death
277, 278	Away in a manger

B

453	Baptized and Set Free
456	Baptized in water
890	Battle Hymn of the Republic
388	Be not afraid
793	Be thou my vision
838	Beautiful Savior
457	Before I can remember
893	Before you, Lord, we bow
649	Behold, how pleasant
425	Behold the host arrayed in white
648	Beloved, God's chosen
338	Beneath the cross of Jesus
326	Bless now, O God, the journey
638	Blessed assurance
250	Blessed be the God of Israel
552	Blessed be the God of Israel
797	Blessed be the name
854	Blessing and honor
433	Blessing, Honor, and Glory
433	Blessing, honor, glory to the Lamb
728	Blest are they
656	Blest be the tie that binds
732	Borning Cry
474	Bread of life from heaven
464	Bread of life, our host and meal
515	Break now the bread of life
301	Bright and glorious is the sky
303	Brightest and best of the stars
700	Bring Peace to Earth Again
670	Build us up, Lord
652	Built on a rock
420, 421	By all your saints
626	By gracious powers
469	By your hand you feed your people

C

794	Calm to the waves
354	Calvary
822	*Cantad al Señor*
555	*Cantemos al Señor*
723	Canticle of the Turning
801	Change my heart, O God
609	Chief of sinners though I be
781	Children of the heavenly Father
715	Christ, Be Our Light
364	Christ has arisen, alleluia

389 Christ is alive! Let Christians sing
372 Christ is arisen
645 Christ is made the sure foundation
382 Christ is risen! Alleluia!
383 Christ is risen! Shout Hosanna!
662 Christ is the king!
370 Christ Jesus lay in death's strong bands
560 Christ, mighty Savior
339 Christ, the life of all the living
373 Christ the Lord is risen today!
369 Christ the Lord is risen today; Alleluia!
304 Christ, when for us you were baptized
553 Christ, whose glory fills the skies
371 Christians, to the paschal victim
299 Cold December flies away
819 Come, all you people
528 Come and fill our hearts
306 Come, beloved of the Maker
804 Come down, O Love divine
799 Come, follow me, the Savior spake
404 Come, gracious Spirit, heavenly dove
395 Come, Holy Ghost, God and Lord
412 Come, join the dance of Trinity
491 Come, let us eat
847 Come, let us join our cheerful songs
720 Come! Live in the light!
816 Come, my way, my truth, my life
247 Come now, O Prince of peace
408 Come, thou almighty King
807 Come, thou Fount of every blessing
254 Come, thou long-expected Jesus
777 Come to me, all pilgrims thirsty
481 Come to the table
687 Come to us, creative Spirit
625 Come, we that love the Lord
501 Come with us, O blessed Jesus
607 Come, ye disconsolate
693 Come, ye thankful people, come
363 Come, you faithful, raise the strain
256 Comfort, comfort now my people
528 *Confitemini Domino*
444 Cradling children in his arm
455 Crashing waters at creation
684 Creating God, your fingers trace
245 Creator of the stars of night
577, 578 Creator Spirit, heavenly dove
855 Crown him with many crowns
725 *Cuando el pobre*

D
790 Day by day
374 Day of arising
594 Dear Christians, one and all, rejoice
520 Dearest Jesus, at your word
443 Dearest Jesus, we are here
298 *Det kimer nu til julefest*
753 Dona nobis pacem

470 Draw us in the Spirit's tether
593 Drawn to the Light
525 *Du är helig*

E
252 Each winter as the year grows older
731 Earth and all stars!
472 Eat this bread
492 Eat this bread, drink this cup
664 *El cielo canta alegría*
538 *Enviado soy de Dios*
756 Eternal Father, strong to save
321 Eternal Lord of love, behold your church
402 Eternal Spirit of the living Christ
761 Evening and morning
354 Every time I think about Jesus

F
812, 813 Faith of our fathers
415 Father most holy
478 Father, we thank you
259 Fling wide the door
419 For all the faithful women
422 For all the saints
427 For all your saints, O Lord
598 For by grace you have been saved
879 For the beauty of the earth
494 For the bread which you have broken
679 For the fruit of all creation
605 Forgive our sins as we forgive
268 From heaven above

G
532 Gather Us In
484 *Gift of Finest Wheat*
770 Give Me Jesus
428 Give Thanks for Saints
428 Give thanks for those whose faith is firm
848 Give to our God immortal praise!
647 Glorious things of you are spoken
540 Go, make disciples
543 Go, my children, with my blessing
290 Go tell it on the mountain
347 Go to dark Gethsemane
536 God be with you till we meet again
891 God bless our native land
738 God created heaven and earth
486 God extends an invitation
526 God is here!
323 God loved the world
795 God, my Lord, my strength
705 God of grace and God of glory
400 God of tempest, God of whirlwind
740 God of the sparrow
736 God the sculptor of the mountains
603 God, when human bonds are broken
564 God, who made the earth and heaven

771	God, who stretched the spangled heavens
673	God, whose almighty word
734	God, whose farm is all creation
678	God, whose giving knows no ending
509	God's word is our great heritage
852	Golden breaks the dawn
288	Good Christian friends, rejoice
385	Good Christian friends, rejoice and sing!
721	Goodness is stronger than evil
401	Gracious Spirit, heed our pleading
784	Grant peace, we pray, in mercy, Lord
358	Great God, your love has called us
733	Great is thy faithfulness
618	Guide me ever, great Redeemer

H

394	Hail thee, festival day!
311	Hail to the Lord's anointed
535	*Haleluya! Pelo tsa rona*
380	Hallelujah! Jesus lives!
535	Hallelujah! We sing your praises
239	Hark, the glad sound!
246	Hark! A thrilling voice is sounding!
270	Hark! The herald angels sing
764	Have no fear, little flock
829	Have you thanked the Lord?
253	He came down
737	He comes to us as one unknown
612	Healer of our every ill
585	Hear us now, our God and Father
664	Heaven is singing for joy
574	Here I Am, Lord
532	Here in this place
483	Here is bread
530	Here, O Lord, your servants gather
797	*Heri ni jina*
637	Holy God, holy and glorious
414	Holy God, we praise your name
473	Holy, holy, holy
762	Holy, holy, holy, holy
413	Holy, holy, holy, Lord God Almighty!
406	*Holy Spirit, come to us*
582	Holy Spirit, ever dwelling
398	Holy Spirit, truth divine
580	How clear is our vocation, Lord
796	How firm a foundation
315	How good, Lord, to be here!
856	How Great Thou Art
698	How long, O God
830	How marvelous God's greatness
636	How small our span of life
620	How sweet the name of Jesus sounds

I

271	I am so glad each Christmas Eve
485	I am the Bread of life
450	I bind unto myself today
482	I come with joy
332, 611	I heard the voice of Jesus say
619	I know that my Redeemer lives!
661	I love to tell the story
477	I received the living God
574	I, the Lord of sea and sky
325	I want Jesus to walk with me
815	I want to walk as a child of the light
732	I was there to hear your borning cry
581	I will come to you in the silence
788	If God himself be for me
788	If God my Lord be for me
769	If you but trust in God to guide you
446	I'm going on a journey
860	I'm so glad Jesus lifted me
834	Immortal, invisible, God only wise
718	In a lowly manger born
615	In all our grief
575	In Christ called to baptize
650	In Christ there is no east or west
699	In deepest night
630	In heaven above
417	In his temple now behold him
744	In my life, Lord, be glorified
429	In our day of thanksgiving
440	In peace and joy I now depart
294	In the bleak midwinter
324	In the cross of Christ I glory
770	In the morning when I rise
466	In the singing
867	In thee is gladness
276	Infant holy, infant lowly
868	Isaiah in a vision did of old
282	It came upon the midnight clear
785	*It is well with my soul*

J

271	*Jeg er så glad hver julekveld*
628	Jerusalem, my happy home
708	Jesu, Jesu, fill us with your love
529	*Jesu, tawa pano*
696	Jesus calls us; o'er the tumult
472	*Jesus Christ, bread of life*
365	Jesus Christ is risen today
312	Jesus, come! for we invite you
345	Jesus, I will ponder now
333	Jesus is a rock in a weary land
808	*Jésus, je voudrais te chanter*
335	Jesus, keep me near the cross
621	Jesus lives, my sure defense
595	Jesus loves me!
317	Jesus on the mountain peak
775	Jesus, priceless treasure
616	Jesus, remember me
755	Jesus, Savior, pilot me
434	Jesus shall reign
624	Jesus, still lead on
754	Jesus, the very thought of you

529	Jesus, we are gathered
297	Jesus, what a wonderful child
267	Joy to the world
836	Joyful, joyful we adore thee
561	Joyous light of heavenly glory
697	Just a closer walk with thee
592	Just as I am, without one plea

K

409	Kyrie! God, Father

L

646	*La paz del Señor*
336	Lamb of God
357	Lamb of God, pure and sinless
768	Lead me, guide me
805	Lead on, O King eternal!
774	*Leaning on the everlasting arms*
490	Let all mortal flesh keep silence
881	Let all things now living
287	Let all together praise our God
717	Let justice flow like streams
291	Let our gladness have no end
710	Let streams of living justice
876	Let the whole creation cry
471	Let us break bread together
641	Let us build a house where love can dwell
802	Let us ever walk with Jesus
523	Let us go now to the banquet
674	Let us talents and tongues employ
841	Lift every voice and sing
660	Lift high the cross
726	Light dawns on a weary world
240	Light one candle to watch for Messiah
307	Light shone in darkness
403	Like the murmur of the dove's song
513	Listen, God is calling
435	Lo! He comes with clouds descending
272	Lo, how a rose e'er blooming
715	Longing for light, we wait in darkness
744	Lord, Be Glorified
727	Lord Christ, when first you came to earth
545	Lord, dismiss us with your blessing
475	Lord, enthroned in heavenly splendor
558	Lord God, we praise you
857	Lord, I lift your name on high
527	Lord Jesus Christ, be present now
599	Lord Jesus, think on me
808	Lord Jesus, you shall be my song
517	Lord, keep us steadfast in your word
512	Lord, let my heart be good soil
752	Lord, listen to your children praying
765	Lord of all hopefulness
716	Lord of all nations, grant me grace
707	Lord of glory, you have bought us
688	Lord of light
766	Lord of our life

730	Lord our God, with praise we come
676	Lord, speak to us, that we may speak
767	Lord, take my hand and lead me
745	Lord, teach us how to pray aright
750	Lord, thee I love with all my heart
463	Lord, who the night you were betrayed
712	Lord, whose love in humble service
579	Lord, you give the great commission
554	Lord, your hands have formed
243	Lost in the night
844	*Louez l'Eternel*
360	Love consecrates the humblest act
631	Love divine, all loves excelling
292	Love has come
397	Loving Spirit

M

837	Many and great, O God
741	*Mayenziwe*
364	*Mfurahini, haleluya*
280	Midnight stars make bright the skies
890	Mine eyes have seen the glory
280	*Mingxing canlan ye wei yang*
649	*Miren qué bueno*
556	Morning has broken
735	Mothering God, you gave me birth
759	My faith looks up to thee
863	My God, how wonderful thou art
596, 597	My hope is built on nothing less
821	My Jesus, my Savior
763	My life flows on in endless song
832	My Lord of light
438	My Lord, what a morning
782	My Shepherd, you supply my need
343	My song is love unknown
723	My soul cries out with a joyful shout
882	My soul does magnify the Lord
573	My soul now magnifies the Lord
251	My soul proclaims your greatness

N

622	Neither death nor life
513	*Neno lake Mungu*
869	*Nimemwona Bwana*
401	*Njoo kwetu, Roho mwema*
367	Now all the vault of heaven resounds
341	Now behold the Lamb
572	Now it is evening
568	Now rest beneath night's shadow
839, 840	Now thank we all our God
570	Now the day is over
379	Now the green blade rises
460	Now the silence
743	Now to the Holy Spirit let us pray
462	Now we join in celebration
500	Now We Remain
486	*Nuestro Padre nos invita*
827	*Nyt ylös, sieluni*

O

888	O beautiful for spacious skies
447	O blessed spring
480	O bread of life from heaven
892	O Canada
604	O Christ, our hope
675	O Christ, our light, O radiance true
610	O Christ, the healer, we have come
760	O Christ the same
431	O Christ, what can it mean for us
722	O Christ, your heart, compassionate
283	O come, all ye faithful
257	O come, O come, Emmanuel
627	O day full of grace
711	O day of peace
521	O day of rest and gladness
886	Oh, for a thousand tongues to sing
880	O God beyond all praising
602	O God, Father in heaven
748	O God in heaven
878	O God of blessings, all praise to you!
713	O God of every nation
507	O God of light
749	O God of love, O King of peace
714	O God of mercy, God of light
632	O God, our help in ages past
806	O God, my faithful God
703	O God, why are you silent
441	Oh, happy day when we shall stand
786	O Holy Spirit, enter in
399	O Holy Spirit, root of life
541	O Jesus, blessed Lord
810	O Jesus, I have promised
658	O Jesus, joy of loving hearts
563	O Light whose splendor thrills
279	O little town of Bethlehem
542	O living Bread from heaven
407	O living Breath of God
751	O Lord, hear my prayer
241	O Lord, how shall I meet you
856	O Lord my God, when I in awesome wonder
313	O Lord, now let your servant
319	O Lord, throughout these forty days
499	O Lord, we praise you
322	Oh, love, how deep
818	O Master, let me walk with you
308	O Morning Star, how fair and bright!
651	Oh, praise the gracious power
562	O radiant Light, O Sun divine
351, 352	O sacred head, now wounded
820	O Savior, precious Savior
555	Oh, sing to God above
822	Oh, sing to the Lord
386, 387	O sons and daughters, let us sing
405	O Spirit of life
559	O Splendor of God's glory bright
833	Oh, that I had a thousand voices
772	Oh, that the Lord would guide my ways
746	O thou, who hast of thy pure grace
571	O Trinity, O blessed Light
316	Oh, wondrous image, vision fair
316	Oh, wondrous type! Oh, vision fair
514	O Word of God incarnate
842	Oh, worship the King
668	O Zion, haste
295	Of the Father's love begotten
274	On Christmas night
787	On Eagle's Wings
249	On Jordan's bank the Baptist's cry
437	On Jordan's stormy bank I stand
811	On my heart imprint your image
537	On our way rejoicing
550	On what has now been sown
273	Once again my heart rejoices
269	Once in royal David's city
701	Once we sang and danced
496	One bread, one body
533	Open now thy gates of beauty
519	Open your ears, O faithful people
247	Osoŏo, osoŏo
602	Otče nebeský, Svoriteľu sveta, Bože
640	Our Father, by whose name
746, 747	Our Father, God in heaven above
606	Our Father, we have wandered
600	Out of the depths I cry to you

P

285	Peace came to earth
381	Peace, to soothe our bitter woes
248	People, look east
593	People who walk in darkness have sought
783	Praise and thanks and adoration
689	Praise and thanksgiving
458	Praise and thanksgiving be to God
884, 885	Praise God, from whom all blessings flow
872	Praise God with the sound of the trumpet
864	Praise, my soul, the God of heaven
865	Praise, my soul, the King of heaven
875	Praise, praise, praise the Lord!
862	Praise, praise! You are my rock
877	Praise the Almighty!
823	Praise the Lord! O heavens
544	Praise the Lord, rise up rejoicing
843	Praise the One who breaks the darkness
844	Praise to the Lord, all of you
858, 859	Praise to the Lord, the Almighty
872	Praise Ye the Lord
773	Precious Lord, take my hand
264	Prepare the royal highway
639	Pues si vivimos

Q

852   *Qing zao qilai kan*

R

682   *Reamo leboga*
430   Rejoice, for Christ is king!
418   Rejoice in God's saints
244   Rejoice, rejoice, believers
873, 874   Rejoice, ye pure in heart
454   Remember and rejoice
328   Restore in us, O God
346   Ride on, ride on in majesty!
548   Rise, O church, like Christ arisen
657   Rise, O Sun of righteousness
665   Rise, shine, you people!
669   Rise up, O saints of God!
623   Rock of Ages, cleft for me

S

590   Salvation unto us has come
473   *Santo, santo, santo*
762   *Santo, santo, santo, santo*
534   Savior, again to your dear name
789   Savior, like a shepherd lead us
263   Savior of the nations, come
601   Savior, when in dust to you
330   Seed that in earth is dying
530   *Sekai no tomo to te o tsunagi*
549   Send me, Jesus
809   Send me, Lord
547   Sent forth by God's blessing
423   Shall we gather at the river
780   Shepherd me, O God
671   Shine, Jesus, shine
821   Shout to the Lord
672   Signs and wonders
281   Silent night, holy night!
355, 356   Sing, my tongue
871   Sing praise to God, the highest good
694   Sing to the Lord of harvest
426   Sing with all the saints in glory
866   *Siyahamba*
608   Softly and tenderly Jesus is calling
878   Soli Deo Gloria
643   *Somos uno en Cristo*
655   Son of God, eternal Savior
310   Songs of thankfulness and praise
439   Soon and very soon
407   *Soplo de Dios viviente*
488, 489   Soul, adorn yourself with gladness
396   Spirit of Gentleness
800   Spirit of God, descend upon my heart
396   Spirit, Spirit of gentleness
663   Spread, oh, spread, almighty Word
348   Stay with me
281   *Stille Nacht, heilige Nacht*
497   Strengthen for service, Lord

T

583, 685   Take my life, that I may be
814   Take, oh, take me as I am
667   Take up your cross, the Savior said
493   Taste and see
293   That boy-child of Mary
384   That Easter day with joy was bright
591   That priceless grace
265   The angel Gabriel from heaven came
298   The bells of Christmas
729   The church of Christ, in every age
654   The church's one foundation
361   The day of resurrection!
569   The day you gave us, Lord, has ended
531   *The feast is ready*
300   The first Noel
320   The glory of these forty days
831   The God of Abraham praise
432   The head that once was crowned
502   The King of love my shepherd is
260   The King shall come
751   *The Lord is my song*
538   The Lord now sends us forth
778   The Lord's my shepherd
683   The numberless gifts of God's mercies
309   The only Son from heaven
646   The peace of the Lord
706   The people walk
889   The right hand of God
390   The risen Christ
861   *The Singer and the Song*
584   The Son of God, our Christ
551   The Spirit sends us forth to serve
366   The strife is o'er, the battle done
798   *The Summons*
531   The trumpets sound, the angels sing
506   The Word of God is source and seed
476   Thee we adore, O Savior
342   There in God's garden
614   There is a balm in Gilead
255   There's a voice in the wilderness
587, 588   There's a wideness in God's mercy
350   They crucified my Lord
376   Thine is the glory
826   Thine the amen
586   This is a day, Lord, gladly awaited
824   This is my Father's world
887   This is my song
448   This is the Spirit's entry now
391   This joyful Eastertide
677   This little light of mine
327   Through the night of doubt and sorrow
809   *Thuma mina*
549   *Thuma mina, Nkosi yam*
613   Thy holy wings
511   Thy strong word

546	To be your presence
682	To God our thanks we give
743	To God the Holy Spirit let us pray
567	To you, before the close of day
266	*Toda la tierra*
583	*Toma, oh Dios, mi voluntad*
739	Touch the earth lightly
334	Tree of Life and awesome mystery
781	*Tryggare kan ingen vara*
817	*Tú has venido a la orilla*
702	*Tú, Señor, que brillas*
849	*Tuya es la gloria*
284	'Twas in the moon of wintertime

U

642	Ubi caritas et amor
653	*Ubi caritas et amor*
706	*Un pueblo que camina*
258	Unexpected and mysterious
498	*Unidos en la fiesta*
498	United at the table
819	*Uyaimose*

V

523	*Vamos todos al banquete*
489	*Vengo a ti, Jesús amado*
406	Veni Sancte Spiritus
602	*Vieme to, pane bože náš*
845	Voices raised to you

W

459	Wade in the water
262	Wait for the Lord
837	*Wakantanka taku nitawa*
436	Wake, awake, for night is flying
445	Wash, O God, our sons and daughters
457	Waterlife
576	We all are one in mission
411	We all believe in one true God
643	We are all one in Christ
692	We Are an Offering
451	We are baptized in Christ Jesus
720	We Are Called
866	We are marching in the light
453	We are people created
479	We come to the hungry feast
617	We come to you for healing, Lord
518	We eat the bread of teaching
686	We give thee but thine own
869	We have seen the Lord
500	We hold the death of the Lord
449	We know that Christ is raised
692	We lift our voices, we lift our hands
467	We place upon your table, Lord
680, 681	We plow the fields and scatter

870	We praise you, O God
690	We raise our hands to you, O Lord
791	We sing to you, O God
635	We walk by faith
495	We who once were dead
625	*We're Marching to Zion*
353	Were you there
633	We've come this far by faith
774	What a fellowship, what a joy divine
742	What a friend we have in Jesus
296	What child is this
487	What feast of love
776	What God ordains is good indeed
524	What is this place
666	What wondrous love is this
803	When I survey the wondrous cross
850, 851	When in our music God is glorified
305	When Jesus came to Jordan
861	When long before time
792	When memory fades
853	When morning gilds the skies
709	When our song says peace
704	When pain of the world surrounds us
785	When peace like a river
725	When the poor ones
566	When twilight comes
639	When we are living
700	Where armies scourge the countryside
359	Where charity and love prevail
719	Where cross the crowded ways of life
642	Where true charity and love abide
653	*Where true charity and love abide*
798	Will you come and follow me
659	Will you let me be your servant
368	With high delight let us unite
425	Who is this host arrayed in white
510	Word of God, come down on earth

Y

424	Ye watchers and ye holy ones
525	You are holy
581	You Are Mine
758	You are the way
817	You have come down to the lakeshore
484	You satisfy the hungry heart
825	You servants of God
787	You who dwell in the shelter of the Lord
702	You, dear Lord
602	Your Heart, O God, Is Grieved
286	Your little ones, dear Lord
336	*Your only Son*
741	Your will be done
849	Yours, Lord, is the glory

Ecumenical Liturgies
School of Theology and Ministry
Seattle University
901 12th Avenue
P.O. Box 222000
Seattle, WA 98122-1090